THE

LEGAL PROCESS

THE

LEGAL

An Introduction

by *Judicial,*

and *Administrative*

BY

CARL A. AUERBACH

Professor of Law,
University of Minnesota

LLOYD K. GARRISON

Member, New York Bar and Formerly Dean of the
University of Wisconsin Law School

Chandler Publishing Company

PROCESS

to Decision-making

Legislative, Executive,

Agencies

WILLARD HURST

Professor of Law,
University of Wisconsin

SAMUEL MERMIN

Professor of Law,
University of Wisconsin

SAN FRANCISCO

PREFACE

This book is designed to introduce the beginning law student and the college upperclassman and graduate student to the operation of our legal system. Its objective is not to teach legal doctrines in any particular area of substantive law, but rather to present the methods and processes of legal decision-making common to all areas. These methods and processes are not considered in a vacuum. They are examined in action, with special reference to how our law-making institutions—the judicial, legislative, executive, and administrative agencies—have dealt with a problem of wide public concern, the allocation of the burden of industrial accidents. The story is told historically, from the first judicial handling of the problem in early 19th-century England through its present-day disposition by workmen's compensation legislation. For realistic appreciation of the American development, as it illustrates the legal process in general, the story centers upon events in a single state jurisdiction—Wisconsin. But developments elsewhere in the United States and the world are not neglected.

The handling of industrial accidents has been chosen as the core problem for illustrative purposes because of the richness of the available materials and because its legal handling typifies the growth of law in many other important areas—initial decision by the courts; followed by legislative intervention; and finally, the choice of a solution which required creation of administrative agencies and continuing efforts of courts, legislatures, administrative agencies, and executive agencies in manifold interrelationships.

But this is not the only problem used for illustrative purposes. The materials presented also raise other problems of concern to the legal order. The basic story is also interrupted frequently with "asides" in the form of Editors' essays, extracts from books, articles, government documents, etc., that serve to develop the broader implications of the materials being studied. In so doing, we have occasionally sacrificed a "logical" order in favor of one more consonant with the sequence of the student's curiosities. The Wisconsin materials, in all, occupy only about an eighth of the total pages.

A few examples may help to clarify our purpose. The judicial decisions which laid down the "fellow-servant" and "safe-place" rules in accident cases are used as a springboard for considering general problems of case analysis, professional ethics, methods of judicial reasoning, the theory of our system of precedents, the adversary nature of our system of litigation, and the role of the judge, jury, and advocate in the development of the common law. Presentation of the role of the judge in these accident cases is accompanied by discussion of the impact upon judicial decisions of political and economic factors, the process of fact determina-

v

tion, and the ever-present choice of ethical values confronting the judge as a maker of policy. So, too, elaboration of the role of custom and private contract in the accident cases is a prelude to analysis of the role of custom in contemporary problems, such as racial desegregation in public education, the relations between law and customary moral attitudes ("Can morality be legislated?"), and the general impact of "public policy" considerations upon the autonomy of private contract.

Similarly, consideration of the functioning of legislatures and administrative agencies in the industrial-accident area leads to probing some basic aspects of our system of legislation and of constitutional and administrative law—including the place of legislative investigations, private interest groups, the role of administrative agencies as organs of adjudication, and the function of judicial review.

Weaving together some fundamentals of public and private law, legal history, legal sociology, legal ethics, and legal philosophy will, we trust, furnish a much-needed perspective to the entering law student. In addition, students of history, politics, economics, sociology, philosophy, and social work may derive particular benefit from the materials, though of course, as John Stuart Mill and Woodrow Wilson among others have urged, anyone seeking a broad liberal education should have some acquaintance with the functioning of the legal system as a social institution.

If we have succeeded in our aim, these materials should give the student an appreciation of the process of legal or authoritative decision-making. We hasten to add that we are not attempting to apply the methods of the modern statistician or game theorist to our field. Chester I. Barnard, explaining the value of the single course in law he took at Harvard, stressed the fact that the study of law "showed how you come to a decision about action where action is required and lack of action would be worse than wrong action." [1] Law, he added, contained "the only body of literature up to within the last fifteen years that has had anything to do with the rationality of decisions for action." [2] Partisans of the new science of "decision-making" will bear with us if we retain this term, in Mr. Barnard's sense, to describe the subject-matter of this volume. It remains most apt. And the legal scholar may even claim priority of use.

Appreciation of the process of legal decision-making may thus benefit the student in ways transcending the particular subject-matter. It may increase the student's sensitivity to the possibility of opposing views and alternative solutions in all problem areas, and sharpen his sense of justice. His critical thinking also should be stimulated by experience with the techniques of comparative case analysis and statutory interpretation, which call for the jurist's essential art of perceiving the general significance of particulars and the particular application of generalities. As Morris R. Cohen said, law and science have a common ideal—"a system that corrects itself by the process of testing principles by their consequences, and conversely, judging actual consequences in the light of principles." [3]

[1] Quoted by Berman, A Report of a Conference on the Teaching of Law in the Liberal Arts Curriculum 22 (Foundation Press, 1956).

[2] Ibid.

[3] M. R. Cohen, Reason and Law 27 (1950).

The present work is the outgrowth of experience with teaching two generations of college upperclassmen and beginning law students. It retains the basic framework of the original Garrison and Hurst materials which were first published, in mimeographed form, in 1941, under the title, *Law in Society*. These materials were thoroughly revised by us in 1956 when the work was published in multilithed form, under its present title. We have again subjected the materials to extensive revision. We have expanded the notes and questions in order to help direct the student's attention to the crucial issues raised by the materials.

This revision has benefited from the suggestions of our colleague Professor William Gorham Rice, Professor Yosal Rogat of the Political Science Department, University of California at Berkeley, the teachers of social science and philosophy who used the earlier revised edition as the basis for their work in the Social Science Research Council Summer Research Training Institute on the Judicial Process held at the University of Wisconsin in 1958 and conducted jointly by Professor William M. Beaney of Princeton University and Professor Auerbach.

Throughout the book, the numbered footnotes from the quoted texts are reproduced without change of number.

CARL A. AUERBACH
SAMUEL MERMIN

Madison, Wisconsin
February 15, 1961

GENERAL OUTLINE

PART 1. The Judicial Process in Common Law Development

CONTENTS

PART 2

The Legislative Process and Its
Relation to the Judicial Process

PART 3

*The Administrative Process and
Its Relation to the Legislative
and Judicial Processes*

Friedmann, Law in a Changing Society (1960)

Llewellyn, The Common Law Tradition—Deciding Appeals (1960)

Symposium, Judicial Administration and the Common Man, 287 Annals of the American Academy of Political and Social Science 1-179 (1953)

Cohen and Cohen, Readings in Jurisprudence and Legal Philosophy, chap. 6 (1951)

Shartel, Our Legal System and How It Operates, chaps. 6 and 7 (1951)

Simpson and Stone, 2 Law and Society 1386-1437 (1949)

Stone, The Province and Function of Law, chap. VII (1946)

Garlan, Legal Realism and Justice (1941)

Radin, The Law as Logic and Experience (1940)

Symposium, The Status of the Rule of Judicial Precedent, 14 University of Cincinnati Law Review 203-355 (1940)

CHAPTER One

The STRUCTURE and PROCEDURE of COURTS

The following is intended to present, in bare outline, sufficient information about the structure of our courts and the procedure of courts in civil (non-criminal) cases to facilitate your reading of the cases. Procedure before administrative agencies will be considered in the part of this book dealing with the administrative process.

Section 1

The STRUCTURE of COURTS

A. *The State Courts*

The courts, taken together, make up one of the three great branches of government; and therefore, as is true of the legislative and executive branches, they are generally provided for in the state constitutions. Generally, the name and "jurisdiction" (i.e., extent of the power) of the principal courts are specified in the constitution. The legislature, by statute, fills in the details concerning the operation of the constitutionally provided courts and exercises the authority usually delegated to it by the constitution to set up additional courts (e.g., for particular municipalities or counties, or for particular purposes).

The fairly standard state pattern includes the following trial courts: (1) a court of *general jurisdiction*—typically called a "district" court or a "circuit" court (so named because in early days, trial judges would travel about "on circuit," holding court in different places)—to handle all cases not reserved for courts of special jurisdiction and sometimes with a jurisdiction overlapping that of the special courts; (2) courts of *special jurisdiction* to handle specified subject matters only—e.g., "probate courts" to take proof of the authenticity and validity of wills and supervise the administration of estates; "family courts" for domestic relations problems; and "juvenile courts"; (3) *small claims* courts (including those held in the office or home of the "Justice of the Peace") to handle lawsuits involving not more than a small amount, e.g., $200, with rather informal procedure.

All states have an *appellate* court of last resort, called the Supreme Court, with some deviations—e.g., in New York, it is called the Court of Appeals and in Connecticut, the Supreme Court of Errors. In most states it is the only court to which appeals may be taken from the trial courts of general

3

jurisdiction. But some states, like New York, have intermediate appellate courts whose decisions are final in some cases but may be appealed to the highest court in others. In cases reachable by the judicial power of the United States, as defined in Article III of the U.S. Constitution, it may also be possible to obtain review of the decisions of state courts of last resort by the U.S. Supreme Court.

B. *The Federal Courts*

Article III of the United States Constitution vests the "judicial power" of the United States "in one Supreme Court and in such inferior courts as the Congress may from time to time ordain and establish." The Constitution does not specify the number of judges to be appointed to the Supreme Court. This always has been decided by the Congress and the number has varied from time to time. The Supreme Court now consists of "a Chief Justice of the United States and eight associate justices," 28 U.S.C.A. 1.

The first Congress exercised its constitutional authority to establish courts "inferior" to the Supreme Court. The system of "inferior" courts has evolved over the years. Today there are federal trial courts in each State, known as *district* courts, and 11 *Courts of Appeals*—one for each of the 11 "Circuits" into which the country is divided. (These are in addition to certain specialized courts set up by the Congress, the courts of the District of Columbia, the territorial courts, the Court of Claims, the Tax Court, the Customs Court, the Court of Customs and Patent Appeals, and the Emergency Court of Appeals). There is at least one judicial district, and usually two or more, in each state. The number of judges in each district varies, depending on the volume of business. A trial is ordinarily presided over by a single judge, but there are situations in which three-judge district courts are required.

In order for a suit to be filed in the federal district court, it must come within one of the classes of cases to which the Constitution extends the federal judicial power. These classes are chiefly two—cases between citizens of different states ("diversity" jurisdiction) and cases involving questions under federal laws or under the United States Constitution ("federal question" jurisdiction). In addition, in most types of cases, a certain minimum amount of money must be involved (generally, $10,000).

Decisions of the district courts are appealable as a matter of right to the appropriate United States Court of Appeals, and in a few cases directly to the Supreme Court of the United States. While the number of Circuit Judges assigned to each circuit varies, court is normally held by three judges at a time. Most of the cases that reach the Supreme Court from the Courts of Appeals come by way of "certiorari." In such cases, the party who lost the case in the Court of Appeals is not given a right to appeal to the Supreme Court, but must persuade the Supreme Court that it should exercise its discretion and take the case for review because of some special importance it has. In only a small fraction of the cases is the petition for a writ of certiorari granted by the Court.

Section 2

PROCEDURE in CIVIL CASES

A. *The Parties to a Lawsuit*

The party who starts the lawsuit is known as the plaintiff, the person who complains; the party against whom the action is brought is known as the defendant. The party appealing is known as the appellant; the other party as the respondent or appellee (in some cases, "petitioner" and "respondent" respectively). Generally, in the published report of a case decided by an appellate court, the name of the plaintiff appears first and the name of the defendant next, regardless of which party becomes the appellant and which the respondent. Thus "Smith v. Brown, 60 Mo. 126" means that in volume 60 of the Reports of the Missouri Supreme Court, at page 126, appears the report of a case decided by that court on appeal, which was started in the trial court by one Smith as plaintiff against one Brown as defendant. But whether it was Smith who appealed, or Brown, you couldn't tell from the title; you would have to get out the volume and look at the case.

B. *The Commencement of an Action*

The job of courts is to settle the controversies which persons bring to them. Courts do not start lawsuits. They have no investigating staff and do not conduct investigations. They do not arrest criminals nor prosecute them. Their sole job is to decide the cases that are brought before them. To get the proceedings going, the plaintiff will have to do three things: he will have to pick the proper court, he will have to see that the defendant or his property is brought before it, and he will have to state his complaint and what he wants the court to do about it.

Picking the Court. This is a technical matter. The point is, as we have seen, that there are various courts with different powers and it is essential to get started in the one whose jurisdiction fits the case.

Catching the Defendant. Courts do not hear lawsuits for the fun of it. It must be clear before they start that if they finally do render a decision it can be enforced. And since the power of every court has territorial limits prescribed by the constitution or the legislature (such as the boundaries of a municipality, a county, a state, or a federal district), it is necessary to demonstrate at the outset that either the defendant or the property involved can be found within those limits, so that the judgment (that is, the court's ultimate decision) can be carried out. In criminal cases, if the defendant is an individual, he is caught quite literally, by being arrested within the territorial jurisdiction of the court, or by being extradited from some other territory. In civil cases the catching is normally symbolic. A "summons" is served on the defendant within the jurisdiction. This demonstrates that he could be arrested if necessary, and also gives him notice that a lawsuit has been started against him, and in what court and by whom. The summons does not, however, compel him to attend court. If it were a subpoena, he would have to obey it or be arrested. But the only result of disregarding a summons is that judgment is likely to be entered against him by default. If the summons cannot be served personally, because the defendant is not there, it may commonly be served by leaving it at his house, if he has one, in the jurisdiction. If he is a non-resident, and does not come into the state, the suit may be started if some property of the defendant can be found and seized, by a proceeding usually called attachment. If none of these things can be done, there may be statutes allowing the lawsuit to be begun in certain situations in which it seems reasonable to do so—e.g., if a non-resident is "doing business" in the state or is a motorist who became involved in an accident in the state. Fixing the precise limitations of the legal doctrines involved in the latter types of cases is beyond our present purposes.

Stating the Claim. The plaintiff must also tell the court and the defendant what it is that he complains of and what he wants the court to do about it. Conceivably this could be done by having the judge orally question the plaintiff in the presence of the defendant. But we have deemed it more expeditious to have the parties, in advance of the trial, attempt to narrow down the issues of fact and law on which they differ by exchanging written statements of their respective claims. This conforms, as we shall see, with our notions of the adversary nature of our litigation. The written statements that are exchanged by the parties are called pleadings. Thus the plaintiff is the first to state his claim and request for relief, in a written document now commonly called the complaint (formerly sometimes called declaration, bill, or petition).

C. *Pleadings and Other Procedures Prior to Trial*

Once the plaintiff has picked his court, caught the defendant or his property, and filed his complaint, the lawsuit is on its way and the next move is up to the defendant. The defendant will no doubt see his lawyer, who will find out from him what the row is all about. The claim may be admitted and paid up, or compromised. If so, the suit will be dismissed by the lawyers, and the court will hear no more about it. Or the claim may be allowed to go by default, in which case, after a certain time lapse, the court will enter judgment for the plaintiff. But if the claim is really in dispute, and is not compromised, the defendant's lawyer will have to file an "Answer."

The answer, too, is a formal document. It states the defendant's position in the controversy, and its first job is to state his position on the things which the plaintiff says in his complaint. If, for example, the complaint states that the defendant owes the plaintiff $1000 for money lent by plaintiff to defendant and not repaid by the defendant on the due date, the answer may deny that the defendant ever borrowed any money of the plaintiff, or it may say the loan is paid, or that it has been discharged by a proceeding in bankruptcy (under the Federal Bankruptcy Act, which permits insolvent debtors, upon surrendering their non-exempt property, to be freed or discharged from their debts by order of a U.S. district court). Whatever the answer says about the plaintiff's claim, it may assert some counterclaim which the defendant has against the plaintiff. Formerly, such additional pleadings could be filed by plaintiff and defendant as were necessary to raise at least one disputed issue of fact or law determinative of the result in the case. But in most states today the pleadings terminate with the answer or with the plaintiff's reply to the defendant's answer.

If the defendant thinks that the complaint fails to state a claim for relief, even though all the statements therein may be true, he may file *a motion to dismiss* the complaint. In many states today, the same objective is achieved by filing a *demurrer*. The demurrer or motion to dismiss may, if appropriate, be used by a plaintiff to attack the answer. This procedural device challenges the *legal* sufficiency of a pleading (i.e., on the temporary assumption that the *facts* alleged in the pleading are true) and the issues it raises will be decided by the judge, not the jury. The defendant need not necessarily choose between the two kinds of responses we have mentioned; he may combine them in one pleading, making his claims in the alternative. He could say: such and such facts alleged in the complaint are not true, but even if they are, the plaintiff's claim for relief is not legally valid.

In addition to the pleadings, other proceedings prior to trial are worth noting. To shorten the trial and reduce the element of surprise, various "discovery" devices are available, including the taking of "depositions" from expected opposing witnesses and asking the court to order production of certain documents by the opposing party. "Pre-trial conferences" of the judge with the opposing attorneys often narrow the issues of fact and law in real dispute, or lead to settlement of the case without trial.

D. *The Trial*

If the only issue on which the parties are in dispute is one of law, the dispute is submitted to the court by the process known as argument. The lawyers appear before the judge, argue the disputed point or points, and perhaps also submit written arguments called briefs. Witnesses and jury are not necessary because there are no disputed facts to pass on. The judge decides the matter himself, on the basis of the arguments and of his own knowledge and study. In most lawsuits, the main dispute disclosed by the proceedings before trial is on the facts. To resolve such a dispute there has to be a trial. This is the familiar courtroom process and consists chiefly of the presentation by the two competing sides of their views of the facts, through documents, physical exhibits, and the oral testimony of witnesses. The decision is based on what is thus offered. Neither the judge nor the jury is supposed to make any independent investigations.

The issues of fact are tried either before the judge alone, or before the judge and a jury, depending on the kind of case. The distinction, for the most part historical, is between cases "at common law" (in which event juries were generally used) or "in equity" (in which event juries were not used). For the present it is enough to say that, in general, in criminal cases, except very minor ones, there will always be a jury (unless, as often happens, the defendant expressly chooses to forgo, or in legal language "waives," a jury); and in civil cases there will be a jury if all the plaintiff wants is money damages (and if he asks for a jury, or the defendant does). But if the plaintiff seeks a remedy which, historically, only a court of equity could grant (e.g., a divorce, or the foreclosure of a mortgage, or an injunction to prevent some threatened wrong) the case is normally tried without a jury. Because of this peculiar and still surviving distinction between cases "at common law" and "in equity," it happens that many very important business cases are regularly tried and decided by a judge alone.

E. *The Judgment*

If the case is tried by a jury, the issues of fact are settled, within limits determined by the judge, by the jury's *verdict*. If it is tried without a jury, they are settled by the judge's findings. The verdict or findings will be followed by a judgment or order of the court. If the defendant has won, the judgment will read substantially as follows: "Adjudged: that the plaintiff recover nothing by this action." If the plaintiff has won, let us say, a judgment for money, it might read: "Adjudged: that the plaintiff recover from the defendant one thousand dollars ($1000.00) with interest thereon at 6% per annum from this date until paid." Other types of judgments will be discussed below and in Chapter 5.

F. *Appellate Review*

The judgment or order of the court is subject to appeal, or to be set aside or corrected by the court that entered it. The time within which either of these steps may be taken is strictly limited. When that time has passed and neither of these steps has been taken or the appellate court of last resort has upheld the judgment or order, it becomes final. The court will generally not hear applications to correct it. Even if the court became convinced, as a result of subsequent disclosures, that the case was wrongly decided, either in fact or law, while that might affect later similar cases between other people, it would not affect the judgment or order previously entered. For that controversy has been settled. "Nothing is settled until it is settled right" is not a maxim of judicial conduct, and for obvious, practical reasons.

When appeal is taken from the judgment or order of the trial court, the appellate court is given a condensed record of the proceedings in the trial court. It will usually contain the pleadings, verdict and judgment and so much of the proceedings at the trial as the attorneys for the parties regard as important. No testimony is heard by the appellate court; just argument by the lawyers as to the pros and cons of what the trial court decided. In addition, the lawyers are permitted to file *briefs* for the parties—printed documents containing legal arguments in much more detailed form than can be presented orally.

G. *Enforcement of the Judgment or Order; Distinction between Legal and Equitable Relief*

The simplest judgment to enforce is one for the defendant. No private or public person need do anything to enforce it, unless the plaintiff continues to assert the same claim or brings another lawsuit on it. If he does that, the defendant will simply plead the prior judgment in defense, and if it is really the same claim and between the same parties he will automatically prevail again. A judgment for the plaintiff for money is more difficult to enforce. You should notice that the court's judgment that the plaintiff recover money is not an order or command by the court to the defendant to pay the money; it is simply a declaration by the court that the law applicable to the facts obligates the defendant to pay the plaintiff a certain sum. The judge does not concern himself personally with seeing to it that the defendant satisfies his legal obligation to the plaintiff; he merely states what the obligation is.

How, then, does the plaintiff collect from the defendant if the defendant refuses to honor the judgment by paying up? He will get from the clerk of the court a writ (order) of "execution," which is a document directing the sheriff to satisfy the judgment out of the defendant's property. (*Note:* The *sheriff* is a county official, generally elected; he is an officer of the court, that is to say, he is subject to judicial supervision in the performance of his duties, which also include various police functions.) When the sheriff (or the United States Marshal in the federal system) receives the "execution" from the plaintiff he will proceed to take into his custody the property of the defendant which has not been exempted by statute from execution; to sell it at public auction; to pay the plaintiff's judgment out of the proceeds; and to remit the balance, if any, to the defendant. All the details of this process are regulated by statute. Judgments for the possession of specific property are enforced in much the same way. The sheriff takes away from the defendant the cow or the car which the defendant has improperly appropriated, and turns it over to the plaintiff. If the defendant has no property out of which the judgment can be satisfied, the plaintiff can do nothing unless and until the defendant acquires property; imprisonment for debt, which used to exist in England and to some extent in this country, has long since been abolished.

So far we have been talking about the enforcement of judgments declaring that the defendant does (or does not) owe the plaintiff money, or has (or has not) in his possession property which belongs to the plaintiff. Judgments of this sort, enforced in this way through the sheriff, were, historically, the product of the English "common law" courts and, subject to some exceptions which need not here be noted, they were the only kind of relief which these courts afforded.

You can see that money damages as a remedy would be ineffective in certain types of cases. Suppose a defendant is infringing a patent owned by the plaintiff and the plaintiff not only wants money damages but also that defendant stop the infringement. Or the defendant has contracted to sell a piece of land to the plaintiff but refuses to go through with the bargain and the plaintiff does not want a judgment for damages but the particular piece of land. Or the defendant is continually trespassing on the plaintiff's land and the plaintiff wants to stop him. To grant the relief sought in these cases, the court would have to forbid (enjoin) the defendant from infringing the plaintiff's patent or trespassing on the plaintiff's land or order the defendant to make out a deed for the land and deliver it to the plaintiff upon receipt of the purchase price. Historically, only the English equity court—the Court of Chancery—could grant this type of "equitable" relief. If the defendant refuses to obey the court's injunction, he will be punished by fine or imprisonment (generally by direction of the judge sitting without a jury) for being in "contempt of court." Since the court has given him a specific command, his disobedience is an affront to the dignity of the court and, indirectly, a challenge to the state; and therefore his disobedience has to be punished.

With the elimination of the dual system of common law and equity courts,* the word "judgment" has gradually come to have a larger meaning and to include equitable orders or decrees as well; and differences in certain procedures followed by the two sets of courts in affording their different remedies have also disappeared. But despite all this, the historical differences in the manner of enforcing the two kinds of relief and in the types of cases in which a plaintiff may obtain one rather than the other kind of remedy, still persist. We have already mentioned perhaps the most significant historical legacy bequeathed by the development of two types of remedies in two separate sets of courts: in the common law courts the facts were ascertained by juries; in the Court of Chancery the judge determined the facts without a jury. Hence today if the plaintiff seeks an ordinary common law judgment, usually either party may demand a jury trial; if the plaintiff seeks

* The English Judicature Act of 1873, as amended, merged the separate "common law" and "equity" courts into one High Court of Justice with three divisions—the King's (or Queen's) Bench Division, the Chancery Division, and the Probate, Divorce, and Admiralty Division. The old English system of strictly separate "common law" and "equity" courts never existed in many states in this country (including Wisconsin) or in the federal structure. But it survived in some states until quite recently.

equitable relief by way of an order or decree (whether or not it is loosely called a "judgment" under modern terminology) neither side is entitled to demand a jury. The constitutional guarantees, state and federal, of the right of trial by jury, do not extend to equity cases but only to common law cases.

So far, we have used the term "common law" merely to distinguish the system of law administered in the common law courts from that administered in the equity court. But we shall be using the term "common law" in this course in a wider sense, to refer to case law or judge-made law as distinguished from statute law or the law made by legislatures.

There is still a third sense of "common law" you will sometimes encounter: the Anglo-American legal system is referred to as a "common law" system in contrast to the "civil law" system derived from Roman law and prevailing today in the non-English-speaking Western world and in Scotland. (This sense of "civil law" is to be distinguished from "civil law" as used in the preceding pages to contrast with "criminal law".)

CHAPTER Two

CASE ANALYSIS—ASPECTS of the DEVELOPMENT of the FELLOW-SERVANT RULE

Section 1

INTRODUCTION to the STUDY of CASES

LLEWELLYN,* *THE BRAMBLE BUSH*
41-45 (Oceana ed., 1951)

Now the first thing you are to do with an opinion is to read it. Does this sound commonplace? Does this amuse you? There is no reason why it should amuse you. You have already read past seventeen expressions of whose meaning you have no conception. So hopeless is your ignorance of their meaning that you have no hard-edged memory of having seen unmeaning symbols on the page. You have applied to the court's opinion the reading technique that you use upon the Satevepost. Is a word unfamiliar? Read on that much more quickly! Onward and upward—we must not hold up the story.

That will not do. It is a pity, but you must learn to *read*. To read each word. To understand *each* word. You are outlanders in this country of the law. You do not know the speech. It must be learned. Like any other foreign tongue, it must be learned: by seeing words, by using them until they are familiar; meantime, by constant reference to the dictionary. What, dictionary? Tort, trespass, trover, plea, assumpsit, nisi prius, venire de novo, demurrer, joinder, traverse, abatement, general issue, tender, mandamus, certiorari, adverse possession, dependent relative revocation, and the rest. Law Latin, law French, aye, or law English—what do these strange terms mean to you? Can you rely upon the crumbs of language that remain from school? Does *cattle levant and couchant* mean *cows getting up and lying down?* Does *nisi prius* mean *unless before?* Or *traverse* mean *an upper gallery in a church?* I fear a dictionary is your only hope—a law dictionary—the one-volume

* Karl Nickerson Llewellyn, Professor of Law, University of Chicago Law School, taught at Yale during 1919-20, 1922-25, and at Columbia during 1925-51. He is an outstanding figure in the fields of jurisprudence and commercial law; was Chief Reporter in drafting the Uniform Commercial Code for the American Law Institute. The Bramble Bush is a collection of his lectures to Columbia law students, first published in 1930. He is the author of The Common Law Tradition—Deciding Appeals (1960) and co-author, with anthropologist E. A. Hoebel, of a study of primitive law, The Cheyenne Way (1942). —Editor

kind you can keep ready on your desk. Can you trust the dictionary, is it accurate, does it give you what you want? Of course not. No dictionary does. The life of words is in the using of them, in the wide network of their long associations, in the intangible something we denominate their feel. But the bare bones to work with the dictionary offers; and without those bare bones you may be sure the feel will never come.

The first thing to do with an opinion, then, is read it. The next thing is to get clear the actual decision, the judgment rendered. Who won, the plaintiff or defendant? And watch your step here. You are after in first instance the plaintiff and defendant *below,* in the trial court. In order to follow through what happened you must therefore first know the outcome *below;* else you do not see what was appealed from, nor by whom. You now follow through in order to see exactly what *further* judgment has been rendered on appeal. The stage is then cleared of form—although of course you do not yet know all that these forms mean, that they imply. You can turn now to what you want peculiarly to know. Given the actual judgments below and above as your indispensable framework—what has the case decided, and what can you derive from it as to what will be decided later?

You will be looking, in the opinion, or in the preliminary matter plus the opinion, for the following: a statement of the facts the court assumes; a statement of the precise way the question has come before the court—which includes what the plaintiff wanted below, and what the defendant did about it, the judgment below, and what the trial court did that is complained of; then the outcome on appeal, the judgment; and, finally the reasons this court gives for doing what it did. This does not look so bad. But it is much worse than it looks.

For all our cases are decided, all our opinions are written, all our predictions, all our arguments are made, on certain four assumptions. They are the first presuppositions of our study. They must be rutted into you till you can juggle with them standing on your head and in your sleep.

1) *The court must decide the dispute that is before it.* It cannot refuse because the job is hard, or dubious, or dangerous.

2) *The court can decide only the particular dispute which is before it.* When it speaks to that question it speaks ex cathedra, with authority, with finality, with an almost magic power. When it speaks to the question before it, it announces law, and if what it announces is new, it legislates, it makes the law. But when it speaks to any other question at all, it says mere words, which no man needs to follow. Are such words worthless? They are not. We know them as judicial dicta; when they are wholly off the point at issue we call them obiter dicta—words dropped along the road, wayside remarks. Yet even wayside remarks shed light on the remarker. They may be very useful in the future to him, or to us. But he will not feel bound to them, as to his ex cathedra utterance. They came not hallowed by a Delphic frenzy. He may be slow to change them; but not so slow as in the other case.

3) *The court can decide the particular dispute only according to a general rule which covers a whole class of like disputes.* Our legal theory does not admit of single

decisions standing on their own. If judges are free, are indeed forced, to decide new cases for which there is no rule, they must at least make a new rule as they decide. So far, good. But how wide, or how narrow, is the general rule in this particular case? That is a troublesome matter. The practice of our case-law, however, is I think fairly stated thus: it pays to be suspicious of general rules which look too wide; it pays to go slow in feeling *certain* that a wide rule has been laid down at all, or that, if seemingly laid down, it will be followed. For there is a fourth accepted canon:

4) *Everything, everything, everything, big or small, a judge may say in an opinion, is to be read with primary reference to the particular dispute, the particular question before him.* You are not to think that the words mean what they might if they stood alone. You are to have your eye on the case in hand, and to learn how to interpret all that has been said *merely* as a reason for deciding *that* case *that* way. . . .

Now why these canons? The first, I take it, goes back to the primary purpose of law. If the job is in first instance to settle disputes which do not otherwise get settled, then the only way to do it is to do it. And it will not matter so much *how* it is done, in a baffling instance, so long as it is done at all.

The third, that cases must be decided according to a general rule, goes back in origin less to purpose than to superstition. As long as law was felt as something ordained of God, or even as something inherently right in the order of nature, the judge was to be regarded as a mouthpiece, not as a creator; and a mouthpiece of the general, who but made clear an application to the particular. Else he broke faith, else he was arbitrary, and either biased or corrupt. Moreover, justice demands, wherever that concept is found, that like men be treated alike in like conditions. Why, I do not know; the fact is given. That calls for general rules, and for their even application. So, too, the "separation of powers" comes in powerfully to urge that general rules are made by the Legislature or the system, not the judges, and that the judge has but to act *according* to the general rules there are. Finally, a philosophy even of expediency will urge the same. Whatever may be the need of shaping decision to individual cases in the juvenile court, or in the court of domestic relations, or in a business man's tribunal for commercial cases—still, when the supreme court of a state speaks, it speaks first to clear up a point of general interest. And the responsibility for formulating general policy forces a wider survey, a more thorough study of the policies involved. So, too, we gain an added guarantee against either sentimentalism or influence in individual cases. And, what is not to be disregarded, we fit with the common notion of what justice calls for. . . .

Back, if I may now, to the why of the two canons I have left: that the court *can* decide only the particular dispute before it; that all that is said is to be read with eyes on that dispute. Why these? I do believe, gentlemen, that here we have as fine a deposit of slow-growing wisdom as ever has been laid down through the centuries by the unthinking social sea. Here, hardened into institutions, carved out and given line by rationale. What is this wisdom? Look to your own discussion, look to any argument. You know where you would go. You reach, at random if hurried, more carefully if not, for a foundation, for a major premise. But never for itself. Its interest lies in leading to the conclusion you are headed for. You shape its words, its content, to an end decreed. More, with your mind upon your object you use words, you bring in illustrations, you deploy and advance and concentrate again. When you have done, you have said much you did not mean. You did not mean, that is, *except* in reference to your point. You have brought generalization up, and discharged it at your goal; all, in the heat of argument, were over-stated. None would you stand to, if your opponent should urge them to *another* issue.

So with the judge. Nay, more so with the judge. He is not merely human, as are you. He is, as well, a lawyer; which you, yet, are not. A lawyer, and as such skilled in manipulating the resources of persuasion at his hand. A lawyer, and as such prone without thought to twist analogies, and rules, and instances, to his conclusion. A lawyer, and as such peculiarly prone to disregard the implications which do not bear directly on his case.

More, as a practiced exponent of the art of exposition, he has learned that one must prepare the way for argument. You set the mood, the tone, you lay the intellectual foundation—all with the case in mind, with the conclusion—all, because those who hear you also have the case in mind, without the niggling criticism which may later follow. You wind up, as a pitcher will wind up—and as in the pitcher's case, it has been known to be intentionally misleading.

With this it should be clear, then, why our canons thunder. Why we create a class of dicta, of unnecessary words, which later readers, their minds now on quite other cases, can mark off as not quite essential to the argument. Why we create a class of *obiter dicta,* the wilder flailings of the pitcher's arms, the wilder motions of his gum-ruminant jaws. Why we set about, as our job, to crack the kernel from the nut, to find the true rule the case in fact decides: the *rule of the case.* . . .

Section 2

EARLY CASES on the FELLOW-SERVANT RULE

PRIESTLEY v. FOWLER
3 Mees. & Wels. 1 (Exchequer, 1837)

CASE.—The declaration stated that the plaintiff was a servant of the defendant in his trade of a butcher; that the defendant had desired and directed the plaintiff, so being his servant, to go with and take certain goods of the defendant's, in a certain van of the defendant then used by him, and conducted by another of his servants, in carrying goods for hire upon a certain journey; that the plaintiff, in pursuance of such desire and direction, accordingly commenced and was proceeding *and being carried and conveyed by the said van,* with the said goods; and it became the duty of the defendant, on that occasion, to use due and proper care that the said van should be in a proper state of repair, that it should not be overloaded, and that the plaintiff should be safely and securely carried thereby; nevertheless, the defendant did not use proper care that the van should be in a sufficient state of repair, or that it should not be overloaded, or that the plaintiff should be safely and securely carried thereby, in consequence of the neglect of all and each of which duties the van gave way and broke down, and the plaintiff was thrown with violence to the ground, and his thigh was thereby fractured, &c. Plea, not guilty.

At the trial before PARK, J., at the Lincolnshire Summer Assizes, 1836, the plaintiff, having given evidence to show that the injury arose from the overloading of the van, and that it was so loaded with the defendant's knowledge, had a verdict for 100 £. In the following Michaelmas Term, ADAMS, Serjt., obtained a rule to show cause why the judgment should not be arrested, on the ground that the defendant was not liable in law, under the circumstances stated in the declaration. In Hilary Term,

GOULBURN, Serjt., and N. R. CLARKE, showed cause. . . .

ADAMS, Serjt., contra. . . . [The reporters' statement of the arguments of counsel is omitted.]

The judgment of the Court was now delivered by

LORD ABINGER, C. B.—This was a motion in arrest of judgment, after verdict for the plaintiff, upon the insufficiency of the declaration. [His lordship stated the declaration.] It has been objected to this declaration, that it contains no premises from which the duty of the defendant, as therein alleged, can be inferred in law; or, in other words, that from the mere relation of master and servant no contract, and therefore no duty, can be implied on the part of the master to cause the servant to be safely and securely carried, or to make the master liable for damage to the servant, arising from any vice or imperfection, unknown to the master, in the carriage, or in the mode of loading and conducting it. For, as the declaration contains no charge that the defendant knew any of the defects mentioned, the Court is not called upon to decide how far such knowledge on his part of a defect unknown to the servant, would make him liable.

It is admitted that there is no precedent for the present action by a servant against a master. We are therefore to decide the question upon general principles, and in doing so we are at liberty to look at the consequences of a decision the one way or the other.

If the master be liable to the servant in this action, the principle of that liability will be found to carry us to an alarming extent. He who is responsible by his general duty, or by the terms of his contract, for all the consequences of negligence in a matter in which he is the principal, is responsible for the negligence of all his inferior agents. If the owner of the carriage is therefore responsible for the sufficiency of his carriage to his servant, he is responsible for the negligence of his coach-maker, or his harness-maker, or his coachman. The footman, therefore, who rides behind the carriage, may have an action against his master for a defect in the carriage, owing to the negligence of the coachmaker, or for a defect in the harness arising from the negligence of the harness-maker, or for drunkenness, neglect, or want of skill in the coachman; nor is there any reason why the principle should not, if applicable in this class of cases, extend to many others. The master, for example, would be liable to the servant for the negligence of the chambermaid, for putting him into a damp bed; for that of the upholsterer, for sending in a crazy bedstead, whereby he was made to fall down while asleep and injure himself; for the negligence of the cook, in not properly cleaning the copper vessels used in the kitchen: of the butcher, in supplying the family with meat of a quality injurious to the health; of the builder, for a defect in the foundation of the house, whereby it fell, and injured both the master and the servant by the ruins.

The inconvenience, not to say the absurdity of these consequences, affords a sufficient argument against the application of this principle to the present case. But, in truth, the mere relation of the master and the servant never can imply an obligation on the part of the master to take more care of the servant than he may reasonably be expected to do of himself. He is, no doubt, bound to provide for the safety of his servant in the course of his employment, to the best of his judgment, information, and belief. The servant is not bound to risk his safety in the service of his master, and may, if he thinks fit, decline any service in which he reasonably apprehends injury to himself: and in most of the cases in which danger may be incurred, if not in all, he is just as likely to be acquainted with the probability and extent of it as the master. In that sort of employment, especially, which is described in the declaration in this case, the plaintiff must have known as well as his master, and probably better, whether the van was sufficient, whether it was overloaded, and whether it was likely to carry him safely. In fact, to allow this sort of action to prevail would be an encouragement to the servant to omit that diligence and caution which he is in duty bound to exercise on the behalf of his master, to protect him against the misconduct or negligence of others who serve him, and which diligence and caution, while they protect the master, are a much better security against any injury the servant may sustain by the negligence of others engaged under the same master, than any recourse against his master for damages could possibly afford.

We are therefore of opinion that the judgment ought to be arrested. Rule absolute.

NOTES AND QUESTIONS

1. The heading of the case: The phrase "3 Mees. & Wels. 1" refers to the names of the persons who published the report of the court's decision; this decision, i.e., is from volume three, page one, of the Reports published by two London barristers named Meeson and Welsby. The word "Exchequer" refers to the fact that the decision reported was rendered by the Court of Exchequer; and 1837 is the year of decision. All of this data would be included, together with the names of the parties, to make up the "citation" of this case, and all of it would be given by a lawyer who wished to refer a court to this decision.

2. The first two paragraphs reprinted from the case of Priestley v. Fowler are written by the Reporters, Meeson and Welsby, and not by the court, and undertake to give a concise statement of how the lawsuit arises. The word "Case" at the outset of the paragraph identifies the form of writ by which the plaintiff began this lawsuit—a writ of "trespass on the case." The "declaration" is the name given at common law to the plaintiff's complaint. The symbol "&c" (et cetera) at the end of the first paragraph is inserted by the Reporters to indicate that the declaration concluded with certain standard assertions and claims to relief by plaintiff, so familiar to lawyers that the Report need

not reproduce them. The phrase "Plea, not guilty" refers to the answer which defendant made to plaintiff's declaration; this plea amounted to a denial that the facts were as plaintiff claimed them to be. Nowadays, the "not guilty" form of plea would be confined to criminal cases. The reference to "the trial before Park, J." shows that there has been a trial of the facts in this lawsuit already before Mr. Justice Park, sitting on circuit, in Lincolnshire. The term "assizes" (Latin, "assideo," to sit together) was the name given to courts held in the country districts outside of London by judges of the three common law courts sent out from Westminster, where the courts sat, to receive indictments presented by grand juries of the localities and try civil and criminal cases with the aid of local juries. The common law courts sat on the bench en banc, in Westminster during four different periods or terms of the year—The Easter, Trinity, Michaelmas and Hilary Terms. Each of the Terms lasted for only a few weeks. The full bench of each court determined all questions within its province arising prior to as well as subsequent to the actual trial (e.g. questions of the sufficiency of the pleadings; whether judgment should be arrested) but not questions which arose during the course of the trial (e.g. admissibility of evidence). Priestley v. Fowler presumably was heard by the full membership of the Court of Exchequer, but the opinion of the court is stated by but one of its members, Chief Baron Lord Abinger.

Adams was the lawyer appearing for the defendant; Goulburn and Clarke the lawyers for the plaintiff; the name "Serjeant" indicates a high rank as barrister.

3. The procedure of bringing the case before the Court of Exchequer: ". . . Adams, Serjt., obtained a rule to show cause why the judgment should not be arrested. . . ." After the jury, at the trial of the facts before Park, J., on circuit, had given verdict for plaintiff, Serjeant Adams, as counsel for defendant, obtained from the full Court of Exchequer an order directed to the plaintiff to appear before the full court and show why he was entitled, as a matter of law, to have judgment entered on the verdict which he had obtained. This court order is the "rule" referred to; when the full court decides in defendant's favor, it makes the rule "absolute," i.e., it enters an unconditional order that the judgment be arrested. If the decision had been for plaintiff, the "rule" would have been recorded as "refused" or "discharged." The significance of arresting judgment is that before the plaintiff could call upon the proper officials to compel defendant to pay, he must have a formal order—the judgment—entered by the court on its records on the basis of the jury's verdict. In the original Report, the Reporters give their summary of the arguments made before the Court of Exchequer by counsel; these summaries are here omitted.

4. Following is a partial summary of common law tort doctrine prevailing at the time that Priestley v. Fowler was decided:

a. *General basis of tort liability:* a defendant was held liable in tort for damages (1) because defendant intentionally inflicted unjustifiable harm upon plaintiff, or (2) because defendant unintentionally inflicted harm upon plaintiff in circumstances in which defendant was deemed at fault; but (3) generally, defendant was not liable to plaintiff for unintentional harm inflicted without fault on the part of defendant. (Such an "absolute" liability was imposed in a few, exceptional situations.)

b. *Nature of liability for unintentional harm:* (1) the "fault" which rendered defendant liable to plaintiff because of harm unintentionally inflicted by defendant on plaintiff consisted in defendant's having behaved in a way in which a reasonable, prudent man would not have behaved in the circumstances; defendant, i.e., was deemed to have been guilty of "negligence" if his conduct fell below the standard of reasonable and prudent conduct in the situation involved; (2) defendant was liable, however, only if his negligence was the cause of the harm done to plaintiff.

c. *Liability of a man for the conduct of another:* there were various social relationships to which the courts attached the consequence that one party to the relation was legally responsible for the behavior of another party to the relation. Before Priestley v. Fowler was decided, it was established that a master was liable to a third person injured by the negligence of the master's servant, in the course of the employment. Put in more general terms, a principal was liable to third persons for negligent conduct of the principal's agent done within the scope of the agency. An "agent" or "servant" was one acting under the control and probably under the pay of another and for the benefit of that other, who was the "master" or "principal." This liability of principal for certain conduct of the agent is often referred to as the doctrine of respondeat superior. ("Let the principal be responsible.")

d. *Defenses to an action for negligent injury:* though plaintiff could show that defendant had negligently inflicted harm on plaintiff, defendant might yet defeat plaintiff's suit by showing certain defenses, the most important of which were (1) contributory negligence: i.e., that plaintiff had himself been guilty of negligent conduct in the situation which contributed to cause the injury; this was a complete defense against plaintiff's action and did not merely operate to reduce the amount of damages plaintiff might recover; (2) assumption of risk: i.e., plaintiff might not recover if it were shown that the injury arose out of a risk in the situation of which plaintiff in fact knew or ought to have known.

e. *Defenses applicable to action against principal for conduct of his agent:* the defenses of contributory negligence and assumption of risk could similarly be invoked to bar recovery by a third person against a principal for injury inflicted on the third person by the negligence of the principal's agent.

5. The Court of Exchequer, in Priestley v. Fowler, rendered a decision as to the legal rights and duties of the parties, on the assumption that certain facts existed. How did the Court of Exchequer discover what were the facts giving rise to plaintiff's claim against defendant? Did the Court of Exchequer make any independent effort of its own to find out what were the facts of the situation involved?

6. Why did the court say that it was not called upon to decide whether the defendant's knowledge that the van was overloaded made him liable? Was the court unfair to the plaintiff in ignoring the evidence at the trial? In interpreting the declaration?

7. What general restrictions upon a court's functioning do the answers to questions 5 and 6 suggest? Were these restrictions violated when the court made its assertions as to the "consequences" of a decision for the plaintiff? Were these restrictions violated when the court stated that the master is "no doubt bound to provide for the safety of his servant . . . to the best of his judgment, information and belief?"

8. Does the decision determine when an employer *is* liable to his injured servant or when he is *not* liable? Why?

9. Where did the rule applied in this case come from?

10. Are the following statements of Lord Abinger statements of law or of fact? (a) "If the master be liable to the servant in this action, the principle of that liability will be found to carry us to an alarming extent." (b) "He is, no doubt, bound to provide for the safety of his servant in the course of his employment, to the best of his judgment, information and belief." (c) "The servant is not bound to risk his safety in the service of his master, and may, if he thinks fit, decline any service in which he reasonably apprehends injury to himself: and in most of the cases in which danger may be incurred, if not in all, he is just as likely to be acquainted with the probability and extent of it as the master." (d) ". . . to allow this sort of action to prevail would be an encouragement to the servant to omit that diligence and caution which he is in duty bound to exercise on behalf of his master, to protect him against the misconduct or negligence of others who serve him. . . ." etc.

11. From what sources of information does the court obtain the bases for the statements quoted in the preceding note? Consider the statements separately. Do you agree with them? Are there any sources today that might assist a court in ascertaining the validity of these statements?

12. Between 1825 and the end of 1835, 54 railway acts of all sorts had been passed by Parliament. By September 1838, about 500 miles of operating public locomotive railway existed, of which one line, the London and Birmingham, accounted for nearly one-half. In 1836-7, 39 more railway bills for new lines in Great Britain received the royal assent, besides a number for Ireland. There was speculative growth and temporary collapse, and fewer railway acts passed for a time after 1838. But the promotions of 1836-7 added over a thousand miles to the English railroads, and in June 1843 there were some 1,900 miles of line open. The railroads operating in 1838 employed at the most about 9,000 men; in 1849 about 56,000 were employed on some 5,000 miles in England and Ireland. This was already a large figure, comparable with the total employment of many old-established industries. Much larger numbers were employed on railroad construction during the period.

At once effect and cause, railway development coincided with an unprecedented development of metallurgy and mining, with annual production rising from 650,000-700,000 tons of iron a year in 1830 to 1,000,000 tons in 1835 and 1,500,000 tons in 1840-1. The blast furnace was growing in size, efficiency and output; from a probable 16,000,000 tons for Great Britain in 1816 to probably 30,000,000 tons in 1836 and 44,000,000 tons in 1846.

In 1834-1835, the cotton industry—the outstanding industrial user of steam power—used 30,000 h.p. of steam and 10,000 h.p. of water. This was on the eve of very rapid development; by 1838 over 15,000 more horsepower of steam had been or were being added in Lancashire and Cheshire alone. Economic difficulties slowed down development, and the power average per firm was still low even in 1850. The increase in output capacity was greater, however, than the increase in power employed, for textile machinery was speeded up greatly between 1830 and 1850. Steam power was much less important in non-textile industries, such as milling and woodworking. In the latter, the circular saw and planing machine did not begin to make real headway until the '30s, and then only in the larger urban works.

This was a period of the growth of cities and towns. The population as a whole was growing fast, and the railways were a powerful influence for urban growth. There was an actual addition to the population of towns with 20,000 inhabitants and upwards in Great Britain; the increase had been 1,100,000 between 1821 and 1831; between 1831 and 1841 it amounted to 1,270,000, and between 1841 and 1851 to no less than 1,800,000.

These data are taken from 1 Clapham, An Economic History of Modern Britain (2d ed. 1930) 387-390, 406, 425, 428, 431, 442-445, 536. Do they verify the picture of 1837 English life suggested by Lord Abinger's opinion? Are they relevant to the legal issue raised by Priestley v. Fowler? What other information might be relevant?

MURRAY v. SOUTH CAROLINA RAILROAD CO.
1 McM. 385 (S.C., 1841)

[The reporter's statement of the case and reprint of the argument of counsel is omitted.—Editor]

Curia, per EVANS, J. In the consideration of the question involved in this case, I shall assume that the verdict established the fact that the plaintiff's injury was the effect of the negligence of the engineer, and then the question arises whether the railroad company is liable to one servant for an injury arising from the negligence of another servant. The business of the company is the transportation of goods and passengers. Its liability in these respects, is, in general, well defined and understood by the profession; and if the plaintiff's case came within any of the principles applicable to these cases, we should have no difficulty in deciding it. The application of steam power to transportation on railroads is of recent origin, but the principle by which the liability of a carrier is fixed and ascertained, is as old as the law itself. There is nothing in the fact that the defendant is a corporation, except that of necessity it must act altogether by agents. The liability is precisely the same as if the defendant was an individual acting by the agency of others. The principle is the same, whether you apply it to a railroad, a steamboat, a wagon, a stage coach, or a ship. If this plaintiff is entitled to recover, I can see no reason why the owner of any of the above modes of conveyance should not be liable under the same circumstances. If the owner of a wagon should employ two men, one to drive and the other to load, and either of them should so negligently perform his work as to injure the other, the owner of the wagon would be liable. The principle will extend to all the vocations of life wherein more than one person is employed to effect a single object; and a new class of liabilities would arise, which I do not think has ever heretofore been supposed to exist. It is admitted, no case like the present has been found, nor is there any precedent suited to the plaintiff's case, unless he stands in the relation of a passenger to the company. In this point of view, his counsel has chosen to regard him, for I understand the declaration alleges he was a passenger. Now, a passenger is everywhere spoken of as one who pays for transportation. In all the operations necessary for this, he is passive. The moment he becomes an operator, for then his character is changed, he becomes the servant of the company, and not its passenger. It would be a confusion of terms so to regard him. He is no more a passenger than a sailor or a stage driver. There is nothing in the definition of bailment, or the classification of the different kinds of liability growing out of that relation, which applies to the plaintiff's case, and if he is entitled to recover, it must be on principles which apply equally to all operations of life in which agents are employed. There is no question that, in general, the principal is liable for the acts of the agent, performed in the execution of his agency, or in and about the business of his principal. Thus, the owners of a railroad would be liable to passengers for an injury sustained by the negligence of any of its servants, superior or subordinate, because it is implied in the undertaking to carry, not only that the road and cars are good, but that the servants employed are competent and will perform their duty. For the loss of goods, the law annexes a still greater responsibility. So, also, if one employ an agent to execute any work whereby an injury may result to a stranger, the law requires it to be done with care, and if a stranger sustain an injury, his principal is liable, as was decided in O'Connel v. Strong, (Dud. Rep. 265). But the plaintiff is neither a passenger nor a stranger, and if he can recover, it must be in his hermaphrodite character as a passenger fireman. In the cases above enumerated, the principal is represented by the agent, and unless he is liable, the great operations of life cannot be carried on—no man would have adequate security for his person or his property. The owner of goods would not trust them on a railroad, or a steamboat, if his only security was the liability of the mere servants employed. No passenger would commit his safety to a railroad, steamboat, or stage coach, if, in case of injury, he could look to none but the agents usually employed about these modes of transportation. So, also, no man would have any guarantee for the security of his property, if his only remedy for negligence was the irresponsible or insolvent agents which another might employ. In all these, and similar cases, the reasons of the liability of the principal are clear, and the law books are full of cases or precedents which apply to them; but it is not so with the plaintiff's case; there is neither authority nor precedent for it.

It was said, in the argument, that if the engineer had been the owner of the road, he would have been liable. Of this I apprehend there would have been no doubt, but then his liability would have arisen, not from his being the owner, but because the injury arose from his own act. That he is now liable, seems to me to admit of no doubt. But it by no means follows as a consequence, that because he is liable, those who employ him are liable also. One acting as agent may subject himself to liability in a variety of cases, for which his principal would not be liable; and this may be as well in cases of contract as in cases of tort. The extent of the liability of the principal, for the acts of the agent, can, in general, be readily ascertained from the object of the contract, and the relative position of the parties. A passenger desires to be transported from one place to another; the carrier undertakes to do this, and is liable if he fails. It is wholly immaterial by whose default the injury resulted. There has been a breach of the contract, and he has a right to look to him with whom his contract was made. With the plaintiff, the defendants contracted to pay hire for his services. Is it incident to this contract that the company should guarantee him against the negligence of his co-servants? It is admitted he takes upon himself the ordinary risks of his vocation; why not the extraordinary ones? Neither are within his contract—and I can see no reason for adding this to the already known and acknowledged liability of a carrier, without a single case or precedent to sustain it. The engineer no more represents the company than the plaintiff. Each in his several department represents his principal. The regular movement of the train of cars to its destination is the result of the ordinary performance, by each, of his several duties. If the fireman neglects his part, the engine stands still for want of steam; if the engineer neglects his, everything runs to riot and disaster. It seems to me, it is, on the part of the several agents, a joint undertaking, where each one stipulates for the performance of his several part. They are not liable to the company for the conduct of each other, nor is the company liable to one for the misconduct of another; and, as a general rule, I would say, that where there was no fault in the owner, he would be liable only for wages to his servants; and so far has this doctrine been carried, that in the case of seamen, even wages are forfeited if the vessel be lost, and no freight earned.

In the above observations, I have endeavored to confine myself strictly to the case before the Court. It is not intended to pre-judge other questions which may arise between the company and its servants; nor do I mean to say, that a case may not occur where the owner, whether an individual or company, will be liable for the acts of one agent to another; but then it must be in such cases as where the owner employs unfit and improper persons as agents, by whose ignorance or folly another is injured. Upon such a case it will be time enough to express an opinion when it arises. The present is not such a case. The engineer, according to the evidence was competent, though he may have been rash in the particular instance in which the plaintiff's injury was sustained. He was known to the plaintiff as well as to the company, for it appears by the report that he selected the engineer under whom he was willing or prepared to serve. It seems to me the plaintiff is not, therefore, entitled to retain his verdict, and a motion for a new trial is granted.

RICHARDSON, EARLE, BUTLER, HARPER, DUNKIN, JJ. and CC., concurred.

JOHNSON, Chancellor. I concur in this opinion, and will only add a word in illustration of my own views of the question.

The foundation of all legal liability is the omission to do some act which the law commands, the commission of some act which the law prohibits, or the violation of some contract by which the party is injured. There is no law regulating the relative duties of the owners of a steam car, and the persons employed by them to conduct it. The liability, if any attaches, must therefore arise out of contract. What was the contract between these parties? The plaintiff, in consideration that the defendants would pay him so much money, undertook to perform the service of fireman on the train. This is all that is expressed. Is there anything more implied? Assuming that the injury done was in consequence of the negligence of the engineer, the defendants would not be liable, unless they undertook to answer for his diligence and skill. Is that implied? I think not. The law never implies an obligation in relation to a matter about which the parties are or may, with proper diligence, be equally informed. No one will ever be presumed to undertake for that which a common observer would at once know was not true. The common case of the warranty of the soundness of a horse, notoriously blind, may be put in illustration. The warranty does not extend to the goodness of the eyes, because the purchaser knew or might have known, with proper care, that they were defective.

Now the plaintiff knew that he was not to conduct the train alone. He knew that he was to be placed under the control of the engineer. He knew that the employment in which he was engaged was perilous, and that its success was dependent on the common efforts of all the hands; and, with proper diligence and prudence, he might have been as well, and it does not follow that he might not have been better, informed than the defendants, about the fitness and security of all the appointments connected with the train. If he was not, it was his own want of prudence, for which defendants are not responsible. If he was he will be presumed to have undertaken to meet all the perils incident to the employment.

There is not the least analogy between this case and that of common carriers of goods or transporters of persons. They are liable in respect to the price paid. Not so here. The plaintiff paid nothing for his transportation; on the contrary, he was to be paid for his labor, and for the perils to which he was exposed, as incident to his employment. No prudent man would engage in any perilous employment, unless seduced by greater wages than he could earn in a pursuit unattended by any unusual danger.

O'NEALL, J., dissenting. This case was tried by myself, and although, had I been on the jury, I should have found for the defendants, yet there were certainly facts in the evidence which might have led another to a different conclusion; and, therefore, I am not disposed to disturb the verdict. This makes it necessary to consider the legal doctrine which I laid down to the jury.

In substance, I held, that if the injury to the plaintiff resulted from the negligence of the engineer, then the plaintiff was entitled to recover. This doctrine, a large majority of my brethren think erroneous, and however much deference is due to their opinions, yet, as I consider them to be wrong, I think it my duty to state my own views.

This case is one of the first arising out of the conveyance of human beings by locomotives on railroads. It goes beyond the ordinary case of a passenger, and presents a claim on the part of a hired servant, against his employers, for an injury sustained in their service. If it arose out of any of the old-fashioned modes of conveyance, managed by the defendants themselves, could there be a doubt that they would be liable, if the injury resulted from negligence? Take the case of a stage coach, driven by the owner, and let it be supposed that the plaintiff was hired as a guard, and that he was injured in that employment, by the careless driving of the defendant, who would hesitate to say that he was entitled to recover? No one who had a proper regard to legal principles.

Is there any distinction in law as to the effect which the employment of the plaintiff is to have, in the different kinds of service in which he may engage? I think there is none. If Mr. Tupper, the able and efficient officer of the company, had, in person, managed the engine, and the plaintiff had been injured by his carelessness, I would most respectfully ask, how could it be pretended that the company was not liable?

I admit here, once and for all, that the plaintiff, like any other servant, took, as consequence of his contract, the usual and ordinary risks of his employment. What is meant by this? No more than that he could not claim for an injury, against which the ordinary prudence of his employers, their agents or himself, could provide. Whenever negligence is made out as the cause of injury, it does not result from the ordinary risks of employment.

How far are the defendants liable for the acts of the engineer? In the language used in Bacon's Abridgment, Tit., Master and Servant, letter R., "it is highly reasonable that they should answer for such substitute, at least *civiliter;* and that his acts, being pursuant to the authority given him, should be deemed the acts of the master." Now, to this authority, it will not do to say the defendants did not authorize the engineer to run his engine so carelessly as to injure the plaintiff. They put him in command of it, and authorized him with it to run the road. If, in the doing of this act, which is according to their authority, he acts negligently, then they are liable for the consequences, for they result from the doing of their business, by one then employed by them. The cases of Drayton ads. Moore, and Parker & Co. vs. Gordon, (Dudley's Rep. 268), and of O'Connell vs. Strong, (Ib. 265), are full to this point. In ordinary cases, this would not be questioned. But it is supposed that this case is not governed by the ordinary rules applicable to cases of liability, arising out of the relation of master and servant. I am at a loss to conceive any just reason for this notion. The law, it seems to me, is to be regarded as a general science, applicable to every case coming within the letter or the reason of the rule. Where it is within neither, it becomes an exception to it. It is only necessary to state this case, to see that it is within both the letter and reason of the rule; for the defendants employ the plaintiff to act under the command of another of their servants. In such a case, the servant in command is in the place of the employers. When they hire another to engage in a service, where neither his own care nor prudence can shield him from injury, which may arise from the act of another of their agents, having the control of him, the question of their liability depends upon the care used by such superior agent. . . .

But, it is said, it would be impolitic to make the defendants liable for any injury accruing to a fireman, from the neglect of the engineer. This would be worth inquiring into with great care in the Legislature; but, in a Court, I think we have nothing to do with the policy of a case; the law of it is our guide. But if we are to look to the policy, then I should argue that the more liability imposed on the railroad company, the more care and prudence would be thereby elicited. This result is what the community desires. For it secures life and property, committed to their care.

I think the motion ought to be dismissed.

Gantt, J., concurred.

[J. Johnston, Ch., concurred in the dissent of O'Neall, J., in a dissenting opinion which is here omitted.—Editor]

NOTES

1. *The opinions in the case:* The opinion of Evans, J., is that of the majority of the court ("*Curia, per* Evans, J." means "The court, by Evans, J.,"), the concurrence of the other members being explicitly noted at the end of the opinion. Chancellor Johnson's separate opinion does not represent disagreement with the result voted for by the majority of the judges, but merely his own analysis of the proper reasons for the decision. Such separate opinions of concurrence are more common in English than in American courts. O'Neall and Gantt, JJ., and J. Johnston, Ch., disagree with the result reached by the majority; two of the three express their reasons in dissenting opinions.

2. *The designations of the judges:* This decision is rendered on an appeal to the Court of Errors of South Carolina. That court was then composed of judges sitting at law and chancellors sitting in equity. These judges presided over lower courts in addition to meeting together to form the Court of Errors; it will be noted that O'Neall, J., had been the presiding judge in this case at the trial below. Today the membership of trial and appellate courts is almost invariably distinct.

FARWELL v. THE BOSTON AND WORCESTER RAILROAD CORPORATION
4 Metc. 49 (Mass., 1842)

[The Reporter's statement of the pleadings is omitted. The excerpts given under the names of Messrs. Loring and Fletcher & Morey are the Reporter's summary of portions of the arguments made by those gentlemen as counsel in the case.— Editor]

* * *

The case was submitted to the court on the following facts agreed by the parties:

"The plaintiff was employed by the defendants, in 1835, as an engineer, and went at first with the merchandise cars, and afterwards with the passenger cars, and so continued till October 30th 1837, at the wages of two dollars per day; that being the usual wages paid to engine-men, which are higher than the wages paid to a machinist, in which capacity the plaintiff formerly was employed.

"On the 30th of October 1837, the plaintiff, then being in the employment of the defendants, as such engine-man, and running the passenger train, ran his engine off at a switch on the road, which had been left in a wrong condition, (as alleged by the plaintiff, and, for the purposes of this trial, admitted by the defendants,) by one Whitcomb, another servant of the defendants, who had been long in their employment, as a switch-man or tender, and had the care of switches on the road, and was a careful and trustworthy servant, in his general character, and as such servant was well known to the plaintiff. By which running off, the plaintiff sustained the injury complained of in his declaration.

"The said Farwell (the plaintiff) and Whitcomb were both appointed by the superintendent of the road, who was in the habit of passing over the same very frequently in the cars, and often rode on the engine.

"If the court shall be of opinion that, as a matter of law, the defendants are not liable to the plaintiff, he being a servant of the corporation, and in their employment, for the injury he may have received from the negligence of said Whitcomb, another servant of the corporation, and in their employment, then the plaintiff shall become nonsuit; but if the court shall be of opinion, as matter of law, that the defendants may be liable in this case, then the case shall be submitted to a jury upon the facts which may be proved in the case; the defendants alleging negligence on the part of the plaintiff."

C. G. LORING, *for the plaintiff.* . . .
The case of Priestley v. Fowler, 3 Mees. & Welsb. 1, on which the defendants will rely, was rightly decided. The case was clearly one of equal knowledge on the part of the two servants, and of voluntary exposure by the plaintiff to a known hazard not required by his duty; and both servants were jointly engaged in the same business when the accident happened to the plaintiff. But the reasoning and dicta of the court went much beyond the case—in undertaking to lay down a general rule, as applying to all cases of damages sustained by a servant in the employment of his master, without discrimination as to the peculiar relations of

the servant, and the causes of the injury received by him—and lead to unsound conclusions.

No general rule can be laid down, which will apply to all cases of a master's liability to a servant. But it is submitted that a master is liable to one servant for the negligence of another, when they are engaged in distinct employments, though he is not so liable, where two servants are engaged jointly in the same service; because, in the latter case, each servant has some supervision and control of every other. . . .

FLETCHER & MOREY, *for the defendants.* . . .

The only cases in which a servant has attempted to recover of a master for another servant's misconduct, are Priestley v. Fowler, 3 Mees. & Welsb. 1, and Murray v. South Carolina Rail Road Company, 1 McMullan, 385; and in both those cases, it was held that the action could not be maintained. In those cases, it is true that both servants were on the same carriage when the accident happened by which one of them was injured. And the counsel for the present plaintiff has invented a rule of law, in order to escape from the pressure of those decisions. But admitting the distinction, and the rule which he advances, to be sound, the case at bar is not thereby affected. The plaintiff and Whitcomb were not engaged in distinct and separate employments, but in the same service. They both were acting to the same end, although they had different parts to perform.

* * *

LORING, *in reply.* In the case in 1 McMullan, 385, the plaintiff, as in the case in 3 Mees. & Welsb. 1, was jointly engaged in the same service with the other servant, whose negligence caused the injury. It therefore does not affect the principle on which the present plaintiff rests his cause.

SHAW, C. J. This is an action of new impression in our courts, and involves a principle of great importance. It presents a case, where two persons are in the service and employment of one company, whose business it is to construct and maintain a railroad, and to employ their trains of cars to carry persons and merchandise for hire. They are appointed and employed by the same company to perform separate duties and services, all tending to the accomplishment of one and the same purpose—that of the safe and rapid transmission of the trains; and they are paid for their respective services according to the nature of their respective duties, and the labor and skill required for their proper performance. The question is, whether, for damages sustained by one of the persons so employed, by means of the carelessness and negligence of another, the party injured has a remedy against the common employer. It is an argument against such an action, though certainly not a decisive one, that no such action has before been maintained.

It is laid down by Blackstone, that if a servant, by his negligence, does any damage to a stranger, the master shall be answerable for his neglect. But the damage must be done while he is actually employed in the master's service; otherwise, the servant shall answer for his own misbehavior. 1 Bl. Com. 431. McManus v. Crickett, 1 East, 106. This rule is obviously founded on the great principle of social duty, that every man, in the management of his own affairs, whether by himself or by his agents or servants, shall so conduct them as not to injure another; and if he does not, and another thereby sustains damage, he shall answer for it. If done by a servant, in the course of his employment, and acting within the scope of his authority, it is considered, in contemplation of law, so far the act of the master, that the latter shall be answerable *civiliter*. But this presupposes that the parties stand to each other in the relation of strangers, between whom there is no privity; and the action, in such cases, is an action sounding in tort. The form is trespass on the case, for the consequential damage. The maxim respondeat superior is adopted in that case, from general considerations of policy and security.

But this does not apply to the case of a servant bringing his action against his own employer to recover damages for an injury arising in the course of that employment, where all such risks and perils as the employer and the servant respectively intend to assume and bear may be regulated by the express or implied contract between them, and which, in contemplation of law, must be presumed to be thus regulated.

. . . As there is no express contract between the parties, applicable to this point, it is placed on the footing of an implied contract of indemnity, arising out of the relation of master and servant. It would be an implied promise, arising from the duty of the master to be responsible to each person employed by him, in the conduct of every branch of business, where two or more persons are employed, to pay for all damage occasioned by the negligence of every other person employed in the same service. If such a duty were established by law—like that of a common carrier, to stand to all losses of goods not caused by the act of God or of a public enemy—or that of an innkeeper, to be responsible, in like manner, for the baggage of his guests; it would be a rule of frequent and familiar occurrence, and its existence and application, with all its qualifications and restrictions, would be settled by judicial precedents. But we are of opinion that no such rule has been established, and the authorities, as far as they go, are opposed to the principle. Priestley v. Fowler, 3 Mees. & Welsb. 1. Murray v. South Carolina Rail Road Company, 1 McMullan, 385.

The general rule, resulting from considerations as well of justice as of policy, is, that he who engages in the employment of another for the performance of specified duties and services, for compensation, takes upon himself the natural and ordinary risks and perils incident to the performance of such services, and in legal presumption, the compensation is adjusted accordingly. And we are not aware of any principle which should except the perils arising from the carelessness and negligence of those who are in the same employment. These are perils which the servant is as likely to know, and against which he can as effectually guard, as the master. They are perils incident to the service, and which can be as distinctly foreseen and provided for in the rate of compensation as any others. To say that the master shall be responsible because the damage is caused by his agents, is assuming the very point which remains to be proved. They are his agents to some extent, and for some purposes; but whether he is responsible, in a particular case, for their negligence, is not decided by the single fact that they are, for some purposes, his agents. It seems to be now well settled, whatever might have been thought formerly, that underwriters cannot excuse themselves from payment of a loss by one of the perils insured against, on the ground that the loss was caused by the negligence or unskilfulness of the officers or crew of the vessel, in the performance of their various duties as navigators, although employed and paid by the owners, and, in the navigation of the vessel, their agents. Copeland v. New England Marine Ins. Co., 2 Met. 440-443, and cases there cited. I am aware that the maritime law has its own rules and analogies, and that we cannot always safely rely upon them in applying them to other branches of law. But the rule in question seems to be a good authority for the point, that persons are not to be responsible, in all cases, for the negligence of those employed by them.

If we look from considerations of justice to those of policy, they will strongly lead to the same conclusion. In considering the rights and obligations arising out of particular relations, it is competent for courts of justice to regard considerations of policy and general convenience, and to draw from them such rules as will, in their practical application, best promote the safety and security of all parties concerned. This is, in truth, the basis on which implied promises are raised, being duties legally inferred from a consideration of what is best adapted to promote the benefit of all persons concerned, under given circumstances. To take the well known and familiar cases already cited; a common carrier, without regard to actual fault or neglect in himself or his servants, is made liable for all losses of goods confided to him for carriage, except those caused by the act of God or of a public enemy, because he can best guard them against all minor dangers, and because, in case of actual loss, it would be extremely difficult for the owner to adduce proof of embezzlement, or other actual fault or neglect on the part of the carrier, although it may have been the real cause of the loss. The risk is therefore thrown upon the carrier, and he receives, in the form of payment for the carriage, a premium for the risk which he thus assumes. So of an innkeeper; he can best secure the attendance of honest and faithful servants, and guard his house against thieves. Whereas, if he were responsible only upon proof of actual negligence, he might connive at the presence of dishonest inmates and retainers, and even participate in the embezzlement of the property of the guests, during the hours of their necessary sleep, and yet it would be difficult, and often impossible, to prove these facts.

The liability of passenger carriers is founded on similar considerations. They are held to the strictest responsibility for care, vigilance and skill, on the part of themselves and all persons employed by them, and they are paid accordingly. The rule is founded on the expediency of throwing the risk upon those who can best guard against it. Story on Bailments, s. 590, & seq.

We are of opinion that these considerations apply strongly to the case in question. Where several persons are employed in the conduct of one common enterprise or undertaking, and the safety of each depends much on the care and skill with which each other shall perform his appropriate duty, each is an observer of the conduct of the others, can give notice of any misconduct, incapacity or neglect of duty, and leave the service, if the common employer will not take such precautions, and employ such agents as the safety of the whole party may require. By these means, the safety of each will be much more effectually secured, than could be done by a resort to the common employer for indemnity in case of loss by the negligence of each other. Regarding it in this light, it is the ordinary case of one sustaining an injury in the course of his own employment, in which he must bear the loss himself, or seek his remedy, if he have any, against the actual wrong-doer.

In applying these principles to the present case, it appears that the plaintiff was employed by the defendants as an engineer, at the rate of wages usually paid in that employment, being a higher rate than the plaintiff had before received as a machinist. It was a voluntary undertaking on his part, with a full knowledge of the risks incident to the employment; and the loss was sustained by means of an ordinary casualty, caused by the negligence of another servant of the company. Under these circumstances, the loss must be deemed to be the result of a pure accident, like those to which all men, in all employments, and at all times, are more or less exposed; and like similar losses from accidental causes, it must rest where it first fell, unless the plaintiff has a remedy against the person actually in default; of which we give no opinion.

It was strongly pressed in the argument, that although this might be so, where two or more servants are employed in the same department of duty, where each can exert some influence over the conduct of the other, and thus to some extent provide for his own security; yet that it could not apply where two or more are employed in different departments of duty, at a distance from each other, and where one can in no degree control or influence the conduct of another. But we think this is founded upon a supposed distinction, on which it would be extremely difficult to establish a practical rule. When the object to be accomplished is one and the same, when the employers are the same, and the several persons employed derive their authority and their compensation from the same source, it would be extremely difficult to distinguish, what constitutes one department and what a distinct department of duty. It would vary with the circumstances of every case. If it were made to depend upon the nearness or distance of the persons from each other, the question would immediately arise, how near or how distant must they be, to be in the same or different departments. In a blacksmith's shop, persons working in the same building, at different fires, may be quite independent of each other, though only a few feet distant. In a ropewalk, several may be at work on the same piece of cordage, at the same time, at many hundred feet distant from each other, and beyond the reach of sight and voice, and yet acting together.

Besides, it appears to us, that the argument rests upon an assumed principle of responsibility which does not exist. The master, in the case supposed, is not exempt from liability because the servant has better means of providing for his safety when he is employed in immediate connexion with those from whose negligence he might suffer; but because the implied contract of the master does not extend to indemnify the servant against the negligence of any one but himself; and he is not liable in tort, as for the negligence of his servant, because the person suffering does not stand towards him in the relation of a stranger, but is one whose rights are regulated by contract express or implied. The exemption of the master, therefore, from liability for the negligence of a fellow servant, does not depend exclusively upon the consideration, that the servant has better means to provide for his own safety, but upon other grounds. Hence the separation of the employment into different departments cannot create that liability, when it does not arise from express or implied contract, or from a responsibility created by law to third persons, and strangers, for the negligence of a servant.

* * *

In coming to the conclusion that the plaintiff, in the present case, is not entitled to recover, considering it as in some measure a nice question, we would add a caution against any hasty conclusion as to the application of this rule to a case not fully within the same principle. It may be varied and modified by circumstances not appearing in the present case, in which it appears, that no wilful wrong or actual negligence was imputed to the corporation, and where suitable means were furnished and suitable persons employed to accomplish the object in view. We are far from intending to say that there are no implied warranties and undertakings arising out of the relation of master and servant. Whether, for instance, the employer would be responsible to an engineer for a loss arising from a defective or ill-constructed steam engine: Whether this would depend upon an implied warranty of its goodness and sufficiency, or upon the fact of wilful misconduct, or gross negligence on the part of the employer, if a natural person, or of the superintendent or immediate representative and managing agent, in case of an incorporated company—are questions on which we give no opinion. In the present case, the claim of the plaintiff is not put on the ground that the defendants did not furnish a sufficient engine, a proper railroad track, a well constructed switch, and a person of suitable skill and experience to attend it; the gravamen of the complaint is, that that person was chargeable with negligence in not changing the switch, in the particular instance, by means of which the accident occurred, by which the plaintiff sustained a severe loss. It ought, perhaps, to be stated, in justice to the person to whom this negligence is imputed, that the fact is strenuously denied by the defendants, and has not been tried by the jury. By consent of the parties, this fact was assumed without trial, in order to take the opinion of the whole court upon the question of law, whether, if such was the fact, the defendants, under the circumstances, were liable. Upon this question, supposing the accident to have occurred, and the loss to have been caused, by the negligence of the person employed to attend to and change the switch, in his not doing so in the particular case, the court are of the opinion that it is a loss for which the defendants are not liable, and that action cannot be maintained.

Plaintiff nonsuit.

QUESTIONS

1. Compare the ways in which the courts were informed about the facts out of which arose the lawsuits in Priestley v. Fowler and the Murray and Farwell cases. Distinguish the procedural devices which were employed for this purpose in each case.

2. What basis is there for Mr. Chief Justice Shaw's assertion in the Farwell case, that the question of the employer's liability for negligent injury inflicted by one of his em-

ployees upon another fits within the "general rule" of assumption of "the natural and ordinary risks and perils incident to the performance of such services"? Where did he get this general rule?

3. Are the South Carolina and Massachusetts decisions based on legal precedent? Consider in this connection the cases referred to in these opinions, regarding an employer's responsibility towards a "stranger" (a non-employee) injured by the negligence of an employee: couldn't they have been treated as "precedent" for the employer's responsibility under the law of tort? Couldn't the "carrier" cases have been treated as precedent for employer responsibility under the law of contract? What is meant when it is said that one case can be distinguished from another?

4. What argumentative strategy did Loring (Farwell's counsel) follow in his treatment of Priestley v. Fowler? What alternative strategy was available; and would it have been wiser?

5. Did the law determine the rights and duties of the parties in these cases or were these rights and duties delimited by the agreements of the parties themselves, with the law seeing to it merely that these agreements were carried out? What evidence is adduced in the opinions as to the precise terms of these agreements? Consider in this connection, Chief Justice Shaw's remarks about "implied promises." In view of these remarks, would you say he did or did not subscribe to the statement of O'Neall, J., dissenting in the Murray case, that "policy" is for the legislature, law for the courts? (Incidentally, is O'Neall's statement consistent with sound "democratic" principle?) On the other hand, when both Shaw and Judge Evans gave some weight, in denying liability, to the absence of precedents imposing liability, were they not leaving "policy" to the legislature? And was not O'Neall himself advocating the particular "policy" embodied in the respondeat superior rule when he urged applicability of that rule to the fellow-servant injury situation?

6. In what ways did the decision of these cases require the specialized training and learning of the lawyer and judge?

7. Regarding what future situations of employee injury do the opinions express "hedging" dicta as to possible employer liability?

Section 3

The LAWYER as OFFICER of the COURT

From the reporter's statement of the argument by Loring (plaintiff's counsel) in the preceding Farwell case, it is apparent that Loring called the court's attention to the case of Priestley v. Fowler even though it was a strong authority for the defendant. This may have been part of a best-defense-is-an-offense strategy by Loring. But even if Loring was certain that the defendant's counsel, as well as the court, did not know of the Priestley case, he may have been under an ethical obligation to call it to the court's attention. The lawyer is an officer of the court. Part of his duty as such officer is candor, including disclosure of some matters that opposing counsel should, in the interest of his client, have brought out but did not. The limits of this duty are not altogether clear. The following materials throw some light on the problem.

DRINKER,* *LEGAL ETHICS*
74-78 (1953)

Canon 22 † is as follows:

". . . The conduct of the lawyer before the Court and with other lawyers should be characterized by candor and fairness.

"It is not candid or fair for the lawyer knowingly to misquote the contents of a paper, the testimony of a witness, the language or the argument of opposing counsel, or the language of a decision or a textbook; or with knowledge of its invalidity, to cite as authority a decision that has been overruled, or a statute that has been repealed; or in argument to assert as a fact that which has not been proved, or in those jurisdictions where a side has the opening and closing arguments to mislead his opponent by concealing or withholding positions in his opening argument upon which his side then intends to rely.

"It is unprofessional and dishonorable to deal other than candidly with the facts in taking the statements of witnesses, in drawing affidavits and other documents, and in the presentation of causes.

"A lawyer should not offer evidence, which he knows the Court should reject, in order to get the same before the jury by argument for its admissibility, nor should he address to the Judge arguments upon any point not properly calling for determination by him. Neither should he introduce into an argument, addressed to the court, remarks or statements intended to influence the jury or bystanders.

"These and all kindred practices are unprofessional and unworthy of an officer of the law charged, as is the lawyer, with the duty of aiding in the administration of justice."

The oath recommended by the American Bar Association contains a pledge that the lawyer "will never seek to mislead the judge or jury *by any artifice* or false statement of fact or law. . . ."

In an Illinois case (People v. Beattie, 137 Ill. 553, 574 (1891)) Judge Magruder said:

"The lawyer's duty is of a double character. He owes to his client the duty of fidelity, but he also owes the duty of good faith and honorable dealing to the judicial tribunals before whom he practices his profession. He is an officer of the court—a minister in the temple of justice. His high vocation is to correctly

---

* Henry S. Drinker, Member of Philadelphia bar; Chairman of the Standing Committee on Professional Ethics and Grievances, American Bar Association; author of The Interstate Commerce Act (1908); The Chamber Music of Johannes Brahms (1933).—Editor

† In 1908, the American Bar Association adopted 32 Canons of Ethics to govern the conduct of lawyers. The latest (47th) Canon was added in 1937. The A.B.A. Ethics Committee issues Opinions from time to time, construing the canons. One of these, Opinion 280, is reproduced herein following the present extract from Drinker. A 1947 volume by the committee collected 274 opinions, and subsequent ones have appeared from time to time in the A.B.A. Journal.—Editor

inform the court upon the law and the facts of the case, and to aid it in doing justice and arriving at correct conclusions. He violates his oath of office when he resorts to deception, or permits his clients to do so. He is under no obligations to seek to obtain, for those whom he represents, that which is forbidden by the law. If he suffers false and perjured testimony to be presented to the presiding judge, with the possible result of inducing the latter to take jurisdiction of a cause, in which there would otherwise be no power to act, and to grant a judgment or decree which the law would prohibit if the real character of the offered testimony were known, he cannot shield himself behind his supposed obligations to his client."

. . . The extent to which it is regarded as counsel's duty to advise the court as to matters relevant to the proper decision of the case of which opposing counsel is ignorant or which he has overlooked turns on the degree to which the old idea that litigation is a game between the lawyers has been supplanted by the more modern view that the lawyer is a minister of justice. Always, however, must be borne in mind the principle that the theory of our system is still that justice is best accomplished by having all the facts and arguments on each side investigated and presented with maximum vigor by opposing counsel, for decision by the court and jury. . . .

A lawyer is bound to tell the court of any decisions directly adverse to any proposition of law on which he expressly relies, of which the lawyer on the other side is apparently ignorant and which would reasonably be considered important by the judge sitting in the case.[46]

OPINION 280, COMMITTEE ON PROFESSIONAL ETHICS, AMERICAN BAR ASSOCIATION
35 American Bar Association Journal 876 (1949)

. . . A member of the Association has asked the Committee to reconsider and clarify the Committee's Opinion 146.

Canons 1, 5, 15, 22—Opinion 146

[Canon 1, entitled "The Duty of the Lawyer to the Courts," reads: "It is the duty of the lawyer to maintain towards the Courts a respectful attitude, not for the sake of the temporary incumbent of the judicial office, but for the maintenance of its supreme importance. Judges, not being wholly free to defend themselves, are peculiarly entitled to receive the support of the Bar against unjust criticism and clamor. Whenever there is proper ground for serious complaint of a judicial officer,

---

[46] See A.B.A. Op. 280 and cases cited; also John C. Harris "Legal Ethics," 69 Albany L. Jour. 300, 303 (1907); Showell Rogers, "The Ethics of Advocacy," 15 L. Quart. Rev. 259, 275, n. (1889); Moody v. Davis, 10 Ga. 403, 410 (1851); also N.Y. City 889 [i.e., Opinion 889 of Ethics Committee of Bar Assoc. of City of N.Y.—Editor] and 35 A.B.A.J. 5 (1949). . . .

it is the right and duty of the lawyer to submit his grievances to the proper authorities. In such cases, but not otherwise, such charges should be encouraged and the person making them should be protected."]

[Canon 5, entitled "The Defense or Prosecution of Those Accused of Crime," reads: "It is the right of the lawyer to undertake the defense of a person accused of crime, regardless of his personal opinion as to the guilt of the accused; otherwise innocent persons, victims only of suspicious circumstances, might be denied proper defense. Having undertaken such defense, the lawyer is bound, by all fair and honorable means, to present every defense that the law of the land permits, to the end that no person may be deprived of life or liberty, but by due process of law.

["The primary duty of a lawyer engaged in public prosecution is not to convict, but to see that justice is done. The suppression of facts or the secreting of witnesses capable of establishing the innocence of the accused is highly reprehensible."]

[Canon 15, entitled "How Far a Lawyer May Go in Supporting a Client's Cause," reads: "Nothing operates more certainly to create or to foster popular prejudice against lawyers as a class, and to deprive the profession of that full measure of public esteem and confidence which belong to the proper discharge of its duties than does the false claim, often set up by the unscrupulous in defense of questionable transactions, that it is the duty of the lawyer to do whatever may enable him to succeed in winning his client's cause.

["It is improper for a lawyer to assert in argument his personal belief in his client's innocence or in the justice of his cause.

["The lawyer owes 'entire devotion to the interest of the client, warm zeal in the maintenance and defense of his rights and the exertion of his utmost learning and ability,' to the end that nothing be taken or withheld from him, save by the rules of law, legally applied. No fear of judicial disfavor or public unpopularity should restrain him from the full discharge of his duty. In the judicial forum the client is entitled to the benefit of any and every remedy and defense that is authorized by the law of the land, and he may expect his lawyer to assert every such remedy or defense. But it is steadfastly to be borne in mind that the great trust of the lawyer is to be performed within and not without the bounds of the law. The office of attorney does not permit, much less does it demand of him for any client, violation of law or any manner of fraud or chicane. He must obey his own conscience and not that of his client."]

[Canon 22, entitled "Candor and Fairness," was quoted in the preceding extract from the Drinker book.—Editor]

The Committee's opinion was stated by Mr. DRINKER. Messrs. Brand, Jackson, Jones, Miller, White and Wuerthner concurring.

Opinion 146 rendered July 17, 1935 was in response to a question by a member of the Association as follows:

"Is it the duty of a lawyer appearing in a pending case to advise the court of decisions adverse to his client's contentions that are known to him and unknown to his adversary?"

Opinion 146, stated by Judge Phillips and concurred in by the other members of the Committee, was as follows:

> A lawyer is an officer of the court. (Ex parte Garland, 4 Wall. 333, 378; People v. Gorman, 346 Ill. 432; Bowles v. United States, C.A. 4th, 50 F. (2d) 848. His obligation to the public is no less significant than his obligation to his client. In Re Bergeron, 220 Mass. 472. His oath binds him to the highest fidelity to the court as well as to his client. In Re Bergeron, supra. It is his duty to aid the court in the due administration of justice. Dodge v. State, 140 Ind. 284; People v. Gorman, supra; United States v. Frank, 53 F. (2d) 128.
>
> The conduct of the lawyer before the court and with other lawyers should be characterized by candor and fairness. (Canon 22.)
>
> We are of the opinion that this Canon requires the lawyer to disclose such decisions to the court. He may, of course, after doing so, challenge the soundness of the decisions or present reasons which he believes would warrant the court in not following them in the pending case.

It will be noted that in the last paragraph the Committee refers to the right of the lawyer to "challenge the soundness of the decisions or present reasons which he believes would warrant the court in not following them in the pending case," but does not refer to his right to "distinguish" them, thus indicating that the Committee had in mind only decisions which were directly adverse.

In the brief summary in the 1947 edition of the Committee's decisions (page 17), Opinion 146 was thus summarized:

> "Opinion 146—A lawyer should disclose to the court a decision directly adverse to his client's cause that is unknown to his adversary."

The lawyer, though an officer of the court and charged with the duty of "candor and fairness," is not an umpire, but an advocate. He is under no duty to refrain from making every proper argument in support of any legal point because he is not convinced of its inherent soundness. Nor is he under any obligation to suggest arguments against his position. His personal belief in the soundness of his cause or of the authorities supporting it, is irrelevant. See Canons 5 and 15.

We would not confine the Opinion to "controlling authorities"—i.e., those decisive of the pending case—but, in acordance with the tests hereafter suggested, would apply it to a decision directly adverse to any proposition of law on which the lawer expressly relies, which would reasonably be considered important by the judge sitting on the case.

Of course, if the court should ask if there are any adverse decisions, the lawyer should make such frank disclosure as the question seems to warrant. Close cases can obviously be suggested, particularly in the case of decisions from other states where there is no local case in point. A case of doubt should obviously be resolved in favor of the disclosure, or by a statement disclaiming the discussion of all conflicting decisions.

Canon 22 should be interpreted sensibly, to preclude the obvious impropriety at which the Canon is aimed. In a case involving a right angle collision or a vested or contingent remainder, there would seem to be no necessity whatever of citing even all the relevant decisions in the jurisdiction, much less those from other states or by inferior courts. Where the question is a new or novel one, such as the constitutionality or construction of a statute, on which there is a dearth of authority, the lawyer's duty may be broader. The test in every case should be, is the decision which opposing counsel has overlooked one which the court should clearly consider in deciding the case? Would a reasonable judge properly feel that a lawyer who advanced, as the law, a proposition adverse to the undisclosed decision, was lacking in candor and fairness to him? Might the judge consider himself misled by an implied representation that the lawyer knew of no adverse authority?

Judge PHILLIPS, who wrote Opinion 146, has authorized the present Committee to state that he concurs in the foregoing.

CURTIS,* *THE ETHICS OF ADVOCACY*
4 Stanford Law Review 3, 9-10, 11 (1951)

. . . Let me give you a case from the autobiography of one of the most distinguished and most conscientious lawyers I or any other man has ever known, Samuel Williston. In his autobiography, Life and Law, he tells of one of his early cases. His client was sued in some financial matter. The details of the claim are not important. Williston, of course, at once got his client's letter file and went through it painstakingly, sorting, arranging, and collating it. The letters, we may well believe, told the whole story, as they usually do in such a case. Trial approached, but the plaintiff's lawyers did not either demand to see the correspondence, nor ask for their production. "They did not demand their production and we did not feel bound to disclose them." At the close of the trial, "In the course of his remarks the Chief Justice stated as one reason for his decision a supposed fact which I knew to be unfounded. I had in front of me a letter that showed his error. Though I have no doubt of the propriety of my behavior in keeping silent, I was somewhat uncomfortable at the time."

This was a letter, a piece of evidence, a fact. Suppose it had been a rule of law. Suppose the Chief Justice had equally mistakenly given as a reason for his decision some statute or regulation which Williston knew had been repealed or amended, and it was not a letter but a copy of the new statute which he had in front of him. Williston would have interrupted the Chief Justice and drawn his attention to it. This is sometimes debated, but it is beyond dispute that this would have been Williston's duty, and there is no doubt at all that he would have performed it as scrupulously as he respected his duty to his client.

. . . The court has priority over the client in matters of law and the client has

---

* Charles P. Curtis, 1891-1959, was a prominent member of the Boston bar, and author of Lions Under the Throne (1947) (a study of the U.S. Supreme Court); It's Your Law (1954); The Oppenheimer Case (1955); A Commonplace Book (1957); The Modern Prudent Investor (1958); and Law as Large as Life (1959); as well as co-author of Hunting in Africa (1925); Introduction to Pareto (1934); and The Practical Cogitator (1945).—Editor

a priority over the court in matters of fact. The distinction is familiar enough to lawyers, and it is a useful distinction once we know what they mean by it, as I will try to make clear later. The point I want to make now is that the relations which a lawyer has with his client on one hand and his court on the other is somewhat bigamous, and it will continue to be until we can find a distinction between his loyalties as marked as their two objects.

Here is what Williston went on to say in his autobiography. "One of the troublesome ethical questions which a young trial lawyer is confronted with is the extent to which he is bound to disclose to the court facts which are injurious to his client's case. The answer is not doubtful. The lawyer must decide when he takes a case whether it is a suitable one for him to undertake and after his decision is made, he is not justified in turning against his client by exposing injurious evidence entrusted to him. If that evidence was unknown to him when he took the case, he may sometimes withdraw from it, but while he is engaged as counsel he is not only not obliged to disclose unfavorable evidence, but it is a violation of his duty to his client if he does so.*

NOTE [ON CURTIS]
4 Stanford Law Review 355, 356-357 (1952)

The Review has received a number of letters containing comments on Mr. Curtis' article. . . .

Professor Lowell Turrentine of the Stanford law faculty, referring to Mr. Curtis' explanation of Williston's refusal to reveal some facts adverse to his client's case says:

A point made by Mr. Curtis in his fascinating article, "The Ethics of Advocacy" in your last issue—namely, that an attorney must not disclose a fact unfavorable to his client even where the court, lacking such disclosure, is in process of making a finding contrary to what the attorney knows to be the fact —needs annotation lest unwarranted inferences be drawn.

A distinction must be made between the client in a defensive position, civil

---

* An article by Drinker in the same volume of the Stanford Law Review and critical of Curtis's article, explained the Williston situation in terms of the "privilege" protecting communications between client and attorney. Curtis replied to this in his book, It's Your Law (1954) (footnote, pp. 17-18): "I do not understand that the files were turned over to Mr. Williston only for examination, but rather for the purpose of using them in the defense of the suit. In that case, if this particular letter was a part of any correspondence in the file which Mr. Williston was to use, as it well might have been, the client would have waived the privilege.

"However, the files were not protected by the privilege. Under the doctrine as set forth by Wigmore this letter file was not a communication to the attorney. This letter was 'a document of the client existing before it was communicated to the attorney,' and so 'not within the present privilege so as to be exempt from [production].' Wigmore, s. 2318, and 2307. A party cannot avoid discovery of a document by giving it to his attorney."

Assuming that Curtis is correct, the question still remains whether the attorney should *voluntarily* disclose either the document or the information in his head communicated to him by the client.—Editor

or criminal, who has a right to cast upon the other side the burden of proving the case—in which situation Mr. Curtis' point is applicable; and on the other hand the client in the position of a plaintiff. If in the course of representing such a client the attorney learns beyond doubt of any fact which if disclosed would be fatal to the client's right of recovery, the attorney must advise his client to discontinue the case. If the client refuses to do so, the attorney must withdraw from it. This appears from No. 44* of the Canons of the American Bar Association.†

EDITORIAL NOTE: THE LAWYER'S DUTY to the COURT and PUBLIC as against the DUTY to HIS CLIENT

It is apparent from the foregoing that the lawyer has conflicting loyalties. While the Canons set forth a duty to court and public, they also embody certain obligations to the client. We cannot here deal with the whole gamut of these conflicts. The preceding materials raise the question of how far, if at all, the protection of his client should lead the lawyer not to inform the court fully. Canon 37 requires the lawyer to "preserve his client's confidences"—a duty analogous to the "attorney-client privilege" recognized by the common law. We shall discuss this privilege below, before dealing with the other problems of client protection considered in the preceding materials.

The attorney-client privilege. Recall the discussion of this privilege in the footnote to the Curtis article above. There are other interesting examples of the collision between the "privilege" of non-disclosure accorded attorney-

* This canon reads: "The right of an attorney or counsel to withdraw from employment once assumed, arises only from good cause. Even the desire or consent of the client is not always sufficient. The lawyer should not throw up the unfinished task to the detriment of his client except for reasons of honor or self-respect. If the client insists upon an unjust or immoral course in the conduct of his case, or if he persists over the attorney's remonstrance in presenting frivolous defenses, or if he deliberately disregards an agreement or obligation as to fees or expenses, the lawyer may be warranted in withdrawing on due notice to the client, allowing him time to employ another lawyer. So also when a lawyer discovers that his client has no case and the client is determined to continue it; or even if the lawyer finds himself incapable of conducting the case effectively. Sundry other instances may arise in which withdrawal is to be justified. Upon withdrawing from a case after a retainer has been paid, the attorney should refund such part of the retainer as has not been clearly earned."—Editor

† Curtis, in his book, It's Your Law (1954), at pp. 19-20, discusses the same point raised by Prof. Turrentine and says: ". . . The reason for this difference between the claim and the defense is, simply that, unless a lawyer presents all the available relevant facts, he would be presenting a different case to the court than the one which his client brought to him. . . . But here we come to the edge of a technical precipice. What is matter of defense? Some things are strictly the business of the defendant to bring up, if he chooses. You bring suit for divorce on the ground of adultery. You tell your lawyer that you have condoned your husband's offense by living with him after you learned of it. The court may very well deny you a divorce because you have, as the law says, condoned his adultery . . . Need your lawyer bring out the fact that you have forgiven your husband? Or should that be left for him to bring up?"—Editor

client communications and the lawyer's duty of disclosure to the court. E.g., A.B.A. Opinion 287 (39 A.B.A.J. 983) ruled on two situations:

(1) A divorce decree had been granted a husband on grounds of the wife's wilful desertion, based on the husband's false testimony as to the date of desertion (the actual date would have made the action premature). The husband subsequently disclosed to his lawyer that the ex-wife was threatening to reveal the true facts unless he paid for her support. The Committee took note of Canon 29, which requires a lawyer to bring perjury to the attention of the prosecuting authorities and Canon 41 which states that when a lawyer discovers a fraud or deception unjustly imposing on the court or a party he should (if the client refuses to forgo the advantage thus gained) inform the injured party or his counsel. The majority of the Committee decided that these canons had not undermined the policy of Canon 37 embodying the attorney-client privilege. The lawyer should urge the client to make the disclosure, and, if the client refused, the lawyer "should have nothing further to do with him, but despite Canons 29 and 41 should not disclose the facts to the Court or to the authorities."

(2) A lawyer knew about his client's prior criminal record, but the court in passing sentence assumed, from the clerk's erroneous statement to him, that there was no prior criminal record. The Committee majority ruled that if the information about the prior record had been communicated to him by the client, the lawyer should *not* disclose it, but "should in due course endeavor to persuade the client to tell the court the truth and if he refuses to do so should sever his relations with the client." The Committee recognized that even if the lawyer's information had not come from the client, the same result might follow because Canon 6 calls upon the lawyer to represent his client with undivided fidelity and not divulge his secrets. The Committee also ruled that if the court asks the lawyer whether the clerk's statement is correct, he should request the court to excuse him from answering and retire from the case, "though this would doubtless put the court on further inquiry as to the truth." Further, if the court doesn't ask about the clerk's statement, but the lawyer believes the court is actually relying on him to corroborate the correctness of the statement, the lawyer should advise the court not to rely on counsel's personal knowledge of the client's record. But if the lawyer is "quite clear" that the court isn't relying on his silence as corroboration, he is "not bound to speak out."

The Canon 37 "privilege" has also been invoked by A.B.A. Opinion 23 to justify a lawyer's refusal to reveal to police, information given him by relatives of a fugitive as to his whereabouts. However, Canon 37 itself says that the lawyer is permitted to disclose a confidence as to the client's intention to commit a crime. Moreover, the lawyer is permitted to disclose client communications as to the whereabouts of a client who jumped bail (Drinker, Legal Ethics (1953) 137, citing A.B.A. Opinions 155, 156) and the subversive activities engaged in by his client (Drinker, *ibid.*, citing opinions of some state and local bar committees). Are these permissions reconcilable with the lack of permission in Opinion 23 concerning the fugitive? The majority in Opinion 287, described above, stated that any inconsistency between Opinions 155, 156 and Opinion 23 should be resolved in favor of Opinion 23.

Other reasons for failing to fully inform the court. We have seen principles other than the attorney-client privilege invoked to excuse failure to be completely candid with the court. Curtis's principle is that while "the court has priority over the client in matters of law" (so as to require disclosure of legal precedents that are "directly adverse"), "the client has a priority over the court in matters of fact" (so as to justify, for instance, Williston's silence about the letter in his file which contradicted the judge's assumption of fact).

According to Turrentine, the lawyer's duty not to disclose adverse facts applies only to facts as to which the client does not have the burden of proof. This was Williston's situation, apparently, because he represented a *defendant* and the plaintiff has the burden of proving his own claims. This may also have been Curtis's hypothetical situation in which the attorney represented a wife who "condoned" the adultery which was the basis for her divorce action. Condonation is usually treated by the courts as a matter of defense to be claimed and proved by the defendant husband. But the "burden of proof" approach has its own difficulties. Curtis's question, "what is matter of defense?", emphasizes that it is often unclear as to which party has the burden on a particular question. Furthermore, the thought persists that the existence of a duty to tell the whole truth should not be made dependent on so technical and often fortuitous a circumstance as location of the "burden of proof" on a particular issue.

And what, precisely, are the disclosure duties of the attorney who does have the burden of proof? Turrentine says that if such an attorney learns of a fact which is "fatal" to his case, he "must advise his client to discontinue the case," and if he refuses, "the attorney must withdraw from the case." (Canon 44 says merely that the attorney "may" withdraw.) But when is a fact "fatal"? It is not easy to say in every case. If the facts are less than fatal (the merely "injurious evidence" referred to in Williston's observations on the duties of the plaintiff's lawyer), even Turrentine, joining Williston and Curtis, would say that the lawyer with the burden of proof has a duty *not* to disclose.

The nub of the difficulty. We cannot help feeling "morally" uncomfortable about the positions taken by all the writers we have presented, including the A.B.A. Committees. Why, after all, shouldn't a lawyer, an officer of the court, be completely candid and cooperative in his relations with the court? Why shouldn't he reveal everything he knows about the case? Isn't that the only way to arrive at a just result? Here we get at the nub of the difficulty, because obligations not to disclose are *also* imposed in the interest of justice. For example, the attorney-client privilege assumes that full, uninhibited communication between attorney and client will promote justice in the individual case. So too, the permission granted a lawyer to withhold facts adverse to his client assumes that on the whole and in the long run, justice will be promoted by the preservation of the "adversary" system of litigation. This system is modelled largely on that of combat, under which the lawyer fights for his client by putting the best possible face on his case, leaving it to opposing counsel to present the adverse side. We in this country think that this is the way to assure vigorous, resourceful presentations on both sides, from which the truth can best be determined by the tribunal. (We shall in a later chapter consider the nature of the adversary system in some detail and you will have an opportunity to evaluate its assumptions.) The system operates within limits, just as there are Marquis of Queensberry rules for pugilistic combats, and even rules of war. These ethical limits, insofar as they are embodied in the Canons, are necessarily couched in broad terms. This means an inevitable uncertainty in their application to particular cases; and many of the interpretive A.B.A. opinions are not unanimous. Neither the exponent of candor at all costs, nor the believer in a lawyer's cagey, cards-close-to-the-chest policy is likely to be satisfied by these bar association opinions. They represent inevitable compromises between conflicting means of achieving an accepted ideal—justice—no one of which we are willing to forgo.

NOTES AND QUESTIONS

1. On the basis of Opinion 280, could it be argued that Loring, plaintiff's counsel in the Farwell case, was not obliged to disclose the Priestley v. Fowler decision?

2. How would you argue against the position of the majority in Opinion 287?

3. Does not the ethical problem posed by Curtis also arise at the pleading stage? Should a lawyer ever deny in a pleading any facts alleged in the opposing pleading which he knows are true? An authority on pleading observes: "It has been a rule coming from the common law that all pleading must be true. That rule should be enforced according to its purpose by striking a clearly false pleading and perhaps by direct action against the party or counsel involved [perjury, if pleadings sworn? disbarment?—Editor]. But beyond this any requirement of truth in pleading is unenforceable, since a party is entitled to present his version of the case to court or jury." Clark, Code Pleading (2d ed., 1947) 632. See also, for related matter in the law of pleading, Michael, The Elements of Legal Controversy (1948) 536-540, 552-571.

Is this truth requirement in pleading inconsistent with the idea we have encountered that at the trial one who doesn't have the burden of proof need *not* disclose the truth but can put the other to his proof? Should it matter that the trial situation involves silence rather than a positive act misrepresenting the true facts?

4. Our ethical problem has an interesting aspect in criminal cases too. Canon 31 provides: "No lawyer is obliged to act either as adviser or advocate for every person who may wish to become his client. He has the right to decline employment." And under Canon 44 he may withdraw from employment, for good cause—which includes his discovery "that his client has no case" or that he is "incapable of conducting the case effectively." At the same time, Canon 5 recognizes "the right of the lawyer to undertake the defense of a person accused of crime, regardless of his personal opinion as to the guilt of the accused; otherwise innocent persons, victims only of suspicious circum-

stances, might be denied proper defense." "Having undertaken such defense," Canon 5 continues, "the lawyer is bound by all fair and honorable means, to present every defense that the law of the land permits, to the end that no person may be deprived of life or liberty, but by due process of law."

Two things should be noted about this right under Canon 5: (1) it is stated as a right, not as a duty; (2) it is concerned with those who in the lawyer's *opinion* are guilty; it does not specifically mention those whom he *knows* to be guilty, e.g., through the client's confession to him. Nonetheless in the latter case too, the right expressed in Canon 5 seems to be generally assumed to apply, though there is remarkably little discussion of the point in the literature. See generally Drinker, Legal Ethics (1953) 142-143. The attorney may properly enter a plea of not guilty and require the prosecutor to discharge his burden of proving the defendant guilty beyond a reasonable doubt. (A person accused of crime is "presumed" to be innocent.) This, then, seems to be an exceptional case, where the law does sanction an untruthful pleading. Is there good reason for making such an exception?

The second paragraph of Canon 5 reads: "The primary duty of a lawyer engaged in public prosecution is not to convict, but to see that justice is done. The suppression of facts or the secreting of witnesses capable of establishing the innocence of the accused is highly reprehensible." Is there good reason for this difference between the duty of the prosecutor and that of the defense attorney?

Section 4

DETERMINING the RULE of the CASE

It will be noted that Loring, plaintiff's counsel in the Farwell case, looked back at Priestley v. Fowler and construed the decision narrowly, so as to apply only to employees in the same "department," whereas Chief Justice Shaw in the Farwell case chose to construe the decision more broadly. The following materials are in large measure concerned with exploring this accordion-like aspect of the process of determining the rule of law in a particular case.

LLEWELLYN, *THE BRAMBLE BUSH*
45-49, 66-69 (Oceana ed., 1951)

Now for a while I am going to risk confusion for the sake of talking simply. I am going to treat as the rule of the case the *ratio decidendi*, the rule *the court tells you* is the rule of the case, the ground, as the phrase goes, upon which the court itself has rested its decision. For there is where you must begin, and such refinements as are needed may come after.

The court, I will assume, has talked for five pages, only one of which portrayed the facts assumed. The rest has been discussion. And judgment has been given for the party who won below: judgment affirmed. We seek the rule.

The first thing to note is this: *no rule can be the ratio decidendi from which the actual judgment* (here: affirmance) *does not follow.* Unless affirmance follows from a rule, it *cannot* be the rule which produced an actual holding of affirmance. But that holding is the decision, and the court speaks ex cathedra only as to the dispute decided, and only as to the decision it has made. At this point, too, I think you begin to see the bearing of the *procedural* issue. There can be a decision (and so an ex cathedra ratio) *only* as to a point which is before the court. But points come before a court of review by way of specific complaint about specific action of the court below, and in no other way. Hence nothing can be held which is not thus brought up.

You will have noted that these two statements are not quite the same. For the losing party may have complained of five, or fourteen, different rulings by the court below, but the final judgment below is affirmed or reversed but once. [The author here asks how we should interpret an appellate court's reversal of the judgment on each of five issues raised in the appeal. Merely because reversal on only one point would have sufficed to reverse the judgment didn't make the rulings on the other points mere dicta, because they were called for by the facts and issues in the case. Still, the ruling on any one of the points carries less weight than it would if it had been on the only issue in the case, perhaps because, as the author says, the court may not have "sweated" over each point in quite the way it would have if it were the only crucial point in the case. Suppose, too, that the judgment below is reversed on one point and affirmed on the other four. The points affirmed are not dicta, but their authority is weak since they do not meet the other test: the actual judgment does not logically follow from them.—Editor]

But our troubles with the ratio decidendi are not over. We meet forthwith a further formal one. Our judge states his facts, he argues his position, he announces his rule. And lo, he seems but to have begun. Once clean across the plate. But he begins again, winds up again, and again he delivers his ratio—this time, to our puzzlement, the words are not the same. At this point it is broader than it was before, there it is narrower. And like as not he will warm up another time, and do the same job over—differently again. I have never made out quite why this happens. A little, it may be due to a lawyer's tendency to clinch an argument by summarizing its course, when he is through. A little, it may be due to mere sloppiness of composition, to the lack, typical of our law and all its work, of a developed sense for form, juristic or esthetic, for what the Romans knew as *elegantia*. Sometimes I get a wry suspicion that the judge repeats because he is uneasy on his ground, that he lifts up his voice, prays his conclusion over loud and louder, to gain and make conviction, much like an advertiser bare of arguments except his slogan. At other times I feel as I read opinions the thrill of adventure in an undiscovered country; the first and second statements of the ratio, with all that has led up to them, are like first and second reconnoiterings of strange hills; like first and second chartings of what has been found and what surmised— knowledge and insight growing as the opinion builds to its conclusion. But whatever the reason, recurrent almost-repetition faces us; also the worry that the repetition seldom is exact. Which phrasing are we then to tie to?

Perhaps in this, as in judging how far to trust a broadly stated rule, we may find guidance in the facts the court assumes. Surely this much is certain. The actual dispute before the court is limited as straitly by the facts as by the form which the procedural issue has assumed. What is not in the facts cannot be present for decision. Rules which proceed an inch beyond the facts must be suspect.

But how far does that help us out? What are *the* facts? The plaintiff's name is Atkinson and the defendant's Walpole. The defendant, despite his name, is an Italian by extraction, but the plaintiff's ancestors came over with the Pilgrims. The defendant has a schnauzer-dog named Walter, red hair, and $30,000 worth of life insurance. All these are facts. The case, however, does not deal with life insurance. It is about an auto accident. The defendant's auto was a Buick painted pale magenta. He is married. His wife was in the back seat, an irritable somewhat faded blonde. She was attempting back seat driving when the accident occurred. He had turned around to make objection. In the process the car swerved and hit the plaintiff. The sun was shining; there was a rather lovely dappled sky low to the West. The time was late October on a Tuesday. The road was smooth, concrete. It had been put in by the McCarthy Road Work Company. How many of these facts are important to the decision? How many of these facts are, as we say, legally relevant? Is it relevant that the road was in the country or the city; that it was concrete or tarmac or of dirt; that it was a private or a public way? Is it relevant that the defendant was driving a Buick, or a motorcar, or a vehicle? Is it important that he looked around as the car swerved? Is it crucial? Would it have been the same if he had been drunk, or had swerved for fun, to see how close he could run by the plaintiff, but had missed his guess?

Is it not obvious that as soon as you pick up this statement of the facts to find its legal bearings you must discard some as of no interest whatsoever, discard others as dramatic but as legal nothings? And is it not clear, further, that when you pick up the facts which are left and which do seem relevant, you suddenly cease to deal with them in the concrete and deal with them instead in *categories* which you, for one reason or another, deem significant? It is not the road between Pottsville and Arlington; it is "a highway." It is not a particular pale magenta Buick eight, by number 732507, but "a motorcar," and perhaps even "a vehicle." It is not a turning around to look at Adoree Walpole, but a lapse from the supposedly proper procedure of careful drivers, with which you are concerned. Each concrete fact of the case arranges itself, I say, as the *representative* of a much wider abstract *category* of facts, and it is not in itself but as a member of the category that you attribute significance to it. But what is to tell you whether to make your category "Buicks" or "motorcars" or "vehicles"? What is to tell you to make your category "road" or "public highway"? The court may tell you. But the precise point that you have up for study is how far it is safe to trust what the court says. The precise issue which you are attempting to solve is whether the court's language can be taken as it stands, or must be amplified, or must be whittled down.

This brings us at last to the case system. For the truth of the matter is a truth so obvious and trite that it is somewhat regularly overlooked by students. *That no case can have a meaning by itself!* Standing alone it gives you no guidance. It can give you no guidance as to how far it carries, as to how much of its language will hold water later. What counts, what gives you leads, what gives you sureness, *that is the background of the other cases* in relation to which you must read the one. They color the language, the technical terms, used in the opinion. But above all they give you the wherewithal to find which of the facts are significant, and in what aspect they are significant, and how far the rules laid down are to be trusted.

Here, I say, is the foundation of the case system. For what, in a case class, do we do? We have set before you, at either the editor's selection or our own, a *series* of opinions which in some manner are related. They may or may not be exactly alike in their outcome. They are always supposedly somewhat similar on their legally relevant facts. Indeed, it is the *aspects in which their facts are similar* which give you your first guidance as to what *classes* of fact will be found legally relevant, that is, will be found *to operate alike,* or to operate *at all,* upon the court. On the other hand, the states of fact are rarely, if ever, quite alike. And one of the most striking problems before you is: when you find two cases side by side which show a difference in result, then to determine, *what* difference in their facts, or *what* difference in the procedural set-up, has produced that difference in result. Those are the two problems which must be in your mind as you examine the language of the opinions. I repeat them. First, what *are* the significant categories of facts, and what is their significance to the court? Second, what *differences* in facts or in procedural set-up produce differences in the court's action when the situations are otherwise alike? . . .

We turn first to what I may call the orthodox doctrine of precedent, with which, in its essence, you are already familiar. Every case lays down a rule, the rule of the case. The express ratio decidendi is prima facie the rule of the case, since it is the ground upon which the court chose to rest its decision. But a later court can reexamine the case and can invoke the canon that no judge has power to decide what is not before him, can, through examination of the facts or of the procedural issue, narrow the picture of what was actually before the court and can hold that the ruling made requires to be understood as thus restricted. In the extreme form this results in what is known as expressly "confining the case to its particular facts." This rule holds only of redheaded Walpoles in pale magenta Buick cars. And when you find this said of a past case you know that in effect it has been overruled. Only a convention, a somewhat absurd convention, prevents flat over-ruling in such instances. It seems to be felt as definitely improper to state that the court in a prior case was wrong, peculiarly so if that case was in the same court which is speaking now. It seems to be felt that this would undermine the dogma of the infallibility of courts. So lip service is done to that dogma, while the rule which the prior court laid down is disembowelled. The execution proceeds with due respect, with mandarin courtesy.

Now this orthodox view of the authority of precedent—which I shall call the *strict* view—is but *one of two views* which seem to me wholly contradictory to each other. It is in practice the dogma which is applied to *unwelcome* precedents. It is the recognized, legitimate, honorable technique for whittling precedents away, for making the lawyer, in his argument, and the court, in its decision, free of them. It is a surgeon's knife. . . .

. . . when you turn to the actual operations of the courts, or, indeed, to the arguments of lawyers, you will find a totally different view of precedent at work beside this first one. That I shall call, to give it a name, the *loose view* of precedent.

That is the view that a court has decided, and decided authoritatively, *any* point or all points on which it chose to rest a case, or on which it chose, after due argument to pass. No matter how broad the statement, no matter how unnecessary on the facts or the procedural issues, if that was the rule the court laid down, then that the court has held. Indeed, this view carries over often into dicta, and even into dicta which are grandly obiter. In its extreme form this results in thinking and arguing exclusively from *language* that is found in past opinions, and in citing and working with that language wholly without reference to the facts of the case which called the language forth.

Now it is obvious that this is a device not for cutting past opinions away from judges' feet, but for using them as a springboard when they are found convenient. This is a device for *capitalizing welcome precedents.* And both the lawyers and judges use it so. And judged by the *practice* of the most respected courts of ordinary stature, this doctrine of precedent is like the other, recognized, legitimate, honorable.

What I wish to sink deep into your minds about the doctrine of precedent, therefore, is that it is two-headed. It is Janus-faced. That it is not one doctrine, nor one line of doctrine, but two, and two which, *applied at the same time to the same precedent, are contradictory of each other.* That there is one doctrine for getting rid of precedents deemed troublesome and one doctrine for making use of precedents that seem helpful. That these two doctrines exist side by side. That the same lawyer in the same brief, the same judge in the same opinion, may be using the one doctrine, the technically strict one, to cut down half the older cases that he deals with, and using the other doctrine, the loose one, for building with the other half. Until you realize this you do not see how it is possible for law to change and to develop, and yet to stand on the past. You do not see how it is possible to avoid the past mistakes of courts, and yet to make use of every happy insight for which a judge in writing may have found expression . . .

Nor, until you see this double aspect of the doctrine-in-action, do you appreciate how little, in detail, you can predict *out of the rules alone;* how much you must turn, for purposes of prediction, to the reactions of the judges to the facts and to the life around them . . .

Applying this two faced doctrine of precedent to your work in a case class you get, it seems to me, some such result as this. You read each case from the angle of its *maximum* value as a precedent, at least from the angle of its maximum value as a precedent *of the first water.* You will recall that I recommended taking down the ratio decidendi in substantially the court's own words. You see now what I had in mind. On the other hand, you will read each case for its *minimum* value as a precedent, to set against the maximum. In doing this you have your eyes out for the narrow issue in the case, the narrower the better. The first question is, how much can this case fairly be made to stand for by a later court to whom the precedent is welcome: You may well add—though this will be slightly flawed authority—the dicta which appear to have been well considered. The second question is, how much is there in this case that cannot be got around, even by a later court that wishes to avoid it?

You have now the tools for arguing from that case as counsel on *either* side of a new case. You turn then to the problem of prediction. Which view will this same court, on a later case on slightly different facts, take: will it choose the narrow or the loose: Which use will be made of this case by one of the other courts whose opinions are before you? Here you will call to your aid the matter of attitude that I have been discussing. Here you will use all that you know of individual judges, or of the trends in specific courts, or, indeed, of the trend in the line of business, or in the situation, or in the times at large—in anything which you may expect to become apparent and important to the court in later cases. But always and always, you will bear in mind that each precedent has not one value, but two, and that the two are wide apart, and that whichever value a later court assigns to it, such assignment will be respectable, traditionally sound, dogmatically correct. Above all, as you turn this information to your own training you will, I hope, come to see that in most doubtful cases the precedents *must* speak ambiguously until the court has made up its mind whether each one of them is welcome or unwelcome. And that the job of persuasion which falls upon you will call, therefore, not only for providing a technical ladder to reach on authority the result that you contend for, but even more, if you are to have *your* use of the precedents made as *you* propose it, the job calls for you, on the facts, to persuade the court your case is sound.

People—and they are curiously many—who think that precedent produces or ever did produce a certainty that did not involve matters of judgment and of persuasion, or who think that what I have described involves improper equivocation by the courts or departure from the court-ways of some golden age—such people simply do not know our system of precedent in which they live.

OLIPHANT,* *A RETURN TO* STARE DECISIS
14 American Bar Association Journal 71-73, 159 (1928)

. . . [A] most profound change . . . has been slowly and imperceptibly creeping into our treatment of problems in Anglo-American law, a fundamental change which merits careful study in order that we may recognize its presence, measure its extent, and judge its consequences. Let me anticipate my conclusions by asserting that we are well on our way toward a shift from following decisions to following so-called principles, from *stare decisis* to what I shall call *stare dictis;* by saying that this shift has far-reaching and unfortunate consequences for both the art of judicial government and the science of law, and by proposing a return toward the ancient doctrine of *stare decisis.*

Stare Decisis Analyzed. Support for this position will be found by examining that doctrine. It asserts not one thing, but two. For one thing, it asserts that prior

* Herman Oliphant, after beginning his teaching career as Professor of English, became a member of the faculty of the University of Chicago Law School in 1914, of Columbia Law School in 1921, and of the Johns Hopkins Institute of Law in 1929. From 1933 to his death in 1939, he was General Counsel to the U.S. Treasury Dept. The article from which portions are here reprinted constituted his presidential address to the Association of American Law Schools in 1927.—Editor

decisions are to be followed, not disregarded. But it also asserts that we are to follow the prior decisions and not something else.

The First Meaning of the Doctrine. Most discussions of the doctrine of *stare decisis* have emphasized the first of these two assertions. In those we are told of the advantages and disadvantages of the doctrine. It has been pointed out how, on the one hand, it makes the law applicable to future transactions certain and the future decisions of judges predictable; and again, how it gives us justice according to law and not according to the whims of men. On the other hand, it has been shown that to follow it gives us a measure of inflexibility in our law, resisting changes needed to meet changing conditions. We are all familiar with these and other broad implications of this branch of the doctrine and have considered the necessary choice between conflicting advantages which its acceptance or rejection involves. The vigor of this branch of the ancient doctrine has been weakened but little. Something in the cases is being followed. This whole aspect of the matter is mentioned here only to be set to one side.

The Second Meaning of the Doctrine. . . . There seems to have been little critical study of this phase of the doctrine,—of just what it is in prior decisions which is to be followed. General statements that the decision is to be looked for, that dicta are of slight weight and offer no certain guide can be turned to at many places in the books and are familiar to all. Students beginning their law study are told these things in a general way and then are left to an apprenticeship among the cases to discover largely for themselves their fuller meaning. Yet this matter is the one most vital and difficult factor conditioning the soundness of their scholarship. It is because the word *decision* may mean any one of many things that it is perilous to leave the matter thus unarticulated.

What Does the Case Decide? In the first place, a court, in deciding a case, may throw out a statement as to how it would decide some other case. Now if that statement is a statement of another case which is as narrow and specific as the actual case before the court, it is easily recognized as dictum and given its proper weight as such. In the second place the court may throw out a broader statement, covering a whole group of cases. . . . But so long as that statement does not cover the case before the court, it is readily recognized as being not a decision, much less the decision of the case. It is dictum, so labeled and appraised. But in the third place, a court may make a statement broad enough to dispose of the case in hand as well as to cover also a few or many other states of fact. Statements of this third sort may cover a number of fact situations ranging from one other to legion. Such a statement is sometimes called the *decision* of the case. Thereby the whole ambiguity of that word is introduced and the whole difficulty presented.

If a more careful usage limits the word *decision* to the *action* taken by the court in the specific case before it, i.e., to the naked judgment or order entered, the difficulty is not met; it is merely shifted. *Stare decisis* thus understood becomes useless for no decision in that limited sense can ever be followed. No identical case can arise. All other cases will differ in some circumstance—in time, if in no other, and most of them will have differences which are not trivial. *Decision* in the sense meant in *stare decisis* must, therefore, refer to a proposition of law covering a group of fact situations . . . as a minimum, the fact situation of the instant case and at least one other.

To bring together into one class even this minimum of two fact situations however similar they may be, always has required and always will require[1] an abstraction. If Paul and Peter are to be thought of together at all, they must both be apostles or be thought of as having some other attribute in common. Classification is abstraction. An element or elements common to the two fact situations put into one class must be drawn out from each to become the content of the category and the subject of the proposition of law which is thus applied to the two cases.

But such a grouping may include multitudes of fact situations so long as a single attribute common to them all can be found. Between these two extremes lies a gradation of groups of fact situations each with its corresponding proposition of law, ranging from a grouping subtending but two situations to those covering hosts of them. This series of groupings of fact situations gives us a parallel series of corresponding propositions of law, each more and more generalized as we recede farther and farther from the instant state of facts and include more and more fact situations in the successive groupings. It is a mounting and widening structure, each proposition including all that has gone before and becoming more general by embracing new states of fact. For example, A's father induces her not to marry B as she promised to do. On a holding that the father is not liable to B for so doing, a gradation of widening propositions can be built, a very few of which are:

1. Fathers are privileged to induce daughters to break promises to marry.
2. Parents are so privileged.
3. Parents are so privileged as to both daughters and sons.
4. All persons are so privileged as to promises to marry.
5. Parents are so privileged as to all promises made by their children.
6. All persons are so privileged as to all promises made by anyone.

There can be erected upon the action taken by a court in any case such a gradation of generalizations and this is commonly done in the opinion. Sometimes it is built up to dizzy heights by the court itself and at times, by law teachers and writers, it is reared to those lofty summits of the absolute and the infinite.

Where on that gradation of propositions are we to take our stand and say "This proposition is the decision of this case within the meaning of the doctrine of *stare decisis?*" Can a proposition of law of this third type ever become so broad that, as to any of the cases it would cover, it is mere dictum?

A Question of Double Difficulty. That would be difficult enough if it ended there. But just as one and the same apple can be thrown into any one of many groups of barrels according to its size, color, shape, etc., so also there stretches up and away from every single case in the books, not one possible gradation of widening generalizations, but many multitudes of radii shoot out from it, each

---

[1] This needs emphasis to avoid any impression that abstractions and generalizations are thought to have no useful part to play. They are always and everywhere indispensable.

pair enclosing one of an indefinite number of these gradations of broader and broader generalizations. For example, a contract for wages contains a stipulation that it shall be non-assignable by the employee. A court holds that the laborer can assign anyway and that his assignee can sue the employer for the wages regardless of the stipulation. This holding can serve as the apex of many triangles of generalizations. At the base of one will be a broad generalization treating the claim as property and asserting the alienability of property; at the base of another will be an equally broad generalization having to do with contractual stipulations opposed to public policy and the base of a third will be a similarly wide generalization concerning the liquidation of claims in the labor market. Others could be enumerated and other cases similarly analyzed. That is not needed, for we all know of at least one case appearing in the case books of more than one subject upon which securely rests more than one inverted pyramid of favorite theory.

A student is told to seek the "doctrine" or "principle" of a case, but which of its welter of stairs shall he ascend and how high up shall he go? Is there some one step on some one stair which is *the* decision of the case within the meaning of the mandate *stare decisis?* That is the double difficulty. Each precedent considered by a judge and each case studied by a student rests at the center of a vast and empty stadium. The angle and distance from which that case is to be viewed involves the choice of a seat. Which shall be chosen? Neither judge nor student can escape the fact that he can and must choose. To realize how wide the possibilities and significant the consequences of that choice are is elementary to an understanding of *stare decisis.* To ask whether there exists a coercion of some logic to make that choice either inevitable or beneficent, searches the significance of *stare decisis* in judicial government and the soundness of scholarship in law. This question is real and insistent. It is one which should be asked explicitly and faced squarely. . . .

But there is a constant factor in the cases which is susceptible of sound and satisfying study. The predictable element in it all is what courts have done in response to the stimuli of the facts of the concrete cases before them. Not the judges' opinions, but which way they decide cases will be the dominant subject matter of any truly scientific study of law. This is the field for scholarly work worthy of best talents because the work to be done is not the study of vague and shifting rationalizations but the study of such tough things as the accumulated wisdom of men taught by immediate experience in contemporary life,—the battered experiences of judges among brutal facts. The response of their intuition of experience to the stimulus of human situations is the subject-matter having that constancy and objectivity necessary for truly scientific study. When we pin our attention to this, we may more freely criticize what courts have said but we shall more cautiously criticize what they have done realizing, as we shall, that they were exposed to the impact of more of the facts than we.

This surer thing for scholarly purpose is also the inner secret of what is soundest in the enfeebled *stare decisis* in judicial government of today. With eyes cleared of the old and broad abstractions which curtain our vision, we come to recognize more and more the eminent good sense in what courts are wont to do about disputes before them. Judges are men and men respond to human situations. When the facts stimulating them to the action taken are studied from a particular and current point of view, which our present classification prevents, we acquire a new faith in *stare decisis*. From this viewpoint we see that courts are dominantly coerced not by the essays of their predecessors but by a surer thing,—by an intuition of fitness of solution to problem,—and a renewed confidence in judicial government is engendered. To state the matter more concretely, the decision of a particular case by a thoughtful scholar is to be preferred to that by a poorly trained judge but the decision of such a judge in a particular case is infinitely to be preferred to a decision of it preordained by some broad "principle" laid down by the scholar when this and a host of other concrete cases had never even occurred to him.

One sampling of this proposed subject-matter of a real science of law must suffice. There are two lines of old cases involving the validity of promises not to compete. They are considered in square conflict. But when the opinions are ignored and the facts re-examined, all the cases holding the promises invalid are found to be cases of employees' promises not to compete with their employers after a term of employment. Contemporary guild regulations not noticed in the opinions made their holding eminently sound. All the cases holding the promises valid were cases of promises by those selling a business and promising not to compete with the purchasers. Contemporary economic reality made these holdings also eminently sound. This distinction between these two lines of cases is not even hinted at in any of the opinions but the courts' intuition of experience led them to follow it with amazing sureness and the law resulting fitted life. That is a sample of the stuff capable of scientific study. . . .

GOODHART,* *DETERMINING THE* RATIO
DECIDENDI *OF A CASE*
40 Yale Law Journal 161-183 (1930)

. . . The initial difficulty with which we are faced is the phrase *"ratio deci- dendi"* itself. With the possible exception of the legal term "malice," it is the most misleading expression in English law, for the reason which the judge gives for his decision is never the binding part of the precedent. The logic of the argument, the analysis of prior cases, the statement of the historical background may all be demonstrably incorrect in a judgment, but the case remains a precedent nevertheless. It would not be difficult to cite a large number of leading cases, both ancient and modern, in which one or more of the reasons given for the decision can be proved to be wrong; but in spite of this these cases contain valid and definite

* Arthur L. Goodhart, born and educated in America, has spent most of his professional life in England. He held various legal and administrative posts at Cambridge University until 1931, when he became professor of jurisprudence at Oxford University. Since 1951 he has been Master of University College at Oxford. His books include Essays in Jurisprudence and Common Law (1931); English Law and the Moral Law (1953).—Editor

principles which are as binding as if the reasoning on which they are based were correct.

In Priestley v. Fowler the famous or infamous doctrine of common employment was first laid down. Of this case it has been well said, "Lord Abinger planted it, Baron Alderson watered it, and the Devil gave it increase." Yet the case is still law in England (although limited in effect by the Employers Liability Act of 1880) in spite of the fact that the two reasons on which Lord Abinger based his judgment are palpably incorrect. The first reason is that any other rule would be "absurd." This argument is always a dangerous one upon which to base a judgment and in this instance, it is, unfortunately, the rule in Priestley v. Fowler which has proved to be not only absurd but also unjust. The second reason given by Lord Abinger is that by his contract of service a servant impliedly consents to run the risk of working with negligent fellow-servants. In fact, of course, a servant does not consent to run the risk; the implication was invented by the judge himself. . . .

For that matter, by what may seem a strange method to those who do not understand the theory of the Common Law, it is precisely some of those cases which have been decided on incorrect premises or reasoning which have become the most important in the law. New principles, of which their authors were unconscious or which they have misunderstood, have been established by these judgments. Paradoxical as it may sound, the law has frequently owed more to its weak judges than it has to its strong ones. A bad reason may often make good law. . . . Our modern law of torts has been developed to a considerable extent by a series of bad arguments, and our property law is in many instances founded on incorrect history. To state this is not, however, to question the authority of that law. It is clear therefore, that the first rule for discovering the *ratio decidendi* of a case is that it must not be sought in the reasons on which the judge has based his decision. . . .

Having stated its reasons for reaching a certain conclusion, the court frequently sums up the result in a general statement of the law on the point at issue. Can we find the principle of the case in this proposition of law, this comprehensive expression of the rule involved, which students underline with such enthusiasm in their casebooks? Thus in the chapter on Judgments in Halsbury's *The Laws of England* (18:210), the rule is given as follows:

> "It may be laid down as a general rule that that part alone of a decision of a court of law is binding upon courts of coordinate jurisdiction and inferior courts which consists of the enunciation of the reason or principle upon which the question before the court has really been determined. This underlying principle which forms the only authoritative element of a precedent is often termed the *ratio decidendi*."

Professor Morgan of the Harvard Law School, in his valuable book *The Study of Law*, says:

> "Those portions of the opinion setting forth the rules of law applied by the court, the application of which was required for the determination of the issues

presented, are to be considered as decision and as primary authority in later cases in the same jurisdiction."

If these statements are to be understood in their literal sense, it is respectfully submitted that the words are misleading, for it is not the rule of law "set forth" by the court, or the rule "enunciated" as Halsbury puts it, which necessarily constitutes the principle of the case. There may be no rule of law set forth in the opinion, or the rule when stated may be too wide or too narrow. In appellate courts, the rules of law set forth by the different judges may have no relation to each other. Nevertheless each of these cases contains a principle which can be discovered on proper analysis.

So also a case may be a precedent, involving an important principle of law, although the court has given judgment without delivering an opinion. At the present time, although occasionally an appellate court will affirm without opinion a case which involves an interesting point, we rarely find a case of any importance in which an opinion has not been written. In the past, however, especially during the Year Book period, we find a great number of cases in which there were no opinions and in which the principle therefore must be sought elsewhere.

Of more frequent occurrence in recent cases is the practice of delivering an opinion, but at the same time being careful not to state any general principle of law . . .

Again, a case may contain a definite principle, although the expression of it in the opinion may not be strictly accurate. In Rex v. Fenton [1 Lew. C.C. 179 (1830)] the prisoner caused the death of a man by wantonly throwing a large stone down a mine. In his charge to the jury Tindal, C. J., said:

> "If death ensues as the consequence of a wrongful act, an act which the party who commits it can neither justify nor excuse, it is not accidental death, but manslaughter."

The principle of the case was correct, although the statement of it was too wide, as was held in the later case of Regina v. Franklin, [15 Cox. C.C. 163 (1883)]. In that case the prisoner threw a box belonging to a refreshment stall keeper into the sea, thereby killing a swimmer. The point at issue was whether, apart from the question of negligence, the prisoner was guilty of manslaughter, his act having been a wrongful one. Field, J., said:

> "We do not think the case cited by the counsel for the prosecution is binding upon us in the facts of this case, and, therefore, the civil wrong against the refreshment-stall keeper is immaterial to this charge of manslaughter." . . .

A striking example of an overstatement of the principle involved in a case may be found in Riggs v. Palmer, [115 N.Y. 506, 22 N.E. 188 (1889)]. The court held that a legatee, who had murdered his testator, could not take under the will, because no one shall be permitted "to take advantage of his own wrong, or to found any claim upon his own iniquity, or to acquire property by his own crime." It would, of course, be possible to give a large number of situations in which this statement would be wrong or doubtful. Would it apply, for example, if the legatee had negligently killed the testator in a motor accident? . . .

On the other hand the rule of law may be stated in too narrow a form. In Barwick v. English Joint Stock Bank [L.R. 2 Ex. 259 (1867)] the defendant's bank manager fraudulently induced the plaintiff to accept a valueless guarantee. In delivering the judgment of the court, Willes, J., said:

> "The general rule is, that the master is answerable for every such wrong of the servant or agent as is committed in the course of the service and for the master's benefit, though no express command or privity of the master be proved."

It was generally believed that this statement of the law was correct until, forty-five years later, the House of Lords in Lloyd v. Grace, Smith & Co. [(1912) A.C. 716] held that it was too narrow. The words "and for the master's benefit" were merely descriptive of the facts in the Barwick case, and not a necessary part of the principle involved. The House of Lords did not disapprove of the principle of the Barwick case, but held that "it is . . . a mistake to qualify it by saying that it only applies when the principal has profited by the fraud."

When we consider the appellate courts it becomes even more obvious that the principle of the case cannot necessarily be found in the rule of law enunciated, for it is not infrequent to find that, although the judges may concur in the result, they differ widely in their statements of the law. . . . Nevertheless these cases cannot be ignored as precedents on the ground that the rules of law set forth cannot be reconciled.

Since, therefore, the principle of the case is not necessarily found in either the reasoning of the court or in the proposition of law set forth, we must seek some other method of determining it. Does this mean that we can ignore the opinion entirely and work out the principle for ourselves from the facts of the case and the judgment reached on those facts? This seems to be the view of a certain American school of legal thought represented by Professor Oliphant. According to him it is what the judge does and not what he says that matters. He writes:

> "But there is a constant factor in the cases which is susceptible of sound and satisfying study. The predictable element in it all is what courts have done in response to the stimuli of the facts of the concrete cases before them. Not the judges' opinions, but which way they decide cases, will be the dominant subject matter of any truly scientific study of law."

Undoubtedly this theory has the attractiveness of simplicity. No longer will we have to analyze the sometimes lengthy and difficult opinions of the judges; all that we are concerned with are the facts and the conclusion. The judge who writes an opinion will be wasting both his own time and ours, for it is not what he says but what he does that matters. We can ignore the vocal behaviour of the judge, which sometimes fills many pages, and concentrate upon his nonvocal behaviour which occupies but a few lines.

Unfortunately I believe that there is a fallacy in Professor Oliphant's argument which will prevent our following this convenient course. The fallacy lies in suggesting that the facts of a case are a constant factor, that the judge's conclusion is based upon the fixed premises of a given set of facts. We do not have to be philosophers to realize that facts are not constant but relative. The crucial question is "What facts are we talking about?" The same set of facts may look entirely different to two different persons. The judge founds his conclusions upon a group of facts selected by him as material from among a larger mass of facts, some of which might seem significant to a layman, but which, to a lawyer, are irrelevant. The judge, therefore, reaches a conclusion upon the facts as he sees them. It is on these facts that he bases his judgment, and not on any others. It follows that our task in analyzing a case is not to state the facts and the conclusion, but to state the material facts as seen by the judge and his conclusion based on them. It is by his choice of the material facts that the judge creates law. A congeries of facts is presented to him; he chooses those which he considers material and rejects those which are immaterial, and then bases his conclusion upon the material ones. To ignore his choice is to miss the whole point of the case. Our system of precedent becomes meaningless if we say that we will accept his conclusion but not his view of the facts. His conclusion is based on the material facts as he sees them, and we cannot add or subtract from them by proving that other facts existed in the case. It is, therefore, essential to know what the judge has said about his choice of the facts, for what he does has a meaning for us only when considered in relation to what he has said. A divorce of the conclusion from the material facts on which that conclusion is based is illogical, and must lead to arbitrary and unsound results.

The first and most essential step in the determination of the principle of a case is, therefore, to ascertain the material facts on which the judge has based his conclusion. Are there any rules which will help us in isolating these material facts? It is obvious that none can be found which will invariably give us the desired result, for if this were possible then the interpretation of cases, which is one of the most difficult of the arts, would be comparatively easy. The following tentative suggestions may, however, prove of some aid to the student faced with his first case-book.

If there is no opinion, or if the opinion does not contain a statement of the facts, then we must assume that all the facts given in the report are material except those which on their face are not. Thus the facts of person, time, place, kind, and amount are presumably immaterial unless stated to be material. As a rule the law is the same for all persons, at all times, and at all places within the jurisdiction of the court. For the purposes of the law a contract made between A and B in Liverpool on Monday involving the sale of a book worth £10 is identical with a similar contract made between C and D in London on Friday involving the sale of a painting worth £100,000. . . .

If there is an opinion which gives the facts, the first point to notice is that we cannot go behind the opinion to show that the facts appear to be different in the record. We are bound by the judge's statement of the facts even though it is patent that he has misstated them, for it is on the facts as he, perhaps incorrectly, has seen them that he has based his judgment. . . .

Two . . . cases illustrate this point in an interesting manner. In Smith v. London and South Western Ry. [L.R. 6 C.P. 14 (1870)] Kelly, C. B., Channell, B., and Blackburn, J., each assumed as a fact "that no reasonable man would have foreseen that the fire would get to the plaintiff's cottage." We lose the whole point of their judgments if we attempt to explain them by showing that a reasonable man should have foreseen that the fire might reach the cottage. . . . Similarly in In Re Polemis and Furness, Withy & Co. [(1912) 3 K.B. 560] the Court of Appeal was bound by the arbitrators' finding of fact that a reasonable man would not have anticipated that a plank falling into the hold of a steamer filled with petrol vapour might cause an explosion. This finding of fact is probably incorrect, but we cannot ignore it if we are to determine the true principle of the judgments based on it. As has already been said, if we are not bound by the facts as stated by the judge it would be wholly illogical to be bound by his conclusion on those facts.

Moreover, such a course would be most inconvenient, for it would then become necessary when citing an important case to go through the record so as to be certain that the facts as given by the court were correct. In view of the vast number of precedents existing on almost any disputed point of law the task of the common law lawyer is sufficiently difficult at the present time; if he must also consult the record in every case to determine the actual facts his work will be overwhelming. The emphasis which American law libraries are now placing on collecting the whole records in the leading cases may prove to be a dangerous one, for such collections tend to encourage a practice which is inconvenient in operation and disastrous in theory.

Although it is comparatively rare to find any real conflict between the facts given in the opinion and those in the record, it is of frequent occurrence to find that the facts in the opinion fail to include some of the facts in the record. Under these circumstances there are two possible explanations of the omission: (1) the fact was considered by the court but was found to be immaterial, or (2) the fact in the record was not considered by the court as it was not called to its attention by counsel or was for some other reason overlooked. Which of the two explanations is the correct one will depend upon the circumstances of the particular case. If counsel have referred to the fact in the course of their arguments this is strong evidence that the fact has not been overlooked but has been purposely omitted. For this reason the practice in the Law Reports of giving a short summary of counsel's speeches is of particular value. But if it is clear that a certain fact, however material it may have been, was not considered by the court, then the case is not a precedent in future cases in which a similar fact appears. . . . It must be noted, however, that the burden of showing that a fact has been overlooked is a heavy one, for as a rule a material fact does not escape the attention of counsel and of the court.

Having, as a first step, determined all the facts of the case as seen by the judge, it is then necessary to discover which of these facts he has found material for his judgment. This is far more difficult than the first step, for the judge may fail to label his facts. It is only the strong judge, one who is clear in his own mind as to the grounds for his decision, who invariably says, "on facts A and B and on them alone I reach conclusion X." Too often the cautious judge will include in his opinion facts which are not essential to his judgment, leaving it for future generations to determine whether or not these facts constitute a part of the *ratio decidendi*. The following guides may, however, be followed in distinguishing between material and immaterial facts.

(1) As was stated above in discussing the principle of a case in which there is no opinion, the facts of person, time, place, kind, and amount are presumably immaterial. This is true to an even greater extent when there is an opinion, for if these facts are held to be material particular emphasis will naturally be placed upon them.

(2) All facts which the court specifically states are immaterial must be considered so. [The author here refers to a case in which the evidence showed that defendant maintained an illegal drinking place, at which acts disturbing the peace occurred. The N.Y. Court of Appeals ruled that the charge of maintaining a public nuisance was sufficiently sustained by proof of an illegal drinking place; that the evidence of disorderly conduct introduced at the trial was immaterial.—Editor]

(3) All facts which the court impliedly treats as immaterial must be considered immaterial. The difficulty in these cases is to determine whether a court has or has not considered the fact immaterial. Evidence of this implication is found when the court, after having stated the facts generally, then proceeds to choose a smaller number of facts on which it bases its conclusion. The omitted facts are presumably held to be immaterial. In Rylands v. Fletcher [L.R. 3 H.L. 330 (1868)] the defendant employed an independent contractor to make a reservoir on his land. Owing to the contractor's negligence in not filling up some disused mining shafts, the water escaped and flooded the plaintiff's mine. The defendant was held liable. Is the principle of the case that a man who builds a reservoir on his land is liable for the negligence of an independent contractor? Why then is the case invariably cited as laying down the broader doctrine of "absolute liability"? The answer is found in the opinions. After stating the facts as above, the judges thereafter ignored the fact of the contractor's negligence, and based their conclusions on the fact that an artificial reservoir had been constructed. The negligence of the contractor was, therefore, impliedly held to be an immaterial fact. . . .

It is obvious from the above cases that it is essential to determine what facts have been held to be immaterial, for the principle of a case depends as much on exclusion as it does on inclusion. It is under these circumstances that the reasons given by the judge in his opinion, or his statement of the rule of law which he is following, are of peculiar importance, for they may furnish us with a guide for determining which facts he considered material and which immaterial. His reason may be incorrect and his statement of the law too wide, but they will indicate to us on what facts he reached his conclusion. . . .

(4) All facts which are specifically stated to be material must be considered material. Such specific statements are usually found in cases in which the judges are afraid of laying down too broad a principle. Thus in Heaven v. Pender [11 Q.B.D. 503 (1883)] the plaintiff, a workman employed to paint a ship, was

injured because of a defective staging supplied by the defendant dock owner to the shipowner. Brett, M. R., held that the defendant was liable on the ground that:

". . . whenever one person is by circumstances placed in such a position with regard to another that every one of ordinary sense who did think would at once recognise that if he did not use ordinary care and skill in his own conduct with regard to those circumstances he would cause danger of injury to the person or property of the other, a duty arises to use ordinary care and skill to avoid such danger."

Cotton and Bowen, L.JJ., agreed with the Master of the Rolls that the defendant was liable, but the material facts on which they based their judgment were: (1) that the plaintiff was on the staging for business in which the dock owner was interested, and (2) he "must be considered as invited by the dock owner to use the dock and all appliances provided by the dock owner as incident to the use of the dock." The principle of the case cannot, therefore, be extended beyond the limitation of these material facts.

(5) If the opinion does not distinguish between material and immaterial facts then all the facts set forth in the opinion must be considered material with the exception of those that on their face are immaterial. There is a presumption against wide principles of law, and the smaller the number of material facts in a case the wider will the principle be. Thus if a case like Hambrook v. Stokes [(1925) 1 K.B. 141], in which a mother died owing to shock at seeing a motor accident which threatened her child, is decided on the fact that a bystander may recover for injury due to shock, we have a broad principle of law. If the additional fact that the bystander was a mother is held to be material we then get a narrow principle of law. Therefore, unless a fact is expressly or impliedly held to be immaterial, it must be considered material.

(6) Thus far we have been discussing the method of determining the principle of a case in which there is only a single opinion, or in which all the opinions are in agreement. How do we determine the principle of a case in which there are several opinions which agree as to the result but differ in the material facts on which they are based? In such an event the principle of the case is limited to the sum of all the facts held to be material by the various judges. A case involves facts A, B and C, and the defendant is held liable. The first judge finds that fact A is the only material fact; the second that B is material, the third that C is material. The principle of the case is, therefore, that on the material facts A, B and C the defendant is liable. If, however, two of the three judges had been in agreement that fact A was the only material one, and that the others were immaterial, then the case would be a precedent on this point, even though the third judge had held that facts B and C were the material ones. The method of determining the principle of a case in which there are several opinions is thus the same as that used when there is only one. Care must be taken by the student, however, to see that the material facts of each opinion are stated and analyzed accurately, for sometimes judges think that they are in agreement on the facts when they concur only in the result.

Having established the material and the immaterial facts of the case as seen by the court, we can then proceed to state the principle of the case. It is to be found in the conclusion reached by the judge on the basis of the material facts and on the exclusion of the immaterial ones. In a certain case the court finds that facts A, B and C exist. It then excludes fact A as immaterial, and on facts B and C it reaches conclusion X. What is the *ratio decidendi* of this case? There are two principles: (1) In any future case in which the facts are A, B and C, the court must reach conclusion X, and (2) in any future case in which the facts are B and C the court must reach conclusion X. In the second case the absence of fact A does not affect the result, for fact A has been held to be immaterial. The court, therefore, creates a principle when it determines which are the material and which are the immaterial facts on which it bases its decision.

It follows that a conclusion based on a fact the existence of which has not been determined by the court, cannot establish a principle. We then have what is called a dictum. If, therefore, a judge in the course of his opinion suggests a hypothetical fact, and then states what conclusion he would reach if that fact existed, he is not creating a principle. The difficulty which is sometimes found in determining whether a statement is a dictum or not is due to uncertainty as to whether the judge is treating a fact as hypothetical or real. When a judge says, "In this case, as the facts are so and so, I reach conclusion X," this is not a dictum, even though the judge has been incorrect in his statement of the facts. But if the judge says, "If the facts in this case were so and so then I would reach conclusion X," this is a dictum, even though the facts are as given. The second point frequently arises when a case involves two different sets of facts. Having determined the first set of facts and reached a conclusion on them, the judge may not desire to take up the time necessarily involved in determining the second set. Any views he may express as to the undetermined second set are accordingly dicta. If, however, the judge does determine both sets, as he is at liberty to do, and reaches a conclusion on both, then the case creates two principles and neither is a dictum. . . . On the other hand, if in a case the judge holds that a certain fact prevents a cause of action from arising, then his further finding that there would have been a cause of action except for this fact is an obiter dictum. By excluding the preventive fact the situation becomes hypothetical, and the conclusion based on such hypothetical facts can only be a dictum.

Having established the principle of a case, and excluded all dicta, the final step is to determine whether or not it is a binding precedent for some succeeding case in which the facts are prima facie similar. This involves a double analysis. We must first state the material facts in the precedent case and then attempt to find those which are material in the second one. If these are identical, then the first case is a binding precedent for the second, and the court must reach the same conclusion as it did in the first one. If the first case lacks any material fact or contains any additional ones not found in the second, then it is not a direct precedent. Thus, in Nichols v. Marsland [(L.R. 10 Ex. 255 (1875)] the material facts were similar to those in Rylands v. Fletcher [supra] except for the additional fact that the water escaped owing to a violent storm. If the court had found that this additional fact was not a material one, then the rule in Rylands v.

Fletcher would have applied. But as it found that it was a material one, it was able to reach a different conclusion.

[The author then rejects the objection that the "material facts" doctrine "leaves us with hardly any general legal principles, for facts are infinitely various . . ." This variety is reduced by categorization (as we have seen Llewellyn demonstrate). Nor do judges nowadays, the author asserts, circumvent precedents by finding, arbitrarily, that additional facts are material. And if judges determine, erroneously, that certain material facts exist, the decision should nevertheless be authoritative in relation to the facts assumed: "it is better to suffer this mistake, which may prove of benefit to the law as a whole, however painful its results may have been to the individual litigant, than to throw doubt on every precedent on which our law is based."—Editor]

Conclusion. The rules for finding the principle of a case can, therefore, be summarized as follows:

(1) The principle of a case is not found in the reasons given in the opinion.

(2) The principle is not found in the rule of law set forth in the opinion.

(3) The principle is not necessarily found by a consideration of all the ascertainable facts of the case and the judge's decision.

(4) The principle of the case is found by taking account (a) of the facts treated by the judge as material, and (b) his decision as based on them.

(5) In finding the principle it is also necessary to establish what facts were held to be immaterial by the judge, for the principle may depend as much on exclusion as it does on inclusion.

The rules for finding what facts are material and what facts are immaterial as seen by the judge are as follows:

(1) All facts of person, time, place, kind and amount are immaterial unless stated to be material.

(2) If there is no opinion, or the opinion gives no facts, then all other facts in the record must be treated as material.

(3) If there is an opinion, then the facts as stated in the opinion are conclusive and cannot be contradicted from the record.

(4) If the opinion omits a fact which appears in the record this may be due either to (a) oversight, or (b) an implied finding that the fact is immaterial. The second will be assumed to be the case in the absence of other evidence.

(5) All facts which the judge specifically states are immaterial must be considered immaterial.

(6) All facts which the judge impliedly treats as immaterial must be considered immaterial.

(7) All facts which the judge specifically states to be material must be considered material.

(8) If the opinion does not distinguish between material and immaterial facts then all the facts set forth must be considered material.

(9) If in a case there are several opinions which agree as to the result but

differ as to the material facts, then the principle of the case is limited so as to fit the sum of all the facts held material by the various judges.

(10) A conclusion based on a hypothetical fact is a dictum. By hypothetical fact is meant any fact the existence of which has not been determined or accepted by the judge.

STONE,* *THE* RATIO *OF THE* RATIO DECIDENDI
22 Modern Law Review 597, 603-608 (1959)

. . . If the *ratio* of a case is deemed to turn on the facts in relation to the holding, and nine facts (a)-(j) are to be found in the report there may (so far as logical possibilities are concerned) be as many rival *rationes decidendi* as there are possible combinations of distinguishable facts in it. What is more, each of these "facts" is usually itself capable of being stated at various levels of generality, all of which embrace "the fact" in question in the precedent decision, but each of which may yield a different result in the different fact-situation of a later case. The range of "facts" of *Donoghue* v. *Stevenson*, [a 1932 House of Lords decision imposing liability upon the manufacturer of an opaque bottle of ginger beer found to contain a dead snail, for injury (shock and gastro-enteritis) to the plaintiff, a Scotch widow who drank from the bottle given her by one who purchased it from a retailer who in turn purchased it from the manufacturer—Editor] standing alone, might be over-simplified into a list somewhat as follows, each fact being itself stated at alternative levels.

(a) *Fact as to the Agent of Harm.* Dead snails, *or* any snails, *or* any noxious physical foreign body, *or* any noxious foreign element, physical or not, *or* any noxious element.

(b) *Fact as to Vehicle of Harm.* An opaque bottle of ginger beer, *or* an opaque bottle of beverage, *or* any bottle of beverage, *or* any container of commodities for human consumption, *or* any containers of any chattels for human use, *or* any chattel whatsoever, *or* any thing (including land or buildings).

(c) *Fact as to Defendant's Identity.* A manufacturer of goods nationally distributed through dispersed retailers, *or* any manufacturer, *or* any person working on the object for reward, *or* any person working on the object, *or* anyone dealing with the object.

(d) *Fact as to Potential Danger from Vehicle of Harm.* Object likely to become dangerous by negligence, *or* whether or not so.

(e) *Fact as to Injury to Plaintiff.* Physical personal injury, *or* nervous or physical personal injury, *or* any injury.

* Julius Stone, Challis Professor of Jurisprudence and International Law, University of Sydney, Australia, is author of The Province and Function of Law (1946); Legal Controls of International Conflict (1954); Aggression and World Order (1958); and co-author of Simpson and Stone, Law and Society (3 vols., 1948-49). —Editor

(f) *Fact as to Plaintiff's Identity.* A Scots widow, *or* a Scotswoman or a woman, *or* any adult, *or* any human being, *or* any legal person.

(g) *Fact as to Plaintiff's Relation to Vehicle of Harm.* Donee of purchaser, from retailer who bought directly from the defendant, *or* the purchaser from such retailer, *or* the purchaser from anyone, *or* any person related to such purchaser or other person, *or* any person into whose hands the object rightfully comes, *or* any person into whose hands it comes at all.

(h) *Fact as to Discoverability of Agent of Harm.* The noxious element being not discoverable by inspection of any intermediate party, *or* not so discoverable without destroying the saleability of the commodity, *or* not so discoverable by any such party who had a duty to inspect, *or* not so discoverable by any such party who could reasonably be expected *by the defendant* to inspect, *or* not discoverable by any such party who could reasonably be expected *by the court or a jury* to inspect.

(j) *Fact as to Time of Litigation.* The facts complained of were litigated in 1932, *or* any time before 1932, *or* after 1932, *or* at any time.

Let us first consider the question of "materiality" *apart from any view on that matter "explicitly" or "implicitly" manifest in the precedent court's opinion.* As to none of these facts (a)-(j), and as to none of the several alternative levels of statement of each of them, could it be said on the basis of the report of *Donoghue* v. *Stevenson* alone that it was on its face not "material" (in the logical sense) to the holding in that case. Even as to the time of litigation, as to which we are most tempted to say that this at least must be "immaterial" on the face of it, we must be careful to avoid a *petitio principii.* Are we really prepared to assert with dogmatism that *Donoghue* v. *Stevenson* should have been and would in fact have been, so decided in 1800? . . .

Does it then overcome this difficulty to define "materiality" as Professor Good-hart in effect does, in terms of the precedent court's explicit or implicit assertion as to which of facts (a)-(j) are material? Or to insist that the question, What are "material facts" by which we determine the prescriptive *ratio* of a case? is always to be determined *according to the view of the precedent court,* and not according to the view of the later court or observer. (Indeed, in defending his position in 1959 [12] this distinction becomes almost its central bastion.) Yet there will often be the gravest doubt as to what facts the precedent court "explicitly or implicitly" "determined" to be material. There will often be inconsistent indications from what is expressed or implicit, even in a one-judge court. Such inconsistencies as between the concurring judgments in appellate courts are notoriously also a consistent and fruitful source of legal uncertainty and change . . .

Yet these are not the most crucial difficulties with Professor Goodhart's system. The crucial ones arise rather from the several alternative levels of statement of each "material fact" of the precedent case, ranging from the full unique concreteness of that actual case, through a series of widening generalizations. . . .

[12] (1959) 22 M.L.R. [Modern Law Review] at 123.

. . . Is it reasonable to assume that courts using language appropriate to the case before them do, or could, address themselves in their choice of language to all the levels of generality at which each "material" fact (a)-(j) of the concrete case is capable of statement, not to speak of the possible combinations and variations of these facts, and the implications of all these for as yet unforeseen future cases? . . . And to admit also that level which might be "implicit" in the former judgment would in most cases be merely to impute to the precedent court a choice of levels of generalised statement (and therefore of the reach of the *ratio* in the instant case) which must in reality be made by the instant later court . . .

NOTES AND QUESTIONS

1. To what extent are Llewellyn, Oliphant, and Stone in agreement?

2. If you asked Goodhart to state the *"ratio decidendi"* of Priestley v. Fowler, what would probably be his formulation? How would Oliphant react to the same question? Llewellyn? Stone?

3. Are there any practical difficulties in the way of acting upon Oliphant's suggestion for ignoring the reasoning of court opinions and concentrating solely on the comparison of the fact situations in different cases?

4. What psychological assumptions is Oliphant making about the process by which judges reach their decisions? Are they warranted?

5. Since Goodhart's critics do not reject the precedent system itself, they agree that an appellate court deciding a case should examine prior opinions. Beyond this point, many questions arise to which answers don't come easily. Do they think a court, in examining precedents, should not look for the things Goodhart would have them look for? If so, what do they think the court should look for? What guidance as "rules of law" do they think precedent opinions offer? Is any guidance to come from other sources? Does the view of Goodhart or any of his critics represent the "correct" or "authoritative" attitude towards the ratio decidendi? We shall attempt to throw some light on these questions below.

(a) We have seen that while Oliphant would examine the prior opinion for facts pertinent to the decision, he would not confine himself to the opinion. He would look at all the facts that seemed material at the time of the prior decision, whether or not treated as material by the court and whether or not present in the record, if they were present in the social setting.

(b) Other writers take a more orthodox view in confining themselves to facts appearing in the prior court's opinion. But *which* facts in the opinion? Can it properly be said that the judge in the instant case takes into account only those facts which the prior opinion indicated were significant or "material"? There are difficulties here: Occasionally, for example, one finds the later court resurrecting some *insignificant* (buried) fact in the earlier opinion because otherwise it cannot follow the prior case, or "distinguish" it, as the case may be. Thus a "buried" fact in Priestley v. Fowler was the fact that the two employees worked closely together in what might be called the "same department" of work; Lord Abinger made no special point of this. Although Loring was unsuccessful in getting the Massachusetts court to distinguish Priestley v. Fowler on this basis, it is significant that many American state courts subsequently adopted this same "departmental distinction" to avoid application of the fellow-servant rule to employees in separate departments. (For another illustration of resurrecting a buried fact, see the observations on Tulk v. Moxhay in Montrose, "The Ratio Decidendi of a Case," 20 Modern L. Rev. 587, 594 (1957).)

As this illustrates, it is not at all clear that an appellate court in actual practice asks itself, as a key question, what facts were deemed material by the prior court. Assuming, however, that it does, certain difficulties, as the critics have emphasized, immediately arise: (1) the rarity of the prior court's explicit labeling, as material, of particular facts set forth in its opinion; (2) rarity of explicit indication of the level of generality or specificity at which each fact is deemed material; (3) rarity of announcement of a rule of law as such (which announced rule, some would say, contrary to Goodhart, ought to be authoritative).

Moreover, why should wise decision in a present case depend on an approach which has its *primary* focus upon the facts deemed material by the *prior* court? True, the rule of the prior court—announced or otherwise—must necessarily go beyond the precise facts before it (e.g., beyond covering cases of butcher boys named Priestley traveling on overloaded vans), and thus has relevance for later courts operating under a precedent system. But assuming even that the prior court has a definite breadth of rule in mind which is ascertainable by the later court, is not the *later* court best able to decide whether the rule should be conceived broadly enough so as to apply to the particular "beyond" area brought before *it* for decision? The later court must determine whether the principles or policies underlying the prior decision are also applicable to the later case—i.e., whether the facts of the two cases are "similar" enough (or the differences without sufficient significance) to justify giving the explicit or implicit "rule" of the earlier case sufficient breadth to "apply" to the later case. To allow that breadth to be *fixed* by what was said in a prior court's opinion without the present situation before it, would be to stultify the process of wise decision. The precedent supplies guidance lines, not a straitjacket.

(c) In general, the critics, and indeed the judges, while necessarily getting some guidance from the prior opinion, are *less rigid* than Goodhart. They would sanction departures from his 5 rules governing determination of the *ratio decidendi* and 10 rules for determining materiality of facts. As Stone has said, "Whatever weight be attached to Professor Goodhart's view that 'most English courts' follow 'the method' to which he is seeking to give a 'guide,' it seems clear both that judicial practice does not consistently do so, and that no rule of law compels them to do so" (Stone, supra, at p. 613). Llewellyn has emphasized this flexibility by saying that "there is not to be found in our system any clear and definite single relation between the cases and the Rule of Case-Law. We have instead a number of relations, any and each of which is authoritative and correct *if* the court chooses to use it." He asserts that judicial practice may recognize as the *ratio decidendi* the rule explicitly laid down as such by the prior court, or any rule regarded by the later court as "necessary" to the decision whether or not explicitly laid down, or the rule laid down by a legal commentator as the rule of the case, etc. "In a word, if one is to see our case-law system as it lives and moves, one must see that the relation between the rule and the cases may move all the way from copying any words printed by anybody in a 'law' book to meticulous reexamination of precise facts, issues, and holdings, in total disregard of any prior language whatsoever. And any degree or kind of operation within that lordly range is correct, doctrinally, if doctrine be taken to be a description of what authoritative courts are doing with and to cases and rules, and doing with effective authority" (Llewellyn, "The Rule of Law in Our Case Law of Contract," 47 Yale L.J. 1244, 1246-7 (1938)).

CHAPTER Three

The JUDGE as POLICY MAKER

The fellow-servant cases thus far encountered have high-lighted the judge's role as policy maker. Ordinarily we tend to think of the legislature rather than the court as being concerned with public policy issues. (Recall the observation of O'neall, J. in the Murray case in South Carolina.) Yet the courts are as significantly—though usually not as openly—concerned with such issues. As a distinguished teacher and writer in the field of tort law recently observed:*

While public policy is the basis of all law, it is sometimes forgotten that it lies at the base of every judicial decision. All that it means is that 'we the people' are a third party to every case in litigation. . . . Ordinarily the weighing of policy is only implicit, for the policy has already been set by constitution, statute or former decision. Ordinarily, any open appeal to public policy is in recognition of some principle likewise established. But implicit or open, an appeal to public policy is not infrequently made when constitution, statute and former decision are silent. It is here that the courts extend, limit or modify some old principle, or recognize some new principle. There is nothing startling in their reliance on public policy. . . .

What is startling, and only because of its rarity, in cases of serious departure from an old principle or of recognition of a new one, is for a court to put its finger on the particular policy relied upon. Here the courts are inclined to talk in terms of the broadest generalities. . . . The policies which the courts most clearly articulate are those which concern the administration of the courts themselves. They hesitate to modify the law if the decision will 'open the door to a flood of litigation,' make it difficult to define definite limits of liability, require an investigation of factual details for which their processes are not well designed, make the re-examination of corollary or subsidiary principles necessary, or threaten to upset an established equilibrium in social conventions, trade practices or property transactions. Nor will courts ordinarily venture openly into a field still troubled by economic or political debate. In all these cases policy dictates no upsetting of the apple cart even though an individual litigant may suffer admitted injustice and hardship. Only when the demand is so urgent or the injustice so blatant in these situations that the pressures of 'we the people' cannot be withstood will courts take notice of the urgency. Even then they will usually refer the problem to the legislature. Thus it is that the open appeal to public policy is more frequently made to justify the court in not taking some bold step than to justify taking the step.

Do Prof. Green's remarks apply to a case like Priestley v. Fowler?

We have seen, in the fellow-servant cases, that the judges were asking themselves what consequences would flow from alternative decisions; mak-

---

* Green, The Study and Teaching of Tort Law, 34 Texas L. Rev. 15-16 (1956).

ing factual assumptions as to such consequences; and evaluating one set of consequences as against another. The editors' past classroom experience suggests that the main focus of student curiosity at this point are questions of this sort: What influenced the courts to make the particular fact-assumptions and value-choices that they did? Were the courts bowing to political, economic, or other social forces? Were they biased? Were they impelled to their conclusion by "legal" considerations and professional traditions? To what extent was judicial ignorance of relevant facts significant? At this early stage in our study, no complete answers can be attempted. The following materials will serve to introduce the student to the nature of the problems raised by these questions. They begin with the problem of political influence on judges, including material bearing on the general issue of judicial selection and tenure, and proceed to a consideration of the other questions raised above.

Section 1

IMPACT of POLITICAL, ECONOMIC, and OTHER INTERESTS

HURST,* THE GROWTH OF AMERICAN LAW
122, 128-131, 133-134, 138-146 (1950)

The methods and ideas concerning the selection and tenure of judges in the United States present a story that can be told briefly. But, for lack of satisfactory evidence by which to weigh the results, the story is disappointingly abstract and barren.

Two pair of opposites were woven together to make up the formal story: appointment versus popular election, as the manner of selection; tenure during good behavior versus tenure for a term of years, as the manner of holding. Appointment and life tenure tended to go together, as did election and limited tenure. The second grouping dominated the long-run trend, up to mid-twentieth century. . . .

Where constitutions provided that judges be appointed they were in fact appointed; there was no de facto conversion of appointment into some disguised practice of popular selection. But in practice the appointing power was often exercised by someone other than those formally invested with it. The prime example was the development in the federal government of that Senatorial "courtesy," under which, if any Senator of the President's party found a nominee personally objectionable, his fellow Senators would join in refusing confirmation. This in effect placed the nomination of federal judges for service within a given state or region in the hands of the administration-party Senators from that area. After

* James Willard Hurst, Professor of Law at the University of Wisconsin, where he has taught since 1937, was law secretary to Justice Brandeis, 1936-37, and a director of the Social Science Research Council, 1948-52. He has authored, in addition to the volume quoted from here, Law and the Conditions of Freedom in the Nineteenth-Century United States (1956), and Law and Social Process in United States History (1960).—Editor

the wry experience of a presidential term, Mr. Taft observed that: "The appointing power is in effect in the Senators' hands, subject only to a veto by the President." Political tradition even broadened this practice, by analogy. Where a judge, especially a district judge, was to be named in a state whose Senators were not of the administration party, the President began to refer the appointment to the local Congressmen of the administration party, or to the state's party leaders, with first voice probably to the national committeeman.

We have no detailed study of practices under the appointing power in the few states in which it prevailed. Impeachment proceedings against a first instance judge in New Jersey in 1934 made a matter of record the accepted operation of "Senatorial courtesy" regarding New Jersey judicial appointments. In Massachusetts, Maine and New Hampshire the governor's judicial appointments must be confirmed by an executive council; the latter was a body distinct from the upper house of the legislature, was popularly elected in Massachusetts and New Hampshire, and elected in joint legislative session in Maine. Haynes* found evidence that in these states there developed some tendency to permit individual councillors to name nominees for local judicial offices, and for the governor to choose nominees for offices of state-wide importance. Political trading entered, where governor and council were of different parties.

With all such qualifications, appointment in form proved to be appointment in practice. Where constitutions provided for popular election of judges, the formal method underwent much more profound changes in operation, and became largely selection by covert appointment. This judgment is framed conservatively. Reliable evidence is spotty, drawn almost wholly from the last thirty years, and consists mostly of opinion. If we treat the available evidence as probably reflecting what went on throughout the United States after 1870, the conclusion must be that popular election of judges became almost wholly a matter of form; and that the form covered two main types of de facto systems of appointment of judges. Both of these de facto appointment systems were products of the rise of the political parties.

Generally, and especially in metropolitan areas after 1870, election of judges meant the formal ratification by popular vote of appointments made by party leaders. A prudent leadership would always reckon with the possibility of popular rebellion at the polls, and this possibility was some check—on prudent leadership —even in the most tightly controlled machines. But experience repeatedly showed that as a rule people were not much interested in judicial elections; this was the more true in proportion as they lived in thickly settled communities where the courts, as well as other more technical aspects of government, seemed remote from daily living.

The most definite influence which the average voter's attitudes had on the de facto system of appointment by party leaders was in the strong presumption which generally favored the renomination and reelection of sitting judges. This was a matter of general feeling and tradition. Only one more or less organized check on

---

* Haynes, The Selection and Tenure of Judges (1944).—Editor

the operation of party appointment developed after 1870. This was through the activity of bar associations in the larger cities, chiefly after 1900; some associations undertook to appraise candidates' qualifications, to offer association support to approved candidates, and opposition to those deemed not qualified. This bar association activity was evidence of the extent to which the most critical problems in judicial elections came out of the shift to an urban society. We shall see later that the modern organized bar itself originated as a response to the shocking levels of politics and legal administration in the great cities in the later nineteenth century. Bar activity in judicial elections was definitely an urban phenomenon. In 1932 a count showed such bar activity in all but 2 cities of 450,000 or more population, and in 27 of the 42 cities of over 200,000 population.

However, the bar associations had only limited effect on the operation of the party appointment system. Their clearest influence was probably in the improvement of the general standards which the law set for qualification to judicial office. Early-nineteenth-century America did not put its faith in courts or lawyers, and distrusted most claims for specialized knowledge or abilities. Thus many states laid down no professional qualifications as requirements even for judges of their highest courts. In the latter part of the century, bar associations began to urge higher standards of legal education and admission to the bar; and as a collateral product of this movement to raise professional standards, the states generally adopted the requirement that all judges except those of some courts of petty jurisdiction must be members of the bar. This was a modest requirement; its minimal nature is emphasized in the fact that up to mid-twentieth century less than a third of the states had adopted any requirement that a man have some experience at the bar before taking judicial office. In their efforts to influence judicial elections, bar associations, it is true, emphasized the quality of candidates' legal education and experience in practice. But at most, the bar's influence was indirect. The bar associations generally did not try directly to influence the party leaders' choice of candidates; frequently, therefore, the bar found itself in the not-too-happy position of publicly recommending that the people accept the lesser evil.

For all of these limitations, judicial elections were not without some quality. As one student of metropolitan judicial elections observed, "The Judiciary is the only group of major elective offices for which progress has been made in requiring specific qualifications other than age or citizenship." . . .

There was a second, less broadly operative, way in which judicial election worked out as a de facto system of appointment. State constitutions commonly gave the governor power to fill vacancies, pending election, both in the supreme court and in the lower courts. Especially where the term of office on the supreme court was a long one, vacancies by death or retirement from illness were frequent, for men were usually already of mature years when they came to the highest court. Thus in some states a high proportion of men who attained the highest court did so originally by the governor's interim appointment following a vacancy. Benefiting by the tradition in favor of returning a sitting judge, they were then likely to win if they ran in the succeeding election, especially if their interim term had been of substantial length. Bar association activity, as in Minnesota and Wisconsin, contributed to this outcome. In Minnesota in 1940, for example, all members of the Supreme Court and thirty-one of the fifty district court judges had come to the bench in the first instance by interim appointment. There seems to be no study which measures for the whole country the practical extent or effect of this combination of interim appointment and ratification by election.

The scheme thus evolved by the accident of events coincided with, and stimulated, what promised to become the model plan advanced by those concerned with improvement of the selection of judges. In 1914 Albert M. Kales, distinguished Illinois practitioner and professor of law, proposed to combine the appointive and elective methods for judicial selection. Kales suggested that some proper appointing authority name the judge for an initial term of years, and that at intervals after the expiration of this first period, the judge submit to popular election on the question of his continuance in office. If the vote were against him, his term would end forthwith. The appointing power would then name a new judge who, after the designated initial period of service, would come before the popular vote. In the election phase of the process, thus, a judge would run only against his own record. The Kales proposal was in substance adopted by constitutional amendment in California in 1934. California applied the new plan directly to judges of the supreme and intermediate appellate courts. It allowed the counties local option as to whether they would adopt the plan for selection of the principal trial judges. In 1940 Missouri likewise adopted the Kales principle, in a somewhat more complicated form than that taken in California. . . .

[While some 35 or so states still use the elective system, the trend of professional thinking is now in the direction of the Missouri or California plans, and a number of states are now considering a shift. The new state of Alaska follows the Missouri type of plan; and the new Hawaii constitution also rejects the elective system by adopting a nomination system similar to that followed in our federal courts.

[Under the Missouri plan, the Governor's appointee is one he has chosen from a panel of three submitted by a "judicial commission." One commission, for the selection of appellate judges, consists of the state Chief Justice; three lawyers elected from each of three districts by the lawyers of the district; and three laymen, one appointed from each such district by the Governor. Separate judicial commissions are used for appointment of circuit, probate, and criminal court trial judges. The judge newly appointed to fill a vacancy serves until the next general election, when his name goes on a separate nonpartisan judicial ballot with the question, "Shall Judge —— be retained in office?" If the vote is favorable, he serves a 12 year term if an appellate judge, and a 6 year term if a trial judge, after which the ballot procedure is repeated if he wishes to run again.

[Under the California plan, the Governor has complete freedom to make his initial selection but the appointment is subject to confirmation by a 3-man commission composed of the Chief Justice, the Attorney General, and presiding judge of one of the state's intermediate appellate courts.

[The English system is not an elective one either. Judicial appointments "are made, for life of course, in the name of the Crown, though actually by the Prime

Minister, and in fact on the recommendation of the Lord Chancellor's office. The latter maintains a small permanent staff which is constantly engaged in accumulating information and preparing files on barristers who may be considered for major judgeships. Recommendations from the Lord Chancellor's office are nonpartisan, and the record shows that appointments are not based on membership in the party in power . . ." Leflar, "The Quality of Judges," 35 Indiana Law Journal 289, 292 (1960).

[Among the other political aspects of the judiciary discussed by Hurst is the question of comparative *quality* of elected judges as against appointed judges. He finds that modern students of the problem agree (though not on the basis of elaborate investigation) that judges appointed for life are on the whole of higher quality than elected judges. The shift in the states, after the 1830's, from an appointive to an elective system was not based upon "any widespread consistent experience of dissatisfaction with the way in which appointed judges handled the day-to-day grist of business"; rather it was part of that broader movement for wider popular control known as Jacksonian Democracy.

[Those who criticize the elective system for not producing high-quality judges are not thinking primarily of judicial corruption (though the known cases of dishonesty seem to have been more prevalent among state than federal judges). There are "subtler means of suborning the administration of justice than through the offer of money." Hurst observes: "Surveys of metropolitan justice in the first half of the twentieth century agreed that by a combination of influences, the elective process had had bad effects upon trial courts; especially, the practical requirements of re-election encouraged types of behavior on the bench that impaired the integrity and dignity of the administration of justice . . . Elected judges must keep in the public eye, must in particular situations defer to national, racial, or religious groups, must find time and energy for recurrent campaigning . . ."

[The elected judge is not usually criticized or praised for being more liberal or radical than the appointed judge. Considering the record of elected state judges and appointed federal judges in dealing with the constitutionality of social welfare legislation in the half century after 1880, Hurst concludes that "appointment did not guarantee a more conservative bench than election. The whole evidence indicated no direct relation between the liberality of the courts toward legislative judgment and the circumstance that the judges were elected or appointed. The ideas and feelings prevailing in any given generation in those levels of the community from which judges came offered far more convincing explanation of judicial policy." *—Editor]

* For a systematic examination of the social and economic background of the 91 Justices appointed to the Supreme Court through 1957, see Schmidhauser, The Justices of the Supreme Court: A Collective Portrait, 3 Midwest J. of Pol. Sci. 1 (1959). See also Frankfurter, The Supreme Court in the Mirror of Justices, 105 U. Pa. L. Rev. 781 (1957).

EDITORIAL NOTE: The CANONS of JUDICIAL ETHICS

Bearing on the matters just considered are the 36 Canons of Judicial Ethics, adopted by the American Bar Association.[1] These include miscellaneous aspects of the standard of impartiality[2] including some specific provisions as to partisan politics. Canon 28 declares that a judge "should avoid making political speeches, making or soliciting payment of assessments or contributions to party funds, the public endorsement of candidates for political office and participation in party conventions. He should neither accept nor retain a place on any party committee nor act as party leader, nor engage generally in partisan activities. Where, however, it is necessary for judges to be nominated and elected as candidates of a political party, nothing herein contained shall prevent the judge from attending or speaking at political gatherings, or from making contributions to the campaign funds of the party that has nominated him and seeks his election or reelection." However, once a judge is in office, then under Canon 30, "he should not become an active candidate either at a party primary or at a general election for any office other than a judicial office. If a judge should decide to become a candidate for any office not judicial, he should resign in order that it cannot be said that he is using the power or prestige of his judicial position to promote his own candidacy or the success of his party."

A recent survey of the operation of these canons reports that Canon 28, above quoted, is "to an alarming degree . . . disregarded throughout the country, largely as a result of the constant need of judges for political support in order to retain their positions." [3]

---

[1] 34 Canons were adopted in 1924, and there have been amendments and additions from time to time.

[2] Thus, Canon 14 requires that a judge "not be swayed by partisan demands, public clamor or considerations of personal popularity or notoriety, nor be apprehensive of unjust criticism." Under Canon 12, a judge's appointments (of trustees, receivers, masters, referees, guardians or others) are not to be made "for personal or partisan advantage." According to Canon 13, he "should not act in a controversy where a near relative is a party; he should not suffer his conduct to justify the impression that any person can improperly influence him or unduly enjoy his favor, or that he is affected by the kinship, rank, position or influence of any party or other person." He must not, under Canons 24, 25, and 26 make investments or incur obligations, pe-

cuniary or otherwise, that would conflict or appear to conflict, with the impartial discharge of his duties. Canon 31 declares that "in superior courts of general jurisdiction," a judge's practice of law "should never be permitted. In inferior courts in some states, it is permitted because the county or municipality is not able to pay adequate living compensation for a competent judge. In such cases one who practices law . . . must be scrupulously careful to avoid conduct in his practice whereby he utilizes or seems to utilize his judicial position to further his professional success."

[3] Blaustein and Porter, The American Lawyer, 266 (1954). This volume is a summary of the reports written over a period of years for the Survey of the Legal Profession. The Survey was financed by the Carnegie Corporation and the American Bar Association.

LASKI,* *THE STATE IN THEORY AND PRACTICE*
161-162, 168, 173-174, 175-177, 183 (1935)

. . . I have pointed out that every society is the theatre of a conflict between economic classes for a larger material benefit, for, that is, a larger share in the results to be distributed from the productive process. Since the power to produce within any society is dependent upon peace, the state must maintain law and order to that end. But, in so doing, it is necessarily maintaining the law and order implied in the particular system of class-relations of which it is the expression. In feudal society, that is, the law and order which the state maintains is the law and order necessary to the preservation of feudal principles. In a capitalist society, the state maintains the law and order necessary to preserve capitalist principles. . . . The state, that is to say, is always at the disposal of that class in the community in which is vested the legal title to the ownership of instruments of production. The law it makes will be law for their interest. The ownership it maintains will be their ownership. If the number of owners, therefore, in a state be few, the bias of the law will be towards the interest of that few. . . .

This view was compressed by the Communist Manifesto into a famous sentence. "The executive of the modern state," wrote Marx and Engels, "is simply a committee for managing the common affairs of the bourgeoisie." . . .

. . . We do not need to argue that all law is a product of the class-struggle. It is clear enough that a good deal of law, in commercial matters, for instance, and, even more, in procedure, represents principles quite remote from it. But it is equally clear, I think, that the idea of the class-struggle permeates legal notions at every point of pivotal importance. . . .

Nor must we forget the fact that wealth is a decisive factor in the power to take advantage of the opportunities the law affords its citizens to protect their rights. The ability to undertake an action in the courts, even with the provision made for legal aid to the poor, remains a grim financial question, and, on the civil side of the law, with its massive hierarchy of appeals, the advantage is solidly with the rich. Broadly, there is equality before the law only when the price of admission to its opportunities can be equally paid; and there is no administrative equity to redress this balance. It is simply inherent in a society with the class-relations of our own. And it is those class-relations also which mean that, as a general rule, the ablest lawyers will be at the service of those only who are able to afford them. The successful lawyer—the class from which, in the Anglo-American system, the members of the judiciary are mostly drawn—spends his life

* Harold J. Laski (1893-1950) was a well-known intellectual leader of the Labor Party and of the left-wing socialist movement in England. His teaching at the London School of Economics and occasional lecture tours made a deep impression upon students of many lands. In America because of his brilliance as a personality and lecturer he had many friends—in spite of their disagreement with his radical views. His friendship with Justice Holmes is interestingly revealed in Howe (Ed.), The Holmes-Laski Letters (1953). Laski's earlier thinking, exemplified by his Grammar of Politics (1925), shifted to a more dogmatic Marxism, exemplified by the extract above.—Editor

in ministering to the dominating class of our society. It is wholly natural, therefore, that he should come, as a general rule, to share its outlook, that his intellectual influence, therefore, should largely be exercised on its behalf. It is a sound instinct that has persuaded the working-classes to look upon the legal profession as one of the protective ramparts of conservatism.

I am not, it must be noted, in any way or in any degree challenging the good will of the lawyer or the legal system. I am merely saying that once the postulates of the society in which they function imply inequality, the main burden of their influence should be towards maintaining it. And when, as with ourselves, so large a part of law is rooted in precedent, it is natural for the lawyer's mind to dwell upon continuity with the past rather than departure from it. Judge-made law is rarely innovating law unless, as with the work of Chief Justice Holt and Lord Mansfield, it deals with a situation in which the guiding precedents are few or non-existent; and where the lawyer, as with Chief Justice Marshall, or Lord Abinger in Priestley v. Fowler, confronts an experiment in which the rights of property are in serious hazard, the emphasis of his work will always tend to be towards supporting them rather than attacking them. That is surely why most great movements for legal reform have either come from outside the profession altogether, or from members of it who, like Bentham, have had a very peripheral connection with it. The business of a legal system is to make the postulates of a society work. It would be remarkable indeed if it could be so worked as to secure their fundamental transformation. . . .

. . . Law, that is to say, is never impartial in the sense of being above the battle, or indifferent to the results which may emerge. The courts, on the contrary, are a fundamental instrument in that battle. They shape the contours of the society, more interstitially, perhaps, because less directly, than either the legislature or the executive; but they are bound to the same purpose. They give effect to the result of the conflicting class-antagonisms which shape the atmosphere in which they have to work. . . .

POUND,* *THE ECONOMIC INTERPRETATION AND*
THE LAW OF TORTS
53 Harvard Law Review 365, 366-367,
373-383 (1940)

. . . With an economic interpretation of the general course of history and so of legal history one can have no quarrel. Nor within limits can one quarrel with

* Roscoe Pound ranks among our most influential legal thinkers. After achieving professional distinction in the field of botany (the fungus Roscoepoundia is named in his honor), he taught law and became Dean at the University of Nebraska Law School, taught at Northwestern, Chicago, and Harvard, and was Dean at Harvard Law School, 1916-36. Jurisprudence or legal philosophy has been the chief area of his scholarship, and "sociological jurisprudence" is generally associated with his name. Among his works are: Introduction to the Philosophy of Law (1922), Interpretations of Legal History (1923), Law and Morals (1924), Social Control Through Law (1942), The Task of Law (1944), New Paths of the Law (1950), and Jurisprudence (5 vols., 1959).—Editor

such an interpretation of certain types of events in legal history. What must give us pause is making it the sole weapon in the jurist's armory or the sole instrument in his tool chest; the reference of every item in the judicial process, of every single decision and every working out of a legal precept by applying the technique of the law to the received materials of decision, to the operation, conscious or unconscious, of the desires and self interest of an economically dominant class.

Undoubtedly what the proponents of the economic interpretation see behind all law is behind many laws framed by legislative law-makers. The legislator is not trained in a technique of referring his action to general principles. He has no settled habits of applying an authoritative technique to authoritatively given materials. Much of legislation can be explained very well by the economic interpretation as developed by our American juristic realists. Yet one has only to read colonial legislation as to certain religious sects (to take an example which cannot be controversial today) in order to see that even legislation need have no economic explanation but may go on deep-seated beliefs or prejudices quite apart from economic considerations. Arbitrary legislative precepts are fitted into the traditional system by interpretation and application. The taught tradition of law is little affected by such details. What stands out in the history of Anglo-American law is the resistance of the taught tradition in the hands of judges drawn from any class you like, so they have been trained in the tradition, against all manner of economically or politically powerful interests. It is not that economic power has dictated decision of particular cases or judicial promulgation of particular rules, but rather that economic progress has led to new wants, new claims, new demands, new desires. As I have said elsewhere, "the pressure of new interests has required that the taught tradition be made to serve new purposes as old doctrines were called on to solve new problems. There has been a gradual shaping of obstinate traditional precepts and traditional doctrines through the need of applying them to new economic conditions in the light of reshaping ideals of the legal order." [2] In this way economic changes have in time a profound effect. But that is another story. Does it follow that single decisions are shaped by class interest? Does the economic status of the parties determine the action of the courts in particular cases? Are legal reasoning, doctrinal exposition, systematic development of authoritative starting points for reasoned decisions mere pretense, mere camouflage of results reached apart from reason solely on the basis of class interest or the social and economic position of the respective parties? [3]

Law is neither wholly reason nor wholly experience. It is experience developed by reason, and reason checked and directed by experience. The strongest single influence both in determining single decisions and in guiding a course of decision is a taught tradition of logically interdependent precepts and of referring cases to principles. Admittedly there are often competing precepts, competing principles, competing starting points for legal reasoning, often of equal authority. It is here that the ideal element in law comes into play, since the results of choosing one

[2] The Formative Era of American Law (1938) 83-84.

[3] See, e.g., Rodell, Woe Unto You, Lawyers!

(1939) c. 10. As to this book, one is tempted to cite St. Paul: 1 Timothy 1, 6-8.

starting point rather than another are measured by the received social ideal, as it has been taught to judges and lawyers.[4] The effect of economic changes upon this ideal is for the most part gradual and slow, no matter what class is affected. The business man and the leader of industry have had quite as much cause of complaint in this respect as the labor leader; and the farmer, long dominant in American politics, no less than either. As Maitland puts it, "taught law is tough law."[5] . . .

Let us see what the proponents of the economic interpretation vouch for their doctrine. Their stock in trade is Priestley v. Fowler, 3 M. & W. 1 (Ex. 1837). A typical pronouncement may be found in Walter Lippmann's Good Society [p. 188]. He says: "Under the old common law of England a workman who was injured could sue the master for damages. If he had been injured by a fellow workman's negligence, he could still sue the master because the law held the master liable for his servant's acts. Under this system of law the state was ready to intervene on behalf of an injured workman and recover damages for him from his employer. In 1837 this system of law was changed in a decision rendered by Lord Abinger. After that, it became the law that the master was not liable for an injury to a working man when the injury was due to a fellow working man." For this positive statement he cites an article in the Encyclopaedia of the Social Sciences. But neither Mr. Lippmann nor the writer in the Encyclopaedia cites or could cite a decision in the English-speaking world before 1837 on the point in question, much less one holding the master liable in such a case. Of this again in a moment.

One can see the realist describing the bench that decided Priestley v. Fowler. Lord Abinger was the son of a rich planter in Jamaica, educated at Cambridge, married to the daughter of a country gentleman, become conservative with advancing years, and a land owner when raised to the bench.[20] Sir James Parke (afterwards Lord Wensleydale) was the son of a merchant, educated at Cambridge, and married to the daughter of a country gentleman. [Id., 497]. Sir William Bolland, also the son of a merchant, also educated at Cambridge, was a protégé of Lord Lyndhurst, the Tory leader. [Id. at 104]. Sir John Gurney was the son of a shorthand writer and a Whig in politics. [Id., 318]. But that did not prevent him from concurring in the decision. Indeed, when one remembers the conditions of the time this was not a bench specially predisposed to formulate as law the self interest of the manufacturers. If anything, the interests of the landed aristocracy or of the mercantile class are suggested and neither of these in 1837 was inclined to take up the cause of the industrialists. We must not forget that the labor legislation of the fore part of the nineteenth century which bettered the condition of workmen in the factories came from Tories. The prime mover in the Factory Acts was one of the nobility.[24] Still . . . a plausible argument might be made from the pre-

---

[4] See my paper, The Ideal Element in American Judicial Decision (1931) 45 Harv. L. Rev. 136.

[5] Maitland, English Law and the Renaissance (1901) 25.

[20] Foss, Judges of England (1870) 590.

[24] Dicey, Law and Public Opinion in England (1905) 228-32. [But compare the comments of Mr. Justice Evatt, of the High Court of Australia, in his article, The

dominantly Tory personnel of the bench. When, however, we read the case we note that it was brought and argued and decided on a contract theory; a theory of what was and what was not implied in a contract of employment. The declaration averred a duty to cause the plaintiff to be safely and securely carried on the wagon of the butcher whose employee he was. The wagon had been overloaded by a fellow employee. The court said that the butcher was not bound to take more care of his servant than he did of himself and that the servant must have known better than his master that the load was too heavy. It is a safe conjecture that in 1837 the butcher and the boy working for him, who presently as he learned the business would set up for himself as a master butcher, were or would be regarded by the court as of the same class. We cannot assume that the court thought of the case in terms of a packing company of today and a laborer, one of some hundreds in the plant.

Mr. Lippmann's version of Priestley v. Fowler proceeds on three false assumptions: (1) That *respondeat superior* is a universal principle of justice, generally recognized as such; (2) that *respondeat superior* is a general principle of law, to be developed and applied wherever the relation of employer and employee exists; (3) that prior to that case it was recognized as applying to hold the master not only for injuries to third persons but also for injuries to his servants without his fault.

Let us see what is behind *respondeat superior* and how far it has been made to extend.

In the article in the Encyclopaedia of the Social Sciences[25] relied upon by Walter Lippmann, it is said that the decision in Priestley v. Fowler was inconsistent with the general proposition of representation of the employer by the employee. The answer to that statement is to be found in an article on Agency by Mr. Justice Holmes.[26] Liability for legal transactions entered into by the agent within the scope of the agency is correlative to a power conferred by the principal upon the agent. Liability without regard to fault for the employee's torts, committed against the instructions of the master, despite all precautions on the part of the

Judges and The Teachers of Public Law (1940) 53 Harv. L. Rev. 1145, 1150: ". . . Lord Abinger . . . is cited by Professor Pound as a judge who apparently decided in favour of the manufacturing interests, although, as a Tory, he belonged to a hostile class. But, whatever the weight of Walter Lippmann's comment upon the origin of the doctrine of common employment, it must be remembered that by the year 1837 Whigs and Tories had frequently combined their forces against the working classes, notably in the case of the Tolpuddle Martyrs, six trade unionists, who, in 1835 were transported to Australia. And a little later, we find Abinger charging a grand jury (in relation to Chartist demands) in terms which are well fitted to be placed alongside the observations of Best, C. J.: '. . . the establishment of any popular Assembly,' said Abinger, 'entirely devoted to democratic principles, elected by persons, the vast majority of whom possess no property, but live by means of manual labour, would be inconsistent with the existence of the monarchy and the aristocracy. Its first aim would be the destruction of property and the overthrow of the throne. . . .' "—Editor]

[25] Berman, Employer's Liability in Encyc. Soc. Sciences (1931) 515.

[26] (1891) 4 Harv. L. Rev. 345 (1891), 5 *id.* at 1.

employer, and although the employer chose the employee with due care, is not correlative to a power conferred. It is imposed by law and has a historical origin.* As Mr. Justice Holmes pointed out, the explanation that the servant represents the master so that what the former does must be treated as done by the latter is a dogmatic fiction. Undoubtedly the historical liability has maintained itself because of the pressure of the social interest in the general security. But the difference between representation in legal transactions and representation in torts contrary to the intent of the employment has been obvious in all connections except to the partisans of the economic interpretation in discussing the fellow servant rule. Mr. Justice Holmes, Dr. Baty,[27] and many others, have pointed out that vicarious liability is the exception to a general principle, not limitation of vicarious liability the exception to the normal type.

"If the law went no further," says Mr. Justice Holmes, "than to declare a man liable for the consequences of acts specifically commanded by him, with knowledge of the circumstances under which those consequences were the natural results of those acts, it would need no explanation and would introduce no new principle." The new principle requiring explanation, he goes on to say, was introduced into the law when the master without fault was treated as if he were the tortfeasor.† There was an old historical liability for the acts of those who were in the household as dependents. In the frankpledge system there was this sort of liability for the acts of others.‡ The master was made to stand as security for the conduct of his servants, to hand them over to justice or pay the fine himself. So far was this carried that the host was liable for the tort of a guest in his house as well as for wrongs done by his servant. Thus liability of the master for the torts of a servant comes down from a primitive liability of the head of a household to buy off the vengeance of the injured person or surrender the wrongdoing dependent.[28] The fellow servant rule, therefore, was not an arbitrary exception to the general principle of liability. It was a refusal to extend an exception to that general principle. In the language of Mr. Justice Holmes, it represents "the revolt of common-sense from the whole doctrine" of identification of the master with the servant "when its application is pushed far enough to become noticeable." [29] It was not at all a unique restriction of vicarious liability. The same question came up with respect to liability of the master for punitive damages for wanton and wilful wrong done by his servant. More than one court, says Mr. Justice Holmes,

---

* I.e., it is clear enough why, in the interests of fair dealing and business reliance, the principal should be legally responsible for deals ("legal transactions . . . within the scope of the agency") which he has instructed his agent to enter into on his behalf. But, Dean Pound is arguing, this analysis does not rest on a general principle broad enough also to explain why the principal should be liable for wrongs ("torts") done without his direction or consent and almost always contrary to his instructions or desires.—Editor

[27] Baty, Vicarious Liability (1916) cc. 1, 5.

† "Tortfeasor": one committing a tort.—Editor

‡ "Frankpledge": the system under which the male members of certain local government units were responsible for the damage done by their fellow members.—Editor

[28] Agency (1891) 4 Harv. L. Rev. 345, 346 et seq.

[29] Agency (1891) 5 Harv. L. Rev. 1, 16.

"impressed by the monstrosity of the result . . . peremptorily declared that it was absurd to punish a man who had not been to blame." [Id., 22]. A historical liability for those who were in the household was made into a liability for the acts of non-dependent employees in order to maintain the general security. But as to fellow servants the idea has not been one of maintaining the general security. It has been one of insuring those who were in no economic position to bear loss at the expense of the nearest person at hand who could bear it. This is a very recent conception as to the requirements of justice, quite out of line with nineteenth-century ideas and one which the judges of 1837 could not reasonably have been expected to grasp. At that time the idea of using litigation as a means to insure what Professor Patten calls bringing about a distribution of the economic surplus had not occurred to any one.

Inability to appreciate the doctrine that when any one has suffered injury there should be some responsible person who can pay the damages, although without fault, has not been confined to the Court of Exchequer in Priestley v. Fowler. In Williams v. Jones [3 H. & C. 256 (Ex. 1864)] a carpenter in the employ of defendant set a fire, by an act not in the course of his employment, but while acting as employee. The court refused to extend the master's liability to such a case, Martin, B., saying: "It is a fallacy with many that because a person employed as Davies was, if responsible, has no means of satisfying the damage, therefore the obligation is cast on his employer." [Id., 263]. This was a case between two neighboring owners so no one brings in the economic interpretation. But suppose a fellow servant had been burned as well as the property of a neighbor destroyed? Then denial of recovery in each case alike would probably be pronounced an arbitrary judicial action dictated by the self interest of the employer class.

As I said above, throughout the law there is a problem of reconciling the general security and the individual life, using the latter term to mean the fullest and freest exercise and development of his powers by each individual. When we seek to maintain justice, as the ideal relation between men, and impose liability to the measure of that ideal, we are continually given pause by the exigencies of the general security.* Hence in the law of torts there is a constant quest of practical adjustment between the two principles; on the one hand the principle of responsibility for culpable conduct, and on the other hand the principle of responsibility as a means of maintaining the general security. The beginnings of the law put the stress upon security. In the eighteenth century, under the influence of natural law

---

* I.e., when one thinks primarily in terms of whether or not a particular individual shall be compelled by law to pay damages to another, considerations of fairness to that individual strongly urge that he should not have to pay unless in some sense he has been guilty of fault (that he has been guilty of "culpable conduct"). On the other hand, consideration for the general peace and efficiency of the community may lead one to think that certain conduct is so dangerous in fact, or that certain damage to a particular individual is so harmful from the community's standpoint, that even though the actor cannot be called "culpable" or guilty of wrong in any moral sense, he ought to engage in such conduct at his own risk, and ought to make good any damage he causes. Dean Pound is here discussing some basic aspects of the choice between liability based on fault and absolute liability for damage caused.—Editor

and humanitarian thinking, the stress shifted to culpability. In the nineteenth century an attempt was made to put the whole law of torts in terms of liability as a corollary of culpability. The French Civil Code (1904) had put the modern Roman law principle of Aquilian *culpa*—the principle that one whose conduct had brought about injury to another must respond to that injury—as the general basis of tort liability [Art. 1382] and this fitted in with the general reference of all legal problems to the idea of free will which governed juristic thinking in the first three quarters of that century. But it was never possible wholly to exclude applications of the principle of security. Thus the French Civil Code left some remnants of liability without fault in connection with injuries by children and by animals. [Arts. 1384, 1385]. In our law absolute liability for trespasses of animals or injuries by vicious animals, in spite of the attempt of Blackstone to reduce it to liability for negligence, persisted into the nineteenth century. [3 Commentaries *211]. It obstinately resisted the endeavors of text writers to bring it into line with the theory of liability as a corollary of culpability by requiring a culpable maintaining or releasing the animals. Only one or two states gave over the historical doctrine,[36] and it would be hard to find an economic interpretation that would differentiate New Jersey from New York or Pennsylvania,[37] and Vermont from New Hampshire in this connection.[38] Likewise in the law as to negligence an objective standard was called for by the exigencies of the general security. In the present century applications of the principle of security have been increasingly numerous and the juristic theory of Continental Europe has been moving away from the theory of liability solely for culpable causation of harm.[39] In the nature of the problem of adjusting human relations there must be this twofold basis of a law of torts. The most that has ever been achieved is a practical balance between the two principles. The only guide to adjustment seems to be to give effect to as much of each as we may with the least infringement of the other. But this had not been learned till long after 1837. At that time, liability without fault was taken to be an obsolete institution of primitive societies.[40]

Equally it would have been too much to expect in 1837, when the whole thought of the time was moving away from thinking of employer and employee as a domestic relation, that a court would hark back to that conception in order to require an employer to answer for the safety of the employee in matters where the employer was in no wise at fault. In general, one has a duty to protect those whom the law makes dependent upon him. But the traditional technique of the law is to generalize and refer cases to principles so as to bring about a body of logically interdependent precepts. When employees were asserting their independence and a contract idea was taking them out of the category of domestic depend-

36 Notably New Jersey, De Gray v. Murray, 69 N.J.L. 458, 55 Atl. 237 (1903).
37 Muller v. McKesson, 73 N.Y. 195 (1878); Mann v. Weiand, 81 Pa. 243 (1875).
38 Worthen v. Love, 60 Vt. 285, 14 Atl. 461 (1888).
39 Duguit, Les Transformations du Droit Privé Depuis le Code Napoléon (1912) 137 et seq.; Pound, Introduction to the Philosophy of Law (1922) 161-64; Triandafil, L'Idée de Risque Comme Fondement de la Responsabilité (1914) c. 2.
40 Pollock, Law of Fraud in British India (1894) 53-54.

ents, no common-law court could have been found, of whomsoever composed, to turn back to the old dependent idea and impose a liability to take care of the employee on that basis. Workmen's Compensation depends upon a wholly different conception of liability from that entertained by any one in the first half of the nineteenth century.

Understand me. I am not arguing for the fellow servant rule as something that should be restored or as something that should have been preserved in the law under the conditions of today. I am simply showing that it was not a setting up of an arbitrary exception to a universally recognized principle of justice. It was not a reversal of a settled proposition of law. It was not inconsistent with the prior course of decision. It was not something adopted wilfully in 1837 by a tribunal consciously expressing in legal doctrine the self interest of a dominant social or economic class. The conception of the employer-employee relation as a domestic relation, which is at the bottom of tort liability of the employer for the fault of the employee, is, as Mr. Justice Holmes has shown, also at the bottom of the fellow servant rule which is charged with being an arbitrary exception to it.

It remains to say something of Farwell v. Boston & Worcester Rail Road Corporation, decided in 1842 [4 Metc. 49] in an opinion by no less a judge than Chief Justice Shaw, which received the doctrine of Priestley v. Fowler for America. Certainly the bench which sat in that case could make an argument for the economic interpretation, since the judges who concurred were old line Federalists of an ultra conservative bringing up, were it not that the same court, the same year, in a case reported in the same volume, rendered the leading decision on the law of conspiracy in favor of the labor unions. Commonwealth v. Hunt [4 Metc. 111 (1842)] to use the words of a leading exponent of the economic interpretation, "overthrew the substructure upon which a Tory criminal law against labor organizations could respectably have been established." [43] If the first decision was a formulation of the interest of the dominant employer class, what of the second? When one studies the history of the law of conspiracy and the origin of the doctrine contended for in the prosecution, it is clear that the same mode of juristic thought that led the judges to follow Priestley v. Fowler led them also to reject a theory of conspiracy out of line with the common law. . . .

An exclusively economic interpretation of single decisions and single items of judicial action leaves out of account the tenacity of a taught tradition. It takes no account of the instinctive tendency of the lawyer to refer every case back to some general principle. It ignores the prevailing mode of thought of the time which often reflects an economic situation of the past when the taught ideal was formative. Specifically in the cases we have been considering it ignores the nineteenth-century attempt to reduce liability to contract and culpable causation of harm. In 1882 this founding of liability upon undertaking and fault seemed to Mr. Justice Holmes the common sense view. [48] No speculation as to class bias is needed

---

[43] Nelles, Commonwealth v. Hunt (1932) 32 Col. L. Rev. 1128, 1151. [See the extract immediately following this one.—Editor]

[48] Agency (1891), 5 Harv. L. Rev. 1, 14 (written in 1882; see the note in (1891), 4 Harv. L. Rev. 345).

to explain how common-law judges of that time in general, where not bound by authority, thought likewise.

NELLES,* *COMMONWEALTH v. HUNT*
32 Columbia Law Review 1128 (1932)

* * *

Shaw, though gruff, was a tender-hearted man. But he had no more liking for democracy or respect for the common man than Hamilton or Webster. At a time when an intelligent Jeffersonian could reasonably hope that juries would continue to correct judicial biases and rigidities often and importantly enough to outweigh their frequent imbecilities, Shaw contributed greatly to depriving jury service of dignity and responsibility. Neither his greatness nor his conscientiousness as a judge is open to the slightest question. His conscience was Tory. The constituency to which his sense of obligation was keenest comprised State Street and Beacon Hill, the bankers, the textile manufacturers, the railway builders. With most of that constituency, he had shifted from Congregationalism to Unitarianism[79]—of the safe and sane variety which looked askance at the audacious social and religious views of Emerson and Theodore Parker.[80] He was often bitterly denounced by radicals. For example Richard Henry Dana, whose abolitionist fervor laid him open to retort in kind, described Shaw as "a man of intense and doting biases in religious, political, and social matters." Though he spoke respectfully of "liberty," he was one of many judges who have found in "license" strict limits to the scope of that flexible concept. Abner Kneeland's "blasphemy" seems to have been an honest and sober statement of religious disbelief; but Shaw sustained his conviction.[82] When Rufus Choate admonished a professional colleague to remember that under Shaw "liberty and property are safe," he meant the extraordinary and perhaps licentious degree of liberty which, since it depends upon successful acquisition, comparatively few can enjoy. Though "property" to Shaw was

---

* Walter Nelles (1883-1937) practiced law in New York 1911-1925, and for some years in the '30s he did research and teaching at the Yale Law School in the area of labor law, legal history, and jurisprudence. Two significant jurisprudential articles of his are called Towards Legal Understanding, 34 Colum. L. Rev. 862, 1041 (1934). In the field of labor history he contributed such important studies as A Strike and Its Legal Consequences, 40 Yale L.J. 507 (1931); The First American Labor Case, 41 Yale L.J. 165 (1931). He has also made scholarly studies of the judicial power to punish for contempt of court. The extract above reproduced is from an historical analysis of an 1842 Massachusetts decision of Shaw's which dealt a substantial blow to the continued use of the "criminal conspiracy" doctrine against labor strikes—Editor

[79] A line of his decisions, commencing with Stebbins v. Jennings, 27 Mass. (10 Pick.) 172 (1830) also shifted church properties to the Unitarian seceders.

[80] It may be evidence that he was tolerant of intellectual idiosyncrasy that Herman Melville, his son-in-law, dedicated Typee to him.

[82] Commonwealth v. Kneeland, 37 Mass. (20 Pick.) 206 (1838).

sacred, he did not conceive its immunities as absolute. He agreed with Taney, as against Marshall and Story, that a merely private interest must yield to interests in industrial expansion.[84] This policy would account more reasonably than the explanation he gave for his position on the fellow servant rule—also for his holding that a railway's insurer's liability ends when it has unloaded freight in its own depot.[85] Railways had yet to establish themselves; and there was much feeling that capital needed encouragement to invest in them.

He was liberal in the sense that another great Tory judge, Lord Mansfield, was liberal; his eyes were wide open to what was going on in the world; he was impatient of narrow legalism, well though he could use it; he wanted law to promote fair dealing in business transactions; he wanted enterprise to prosper; he was sagaciously alert to promote these and other interests which seemed to him to be those of the supposed entity called "society." Holmes wrote of him: "The strength of that great judge lay in accurate appreciation of the requirements of the community whose officer he was. Some, indeed many, English judges could be named who have surpassed him in accurate technical knowledge; but few have lived who were his equals in their understanding of the grounds of public policy to which all laws must ultimately be referred." [86] Holmes himself owes much to him. Shaw anticipated him, for example, when he said: "In considering the rights and obligations arising out of particular relations, it is competent for courts of justice to regard considerations of policy and general convenience." The context in which Shaw said this, however, distinguishes him from Holmes—whose Toryism is greatly modified, much as John Adams' was, by Jeffersonian values. It was said as preface to Shaw's argument of the sound policy in the fellow servant rule.

[Concluding his discussion of Commonwealth v. Hunt, Nelles expresses the opinion that "the campaign for tariff protection may have had a larger share of responsibility for the decision of Commonwealth v. Hunt than the reasons stated in the opinion." (p. 1162) He suggests that Chief Justice Shaw was "subconsciously if not consciously influenced" by the thought that a decision against the interests of the workers would have alienated workers' support for the tariff legislation the New England textile industries desperately needed for their survival. Pound, in the article preceding the Nelles extract above, makes no mention of this explanation. He does criticize as "extravagant" the alleged view of Nelles that Shaw had feared "the people would take away the life tenure of the bench and make it elective if some case was not decided in favor of workingmen at an early opportunity." No statement of the latter view has been found in the Nelles article. —Editor]

---

[84] Commonwealth v. Alger, 61 Mass. (7 Cush. 53 (1851). Cf. Taney in Charles River Bridge v. Warren Bridge, 36 U.S. (11 Pet.) 420 (1837); in that case Shaw had as counsel in the Massachusetts courts argued for the side which would have pre-vailed had Marshall survived.

[85] Norway Plains Co. v. Boston & Providence R. Co., 67 Mass. (1 Gray) 282 (1854).

[86] Holmes, The Common Law (1881) 106.

FREUND,* *ON UNDERSTANDING THE SUPREME COURT*
45-47 (1949)

. . . A crude economic interpretation of the judicial office ignores too many elements of character. The taking of the robe, an experience at once emancipating and humbling, is apt to dissolve old ties and to quicken the sense that there is no escape from that judgment of one's successors which is called history.

The record of the Court supplies many cautions against the generalization that the lawyer is father to the judge. It was a successful lawyer for shipping interests, Henry Billings Brown, who as Mr. Justice Brown delivered a memorable dissent in the income-tax cases: ". . . the decision involves nothing less than a surrender of the taxing power to the moneyed class. . . . I hope it may not prove the first step toward the submergence of the liberties of the people in a sordid despotism of wealth." . . . It was [a] railroad lawyer, Joseph P. Bradley, who as Mr. Justice Bradley protested against the use of the due-process clause to review the regulation of railroad rates by the states, and who would have permitted the states to regulate interstate rates until Congress assumed the responsibility. And it was Harlan F. Stone, whose record in sustaining the validity of social legislation needs no comment, who had written in 1916 by way of commentary on Herbert Spencer's "The Sins Of Legislators" that "Spencer's vigorous warning furnishes food for thought and will perhaps inspire with caution the zealous advocates of such sweeping legislative changes as are involved in the many proposals for the various types of pension law, and minimum wage statutes, and modern legislation of similar character." The list could be extended . . .

NOTES AND QUESTIONS

1. In what way, if any, does Laski's version of the economic interpretation of legal history differ from Pound's? Which is more faithful to the thought of Karl Marx? Which more plausibly accounts for Priestley v. Fowler?

2. Does the validity of the "economic interpretation" of Priestley v. Fowler depend upon acceptance of Lippmann's views as to the state of the law at the time this case was decided?

3. How, according to Pound, does the "taught tradition of the law" explain the fellow-servant cases? Were you satisfied by this explanation? Why?

4. We have seen much attention paid by the writers to judicial motives for the fellow-servant decisions. Why should we be concerned about a judge's motives for decision, as distinguished from (a) the reasons he gives for his decision and (b) its consequences?

5. It is generally assumed that the "considerations of policy" invoked by Shaw in the

* Paul A. Freund, professor of law at Harvard since 1940, was law secretary to Mr. Justice Brandeis 1932-33, and was a government attorney for many years thereafter. He served in the Solicitor-General's Office, Department of Justice (1935-39, 1942-46), briefing and arguing Supreme Court cases. He is co-editor of a casebook on constitutional law; contributed to Cahn (ed.), Supreme Court and Supreme Law (1954); and is Editor-in-Chief of a forthcoming History of the U.S. Supreme Court. The book quoted from above consists of lectures given at Northwestern in 1949 under auspices of the Julius Rosenthal Foundation.—Editor

Farwell case were those in favor of the promotion of railroad and industrial expansion. Charles Warren, in A History of the American Bar 486-487 (1911), observed that railroads began to operate only 8 years before the Farwell decision and quoted an 1883 writer to the effect that the decision was "a species of protective tariff for the encouragement of infant railway industries." The United States Supreme Court has said that the "assumption of risk" doctrine was "a judicially created rule . . . developed in response to the general impulse of common law courts . . . to insulate the employer as much as possible from bearing the 'human overhead' which is an inevitable part of the cost—to someone—of the doing of industrialized business." "The general purpose behind this development in the common law," the Court continued, "seems to have been to give maximum freedom to expanding industry." Tiller v. Atlantic Coast Line Railroad, 318 U.S. 54, 58-59 (1943). Woodrow Wilson expressed similar views in The New Freedom 14-15 (1916).

Professor Leonard Levy, in The Law of the Commonwealth and Chief Justice Shaw 178-80, 192-206 (1957), concurs in this reading of the Farwell case. But he rejects Nelles' tariff-support explanation of Commonwealth v. Hunt, pointing to evidence that Shaw espoused free trade. The most plausible explanation of Commonwealth v. Hunt, he thinks, is that "Shaw regarded combinations, whether by entrepreneurs or workers, as inherent in a free, competitive society, and he saw a social gain in competition" between the organized interests.

EDITORIAL NOTE: The MATERIALIST INTERPRETATION

It should be noted that many historians and theorists who are sympathetic to an "economic determinist" philosophy use "economic" in a broad sense —so as to refer not only to the influence of economic class-antagonisms, but also to the impact of all the *material conditions* of life. One can plausibly correlate factors in the material environment in America with developments in American law, law enforcement, and public attitudes towards law. For instance, the fact of abundant land permitted a legal policy of liberal disposition of the public domain; led to habits of wastefulness, ultimately requiring legislation on conservation; and promoted an American tendency to thumb one's nose at legal authority (one could if necessary, move on). A difference in the availability of water, as between the arid western states and the eastern states, correlates with clear differences in the legal doctrines governing the use of water in the various states. Although the Supreme Court held in 1825 that the federal admiralty and maritime jurisdiction extended only to tidewater, it overruled itself in 1851, recognizing explicitly that the effects of the invention of the steamboat and settlement of the Mississippi Valley upon commerce on navigable streams made it necessary that the federal jurisdiction apply to all navigable waters. Technological change in such fields as printing and telegraphy produced new legal problems, in areas of trademark and copyright, libel, and freedom of speech. Urbanization, the coming of the automobile, mass production, meant new problems for legal solution, and new doctrines in auto negligence law, legislation on health, safety, fair dealing, employer-employee relations, monopolies, and many other subjects. Technological change also affected law enforcement: it made enforcement in some ways more difficult (e.g., the auto provided a fast means of escape) but in many ways easier (officials had not only fast transport and quick communication, but many scientific weapons of crime detection).

For discussion of these and other material factors, and their interplay with ideas, interests, and habits, in influencing the development of American legal agencies, see Hurst, The Growth of American Law (1950) 3-19, 439-446. Many non-Marxists, such as Hurst, stress the economic (in the broad sense) but do not ignore the complementary role of other factors.

Pound and the Interest-Analysis. As the previously quoted passages from Pound on the economic interpretation show, he was not unaware of the significance of economic factors in shaping the course of the law, though he tended to emphasize other factors as well. Thus he has called attention not only to the "taught tradition" and the "received ideals" as to rightness and wrongness, but also to the variety of conflicting interests or claims in society, economic and otherwise, which law must seek to adjust. This "interest-analysis," which Pound has elaborated at great length provides a valuable tool for legal and social analysis and is one of the most important features of his thought. The following extract gives a substantial outline of the analysis.*

POUND, *SOCIAL CONTROL THROUGH LAW*
68-81 (1942)

Interests, that is, the claims or demands or desires for which or about which the law has to make some provision if civilization is to be maintained and furthered, are asserted by individual human beings. But they are not for that reason all of them individual interests. We must not confuse interest as claim, as jurists use the term, with interest as advantage, as economists use it. Thinking of the claims or demands men make, interests fall into three classes, individual interests, public interests, and social interests. Some are claims or demands or desires involved immediately in the individual life and asserted in title of that life. These may be called individual interests. Others are claims or demands or desires involved in life in a politically organized society and asserted in title of that organization. Others, or some of the same in other aspects, are claims or demands or desires involved in social life in civilized society and asserted in title of that life.

Every claim does not necessarily go once and for all in one of these categories. The same claim may be asserted in different titles and may have to be looked at from different standpoints. It may be asserted in title of more than one aspect of

* For a more detailed exposition of his theory of interests, see Pound, A Survey of Social Interests, 57 Harv. L. Rev. 1 (1943); A Theory of Social Interests, 15 Proc. Am. Soc. Society 1 (1943); and A Survey of Public Interests, 58 Harv. L. Rev. 909 (1945); or Vol. III, pt. 4 of Pound, Jurisprudence (1959). For a comprehensive critique and application of Pound's theory, see Stone, The Province and Function of Law (Harvard ed. 1950), 487-646. A shorter critique is Patterson, Pound's Theory of Social Interests, in Sayre (ed.), Interpretations of Modern Legal Philosophies (1947), 558-573.

life. Thus my claim to my watch may be asserted as an individual interest of substance when I sue someone who walks off with it without my consent, either to recover possession of it or to obtain its money value as damages for depriving me of it. But my claim may be looked at also as coincident with a social interest in the security of acquisitions and may be asserted as such when I by making due complaint procure the district attorney to prosecute for larceny someone who has stolen it from me.

It will be enough to give a general sketch of the scheme of interests which have pressed for recognition and security in the past. Individual interests may be classified as interests of personality, interests in domestic relations, and interests of substance. Interests of personality are those involved in the individual physical and spiritual existence. One form is the interest in security of one's physical person and bodily health. Another is in free exertion of one's will—freedom from coercion and from deception whereby one is led to do by force or trickery what he would not do freely or with knowledge of the facts. Another is in free choice of location, the claim to choose where he will go and where he will stay. Another is to one's reputation, to be secure against defamation and other aggressions upon his standing among his neighbors. Another is in free contract and freely entering into relations with others and, a closely related interest, in freely employing himself or gaining employment in any occupation for which he is or is thought to be qualified. Still another is in free belief and opinion. But each of these comes into competition with other recognized interests and requires limitation. Thus, for example, the interests in freedom of contract and freedom to follow an occupation come into competition with claims of laborers, asserted through trade-unions, and have raised typically difficult questions for the courts and for legislation for more than a generation.

Individual interests in the domestic relations make many difficult problems. Husband and wife have each a claim or demand which they assert against the whole world that outsiders shall not interfere with the relation. Yet such abuses have proved to go along with the actions by which these claims were vindicated, that on a weighing of all the interests involved many states have been led to abrogate those actions. The interest is still recognized, but effective security is now denied it. Also the relation involves reciprocal claims or demands which husband and wife assert against each other. The claims of the husband to the society of the wife and to her services for the benefit of the household, which were formerly well secured, have come to be deprived of all substantial legal security on a weighing in comparison with the individual interest of the wife in individual free self-assertion. On the other hand, the claim or demand of the wife for support and maintenance by the husband is not only recognized but is provided for in a variety of ways which make it one of the best secured interests known to the law. As to the interests involved in the relation of parent and child, formerly the claims of the parent were given effect by privilege of "correction" (i.e., corporal punishment), by control of the child's earnings, and by a wide authority of shaping the training and bringing up of the child in every phase. But everywhere today individual interests of the child and a social interest in dependents have been weighed against the claims of parents; and juvenile courts, courts of domestic relations, and family courts in our large cities have greatly changed the legal balance of these interests.

Those claims or demands which are asserted by individuals in title of the individual economic existence are called interests of substance. You will think at once of claims to control corporeal things, the subject of the law of property; and of claims to the fulfilment of promised advantages, the subject of the law of contracts. But let us look instead at a group of interests in economically advantageous relations with others. Such relations may be social or domestic or official or contractual. If a man is wrongfully and maliciously expelled from a social club the injury to his reputation and his social standing in the community may have a serious economic effect upon him. Yet other claims must be thought of. The claims of other members to free determination of their own associations cannot be ignored. They cannot be compelled to associate with him as a fellow clubman if they persist in refusing to do so. In one case where a court ordered a wrongfully expelled member restored to membership, the club reinstated him and then dissolved and formed a new club, leaving him out.

I have already pointed out how claims of the husband to the society and affection of the wife and to her services for the benefit of the household have ceased to be effectively secured either against outside interference with the relation or the wife's refusal to adhere to it. Other interests have come to be recognized and be conceded a higher value. As to official relations, public interests have to be weighed and the older conception of property in a profitable office has been given up. But the most significant questions for our purpose have arisen with respect to contractual relations. If one has a contract with another, he makes a claim against the whole world that third persons shall not interfere to induce the other to break the contract. Yet the third person may assert claims which must be taken account of in this connection. In the immediate past some of the hardest questions in labor law have turned on recognition of claims of labor organizations to induce breaking of contracts of employment and what should be regarded as giving a privilege to interfere with such contracts.

Turning to public interests, one example of difficult questions of weighing will suffice. When political organization of society was struggling with kin organization and later with religious organization for the primacy in social control, the dignity of the state was a very serious matter. Recognizing this interest, it became settled that the state could not be sued without its consent, that its debts could not be set off against its claims, that it was not estopped by what was done by its officials, and that its claims were not lost by official neglect to assert them nor barred by limitation. There were other bases for some of these propositions. An interest in unimpaired efficiency of the political organization was also put in the scale. But now we are asking how far the dignity of the political organization of society is an interest entitled to weight. The extent to which the foregoing propositions should be maintained today, in view of changed ideas as to the dignity of the state, is a controversial subject in public law.

A whole lecture might be given up to a catalogue of social interests. The one which has seemed most obvious in the past is the general security. This includes claims to peace and order, the first social interest to get legal recognition, the general safety, long recognized in the maxim that the public safety is the highest law, the general health, the security of acquisitions, and the security of transactions. One example of conflict or overlapping of recognized interests must suffice here. From the standpoint of the security of acquisitions one who wrongfully takes and holds another's property should not be able to transfer to a third person a better title than he has. But from the standpoint of the security of transactions, people generally who have no knowledge or notice of the owner's claim and, acting in good faith, part with value in a business transaction with one in possession of the property ought to be protected. It is claimed that possession, even if wrongful, ought to give a power of entering into business transactions as to the thing possessed and apparently owned. This question as to the limits of what is called negotiability has been coming up all over the world and recent legislation has been giving greater weight to the security of transactions in comparison with the security of acquisitions.

Closely related and hardly less important is the social interest in the security of social institutions, domestic, religious, political, and economic. Vexed questions as to divorce legislation turn on the relative weight to be given to the individual claims of husband and wife or to the social interest in marriage as a social institution. Vexed questions as between legislation against sedition and judicial maintenance of guarantees of free speech turn on the relative weight to be given to individual interests in free belief and opinion, subsumed under a social interest in general progress and in the individual life, or the social interest in the security of social institutions. Recent legislation is full of examples of the necessity of reconciling the security of economic institutions with the individual life.

Some other important social interests, namely, in the general morals, in the use and conservation of social resources, and in general progress, social, political, economic, and cultural, can only be mentioned in passing. But finally, and by no means least, there is the social interest in the individual life—the claim or demand asserted in title of social life in civilized society that each individual be secure in his freedom, have secured to him opportunities, political, social, and economic, and be able to live at least a reasonably minimum human life in society. Here, too, all manner of overlappings and conflicts are continually encountered and have to be adjusted. It is enough to say that every item in the catalogue must be weighed with many others and that none can be admitted to its full extent without impairment of the catalogue as a whole.

Nor is the task of the law finally achieved as to any claim or demand when it has been denied recognition or has been recognized and delimited. There is a constant pressure to recognize claims which have not been admitted. There is a constant struggle to obtain a higher valuing of claims which have obtained recognition. For example, the case pressed upon the legal order by organized labor has not been that laborers in such organizations and labor organizations were not treated as other litigants and litigant organizations were but that they were so treated. They considered that their claims were entitled to a higher value than that accorded by legal formulas which put them on the same plane with individuals generally and treated their disputes as ordinary controversies about trespass, breach of contract, and interference with contracts and business relations. Moreover, there are claims and conflicts of claims which have given rise to standing puzzles of the law. In one notable case lawmakers and jurists have debated and exercised their ingenuity since the time of Cicero and the problem is no nearer to a wholly satisfactory solution than it was then.

It is clear, then, that when an inventory of the claims or demands pressing for recognition has been made, the next step is to recognize or partially recognize or refuse to recognize them and to fix the limits of those which are recognized. Conceivably this may be done arbitrarily. But arbitrary adjustments of interests do not maintain themselves. Men feel a double grievance when not only are their claims and demands denied but they are denied otherwise than on a basis of reason. Ultimately recognition or denial of recognition of interests and delimitation of those recognized is done in accordance with an established measure of values—something which I shall discuss in the last chapter. Then comes the question how to secure the interests recognized and delimited, and this brings us to the much-vexed question of rights. We secure interests chiefly by attributing to the one who asserts them what we call legal rights.

What is a right? It is said that an Irish jury in a manslaughter prosecution sent in a communication to the trial judge asking whether a man who had a spot in his skull where it was no thicker than an eggshell did not have a right to get killed if he went to the pig fair. Here "right" meant reasonable expectation. Apart from philosophical or metaphysical ethical considerations, a person may have reasonable expectations based on experience, or on the presuppositions of civilized society, or on the moral sentiment of the community. Some one or all of these may be recognized and backed by the law whereby they become the more reasonable. We say that a natural or a moral right has been made also a legal right. But the expectation may arise simply and solely from the law, in which case we say there is a legal right only. It is seldom that a legal right is conferred consciously and intentionally otherwise than as a recognition of reasonable expectations, or what are believed to be reasonable expectations, expressing presuppositions of civilized life. . . .

Section 2

DETERMINATION of the FACTS NECESSARY for POLICY JUDGMENT

As stated in the quotation from Professor Leon Green at the opening of this chapter, our law—including our judicial decisions—embodies policy judgments and has policy consequences. Even if a court merely cites precedent and (unlike the court in Priestley v. Fowler) is silent about what interests or values will be served by its decision, it is clear that (a) the decision nonetheless has social consequences, (b) the same can be said of the precedents relied upon, whether or not they in turn explicitly consider policy issues, and (c) the law would have little reason for existence apart from its social consequences. The law is made for man, not man for the law. Obviously, then, reliable methods of determining factual consequences of alternative decisions would greatly improve the judicial process. Occasionally, but only occasionally, jurists have interrupted their professional labors to note the significance of this fact. In a famous lecture to law students in 1897, Justice Holmes pointed out that "a body of law is more rational and more civilized when every rule it contains is referred articulately and definitely to an end which it subserves, and when the grounds for desiring that end are stated or are ready to be stated in words. . . . For the rational study of the law the black-letter man may be the man of the present, but the man of the future is the man of statistics and the master of economics. It is revolting to have no better reason for a rule of law than that so it was laid down in the time of Henry IV. It is still more revolting if the grounds upon which it was laid down have vanished long since, and the rule simply persists from blind imitation of the past. . . . What have we better than a blind guess to show that the criminal law in its present form does more good than harm?" [1]

A generation later, the Dean of the University of Pennsylvania Law School voiced a similar dissatisfaction (which, unfortunately, could appropriately be voiced today as well): ". . . We really know very little about how our legal rules affect the conduct and welfare of the men and women to whom they are applied. We do not even know very much about the operation of the procedural machinery of the law, except that, in general, it is slow, cumbersome and expensive. Judges have laid down rules on the basis of public policy without the slightest support for the policy except preconceived opinion, and without either knowing or having means of knowing whether the policy declared was or was not aided by the particular decision rendered. . . ." [2]

The following readings deal with some of the problems involved in determining fact consequences of decisions, as well as in determining certain other facts necessary for the making of policy judgments. Solution of these problems will require imaginative collaboration between lawyers and social scientists.

M. R. COHEN,* *LAW AND THE SOCIAL ORDER*
186-187 (1933)

Law and Scientific Method. If scientific method be a way of avoiding certain human pitfalls in the search for truth, then the law surely compares favorably in

---

[1] Holmes, The Path of the Law, 10 Harv. L. Rev. 457, 468, 469, 470 (1897).

[2] Goodrich, The Improvement of the Law, 4 Temple L. Quar. 324 (1930).

* Morris R. Cohen (1880-1947) was rare among modern professional philosophers for his interest in legal theory. He taught

philosophy in the College of the City of New York, 1912-1938 and at the University of Chicago thereafter, and also lectured in jurisprudence at law schools from time to time. Among his studies in philosophy and logic are Reason and Nature (1931); Introduction to Logic and Scientific Method

this respect with other human occupations. Court procedure to determine whether A and B did make a contract, or whether C did commit a criminal act, shows a regard for orderly attainment of truth that compares very favorably with the procedure of a vestry board in determining the fitness of a minister, or of a college in selecting a professor.

When we come, however, to the appellate work of higher courts, in which new public policies are decided under the guise of their legality or constitutionality, we find courts making all sorts of factual generalizations without adequate information. The facilities of our courts for acquiring information as to actual conditions are very limited. Courts have to decide all sorts of complicated issues after a few hours of oral argument and briefs by lawyers. Are ten hours per day in the old-type bakery a strain on the baker's health? Will a workmen's compensation act or a minimum wage law take away the property of the employer or of the worker that receives less than the minimum of subsistence? It is not to the credit of any system that its chief exponents can put their amateurish opinions against those of physicians or economists who have given these questions careful scientific study. Yet the law cannot simply and uncritically accept all the opinions of economists or sociologists. After all, on many important points social scientists are not agreed among themselves; and certainly the social sciences do not demonstrate their results as rigorously as do the natural sciences. Much of what passes as social science is just exercise in technical vocabulary, or mere plausible impressionism, without any critical methods for testing data or accurately determining whether certain assumed results are really true. A good deal of psychology, normal and abnormal, is still in that condition. This, of course, is no argument for the law's ignoring what experts in these fields have to say. But it should impress upon us the necessity for the law itself—in the persons of jurists, judges, and advocates —to have a trained sense of scientific method. . . .

BIKLÉ,* *JUDICIAL DETERMINATION OF QUESTIONS OF FACT AFFECTING THE CONSTITUTIONAL VALIDITY OF LEGISLATIVE ACTION*
38 Harvard Law Review 6-9, 11-16, 18-19, 21-22 (1924)

In discussions involving the authority of the judiciary to determine the constitutional validity of legislation, it is assumed, not infrequently, that the question for decision is a relatively simple one involving merely the determination of the

(1934) (with Ernest Nagel); Preface to Logic (1934). Important jurisprudential studies of his were Law and the Social Order (1933) and two posthumously published volumes, Reason and Law (1950) and Readings in Jurisprudence and Legal Philosophy (1951) (with his son, Felix S. Cohen). Some other works were: The Faith of a Liberal (1945), The Meaning of Human History (1947), American Thought (1954), A Dreamer's Journey (1949)

(autobiographical). The essay on Law and Scientific Method was first published in 1930 (6 Am. L. Sch. Rev. 231) and was reprinted in the 1933 volume.—Editor

* Henry Wolf Biklé (1877-1942), a Philadelphia lawyer, taught at U. of Pa. Law School 1901-1929, was for many years counsel to the Pennsylvania R.R., and was president of the Assoc. of Practitioners Before the I.C.C., 1931-32.—Editor

existence of harmony or conflict between two legal texts, viz., the constitution and the challenged statute; or, in other words, presenting only the not unusual difficulty met with "if two laws conflict with each other," in which event "the courts must decide on the operation of each." It was thus that Chief Justice Marshall described it in Marbury v. Madison.[1]

While this is undoubtedly a correct description of one class of cases arising out of a claimed conflict between a statute and the fundamental law, the development of constitutional doctrines has rendered it quite inadequate as applied to another and highly important class. In this latter class of cases, [the judge] . . . must first be informed as to the truth of some question of fact which the statute postulates or with reference to which it is to be applied; and . . . there is no . . . basis for assumption that he is specially qualified—unless the relevant information is properly developed in the case before him—to determine these underlying questions of fact. . . .

[Thus] the layman may be quite ready to defer to the opinion of the court when the decision requires a definition of the legal significance of the phrase "ex post facto law";* but when the court decides that a law limiting the hours that people may work in bakeshops has no substantial relation to the promotion of the public health,[2] he is inclined to doubt the finality of this finding, since he knows of no particular reason for supposing that the judges are better able to decide such a question than other intelligent persons, unless their determination is based upon evidence produced before them in the usual way, carefully weighed and considered. . . .

Obviously, the underlying question on which the case turns is one of fact, namely, whether, having regard to the workman's physical equipment and the facts of industrial life, this legislation has the described relation—a question of fact on which there seems to be no reason for believing that judges are capable of expressing expert opinions in the absence of evidence. . . .

The validity of the Massachusetts vaccination statute turned essentially on the question whether such a requirement was an arbitrary interference with personal liberty and therefore a violation of the due process clause of the Constitution; and, as in the bakeshop case, this question could only be resolved by an intelligent consideration of the efficacy of vaccination.[16]

---

[1] Cranch (U.S.) 137, 177 (1803). [Cf. Roberts, J., for the Court, in United States v. Butler, 297 U.S. 1, 62 (1935): ". . . When an act of Congress is appropriately challenged in the courts as not conforming to the constitutional mandate, the judicial branch of the Government has only one duty—to lay the article of the Constitution which is invoked beside the statute which is challenged and to decide whether the latter squares with the former. . . . The court neither approves nor condemns any legislative policy. Its delicate and difficult office is to ascertain and declare whether the legislation is in accordance with, or in contravention of, the provisions of the Constitution; and, having done that, its duty ends. . . ." —Editor]

* "Ex post facto law": a law declaring illegal past action which was lawful when performed.—Editor

[2] Lochner v. New York, 198 U.S. 45, 64 (1905).

[16] Jacobson v. Massachusetts, 197 U.S. 11 (1905).

Frequent additional illustrations of cases where the validity of statutes depends on questions of fact are found in cases involving the validity of price-fixing or rate-regulating statutes, and the determination whether such statutes allow the fair return on the value of the property devoted to the public service, which is secured by the Constitution. Such cases, as well as certain others, include the statutes which may be without inherent constitutional invalidity, but may be open to attack in their application in particular situations. Thus a statute regulating the level of railroad passenger fares may be valid as applied to one railroad and not as applied to another; and a statute not generally arbitrary may be arbitrary as applied to some specific person. But it is clear that the question of validity or invalidity is dependent upon the decision in the first instance of some question of fact.

In passing upon these and similar underlying questions of fact which condition the validity of certain statutes, the Supreme Court of the United States has relied upon information derived in sundry ways.

(a) In the first place, it has dealt with the question just as it deals with the usual question of law, as a matter dependent upon reasoning and precedent, and not upon facts disclosed upon the record . . . It seems clear that a substantial part of the criticism which [the bakeshop decision] aroused was due to the Court's undertaking to decide for the country the controlling questions of fact on the basis of a priori reasoning. . . .

(b) A second method of informing the Court as to the considerations which bear upon questions of fact underlying the validity of legislation is the method used on a large scale by Mr. Brandeis when he appeared as counsel in Muller v. Oregon[25] in support of an hours-of-service law for women. This method has since been followed in [other cases]. It undertakes to bring before the Court, by inclusion in the brief of counsel, pertinent statistical data, legislative practice, scientific discussions by persons of eminence in their professions, departmental reports, and so forth, and to ask the Court to take judicial notice of the material so presented.* Of this material the Supreme Court said, in Muller v. Oregon [pp. 420-421]:

---

[25] 208 U.S. 412 (1908). [Louis D. Brandeis subsequently became an Associate Justice of the Supreme Court of the United States.—Editor]

* "The doctrine of judicial notice" in its orthodox form (as distinct from a more liberal form referred to later in these pages) says that it is unnecessary to introduce evidence to prove the existence of facts of common knowledge or facts required to be recorded in offices of the government. Thus it is proper for the judges, when it appears that such a fact is relevant to a case before them, to resort to dictionaries, or authoritative scientific, historical, or sociological works or to government records

to determine the fact. So a court may take judicial notice of the fact that water freezes at a temperature of 32 degrees Fahrenheit, or that the City of Milwaukee is located on Lake Michigan, and a Wisconsin court will take judicial notice of the existence of a law on the statute books of Wisconsin. Men may differ, however, as to when a point is a matter of "fact" and when of "opinion," and as to when a "fact" has become so well established in a field of natural or social science that it can be deemed part of the community's stock of "common knowledge." These opportunities for disagreement will always exist at the borderlines of the doctrine

"The legislation and opinions referred to in the margin may not be, technically speaking, authorities, and in them is little or no discussion of the constitutional question presented to us for determination, yet they are significant of a widespread belief that woman's physical structure, and the functions she performs in consequence thereof, justify special legislation restricting or qualifying the conditions under which she should be permitted to toil. . . ."

. . . It may perhaps be suggested that in the group of cases discussed above under "(a)" the Court is really proceeding on the basis of facts of which it takes judicial notice; but there seems to be this justifiable distinction, that the Court is not so much taking judicial notice of concrete and specific facts upon which it may base its conclusion, as assuming to determine, as a matter of general information, the essential question of fact in dispute. This involves the risk, so aptly characterized in the oft-quoted words of Mr. Justice Holmes, that "the decision will depend on a judgment or intuition more subtle than any articulate major premise." [31]

In addition, the underlying evidential facts are not brought to the Court's attention for the purpose of judicial notice with the completeness and formality which is desirable, if the Court's opinion is to find an adequate foundation in the record and to command on this account the approval of the community—a consummation devoutly to be wished.

(c) In certain cases evidence has been submitted at the trial with reference to the underlying question of fact . . . In Smith v. Texas [233 U.S. 630 (1914)] the Court relied in part on the evidence submitted to support its decision that a statute was arbitrary which prohibited any person from acting as a conductor on a railroad train without having for two years prior thereto worked as a brakeman or conductor of a freight train. In the very recent case of The Chastleton Corporation v. Sinclair [264 U.S. 543 (1924)] the Court, considering a case arising under the Rent Law of the District of Columbia, which had been sustained as an emergency measure in Block v. Hirsh [256 U.S. 135 (1921)] and referring to the question whether the regulation could continue to be upheld against the contention that the emergency [declared by the statute to exist] no longer existed, [ruled that the legislative finding was subject to rebuttal by evidence, and remanded the case for the taking of evidence on plaintiffs' allegations that the emergency no longer existed] . . .

(d) The [opinion in] The Chastleton Corporation v. Sinclair indicates that a legislative declaration as to the underlying question of fact is entitled to great respect on the part of the Court; . . .

Manifestly, therefore, the Court may receive information as to the underlying facts justifying legislation from declarations contained in the legislation itself, and such declarations are entitled to "great respect"; but it may be doubted whether

of judicial notice. See generally, Morgan, Judicial Notice, 57 Harv. L. Rev. 269 (1944); McCormick, Judicial Notice, 5 Vand. L. Rev. 296 (1952); Davis, Judicial Notice, 55 Colum. L. Rev. 945 (1955).—Editor

[31] Dissenting opinion in Lochner v. New York, 198 U.S. 45, 76 (1905).

this is much more than the presumption which arises in favor of the validity of all legislation because of the respect due the legislature.

It is clear that the legislative finding as to the fact upon which the validity of the legislation depends cannot be allowed to be binding upon the courts, since this would furnish a simple means of preventing judicial review of such legislation in this class of cases . . .

(e) But the report of the committee in charge of a bill is likely to set forth with somewhat greater detail than the legislation itself the basis of fact upon which it rests, and that this is a proper source of information for the court is recognized in the recent decision in James Everard's Breweries v. Day [265 U.S. 545 (1924)] . . .

It is manifest that the litigant who attacks legislation is not likely to find support for his contention as to the underlying question of fact in either the reports of the committees in charge of the bill or in the declarations of fact in the legislation itself; they are more likely to contain matter that he must overcome. Consequently he is relegated to the proof of the facts on which he relies or to the presentation in proper form of matters of which the Court may take judicial notice, or, possibly, to the contention that reason and precedent resolve the issue in his favor.

Now, it is submitted that, where there is room to debate the underlying question of fact, this last method—which is the first of those enumerated above—should not be adequate to overthrow the legislation. The reason is the one already outlined, viz., that while the training and experience of the judges have qualified them to deal with strict questions of law, the same training and experience have not qualified them to deal in an expert way with such questions of fact, and they should not undertake to do so except when the relevant facts are properly brought before them either by means of direct evidence or through such presentation as justifies judicial notice. . . .

If this is the correct legal conclusion, it would seem to insure a satisfactory basis for the Court's decision. It would then stand or fall on the record before the Court and not on the information the Court might secure from other sources or the assumptions that it might make in the absence of proof. The statute would be sustained as a matter of course, unless the record disclosed its infirmity; and decisions invalidating statutes because of the Court's conclusions as to some underlying question of fact would afford much less ground for criticism and would be far more likely to strengthen the Court's position if these decisions were founded upon a definite record than if based on a priori reasoning.

It may be that this rule might increase the difficulty of invalidating certain legislation, but it is not perceived that this is an argument against it. . . .

NOTES AND QUESTIONS

1. In what respects do the "facts" that concern Cohen and Biklé differ from the "facts" we have in mind when we speak of the facts in a particular case before the court?

2. Is there any reason why the parties to litigation should not be expected to present evidence on the questions of fact underlying issues of law in fields other than constitutional law? Recall, again, the fact questions underlying the legal issue in Priestley v. Fowler.

3. According to Biklé, what alternative techniques are available to bring before the tribunal the facts underlying questions of law? Appraise the relative merits, in different situations, of the alternative techniques. In doing so, consider the following materials (a to d):

a. It has been observed that under "the guise of judicial notice, some courts have conducted independent researches on their own in order to learn social facts not so notorious or indisputable as to be capable of true judicial notice. They have not usually obtained the information from the primary source but rather have had resort to libraries, experts, government agencies, or even employees of an agency which is a party to the case. The greatest objection to such practice is the disregard of the parties to the litigation, who are given no opportunity to be heard." Note, Social and Economic Facts—Appraisal of Suggested Techniques for Presenting Them to the Courts, 61 Harv. L. Rev. 692, 697 (1948).

b. An interesting recent illustration of this observation is United States v. Roth, 237 F. 2d 796 (C.A. 2, 1956), aff'd 354 U.S. 476 (1957) involving the constitutionality of the federal statute against mailing obscene matter. Judge Jerome Frank's concurring opinion and appendix referred to the existing state of psychological research and concluded that "no one can now show that, with any reasonable probability obscene publications tend to have any effects on the behavior [as distinct from the thoughts] of normal average adults. . . ." He made similar observations as to the alleged effect of certain comic books and other violent and obscene literature in causing juvenile delinquency. (pp. 802, 812-817) He placed great reliance on a letter to him from Marie Jahoda, editor of a research study relied on by the majority, which letter, he argued, interpreted the study report differently from the majority. In justifying use of such unorthodox material, he cited the (dissenting) opinion of Justice Jackson in F.T.C. v. Ruberoid Co. 343 U.S. 470, 485 (1952) which made use of an unpublished treatise in interpreting the role of the F.T.C. under its statute.

How could Justice Jackson and Judge Frank have obviated any objection to what they did?

c. Justice Currie of the Wisconsin Supreme Court has surveyed the rather liberal Wisconsin practice in this connection, in Appellate Courts' Use of Facts Outside of the Record by Resort to Judicial Notice and Independent Investigation, 1960 Wis. L. Rev. 39. Justice Currie refers to the suggested codes of evidence drafted by the American Law Institute and the Commissioners on Uniform State Laws which require that the parties be given an opportunity to present information relative to the propriety of a proposed taking of judicial notice. He agrees with Prof. Kenneth Davis that such an advance-notice requirement would be silly when applied to some matters of common knowledge, and also that the requirement should not be applied to "legislative" facts (those underlying legal issues) as distinguished from "adjudicative" facts (those determining what happened in the particular case before the court). See Davis, An Approach to Problems of Evidence in the Administrative Process, 55 Harv. L. Rev. 364, 402-406 (1942).* Justice Currie writes: "when an appellate court is faced with the issue of determining what rule of law to adopt, it should be free to rely on whatever social and economic data it, in its discretion, deems dependable without any obligation to give advance notice thereof to the parties. . . . An appellate court likewise should not be required to give the parties advance notice

---

* That the doctrine of judicial notice has been more broadly or loosely applied in the case of "legislative" as against "ad- judicative" facts, see 9 Wigmore, Evidence, Sec. 2555d, 3rd ed., 1940; Davis, supra. —Editor

of the intended use of economic or social data to uphold the constitutionality of a statute. . . . However, it is questionable if judicial notice should be taken of such data in order to hold a statute unconstitutional."

(c.1) Consider first Justice Currie's position regarding constitutional cases. Note that it relies on the presumption of constitutionality and the burden it imposes on the party asserting unconstitutionality to overcome the presumption by coming forth with pertinent evidence. Justice Currie thinks concerning the data judicially noticed in this situation, that "the legislature may be deemed to have relied, or could reasonably have relied, on the same data." The risk that judicial notice will be taken of the data is deemed properly borne by a party who failed to overcome the presumption of constitutionality. This position is not as extreme as that taken in Jacobson v. Massachusetts, 197 U.S. 11 (1905), cited by Biklé. There the Supreme Court held that the state compulsory vaccination law was constitutional and upheld the *exclusion* of medical testimony, offered by the defendant, on the general danger of vaccination. "What everybody knows the court must know, and therefore the state court judicially knew, as this court knows, that an opposite theory accords with the common belief and is maintained by high medical authority." *Id.* at 11. The Court quoted from encyclopedias, treatises, and a Royal Commission. Should the defendant's testimony, however, have been excluded?

Such exclusion has been justified on a ground related to that justifying judicial notice where the party attacking the statute has introduced *no* evidence overcoming the presumption of constitutionality; i.e., the Court interpreted the presumption as not requiring it to ascertain whether vaccination, in fact, was efficacious and safe but only whether the Massachusetts legislature had a rational basis for thinking so. Nevertheless, could the Court properly determine this question without at least considering the evidence which the defendant offered in the attempt to prove that "common belief," even if "maintained by high medical authority" was without a rational basis?

(c.2) In non-constitutional cases, too, Justice Currie's position is not that pertinent evidence on facts underlying the legal issue should be excluded, but rather—assuming that the parties have introduced no evidence or inadequate evidence on such "legislative facts"—that the court need not give the proposed "advance notice." Is the position more debatable here than in the constitutional case?

In any event, it should be noted that a liberal view—defended by Justice Currie—of the kinds of data which may be judicially noticed need not necessarily be accompanied by (a) a practice of not giving the above "advance notice" (a practice also defended by him) or (b) the exclusion of the parties' offered evidence on the legislative facts.

Judge Wyzanski urges that whenever a judge relies upon data outside the record to help him formulate a rule of law, he should lay these data and the conclusions he derived therefrom before the parties for their criticism—either by submitting the data at the trial "for examination, cross-examination and rebuttal evidence" or, "where expert criticism has primarily an argumentative character, it can be received better from the counsel table and from briefs than from the witness box." Wyzanski, A Trial Judge's Freedom and Responsibility, 65 Harv. L. Rev. 1281, 1295-6 (1952). "This opportunity is owed as a matter of fairness and also to prevent egregious error." Id. at 1296. Wyzanski goes so far as to suggest that it "may be the responsibility of the judge to present [novel arguments made to him by his law clerk] to counsel for examination." Id. at 1296, n. 71.

d. In addition to the parties' presentation of evidence during the trial (either originally or upon remand by the appellate court), and the use of judicial notice with its sometimes accompanying judicial investigation, there are other techniques by which the court may become aware of legislative facts.

(d.1) Professor Jacob Beuscher suggests that every court has the inherent authority to appoint an expert in the particular field of knowledge to report to the court, or give evidence as a witness in the litigation; or even serve as a "master" or "referee" who would take evidence and file with the court a report which would be open to attack by the parties. Beuscher, "The Use of Experts by the Courts," 54 Harv. L. Rev. 1105, 1117 (1941). Federal District Judge Wyzanski appointed Harvard Economics Professor Carl Kaysen as his personal clerk to assist him in the complex United Shoe Machinery anti-trust case—though it appears that he did not follow all the suggestions of his expert. See Freund, "The Supreme Court and American Economic Policy," 4 The Juridical Review 142, 159 (1959); United States v. United Shoe Machinery Corp., 110 F. Supp. 295 (D. Mass. 1953), aff'd per curiam, 347 U.S. 521 (1954); and Kaysen, United States v. United Shoe Machinery Corporation: An Economic Analysis of an Anti-Trust Case (1956).

(d.2) The suggestion has also been made for the use of "an independent research agency under the control of the courts." Note, 61 Harv. L. Rev. 692, 700, citing Professor Frederick Beutel and Dean Roscoe Pound. As early as 1923, Professor E. S. Corwin suggested that "some agency be created for enlightening the court as to such matters, upon whose results the court could depend." Reports of the National Conference on the Science of Politics, 18 Am. Pol. Sci. Rev. 119, 153 (1924). Do you agree with these suggestions? What provisions would you make for the composition, mode of selection, tenure, and power of such an agency?

4. We have seen from Cohen's remarks, why the lawyers and judges cannot completely abdicate to the experts in seeking answers to social-economic questions underlying issues of legality and constitutionality. It also makes sense that they should not abdicate to the layman—i.e., the jury—in handling such questions. Where such underlying social-economic facts are in dispute and a jury (which has the traditional "fact-finding" function) is sitting, the judge rather than jury is regarded as the proper determiner thereof. 9 Wigmore, Evidence, Sec. 2555d, 3rd ed. 1940. For a prominent case example, see the Supreme Court decision that the determination of whether a "clear and present danger" existed so as to justify holding the anti-Communist Smith Act constitutional was a question for the judge rather than the jury. Dennis v. United States 341 U.S. 494 (1951).

BROWN v. BOARD OF EDUCATION OF TOPEKA
347 U.S. 483 (1954)

[This is the celebrated school desegregation decision delivered by a unanimous Supreme Court, speaking through Chief Justice Warren.—Editor]

. . . In each of the [4] cases, minors of the Negro race, through their legal representatives, seek the aid of the courts in obtaining admission to the public schools of their community on a nonsegregated basis. In each instance, they had been denied admission to schools attended by white children under laws requiring or permitting segregation according to race. This segregation was alleged to deprive the plaintiffs of the equal protection of the laws under the Fourteenth Amendment. In each of the cases other than the Delaware case, a three-judge federal district court denied relief to the plaintiffs on the so-called "Separate but equal" doctrine announced by this Court in Plessy v. Ferguson, 163 U.S. 537 [1896]. Under that doctrine, equality of treatment is accorded when the races are provided substantially equal facilities, even though these facilities be separate. In the Delaware case, the Supreme Court of Delaware adhered to that doctrine, but ordered that the plaintiffs be admitted to the white schools because of their superiority to the Negro schools.

The plaintiffs contend that segregated public schools are not "equal" and cannot be made "equal," and that hence they are deprived of the equal protection of the laws. . . . Argument was heard in the 1952 Term and reargument was heard this Term on certain questions propounded by the Court.[3]

Reargument was largely devoted to the circumstances surrounding the adoption of the Fourteenth Amendment in 1868. It covered exhaustively consideration of the Amendment in Congress, ratification by the states, then existing practices in racial segregation, and the views of proponents and opponents of the Amendment. This discussion and our own investigation convince us that, although these sources cast some light, it is not enough to resolve the problem with which we are faced. At best, they are inconclusive. The most avid proponents of the post-War Amendments undoubtedly intended them to remove all legal distinctions among "all persons born or naturalized in the United States." Their opponents, just as certainly, were antagonistic to both the letter and the spirit of the Amendments and wished them to have the most limited effect. What others in Congress and the state legislatures had in mind cannot be determined with any degree of certainty.

An additional reason for the inconclusive nature of the Amendment's history, with respect to segregated schools, is the status of public education at that time. In the South, the movement toward free common schools, supported by general taxation, had not yet taken hold. Education of white children was largely in the hands of private groups. Education of Negroes was almost nonexistent, and practically all of the race were illiterate. In fact, any education of Negroes was forbidden by law in some states. Today, in contrast, many Negroes have achieved outstanding success in the arts and sciences as well as in the business and professional world. It is true that public education had already advanced further in the North, but the effect of the Amendment on Northern States was generally ignored in the congressional debates. Even in the North, the conditions of public education did not approximate those existing today. The curriculum was usually rudimentary; ungraded schools were common in rural areas; the school term was but three months a year in many states; and compulsory school attendance was virtually unknown. As a consequence, it is not surprising that there should be so little in the history of the Fourteenth Amendment relating to its intended effect on public education.

In the first cases in this Court construing the Fourteenth Amendment, decided shortly after its adoption, the Court interpreted it as proscribing all state-imposed discriminations against the Negro race. The doctrine of "separate but equal" did not make its appearance in this Court until 1896 in the case of Plessy v. Ferguson, supra, involving not education but transportation.[6] American courts have since

---

[3] 345 U.S. 972. The Attorney General of the United States participated both Terms as amicus curiae.

[6] The doctrine apparently originated in Roberts v. Boston, 5 Cush. 198, 206 (1849, Mass.), upholding school segregation against attack as being violative of a state constitutional guarantee of equality. Segregation in Boston public schools was eliminated in 1855. Mass. Acts 1855, ch. 256. But

labored with the doctrine for over half a century. In this Court, there have been six cases involving the "separate but equal" doctrine in the field of public education. In Cumming v. County Board of Education, 175 U.S. 528 and Gong Lum v. Rice, 275 U.S. 78, the validity of the doctrine itself was not challenged. In more recent cases, all on the graduate school level, inequality was found in that specific benefits enjoyed by white students were denied to Negro students of the same educational qualifications. Missouri ex rel. Gaines v. Canada, 305 U.S. 337; Sipuel v. University of Oklahoma, 332 U.S. 631 . . . ; Sweatt v. Painter, 339 U.S. 629; McLaurin v. Oklahoma State Regents, 339 U.S. 637. In none of these cases was it necessary to reexamine the doctrine to grant relief to the Negro plaintiff. And in Sweatt v. Painter, supra, the Court expressly reserved decision on the question whether Plessy v. Ferguson should be held inapplicable to public education.

In the instant cases, that question is directly presented. Here, unlike Sweatt v. Painter, there are findings below that the Negro and white schools involved have been equalized or are being equalized, with respect to buildings, curricula, qualifications and salaries of teachers, and other "tangible" factors. Our decision, therefore, cannot turn on merely a comparison of these tangible factors in the Negro and white schools involved in each of the cases. We must look instead to the effect of segregation itself on public education.

In approaching this problem, we cannot turn the clock back to 1868 when the Amendment was adopted, or even to 1896 when Plessy v. Ferguson was written. We must consider public education in the light of its full development and its present place in American life throughout the Nation. Only in this way can it be determined if segregation in public schools deprives these plaintiffs of the equal protection of the laws.

Today, education is perhaps the most important function of state and local governments. Compulsory school attendance laws and the great expenditures for education both demonstrate our recognition of the importance of education to our democratic society. It is required in the performance of our most basic public responsibilities, even service in the armed forces. It is the very foundation of good citizenship. Today it is a principal instrument in awakening the child to cultural values, in preparing him for later professional training, and in helping him to adjust normally to his environment. In these days, it is doubtful that any child may reasonably be expected to succeed in life if he is denied the opportunity of an education. Such an opportunity, where the state has undertaken to provide it, is a right which must be made available to all on equal terms.

We come then to the question presented: Does segregation of children in public schools solely on the basis of race, even though the physical facilities and other "tangible" factors may be equal, deprive the children of the minority group of equal educational opportunities? We believe that it does.

In Sweatt v. Painter . . . supra, in finding that a segregated law school for Negroes could not provide them equal educational opportunities, this Court relied

elsewhere in the North segregation in public education has persisted until recent years. It is apparent that such segregation has long been a nationwide problem, not merely one of sectional concern.

in large part on "those qualities which are incapable of objective measurement but which make for greatness in a law school." In McLaurin v. Oklahoma State Regents . . . supra, the Court, in requiring that a Negro admitted to a white graduate school be treated like all other students, again resorted to intangible considerations: ". . . his ability to study, to engage in discussions and exchange views with other students, and, in general, to learn his profession." Such considerations apply with added force to children in grade and high schools. To separate them from others of similar age and qualifications solely because of their race generates a feeling of inferiority as to their status in the community that may affect their hearts and minds in a way unlikely ever to be undone. The effect of this separation on their educational opportunities was well stated by a finding in the Kansas case by a court which nevertheless felt compelled to rule against the Negro plaintiffs:

"Segregation of white and colored children in public schools has a detrimental effect upon the colored children. The impact is greater when it has the sanction of the law; for the policy of separating the races is usually interpreted as denoting the inferiority of the Negro group. A sense of inferiority affects the motivation of a child to learn. Segregation with the sanction of law, therefore, has a tendency to retard the educational and mental development of Negro children and to deprive them of some of the benefits they would receive in a racially integrated school system." [10]

Whatever may have been the extent of psychological knowledge at the time of Plessy v. Ferguson, this finding is amply supported by modern authority.[11] Any language in Plessy v. Ferguson contrary to this finding is rejected.

We conclude that in the field of public education the doctrine of "separate but equal" has no place. Separate educational facilities are inherently unequal. Therefore, we hold that the plaintiffs and others similarly situated for whom the actions have been brought are, by reason of the segregation complained of, deprived of the equal protection of the laws guaranteed by the Fourteenth Amendment. . . .

Because these are class actions, because of the wide applicability of this decision, and because of the great variety of local conditions, the formulation of decrees in these cases presents problems of considerable complexity. On reargument, the consideration of appropriate relief was necessarily subordinated to the primary question—the constitutionality of segregation in public education. We have now announced that such segregation is a denial of the equal protection of the laws. In order that we may have the full assistance of the parties in formulating decrees,

[10] A similar finding was made in the Delaware case. . . .

[11] K. B. Clark, Effect of Prejudice and Discrimination on Personality Development (Midcentury White House Conference on Children and Youth, 1950); Witmer and Kotinsky, Personality in the Making (1952), ch. VI; Deutscher and Chein, The Psychological Effects of Enforced Segregation: A Survey of Social Science Opinion, 26 J. Psychol. 259 (1948); Chein, What Are the Psychological Effects of Segregation Under Conditions of Equal Facilities?, 3 Int. J. Opinion and Attitude Res. 229 (1949); Brameld, Educational Costs, in Discrimination and National Welfare (McIver, ed., 1949), 44-48; Frazier, The Negro in the United States (1949), 674-681. And see generally Myrdal, An American Dilemma (1944).

the cases will be restored to the docket, and the parties are requested to present further argument on Questions 4 and 5 previously propounded by the Court for the reargument this Term.[13] The Attorney General of the United States is again invited to participate. The Attorneys General of the states requiring or permitting segregation in public education will also be permitted to appear as amici curiae upon request to do so by September 15, 1954, and submission of briefs by October 1, 1954.

It is so ordered.

* * *

Subsequently, after submissions of briefs and argument, the Court on May 31, 1955 remanded the cases to the District Courts* "to take such proceedings and enter such orders and decrees consistent with this opinion as are necessary and proper to admit to public schools on a racially nondiscriminatory basis with all deliberate speed the parties to these cases." 349 U.S. 294, 301 (1955). In explaining this decree, Chief Justice Warren, speaking for the unanimous Court, said (at 299-301):

> Full implementation of these constitutional principles [announced in the 1954 case] may require solution of varied local school problems. School authorities have the primary responsibility for elucidating, assessing, and solving these problems; courts will have to consider whether the action of school authorities

---

[13] "4. Assuming it is decided that segregation in public schools violates the Fourteenth Amendment

"(a) would a decree necessarily follow providing that, within the limits set by normal geographic school districting, Negro children should forthwith be admitted to schools of their choice, or

"(b) may this Court, in the exercise of its equity powers, permit an effective gradual adjustment to be brought about from existing segregated systems to a system not based on color distinctions?

"5. On the assumption on which questions 4 (a) and (b) are based, and assuming further that this Court will exercise its equity powers to the end described in question 4 (b),

"(a) should this Court formulate detailed decrees in these cases;

"(b) if so, what specific issues should the decrees reach;

"(c) should this Court appoint a special master to hear evidence with a view to recommending specific terms for such decrees;

"(d) should this Court remand to the courts of first instance with directions to frame decrees in these cases, and if so, what general directions should the decrees of this Court include and what procedures should the courts of first instance follow in arriving at the specific terms of more detailed decrees?"

* The Delaware case (in which the state court judgment ordering admission of Negro students had been affirmed) was remanded to the state court for further proceedings.—Editor

constitutes good faith implementation of the governing constitutional principles. Because of their proximity to local conditions and the possible need for further hearings, the courts which originally heard these cases can best perform this judicial appraisal. Accordingly, we believe it appropriate to remand the cases to those courts.

In fashioning and effectuating the decrees, the courts will be guided by equitable principles. Traditionally, equity has been characterized by a practical flexibility in shaping its remedies and by a facility for adjusting and reconciling public and private needs. These cases call for the exercise of these traditional attributes of equity power. At stake is the personal interest of the plaintiffs in admission to public schools as soon as practicable on a nondiscriminatory basis. To effectuate this interest may call for elimination of a variety of obstacles in making the transition to school systems operated in accordance with the constitutional principles set forth in our May 17, 1954, decision. Courts of equity may properly take into account the public interest in the elimination of such obstacles in a systematic and effective manner. But it should go without saying that the vitality of these constitutional principles cannot be allowed to yield simply because of disagreement with them.

While giving weight to these public and private considerations, the courts will require that the defendants make a prompt and reasonable start toward full compliance with our May 17, 1954, ruling. Once such a start has been made, the courts may find that additional time is necessary to carry out the ruling in an effective manner. The burden rests upon the defendants to establish that such time is necessary in the public interest and is consistent with good faith compliance at the earliest practicable date. To that end, the courts may consider problems related to administration, arising from the physical condition of the school plant, the school transportation system, personnel, revision of school districts and attendance areas into compact units to achieve a system of determining admission to the public schools on a nonracial basis, and revision of local laws and regulations which may be necessary in solving the foregoing problems. They will also consider the adequacy of any plans the defendants may propose to meet these problems and to effectuate a transition to a racially nondiscriminatory school system. During this period of transition, the courts will retain jurisdiction of these cases.

In the companion case, Bolling v. Sharpe, 347 U.S. 497 (1954), the Court held that the due process clause of the Fifth Amendment prohibited racial segregation in the public schools of the District of Columbia. The Court noted that the Fifth Amendment, which is applicable in the District, does not contain an equal protection clause as does the Fourteenth Amendment, which applies only to the states. But it concluded that segregation imposed on the Negro children of the District "a burden that constitutes an arbitrary deprivation of their liberty in violation of the Due Process Clause."

APPENDIX TO APPELLANTS' BRIEFS IN ABOVE CASES: "THE
EFFECTS OF SEGREGATION AND THE CONSEQUENCES OF
DESEGREGATION: A SOCIAL SCIENCE STATEMENT" *
Reprinted in 37 Minnesota Law Review 427-439 (1953)

I

The problem of the segregation of racial and ethnic groups constitutes one of
the major problems facing the American people today. It seems desirable, therefore,
to summarize the contributions which contemporary social science can make toward
its resolution. There are, of course, moral and legal issues involved with respect to
which the signers of the present statement cannot speak with any special authority
and which must be taken into account in the solution of the problem. There are,
however, also factual issues involved with respect to which certain conclusions
seem to be justified on the basis of the available scientific evidence. It is with these
issues only that this paper is concerned. Some of the issues have to do with the
consequences of segregation, some with the problems of changing from segregated
to unsegregated practices. These two groups of issues will be dealt with in separate
sections below. It is necessary, first, however, to define and delimit the problem to
be discussed.

Definitions. For purposes of the present statement, segregation refers to that
restriction of opportunities for different types of associations between the members of one racial, religious, national or geographic origin, or linguistic group and
those of other groups, which results from or is supported by the action of any
official body or agency representing some branch of government. We are not here
concerned with such segregation as arises from the free movements of individuals
which are neither enforced nor supported by official bodies, nor with the segregation of criminals or of individuals with communicable diseases which aims at
protecting society from those who might harm it.

Where the action takes place in a social milieu in which the groups involved do

* This statement was drafted and signed by
the following sociologists, anthropologists,
psychologists and psychiatrists, who have
worked in the area of American race
relations:

Floyd H. Allport, Syracuse, New York;
Gordon W. Allport, Cambridge, Massa-
chusetts; Charlotte Babcock, M.D., Chicago,
Illinois; Viola W. Bernard, M.D., New
York, New York; Jerome S. Bruner, Cam-
bridge, Massachusetts; Hadley Cantril,
Princeton, New Jersey; Isidor Chein, New
York, New York; Kenneth B. Clark, New
York, New York; Mamie P. Clark, New
York, New York; Stuart W. Cook, New
York, New York; Bingham Dai, Durham,
North Carolina; Allison Davis, Chicago,
Illinois; Else Frenkel-Brunswik, Berkeley,
California; Noel P. Gist, Columbia, Mis-
souri; Daniel Katz, Ann Arbor, Michigan;
Otto Klineberg, New York, New York;
David Krech, Berkeley, California; Alfred
McClung Lee, Brooklyn, New York; R. M.
MacIver, New York, New York; Robert
K. Merton, New York, New York; Gardner
Murphy, Topeka, Kansas; Theodore M.
Newcomb, Ann Arbor, Michigan; Robert
Redfield, Chicago, Illinois; Ira DeA. Reid,
Haverford, Pennsylvania; Arnold M. Rose,
Minneapolis, Minnesota; Gerhart Saenger,
New York, New York; R. Nevitt Sanford,
Poughkeepsie, New York; S. Stanfield
Sargent, New York, New York; M. Brewster
Smith, New York, New York; Samuel A.
Stouffer, Cambridge, Massachusetts; Well-
man Warner, New York, New York;
Robin M. Williams, Ithaca, New York.

not enjoy equal social status, the group that is of lesser social status will be referred to as the segregated group.

In dealing with the question of the effects of segregation, it must be recognized that these effects do not take place in a vacuum, but in a social context. The segregation of Negroes and of other groups in the United States takes place in a social milieu in which "race" prejudice and discrimination exist. It is questionable in the view of some students of the problem whether it is possible to have segregation without substantial discrimination. Myrdal [1] states: "Segregation . . . is financially possible and, indeed, a device of economy only as it is combined with substantial discrimination" (p. 629). The imbeddedness of segregation in such a context makes it difficult to disentangle the effects of segregation per se from the effects of the context. Similarly, it is difficult to disentangle the effects of segregation from the effects of a pattern of social disorganization commonly associated with it and reflected in high disease and mortality rates, crime and delinquency, poor housing, disrupted family life and general substandard living conditions. We shall, however, return to this problem after consideration of the observable effects of the total social complex in which segregation is a major component.

II

At the recent Mid-century White House Conference on Children and Youth, a fact-finding report on the effects of prejudice, discrimination and segregation on the personality development of children was prepared as a basis for some of the deliberations.[2] This report brought together the available social science and psychological studies which were related to the problem of how racial and religious prejudices influenced the development of a healthy personality. It highlighted the fact that segregation, prejudices and discriminations, and their social concomitants potentially damage the personality of all children—the children of the majority group in a somewhat different way than the more obviously damaged children of the minority group.

The report indicates that as minority group children learn the inferior status to which they are assigned—as they observe the fact that they are almost always segregated and kept apart from others who are treated with more respect by the society as a whole—they often react with feelings of inferiority and a sense of personal humiliation. Many of them become confused about their own personal worth. On the one hand, like all other human beings they require a sense of personal dignity; on the other hand, almost nowhere in the larger society do they find their own dignity as human beings respected by others. Under these conditions, the minority group child is thrown into a conflict with regard to his feelings about himself and his group. He wonders whether his group and he himself are worthy of no more respect than they receive. This conflict and confusion leads to self-hatred and rejection of his own group.

[1] Myrdal, G., An American Dilemma, 1944.
[2] Clark, K. B., Effect of Prejudice and Discrimination on Personality Development, Fact Finding Report, Mid-century White House Conference on Children and Youth, Children's Bureau, Federal Security Agency, 1950 (mimeographed).

The report goes on to point out that these children must find ways with which to cope with this conflict. Not every child, of course, reacts with the same patterns of behavior. The particular pattern depends upon many interrelated factors, among which are: the stability and quality of his family relations; the social and economic class to which he belongs; the cultural and educational background of his parents; the particular minority group to which he belongs; his personal characteristics, intelligence, special talents, and personality pattern.

Some children, usually of the lower socio-economic classes, may react by overt aggressions and hostility directed toward their own group or members of the dominant groups.[3] Anti-social and delinquent behavior may often be interpreted as reactions to these racial frustrations. These reactions are self-destructive in that the larger society not only punishes those who commit them, but often interprets such aggressive and anti-social behavior as justification for continuing prejudice and segregation.

Middle class and upper class minority group children are likely to react to their racial frustrations and conflicts by withdrawal and submissive behavior. Or, they may react with compensatory and rigid conformity to the prevailing middle class values and standards and an aggressive determination to succeed in these terms in spite of the handicap of their minority status.

The report indicates that minority group children of all social and economic classes often react with a generally defeatist attitude and a lowering of personal ambitions. This, for example, is reflected in a lowering of pupil morale and a depression of the educational aspiration level among minority group children in segregated schools. In producing such effects, segregated schools impair the ability of the child to profit from the educational opportunities provided him.

Many minority group children of all classes also tend to be hypersensitive and anxious about relations with the larger society. They tend to see hostility and rejection even in those areas where these might not actually exist.

The report concludes that while the range of individual differences among members of a rejected minority group is as wide as among other peoples, the evidence suggests that all of these children are unnecessarily encumbered in some ways by segregation and its concomitants.

With reference to the impact of segregation and its concomitants on children of the majority group, the report indicates that the effects are somewhat more obscure. Those children who learn the prejudices of our society are also being taught to gain personal status in an unrealistic and non-adaptive way. When comparing themselves to members of the minority group, they are not required to evaluate themselves in terms of the more basic standards of actual personal ability and achieve-

---

[3] Brenman, M., The Relationship Between Minority Group Identification in A Group of Urban Middle Class Negro Girls, J. Soc. Psychol., 1940, 11, 171-197; Brenman, M., Minority Group Membership and Religious, Psychosexual and Social Patterns in A Group of Middle-Class Negro Girls, J. Soc. Psychol., 1940, 12, 179-196; Brenman, M., Urban Lower-Class Negro Girls, Psychiatry, 1943, 6, 307-324; Davis, A., The Socialization of the American Negro Child and Adolescent, J. Negro Educ., 1939, 8, 264-275.

ment. The culture permits and, at times, encourages them to direct their feelings of hostility and aggression against whole groups of people the members of which are perceived as weaker than themselves. They often develop patterns of guilt feelings, rationalizations and other mechanisms which they must use in an attempt to protect themselves from recognizing the essential injustice of their unrealistic fears and hatreds of minority groups.[4]

The report indicates further that confusion, conflict, moral cynicism, and disrespect for authority may arise in majority group children as a consequence of being taught the moral, religious and democratic principles of the brotherhood of man and the importance of justice and fair play by the same persons and institutions who, in their support of racial segregation and related practices, seem to be acting in a prejudiced and discriminatory manner. Some individuals may attempt to resolve this conflict by intensifying their hostility toward the minority group. Others may react by guilt feelings which are not necessarily reflected in more humane attitudes toward the minority group. Still others react by developing an unwholesome, rigid, and uncritical idealization of all authority figures—their parents, strong political and economic leaders. As described in The Authoritarian Personality,[5] they despise the weak, while they obsequiously and unquestioningly conform to the demands of the strong whom they also, paradoxically, subconsciously hate.

With respect to the setting in which these difficulties develop, the report emphasized the role of the home, the school, and other social institutions. Studies[6] have shown that from the earliest school years children are not only aware of the status differences among different groups in the society but begin to react with the patterns described above.

Conclusions similar to those reached by the Mid-century White House Conference Report have been stated by other social scientists who have concerned themselves with this problem. The following are some examples of these conclusions:

Segregation imposes upon individuals a distorted sense of social reality.[7]

Segregation leads to a blockage in the communications and interaction between the two groups. Such blockages tend to increase mutual suspicion, distrust and hostility.[8]

Segregation not only perpetuates rigid stereotypes and reinforces negative at-

[4] Adorno, T. W.; Frenkel-Brunswik, E.; Levinson, D. J.; Sanford, R. N., The Authoritarian Personality, 1951.
[5] [Ibid.—Editor.]
[6] Clark, K. B. & Clark, M. P., Emotional Factors in Racial Identification and Preference in Negro Children, J. Negro Educ., 1950, 19, 341-350; Clark, K. B. & Clark, M. P., Racial Identification and Preference in Negro Children, Readings in Social Psychology, Ed. by Newcomb & Hartley, 1947; Radke, M.; Trager, H.; Davis, H., Social Perceptions and Attitudes of Chil-

dren, Genetic Psychol. Monog., 1949, 40, 327-447; Radke, M.; Trager, H., Children's Perceptions of the Social Role of Negroes and Whites, J. Psychol. 1950, 29, 3-33.
[7] Reid, Ira, What Segregated Areas Mean; Brameld, T., Educational Cost, Discrimination and National Welfare, Ed. by MacIver, R. M., 1949.
[8] Frazier, E., The Negro in the United States, 1949; Krech, D. & Crutchfield, R. S., Theory and Problems of Social Psychology, 1948; Newcomb, T., Social Psychology, 1950.

titudes toward members of the other group, but also leads to the development of a social climate within which violent outbreaks of racial tensions are likely to occur.[9]

We return now to the question, deferred earlier, of what it is about the total society complex of which segregation is one feature that produces the effects described above—or, more precisely, to the question of whether we can justifiably conclude that, as only one feature of a complex social setting, segregation is in fact a significantly contributing factor to these effects.

To answer this question, it is necessary to bring to bear the general fund of psychological and sociological knowledge concerning the role of various environmental influences in producing feelings of inferiority, confusions in personal roles, various types of basic personality structures and the various forms of personal and social disorganization.

On the basis of this general fund of knowledge, it seems likely that feelings of inferiority and doubts about personal worth are attributable to living in an underprivileged environment only insofar as the latter is itself perceived as an indicator of low social status and as a symbol of inferiority. In other words, one of the important determinants in producing such feelings is the awareness of social status difference. While there are many other factors that serve as reminders of the differences in social status, there can be little doubt that the fact of enforced segregation is a major factor.[10]

This seems to be true for the following reasons among others: (1) because enforced segregation results from the decision of the majority group without the consent of the segregated and is commonly so perceived; and (2) because historically segregation patterns in the United States were developed on the assumption of the inferiority of the segregated.

In addition, enforced segregation gives official recognition and sanction to these other factors of the social complex, and thereby enhances the effects of the latter in creating the awareness of social status differences and feelings of inferiority.[11] The child who, for example, is compelled to attend a segregated school may be able to cope with ordinary expressions of prejudice by regarding the prejudiced person as evil or misguided; but he cannot readily cope with symbols of authority, the full force of the authority of the State—the school or the school board, in this instance—in the same manner. Given both the ordinary expression of prejudice and the school's policy of segregation, the former takes on greater force and seemingly becomes an official expression of the latter.

Not all of the psychological traits which are commonly observed in the social complex under discussion can be related so directly to the awareness of status differences—which in turn is, as we have already noted, materially contributed to by the practices of segregation. Thus, the low level of aspiration and defeatism so commonly observed in segregated groups is undoubtedly related to the level of

[9] Lee, A. McClung and Humphrey, N. D., Race Riot, 1943.

[10] Frazier, E., The Negro in the United States, 1949; Myrdal, G., An American Dilemma, 1944.

[11] Reid, Ira, What Segregated Areas Mean, Discrimination and National Welfare, Ed. by MacIver, R. M., 1949.

self-evaluation; but it is also, in some measure, related among other things to one's expectations with regard to opportunities for achievement and, having achieved, to the opportunities for making use of these achievements. Similarly, the hypersensitivity and anxiety displayed by many minority group children about their relations with the larger society probably reflects their awareness of status differences; but it may also be influenced by the relative absence of opportunities for equal status contact which would provide correctives for prevailing unrealistic stereotypes.

The preceding view is consistent with the opinion stated by a large majority (90%) of social scientists who replied to a questionnaire concerning the probable effects of enforced segregation under conditions of equal facilities. This opinion was that, regardless of the facilities which are provided, enforced segregation is psychologically detrimental to the members of the segregated group.[12]

Similar considerations apply to the question of what features of the social complex of which segregation is a part contribute to the development of the traits which have been observed in majority group members. Some of these are probably quite closely related to the awareness of status differences, to which, as has already been pointed out, segregation makes a material contribution. Others have a more complicated relationship to the total social setting. Thus, the acquisition of an unrealistic basis for self-evaluation as a consequence of majority group membership probably reflects fairly closely the awareness of status differences. On the other hand, unrealistic fears and hatreds of minority groups, as in the case of the converse phenomenon among minority group members, are probably significantly influenced as well by the lack of opportunities for equal status contact.

With reference to the probable effects of segregation under conditions of equal facilities on majority group members, many of the social scientists who responded to the poll in the survey cited above felt that the evidence is less convincing than with regard to the probable effects of such segregation on minority group members, and the effects are possibly less widespread. Nonetheless, more than 80% stated it as their opinion that the effects of such segregation are psychologically detrimental to the majority group members.[13]

It may be noted that many of these social scientists supported their opinions on the effects of segregation on both majority and minority groups by reference to one or another or to several of the following four lines of published and unpublished evidence.[14] First, studies of children throw light on the relative priority of the awareness of status differentials and related factors as compared to the awareness of differences in facilities. On this basis, it is possible to infer some of the consequences of segregation as distinct from the influence of inequalities of facilities. Second, clinical studies and depth interviews throw light on the genetic

---

[12] Deutscher, M. and Chein, I., The Psychological Effects of Enforced Segregation: A Survey of Social Science Opinion, J. Psychol., 1948, 26, 259-287.

[13] Deutscher, M. and Chein, I., The Psychological Effects of Enforced Segregation: A Survey of Social Science Opinion, J. Psychol., 1948, 26, 259-287.

[14] Chein, I., What Are the Psychological Effects of Segregation Under Conditions of Equal Facilities?, International J. Opinion and Attitude Res., 1949, 2, 229-234.

sources and causal sequences of various patterns of psychological reaction; and, again, certain inferences are possible with respect to the effects of segregation per se. Third, there actually are some relevant but relatively rare instances of segregation with equal or even superior facilities, as in the cases of certain Indian reservations. Fourth, since there are inequalities of facilities in racially and ethnically homogeneous groups, it is possible to infer the kinds of effects attributable to such inequalities in the absence of effects of segregation and, by a kind of subtraction to estimate the effects of segregation per se in situations where one finds both segregation and unequal facilities.

III

Segregation is at present a social reality. Questions may be raised, therefore, as to what are the likely consequences of desegregation.

One such question asks whether the inclusion of an intellectually inferior group may jeopardize the education of the more intelligent group by lowering educational standards or damage the less intelligent group by placing it in a situation where it is at a marked competitive disadvantage. Behind this question is the assumption, which is examined below, that the presently segregated groups actually are inferior intellectually.

The available scientific evidence indicates that much, perhaps all, of the observable differences among various racial and national groups may be adequately explained in terms of environmental differences.[15] It has been found, for instance, that the differences between the average intelligence test scores of Negro and white children decrease, and the overlap of the distribution increases, proportionately to the number of years that the Negro children have lived in the North.[16] Related studies have shown that this change cannot be explained by the hypothesis of selective migration.[17] It seems clear, therefore, that fears based on the assumption of innate racial differences in intelligence are not well founded.

It may also be noted in passing that the argument regarding the intellectual inferiority of one group as compared to another is, as applied to schools, essentially an argument for homogeneous groupings of children by intelligence rather than by race. Since even those who believe that there are innate differences between Negroes and whites in America in average intelligence grant that considerable overlap between the two groups exists, it would follow that it may be expedient to group together the superior whites and Negroes, the average whites and Negroes, and so on. Actually, many educators have come to doubt the wisdom of class groupings made homogeneous solely on the basis of intelligence.[18] Those who are

[15] Klineberg, O., Characteristics of American Negro, 1945; Klineberg, O., Race Differences, 1936.

[16] Klineberg, O., Negro Intelligence and Selective Migration, 1935.

[17] Klineberg, O., Negro Intelligence and Selective Migration, 1935.

[18] Brooks, J. J., Interage Grouping on Trial-Continuous Learning, Bulletin No. 87, Association for Childhood Education, 1951; Lane, R. H., Teacher in Modern Elementary School, 1941; Educational Policies Commission of the National Education Association and the American Association of School Administration Report, in Education for All Americans, published by N.E.A. 1948.

opposed to such homogeneous grouping believe that this type of segregation, too, appears to create generalized feelings of inferiority in the child who attends a below average class, leads to undesirable emotional consequences in the education of the gifted child, and reduces learning opportunities which result from the interaction of individuals with varied gifts.

A second problem that comes up in an evaluation of the possible consequences of desegregation involves the question of whether segregation prevents or stimulates interracial tension and conflict and the corollary question of whether desegregation has one or the other effect.

The most direct evidence available on this problem comes from observations and systematic study of instances in which desegregation has occurred. Comprehensive reviews of such instances[19] clearly establish the fact that desegregation has been carried out successfully in a variety of situations although outbreaks of violence had been commonly predicted. Extensive desegregation has taken place without major incidents in the armed services in both Northern and Southern installations and involving officers and enlisted men from all parts of the country, including the South.[20] Similar changes have been noted in housing[21] and industry.[22] During the last war, many factories both in the North and South hired Negroes on a non-segregated, nondiscriminatory basis. While a few strikes occurred, refusal by management and unions to yield quelled all strikes within a few days.[23]

Relevant to this general problem is a comprehensive study of urban race riots which found that race riots occurred in segregated neighborhoods, whereas there was no violence in sections of the city where the two races lived, worked and attended school together.[24]

[19] Delano, W., Grade School Segregation: The Latest Attack on Racial Discrimination, Yale Law Journal, 1952, 61, 5, 730-744; Rose, A., The Influence of Legislation on Prejudice; Chapter 53 in Race Prejudice and Discrimination, Ed. by Rose, A., 1951; Rose, A., Studies in Reduction of Prejudice, Amer. Council on Race Relations, 1948.

[20] Kenworthy, E. W., The Case Against Army Segregation, Annals of the American Academy of Political and Social Science, 1951, 275, 27-33; Nelson, Lt. D. D., The Integration of the Negro in the U.S. Navy; 1951; Opinions About Negro Infantry Platoons in White Companies in Several Divisions, Information and Education Division, U.S. War Department Report No. B-157, 1945.

[21] Conover, R. D., Race Relations at Codornices Village, Berkeley-Albany, California: A Report of the Attempt to Break Down the Segregated Pattern on a Directly Managed Housing Project, Housing and Home Finance Agency, Public Housing Administration, Region I, December 1947 (mimeographed); Deutsch, M. and Collins, M. E., Interracial Housing, A Psychological Study of a Social Experiment, 1951; Rutledge, E., Integration of Racial Minorities in Public Housing Projects: A Guide for Local Housing Authorities on How to Do It, Public Housing Administration, New York Field Office (mimeographed).

[22] Minard, R. D., The Pattern of Race Relationships in the Pocahontas Coal Field, J. Social Issues, 1952, 8, 29-44; Southall, S. E., Industry's Unfinished Business, 1951; Weaver, G. L. P., Negro Labor, A National Problem, 1941.

[23] Southall, S. E., Industry's Unfinished Business, 1951; Weaver, G. L. P., Negro Labor, A National Problem, 1941.

[24] Lee, A. McClung and Humphrey, N. D., Race Riot, 1943; Lee, A. McClung, Race Riots Aren't Necessary, Public Affairs Pamphlets, 1945.

Under certain circumstances desegregation not only proceeds without major difficulties, but has been observed to lead to the emergence of more favorable attitudes and friendlier relations between races. Relevant studies may be cited with respect to housing,[25] employment,[26] the armed services[27] and merchant marine,[28] recreation agency,[29] and general community life.[30]

Much depends, however, on the circumstances under which members of previously segregated groups first come in contact with others in unsegregated situations. Available evidence suggests, first, that there is less likelihood of unfriendly relations when the change is simultaneously introduced into all units of a social institution to which it is applicable—e.g., all of the schools in a school system or all of the shops in a given factory.[31] When factories introduced Negroes in only some shops but not in others the prejudiced workers tended to classify the desegregated shops as inferior, "Negro work." Such objections were not raised when complete integration was introduced.

The available evidence also suggests the importance of consistent and firm enforcement of the new policy by those in authority.[32] It indicates also the

[25] Deutsch, M. and Collins, M. E., Inter-racial Housing, A Psychological Study of a Social Experiment, 1951; Merton, R. K., West, P. S., Jahoda, M., Social Fictions and Social Facts: The Dynamics of Race Relations in Hilltown, Bureau of Applied Social Research, Columbia Univ., 1949 (mimeographed); Rutledge, E., Integration of Racial Minorities in Public Housing Projects; A Guide for Local Housing Authorities on How to Do It, Public Housing Administration, New York Field Office (mimeographed); Wilner, D. M.; Walkley, R. P.; and Cook, S. W., Intergroup Contact and Ethnic Attitudes in Public Housing Projects, J. Social Issues, 1952, 8, 45-69.

[26] Harding, J., and Hogrefe, R., Attitudes of White Department Store Employees Toward Negro Co-workers, J. Social Issues, 1952, 8, 19-28; Southall, S. E., Industry's Unfinished Business, 1951; Weaver, G. L. P., Negro Labor, A National Problem, 1941.

[27] Kenworthy, E. W., The Case Against Army Segregation, Annals of the American Academy of Political and Social Science, 1951, 275, 27-33; Nelson, Lt. D. D., The Integration of the Negro in the U.S. Navy, 1951; Stouffer, S., et al., The American Soldier, Vol. I, Chap. 19, A Note on Negro Troops in Combat, 1949; Watson, G., Action for Unity, 1947; Opinions About Negro Infantry Platoons in White Compa-

nies in Several Divisions, Information and Education Division, U.S. War Department, Report No. B-157, 1945.

[28] Brophy, I. N., The Luxury of Anti-Negro Prejudice, Public Opinion Quarterly, 1946, 9, 456-466 (Integration in Merchant Marine); Watson, G., Action for Unity, 1947.

[29] Williams, D. H., The Effects of an Interracial Project Upon the Attitudes of Negro and White Girls Within the Young Women's Christian Association, Unpublished M.A. thesis, Columbia University, 1934.

[30] Dean, J. P., Situational Factors in Intergroup Relations: A Research Progress Report, Paper Presented to American Sociological Society, 12/28/49 (mimeographed); Irish, D. P., Reactions of Residents of Boulder, Colorado, to the Introduction of Japanese Into the Community, J. Social Issues, 1951, 8, 10-17.

[31] Minard, R. D., The Pattern of Race Relationships in the Pocahontas Coal Field, J. Social Issues, 1952, 8, 29-44; Rutledge, E., Integration of Racial Minorities in Public Housing Projects; A Guide for Local Housing Authorities, on How to Do It, Public Housing Administration, New York Field Office (mimeographed).

[32] Deutsch, M., and Collins, M. E., Inter-racial Housing, A Psychological Study of a Social Experiment, 1951; Feldman, H., The Technique of Introducing Negroes

importance of such factors as: the absence of competition for a limited number of facilities or benefits;[33] the possibility of contacts which permit individuals to learn about one another as individuals;[34] and the possibility of equivalence of positions and functions among all of the participants within the unsegregated situation.[35] These conditions can generally be satisfied in a number of situations, as in the armed services, public housing developments, and public schools.

IV

The problem with which we have here attempted to deal is admittedly on the frontiers of scientific knowledge. Inevitably, there must be some differences of opinion among us concerning the conclusiveness of certain items of evidence, and concerning the particular choice of words and placement of emphasis in the preceding statement. We are nonetheless in agreement that this statement is substantially correct and justified by the evidence, and the differences among us, if any, are of a relatively minor order and would not materially influence the preceding conclusions.

CAHN,* *A DANGEROUS MYTH IN THE SCHOOL SEGREGATION CASES*
30 New York University Law Review 150, 153-154, 157-168 (1955)

. . . *The Brandeis-Brief Dilemma.*—Professor Paul Freund has indicated more than once that while the Brandeis brief, filled with sociological and economic data for the judges' information, is an excellent device for upholding legislation, it creates an awkward logical predicament when the objective becomes one of overturning legislation.[9] If statistics, expert opinions, graphs, and similar data are sufficient to establish that the legislative or administrative authorities have acted

Into the Plant, Personnel, 1942, 19, 461-466; Rutledge, E., Integration of Racial Minorities in Public Housing Projects; A Guide for Local Housing Authorities on How to Do It, Public Housing Administration, New York Field Office (mimeographed); Southall, S. E., Industry's Unfinished Business, 1951; Watson, G., Action for Unity, 1947.

[33] Lee, A. McClung and Humphrey, N. D., Race Riot, 1943; Williams, R., Jr., The Reduction of Intergroup Tensions, Social Science Research Council, New York, 1947; Windner, A. E., White Attitudes Towards Negro-White Interaction in an Area of Changing Racial Composition. Paper delivered at the Sixtieth Annual Meeting of the American Psychological Association, Washington, September 1952.

[34] Wilner, D. M.; Walkley, R. P.; and Cook, S. W., Intergroup Contact and

Ethnic Attitudes in Public Housing Projects, J. Social Issues, 1952, 8, 45-69.

[35] Allport, G. W., and Kramer, B., Some Roots of Prejudice, J. Psychol., 1946, 22, 9-39; Watson, J., Some Social and Psychological Situations Related to Change in Attitude, Human Relations, 1950, 3, 1.

* Edmond Cahn practised law in New York City, 1927-50; and has been a law professor at New York University since 1946. He is the author of The Sense of Injustice (1949); The Moral Decision (1955) and is editor and contributor, Supreme Court and Supreme Law (1954).

[9] Freund, "Review of Facts in Constitutional Cases" in Supreme Court and Supreme Law 49-50 (Cahn ed. 1954). For another analysis by the same gifted author, see On Understanding the Supreme Court 88 et seq. (1951).

rationally, then is it ever possible to prove that they have acted otherwise? Shrewd, resourceful lawyers can put a Brandeis brief together in support of almost any conceivable exercise of legislative judgment. Moreover, the mere fact that the legislature has acted in the premises ought normally to imply that the action had some rationally explicable basis.

The Brown and Bolling records, for example, included considerable evidence to show that school segregation was not unreasonable. In addition to explicit provisions in the respective state constitutions and statutes, there was the testimony of experienced school administrators, supported to some extent by the expert opinions of psychological and psychiatric witnesses (especially in the case from Virginia). Hence, whatever else the Supreme Court's action may accomplish, it does demonstrate satisfactorily that a challenge to constitutionality *can* overcome the kind of defense which is implicit in a Brandeis brief.

It is fair to suspect that the impact of the Brandeis brief is no longer so great as when the device was novel and judges were more readily impressed by the paraphernalia of science or pseudoscience. In the last two decades, many Brandeis briefs have been conspicuously vulnerable in respect of statistical method, rationality of inferences from assembled data, adequacy of sampling, and failure to allow for—or to disclose—negative instances. Perhaps their quality will improve with a more critical attitude on the judges' part. . . .

A Dangerous Myth.—In the Virginia case[14] and to a lesser extent in the other litigations, various psychiatrists, psychologists, and social scientists gave expert testimony concerning the harmful effects of segregation on Negro school children. In addition, some of appellants' witnesses prepared an elaborate statement on the subject, which, signed by a total of thirty-two experts, was submitted to the Supreme Court as an appendix to appellants' brief. In the months since the utterance of the Brown and Bolling opinions, the impression has grown that the outcome, either entirely or in major part, was caused by the testimony and opinions of the scientists, and a genuine danger has arisen that even lawyers and judges may begin to entertain this belief.[16] The word "danger" is used advisedly, because I

[14] Davis v. County School Board, 103 F. Supp. 337 (E.D. Va. 1952), No. 4 in the Supreme Court.

[16] For example, Will Maslow, Director of the Commission on Law and Social Action of the American Jewish Congress, said: "The NAACP struggled for sixteen years to convince the United States Supreme Court that segregation in and of itself was a form of inequality forbidden by the Fourteenth Amendment. As long as the argument revolved about the size of classes, the length of school terms, the salaries of teachers, the physical condition of the school plant or the distance required to travel to school, little headway was made in convincing the court. But when the psychologists began to argue about the injury to pupil morale caused by governmentally imposed segregation, the sense of inferiority occasioned thereby and the hampering of the learning process, the Court pricked up its ears. When the final decision was handed down in the public school segregation cases, it rested not on conceptual legal principles or the legislative history of the Fourteenth Amendment or even on the sociological demonstration that in practice segregation results in inferior schools but on the psychological finding of thwarted intellectual development." Address, The Uses of Law in the Struggle for Equality, Atlantic City, N.J., December, 1954.

would not have the constitutional rights of Negroes—or of other Americans—rest on any such flimsy foundation as some of the scientific demonstrations in these records.[17]

The moral factors involved in racial segregation are not new—like the science of social psychology—but exceedingly ancient. What, after all, is the most elementary and conspicuous fact about a primitive community if not the physical proximity of human beings mingling together? When the members of a community decide to exclude one of their number from the group life without killing him outright, what else can they do but force him to remove himself physically (as in the case of Cain), ostracize him for what they consider the general welfare (as the Athenians did), banish him from the cluster of community dwellings (as in outbreaks of leprosy or other plague), assign him a fixed area or ghetto to occupy (as with the Jews in medieval times), or lock him in a penitentiary (as we do with convicted criminals)? Hardly anyone has been hypocritical enough to contend that no stigma or loss of status attaches to these forms of physical separation. Segregation does involve stigma; the community knows it does. It knows full well that if "Stone walls do not a prison make nor iron bars a cage," they certainly do hamper a person's freedom to move about and consort with whom he pleases. Possibly, as the poet said, the walls can be understood as a "hermitage" or retreat or monastery, but only for those who choose them without being compelled by the social group.

There are people who argue, sometimes quite sincerely, that racial segregation is not *intended* to humiliate or stigmatize. On first impression, the argument seems to have some slight mitigative value, for surely a deliberate insult is liable to cut deeper than one inflicted out of mere crudeness or insensibility. But the mitigation comes too late. An excuse that one did not intend to injure does not stand much chance of reception when the offender, having been informed of the damage he has done, continues and persists in the same old callous insults. As is observed in the ancient Babylonian Talmud, to shame and degrade a fellow-creature is to commit a kind of psychic mayhem upon him. Like an assailant's knife, humiliation slashes his self-respect and human dignity. He grows pale, the blood rushes from his face just as though it had been shed.[18] That is why we are accustomed to say he feels "wounded."

Moreover, if affronts are repeated often enough, they may ultimately injure the victim's backbone. We hear there are American Negroes who protest they do not feel insulted by racially segregated public schools. If there are any such Negroes, then they are the ones who have been injured most grievously of all, because segregation has shattered their spines and deprived them of self-respect.

So one speaks in terms of the most familiar and universally accepted standards

[17] Clearly, counsel followed the right strategy in offering the expert testimony for whatever the several courts or judges might find it worth. The younger Pliny, an extraordinarily successful advocate, insisted at some length that since different minds may be persuaded by different arguments, the advocate ought to develop and present them all, neglecting none. Pliny, Letters I. xx (Loeb ed. 1931) I, 70-2. . . .

[18] Baba Mezia 58b in The Babylonian Talmud, Seder Nezikin II 348-49 (Soncino trans. 1935).

of right and wrong when one remarks (1) that racial segregation under government auspices inevitably inflicts humiliation, and (2) that official humiliation of innocent, law-abiding citizens is psychologically injurious and morally evil. Mr. Justice Harlan and many other Americans with responsive consciences recognized these simple, elementary propositions before, during, and after the rise of "separate but equal." For at least twenty years, hardly any cultivated person has questioned that segregation is cruel to Negro school children. The cruelty is obvious and evident. Fortunately, it is so very obvious that the Justices of the Supreme Court could see it and act on it even after reading the labored attempts by plaintiffs' experts to demonstrate it "scientifically."

Claims and Facts.—When scientists set out to prove a fact that most of mankind already acknowledges, they may provide a rather bizarre spectacle. Fifty years ago, certain biologists who were engaged in just this sort of enterprise, provoked George Bernard Shaw to denounce their "solemnly offering us as epoch-making discoveries their demonstrations that dogs get weaker and die if you give them no food; that intense pain makes mice sweat; and that if you cut off a dog's leg the three legged dog will have a four-legged puppy." [19] Then Mr. Shaw called the scientists a number of fearful names (beginning with "dolts" and "blackguards"), none of which would be remotely applicable to the psychologists and psychiatrists who testified in the desegregation cases. So far as I can judge, all of these are fine, intelligent, dedicated scholars. Yet one can honor them as they deserve without swallowing their claims.

Professor Kenneth B. Clark of the psychology department of City College acted as general social science consultant to the NAACP legal staff and served as liaison between the lawyers and the scientists. His endeavors having been long and arduous, perhaps it was natural that he should exaggerate whatever the experts contributed to the case. In an article written while the country was waiting for the Supreme Court's decisions, he asserted, "*Proof* of the arguments that segregation itself is inequality and that state imposed racial segregation inflicts injuries upon the Negro *had to come from the social psychologists and other social scientists.*" [20] (Emphasis supplied.)

When Professor Clark wrote thus, he could not know that Chief Justice Warren's opinions would not mention either the testimony of the expert witnesses or the submitted statement of the thirty-two scientists. The Chief Justice cushioned the blow to some extent by citing certain professional publications of the psychological experts in a footnote, alluding to them graciously as "modern authority." [21] In view of their devoted efforts to defeat segregation, this was the kind of gesture a magnanimous judge would feel impelled to make, and we are bound to take satisfaction in the accolade. Yet, once the courtesy had been paid, the Court

[19] From a lecture prepared by Shaw in 1906 for delivery before the Fabian Society. This is one of several excerpts which he used later in the Preface to Back to Methuselah.

[20] Clark, Desegregation: An Appraisal of the Evidence, 9 J. Social Issues No. 4, p. 3 (1953). It would relieve me to learn that I have read Professor Clark too literally, but general opinion indicates that I have not.

[21] 347 U.S. 483, 494 and n. 11 (1954).

was not disposed in the least to go farther or base its determination on the expert testimony.

As I have said, these developments Professor Clark could not have known when he staked so wide a claim for his profession. But he did know that circumstances in the Virginia litigation—the one he participated in most actively—had reflected very directly on his assertion. The Virginia school board had offered the testimony of three expert witnesses, and all three (psychiatrist Kelly, psychologist Buck, and Professor Clark's own former teacher, Professor Garrett of Columbia) had *admitted,* in one way or another, that racial segregation in the schools does injure Negro children's personalities.[22] They admitted, as we have said, a fact of common experience. On the defendants' behalf, they testified as persuasively as they could against the Court's adopting what they called "disruptive" or "coercive" measures, and they spoke regretfully about the firmness of established regional customs. Buck summarized their attitude in two statements: "I feel that as an abstract idea, segregation is bad," and "I think the whole society is sick." [23]

When we come to explain why the statement signed by the thirty-two social scientists went without mention by Chief Justice Warren, I find myself at a disadvantage. Only the reader's assistance can rescue me. I have examined the text of this statement, which has become easy of access by being reprinted in a law review. My personal, subjective reaction is that the text conveys little or no information beyond what is already known in "literary psychology" (by which I mean such psychological observations and insights as one finds continually in the works of poets, novelists, essayists, journalists, and religious prophets). The statement's vocabulary and style would not be called "literary"; I refer only to its substance. If my readers will inspect the statement for themselves, they will ascertain whether it impresses them as it did me. At that, my reaction may be due to a lack of technical training in scientific psychology and psychological testing.

The "Generally Accepted" Test.—When a scientist is engaged in demonstrating a fact of common knowledge (e.g., that fire burns, that a cold causes sniffles, or that segregation degrades), it is not easy to pass a fair judgment on the validity of his proof. Our minds tend to supply his conclusion before he is ready to deduce it. Subconsciously we reinforce his evidence with the facts and feelings of our own experience, and if his reasoning should contain a flaw, we are too preoccupied with reaching the familiar destination to detect it. Moreover, in the present situation, men who specialize in conducting psychological tests might discover all sorts of weak assumptions and fallacies that mere lawyers would never notice. Under these

---

[22] No. 4, Davis v. County School Board (the Va. case), Transcript of Record: Kelly testifying at p. 529; Buck at pp. 538, 544; and Garrett at p. 550. Professor Garrett said: "I do not think that one can possibly defend separation of one group from another, if the separated group is stigmatized or put into an inferior position. Separation can be of different sorts which does not involve, necessarily, any feeling of inferiority or any stigma." And then he went on to instance, as examples of separation without stigma, the following: (1) separate schools for boys and girls, (2) parochial schools, (3) classes for "children who are slow," and (4) classes for "children who are bright." (May all the opposers of equality have witnesses like these!)

[23] *Id.* at 538, 544.

several disadvantages, the most I can do here is present Professor Clark's evidence concerning the "generally accepted" test,[25] together with the comments that suggest themselves to an untrained but interested observer.

Professor Clark testified as an expert in the South Carolina, Delaware, and Virginia litigations. The clearest description of the test appears in his testimony in the South Carolina case. He said:[26]

> A. I made these tests on Thursday and Friday of this past week at your request, and I presented it to children in the Scott's Branch Elementary school, concentrating particularly on the elementary group. I used these methods which I told you about—the Negro and White dolls—which were identical in every respect save skin color. And, I presented them with a sheet of paper on which there were these drawings of dolls, and I asked them to show me the doll— May I read from these notes?
>
> JUDGE WARING: You may refresh your recollection.
>
> THE WITNESS: Thank you. I presented these dolls to them and I asked them the following questions in the following order: "Show me the doll that you like best or that you'd like to play with," "Show me the doll that is the 'nice' doll," "Show me the doll that looks 'bad,' " and then the following questions also: "Give me the doll that looks like a white child," "Give me the doll that looks like a colored child," "Give me the doll that looks like a Negro child," and "Give me the doll that looks like you."
>
> By MR. CARTER:
>
> Q. "Like you?"
>
> A. "Like you." That was the final question, and you can see why. I wanted to get the child's free expression of his opinions and feelings before I had him identified with one of these two dolls. I found that of the children between the ages of six and nine whom I tested, which were a total of sixteen in number, that ten of those children chose the white doll as their preference; the doll which they liked best. Ten of them also considered the white doll a "Nice" doll. And, I think you have to keep in mind that these two dolls are absolutely identical in every respect except skin color. Eleven of these sixteen children chose the brown doll as the doll which looked "bad." This is consistent with previous results which we have obtained testing over three hundred children,[27] and we interpret it to mean that the Negro child accepts as early as six, seven or eight the negative stereotypes about his own group. And, this result was confirmed in Clarendon County where we found eleven out of sixteen children picking the brown doll as looking "bad," when we also must take into account that over

[25] For Professor Clark's testimony that this is the test "generally accepted as indications of the child's sensitivity to race as a problem," see No. 2, Briggs v. Elliott (the S.C. case), Transcript of Record, p. 86. Professor Clark suffered from inflicting the test on the Negro children. No. 4, Davis v. County School Board (the Va. case), Transcript of Record, p. 251.

[26] No. 2, Briggs v. Elliott (the S.C. case), Transcript of Record, pp. 87-90.

[27] A bit later, the number was stated as "400 times." Id. at 96.

half of these children, in spite of their own feelings,—negative feelings—about the brown doll, were eventually required on the last question to identify themselves with this doll which they considered as being undesirable or negative. It may also interest you to know that only one of these children, between six and nine, dared to choose the white doll as looking bad. The difference between eleven and sixteen was in terms of children who refused to make any choice at all and the children were always free not to make a choice. They were not forced to make a choice. These choices represent the children's spontaneous and free reactions to this experimental situation. Nine of these sixteen children considered the white doll as having the qualities of a nice doll. To show you that that was not due to some artificial or accidental set of circumstances, the following results are important. Every single child, when asked to pick the doll that looked like the white child, made the correct choice. All sixteen of the sixteen picked that doll. Every single child, when asked to pick the doll that was like the colored child; every one of them picked the brown doll. My opinion is that a fundamental effect of segregation is basic confusion in the individuals and their concepts about themselves conflicting in their self images. That seemed to be supported by the results of these sixteen children, all of them knowing which of those dolls was white and which one was brown. Seven of them, when asked to pick the doll that was like themselves; seven of them picked the white doll. This must be seen as a concrete illustration of the degree to which the pleasures[28] which these children sensed against being brown forced them to evade reality—to escape the reality which seems too overburdening or too threatening to them. This is clearly illustrated by a number of these youngsters who, when asked to color themselves— For example, I had a young girl, a dark brown child of seven, who was so dark brown that she was almost black. When she was asked to color herself, she was one of the few children who picked a flesh color, pink, to color herself. When asked to color a little boy, the color she liked little boys to be, she looked all around the twenty-four crayons and picked up a white crayon and looked up at me with a shy smile and began to color. She said, "Well, this doesn't show." So, she pressed a little harder and began to color in order to get the white crayon to show. These are the kinds of results which I obtained in Clarendon County.

Q. Well, as a result of your tests, what conclusions have you reached, Mr. Clark, with respect to the infant plaintiffs involved in this case?

A. The conclusion which I was forced to reach was that these children in Clarendon County, like other human beings who are subjected to an obviously inferior status in the society in which they live, have been definitely harmed in the development of their personalities; that the signs of instability in their personalities are clear, and I think that every psychologist would accept and interpret these signs as such.

Q. Is that the type of injury which in your opinion would be enduring or lasting?

---

[28] Thus in original; probably should be "pressures."

A. I think it is the kind of injury which would be as enduring or lasting as the situation endured, changing only in its form and in the way it manifests itself.

MR. CARTER: Thank you. Your witness.

General Comments.—We are not provided here with any proof of the numerical adequacy of the sampling or of its being a representative cross-section. We have no demonstration that abnormal or eccentric backgrounds of the individual children have been investigated. Among these 16 children (or 300, including the other groups mentioned) there would probably be a certain proportion with untypical private experiences. In such a strikingly small sample, the results could easily mislead.

Moreover, if one follows the arithmetic in Professor Clark's testimony—which is not easy for me—some of his interpretations seem to be predetermined. For example, if Negro children say a *brown* doll is like themselves, he infers that segregation has made them conscious of race; yet if they say a *white* doll is like themselves, he infers that segregation has forced them to evade reality.

Perhaps the main point is that this test does not purport to demonstrate the effects of *school* segregation, which is what the court was being asked to enjoin. If it disclosed anything about the effects of segregation on the children, their experiences at school were not differentiated from other causes. Considering the ages of the children, we may conjecture they had not been long at school.

Comment on the Opening Questions.—We do not know how the children took these questions. If Professor Clark had offered to give real dolls instead of showing pictures of dolls, the reaction might have been more serious. In any case, I do not think any certain inference follows from 10 out of 16 pointing to the picture of the white doll. Habituation with *dolls* (as distinguished from people) should be allowed for. Manufacturers and commercial fashions practically restrict a child's concept of what a "nice" doll would look like. Many white children of certain generations were taught to prefer "Topsy" or other colored dolls;[29] some children would say that there is no really "nice" doll but a teddy-bear. At this point, the response seems uninformative.

Comment on the "Bad Doll" Question.—Here, it seems to me, the children were tricked. Perhaps that is how some of them felt. There had been no previous question about a "good doll," only about a "nice" one, which the children clearly understood meant one "you'd like to play with." What is a "bad doll"? Some children might consider this a term of preference for play purposes: all little "mothers" love to rebuke and punish naughty dolls. Other children, on hearing the question, would be simply bewildered by the sudden, unexpected introduction of moral or disciplinary references. Some may have responded by pointing to the

[29] Professor Clark testified that a graduate student at Columbia had used the test on white children with his permission, but he had not obtained the results. No. 2, Briggs v. Elliott (the S.C. Case), Transcript of Record, p. 96. Yet it would seem that trying the test on white children would be the very first and most obvious way to begin ascertaining whether it had any probative value when given to Negro children.

brown doll because the question seemed to imply that a process of elimination was contemplated. But I hope the children asked themselves: Why must there be a "bad" doll at all? Why cannot both dolls be "nice"? We observe that five children declined to answer this question. Probably they felt it unfair or at least very confusing in the circumstances.

Comment on the Remaining Questions.—It is noteworthy that seven Negro children picked the white doll "when asked to pick the doll that was like themselves." Professor Clark leaps to infer that they were evading reality. This I doubt. Although his testimony does not make me clear on the point, I gather that these seven children were among the ten who had previously chosen the white doll as "nice." Were they wrong, then, to claim that the white doll was very much "like themselves" because they too were "nice"? No one can state positively what these children were thinking at the time; but if they did have perception enough to insist to themselves that the "niceness" was decisive and not the color, lo and behold! This would be wisdom indeed! "Out of the mouths of babes and sucklings—"? Perhaps, merely perhaps. In any event, I cannot see that the opposite interpretation (Professor Clark's) is so evident that it deserves to rank as scientific proof.

Aid from an Unexpected Quarter.—Fortunately, the outcome of the Brown and Bolling cases did not depend on the psychological experts' facing and answering the objections, queries, and doubts I have presented. It is possible that if the questions had been put to Professor Clark on cross-examination, he would have come forward with convincing answers. But, to all intents and purposes, the questions were not put. The doll test was not analyzed in suitable detail by any of the cross-examiners, probably because they, too, realized that segregation does degrade and injure Negro school children.

In the Virginia trial, the defense appeared particularly inept. Far from caring to concentrate on the doll test and its scientific validity, the lawyer for the defendants was preoccupied with other lines of cross-examination. He had a different set of values to display. Why concern himself with dissecting the experts' logic and the correctness of their inferences? Instead, questions were asked which would convey disparaging insinuations about a professor's parents, his ancestral religion, the source of his surname, the pigmentation of his skin, or the place of his birth. If these items did not discredit him satisfactorily, then one went on to inquire how many years he had spent in the South; if he had lived in the South, how long in Virginia; and so on—implying all the while that science, common sense, and human nature would not dare to cross Virginia county lines.[30] And, of course, there would be continual hints that what the plaintiffs' witnesses really desired to achieve was miscegenation and a mixed race.

As any healthy-minded person reads the Virginia trial record, it is impossible not to contrast the altruism and sober dignity of the scientists with the behavior of defendants' counsel, who, by his manner of espousing the old order, exposed its cruelty and bigotry. Here was a living spectacle of what racial segregation can do

[30] No. 4, Davis v. County School Board (the Va. Case), Transcript of Record, pp. 214, 262, 265. . . .

to the human spirit. The segregated society, as defendants' own expert had said, was "sick"; and the tactics of cross-examination used by defendants' lawyer showed how very sick it was. I suggest that these pages of the record did not fail of notice in the deliberations of the United States Supreme Court.

Without Salt, No Science.—We may as well resign ourselves to letting the troglodytes remain troglodytes, and turn our attention back to our civilized friends, the social psychologists. As the courts' exclusionary rules of evidence tend to relax more and more, the scientists will appear more frequently to testify as expert witnesses. How much respect should the judges extend to their testimony?

The answer depends in large measure on the scientists. If I have been right in suggesting that their evidence in the desegregation cases seemed persuasive because it happened to coincide with facts of common knowledge, they surely cannot rely on having the same advantage in every future litigation. It is predictable that lawyers and scientists retained by adversary parties will endeavor more aggressively to puncture any vulnerable or extravagant claims. Judges may learn to notice where objective science ends and advocacy begins.[31] At present, it is still possible for the social psychologist to "hoodwink a judge who is not overwise" without intending to do so; but successes of this kind are too costly for science to desire them.

For one thing: Merely translating a proposition of "literary" psychology into the terms of technical jargon can scarcely make it a scientific finding. For another: Just because social psychology is in a youthful and somewhat uncertain stage, the utmost rigor should be imposed on its intermediate processes.

The point is vital, involving as it does not only social psychology's prestige in the courts but—what is ultimately more valuable—its capacity to evolve and progress as a cumulative body of tested knowledge and approved method. Among

---

[31] In the attractive account cited in note 20 supra, Professor Clark described the close collaboration between the NAACP lawyers and the scientists, and went on to remark: "In fact, there were times when the lawyers could speak as social psychologists and the social psychologists began to sound like lawyers. In spite of this mutual accommodation, however, a clear distinction of roles and responsibilities had to be maintained for effective collaboration." Clark, supra, note 20, at 6. It seems possible that the distinction of roles would be maintained more satisfactorily if the social psychologist's primary motive in maintaining it were strict fidelity to objective truth rather than "effective collaboration."

For an example of the kind of methodological criticism we need from the social scientists, see Hoebel, The Law of Primitive Man 272-74 (1954). The instance discussed by Professor Hoebel likewise involved a very flabby attempt to "demonstrate" an assertion that on its face would seem entirely plausible to the lay mind.

Under the circumstances, some readers may feel inclined to credit Chief Justice Warren with Mephistophelean wit in that famous "footnote 11" (the accolade to the social psychologists which we have already mentioned). In the footnote, the Chief Justice lists various works published between the years 1944 and 1952. The latest of these discloses: "*Unfortunately for scientific accuracy and adequacy, thoroughly satisfactory methods of determining the effects of prejudice and discrimination on health of personality have not yet been devised, nor has a sufficient number of studies dealing with the various minority groups been made.*" (Emphasis supplied.) Witmer and Kotinsky, Personality in the Making 139-40 (1952).

the major impediments continually confronting this science are (1) the recurrent lack of agreement on substantive premises, and (2) the recurrent lack of extrinsic, empirical means for checking and verifying inferred results. As long as these disadvantages remain, and they are likely to remain in some measure for a very long time, social psychology will need, above all things, the use of scrupulous logic in its internal, intermediate processes. If the premises must be loose, the reasoning from them should be so much tighter; and if the final results cannot be validated precisely by external tests, then the methods of inference should be examined and re-examined all the more critically. It is meticulous standards that bring respect and credence to scientific testimony. When a social psychologist is called to serve as a "friend of the court," he should be able to assume our belief that his best friend, his premier loyalty, is always the objective truth.

Some of the Consequences.—Obviously, the Brown and Bolling opinions are susceptible of more than one interpretation. My views do not agree with those of some very able commentators, who consider that the opinions show important marks of the psychologists' influence. Granting this variety of interpretations, does it really matter whether the Supreme Court relies or does not rely on the psychologists' findings? Does it make any practical difference?

I submit it does. In the first place, since the behavioral sciences are so very young, imprecise, and changeful, their findings have an uncertain expectancy of life. Today's sanguine asseveration may be cancelled by tomorrow's new revelation —or new technical fad. It is one thing to use the current scientific findings, however ephemeral they may be, in order to ascertain whether the legislature has acted reasonably in adopting some scheme of social or economic regulation; deference here is shown not so much to the findings as to the legislature. It would be quite another thing to have our fundamental rights rise, fall, or change along with the latest fashions of psychological literature. Today the social psychologists—at least the leaders of the discipline—are liberal and egalitarian in basic approach. Suppose, a generation hence, some of their successors were to revert to the ethnic mysticism of the very recent past; suppose they were to present us with a collection of racist notions and label them "science." What then would be the state of our constitutional rights? Recognizing as we do how sagacious Mr. Justice Holmes was to insist that the Constitution be not tied to the wheels of any economic system whatsoever, we ought to keep it similarly uncommitted in relation to the other social sciences.

There is another potential danger here. It concerns the guarantee of "equal protection of the laws." Heretofore, no government official has contended that he could deny equal protection with impunity unless the complaining parties offered competent proof that they would sustain or had sustained some permanent (psychological or other kind of) damage. The right to equal protection has not been subjected to any such proviso. Under my reading of the Brown and Bolling opinions, this would remain the law. But if, in future "equal protection" cases, the Court were to hold that it was the expert testimony that determined the outcome of Brown and Bolling, the scope of the constitutional safeguard might be seriously restricted. Without cataloguing the various possibilities, one can discern at least that some of them would be ominous. It is not too soon to say so, for basic rights need early alarms. . . .

Garfinkel,* *SOCIAL SCIENCE EVIDENCE AND THE SCHOOL SEGREGATION CASES*
21 Journal of Politics 37, 51-58 (1959)

. . . We turn to the effort to demonstrate that racial segregation in elementary schools, whether tangible facilities are equal or not, provides a *psychological handicap* to the pursuit of curricular objectives. If this could be established, the conclusion would necessarily follow that "separate" cannot be "equal" in public education.

If all that were required is to weigh the sheer bulk of social science *opinion* as "modern authority" on this matter, the conclusion would be incontrovertible. In addition to the substantial number of expert witnesses in the lower-court trials and those who signed the appendix of the appellants' brief, a survey was conducted of social science opinion.[36] Over five hundred anthropologists, sociologists and psychologists returned a mailed questionnaire revealing that ninety per cent agreed that "enforced segregation has detrimental psychological effects *on the segregated groups*"; only two per cent disagreed, the others expressed no opinion. "Eighty-three per cent . . . believe that enforced segregation has detrimental psychological effects *on the group which enforces the segregation*." Four per cent disagreed, the rest had no opinion.

Of course, it is traditional that expert witnesses, unlike ordinary witnesses, are permitted to offer *opinions* in court and are not restricted to recounting *facts*. However, social scientists who are concerned with more than scoring a partisan point, even for a deeply felt moral commitment, will not wish to rest their case purely on professional "opinion." Clearly, this survey is no substitute for research-supported conclusions, and such a purpose is explicitly disclaimed by the authors. Moreover, the respondents have either neglected to publish their findings, or they have exaggerated the extent to which they have been directly involved in such research. Morroe Berger reports that one of the authors of the survey-analysis thought it odd that twenty-nine per cent of his respondents should claim their own research as the basis for their conclusions. How could ". . . so many social scientists . . . have claimed to have done research on the subject when only a 'negligible' amount of material had appeared in print"?[37]

A recent report of the Group for the Advancement of Psychiatry on "Psychiatric Aspects of School Desegregation" also maintains that there are "psychosocial ills

* Herbert Garfinkel, Assistant Professor of Government, Michigan State University, taught at Illinois Institute of Technology and Dartmouth College. He is the author of When Negroes March (1959).—Editor

[36] M. Deutscher and I. Chein, "The Psychological Effects of Enforced Segregation: A Survey of Social Science Opinion," Journal of Psychology XXVI (1948), 259-287. This was cited by the Court in Brown v. Topeka.

[37] "Desegregation, Law, and Social Science," [Commentary, XXIII (May, 1957)], p. 475.

arising from segregation." [38] It is interesting that, although a separate paragraph is devoted to the statement declaring, "For the segregating group, in this case the whites, the reactions, though less obvious, are nonetheless serious," not a single reference is cited to support the point. At least the paragraph dealing with the effects of segregation on *Negro* personality is footnoted with five items from the literature.[39]

There is an interesting psychological literature, beginning with the work of Erich Fromm,[40] which has attempted to study the personality characteristics of prejudiced persons. However, these studies (e.g., the Adorno group's research on the *Authoritarian Personality*)[41] are very remote from a definitive finding that *white* children suffer personality damage that impairs their ability to receive an education in public schools from which Negroes are excluded. We must agree with the conclusion of the Fact-Finding Report of the Midcentury White House Conference on Children and Youth:

> ". . . it seems doubtful that objections to racial and religious prejudice can be based to any large extent on the grounds of demonstrated detrimental effect on the feelings, values, ideas, or behavior of those who practice discrimination.[42]

. . . In [their] experiment, the Clarks found that the children were quite capable of making correct identifications; 94 per cent know the "white" doll, 93 per cent know the "colored" doll, 72 per cent know the "Negro" doll. A majority of the children definitely reveal patterns of self-alienation; they "prefer the *white* doll and reject the colored doll." They prefer to play with the white rather than with the colored doll (67 per cent to 32 per cent). The majority (59 per cent) think the white is the "nice" doll (38 per cent choose the colored). The doll which "looks bad" is the colored (59 per cent compared with 17 per cent who think the white doll "looks bad"); and 60 per cent choose the white doll as the one "that is a nice color" compared with only 38 per cent who choose the colored doll.

These data have been replicated in subsequent experiments and, by way of contrast, a study involving both white and Negro children as subjects found 89 per cent of the whites and 57 per cent of the Negroes preferred the white doll.[45] . . .

The question is whether one of these ways [in which prejudice and discrimination work very much to the disadvantage of the personality development of most minority-group members] is directly connected with the effects of school segregation per se, and whether this impairs equal educational opportunity. Counsel for the defense in the South Carolina case was sharp enough in cross-examination to

[38] *Op. cit.*, p. 10.
[39] *Ibid.*
[40] Escape From Freedom (New York, 1941).
[41] (New York, 1950).
[42] H. L. Witmer and R. Kotinsky (eds.), Personality in the Making: The Fact-Find-ing Report of the Midcentury White House Conference on Children and Youth (New York, 1952), p. 153.
[45] M. Radke and H. G. Trager, "Children's Perceptions of the Social Roles of Negroes and Whites," Journal of Psychology, IIXI (1950), 3-33.

reveal that Dr. Clark could not answer this from the scientific literature. The exchange was as follows:

Q. And then you say you were forced to the conclusion, after talking to these children, that they had suffered harm by attending the Scott's Branch School?

A. I was forced to the conclusion that they have definite disturbances and problems in their own self-esteem; that they had feelings of inferiority that related to race.

Q. Because they had attended the Scott's Branch School?

A. No, because they perceived themselves in an inferior status—generally inferior.

Q. Well, the Scott's Branch School had nothing to do with it?

A. Well, I wouldn't say that, Counsellor.

Q. Well what would you say?

A. Well, I would say it would definitely.

Q. And why?

A. Because of some information which I got from the children between the ages of twelve and seventeen. As you can see, this method is not as sensitive for older children as it would be for younger children. So, it became apparent to me as I talked to the older children that I could get similar data by a different method, namely the interviewer method . . .[48]

Actually, had the southern counsel taken the trouble to peruse Clark's research publications, they could have asked some embarrassing questions. For example, Clark reported, ". . . although the majority of Negro children at each age prefer the white doll to the brown doll, this preference decreases gradually from four through seven years." [50] But that is when the children are beginning school: what, then, is the effect of segregated as against integrated schools? The data are not broken down by geography plus age so we cannot compare North and South here. It would be interesting to see these data.

There is a presentation of North-South differences, however, without respect to age. Clark reports, ". . . it is clear that the southern (Negro) children in segregated schools are less pronounced in their preference for this [white] doll." [51] This information is supplied in the original study report but not in the Clark report to the White House Conference, or in the Conference's report either. Thus, it is in none of the Court's cited works.

A book published by Clark *after* the Supreme Court's decision, based upon his fact-finding report to the Midcentury Conference, does deal with the point. There he states:

On the surface, these findings might suggest that northern Negro children suffered more personality damage from racial prejudice and discrimination than

[48] Transcript of Record, Briggs v. Elliott, U.S. Sup. Ct., Oct. Term 1953, No. 2, pp. 91-92.

[50] "Racial Identification and Preference in Negro Children," [in Swanson, et al., Readings in Social Psychology, rev. ed. 1952, p. 557].

[51] *Ibid.*, p. 559.

southern children. However, this interpretation would seem to be not only superficial but incorrect. The apparent emotional stability of the southern Negro child may be indicative only of the fact that through rigid racial segregation and isolation he has accepted as normal the fact of his inferior social status. Such an acceptance is not symptomatic of a healthy personality. The emotional turmoil revealed by some of the northern children may be interpreted as an attempt on their part to assert some positive aspect of the self.[52]

As Clark says, this "may be." However, he cannot have it both ways. The application of the tests to the plaintiff children was interpreted to the South Carolina court as meaning "that the Negro child . . . accepts the negative stereotypes about his own group." If the amount of preference for the white doll over the colored is an index of self-alienation, for whatever reason, the data still show less of that effect in the segregated school situation. The weakness of basing broad generalizations on meagre research is apparent in the psychological evidence on this point. . . .

[A]dequate research techniques are yet to be devised which can distinguish between the broad effects of minority group status and the specific psychological consequences of institutionalized segregation. . . .†

CLARK,* *THE SEGREGATION CASES: CRITICISM OF THE SOCIAL SCIENTIST'S ROLE*
5 Villanova Law Review 224, 231-232, 234-239 (1959-60)

. . . Whatever might be one's degree of agreement or disagreement with Professor Cahn's estimate of the worth of the social scientists' testimony in these cases or the degree of the Court's regard for the social scientists' material presented in the brief or in the trial records, one must take seriously his argument that the constitutional rights of Negroes or other Americans should not rest on social scientists' testimony alone. If he had concentrated and elaborated on this issue on a high level of academic discourse, he might have made an important contribution

---

[52] K. B. Clark, Prejudice and Your Child (Boston, 1955), pp. 45-46. Clark does add a footnote reporting a study of admissions to mental hospitals in New York which he uses to conclude that the "future personality adjustment of the northern Negro is healthier than that of the southern Negro. . . ." Myrdal, however, in his An American Dilemma throws considerable cold water on any effort to establish this as conclusively demonstrated: "It is impossible, for example, to present meaningful figures comparing Negroes and whites in the whole country (or in the South alone), Southern Negroes with Northern Negroes, or rates at present with rates a few decades ago." (*Op. cit.*, p. 981, footnote a.)

† See further on the nature of the research on the effects of segregation, Note, Grade School Segregation: The Latest Attack on Racial Discrimination, 61 Yale L.J. 730 (1952).—Editor

* Kenneth B. Clark has been associated with the psychology department of the College of the City of New York since 1942. He has been research director, Northside Center for Child Development since 1946; social science consultant to the NAACP since 1950; member of various New York City and state educational agencies. He is the author of Desegregation: An Appraisal of the Evidence (1953); Prejudice and Your Child (1955).—Editor

to thought in a field in which he is competent. When he leaves the area of the law, constitutional rights, and matters of jurisprudence and invades the area of social sciences, making broad and general comments about the validity of social science methods, premises, approaches, findings and conclusions, and when he explicitly or implicitly attacks or suggests that the social scientists who participated in these cases as witnesses and consultants did not do so with the utmost personal and scientific integrity, he gratuitously leaves his field of competence and communicates his personal opinions, biases and misconceptions as if they were facts. His prestige in a field in which he has been trained thereby disguises his ignorance in a field in which he has no training. For these reasons, it is necessary to answer these charges and generalizations with clarity.

Before one enters a general appraisal of the validity of some of the many assumptions, implications, and charges raised by Professor Cahn, it is necessary to clarify certain points of fact which are relevant to opinions about the role of social scientists in these cases:

(1) The social scientists who participated in these cases were invited to do so by the lawyers of the NAACP . . . The social scientists were asked whether there were any relevant scientific studies of the psychological effects of racial segregation . . .

(2) . . . The White House Conference manuscript, which was cited by the United States Supreme Court in footnote 11 in the *Brown* decision, was a compilation of all of the available knowledge of the effects of prejudice and discrimination on personality development in children and was prepared by this writer months before he was aware of the fact that the NAACP intended to bring cases before the federal courts challenging the validity of segregated schools.

(3) The studies cited in this White House Conference manuscript and the joint primary research of this writer and his wife formed the bulk of his testimony in three of these five cases. The primary research studies were conducted ten years before these cases were heard on the trial court level. Professor Cahn's allegation that the writer served in the role of advocate rather than that of an objective scientist in his participation in these cases seems difficult to sustain in the face of testimony given on the basis of research conducted ten years before these cases were heard. . . .

(4) The use of the "Dolls Test" (actual dolls, not pictures of dolls, were used in this research) on some of the plaintiffs was to determine whether the general findings from the larger number of Negro children who had been tested years before were true also for the children who were the actual plaintiffs in these cases. The decision to test some of these plaintiffs was a legal one made by the lawyers of the NAACP. It was their assumption as lawyers that general scientific findings would have more weight in a courtroom if it could be demonstrated that they also applied in the specific cases and for the particular plaintiffs before the court. When these plaintiff children were tested and interviewed by this writer, it was his judgment that some of these children showed evidence of the same type of personality damage related to racial prejudice, segregation, and discrimination which was found in the larger number of subjects who were studied in the original,

published research. This opinion was presented to the courts in the form of sworn testimony. . . .

When the lawyers of the NAACP, in their understandable zeal to develop the strongest possible case, asked the social scientists whether it was possible to present evidence showing that *public school segregation*, in itself, damaged the personalities of Negro children, it was pointed out to them that the available studies had so far not isolated this single variable from the total social complexity of racial prejudice, discrimination, and segregation. It was therefore not possible to testify on the psychologically damaging effects of segregated schools alone. Such specific evidence, if available at all, would have to come from educators and educational philosophers. Some of the more insistent lawyers felt that only this type of specific testimony would be of value to them in these cases. It was pointed out to these lawyers that if this were so then the social psychologists and other social scientists could not be of any significant, direct help to them. A careful examination of the testimony of the social scientists, found in the record of these cases and the Social Science appendix submitted to the United States Supreme Court, will show that the social scientists presented testimony, opinions, and information consistent with the available empirical studies, conclusions, and observations. . . .

. . . Professor Cahn contends, however, that when scientists attempt to demonstrate . . . "well-known facts" through their use of the methods and approaches of science, they "provide a rather bizarre spectacle." What is more, he maintains they exaggerate their role, their methods are questionable, their logic and interpretation weak and fallacious, and they distort their findings as they become advocates who seek to "hoodwink" the judges. A serious question would be: How could the social scientists be so unreliable yet nonetheless come out with a picture of social reality which Professor Cahn and everyone else "already knew"? [5] . . .

. . . [T]his was not the first time that the lawyers of the NAACP had sought to convince the United States Supreme Court that segregation in and of itself was unconstitutional. In the *Sweatt*[7] and *McLaurin*[8] cases they sought a decision on the issue of segregation *per se* by relying on the traditional legal approach. Substantially the same United States Supreme Court which handed down the *Brown* and *Bolling* decisions, however, decided the *Sweatt* and *McLaurin* cases within the framework of the *Plessy* "separate but equal" doctrine. It may merely be coincidental that the lawyers of the NAACP succeeded in overruling the Plessy doctrine

[5] It may be noted parenthetically that it is questionable whether all judges share this "common knowledge," as is evidenced by the prior decision that upheld the "separate but equal" doctrine. At any rate, Professor Cahn does not explain why these judges did not act upon their knowledge. In fact, he does not explain how a person not gifted with superior insights can determine what is and what is not "common knowledge" as distinct from the personal biases of judges. Nor does Professor Cahn suggest any means, other than through the medium of expert witnesses, for getting "common knowledge," critically examined, into the court record so that it may be considered by judges who have the responsibility for the final decision.

[7] Sweatt v. Painter, 339 U.S. 629 (1950).
[8] McLaurin v. Oklahoma State Regents, 339 U.S. 637 (1950).

only after they enlisted an impressive array of social science testimony and talent and attacked this problem with this approach. . . .

NOTES AND QUESTIONS

1. Which of the following views about the weight the Supreme Court gave to the social-psychological data in the School Segregation Cases is justified by a reading of the Court's opinion: Professor Cahn's? Professor Clark's? That of the editor of the Montgomery Advertiser who described the Supreme Court Justices as "the nine most famous and puissant sociologists in the republic—protégés grateful of the Swede Myrdal—(who) have ruled that the Negro cannot develop without exposure to the superior white" (Quoted by Garfinkel, *supra*)? That of Professor Charles Black of the Yale Law School who writes that it is a "canard" to say that "principal reliance was placed on the formally 'scientific' authorities, which are relegated to a footnote and treated as merely corroboratory of common sense" (Black, "The Lawfulness of the Segregation Decisions," 69 Yale L.J. 421, 430, n. 25)?

2. What is it about the use of the social-psychological data in these cases that worries Professor Cahn?

a. Is Cahn concerned only with the *poor quality*, in his judgment, of the work of the social-psychologists in the School Segregation Cases? Would we not agree that if their work was an attempt to "hoodwink" the Court, resort to social science data in such cases will be generally discredited to the detriment of the development of the discipline itself? Is Cahn's estimate of the work of the social psychologists fair? Does Clark adequately meet Cahn's and Garfinkel's objections?

If the social scientists thought that the NAACP lawyers were asking a question which, on the basis of their empirical studies, they were unable to answer (i.e., whether, in Clark's words, public school segregation in itself, "isolated . . . from the total social complexity of racial prejudice, discrimination and segregation," damaged the personalities of Negro children) should they have undertaken to express their opinions on the question? How seriously should the Court have taken such opinions?

b. Is Cahn arguing that the consequences of segregated schools for Negro children were not *material* (legally significant) for the constitutional issue before the courts and, therefore, the data bearing on these consequences should not have been admitted as evidence? Would such a position have been similar to that taken by the Supreme Court when it excluded scientific evidence in the vaccination case, previously referred to?

(b.1) Is not the psychological evidence made relevant by the language of Plessy v. Ferguson itself? In that case the Court said: "We consider the underlying fallacy of the plaintiff's argument to consist in the assumption that the enforced separation of the races stamps the colored race with a badge of inferiority. If this be so, it is not by reason of anything found in the act (requiring segregation), but solely because the colored race chooses to put that construction upon it. . . . The argument also assumes that social prejudice may be overcome by legislation. . . . Legislation is powerless to eradicate racial instincts or to abolish distinctions based upon physical differences." 163 U.S. at 551.

Should the NAACP lawyers have gone to trial in these cases without the data to rebut these statements in the Plessy opinion? What data, other than those referred to in the Appendix reprinted above, should they have gathered and used?

(b.2) On what basis, if any, could the Supreme Court have concluded that racial segregation in the public schools is unconstitutional, even when the separate facilities are equal, *in the absence of data in the record* showing that enforced segregation has harmful psychological effects upon Negro children—because it implies their inferiority and thereby retards their educational and mental development?

Assume that it is shown that Negro children have even more serious personality problems in an integrated school in which they are received with hostility than in a segregated school in which, at least, they have a sense of security. Would the basis of the Supreme Court's decision be destroyed by such a showing?

(b.3) Professor Louis Pollak of the Yale Law School does not think the Court was called upon to decide whether segregation had harmful effects upon Negro school children. Pollak, "Racial Discrimination and Judicial Integrity: A Reply to Professor Wechsler," 108 U. of Pa. L. Rev. 1, 26-30 (1959). He relies largely upon the presumption of unconstitutionality which the Court has sometimes attached to legislation curtailing the civil rights of racial minorities and which we shall have occasion to consider in Chapter 11. Pollak argues that the Court was obligated to hold the public school segregation laws unconstitutional unless the constitutional doubts which they generated were allayed by their defenders. According to him, the record built by the defenders was insufficient to allay these doubts.

Would it have been proper for the Court to attach a presumption of unconstitutionality to segregation laws which had been held constitutional since the Plessy case, a precedent of more than 50 years' standing? And to duck the question of the consequences of segregation in this manner?

c. Is Cahn arguing that the Court had to decide whether enforced segregation has harmful effects upon Negro children but that it is a fact of "common experience" that segregation has such effects—a fact, therefore, which needed no proof because no one denied it and of which the Court could properly have taken *judicial notice*? (Recall the material on judicial notice in the Notes following the Biklé article.)

(c.1) Professor Black presents essentially this argument in the article cited above. To prove his point, he describes, briefly, the "broad societal patterns" which determined the "facts of life" for the Negro in the South in the past and do so today. As if in answer to the question raised by Professor Clark in note 5 of the article reprinted above, Black says: "I have stated all these facts shortly (the "fact that the social meaning of segregation is the putting of the Negro in a position of walled-off inferiority—or the equally plain fact that such treatment is hurtful to human beings") because they are matters of common notoriety, matters not so much for judicial notice as for the background knowledge of educated men who live in the world. A court may advise itself of them as it advises itself of the facts that we are a 'religious people,' that the country is more industrialized than in Jefferson's day, that children are the natural objects of fathers' bounty, that criminal sanctions are commonly thought to deter, that steel is a basic commodity in our economy, that the imputation of unchastity is harmful to a woman. Such judgments, made on such a basis, are in the foundations of all law, decisional as well as statutory. . . ."

Would the NAACP lawyers have been better advised to ask the Court to take judicial notice of these "matters of common notoriety" instead of the social-psychological data questioned by Professor Cahn? Black's article shows what a "Brandeis-brief" along these lines might have looked like. Black charges that "the venial fault" of the Court's opinion in the School Segregation Cases "consists in its not spelling out that segregation . . . is perceptibly a means of ghettoizing the imputedly inferior race." He conjectures "that the motive for this omission was reluctance to go into the distasteful details of the southern caste system." "That such treatment is generally not good for children needs less talk than the Court gives it."

Thus, Black seems to think that the social scientists undertook a task that was as unnecessary as it was difficult. He writes: "It is true that the specifically hurtful character of segregation, as a net matter in the life of each segregated individual, may be hard to establish. . . . It seems enough to say of this . . . that no such demand is made as to other constitutional rights. To have a confession beaten out of one might in some particular case be the beginning of a new and better life. To be subjected to a racially differentiated curfew might be the best thing in the world for some individual boy. A man might ten years later go back to thank the policeman who made him get off the platform and stop making a fool of himself. Religious persecution proverbially strengthens faith. We do not ordinarily go that far, or look so narrowly into the matter. That a practice, on massive historical evidence and in common sense, has the designed and generally apprehended effect of putting its victims at a disadvantage, is enough for law. At least it always has been enough."

Would such a view be inconsistent with Justice Currie's analysis giving a very restricted role to judicial notice *in overcoming the presumption* of constitutionality (assuming, contrary to Pollak, that the normal presumption of constitutionality should apply to the educational segregation law)?

d. Professor Herbert Wechsler of Columbia University Law School doubts that the Supreme Court's decision turned on "the sufficiency of evidence or of judicial notice to sustain a finding that the separation harms the Negro children who may be involved." Wechsler, "Toward Neutral Principles of Constitutional Law," 73 Harv. L. Rev. 1, 32 (1959). He thinks it "must have rested on the view that racial segregation is, in principle, a denial of equality to the minority against whom it is directed; that is, the group that is not dominant politically, and, therefore, does not make the choice involved."

Wechsler, however, sees difficulties with this ground for decision. He argues that the provision of equal, but separate, facilities does not *discriminate* against the Negro any more than it discriminates against the white person. "Is a prohibition of miscegenation a discrimination against the colored member of the couple who would like to marry?" He maintains that state-enforced segregation, assuming equal facilities, does not raise the question of discrimination at all, but of "the denial by the state of freedom to associate, a denial that impinges in the same way on any groups or races that may be involved." But if so, "integration forces an association upon those for whom it is unpleasant and repugnant." "Is there," Wechsler asks, "a basis in neutral principles for holding that the Constitution demands that the claims for association should prevail?" "I should like to think there is, but I confess that I have not yet written the opinion. To write it is for me the challenge of the school segregation cases."

Even if Wechsler correctly states what was really at issue in these cases, would the Supreme Court not have needed data on the alternative empirical consequences of deciding in favor or against the claim for association?

Writing a year before Wechsler hurled his challenge, Professor Sidney Hook had this to say about the position that it is wrong to force white parents to send their children to an integrated school: "If it is wrong to force white parents to send their children to an integrated school . . . it is wrong to force Negro parents to send *their* children to segregated schools, and wrong to force white parents who do not object to *their* children associating with Negro children to do the same. The same principle obviously obtains with respect to the feelings of parents toward the children of *any* minority. It is wrong to force parents to send their children to legally unsegregated public schools if they do not wish *their* children to associate with the children of religious, racial or ethnic minorities. Since most of these critics do not propose to abolish our compulsory education laws, and rule out private education as economically unfeasible, they must require the state or community to build separate schools for any group of parents who wish to safeguard their children from any kind of context and association they regard as seriously undesirable.

"Educational context and association, however, extend far beyond the classroom into school buses, lunchrooms, playgrounds, pools, gymnasiums. . . . Since these are normally incidental to public education, special facilities would have to be provided for the entire gamut of parental fastidiousness. What holds for public education must by these principles also hold for public health and medical facilities . . .

"Actually, parents are *not* forced to send their children to an integrated school. Parents may choose to send their children to private schools which are not integrated. Or, in most states, they may provide education at home. This the law permits . . . [Pierce v. Society of Sisters, 268 U.S. 510 (1925)].

"The difficulty with this kind of analysis, however, is that it cannot convince those who are prepared to swallow one absurdity to defend another. I therefore focus directly on some of the basic premises of their position." Hook, "Democracy and Desegregation," The New Leader, April 21, 1958, reprinted as c. 8 in Hook's Political Power and Personal Freedom (1959).

Hook concludes: "If there is any relation between morality and law, the existence of certain evil social practices *may* (not must) justify us in taking legal action to prevent them. And if this is of necessity an abridgment of some human freedom, as is true of every law, it is taken in behalf of other human freedoms. The human freedoms we safeguard by legal action against segregation and unfair discrimination are more important than those we restrict."

3. The testimony of more than 40 social scientists and educators introduced in 4 of the 5 School Segregation Cases (all except the District of Columbia case) filled about 4 volumes and was also directed at showing, as indicated in the Appendix to Appellants' Brief, that (a) classification of pupils on a racial basis did not fulfill a reasonable educational purpose (i.e., that the assumption of innate intellectual differences between races is scientifically unsound), and (b) that desegregation can be accomplished without undue conflict or violence, provided that strong government leadership was exercised.

4. How, then, would you summarize the views on (a) what were the actual bases of the Supreme Court opinion in the School Segregation Cases, and (b) what the bases should have been?

Among still further discussions that are relevant and interesting are: Cahn, Jurisprudence, 31 N.Y.U.L. Rev. 182 (1956); Van den Haag, Social Science Testimony in the Desegregation Cases—A Reply to Professor Kenneth Clark, 6 Villanova L. Rev. 69 (1960).

See generally, Karst, Legislative Facts in Constitutional Litigation, The Supreme Court Review 75 (1960); Kohn, Social Psychological Data, Legislative Fact, and Constitutional Law, 29 G. Wash. L. Rev. 136 (1960).

EDITORIAL NOTE: FURTHER JUDICIAL ATTITUDES toward the LEGAL USE of SCIENTIFIC DATA

It is difficult, merely on the basis of the School Segregation Cases, to generalize about the attitudes of the courts toward the legal use of scientific data. So much depends upon the nature of the issue before the court, the particular data deemed relevant, and the state of the science involved.

Psychological data were admitted in evidence in Tudor v. Board of Education, 14 N.J. 31, 100 A. 2d 857 (1953), which held that a particular system for the free distribution of Gideon Bibles to school children violated the constitutional principle that church and state must be separated. The data were admitted in evidence to show that the system of distribution exerted psychological pressure upon the children to accept the Bibles.

When the California Supreme Court invalidated a statute forbidding interracial marriages, both the majority and dissenting opinions relied upon anthropological findings. Perez v. Lippold, 32 Cal. 2d 711, 198 P. 2d 17 (1948). Judge Traynor's majority opinion cited anthropologists and other social scientists as authority for the propositions that (1) "the progeny of marriages between persons of different races are not inferior to both parents"; (2) the alleged physical and mental inferiority of non-Caucasians lacks scientific proof; (3) segregation in an inferior environment is a factor increasing liability to physical ailments; and (4) there "are now so many persons in the United States of mixed ancestry that the tensions upon them are already diminishing and are bound to diminish even more in time." Dissenting Judge Shenk relied on scientific authority for the proposition that "the crossing of the primary races leads gradually to retrogression and to eventual extinction of the resultant type unless it is fortified by reunion with the parent stock." See generally, Cummins and Kane, Miscegenation, the Constitution and Science, 38 Dicta 24 (1961).

Sometimes a court may be misled by the existing state of knowledge. On the assumption that individuals are likely to transmit tendencies to feeble-mindedness to their offspring, the Supreme Court upheld a state law under which the sterilization of a feeble-minded inmate of a state institution was ordered. Buck v. Bell, 274 U.S. 200 (1927). Yet it is doubtful whether this assumption is supported by current knowledge in the field of eugenics.[1] It is possible, of course, to raise the question of the constitutionality of the eugenical sterilization laws once again.

Nor is there unanimity of opinion about the use of scientific data in the trial of non-constitutional issues. While the results of public opinion polls or "survey research" have been admitted as evidence in the trial of many issues (e.g., whether one trademark or design patent is "confusingly similar" to another; whether particular advertising or branding of food, drugs, or cosmetics is "misleading"; whether the public is so prejudiced against a person accused of crime that he will not get a fair trial, unless the place of trial—venue—is changed),[2] recently the hidden uncertainties and possible deceptions in opinion-poll data have been pointed out and the question raised as to how much probative value judges should accord them.[3]

So too not all kinds of natural science evidence have a strong evidentiary

---

[1] See O'Hara and Sanks, Eugenic Sterilization, 45 Geo. L.J. 20 (1956); Cook, Eugenics or Euthenics, 37 Ill. L. Rev. 287 (1943); Myerson, Certain Medical and Legal Phases of Eugenic Sterilization, 52 Yale L.J. 618 (1943); Berns, Buck v. Bell: Due Process of Law?. 6 Western Pol. Q. 762 (1953); Note, 35 Iowa L. Rev. 251 (1950).

[2] See generally, Barksdale, Use of Survey Research Findings As Legal Evidence (1957); Sorenson and Sorenson, The Ad-

missibility and Use of Opinion Research Evidence, 28 N.Y.U.L. Rev. 1213 (1953); Kohn, Social Psychological Data, Legislative Fact, and Constitutional Law, 29 Geo. Wash. L. Rev. 136 (1960); and Note, 66 Harv. L. Rev. 498.

[3] See, for example, Eysenck, Psychology of Politics, c. 2 (1955); and Blum and Kalven, The Art of Opinion Research: A Lawyer's Appraisal of an Emerging Science, 24 U. Chi. L. Rev. 1 (1956).

status. In cases in which it is crucial to determine whether a particular person is the father of a particular child, many state statutes require the court to accept as *conclusive* the results of a blood-test purporting to show nonpaternity. On the other hand, lie detector data are thought to lack general scientific acceptance and are *excluded* as evidence that a person is or is not telling the truth.[4] The results of chemical tests for intoxication have been accepted in evidence, but have not been made conclusive by law. In the field of psychiatry, particularly in insanity cases, the familiar "battle of the experts" and alleged lack of scientific soundness of expert opinion have provoked a sociologist to suggest, seriously, that psychiatric testimony be entirely excluded from evidence.[5]

Judicial uneasiness about the use of "expert" witnesses is reflected in Commonwealth v. Isenstadt, 318 Mass. 543, 62 N.E. 2d 840 (1949), which involved the question whether the sale of the book "Strange Fruit" by Lillian Smith violated the anti-obscenity law. The Massachusetts Supreme Court upheld the trial court's exclusion of the testimony of a writer and teacher of literature, a child psychiatrist and a theology professor, which had been offered largely to show that the book would "elevate rather than corrupt morals." In the court's opinion, the testimony concerned "nothing more than the reaction of normal human beings" and "there is reason to believe that a jury, being composed of men drawn from the various segments of the public, would be as good a judge of the effect as experts in literature or psychiatry, whose . . . mental reactions . . . are likely to be entirely different from those of the general public." If evidence of this sort were admissible, the court feared, many cases could not be "adequately tried without an expensive array of experts on both sides." "Experience in those fields in which expert testimony is now admittedly necessary does not lead us to look with favor upon such a sweeping extension. Without prejudging the indefinite future, we are not convinced that the time has come for it."

What does all this add up to? We think Alexander Pekelis answered this question most succinctly in his essay on "The Case for a Jurisprudence of Welfare"[6] when he said: "An enlightened welfare jurisprudence providing the judge with intelligible findings reached by the social studies, and keeping him in contact with an informed public opinion, would enable the courts to weigh the conflict before them intelligently, to state their reasons,

---

[4] McCormick disagrees with this judicial approach to the problem. He writes: " 'General scientific acceptance' is a proper condition upon the court's taking judicial notice of scientific facts, but not a criterion for the admissibility of scientific evidence. Any relevant conclusions which are supported by a qualified expert witness should be received unless there are other reasons for exclusion." Handbook of the Law of Evidence 363-364 (1954). He believes that

the "lie-detector" has proved to be a fertile means of ascertaining the truth.
[5] Hakeem, A Critique of the Psychiatric Approach to Crime and Correction, 23 Law and Contemp. Prob. 650, 681 (1958). This is one of the articles in a symposium on crime and correction.
[6] Law. Guild Rev. 611, 625-626 (1946), reprinted from Social Research, Vol. II, No. 3.

and to *adjudge* the conflict, thus truly performing the function entrusted to them. . . .

"We cannot turn back the clock. Social scientists are with us for good, and are going to remain in the very midst of government. . . . Judges may and should become acquainted with the various non-legal disciplines. But because of the variety of these disciplines, and of the variety of their judicial tasks, they will always remain intelligent *laymen,* as far as these disciplines are concerned. And intelligent lay control . . . seems the best defense against the tyranny of experts. . . .

"A judge should know more about social studies precisely in order to acquire the conviction that they can furnish no more certainty than constitutions, statutes or precedents. . . . A better knowledge of social sciences will enable judges to use their findings without abdicating the responsibility of the final choice of policy, which must rest with lay society represented by its lawmakers."

Section 3

The CHOICE of VALUES

F. S. Cohen,* *ETHICAL SYSTEMS AND LEGAL IDEALS*
2-7, 15-19, 25-26, 30-33 (1933)

. . . Fundamental to all adequate thought on politics and society lies the question of what law ought to do, the search for valid standards of legal criticism.

The problem is, in the first place, an ethical one, since legal criticism is a passing of judgments of good and bad, right and wrong, upon human acts and works. This has led to a tendency apparent in most modern "scientific" studies of law to disclaim responsibility for its solution, to pass the buck to the ethical philosopher. But in the second place, the problem involves a calculation of the nature, effects, and potentialities of legal machinery which only the jurist or social scientist as such can attempt, and this has led most ethical philosophers to ignore crucial legal problems, throwing responsibility back to the jurist. This game of battledore and shuttlecock, or, to put the analogy in modern terms, volley ball, is carried on through most of the social sciences today. The historian, the economist, the political scientist, the sociologist, all argue that science is non-moral, and that their task is done when they have portrayed the facts. Ethical philosophers, on the other hand, are seldom anxious to descend from the ethereal realm of abstract duties and intrinsic goods to the mud of social statistics. . . .

Shunned alike by scientists and philosophers, most social-ethical questions are left today in a No Man's Land where only those with strong practical and emotional

* Felix S. Cohen (1907-1953) also wrote Handbook of Federal Indian Law (1941), Readings in Jurisprudence and Legal Philosophy (1953) (with M. R. Cohen), and numerous contributions to legal and other journals. He served in the Solicitor's Office, Dept. of Interior 1933-47 and for some years was Associate Solicitor. He re-entered the practice of law in 1948 and did some part-time teaching at Yale Law School and City College of New York.—Editor

interests will make a stand. This arbitrary and inadequate division of intellectual labor would be pitiable enough if the limitations it imposes upon social thought were regularly recognized. But the moral philosopher who disdains the data sheets of social science as irrelevant to questions of value continues to assume human desires and human abilities which those data refute; and the social scientist (not least of all the jurist) continues to assume ethical norms which have not withstood the test of philosophical analysis.

An ethics, like a metaphysics, is no more certain and no less dangerous because it is unconsciously held. There are few judges, psychoanalysts, or economists today who do not begin a consideration of their typical problems with some formula designed to cause all moral ideals to disappear and to produce an issue purified for the procedure of positive empirical science. But the ideals have generally retired to hats from which later wonders will magically arise. A historical school of law disclaims concern with ethics and repeatedly invokes a Zeitgeist or a Volksgeist to decide what the law ought to be. An analytical school of jurisprudence again dismisses questions of morality, and again decides what the law ought to be by reference to a so-called logical ideal, which is not an ideal of logic at all, but an aesthetic ideal of symmetrical analogical development. Those who derive the law from the will of the sovereign usually introduce without further justification the premise that it is good to obey that will. And those who define law in terms of actually prevailing social demands or interests make frequent use of the undisclosed principle that these demands ought to be satisfied.[6]

The objection, then, is not that jurists have renounced ethical judgment but that they have renounced ethical science. Ethical science involves an analysis of ethical judgments, a clarification of ethical premises. Among the current legal crypto-idealisms there can be no edifying controversy, since there is no recognition of the moral issues to which their differences reduce. One looks in vain in legal treatises and law-review articles for legal criticism conscious of its moral presuppositions. The vocabularies of logic and aesthetics are freely drawn upon in the attempt to avoid the disagreeable assertion that something or other is intrinsically better than something else. Particular decisions or legal rules are "anomalous" or "illogical," "incorrect" or "impractical," "reactionary" or "liberal," and unarguable ethical innuendo takes the place of critical analysis. Little wonder then that on a more abstract plane of thought the classification of ideas has taken the place of

---

[6] "In the actual practice of courts and jurists, after stating claims or demands in general terms as social interests, attempt is made, more or less consciously, to secure as much as possible of the whole scheme of social interests with the least sacrifice. This is the pragmatist ethical principle stated by William James. How far it is a sound ethical criterion we need not inquire. . . . The task of the jurist is to make us conscious of the method that actually obtains and to give it more precision. He should aim at all times, and in all the compromises and adjustments and reconcilings involved in the legal order, to give effect to as much of the whole body of social interests as possible." Pound, "Jurisprudence" in History and Prospects of the Social Sciences (1925) p. 472. See also Pound, Introduction to the Philosophy of Law (1922) pp. 95-99.

legal philosophy, while Hegelian pictures of inevitable trends are offered as substitutes for the delineation of the desirable.

But the relevance of ethics to the philosophy of law would be clear even if it were not unconsciously assumed by those who appear to deny or to ignore the connection. For ethics is the study of the meaning and application of judgments of good, bad, right, wrong, etc., and every final valuation of law involves an ethical judgment. When we say, for instance, that a given law is bad, that one judicial decision is better than another, that the American constitution ought to be revised, or that laws ought to be obeyed, we are passing judgments whose truth or falsity cannot be established without a consideration of ethics. That portion of jurisprudence which is not concerned merely with the positive nature of law or with its technical relation to assumed ends is, accordingly, a part of the domain of ethics.

There is no way of avoiding this ultimate responsibility of law to ethics. Every final determination of the general end of law, the standard of legal criticism (whether this be labeled "justice," "natural law," "the protection of natural rights," or "the organization of social interests"), must reduce to the general form, "The law ought to bring about as much good as it can." . . .

By ethics we shall mean the science of the significance and application of judgments of good, bad, right, wrong, better, worse, best, worst, ought, and their derivatives in so far as these terms are applied categorically. By this qualification we exclude only such use of these terms as is exemplified when we say that medicine is good for colds without implying any judgment as to the value of colds or of the curing of colds. We do not thereby exclude the judgment that medicine is good because it cures colds. That is to say, ethics deals with instrumental as well as intrinsic values, but it does not deal with physical causality as such. . . .

We may decide whether law is good for strengthening social bonds or bad for the peace of mind of criminals, without any appeal to ethics, but when we come to the question of whether the strengthening of social bonds or the peace of mind of criminals is good, and whether law which has the described effects is good, we are in the realm of ethics. Thus every valuation of law, every formulation of the ideal object or end of law, must be either categorical and ethical, or conditional, in terms of some ulterior aim which can itself be valued ethically. In either case, there is no way of escaping the final responsibility of law to ethics, and, since the field of law lies within the field of human conduct, to morality. . . .[20]

This position, . . . has been attacked on two grounds. In the first place, it is claimed, we do not know what the effects of law will be. And in the second place, we do not know what the good life is.

Both of these objections are true in a certain sense, but in that sense they do not

[20] Cf. Laird, Study in Moral Theory (1926) pp. 26-29; Demogue, Analysis of Fundamental Notions (1911, trans. by Scott and Chamberlain 1916), in Modern French Legal Philosophy, Modern Legal Philosophy Series, vol. 7, ss. 206-221; Pound: "Jurisprudence," in History and Prospects of the Social Sciences (1925) p. 472.

contradict our conclusion. It is certainly true that we cannot calculate all the effects of law or of anything else. And it is equally obvious that our knowledge of ethics and of human nature is not great enough to permit us to describe completely and in detail what constitutes the good life for each person or even for man in the abstract. But if there is any such thing as human knowledge, we certainly have enough of it upon both these subjects to formulate definite problems and to reject unsatisfactory solutions. And, as a great French jurist, M. Pierre Tourtoulon, has said, "There is no need to throw to the dogs everything that is not fit for the altars of the gods." A recognition of the inadequacy of our knowledge in these fields can bring a sweet scepticism into our political beliefs but it cannot deny them. To quote again from Tourtoulon, "The greatest jurist has only very vague ideas concerning the services that the laws which he expounds and explains render to society. . . . The first step toward wisdom is the knowledge that we are ignorant of nearly all the functions of our laws, or of the evil or the good which they may bring us." [24] And one more quotation: "A little scepticism will render him (the judge) more scrupulous, more indulgent to every one and consequently more just." [25]

The inadequacy of human knowledge, we may fairly assume, does not destroy the usefulness of our fundamental principle of legal criticism. In fact, a judgment of ethical values the truth of which is recognized to be partially dependent upon the accuracy of human scientific knowledge seems to be far more useful than the sort of judgment which assumes that, however uncertain the physical results of an act may be, we can know clearly in advance whether they will be good or bad. . . .

The abduction of law from the domain of morality is defended by Professor Morgan. . . . "It must be remembered," he writes, "that the law does not have the same purpose as religion or ethics or morals. It is not concerned with developing the spiritual or moral character of the individual but with regulating his objective conduct toward his fellows. Consequently courts will have to formulate and apply some rules which have no relation at all to morals, some which have to place a loss upon one of two equally blameless persons, some which impose liability regardless of fault and some which refuse to penalize conduct denounced by even the morally blind. It must be apparent that the moral law has no mandate upon the content of the rules of the road." [36]

This position is so representative of the class of theories we are considering, and so generally accepted, at least in our American law schools, that it may be worth while to point out in detail some of the ambiguities and fallacies it involves. In the first sentence we are told that law does not have the same *purpose* as religion or ethics or morals. It is upon the ambiguity of this word that the specious force of the rest of the argument depends. If the word refers to the state of mind of judges or legislators, the assertion that this differs from the state of mind of

[24] Tourtoulon, Philosophy in the Development of Law (1919, trans. by Read 1922), Modern Legal Philosophy Series, vol. 13, p. 24.

[25] *Ibid.*, p. 487.

[36] E. M. Morgan, Introduction to the Study of Law (1926), pp. 32-33.

moralists, ethical philosophers and religious leaders is perhaps true, but it is completely irrelevant to Professor Morgan's ethical conclusions as to what the law ought to do. If by the *purpose* of law is meant that at which law *ought* to aim, the statement is relevant, indeed basic, to his further conclusions, but obviously false. For the law ought to secure the good life, which is the *ideal* purpose of moral and religious rules as well.

In the second sentence of this excerpt we are told that law is *not concerned* with certain noble ends. Again, the same basic ambiguity. If the law is not actually concerned with man's spiritual or moral character, that is an unfortunate fact which we ought to remedy. But if this assertion means that the law ought not to be determined by such factors, it is simply false. Man's moral life is fundamentally moulded by rules of property law, family law, etc., and the refusal to follow the meaning of such legal rules into their ultimate moral or spiritual implications is the essence of legalistic obscurantism.

In the next sentence, we are told that *consequently* courts *have to* formulate rules which have no relation at all to morals, and here the confusion between the *is* and the *ought* bears its first fruits. Thus far Morgan's statements can be justified on a positive interpretation, but if that interpretation be given, the inference of *have to* (apparently ethical) from *does* and *is* is clearly fallacious. Here an ethical interpretation of the foregoing premises is required, and that, we have seen, results in patent error. . . .

. . . Even the rule of the road, the favorite example of non-moral law, is full of moral values. When there is a law on the subject, my disobedience of it, involving the possibility of injuring myself and others, certainly entails some moral evil. The question of whether or not I ought to obey such a law is therefore a moral question. Finally, the question of whether or not there ought to be such a law is a moral question. It is not generally true that no moral values are involved in the choice between a rule keeping traffic to the left and one keeping it to the right. Where such a choice is enacted into law, there are regularly physiological peculiarities or social habits which make one rule preferable to the other. But even if the choice were morally indifferent the law chosen would not be morally indifferent,—that is to say, the demand that the law enact at least one of the two possible rules would be no less a moral demand because of the indeterminateness of the alternative. The demand that I save a friend's life and the act by which this is accomplished do not cease to be moral if there are a number of slightly different ways of attaining this result, among some of which my choice is morally indifferent. . . .

. . . The question which a judge faces in coming to a decision, it is argued, is purely legal, not moral. Legislatures may endeavor to decide what the law ought to be, but it is for the judge to decide what, in any particular case, the law is. It is apparently in this vein that Maine, distinguishing the philosophy of law from the philosophy of legislation, says, "The jurist, properly so called, has nothing to do with any ideal standard of law or morals." And in the same vein Dean Pound has said, "The utilitarian theory of Bentham was a theory of legislation. The social theory of the present is a theory of legal science." So, in the general philosophy of the Anglo-American bench and bar, "public policy" (the legal equivalent for "morality") seems to be relevant to the decision of a case only when precedents and statutes fail and the function of the judge becomes "legislative."

. . . The [effect of the] theory we are attacking . . . is to exclude the conscious consideration of ethical issues from the judicial mind and to lend weight to the unconscious and uncriticized value standards by which judges decide what they *ought* to do. Fundamentally it attempts to set up as a standard of legal criticism *truth* or *consistency* rather than *goodness*. But neither truth nor consistency can be rivals to goodness, in legal criticism or anywhere else. Truth and consistency are categories which apply to propositions or to sets of propositions, not to actions or events. A judicial decision is a command, not an assertion. Even if any sense could be found in the characterization of a decision as true or false (or, in the non-ethical sense of the terms, right or wrong, correct or erroneous), such truth or falsity could not determine what decision, in any case, ought to be given. That is a question of conduct and only the categories of ethics can apply to it. In answering such a question, the ethical value of certainty and predictability in law may outweigh more immediate ethical values, but this is no denial of the ethical nature of the problem. *Consistency*, like *truth*, is relevant to such a problem only as an indication of the interest in legal certainty, and its value and significance are ethical rather than logical. The question, then, of how far one ought to consider precedent and statute in coming to a legal decision is purely ethical. The proposition that courts ought always to decide "in accordance with precedent or statute" is an ethical proposition the truth of which can be demonstrated only by showing that in every case the following of precedent or statute does less harm than any possible alternative. . . .

Pound, *SOCIAL CONTROL THROUGH LAW*
103, 113-117 (1942)

Difficult as it may be, the problem of values is one from which the science of law cannot escape. Even the crudest or most blundering or most capricious adjustment of relations or ordering of conduct has behind it some canon of valuing conflicting and overlapping interests. . . .

A generation ago I sought to formulate the jural postulates of civilized society in our time and place, for the purposes of systematic exposition of private law (i.e., the law governing individual interests and relations of individuals with their fellows) in five propositions, with certain corollaries. For the present purpose we need not look at the corollaries. What I sought to do was to formulate what was presupposed by the law as to possession, as to property, as to legal transactions and resulting relations, and as to wrongs. As I should put them now they read:

1. In civilized society men must be able to assume that others will commit no intentional aggressions upon them.

2. In civilized society men must be able to assume that they may control for beneficial purposes what they have discovered and appropriated to their own use,

what they have created by their own labor, and what they have acquired under the existing social and economic order.

3. In civilized society men must be able to assume that those with whom they deal in the general intercourse of society will act in good faith and hence

(a) will make good reasonable expectations which their promises or other conduct reasonably create;

(b) will carry out their undertakings according to the expectations which the moral sentiment of the community attaches thereto;

(c) will restore specifically or by equivalent what comes to them by mistake or unanticipated or not fully intended situation whereby they receive at another's expense what they could not reasonably have expected to receive under the circumstances.

4. In civilized society men must be able to assume that those who are engaged in some course of conduct will act with due care not to cast an unreasonable risk of injury upon others.

5. In civilized society men must be able to assume that those who maintain things likely to get out of hand or to escape and do damage will restrain them or keep them within their proper bounds.

Professor Hocking considered that these postulates established "the liaison between philosophy and the science of law." [3] At any rate, they seemed to be borne out by the law as it stood at the end of the last century and to afford a measure of value for newly asserted claims. But it has been becoming more and more evident that the civilization of the time and place presupposes some further propositions which it is by no means easy to formulate, since the conflict of interests involved has by no means been so thoroughly adjusted that one may be reasonably assured of the basis upon which the adjustment logically proceeds.

In general, a postulated claim of the job holder to security in his job is becoming recognized. But exactly in what sort of job holders and in what sort of jobs a right is to be recognized is far from clear. Moreover, the regime of collective bargaining with organizations commanding a majority of votes in a plant seems to involve a proposition that the minority are not to have a recognized right to their jobs as against the prevailing majority organization. The most that can be said at present is that the employer-employee relation is being removed from the domain of contract and is coming to involve a security of tenure not depending upon agreement.

Another emerging jural postulate appears to be that in the industrial society of today enterprises in which numbers of men are employed will bear the burden of what might be called the human wear and tear involved in their operation. Some such postulate is behind workmen's compensation laws. But in the administration of those laws there is much to suggest a wider proposition. There are also other indications of a third proposition, which may come to include the second, namely, that the risk of misfortune to individuals is to be borne by society as a whole. Some such postulate seems to be behind what has been called the insurance theory

[3] Hocking, The Present Status of the Philosophy of Law and of Rights, p. 95.

of liability and is behind much social security legislation. Perhaps a reaching out for something of the sort has been behind a tendency of juries to hold that, whenever anyone has been hurt, someone able to respond in damages ought to pay. . . .

PATTERSON,* *POUND'S THEORY OF SOCIAL INTERESTS*
in Interpretations of Modern Legal Philosophies 568-569   (Sayre ed., 1947)

Should appellate courts be invited to discard rules and precedents and to decide cases by the use of Pound's (or some other) scheme of social interests? I believe that an unqualified affirmative answer should not be given. Despite all that Holmes and others have said about the illusive certainty of the law, the formulation of legal rules increases the area of operation in which the law is a reliable guide for the future conduct of lawyers and laymen, as compared with the reliability of such broad policies as Pound's major social interests. To the extent that legal rules are reliable, they promote impartiality and equality of treatment among litigants. In the criminal law especially, legal rules are safeguards for the individual against governmental oppression. In other fields, such as real property law, legal rules have historical explanations which maintain their continuity with the past. All of these are values which have, I think, a place in Pound's scheme of social interests. To them must be added certain values of economy and expediency in the judicial process. It is usually easier for judges to agree on a rule for a concrete type of situation than on a statement of the policy or policies which justify that rule, for it is ordinarily easier, as Holmes said, to drill a squad than to maneuver an army. The generosity of American law in permitting appeals does not allow appellate courts the time and energy to overhaul the basic policies of the legal order in every case. To these must be added the limited range of inquiry, in ordinary litigation, into the factual bases of public policies; except in cases involving constitutionality, the social consequences of a judicial decision, considered as a guide to the decision of future cases, are not open to investigation as a part of the factual issues in a case.

Yet the policy-method of adjudication in appellate courts is making considerable headway. For one thing, the body of citable judicial precedents is becoming unmanageable, and the extrication of legal rules from them is becoming Herculean. More and more appellate courts will, I believe, have to turn to the underlying policies of a litigated situation as a means of solution more just and efficient than trying to read and reconcile and use all of the citable precedents. The rule-method will still provide a framework within which the policy-method will operate—and not the other way around. The underlying policies of legal rules will indicate which should be discarded, how those retained should be interpreted, and what

* Edwin W. Patterson, Professor of Law at Columbia, has taught at Texas, Colorado, and Iowa, practiced law in Missouri 1911-15, was in charge of New York Insurance Law Revision, 1935-39 and Deputy Supt. of Insurance of New York, 1936. He is the author of The Insurance Commissioner in the United States (1927); Jurisprudence—Men and Ideas of the Law (1953); co-editor of Materials for Legal Method (1946), and editor of casebooks in the fields of contracts and insurance.—Editor

should be done in the gap-areas which one can always find—some lawyers more frequently than others—outside the area of rules. The policy-method can thus supplement the rule-method without superseding it. If it be said that Pound's theory of social interests introduces uncertainty into the law, the answer is that to a considerable extent the uncertainty was there already. The choice of interests to be protected and of policies to be promoted or effectuated was made by appellate courts, even though in many cases, I believe, the balancing of interests or weighing of policies was not a conscious deliberative process. Pound's theory of social interests gives persuasive proof that the choice must be made, and that it will be better made if it is a reflective and deliberate choice. By including in his inventory the social interests which call for certainty and security, Pound has made the choice between following an 'established rule' and discarding it for a supposedly paramount policy, itself a process of balancing interests. That this balancing goes on, behind the scenes, in an appellate court which is struggling with the problem of overruling its precedents, we have reliable evidence. So despite the procedural limitations referred to above, courts will continue to make prophecies as to the consequences that will follow one or another line of decision . . . These prophecies will become more reliable if the judges who make them realize that, as Pound's theory of social interests seems to tell us, the making of them involves judgments of fact as well as of value. . . .

NOTES AND QUESTIONS

1. Should we accept Patterson's flat statement that "except in cases involving constitutionality, the social consequences of a judicial decision, considered as a guide to the decision of future cases, are not open to investigation as a part of the factual issues in a case"? Why aren't they?

2. Is Dean Pound's explanation of Priestley v. Fowler consistent with his view that courts should decide cases by reference to "some canon of valuing conflicting and overlapping interests"?

3. What are the canons of evaluation to which Dean Pound refers? Are you helped by his jural postulates? Are the postulates which he added in 1942 entirely consistent with those he formulated earlier? [See Stone, The Province and Function of Law 366-368, 337-338, 359-360 (1950).] Would any of these postulates have helped the Supreme Court to decide the School Segregation Cases?

4. Is there any danger that the effort of judges to ascertain and weigh the consequences of alternative decisions and to be rational in their choice of values (see the following Editorial Note) may make them so self-conscious as to paralyze or impair their ability to decide? Can we afford to expect less of our judges?

EDITORIAL NOTE: M. R. COHEN'S RATIONALISTIC VALUE-ANALYSIS and PRIESTLEY V. FOWLER

A leading exponent of a rational approach to the ethical problem implicit in legal judgment has been M. R. Cohen. Before attempting to apply this approach to Priestley v. Fowler as a case example, we shall first set forth a summary of the approach as contained in Mermin, Book Review, M. R. Cohen, Reason and Law (1950), 59 Yale L.J. 1373, 1378-1379 (1950):

". . . The outlines of Cohen's position are quite clear: (1) The ethical *ought* is to be distinguished from the *is,* and cannot logically be deduced from the latter (since an ought-conclusion of a syllogism cannot logically be deduced from premises containing no ought) (pp. 6-7; 179). (2) The usual ethical maxims (e.g., equality, giving each man his due, etc.) are too indeterminate or ambiguous to be very valuable (pp. 7, 21-23). (3) The values and interests to be compared and harmonized are incommensurable; we not only lack a common denominator for the different values or interests but we do not regard every individual's interest on the same basis (those remote in time, space, social group, etc. are normally regarded differently) (pp. 28, 93-97). (4) Even if ethical maxims were not ambiguous, they are not unchanging, but rather exhibit great variety in different times and places (pp. 23-26). (5) There are limitations on the capacity of law to bring about a just social order (e.g., because of diversity of interests between the governing and the governed)[1] (pp. 97-101). (6) In spite of these difficulties it is both possible (p. 181) and necessary (p. 97) to organize logically an ethical system which involves (a) 'knowledge of natural causal relations which determine what means are necessary for certain ends,'[2] and (b) 'a critical consideration of what is ultimately good or worthwhile and for which we ought to strive. Such a system may be called a rational art rather than science.' (p. 181). (7) Such a system will enable us to determine whether we are 'mistaken as to what ends we really think worthy of achievement,' and 'we can make progress at least in the clarification of our ideas.' (pp. 90, 91). (8) The foregoing necessarily means a rejection of any absolute standards unrelated to the postulated needs of the particular society. 'To kill the patient in order to follow the rules of hygiene is no more absurd than to ruin a society for the sake of observing a supposed rule of justice. Even the divinely ordained Sabbath was made for man, not man for the Sabbath.' (p. 101).

"Note the limited character of the claims for this proposal. Cohen knows there

[1] This had been elaborated in Reason and Nature (1931) as "the intractability of human materials" (p. 420). Cohen there included in his discussion the lack of necessary knowledge on the part of the legislators and their imperfect power to control judicial interpretation; resistance on the part of the governed to law enforcement in certain fields of human life; the frailties of human officials; and the possibility that an attempt to effectuate an apparently just objective may on the whole do more harm than good. In addition to the intractability of human materials, Cohen listed among the difficulties in evolving a theory of justice, the "indeterminateness of jural ideals" (pp. 415-420), . . . and the "abstractness of legal rules" (pp. 425-426)—the inability of the law to depart much from an abstract uniformity in spite of individual differences among the governed. . . .

[2] The point had been explained in Reason and Nature as follows (pp. 441-442): "If I wish to preserve my health I must take account of the laws of physiology. But ought I always to preserve my health? That depends on some further assumptions. If I value the safety of my country, my family, or my own creative artistic activity, I may answer in the negative. And so, ethics may be viewed as dealing with hypothetical imperatives which condition a rationally coherent plan of life. Such a science directly enlightens us only as to necessary means, but in so doing it clarifies the choice of ends by showing what is involved in such choice. We can better decide what road to take if we know what we can reasonably expect on the way. While, therefore, rational science cannot give us absolute moral rules, it is, like mathematics, inherently applicable to the actual world."

is a role for science in the field of instrumental oughts in 6 (a) above—i.e., in verifying whether a particular ought will in fact achieve a particular desired end—but that the determination of the ultimate oughts (i.e., what these desired ends shall be) is not a matter of science at all. All that he can say of this determination is that it demands a 'critical consideration' (and presumably it should pay some heed, in a democratic society, to majority feelings and needs in the matter). This is a matter of 'free' choice rather than scientific evidence; nor are we able to make the choice between competing ultimate oughts (e.g., economic vs. spiritual values) on the basis of any common denominator of ultimate oughtness. It is possible, however, that 'ethical judgments can be verified if applied to long spans of human experience.' (p. 181). . . ."

The meaning of Cohen's views, as above summarized, might be clarified through their application to a specific judicial decision like that of Lord Abinger in Priestley v. Fowler. It will be recalled that Lord Abinger considered the probable consequences of alternative decisions, before deciding against the injured plaintiff. For instance, he thought that a decision for the plaintiff would make workers less careful, and would put an absurd and alarming economic burden upon employers. Thus, the conclusion that the defendant in the case ought to be free from liability was an "instrumental" ought, based on a prediction, in Cohen's language, of "what means are necessary for certain ends." The "ends" in question would be: maximizing the carefulness of workers, and avoiding too heavy a burden upon employers. Evidently these ends were not of the "ultimate" variety; they seemed to be desired not for their own sake, but because they would serve in turn as means for further ends. What further ends? Lord Abinger did not tell us, and probably did not even have them consciously in mind, beyond perhaps a vague ideal of a growingly prosperous society.

In what ways could this process of value-choice be made more of a "rational art," in Cohen's analysis?

(1) Consider first the matter of ultimate ends. A "critical consideration of the ultimately good or worthwhile" would have required Abinger to ask himself what his more remote ends were; to state why he wanted to make workers more careful and employers free from heavy economic burdens; and if the answer was in some such terms as a growingly prosperous society, then to analyze the precise components of this vague ideal. Did it involve, and should it involve, economic prosperity only? Prosperity of employers only? What kind of balance should be struck as between the human costs and money costs of achieving the end? Is this weighing of costs to be done in the light of effects upon psychic states (e.g., "happiness") and if so, whose? This "critical consideration" directed at making vague ultimate ideals more precise and explicit is of course analytically helpful.

(2) How does Cohen's analysis affect the less ultimate value-judgments (the means-ends assumptions) that Lord Abinger explicitly made: that judgment ought to be for the defendant, because we ought to make workers more careful and ought to avoid a heavy burden upon employers? Here reliable knowledge was not at hand; experience could yield only the roughest

kind of "verification." Will the means actually produce the ends envisaged? Might freedom from liability make the employer more careless and thus produce more employee injuries and thus impose a heavier economic burden through absenteeism and labor turnover? Moreover, might this means-end inquiry turn up the fact that even if the means under consideration (freedom from liability) was efficacious in producing the contemplated end of freeing employers from heavy economic burdens, the means were too costly, i.e., they had other *additional* results, e.g., high human costs which were too undesirable (enter another value judgment). In this way the inquiry into means affects the choice of the ends themselves. For it, in Cohen's words, "clarifies the choice of ends by showing what is involved in such choice." Further, to the extent that the means-ends inquiry is not merely theoretical but is supplemented by actual human *experience* of the projected consequences, it may be found that these consequences are not as desired or desirable as supposed—e.g., they are not psychically satisfying, or produce a train of still further consequences that are undesirable. (This is apparently what Cohen meant by "verification" of value-judgments over "long spans of human experience").

Today, of course, more "experience" is available than was available to Lord Abinger if he had asked himself questions of the kind we have posed. For example, should Lord Abinger have anticipated the possibility of an insurance system which would not impose unduly heavy economic burdens upon employers absolutely liable under workmen's compensation laws? Also, statistics seem to show a declining accident rate in industry since the enactment of these laws. Does this show Lord Abinger was wrong in asserting that the employer liability contended for by the plaintiff would make workers more careless? Has this declining rate been caused by the fact that employers' liability has been increased? Doubtless other factors were at work, e.g., improved safety devices, but to what extent were these in turn stimulated by the increased liability of employers, rather than by, e.g., an increased humanitarianism? The problem of causation is obviously complex. The "verification" of means-ends judgments is still a rough one.

Thus, the "rational" ethics championed by Cohen (and of course by numerous other ethical thinkers) puts a premium on reliable social knowledge, which still seems woefully inadequate. But Cohen would answer that a persistent effort to perfect the application of a rational method is clearly preferable to complacent acquiescence in guesswork, intuition, and "inarticulate major premises."

CHAPTER Four

The AUTHORITY of PRECEDENT—the
WISCONSIN FELLOW-SERVANT and
SAFE-PLACE RULES

CHAMBERLAIN v. MILWAUKEE & MISSISSIPPI RAILROAD CO.
11 Wis. 248 (1860)

By the Court, PAINE, J. . . .

The general rule is conceded, that every person is responsible for injuries occurring to others by the negligence of his servants, while in the execution of his employment. This rule settles the question, unless the fact that the person injured is also a servant of the same employer, is just ground for making it an exception. That the majority of the cases which have passed upon the point, both in this country and in England, have recognized this as an exception, cannot be denied. And if it is only that duty of a court to count the cases on each side of a question, and decide in favor of the majority, this matter could be very readily determined; though upon some questions, with the rapidity with which judicial decisions are multiplying, this rule might require considerable arithmetical capacity. But if the reason of the law be the soul of the law, and such we understand to have ever been its proudest boast, then a court has, although a more difficult, yet a more worthy task, and has not only to count but to weigh the cases, and by this test the majority do not always rule. And such we think to be the result here.

The question has been very thoroughly examined in the following cases: Gillentwater v. The Madison & Indianapolis R.R. Co., 5 Port. (Ind.), 339; Fitzpatrick v. New Albany & Salem R.R. Co., 7 id., 436; Little Miami R.R. Co. v. Stevens, 20 Ohio, 415; and Railroad Company v. Keary, 3 Ohio St. Rep., 201. . . . But in the cases in Indiana the servant injured was not engaged in the same department of business, as the one by whose negligence the injury was caused; and the court states this as a reason for distinguishing them from those which had decided against any liability. While the cases in Ohio, which are themselves authorities against this distinction, profess, or at least the later cases do, to recognize another, and while holding the company liable for an injury to a subordinate, occasioned by the negligence of his superior, admit that such liability would not exist, when the one injured occupied the position of an equal in the employment, with respect to the one causing the injury. While recognizing, therefore, the reasoning of these courts, as stating clearly the grounds upon which liability in such cases rests, we shall attempt to show that that reasoning is entirely inconsistent with the distinctions they profess to admit, and necessarily establishes the liability without reference to those distinctions. And that the latter must have been suggested out of deference to authorities, from which they did not care to depart, further than the facts of the case made necessary.

And first, as to the distinction suggested by the cases in Indiana, exempting the principal from liability where the negligence was committed by a servant working in the same department as the one injured. Can this be sustained without overturning the very principles on which the court sustained the liability, where the negligence occurred in a different department? We think not. The only view in which that circumstance should be material would seem to be this. Where the servant injured was himself engaged at the immediate point where the negligence occurred, that might furnish some grounds to implicate him in the negligence. And for the purpose of determining whether his own negligence contributed to the injury, it would be proper to inquire whether he was working at the point where it occurred. But, conceding the one injured to have performed his whole duty with skill and care, it seems entirely immaterial whether he is injured by the negligence of one working in the same department or in another. The company is held liable, because, in setting a force in motion, to be used for its benefit, it is bound to see to it that it is employed with proper care and skill. But does not this obviously extend to the different duties in the same department, as well as to those of different departments? The great object of this common law principle is not to protect those in one department as against those in another, but to protect every one from injury by the negligence of another. Now, the court classes all whose duties are connected with the running of the cars, as engaged in the same department. Yet, everybody knows that this department requires various duties entirely separate and distinct in their character. So that a servant performing one can, by no just reasoning, be held responsible for the negligence of another. A brakeman has to act in obedience to signals by the engineer; but he has no connection whatever with the performance of the duties of the engineer. Where it is conceded, therefore, that the company is bound to conduct the force it sets in motion with proper care and skill, upon what principle can it be maintained that they may, through their engineer, so negligently manage the engine as to mangle the brakeman and all their other servants on the train, and yet be entirely irresponsible? In our judgment, no rational answer has been or can be given to this question.

It has been said that the servant, in undertaking the business, has, by his contract, agreed to assume all risks; that of negligence as well as others. But the court of Indiana justly repudiates this idea. It says: "True, there are authorities for the position, that when a party contracts to perform services, he takes into account 'the dangers and perils' incident to the employment, but this can only be intended to mean such 'dangers and perils' as necessarily attend the business when conducted with ordinary care and prudence. He cannot be presumed to contract with reference to injuries inflicted on him by negligence."

That court, therefore, would not sustain their distinction, by which a servant would be remediless for an injury by the negligence of another in the same department, on the ground that by his contract he had assumed the risk of such negligence. They say he does not contract with reference to any injuries to be inflicted on him by negligence. They therefore deprive themselves of all support for their distinction from one of the strong grounds relied on by all the cases in favor of the exemption from liability.

The only other ground upon which this exemption is claimed at all is, that public policy requires it. It is rather faintly suggested by the court of Ohio, in Railroad v. Keary, that "public policy may be concerned in their keeping a supervision over each other," etc. And if this is true, then the distinction between those serving in different departments might be valid, for the reason that those in the same department might supervise each other, and not those in other departments. But there seems to be no solid foundation for the idea that public policy requires this exemption. The only possible ground upon which it could rest, would be the supposition that employes upon railroads and other improvements which the public use, would be more vigilant to prevent injuries from the negligence of each other, if they knew they could not recover damages, against the company, than they would with the opposite belief. But this notion is based upon a false estimate of the motives which govern human action. The lives and limbs of these employes are at hazard along with those of the public, and all human experience and consciousness, abundantly testify that to the motives which these furnish, the right to an action for damages could add nothing. There seems, therefore, no reason for sustaining the doctrine upon that ground. In truth, the argument to be derived from public policy is the other way. *First.* These employes are a portion of the public, and the safety of the rest not requiring it, there can be no just reason for excluding them from that protection, which it is the policy of the law to furnish to every one, against injury by the negligence of others. *Next,* by just so much as the liability of the employer for the negligence of his servants is reduced, by just so much are the motives diminished which induce him to employ servants of the greatest skill and vigilance. And if from this relaxation, negligent servants are employed, the public at large, as well as the other employes, run the hazard of the calamities arising from it.

And it is proper, in connection with this view, to consider the suggestion made in some of the cases, that an employe, where he sees that other negligent persons are employed, may leave the service. This suggestion is made in Farwell v. Railroad Co., 4 Met., 59. Now suppose this view practically carried out, those employes who are themselves vigilant and attentive, find that there are some others negligent or reckless. The law furnishes them no protection against injuries by these and the employer not being liable except as to the public chooses to run the risk. The prudent and faithful servants, in obedience to the advice of the supreme court of Massachusetts, leave the service. What position would the public then be in? The faithful, careful servants have left in obedience to the law, whose policy would not protect them by holding their employer under the strongest possible inducements to employ the most faithful and careful servants with them, and so by the operation of public policy the public are left to the mercy of the negligent. This doctrine, therefore, seems to rest only on a purely imaginary influence of the absence of any right of action to create additional vigilance on the part of employes, while it overlooks the real influence which the liability to an action has upon the company to induce it to employ the most skillful and careful servants. And, indeed, this suggestion of public policy seems to have been made with some hesitation in the later cases, while following the English cases, which first established the exemption from liability upon other grounds.

In Priestley v. Fowler, 3 M. and W., 1, which was the first case upon the subject, although the court dwells upon the inconvenience which masters might suffer, they do not place their decision upon public policy. And such a suggestion would have been somewhat ludicrous in that case, as it is difficult to see how public policy could be very deeply interested in the loading of a private cart.

We think, therefore, that the cases in Ohio and Indiana, following the dissenting opinion of Judge O'NEALL in the case in South Carolina, 1 McMullan, have overturned the only two grounds upon which this exception has ever been placed, and having overturned them, they leave no foundation for the distinctions which they admit.

Thus the cases in Ohio ignore the distinction implied in Indiana, and hold the company liable to the engineer for the negligence of the conductor, though both were in the same department. But then they place it upon the ground that the engineer was subordinate to the conductor. But what bearing does that have upon the principles upon which they assert the liability? None at all that we can possibly discover. They hold the company liable, because having set a force in motion for their own benefit, they are bound to see that it is conducted with proper care and skill, so as not to injure others. In order to do that, it is necessary that proper directions should be given. And if the company choose to give these directions through a conductor, and he was negligent, that was their negligence, and they had failed in their duty and should be responsible. But if these principles are correct, as they undoubtedly are, is it not equally clear that, in order to manage the force which they have set in motion properly, the proper directions must be properly executed as well as given? This is too obvious for question. Can the same court which has said to one brakeman that the company is bound so to manage the force it sets in motion, as not to injure him by negligence, and has given him a judgment for the negligence of the conductor, and with any consistency say to another who has been injured by the negligence of the engineer, that he cannot recover, because he was not subordinate? Suppose the conductor himself, having used every care and vigilance, is injured by the negligence of the engineer, whom he did not employ, but the company did, is he without remedy? If so, the court must abandon its general principle, that he who set a force in motion is bound so to control it as not to injure others. That principle and the distinction cannot both stand. For the question whether the one injured stood in the relation of equal, subordinate, or superior to the one whose negligence committed the injury, except so far as it might tend to show whether his own negligence contributed thereto, is entirely immaterial.

We are satisfied, therefore, that the general principles of the common law sustain this liability, and that those cases which have attempted to establish an exception, do not rest upon solid ground. If the plaintiff was injured by the negligence of the engineer, even though he was at the time a servant of the company, he himself being guilty of no negligence which contributed to the injury, he is entitled to recover.

For these reasons the judgment must be reversed, and the cause remanded for a new trial.

COLE, J. I do not wish to be understood as expressing any opinion whatever upon one question so fully discussed in the opinion of Justice PAINE, filed in this case, namely, as to whether one servant or employe can maintain an action against his principal for injuries which he has sustained by or through the carelessness of another servant, in the employ of the same principal, while engaged in the same common service. I think the case should be reversed for the reason that the circuit court improperly instructed the jury as to the effect and meaning of the former decision. . . .

But whether the appellant could recover if it appeared that he was an employe of the company at the time he received the injuries complained of, I will express no opinion. That is a very interesting and important question, which I have not had time fully to consider; and the decisions upon that point, in this country and in England, are quite unanimous that a recovery could not be had under such circumstances. But whether these decisions rest upon sound reason and an enlightened public policy, I will not now undertake to say.

MOSELEY v. CHAMBERLAIN
18 Wis. 700 (1861)

By the Court, DIXON, C. J. The action was commenced in the county court of the county of Milwaukee by the plaintiff, a citizen and resident of this state, against the defendant, a citizen and resident of the state of Ohio. The defendant applied under the twelfth section of the judiciary act of 1789 (U.S. Stat. at Large, p. 79), for the removal of the cause into the district court of the United States for this district, which was refused. I hold that the defendant's petition and proceedings for that purpose were regular, and that the cause ought to have been removed. I think, therefore, that the county court lost jurisdiction of the case, and that the judgment should for that reason, be reversed. My brethren, however, are of a different opinion. They hold that congress has no power to provide for the removal of a cause from a state to a federal court, and consequently, that the application was properly denied. But upon the law governing the merits of the case they disagree. Justice PAINE adheres to his opinion expressed in Chamberlain v. Mil. & Miss. R.R. Co., 11 Wis., 238, that an employee can recover of his employer for an injury occasioned by the negligence of another employee engaged in the same business; while Justice COLE thinks that he cannot. This diversity of opinion between them makes it necessary for me to express my opinion upon this question, in order that the cause may be determined, although upon the merits I think we have no jurisdiction of it. I recede from the opinion of the majority, in which I then concurred, in Chamberlain v. Mil. & Miss. R.R. Co., and agree with Justice COLE that the doctrine of that case must be overruled.

In coming to this conclusion I have no words of apology to offer, and but few observations. The argument on both sides was long since exhausted. I recede more from that deference and respect which is always due to the enlightened and well considered opinions of others, than from any actual change in my own views. The judgment of a majority in that case is sustained by weighty and powerful reasons. Like reasons are not wanting on the other side, and that side is sustained by the almost unanimous judgments of all the courts both of England and this country. I think I am bound to yield to this unbroken current of judicial opinion. At the time that decision was announced, it was supposed that the doctrine had been or would be sustained by the courts of Ohio and Indiana; but by the reports which have more recently reached us, it appears that they hold the very opposite (Whaalan v. The Mad River & Lake Erie R.R. Co., 8 Ohio St., 249; The Ohio & Miss. R.R. Co. v. Tindall, 13 Ind., 366); so that now the case stands alone, in opposition to the decisions of all the courts of both countries, and I think, with Justice COLE, that it must be overruled.

Judgment reversed, and a new trial awarded.

NOTES AND QUESTIONS

1. Wisconsin Constitution, Art. XIV, sec. 13: "Such parts of the common law as are now in force in the territory of Wisconsin, not inconsistent with this constitution, shall be and continue part of the law of this state until altered or suspended by the legislature." (Adopted 1848.)

Did this constitutional provision require the Wisconsin Supreme Court in the 1860 case to follow Priestley v. Fowler? The following extracts and comments dealing with the American "reception" of English common law should help to answer this question.

Reinsch,* The English Common Law in the Early American Colonies (Bulletin of the Univ. of Wis., Historical Series, II, No. 4 (1899), reprinted in 1 Select Essays in Anglo-American Legal History 367 (1907)):

"The earliest settlers in many of the colonies made bodies of law, which, from every indication, they considered a complete statement of the needful legal regulations. Their civilization being primitive, a brief code concerning crimes, torts, and the simplest contracts, in many ways like the dooms of the Anglo-Saxon kings, would be sufficient. Not only did these codes innovate upon, and depart from, the models of common law, but, in matters not fixed by such codes, there was in the earliest times no reference to that system. They were left to the discretion of the magistrates.

"In many cases the colonists expressed an adhesion to the common law, but, when we investigate the actual administration of justice, we find that usually it was of a rude, popular, summary kind, in which the refined distinctions, the artificial developments of the older system have no place. A technical system can, of course, be administered only with the aid of trained lawyers. But these were generally not found in the colonies during the 17th century, and even far down into the 18th we shall find that the legal administration was in the hands of laymen in many of the provinces. Only as the lawyers grow more numerous and receive a better training, do we find a general reception and use of the more refined theories of the common law. It is but natural that, with increased training, the courts and practitioners should turn to the great reservoir of legal experience in their own language for guidance and information;

* Paul S. Reinsch (1870-1923) was Professor of Political Science for many years at the University of Wisconsin, where he taught and wrote in the area of American legislation as well as international relations.—Editor

the courts would be more ready to favor the theory of the adoption of the common law, as it increased their importance, virtually giving them legislative power. The foregoing statements are especially true of New England. . . ."

Kent,* Commentaries (7th ed., 1851) 523-526:

"The common law, so far as it is applicable to our situation and government, has been recognized and adopted, as one entire system, by the constitutions of Massachusetts, New York, New Jersey, and Maryland. [Also by the Wisconsin Constitution.— Editor] It has been assumed by the courts of justice, or declared by statute, with the like modifications, as the law of the land in every state. It was imported by our colonial ancestors, as far as it was applicable, and was sanctioned by royal charters and colonial statutes. It is also the established doctrine, that English statutes, passed before the emigration of our ancestors, and applicable to our situation, and in amendment of the law, constitute a part of the common law of this country.

"The best evidence of the common law is to be found in the decisions of the courts of justice, contained in numerous volumes of reports, and in the treatises and digests of learned men, which have been multiplying from the earliest periods of the English history down to the present time. The reports of judicial decisions contain the most certain evidence, and the most authoritative and precise application of the rules of the common law. . . ."

Wisconsin became a territory in 1836 and a state in 1848. Under Art. XIV, sec. 13 of the Constitution, the State took over the common law of the territory. But where did the territory get its common law from? Its common law consisted of (a) the English common law as of the eve of the American Revolution [see Coburn v. Harvey, 18 Wis. 147 (1864)], plus (b) such changes therein or additions thereto as time had brought and as the first territorial lawyers and judges conceived to be applicable; plus, as the territory continued in existence, (c) such further changes and additions as the territorial judges effected. The State took over also the territorial statutory law,—Art. XIV, sec. 2 of the Constitution providing that "all laws now in force in the territory of Wisconsin which are not repugnant to this constitution shall remain in force until they expire by their own limitation or be altered or repealed by the legislature."

See also Ford, The Common Law: An Account of Its Reception in the United States, 4 Vand. L. Rev. 791 (1951).

2. Why did not the Wisconsin Supreme Court in the 1860 case follow the current of judicial decision on the question before it? Did this current of decision constitute "precedent" binding upon it? Did the court admit that in this case it was departing from the "taught tradition of the law"? Is its view of the state of the common law at the time closer to Lippmann's or Dean Pound's?

3. Did the court in the 1860 case recognize that it had complete latitude to decide the case one way or the other? Do you think it raised all the questions of fact which had to be answered to make an intelligent choice between the alternatives open to it? How did it get the information necessary to answer the questions of fact which it did raise? How did the court, for example, know that an employee does not assume the risk of a fellow employee's negligence as part of his contract of employment with his employer? How did

---

* James Kent (1763-1847) was admitted to the bar in New York, was several times elected to the New York legislature, lectured at Columbia Law School, and published the first edition of his famous Commentaries On American Law during 1826-1830. The latter work, which became the standard, general treatise in its field, was mainly devoted to constitutional law and to real property. The 12th edition (1873) was edited by a young Boston lawyer who was later to become the celebrated Mr. Justice Holmes.—Editor

it know whether employees would be more or less "vigilant to prevent injuries from the negligence of (their fellow employees) if they knew they could not recover damages against" their employers? Does its opinion reflect any more information on this subject than is reflected in the opinions we have previously read which reached a contrary conclusion?

4. Is the separate opinion of Cole, J. in the 1860 case a dissenting opinion? What conclusions would you have drawn about Cole's views on the merits of the fellow-servant rule if you were a lawyer reading his opinion the day it was made public?

5. The following is an explanation of the "removal" issue in the 1861 case. Article III of the United States Constitution extends the judicial power of the United States to controversies between citizens of different states. The Judiciary Act of 1789 gave the lower federal courts jurisdiction "concurrent with" the state courts "of all suits of a civil nature . . . where the matter in dispute exceeds, exclusive of costs, the sum or value of five hundred dollars, and . . . the suit is between a citizen of the state where the suit is brought, and a citizen of another state." Since 1789 the "jurisdictional amount" has been increased until it is now $10,000. It was $500 at the time the Wisconsin cases in question were decided. The Judicial Code presently gives the federal district courts "original jurisdiction of all civil actions where the matter in controversy exceeds the sum or value of $10,000 exclusive of interest and costs, and is between: (1) citizens of different states . . ." 28 U.S.C. 1332. This jurisdiction is still concurrent with that of the states.

Since 1789, too, the judiciary acts have provided for the removal of a case from a state to a lower federal court for trial in the first instance. The Judiciary Act of 1789 extended the removal privilege to a defendant who was sued by a citizen of the state where the suit was brought, if the defendant was a citizen of another state and more than $500 was in dispute. It was this provision which the defendant in the 1861 case sought to use.

Congress's power to provide for removal in this type of case was upheld by the United States Supreme Court in Railway Co. v. Whitton, 13 Wall. 270 (U.S. 1872), which thereby vindicated the position of Dixon, C. J. in the 1861 case. The Judicial Code presently authorizes the defendant to remove to a federal district court any action brought in a state court of which the federal district courts have original jurisdiction. 28 U.S.C. 1441 (a). The code also contains other removal provisions which do not concern us at this point.

The defendant sought to remove the 1861 case to the federal court in the hope that it would not apply Wisconsin law, as laid down in the 1860 case, but the contrary current of judicial decisions. The federal court at this time was not required to apply the rule of liability applicable in the state court from which the case was removed. Section 34 of the Judiciary Act of 1789—the so-called Rules of Decision Act—declared that the "laws of the states" shall apply in the federal courts, unless the federal constitution or statutes required otherwise. But in the famous case of Swift v. Tyson, 10 L. Ed. 865 (U.S. 1842), the Supreme Court held that "laws of the states" referred to statutes—acts of the legislature—and not to the body of judicial decisions making up the general common law. The federal court, therefore, was free to develop its own common law in the fields of torts, contracts, and commercial relations not covered by state statutes.

Almost a century after it was decided, Swift v. Tyson was overruled. In Erie R.R. v. Tompkins, 304 U.S. 64 (1938), the Supreme Court said: "Except in matters governed by the Federal Constitution or by Acts of Congress, the law to be applied in any case is the law of the state. And whether the law of the state shall be declared by its Legislature in a statute or by its highest court in a decision is not a matter of federal concern. . . ."

So today, the rules of tort liability applied by the highest state court would be applied by the federal courts in the state in a diversity-of-citizenship suit, whether the suit was originally brought in the federal court or removed there from a state court.

6. Why did not the Wisconsin Supreme Court in 1861 follow the precedent of the

1860 case? Was the court in 1861 merely bowing to the current of judicial decision outside Wisconsin?

7. Note that the same judges decided the 1860 and 1861 cases. The difference in result is due to the fact that Dixon, C. J. changed his vote. But is not Dixon failing to perform his judicial duty when he recedes "more from that deference and respect which is always due to the enlightened and well considered opinions of others than from any actual change in my own views?" Compare Sutherland, J., dissenting in West Coast Hotel Co. v. Parrish, 300 U.S. 379, 401 (1937):

". . . rational doubts must be resolved in favor of the constitutionality of the statute. But whose doubts, and by whom resolved? Undoubtedly it is the duty of a member of the court, in the process of reaching a right conclusion, to give due weight to the opposing views of his associates; but in the end, the question which he must answer is not whether such views seem sound to those who entertain them, but whether they convince him that the statute is constitutional or engender in his mind a rational doubt upon that issue. The oath which he takes as a judge is not a composite oath, but an individual one. And in passing upon the validity of a statute, he discharges a duty imposed upon *him*, which cannot be consummated justly by an automatic acceptance of the views of others which have neither convinced, nor created a reasonable doubt in, his mind. If upon a question so important he thus surrenders his deliberate judgment, he stands forsworn. He cannot subordinate his convictions to that extent and keep faith with his oath or retain his judicial and moral independence."

By which of these two views should a judge be guided? May there be a basis for a difference in judicial attitude depending upon whether a judge is passing on the constitutionality of a statute or contributing to the development of the common law? We shall have occasion to return to this question in Chapter 11.

8. Compare Dwyer v. Express Co., 82 Wis. 307, 312 (1892), regarding the fellow-servant doctrine: "Whatever may be thought of the reason or justice of the rule, it is now too deeply imbedded in our jurisprudence to be repudiated or shaken by judicial determination. If any change of the rule is desirable, it should be made by the legislature—not by the courts."

Is this attitude consistent with what the court did in the 1861 case?

9. Did the legal developments in Ohio and Indiana prove, in retrospect, that the strategy of Loring, plaintiff's lawyer in the Farwell case, was justified?

10. Should Dixon, C. J., in the 1861 case, have abstained from giving his opinion on the law relative to the fellow-servant rule when he believed that the Wisconsin courts had lost jurisdiction of the law suit because of what he deemed a valid removal of the case to the federal courts on diversity of citizenship?

How would the case have come out if he had done so?

EDITORIAL NOTE: COUNSEL'S ARGUMENTS
in the FOREGOING TWO CASES

Lawyers present their views of the evidence and the applicable law to a court by oral and by written argument. Many cases are presented in the trial courts only on oral argument, although written arguments ("briefs") are generally also given the court in important or difficult cases, either on the attorneys' own initiative, or perhaps at the request of the court after it has heard oral argument. When a case is appealed to a higher court, written arguments are invariably presented to the court. Oral argument will generally be heard also, although cases are sometimes presented simply on the briefs; when this is done the case is said to be "submitted." In addition, as many of the formal papers in the record (the summons, pleadings, motions, etc.), and a full or summary report of as much of the evidence taken in the trial court, as the respective parties deem necessary, will accompany the briefs on appeal.

The official Reports of decisions of appellate courts often contain, at least for cases the Reporter thinks sufficiently important to justify the effort, brief summaries of the main arguments and citations of opposing counsel. See, e.g., the excerpts from such summaries reprinted above in connection with the Farwell case.

The volumes of records and briefs present a rich mine of information to one who knows how to use them, whether his interest is that of the practicing lawyer, legal scholar, or social scientist. An opinion of the court may take on new or added significance when it is read in comparison with the records and briefs. Close study of the record may tell the reader more precisely than the opinion the factual context in which the issues were presented to the court, and may give the careful and imaginative observer some "feel" of the living case as it may have touched the sympathies or antipathies of the judges who heard it. Comparison of briefs and opinion may disclose the extent to which the court itself broke new ground and the extent to which it followed the lead of able counsel; reveal that issues were argued by counsel which were scantily treated or ignored by the opinion; indicate to the appraising eye how far counsel performed their professional obligation of informing the court and how far counsel for one side may have outmatched counsel for the other side in the ability of presentation. These and many other factors have obvious pertinence in a well-rounded appraisal of the importance, justification and probable future significance of an opinion of the court. The busy practitioner cannot of course undertake exhaustive research in such materials for every brief which he has to prepare; but he should be aware of the availability and potential usefulness of these documents. For the research student in law, to resort to such materials should become a regular step in workmanlike procedure.

For the social scientist, the records and briefs of cases may, in addition, contain valuable factual information about contemporary life not as easily accessible in any other way.

The following passages present the entire argument on the basic question of recognition of the "fellow-servant rule," involved in the two Wisconsin cases, as that argument was made to the Supreme Court in the briefs of counsel. Careful effort was made, where reasons of space required some omissions, to omit only what seemed repetitious, so that the following excerpts may be taken to indicate the full extent of the substance of the briefed arguments of counsel. Editorial comments regarding the extent of omissions are added at the end of each passage.

Brief of Brown & Ogden for appellant, plaintiff-employee, in Chamberlain v. Milwaukee & Mississippi Railroad Co., 11 Wis. 245 (1860):

". . . The defendant relies on a class of cases starting from a decision in England (Priestley v. Fowler, 3 Mees and Welsby 1,) in which by gradual judicial encroachment, doctrines not only foreign to the common law but never contemplated by the Court in the original case, have been introduced. . . . We deny that the doctrine maintained in that series of cases is supported by the case, above referred to, in England, or that it should be adopted in Wisconsin. Each subsequent case in the series goes beyond the one immediately preceding, until the well established rule of liability of the master for acts of his servants is entirely destroyed. We call the attention of the Court to the confession in many of the decisions, that the principle decided is new, and to the entire insufficiency of the reasoning to support the conclusions.

"The well established doctrine of the common law is, that the master is responsible for all injuries to others happening through the neglect of a servant in the course of his employment; and we maintain that the common law on that subject, always has been and by the provision of the Constitution hereinafter referred to, continues to be in force in this State. . . . Both in Ohio and Indiana, the common law on this subject is followed. . . ." [citing 20 Ohio 415, 3 id. 625; 5 Ind. 340; 7 Porter (Ind.) 436.]

The foregoing is the entire discussion in plaintiff's brief, with the omission of some inconsequential phrasing.

Brief of Finches, Lynde & Miller for appellee, defendant-railroad, in 11 Wis. 245:

". . . If repeated decisions arising under almost every variety of circumstances can settle and determine the law, then the principle [the fellow-servant rule] cannot be disputed. It has been decided by the highest courts of England, New York, Pennsylvania, Massachusetts, Illinois and South Carolina, and the decisions have been numerous. . . ."

The brief then presents a list of citations of cases. The only other matter on the subject omitted in this excerpt is the brief's quotation of a standard statement of the fellow servant rule.

Brief of Finches, Lynde & Miller, for appellant, defendant-railroad, in Moseley v. Chamberlain, 18 Wis. 700 (1861):

". . . The decision in that case [11 Wis. 245] has the merit of standing alone. In the hope of inducing this Court to reconsider that decision, and believing that a re-examination of the authorities will lead the Court to reconsider that opinion, we have taken the objection to the complaint. We have supposed that when a question had been repeatedly before the Courts, and as often and as repeatedly decided, and the same principle affirmed, that it not only was *prima facie* evidence of the law, but *conclusive.* The maxim of the law so well known, understood and appreciated by intelligent judges, *stare decisis,* [i.e., that precedent should be followed] seems to have been overlooked and forgotten in the decision of that case. If any principle of law was, or ever could be settled by *judicial decisions,* the principle that one employee could maintain no action against his principal, for injuries received by the carelessness or negligence of his co-employee, while engaged in the same common service, must be deemed to have been settled. We ask the Court to see what a sweeping away and wiping out of authority this Court has made, by its decision in that case. In every case in this country, or in England, where the question has been raised, the decision has been directly the reverse of the decision made by this Court! and see the number and variety of those decisions. [The brief here cites seven English and 29 American decisions].

". . . we submit that where there is found such a unanimous and unvarying amount of authority, that this Court ought to hesitate and ponder well before placing itself upon the record in opposition to all these Courts. . . . Nor do we ask this Court merely to count the cases, and by the *mere number* of cases to determine the question. But we do ask this Court, where there is an unbroken current of authority, and where that current of authority is the judicial determination of some of the ablest and most renowned Courts of this country and England, to adhere to the maxim of the law, *stare decisis*. And we insist that even if the 'reasoning' of some of the Judges in giving their opinions is not entirely satisfactory to every member of this Court, that it is more in accordance with the maxims of the law for this Court to abide by former precedents *stare decisis,* where the same points come again in litigation, as well to keep the scale of justice even and steady and not liable to waver with every new Judge's opinion, as also because the law in that case, being solemnly declared and determined, what before was uncertain and perhaps indifferent, is now become a permanent rule which *it is not in the breast of any subsequent Judge to alter or swerve from, according to his own private judgment, but according to the known laws and customs of the land,—*NOT DELEGATED TO PRONOUNCE A NEW LAW, BUT TO MAINTAIN AND EXPOUND THE OLD ONE.

"Where a rule has become settled law, it is to be followed although some possible inconvenience may grow from a strict observance of it, or although a satisfactory reason for it is wanting, or although the principle and policy of the rule may be questioned. (8 Bing. 557). If judicial decisions are to be swept away, and all the principles determined by such decisions, overturned by the whim or caprice of every new Judge, then the successful practice of law is at an end. . . .

". . . The Court starts out, in its opinion [in 11 Wis. 245], with the enumeration of a principle, which is not good law, to the full extent which the Court announces, and that principle as announced by the Court is, 'that the Company is held liable, because by setting a force in motion, to be used for its benefit, it is bound to see to it that it is employed with proper care and skill.' This assumes, as the liability of the Company, just the very thing which is denied. It is bound to see that the 'force in motion' is employed with 'care and skill' only under certain circumstances, and with certain restrictions. It is so bound to the public, who have no control over, and are not engaged in managing . . . that 'force in motion'. But, it is bound to use such 'care and skill' towards one who is managing . . . or aiding in the management . . . of such 'force in motion'? No elementary writer, no judicial decision, with the exception of the Scottish Justices [referring to a Scottish case cited in 11 Wis. 245, omitted in the portion of that case reprinted above], and the dissenting opinion of Justice O'Neil [*sic*] in the South Carolina Report, and the decision of this Court in the case of Chamberlain v. M. & M. R. Co., has been furnished or referred to, as sustaining or upholding such a principle. . . . The reason of the rule for which we contend is clearly perceptible in the very nature of things. It is to be presumed that every human being has some little common sense, and some appreciation of things around and about him. Man . . . sees everywhere the evidence of forces over which he has no control, and in and of themselves destructive.—Every step of his life is one of danger and hazard. . . . And if true in the natural world, how much more true when brought in contact with and compelled to act in concert with numbers of his fellow men! He has discrimination and observation to know and to see that there are men proverbially reckless, careless and indifferent, and men the reverse of this. And what intelligent man does not know that he stands in far more danger of his life, when associated with and operating with his fellow men, than when alone? This is understood by all men. Every kind of business has its hazards and dangers; and no kind of business is more hazardous or dangerous than being engaged in running or assisting with the running of Rail Road trains. The man who engages to assist in running or operating a railroad train knows that he is placing himself in a position, and that too voluntarily, where he is liable to, and oftentimes is, endangered in life and limb, by the carelessness or negligence of his co-employees. And does he assume no risks? Is it understood between him and his employer, that in such service he assumes no risks? That the extraordinary liability which the law imposes upon the Railroad Company as to passengers, is guaranteed to him? . . . To our minds, reasoning from the 'course of human actions,' we should say that Willis Moseley, when he went into the service, did assume some risks. *He assumed the risks incident to his employment.*

". . . In Indiana and Ohio, the principle announced by the decisions above cited, have been directly sustained in . . . 8 Ohio State Rep. 249; and the 6 Ind. 205; and the 13th Ind. 366. So that the decision of this Court in [11 Wis. 245] is sustained by no authority—English or American—and by no opinion except that of the Scottish Justices, and the dissenting opinions of the South Carolina Justices, in the case in McMullin.

". . . Ought not this Court, under this great weight of authority, to yield its individual and private opinions to the judgment of all the Courts of this Country and England? We trust that our Court will not stand solitary and alone, and in opposition to all Courts upon this question. We have a pride that the decisions of this Court may be regarded by its sister States, but if the case of Chamberlain vs. the M. & M. R.R. Co., is to be re-affirmed, and the principles there laid down persistently maintained in opposition to, and against all the decisions of this country and England, we fear that Wisconsin Reports will be valueless and worthless in every State save and except Wisconsin. No lawyer, professing to be governed by, or recognizing the binding authority of established precedent, can examine that case by the light of the authorities presented to this Court, and hold the same good law. It is not law, if the authorities presented are entitled to due consideration.

"We leave this point, upon the authorities here presented."

The foregoing passages are thought fairly to present the argument made in 10 close-printed pages of brief. Substantial omissions were made to save space. All marks of emphasis are those of the original brief.

Brief of Smith & Salomon, for appellee, plaintiff-employee, in 18 Wis. 700:

". . . that decision is our authority for the right to bring the action on account of injury to the employee of the defendant. We do not know how to add force to the argument in that opinion, and have no intention to try." [This is the only direct reference to 11 Wis. 245 or the issue of the fellow-servant rule, in the brief.]

QUESTIONS

1. How helpful to the court do you think these briefs were? To what extent, if at all, do you think they influenced the result in each case?

2. Did the briefs attempt to give the court any help on the factual assumptions made by both the proponents and opponents of the fellow-servant rule? Do you think the lawyers could have done any better at this time? How?

3. Does the brief for the employer in the 1861 case show that the lawyers benefitted from their experience in the 1860 case? How?

4. Did the attorneys for the injured employee in the 1861 case plan their argument wisely? What else could they have done?

WEDGWOOD v. CHICAGO & NORTHWESTERN RY. CO.
41 Wis. 478 (1877)

APPEAL from the Circuit Court for Sauk County. . . .

"The complaint states in substance, that the plaintiff was in the employ of the defendant as brakeman on a freight train over a division of its road; that it was his duty, whenever occasion should require, to go between the freight cars and couple them together with such machinery, appliances and fixtures as the defendant provided; and that in operating its road it was the duty of the defendant to see that the cars and other rolling stock used on its road were safe and suitable for the business, so as not to unnecessarily endanger the lives and limbs of its employees and servants. It is then alleged that the defendant did, on or about the 31st of May, 1875, carelessly and negligently, and contrary to its duty, take upon its track, use and operate a freight car, upon the brake-frame or brake-beam of which, at the end of the car, was a large and long bolt, out of place, and which unnecessarily, carelessly and unskillfully projected beyond the frame, beam or brakehead, in the way of the brakeman going to couple the cars; that the defendant negligently suffered the bolt to remain, without cutting off the projecting part thereof, and without informing the plaintiff of its dangerous condition; that the plaintiff, while going between said car and another to couple them together, was tripped and thrown down by this projecting bolt, so allowed by the defendant to remain, and sustained the injuries of which he complains." *

The defendant answered by a general denial, and an averment of contributory negligence on plaintiff's part.

At the trial, defendant objected to the introduction of any evidence by the plaintiff, on the ground that the complaint did not state facts sufficient to constitute a cause of action. The objection was sustained, and the complaint dismissed. From this judgment the plaintiff appealed. . . .

COLE, J. It seems to us that the complaint states a good cause of action. It is a settled principle that the law imposed upon the defendant the duty of supplying and maintaining suitable cars and appliances for operating its road; and the company was bound to take due care, and use all reasonable means, to guard against defects in its locomotives and cars, which would endanger the lives and limbs of its servants and employees while in the performance of their duties. Numerous authorities might be cited on this point, if necessary; but many of the cases will be found in the brief of respondent's counsel in Brabbits v. The Chicago & Northwestern Railway, 38 Wis., 290. See also Strahlendorf v. Rosenthal, 30 Wis., 674. It has often been made a question whether the master was liable to his servant for

---

* This statement of the contents of the complaint is taken from the opinion of   Mr. Justice Cole herein, as originally prepared.

injuries caused by the negligence of a fellow servant in the same employment; but we did not suppose the master's responsibility was denied where, by his own negligence or malfeasance, he has enhanced the risk to which the servant is exposed beyond the natural risks of the employment; or has knowingly, and without informing the servant of the fact, used machinery defective in its construction, which has caused the injury. . . .

Now, from the matters stated in the complaint, we must assume that the defendant, carelessly, negligently and contrary to its duty, took upon and used on its road a freight car defectively constructed, which rendered the employment of the plaintiff in coupling this car to others unnecessarily hazardous and unsafe. It is charged that the company carelessly and negligently omitted the usual and proper inspection of the car, or improperly inspected it, and also allowed the projecting bolt at the end of the car to remain without being cut off. The plaintiff was wholly unaware of the dangerous position of this bolt, and, while performing his duty, was thrown down by it and injured. These facts would seem to bring the case within the rule which imposes liability on the master for an injury to the servant occasioned by a defect in machinery furnished the servant to operate, where the master has been guilty of negligence in furnishing such machinery, or, knowing of a defect therein, fails to notify the servant of its existence. It is true, the defendant in the present case is a railroad corporation, and can only act through officers or agents. But this does not relieve it from responsibility for the negligence of its officers and agents whose duty it is to provide safe and suitable machinery for its road which its employees are to operate.

By the Court.—The judgment of the circuit court is reversed, and the cause remanded with directions to proceed herein according to law.

QUESTIONS

1. Is the Wedgwood decision consistent with the fellow-servant doctrine accepted in the 1861 Wisconsin case? Are you satisfied by the manner in which the court "distinguished" the Wedgwood situation? Why is not liability in this case foreclosed by the implied agreement of the employee to assume the risk of his injury?

2. Would it be proper to read the Wedgwood case as inaugurating the "different-department" exception to the fellow-servant rule? Did the court say that it was doing so?

3. Was the result in the Wedgwood case foreshadowed in any of the previous cases beginning with Priestley v. Fowler?

4. How would you state the ratio decidendi of the 1861 case now that the Wedgwood case has been decided? Would you have stated it the same way before having read the Wedgwood case? Which of the different conceptions of the rule of a case do you think is supported by our reading of cases up to this point? Goodhart's? Oliphant's? Llewellyn's?

HEINE v. CHICAGO & NORTHWESTERN RY. CO.
58 Wis. 525, 17 N.W. 420 (1883)

TAYLOR, J. This action was brought by the appellant to recover damages for injuries received while at work for the respondent as a common laborer. The appellant, with a large number of other men, was at work for the respondent near

Cottage Grove "surfacing track"; that is, filling the dirt and gravel between the ties, and dressing up the surface. The gravel used was brought by a train of flat cars in charge of a conductor and the usual train hands. It was the duty of the men engaged in "surfacing" to get upon the cars, when the gravel train came up, and shovel off the gravel. The men engaged in "surfacing" were not otherwise connected with the train. The appellant claims he was injured in the following manner: When the gravel train came up with its load of gravel to the place where he and the others engaged in "surfacing" were at work, the conductor of the gravel train stopped the train, and ordered the appellant and the men working with him to get on the train for the purpose of being taken to the place where the gravel was to be unloaded, and then unload the same; that while he was engaged in getting on the train, and before he had time to do so, the conductor carelessly and negligently started the train without warning, and he was thrown upon the track and injured.

Upon the trial there was conflicting evidence as to how the injury occurred, and the weight of the evidence would seem to show that the appellant was injured by attempting to get on the train while it was in motion, without being ordered to do so by any one in charge thereof. There is perhaps some evidence tending to prove the appellant's version of the matter; and, as the learned circuit judge ordered a nonsuit, we must, upon this appeal, consider the case in the light of the appellant's version of the cause of his injury. Taking it for granted that the conductor of the gravel train stopped the same, and directed the appellant and the other men whose duty it was to unload the gravel to get upon the train for that purpose, and that while the appellant was obeying such order, and before he had time to do so, the conductor negligently and carelessly started the train without giving proper warning, and thereby the appellant was injured, was it error on the part of the circuit judge to order a nonsuit?

The answer to this question depends upon the other question, whether the conductor of the train and the appellant were co-employees of the respondent in the business then in hand, within the meaning of the law which relieves the respondent from liability to answer in damages for an injury to its servant or employee, while in its employment, which results solely from the carelessness or negligence of another employee. The answer to this question would not be free from difficulty if we were called upon to determine it upon the authority of the decisions of the courts of other states; but as this question has received the consideration of this court in several decided cases, the authority of which we are bound to respect, and which we think are fully supported by at least a preponderance of the authority, we feel no hesitancy in holding that the nonsuit was properly ordered in this case.

The distinction which some of the courts have made in favor of the employee, who by the nature of his employment is under the orders or directions of some other employee as to the way or manner in which he shall perform his part of the common work in hand, and holding that employees having such relations to each other are not co-employees within the meaning of the law above stated, and that the principal is liable for an injury resulting to the subject employee through the negligence of the employee having the power to direct his movements and acts, is not sustained by the weight of authority outside of this state, and has not been adopted by this court. . . .

[The court then quotes from the Brabbits case (cited in the Wedgwood opinion) and cites the Wedgwood case, among others, as establishing an "exception" from the fellow-servant rule.—Editor]

It will be seen that these cases all go upon the ground that the company owes an absolute duty to its employees to furnish them with reasonably suitable and safe machinery and other appliances with which they are required to do their work, or with which they may come in contact while doing their work, as well as a reasonably suitable and safe place for doing the same, and this duty being one which the company is bound to perform, it cannot be excused from its performance by intrusting it to an employee or officer who may neglect to perform such duty. The duty to see to its performance rests upon the company, notwithstanding it has appointed a suitable person or persons whose duty to the company is to see that such duty is performed. It is a duty that cannot be evaded by the appointment of a suitable agent to perform the same. The duty of performance rests upon the company, as much after the appointment of such agent as it did before, and the neglect of the agent is therefore attributed to the principal.

There is no case that holds that a corporation or other master owes a duty to its employees that the machinery or appliances which it uses in the performance of its work shall be so used as to do no injury to them. In that respect the duty of the master or principal is that he must use ordinary care in selecting men who are competent to work and manage such machinery and appliances, and he does not guaranty his employees that the men so employed by him will in all cases use the utmost care in working and managing the same. . . .

The cases above cited in this court clearly establish the rule that an employee cannot recover of his principal or employer for an injury caused by the negligence of another employee engaged in the same business; and the fact that the negligent employee has the power to direct and order the acts and movement of the one injured does not take the case out of such general rule.

In this case, taking the statement of the evidence most favorable to the appellant, it shows that he and the conductor of the train upon whom he charges the negligence were employed in the same business at the time the injury was received. The work to be done at the time was unloading the gravel cars. It was, as the evidence shows, the duty of the appellant, with others, to get on the cars and ride to the place of unloading, and then unload the same, and it was the duty of the conductor to stop the train and permit them to get on board for such purpose. He stopped the train for that purpose, and his carelessness in starting up too quick was the carelessness complained of by the appellant. Unless we disregard all that has been said upon this question by this court, we must hold that the appellant and the conductor on the gravel train were, at the time the injury was received, co-employees engaged in the same business, and the negligence of the one, which causes an injury to the other, cannot render the common master or employer liable for such injury.

There is no pretense in the evidence in this case that the employer was guilty of any negligence in employing a careless or incompetent conductor, or in retaining him in its service after having knowledge of his incompetency or carelessness. We refer to the brief of the learned counsel for the respondent for a collection of a large number of cases in other courts sustaining the rule adopted by this court in this case.

By the Court.—The judgment of the circuit court is affirmed.

NOTES AND QUESTIONS

1. The form of citation: By the time this case was decided, an unofficial, commercial publisher had begun to issue volumes of decisions of state appellate courts, in sets grouped according to geographical sections of the country. Thus this opinion may be found printed not only in the official Wisconsin Reports, but also in the so-called North Western Reporter.

2. Were plaintiff and the conductor in this case in fact co-employees? Were not the plaintiff and the employees charged with maintenance of the rolling stock in the Wedgwood case co-employees in fact also? Why is recovery denied in the Heine case because plaintiff was injured by a "co-employee," and allowed in the Wedgwood case? Do you think the two cases make for a consistent and understandable set of rules concerning employers' liability?

3. What does the court in the Heine case mean when it says that the company "owes an absolute duty to its employees to furnish them with reasonably suitable and safe machinery, etc."? Is it suggesting that the company may be liable irrespective of anybody's negligence?

Catlett,* *THE DEVELOPMENT OF THE DOCTRINE OF STARE DECISIS AND THE EXTENT TO WHICH IT SHOULD BE APPLIED*
21 Washington Law Review 158-164, 167-169 (1946)

. . . The doctrine of stare decisis, which means "to stand by decisions and not to disturb settled matters," is of ancient lineage. Some writers find evidences of it in Bracton and in the Year Books,[5] although one very careful scholar, who has gone through the Year Books for the special purpose of determining to what extent the doctrine of stare decisis was recognized in that early period, concludes that it cannot be said that the doctrine was firmly established then.[6] Other writers have been of the opinion that the essence of the doctrine can be found in the Roman Civil Law and even in the Code of Justinian.[7]

The exact time when the doctrine first appeared or was definitely accepted in English Law is of small practical importance. It appeared early and is certainly a very useful and a natural doctrine of any system of law which is based upon usage

* Fred W. Catlett, member of the Seattle, Washington bar, was a member of the Federal Home Loan Bank Board, 1934-42 and taught law at Washington University, 1914-18.—Editor

[5] Robert Von Moschzisker, Stare Decisis . . . (1929).

[6] T. Ellis Lewis, The History of Stare Decisis (1931) 47 L.Q. Rev. 411.

[7] Daniel H. Chamberlain, The Doctrine of Stare Decisis . . . (1885).

and custom. Unlike some of the other early doctrines of the common law, it is still easy to perceive the reasons lying at the base of stare decisis. Those reasons are stability and certainty in the law, convenience, and uniformity of treatment of all litigants. To the English or American mind, a system of law which lacks certainty and stability would be faulty and undesirable. It would be exceedingly difficult for a citizen to conduct his business or to deal with his property or to carry on satisfactorily many of the affairs of life, if he could not count upon the continued recognition of the principles of law in effect when he is compelled to act. It would be impossible for a lawyer to give any dependable advice to a client. If the courts were free to apply to each particular case the personal views of the particular judge or judges sitting, or if a judge were free to settle controversies in accordance with his own personal desires, the conduct of business would involve an added hazard and the decision of controversies between litigants would lose all semblance of justice or fairness. Confidence in the honesty and integrity of the courts and in their impartiality could not be maintained. We should have a government of men and not of laws.

The acceptance of the doctrine of stare decisis was a gradual one. . . . It was not . . . until the latter half of the nineteenth century that even in England the doctrine became established in its most rigid form.[10] At the present time, a decision by the final court of appeal in England upon a point raised in a case before the court and actually passed upon and decided by the court, is regarded as binding, not only upon all inferior courts but upon the appellate court itself, if and when the same point is presented to it. The rule established can be changed only by an act of Parliament. The real test of the doctrine arises, of course, only when the judges in a given case are convinced that the rule established by the earlier decision is wrong and yet apply it in the case before them. Contrary to the weight of authority in the United States, the House of Lords has applied its rigid doctrine of stare decisis even where the earlier decision was made by an evenly divided court, the effect of the even division being an affirmance of the judgment of the lower court.[11]

It does not appear that the courts of the United States ever accepted the rigid doctrine now held by the English courts.[12] A distinguished scholar, nevertheless, is authority for the statement that, on the whole, the stare decisis doctrine in the United States approximated that of the English courts up to the beginning of the twentieth century. He says that, beginning with that century, a decided difference appeared in the attitude of the courts towards the maxim, and that this change of attitude may be attributed to what Dean Pound characterizes as the "socialization of the law." [13]

---

[10] Attorney Gen. v. Windsor, 8 H.L. Cases 389; 11 Eng. Rep. 481 (1860). Beamish v. Beamish, 9 H.L. Cases 274; 11 Eng. Rep. 481 (1861). London Street Tramways, Ltd. v. The London County Council, 1898 App. Cas. 375.

[11] Beamish v. Beamish, *supra*.

[12] Gray, Judicial Precedents (1895) 9 Harv. L. Rev. 27.

[13] Albert Kocourek and Harold Koven, Renovation of the Common Law Through Stare Decisis (1934) 29 Ill. L. Rev. 971; Arthur L. Goodhart, Case Law in England and America (1929) 15 Corn. L.Q. 173.

If the doctrine of the American courts is not the rigid one of the English courts, it becomes important to determine just what the American doctrine is. There have been various attempts to phrase it. Two of those attempts seem to have been more successful than the others and have produced definitions which have received wide approval. The first is the definition by Kent:[14]

"A solemn decision upon a point of law arising in any given case becomes an authority in a like case because it is the highest evidence which we can have of the law applicable to the subject, and the judges are bound to follow that decision so long as it stands unreversed, unless it can be shown that the law was misunderstood or misapplied in that particular case."

The second definition, formulated by Daniel H. Chamberlain in a prize essay written in 1885 for the New York State Bar Association, reads as follows:

"That a deliberate or solemn decision of a court or judge made after argument on a question of law fairly arising in a case and necessary to its determination is an authority or binding precedent in the same court or in other courts of equal or lower rank in subsequent cases where 'the very point' is again in controversy; but that the degree of authority belonging to such a precedent depends of necessity on its agreement with the spirit of the times or the judgment of subsequent tribunals upon its correctness as a statement of the existing or actual law; and that the compulsion or exigency of the doctrine is, in the last analysis, moral and intellectual rather than arbitrary or inflexible." [15]

This last statement, it will be observed, was framed prior to the lessened emphasis upon the maxim observed in the decisions after the beginning of the twentieth century. An examination of the authorities leads to the conclusion that this statement rather accurately summarizes the American doctrine then and today.

The acceptance of this statement, however, as the true rule of stare decisis in this country will lead to confusion in thought unless one is careful to observe that on many occasions a judge or an author, when referring to the rule by name, has in mind the inflexible rule of the English courts. When the United States Supreme Court, for instance, has said, as it frequently has, that the doctrine is not inflexible or inexorable, it has reference to the strict rule, for the flexibility of the stated rule is perfectly obvious.

The American rule, then, does not destroy the value of prior decisions nor deny that they should be regarded as controlling until authoritatively reversed. Mr. Justice Brandeis, one of the early leaders in the attack upon the rigid rule, has said:

"Stare decisis is usually the wise policy because in most matters it is more important that the applicable rule of law be settled than that it be settled right.

---

[14] I Kent's Commentaries (14th ed. 1896) 475. If the previous decision has been made in the same case, it becomes the "law of the case" and is generally regarded as absolutely binding. Gange Lumber Co. v. Rowley 22 Wn. (2d) 250, 155 P. (2d) 802 (1945). But see Johnson v. Cadillac Motor Co., 261 Fed. 878, 886 (1919). It is also almost the universal rule that an inferior court is bound by the decisions of the superior court until it is overruled . . .

[15] *Supra* note 7.

This is commonly true, even where the error is a matter of serious concern, provided correction can be had by legislation." [16]

And Mr. Justice Cardozo, another acknowledged liberal, has written in his masterful essay on "The Nature of the Judicial Process":

"I think adherence to precedent should be the rule and not the exception." [17]

If, then, the binding effect of precedent is to be recognized as the general rule, when or under what circumstances is it to be disregarded?

In the first place, it is agreed that a previous decision, to be binding, must be upon the identical point of law involved in the succeeding case. In the English courts, the emphasis seems to have been placed upon the decision of the earlier court and not upon the reasons given for it. In the United States, although greater consideration has been given to the opinion, it is likewise the actual decision which governs.[18] As a corollary, it is also generally agreed that the decision of the court upon a point not properly before it and not actually raised in the case is not binding as a precedent; obiter dicta are in no wise controlling. It would seem that one decision on a particular point should constitute a sufficient precedent,[20] but that has not been the view of some courts.[21] . . . If it be a single decision,[23] a case of first impression, or one of a line of cases, if it be a decision of long standing, or a recent one upon which the public has had no time to act, if the opinion is written by a judge of acknowledged ability or eminence, its importance as a precedent may be increased or diminished.

In addition, the weight to be given to a previous decision is affected greatly by the character of the question which has been decided. If the rule in question is a rule of property or a rule affecting trade, business or commerce, in reliance upon which the people have acted for a long period of time, the courts are slow to upset it. If the matter is one which can be easily changed by the legislature and the legislature has had an opportunity to act and has not done so, the courts will assume that the earlier rule has not been found unsatisfactory.[25]

In criminal cases, a change in an applicable rule has the appearance of *ex post facto* legislation. In interpreting a criminal statute, therefore, the court is very

---

[16] Burnet v. Coronado Oil & Gas Co., 285 U.S. 405 (1931). See Smith v. Allwright, 313 U.S. 299 (1944); Louis B. Boudin, The Problem of Stare Decisis in Our Constitutional Theory (1931) 8 N.Y.U.L.Q. Rev. 589.

[17] Benjamin Cardozo, The Nature of the Judicial Process (1921) 149.

[18] Max Radin, Case Law and Stare Decisis (1933) 33 Col. L. Rev. 210; John C. Gardner, A Comparison of the Doctrine of Judicial Precedent in American Law and in Scots Law (1940) 52 Juridical Rev. 144; Herman Oliphant, A Return to Stare Decisis (1928) 14 A.B.A.J. 71, 159.

[20] Max Radin, Case Law and Stare Decisis (1933) 33 Col. L. Rev. 201.

[21] Quaker Realty Co. v. Labasse, 131 La. 996, 60 So. 661, 665 (1913); McDonald v. Davey, 22 Wash. 366, 60 Pac. 1116 (1900).

[23] Raphael v. Morris Plan Industrial Bank (C.C.A., 2d Cir.), 146F. (2d) 340 (1944).

[25] But see criticism of this assumption by Mr. Justice Frankfurter in Helvering v. Hallock, 309 U.S. 106 (1934). [Note: Courts have often *not* made the assumption, and gone on to overrule—as we shall later see.—Editor]

likely to regard the former interpretation as having become in effect a part of the statute and not thereafter subject to change by the court.[26] The same principle has been applied to the interpretation of other types of statutes upon which the business community can be said to have relied.[27] On the other hand, on questions of procedure or evidence, our courts have felt less firmly bound by prior decisions.[28]

It is on questions of constitutional law, however, that the courts of this country have been most ready to decline to follow precedent. Justice Brandeis has expressed the feeling of many of the judges, including the majority of the present United States Supreme Court:[29]

"But in cases involving the Federal Constitution, where correction through legislative action is practically impossible, this court has often overruled its earlier decisions. The court bows to the lessons of experience and the force of better reasoning, recognizing that the process of trial and error so fruitful in the physical sciences is appropriate also in the judicial functions.

"In cases involving the Federal Constitution, the position of this court is unlike that of the highest court of England, where the policy of stare decisis was formulated and is strictly applied to all classes of cases. Parliament is free to correct any judicial error and the remedy may be promptly invoked. . . ."

*   *   *

An unfortunate logical consequence of an overruling decision under present legal theory is its retroactive effect. Parties who have dealt in reliance upon the earlier decision suddenly find that the law upon which they had a right to rely has been changed. Acts which were at the time they were committed legal may suddenly turn out to have been illegal.[39]

The courts have tried to avoid this injustice in various ways. In the case of the interpretation of statutes, they have established the doctrine that the construction of a statute by the court becomes in effect a part of that statute.[41] It cannot be changed except by act of the legislature. This is particularly true of penal statutes. Some courts have applied the old law to the case at bar but announced that in

---

[26] Robert Freeman, *The Protection Afforded Against the Retroactive Operation of an Overruling Decision* (1918) 18 Col. L. Rev. 230; Florida Forest & Park Service v. Strickland, 154 Fla. 472, 18 S. (2d) 152 (1944); State v. Mellenberger, 163 Ore. 103, 95 P. (2d) 709 (1944); 128 A.L.R. 1506 . . . ; Commonwealth v. Trousdale, 297 Ky. 724, 181 S.W. (2d) 254 (1944).
[27] Pouch v. Prudential Ins. Co., 204 N.Y. 281, 97 N.E. 731 (1912); Yakima Valley Bank & Trust Co. v. Yakima County, 149 Wash. 552, 271 Pac. 820 (1928); Falconer v. Simmons, 51 W. Va. 172, 41 S.E. 193 (1902).

[28] State v. Brunn, 22 Wn. (2d) 120, 154 P. (2d) 826 (1945), overruling earlier cases on the meaning of "double jeopardy." Whittaker v. Lane, 128 Va. 317, 104 S.E. 252 (1920).
[29] *Supra,* note 16.
[39] *Supra,* note 28.
[41] Henges v. Dentler, 33 Pa. 496 (1858); Farrior v. New England Mort. Security Co., 92 Ala. 176, 9 So. 532 (1891); Gelpcke v. Dubuque, 1 Wall. 175 (U.S. 1864); Douglas v. Pike County, 25 L. ed. 968 (1880); Loeb v. Trustees of Columbia Township, 179 U.S. 472 (1900). [Note: Not all courts accept such a doctrine.—Editor]

the future they would apply a new rule.[42] Sometimes the courts have clung to the old rule in the case before them but called the attention of the legislature to the fact that the court believed the rule to be wrong and suggested its change by the legislature.

It has been advocated also by certain writers that the courts can protect against such injustices, either by changing their view that the decision of a court is merely evidence of the law and regarding their decision as actually establishing the law, in which case a change of decision would merely mean a change of the law in the future; or, without changing their view of the nature of court decisions, they could adopt the principle that their decisions as to the law should have no retroactive effect. The great objection voiced to the latter suggestion is that such action would be nothing but sheer judicial legislation, to which, however, the rather effective answer has been made:

"If overruling a prior decision has not been condemned as amounting to judicial legislation, it is difficult to see how giving an overruling decision prospective effect only would be any more a matter of legislation." [43]

. . . It has been suggested in high quarters that the cause for [present] lessened respect for precedent is the tremendous output of judicial decisions. It is said that the multiplication of precedents is having the same effect upon their value as inflation has, or would have, upon the value of the dollar.[45] It is doubtless true that the great increase in the number of judicial opinions has had the effect of depreciating the value of precedent. The real cause, however, would seem to lie much deeper. We are in a period of great social and political change. Conceptions which have seemed to many established and fundamental have been questioned and modified or discarded. There is no longer, even among lawyers, a general agreement as there was in the earlier days upon fundamental legal and political principles. These changes were beginning to be felt in the latter part of the last century, but it has not been until comparatively recent years that individuals imbued with the new views have, in large numbers, obtained positions on our courts . . .

Undoubtedly, too, the methods of teaching in our law schools have tended to produce the result we are observing. The case system and the critical analysis of all decisions and the thorough examination of the reasons which lie behind them, all tend to lessen the respect for the omniscience of judges and the authority of precedent.

If one is to judge from the opinions of our courts, no change in the doctrine of stare decisis, as formulated in America, is likely. It is possible that the courts will go further than they have gone in protecting against the unjust retroactive effect of overruling decisions. . . .

---

[42] State v. Bell, 136 N.C. 674, 49 S.E. 163 (1904); State v. Longine, 109 Miss. 125, 67 So. 902 (1915). See also Great Northern Ry. Co. v. Sunburst Oil & Refining Co., 287 U.S. 358 (1932).

[43] Albert Kocourek and Harold Koven, Renovation of the Common Law Through Stare Decisis (1945) 29 Ill. L. Rev. 971, at 996.

[45] Mr. Justice Jackson in (1944) 30 A.B.A.J., 334-5.

EDITORIAL NOTE: The PROBLEM of the RETROACTIVE EFFECT
of the OVERRULING of PRIOR DECISIONS

It has been asserted that courts in our time, particularly the United States
Supreme Court, are overruling precedents to a greater extent than they once
did. Supreme Court statistics support this assumption, but not overwhelm-

The following table is from Ulmer, An Empirical Analysis of Selected Aspects
of Lawmaking of the United States Supreme Court, 8 J. Pub. L. 414, 432 (1959):

TABLE VI. TOTAL CASES DISPOSED OF, APPELLATE DOCKET
UNITED STATES SUPREME COURT, AS COMPARED TO TOTAL
OVERRULING CASES, 1880-1955 TERMS *

Term Year	OR†	Cases	Term Year	OR†	Cases	Term Year	OR†	Cases
1880	2	365	1906	0	438	1932	0	906
1881	0	400	1907	0	393	1933	1	1025
1882	2	390	1908	0	430	1934	0	926
1883	0	450	1909	0	395	1935	1	986
1884	1	464	1910	0	455	1936	1	941
1885	0	440	1911	0	499	1937	2	1004
1886	2	451	1912	0	576	1938	3	922
1887	2	414	1913	1	593	1939	3	942
1888	0	417	1914	0	539	1940	6	979
1889	1	458	1915	1	547	1941	3	1166
1890	0	610	1916	1	637	1942	4	992
1891	1	496	1917	2	619	1943	5	960
1892	0	414	1918	0	669	1944	0	1249
1893	1	500	1919	1	602	1945	1	1161
1894	1	406	1920	0	598	1946	1	1366
1895	0	499	1921	1	595	1947	1	1172
1896	0	434	1922	1	760	1948	3	1199
1897	0	372	1923	0	655	1949	1	1182
1898	0	529	1924	1	758	1950	0	1216
1899	1	371	1925	0	844	1951	1	1223
1900	0	368	1926	0	885	1952	0	1288
1901	0	375	1927	0	857	1953	0	1307
1902	0	423	1928	1	822	1954	0	1363
1903	0	449	1929	1	790	1955	0	1637
1904	0	402	1930	1	893			
1905	0	463	1931	1	883			

* Source of the appellate data: Annual Report of the Attorney General
of the United States (various years).
† OR = Number of Overruling Cases—Editor

ingly (see table page 172), and the issue is complicated by the fact that the Supreme Court, like other courts, has been apt to effect a sub rosa over-ruling by "distinguishing" prior cases on dubious grounds.

Since socio-economic conditions have been changing more rapidly, we should expect judge-made law to change faster too. But, it is sometimes argued, courts should look to legislatures to make the necessary changes. One of the reasons advanced in support of this position is that legislative change will generally be prospective—it will look to the future only—but the judicial overruling of precedent will have retrospective impact on all claims arising out of transactions and events which took place prior to the overruling, including the claim involved in the very lawsuit which culmi-nated in the overruling decision.[1] The 1861 Wisconsin case is, of course, an example of such retroactivity.

Constitutional Limits in General. There are constitutional limits upon the power of every law-making agency—legislatures, executive, and ad-ministrative agencies, as well as courts—to give retroactive effect to changes in the law which it makes. Article I, section 9 of the United States Constitution prohibits Congress, and section 10 prohibits the states, from passing any "ex post facto" law or bill of attainder. Since early days, the ex post facto prohibition has been confined to retroactive penal legislation[2] —the legislature may not make an act criminal which was not criminal when committed. The bill of attainder provision, according to the Supreme Court, prohibits all "legislative acts, no matter what their form, that apply either to named individuals or to easily ascertainable members of a group in such a way as to inflict punishment on them without a judicial trial." United States v. Lovett, 328 U.S. 303, 315 (1946).

Retroactive legislation which is not penal may raise questions under other provisions of the United States Constitution. Article I, section 10 prohibits the states from passing any law impairing the obligation of contracts. The Fifth Amendment forbids Congress, and the Fourteenth the states, to deprive any person of life, liberty, or property without due process of law. It is a rare case, however, in which the legislature seeks to act retroactively, even in the non-penal field.[3]

On the other hand, changes in law effected by judicial decision normally apply retroactively. Yet neither the ex post facto law prohibition nor the contract clause of the Constitution has been held to apply to retroactive deci-

---

[1] See, e.g., Knecht v. Saint Mary's Hospital, 392 Pa. 75, 140 A. 2d 30 (1958) where the court deemed prospective legislative change preferable to judicial overruling of an established common-law rule—the im-munity of charitable hospitals from liability for employees' torts against hospital pa-tients.

[2] Calder v. Bull, 3 Dall. 386 (U.S. 1798); cf. Cummings v. Missouri, 4 Wall. 277,

316 (U.S. 1867) with Harisiades v. Shaugh-nessy, 342 U.S. 580, 595 (1952).

[3] For a discussion of the limits imposed by the due process clause upon the power of the legislature to pass retroactive non-penal legislation, see Hochman, The Supreme Court and the Constitutionality of Retro-active Legislation, 73 Harv. L. Rev. 692 (1960).

sions by the courts.[4] And only in very rare cases has the retrospective application of judicial decisions been held to violate the due process clause. One of these rare cases was Brinkerhoff-Faris Co. v. Hill, 281 U.S. 673 (1930), wherein a taxpayer sued in a state court to enjoin the collection of a tax it contended was discriminatory and therefore violative of the Fourteenth Amendment. The highest state court had previously construed the state statutes to give the taxpayer no remedy before the State Tax Commission but to confine him to the type of court action brought in this case. Now the highest state court overruled its earlier interpretation and held that the taxpayer's remedy was before the Tax Commission in the first instance. So it dismissed the suit. By this time, an application to the Tax Commission for relief was barred by the Statute of Limitations. The United States Supreme Court unanimously reversed the dismissal on the ground that it constituted a violation of due process. "If the judgment is permitted to stand, deprivation of plaintiff's property is accomplished without its ever having had an opportunity to defend against the exaction . . ."

Barriers to Retroactive Application to Other Claimants. What about the impact of judicial retroactivity on persons with claims similar to those of the particular litigants? Here, too, the judicial decision is normally retroactive, though again the due process limitation may be applied. There are additional limitations, too. One is the doctrine of res judicata. Thus if the similar claim has already been brought to court and adjudicated and the time for appeal has expired (or the appeal itself has been finally adjudicated), the decision will generally be unaffected by the overruling decision. So, for example, the injured employee who collected damages in the 1860 Wisconsin case did not have to return the money to his employer when the overruling 1861 case was decided. If he had been sued for the return of the money, he could have pleaded "res judicata"—the matter has been adjudicated—and won. Otherwise, there would never be an end to any lawsuit.

Still, a concern for the individual has barred the rigid application of the res judicata doctrine in the administration of criminal justice. Prisoners have been released from confinement upon a showing, in a habeas corpus proceeding, that they would not have been convicted in the light of subsequent judicial decisions. See the cases cited by Field, The Effect of an Unconstitutional Statute 153, n. 7 (1935), and Eskridge v. Washington State Board of Prison Terms and Paroles, 357 U.S. 214 (1958), which we shall consider shortly.

There have also been occasional departures from the res judicata doctrine in non-criminal cases. For example, in United States v. Ohio Power Co., 353 U.S. 98 (1957), a taxpayer, Ohio Power, filed suit in the United States Court of Claims to recover an alleged overpayment of taxes and won a judgment in its favor. The Supreme Court denied the Government's petition for certiorari in October 1955, its petition for rehearing in December 1955 and its second petition for rehearing in May 1956. But in June 1956 the

---

[4] Ross v. Oregon, 227 U.S. 150 (1913); Tidal Oil v. Flanagan, 263 U.S. 444 (1924).

Court, on its own motion, granted the Government a rehearing so that the case could be considered by it together with two other cases then pending and presenting the same question. These two cases were decided against the taxpayer and so in 1957 the Court in a 4 to 3 decision reversed the Court of Claims judgment in favor of the Ohio Power Co. In a per curiam opinion, the majority simply said: "We have consistently ruled that the interest in finality of litigation must yield where the interests of justice would make unfair the strict application of our rules."

The dissenting opinion, written by Justice Harlan, recognized that "finality of adjudication in this Court ultimately depends on the Court's self-restraint" but stressed the law's "deep-rooted policy that adjudication must at some time become final." Justice Harlan continued: "I can think of nothing more unsettling to lawyers and litigants, and more disturbing to their confidence in the evenhandedness of the Court's processes, than to be left in the kind of uncertainty which today's action engenders, as to when their cases may be considered finally closed in this Court." The Justice acknowledged that criminal cases presented considerations not found in civil cases.

A second doctrine—in addition to res judicata—which may bar the retroactive application of an overruling decision to other claims is that represented by the Statute of Limitations. Such a statute is an act of the legislature which prescribes the period of time, after the events or transaction giving rise to a claim took place, within which a lawsuit must be brought to enforce the claim. If the lawsuit is not brought within the specified time, the claimant usually loses his right to any remedy he might otherwise have.[5] Thus, the specified period (e.g., one, two, or three years) for many claims may have expired by the time the overruling decision is handed down.

"Prospective Overruling": the Sunburst Technique and Its Variant. Even in cases where a judge knew that none of the foregoing barriers—due process, res judicata, statute of limitations—would apply so as to bar the retroactive impact of his overruling decision, he might still hesitate to impose retroactive liabilities and consequent hardships upon an indefinite number of persons who acted in reliance upon the old law. (This concern in itself is a factor which induces judges to follow precedent.) Hence, to facilitate change and yet satisfy the expectations which existing law engenders, some courts have applied their overruling decisions prospectively only. The United States Supreme Court upheld the power of a state court to do so in Great Northern Railway Co. v. Sunburst Oil and Refining Co., 287 U.S. 358 (1932).

Prior to this decision, the Montana Supreme Court had ruled, in 1921,

---

[5] The purpose of a statute of limitations is to prevent the prosecution of stale, and possibly fraudulent, claims which are difficult to defend against after a great lapse of time because of the disappearance of witnesses, faulty memories of events long past, etc. The statute gives every individual the security of knowing that after the lapse of a specified period of time, he is free of any claims that might otherwise be made against him.

that if railroad freight charges paid by a shipper are later found to be excessive by the state railroad commission, the shipper could sue to recover the excess. Some years later, Sunburst, a shipper, sued a railroad in such a situation. The Montana Supreme Court then announced that its 1921 ruling was erroneous and would not be followed in the future, but that the plaintiff-shipper in the case before it would be permitted to recover because it had relied on the 1921 holding. In the Supreme Court, the railroad maintained that it was being deprived of due process of law, in violation of the Fourteenth Amendment, because the Montana court was applying a rule of law it admitted to be wrong. The United States Supreme Court was unanimous in rejecting this argument in the Sunburst case. Justice Cardozo wrote: "We think the federal constitution has no voice upon the subject. A state in defining the limits of adherence to precedent may make a choice for itself between the principle of forward operation and that of relation backward. It may say that decisions of its highest court, though later overruled, are law none the less for intermediate transactions. Indeed there are cases intimating, too broadly . . . that it *must* give them that effect; but never has doubt been expressed that it *may* so treat them if it pleases, whenever injustice or hardship will thereby be averted. . . . On the other hand, it may hold to the ancient dogma that the law declared by its courts had a Platonic or ideal existence before the act of declaration, in which event the discredited declaration will be viewed as if it had never been, and the reconsidered declaration as law from the beginning . . . The alternative is the same whether the subject of the new decision is common law . . . or statute. . . ."

Though prospective overruling has thus been sanctioned by the United States Supreme Court, Justice Traynor of the California Supreme Court complained in 1959: "We have not begun to make use as we should of the sensible solution approved nearly a generation ago in the Sunburst case. . . . One who has invoked this solution to no avail may be permitted to lament that it has met with such resistance [citing California cases]. The alternative is to live uneasily with an unfortunate precedent by wearing it thin with distinctions that at last compel a cavalier pronouncement, heedless of the court's failure to make a frank overruling, that it must be deemed to have revealed itself as overruled by its manifest erosion. It must be cold comfort to bewildered counsel to ruminate that the precedent on which he relied was never expressly overruled because it so patently needed to be." [6]

The fear is sometimes expressed that adoption of the policy of prospective overruling will discourage the bringing or defense of lawsuits in order to get a change of law since the party that will be successful in securing the change will also be deprived of its benefit. This fear is probably exaggerated. We are told that in "one jurisdiction which has consistently given over-

[6] Traynor, Comment on Courts and Law-making, in Legal Institutions Today and Tomorrow 54, The Centennial Conference Volume of the Columbia Law School (Paulsen ed. 1959).

ruling decisions only prospective effect, there have been at least twelve appeals in the last ten years which successfully obtained the overruling of prior decisions." [7] One or another party may have an incentive to secure a change in law, even if only for the future, because he wishes to engage in a future course of conduct which he would like to see governed by the changed rule he seeks.

Nevertheless, to allay the fear of discouraging litigation seeking change, some courts have applied the overruling decision to the case which occasioned it, but have otherwise given it only prospective effect. For example, in Molitor v. Kaneland Community Unit District No. 302, 163 N.E. 2d 89 (Ill. 1959), a pupil riding in a school bus was injured when the bus left the road, hit a culvert, exploded and burned. He sued the school district, claiming that the negligence of its employee, the bus driver, caused the accident. In reversing a long-standing rule that school districts were immune from such liability, the Illinois Supreme Court said:

> In here departing from stare decisis because we believe justice and policy require such departure, we are nonetheless cognizant of the fact that retrospective application of our decision may result in great hardship to school districts which have relied on prior decisions upholding the doctrine of tort immunity of school districts. For this reason we feel justice will best be served by holding that, except as to the plaintiff in the instant case, the rule herein established shall apply only to cases arising out of future occurrences. . . . At least two compelling reasons exist for applying the new rule to the instant case while otherwise limiting its application to cases arising in the future. First, if we were to merely announce the new rule without applying it here, such announcement would amount to mere dictum. Second, and more important, to refuse to apply the new rule here would deprive appellant of any benefit from his effort and expense in challenging the old rule which we now declare erroneous. Thus, there would be no incentive to appeal the upholding of precedent since appellant could not in any event benefit from a reversal invalidating it. . . .
>
> Although ordinarily the cases which have invoked the doctrine of prospective operation have involved contract or property rights or criminal responsibility, the basis of the doctrine is reliance upon an overruled precedent. Despite the fact that the instant case is one sounding in tort, it appears the 'reliance test' has been met here. We do not suggest that the tort itself was committed in reliance on the substantive law of torts, i.e., the bus driver did not drive negligently in reliance on the doctrine of governmental immunity, but rather that school districts and other municipal corporations have relied upon immunity and that they will suffer undue hardship if abolition of the immunity doctrine is applied retroactively. In reliance on the immunity doctrine, school districts have failed to adequately insure themselves against liability. In reliance on the immunity doctrine, they have probably failed to investigate past accidents which they would have investigated had they known they might later be held responsible therefor. Our present decision will eliminate much of the hardship which might be incurred by school districts as a result of their reliance on the overruled doctrine, and at the same time reward appellant for having afforded us the opportunity of changing an outmoded and unjust rule of law. . . .

[7] Note, 60 Harv. L. Rev. 437, 440 (1947), citing, as examples, Button v. Drake, 302 Ky. 517, 195 S.W. 2d 66 (1946); Prewitt v. Supreme Council of Royal Arcanum, 302 Ky. 301, 194 S.W. 2d 633 (1946).

A dissenting opinion argued that the majority "included within the ambit of its opinion the action of the plaintiff, while the elements of reliance and ensuing hardship were as real and present with this defendant as with other potential defendant school districts which escaped liability by virtue of the prospective application of the court's opinion." It continued:

> The principle announced by the court is an aborted offspring of the Sunburst theory. It is without legal justification other than that the plaintiff should be rewarded for bringing the action, and it has thwarted the reasonable expectations of the well-intentioned governing body of defendant school district. . . .
>
> Eighteen pupils of defendant school district were riding on its bus on March 10, 1958, when the bus crashed into a culvert which resulted in an explosion of the gasoline tank whereby most of them were burned and injured. . . . When we consider that under the court's decision only Thomas Molitor can recover even though the other pupils were similarly injured in the same accident, the position of the court becomes even less tenable. . . .[8]

It is a striking fact that the United States Supreme Court, in overruling its own decisions, has not experimented with the Sunburst doctrine. For example, in Griffin v. Illinois, 351 U.S. 12 (1956), the Court, for the first time, held that it was a violation of the constitutional guarantee of the equal protection of the laws for Illinois to limit full direct appellate review of criminal convictions to cases in which the appellate court was furnished with a stenographic transcript of the trial proceedings, without in some way taking care of indigent defendants who were unable to pay for such a transcript. The Court extended the benefit of the new rule to the criminal defendant before it and apparently contemplated that it would also retroactively benefit all convicted prisoners similarly deprived of their constitutional rights. In a concurring opinion, Justice Frankfurter, citing Sunburst, urged the Court to foreclose this possibility but to give the instant defendant the benefit of the new doctrine (thus actually favoring a Molitor rather than a Sunburst approach). Two years later, the Griffin rule was applied to benefit a prisoner who, twenty-one years before, had been denied the right to appeal to the Washington Supreme Court because he had failed to furnish his own transcript; his claim of right to a free transcript, because of indigence, had been denied. Eskridge v. Washington State Board of Prison Terms and Paroles, 357 U.S. 214 (1958). Justices Harlan and Whitaker dissented, urging that "the Griffin case, decided in 1956, should not be applied to this conviction occurring in 1935."

Legislative Nullification of Judicial Retroactivity. On occasion, the Congress has intervened to mitigate hardships it thought would be inflicted by the retroactive application of the Supreme Court's overruling decisions.

---

[8] The policy followed in the Molitor case was also adopted in Michigan and Wisconsin (Parker v. Port Huron Hospital, 361 Mich. 1, 105 N.W. 2d 1 (1960); Kojis v. Doctors' Hospital, 107 N.W. 2d 131, supp. opinion 107 N.W. 2d 292 (Wis. 1961). On Illinois legislative reaction to the Molitor decision, see 54 Nw. L. Rev. 588 (1959).

The Molitor policy was also employed in Durham v. United States, 214 F. 2d 862 (D.C. Cir. 1954), which established a new test to determine the sanity of the accused in a criminal case. See, too, Warring v. Colpoys, 122 F. 2d 642 (D.C. Cir. 1941), cert. den., 314 U.S. 678 (1942).

Examples of such decisions are Helvering v. Gerhardt, 304 U.S. 405 (1938) and Graves v. New York ex rel. O'Keefe, 306 U.S. 466 (1939), where the Supreme Court overruled prior decisions holding that (1) salaries of officers and employees of the federal government and its instrumentalities were immune from state income taxation and (2) a similar immunity from federal income taxation attached to state salaries. Though requested to do so, the Court refused to give the overruling decisions only prospective effect. To relieve the government employees from accumulated tax liability for the preceding years when their salaries supposedly had been immune, Congress, less than 3 weeks after the O'Keefe case, passed the Public Salaries Taxing Act, 53 Stat. 574. This law exempted state employees from liability under the federal income tax for past years, if their state exempted federal employees from liability under the state income tax for past years. Naturally, the states reciprocated.

Court or Legislature. Courts are more reluctant to overrule prior decisions when the fear of the retroactive effect of such action is combined with the fact that the legislature considered the matter and failed to make any change. A good example is the case of professional baseball under the antitrust laws. In Federal Baseball Club of Baltimore v. National League of Professional Baseball Clubs, 259 U.S. 200 (1922), the Court decided that professional baseball was not a business in interstate commerce within the scope of the federal antitrust laws. More than 30 years later, the Court admitted that the 1922 baseball ruling was at best of dubious validity and that it would hold the other way if it were free to do so. But it refused to overrule the 1922 decision, saying: "Congress has had the ruling under consideration but has not seen fit to bring such business under the antitrust laws by legislation having prospective effect. The business has thus been left for thirty years to develop, on the understanding that it was not subject to existing antitrust legislation. The present cases ask us to overrule the prior decision and, with retrospective effect, hold the legislation applicable. We think that if there are evils in this field which now warrant application to it of the antitrust laws it should be by legislation." Toolson v. New York Yankees, 346 U.S. 356 (1953). The Court gave no consideration to the possibility of overruling the 1922 precedent prospectively.

Yet, apparently, the Court was not concerned about the element of retroactivity in its decisions holding the antitrust laws applicable to professional boxing and professional football. United States v. International Boxing Club, 348 U.S. 236 (1955) and Radovich v. National Football League, 352 U.S. 445 (1957). In Radovich, the Court pointed out that bills had been introduced to exempt organized professional sports from the antitrust laws but that none had passed. Again, the Court took the position that "the orderly way" to eliminate the discrimination between baseball and the other sports, "if any there be," was by legislation and not by court decision.

Justice Frankfurter among others dissented in the Boxing and Football cases, asserting in the former case: "I cannot translate even the narrowest conception of stare decisis into the equivalent of writing into the Sherman

Law an exemption of baseball to the exclusion of every other sport different not one legal jot or tittle from it." Thus, he regarded the second baseball case as precedent for treating boxing and football as also exempt. But neither he nor the majority even mentioned the possibility of applying the Sunburst doctrine in the Football and Boxing cases, even though these businesses undoubtedly relied upon the baseball case in arranging their affairs.

Not all courts have hesitated to overrule prior decisions because of the failure of the legislature to make the change in the interim. Thus, when the New Jersey Supreme Court overruled its decisions holding charitable hospitals to be immune from tort liability and applied the overruling decision retroactively [Collopy v. Newark Eye and Ear Infirmary, 27 N.J. 29, 41 A. 2d 276 (1958)], it was not dissuaded from this course of action by the fact that a bill had failed of passage in 1955 which would have subjected hospitals and similar charitable institutions to tort liability for damages up to $10,000. (The dissenting opinion stressed the superiority of a legislative solution by pointing out that the bill not only would have avoided retroactivity but, by its $10,000 damage limit, also would have mitigated the consequences of the change in law.) The majority curtly remarked that the bill "has no bearing here."

The latter sentiment has a vigorous defender in Professor Henry M. Hart, Jr. He vigorously criticizes as a "fallacy" the view that "a legislature can legislate by not legislating." [9] He argues: "When the courts accord significance to the inaction of the legislature, what they are really doing, I suggest, is avoiding responsibility. They do so by shifting the responsibility to an institution which has already evaded it, or at least refrained from assuming it. . . . What, in the end, is crucial here is one's judgment about the distinctive value in the growth of the law of the judicial process of reasoned development of principle. If we value this process of growth as highly as I have urged that we ought, then we should always be reluctant to conclude that the legislature, in relation to any matter, has tried to paralyze the process. We should welcome a doctrine which says that the legislature can do this, if it can do it all, not by silence but only by unmistakable words. Only by adherence to such a doctrine can the resources of the judicial process for the infusion of reason into the law be fully utilized." [10]

[9] Hart, Comment on the Courts and Law-making, in Legal Institutions Today and Tomorrow 46-48, The Centennial Conference Volume of the Columbia Law School (Paulsen ed. 1959).

[10] Cf. the observations of the Supreme Court in overruling the long-standing rule that the wife of a defendant in a federal criminal case could not testify in his behalf: "It may be said that the court should continue to enforce the old rule, however contrary to modern experience and thought, and however opposed, in principle, to the general current of legislation and of judicial opinion it may have become, leaving to Congress the responsibility of changing it. Of course, Congress has that power; but if Congress fails to act, as it has failed in respect of the matter now under review, and the court be called upon to decide the question, is it not the duty of the court, if it possess the power, to decide it in accordance with present-day standards of wisdom and justice rather than in accordance with some outworn and antiquated rule of the past? . . ." Funk v. United States, 290 U.S. 371, 381 (1933).

Professor Hart here raises the general question of the respective uses of legislature and court—a question which in its total breadth transcends the bounds of this Note. However, the reference to the problem in this Note is supplemented by later materials in this volume throwing further light on the court v. legislature problem.

Indeed we considered one aspect of the problem at the very outset of this volume: the fact that the courts did not wait upon the legislature to decide the cases of first impression which laid down the fellow-servant doctrine. In this situation—as well as the situation in which courts are asked to overrule their decisions—the legislative alternative to judicial action may *sometimes* be preferable. It is worth remembering that for some matters, even Justice Brandeis, who never failed to appreciate the creative role of the judge, thought that the legislature was better suited to handle a new problem in the first instance. He dissented when the Supreme Court for the first time recognized a kind of property right in the news and enjoined the International News Service from copying and distributing as its own, news items which appeared in the early editions of newspapers belonging to the Associated Press or in publicly-posted AP news bulletins. Justice Brandeis acknowledged that the "unwritten law possesses capacity for growth; and has often satisfied new demands for justice by invoking analogies or by expanding a rule or principle." This process was generally satisfactory if "private interests only are involved," but "with the increasing complexity of society the public interest tends to become omnipresent" and "the creation or recognition by courts of a new private right may work serious injury to the general public, unless the boundaries of the right are definitely established and wisely guarded." This was precisely what the Court could not do in this particular case, explained the Justice. "Courts are ill-equipped to make the investigations which should precede a determination of the limitation which should be set upon any property right in news or of the circumstances under which news gathered by a private agency should be deemed affected with the public interest. Courts would be powerless to prescribe the detailed regulations essential to full enjoyment of the rights conferred or to introduce the machinery required for enforcement of such regulations. Considerations such as these should lead us to decline to establish a new rule of law in the effort to redress a newly discovered wrong, although the propriety of some remedy appears to be clear." International News Service v. Associated Press, 248 U.S. 215, 262-263, 267 (1918).

NOTES AND QUESTIONS

1. Did the 1861 overruling of the 1860 Wisconsin case have an unfair retroactive effect upon the plaintiff-employee in the 1861 case? In what way, if at all, did the 1861 plaintiff rely upon the 1860 case? Compare the kind of reliance referred to by the court in the Molitor case.

2. Didn't Priestley v. Fowler have retroactive effect? Wouldn't it have had such effect whichever way it was decided? Is there any way of avoiding the retroactive effect of a case of first impression?

3. Does the Molitor policy put a justifiable premium on a party's speed in getting a suit to court and adjudicated?

4. Should the Molitor policy apply if neither party asks for a change of law, but the change is wholly the court's idea? In Erie R.R. v. Tompkins, referred to earlier in this chapter and decided six years after the Sunburst case, the overruling of Swift v. Tyson was applied retroactively to the advantage of the defendant railroad which did not even suggest the departure from Swift v. Tyson. Should such a defendant benefit by the Molitor policy, assuming that the court would otherwise apply it?

5. What do you think of the following suggestion made by Terrell, J., concurring in State ex rel. Hawkins v. Board of Control, 83 So. 2d 20, 26 (Fla. 1955), which refused to order the immediate admission of a Negro applicant to the State University Law School who had been refused admission solely because of his race:[1] "Now after generations the same court which decided Plessy v. Ferguson, and after the states with segregated school systems in reliance on it had spent many billions of dollars in providing the latest approved school equipment, has decided that it is unconstitutional and **must** be discarded. This is in the face of the fact that there is no local agitation for the change. It seems to me that these circumstances suggest equity enough to stay desegregation until the schools provided in reliance on the doctrine of Plessy v. Ferguson have ceased to be adequate and must be replaced by others to meet the new requirement."

In its brief as amicus curiae in the School Segregation cases, which we considered in Chapter 3, the Solicitor General, on behalf of the United States, cited the Sunburst case in suggesting the possibility of integration on a grade-by-grade basis—i.e., that the first grades be integrated immediately and that one additional grade be integrated each succeeding year. This plan of integration is being attempted in certain localities.

6. If prospective overruling is resorted to, different rules of law will govern similar transactions and events, depending upon when the particular transaction or events occurred. Will this result in too confusing a system of precedent for the courts to administer? Will it make the counseling task of the lawyer too burdensome?

7. Consider whether preference should be given to (1) completely retroactive overruling (as in Erie Railroad and in Eskridge); (2) partially retroactive overruling (as in Molitor); (3) wholly prospective overruling (as in Sunburst); or (4) no overruling, prospective or otherwise, because of the assumption or even overt recommendation that a prospective change should be made by the legislature.

8. On the problems of stare decisis in general, see Douglas, "Stare Decisis," 49 Col. L. Rev. 735 (1949); Lobingier, "Precedent in Past and Present Legal Systems," 44 Mich. L. Rev. 955 (1946); Radin, "The Trail of the Calf," 32 Corn. L.Q. 137 (1946); Sprecher "The Development of the Doctrine of Stare Decisis and the Extent to Which It Should Be Applied," 31 A.B.A.J. 501 (1945); Pound, "What of Stare Decisis?" 10 Fordham L. Rev. 1 (1941); Kocourek and Koven, "Renovation of the Law Through Stare Decisis," 29 Ill. L. Rev. 971 (1935); Blaustein and Field, " 'Overruling' Opinions in the Supreme Court," 57 Mich. L. Rev. 151 (1958); Note, 60 Harv. L. Rev. 437 (1947); Note, 46 Iowa L. Rev. 600 (1961); Levy, "Realist Jurisprudence and Prospective Overruling," 109 U. of Pa. L. Rev. 1 (1960).

For similar problems in the administrative process, see Davis, Administrative Law Text 317-325 (1959); Newman, Should Official Advice Be Reliable?—Proposals as to Estoppel and Related Doctrines in Administrative Law, 53 Col. L. Rev. 374 (1953).

---

[1] The United States Supreme Court overruled the Florida court, holding, in a per curiam opinion, that "as this case involves the admission of a Negro to a graduate professional school there is no reason for delay." 350 U.S. 413 (1956).

EDITORIAL NOTE: MAY a LOWER COURT ANTICIPATE
by ITS DECISION the OVERRULING of PRECEDENT
by the HIGHEST COURT?

The answer to this question is yes and some examples of such anticipatory overruling follow.

In Fujii v. California, 38 Cal. 2d 718, 242 P. 2d 617 (1952), the California Supreme Court invalidated the state's Alien Land Law because it denied aliens the equal protection of the law in violation of the Fourteenth Amendment. Prior decisions of the United States Supreme Court, as well as of the California Supreme Court, had upheld this law which prohibited aliens then ineligible for citizenship (for the most part, Japanese) from owning agricultural land. See, for example, Terrace v. Thompson, 263 U.S. 195 (1923). But in the Fujii case, the California Supreme Court concluded that Oyama v. California, 332 U.S. 633 (1948)[1] and Takahashi v. Fish and Game Commission, 334 U.S. 410 (1948)[2] reflected a change of position on the part of the United States Supreme Court which would require it to overrule the Terrace v. Thompson line of cases if the issue were again squarely presented. In Oyama and Takahashi the Supreme Court said that it was unnecessary to reconsider Terrace v. Thompson in order to decide these cases. The state of California did not seek Supreme Court review of the decision in the Fujii case.

In 1940, with only Chief Justice Stone dissenting, the Supreme Court decided that West Virginia could validly require children of the Jehovah's Witnesses faith to salute the flag in the public schools, even though saluting was contrary to their religious scruples. Minersville School District v. Gobitis, 310 U.S. 586. Two years later, three of the justices making up the majority in Gobitis (Black, Douglas, and Murphy) announced in their dissenting opinion in Jones v. Opelika, 316 U.S. 584 (1942), that they thought Gobitis had been decided incorrectly. (In Jones v. Opelika, the Court upheld a municipal ordinance exacting a fee for the privilege of distributing Jehovah's Witnesses tracts on public streets.)

When the flag-salute issue was raised again in a three-judge district court in West Virginia, the court refused to follow the Gobitis precedent. The opinion by the highly respected Circuit Court Judge Parker, 47 F. Supp. 251, pointed out that at least four justices were now opposed to the Gobitis decision and that the majority in Jones v. Opelika distinguished Gobitis instead of relying upon it. It concluded: "Under such circumstances, and believing as we do that the flag salute here required is violative of religious

---

[1] This case invalidated the California land law provision that a transfer of realty to an eligible landholder with the consideration paid by the ineligible alien would be regarded, presumptively, as an evasion of the law. The ineligible alien had paid the consideration for a transfer to his minor son and the statutory presumption was invalidated on the ground that it deprived the child of the equal protection of the law and abridged his privileges as a citizen.

[2] This case invalidated a California law denying commercial fishing licenses to aliens ineligible for citizenship.

liberty when required of persons holding the religious views of plaintiffs, we feel that we would be recreant to our duty as judges if through a blind following of a decision which the Supreme Court itself has thus impaired as authority, we should deny protection to rights which we regard as among the most sacred of those protected by constitutional guaranties." Judge Parker correctly anticipated that the Supreme Court would affirm his decision. The Court overruled Gobitis by a 6 to 3 vote. West Virginia Board of Education v. Barnette, 319 U.S. 624 (1943). The majority was composed of Chief Justice Stone and Justices Black, Douglas, and Murphy, plus Justices Rutledge and Jackson who replaced Justices Hughes and McReynolds in the three-year interval between the two decisions. (In the same year, the Court vacated the judgment in Jones v. Opelika and invalidated the ordinance in question.)

Note also the following observations of Clark, J., in Spector Motor Service v. Walsh, 139 F. 2d 809 (2d Cir. 1944) at 814: ". . . our function cannot be limited to a mere blind adherence to precedent. We must determine with the best exercise of our mental powers of which we are capable that law which in all probability will be applied to these litigants or to others similarly situated. If this means the discovering and applying of a 'new doctrinal trend' . . . this is our task to be performed directly and straightforwardly, rather than 'artfully' dodged. . . ."

Dissenting in the same case, L. Hand, J. maintained (p. 823): "It is always embarrassing for a lower court to say whether the time has come to disregard decisions of a higher court, not yet explicitly overruled, because they parallel others in which the higher court has expressed a contrary view. I agree that one should not wait for formal retraction in the face of changes plainly foreshadowed; the higher court may not entertain an appeal in the case before the lower court, or the parties may not choose to appeal. In either event the actual decision will be one which the judges do not believe to be that which the higher court would make. But nothing has yet appeared to satisfy me that the case at bar is of that kind. . . . Nor is it desirable for a lower court to embrace the exhilarating opportunity of anticipating a doctrine which may be in the womb of time, but whose birth is distant; on the contrary, I conceive that the measure of its duty is to divine, as best it can, what would be the event of an appeal in the case before it."

See, generally, Note, Stare Decisis and the Lower Courts, 59 Colum. L. Rev. 504 (1959).

GARRISON,* *THE NATIONAL RAILROAD ADJUSTMENT BOARD*
46 Yale Law Journal 567, 583-584 (1937)

[The Board which is discussed in this article was created by a 1934 amendment to the Railway Labor Act of 1926, for the purpose of rendering judicially enforce-

* Lloyd K. Garrison practised law in New York, 1922-32, was Dean of the University of Wisconsin Law School, 1932-45, chair- man in 1934 of the National Labor Relations Board, president of the Association of American Law Schools in 1937, served with

able decisions in controversies arising out of labor contracts between railroads and labor unions.—Editor]

. . . In these various ways the Divisions [of the Adjustment Board] are busy building up their own common law, and it is curious to note how seriously their lay members treat the precedents and with what skill they are able to urge that this case should be distinguished or that analogy applied. It is interesting also to note that the "equities," save in the relatively rare "grievance" cases, of discipline or refusal to promote, are not, in theory at least, considered. All the members agree that the question in every case (save the ones just mentioned) is what the contract means, and this question must be answered as a cold-blooded matter of construction, however inequitable the outcome. That a referee, or a Division without a referee, should reach a manifestly unfair result in a particular case by strict application of the rules and precedents is considered far better than to do equity by glossing over or reading exceptions into the rules or by disregarding clear precedents.

I have received the distinct impression that laymen in a judicial position are quite as eager as lawyers in pursuing, and quite as contentious in dissecting, the available precedents; and that precedents are thus magnified not because of any notion of the social desirability of certainty but because they are a godsend to men harassed by the necessity of making up their minds in close cases and of justifying their decisions when made. I have concluded also that lay judges are fully as hardboiled as ordinary judges in cleaving to the result, however harsh, which precedent or the letter of the contract dictates, and are equally loath to commit themselves upon moot or hypothetical questions.

GRAY,* SOME THOUGHTS ON THE USE OF PRECEDENTS IN LABOR ARBITRATION
6 Arbitration Journal (new series) 135-139 (1951)

Does the doctrine of stare decisis have a place in the disposition of labor disputes through arbitration? Should decisions reached by arbitrators become precedents to be followed by other arbitrators confronted by like or similar issues? Is it desirable in that way to build what might be considered a body of common law of the collective labor agreement?

Much can be said on both sides of this question. The debate has been going on for some time and the conflicting viewpoints have been presented with clarity and vigor. Perhaps here, as elsewhere in the affairs of men, the truth lies in neither extreme. Sound policy would indicate a middle course.

Clearly, disputes commonly arise in the course of labor relations which simply cannot be resolved on the basis of rulings made elsewhere between other parties.

the National War Labor Board as general counsel and in other capacities, 1942-45, became a member of the New York firm of Paul, Weiss, Rifkind, Wharton and Garrison in 1946, and since then has often been a part-time lecturer in corporation law at N.Y.U. Law School. He has been appointed from time to time to governmental arbitration and investigatory posts.—Editor

* Herman A. Gray, Member of New York Bar; Associate Professor, New York University.

Was there "just cause" for a particular charge? Is a given employee eligible for vacation pay and, if so, for what amount? Are the machines over-manned? Or, are the men being asked to carry a work-load unreasonably burdensome? Should wage rates be adjusted upwards or downwards, and, if so, to what degree?

The determination of such questions must depend entirely on the exact wording of the particular agreement involved. Or, on the policy which should control the application of the agreement in the light of the special conditions and practices prevailing in the given plant. Little or no aid can be derived from precedents. On the contrary, reliance on precedent may produce a decision empty of reality and disruptive in its effect.

These questions are set forth merely as illustrations. Others of the same nature and which likewise do not lend themselves to successful disposition through the use of precedents will readily suggest themselves.

Yet, it is equally clear that issues of this type do not exhaust the gamut of labor controversy. There are other disputes in the determination of which the use of prior decisions not only has validity but positive value. Take the matter of wage reopenings. Such a clause usually provides that at stated intervals either party may reopen the matter of wages and, on failure to agree, the question shall be disposed of through arbitration. The operation of a provision of this kind involves two subsidiary issues.

First, what is included within the word "wages"? Is it limited to going wage rates or does it include the scale of minimum rates as well? And, to what extent may the union under a "wage" reopening clause bring in matters which bear on "take-home" pay and other economic benefits, as, for example, premium pay, bonus arrangements, welfare and pension plans?

Secondly, what are the factors which can legitimately be considered on a reopening? Does a reopening permit a general renegotiation of wages? Or, is reopening a limited proceeding designed to do no more than to keep the stipulated wage rates adjusted to shifting economic conditions so that the standards as agreed to by the parties may be maintained for the life of their collective agreement, neither lowered nor improved?

Different arbitrators have ruled differently on these questions depending on their personal views as to the purpose and function of a wage reopening clause. Such a result is not desirable. It creates uncertainty for the parties and an extreme hazard. It often leads to defeating their intent in agreeing to a wage reopening with a resultant reaction against the arbitration process as capricious, haphazard, and untrustworthy.

Here is a place where uniformity of interpretation would make for confidence and stability. If the scope of a wage reopening clause were to be settled on the basis of a line of precedents, the parties could agree to such a clause knowing in advance the nature of the obligation they were undertaking and the degree of the risk they were running.

Many arbitrations have been held over the question whether holiday pay is due when the holiday falls on a Saturday, a Sunday or some other day when the plant is normally shut down irrespective of the holiday. Arbitrators have ruled both ways. Parties cannot be sure what their rights are. It will depend on the particular person who is selected to make the decision.

There is neither reason nor justification for diversity on this question. It can well be settled by a general principle universally applicable. It makes little difference whether it is settled one way or the other so long as the rule is fixed and followed uniformly. Once that is done, parties and their counsel will know how to guide themselves and they can enter upon agreements with assurance that on this point at any rate their intentions will not be frustrated.

Or, take a new kind of dispute which is beginning to arise. The collective agreement declares that there shall be no discharge except for just cause. It is silent on the question of retirement for old age. The company institutes a rule that it will retire all workers reaching the age of sixty-five, irrespective of physical capability to continue to do the required work. Is the retirement of a worker under this rule a "discharge" within the meaning of the agreement so that it can be made a subject of grievance and arbitration? If so, is old-age "good cause"? These are issues obviously of major importance to both sides. Also, they are issues which can be successfully dealt with through principles having general applicability.

With increasing frequency we find the same provisions appearing in collective agreement after collective agreement, sometimes with only insubstantial changes in wording and often with none at all. The parties by this practice give evidence that there are areas in which uniformity and standardization are not only possible but desirable. This development should not be frustrated by diversity in interpretation and application resulting from differences in the views and attitudes of arbitrators.

To the degree that we can give in advance understanding and certainty as to the commitments which are being undertaken, we strengthen the collective agreement as an instrument for ordering and stabilizing labor relations. To the extent that we are able to free the operation of the agreement from the personality of the arbitrator, we reduce the incentive for shopping around in the selection of arbitrators. Those who are critical of labor arbitration, and not without much reason, will, on an analysis of their complaints, discover that the root of most of the present deficiencies is the continuous search carried on by the parties for arbitrators who on the basis of past performance or supposed predilections give promise of a favorable ruling.

[See also Rubin and Ponder, The Ostrich and the Arbitrator: The Use of Precedent in Arbitration of Labor Management Disputes, 13 La. L. Rev. 208 (1957); Note, Case Law or "Free Decision" in Grievance Arbitration, 62 Harv. L. Rev. 118 (1948).—Editor]

CHAPTER Five

The ADVERSARY SYSTEM

Section 1

RATIONALE of the ADVERSARY SYSTEM
and the LAWYER'S ROLE in IT

As we have seen, the adversary system of litigation is used not only to develop the rules of law applicable to the particular case but also to ascertain the facts in the case. The extent to which justice is served or defeated by relying upon the adversary system to accomplish these purposes has long been the subject of controversy. After presenting a general justification of our adversary system and some notes on the central role of the advocate in the system, we shall, in succeeding sections, proceed to an examination of the controversy.

REPORT OF THE JOINT CONFERENCE ON PROFESSIONAL RESPONSIBILITY, OF THE ASSOCIATION OF AMERICAN LAW SCHOOLS AND THE AMERICAN BAR ASSOCIATION
44 American Bar Association Journal 1159, 1160-1161 (1958) *

[A]ny arbiter who attempts to decide a dispute without the aid of partisan advocacy . . . must undertake, not only the role of judge, but that of representative for both of the litigants. Each of these roles must be played to the full without being muted by qualifications derived from the others. When he is developing for each side the most effective statement of its case, the arbiter must put aside his neutrality and permit himself to be moved by a sympathetic identification sufficiently intense to draw from his mind all that it is capable of giving,—in analysis, patience and creative power. When he resumes his neutral position, he must be able to view with distrust the fruits of this identification and be ready to reject the products of his own best mental efforts. The difficulties of this undertaking are obvious. If it is true that a man in his time must play many parts, it is scarcely given to him to play them all at once.

It is small wonder, then, that failure generally attends the attempt to dispense with the distinct roles traditionally implied in adjudication. What generally occurs in practice is that at some early point a familiar pattern will seem to emerge from the evidence; an accustomed label is waiting for the case and, without awaiting further proofs, this label is promptly assigned to it. It is a mistake to suppose that

* This Report was approved by the A.B.A. House of Delegates in February 1959 and by the A.A.L.S. in December 1958.—Editor

this premature cataloguing must necessarily result from impatience, prejudice or mental sloth. Often it proceeds from a very understandable desire to bring the hearing into some order and coherence, for without some tentative theory of the case there is no standard of relevance by which testimony may be measured. But what starts as a preliminary diagnosis designed to direct the inquiry tends, quickly and imperceptibly, to become a fixed conclusion, as all that confirms the diagnosis makes a strong imprint on the mind, while all that runs counter to it is received with diverted attention.

An adversary presentation seems the only effective means for combatting this natural human tendency to judge too swiftly in terms of the familiar that which is not yet fully known. The arguments of counsel hold the case, as it were, in suspension between two opposing interpretations of it. While the proper classification of the case is thus kept unresolved, there is time to explore all of its peculiarities and nuances.

These are the contributions made by partisan advocacy during the public hearing of the cause. When we take into account the preparations that must precede the hearing, the essential quality of the advocate's contribution becomes even more apparent. Preceding the hearing inquiries must be instituted to determine what facts can be proved or seem sufficiently established to warrant a formal test of their truth during the hearing. There must also be a preliminary analysis of the issues, so that the hearing may have form and direction. These preparatory measures are indispensable whether or not the parties involved in the controversy are represented by advocates.

Where that representation is present there is an obvious advantage in the fact that the area of dispute may be greatly reduced by an exchange of written pleadings or by stipulations of counsel. Without the participation of someone who can act responsibly for each of the parties, this essential narrowing of the issues becomes impossible. But here again the true significance of partisan advocacy lies deeper, touching once more the integrity of the adjudicative process itself. It is only through the advocate's participation that the hearing may remain in fact what it purports to be in theory: a public trial of the facts and issues. Each advocate comes to the hearing prepared to present his proofs and arguments, knowing at the same time that his arguments may fail to persuade and that his proofs may be rejected as inadequate. It is a part of his role to absorb these possible disappointments. The deciding tribunal, on the other hand, comes to the hearing uncommitted. It has not represented to the public that any fact can be proved, that any argument is sound, or that any particular way of stating a litigant's case is the most effective expression of its merits.

The matter assumes a very different aspect when the deciding tribunal is compelled to take into its own hands the preparations that must precede the public hearing. In such a case the tribunal cannot truly be said to come to the hearing uncommitted, for it has itself appointed the channels along which the public inquiry is to run. If an unexpected turn in the testimony reveals a miscalculation in the design of these channels, there is no advocate to absorb the blame. The deciding tribunal is under a strong temptation to keep the hearing moving within the boundaries originally set for it. The result may be that the hearing loses its character as an open trial of the facts and issues, and becomes instead a ritual designed to provide public confirmation for what the tribunal considers it has already established in private. When this occurs adjudication acquires the taint affecting all institutions that become subject to manipulation, presenting one aspect to the public, another to knowing participants.

These, then, are the reasons for believing that partisan advocacy plays a vital and essential role in one of the most fundamental procedures of a democratic society. But if we were to put all of these detailed considerations to one side, we should still be confronted by the fact that, in whatever form adjudication may appear, the experienced judge or arbitrator desires and actively seeks to obtain an adversary presentation of the issues. Only when he has had the benefit of intelligent and vigorous advocacy on both sides can he feel fully confident of his decision.

Viewed in this light, the role of the lawyer as a partisan advocate appears, not as a regrettable necessity, but as an indispensable part of a larger ordering of affairs. The institution of advocacy is not a concession to the frailties of human nature, but an expression of human insight in the design of a social framework within which man's capacity for impartial judgment can attain its fullest realization.

When advocacy is thus viewed, it becomes clear by what principle limits must be set to partisanship. The advocate plays his role well when zeal for his client's cause promotes a wise and informed decision of the case. He plays his role badly, and trespasses against the obligations of professional responsibility, when his desire to win leads him to muddy the headwaters of decision, when, instead of lending a needed perspective to the controversy, he distorts and obscures its true nature. . . .

EDITORIAL NOTE: FURTHER ASPECTS
of the ADVOCATE'S ROLE

In addition to the foregoing indication of the advocate's role, there have been previous instances in which we have noted the part played by lawyers in our story. We considered the implications of the lawyer's status as officer of the court and the contributions of the lawyers' briefs in the Wisconsin fellow-servant cases.

Our emphasis upon litigation, however, has obscured the lawyer's function as a counsellor to his client. The significance of this function must be appreciated if we are to comprehend the nature of our legal system fully. Litigation is a last resort for both client and lawyer. In his capacity as counsellor, the lawyer generally strives to advise, plan, and effectuate a course of action that will keep his client out of litigation. In this role, the lawyer is the agency through which the parties are able to order their own affairs, within the limits permitted by law.[1] The lawyer in a real sense "makes" and "administers" the law. "In carrying out his work as lawmaker, the lawyer is

---

[1] See Brown, Preventive Law (1950); Brown, Preventive Law and Public Rela-   tions: Improving the Legal Health of America, 39 A.B.A.J. 556 (1953).

at once the architect and builder of human relationships. He draws on his legal learning for knowledge of the legal tools and materials he can use and their capacity to bear loads and withstand stresses. At the same time he draws on his knowledge of human nature and of business practice to gauge the workability of the arrangements he is considering. In addition, he employs his skill in analyzing problems and in using language effectively to make sure that the documents embodying the arrangements he has designed cover all significant contingencies and, at the same time, do not create other risks by ambiguities of plan or language.

"Books and articles have been and are continuing to be written about the judicial process, the legislative process, the administrative process. But I suspect the first book has yet to be written about the process whereby a couple of lawyers bring two militantly hostile parties together in an office, adjudicate their disputes, draw a decree or statute called a contract to govern their conduct for the next ten years, and thereafter administer the law they have written in a way that will sensibly and faithfully carry out the legislative intent." Cavers, Legal Education and Lawyer-Made Law, 54 W. Va. L. Rev. 177, 179-181 (1952).[2]

In thus operating as a kind of judge, legislator, and administrator combined, the lawyer may be called upon to exercise great skill in the process of negotiation and compromise. He is indeed required by the A.B.A. ethical canons governing his profession to prefer such methods, when reasonably feasible, to litigation.[3] We tend also to overlook the extent to which legal disputes are disposed of by means other than litigation even after court proceedings have been initiated. A famous study by Clark and Shulman of

---

[2] Cf. Horsky, The Washington Lawyer 137 (1952): "He is consulted by his clients on a proposed course of action, a proposed contract, a proposed form of advertising, a proposed almost everything. He says no, and the proposal is abandoned or modified. To me that is just as significant as an injunction obtained by the government against the same proposal. For every occasion on which the government itself prevents some unlawful course of dealing, either in limine or after it has begun, there must be a dozen which have been prevented by the refusal of a lawyer to approve them. I am convinced that my generalization holds: private lawyers, such as the Washington lawyers who specialize in the antitrust field, do more toward enforcing the antitrust laws than ten times as big a government could ever do."

[3] Drinker, Legal Ethics, 101 (1953): "The last sentence of Canon 8 provides: 'Whenever the controversy will admit of fair ad-

justment, the client should be advised to avoid or to end the litigation.' For a lawyer whose mind is eagerly fixed on his compensation there very often occur situations where this tends to cloud his judgment as to what is best for the client. Unless a principle is involved which it is essential that the client maintain, a settlement on a reasonable basis, on a fair estimate of the relative chances of the parties, is always better for the client than litigation, involving time, expense and ill feeling, though often considerably less fees to the lawyers. Nevertheless, the lawyer will be better off in the long run in giving sound advice and good service to his client. A clause in a retainer agreement prohibiting the client from settling without the attorney's consent [has been held] void as against public policy; as [has] an agreement with the client that no part of the retainer shall be refunded in the event of a reconciliation between the parties."

judicial proceedings in New Haven County during 1919-1932, showed that only 17% of contract cases, 16% of automobile negligence cases, 21% of negligence cases other than auto, and 36% of other miscellaneous suits were finally terminated by court consideration.[4] Thus, negotiation and compromise—occurring sometimes before and sometimes after the institution of suit—seem even more significant than actual litigation in the resolution of legal disputes.

When for some reason private arrangements break down and a compromise settlement is not reached, so that litigation is resorted to, the advocate influences the outcome in a number of ways we should like to explore still further. The lawyer's creative role is manifest in the strategic choices he is called upon to make. Recall Loring's suggestion in the Farwell case. Though he was not successful in that case, Loring contributed to the development of legal doctrine because his views were ultimately accepted by a number of American courts.

Moreover, the advocate must imaginatively shape his presentation in the light of what he thinks will be most persuasive with the particular judge or jury. Skills among lawyers in this respect will vary; and different types of cases will demand different skills. Hence, a client's or law firm's choice of the man to handle a particular piece of litigation may have important consequences. As far as Government lawyers are concerned, significant variations in their qualities have been pointed out by Swisher, who contrasts a more cautious, conservative type in the Department of Justice with a more zealous, impatient type in the early New Deal agencies.[5] Freund and Stern have given us excellent accounts of the nature and consequences of the strategies of counsel in constitutional litigation over the New Deal program.[6] In Chapter 11, we refer to the influence upon the critical vote of Justice Roberts in the 1936 New York minimum wage case, of the decision of counsel to argue that the unfavorable precedent case be distinguished rather than overruled.

Wiener attributes the Supreme Court's "historic blunder" in the Cramer treason case to the Government's strategic decision not to file an "advocate's brief after the Court set the case down for reargument" but, instead, to submit a 404-page historical study of the law of treason prepared independently at the Solicitor-General's request, together with "an 88-page Government brief that was in the nature of a commentary on The Appendix."[7] It

---

[4] The study is summarized in Hurst, The Growth of American Law, 172-173 (1950). See also Note, Settlement of Personal Injury Cases in the Chicago Area, 47 Nw. U.L. Rev. 895-914 (1953).

[5] Swisher, Federal Organization of Legal Functions, 33 Am. Pol. Sci. Rev. 973 (1939).

[6] See Freund, On Understanding the Supreme Court, Chap. III (1950); Stern, The Commerce Clause and the National Economy, 59 Harv. L. Rev. 645, 883 (1946).

[7] Wiener, Effective Appellate Advocacy (1950) 9-10. Wiener points out that the Supreme Court in its Cramer decision (325 U.S. 1) treated the constitutional clause requiring two witnesses' testimony to the same overt act for a treason conviction as being a *departure* from English law—"in the face of Mr. Justice Wilson's statement

is a corollary of the adversary system, he argues, that "when the opposing positions are not strongly or argumentatively presented, the tribunal does not necessarily reach a sound result, does not necessarily ascertain the truth and may be led into egregious error." "It is my own considered view, reached after a good deal of searching cogitation, that the Cramer case stands as a living monument to that corollary."

While the advocate at the trial level is primarily influential in the fact-determination process, he must be alert about legal issues at this stage as well as at the appellate stage. The appellate court will refuse to consider issues which were not presented during the trial. For a critical discussion of this general principle, see Note, 64 Harv. L. Rev. 652 (1951). (Some aspects of the trial lawyer's role in the fact-finding process will be considered in the next section.)

Not only the substance but even the form of a court's opinion may bear the imprint of the advocate. We have seen that it is the lawyer's duty to call the court's attention to authorities that it might otherwise overlook. The diligence which counsel show in this respect will often be reflected in the court's opinion.[8] Then, too, whole sentences and paragraphs in a court's opinion may be "lifted" from the successful lawyer's brief.

Judges themselves have been quick to acknowledge the advocate's contribution to the judicial process. Federal Circuit Judge Joseph C. Hutcheson has said: "If you have ever been [a judge] you know how difficult a thing it is for a judge to decide a case which has not been well argued at the Bar. . . . If we stop to think that courts cannot make law by issuing abstract and general proclamations, that all that judges under the Constitution of the United States can do is deal with litigated cases, we are bound to see how tremendously important it is to the life and growth of the law that the lawyer be learned and able in the law; that by living it, and reading of it he be learned of life and its history, and more, that through skill and zeal in advocacy he know how to drive for his client's cause." Hutcheson, Some Observations on Stare Decisis, 32 Reports of La. State Bar Ass'n 17 (1932).

In his first year as a federal appellate judge, Harold Medina gave an address in which he explained that as an appellate lawyer he had thought that "the function of the lawyer ceased with the clarification of the question, a discussion of the authorities and a comprehensive and absolutely accurate

---

in 1790—and he had drafted the clause in 1787—that the old language was employed because of a desire to carry over the old interpretations." Neither the old English statute nor Mr. Justice Wilson's statement was referred to in either of the Cramer opinions. They had been, in Wiener's words, "lost, literally lost somewhere in the 404 pages of 'fair, dispassionate, and informative analysis.'" The 404-page historical study was written by Pro-

fessor Hurst and published as Treason in the United States, 58 Harv. L. Rev. 226-72, 395-444, 806-857 (1945).

[8] Professor Allen, however, cites numerous English cases in which the relevant authorities were not put forward by counsel. See C. K. Allen, Law in the Making, 293-297, 343-354 (5th ed. 1951). There is no reason to assume that this failing is peculiar to the English bar.

statement of the facts." He had not thought that a lawyer could persuade a judge to decide a case his way. As a judge, "my surprise number one came when I discovered that the lawyers were doing this very thing to me and I want to confess it openly and to say that in my judgment that is one of the things a good lawyer is supposed to do." "I do not mean that I am bamboozled into deciding wrongly—although that could be. I merely wish to admit that the cogency of a lawyer's argument, the skill and ingenuity with which he built up his propositions in logical sequence and the research he brought to bear upon his presentation of the case really did much more than merely clarify the issues and then leave the case for me to decide. After all, as I view the administration of American justice, it is a cooperative effort in which the best results are obtained by the interaction of the minds of the court and counsel, and it is silly to suppose that the judge loses any of his dignity or authority when he admits that the art of persuasion still flourishes." Medina, Some Reflections on the Judicial Function, 38 A.B.A.J. 107-108 (1952).

Does the adversary system put too high a premium on the abilities of a litigant's lawyer? A negative answer is commonly defended by saying that if the talents of opposing counsel are too disparate, the judge will try to correct the imbalance. Judge Hutcheson has said: "The resultant of these two equal offensive forces [the opposing attorneys] if they are equal, is good law. The resultant of these two forces, if they are not equal, is apt to be ill considered law, unless the state is fortunate enough to have on the Bench men minded like advocates who, loving the law, will, when the fight is wavering, through the weakness of a hard pressed side, throw their strength to the weaker side to hold the line of the law until the case is fully put." Hutcheson, supra at 17, 25.

It is also true, as we saw in Chap. 2, Sec. 3, that the "fight" between advocates is not of the sort which is waged with no holds barred, but rather involves numerous ethical restraints upon the antagonists. Nevertheless, as a distinguished lawyer once concluded, "The influence of powerful counsel on courts, and the unequal chances of success which follow from this alone, irrespective of the merits of a cause, are so far a result of that partiality in distributing talents for which nature is responsible that it can hardly be considered as any other than an unavoidable disturbance in the cause of justice." Warner, The Responsibilities of the Lawyer, 19 A.B.A. Reports 319, 326 (1896). The adversary system magnifies this "unavoidable disturbance."

For discussion of the lawyer's social role, as a sociologist might view it, see Hurst, The Growth of American Law c. 12, 13 (1950); Blaustein and Porter, The American Lawyer 1-63 (1954). See also Gower and Price, The Profession and the Practice of the Law in England and America, 20 Modern L. Rev. 317 (1957).

Section 2

FACT-FINDING UNDER OUR ADVERSARY SYSTEM: SOME CRITICAL VIEWS

EDITORIAL NOTE: The VIEWS of JEROME N. FRANK

As typical of the iconoclastic ideas about the worthiness of our adversary system, this chapter will present the views of Jerome Frank* and Thurman Arnold† (Frank's at this point and Arnold's in the next section). While they had their differences, they also had many things in common, in addition to ebullient personalities and a talent for putting their many and stimulating ideas into readable prose. Both were active in academic life, in political affairs, and as judges of federal Courts of Appeals. Frank had an active career at the bar and Arnold is today a busy practicing lawyer.

In his voluminous writings, of which on the present subject Courts on Trial (1949) will repay reading in its entirety, Judge Frank indicted our system of litigation for its failures in the process of fact-finding. His criticism is two-fold—(1) our system does not ensure that all the pertinent true facts in the case will be made available to the tribunal (judge and jury) and (2) the tribunal—the jury in particular—is not a competent fact-finding agency. (The next chapter, in a general analysis of the jury system, deals with his second criticism.)

Judge Frank blamed our adversary system for the fact that not all the practically available evidence was procured by the tribunal. Like Thurman Arnold, he emphasized that our system of litigation, reflecting the doctrines of individualism and laissez-faire, is based on the "fight" theory—the

---

* Jerome N. Frank (1889-1957) was Associate Judge of the United States Court of Appeals for the Second Circuit from 1941 to 1957. He was General Counsel to the Agricultural Adjustment Administration and the Federal Surplus Relief Corporation, 1933-35; Special Counsel to the Reconstruction Finance Corporation, 1935 and to the Public Works Administration, 1936-37; and Member and Chairman of the Securities and Exchange Commission, 1937-41. In the latter part of his life, he was also visiting lecturer at the Yale Law School. He was the author of Law and the Modern Mind (1930), Save America First (1938), If Men Were Angels (1942), Fate and Freedom (1945), Courts on Trial (1949) and co-author with his daughter of Not Guilty (1957).

† Thurman W. Arnold is a member of the Washington, D.C. law firm of Arnold, Fortas and Porter. He practiced law in Chicago and Laramie, Wyoming, 1914-27. He was a member of the Wyoming legislature in 1921, mayor of Laramie, 1923-24, and law lecturer at the University of Wyoming, 1921-26. He continued his academic career as Dean of the West Virginia College of Law, 1927-30 and professor of law at Yale, 1930-38. As Assistant Attorney General, 1938-43, he greatly stepped up the Government's antitrust activities, after which he served as Associate Judge of the United States Court of Appeal for the District of Columbia, 1943-45. He resigned to re-enter the practice of law. His books include Symbols of Government (1935), Folklore of Capitalism (1937), Bottlenecks of Business (1940) and Democracy and Free Enterprise (1942).

Upon Frank's death, Arnold contributed a eulogistic analysis of him as theorist and judge to a symposium on Frank, in 24 U. Chi. L. Rev. 625, 633-642 (1957).

theory that the facts in a case can best be ascertained if each side strives "as hard as it can, in a keenly partisan spirit, to bring to the court's attention the evidence favorable to that side." (Courts on Trial at 80.) Though he agreed that this theory "has invaluable qualities with which we cannot afford to dispense," Frank argued that frequently "the partisanship of the opposing lawyers blocks the uncovering of vital evidence or leads to a presentation of vital testimony in a way that distorts it." (*Ibid.* at 81.) Typical and accepted features of court-room procedure and practice are responsible, said Frank, pointing out that (1) the whole atmosphere of the courtroom bewilders witnesses; (2) lawyers, before trial, "coach" the witnesses who will appear for their clients, not only with regard to the story they will tell but also the demeanor they should assume in testifying so as to give the most favorable personal impression; (3) dishonest lawyers use this accepted practice to encourage perjury; (4) lawyers attempt to discredit adverse witnesses through exercise of the art of cross-examination, regardless of the truth of what these witnesses may be saying; (5) lawyers refuse to concede facts harmful to their clients if they think the adversary cannot prove them, and they will not help to correct inaccurate statements of witnesses favorable to their clients;[1] (6) lawyers rely, wherever possible, upon surprise as a tactic to keep the adversary from preparing to rebut particular testimony favorable to their clients; and (7) a party may not have the funds to pay for an investigation, before trial, to assemble evidence on his behalf and rebut evidence on which the other party may rely. Frank did not blame the lawyers for using the techniques mentioned, but the system of litigation which makes it their prime duty to try to win the case rather than aid the court in a mutual search for truth. (*Ibid.* at 81-85, 94-96.)

Frank recognized that the "fight" theory is mitigated in some respects. He called attention to the recent development of "discovery" procedures which in civil cases require litigants to disclose, before trial, evidence in their possession. (*Ibid.* at 93.) Thus, under the federal rules of procedure, either party may, before trial, (1) take a deposition of any person upon *oral examination* or *written interrogatories* "for purpose of discovery or for use as evidence in the action or for both purposes," but unless otherwise agreed by the parties, this sworn statement is inadmissible as evidence at the trial unless the witness making it cannot be produced in court or unless it is used to contradict or impeach the witness; (2) request from the other party an *admission* of the genuineness of "relevant documents" or "the truth of any relevant matters of fact set forth in the request"; and (3) seek a court order allowing *inspection* of documents, persons or things. In addition to these "discovery" devices, the federal rules also provide for "pre-trial conferences"

---

[1] That every lawyer is an "officer of the court" means only, said Frank, that "a lawyer must not affirmatively mislead a court, must not introduce in evidence, at a trial, documents which he knows to be false, testimony which he knows to be perjured." *Ibid.* at 89. In this connection read again the material in Chapter 1, Section 3, dealing with the controversy about Professor Williston's tactics as trial counsel.

which permit the judge to confer with counsel in order to simplify issues, limit the trial to actually contested issues and, possibly even, bring about settlement of the case. Discovery procedures and the pre-trial conference have become part of the civil procedure of most states.

Frank also discussed other mitigating features—(1) recognition of the power and right of trial judges to participate in the questioning of witnesses and even to call witnesses whom neither party has produced, though, he noted, few judges exercise this power; and (2) the growth of legal aid services for needy litigants. We shall have occasion shortly to consider other mitigating factors. The principal recommendation Frank made was that the court assume some of the burden of producing in civil suits, as it does to some extent in criminal cases, and as administrative agencies do, evidence not presented by either party. Going further, he called for consideration of the suggestion that "a public prosecutor of civil actions" be appointed to bring suit on behalf of any party who wishes to employ him. (*Ibid.* at 98-99.)

REISS,* *LESSONS IN JUDICIAL ADMINISTRATION FROM EUROPEAN COUNTRIES*
37 Journal of the American Judicature Society 104-106 (1953)

[Reiss shares Judge Frank's views concerning the shortcomings of our judicial administration and in this article proposes the following reforms which he states were embodied in the pre-World War I Austrian code drafted by the pioneer legal reformer, Franz Klein. Reiss's use of the present tense presumably describes the situation in general under this Austrian Code.—Editor]

Preparation for Trial. . . . The parties are required to inform the court from the beginning not only of all relevant facts but also of all means of proof at their disposal. They have to present to the court along with the complaint or answer, at least copies of all documents, including the entire correspondence. Copies of the documents must be furnished to the other party at the same time. This prevents a malicious defendant from repeatedly postponing the trial by presenting facts and producing evidence in piecemeal fashion. It is the function of the court to make sure that all the evidence is ready for trial. The court calls the witnesses, experts and parties. Simple arrangements between the courts and the post office department ensure service of papers, eliminating the complicated procedures with process servers and so forth. . . .

Pre-Trial. . . . The "Erste Tagsatzung" (first day in the court) was one of the great achievements of the Klein reform. It necessarily takes place a few days, not months or years, after the complaint is filed. Jurisdictional and all other technical obstacles are removed at this stage. Settlement is procured where the actual aim of the defendant is merely to postpone the judgment. In many cases

* Leo J. Reiss, a practicing lawyer in Vienna, Austria until 1939, now practices law in New York City and is professor of Roman law and comparative law at the Brooklyn Law School.—Editor

judgment can be made at once when one party is obviously in the right; further procedures are not then required. . . .

Conduct of the Trial. . . . The judge conducts the trial. As has been already mentioned, the court is from the very beginning in possession of all the allegations of all the facts and all the means of proof at the disposal of the parties. The judge has studied the file during the preparation for trial and has made sure that all the evidence is ready for trial. The court calls the witnesses, experts and parties to the trial. Immediately before trial, the judge again carefully reviews the files. . . .

Witnesses of the Parties. . . . One of the main obstacles to any reform in this respect consists in convincing people that the custom of interviewing witnesses should be abolished. How difficult this will be can be seen from the remarks of Judge Learned Hand, who has expressed his view that the practice of interviewing witnesses and reducing their proposed testimony to writing is "universal" and who calls it a "fantastic extreme" to consider such custom unprofessional for a lawyer.[6] Likewise, Judge Jerome Frank says that "every sensible lawyer, before a trial, interviews most of the witnesses."[7] From my lectures to American lawyers on comparative law, I know that this "method of finding the truth" is so much "inherited like some eternal disease" that lawyers accustomed to it cannot imagine what the principal function of the lawyer should be in preparing for trial if it were not for the interviewing of witnesses. . . .

A witness is a person at the disposal of the court. He is not the witness of either party, and he serves the court so that it may learn the truth. Since a person ceases to be a reliable witness for the court after he has been interviewed or examined by a lawyer of one of the parties, it is considered unethical for an attorney to discuss the facts of a case with a prospective witness.

Testimony. . . . After the parties have presented the whole story, the witnesses are heard. They are the court's witnesses. Everybody has a chance to speak freely in his own language, without unnecessary interruption. The judge assists by asking questions. Thereafter, the lawyers ask additional questions in order to bring out the facts more clearly. Prepared statements are not admitted. Depositions represent the witnesses' own views and are not influenced by the suggestions of the lawyers of the party who called them.

Experts. . . . In all cases the court has the power to call for experts, even before trial. Direct inspection by experts in the presence of the judge, the parties and their lawyers, is the backbone of the procedure. This inspection is particularly meaningful in negligence cases, and may take place within a few days after the filing of the complaint, not months or years thereafter. With this method, experience has showed that in most instances only one expert is needed. To consult another expert usually is superfluous, since impartial experts as a rule share the same opinion. Many cases have been settled as soon as the expert has given his opinion.

Experts are taken from a panel of qualified persons who are nominated by responsible agencies in every specialized field. Great care is taken to have the

[6] Becker v. Webster, 171 F. 2d. 762, 765. See also, Rudolf Schlesinger, Comparative

Law, Cases and Materials (1950), p. 208.
[7] Jerome Frank, Courts on Trial, p. 86.

panel composed of outstanding and honest persons. The parties may agree in advance on one or more persons taken from this panel who are to serve as experts. They may even agree on one or more experts who are not listed on the panel but whose qualifications and impartiality they trust. The fees·for the expert are deposited beforehand by the parties. The expert is paid by the court and not hired by the parties. His fees are finally charged to the losing party.

[Reiss takes note of a recent plan instituted in New York City to eliminate the delay and confusion in trials of personal injury actions resulting from the conflicting testimony of doctors on the nature and extent of plaintiffs' injuries. Under this plan, if during the pre-trial conference on a case it appears that the parties will dispute a medical issue, the case is referred to the panel of medical experts named by the medical societies in New York. A panel doctor examines the injured party and reports on his diagnosis and prognosis. If the case goes to trial, the panel doctor may be called to testify by either party or by the court; but either party may also call his own expert to contradict the panel doctor. During the two-year experimental period, the panel doctors were paid from funds granted by the Alfred P. Sloan Foundation and the Ford Fund. The experiment was so successful that New York made the doctors' panel a permanent feature of its judicial administration and pays its costs out of the regular court budget. The plan has been endorsed by the American Bar Association. See Impartial Medical Testimony, A Report by a Special Committee of the Association of the Bar of the City of New York (1956); the analysis and praise of the plan by former N.Y. Supreme Court Justice David W. Peck, in 22 Fed. Rules Decis. 21 (1958) and 42 A.B.A.J. 931 (1956); and critical comment by Zeisel in 8 Stanford L. Rev. 730 (1956). Responding to some lawyers' objections that juries would give more weight to the impartial expert's testimony than to a party's own expert, Justice Peck reminded the profession "that a trial is a search for truth, not a game of chance." 22 Fed. Rules Decis. 21, 25 (1958).—Editor]

The Parties. . . . A hearing of the parties for information is indispensable in many cases. It is hard to get a picture of the facts without having heard the parties concerned speaking in their every-day language. Formal testimony of the parties (if necessary under oath) is used to elucidate contradictory points of evidence.

Rules of Evidence. . . . Rules of evidence are almost abolished. Free evaluation of evidence is the rule. Surprise of the opponent is hardly possible, as explained before.

NOTES AND QUESTIONS

1. Would the system of judicial administration briefly outlined by Reiss be subject to the criticism levelled at non-adversary systems in the Report of the Joint Conference on Professional Responsibility, reprinted in part in Section 1 above? Is this criticism warranted?

2. Is it helpful to say that one's views for or against the adversary system should be determined by whether one thinks the lawyer's principal obligation should be to try to win his client's case or aid the court in a mutual search for truth? Is the

adversary system incompatible with the "search for truth"? How would you state the issue?

3. For a detailed analysis of German civil procedure, revealing the same dominant role of the judge indicated by Reiss (e.g., the judge doing the major questioning of witnesses; counsel not interviewing witnesses before trial), see Kaplan, von Mehring and Schaefer, Phases of German Civil Procedure, 71 Harv. L. Rev. 1193, 1443 (1958).

See also Hartshorne, Court Procedures Compared, 41 J. Am. Jud. Soc. 166 (1958).

Section 3

The ADVERSARY SYSTEM as a CONDITION for the DEVELOPMENT of LAW

EDITORIAL NOTE: The CASE or CONTROVERSY DOCTRINE; WHO ARE the ADVERSARIES?

1. Article III, Section 2 of the United States Constitution extends the judicial power of the United States to specified categories of "cases" and "controversies." From the earliest days, this provision has been interpreted not only as granting but also as limiting the federal judicial power, i.e., confining federal judges to the business of deciding disputes between adversary parties. Many state constitutions contain a similar definition of the judicial power. But even in the absence of such a constitutional definition, state courts have accepted the same limitation as part of the traditional concept of the judicial function. As Judge Hutcheson emphasized, courts "cannot make law by issuing abstract and general proclamations." Judges may not determine the legal rights and duties of persons who are not parties to the "case" or "controversy" before them. And the courts themselves will decide what is a "case" or "controversy" and who are the parties to it who therefore have "standing to sue"—that is, the right to set the court in motion.

2. However, the constitutions of several states authorize courts, in certain narrowly confined situations, to render "advisory opinions"—opinions which do not accompany the decision of any "case" or "controversy." [1] As observed in a recent survey, the "advisory opinion is not available to private or corporate or group parties generally. It is restricted, usually to the two houses of the legislature and the executive. . . . Private parties injured may not initiate a request under existing constitutional provisions. Nor are advisory opinions binding upon private parties. . . . The advisory opinion is designed for use during the process of legislation, or in the process of executive action." Field, The Advisory Opinion—An Analysis, 24 Ind. L.J. 203, 222 (1949).[2]

[1] For example, the Massachusetts constitution, Art. 2, chap. 3, provides: "Each branch of the legislature as well as the governor and council, shall have authority to require the opinions of the justices of the supreme judicial court upon important questions of law, and upon solemn occasions."

[2] "The advisory opinion has been used in other legal systems. For a history of the

3. The courts have distinguished justiciable "cases" and "controversies" from differences of a hypothetical character and disputes that have become academic or "moot." As Justice Jackson said in Public Service Commission v. Wycoff Co., 344 U.S. 237 (1952): "The disagreement must not be nebulous or contingent but must have taken a fixed and final shape so that a court can see what legal issues it is deciding, what effect its decision will have on the adversaries and some useful purpose to be achieved in deciding them." [3]

4. For some time it had been supposed that a justiciable controversy existed only if the plaintiff sought the payment of damages by, or an injunction against, or some other kind of specific relief from, the defendant. But the Supreme Court finally decided that this was not so when it upheld the constitutionality of the federal Declaratory Judgment Act of 1934 in Aetna Life Insurance Co. v. Haworth, 300 U.S. 227 (1937). The essentials of this relatively new type of lawsuit in this country (and note that it too can be used only if there is an actual controversy between genuinely adverse parties) have been set forth by Potts, The Declaratory Judgment, 28 J. Am. Jud. Soc'y 82-84 (1944) as follows:

. . . The Declaratory Judgment statute empowers the court to enter a final judgment between litigants, defining their respective rights in the subject matter, without attaching to that judgment any consequential or coercive relief. It proceeds on the theory that men in their business relations are generally honest, and that they are willing to discharge their obligations when they are authoritatively informed as to what those obligations are. The court merely declares the rights of the litigants upon formal petition or complaint, just as in other suits, but does not assume that force will be needed to make its decision effective. If on subsequent complaint it appears that the defeated party has refused to perform, the court issues execution or other proper compulsory process as a matter of course, and that, too, of course, without opening up the matter on its merits. All that has to be shown in such a motion is that judgment has been declared, that the defendant has not performed, and, therefore, that the plaintiff is entitled to have execution issued.

device in Canada, and its use in determining the constitutionality of Canadian experimental legislation during the 1930's compared with the resolution of the contemporaneous problems in the United States, see Davison, The Constitutionality and Utility of Advisory Opinions, 2 U. of Toronto L.J. 254 (1938). The Permanent Court of International Justice rendered twenty-seven advisory opinions from 1922 to 1935. Its successor, the International Court of Justice, is authorized to answer interrogatories by the General Assembly, the Security Council, and other organs and agencies of the United Nations. It has been pointed out, however, that the advisory opinions given by the old World Court were for the most part analogous to what we would call declaratory judgments, since there were actual disputes, and adverse parties argued the points involved." Hart and Wechsler, The Federal Courts and the Federal System (1953) 81.

See, too, Note, Advisory Opinions on the Constitutionality of Statutes, 69 Harv. L. Rev. 1302 (1956).

[3] On the doctrine of mootness, see Note, Cases Moot on Appeal: A Limit on the Judicial Power, 103 U. Pa. L. Rev. 772 (1955); Note, Disposition of Moot Cases by the United States Supreme Court, 23 U. Chi. L. Rev. 77 (1955); Diamond, Federal Jurisdiction to Decide Moot Cases, 94 U. Pa. L. Rev. 125 (1946).

This process, it will be noted, is a distinct departure from the usual procedure at common law and under statutes based on the common law. With some exceptions, the machinery of the courts in common law jurisdictions can only be set in motion when a wrong has actually been committed or is immediately threatened. . . .

It follows that under the old procedure, if A and B differ as to the meaning of a contract, or a deed, or a lease, or a will, one of them must act upon his interpretation of it and run the risk of incurring a heavy liability to the other, before the court will take jurisdiction and inform them of their rights. But by means of the declaratory judgment, without incurring such risks, either A or B has a right to go into a court and ask for an interpretation of the instrument. He has a legal right to know his legal rights. With both parties present before the court, and with the parties having a substantial interest in the subject matter and each contending for his own interpretation of the instrument, the court has before it a real case or controversy and its decision on the issues presented is final as between the parties.

The advantages of this form of procedure are obvious. In the first place, the issues presented to the court for its decision are usually simple and there are few if any issues of fact. A contract or other written instrument, or a statute, is to be interpreted, and the cases are often submitted on an agreed statement of facts. That fact enables the court in many cases to dispense with the services of a jury. Then, too, the controversy being in its initial stage, no wrong or violence has yet been committed, or if so, the plaintiff waives any injury he may have sustained as a result of such wrong, and only asks for a declaration of his rights for the future guidance of the parties. As a result, the court is relieved of all perplexing questions as to the amount of damages. And, most important of all, since no wrong is charged against the defendant and no damages are asked for, there is present in such a case a notable absence of the bitterness and hostility frequently present in ordinary damage suits, and the litigants are able to continue their business relations. In this way is obviated one of the most serious consequences of litigation under the old procedure, the loss of a good customer or business associate. . . .

. . . While a declaratory judgment is advisory in character, since it looks to the future and does not seek to redress past wrongs, it . . . is a very different thing from . . . advisory opinions. . . . In the advisory opinion, a legislative body or an executive office is authorized to call upon the court to pass upon the constitutionality of a measure under consideration. There is no concrete case before the court, no res or rights of parties to be disposed of, no adversary parties, and usually no counsel, no oral arguments and no briefs. If any counsel at all appear, it is usually as *amici curiae.* They have only a general social interest in the result, and not a vital interest as the representative of a party whose property rights are at stake. As there are no parties, no one is bound. Such advisory opinions are not *res judicata,* and the courts, when concrete cases arise, do not hesitate to overturn them. . . .

The modern declaratory judgment is said to be an evolution from Roman legal procedure. This form of procedure is found in a number of modern European states, and has been in use in Scotland for more than three hundred years. . . .

The constitutionality of the state declaratory judgment acts has been upheld by the supreme court of every state in which the question has been raised. . . .[4]

[4] The statutes of some 44 states and territories provide for the use of the declaratory judgment and a uniform declaratory judgment act has been adopted in 28 of these jurisdictions. Clark, Code Pleading (2d ed., 1947) 333. It should further be

5. It should also be recalled at this point that courts, as the fellow-servant cases demonstrated, will rule only on the facts and legal issues presented in the record made by the parties in controversy and governed by the applicable rules of procedure. But who are the "adverse parties" to a "case" or "controversy" who have "standing" to compel the court to rule on particular issues?

To have such standing, the party plaintiff or defendant must himself be legally and in fact interested in the court's decision. He must be affected, directly and substantially, by the legal rule he is asking the court to pronounce or apply and by the remedy or judgment he is asking the court to give. He must be seeking to vindicate his own claims, not someone else's.

Tileston v. Ullman, 318 U.S. 44 (1943) is a good example of the application of this requirement. A Connecticut statute prohibited the use of contraceptive drugs and instruments and made it illegal for physicians to prescribe or assist in their use. The plaintiff, a physician, tried to challenge the constitutionality of the statute. His complaint set out in detail the danger to the lives of three of his women patients if they should bear children and alleged that he would run the risk of criminal prosecution by giving them professional advice concerning the use of contraceptives. The doctor sought a declaratory judgment that the statute deprived his patients of their lives without due process of law in violation of the 14th Amendment. His complaint did not contend that the statute infringed his own liberty or property rights. The highest court in Connecticut ruled that the statute prohibited the proposed advice and that it was constitutional. The United States Supreme Court dismissed the doctor's appeal, saying: "We are of the opinion that the proceedings in the state courts present no constitutional question which appellant has standing to assert. The sole constitutional attack upon the statutes under the Fourteenth Amendment is confined to their deprivation of life—obviously not appellant's but his patients'. There is no allegation or proof that appellant's life is in danger. His patients are not parties to this proceeding and there is no basis on which we can say that he has standing to secure an adjudication of his patients' constitutional right to life, which they do not assert in their own behalf. . . ." For the failure to obtain a decision on the merits even after these deficiencies had been remedied, see Poe v. Ullman, 81 S. Ct. 1752 (1961).

The Supreme Court has subsequently referred to this "standing" doctrine as a "rule of practice" which is "weighty" but not rigid. Barrows v. Jackson, 346 U.S. 249 (1953) and United States v. Raines, 80 S. Ct. 519 (1960). In the former case, owners of property in a Los Angeles residential neighborhood entered into an agreement—a "covenant running with the land"—

---

noted that a "plaintiff may ask for a declaration either as his sole relief or in addition or auxiliary to other relief, and a defendant may similarly counterclaim therefor." *Ibid.* at 337.

The Supreme Court upheld the Uniform Declaratory Judgment Act of Tennessee in Nashville, Chattanooga, and St. Louis Railway Co. v. Wallace, 288 U.S. 249 (1933).

which restricted ownership and occupancy to members of the white or Caucasian race. Jackson, a Caucasian subject to the restrictive covenant, was sued by the other landowners for damages because she violated the agreement by selling to a Negro. Thus it was not the same sort of case as the famous case of Shelley v. Kraemer, 334 U.S. 1 (which we shall consider in Chapter 7) in which the Supreme Court had decided that the judgment of a state court ousting Negroes from possession of property sold to them in violation of a restrictive covenant would deprive the Negroes of the equal protection of the law guaranteed them by the 14th Amendment. While Mrs. Jackson could of course show that a court judgment for damages would injure her, she could not show that such a judgment would deprive her of the equal protection of the laws. Nor would such a judgment inflict any injury upon the particular Negro who purchased from Mrs. Jackson and who remained in possession. Nevertheless, the Court sustained her claim of unconstitutionality. It held that a judgment of damages against Mrs. Jackson would unconstitutionally discriminate against Negroes seeking to buy real estate in the future because landowners, under threat of a suit for damages, would either refuse to sell to them or else demand higher prices from them. "Under the peculiar circumstances of this case," explained the Court, "we believe the reasons which underlie our rule denying standing to raise another's rights, which is only a rule of practice, are outweighed by the need to protect the fundamental rights which would be denied by permitting the damages action to be maintained."

The Supreme Court took a similar position recently in National Association for the Advancement of Colored People v. Alabama, 357 U.S. 449 (1958) in which it held that it was a violation of the Due Process Clause of the Fourteenth Amendment for Alabama to compel the NAACP to reveal to the state's Attorney General the names and addresses of all its Alabama members and agents, without regard to their positions or functions in the Association. The Court rejected the argument that the NAACP had no standing to assert the constitutional rights of its members and held that the NAACP's "nexus with [its members] is sufficient to permit that it act as their representative before this Court." Writing for the Court, Justice Harlan pointed out that to require NAACP members to sue in order to vindicate their claimed right not to disclose their membership in the NAACP "would result in nullification of the right at the very moment of its assertion."

In United States v. Raines, *supra,* the Court reaffirmed the doctrine of Tileston v. Ullman and barred a challenge by state *officials* to the constitutionality of the Civil Rights Act of 1957. The challenge had been on the ground that the Act might be construed to prohibit *private* persons from interfering with the Negroes' right to vote in state and local elections—a result beyond the reach of the Fifteenth Amendment. Barrows v. Jackson and NAACP v. Alabama were exceptional cases, the Court now explained, involving a situation where "as a result of the very litigation in question, the constitutional rights of one not a party would be impaired, and he has no effective way to preserve them himself."

How directly and substantially must a party be affected to have the necessary standing? In Frothingham v. Mellon, 262 U.S. 447 (1923), the Court held that a federal taxpayer lacked standing to enjoin the enforcement of the federal Maternity Act, which set up a program to protect the health of mothers and infants and, to this end, authorized annual appropriations to be apportioned among the states willing to comply with certain federal conditions. She lacked standing because her "interest in the moneys of the treasury—partly realized from taxation and partly from other sources —is shared with millions of others, is comparatively minute and indeterminable, and the effect upon future taxation of any payment out of the funds, so remote, fluctuating, and uncertain, that no basis is afforded for an appeal to the preventive powers of a court of equity." To entertain such suits would permit taxpayers to harass government unduly by challenging the validity of "every . . . appropriation act and statute whose administration requires the outlay of public money." In the last analysis, a "matter of public and not of individual concern" was here involved, the resolution of which was not within the province of the judiciary.

"On the other hand," added the Court in Frothingham v. Mellon, "the interest of a taxpayer of a municipality in the application of its moneys is direct and immediate and the remedy by injunction to prevent their misuse is not inappropriate." In fact, the taxpayer's suit "is currently available to challenge state action in at least thirty-four states, and municipal action in virtually every jurisdiction." Note, Taxpayers' Suits: A Survey and Summary, 69 Yale L.J. 895 (1960).

Which rule of standing applies if a taxpayer attacks state or municipal expenditures on the ground that they violate federal law (constitutional or statutory) and comes before the federal Supreme Court for review?

The Supreme Court has been known to pass on the merits of a constitutional issue without discussing this question. It did so in Everson v. Board of Education, 330 U.S. 1 (1947), in which it permitted a local taxpayer to challenge the local spending of public funds for the transportation of parochial school children as a violation of the First Amendment. But in Doremus v. Board of Education, 342 U.S. 429 (1952), the Court dismissed an appeal by local taxpayers from a state court decision upholding the validity, under the First Amendment, of a New Jersey law requiring verses of the Old Testament to be read, without comment, at the opening of each public school day. The Court held that the taxpayers did not have standing to raise the federal constitutional issue.[5] Professor Freund has

---

[5] The Court pointed out: "There is no allegation that this [Bible-reading] activity is supported by any separate tax or paid for from any particular appropriation or that it adds any sum whatever to the cost of conducting the school" or to the taxes paid by the plaintiff taxpayers.

As for one plaintiff's claim of a litigable interest as *parent*, not only had the child graduated before the case came to the

welcomed the line taken by Doremus but does not think it goes far enough. He writes: "In Doremus, as I understand it, the Court said, regardless of what the state court thinks about a tax-payer's suit as a vehicle for raising this constitutional question, we will not accept the case on review. I think it is a needed change to make standing to raise a federal constitutional question, itself a federal question, so that it will be decided uniformly throughout the country. I disagree with the Doremus case in so far as it lets the state judgment stand and merely declines review. It seems to me that the Court should have gone the full way, holding that standing to raise a constitutional question is itself a federal question, that there was no standing, and, therefore, the petition should stand dismissed in the state court and the decree vacated so that it would not be a precedent even in the state court." Freund in Supreme Court and Supreme Law 35 (Cahn ed. 1954).[6]

For a general discussion of the standing doctrine, see Justice Frankfurter's concurring opinion, Joint Anti-Fascist Refugee Committee v. McGrath, 341 U.S. 123, 149 (1949); Davis, Administrative Law Text c. 22 (1959); and Note, 69 Yale L.J. 895, 919-924 (1960).

6. The "case" or "controversy" must be genuine and not feigned or collusive. In United States v. Johnson, 319 U.S. 302 (1943), a tenant brought an action against his landlord under the Emergency Price Control Act of 1942 to recover, as the law allowed, three times the amount by which his rent exceeded the maximum rent the landlord could lawfully charge under the Act. The landlord challenged the constitutionality of the statute. The United States intervened, as it has a statutory right to do in such cases under 28 U.S.C.A. §2403 and filed a brief in support of the Act. The federal district court held the Act to be unconstitutional and dismissed the action. Before the order of dismissal was entered, the Government ascertained the following facts. The tenant, using a fictitious name, had brought the suit at the request of the landlord who assured the tenant that he would incur no expense in doing so. The landlord's attorney procured the tenant's attorney; the tenant did not pay or even meet his attorney; he was assured by the landlord's attorney that his presence in court during the trial would not be necessary. The tenant did not know who paid the $15 filing fee in the district court; he did not read the complaint which was filed in his name; he conferred with the landlord and the landlord's attorney about the suit but nothing was said in their conferences about treble damages; in fact, the

Supreme Court (thereby making this claim "moot") but the pleading allegations were insufficient to sustain a litigable interest as parent. "There is no assertion that [the child] was injured or even offended thereby or that she was compelled to accept, approve or confess agreement with any dogma or creed or even to listen when the Scriptures were read. On the contrary there was a pretrial stipulation that any student, at his own or his parent's request, could be excused during Bible reading and that in this case no such excuse was asked."

[6] Professor Freund's point would not apply if the state court also ruled on the constitutionality of the challenged statute under the *state* constitution. To that extent, the state court's decision would have to stand.

tenant did not know of the amount of the judgment asked for in the complaint until he read of it in a local newspaper. No brief was filed on the tenant's behalf in the district court.

The Government made these facts known to the district court and moved that it reopen the case and dismiss it as collusive. When its motion was denied, the Government took a direct appeal to the Supreme Court under a statute, now 28 U.S.C.A. §1252. The Supreme Court dismissed the suit, even though the Government admitted that the facts submitted by the parties were neither false nor fictitious. There was no " 'honest and actual antagonistic assertion of rights' to be adjudicated—a safeguard essential to the integrity of the judicial process, and one which we have held to be indispensable to adjudication of constitutional questions by this Court."

A collusive case is to be distinguished from a "test case" in which, though both parties welcome the "test," a genuine controversy exists between them. Further, the action of a court may sometimes be necessary even if one party agrees with the position taken by another—e.g., a defendant in a divorce case may not contest it but that fact alone will not prevent entry of judgment. However, this non-adversary situation may prompt the court to take special precautions. In a recent case involving the validity of a "quickie" Virgin Islands divorce law, the Supreme Court said: "In view of the lack of genuine adversary proceedings at any stage in this litigation, the outcome of which could have far-reaching consequences on domestic relations throughout the United States, the Court invited specially qualified counsel 'to appear and present oral argument as *amicus curiae* in support of the judgment below'. . . ." Granville-Smith v. Granville-Smith, 349 U.S. 1, 4 (1955).

ARNOLD, *TRIAL BY COMBAT AND THE NEW DEAL*
47 Harvard Law Review 913-922, 944-947 (1934)

[This article reflects the legal difficulties encountered by Thurman Arnold in attempting to help administer and validate the New Deal agricultural program in 1933 when he served as special assistant to the general counsel of the Agricultural Adjustment Administration.—Editor]

Anglo-American judicial theory constantly emphasizes that only the particular and narrow issues brought before courts by contesting parties may be the basis of judge-made law. Judicial language not necessary for the decision of those narrow issues is called by the uncomplimentary name of dicta. The impression is given that legal rules and principles based on mere dicta are of doubtful validity. A court is not supposed to regulate situations merely because regulation is badly needed. A court should never approve, disapprove, or clarify an entire set of rules governing a general business situation. A court should never answer questions. The limits of their power in this direction is to produce parables out of which further arguments may be spun.

What the issues of a case are depends upon the record, beyond the limits of which no court should go. The pronouncement that assuming certain facts to be true, such would be the law applicable, which is familiar to continental judges, is supposed in this country to indicate loose judicial thinking. The court might be aware, as men of common sense, that the parties desired a general rule to be adopted or rejected, or the parties might even stipulate that such was their desire. Nevertheless, the court would be powerless to discuss the rule or principle if the record, judged in the light of certain technical rules, did not raise those precise issues.

Typical Results of Emphasis on "Issues." The most frequent illustration of this attitude is found in the repeated exhortation of appellate courts that counsel stay within the record. The doctrine of judicial notice becomes at times a convenient escape from this limitation but counsel can never know how far they may rely on it. Oral arguments are filled with remarks which indicate how fixed the attitude is in the minds of the court. For example, in the recent case of Nebbia v. People of the State of New York,[1] a case designed to test the constitutionality of far-reaching legislation, argument before the Supreme Court of the United States on the question of the power of the state to fix prices was stopped while counsel was asked to point out in the record where it appeared that the defendant was a milk dealer, rather than a person who had just happened to sell a quart of milk for the first and last time in his life. It was apparent that the sole purpose of the case was to test the power of a state to fix prices. There was a deliberate attempt to exclude all other issues. One hearing the argument might easily have gained the impression that a careless omission in the record might prevent the court from making a decision for which vast interests were anxiously waiting. . . .

We may at times even transcend the limits of the record provided our purpose is not to remedy inadequate presentation of issues, but to show that the parties desire information on the law without going through the risks of a combat. Thus in the recent Lake Cargo Rate case, the entire coal industries of Pennsylvania and West Virginia were awaiting an interpretation of the Interstate Commerce Act. A bitter dispute was in process of litigation. The Interstate Commerce Commission had been enjoined from requiring a certain differential between West Virginia and Pennsylvania coal mines. In order to clarify the situation pending an appeal, a compromise rate had been approved. This was considered by the parties to be only a necessary compromise until the Supreme Court could make its decision. Instead of deciding the question which had required so much time and effort to bring before them, the Supreme Court held that no "issues" were before it. Because a new rate had been approved in the interim the case was "moot." Therefore the Court could not speak. The whole litigation had to be begun over again. . . .

The Department of Agriculture was engaged in negotiating a milk agreement and license in the state of New York. The Attorney General of New York examined the cases and announced that the proposed action by the Department was unconstitutional. The government proceeded with its negotiations. When the action is taken, there will be no way in which judicial approval or disapproval

[1] 291 U.S. 502 (1934). This case involved the validity of legislation fixing minimum prices for milk.—Editor

of its terms can be obtained. The parties must operate under a cloud until one of them decides to litigate. . . . The courts are a necessary part of the system which finally approves marketing agreements, licenses, and codes. Yet their participation in this system is based on a sort of catch-as-catch-can philosophy.

The major points of constitutionality of the recovery legislation will soon be decided. Yet the particular provisions of the hundreds of codes[2] will always be in question. A tentative or qualified judicial approval during the period of experiment, while such provisions are in operation, is made very difficult by the notion that courts can finally decide only on issues brought before them, because time, and place, the parties, and the scope of the decision are all left to Providence, aided by prevailing conceptions of pleadings, the record, and res judicata.

Of course, cases may be fixed up to assist Providence in minor ways, but this process presents troubling and unsolvable ethical problems. In a recent instance the government desired an interpretation of an agricultural adjustment license. It was suggested that a corporation be formed which would violate the specific terms of the license on which a decision was wanted and thus present the question at the time, and in the place which administrative convenience considered advisable. The scheme was thought dangerous. No one quite knew whether it was ethical or not. It was argued that this was the most orderly way of getting the precise questions before the court to which answers were imperatively required by a waiting agricultural industry. Yet the spectacle of the government manufacturing a case to accomplish this violated a traditional attitude. It was, therefore, thought better to wait, in spite of the administrative confusion which resulted, until Providence in its infinite wisdom should send the right kind of a case. The difference between a moot case and a test case has never been defined and never will be. The only sure thing is that the one is bad, and the other perfectly proper. . . .

Assumptions Underlying the Search for Issues. The suggestion that a court should be permitted to speak without a contested case before it has been met with an air of shocked surprise by such persons learned in the law as the writer has interviewed on the subject. It is considered dangerous in spite of the fact that in large areas of judicial participation in business, such as consent receiverships,[3] this

[2] The reference is to the National Industrial Recovery Act and the codes of fair competition adopted thereunder by many industries and trades at the outset of the New Deal.—Editor

[3] If he could show certain facts to exist, a creditor of a corporation in financial difficulties might obtain from a court of equity the appointment of a court officer, called a receiver, to administer the affairs of the corporation and prevent the dissipation of its assets, with a view generally to reorganization of the business on a sounder financial basis. Those in control of the corporation might themselves wish the advantages of such a reorganization.

They might bring this about by inducing a friendly creditor to ask the court of equity to appoint a receiver, and then causing the corporation, which was always formally a party defendant to such a proceeding, to admit the existence of those facts necessary to establish the creditor's right to have a receiver appointed. This was known as a "consent receivership." For years prior to the enactment of the present federal legislation extending the federal bankruptcy law to cover problems of corporate reorganization, this device was used in the very important volume of court business having to do with the financial difficulties of corporate enterprise. In the

is exactly what the courts have been compelled to do. Courts for a long time have regulated insolvent business on the sensible lines of control instead of the romantic technique of battle. The difficulties have arisen only because the older tradition keeps courts from exercising enough control. Today, when something of the same type of regulation is being imposed upon solvent business, the notion of groups of individuals getting up plans and regulations for the approval of the court becomes a necessary development. Yet we still prefer a two-party injunction suit to test the operation of a code to a more sensible impartial examination at the request of interested groups who are not necessarily fighting each other. The reasons for this preference are worth examining.

The philosophical rationalization of why courts may not be trusted to clarify rules in confused situations, except by the hit-or-miss method of the occasional decision after a contest, is of course contradictory. That is to be expected. Every human institution is the embodiment of all sorts of contradictory ideals going in different directions. To each important institution is attached a priesthood devoted to the task of proving that which is necessarily false, namely, that the institutional ideals are not contradictory, and that they are not going in different directions. In the law this is accomplished by a science known as jurisprudence. This science takes the simple emotional ideals to which the judiciary owes its popular acceptance and elaborates them into a literature with which it takes years to become thoroughly familiar. Few connected with the judicial institution know anything about this literature, and when, from a sense of duty, lawyers or judges peruse works which claim to be jurisprudence, they get a distinctly fuzzy feeling which they humbly attribute to their own incompetence. They are, however, profoundly grateful that a little group of scholars are taking over the task of examining the nature and sources of the law and finding them to be, on the whole, sound. Therefore, the fact that the assumptions underlying the science of jurisprudence, while pretending to be rational, are as a matter of fact completely irrational, escapes their attention. In the same way the complete irrationality of the theology preached in this country from 1800 to 1880, always escaped the "good" churchgoers because the length and complexity of the sermons convinced them that it must be rational. Where there is so much language there must be some truth.

The task of jurisprudence has been to make rational in appearance the operation of an institution which is actually mystical and dramatic, and which maintains its hold upon popular imagination by means of emotionally relevant symbols. If one were compelled to summarize the assumptions underlying the ideal of a lawmaking body, which never speaks except to settle a combat properly brought before it, the result would be somewhat as follows:

(1) Every trial should be a contest over issues presented by the parties and

course of such a receivership, detailed and often very complex plans for the financial reorganization and continuing operation of the embarrassed corporation would be presented to the court by interested groups, discussed, fought over, and more or less surveyed by the court for their "fairness" to the different parties concerned; and, if possible, a plan would finally be adopted under court approval.—Editor

not an investigation of what the facts were which created the necessity of the suit.

(2) The unskillful antagonist should lose, because the rules should be so simple that it is his own fault if he does. Simplicity of rules is obtained by not permitting courts to clarify these rules except by penalizing one of the antagonists. To permit anyone to find out about them in advance would destroy the idea of a combat.

(3) Courts are not permitted to plan their participation in a new situation, such as is presented by the recovery acts, any more than they were permitted to plan their participation in arbitration, rate making, or administrative law. This participation is rather to be determined by a series of battles. Each particular battle is a war to end war.

(4) Rules governing human conduct will be better and more consistent if only a small section of that conduct is considered at a time. It is a mistake for a rule-making body to consider a situation as a whole.

(5) The best way to avoid litigation is to make the power to promulgate rules and regulations exclusively dependent upon litigation.

(6) Courts should keep their eyes fixed on the past and follow precedent. Legislatures should look to the future, and disregard it. Thus the two extremes will correct each other, if courts in making their decisions will only keep future policies in mind, and if legislatures will only have more respect for the past. Thus the legislative and judicial functions will nicely balance each other, provided we set up enough administrative tribunals actually to do the work required.

These assumptions are reconciled with practical efficiency by the notion that courts are more apt to formulate or apply rules soundly if the opposite sides are prevented from sitting around a table together in friendly conference. Mutual exaggeration is supposed to create lack of exaggeration. Bitter partizanship in opposite directions is supposed to bring out the truth. Of course no rational human being would apply such a theory to his own affairs nor to other departments of the government. It has never been supposed that bitter and partizan lobbying assisted legislative bodies in their lawmaking. No investigation is conducted by hiring persons to argue opposite sides. The common law is neither clear, sound, nor even capable of being restated in areas where the results of cases are being most bitterly contested. And particularly with reference to administrative regulation does mutual exaggeration of opposing claims negative the whole theory of rational, scientific investigation. Yet in spite of this most obvious fact, the ordinary teacher of law will insist (1) that combat makes for clarity, (2) that heated arguments bring out the truth, and (3) that anyone who doesn't believe this is a loose thinker. The explanation of this attitude lies in the realm of social anthropology. . . .

The requirements necessary for an orderly review of administrative tribunals are relatively simple once we rid them of their philosophical trappings. The machinery for satisfying these requirements is already at hand, having been developed *sub rosa* out of the necessities of the past. We will briefly enumerate them.

(1) There must be a method by which judicial approval of a regulation may be tentatively given during an experimental period. We have instances of this already. In the Appalachian Coals case[4] the Supreme Court indicated that its decision was operative for the time being only, and might be modified by subsequent changes of conditions. The case was kept alive expressly for that purpose. . . .

(2) Cases involving approval or disapproval of administrative regulations must be considered in the light of interests of whole groups of people. Two parties must not be permitted to control the entire litigation. The analogy of the creditors' suit which begins a corporate reorganization may be useful here. Such a suit is supposed to be representative. All sorts of conflicting interests have a standing for appeal. Suits for injunctions against provisions of NRA codes may be twisted into the same form, to enable courts to treat such litigation as determining the broad principles under which whole groups of conflicting interests must be reconciled.

(3) There must be speedy methods of appealing precise questions to the Supreme Court of the United States, unencumbered with procedural formulae. The method of certifying questions to be answered is suggested here as a useful analogy.[5]

(4) There must be some planned participation of federal courts in governmental regulation. . . .

A period of confusion, during which the judicial participation will be confused and uncertain, is inevitable. Yet in an age when orderly planning is regarded everywhere as a possibility, where *laissez faire* is no longer the ultimate ideal, it is probable that courts also will be driven to intelligent procedural planning. The hit-or-miss methods of waiting until Providence leaves just the right case at the judicial doorstep before giving a waiting industry any enlightenment is apt to appear in the future less rational than it did in the past. . . .

Conclusion. . . . On the New York post office is the motto: "Neither snow nor rain nor heat nor gloom of night shall stay these messengers from the swift completion of their appointed rounds." Common sense tells us that this means only that mail will be delivered even in bad weather. A longer motto on the Washington post office means that mail is only delivered to nice people for laudable purposes. Yet who wants to strip these mottoes of their decorative quality so long

---

[4] United States v. Appalachian Coals, Inc., 1 Fed. Supp. 339 (W.D. Va. 1932), reversed, 288 U.S. 344 (1933). The Government here attacked the validity of an agreement by a group of producers of coal to maintain a common selling agency, on the ground that the arrangement violated the anti-trust laws. The selling agency was not yet in operation, and the Supreme Court found that on the facts then appearing, the arrangement could not be held to involve either a purpose to restrain competition unlawfully, or the power to do so. The Court left its decree open for subsequent application by the Government for relief if the sales agency should, in operation, prove to work out as a combination in restraint of trade.—Editor

[5] A provision of the Federal Judiciary Act gives to the Courts of Appeals the right to certify to the Supreme Court of the United States at any time any question of law concerning which instructions are desired. It has been decided repeatedly that a Court of Appeals cannot certify an entire record or case, but is confined to certifying specific questions of law which can be answered by the Supreme Court without examination of the whole case.—Editor

as they tend to create loyalties and enthusiasm? The same may be said of the elaborate formulae surrounding trial by combat. So long as they met a deeply felt emotional want, the mere fact that they were not what they pretended to be, that they could not be a sensible way of investigating the truth or a rational way of making a system of regulations, in no way affected their vitality as an ideal. . . .

Yet, if the American people once accept regulation as a normal function of government, we may no longer feel the emotional need of trial by combat.

FRANKFURTER* and HART,† THE BUSINESS OF THE SUPREME COURT AT OCTOBER TERM, 1934
49 Harvard Law Review 68, 94-107 (1935)

In all constitutional cases, whether on review from the state or federal courts, jurisdictional limitations assume peculiar importance, intensified where the . . . adjudication [by the Supreme Court of the United States] resolves what is in effect a controversy between itself and the Congress, or between itself and the Executive. Into the tradition of constitutional adjudication has gone the accumulated experience of a century and a half. Conventions and practices too subtle and flexible to be adequately summarized into rules determine the everyday administration of the Court. They express the sensibilities of statesmen, not the formulation of technicians. Such conventions and practices derive from an insight into conditions essential for the effective administration of the "peculiar jurisprudence" of the Supreme Court, because they are essential to the continuance of the Court's traditional share in the government of our democratic society.

And so the threshold requirement of the existence of a "case" or "controversy" is basic to the assumption of authority by all United States courts. It has the liveliest public importance, and not merely technical relevance, when the scope of the Constitution is an issue. It is neither intellectual timidity nor adherence to the mumbo-jumbo of legal jargon that has made the Supreme Court from the very outset, on appeals to it, give very restricted scope to the concept of a "case" or "controversy." The instinct of statesmen who were either participants in or

---

* Felix Frankfurter taught law at the Harvard Law School from 1914 until 1939, when he became an Associate Justice of the United States Supreme Court. His writings include The Case of Sacco and Vanzetti (1927), The Business of the Supreme Court (with James M. Landis) (1928), The Labor Injunction (with Nathan Greene) (1930), The Public and Its Government (1930), The Commerce Clause Under Marshall, Taney and Waite (1937), Mr. Justice Holmes and the Supreme Court (1939), Law and Politics (1939), Of Law and Men (1958). He edited a volume on Mr. Justice Holmes (1931), as well as a number of case-books. A series of recorded interviews which he gave were published as Felix Frankfurter Reminisces (1960).—Editor

† Henry M. Hart, Jr. has taught law at Harvard since 1932. He was secretary to Mr. Justice Brandeis, 1931-32, a member of the Attorney General's Committee on Administrative Procedure, 1939-41, and a federal government attorney in responsible posts during 1937-38 and 1940-46. He is co-editor (with Herbert Wechsler) of The Federal Courts and the Federal System (1953) and (with Albert Sacks) of the forthcoming work, The Legal Process.—Editor

witnesses to the fashioning of the Constitution decisively rejected any practice which would make of the Court a standing body of expert expounders of the Constitution.* If the Court was to have the vital function which it evolved for itself, the occasions for its authoritative intervention had to be severely circumscribed.

What the earliest judges felt by instinct has from time to time been translated into unquestioned canons for constitutional administration. It is not enough that a conflict should be in the offing. Judicial abstention is imperative unless real conflicting interests have reached a point of immediate litigious ripeness. Appeals to the Court must be denied until appeals to the Constitution can no longer go unheeded. . . .

The importance of having a concrete issue derives partly from the importance of having data relevant and adequate to an informed judgment. Data must always be relevant to something. They depend upon the presence of a specific issue for determination. The untutored assumption that adjudication in the most difficult areas of constitutional conflict requires only an effort of the mind and a reading of prior judicial decisions receives scant recognition in the practice of the Court. Constitutionality is not a fixed quantity. The decision in Nashville, C. & St. L. Ry. v. Walters [294 U.S. 405, 415 (1935)] at the last term is a reminder that a statute valid as to one set of facts may be invalid as to another, and hence of the necessity of a full presentation of the context of circumstances under which the issue of validity is posed. . . .

The Court's sense of its position and function as an appellate tribunal leads it to emphasize not only the necessity of adequate data but of data already explored and sifted by trial and intermediate tribunals. This insistence rests not merely upon administrative considerations of the pressure of business. It rests also upon awareness of adjudication as a process, as a process in which the deliberations of successive tribunals serve to illumine final judgment and in which particularly "the special knowledge of local conditions" possessed by local tribunals may be indispensable. . . .

Judged from the unworldly heights of "pure law," all these instances present the familiar process of pouring new wine into old bottles, if they do not have the worse appearance of finicky observance of dry technicality. The technicality is the avoidance of a decision on what is loosely called the merits. The old bottle— the very old bottle—is the common law instinct for empiricism in deciding live, concrete, real adversary issues, sticking close to fact, avoiding abstraction and the enunciation of premature generalization. But this healthy pragmatic instinct, this concentration on the complications of the present and not heedlessly borrowing trouble by seeking to discern the too dim image of the future, will be disdained only by those who have not adequately experienced the serious clash of forces so often embedded in the procedural interstices of constitutional litigation, or who

* In the course of the framing of the Constitution a proposal was made and rejected to link the Court and the Executive together as a Council of Revision to exercise a general veto power over all legislation passed by the Congress.—Editor

do not appreciate to what extent the Supreme Court's prestige has been won through its self-denying ordinances.

The wisdom of the attitudes disclosed in the day-to-day practice of the Court appears most clearly in occasional departures. At least three opinions of the last term collide, in essential respects, with the Court's own statements of its functions and with its avowed criteria for their discharge. That these opinions were all rendered in cases freighted to an uncommon degree with implications for the national destiny sharpens the questions of procedural responsibility which they raise.

The decision of the Court in the Liberty Bond Gold Clause Case[80] was that the plaintiff Perry, under the circumstances presented, had suffered no damage and could not recover. Whatever the grounds of this conclusion,[81] a judgment that the Joint Resolution of June 5, 1933[82] was unconstitutional was plainly not among them. Perry's failure to recover was in spite of and not because of the invalidity of the Resolution. Yet the opinion pronounced the Resolution void.[83] In the Railway Pension Case,[84] an Act of Congress was attacked upon the double ground that it offended the due process clause of the Fifth Amendment and that it overstepped the bounds of Congressional power under the commerce clause. The Court's opinion upheld the first contention, a decision wholly adequate to dispose of the controversy. Nevertheless it then proceeded to sustain also the second. And in so doing it used language which not only condemns the particular statute in question but which, in the words of the Chief Justice, "denies to Congress the power to pass any compulsory pension act for railroad employees." [295 U.S. at 374-75.] Similarly, in A.L.A. Schechter Poultry Corp. v. United States,[86]

[80] Perry v. United States, 294 U.S. 330 (1935). [This case involved the validity of the Congressional Resolution declaring that payments under government bonds should be made in any currency which is legal tender, even though the terms of the bonds specified payment in gold. The Court's opinion declared that the Resolution was unconstitutional, but also decided that the bondholder was not entitled to judgment in his suit on his bond to collect the gold value of the bond, because he had not shown that as a result of the Resolution of Congress he had suffered any damage. The theory of this ruling was that even if he had received gold in payment, his use of the gold was so restricted by other gold legislation of Congress, which was found to be constitutional legislation, that the gold would not have been worth any more to him than the paper money which the government insisted he take in payment of the bond.—Editor]

[81] See Hart, The Gold Clause in United States Bonds (1935) 48 Harv. L. Rev. 1057.
[82] 48 Stat. 112, 31 U.S.C.A. § 463 (Supp. 1934).
[83] "We conclude that the Joint Resolution of June 5, 1933, in so far as it attempted to override the obligation created by the bond in suit, went beyond the congressional power." 294 U.S. at 354. Compare the concurring opinion of Mr. Justice Stone, id. at 358.
[84] Railroad Retirement Board v. Alton R.R., 295 U.S. 330 (1935).
[86] 295 U.S. 495 (1935). [The National Industrial Recovery Act provided for the adoption of codes of fair competition drawn by members of industries engaged in interstate commerce and approved by the President. The Schechter case was a prosecution by the United States to enforce the code of fair competition thus adopted for the live poultry industry. The Court held the Recovery Act unconstitutional because, in

the Court began by invalidating the poultry code in litigation upon the ground that it had been adopted pursuant to an unconstitutional delegation of legislative power to the President. It then condemned the code a second time under the commerce clause. Not only did the Court in this branch of the opinion fail to confine its declaration to the poultry code, so that its decision was widely understood as concluding analogous questions under other codes, but it did so in language seemingly applicable, especially in the political and emotional context of the times, to many other and widely different types of legislation.

The substantive problems in all these decisions are quite outside the province of this paper. With the broader issues of jurisdiction and procedure—of the process of adjudication underlying all decisions—we are directly concerned. Those issues are implied in the classic statement of Mr. Justice Matthews:

> "[This Court] has no jurisdiction to pronounce any statute, either of a State or of the United States, void, because irreconcilable with the Constitution, except as it is called upon to adjudge the legal rights of litigants in actual controversies. In the exercise of that jurisdiction, it is bound by two rules, to which it has rigidly adhered, one, never to anticipate a question of constitutional law in advance of the necessity of deciding it; the other never to formulate a rule of constitutional law broader than is required by the precise facts to which it is to be applied." [87]

Let us apply these canons—and every member of the Court unquestionably yields abstract fealty to them—to the great constitutional cases of the last term. The bearing of the second of Mr. Justice Matthews' canons on the Railway Pension Case is sufficiently underscored by the Chief Justice's own statement, rendered in dissent, that the opinion "denies to Congress the power to pass *any* compulsory pension act for railroad employees." No such question, of course, was or could have been before the Court. The corresponding aspect of the Schechter decision requires fuller comment. The business of the Schechters was part of the network of distribution; and the opinion is in terms applicable—without differentiation—to the regulation of hours and wages in all such businesses, if their operations are likewise outside the technical " *'current' or 'flow'* of interstate commerce." Whether large abstract concepts—involving the dual nature of our political society and, what is more relevant, questions of degree in the application of those vast concepts—should abstractly be applied to situations not before the Court is

---

permitting the industry under the President's approval to draft a code of rules of competition, the Congress was thought to have abdicated its legislative duty and to have permitted persons not constitutionally entrusted with legislative power to make laws. Secondly, the Court ruled the Recovery Act unconstitutional on the ground that the parties involved in the suit (New York City poultry wholesalers) were not in interstate commerce and that the rules of competition involved in the code (regulations of hours and wages) were not of a sort which could be deemed regulations of interstate commerce, and that therefore the statute could not be held authorized by the constitutional grant to Congress of the power to regulate interstate commerce.—Editor]

[87] Liverpool, N.Y. and P.S.S. Co. v. Commissioners of Emigration, 113 U.S. 33, 39 (1885). . . .

sufficiently doubtful. And the tendering of some such issue by the Government does not of itself justify a yielding to the temptation. But in any event the Court's opinion did not confine itself to distributive businesses.[91] So far at least as it invites the reading that it bears also upon similar regulation of factors in production for interstate shipment, plainly it "formulate[s] a rule . . . broader than is required by the precise facts to which it is to be applied."

To be sure, every judicial opinion contains the implicit qualification—commonplace to a sophisticated bar—that it is to be read as applying only to the circumstances of the case before the court. But the relevance of this convention to a Schechter opinion implies a degree of precision in the application of precedent in case law which is foreign to the discipline even of lawyers. Nor are constitutional opinions written only for the legal profession. Questions of the liveliest concern not only to members of the coordinate branches of government but to the public at large ought not to be left to be resolved by the subtlest and least determinate of the lawyer's arts. The whole force of Mr. Justice Matthews' canon is that in constitutional cases the Court should not be content with the usual inference but, out of respect for the delicacy of its function and in view of the touchiness of the subject matter, should expressly confine itself to what is needed to dispose of the controversy before it and not stray outside the strict circumference of the record.

Mr. Justice Matthews' warning against deciding more than is required is of secondary importance compared with his warning against deciding when no decision is required at all. The conclusion that the Perry opinion anticipated a question of constitutional law in advance of the necessity of deciding it seems unescapable. So is it, if less palpably, with the pension and Schechter opinions. Specifically, the inappropriateness in both cases of considering the scope of Congressional power under the commerce clause seems manifest. The Court has perhaps formulated no express canon that of two constitutional issues the lesser, that is, that which involves a narrower circumscription of Congressional power, shall be decided before the greater.[92] Yet surely such a canon is implicit, if not in the theoretical bases of the power to review legislation, at least in the practical conventions of decision according to which in wisdom that power has been employed. The defects of due process and delegation in the pension and recovery legislation were in part at least curable.* The commerce clause questions were entangled, in

---

[91] See, especially, 295 U.S. at 549: "The argument of the Government proves too much. If the federal government may determine the wages and hours of employees in the internal commerce of a State, because of their relation to cost and prices and their indirect effect upon interstate commerce, it would seem that a similar control might be exerted over other elements of cost, also affecting prices. . . . All the processes of *production* and distribution that enter into cost could likewise be controlled." (Italics ours.)

[92] But *cf.* Miller, J., in The Trade-Mark Cases, 100 U.S. 82, 85 (1879).

* I.e., when the objection is that the Congress has left too wide a range of discretion to executive officials and has thus evaded its legislative responsibility to define the public policy of the community, this may be cured by passing a more definite statute. So when the objection is that the statute violated the constitutional guaranty that no person shall be deprived of life, liberty or property without due process of law, this may often mean, not that Congress

a quite different manner, with ultimate issues of governmental power. These questions "are not to be lightly treated," said Mr. Justice Miller of a matter far less complex and extensive in its ramifications, "nor are we authorized to make any advances to meet them. . . ." [93] That observation was in the traditional spirit of American constitutional law. It applies with peculiar force to a question of such breadth of impact—so resistant to final justiciability—as that of the extent of federal power over the national economy.

Logical difficulty there may be, when a decision is rested upon two constitutional grounds, in singling out either one as unnecessary. What at least is clear is that both are not necessary. In the pension case and in the Schechter case alike the ground of decision first stated not only disposed of the controversy before the Court, but it was conclusive of the entire invalidity of the Statute in question. In the Schechter case the entire code structure which had given rise to the litigation was destined in any event to expire in twenty days.[95] Further discussion of any constitutional issue, being wholly prospective in its bearing, was thus relevant only to future exertions of legislative power. Against such advisory pronouncements the constitutional theory and practice of a century and a half unite in protest, howsoever strong may be the eagerness for guidance on the part of draftsmen of potential legislation or the cooperative desire on the part of the Court to give light.

The critical problem of American constitutional law was never more acutely stated than it was by Judge Pendleton in Virginia before ever the Constitution was adopted:

> "How far this court, in whom the judiciary powers may in some sort be said to be concentrated, shall have power to declare the nullity of a law passed in its forms by the legislative power, *without exercising the power of that branch,* contrary to the plain terms of that constitution, is indeed a deep, important, and I will add, a tremendous question, the decision of which would involve consequences to which gentlemen may not have extended their ideas." [96]

The well understood tradition of the common law, whereby for centuries common law judges had occupied themselves exclusively with settling the rights of parties to lawsuits, provided the foundation for the answer to Judge Pendleton's question. The incorporation into the law of the Constitution of the concept of a

tried to do something it cannot do at all, but simply that it adopted the wrong means; it can try again to accomplish the same purpose with more reasonable means. It is a far more fundamental objection, to urge that, however definite the standards set and however reasonable the means adopted, the purpose of the legislation is one which Congress lacks constitutional authorization to pursue.—Editor

[93] Bartemeyer v. Iowa, 18 Wall. 129, 134 (U.S. 1873). The question here reserved, the power of a state to forbid the sale of liquor owned before the law took effect, was not resolved for another fourteen years. Mugler v. Kansas, 123 U.S. 623 (1887).

[95] The decision was rendered on May 27, 1935; the Act was to expire on the succeeding June 16. See Act of June 16, 1933, c. 90, 48 Stat. 195, 196, 15 U.S.C.A. § 701 (c) (Supp. 1934).

[96] In Commonwealth v. Caton, 4 Call 5 (Va. 1782).

"case" or "controversy" reënforced that tradition, just as the adoption of the Constitution, with its formal division and limitation of the powers of government, made it doubly significant. In turn, the existence of a controversy between parties before the Court, and the necessity of resolving it, became the avowed and exclusive basis of the power of judicial review. Finally, the avoidance, by leaning backwards, of encroachment upon the legislative province became the common theme of all those conventions of administration, evolved by the Court in the exercise of that power, of which the chief are the canon which requires every doubt to be resolved in favor of the validity of legislation[98] and that which forbids the issue of validity to be considered at all "unless by the case presented its consideration is imperatively required." [99] It is but a confirmation of Judge Pendleton's prophetic insight to say that the gravest of the Court's "self-inflicted wounds" [100] have invariably been associated with laxity in the observance of these standards.

Even with standards the most rigorous and their observance the most austere, judges are bound to render decisions which—unless the judicial process becomes petrified—will require modification. For facts change, insight deepens, or a different balance is struck in the choice of values which underlies decisions. The history of the Supreme Court has been the history of a dynamic process, partly revealed by explicit overruling of earlier decisions.* Even more inevitable in such a judicial history have been corrections of lapses into dicta. In most instances the dicta have been retrospective, as it were; later cases have disclosed an unintended and inadmissible breadth of application implicit in the language of an earlier opinion. The extent to which such lapses are avoided varies, of course, with the felicity of style of individual authors of opinions, with their literary sensitiveness, their prophetic instinct for future contingencies, and the intensity of their conviction regarding the importance of sticking in the bark of the particular litigation. These are limitations of fallibility of even the greatest judges. But it is precisely because of these limitations that the Court has evolved its doctrines of constitutional administration as barriers against avoidable excesses in adjudication. The occasional disregard of these barriers has usually been followed by an awakening to renewed consciousness of the wisdom of adhering to them. For permeating confidence in the judicial process is weakened by important retractions. More concretely, political action is often taken on the basis of weighty dicta, and its dislocation by later decisions erasing the dicta adds needlessly to the frictions of government.

The practical importance of all this was illustrated in a case decided the very

[98] For impressive justification of this doctrine, see James Bradley Thayer, *The Origin and Scope of the American Doctrine of Constitutional Law* (1893) 7 Harv. L. Rev. 129.

[99] Mr. Justice Field, in San Bernardino County v. Southern Pac. R.R., 118 U.S. 417, 423 (1886).

[100] See Hughes, The Supreme Court of the United States (1928) 50.

* Since this article was written, the Court has substantially repudiated its broad declarations regarding the scope of the commerce power in the Railroad Retirement and Schechter decisions. See especially: Mulford v. Smith, 307 U.S. 38 (1939); United States v. Rock Royal Co-operative, Inc., *id.* 533 (1939); United States v. Lowden, 308 U.S. 225 (1939).—Editor

day the Schechter opinion was handed down.[102] The constitutional issue there presented concerned the power of Congress to restrict the President's power to remove a member of the Federal Trade Commission. The President had relied in his action, and the Government relied in argument, upon the Court's opinion in Myers v. United States,[103] in the course of which Mr. Chief Justice Taft had said:

> "Then there may be duties of a quasi-judicial character imposed on executive officers and members of executive tribunals whose decisions after hearing affect interests of individuals, the discharge of which the President can not in a particular case properly influence or control. But even in such a case he may consider the decision after its rendition as a reason for removing the officer, on the ground that the discretion regularly entrusted to that officer by statute has not been on the whole intelligently or wisely exercised. Otherwise he does not discharge his own constitutional duty of seeing that the laws be faithfully executed." [104]

The context of this utterance, and other observations in the opinion,[105] left no doubt that it included and was intended to include removal of members of the Federal Trade Commission. The weight of the utterance, particularly as a solemn injunction to the President as to his constitutional duty as well as his constitutional power, can only be appreciated in the light of the extraordinary circumstances attending the rendition of the Myers decision. Few, if any, constitutional issues have ever been decided by the Court with more focused attention or after more elaborate consideration. The controversy—specifically, the scope of the President's power to remove a first-class postmaster—was a phase of a debate which had been waged intermittently since early in the first session of the First Congress and to which had contributed virtually all the great figures of American political history. From the beginning, and particularly since the question had been made acute by the Tenure of Office Act, 1867,[106] the Supreme Court had "studiously avoided deciding the issue until it was presented in such a way that it could not be avoided." [107] The Court first heard argument in the Myers case on December 5, 1923. Thirteen months later it restored the case to the calendar for reargument; and invited one of the most distinguished lawyers of the time, Senator George Wharton Pepper of Pennsylvania, to participate as *amicus curiae* and present the constitutional position of the Congress. The reargument extended over two days, April 13 and 14, 1925, and this time the Court held the case under consideration for a year and a half. When at length the case was decided, on October 25, 1926, four Justices delivered opinions, the report occupying 243 pages in the United States Reports. The judgment of the Court was pronounced by the Chief Justice, whose unique experience as a former President gave him unparalleled insight as judge into the great issues of government at stake. His opinion, which is 72 pages

---

[102] Rathbun v. United States, 55 Sup. Ct. 869 (1935).

[103] 272 U.S. 52 (1926).

[104] *Id*. at 135.

[105] See, especially, *id*. at 171-72.

[106] Act of March 2, 1867, 14 Stat. 430, c. 154.

[107] See 272 U.S. at 176.

in length, instead of restricting itself to the *ad hoc* situation, undertook to pronounce authoritatively upon the whole subject of the removal power.

Less than nine years later we find Mr. Justice Sutherland stating on behalf of a unanimous Court:

> "Nevertheless, the narrow point actually decided was only that the President had power to remove a postmaster of the first class, without the advice and consent of the Senate as required by act of Congress. In the course of the opinion of the court, expressions occur which tend to sustain the government's contention, but these are beyond the point involved and, therefore, do not come within the rule of stare decisis. In so far as they are out of harmony with the views here set forth, these expressions are disapproved." [108]

Pressure of work has greatly stimulated the invention of procedural devices and accelerated the tempo in the despatch of business by the Court. The volume of litigation of which the Court now disposes at a single term, the smoothness of the administrative mechanism by which this is accomplished, the extent to which argument has become a Socratic dialogue between Court and counsel, would startle the shades of Marshall and Taney even as they would have hampered the eloquence of Clay and Webster. While great changes have thus ensued during the course of a century in the details for coping effectively with the vast changes in the amount of business that has come to the Court, the essential conditions remain the same under which the ultimate issues of our federalism—the distribution of power as between the nation and the states—added to the ultimate issues of every government—the conflict between authority and liberty—are with us left for settlement by the Supreme Court through the form of an ordinary lawsuit. As governmental problems become more and not less complicated, as the dislocating impact of technological advances becomes more powerful and less imperceptible, as the forces of economic interdependence demand more and more determination and ingenuity for the maintenance of a simpler but perhaps socially more satisfying society, the deep wisdom of the Court's self-restraint against undue or premature intervention, in what are ultimately political controversies, becomes the deepest wisdom for our times.

EDITORIAL NOTE: LATER INTERCHANGES of ARNOLD, FRANKFURTER, and HART

1. Some twenty years after the above articles were written, Thurman Arnold argued before the Supreme Court, which included Justice Frankfurter, a case which tested some of the Arnold and Frankfurter views on the adversary system. Dr. J. P. Peters, a Yale professor of medicine was in 1951 appointed for a two-and-one-half-year term as Special Consultant to the Public Health Service in the Federal Security Agency. After he had twice been cleared by the F.S.A. Board of Inquiry on Employee Loyalty, the

---

[108] Rathbun v. United States, 55 Sup. Ct. 869, 873 (1935). . . . [We shall have   occasion to consider this case again in Part III.—Editor]

Loyalty Review Board of the Civil Service Commission on its own motion conducted a "post audit" of the Agency Board action. It concluded there was a reasonable doubt as to Dr. Peters' loyalty to the United States and barred him from Government service for 3 years. (An Executive Order of the President gave the Loyalty Review Board jurisdiction to review cases of persons recommended for dismissal and power to make rules and regulations, not inconsistent with the Executive Order, which it deemed necessary to implement the statutes and Executive Orders relating to employee loyalty. The Board issued a regulation indicating it would make "post-audits" of cases of cleared employees.)

A portion of the oral argument (as reported in 23 U.S. Law Week 3265-66 (1955)) is as follows:

"At the outset of his argument on behalf of Dr. Peters, Thurman Arnold, of Washington, D.C., made it clear that the only point he was interested in making was the right to confrontation of witnesses.

"Immediately, Mr. Justice Frankfurter wanted to know whether there was any question that the administrative procedural requirements had been complied with.

"Mr. Arnold referred to the contention in his brief, that, because the Loyalty Review Board acted on the basis of evidence whose source was unknown to it, it did not comply with Executive Order 9835's requirement that findings be made on the basis of all the evidence. But he added: 'We raise the point, but we don't argue it.' . . .

"Mr. Justice Reed: . . . 'Do you say that the Review Board did not have authority to review the case?'

" 'No, we are not raising that question.' "

[After Justices Harlan, Frankfurter and Reed had pressed him on the same point, Mr. Arnold said]:

" 'I would not like to win the case on that ground.'

" 'The question is not whether you want to win the case on that ground or not,' Mr. Justice Frankfurter observed. 'This Court reaches constitutional issues last, not first.'

" 'If the Court holds that the Review Board had no authority to pass on the loyalty of an employee already cleared by his agency board, then the case might be decided on that ground. But that, your Honor, is not the issue of this case as I see it. We say the Government cannot, with a formal hearing, condemn a citizen for disloyalty without complying with the requirements of due process of law.' . . .

"Later, Mr. Justice Minton interrupted to ask: 'This man wasn't a government employee, was he?'

" 'He had an appointment as a consultant which would have expired about two months later if he had not been discharged.'

"Mr. Justice Reed: 'Then he cannot be restored to his job?'

" 'No.'

" 'That is moot?'

" 'That's right.' "

The actual decision in this case (Peters v. Hobby, 349 U.S. 311 (1955)) was foreshadowed by the judicial views above expressed during oral argument. It was held that the Loyalty Review Board's review, on its own motion, of the agency board's ruling for Peters, exceeded the powers conferred upon it by the Executive Order. Chief Justice Warren observed for the majority (p. 338): "From a very early date, this Court has declined to anticipate a question of constitutional law in advance of the necessity of deciding it. . . . Applying this rule to the instant case, we . . . conclude that the Loyalty Review Board's action was so patently in violation of the Executive Order —in fact, beyond the Board's delegated jurisdiction under the Order—that the constitutionality of the Order itself does not come into issue." On the matter of relief, the Chief Justice stated: "Initially, petitioner is entitled to a declaratory judgment that his removal and debarment were invalid. He is further entitled to an order directing the respondent members of the Civil Service Commission to expunge from its records the Loyalty Review Board's finding that there is a reasonable doubt as to petitioner's loyalty and to expunge from its records any ruling that petitioner is barred from federal employment by reason of that finding. His prayer for reinstatement, however, cannot be granted, since it appears that the term of petitioner's appointment would have expired on Dec. 31, 1953, wholly apart from his removal on loyalty grounds."

Justice Black, concurring, agreed with the principle against needless decision of constitutional issues, but reminded his brethren that it was not "an inflexible rule to be inexorably followed under all circumstances." He favored decision of the constitutional issues in question, including the President's authority to issue the Executive Order—about which he expressed "grave doubt." Justice Douglas also concurred, saying: "The construction urged by the Attorney General is buttressed by a history of administrative practice. . . . The question of construction of the Executive Order was so well settled that neither the Government nor Dr. Peters suggested the absence of authority in the Review Board to take jurisdiction of this case on its own motion. I agree that it had such authority. It therefore becomes necessary for me to reach the constitutional issue." He then concluded that the use of "faceless informers" was unconstitutional. Justice Reed (joined by Justice Burton) dissented from the majority view that the Review Board's action was unauthorized by the Executive Order but expressed no opinion on the constitutional issues.

2. Arnold tangled with Hart, too—in an exchange of articles in 1960, which we shall consider at greater length in Chapter 8. Hart analyzed the time spent by members of the Supreme Court in studying a case, listening to argument, and conferring on the decision, and found the time inadequate to develop that "underpinning of principle which is necessary to illumine large areas of the law and thus to discharge the function which has to be discharged by the highest judicial tribunal of a nation dedicated to exemplifying the rule of law not only to itself but to the whole world." The Supreme Court, Hart argued, must be "a voice of reason, charged with the creative function of discerning afresh and of articulating and developing

impersonal and durable principles of constitutional law and impersonal and durable principles for the interpretation of statutes and the resolution of difficult issues of decisional law." Hart, The Time Chart of the Justices: Foreword to The Supreme Court, 1958 Term, 73 Harv. L. Rev. 84, 99 (1959). Arnold replied: "Since even Justices cannot foresee everything that may happen in the future, the opinion which 'illumines' the largest possible area of the law is not necessarily the wisest opinion. . . . Attempts to settle many issues not involved in a particular case have all too often led to untenable pronouncements from which later courts withdraw stealthily but steadily. Professor Hart's own teacher, Mr. Justice Frankfurter, has repeated over and over again that courts should avoid deciding any question not directly and unavoidably in issue." Arnold, Professor Hart's Theology, 73 Harv. L. Rev. 1298, 1311-12 (1959).

NOTES AND QUESTIONS

1. What is the justification for each of the elements of the case or controversy (including standing to sue) doctrine? Consider and evaluate the criticisms which have been directed at the various aspects of the doctrine.

Do you, for example, think that the Lake Cargo Rate case criticized by Thurman Arnold was a reasonable application of the rule that the court will not decide issues that have become moot? Is it proper to criticize a doctrine because it has been applied unreasonably in a particular case?

2. Is there reason to apply the case or controversy doctrine more strictly or less so, when statutes passed by Congress are sought to be attacked as unconstitutional? Why?

In view of the fact that the Government intervened in United States v. Johnson to uphold the constitutionality of the Emergency Price Control Act and it did not contend that the facts presented by the private parties were false or fictitious, why did it matter that the suit was "collusive"? Why should the Supreme Court have dismissed the action?

3. What rules, other than those expounding the case or controversy doctrine, limit the scope of judicial discretion to pass upon the constitutionality of statutes?

4. Are the 1934-35 views expressed by Arnold and Frankfurter consistent with their respective views in the Peters case?

5. Are the 1934-1935 views expressed by Arnold and Hart consistent with their respective views in their most recent exchange?

6. List and consider the various ways in which it may be said that courts in fact depart from a strict adherence to the doctrines limiting the exercise of the judicial power.

7. The tenant in United States v. Johnson also appealed to the Supreme Court and his appeal was consolidated with that of the Government and heard at the same time. Suppose, however, that the tenant had not appealed. Would the Government have had standing to appeal alone? The Supreme Court has never had to decide this question. Why should there be any doubt about it? Note that (1) the statute under which the Government intervened, 28 U.S.C.A. 2403, provides that the "United States shall, subject to applicable provisions of law, have all the rights of a party. . . ." and (2) the statute under which the Government appealed, 28 U.S.C.A. 1252, allows direct appeals to the Supreme Court by any party if the decision below is against the con-

stitutionality of an Act of Congress and the United States or any of its agencies is a party to the litigation below.

FULLER,* *AMERICAN LEGAL REALISM*
82 University of Pennsylvania Law Review 429, 438-442 (1934)

. . . How does it come about that a system of law which develops out of fortuitously selected cases can develop in a way that is tolerable from a political or social point of view? Why does not such a legal system become a planless, orderless chaos of doctrine?

Under our precedent system courts do not regard themselves as free to anticipate the need for legal rules; they manufacture rules *ad hoc* only, for the particular case in litigation. But what issues will get into litigation? This depends on the interest of individual litigants, and there is, therefore, no way of predicting or controlling the kind of questions which will be the subject of adjudication. In consequence it might appear inevitable that our case law would be spotty and incomplete. A developing field of business practice may be in urgent need of legal direction and control, yet the purely fortuitous circumstance that no individual happens to have an interest in litigation may bring it about that no cases are decided in the field and in consequence no "law" is made.

Now as a matter of fact we know that things do not work out quite as badly as this theory would make it appear. Where legal direction is needed it is generally forthcoming. There are hiatuses in our law, to be sure, but they are neither so numerous nor so extensive as one might be led to suppose in view of the apparently planless way in which our law grows. In spite of its dependence on the past, in spite of the lack of conscious direction over its growth, our system of case law has generally proved itself capable of meeting new social conditions. How does this come about?

Llewellyn solves this problem in a way one might have anticipated. Litigation is not purely a matter of chance and individual interest. Litigation arises out of conflict. Conflict in turn arises in those fields of social activity where growth is taking place, where the relative strength of interest-groups is changing. Things are so arranged that where changing social practice demands new law individual interest will see to it that suits will be brought which will furnish a substratum for the elaboration of the needed doctrine. There is happily a kind of automatic correlation between the interest of the individual and the social need for new law.

That there is an element of truth in Llewellyn's solution of this problem is pretty obvious. It is equally obvious that the solution is partial and incomplete. The correlation between the interest of the individual litigant and the interest of society in legal development—like the correlation assumed by classical economics between

---

* Lon L. Fuller, professor of law at Harvard since 1940, has also taught law at Univ. of Oregon, 1926-28, Univ. of Illinois, 1928-31, Duke, 1931-39, and practiced with a Boston law firm, 1942-45. He is the author of The Law in Quest of Itself (1940), editor of case-books on contracts and jurisprudence, and a prominent figure in American legal philosophy. The article from which the above extract is taken was awarded a prize by the American Philosophical Association.—Editor

the individual economic interest and the common good—is unfortunately far from complete. It is scarcely necessary to demonstrate that our courts' piece-meal and backward-looking system of legislating frequently proves inadequate to meet the need for legal control in fields where social practices are changing rapidly. There are many reasons why this should be so. If the growth in social practice is at all rapid it is likely that with our crowded court calendars case law cannot keep up with it. Again, though the change in social life may involve the interests of whole sections of the population, the pecuniary interest of any individual may be so slight as to make litigation (or at least appeal to the upper courts) impracticable.[25]

I do not for a moment believe that Llewellyn meant to assert any complete and nature-given coincidence between the interest of the individual litigant and the social need for new law. Perhaps he would recognize the need for the qualifications suggested here. But if that is so it must be confessed that his own treatment of the subject leaves too much to inference and presents, at most, intimations of the darker side of case law.

After proving that case law will, or is likely to, grow to meet new social conditions, Llewellyn points out that there are things which may operate to prevent that growth from being a healthy one. Often a whole field of law is influenced permanently by the particular turn taken by the first case arising in

---

[25] An example of this is to be found in the field of what is called "industrial insurance."

The history of regular life insurance, on the other hand, justifies pretty well Llewellyn's optimism concerning the ability of case law to deal with new situations. A whole new field of social practice grew up with life insurance and, as was inevitable, all sorts of abuses grew up with it. *A priori* one might argue that this is the kind of situation case law is not adequate to meet. Yet we know that, in general, the courts saw that the problem of life insurance was really a *new* problem, and they remade the law to fit this new field. They refused to apply in this new field the supposedly fundamental principles of contract, tort and agency law—not, to be sure, without causing some distress to the student writers of law review notes.

The history of standard life insurance is repeating itself, so far as social practice is concerned, in what is called "industrial insurance." Industrial insurance is written in small amounts (say $100 to $500). Premiums are collected weekly. The policy is issued without a medical examination, though not without warranties concerning the health of the insured sufficiently inclusive to make most of the policies issued void if these warranties were taken literally. It is no exaggeration to say that the abuses which have arisen out of this type of insurance are appalling. Many of the policies are so worded as to bind the companies to practically nothing. Not infrequently a large portion of the premium is paid for disability insurance which *is cancellable at any time by the company.* Of course, the practice is not as bad as these provisions might imply. But it is bad enough. And all of these social abuses are growing up without judicial curb. Why? For the very obvious reason that the amounts involved are too small to attract lawyers to undertake litigation. The man of moderate means, who takes out regular life insurance, has been freed from abuses of this sort by the courts—even if the courts have had to hurt the juristic sensibilities of legal theorists in order to do it. But the poor man remains a victim of the rapaciousness of the less responsible insurance companies. Is not the general indifference toward his plight in some part the product of our faith in the capacity of case law to take care of new problems? We think in terms of case law, and *we assume that the need for statutory reform is not really pressing until it makes itself manifest in the decisions.*

the field. This case may have carried a certain factual and ethical complexion which was actually the determinative element in its decision. The court in deciding it, however, may lay down a categorical rule which subsequently becomes divorced from the particular circumstances of its first utterance and controls perhaps hundreds of cases which from an ethical or "factual" viewpoint are quite different from the first and "critical" case. There is an even more sinister possibility. Organized interest-groups, aware of the importance of such critical cases, may see to it that these cases "come up in the right way." Thus by the expenditure of a little money and effort at the right time the whole future development of a field of law may be influenced.

Llewellyn fails to mention another element of contingency in the growth of case law which it seems to me is necessary to complete the picture. I refer to the fact that it is a matter of chance *in what order* cases will arise, and what the *doctrinal* connection will be between the cases which do arise and those already decided. Just as a whole field of law may be influenced by the accidental *presence* of a particular case at a particular stage of its development, so a whole field of law may be influenced by the accidental *absence* of a decision which might serve as a sort of *doctrinal bridge* between existing rules and needed new law.

The case of Shuey v. United States [92 U.S. 73 (1875)] decided that the published offer of a reward might be effectively revoked by an announcement given equal publicity. Pollock in his treatise on contracts admits the reasonableness of the decision but adds the remark that it "seems a rather strong piece of judicial legislation." [28] Why this? Because previous decisions had declared that a revocation takes effect only when "communicated." This revocation had not been "communicated" since it had never come to the knowledge of the claimant of the reward. Now suppose that there had intervened between these previous decisions and the case of Shuey v. United States a case in which a letter of revocation had been promptly delivered at the place of business of the offeree and had been allowed to remain unopened on his desk. Without much question a court would have held that such a revocation was "communicated" so soon as the offeree had had a fair opportunity to become familiar with it. And had such a case existed before the Shuey case is it likely that anyone would have regarded that decision as a "strong piece of judicial legislation"? Pollock's attitude was influenced by the purely fortuitous circumstance that there did not exist a case which could operate to carry his mind, without shock, from the older cases to the decision in the Shuey case.

The possibility that a doctrinal bridge may be lacking represents, then, an additional element of fortuity in the development of case law, operating to make the litigant's rights depend on the chronological order in which his case comes up. Furthermore it is an element which is especially likely to be operative in fields where social practice is changing rapidly. Social practice may change so rapidly that by the time cases actually get into litigation they are so far removed from what the court is familiar with that the court is left without any intellectual conduit to carry it from the old to the new. . . .

Incidentally this whole discussion gives point to a statement once made by

[28] Principles of Contract (4th ed. 1885) *20.

Ihering which would probably be disturbing to the orthodoxy of most realists.[29] The statement was that Roman law was great because it was built upon a system of "case law" which did not discriminate between real and hypothetical cases. The jurisconsults gave answer to all cases put to them, without inquiring whether they were real. This gave a continuity to the body of doctrine which they developed which cannot exist where only "real" cases are dealt with. . . .

Section 4

FEATURES of OUR SYSTEM MITIGATING ITS ADVERSARY NATURE

There are many features of our system of litigation which serve to prevent the extreme consequences which might otherwise follow from its adversary nature. We shall here attempt to summarize these features, some of which have been considered previously, and mention the procedures outside the courtroom which are available for the settlement of disputes by persons other than the parties thereto. These are noted under the headings of procedural reform, participation of organized interest groups and government, aids for litigants of limited resources, and arbitration.

1. *Procedural reform.* As we have seen was conceded by Judge Jerome Frank, modern procedural reform, principally through the pre-trial discovery devices and the pre-trial conference, has tended to make the trial less of a battle of wits and more of a search for truth. The increasing willingness of judges to call witnesses and rely upon independent experts has had the same effect.

2. *Participation of organized interest-groups and government.* The view of a trial as a battle between isolated *individual* interests must be modified to the extent that larger interests may be playing a role behind the scenes or may be permitted by the court to participate in the proceeding.

In the first place, the Government itself has sometimes appeared as amicus curiae (friend of the court).[1] And Government intervention as a *party* in litigation between private parties has often occurred, sometimes by judicial permission,[2] and sometimes under statutory right.[3] In addition, there are

[29] Geist Des Römischen Rechts (4th ed. 1858) II. 2, 385-6.

[1] Famous instances are the Government's amicus brief and argument in the restrictive covenant cases, Shelley v. Kraemer, 334 U.S. 1 (1948); Hurd v. Hodge, 334 U.S. 24 (1948), and in the school segregation cases, Brown v. Bd. of Education; Bolling v. Sharpe, 347 U.S. 483 (1954), 349 U.S. 294 (1955).

[2] In the federal courts, when a party relies

for a ground of claim or defense upon a statute or executive order (or regulation or order or agreement pursuant thereto) administered by a federal or state officer, such officer may be permitted to intervene as a party to the action, in the court's discretion. Rule 24(b), Federal Rules of Civil Procedure.

[3] Under a 1937 statute, 28 U.S.C. § 2403 (encountered previously in connection with our discussion of the landlord-tenant col-

important cases in which the Government is authorized, initially, to bring suit to see to it that private interests are afforded the legal protection to which they are entitled—e.g., Government suits to protect voting rights under the Civil Rights Act of 1957, 42 U.S.C. §1971, and suits under the Fair Labor Standards Act to obtain redress for workers who are not paid the wages to which they are entitled under the statute, 29 U.S.C. §216.

In the second place, the growing desire of interest groups—the labor unions, the National Association for the Advancement of Colored People, the trade associations, etc.—to participate in litigation ostensibly between individuals but involving their group interests, has been met with judicial liberality in allowing appearances as amici curiae. A study of this practice, by Prof. C. E. Vose of Wesleyan University, observes:[4]

The appearance of organizations as amici curiae has been the most noticed form of group representation in Supreme Court cases. This does not concern the technical office of amicus curiae for which an attorney is appointed to assist the court in deciding complex and technical problems. Today, the Supreme Court does sometimes, as in formulating its decree in the School Segregation Cases, issue a special invitation to the Solicitor General or to state Attorneys General to act as amici curiae. Of interest here is the rule under which individuals, organizations, and government attorneys have been permitted to file briefs and/or make oral argument in the Supreme Court. During the last decade amici curiae have submitted an average of sixty-six briefs and seven oral arguments in an average total of forty cases a term. . . .

Many amici curiae briefs are workmanlike and provide the Court with helpful legal argument and material. Yet writers who favor their use by organizations and recognize that "the amicus curiae has had a long and respected role in our own legal system and before that, in the Roman law" believe that many briefs in recent years display a "timewasting character."[38] Another authority has said that after 1947 there were multiplying signs "that the brief amicus curiae had become essentially an instrumentality designed to exert extra-judicial pressure on judicial decisions."[39] Concern over this by the members of the Supreme Court was shown in 1946 when Justice Robert H. Jackson, in a dissenting opinion, criticized an amicus curiae brief by the American Newspaper Publishers Association:[40]

". . . Of course, it does not cite a single authority not available to counsel for the publisher involved, and does not tell us a single new fact except this one: 'This membership embraces more than 700 newspaper publishers whose publications represent in excess of eighty per cent of the total daily and Sunday circulation of newspapers published in this country. The Association is vitally interested in the issue presented in this case, namely, the right of newspapers to publish news stories and editorials on cases pending in the courts.' "

lusive suit, U.S. v. Johnson) the Government has an absolute right of intervention in a private action "wherein the constitutionality of a federal act affecting the public interest is drawn in question."
[4] Vose, Litigation as a Pressure Group Activity, 282 Annals 20, 27-30 (1958).
[38] Harper and Etherington, [Lobbyists Before the Court, 101 U. Pa. L. Rev. 1172 (1953)].
[39] Frederick Bernays Wiener, [The Supreme Court's New Rules, 68 Harv. L. Rev. 20, 80 (1954)].
[40] Craig v. Harney, 331 U.S. 367, 397 (1946).

Justice Jackson told his colleagues, "this might be a good occasion to demonstrate the fortitude of the judiciary" . . . [The remark had a special thrust. The majority, in holding invalid the contempt punishment imposed by a State judge on a newspaper publisher, editorial writer, and news reporter for strong comments on the judge's handling of an eviction case, had observed: ". . . the law of contempt is not made for the protection of judges who may be sensitive to the winds of public opinion. Judges are supposed to be men of fortitude, able to thrive in a hardy climate." (Craig v. Harney, supra at 376).—Editor]

Supreme Court rules long provided that a "brief of an amicus curiae may be filed when accompanied by written consent of all parties to a case." [45] Until 1949 permission was freely granted. In that year, the filing of briefs by forty organizations in the case of the "Hollywood Ten" who had declined to testify before the House Un-American Activities Committee was widely regarded as an excessive use of the amici curiae procedure.[46] The Supreme Court thereupon called attention to the "rule of consent" by elaborating the procedures and permitting persons denied consent by a party to seek leave from the Court itself to act as amicus curiae. The Solicitor General, as the legal representative of the United States in the Supreme Court, took the 1949 rule change to mean that he should exercise the "rule of consent" against persons or groups wishing to be amici curiae in all cases. Since the United States government is a party in approximately 50 per cent of all cases before the Supreme Court the universal refusal of consent cut the number of organizations filing amici curiae briefs rather drastically. This rigid policy was adhered to by a succession of Solicitors General until August 1952. Complaints by Justices Black and Frankfurter then led the Solicitor General to modify the practice and exercise administrative discretion in passing upon requests of organizations to file briefs amici curiae.[47] This practice satisfied a majority of the Supreme Court for its 1949 rule change was incorporated into the full revision of the Court's rules which went into effect on July 1, 1954. However, Justice Black was still dissatisfied and, on adoption of the 1954 rules, declared:

". . . I have never favored the almost insuperable obstacle our rules put in the way of briefs sought to be filed by persons other than the actual litigants. Most of the cases before this Court involve matters that affect far more than the immediate record parties. I think the public interest and judicial administration would be better served by relaxing rather than tightening the rule against amicus curiae briefs." [48]

The standard governing grant or denial of consent to file amicus curiae briefs has been elaborated upon in a statement of policy issued by the Office of the

[45] In the old Supreme Court Rules, effective Feb. 27, 1939, section 27 (9), 306 U.S. 708-09 (1939). This section was amended on Nov. 14, 1949, 338 U.S. 959-60 (1949). All existing provisions were rescinded when new Supreme Court Rules became effective on July 1, 1954, 346 U.S. 951 (1954). Rules 42 and 44 govern *amicus curiae* procedure, 346 U.S. 951, 993, 996.

[46] Lawson v. United States, 339 U.S. 934 (1949); Marshall v. United States, 339 U.S. 933 (1949). See Harper and Ethering-

ton, *op. cit.,* p. 1173.

[47] Sonnenfeld, ["Participation of *Amici Curiae* . . . In Decisions of the Supreme Court, 1949-1957," Gov't. Research Bureau, Working Papers No. 2, East Lansing, Mich., 1958] pp. 2, 3, 8, 10. For criticism by the justices, see Lee v. United States, 343 U.S. 924 (1952); United States v. Lovknit, 342 U.S. 915 (1952).

[48] Justice Black's objection is appended to the Order Adopting Revised Rules of the Supreme Court, 346 U.S. 947 (1954).

Solicitor General.[49] While espousing a liberal attitude, the Solicitor General frowns on applicants with "a general, abstract or academic interest" in a case and on "a brief which is a vehicle for propaganda efforts." Nor is a brief that merely repeats the arguments of the parties well regarded. On the other hand, consent is given "where the applicant has a concrete, substantial interest in the decision of the case, and the proposed brief would assist the Court by presenting relevant arguments or materials which would not otherwise be submitted." Furthermore, in recent years when the Solicitor General has refused consent, the Supreme Court in some cases has granted permission to an organization to file a brief amicus curiae.

Efforts to regulate the indiscriminate filing of amici curiae briefs prevent organizations on about ten occasions each term from participating in cases. For example, an American Legion post was refused consent to file an amicus curiae brief in the Steel Seizure Case while the Congress of Industrial Organizations was permitted to do so.[50] The most active organizations in filing amici curiae briefs in recent years have been the American Civil Liberties Union, the American Federation of Labor-Congress of Industrial Organizations, the American Jewish Congress, and the National Lawyers Guild. Yet under the "rule of consent" by parties to the case each of these organizations has sometimes been denied leave to file briefs.

In spite of the increasing use of the amicus curiae brief, the judicial process will continue to retain its distinctive attribute—a forum in which an individual litigant—a one man's lobby—may force consideration of his claims in a way he may lack the means to do before the legislative branch of Government. As Professor Hurst has written: "In the second half of the twentieth century the courts have distinctive importance because they are the forum in which individuals and small groups, of their own resources, can best call organized power to account." Hurst, The Law in United States History, 104 Proc. of Amer. Phil. Soc. 518, 522 (1960).

See generally, Horn, Groups and the Constitution (1956); Vose, Caucasians Only: The Supreme Court, the NAACP and the Restrictive Covenant Cases (1959); Note, Private Attorneys General: Group Action in the Fight For Civil Liberties, 58 Yale L.J. 574 (1949); Comment, The Amicus Curiae, 55 Nw. L. Rev. 469 (1961).

3. *Aids for litigants of limited resources.* For the individual of small or no means asserting a claim which no organized group shares, our adversary system seems to function unjustly, i.e., without taking account of the resources, or relative resources, of the adversaries. However, here too, as we shall see, reforms are making some headway.

In his pioneer study, Justice and the Poor (3d ed., 1924), Reginald Heber Smith concluded that the "existing denial of justice to the poor is not attributable to any injustice in the heart of the law itself" but to defects in the machinery of justice, particularly delay ("which gives the monied might the means abundantly of wearing out the right") and the inability of the

[49] Statement of the Office of the Solicitor General, issued May 1957, quoted in Sonnenfeld, *op. cit.* [Note 47 *supra*], Appendix C, pp. 25-26.

[50] Youngstown Sheet and Tube Co. v. Sawyer, 343 U.S. 579 (1952).

poor to pay for the services of counsel. At the time he wrote, Mr. Smith calculated that there were in the United States over 35,000,000 men and women and children whose financial condition rendered them unable to pay any appreciable sum for attorney's services.[5] A 1951 study (Brownell, Legal Aid in the United States (1951), 76 et seq.) puts the figure at about 30,000,000. One means of dealing with this problem has been the familiar "legal aid" bureau, offering free or almost free legal services to the indigent. "Of the ninety legal aid offices operating in the United States in 1950 (not including volunteer facilities), thirty-seven of them were organized in the form of independent legal aid societies, thirteen were departments of social agencies, twenty were bar-association offices, eleven were public bureaus, and nine were law-school clinics. . . . Throughout the nation, the greatest single source of legal aid support is the Community Chest system."[6] The lawyers are generally paid less than salaried lawyers in private practice, and many are on a part-time basis. While legal aid services have multiplied, so has the need, so that little more than half the need is being met—which is not much improvement over the 1917 situation.[7]

For the person whose economic means are just above the level of eligibility for legal aid, but who cannot afford the typical cost of legal service, other plans are in operation. "In the 1930's imaginative young Philadelphia lawyers experimented with the creation of supervised, low-cost 'neighborhood' law offices, designed to bring legal service closer to the average person in the large city. The neighborhood law office was aimed to serve the client who could pay a moderate fee, but who through fear or ignorance was unlikely to go 'downtown' for the help he needed. In 1940 the Chicago Bar Association established a referral service, with panels of lawyers passed upon by the Association, and a referral officer, to bring together people looking for competent legal advice at reasonable fees and lawyers prepared to offer

---

[5] This figure was not intended to apply to criminal cases. Usually, the indigent accused will be defended either by counsel assigned by the court, or by a "public defender" or a "voluntary defender." Provision may or may not be made for compensation—which in any event is generally meagre. In only about one-third of the states is assignment of counsel mandatory in felony cases other than capital offenses. See generally, Blaustein and Porter, The American Lawyer (1954) 72-73, 78-81; Beaney, The Right to Counsel in American Courts (1955); Slovenko, Representation for Indigent Defendants, 33 Tul. L. Rev. 363 (1959); Equal Justice for the Accused (1959) (Report of the Joint Committee of the National Legal Aid and Defender Association and the Association of the Bar

of the City of New York).

[6] Blaustein and Porter, supra at 75, 86. Of the total support, 60% comes from community chests, 14% from other contributed funds, 9.5% from tax funds, 8.5% from bar associations and lawyers, 6% from clients, 2% from capital income. The American Bar Association has urged the extension of legal aid, both as an expression of the bar's "devotion to the ideal of equal justice for all, and in order to forestall the threat to individual freedom implicit in growing efforts to socialize the legal profession." Viewing government support as an entering wedge for socialization of the profession, the A.B.A. urged that legal aid be a "privately supported community service." Ibid., 89-90.

[7] Ibid., 67.

it. The Philadelphia and Chicago experiments together suggested that bar associations might guide the development of low-cost legal service offices in large cities." [8] The American Bar Association has endorsed the setting up of bar association "lawyers' referral plans and low cost legal service methods for . . . cases of persons who might not otherwise have the benefit of legal advice"; and by 1948 about 20 referral plans were operating.[9]

Related efforts at solution of our problem have appeared in the creation of small claims[10] and domestic relations[11] courts to dispense justice speedily and cheaply. The growth of the administrative process has also had the effect of making it unnecessary in the areas in which administrative agencies[12] are entrusted with the task of enforcing private claims (e.g., workmen's compensation, wage collection) for individuals with limited means to resort to court litigation to enforce these claims.

4. *Arbitration.* Substitutes for courtroom litigation are available whereby parties to a controversy may have it adjudged by persons other than themselves. We have mentioned the administrative agency, to which all of Part III of this book is devoted. It may be appropriate at this point also to con-

---

[8] Hurst, The Growth of American Law (1950) 326. "The lawyer-secretary of the Chicago Bar Association's referral office was able to dispose of about 80% of the inquiries that came to his office every year, without need to refer the matter to further counsel. The fact indicated how much simple consultation business there was to be done, in a volume which should make possible the self-sustaining operation of a new type of city law office, adapted to handling it for relatively small fees." *Ibid.*
[9] *Ibid.* at 327; and see Blaustein and Porter, *supra* at 92-96.
[10] In small claims courts, generally "the plaintiff did not have to file a complaint or serve the defendant, since the clerk of court would attend to both matters, on the basis of the facts given him by the plaintiff. Service was frequently by registered or ordinary mail, or even by telephone. Usually the defendant was not required to file an answer. . . . Action was fast. Ten days would ordinarily be enough to bring a claim through the whole process of trial. Some laws required no payment of court costs. Where costs were assessed, they were very low as compared with those familiar in justice courts; Boston showed small claims court costs as low as $1.20, Cleveland $1.40, Milwaukee $1.70, and the state of Vermont $2.00. The extreme simplicity of procedure and the help which the court and its staff gave the parties further cut expense, by almost completely eliminating the need of lawyers; in half a dozen states, the statutes, with unwise rigidity, went so far as to forbid the appearance of counsel in the small claims court." Hurst, The Growth of American Law, 161-162 (1950).
[11] "After the opening of the twentieth century, the criminal law broadened to cover more adequately the matter of non-support and desertion. This meant that the aggrieved wife who lacked means could have a possible remedy through the help of the district attorney and the follow-up of the probation officer; and this assistance she could have without cost to herself, with comparatively little delay, and generally without need of private counsel. Similarly, the provision of domestic relations courts, staffed with their own investigators, foretold a lessened need for lawyers' services in handling the more complex questions of divorce, separate maintenance, and custody of children. Such developments in the interest of the domestic relations litigant of small means were the more important since from the start legal aid societies usually adopted the policy of defending, but not initiating divorce proceedings." *Ibid.*, 155-156.
[12] *Ibid.* at 158-159.

sider another substitute—the process of arbitration which perhaps is best known to the public in the area of collective labor agreements. In this area, disputes arising under the agreements are usually settled by arbitration—which is provided for by almost all of the existing 100,000 or so collective labor agreements. At common law, though the arbitration awards themselves were enforceable, agreements to arbitrate were not specifically enforceable by a court order to arbitrate,—but many state statutes have made this possible. More significant than state laws in this area is the federal Labor-Management Relations Act, under which, the Supreme Court has held, the federal courts can enforce agreements to arbitrate, if the Act is otherwise applicable because interstate commerce is affected. On labor arbitration generally, see Justin, Arbitration Under the Labor Contract—Its Nature, Function and Use, 2 Lab. L.J. 908-928 (1951); Ferguson, Cooper and Horvitz, Appraisal of Labor Arbitration, 8 Ind. and Lab. Rel. Rev. 79-89 (1954); Jones, Standards in Labor Arbitration, 6 Lab. L.J. 743 (1955).

Commercial arbitration—the resolution of disputes among businessmen by arbitration—has been utilized for at least two centuries and has undergone a rapid and extensive development in modern times, largely due to conditions which surround court litigation—e.g., the delays and technicalities of court procedure and unfamiliarity of judges and juries with many specialized business controversies.[13] "Commercial arbitration, on the other hand, contemplates that the parties to a dispute shall choose one or more persons specially qualified to decide their particular case. There are no pleadings. Each party may tell his side of the case and present his testimony and other evidence informally. An arbitral hearing is held in private and at such time and place as meet the conveniences of the parties and arbitrators. Experience teaches that an arbitral adjustment of a business dispute leaves the parties susceptible to further business dealings. What is more significant, the use of future-disputes clauses often induces the parties to resolve their own misunderstandings before they require a formal arbitration." Sturges, "Commercial Arbitration," 2 Encyclopedia of the Social Sciences, 152 (1930).

It has been estimated that "if we lay aside first the cases in which the

---

[13] "Congestion of trial court calendars has been a factor. Capital is thereby unduly tied up, bankruptcies intervene and witnesses forget, die or move away before the case is tried. The records of a case are promiscuously published, to the prejudice of the credit and trade reputation of the parties. When the date for trial finally arrives, there is frequently delay in proceeding with the case, even if one or more continuances are not granted. The jurymen have often had little experience and no training in the business out of which the particular case arises. Judges are likewise frequently unqualified to try the highly technical matters involved in modern business controversies. Trial court practice seems technical and treacherous, and tends to involve unnecessary bickering. Complex rules of procedure and of the law of evidence, as well as the practise of opposing attorneys to assume no common responsibility with the trial judge to keep the case free from legal errors, often enable the losing party to appeal the case and to procure a reversal and a new trial, with delays and expenses repeated." Sturges, Commercial Arbitration, 2 Encyclopedia of the Social Sciences 152 (1930).

government is a party and second the accident cases, then the matters going to arbitration rather than to the courts represent 70 per cent or more of our total civil litigation. This suggests that the major decisional process of dispute settlement may be the arbitration and not the formal legal process. If, as further appears to be the case, the trend to arbitration seems to be increasing, then we are now living through a more violent change of judicial machinery than was present when equity emerged into conflict with the common law courts. It is not impossible to envisage a future in which the adjudicatory work of the formal legal system will be limited to the regulatory type of litigation while the resolution of private disputes becomes almost entirely a matter of consensual tribunals." Mentschikoff, The Significance of Arbitration—A Preliminary Inquiry, 17 Law & Contemp. Prob. 698 (1952). See generally on commercial arbitration the symposium in 17 Law & Contemp. Prob. 471-710 (1952).

Mention should also be made of the process of "conciliation,"—a word sometimes used synonymously with arbitration, sometimes in the sense of mediation (as where a governmental labor-disputes agency attempts to resolve differences between the disputants without imposing any compulsory settlement), sometimes in the sense of the work done by "courts of conciliation" in some European countries.[14]

---

[14] See the description of the successful use of these informal, lawyer-less courts in Norway, in Grevstad, Courts of Conciliation, 2 J. Am. Jud. Soc'y. 5 (1918). Some American state constitutions provide for courts of conciliation. Thus the Wisconsin provision (Art. VII, Sec. 16) declares: "The legislature shall pass laws for the regulation of tribunals of conciliation, defining their powers and duties. Such tribunals may be established in and for any township, and shall have power to render judgment to be obligatory on the parties, when they shall voluntarily submit their matter in difference to arbitration and agree to abide the judgment or assent thereto in writing." This provision seems as yet unexecuted in Wisconsin, though statutes have been passed governing the submission of disputes to arbitrators. See Wis. Stats., chap. 298.

CHAPTER Six

The JURY and ITS RELATION to the JUDGE: the PROCESS of FACT FINDING

Up to now we have examined some fundamental questions about the role of judges in the process of determining the public policy, standards and rules of the community. In this part we shall consider the role of the jury in this process.

We have already had reason to doubt that the only significant job of our tribunals is to determine questions of "law." Before any decision can be reached, the "facts" of the case must be ascertained and this often if not generally is the hardest task of all. There are two aspects of the job of fact ascertainment which should be evaluated separately. One is the process, which we have already referred to, of selecting from all the facts that occurred in connection with the controversy those which are deemed to be legally significant, that is, those which are material or call into operation the legal rule or rules which it is thought should govern the case. The other aspect of the process is that of finding what "facts" actually did occur.

The following materials, therefore, will deal not only with the jury's contribution to "law-making" but also with its functioning as a fact finding institution subject to judicial supervision.

WEDGWOOD v. CHICAGO & NORTHWESTERN RY. CO.
44 Wis. 44 (1878)

COLE, J. This case has been once before this court, on appeal from a judgment dismissing the complaint, and will be found in 41 Wis. 478. We then held that the facts stated in the complaint showed an actionable injury, and reversed the judgment. The cause went back for trial, and, on the trial, when the plaintiff rested, the defendant moved for a nonsuit, which was denied. Again, at the close of the testimony on both sides, the defendant moved to dismiss the complaint and for judgment of nonsuit, which was also denied. The first and second errors assigned are these rulings of the court.

We are very clear in the opinion that the court was right in refusing to withdraw the case from the consideration of the jury, on the question of defendant's negligence. It is said by the learned counsel for the defendant, that there was no evidence to go to the jury upon the question of the failure of the company to perform any duty which it owed the plaintiff, or that the injury complained of was caused by a defect in the freight car, or in the braking machinery furnished the plaintiff to operate, or that the cars were not in perfect order. The contention of the plaintiff was, that the bolt in the brake beam, or draw-bar, unskillfully projected in the way of a brakeman coupling the cars, and was suffered so to remain out of place, thereby increasing the danger of his employment. We think there was evidence from which the jury might well have found that this bolt did project through the bar or beam farther than was necessary, so as to make the act of coupling the cars unnecessarily hazardous. The conductor, Stockwell, testified that he was present when the accident happened, and had his attention called to this bolt by the fireman; that he measured it with his hands, and that it extended through the draw-bar about twelve inches. The employee, McGilvera, testified substantially to the same fact, that the bolt was out very nearly even with the draw-bar, or nearly twelve inches. It was a question for the jury, upon all the evidence, whether this condition of the bolt constituted a defect in the braking machinery, which enhanced the risk of the plaintiff in coupling the cars, and which the company was under obligation to remedy.

There was abundant evidence that this bolt caused the injury. The plaintiff in his testimony says, that as he went to pass between the moving and stationary car to the opposite side of the track, to give the engineer the signal to stop, he struck his leg against this bolt, and was thrown and injured. And McGilvera also testified, that when the plaintiff was going around the draw-bar, that rod caught the leg of his pants, and made him stumble; that he examined the end of the bolt, after the accident, and found ravelings of thread on it. We do not attempt to give the precise words of the witnesses, but this is the substance of their testimony on this point. In view of this testimony, it cannot be said that there was no evidence to go to the jury on the question whether there was a defect in the braking appliances of the car, which the company ought to have known, and remedied; or whether this defect did or did not cause the injury. Of course, it was not the province of the circuit court, any more than it is of this court, to pass upon the weight or effect of this testimony, but only to determine whether there was any evidence of negligence on the part of the defendant, which should be submitted to the jury. And it seems to us plain that there was. . . .

The last error assigned is the refusal of the court to grant a new trial. If we are correct in the views already expressed, a new trial was properly denied.

By the Court.—The judgment of the circuit court is affirmed.

LYON, J., took no part.

NOTES AND QUESTIONS

1. Explanation of court orders requested by defendant railroad: A "motion" is a formal request by a party that the judge take some official action in his behalf. When the plaintiff "rested" (i.e., when the plaintiff had finished presenting his evidence to the jury), the defendant "moved" (made a motion) for a "nonsuit" or judgment of nonsuit. The defendant made a similar motion after all the evidence of both parties had been presented to the jury. These are motions based on the claim that plaintiff has not produced evidence sufficient to support a jury verdict in his favor.

2. State the questions of fact which the jury in this case was called upon to decide. As a juryman in this case, how would you go about making up your mind about each

of these questions? Would the process by which you came to a decision about each of them be the same?

3. Does it satisfactorily describe the relative functions of court and jury in this case, to say that the court stated the law governing the case, and the jury found the facts in the case? In what respect might it be said that the jury was making a determination of law?

Compare Guinard v. Knapp-Stout & Co., 95 Wis. 482, 484 (1897): "The defendant also requested the court to instruct the jury that no statute law in this state required the defendant to cover or guard the set screw on which the plaintiff was caught. This, also, the court refused. Whether the statute requires such machinery to be covered or guarded depends upon whether it is 'so located as to be dangerous to employees when engaged in their ordinary duties.' . . . That is a question of fact for the jury. It was not error to refuse the instruction." Compare also Kreider v. Wisconsin River Paper & Pulp Co., 110 Wis. 645, 657, 86 N.W. 662, 667 (1901) (under the same statute): ". . . Most of these cases leave it to the jury to say whether the unguarded shafting or gearing was so located as to be dangerous. Of course, where there is no room for conflicting inferences, it is for the court. . . ."

Would you agree that the question left to the jury in these cases is a question of fact?

4. The typical form of jury verdict in a negligence case is the so-called "general verdict." After the judge instructs it as to the applicable "law," the jury finds for the plaintiff or defendant without specifying the facts it found or how it applied the law to these facts. When asked to render a "special verdict," the jury is confined to answering specific questions of fact put to it—after which the judge applies the law to the facts thus found by the jury and renders judgment. See Sunderland, Verdicts, General and Special, 29 Yale L.J. 253 (1920).

5. Would it have been proper for the trial judge in the Wedgwood case not to have permitted the case to go to the jury, or to have entered judgment for the defendant notwithstanding the jury's verdict, because he did not think that the plaintiff had tripped over the bolt? Or because he did not think that the defendant was negligent? May a judge ever take such action? When? How does the Wedgwood opinion delineate the proper extent of judicial review of the work of the jury? Does the line it draws make sense? Does it apply in the case of both of the above questions?

6. Would the judge in the Wedgwood case be deciding a question of fact or of law if he overturned the jury's verdict because he did not think there was sufficient evidence to go to the jury on the issues (a) whether the plaintiff tripped over the bolt; and (b) whether the defendant was negligent?

7. Does the judicial determination of whether there is sufficient evidence to go to the jury violate the provisions of state constitutions like that of Wisconsin and, in the case of a federal trial, of the United States Constitution?

The Wisconsin Constitution, I, 5 provides: "The right of trial by jury shall remain inviolate, and shall extend to all cases at law without regard to the amount in controversy. . . ."

The Seventh Amendment to the United States Constitution provides: "In suits at common law, where the value in controversy shall exceed $20, the right of trial by jury shall be preserved and no fact tried by a jury, shall be otherwise reexamined in any Court of the United States, than according to the rules of the common law."

In answering this question, consider the Kiley opinion quoted in the next question.

8. Article VII, 2 of the Wisconsin Constitution declares that "The judicial power of this state, both as to matters of law and equity, shall be vested in a supreme court, circuit courts, courts of probate, and in justices of the peace."

In Kiley v. C.M. & St. P. Ry. Co., 138 Wis. 215, 226, 119 N.W. 309, 314 (1909), holding constitutional a statute (considered later in these materials) making a railroad liable for injury caused one employee by the negligence of another employee, the court said:

"Under the system of law as it then existed it devolved on the court to determine the legal sufficiency of the evidence tending to prove a fact; and when the court had judicially ascertained that the evidence adduced tended to establish the constituent facts of the matter at issue, it then devolved on the jury to determine whether, upon the evidence, the fact was satisfactorily proven. The powers of the court and jury in the administration of the law in these respects were distinct and well defined at the time of the adoption of our constitution and became vested in the court and jury by its provisions. They cannot be abrogated or modified by legislative action to the extent of impairing, in any degree, the judicial power. Under the constitution, courts have become vested with the judicial power to determine the questions of the legal sufficiency of the evidence to establish the rights of the parties at issue and to apply the law to the facts when found, and this power cannot be withdrawn from them and conferred on juries.

"Did the legislature intend by the provisions of subd. 5 of sec. 1816, as amended, to confer judicial power, vested in the court, on the jury? It declares: 'In all cases under this act the question of negligence and contributory negligence shall be for the jury.' In their general sense the words are but a declaration of the law as it exists, namely, that when the court has found that there is legal evidence tending to show negligence or contributory negligence, it is for the jury to determine from the evidence adduced whether negligence or contributory negligence exists. This interpretation of the provision does not make a change in the law and cannot affect the rights of any person."

9. Do you agree with the following comment made by the late Professor Jerome Michael? The court, Professor Michael said, "is supposed to submit an issue to the jury if, as the judges say, the jury can decide reasonably either way. But to say that I can decide an issue of fact reasonably either way is to say, I submit, that I cannot, by the exercise of reason, decide the question. That means that the issue we typically submit to juries is an issue which the jury cannot decide by the exercise of its reason.

"The decision of an issue of fact in cases of closely balanced probabilities, therefore, must, in the nature of things, be an emotional rather than a rational act. . . ." Discussion following Michael, The Basic Rules of Pleading, 5 Record of N.Y.C.B.A. 175, 199-200 (1950).

HOLMES,* THE COMMON LAW
111-112, 120-129 (1881)

. . . If, now, the ordinary liabilities in tort arise from failure to comply with fixed and uniform standards of external conduct, which every man is presumed

* Oliver Wendell Holmes, Jr. (1841-1935) was Associate Justice, U.S. Supreme Court, 1902-32, having previously served on the Massachusetts Supreme Court, 1882-1902 (Chief Justice from 1889). He came out of the Civil War a Lieutenant-Colonel at 23, edited the American Law Review, 1870-73 and did some lecturing at Harvard. He wrote The Common Law (1881) and a number of essays and addresses collected in Collected Legal Papers (1920). His correspondence with Sir Frederick Pollock has been edited by Prof. Mark D. Howe, as has also his correspondence with Harold Laski. Many of his important writings and judicial opinions are reproduced, with helpful editorial commentary in Lerner (ed.), The Mind and Faith of Justice Holmes (1943). Holmes is generally acknowledged to be a central figure in American jurisprudential thought, and forerunner of the subsequent school of thought labelled "legal realism."—Editor

and required to know, it is obvious that it ought to be possible, sooner or later, to formulate these standards at least to some extent, and that to do so must at last be the business of the court. It is equally clear that the featureless generality, that the defendant was bound to use such care as a prudent man would do under the circumstances, ought to be continually giving place to the specific one, that he was bound to use this or that precaution under these or those circumstances. The standard which the defendant was bound to come up to was a standard of specific acts or omissions, with reference to the specific circumstances in which he found himself. If in the whole department of unintentional wrongs the courts arrived at no further utterance than the question of negligence, and left every case, without rudder or compass, to the jury, they would simply confess their inability to state a very large part of the law which they required the defendant to know, and would assert, by implication, that nothing could be learned by experience. But neither courts nor legislatures have ever stopped at that point.

From the time of Alfred to the present day, statutes and decisions have busied themselves with defining the precautions to be taken in certain familiar cases; that is, with substituting for the vague test of the care exercised by a prudent man, a precise one of specific acts or omissions. The fundamental thought is still the same, that the way prescribed is that in which prudent men are in the habit of acting, or else is one laid down for cases where prudent men might otherwise be in doubt. . . .

The principles of substantive law* which have been established by the courts are believed to have been somewhat obscured by having presented themselves oftenest in the form of rulings upon the sufficiency of evidence. When a judge rules that there is no evidence of negligence, he does something more than is embraced in an ordinary ruling that there is no evidence of a fact. He rules that the acts or omissions proved or in question do not constitute a ground of legal liability, and in this way the law is gradually enriching itself from daily life, as it should. Thus, in Crafton v. Metropolitan Railway Co.,[1] the plaintiff slipped on the defendant's stairs and was severely hurt. The cause of his slipping was that the brass nosing of the stairs had been worn smooth by travel over it, and a builder testified that in his opinion the staircase was unsafe by reason of this circumstance and the absence of a hand-rail. There was nothing to contradict this except that great numbers of persons had passed over the stairs and that no accident had happened there, and the plaintiff had a verdict. The court set the verdict aside, and ordered a non-suit. The ruling was in form that there was no evidence of negligence to go to the jury; but this was obviously equivalent to saying, and did in fact mean, that the railroad company had done all that it was bound to do in maintaining such a staircase as was proved by the plaintiff. A hundred other equally concrete instances will be found in the text-books.

On the other hand, if the court should rule that certain acts or omissions

---

* "Substantive law": i.e., the general body of rules undertaking to define the rights and duties of persons, as distinguished from rules pertaining to court procedure, including the rules regarding the introduction of evidence. —Editor

[1] L.R. 1 C.P. 300.

coupled with damage were conclusive evidence of negligence unless explained, it would, in substance and in truth, rule that such acts or omissions were a ground of liability, or prevented a recovery, as the case might be. Thus it is said to be actionable negligence to let a house for a dwelling knowing it to be so infected with small-pox as to be dangerous to health, and concealing the knowledge.[2] To explain the acts or omissions in such a case would be to prove different conduct from that ruled upon, or to show that they were not, juridically speaking, the cause of the damage complained of. The ruling assumes, for the purposes of the ruling, that the facts in evidence are all the facts.

The cases which have raised difficulties needing explanation are those in which the court has ruled that there was *prima facie** evidence of negligence, or some evidence of negligence to go to the jury.

Many have noticed the confusion of thought implied in speaking of such cases as presenting mixed questions of law and fact. No doubt, as has been said above, the averment that the defendant has been guilty of negligence is a complex one: first, that he has done or omitted certain things; second, that his alleged conduct does not come up to the legal standard. And so long as the controversy is simply on the first half, the whole complex averment is plain matter for the jury without special instructions, just as a question of ownership would be where the only dispute was as to the fact upon which the legal conclusion was founded. But when a controversy arises on the second half, the question whether the court or the jury ought to judge of the defendant's conduct is wholly unaffected by the accident, whether there is or is not also a dispute as to what that conduct was. If there is such a dispute, it is entirely possible to give a series of hypothetical instructions adapted to every state of facts which it is open to the jury to find. If there is no such dispute, the court may still take their opinion as to the standard. The problem is to explain the relative functions of court and jury with regard to the latter.

When a case arises in which the standard of conduct, pure and simple, is submitted to the jury, the explanation is plain. It is that the court, not entertaining any clear views of public policy applicable to the matter, derives the rule to be applied from daily experience, as it has been agreed that the great body of the law of tort has been derived. But the court further feels that it is not itself possessed of sufficient practical experience to lay down the rule intelligently. It conceives that twelve men taken from the practical part of the community can aid its judgment. Therefore it aids its conscience by taking the opinion of the jury.

But supposing a state of facts often repeated in practice is it to be imagined that the court is to go on leaving the standard to the jury forever? Is it not manifest, on the contrary, that if the jury is, on the whole, as fair a tribunal as it is represented to be, the lesson which can be got from that source will be learned? Either the court will find that the fair teaching of experience is that the conduct complained of usually is or is not blameworthy, and therefore, un-

[2] Minor v. Sharon, 112 Mass. 477, 487.
* "*Prima facie* evidence": enough evidence, if unrebutted by the opposing party, to support the claim of the party introducing the evidence.—Editor

less explained, is or is not a ground of liability; or it will find the jury oscillating to and fro, and will see the necessity of making up its mind for itself. There is no reason why any other such question should not be settled, as well as that of liability for stairs with smooth strips of brass upon their edges. The exceptions would mainly be found where the standard was rapidly changing, as, for instance, in some questions of medical treatment.[3]

If this be the proper conclusion in plain cases, further consequences ensue. Facts do not often exactly repeat themselves in practice; but cases with comparatively small variations from each other do. A judge who has long sat at *nisi prius** ought gradually to acquire a fund of experience which enables him to represent the common sense of the community in ordinary instances far better than an average jury. He should be able to lead and to instruct them in detail, even where he thinks it desirable, on the whole, to take their opinion. Furthermore, the sphere in which he is able to rule without taking their opinion at all should be continually growing.

It has often been said, that negligence is pure matter of fact, or that, after the court has declared the evidence to be such that negligence *may* be inferred from it, the jury are always to decide whether the inference shall be drawn. But it is believed that the courts, when they lay down this broad proposition, are thinking of cases where the conduct to be passed upon is not proved directly, and the main or only question is what that conduct was, not what standard shall be applied to it after it is established.

Most cases which go to the jury on a ruling that there is evidence from which they may find negligence, do not go to them principally on account of a doubt as to the standard, but of a doubt as to the conduct. Take the case where the fact in proof is an event such as the dropping of a brick from a railway bridge over a highway upon the plaintiff; the fact must be inferred that the dropping was due, not to a sudden operation of weather, but to a gradual falling out of repair which it was physically possible for the defendant to have prevented, before there can be any question as to the standard of conduct.

So, in the case of a barrel falling from a warehouse window, it must be found that the defendant or his servants were in charge of it, before any question of standard can arise. It will be seen that in each of these well-known cases the court assumed a rule which would make the defendant liable if his conduct was such as the evidence tended to prove. When there is no question as to the conduct established by the evidence, as in the case of a collision between two trains belonging to the same company, the jury have, sometimes at least, been told in effect that, if they believed the evidence, the defendant was liable.

[3] In the small-pox case, Minor v. Sharon, 112 Mass. 477, while the court ruled with regard to the defendant's conduct as has been mentioned, it held that whether the plaintiff was guilty of contributory negligence in not having vaccinated his children was "a question of fact, and was properly left to the jury." p. 488.

* "A judge . . . at *nisi prius*": a judge sitting on trial with a jury. The phrase is derived from old writs, which used to summon jurors for service at Westminster, unless before (nisi prius) the time assigned, a judge should arrive at the particular locality, in the course of riding circuit, to try the case there.—Editor

The principal argument that is urged in favor of the view that a more extended function belongs to the jury as matter of right, is the necessity of continually conforming our standards to experience. No doubt the general foundation of legal liability in blameworthiness, as determined by the existing average standards of the community, should always be kept in mind, for the purpose of keeping such concrete rules as from time to time may be laid down conformable to daily life. No doubt this conformity is the practical justification for requiring a man to know the civil law, as the fact that crimes are also generally sins is one of the practical justifications for requiring a man to know the criminal law. But these considerations only lead to the conclusion that precedents should be overruled when they become inconsistent with present conditions; and this has generally happened, except with regard to the construction of deeds and wills. On the other hand, it is very desirable to know as nearly as we can the standard by which we shall be judged at a given moment, and, moreover, the standards for a very large part of human conduct do not vary from century to century.

The considerations urged in this Lecture are of peculiar importance in this country, or at least in States where the law is as it stands in Massachusetts. In England, the judges at *nisi prius* express their opinions freely on the value and weight of the evidence, and the judges *in banc,* by consent of parties, constantly draw inferences of fact. Hence nice distinctions as to the province of court and jury are not of the first necessity. But when judges are forbidden by statute to charge the jury with respect to matters of fact, and when the court *in banc* will never hear a case calling for inferences of fact, it becomes of vital importance to understand that, when standards of conduct are left to the jury, it is a temporary surrender of a judicial function which may be resumed at any moment in any case when the court feels competent to do so. Were this not so, the almost universal acceptance of the first proposition in this Lecture, that the general foundation of liability for unintentional wrongs is conduct different from that of a prudent man under the circumstances, would leave all our rights and duties throughout a great part of the law to the necessarily more or less accidental feelings of a jury.

It is perfectly consistent with the views maintained in this Lecture that the courts have been very slow to withdraw questions of negligence from the jury, without distinguishing nicely whether the doubt concerned the facts or the standard to be applied. Legal, like natural divisions, however clear in their general outline, will be found on exact scrutiny to end in a penumbra or debatable land. This is the region of the jury, and only cases falling on this doubtful border are likely to be carried far in court. Still, the tendency of the law must always be to narrow the field of uncertainty. That is what analogy, as well as the decisions on this very subject, would lead us to expect.

The growth of the law is very apt to take place in this way. Two widely different cases suggest a general distinction, which is a clear one when stated broadly. But as new cases cluster around the opposite poles, and begin to approach each other, the distinction becomes more difficult to trace; the determinations are made one way or the other on a very slight preponderance of feeling, rather than of articulate reason; and at last a mathematical line is arrived at by the contact of contrary decisions, which is so far arbitrary that it might equally well have been drawn a little farther to the one side or to the other, but which must have been drawn somewhere in the neighborhood of where it falls. . . .

An example of the approach of decisions towards each other from the opposite poles, and of the function of the jury midway, is to be found in the Massachusetts adjudications, that, if a child of two years and four months is unnecessarily sent unattended across and down a street in a large city, he cannot recover for a negligent injury; that to allow a boy of eight to be abroad alone is not necessarily negligent; and that the effect of permitting a boy of ten to be abroad after dark is for the jury; coupled with the statement, which may be ventured on without authority, that such a permission to a young man of twenty possessed of common intelligence has no effect whatsoever. . . .

The same principle applies to negligence. If the whole evidence in the case was that a party, in full command of his senses and intellect, stood on a railway track, looking at an approaching engine until it ran him down, no judge would leave it to the jury to say whether the conduct was prudent. If the whole evidence was that he attempted to cross a level track, which was visible for half a mile each way, and on which no engine was in sight, no court would allow a jury to find negligence. Between these extremes are cases which would go to the jury. But it is obvious that the limit of safety in such cases, supposing no further elements present, could be determined almost to a foot by mathematical calculation.

The trouble with many cases of negligence is, that they are of a kind not frequently recurring, so as to enable any given judge to profit by long experience with juries to lay down rules, and that the elements are so complex that courts are glad to leave the whole matter in a lump for the jury's determination. . . .

QUESTIONS

1. Why, in spite of the fact that the judge instructs the jury on the meaning of negligence should Holmes regard the judge as surrendering his function when he submits the question of negligence to the jury?

2. How does Holmes justify the "surrender"? To what extent does he advocate that it be merely a temporary surrender? Are there any constitutional obstacles in the way of effectuating Holmes's suggestion? Does it support Holmes's suggestion to point out that there is more likelihood that judges, rather than successive juries, will apply the same standard to essentially similar conduct involved in successive cases? Is this desirable? What are the counterarguments, if any, for leaving the question of standards to successive, ad hoc juries? Do these considerations apply also to the determination of the "adjudicative" facts?

PECK,* *CRISIS IN THE COURTS*
(1955)

Everyone would agree that the administration of justice is a prime function of government. Indeed, tribunals for the adjustment and adjudication of the disputes

* David W. Peck, member of the New York bar, was until his resignation a Justice of the Supreme Court of New York, 1943-57, and Presiding Justice of the Appellate

and differences of men are the foundation of a peaceful society. Yet the courts and the administration of justice have been neglected and allowed to fall behind the general progress. . . .

As for the processes or mechanics of court operations, we find nothing corresponding to the improvements made in every other sphere. In medicine, all the sciences, engineering, business, and the practice of law outside of the courts, we have witnessed amazing advances. But in the courts, methods and techniques are practically the same in the automobile age as in the age of the oxcart. It is not surprising, therefore, that the court story is one of delay and that the time courts are behind in reaching cases for trial is reckoned in the terms of years. That, bad as it is, is at least measurable. What is not measurable is the cost and loss in economic and human terms of a court system which is excessively expensive and inordinately slow. . . .

We must also re-examine and re-appraise the jury system as the basis of the trial process. The jury system has been taken for granted and assumed to be good, although ours is the only country in the world which any longer attempts to handle the bulk of its civil litigation by jury trial. There is still good reason to adhere to the jury system in serious criminal cases. But on the civil side, it is quite time to question the value of the jury system and at least see what effect it is having on the administration of justice. I would not undertake in this short period to debate the merits of the jury system in civil cases, but I would point out that the process of jury trial, more than any other factor, is the root of delay in the courts. The process is so slow that it creates a bottleneck in any court with a large volume of cases. Automobile accident cases are the principal problem. Traffic congestion and court congestion go together. The flood of personal injury cases coming into court is too great to be funneled through the jury process with the present complement of judges and jurors. The cases back up just like traffic backs up at a roadblock.

Consider, also, what the jury system means in the terms of multiple hours or days of jurors' time required to do the same work that a judge alone could do. The coefficient of jurors' time to a judge's time is 108 to 1; it requires 108 jurors over any period to do what one judge could do in the same time. The mathematics are simple and have been proved over and over again in the Supreme Court of New York County. First, there is the base of twelve jurors to one judge. Then there are two additional multiples of three which must enter into the question. It takes three times as long to try a case with a jury as without a jury, meaning that in the actual trial process the time of 36 jurors is taken to do what a single judge could do. But, preliminarily, in the process of assembling jurors, keeping them available in sufficient numbers for possible need, and in examining them and accepting or rejecting them for actual service, two-thirds of a jury panel's time

Division, First Department, 1947-57. He was a member of the Task Force On Legal Services, Hoover Commission, 1954. The excerpts are from an address delivered by Justice Peck before the alumni of the Graduate Schools of Harvard University, June 15, 1955, and published in the Harvard Law Record, from which this text is reprinted.—Editor

is lost; or, to put it another way, only a third of a panel's time is actually employed in the trial of cases. The cost of this time-consuming trial process can hardly be calculated, but it is surely staggering. A jury trial is not only slow and expensive in itself, but the accumulative delay, increasing the lawyer's burden and the risk of a miscarriage of justice and postponing realization on just claims, is undoubtedly reflected in excessive contingent fee arrangements, inflated verdicts, excessive insurance premiums and the public expense of maintaining the court system.

So uneconomic is the whole procedure, aggravated by uncertainty and delay, that the public might be better served by taking automobile accident cases at least out of the courts and putting them on a compensation basis like workmen's compensation. Thoughtful persons, observing the incidents of court operations, are increasingly recommending a compensation system for automobile accidents. . . .

Perhaps I should give some explanation of why automobile accident cases are singled out for so much attention, when they are not very interesting on the intellectual level of the law. The reason is that such cases constitute the bulk of the work in the courts. It is the automobile cases which clog the calendars and tie up court operations. Automobile cases also are the bread and butter of a large part of the bar. You can imagine, therefore, how popular the suggestion of a compensation system is in legal circles.

Clearly some constitutional or radical reforms are required in the organization and functioning of the courts. . . .

SKIDMORE v. BALTIMORE & O. R. CO.
167 F. 2d 54 (2d Cir. 1948)

FRANK, Circuit Judge.

[In this case, the court affirmed a judgment for the plaintiff under the Federal Employers' Liability Act and, in so doing, upheld the trial court's denial of a request for a special verdict. In his opinion (there were separate concurrences in the affirmance, by Judges Learned Hand and Swan) Judge Frank took the opportunity to restate his views about the jury system, and indicated greater optimism than his earlier views reflected about the possibilities of the special verdict as the cornerstone of desirable reform of the jury system.—Editor]

. . . Undeniably, the verdict affords no satisfactory information about the jury's findings. But almost every general verdict sheds similar or even greater darkness. Such verdicts account for much (not all) of the criticism of the civil jury. Some revaluation of the jury system seems not unjustified in the light of the fact that ours is the only country in the world where it is still highly prized. Lauded as essential to individual liberty and democracy, and imported in the late eighteenth and nineteenth centuries from England and the United States, trial by jury was adopted in criminal cases on the European continent, but subsequently ceased there, in pre-Hitler days, to maintain its popularity. Nor can that attitude be explained as a symptom of decreased interest in democracy and individualism. For Scotland, surely long a land of liberty-loving individualists, having in the sixteenth century virtually rejected the civil jury, re-adopted it in 1815, and, still later, all but gave it up. In England, whence trial by jury came to us, it is now seldom employed in civil suits, has been abandoned in criminal prosecutions other than for major crimes, and even there is used decreasingly. In the United States, the number of jury-waivers indicates the jury's slowly waning popularity. But here, especially in the federal courts, the civil jury, in many cases, cannot be eliminated except by constitutional amendments. We must, then, as to some kind of cases, assume that it will long be with us.

But what many persons regard as its major defects can be mitigated. One device which will help to achieve that end is the special or fact verdict. Those who resent any reform which invades the jury's province should be reassured by the historians who teach that the special verdict is no new-fangled idea, but one almost as old as the jury itself, older indeed than the modern jury. In those early days, Morgan tells us, jurors often successfully insisted upon the right to render such verdicts against the desires of the judges who wanted general verdicts.[7] To be sure, in this country, during the latter part of the eighteenth and the early part of the nineteenth centuries, the right to return a general verdict was highly esteemed as the jury's prerogative, especially in criminal cases; the judges then instructed the juries that they were to decide both "the law" and the facts, not being bound by the opinion of the trial judge. Most jurisdictions later repudiated that doctrine. The courts and legal writers declared that, if juries had the right to ignore the judges' instructions as to the applicable legal rules, the "law" would "become as variable as the prejudices, the inclinations and the passions of men"; "the parties would suffer from an arbitrary decision"; "decisions would depend entirely upon juries uncontrolled by any settled, fixed, legal principle," and would be "according to what the jury in their own opinion suppose the law is or ought to be"; "our government" would "cease to be a government of laws and become a government of men"; "jurors would become not only judges but legislators as well"; the "law" would "be as fluctuating and uncertain as the diverse opinions of different juries in regard to it"; jurors would be "superior to the national legislature, and its laws . . . subject to their control" so that a "law of Congress" would "be in operation in one state and not in another." [10]

Yet no amount of rave talk can do away with the fact that, when a jury returns an ordinary general verdict, it usually has the power utterly to ignore what the judge instructs it concerning the substantive legal rules, a power which, because generally it cannot be controlled,[11] is indistinguishable for all practical purposes, from a "right." Practically, then, for all we may say about the jury's duty when it renders a verdict, we now do have the very conditions which we were warned would result if the jury had the right to decide legal propositions: cases are often decided "according to what the jury suppose the law is or ought to be"; the "law,"

[7] Morgan, A Brief History of Special Verdicts and Special Interrogatories, 32 Yale L.J. (1923) 575, 588.

[10] Most of these statements are quoted in the majority opinion in Sparf and Hansen v. United States, [156 U.S. 51 (1895)]. . . .

[11] . . . [The trial judge, of course, can grant a new trial in any civil case, and in a criminal case where the verdict is against the defendant. But he thus exercises merely a temporary veto, since another jury, with like power, again hears the case. Except in unusual circumstances, there is a limit to the number of new trials which may be granted. . . .]

when juries sit, is "as fluctuating and uncertain as the diverse opinion of different juries in regard to it"; and often jurors are "not only judges but legislatures as well." Indeed, some devotees of the jury system praise it precisely because, they say, juries, by means of general verdicts, can and often do nullify those substantive legal rules they dislike,[13] thus becoming ad hoc ephemeral (un-elected) legislatures (a state of affairs singularly neglected by most writers on jurisprudence, who would do well to modify their ideas by recognizing what might be called "juries-prudence"). Surprisingly, that sort of defense of the general verdict is not seldom voiced by lawyers who, in the next breath, demand strict adherence to the legal precedents. . . .

The general verdict enhances, to the maximum, the power of appeal to the biases and prejudices of the jurors, and usually converts into a futile ritual the use of stock phrases about dispassionateness almost always included in judges' charges. Many books on trial tactics, written by experienced trial lawyers, which give advice as to how to arouse juries' emotions, make the point that a jury tries the lawyers rather than the case, and that the lawyers, in jury trials, must recognize themselves as actors or stage-managers engaged in theatrical performances.[16] In a series of pamphlets on trial practice, recently published under the auspices of the American Bar Association, one author writes that "the advocate . . . must always recognize that the jury is judging the lawyer as well as the witnesses, quick to take sides because of the protagonists rather than their opinion of the testimony";[17] another says that the jurors' reaction to trial counsel "may be more important than the reaction to the client, for the client appears on the stand only during a relatively brief period, while the lawyer is before the jury all the time"; this same author gives detailed suggestions of means by which a lawyer may "ingratiate himself" with the jury.[18] A court has solemnly decided that "tears

---

[13] See, e.g., Wigmore, A Program For the Trial of a Jury Trial, 12 Am. Jud. Soc. (1929) 166. . . . See Pound, Law In Books and Law In Action, 44 Am. L. Rev. (1910) 12, 18, 19: "Jury lawlessness is the great corrective law in its actual administration. The will of the state at large imposed on a reluctant community, the will of a majority imposed on a vigorous and determined minority, find the same obstacle in the local jury that formerly confronted kings and ministers. . . . What is the purpose and what the occasion of the extensions of the powers of juries to which I have referred? Practically the purpose is, in largest part, to keep the letter of the law the same in the books, while allowing the jury free rein to apply different rules or extra-legal considerations in the actual decision of causes—to create new breaches and widen existing breaches between law in the books and law in action. The occasion

is that popular thought and popular action are at variance with many of the doctrines and rules in the books, and that the law is trying to save the latter and accommodate itself to the former. . . . If the ritual of charging the jury on the law with academic exactness is preserved, the record will show that the case was decided according to law, and the fact that the jury dealt with it according to extra-legal notions of conformity to the views of the community for the time being, is covered up." . . .

[16] See, e.g., Goldstein, Trial Technique (1935); Harris, Hints On Advocacy (1943 ed.); Longenecker, Hints On The Trial of A Law Suit (1927).

[17] Gair, The Trial of a Negligence Action (1946) 36.

[18] Bodin, Selecting a Jury (1945) 50 ff. See also, in the same series, Hays, Tactics in Cross-Examination (1946) 18 ff. Cf. Bodin, Pleading and Practice (1946) 50-51.

have always been considered legitimate arguments before a jury," that such use of tears is "one of the natural rights of counsel which no court or constitution could take away," and that "indeed, if counsel has them at command, it may be seriously questioned whether it is not his professional duty to shed them whenever proper occasion arises. . . ."[19] Harris, in his well known book on advocacy, says, "It may be that judgment is more easily deceived when the passions are aroused, but if so, you [the lawyers] are not responsible. Human nature was, I presume, intended to be what it is, and when it gets into the jury-box, it is the duty of the advocate to make the best use of it he fairly can in the interests of his client."[19a] This is no laughing matter. For prejudice has been called the thirteenth juror,[19b] and it has been noted that "Mr. Prejudice and Miss Sympathy are the names of witnesses whose testimony is never recorded, but must nevertheless be reckoned with in trials by jury."[19c]

Small wonder that Thayer commented that jury trials are "a potent cause of demoralization to the bar,"[20] or that Morgan, well versed in trial tactics, in reviewing a book on jury trial techniques, recently wrote:[21] "If only some lawyer could rise up and honestly denounce Mr. Goldstein as a defamer of his profession. . . . If only a reviewer could assert that this book is a guide not to the palaces of virtue but to the red-light districts of the law. But a decent respect for the truth compels the admission that Mr. Goldstein has told his story truly. He has told it calmly, without a pretense of shame and [God save us!] without the slightly suspicion of its shamefulness. He has shown by his own unperturbed frankness with what compliance the profession, which would smile the superior smile of derision at the suggestion of a trial by battle of bodies, accepts trial by battle of wits. In all innocence, he has produced a volume which is a devastating commentary upon an important aspect of our administration of justice." Not that lawyers, trying to protect their clients, should be censured for employing the stratagems described in such a book—as long as we retain the general-verdict jury system. But, with the general verdict in operation, and those stratagems as its usual concomitants, it should not be surprising that one of the members of this court said, "I am by no means enamored of jury trials, at least in civil cases

---

19 Ferguson v. Moore, 98 Tenn. 342, 39 S.W. 341, 343.

The court also said: "Perhaps no two counsel observe the same rules in presenting their cases to the jury. Some deal wholly in logic,—argument without embellishments of any kind. Others use rhetoric, and occasional flights of fancy and imagination. Others employ only noise and gesticulation, relying upon their earnestness and vehemence instead of logic and rhetoric. Others appeal to the sympathies—it may be the passions and peculiarities—of the jurors. Others combine all these with variations and accomplishments of different kinds."

19a Harris, Hints On Advocacy, 1943 Ed. 275.

Aristotle, in his Rhetoric, gave similar advice, in great detail, as to how to win cases before Greek juries. Those juries, we are told, "judged both the law and the facts"; but, in truth, so, too, do ours when they render general verdicts.

19b Osborn, The Mind of the Juror (1937) 92.

19c Osborn, The Problem of Proof (2d Ed. 1926) 112.

20 Thayer, A Preliminary Treatise on Evidence (1898) 535. . . .

21 Morgan, Book Review, 49 Harv. L. Rev. (1936) 1387, 1389.

. . .," [22] and that Mr. Justice Cardozo, speaking for the Supreme Court, remarked, "Few would be so narrow or provincial as to maintain that a fair and enlightened system of justice would be impossible without" trial by jury.[22a]

That is not to say that, by way of contrast with juries, all trial judges are free of all susceptibility to emotional appeals, or that—although most trial judges, because of experience, are more skilled in fact-finding than juries and better armored against the seductive wiles of lawyers—any trial judge can (or should) slough off all predilections. (Lord Bramwell observed, "One third of a judge is a common law juror if you get beneath his ermine"; and Mr. Justice Riddell added that "the other two thirds may not be far different." [23a] Nor is it to say that, where constitutional or statutory provisions require jury trials, judges do not have the highest obligation to see that such trials are conducted in accordance with the basic principles which govern such proceedings.[24] But, as reasonable modifications

[22] L. Hand, The Deficiencies of Trials to Reach The Heart of The Matter, 3 Lectures on Legal Topics (1926) 89. Judge Hand has often elsewhere recognized important policy reasons for retaining the criminal jury.

[22a] Palko v. Connecticut, 302 U.S. 319, 325, 58 S. Ct. 149, 152, 82 L. Ed. 288. See also Adams v. United States ex rel. McCann, 317 U.S. 269, 279, 63 S. Ct. 236, 87 L. Ed. 268, 143 A.L.R. 435.

[23a] Riddell, Common Law and Common Sense, 27 Yale L.J. (1918) 993, 996. In Huskie v. Griffin, 75 N.H. 345, 74 A. 595, 598, 27 L.R.A., N.S., 966, 139 Am. St. Rep. 718, the court said: "Judges are men, and their decisions upon complex facts must vary as those of jurors might on the same facts. Calling one determination an opinion and the others a verdict does not . . . make that uniform and certain which from its nature must remain variable and uncertain."

Nevertheless, the trial judge has distinct advantages. So far as he is a juror, his experience with many trials gives him a training for his job: the distractions and interruptions do not confuse him as they are likely to confuse the ordinary juryman. And obviously, the trial judge is far better able to understand the legal rules and the method of applying them to the facts.

Moreover, the character of a trial is different when only a trial judge sits. Says Green, "If the jury is taken out of the courthouse, the drama is gone. The court-room is not the same place. There is no tenseness. The lawyers are not the

same; they no longer glare at one another. Even the parties are docile. The judge returns to himself. The attendants drop back into their humdrum ways. The crowd is made up of a few parties at interest and the habitual loungers. The place is dead. There is no haranguing in choosing the arbiter, nothing more than a brief statement of the issues, and seldom that; the examination of the witnesses proceeds with calmness, barring the most exceptional case; objections to evidence are seldom made, and when made, if there is the slightest uncertainty, the judge hears the evidence and states that if it appears to be inadmissible he will ignore it in his findings. The argument on the issues is brief and pointed. There are no instructions to prepare, no verdict, no motion for a new trial except in the rarest instance. The judge either announces his conclusion, or else takes it under advisement for further study and later announcement. He may then file the findings which support his decision. The whole process is deflated until there is little left to do save get down to business. The trial of the same case before a judge and before the same judge with a jury, with the same lawyers, reflects the most startling differences. . ." Green, Judge and Jury, 403, 404.

[24] The writer of this opinion has expressed his own views on this subject in a dissenting opinion in United States v. Antonelli Fireworks Co., 2 Cir., 155 F. 2d 631, 642, 665, as follows: "It has been suggested that a judge (like me) who shares the doubts about the wisdom of the jury system is

of the jury system are not thereby precluded, a vigorous revival of a traditional adjunct of that system, i.e., the special verdict, represents no deviation from judicial obligations.

Perhaps the least desirable feature of the general verdict, a feature which the fact verdict wipes out, is this: The theory of the general verdict involves the assumption that the jury fully comprehends the judge's instructions concerning the applicable substantive legal rules. Yet, often the judge must state those rules to the jury with such niceties that many lawyers do not comprehend them, and it is impossible that the jury can. Judge Bok notes that "juries have the disadvantage . . . of being treated like children while the testimony is going on, but then being doused with a kettleful of law during the charge that would make a third-year law-student blanch." [25b] Nevertheless, the patently fictitious assumption that the jurors have more legal wisdom than third-year law-students requires the upper court to reverse when a trial judge fails to state the pertinent substantive rules with sufficient particularity. Such faulty instructions, it has been said, "are the greatest single source of reversible error." [25c] Judge Rossman says: "The general verdict is responsible for the elaborate instructions given to the jury. . . . The necessity for [these] instructions creates pitfalls which may trap the trial judge

---

inconsistent if he urges that the courts be vigilant in preserving the jury's function. I do not understand that criticism. It is the sworn duty of judges to enforce many statutes they may deem unwise. And so, when on the bench, our private views concerning the desirability of the jury system are 'as irrelevant as our attitudes towards bimetallism or the transmigration of souls.' Consequently, as long as jury trials are guaranteed by constitutional or statutory provisions, it is the obligation of every judge, no matter what he thinks of such trials, to see that they are fairly conducted and that the jury's province is not invaded. That does not mean that a judge may not freely express his skepticism about the system, may not seek to bring about constitutional and statutory changes which will avoid or reduce what he considers its unfortunate results as it now operates."
[25b] Bok, I, Too, Nicodemus (1946).

There are at least three theories of how the general-verdict-jury-system works: (1) According to a naive theory, the judge conclusively determines the pertinent substantive legal rules, and the jury confines itself to finding the facts. (2) A more sophisticated theory runs thus: The judge has one function and the jury two. The judge announces authoritatively the perti-

nent rules of law. The jury (a) ascertain the facts and (b) apply to these facts the rules of law laid down by the judge and (c) thus arrive at their general verdict. The judge, that is, supplies the major premises, consisting of the abstract rules of law; the jury determine the minor premise from the evidence, and then work out the syllogism to its logical conclusion in the verdict which they report to the judge. Some of those who accept this theory assert that juries often circumvent the legal rules by misfinding the facts; the facts, it is said, are "found in order to reach the result." [See, e.g., Pound, Introduction to the Philosophy of Law (1921) 133; cf. 121.] That thesis assumes that the jurors, understanding what the judge told them about the substantive legal rules, proceed with consummate skill and cunning to devise the exact finding of facts which, when correlated with those rules, will logically compel the judgment the jurors desire. (3) A more realistic theory maintains that jurors often do not understand the judge's instructions and simply bring in an unexplained verdict for the party they favor. See Frank, Law and The Modern Mind (1930) Part One, Chapter 16, and Appendix V.
[25c] Green, Judge and Jury (1930) 351. . . .

and which in turn may result in new trials, appeals and reversals." [25d] In many instances, such a reversal means merely another trial at which the judge will intone to another uncomprehending jury a revised version of those legal rules. There results an enormous waste of time and money. Indeed, the prospect of a prolonged new trial undoubtedly often induces a litigant of modest means to accept an unfair settlement. The fact verdict provides an obvious escape from these wasteful or unfair consequences of the general verdict.

The finding of facts, says Sunderland, "is much better done by means of the special verdict. Every advantage, which the jury is popularly supposed to have over the court as a trier of facts, is retained, with the very great additional advantage that the analysis and separation of the facts in the case which the court and the attorney must necessarily effect in employing the special verdict, materially reduces the chance of error. It is easy to make mistakes in dealing at large with aggregates of facts. The special verdict compels detailed consideration. But above all it enables the public, the parties and the court to see what the jury has really done. . . . The morale of the jury also is aided by throwing off the cloak of secrecy, for only through publicity is there developed the proper feeling of responsibility in public servants. So far, then, as the facts go, they can be much more effectively, conveniently and usefully tried by abandoning the general verdict and substituting the special verdict. . . . The special verdict is devised for the express purpose of escaping the sham of false appearances." [26]

When using a special verdict, the judge need not—should not—give any charge about the substantive legal rules beyond what is reasonably necessary to enable the jury to answer intelligently the questions put to them. As, accordingly, the jury is less able to know whether its findings will favor one side or the other, the appeal to the jurors' cruder prejudices will frequently be less effective. "A perverse verdict may still be returned, granted a jury clever enough to appreciate the effect of its answers, and to shape them to harmonize with its general conclusions. But it is much more difficult . . . and by requiring the jury to return the naked facts only we may fairly expect to escape the results of sympathy, prejudice and passion." [26b] That may be too sanguine a hope; but the fact verdict may often reduce the more undesirable sway of emotions. It is suggested, too, that a special verdict "searches the conscience of the individual juror, as a general verdict does not," because "such are the contradictions in human nature that many a man who will unite in a general verdict for a large and unwarranted sum of money will shrink from a specific finding against his judgment and sense of right and wrong." . . .[26c]

True, the common-law type of special verdict, when utilized in this country, frequently caused so many complications that it fell into disrepute.[27] But in three

[25d] Rossman, The Judge-Jury Relationship In the State Courts, 3 F.R.D. 98, 109. See Farley, Instructions to Juries, 42 Yale L.J. (1932) 194, 208, 215-216; Cornelius, Trial Tactics (1932) 291 . . .

[26] Sunderland, [Verdicts, General and Special, 29 Yale L. J. 253 (1920)].

[26b] Clementson, Special Verdicts and Special Findings by Juries (1950) 12.

[26c] Clementson, loc. cit., 15. . . .

[27] See, e.g., Dobie, The Federal Rules of Civil Procedure, 25 Virginia L. Rev. 261, 287 (1939).

states, North Carolina, Wisconsin and Texas, the special-verdict practice in civil cases was so modified as to avoid most of those complications.[27a] The Wisconsin* and Texas procedures, apparently the most effective, seem to have been the model for Rule 49 (a) of the Federal Civil Rules of Procedure, 28 U.S.C.A. following section 723c, which authorizes the trial judge to dispense with a general verdict and, instead, to require the return of special written findings. Rule 49 (b) also authorizes the judge to call for a general verdict accompanied by written interrogatories.[29] But, unlike the Texas trial judge, the federal district judge, under the Rule, has full, uncontrolled discretion in the matter. He may still require merely the old-fashioned general verdict.

Accordingly, we cannot hold that a district judge errs when, as here, for any reason or no reason whatever, he refuses to demand a special verdict, although we deem such a verdict usually preferable to the opaque general verdict. Perhaps some day soon Rule 49 will be amended to make compulsory either special verdicts or written interrogatories in civil jury cases. Meanwhile, we can but hope that, in such cases, the district judges will require one or the other, on their own motion or when asked to do so.

The fact verdict will furnish no panacea. Among other things, as previously noted, it will still be true that, in a relatively simple case, the jury will still be able to foresee what answers to the questions will produce a judgment for the side it favors. There is this, too, to consider: Some persons oppose the requirement that trial judges in non-jury cases shall file special findings of fact.[32] As such findings closely resemble a jury's special verdict, it is therefore pertinent here that some of those opponents suggest, in effect, that a trial judge's decision is a unique composite reaction to the oral testimony, a composite which ought not—or, rather, cannot without artificiality—be broken down into findings of fact and legal conclusions. Back of this suggestion there lurks something like the notions of gestalt psychology: A judge's reaction to the evidence at a trial is apparently considered a "whole" (a "gestalt" or "pattern") which cannot adequately be analyzed. Separation of a decision in "law" and "fact" components, it seems to be asserted, will be "too logical," in the sense that it excludes the "intuition of experience which outruns analysis and sums up many unnamed and tangled impressions, impressions which may lie beneath consciousness without losing their worth."[36] Some support

---

[27a] See Green, Judge and Jury (1930) 350. . . .

* For the Wisconsin system, see Volz, The Wisconsin Method for Submission of Fact Issues to Juries—the Special Verdict, 23 U. Kan. City L. Rev. 206 (1955).—Editor

[29] As to interrogatories, see Wicker, Special Interrogatories to Juries in Civil Cases, 35 Yale L.J. (1926) 296; Green, loc. cit., 354, 355.

Clementson, Special Verdicts and Findings By Juries (1905) 45, 46, says: "The submission of interrogatories . . . is a sort

of 'exploratory opening' into the abdominal cavity of the general verdict . . . by which the court determines whether the organs are sound and in place, and the proper treatment to be pursued."

[32] Sunderland, Findings of Fact and Conclusions of Law, 4 U. Chi. L. Rev. (1937) 218; Davis v. Boston Elevated Ry. Co., 235 Mass. 482, 494, 126 N.E. 841, 842, 843; cf. Guiseppi v. Walling, 2 Cir., 144 F. 2d 608, 622, 155 A.L.R. 761.

[36] Holmes, J., in Chicago, B.&Q. Ry. Co. v. Babcock, 204 U.S. 585, 598, 27 S. Ct. 326,

for this position might be sought in recent writings to the effect that logic stems from language which, in turn, because of its inherent character, cannot fully express or symbolize "feelings," and that feelings have a rational validity, expressive of "wordless knowledge," which must not be disregarded.[37] While, on net balance, however, a logical assaying by a trial judge of his decision has immense value, so that in a non-jury case special findings of fact by a trial judge are eminently desirable, the argument against special findings of fact by trial judges might perhaps be applied with somewhat greater effectiveness against fact verdicts by juries: It might be said that some *one* person or body, either a trial judge or a jury, should be entrusted in each case with reaching a composite reaction to the evidence, and that therefore a division of functions into explicit fact-finding by a jury and "law-finding" by a judge will yield an undesirable artificiality. Nonetheless, even assuming that that argument has some cogency, fact verdicts seem clearly better than general verdicts.

NOTES AND QUESTIONS

1. In The Law and the Modern Mind (1930) 176 (footnote), Judge Frank cited the "refusal of juries to apply the harsh fellow-servant rule which the courts evolved" as an example of jury "lawlessness" designed to liberalize strict law. Recall the Heine case in Chapter 4. Does this case indicate that Frank has chosen an apt example? As illustrated by the Heine case, how do legal rules enable the judge to impose effective limits upon the scope of jury lawlessness?

2. Judge Frank went on to ask: "But is it not possible that the courts failed to abolish the fellow-servant rule by 'judicial legislation' just because the juries made that abolition unnecessary?" Does the Heine case justify an affirmative reply to this question?

3. Whatever the extent, in fact, of jury lawlessness, is there any question but that the general verdict affords greater opportunity than the special verdict for this practice?

51 L. Ed. 636. Cf. Perkins v. Endicott Johnson Corporation, 2 Cir., 128 F. 2d 208, 221 and note 49.

For discussion of the difficulty of nicely separating "law" and "facts," and as to interactions between them, see Wurzel, Methods of Juridical Thinking (1904) in The Science of Legal Method (1917) 390, 396; Orfield, Criminal Appeals in America (1939) 85; Paul, Dobson v. Commissioner: The Strange Ways of Law and Fact, 57 Harv. L. Rev. (1944) 753; Isaacs, The Law and the Facts, 22 Col. L. Rev. (1922) 1, 11; Fox, Law and Fact, 12 Harv. L. Rev. (1899) 545; Thayer, A Preliminary Treatise on The Law of Evidence (1898) 183 ff, 249 ff; Green, Judge and Jury (1930) 270; Dickinson, Administrative Justice and The Supremacy of Law (1927) 52-55, 168-170, 203, 313-319; Morris, Law and Fact, 55 Harv. L. Rev. (1942) 1303; Cook, 'Facts' and 'Statements of Fact,' 4 U. Chi. L. Rev. (1937) 233; Green, Mixed Questions of Law and Fact, 15 Harv. L. Rev. (1901) 271; Clark and Stone, Review of Findings of Fact, 4 U. Chi. L. Rev. (1937) 190, 211 note 93. Compare Pound, Appellate Procedure in Civil Cases (1941) 28 with Pound, Justice According to Law, 14 Col. L. Rev. (1914) 103, 104.

[37] See, e.g., Langer, Philosophy In A New Key (1942), Pelican ed. (1948) passim; Sullivan, Beethoven (1927) 32-35; cf. Ortega, Concord and Liberty (1946) 61-63; MacMillan, Law and Other Things (1937) 319-330; Huxley, Science, Liberty and Peace (1946) 35-39; Forster, On Criticism of The Arts, Harpers' Magazine, July 1947, p. 9; Pascal, Pensees (1670) Nos. 1-4, 36, 253, 276, 282, 283, 358.

EDITORIAL NOTE: FURTHER VIEWS of JUDGE FRANK on the FACT-FINDING PROCESS and the JURY'S ROLE

Judge Frank has emphasized repeatedly that the inability of lawyers to predict future decisions of courts is due not only to the indefiniteness of the rules of law but also, and even in greater measure, to the inevitable doubt about what the tribunal will find were the facts in the case. (See e.g., Courts On Trial, at 14-36.)

For purposes of a lawsuit, says Frank, the facts are not what actually happened, but only what the trial judge and jury come to think happened. The actual events, of course, happened in the past; the tribunal "can learn of those facts only as an historian learns of facts—at second or third hand, through the stories of witnesses." (Frank, Judicial Fact-Finding and Psychology, 14 Ohio St. L.J. 183 (1953)). The "facts" of a lawsuit, therefore, maintains Frank, are only "guesses" about the facts by the trial judge and jury. Since these guesses must be based usually on the oral testimony of witnesses, their soundness depends upon the reliability of that testimony. Yet, says Frank, it "is a commonplace that a witness may be seriously mistaken in one or all of three ways: (1) He may have erred in his original observation of the past event, (2) or in his subsequent memory of what he observed, (3) or in the way his memory of his original observation is communicated to the trial court" (14 Ohio St. L.J., at 184).

These are difficulties inherent in the testimony even of honest and unprejudiced witnesses. But some witnesses, Frank also reminds us, are liars, and others are prejudiced, consciously and unconsciously, for or against one of the parties to the lawsuit and this bias colors the testimony offered. (Courts on Trial, at 18, 19). Difficulties are further compounded by the possibility that for any number of reasons a truthful witness may make an unfavorable personal impression upon the tribunal while an untruthful witness may make a favorable one. The path to truth may also be blocked because an important witness is dead or missing and important written evidence destroyed or unavailable. Finally, Frank points out, the trial judge and jury are themselves witnesses of what goes on in the courtroom and, as such, subject to all the infirmities of other witnesses in determining what the witnesses appearing before them said and how they behaved. "A trial court's finding of fact," he concludes, "is then, at best, its belief or opinion about someone else's belief or opinion." (*Id.* at 22). Yet a trial court's mistakes about facts based on oral testimony are rarely corrected by an appellate court because only the trial court saw and heard the witnesses and was able to judge their demeanor, without which their testimony cannot be evaluated intelligently.

In his talk before a meeting of the special committee on law and psychology of the Association of American Law Schools, held at Columbia University, November 28, 1952 (reprinted in the article in the Ohio State Law Journal cited above), Frank urged that psychological and psychiatric experiments as to errors in perception, memory, and communication, under court-room conditions, be conducted jointly by lawyers and psychologists (Ohio St. L.J., at 184). As practical measures, he recommended (1) that a psychologist and a psychiatrist examine each witness and report to the trial court whether the witness had any marked defects in perception, memory, and communication, with particular reference to the specific matters about which the witness testified; (2) further study of such devices as lie detectors and truth serums, which he recognized would not meet the problem of honest but unreliable witnesses; (3) drastic modification of the exclusive use of the question-and-answer method of interrogating witnesses; (4) reconsideration of present judicial reliance upon "demeanor evidence"; and (5) education of trial judges about their own biases by making available psychiatrists whom the judges could consult from time to time. (*Id.* at 185-189).

Even if measures are adopted to enable the tribunal to evaluate the testimony of witnesses intelligently, Judge Frank points out that the reliability of the fact-finding process will also depend upon the ability of juries to do the evaluating. But, he argues, many "experienced persons believe," as he does, "that of all the possible ways that could be devised to get at the falsity or truth of testimony, none could be conceived that would be more ineffective than trial by jury." (Courts on Trial, at 20).

Still, as we saw in the Skidmore case, Judge Frank believed that improvements in the jury system were possible and in Courts on Trial, pp. 143-146, he summarized his suggestions for improvement. In addition to the more widespread use of special verdicts, his recommendations include (1) use of special juries consisting of persons conversant with the subject matter of the litigation; (2) referral of complex matters in dispute in a civil suit to experts whose report on the facts, together with the evidence on which it was based, should be presented to the jury; (3) revision of the exclusionary rules of evidence, which Frank discussed briefly in his Skidmore opinion; (4) consideration of the suggestion made by Judge Galston, in Civil Jury Trials and Tribulations, 29 A.B.A.J. 195 (1943), that jury-room deliberations be recorded and the record made available to the trial judge for use by him in reviewing the jury's verdict; and (4) training of prospective jurors through the medium of courses in the public schools and adult education classes which will deal with the function of the jury and the nature of trial court fact-finding. Frank would bar from jury service any person who has not taken such a course and passed the examination in it. Elsewhere, Frank has recognized that educating prospective jurors, psychologically and psychiatrically, to deal with testimony, is an "even more horrendous problem" than so educating future judges. (Judicial Fact-Finding and Psychology, 14 Ohio St. L.J. 183, 189 (1953)).

If all these reforms were adopted, Frank concludes, jury trials would be less hazardous for litigants than at present, but "they would still be far less desirable than jury-less trials before well-trained honest trial judges." (Courts on Trial, at 145).

BOTEIN,* *TRIAL JUDGE*
182-185, 187-191, 193-194, 208-210 (1952)

I cannot join in a criticism leveled frequently at our jury system: that the emotional content of juries is much higher than that of judges—and too high to permit of sound verdicts. The verdicts resulting from jury lawmaking are sometimes dramatic and startling, because they vary so drastically from the verdicts indicated by a strict application of the law. The tendency is to attribute these variations to emotional susceptibility and sentimentality, and not to a conscious desire to reject a law which the jury regards as unfair and impractical.

The average jury may contain members whose reason sometimes yields to their emotions. But as a jury, as an entity, it seldom succumbs to such influences. At least, I find little evidence of it in the trial of civil cases.

Jurors may be lawless, but they are not irrational. They may not realize all of the influences and forces which affect their decisions; but then, neither does a judge. I believe jurors do require that a law square with their ideas of morality and fair play. . . .

The critics who urge elimination of the jury seldom extend this recommendation to criminal trials. One compelling reason is that the jury institution in criminal cases is traditionally associated with the protection of the civil liberties of the individual.

Yet the tendency to emotion-laden verdicts would appear to be stronger in criminal cases than in civil cases. Loss of freedom would impress jurors as being much more devastating than loss of dollars. Still, many prosecuting officers boast a conviction average in excess of eighty per cent and even ninety per cent of the cases tried. Surely, in rendering many of those verdicts of conviction jurors had to steel themselves against their apprehensions of the misery that would flow from their verdicts—often upon the innocent family of the accused. It may be that the basic standards of morality written into our criminal law conform closely to the standards of the man in the street.

It is curious that the "lawlessness" of juries should be the focal point of modern criticism of the jury system, since it was just such "lawlessness" which in earlier times made the jury, in the words of Blackstone, "the grand bulwark of every Englishman's liberties." It was jury "lawlessness" when seventeenth-century English jurors disregarded repressive legislation and acquitted of charges of sedition and libel men whose only crime was political dissent.

A major argument of those who would eliminate juries is that a trained and experienced judge, unlike most jurors, will hew to the line of the relevant and not be led astray by the extraneous. This argument I believe to be valid without agreeing with the suggested remedy.

An experienced judge is a disciplined sifter of the facts. He is, nevertheless, just an expert in his field. An automobile mechanic is an expert in another field. I

* Bernard Botein has been a member of the Supreme Court of New York since 1941. He was Assistant District Attorney, New York City, 1929-36; was in charge of public investigations of accident frauds, 1936-37, insurance funds, 1938-40, and printing, 1940-41; and is the author of The Prosecutor (1956).—Editor

drive my car and hear all sorts of rattles, creaks, and squeaks. I don't know whether they come from the vitals underneath the hood, where they would be material and relevant, or whether they come from the door and windows, where they would be irrelevant and immaterial. So I take the car to an expert—an automobile mechanic. His trained ear sorts out the noises more surely than does mine. The trained ear of the judge sorts out admissible and inadmissible evidence, with comparable expertness. And, of course, both experts will be wrong at times.

In reserve, if it affords any comfort to litigants, resides the limited power of the court, to correct jury excesses. It is not uncommon, as indicated earlier in this chapter, for a judge to set aside or reduce a verdict which he regards as excessive. A judge may also set aside a verdict in a civil case which is contrary to the weight of the evidence.

Of course, a judge will direct the verdict for either party and take the case out of the hands of the jury when it becomes evident that there are no facts in dispute and that only questions of law are involved. The court will also nullify a jury verdict which is palpably based on a mistaken notion of the law. . . .

There is a certain inscrutability about the general verdict of a jury. Often defying external analysis, it cannot be shrugged off as an emotional distortion of fact and law. On the rare occasions when the veil is lifted from the deliberations, one may ascertain whether the consideration given all factors was deep and not superficial, practical and not whimsical. For example, we know that often, in fixing damages, a jury will estimate the lawyer's fee and include it in the verdict. Although it is not a proper item of damage legally, the jurors know that practically it is an item that must be paid. A jury's verdict is sometimes an amalgam of a shrewd appraisal of the facts squared with community values. . . .

I believe that the fears that jurors are led away from the main issues by trivia and irrelevancies are largely unfounded, although it will happen in an occasional case—particularly with a substandard jury. Juries are excellent, good, bad, and indifferent—just like judges.

But generally the judge will so conduct the trial that only evidence bearing properly upon the issues will be submitted to the jury. He presides over a conveyer belt transmitting factual material to the minds of the jurors. Before the belt reaches its destination he will extract any defective materials. It is a problem in administration. The problem is not only to rule out hearsay and self-serving declarations, but to control lawyers so that they will not offer the jury forbidden tidbits within the framework of improper questions.

Preoccupation with the sterilization of the data fed to jurors has resulted in many of our trial rules for the admission and exclusion of evidence—rules which, if they err, err on the side of repression rather than full disclosure. It is, therefore, not surprising that a discernible correlation exists between the elaborate evidentiary rules developed in Anglo-American jurisprudence and the preeminence of the jury system in that same jurisprudence.

The thinking of a judge who reviews steadily a passing parade of varied cases may become grooved. He may not bring to each case the eager, fresh consideration of a juror. From long experience, his attitude toward certain types of witnesses and certain types of cases may understandably have become frozen. The judge will have to admonish himself constantly in order to do justice in the particular case before him. Conceivably, if our attitudes have frozen hard, we may be unfair to an honest claimant in some cases. One is hard put to choose between the initial skepticism of judges and the initial gullibility of jurors.

A judge may know from hearing him testify frequently, and from the hearsay process of comparing notes with other judges, that a certain doctor's testimony will always be weighted heavily in favor of the side that retains him. He may know from similar sources that another doctor will always testify with complete honesty. If a prospective juror knew or had similar knowledge about a party or a key witness, one of the lawyers would see to it that he would be challenged and excused from serving in the case. But a judge may not be disqualified for such reasons. This, of course, is knowledge acquired outside the evidence in a particular case. It is not available to the jury, which may be more impressed by the testimony of the charlatan than by that of the ethical physician.

It would be desirable, and dramatic, to expose the knave while he is on the witness stand. But the judge may not convey his inbred suspicion to the jury. Experience has proved that in the long run it is better to contain the evidence within well-defined rules, even if injustice occasionally follows in an individual case. An astute opposing lawyer, however, could convey some of his misgivings to the jury by cross-examining the doctor as to how many times he appears in court yearly, how many examinations he has conducted in the past for the other side's lawyer, whether he generally testifies for plaintiffs or defendants, whether he was brought into the case by the lawyer, his charges for court appearances, etc.

There are lawyers whom judges have grown to distrust, and who must document every assertion they make before a judge will accept it. There is the overwhelming majority of lawyers, whose word will be accepted without question by judges.

When cases are tried by a judge without a jury, he must be on guard lest his previously formed opinion about a familiar expert witness or lawyer prejudice his deliberations in the individual case.

Judges, like jurors, have their strengths and weaknesses in comprehending and appraising testimony. They are much better qualified than most jurors to understand commercial transactions. Bills of lading, negotiable instruments, debentures, voting trust agreements, invoices are all familiar words to judges. They have heard of them for a mature lifetime—as practicing lawyers and sitting judges. Such terms might be so much Greek to housewives, mechanics, shopkeepers, and others inexperienced in commercial usages.

On the other hand, there are areas of litigation in which a judge has to grope to follow the evidence. Some judges have little mechanical aptitude or understanding. They have great difficulty in coping with a case involving problems of engineering, construction, chemical processes, manufacturing processes, patents, and the like. The average jury will often contain a few members whose grasp of these problems will be better than that of the judge.

The recent proliferation of administrative agencies in American law may, at least in part, be attributed to the recognized difficulties of judges as well as juries in understanding the complex factual situations which arise in such fields.

Then, just like jurors, I suppose judges labor under psychological blocks. I am not qualified to discuss their nature, how effectively they are offset by conditioning, and to what extent, if at all, they distort the fact-finding and decision-making process. When I was a practicing attorney I recall that the bar employed rough psychology in seeking or avoiding assignments before certain judges. Lawyers representing wives in matrimonial matters shunned a judge who had borne a heavy domestic cross for many years. And lawyers representing husbands avoided a judge who had a reputation as a ladies' man. Some judges were labeled "plaintiffs' judges." Presumably their sympathies were drawn to plaintiffs in accident cases. Other judges were labeled "defendants' judges," particularly if they had represented casualty insurance companies before ascending the bench. I suspect that upon investigation these alleged prejudices would prove to be greatly exaggerated.

But if psychological or emotional blocks do tend to cloud one's judgment in deciding litigated issues, less damage will be done if they affect jurors. Except for rare occasions, where prejudice is communal, they will cancel out one another's prejudices and obsessions, as it is most unlikely that all twelve jurors will suffer the same blocks. The very efforts of opposing lawyers to select jurors with leanings and sympathies toward their contending clients help to stabilize a jury.

There is no doubt that both time and money could be saved by the elimination of juries. The judge has to sit through every stage of the case in any event. If he is better qualified to render a verdict, the jurors are just so much expensive surplus. Their period of service represents a loss of manpower to the national economy and some consequent dislocation of industry. They represent also a more direct cost to the government: jury fees. From the time they are summoned to the time of their discharge they engage a good part of the courts' facilities and of the courts' personnel—judges, clerks, and bailiffs.

Without juries, there would be no prolonged conditioning of jurors under guise of inquiring into their qualifications. The flourishes and devices which lawyers so fondly believe impress jurors would be abandoned before judges. So would evidence of dubious materiality. For some reason most trial lawyers believe that a jury will smile favorably upon their clients if they put on a good show. In other words, reward them for the entertainment. They also believe conversely that such histrionics annoy a judge—an unquestionably sound belief.

Concessions as to inevitable proof are given freely in a nonjury case. There is no doubt that the elimination of the jury would speed the judicial processes. The decisive question is: How would it affect the administration of justice? And, correlative to that question, would it weaken public confidence in the administration of justice? If so, the most substantial economies in time and money would not justify the change.

There can be no compromise with the quality of justice in a democracy. If in fact the jury serves a useful purpose, it must be preserved at any cost. But if in fact the jury is neither affirmatively helpful nor harmful, or if the factors involved are too nebulous to permit of an assured answer, then it might still be desirable as a matter of public policy to preserve the system because of the reverence in which it is held by the public.

It must be repeated that the jury system has always drawn nourishment as the defender of the individual against tyranny and oppression. Those who cherish it in that role are willing to yield a bit on its efficacy as a truth finder and still maintain it to be an essential pillar of good government. Of course, they cannot concede any great margin of inefficiency, because a system which is not geared to search out the truth with a reasonable measure of competency and consistency is a poor protector of the weak and oppressed.

But this has been a dominant consideration in the development of the jury. While there have been ignoble passages in its history, there have also been glorious and stirring episodes. . . .

It is very difficult to take an unqualified position in the controversy between those who would abolish and those who would retain the jury system. Certainly, it has many infirmities, but it also retains a good deal of vigor. I experience no great embarrassment or difficulty in meshing my functions with those of jurors, and I even derive stimulation from their collaboration.

Intrinsically, jury trials are unquestionably more expensive, more protracted, and more apt to be blown off their course by irrelevancies, emotions, and professional guile than trials before judges only. On the other hand, the jury can offer a composite shrewdness, general and specific knowledge, and balanced community thinking, to supplement the expert and experienced leadership of the judge. This is the team conceived by our Anglo-American jurisprudence as best qualified to find the truth in litigation. It is a long way from the tribal chase upon mere accusation, and should not be discarded lightly.

In any event, I would oppose immediate and radical surgery on the jury system. It is not so diseased as to require drastic measures, and it has a certain therapeutic value for the parties. To many litigants their day in court means only trial by a jury of their peers. . . .

What can be done about training jurors so that they can hold down their positions on the team with competence?

Theoretically, the courts should be able to turn to the educators and say, "Look here, we've been hearing a lot of talk about educating our youth for citizenship. What function of citizenship is more important than intelligent, courageous, and honest jury service?"

As a practical matter, however, our jury system might well flounder before such an educational program would make an impression upon our population. It is, therefore, a job in education which the courts themselves must undertake.

Jurors are generally summoned to serve a two-week term. For the first few days they should go to school in the courthouse. A juror need take such a course only once in a lifetime.

The instructors should be employed on a permanent basis. There would be no point in setting forth a full curriculum in this chapter. It could, however, include the structure of the court, its various parts and functions. The jurors should be cautioned, in terms of the law, against harboring prejudice because of a party's race, creed, color, or national origin. The democratic beginnings and concepts of the jury system should be stressed.

The function of the pleadings should be illustrated, from actual samples. The major rules of evidence and those most commonly resorted to should be explained. Similar study should be made of those portions of a judge's charge which are fixed and mandatory, such as burden of proof, preponderance of evidence, etc.

The jurors should be taught the rudiments of the law specially applicable to the types of cases which will be presented to them most frequently, such as accident and breach of contract. What constitutes negligence, actual and constructive notice, measure of damages, and similar aspects of such cases would be explained.

A short history of the development of the jury system should be given. It would help orient the juror as to the necessity and importance of his functions. If he is critical or cynical about these functions it will pose him the problem of suggesting a better medium for safeguarding his personal and property rights and ascertaining the truth without fear or favor. He will derive a sense of dignity in the performance of duties rooted in the traditions of centuries, and a sense of inspiration from the stirring and courageous achievements of the past. The instructors can collaborate with the jury officials in striking off the rolls persons who are clearly incompetent to serve. For example, morons, persons who are physically incapacitated or who suffer aberrations which prevent them from serving adequately, should be disqualified.

Jurors should be afforded physical facilities which will make their service as comfortable as possible. Their waiting periods, when not engaged in trials, should be made less irksome than they now are in most jurisdictions.

Chief Judge Laws, of the United States District Court for the District of Columbia, thus described model juror accommodations during the recent dedication of the new Federal Courthouse in his district:

> ". . . in this new building we have provided for him a luxurious waiting room, one comparable to those in club quarters. We have provided parking for his automobile, which is no small item. We have provided for him during the necessarily enforced periods of his idleness, which no court system has been able to work out a means to prevent, a private, sound-proof room, where he can bring his secretary or his associates and carry on business uninterruptedly, perhaps for hours in the day, until he is called as juror to serve in a specific case. We have provided for him a message center, where a message can be delivered to him by an officer of the court at any time. We have provided for him private sleeping quarters, where he can spend in comfort the overnight sessions which jurors oftentimes are compelled to hold."

I believe jurors should be paid adequately for their services. There is a school of thought which holds that if the jury fees are made high they will attract an undesirable type of juror. This is a danger only if the enforcement of jury service is lax.

Formal or higher education will not necessarily prepare a juror for his duties. An alert day laborer may be a more valuable and perspicacious juror than a sluggish college professor or business executive. But all must be educated to an awakened and understanding interest in the scope and importance of their jobs as jurors. They must be trained for the particular job on hand. The incompetents must be weeded out and the remaining eligibles groomed to serve intelligently, expertly, and cheerfully.

WYZANSKI,* *A TRIAL JUDGE'S FREEDOM AND RESPONSIBILITY*
65 Harvard Law Review 1281, 1282-1290 (1952)

I. *Judge and Jury*

The trial judge's first problem is his relationship to the jury. Much of the debate about the jury system rests on political premises as old as the eighteenth century. Montesquieu,[6] Blackstone[7] and their followers contended that lay tribunals with a plurality of members were the safeguard of liberty. Bentham[8] and more modern reformers replied that when the rule of law itself is sound, its integrity requires that its application be entrusted to magistrates acting alone. In their view responsibility is the secret of integrity, and a reasoned choice is the secret of responsibility.

Experience will not give a sovereign answer to these warring contentions. Yet the disagreement can be narrowed if the question of the jury's utility is subdivided with specific emphasis on separate types of suits.

The importance of this subdivision may be concealed by the striking phrase that a federal judge is the "governor of the trial." [9] Some regard this as an implied acceptance of the practice of English courts.[10] And others construe it as a broad invitation to exercise in all types of cases a right to comment upon the evidence, provided of course that the judge always reminds the jury in his charge that they are not bound to follow the court's view of the facts or the credibility of the witnesses. But such boldness is not the surest way to end disputes in all types of cases.

A. Tort Cases. The trial judge's comments upon evidence are particularly unwelcome in defamation cases. In 1944 a discharged OPA official brought a libel

---

* Charles E. Wyzanski, Jr. has been U.S. District Judge in Massachusetts since 1942. He was law clerk to federal Circuit Judges Augustus N. Hand and Learned Hand, 1930-32, practiced law in Boston, lectured at Harvard and some other universities, was Solicitor, U.S. Department of Labor, 1933-35 and Special Assistant to the U.S. Attorney General, 1935-37.—Editor

[6] Montesquieu, Spirit of the Laws VI, c. 6, pp. 79-80 (Nugent's transl. 1949).

[7] 3 Bl. Comm. *349-350; 4 *id.* *349.

[8] See Halevy, The Growth of Philosophic Radicalism 397-403 (1928).

[9] The phrase comes from several Supreme Court opinions, the most notable being that of Hughes, C.J., in Quercia v. United States, 289 U.S. 466, 469 (1933).

[10] Yet no federal judge would be likely to give as detailed, as long or as leading a charge as say Lord Wright's admirable summing up in The Royal Mail Case, see Notable British Trials, The Royal Mail Case 222-262 (Brooks ed. 1933); or Lord Chief Justice Goddard's summing up in The Laski Libel Action, see The Laski Libel Action 367-98 (1947). Lord Wright's charge must have lasted at least four hours and Lord Goddard's two.

suit against the radio commentator, Fulton Lewis, Jr.[11] At one stage in the examination I suggested that Mr. Lewis' counsel was throwing pepper in the eyes of the jury; and at the final summation I indicated plainly enough that, although the jury was free to reject my opinion, I thought Mr. Lewis had been reckless in his calumnious charges against the ex-OPA official. It makes no difference whether what I said was true; I should not have said it, as the reaction of the bar and public reminded me. A political libel suit is the modern substitute for ordeal by battle. It is the means which society has chosen to induce bitter partisans to wager money instead of exchanging bloody noses. And in such a contest the prudent and the second-thinking judge will stand severely aside, acting merely as a referee applying the Marquis of Queensberry rules.[12] In a later trial of a libel suit brought by James Michael Curley the gravamen of the complaint was that the Saturday Evening Post had said that Mr. Curley was a Catholic of whom His Eminence, Cardinal O'Connell would have no part.[13] Who knew better than the Cardinal whether that charge was true? Mr. Curley, the plaintiff, did not call the Cardinal to the stand. The defendant's distinguished counsel did not desire to find out what would be the effect upon a Greater Boston jury if a Protestant lawyer should call a Catholic prelate to the witness stand. Should the court have intervened and summoned the Cardinal on its own initiative? The Fulton Lewis case gave the answer. In a political[14] libel suit the judge is not the commander but merely the umpire.

Those tort cases which involve sordid family disputes also are better left to the jury without too explicit instructions. Plato implied[15] and Holmes explicitly stated[16] that judges are apt to be naive men. If judges seem to comment on the morality of conduct or the extent of damages, they may discover that the jurors entirely disregard the comment because they believe that their own knowledge of such matters is more extensive than the judges'. At any rate when brother sues brother,[17] or when spouse sues paramour,[18] the very anonymity of the jury's judgment often does more to still the controversy than the most clearly reasoned opinion or charge of an identified judge could have done.

What of the trial judge's role in accident cases? How far should he go in requiring available evidence to be produced,[19] in commenting on the testimony,

[11] Balsam v. Lewis, Civil No. 2259, D. Mass., Jan. 27, 1944.

[12] See the introductory remarks of Lord Chief Justice Goddard in his summing up in The Laski Libel Action. The Laski Libel Action 367 (1947).

[13] Curley v. Curtis Publishing Company, Civil No. 1872, D. Mass., Feb. 25, 1944.

[14] In a libel suit where political and like emotional elements are absent, a judge may do as well as a jury. Cf. Kelly v. Loew's, Inc., 76 F. Supp. 473 (D. Mass. 1948).

[15] Plato, The Republic III.

[16] Holmes, Law and the Court in Collected Legal Papers 291, 295 (1920).

[17] Hegarty v. Hegarty, 52 F. Supp. 296 (D. Mass. 1943).

[18] Gordon v. Parker, 83 F. Supp. 40, 43, 45 (D. Mass.), aff'd, 178 F. 2d 888 (1st Cir. 1949). It may be said that divorce cases are contrary to my thesis. But is it not true that most divorce cases involve either no contest or an attempt by the judge to act as conciliator? Where there is a bitter contest, many divorce court judges, I believe, would rather have the issue put to a jury, if that were possible.

[19] See the suggestion of Frankfurter, J., dissenting in Johnson v. United States, 333 U.S. 46, 54-55 (1948).

and in using special verdicts and like devices to seek to keep the jury within the precise bounds laid down by the appellate courts? There are some who would say that the trial judge has not fulfilled his moral obligation if he merely states clearly the law regarding negligence, causation, contributory fault and types of recoverable damage. In their opinion it is his duty to analyze the evidence and demonstrate where the evidence seems strong or thin and where it appears reliable or untrustworthy.[21] But most federal judges do not make such analyses. They are not deterred through laziness, a sentimental regard for the afflatus of the Seventh Amendment or even a fear of reversal.[22] They are mindful that the community no longer accepts as completely valid legal principles basing liability upon fault. They perceive a general recognition of the inevitability of numerous accidents in modern life, which has made insurance widely available and widely used. Workmen's compensation acts and other social and economic legislation have revealed a trend that did not exist when the common law doctrines of tort were formulated. And the judges sense a new climate of public opinion which rates security as one of the chief goals of men.

Trial judges cannot, without violating their oaths, bow directly to this altered policy. In instructions of law they must repeat the doctrines which judges of superior courts formulated and which only they or the legislatures can change. But trial judges are not giving "rein to the passional element of our nature" [26] nor forswearing themselves by following Lord Coke's maxim that "the jurors are chancellors." [27] Traditionally juries are the device by which the rigor of the law is modified pending the enactment of new statutes.

Some will say that this abdication is not merely cowardly but ignores the "French saying about small reforms being the worst enemies of great reforms." [28] To them the proper course would be to apply the ancient rules with full rigidity in the anticipation of adverse reactions leading to a complete resurvey of accident law; to a scrutiny of the costs, delays and burdens of present litigation; to a comparative study of what injured persons actually get in cash as a result of lawsuits, settlements out of court, administrative compensation proceedings and other types of insurance plans; and ultimately to a new codification. To this one answer is that in Anglo-American legal history reform has rarely come as a result of prompt, comprehensive investigation and legislation. The usual course has been by resort to juries,[29] to fictions,[30] to compromises with logic. Only at the last

---

[21] Cf. Frankfurter, J., concurring in Wilkerson v. McCarthy, 336 U.S. 53, 65 (1949): "A timid judge, like a biased judge, is intrinsically a lawless judge."

[22] It would, however, be less than candid for an inferior federal judge to deny the indirect, as well as the direct, effect of recent decisions of the Supreme Court of the United States tending toward leaving large scope to juries in accident cases. See Wilkerson v. McCarthy, 336 U.S. 53 (1949); Bailey v. Central Vermont Ry.,

319 U.S. 350 (1943), and the cases there collated.

[26] L. Hand, J., in Skidmore v. Baltimore & Ohio R.R., 167 F. 2d 54, 70 (2d Cir. 1948).

[27] Quoted from Pound, An Introduction to the Philosophy of Law 133 (1922).

[28] Morley, On Compromise 185 (rev. ed. 1877).

[29] In Chapters VIII and IX of Courts on Trial (1949), Judge Frank, while admitting that some reforms are attributable to jury

stages are outright changes in the formal rules announced by the legislators or the appellate judges. This is consistent with Burke's principle that "reform is impracticable in the sense of an abrupt reconstruction of society, and can only be understood as the gradual modification of a complex structure." [31]

Parenthetically, let me say that I am not at all clear that it would be a desirable reform in tort cases to substitute trial by judges for trial by juries. Just such a substitution has been made in the Federal Tort Claims Act.[32] And experience under that statute does not prove that in this type of case a single professional is as satisfactory a tribunal as a group of laymen of mixed backgrounds. In estimating how a reasonable and prudent man would act, judges' court experience counts for no more than juries' out-of-court experience. In determining the credibility of that type of witness who appears in accident cases an expert tribunal is somewhat too ready to see a familiar pattern. Shrewdness founded on skepticism and sophistication has its place in scrutinizing the stories of witnesses. But there is a danger that the professional trier of fact will expect people of varied callings and cultures to reach levels of observation and narration which would not be expected by men of the witness' own background. Moreover, when it comes to a calculation of damages under the flexible rules of tort law the estimate of what loss the plaintiff suffered can best be made by men who know different standards of working and living in our society. Indeed I have heard federal judges confess that in a Federal Tort Claims Act case they try to make their judgments correspond with what they believe a jury would do in a private case. And not a few judges would prefer to have such cases tried by juries.[34]

B. *Commercial Litigation.* In commercial cases and those arising under regulatory statutes there is reason to hold a jury by a much tighter rein than in tort cases. This is not because the rules of law are more consonant with prevailing notions of justice. In these controversies judges have a specialized knowledge. Parties have usually acted with specific reference to their legal rights,[36] and departures

lawlessness, in general distrusts such methods. He suggests that certainty and equality are impossible because one jury differs so much from another. This difference he says is recognized by the bar which gives great attention to the selection of jurors (pp. 120-21). This argument may be overstated. In the Massachusetts District there are rarely more than two or three challenges to jurors in any but criminal cases. It ordinarily takes less than five minutes and in the last decade has never taken more than half an hour to select a jury. And these juries tend to act so uniformly that the court officers and attendants who have sat with hundreds of juries can make a substantially accurate prediction of how any given jury will act. Indeed, their prediction of jury action is much closer to the ultimate result than

their prediction of judicial actions.
[30] M. Cohen, The Process of Judicial Legislation, in Law and the Social Order 112, 126 (1933).
[31] Quoted in 2 L. Stephen, A History of English Thought in the Eighteenth Century 230 (1881).
[32] 28 U.S.C. ss. 2671 et seq. (Supp. 1951).
[34] This paragraph is admittedly contrary to the views expressed by Judge Frank in Courts on Trial (pp. 137-38). He assumes that no judge would give juries jurisdiction over types of cases that are now tried without a jury.
[36] Although there are some exceptions, usually parties to an accident case have acted without reference to the law, whereas the law has been one of the considerations in contemplation when parties to a commercial transaction took their action. The chief

from the declared standard would undermine the legislative declaration and would be likely to produce confusion and further litigation rather than reform. An extreme example will serve as an illustration. In a tax case[37] tried before a jury at the suit of one holder of International Match Company preference stock, the issue was whether for tax purposes those certificates had become worthless in the year 1936. In another taxpayer's case the Second Circuit Court of Appeals had affirmed a ruling of the Board of Tax Appeals that similar stock had become value-less in the year 1932.[38] Technically this adjudication did not bind the jury, though the evidence before it was substantially the same as that in the earlier case. To preserve uniformity on a factual tax problem of general application I had no hesitation in strongly intimating to the jury that they should reach the same result as the Second Circuit.

In sales cases, moreover, something close to a scientific appraisal of the facts is possible. There are strong mercantile interests favoring certainty and future litigation can be reduced by strict adherence to carefully prescribed statutory standards. These considerations sometimes warrant giving juries written instructions or summaries[39] and often warrant the use of special verdicts.[40] Either method makes jurors focus precisely on the formalities of the contract, the warranties alleged to have been broken, the types of damage alleged to have been sustained, and the allowable formulae for calculating those damages. Indeed, except for tort cases, I find myself in agreement with Judge Frank that the trial judge ought to use special verdicts to a much larger extent, though it is more difficult than may at first be realized to frame questions to the satisfaction of counsel and to the com-prehension of juries. Once when I used what I thought simple questions, a fellow judge, half in jest, accused me of trying to promote a disagreement of the jury and thus to force a settlement.

The arguments supporting special verdicts in commercial or statutory cases also support a trial judge in giving in such cases a more detailed charge and more specific guidance in estimating the testimony. In complicated cases or those in fields where the experience of the average juror is much less than that of the average judge, there is a substantial risk of a miscarriage of justice unless the judge points rather plainly to the "knots" in the evidence and suggests how they can be unravelled. The only time I have ever entered judgment notwithstanding a verdict was in a private antitrust suit.[44] The jury had awarded damages of over one million dollars due, I believe, to the generality of my instructions. I should have spent as much time on my charge in helping them understand the testimony

exceptions are where the tort defendant failed to take out insurance because he sup-posed there was no risk of liability save for misconduct, and the rare case where a con-tract defendant made or broke his promise without attention to the written rules of law.

[37] Clark v. Welch, Civil No. 3944, D. Mass., April 7, 1943, aff'd, 140 F. 2d 271, 274 (1st Cir. 1944).

[38] Young v. Commissioner, 123 F. 2d 597 (2d Cir., 1941).

[39] Perry Sportswear, Inc. v. O'Keefe Tan-ning Corp., Civil No. 1871, D. Mass., Jan. 21, 1944.

[40] Boyce v. Fowler, 87 F. Supp. 796 (D. Mass. 1949).

[44] Momand v. Universal Film Exchange, Inc., 72 F. Supp. 469 (D. Mass. 1947), aff'd, 172 F. 2d 37 (1st Cir. 1948).

as I later spent on the memorandum in which I analyzed the evidence for an appellate court. And one of the few totally irrational awards that I have seen a jury make came in a compromise verdict in a breach of contract case[45] brought by a plaintiff of foreign birth against a defendant who came from the dominant local group. The charge had stopped with broad, though probably correct, statements of the substantive law. The jury should have been told that their choice lay between only two alternatives—either to find for the plaintiff for the full amount claimed or to find for the defendant. Any intermediate sum could be attributable only to a discount for prejudice or a bounty for sympathy.

C. Criminal Prosecutions. At the trial of criminal cases the judge's role more closely resembles his role in tort cases than in commercial litigation. . . .

BROEDER,* *THE UNIVERSITY OF CHICAGO JURY PROJECT*
38 Nebraska Law Review 744 (1959)

I. *Introduction*

The purpose here is briefly to set forth some of the tentative conclusions and findings of the University of Chicago jury project. In the main the work reported out is the property of others; the writer's own reflects but a small segment of the total. Some errors in reporting the data therefore are bound to have crept in. For them of course the writer accepts full responsibility.

The jury project was initially financed out of a $400,000 grant by the Ford Foundation to the University of Chicago Law School. Not all of this money was spent on the jury project; there were other projects, too, chief among them a study of arbitration. The broad purpose of the grant was to further research in the law and behavioral sciences. Social science techniques, in other words, were to be used in studying legal phenomena. But in 1956 the money gave out. Research of this kind is very expensive and so back the law school went to the foundation which suspiciously wanted to see how we had been doing. They sent some very distinguished men to find out—judges, lawyers, social scientists and, it is to be hoped not significantly, at least one psychiatrist. As a result of the reports made by these men, one of the projects, a study of public attitudes towards our federal tax laws, was knocked out. The jury and arbitration projects, however, were given additional money, enough to carry them through to September, 1959, which is the target date for final publication.

Confining ourselves to the jury project, now, how is it organized and composed? From the beginning we have had about an equal number of lawyers—several with years of actual jury trial experience—and social scientists. Final responsibility, however, rests with a lawyer-academician, Professor Harry Kalven, Jr. Working very closely and on a policy level with Professor Kalven have been two distinguished social scientists—Professor Hans Zeisel, former president of the American Statistical

[45] Schleifer v. Killion, Civil No. 8030, D. Mass., Nov. 22, 1949, aff'd, 183 F. 2d 237 (1st Cir. 1950).
* Dale W. Broeder, a 1953 graduate of the University of Chicago Law School, is Associate Professor of Law, University of Nebraska.—Editor

Society, and Professor Fred Strodtbeck, an expert on the behavior of small groups. Even with such capable men at the helm, however, there were many difficulties. The lawyers could not always understand the social scientists and the opposite was also true. These difficulties unfortunately have never wholly been overcome but much progress has been made and the experience of just trying has been rich and rewarding.

Doubtless much of the credit for this is due to the institution under study. It is a fascinating and important institution and one deeply rooted in our traditions. Each year in the United States there are more than 100,000 jury trials and more than one million persons are called upon to report for jury duty. Furthermore, the jury is and long has been a controversial institution, particularly in relation to civil cases. There is a vast literature debating the merits of the jury and it is pertinent to add in this connection that for every charge leveled against the jury in this debate there is likewise to be found a vigorous defense. Of course, much of the debate has necessarily been conducted in a vacuum; we know precious little about the jury.

II. *Conventional Research*

Perhaps it is best to begin with the place of conventional legal research in the project. We first thought of writing a sort of Wigmore on the jury. This however proved too big a job and one which did not urgently need doing anyway. Much of the writing in the field is excellent. A substantial number of original research memoranda, however, have been prepared and all published field studies will be supported by studies of the directly relevant law. A comprehensive bibliography of the existing literature on the jury has been compiled and a limited number of studies in comparative law have been undertaken, including one on the lay judge under German law, one of the Scottish jury and one on the awarding of lawyer fees. A study has also been done on the notable decline of the civil jury in England. This decline, it should be noted, long antedates the recent Parliamentary legislation drastically limiting the number of civil cases in which a jury trial is available in England. It is a striking fact that the country which gave us our jury now has less than 200 jury trials per year.

The debate about the merits of trial by jury has been carefully reviewed and has served in part as a source of hypotheses for study. This undertaking has likewise provided us with a unit scheduled for inclusion in our report on the public's image of the jury.

One aspect of the law will receive special emphasis. There is good reason to believe that although we inherited the jury from England it has developed in many respects into a distinctive American institution. The changes in the various rules defining the respective spheres of judge and jury, for example, can be traced against other developments in American politics over the past century and a half. Such a study has been undertaken and will form an integral part of the final project publication.

Midway between our own field research and the more or less orthodox research just described is the work we have done in collecting and refining the jury trial statistics gathered by others. There is, for example, a large body of statistics on the extent to which defendants charged with felony waive jury trials in favor of bench trials. Historically, of course, waiver was never permitted in such cases even with the consent of the government and the trial judge and this is still the rule in a few jurisdictions. In many states, however, a defendant is entitled to a bench trial in a felony case either absolutely upon request or with the consent of the government and/or the trial judge. The data from such states are interesting and exhibit a marked disparity in the extent of jury trial waiver from one state to another. Thus in New York practically no one accused of felony ever waives a jury while in Chicago almost two-thirds of the felony trials are bench trials. And in Maryland the percentage of jury trial waiver is even higher. Unfortunately the reasons for such wide regional disparities are still very obscure.

We also have figures on jury trial waiver in civil cases and have conducted a series of intensive interviews with lawyers as to why they waived the jury in particular cases. Such data contribute importantly to any statement of the lawyers' image of the jury. More broadly, of course, our interest in waiver stems from a desire to make a meaningful statement about the extent to which the jury is currently used.

We have likewise gathered data on the percentage of hung juries in civil cases in various states. Overall the picture is encouraging. Hung juries are rare, occurring in only four and one-half percent of the cases. The interesting finding however is that the percentage of hung juries is only slightly lower in jurisdictions where the verdict does not have to be unanimous. Three percent of the juries hang in non-unanimity jurisdictions and only six percent in jurisdictions requiring unanimity. Abolition of the unanimity requirement, it would appear, is not going to have much effect in reducing the number of hung juries which, statistically speaking, are not much of a problem anyway.

A final example of our use of available statistics is in connection with our study of congested court dockets. Much of this congestion has in many areas been blamed solely on the jury. This has particularly been true in New York City where various people with little affection for the jury have compiled statistics purporting to show that civil jury trials take from two and one half to three times as long as bench trials. Hence, these people say, the civil jury should be done away with. We have taken those statistics and refined them, grouping the various cases according to the nature and complexity of the issues involved. The result is a quite different picture. We find that juries, at least in New York City, are on the average given more difficult cases to try than are judges and that for comparable cases jury trials require only slightly more time than bench trials. Preliminary analysis of similar statistics from Chicago indicate that this is likewise the situation there.

III. *Varied Field Studies*

So much then for our analysis and refinement of the statistics of others. Let us now turn to certain of our own field research. One thing we wanted to know was the importance of deliberations in criminal cases. How often is it, for example, that a minority of jurors persuade the majority to change their votes? In order to find out we interviewed more than 1500 jurors who served on 213 different criminal cases in Chicago and Brooklyn. They were asked for certain information concerning their backgrounds, how they voted on the first ballot, the results of the first ballot, when the first ballot was taken and the final verdict. The results were as follows. In virtually all of the cases a ballot was taken immediately. In thirty percent of the cases the first ballot was unanimous and that ended it. In seventy percent of the total cases, however, there was some division of opinion on the first ballot. And the striking fact about such cases is that the majority on the first ballot almost always won. The majority won in approximately ninety percent of such cases. Furthermore, it did not make any difference who comprised the minority—wealthy persons, poor persons, men or women. Being in the minority was the determinative factor. The broad point suggested, of course, is that most criminal cases are decided during the trial and not during the deliberations.

There is, of course, ten percent of the cases left over. In six percent of the cases the jury hanged and in four percent of the cases the initial minority prevailed. In almost all of the cases where the minority prevailed, however, it was a large minority—three or more jurors. To return now to the cases where the jury hanged. Hung juries, it is often assumed, are generally due to a supposed single stubborn juror. The data, on the contrary, suggest that the hung jury results from the closeness of the case itself and perhaps also from the moral support that a man feels when his minority view has at least several other supporters. Thus of the twenty hung juries in the sample, constituting, it will be recalled, but six percent of the total cases studied, not a single jury hung with a minority of less than three.

A second aspect of this survey has been to give information relevant to one of the central questions about the jury: "How much do jurors differ from one another as decision makers?" A couple of illustrations will have to suffice. Persons with German and British backgrounds were more likely to favor the government whereas Negroes and persons of Slavic and Italian descent were more likely to vote for acquittal. Probably this comes as no surprise. Certainly it was in accord with the expectations of a large number of lawyers we interviewed on the subject.

One final illustration. The interview also asked the three questions used in New York to qualify "blue ribbon" jurors, jurors used in serious and sensational criminal cases: 1) Do you have scruples against the death penalty?; 2) Would you convict on circumstantial evidence?; and 3) Would you draw a negative inference if the defendant failed to take the stand? One by-product was the discovery of how few jurors understood what circumstantial evidence was. But the main point was to compare the first ballot votes of the jurors who "qualified" under these three questions and thus could have become blue ribbon jurors with the first ballot votes of the jurors who would not have qualified. The finding was that the blue ribbon jurors were considerably more prone to convict. Such a finding, of course, by no means decides the difficult policy questions raised by the blue ribbon jury.

Another study is an effort to get more systematic knowledge about the regional variations in jury awards throughout the United States. It is, of course, well known that there are high and low award areas but the problem has been to get an accurate measurement of the variations. The study uses the estimates of liability insurance adjusters as circumstantial evidence of the level of jury awards in their immediate areas. Six model cases have been submitted to the adjusters of three large insurance companies doing a national business. These adjusters, approximately 600 in all, were asked to indicate the most likely verdict for each of the six cases in a particular local court which we specify. The results were as follows. Taking the average award as 100, ten percent must be added to the award if the court is located either on the Eastern or Western seaboard and an additional ten percent if the court is situated in a large city. If, on the other hand, the court is situated in the South or the Midwest, ten percent must be subtracted from this average award of 100 and another ten percent subtracted if the court is located in a rural as contrasted with an urban community. To put it in another way: The award in a court situated in an Eastern metropolis will be from forty to fifty percent higher than if the court is situated in a rural community in either the Midwest or the South.

A more significant block of research is designed to cast light on the question: "What difference would it make if we had no jury trials and all of our trials were bench trials?" Five hundred trial judges throughout the nation cooperated in the research by filling out a questionnaire for each jury trial over which they presided. There were many questions on the questionnaire but the one of greatest interest here requested them to say how they would have decided the case had there been no jury, had the trial instead been a bench trial. It should be noted that the judges were asked to do this prior to the rendition of the verdict. In all, we received back some 3,000 questionnaires, 1500 criminal cases questionnaires and an equal number of personal injury case questionnaires.

The criminal cases are less involved and better dealt with first. In eighty-one percent of the cases the judge and jury agreed. In only nineteen percent of the cases was there a disagreement. Now, what was its nature? Did the judges want to convict when the jury acquitted or was it the other way around? The answer is that the judges were considerably more prone to convict. If all the defendants in our 1500 cases had been tried by a judge, the number of acquittals in such cases would have been cut almost in half, from approximately 500 to approximately 250.

The nature of the cases where the judge and jury disagreed is perhaps also of interest. The greatest percentage of disagreement came in the statutory rape cases. Here the judge and jury disagreed forty percent of the time. And when they did disagree, the jury acquitted in ninety percent of the cases where the judge would have convicted. On the other hand, the judges and juries saw eye to eye in the narcotic cases. In not one of such cases did the judge and jury disagree. One further point. In the first offense drunk-drive cases juries frequently acquitted where the judge would have convicted. Juries, in other words, were willing to give such defendants another chance whereas the judges would have felt obliged to uphold the law. Interestingly, several of the judges commented on their questionnaires in such cases that they were pleased the jury had acquitted notwithstanding that they themselves would have found it necessary to convict. The picture is different when one turns to the second or third offense drunk-drive cases. Here the judge and jury practically never disagreed. The suggestion, of course, is this: Juries, while frequently willing to give a drunk-drive defendant one break, think that the second and certainly the third offense deserves punishment.

The personal injury case questionnaires found the judge and jury agreeing on the question of liability in eighty-three percent of the cases. Disagreement occurred on this question then in only seventeen percent of the cases. In nine percent of the cases where there was disagreement the jury found for the plaintiff, the judge for the defendant. But in eight percent of the cases where the judge found for the plaintiff the jury found for the defendant. The message, of course, is that so far as the question of liability is concerned and looking at the data as a whole there was hardly any difference. The judge found for the plaintiff in fifty-seven percent of the cases and the jury in fifty-eight percent. This means that the jury found for the defendant in forty-two percent of the cases, an important point and one which goes far to dispel the popular idea that juries are forever holding the defendant liable and returning a reduced award.

When the cases are classified as to the type of defendant involved however and the question of damages is examined the result is a slightly different picture. If the defendant is an individual, the judge and jury practically never differ on the question of liability but the jury's award where the verdict is for plaintiff is approximately ten percent higher than that of the judge. If the defendant is a corporation there begins to be a difference even on the question of liability. The jury finds against corporations two percent more often than does the judge. And if the defendant is a city or state, the jury finds liability in eight percent more of the cases. The situation on the damage side is similar. Where the defendant is a corporation or a city or state and the verdict is for plaintiff, the jury awards approximately twenty-five percent more than does the judge. Railroad defendants are even more poorly situated. If the jury finds a railroad liable, the award is about thirty percent higher than that of the judge. The central finding seems very clear: Juries find against wealthy defendants more often than do judges and adjust their awards according to the defendant's ability to pay. The more wealthy the defendant, the higher the verdict will prove to be. Judges, on the other hand, seem not to pay as much attention to the ability-to-pay factor.

The data were run for state and federal judges separately and show no significant change in the amount of agreement and disagreement. The percentage of agreement likewise remains almost constant whether or not written instructions are given the jury, whether or not the judge summarizes the evidence; and whether or not the judge comments on the weight of the evidence. These have been highly controversial issues in recent years but the data strongly suggest that at least in personal injury cases these procedural controls make the jury neither more nor less like the judge.

Another segment of the study is concerned with attitudes toward jury service. Briefly, the results show that of the jurors who actually sat on a case and suffered no economic hardship, some eighty percent would like to serve again. However, of the jurors suffering economic hardship and who did not get to serve, only forty-eight percent would like to serve again. These figures, then, generally indicate an affirmative response to jury service and point up the two well known burdens of such service: the waste of time of the person who is called but repeatedly challenged and the economic loss that jury duty involves for some persons.

There are additional data on this question. One source has been an intensive public opinion survey of attitudes toward the court and jury in a moderately-sized city. A sample of those who had had jury service in the last year and a sample of the general population were interviewed. The survey discloses that some six percent of the general population had had jury service at some time during their lives and that three percent had their only direct contact with the courts as a result of jury service. On the other hand, some fifty-five percent of the public had known someone who had been a juror. It would appear from this that jury service is no longer, if ever it was, a major source of direct citizen contact with the courts but that it is an important source of indirect contact.

The study also provides data on the impact of jury service. Among those who had never served, only thirty-six percent said they would like to serve, sixteen percent were undecided and some forty-eight percent said they would not like to serve. However, among those who had served within the last year ninety-four percent said they would like to serve again, three percent were willing to serve again as a duty and only three percent said they would dislike it. Our tentative conclusion from this is that though in many communities people notoriously seek to avoid jury service, once they serve they like it and want to serve again.

The respondents were also asked: "Which do you think is the better way to have a case decided, by a judge or by a jury?" Among the general public some seventy percent favored the jury, twenty-one percent were undecided, and only nine percent favored trial by judge alone. Among those who had had jury service within the past year seventy-seven percent favored jury trial while those favoring bench trial rose to fifteen percent.

The respondents showed a tendency to discriminate the type of case in which they preferred a jury. Thus when asked specifically, only ten percent of the sample of the general public preferred a judge in criminal cases as against twenty-eight percent in contract cases. And for those with recent jury service, five percent preferred a judge in criminal cases as against fifty-five percent in contract cases. These refinements, of course, suggest that the general question about preference for judge or jury trial may frequently be understood as a question about criminal trials and further that jury service tends to make one more enthusiastic about the jury in a criminal case and less enthusiastic about it in the contract case.

Finally, there is some evidence coming from our use of experimental juries which will be discussed momentarily. The jurors who were given an experimental negligence case to decide were asked whether they would prefer judge or jury trials in a negligence case first if they were the plaintiff and then if they were the defendant. Those who would prefer trial by judge in both situations favored an average award in the experimental case of $14,000. Those who would prefer trial by jury in both situations favored an average award of $38,000. Liking the jury, then, makes for a plaintiff's juror, disliking it for defense juror.

Two other studies concern jury selection. Without pausing for details, it might be noted that the population of those who actually serve differs considerably from the population initially contacted for jury duty. There is a marked increase of women over men, a marked reduction in both those with much and those with little education, and some increase in the relative percentage of lower income groups as against middle income groups.

An intensive study has also been made of the voir dire examinations for twenty cases and lawyers have been interviewed concerning their detailed reasons for challenging particular jurors and for retaining others. An attempt was also made to determine the amount of time the lawyer spends indoctrinating jurors as compared with sifting out unfavorable jurors. Sixty percent of the lawyer's voir dire time, it was found, was spent in indoctrining jurors and only forty percent in asking questions designed to separate the favorable from the unfavorable jurors. A study has also been done on the extent to which lawyers conduct pre-voir dire investigations into the backgrounds of the veniremen. In some sections of the country this practice is widespread. Indeed, there is a commercial agency in Los Angeles which supplies its lawyer subscribers with detailed information on the backgrounds of veniremen.

IV. *Experimental Juries*

Let us now turn to the most important facet of the project, the development of the experimental jury. Tape recordings of mock trials based on actual trials have been prepared and with the consent of the court and of the jurors themselves— these are persons actually on jury duty at the time—have been played to the jurors. By means of this experimental technique we are able to repeat the same trial before several juries and by comparing the verdicts and the deliberations of groups which have heard different versions of the same trial to test the effects of a given change. In addition, and with the consent of the jurors, the experimental jury has made possible the full recording of the deliberations. Finally the set-up has enabled us to interview the jurors at various stages of the case. Thus they have been asked for their individual decisions at the end of the trial and just before the deliberations and again after the deliberations. Four moot cases have been developed thus far and have been played to over 100 juries.

Only a few illustrations will be attempted from the data and these are drawn from the first experimental case. The case involved an auto-accident in which plaintiff, a forty year old stenographer, was injured when the car in which she was riding as a passenger collided with a car driven by defendant.

The design permitted us to test the effect of several variables at the same time. In three treatments, defendant's liability was very clear; in three it was a little doubtful. These versions were then combined with three different treatments of defendant's liability insurance. In the first, defendant reveals he has no insurance but there is no objection or further attention paid to the disclosure; in the second, the defendant reveals that he has insurance, defense counsel objects and the court directs the jury to disregard; in the third treatment, the defendant again discloses insurance but there is no objection and no further notice is taken. The tapes were then played to sets of juries operating under the unanimity rule and to sets of juries operating under the three-fourths majority rule. In all, the experiment was given to thirty juries.

Here briefly are some of the results. First, twenty-eight verdicts were for plaintiff, one jury hung on the damage issue and one jury found for the defendant. Second, the average award of all verdicts where liability was very clear was $41,000; the average award of all verdicts where liability was somewhat ambiguous was $34,000, $7,000 less. This, of course, supports the suspicion long entertained by the bar that the weaker the proof on liability the lower the verdict is apt to be. However, no significant difference in award level resulted between juries operating under the unanimity rule and juries operating under the three-fourths majority rule.

Then there are the results of the three insurance treatments. Where the defendant disclosed that he had no insurance the average award of all verdicts was $33,000. Where defendant disclosed that he had insurance but there was no objection the average award rose to $37,000. Where, however, the defendant said he had insurance and there was an objection and an instruction to disregard, the average award rose to $46,000, $13,000 more than when the defendant said he was not insured, and $9,000 more than when he said he was insured but where there was no objection or instruction to disregard. The conclusion appears to be two-fold: First, that juries tend to award less when they know that an individual defendant is not insured; and, second, that where they know defendant is insured and a fuss is made over it the verdict will be higher than when no such fuss is made. The objection and the instruction to disregard, in other words, sensitize the jurors to the fact that defendant is insured and thereby increase the award. However, the instruction to disregard at least served the purpose of keeping the jurors from talking about insurance during the deliberations.

As previously noted four experimental cases have been developed thus far. A second involves the defense of insanity in a prosecution for housebreaking and the facts of the case are substantially identical with those of *Durham v. United States*, 214 F. 2d 862 (App. D.C. 1954), the now famous decision by the Court of Appeals for the District of Columbia. *Durham* of course holds that the test for criminal insanity is not only whether defendant knows the difference between right and wrong or even whether he was irresistibly impelled to commit the act but simply whether his act resulted from a mental disease or defect. The basic purpose of the experiment was to test the difference in jury response to these varying legal tests of insanity. The central finding can be stated simply: Varying the instruction made almost no difference. In fact, the supposedly harsh "right and wrong" test produced a few more acquittals than the supposedly more liberal "mental disease" or "mental defect" test.

A third case involves question of manufacturer and retailer liability where a vaporizer allegedly causes a fire and severely burns a young child. The principal variable sought to be tested here is the effect of the special verdict procedure. In one set of runs the jury operates under the conventional general verdict procedure;

in a second set the special verdict is employed and the jury is given sixteen inter-rogatories; while in the third the jury, again operating with a general verdict, is given no instruction at all other than the instruction to do justice and equity.

Finally, we have a case where the plaintiff is injured due to defendant's alleged negligence in leaving his car keys in the ignition. The car is stolen by a thief who negligently runs into plaintiff. The case was chosen chiefly in order to get a set of deliberations where the jury would be forced to concentrate primarily on what constitutes negligence. One tentative finding will have to do: The experimental jurors were on the whole prone to find the defendant liable. The jury verdicts in this regard form an interesting contrast to the numerous appellate court opinions holding either that defendant is not negligent as a matter of law or that his negligence, if any, is not proximately connected with the theft of the car and the resulting injury to plaintiff. The experimental jurors thought the connection was very direct. This particular experimental case has been played to two sets of jurors, one set operating under a comparative negligence instruction, the other under con-ventional contributory negligence instructions.

V. *Intensive Jury Interviews*

Finally there is the work for which the writer had the principal responsibility, the observation of a series of twenty jury trials and the intensive court-approved interviewing of the jurors who served in them. These interviews were conducted as soon as possible after the trial. The average interview lasted about one and one-half hours and a considerable number lasted for three hours or more. In all, 225 dif-ferent jurors were interviewed. There were thirteen civil cases, all of them personal injury actions, and seven criminal cases. The central problem with such an under-taking, of course, is that all of these cases are different; and, further, that twenty cases is not very many cases. Obviously one cannot produce findings from such data which are statistically significant. But while no conclusive answers can be provided by the technique it has at least given us some worthwhile insights.

Approximately fifty essays have been written on points common to several or all of the cases, the jurors' use of their out-of-court knowledge and experiences, for example, the effectiveness of the voir dire, the impact of the lawyers and of the judge, the extent to which jurors consider defendant's wealth or insurance protec-tion, the effect of a criminal defendant's failure to take the stand and many others. Aside from this, one of the civil cases has been written up in full, trial and all, and an effort made to reconstruct the sequence of events occurring during the deliberations. The case chosen was a wrongful death action brought for the benefit of a young trucker's widow and two baby girls. Throughout, of course, all names have been changed as well as anything else which would readily identify a person or place.

Perhaps the intensive interview data is best illustrated by giving a brief account of one of the cross-case essays. The essay chosen concerns the effect of the sum plaintiff's counsel requests as damages which, in some places at least. is called the ad damnum. Does its size make a difference and, if so, why? The question was studied in eleven of the thirteen negligence cases in the series. Plaintiff prevailed in seven cases, defendant in four.

In brief, plaintiff's damage request did yeoman service as a kind of damage jumping-off place for the jurors. Thus damages were to some degree determined with reference to it in six of the seven cases where it was necessary for the jury to assess damages. The only exception was a case where the jurors sharply divided on liability and where plaintiff's counsel had apologized to the jury for requesting "as much as $50,000."

The ad damnum had its greatest impact as a determinant of damages in a case we will call the *Landis* case. Plaintiff sought $2,400 for the "loss of use" of his tractor while it was being repaired and $50,000 for personal injuries. Defense counsel did not argue damages. After agreeing on liability the jurors' attention was first directed to the "loss of use" item the assessment of which was entirely given over to one juror, the owner of a large auto-truck agency and garage whose exposed expertise in the premises had been made the subject of a closing argument reference by plaintiff's counsel. This juror possessed expertise, all right, but there were certain difficulties and he therefore proposed that the jury cut the $2,400 figure in half and agree on a verdict for $1,200. The reason for this, he said, was because lawyers always ask for about twice what they really expect. There was instant agreement and the foreman promptly recorded $1,200 on the appropriate line of the verdict-form. The precedent thus established with regard to "loss of use" was later to prove of great significance.

But this is to anticipate. When the jurors turned to the question of personal injury damages, attention first focused upon a $37,500 figure which was generally but mistakenly regarded as the lowest aggregate sum plaintiff's counsel had requested for personal injuries. Actually, $37,500 was merely the suggested compensation for plaintiff's "future pain and suffering" and only constituted a part of counsel's over-all damage request, which, as previously noted, was $50,000. For some reason, however, the jurors did not so understand him and the $37,500 figure was accordingly regarded as an outside limit upon recovery. And there was an immediate consensus that this was too much. Plaintiff was not that sick and lawyers always ask for much more than they expect.

Considerable discussion of the evidence followed and an oral ballot on damages which revealed marked differences of opinion. It was now almost 10:00 p.m., seven hours from the start of the deliberations. Everyone was exhausted. Solution came however with the resurrection of counsel's abused $37,500. A juror who favored about $25,000 referred again to the well-known practice of attorneys asking for twice what they expect, and to the deliberation precedent already established by halving the amount counsel had requested for "loss of use" of the tractor. Why not, then, divide $37,500 by two and return that as the verdict? There was almost immediate agreement and the foreman announced that the deliberations had ended.

A slightly different twist on the jurors' use of the ad damnum in calculating damages is presented by the wrongful death action mentioned previously. Plaintiff asked for $168,000, counsel arguing that the widow and children would have received such sum during deceased's lifetime. Defense counsel hardly referred to the question of damages. Unfortunately the jurors were not systematically questioned concerning their use of the $168,000 figure. In passing, however, two of them stated that the $168,000 request was a reliable index of the legitimate damage expectations of plaintiff and her counsel. This was on the theory that $168,000 really meant $75,000, as one of the jurors thought, or $100,000, as the other thought, and that a verdict for any small sum would be interpreted by everyone as a victory for defendant which would mar the reputation of plaintiff's counsel whom they very much admired. Accordingly, they strongly pressed for $75,000 and $100,000 awards during the deliberations. The theory's underpinning, of course, was the thought that lawyers always ask for considerably more than they expect, one of them said "twice what they expect." . . .

On the question of damages, therefore, the ad damnum was clearly of importance. But this was only as it turned out. Suppose defense counsel, instead of ignoring the question of damages or discussing it generally, had instead argued specific amounts to the jury. None of them did so. This points up a very serious limitation of the data, for if the ad damnum makes a difference, so should defendant's suggestion of a specific amount. Especially is this true in the light of what probably constitutes the basic explanation of the ad damnum's importance—the difficulties involved in assessing damages and the consequent need felt by many jurors for a concrete dollar basis from which to begin. If defendant fails to supply an alternative basis, such jurors must of necessity rely exclusively on plaintiff's.

Seemingly implicit in all this is the suggestion that the higher the ad damnum the higher the verdict. And, to a degree, this seems to have been the case. But common sense tells us that there are limits. Indeed, an ad damnum thought by the jurors to be excessive may under some circumstances even become an important factor in causing a verdict for the defendant.

Plaintiff's counsel in the *Landis* case at one point mentioned $75,000 as a reasonable award for his client's future pain and suffering though he later cut such figure in half. Defense counsel, it will be recalled, completely ignored the question of damages. All four of the jurors originally voting against liability indicated that they did so in part on account of the $75,000 figure. First of all was the notion that plaintiff and his lawyer were simply out to line their pockets without regard to the evidence and other important considerations, such as defendant-employer's insurance costs and the truck-driving reputation of defendant's employee. In sum, the $75,000, regarded by the minority jurors as excessive, made them mad and thus less willing to find liability.

More important however was the impact of the request in exciting their fears that the other jurors would favor a verdict for $75,000 in the event liability was agreed to. Rather than "risk" later having to assent to a verdict for $75,000, they voted against liability. It must be remembered that defense counsel had not argued damages. Furthermore, there appears to have been no pre-deliberation discussion of damages among the jurors. Consequently, plaintiff's damage figures—and for some reason only the $75,000 figure stuck in the minds of the minority—was, as stated by one juror, "all we had to go on until somebody said something." Ultimately the majority did say something, namely, that they did not favor $75,000 and this eventually brought about agreement on liability.

There are other facets to the data but what has been said will have to suffice as a sample both of the ad damnum essay and of what has been done with the data obtained through intensive interviewing of jurors. There is just one caveat: Most of the other essays and most of the project's findings show the jury in a far more favorable light.

VI. *Conclusion*

A conclusion will be foregone except to note that, in addition to the studies mentioned, we are currently engaged in the brief interviewing of several hundred civil case jurors as to various aspects of their behavior—their first ballot votes on liability and damages, for example, and whether and to what extent they considered the defendant's ability to pay. We also plan to conduct a public opinion survey of judges, lawyers and law teachers concerning their respective images of the jury and to do a content analysis of the way the jury is spoken of in various of our leading newspapers and periodicals.

NOTES AND QUESTIONS

1. Another interesting, but later discontinued, activity of the Chicago researchers was to record actual jury deliberations in four civil cases tried in the Tenth Federal Circuit Court at Wichita, Kansas in May, 1954. This was done with the prior consent and approval of the Chief Judge of the Circuit, the trial judge and attorneys for all parties, including an assistant United States District Attorney. Permission was granted on condition that the cases and the names of participants would not be disclosed. But the jurors were not informed that their deliberations would be recorded. Selections from the recordings were played by the Federal judges of the Tenth Circuit at their regular judicial conference at Estes Park, Colorado, in the summer of 1955.

When this became known, Attorney-General Herbert Brownell Jr. reprimanded the University of Chicago Law School, saying that the Department of Justice was "unequivocally opposed to any recording or eavesdropping on the deliberations of a jury under any conditions regardless of the purpose" and that he would ask Congress for a law to prevent any such intrusions upon jury privacy. The Senate Sub-Committee on Internal Security held hearings on Chicago's Jury Project. At the conclusion of the hearings, Senators James O. Eastland and William E. Jenner issued a statement condemning the "bugging" of jury deliberations as "a flagrant abuse of authority, a violation of the constitutional guarantee, under the Seventh Amendment, of the right of trial by jury, and a serious threat to such right for the future as long as there is no guarantee that incidents of this nature will not again occur. . . . The jury system is a fundamental of our judicial structure, and is basic to a free society under law as we know it. If the jury system is destroyed or substantially weakened, a bitter blow will have been struck at the liberties of the people. . . ." The eavesdropping was similarly attacked by the Washington office of the American Civil Liberties Union. N.Y. Times, Oct. 19, 1955, p. 32, col. 6.

Recommending a bill punishing such eavesdropping, H. Report 2807, accompanying S. 2287, 84th Cong., 2 sess., reproduced a Feb. 20, 1956 Department of Justice letter to the Senate Judiciary Committee which quoted the Attorney-General's earlier statement, and observed: "Such practices, however well intentioned, obviously and inevitably stifle the discussion and free exchange of ideas among jurors. They tend to destroy the very basis for common judgment among the jurors, upon which the institution of trial by jury is based, and are inconsistent with the purposes of the seventh amendment to the Constitution . . . which requires that trial by jury shall be preserved." The Department letter also pointed out that the Judicial Conference of the United States had in March 1956 approved the principle of the bill.

Although many prominent judges, lawyers and law teachers defended the recordings because they were made under proper safeguards and as a significant part of the over-all study of the jury system, the criticized activity was discontinued; and the bill in question became effective on August 2, 1956 (18 U.S.C. 1508). The law imposed a penalty of up to $1,000 fine and/or up to 1 yr. imprisonment upon anyone who "knowingly and wilfully, by any means or device whatsoever" attempts to, or actually does (a) record the deliberations or voting of a federal grand or petty jury, or (b) listen to or observe such proceedings of a jury of which he is not a member. (Nothing in the Act was to be construed as prohibiting a federal juror from taking notes to assist him in his duties as juror).

2. In the light of the material presented in this chapter, what position do you take on whether the jury system should be (a) abolished or (b) retained completely, or (c) retained in some modified form; and whether any differentiation should be made in these respects between civil and criminal cases and between different kinds of civil cases?

3. On the jury system in general, see Williams, The Proof of Guilt 190-272 (1st ed. 1955); Lummus, The Trial Judge (1937); Ulman, A Judge Takes the Stand (1936); Wellman, Gentlemen of the Jury (1931); Green, Judge and Jury (1930); Kalven, The Jury, The Law and the Personal Injury Damage Award, 19 Ohio St. L.J. 158 (1958); Jury Trial On Trial—A Symposium, 24 N.Y. State Bar Bull. 322 (1956); Broeder, Functions of the Jury, 21 U. Chi. L. Rev. 386 (1953); Hoffman and Brodley, Jurors on Trial, 17 Mo. L. Rev. 235 (1952); Goodman, In Defense of Our Jury System, 177 Colliers 24 (1951); James, Functions of Judge and Jury in Negligence Cases, 58 Yale L.J. 667 (1949); Hartshorn, Jury Verdicts: A Study of Their Characteristics and Trends, 35 A.B.A.J. 113 (1949).

CHAPTER Seven

CUSTOM, CONTRACT, and LAW—ARE LAYMEN LAWMAKERS TOO?

Section I

A GENERAL VIEW

Cardozo,* *THE NATURE OF THE JUDICIAL PROCESS*
58-64 (1921)

If history and philosophy do not serve to fix the direction of a principle, custom may step in. When we speak of custom, we may mean more things than one. "Consuetudo," says Coke, "is one of the maine triangles of the lawes of England; these lawes being divided into common law, statute law and customs." [9] Here common law and custom are thought of as distinct. Not so, however, Blackstone: "This unwritten or Common Law is properly distinguishable into three kinds: (1) General customs, which are the universal rule of the whole Kingdom, and form the Common Law, in its stricter and more usual signification. (2) Particular customs, which for the most part affect only the inhabitants of particular districts. (3) Certain particular laws, which by custom are adopted and used by some particular courts of pretty general and extensive jurisdiction." [10]

Undoubtedly the creative energy of custom in the development of common law is less today than it was in bygone times.[11] Even in bygone times, its energy was very likely exaggerated by Blackstone and his followers. "Today we recognize," in the words of Pound,[12] "that the custom is a custom of judicial decision, not of popular action." It is "doubtful," says Gray,[13] "whether at all stages of legal history, rules laid down by judges have not generated custom, rather than custom

---

* Benjamin Nathan Cardozo (1870-1938) was Associate Justice, U.S. Supreme Court 1932-38, having been appointed by President Hoover upon Holmes' retirement. After practicing law in New York for some 22 years, he was elected to the N.Y. Supreme Court in 1914, but was almost immediately appointed to the N.Y. Ct. of Appeals (to which he was later elected) where he served 1914-32 and was Chief Judge from 1927. His chief works are The Nature of the Judicial Process (1921); The Growth of the Law (1924); Paradoxes of Legal Science (1928); Law in Literature and Other Essays (1931). All of these to-

gether with other addresses and essays are available in a single volume, Selected Writings of B. N. Cardozo (Hall ed., 1947). The book from which extracts are quoted above is a collection of four lectures given at the Yale Law School in 1921.—Editor

[9] Coke on Littleton, 62a; . . .

[10] Blackstone, Comm., pp. 67, 68; Gray, "Nature and Sources of the Law," p. 266, sec. 598. . . .

[11] Cf. Gray, *supra*, sec. 634. . . .

[12] "Common Law and Legislation," 21 Harvard L.R. 383, 406.

[13] *Supra*, sec. 634

generated the rules." In these days, at all events, we look to custom, not so much for the creation of new rules, but for the tests and standards that are to determine how established rules shall be applied. When custom seeks to do more than this, there is a growing tendency in the law to leave development to legislation. Judges do not feel the same need of putting the *imprimatur* of law upon customs of recent growth, knocking for entrance into the legal system, and viewed askance because of some novel aspect of form or feature, as they would if legislatures were not in frequent session, capable of establishing a title that will be unimpeached and unimpeachable. But the power is not lost because it is exercised with caution. "The law merchant," says an English judge, "is not fixed and stereotyped, it has not yet been arrested in its growth by being moulded into a code; it is, to use the words of Lord Chief Justice Cockburn in Goodwin v. Roberts, L.R. 10 Exch. 346, capable of being expanded and enlarged to meet the wants of trade." In the absence of inconsistent statute, new classes of negotiable instruments may be created by mercantile practice. The obligations of public and private corporations may retain the quality of negotiability, despite the presence of a seal, which at common law would destroy it. "There is nothing immoral or contrary to good policy in making them negotiable if the necessities of commerce require that they should be so. A mere technical dogma of the courts or the common law cannot prohibit the commercial world from inventing or issuing any species of security not known in the last century." [16] So, in the memory of men yet living, the great inventions that embodied the power of steam and electricity, the railroad and the steamship, the telegraph and the telephone, have built up new customs and new law. Already there is a body of legal literature that deals with the legal problems of the air.

It is, however, not so much in the making of new rules as in the application of old ones that the creative energy of custom most often manifests itself today. General standards of right and duty are established. Custom must determine whether there has been adherence or departure. My partner has the powers that are usual in the trade. They may be so well known that the courts will notice them judicially. Such for illustration is the power of a member of a trading firm to make or indorse negotiable paper in the course of the firm's business. They may be such that the court will require evidence of their existence. The master in the discharge of his duty to protect the servant against harm must exercise the degree of care that is commonly exercised in like circumstance by men of ordinary prudence. The triers of the facts in determining whether that standard had been attained, must consult the habits of life, the everyday beliefs and practices, of the men and women about them. Innumerable, also, are the cases where the course of dealing to be followed is defined by the customs, or, more properly speaking, the usages, of a particular trade or market or profession. The constant assumption runs throughout the law that the natural and spontaneous evolutions of habit fix the limits of right and wrong. A slight extension of custom identifies it with customary morality, the prevailing standard of right conduct, the *mores* of the time.

[16] Mercer County v. Hacket, 1 Wall. 83; cf. Chase Nat. Bank v. Faurot, 149 N.Y. 532.

This is the point of contact between the [judicial] method of tradition and the method of sociology. They have their roots in the same soil. Each method maintains the interaction between conduct and order, between life and law. Life casts the moulds of conduct, which will some day become fixed as law. Law preserves the moulds, which have taken form and shape from life.

FULLER, *AMERICAN LEGAL REALISM*
82 University of Pennsylvania Law Review 429, 448-460 (1934)

The Relation of Law and Society

One of the fundamental problems which any social philosophy must face may be stated in a somewhat vague way as the problem of the relation between law and society,—or, if one prefers, of the relation of Law to Life. Many of the problems of ethical philosophy, in whatever terms they may have been expressed, will be found to center about this relationship. The most imposing legal philosophies will often disclose themselves as involving fundamentally nothing more than a bias concerning this relation,—a bias in favor of "law," or in favor of "society." . . .

I shall begin by quoting a series of statements which will furnish the background for what I have to say:*

"Law and the law official are not therefore in any real sense what *makes* order in society. For them society is given and order is given because society is given. . . . The law then, the interference of officials in disputes, appears as the means of dealing with disputes which do not otherwise get settled. Not as *making* order, but as *maintaining* order when it has gotten out of order. . . . By and large the *basic order* of our society, and for that matter in any society, *is not produced by law*. . . . Law plays only upon the fringes."

Certainly, the emphasis is here placed on the "society" side of the relation. Law, the principle of conscious guidance, is relegated to the background, and becomes a kind of midwife called in occasionally to assist the processes of nature, but having no hand in the act of creation itself.

I do not contend, of course, that Llewellyn denies altogether any creative role to law. Though he emphasizes the "power of society over courts," he admits that there is another side to the thing which occasionally manifests itself: "the power of courts over society." He recognizes that sometimes even a single legal decision may shape the growth of an institution, and that men "often do orient the action which they take *apart from* litigation" on the basis of legal rules. Llewellyn himself, then, qualifies the broad statements I have quoted previously. It cannot be asserted that he does not see the whole picture. What I fear is that he may suffer from a species of color blindness which causes him to see one part of the picture with especial vividness while the rest fades into an indistinct background. The

---

* Professor Fuller here quotes from writings of Professor Karl Llewellyn and much of the following discussion is in terms of a criticism of Professor Llewellyn's views.—Editor

aspect of the relation of law and society which he constantly chooses for categorical assertion is "the power of society over courts." The qualifications come later, too late to restore a proper balance of emphasis.

This bias on the side of "society" is evidenced in many parts of Llewellyn's work. It is illustrated in his theory that case law will, in a more or less automatic fashion, develop in those places where social change demands it. It is found in his conception of the "pathological case" as the case "so exceptional that the normal ways of society afford . . . no solid basis for deciding [it]. . . ." The implication is that the ordinary, "non-pathological" case can and should find its regulation in the "normal ways of society." The same attitude is found in his discussion of legal certainty. "Layman's legal certainty" is identified with the congruence of law and social norms, and it is assumed, not only that law should generally conform to the "ways of life," but that these ways afford a substantial basis for judicial decision.

This emphasis on the society side of the relation is also found in Llewellyn's constant insistence that the legal scholar's first task must be to master in its last detail the whole pattern of human behavior before he attempts to prescribe regulations for it. This insistence that "value judgments" be postponed until we have traced out exhaustively the whole labyrinth of social norms certainly involves itself a "value judgment," however much Llewellyn may protest the rigid exclusion of "ought" from his approach. If I tell a sculptor that he must spend twenty years investigating the physical and chemical structure of the clay used in modelling before he takes up the study of modelling itself, it will hardly do for me to say I am not teaching sculpture. I shall be judged by the effects of my instructions. The man who has spent most of his life studying clay will be a different kind of sculptor from the man who has devoted more of his time to the art of modelling. There is no *a priori* reason for supposing he will be a better sculptor. If I assume he will be, it must be because of some notion I have concerning the relative importance of clay and modelling in the process of sculpturing.

If I have to choose someone to draft a statute regulating the banking business I may put a high value on a knowledge of banking practice. I may regard as the ideal man for the task the man who knows the practices of the banking world so thoroughly that he can predict with certainty the psychological reactions which the sight of a postdated check will invoke in any banking employee, from messenger boy to president. I may prefer him to a man who, though less familiar with the behavior of bank employees, has spent his life studying the history and theory of banks and banking law, and many hours in arm-chair reflection on the possible ways of organizing and controlling the banking business. I am entitled to my preference. But I am not entitled to escape responsibility for it by saying it involves no "value judgment," no philosophy of what ought to be.

I do not deny that Llewellyn's bias for the society side of the relation may answer to a real need in our law. Lawyers have been too prone to think of society as mere clay in the hands of the "Law." Our courts too often talk as if their task were merely to cut channels, largely after a design of their own fancy, through which the waters of life are expected to flow inertly and complaisantly. To this conception Llewellyn offers a needed antidote. But it is wise to remember that antidotes can be administered too liberally, and that in the case at hand there is danger we may escape one simplification only to fall victims to another.

There are two extreme, and therefore simple, ways of conceiving of the relation of law and society. "Law" can be conceived of as the active principle operating to shape an inert element "society." This is the view toward which the imperative school tends,* and it is the view tacitly assumed by most legal writers not of a particularly philosophic turn of mind.

At the other extreme is the view that "society" is the active principle and that "law" is simply a function of this principle. This is the view toward which Maine, Savigny, Ehrlich and Duguit tend. Llewellyn seems to me to place himself in this class, though his closest affinity is with the last two mentioned.

These are the extreme views. Each of them has a value,—as a corrective of the other. Indeed it is often difficult to say whether the emphasis made by a given writer is intended to convey his conception of an ultimate truth, or is intended simply to restore a balance which he considers to have been disturbed by extremists on the other side. But fighting fire with fire is always attended by hazards. We avoid the difficulties which arise from these extreme simplistic positions if we recognize frankly that the relation is one of mutual action and reaction. In the relation of law and society neither element is wholly determinative, neither wholly determined. This intermediate view seems to me to represent the position of such scholars as Ihering, Pound, Geny, Stammler and Cohen.

In dealing with this problem we can employ with advantage Cohen's principle of polarity. Law and Society are polar categories. Though we are under the necessity of opposing them to one another we must recognize that each implies the other. If we deny one, the other becomes meaningless. We may picture Law and Society as the two blades of a pair of scissors. If we watch only one blade we may conclude it does all the cutting. Savigny kept his eye on the Society blade and came virtually to deny the existence of the Law blade. With him even the most technical lawyer's law was a kind of glorified folk-way. Austin kept his eye on the Law blade and found little occasion in a book of over a thousand pages to discuss the mere "positive morality" which social norms represent. Blackstone shifted his eye from one blade to the other and gave us the confused account in which, on the one hand, he bases the common law on custom, and, on the other, informs us that the authoritative statement of this custom is to be found only in court decisions. As if to add to the confusion, he then lays down rules for determining when a custom should be recognized by the law. We avoid all these difficulties by the simple expedient of recognizing that both blades cut, and that neither can cut without the other.

By saying that we avoid difficulties by adopting the "polar" view of the relation of law and society, I do not mean to imply that the adoption of this view renders the problem a simple one. On the contrary, the advantage of this view lies precisely in the fact that it reveals the difficulties which exist and enables us to prepare to

---

* "The imperative school": the juristic theory that "the law" consists in the commands of a sovereign, and in nothing else. —Editor

meet them. This view makes it clear that the problem of the relation of law and society is not the sort of issue which can be "solved" by some "theory" and then passed over. It is, to use Radin's suggestive phrase, one of the "permanent problems of the law." But while we may not have disposed of the question, we shall at least have divested it of a specious simplicity which is itself the source of endless difficulty.

The "Institutional Approach" of Underhill Moore

What these difficulties are becomes apparent when an attempt is made to apply in a practical way a simplistic conception of the relation of law and society. One of the most recent and most thoroughgoing attempts to do this is to be found in Underhill Moore's "institutional approach." Professor Moore starts with the question, What actually controls judicial decisions? The judge moves in a complex environment—moral, intellectual, and physical—and his decisions may be regarded as reactions to that environment. But of the numberless factors of this environment, which are the most significant? The traditional theory supposed, or pretended to suppose, that the judge was influenced solely by a segment of his intellectual environment, that represented by "law" and legal theory. This view is no longer tenable. We now realize that rules are impotent to exercise any real control over the judicial process. Even when they seem to chart a definite course (which is seldom because of their vagueness) frequent judicial aberrations from the charted course remind us that there must be other, more significant factors in the judge's environment. Professor Moore then sets about to discover what these more significant factors are. One item after another is rejected. Common sense rejects the assumption that the physical environment has any very important, or at least measurable, influence over judicial decisions. A poorly ventilated court room may conceivably affect the judicial process,—but this is a remote and conjectural possibility. The notion that prevailing philosophic notions, conceptions of the good life, may have any very great influence is rejected because these things are matters of "intuition" and are therefore incapable of scientific treatment. The search for some ultimately determinative element begins to look futile. But let us not give up hope. There is one constant in our shifting firmament. We still have the "institutional patterns of behavior" which prevail in the community. We know that "men's actions move along the well-cut channels or straggling ruts of habits,"—this is, indeed, "the conclusion of the philosopher, the psychologist and the common man." These folk-ways, these institutional patterns of behavior, become then, like "the sun, the tides, the rain, one of the constant factors among the welter of variables." Can we not assume that the judicial process is controlled by them, that judicial decisions turn ultimately on the institutional or non-institutional character of the litigants' behavior? [62] *

[62] This paragraph is intended to summarize the arguments found in Rational Basis of Legal Institutions (1923) 23 Col. L. Rev. 609, and An Institutional Approach to the Law of Commercial Banking (1929) 38 Yale L.J. 703.

It may be objected at this point that Moore's study is not pertinent to the present

Professor Moore does not rest content with enunciating a theory; he proceeds to test his theory in practice. Do the decisions actually reveal that judges are primarily controlled by the patterns of behavior which prevail in the community? To determine this three cases were selected for study. All three related to the same point of banking law.† Two cases (from New York and Pennsylvania) decided the point in one way;[63] the other case (from South Carolina) decided it in another way.[64] Can we explain this difference as arising, not from a different conception of "law," not from a different philosophy of life or from other such imponderables, but from an *observable* difference in the banking practices of South Carolina as compared with those of New York and Pennsylvania? An elaborate investigation was undertaken to answer this question.[65]

Now before undertaking such an investigation, one has to consider at least four questions. How do you ascertain what social institutions exist, or, to use Moore's own phrase, how do you go about "ethnologizing a particular present day culture"? How do you extract out of the social institutions so ascertained a norm of decision? Can you be sure that the courts will be familiar with existing social insti-

inquiry because he clearly disclaims any intent to say what law ought to be. He does not say how courts *ought* to decide cases; he only describes how they *must* decide them. It would be easy to answer this objection by pointing out that it is no unheard of thing for moralists to present their Utopias as necessities, their "oughts" as "musts." But let us give Professor Moore the benefit of the doubt and assume that he is not a preacher disguised as a scientist. His study still remains pertinent to our discussion. Moore is at least disposing of other people's "oughts" whether he is setting up one of his own or not. If courts *must* decide cases by a reference to prevailing behavior patterns, then those who argue that they ought to decide them on some other basis are wasting their breath. For this reason the ethical philosopher cannot avoid bringing Moore into his discussions, however little Moore may feel inclined to return the compliment.

* The question posed is this: does not the court in deciding whether defendant legally wronged plaintiff, decide simply whether defendant departed from the prevailing habits or patterns of conduct which are in fact followed by people in the community in the circumstances involved?—Editor

† The question was whether a bank depositor can recover from the bank for damages due to the bank's failure to honor his check because the bank applied an overdue note against the deposited funds.—Editor

[63] Delano v. Equitable Trust Co., 110 Misc. 704, 181 N.Y. Supp. 852 (1920); Goldstein v. Jefferson Title & Trust Co., 95 Pa. Super. 167 (1928).

[64] Callahan v. Bank of Anderson, 69 S.C. 374, 48 S.E. 293 (1904). [I.e., this court allowed recovery by the depositor. And Moore's investigation purported to show that the bank's debiting of the deposit account was a *deviation* from South Carolina banking practice.—Editor]

[65] Moore and Sussman [Legal and Institutional Methods Applied to the Debiting of Direct Discounts, 40 Yale L.J. 381, 555, 752, 928, 1055, 1219 (1931)] a total of 145 pages. The method succeeded in explaining the South Carolina decision, and Moore therefore concludes that "the study probably justifies the inference of a causal relation" between judicial decisions and the institutional or deviational character of the litigants' behavior. *Id.* at 1249. Aside from the question whether the ability to explain a single decision is a very impressive demonstration of the validity of a method, it is interesting to observe that the South Carolina case was decided by an equally divided court. So while Moore succeeded in explaining why two of the judges voted to affirm the decision of the lower court, he has yet to explain why the other two members of the court voted the other way.

tutions and will extract from them the same norm of decision that you do? Can you be sure that the courts will necessarily regard the norm of decision implied in a given social institution as the best one? Moore's study involves an answer to each of these questions and, it seems to me, in each case the answer which he gives is erroneous.

First of all, how do you go about determining what social institutions, what folk-ways, exist? Professor Moore's answer is that you simply observe the way people behave. If you are investigating banking practice with reference to notes, you send an investigator into the cage of the note teller to make a record of what he does. Or, you put a hypothetical situation to an experienced banker and ask him how he would conduct himself in such a case. The emphasis is on behavior. The purpose back of that behavior, the rationalizations and intellectual activity which accompany it are ignored.

This, it seems to me, constitutes the fundamental fallacy of the "institutional approach" of Moore—the assumption that the significance of institutions is exhausted in behavior. In an early article he writes, "To say that a legal institution,—private property, the federal government of the United States, Columbia University,—exists is to say that a group of persons is doing something, is acting in some way." [66] Now many people would say that a legal institution consists not of actions, but of attitudes of mind to which actions merely give external expression. This view is rejected by Moore on the ground, I take it, that these attitudes of mind are usually simply rationalizations of the behavior which they accompany, and are therefore the effect of the behavior, not the cause of it. *Now it is quite true that this is often the case.* But the truth here happens to be complex, and it is also true that behavior is, at least sometimes, the expression of mental attitudes. This fact is enough to vitiate any purely "behavioristic" approach to social institutions.

Bankers were never asked by Professor Moore's investigators what they were trying to accomplish, or why they acted as they did. They were only "observed," or were asked to state how they would react to certain situations selected by Professor Moore and phrased in his own language. The fallacy of this procedure becomes apparent when we realize that it is impossible to define what the "situation" is to which the banker reacts unless we know what is going on in his mind. We observe that a banker, whose customer's note is due and unpaid, refrains from charging the amount of the note against the customer's checking account until the consent of the customer has been obtained. What is the situation which called forth this reaction? Moore defines the situation entirely in terms of "observables." Was the note secured? How did the note come into the hands of the bank? Had the note just come due, or had it been overdue for some time? Yet from the standpoint of the banker, these were perhaps the least significant elements in the situation. The most significant factor from the standpoint of the banker may have been the fact that the customer's default on the note was obviously due to an oversight, or the fact that the customer was a man of good credit standing, or some other fact not stated in Moore's hypothetical "situation."

[66] Moore, *supra* note 62, at 609.

The realists regard as one of the fundamental fallacies of the traditional method its assumption that the judge reacts only to those facts of the case which are visible through the prism of legal theory. In truth, the judge's decision represents a reaction to the whole situation, including many facts which from the standpoint of legal theory are irrelevant. The realist condemns the traditional method for its mistaken assumption that you can limit the influence of facts to those tagged as legally relevant, and for the corollary assumption that it is profitable to discuss the solution of controversies on the basis of textbook outlines of the facts. Yet precisely the same fallacy, if it is a fallacy, is contained in Moore's approach. He adopts toward bankers the same attitude the traditional theory adopts towards judges,—a procedure which could only be justified on the doubtful assumption that bankers possess less complicated personalities than judges. He assumes that there are principles guiding the practice of banking which one can discover merely by asking a banker how he would react in certain skeletonized "situations." [67] He seems aware of the temerity of this procedure and of the need for justifying it for he is at pains to report that the answers which bankers gave to his questions were "stated with the positive assurance with which are given descriptions of the way everyday situations are met." [68] This may seem to prove that he had accurately stated the "situations" to which bankers react, but I think that this inference is wholly without justification. If some earnest sociologist were to attempt a "scientific" investigation into the folkways of lawyers, and were to ask one hundred unselected lawyers, "Can a man who has rescinded a contract, sue on it?" I suspect that most of his answers would be in the negative and would be given with "positive assurance." The "positive assurance" would exist precisely because the lawyer was asked about a skeletonized, "conceptual" situation. If he were put a series of actual cases his assurance would probably diminish to the vanishing point. Professor Moore asked his bankers if, when a customer's note was due, they charged the note against his account without authority from him. They gave, for the most part, ready answers. Would the answers have been so ready if the situation had been filled out with such pertinent facts as the credit standing of the customer, the availability or non-availability of legal advice inside the bank, the apparent reason for the customer's default (oversight, insolvency, temporary stringency, etc.) and the purpose for which the account was being used? And if not, does the uniformity of the banker's reactions to skeletonized fact situations represent a really significant "institution"?

An uncritical adherence to the behavioristic approach leads to another erroneous assumption, that norms of decision may be extracted directly from regularities of behavior, and that where you have a definite "behavior pattern" you necessarily

[67] For the purpose of making clear my own attitude, I should say that I do not share unqualifiedly the realist's antipathy toward skeletonized cases. I think such cases have both a dialectic and a pedagogical utility. But the "skeletonizing" of cases is a delicate business, and necessarily anticipates the analysis which will be applied to the simplified situation. This means that when you "skeletonize" situations for bankers you have to do so with reference to the principles on which bankers act in the conduct of their business. This is what Moore made no attempt to do.

[68] Moore and Sussman, *supra* note 65, at 759.

have a correspondingly definite norm of decision. Now this is demonstrably untrue. It may be the practice of department stores generally to accept goods returned by customers. This behavior pattern may be exemplified in literally thousands of instances. But what norm of decision is implied in this practice? The department store, we shall assume, refuses to accept goods returned by the customer and the customer sues. Now we cannot decide this case simply by referring to the existence of a pattern of behavior. The mere fact that people habitually act in certain ways in certain situations is not itself a criterion on the basis of which lawsuits may be decided. If a folk-way is relevant to decision, it must be because it has a "normative" aspect. But we cannot discover this normative aspect by a mere statistical investigation, by inquiring, in the case I have supposed, how many times department stores have accepted returned goods. We have to discover whether this practice is merely a matter of accommodation ("the customer is always right"), or has established an attitude of expectancy, a sentiment of "ought," which can serve as a norm of decision. The interesting thing is that we can get the most light on this normative aspect of the practice from the way in which the department store acts in what Professor Moore calls "deviational" cases, for example, where the customer's dissatisfaction with the goods is patently unreasonable. The essence of an "institution" will generally be found, not in "behavior," but in mental attitudes, and frequently the nature of these attitudes is revealed and defined only in "non-institutional" situations. Often it is the observation of behavior in the unusual case which gives definiteness to the contour of an institution.

So soon as we abandon the attempt to stick to a purely behavioristic approach, and begin to take into account the intellectual processes which accompany and guide behavior, we see at once the absurdity of the view that the law should (or does) simply take over social institutions as a ready-made norm of decision. We see that our note teller's patterns of behavior may be shaped, not by an invisible psychological force which confines him to some "straggling rut of habit," but by his own imperfect notions of the law, so that to take over his patterns of behavior as a norm of decision is simply to put the judicial ermine on the bank teller and to substitute second-hand knowledge and rumor for the researches of judge and counsel. We see also that "law" and "institutional patterns of behavior" often derive from a common emotional and intellectual source—for example, from current conceptions of business expediency and social justice.[70] For assistance in

[70] The South Carolina deviation from the rule obtaining in Pennsylvania and New York might conceivably have been explained on the basis of Southern business *mores*. My own experience in the South would lead me to believe that the Southerner does not typically regard the debtor-creditor relationship in the impersonal, "businesslike" way it is regarded in the North. It is a personal relation, involving a duty of consideration not only of debtor toward creditor, but of creditor toward debtor. This makes it understandable why a Southern judge would feel a resentment toward a banker who suddenly began turning down his customer's checks, after allowing his note to remain overdue without action for a considerable period. Professor Moore would, of course, scoff at any such explanation as resting on "intuition." But is any more "intuition" involved in this explanation than is involved in his assumption that, in some mysterious way, judges know or "sense" the institutional patterns of behavior prevailing in their communities? But then, this assumption probably rep-

understanding these intangibles we shall be forced to call back the "brilliant intuitionalists" whom Professor Moore so cavalierly dismissed at the beginning of his study.

Professor Moore claims for his method that it corresponds to the method actually employed by courts, whether they are aware of that fact or not. This necessarily assumes that courts are familiar with the behavior patterns of the community. For the culture patterns of life inside the bank teller's cage can influence the judge only if he knows of them. Yet there seems a certain temerity in the assumption that the justices of the Supreme Court of South Carolina (whose biographies incidentally reveal no practical banking experience) [71] already knew what Moore's investigators took months to learn. Moore meets this point only by saying that the judge's "attitudes and ideas are molded by a cultural matrix whose patterns are engraved by frequency. Put in another way, if the court [the judge?] is not conditioned by frequent contact with the behavior itself, it is conditioned by verbal behavior which will be found, on last analysis, to be causally related to the patterns or institutions." [72] I am not quite sure that I understand this. It seems to mean that the judge in the contacts of daily life will inevitably hear turns of expression which, in some subtle way, will convey to him an insight into what note tellers are doing about debiting direct discounts. But it is hard to believe Professor Moore meant anything quite so preposterous as that. In view of the uncertainty of his meaning, perhaps it would be best to let this point go without refutation.

Let us, then, grant Professor Moore his point about the "cultural matrix," even if we remain a little obscure as to what it is we are granting. Let us assume that there exists a definite pattern of behavior, that the court knows of it, and that the court has been able to extract from it a norm of decision. Still it by no means follows, as Moore seems to assume, that the court will or should regard the norm so obtained as the most desirable basis of decision. Obviously where a court disapproves the end toward which a social practice is directed, it may refuse to accept the practice as a norm of decision. A court may decline to enforce a gambling debt, though it be admitted that the norms of society call for the payment of such debts. Courts exercise at least a veto power over folk-ways. This qualification of the "institutional method" is so obvious that we would be unfair if we did not assume that the proponents of the method had it tacitly in mind. Let us turn to a less obvious point. Does the institutional method remain valid in those situations where the court regards as innocent the purpose which the parties are attempting to achieve? I think not. To accept the "institutional approach" uncritically even in these cases is to overlook the fact that a court may refuse to conform to a folkway, not because it disapproves of the object toward which it is directed, but

---

resents an example of the "qualitative subjective judgment" which Moore admits is involved in his method; it cannot be mere "intuition" for that is presumably excluded from his approach.

[71] See Brooks, South Carolina Bench and Bar (1908) for biographical sketches of the four justices involved. Incidentally there is nothing in the biographies of the two dissenting judges which would explain why the cultural matrix failed to make an impression on them.

[72] Moore and Sussman, *supra* note 65, at 1219.

because it considers it ill-adapted to achieve that object. It is to ignore the possibility that a court may undertake to reshape a "behavior pattern" to assist it in reaching its own end. If it were true, for example, that laymen generally regarded the ceremony of "shaking on it" as creating a binding contract, it would not follow that a court would have to accept this ceremony as a valid legal formality if it considered that it offered insufficient safeguards against the dangers which legal formalities are supposed to avert.[73] The law has always to weigh against the advantages of conforming to life, the advantages of reshaping and clarifying life, bearing always in mind that its attempts to reshape life may miscarry, or may cost more than they achieve.[74] . . .

M. R. COHEN, *LAW AND THE SOCIAL ORDER*
124-125, 189-190 (1933)

Custom as such does not give one a legal right. Courts, however, do frequently give legal sanction to certain customary ways of doing things and thus transform them into legal rules.

*   *   *

The study of "living law" (for which Llewellyn has called so eloquently) is a study of custom—a very important condition of law, but not a sufficient determinant of it. For actual practices may be contrary to the policy of the law. The law cannot accept anything as legal merely because it is the practice of a large number of people. Custom must meet certain criteria before the law will sanction it. It is doubtless of the utmost importance to know the actual conditions under which a legal rule is to be applied. But it cannot be too strongly insisted that the knowledge of such social conditions belongs to economics, or to some branch of descriptive social science. Law is a method of regulating social action, and the science of law has a content over and above that met in the knowledge of actual conditions. . . . [Law] is essentially concerned with norms that regulate, rather than with uniformities that describe, human conduct.

---

[73] Our courts probably made a mistake in following lay practice in the "liberalization" of the requirement of a seal. In this way they frittered away, perhaps irretrievably, a valuable social practice. [In the earlier common law, it was frequently required that a document, to be legally effective, have attached to it a waxed, or gummed paper, or a piece of wax bearing the distinctive sign of the party to be bound. This was the "seal," the requirement of which, as the author notes, has been dispensed with increasingly.—Editor]

[74] Ihering speaks of the close relation which existed between law and business in ancient Rome. He goes on to say, "The intimacy of the relation between legal science and business redounded to the benefit of both. To the benefit of business, because the lawyer had his hand constantly on its pulse and knew what it needed and how it could be helped. To the benefit of jurisprudence because, without denying in any material respect the demands of business, it could bring business into that form which was, from the legal standpoint, the most desirable one." . . . American "institutionalists" should, I think, ponder the last sentence, to see whether it may not describe a desideratum they have fallen into the habit of overlooking.

NOTES AND QUESTIONS

1. When Oklahoma was a "dry" state, it was apparently illegal to serve liquor to business guests, even in one's own home. A lawyer served liquor for entertainment which the trial court found appropriate and helpful for development of the lawyer's clientele, in accordance with the usual practice of lawyers in the State. The lawyer sought to have the liquor expenditures deducted from his gross income as a business expense for income tax purposes. Applying the established doctrine that business expenses which violate or frustrate sharply defined national or state policies are not deductible, the Tenth Circuit refused to allow the deduction. United States v. Winters, 261 F. 2d 675 (10 Cir., 1958). Judge Murrah's dissent, after pointing out that no criminal charge for serving liquor to business guests in one's own home had been reported in more than fifty years of Oklahoma prohibition, declared:

> "When the Oklahoma law is thus construed in the context of human conduct, it is extremely doubtful that the taxpayer has severely and immediately frustrated any very well defined public policy of Oklahoma . . . As one living in the state since the very inception of the [prohibition] law, and as one claiming some acquaintance with the mores of the community, I certainly cannot say so.
>
> "This is not to say that the letter of the law is subordinate to its observance so that a law honored in its breach does not reflect public policy. It is to say that the law is interpreted not only by the courts, but also by the mores of the community wherein it is effective. Indeed, the people make the law, and by their conduct construe it to reflect the public policy of the state."

Do you agree with the dissent? How does it fit in with the ideas expressed in the preceding articles? Would Fuller and Cohen agree or disagree with Murrah's dissent?

2. Could a sociologist who believed that the most important force in maintaining order in the society is the force of customs, habits, or tradition, still disagree with Underhill Moore's thesis?

3. For miscellaneous general discussions of the relationship between custom and law, see Allen, Law In the Making (5th ed. 1951) 61-153; Stone, Province and Function of Law (1946) c. XXIV; Braybrooke, Custom As a Source of English Law, 50 Mich. L. Rev. 71 (1951); Note, Custom and Trade Usage: Its Application to Commercial Dealing and to Commercial Law, 55 Colum. L. Rev. 1192 (1955).

EDITORIAL NOTE: The ASCERTAINMENT and LEGAL RELEVANCE of PREVAILING IDEALS and ATTITUDES

As Fuller pointed out, the study of behavior alone gives no insight into the (1) ought-sentiments or ideals of the actors or (2) the ideals which should be translated into law by the lawmaker who would channel behavior into ideal paths. What, then, is the appropriate way to ascertain the ideals which prevail in the society on any particular issue? And once ascertained, what is their relevance for the lawmaker? Should the lawmaker be governed by prevailing ideals and attitudes any more than by customary behavior?

1. *Is a Person Who Commits Euthanasia of "Good Moral Character"?* The different views held about these questions is illustrated by the split decision in Repouille v. United States, 165 F. 2d 152 (2d Cir. 1947). For the majority, Judge Learned Hand observed:

The District Attorney, on behalf of the Immigration and Naturalization Service, has appealed from an order naturalizing the appellee, Repouille. The ground of the objection in the district court and here is that he did not show himself to have been a person of "good moral character" for the five years which preceded the filing of his petition.[1] The facts were as follows. The petition was filed on September 22, 1944, and on October 12, 1939, he had deliberately put to death his son, a boy of thirteen, by means of chloroform. His reason for this tragic deed was that the child had "suffered from birth from a brain injury which destined him to be an idiot and a physical monstrosity malformed in all four limbs. The child was blind, mute, and deformed. He had to be fed; the movements of his bladder and bowels were involuntary, and his entire life was spent in a small crib." Repouille had four other children at the time towards whom he has always been a dutiful and responsible parent; it may be assumed that his act was to help him in their nurture, which was being compromised by the burden imposed upon him in the care of the fifth. The family was altogether dependent upon his industry for its support. He was indicted for manslaughter in the first degree; but the jury brought in a verdict of manslaughter in the second degree with a recommendation of the "utmost clemency"; and the judge sentenced him to not less than five years nor more than ten, execution to be stayed, and the defendant to be placed on probation, from which he was discharged in December 1945. Concededly, except for this act he conducted himself as a person of "good moral character" during the five years before he filed his petition. Indeed, if he had waited before filing his petition from September 22, to October 14, 1944, he would have been admitted without question.

Very recently we had to pass upon the phrase "good moral character" in the Nationality Act; and we said that it set as a test, not those standards which we might ourselves approve, but whether "the moral feelings, now prevalent generally in this country" would "be outraged" by the conduct in question: that is, whether it conformed to "the generally accepted moral conventions current at the time." [2] In the absence of some national inquisition, like a Gallup poll, that is indeed a difficult test to apply; often questions will arise to which the answer is not ascertainable, and where the petitioner must fail only because he has the affirmative. Indeed, in the case at bar itself the answer is not wholly certain; for we all know that there are great numbers of people of the most unimpeachable virtue, who think it morally justifiable to put an end to a life so inexorably destined to be a burden to others, and—so far as any possible interest of its own is concerned—condemned to a brutish existence, lower indeed than all but the lowest forms of sentient life. Nor is it inevitably an answer to say that it must be immoral to do this, until the law provides security against the abuses which would inevitably follow, unless the practice were regulated. Many people—probably most people—do not make it a final ethical test of conduct that it shall not violate law; few of us exact of ourselves or of others the unflinching obedience of a Socrates. There being no lawful means of accomplishing an end, which they believe to be righteous in itself, there have always been conscientious persons who feel no scruple in acting in defiance of a law which is repugnant to their personal convictions, and who even regard as martyrs those who suffer by doing so. In our own history it is only necessary to recall the Abolitionists. It is reasonably clear that the jury which tried Repouille did not feel any moral repulsion at his crime. Although it was inescapably murder in the first degree, not only did they bring in a verdict that

---

[1] Sec. 707(a) (3). Title 8 U.S.C.A.   [2] United States v. Francisco, 2 Cir., 164 F. 2d **163.**

was flatly in the face of the facts and utterly absurd—for manslaughter in the second degree presupposes that the killing has not been deliberate—but they coupled even that with a recommendation which showed that in substance they wished to exculpate the offender. Moreover, it is also plain, from the sentence which he imposed, that the judge could not have seriously disagreed with their recommendation.

One might be tempted to seize upon all this as a reliable measure of current morals; and no doubt it should have its place in the scale; but we should hesitate to accept it as decisive, when, for example, we compare it with the fate of a similar offender in Massachusetts, who, although he was not executed, was imprisoned for life. Left at large as we are, without means of verifying our conclusion, and without authority to substitute our individual beliefs, the outcome must needs be tentative; and not much is gained by discussion. We can say no more than that, quite independently of what may be the current moral feeling as to legally administered euthanasia, we feel reasonably secure in holding that only a minority of virtuous persons would deem the practise morally justifiable, while it remains in private hands, even when the provocation is as overwhelming as it was in this instance.

However, we wish to make it plain that a new petition would not be open to this objection; and that the pitiable event, now long passed, will not prevent Repouille from taking his place among us as a citizen. The assertion in his brief that he did not "intend" the petition to be filed until 1945, unhappily is irrelevant; the statute makes crucial the actual date of filing.

Order reversed; petition dismissed without prejudice to the filing of a second petition.

In dissent, Judge Jerome Frank declared:

This decision may be of small practical import to this petitioner for citizenship, since perhaps, on filing a new petition, he will promptly become a citizen. But the method used by my colleagues in disposing of this case may. as a precedent, have a very serious significance for many another future petitioner whose "good moral character" may be questioned (for any one of a variety of reasons which may be unrelated to a "mercy killing") in circumstances where the necessity of filing a new petition may cause a long and injurious delay.[3] Accordingly, I think it desirable to dissent.

The district judge found that Repouille was a person of "good moral character." Presumably, in so finding, the judge attempted to employ that statutory standard in accordance with our decisions, i.e., as measured by conduct in conformity with "the generally accepted moral conventions at the time." My colleagues, although their sources of information concerning the pertinent mores are not shown to be superior to those of the district judge, reject his finding. And they do so, too, while conceding that their own conclusion is uncertain, and (as they put it) "tentative." I incline to think that the correct statutory test (the test Congress intended) is the attitude of our ethical leaders. That attitude would not be too difficult to learn; indeed, my colleagues indicate that they think such leaders would agree with the district judge. But the precedents in this circuit constrain us to be guided by contemporary public opinion about which, cloistered as judges are, we have but vague notions. (One recalls Gibbon's remark that usually a person who talks of "the opinion of the world at large" is really referring to "the few people with whom I happened to converse.")

[3] Consider, e.g., the case of a professional man, unable during a long delay, incident to his becoming a citizen, to practice his profession in certain states of this country.

Seeking to apply a standard of this type, courts usually do not rely on evidence but utilize what is often called the doctrine of "judicial notice," which, in matters of this sort, properly permits informal inquiries by the judges. However, for such a purpose (as in the discharge of many other judicial duties), the courts are inadequately staffed, so that sometimes "judicial notice" actually means judicial ignorance.

But the courts are not utterly helpless; such judicial impotence has its limits. Especially when an issue importantly affecting a man's life is involved, it seems to me that we need not, and ought not, resort to our mere unchecked surmises, remaining wholly (to quote my colleagues' words) "without means of verifying our conclusions." Because court judgments are the most solemn kind of governmental acts—backed up as they are, if necessary, by the armed force of the government—they should, I think, have a more solid foundation. I see no good reason why a man's rights should be jeopardized by judges' needless lack of knowledge.

I think, therefore, that, in any case such as this, where we lack the means of determining present-day public reactions, we should remand to the district judge with these directions: The judge should give the petitioner and the government the opportunity to bring to the judge's attention reliable information on the subject, which he may supplement in any appropriate way. All the data so obtained should be put on record. On the basis thereof, the judge should reconsider his decision, and arrive at a conclusion. Then, if there is another appeal, we can avoid sheer guessing, which alone is now available to us, and can reach something like an informed judgment.[4]

2. *Proposal for a More Scientific Ascertainment of Prevailing Ideals.* Cohen, Robson and Bates* argue that polls can and should be used to ascertain prevailing ideals and criticize the majority's attitude in the Repouille case as follows:

. . . In Repouille v. United States, the test of "good moral character" was not [Judge Hand's] own belief, but whether "the moral feelings now generally prevalent in this country would be outraged."

In Johnson v. U.S., he again stated:[18]

Our duty in such cases, as we understand it, is to divine what the "common conscience" prevalent at the time demands; and it is impossible in practice to ascertain what in a given instance it does demand. . . . Nor is it possible to make use of general principles, for almost every moral situation is unique. . . . Theoretically, perhaps, we might take as the test whether those who would approve the specific conduct would outnumber those who would disapprove; but it would be fantastically absurd to try to apply it. So it seems to us that we are confined to the best guess we can make of how such a poll would result.

. . . Now granted that such a "poll" as suggested by Judge Hand would not yield any general principles covering all moral situations; granted, also, that it would be impracticable to poll the community concerning *each* specific moral issue raised in litigious controversies—would it not be more reliable to develop analogically from a poll of sentiment of *several* concrete moral issues, concerning which the views of the community are relevant, than it is to

---

[4] Of course, we cannot thus expect to attain certainty, for certainty on such a subject as public opinion is unattainable.

* Cohen, Robson and Bates, Ascertaining

the Moral Sense of the Community, 8 J. Legal Ed. 137, 140-141, 144-145, 148-149 (1955).—Editor

[18] 186 F. 2d 588, 590 (2d Cir. 1951).

develop analogically from a surmise or "guess" by a judge as to the nature of the community sentiment regarding those issues? [20] Take the situation in the Johnson case. Johnson had failed to support his legal wife; for years he had been living with a paramour. Was he of "good moral character" within the meaning of the naturalization statute? Judge Hand held in the negative because of his belief that it conformed to his "best guess" of what the "common conscience" would be on the facts of the case. Now, suppose that Judge Hand were confronted with another case, the facts of which varied slightly from the Johnson case. Would he not be on firmer ground in the second case if he had at his disposal an accurate "poll" of the community's reaction to the situation in the Johnson case than he would be upon his "guess" of what the moral sense of the community would be with respect to it? We think he would be. For if he erred in his judgment in the first case, the error would be pyramided in the second, in the third, and in the other analogical extensions that would follow . . .

[In an experiment being conducted at the University of Nebraska] the state of existing law and the community values concerning what the law ought to be were sought with respect to the following issues (concerning these, we hypothesized a fairly wide variation in the homogeneity and heterogeneity of community values): (1) the parents' right to transfer the custody of their child without legal supervision; (2) their right to obtain a return of their child once custody has been voluntarily relinquished by them; (3) their right to control the earnings of the child and (4) gifts to the child; (5) their liability for the torts of the child; (6) their duty concerning the health of the child; (7) their duty to provide for the support of the child after their death; (8) the child's right to sue his parents for harmful injury; (9) the child's right to sue third parties for the alienation of parental affections; (10) the parents' duty to support indigent emancipated children; (11) the child's duty to support indigent parents; and (12) the extent of parental control with respect to the adolescent child. Stated in more general terms, these deal broadly with the issue of parental versus governmental control over children; with the question of the extent of the child's freedom from parental authority; with the nature of the obligations of the parent to the child and of the child to the parent; and with the obligations of third parties to children and of children to third parties. To obtain the sense of community values as they relate to these selected issues, it was necessary to interview the representative members of the community, chosen on the basis of a rigorously-designed sampling procedure. . . .

. . . We hope that this study will contribute to the development of a model for research in other areas where the moral sense of the community is a relevant factor in the decisional process. We hope, too, that out of it will come a more reliable method than is now in use for those who seek to narrow the distance between lawmakers and their subjects. Lawmakers who equate public acquiescence in a decision with agreement with its substantive content should take note of John Dickinson's observation that such acquiescence does not mean "that the community would not have acquiesced in a decision of a contrary tenor." Indeed, it might be due merely to "willingness to accept an authoritative decision merely because it is authoritative." [28] To those lawmakers who seek greater acquiescence in the substantive content of their decisions, it is our belief that

---

[20] We shall be able to demonstrate later (in our final report) that it would not be economically or otherwise infeasible to undertake such a poll of sentiment in key areas of policy where the views of the community are crucial to the decisional process.

[28] Dickinson, Social Order and Political Authority, 30 Amer. Pol. Sci. Rev. 593, 615 (1929).

modern social science can offer a better device than the primitive divining rod for fulfilling so important a task.*

3. *Further Reflections on the Legal Relevance of Prevailing Ideas and Attitudes.* Cohen, Robson, and Bates also referred to the exchange between Judge Learned Hand of the Second Circuit and Judge John Parker of the Fourth Circuit during the American Law Institute debates over whether homosexual relations between consenting adults should be made criminal in the Model Penal Code. The authors wrote:

Judge Parker urged that private homosexuality should be prohibited by law because such conduct flies "in the face of public opinion as evidenced by the code of every state in the union." Judge Hand supported the opposite view on the ground that "criminal law which is not enforced practically is much worse than if it was not on the books at all," and that sodomy "is a matter very largely of taste, and is not a matter that people should be put in prison about." How was the issue resolved? By consulting the community concerning its own moral sense? Not at all. According to the report, the Institute settled it by *voting* "35 to 24 to uphold Judge Hand's . . . view" that sodomy be recommended for removal from the list of crimes.

Responding to this implied criticism of the Institute proceedings, Prof. Louis Schwartz, Associate Reporter for the Model Penal Code, wrote as follows:*

The authors are plainly horrified that the state of public opinion would have been determined in this crude fashion. Later in the article, after describing their model for opinion research, the authors refer to its superiority over "primitive divining rod" methods and express the hope that "those who seek to lessen the distance between lawmakers and their subjects" will have better tools.
It should be noted, however, that the Institute's vote had practically none of the significance which Professors Cohen, Robson, and Bates attribute to it. The Institute was asked to vote neither on the morality of sodomy nor on public opinion of sodomy. Many things that are immoral are, nevertheless, not proper subjects for criminal punishment. And some things that unthinking public opinion has put in the criminal codes ought now to be taken out. It is obvious from the quotation that Judge Hand was talking about his own views of morality and penal policy, not public opinion. Judge Parker's observation does indeed refer to public opinion, but the record will show that his basic position was in favor of punishing sodomy as a socially harmful practice. His reference to public opinion was a secondary argument that, aside from the merits, a Model Code that fails to punish this behavior will be unacceptable to legislatures. Neither of these wise and eminent men conceived the task of drafting a Penal Code as an effort to "narrow the distance between lawmakers and their subjects"; i.e., to make "popular" law. On the contrary, the Institute is trying to narrow the distance between lawmakers and such "unpopular" people as psychiatrists and sociologists. We are engaged in making rational, useful law which we hope can be popularized by education.

* The study referred to has been published as Cohen, Robson, and Bates, Parental Authority: The Community and the Law (1958).—Editor

* Schwartz, Ascertaining the Moral Sense of the Community: A Comment, 8 J. Legal Ed. 319-320 (1955).

Quantification of public opinion will be useful, for example, to persuade legislators that the voters are not as benighted as some suppose. I'm for the project anyway, since it is another manifestation of that endless curiosity that we call science. But as respects law reform, precise knowledge of prevailing public attitudes can hardly do more than indicate the limit of mass tolerance for immediate changes.

That the Institute Advisory Committee assigned less than controlling weight to public reactions deemed strongly adverse to homosexuality is revealed by the following Comment accompanying the tentative Model Penal Code:*

In varying degrees deviate sexuality has been regarded with intense aversion in nearly all times and civilizations, and subject to condemnation by religious interdict or severe secular punishment. . . .

Our proposal to exclude from the criminal law all sexual practices not involving force, adult corruption of minors, or public offense is based on the following grounds. No harm to the secular interests of the community is involved in atypical sex practice in private between consenting adult partners. This area of private morals is the distinctive concern of spiritual authorities. . . .

As in the case of illicit heterosexual relations,† existing law is substantially unenforced, and there is no prospect of real enforcement except against cases of violence, corruption of minors and public solicitation. Statutes that go beyond that permit capricious selection of a very few cases for prosecution and serve primarily the interest of blackmailers. Existence of the criminal threat probably deters some people from seeking psychiatric or other assistance for their emotional problems; certainly conviction and imprisonment are not conducive to cures. Further, there is the fundamental question of the protection to which every individual is entitled against state interference in his personal affairs when he is not hurting others. Lastly, the practicalities of police administration must be considered. Funds and personnel for police work are limited, and it would appear to be poor policy to use them to any extent in this area when large numbers of atrocious crimes remain unsolved. Even the necessary utilization of police in cases involving minors or public solicitation raises special problems of police morale, because of the entrapment practices that enforcement seems to require, and the temptation to bribery and extortion.

---

* Tentative Draft No. 4, Model Penal Code (1955), 276-278.

† As to these relations (fornication and adultery), the Comment had been (*Id.* at 207-208): "The Code does not attempt to use the power of the state to enforce purely moral or religious standards. We deem it inappropriate for the government to attempt to control behaviour that has no substantial significance except as to the morality of the actor. Such matters are best left to religious, educational and other social influences. Apart from the question of constitutionality which might be raised against legislation avowedly commanding adherence to a particular religious or moral tenet, it must be recognized, as a practical matter, that in a heterogeneous community such as ours, different individuals and groups have widely divergent views of the seriousness of various moral derelictions." The Comment then considered possible "secular" aims of punishing illicit intercourse (preserving the marital institution; preventing peace disturbances caused by seduction of female relatives; preventing behavior which openly and provocatively flouts the moral standards of others; preventing illegitimacy; preventing disease) and concluded that the prohibition should not be made except in certain narrowly restricted situations, notably where "the behavior is open and notorious."—Editor

However, these views of the Institute Advisory Committee were not accepted by the Institute Council, which voted in favor of criminal punishment. "Some members believe that the Reporters' [and Advisory Committee's] position is the rational one but that it would be totally unacceptable to American legislatures and would prejudice acceptance of the Code generally. Other members of the Council [assert] that sodomy is a cause or symptom of moral decay in a society and should be repressed by law." (*Id.*, 276). The Institute membership voted to uphold the Council in May 1961.

It is still fair to say, however, that the Council believed that even if a practice meets with general moral condemnation (which it thought was the usual basis of the typical criminal prohibition) the practice need not necessarily be made criminal. Accordingly, when it came to deal with the problem of abortion, and regarded prevalent "opinion among reasonable men" as less than strongly and uniformly adverse to the practice, this was an a fortiori case for the law's abstention. The Institute Council was willing to "recommend a policy of cautious expansion of the categories of lawful justification of abortion." *

The 1957 Wolfenden Report in England † paralleled the Institute Advisory Committee's attitude towards homosexuality. It recommended "that homosexual behavior between consenting adults in private should no longer be a criminal offence," stressing "the importance which society and the law ought to give to individual freedom of choice and action in matters of private morality." "Unless a deliberate attempt is to be made by society, acting through the agency of the law, to equate the sphere of crime with that of sin, there must remain a realm of private morality and immorality

---

* Model Penal Code, Tentative Draft No. 9, 150-151: "The criminal law in this area cannot undertake or pretend to draw the line where religion or morals would draw it. Moral demands on human behavior can be higher than those of the criminal law precisely because violations of those higher standards do not carry the grave consequences of penal offenses. Moreover, moral standards in this area are in a state of flux, with wide disagreement among honest and responsible people. The range of opinion among reasonable men runs from deep religious conviction that any destruction of incipient human life, even to save the life of the mother, is murder, to the generally fervent belief that the failure to limit procreation is itself unconscionable and immoral, if offspring are destined to be idiots, or bastards, or undernourished, mal-educated rebels against society. For many people, sexual intercourse divorced from the end of procreation is a sin; for multitudes of others it is one of the legitimate joys of living. Those who think in utilitarian terms on these matters can differ among themselves as widely as moralists. Voluntary limitation of population can be seen as national suicide in a world-wide competition for numerical superiority, while to others uncontrolled procreation appears equally suicidal as tending to aggravate the pressure of population on limited national resources and so driving nations to mutually destructive wars. To use the criminal law against a substantial body of decent opinion even if it be minority opinion, is contrary to our basic traditions. Accordingly, here as elsewhere, criminal punishment must be reserved for behavior that falls below standards generally agreed to by substantially the entire community."

† Report of the Committee on Homosexual Offences and Prostitution, para. 61 (1957).

which is, in brief and crude terms, not the law's business. To say this is not to condone or encourage private immorality."

Commenting on this Report, the Hon. Sir Patrick Devlin, one of Her Majesty's Judges in the High Court of Justice, cautioned† that the moral standards to be reflected in the law are those of the "reasonable man," the "man in the Clapham omnibus," the "man in the jury box"; and if he has a "real feeling of reprobation" towards homosexuality, this is "a good indication that the bounds of toleration are being reached." "Not everything is to be tolerated. No society can do without intolerance, indignation and disgust; they are the forces behind the moral law. . . ." Sir Patrick recognized, however, that "before a society can put a practice beyond the limits of tolerance there must be a deliberate judgment that the practice is injurious to society." "There is, for example, a general abhorrence of homosexuality. We should ask ourselves in the first instance whether looking at it calmly and dispassionately, we regard it as a vice so abominable that its mere presence is an offence. If that is the genuine feeling of the society in which we live, I do not see how society can be denied the right to eradicate it. Our feeling may not be so intense as that. We may feel about it that, if confined, it is tolerable, but that if it spread, it might be gravely injurious; it is in this way that most societies look upon fornication, seeing it as a natural weakness which must be kept within bounds but which cannot be rooted out. It becomes then a question of balance, the danger to society in one scale and the extent of the restriction in the other . . ."

Another reason, Devlin noted, for not immediately translating into law a strong popular aversion is the fact that "in matters of morals the limits of tolerance shift. Laws, especially those which are based on morals, are less easily moved. It follows . . . that in any new matter of morals, the law should be slow to act. By the next generation the swell of indignation may have abated and the law be left without the strong backing which it needs. But it is then difficult to alter the law without giving the impression that moral judgment is being weakened. This is now one of the factors that is strongly militating against any alteration to the law on homosexuality."

NOTES AND QUESTIONS

1. Was the court in the Repouille case wise to interpret the statute as embodying the "moral feelings, now prevalent generally in this country"? Would they have been wiser to embody their own moral conceptions in the statute? Or those of the community's "ethical leaders"? Who are they?

2. Is Judge Hand's attitude in the Repouille case consistent with his attitude in the ALI deliberations on homosexuality described by Professor Schwartz?

3. Should society make criminal whatever it abhors? What if there is a discrepancy between society's articulated moral standards and its actual practices? For example, should all the sexual practices Kinsey found to be prevalent be left alone by the law simply

† Devlin, The Enforcement of Morals (Maccabaean Lecture in Jurisprudence of the British Academy, 1959).

because they are prevalent? Would Fuller, Judge Frank, Schwartz, and Sir Patrick Devlin agree or disagree in answering these questions? For some further discussion of the homosexuality problem, see Note, Private Consensual Homosexual Behavior: The Crime and Its Enforcement, 70 Yale L.J. 623 (1961); H.L.A. Hart, The Use and Abuse of the Criminal Law, 4 The Oxford Lawyer 7 (1961).

4. How is the line to be drawn between "private" and "public" morality? Consider this observation of Sir Patrick Devlin in the lecture above cited: "I think there can be no theoretical limits to legislation against immorality. You may argue that if a man's sins affect only himself, it cannot be the concern of society. If he chooses to get drunk every night in the privacy of his own home, is anyone except himself the worse for it? But suppose quarter or a half of the population got drunk every night, what sort of society would it be? . . ."

5. The Repouille case is discussed in Cahn, The Moral Decision 300-312 (1955) and Note, 16 Univ. Chi. L. Rev. 138 (1948). The general problem of the relation of the judge's values to those he deems prevailing in the community is treated in Cahn, Authority and Responsibility, 51 Colum. L. Rev. 838 (1951); Cardozo, The Nature of the Judicial Process 105-111 (1921).

6. On the divergence between the "law in books" and the "law in action" (exemplified in the text by the law and practice with respect to illicit sex relations discussed by the ALI), see Pound, The Law In Books and the Law In Action, 44 Am. L. Rev. 12 (1910); Stone, The Province and Function of Law 406-410; 414-417 (1946).

Section 2

CUSTOM and PRIVATE RULES: THEIR RELEVANCE in NEGLIGENCE CASES

BOYCE v. WILBUR LUMBER CO.
119 Wis. 642, 97 N.W. 563 (1903)

[Plaintiff, night yardmaster for a railroad company, was injured when he was knocked from the side of a freight car on which he was riding during switching operations. He was struck by another car which employees of defendant had left standing on a siding at a point close to the track on which plaintiff's train was moving. The case was heard before a jury, which returned a verdict on the basis of which the trial court rendered judgment for plaintiff. The Supreme Court of Wisconsin reversed this judgment, but on other grounds than are involved in the passage here reprinted.—Editor]

Winslow, J. . . . Testimony was admitted, under objection and exception, to the effect that it was customary for yardmasters and switchmen upon railroads to ride upon the ladders of freight cars while setting in and taking out cars from the switch tracks in the yards, and error is claimed in this ruling. The question as to the admissibility of evidence of customary methods of doing business, as bearing on the question of negligence, either original or contributory, has been much discussed, and the decisions even in this state are not entirely harmonious. Inasmuch as negligence ordinarily consists simply of lack of ordinary care, and ordinary care is that care which the great majority of people are accustomed to exercise under the same or similar circumstances, it was, in substance, held in Guinard v. Knapp-

Stout & Co., 95 Wis. 482, 70 N.W. 671, that in determining whether an employer was negligent in furnishing an unsafe place to work, because of the proximity of uncovered machinery, the test was whether the defendant had come up to the standard of employers generally in the same business and under similar circumstances, and this test has been approved several times since that decision was rendered. Innes v. Milwaukee, 96 Wis. 170, 70 N.W. 1064; Prybilski v. N.W.C.R. Co., 98 Wis. 413, 74 N.W. 117; Kreider v. Wis. River P. & P. Co., 110 Wis. 645, 86 N.W. 662. While the question of the admissibility of evidence to show the usual or ordinary methods of others in the same business was not directly raised in these cases, it is very manifest that the legal principle adopted, and which must be considered as settled, necessarily calls for the admission of just such evidence; and in Pier v. C., M. & St. P.R. Co., 94 Wis. 357, 68 N.W. 464, it was said that the customary way of doing certain things in a railroad switchyard was a fact proper to be considered in determining the question of negligence of an employee while doing those things. In Jochem v. Robinson, 72 Wis. 199, 39 N.W. 383, and Nadau v. White River L. Co., 76 Wis. 120, 43 N.W. 1135, it was directly held that evidence of the customary manner of doing certain things was competent on the question of negligence of a party to the action, where the doing of those things was involved.

On the other hand, in the case of Propson v. Leatham, 80 Wis. 608, 50 N.W. 586, where the question was whether a lumber dock was negligently defective, so as to be dangerous to employees, it was held that evidence as to how it compared with other docks used for the same purposes was incompetent; and in Molaske v. Ohio Coal Co., 86 Wis. 220, 56 N.W. 475, where the question was whether the defendant was negligent in employing a boy twelve years of age to give signals for the hoisting of coal buckets upon a coal dock, it was held that no custom or usage of employing boys of such tender years in such a position could be upheld. Again, in Colf v. C., St. P., M. & O.R. Co., 87 Wis. 273, 58 N.W. 408, where the question was whether a brakeman was negligent in jumping from a moving engine in the freightyard, it was held that evidence of a custom on the part of employees in the yard to jump from moving engines was not admissible; and in Simonds v. Baraboo, 93 Wis. 40, 67 N.W. 40, while the general rule that evidence of custom is admissible on the question of negligence was recognized, it was held that it was not admissible as to acts the manner of doing which is matter of common knowledge, and this rule was quoted approvingly in Crouse v. C. & N.W.R. Co., 104 Wis. 473, 80 N.W. 752. In Dorsey v. Phillips & C.C. Co., 42 Wis. 583, it was questioned whether a custom on the part of railway companies to locate structures so near the track as to be necessarily dangerous to employees could be held to excuse the danger, while in Mulcairns v. Janesville, 67 Wis. 34, 29 N.W. 565, evidence of a custom as to the bracing of cistern walls was held inadmissible because it was not specially directed to a cistern wall of the kind under consideration.

While these cases can hardly be considered as entirely in accord, it seems clear that the general rule that evidence of the general business custom is admissible upon the question of negligence is well recognized in this state, as stated in Simonds v. Baraboo, supra, but that it is subject to exceptions, among which are that it cannot be allowed to contradict common knowledge, nor is it admissible to prove a custom which is so obviously dangerous to life and limb as to be at once recognized as such by all intelligent persons. Innes v. Milwaukee, 96 Wis. 170, 70 N.W. 1064. Under this rule, all the cases cited may perhaps be substantially harmonized, unless it be the Colf Case; and, so far as that case disagrees with the conclusion now reached, it must be considered as overruled. It cannot be said that the act of a brakeman or yardmaster in riding on the ladder on the side of a freight car in the course of switching operations is such an obviously dangerous act as to preclude proof that it is customary. Therefore the evidence in question was properly received.

POLASKI v. PITTSBURGH COAL DOCK CO.
134 Wis. 259, 114 N.W. 437 (1908)

Appeal from a judgment of the circuit court for Douglas county: A. J. VINJE, Circuit Judge. *Reversed.*

The defendant maintained a coal dock at the city of Superior about 900 feet in length and 300 feet in width, in the center whereof were three longitudinal railroad tracks for the loading and moving of railroad cars, upon which cars were frequently in motion, usually moved by attaching a hook to them and gripping unto a moving cable beside each track. It was necessary and customary for the workmen on the dock to pass frequently across these tracks, which were in a depression about four feet deep. The plaintiff was a common laborer and had, with six other men, just completed the loading of a car on one of these tracks, when the gang was ordered by the foreman to cross the tracks to the other side of the dock. One after another they jumped down and started across in front of this car, which plaintiff's testimony tends to show was stationary, with nothing to indicate that it was about to be moved. As plaintiff passed in front of it, somewhat diagonally across the track, having seen it stationary as he started, it was put in motion and overtook him just as he reached the furthest or west rail of the track, knocked him down, and passed over one of his legs. There was evidence that no rule had been promulgated by the defendant in any wise tending to guard against the running down of employees by these cars; that the gripman who had charge of moving them was accustomed indiscriminately to fasten on either the front or back end; that under some circumstances there would be a man on top of the cars to set the brakes, at other times not; that the gripman's habit was irregular; that sometimes he looked in front of the car or shouted warning of its approach and sometimes he did not, and that in the present instance he had fastened his grip to the rear end of the car, had not looked in front, and gave no warning. The negligence alleged in the complaint was the failure on the part of the defendant to promulgate any rule or regulation or to give any instruction tending in any wise to protect its employees from the peril of these moving cars, either by requiring signal and warning or the presence of any person in front of the car when moving; also in employing the plaintiff in an unsafe place without any such regulations, and in ordering him to cross the track after having directed the gripman to start the car. At the close of the plaintiff's evidence the trial court granted a nonsuit from judgment in accordance with which the plaintiff brings this appeal. . . .

DODGE, J. In a business conducted by many employees performing work independently of each other and in which the work of one becomes periodically dangerous to another, it is the duty of the master to provide reasonable precautions against such danger, and amongst these is promulgating rules and regulations for the giving of warning to the persons likely to be endangered when such dangerous acts are about to be performed. . . . In some instances the danger is so obvious and imminent and the making of regulations so easy that their absence might be considered negligence as a matter of law. In other cases of more doubt it becomes a question for the jury whether the omission of them is a failure of that due care which the employer owes his employees to guard them from injury. In the present case we have no doubt that as cars were likely at any moment to be set in motion by some employees, and other employees, whose work was wholly independent except that it promoted the general operation of the dock, were likely at any moment to be upon the tracks engrossed with their work so that an injury to them from a silently moving car was within imminent probability, it might well be thought by reasonable men that the duty of ordinary care required that some precaution, either by warning or lookout, be exercised. It is also obvious that those precautions were entirely easy and feasible. A lookout might be stationed on the forward end of the car, a bell or other signal sounded or given, but more easy and natural still would have been the precaution that the gripman should uniformly attach the moving apparatus to the front end and thus be in a position where he could see the track ahead of him. The evidence tended to prove that absolutely no instructions or regulations requiring any precautions whatever had ever been promulgated, and such is the negligence charged by the complaint. We deem it clear that a jury might properly decide that such omission constituted a want of due care on the part of the employer, nor can we doubt that they might reach the conclusion that such negligence was the proximate cause of the injury to the plaintiff, who was in a place required by his duty and by the command of his superior. Hence we must conclude that a prima facie case of negligence and liability was made out. . . .

LUEBKE v. CHICAGO, MILWAUKEE & ST. PAUL RY. CO.
63 Wis. 91, 23 N.W. 136 (1885)

LYON, J. . . . It was abundantly proved—indeed there is no evidence to the contrary—that while the plaintiff was under the car three train-men in the employ of the defendant were standing by the car, and that it was the duty of each of them, incident to his employment, to act as a watchman to protect the plaintiff from injury.

True, no written or published regulation of the company to that effect was shown; neither did any witness in the employ of the company testify that he had been charged by any officer of the company with the duty of watching for the safety of other employees working under cars upon the tracks; but many such witnesses testified that their duty in that behalf was well understood by them and other employees of the company. It was a sort of common law of the company, obligatory upon its employees, and as thoroughly understood by them as though it had been embodied in the printed regulations and read by the officers of the company to them. It thus became a rule or custom of the company, as well as an understanding between its employees.

The jury found that it was not a rule or custom of the company, imposed by it upon its employees, that they should watch for the safety of their fellow-workmen in positions of danger. This finding is the basis of the judgment for the plaintiff, and yet, as we understand the evidence, it is entirely unsupported by the testimony. The undisputed evidence establishes a perfect defense to the action, and the court should have directed a verdict for the defendant, or at least should have granted the motion of the defendant for a new trial. . . .

COLLINS v. MINERAL POINT & NORTHERN RY. CO.
136 Wis. 421, 117 N.W. 1014 (1908)

WINSLOW, C. J. It appeared by the plaintiff's own evidence that he had worked as brakeman or trainman in the employ of various railroad companies since boyhood, and was well acquainted with the ordinary methods of performing such work as well as with the ordinary dangers. For a considerable length of the time he was employed by the Chicago, Milwaukee & St. Paul Railway Company and was familiar with its printed rules, one of which, directed to all trainmen and switchmen, was as follows:

"(2) You are forbidden to work on the side of cars or trains where there are buildings, sheds, cattle chutes, or other projecting structures. Always work on that side where there are no buildings or structures, and in getting on or off or riding on the side of moving cars, do so only at places where there are no obstructions alongside the tracks, such as buildings, structures, lumber piles, etc., that will make such work hazardous."

It further appeared without contradiction that the plaintiff was employed as conductor by the defendant company from January, 1905, when it first began to do business, up to the time of the accident; that the defendant company formally adopted the foregoing rule with other rules of the St. Paul Company at the very beginning of its active business, and gave notice to the plaintiff to that effect, and that the plaintiff fully understood that the rule was in force. . . .

There is no doubt from the evidence that the plaintiff knowingly disobeyed a rule intended for his protection and suffered his injury by reason of such disobedience. Under such circumstances he cannot recover unless he shows either that the rule is impracticable in the due discharge of duty, or that it has been waived or abrogated by habitual disobedience of the employees with the knowledge and tacit consent of the master, or for such a length of time that the master must be presumed to have become aware of such disobedience and acquiesced therein. . . . In the present case we find no evidence which would suffice to take to the jury the question of impracticability. It was shown that the switch stand was on the north side of the track, and that it was more convenient to do the signaling to the engine from the north side of the train, and thus that it would take somewhat longer to perform the switching operation if the conductor rode on the south side of the car, but there was absolutely no evidence of impracticability, or that the plaintiff did not have ample time to perform the duty in hand in accordance with the provisions of the rule. . . . We find no tangible evidence of any such habitual and open violation of the rule by defendant's employees known to and acquiesced in by the defendant's responsible officials, or existing for such a length of time as to raise a presumption of knowledge and acquiescence. A verdict should therefore have been directed for the defendant upon the evidence. . . .

NOTES AND QUESTIONS

1. To what specific legal issue was the customary practice of yardmasters legally relevant in the Boyce case? How was the question of its legal relevance raised? Who decided it? How was it decided whether there was a customary practice and precisely what its nature was?

2. What was the significance of the reversal of the judgment of the circuit court nonsuiting the plaintiff in the Polaski case? Did it ensure that Polaski would thereafter recover damages?

3. To what specific legal issue was the existence of a rule or custom legally relevant in the Luebke case? How was it decided whether such a rule or custom existed?

4. What was the legal consequence, according to the Collins case, of a violation by an employee of a safety rule promulgated by the employer? Would this consequence follow the violation of *any* safety rule? If not, who would determine which safety rules should carry such a consequence in the event of their violation?

5. Is it an accurate summary of the practical effect of these four cases to say that under them the business of law-making or rule-making for the community has been *in part* delegated to private parties? If so, can the delegation to any extent be justified in any of these cases? In this connection, consider the following extracts from a brief submitted to the legislature in 1905 by Mr. F. W. Hall, attorney for the Legislative Council of the Brotherhood of Locomotive Engineers, pp. 22, 23 (on deposit in the Wisconsin Legislative Reference Library):

"These general rules cover five large pages of printed matter and are over four hundred in number, and include the time tables, rules for trainmen, enginemen, rules with respect to safety of passengers, standard time, time tables, standard signals, lamp signals, fixed signals, bell cord signals, whistle signals, train signals, classification of trains and trainmen, instructions to train and enginemen, movements of trains by telegraph, instructions to track and bridge men, instructions to station agents. . . ." Arguing that many of the rules were not made in good faith, Mr. Hall claimed as an example a rule declaring to trainmen, 'You are prohibited from using any tools or appliances of any kind that are not safe to be used and are required to report promptly when tools or appliances are out of order.' Of these and related rules, he argued: "Employees complain that it is absolutely impossible to comply wholly with the above notice, and that any attempt to comply with the same would cost an employee his place upon the road; that it is not expected or intended that the rules should be complied with, but that the rules are a protection to the company, in that prima facie they throw responsibility upon the employee for the largest parts of the accidents which occur on account of defective machinery, on account of dangerous passages, under bridges and tunnels, and through the yards, and dangers on account of couplings on foreign cars. . . ."

Cf. Milwaukee Free Press, May 21, 1905.

6. Which of the writers whose views on the relation between custom and law are presented in this chapter (Underhill Moore and M. R. Cohen for example) could look to these four cases for support?

7. Note, again, the limits on "jury lawlessness" imposed by cases like Luebke and Collins.

Section 3

CUSTOM, the DESEGREGATION CASES, and the PROBLEM of ENFORCEMENT

Before beginning this section, the student should re-read the materials on the School Segregation Cases, including the Supreme Court opinions, set out in Chapter 3 and reflect upon the following questions. How did the Supreme Court show its awareness of the fact that its decisions might meet with the resistance of strongly-entrenched custom? Was the Court wise to try to alter the pattern of public segregation in the South by interpreting the Constitution as prohibiting it? What are the prevailing attitudes about the morality of segregation in the South? In the North? Should the Court have tried to ascertain these attitudes before deciding the cases? What if Southern attitudes were found to be different from Northern ones? Have the Supreme Court opinions, in fact, done more good than harm? How shall we judge?

DECLARATION OF CONSTITUTIONAL PRINCIPLES ISSUED BY 19 SENATORS AND 17 REPRESENTATIVES *

The unwarranted decision of the Supreme Court in the public school cases is now bearing the fruit always produced when men substitute naked power for established law.

The Founding Fathers gave us a Constitution of checks and balances because they realized the inescapable lesson of history that no man or group of men can be safely entrusted with unlimited power. They framed this Constitution with its provisions for change by amendment in order to secure the fundamentals of government against the dangers of temporary popular passion or the personal predilections of public officeholders.

We regard the decision of the Supreme Court in the school cases as clear abuse

* The Congressmen represented 11 Southern states—Alabama, Arkansas, Florida, Georgia, Louisiana, Mississippi, North Carolina, South Carolina, Tennessee, Texas, and Virginia. Senators Estes Kefauver and Albert Gore of Tennessee refused to sign the document. Senator Lyndon C. Johnson of Texas, then Senate Majority Leader, was not asked to sign. The Declaration was published in the New York Times, March 12, 1956, p. 21.—Editor

of judicial power. It climaxes a trend in the Federal judiciary undertaking to legislate, in derogation of the authority of Congress, and to encroach upon the reserved rights of the states and the people.

The original Constitution does not mention education. Neither does the Fourteenth Amendment nor any other amendment. The debates preceding the submission of the Fourteenth Amendment clearly show that there was no intent that it should affect the systems of education maintained by the states.

The very Congress which proposed the amendment subsequently provided for segregated schools in the District of Columbia.

When the amendment was adopted in 1868, there were thirty-seven states of the Union. Every one of the twenty-six states that had any substantial racial differences among its people either approved the operation of segregated schools already in existence or subsequently established such schools by action of the same law-making body which considered the Fourteenth Amendment.

As admitted by the Supreme Court in the public school case (Brown v. Board of Education), the doctrine of separate but equal schools "apparently originated in Roberts v. City of Boston (1849), upholding school segregation against attack as being violative of a state constitutional guarantee of equality." This constitutional doctrine began in the North—not in the South—and it was followed not only in Massachusetts but in Connecticut, New York, Illinois, Indiana, Michigan, Minnesota, New Jersey, Ohio, Pennsylvania and other northern states until they, exercising their rights as states through the constitutional processes of local self-government, changed their school systems.

In the case of Plessy v. Ferguson in 1896 the Supreme Court expressly declared that under the Fourteenth Amendment no person was denied any of his rights if the states provided separate but equal public facilities. This decision has been followed in many other cases. It is notable that the Supreme Court, speaking through Chief Justice Taft, a former President of the United States, unanimously declared in 1927 in Lum v. Rice that the "separate but equal" principle is ". . . within the discretion of the state in regulating its public schools and does not conflict with the Fourteenth Amendment."

This interpretation, restated time and time again, became a part of the life of the people of many of the states and confirmed their habits, customs, traditions and way of life. It is founded on elemental humanity and common sense, for parents should not be deprived by Government of the right to direct the lives and education of their own children.

Though there has been no constitutional amendment or act of Congress changing this established legal principle almost a century old, the Supreme Court of the United States, with no legal basis for such action, undertook to exercise their naked judicial power and substituted their personal political and social ideas for the established law of the land.

This unwarranted exercise of power by the court, contrary to the Constitution, is creating chaos and confusion in the states principally affected. It is destroying the amicable relations between the white and Negro races that have been created through ninety years of patient effort by the good people of both races. It has planted hatred and suspicion where there has been heretofore friendship and under-standing.

Without regard to the consent of the governed, outside agitators are threatening immediate and revolutionary changes in our public school systems. If done, this is certain to destroy the system of public education in some of the states.

With the gravest concern for the explosive and dangerous condition created by this decision and inflamed by outside meddlers:

We reaffirm our reliance on the Constitution as the fundamental law of the land.

We decry the Supreme Court's encroachments on rights reserved to the states and to the people, contrary to established law and to the Constitution.

We commend the motives of those states which have declared the intention to resist forced integration by any lawful means.

We appeal to the states and people who are not directly affected by these deci-sions to consider the constitutional principles involved against the time when they too, on issues vital to them, may be the victims of judicial encroachment.

Even though we constitute a minority in the present Congress, we have full faith that a majority of the American people believe in the dual system of gov-ernment which has enabled us to achieve our greatness and will in time demand that the reserved rights of the states and of the people be made secure against judicial usurpation.

We pledge ourselves to use all lawful means to bring about a reversal of this decision which is contrary to the Constitution and to prevent the use of force in its implementation.

In this trying period, as we all seek to right this wrong, we appeal to our people not to be provoked by the agitators and troublemakers invading our states and to scrupulously refrain from disorder and lawless acts.

ROCHE* *and* GORDON,* *CAN MORALITY BE LEGISLATED*
New York Times Magazine, May 22, 1955, p. 10

The Supreme Court is pondering its decision on how and when to carry out its ruling of a year ago that public school segregation is unconstitutional. It is there-fore timely to examine the relationship between law and mores, between the decrees of courts and Legislatures and the vast body of community beliefs which shape private action.

While it is not perhaps customary to think of the Supreme Court as a legislative body, the cold fact is that in the desegregation cases, the nine justices have under-taken to rewrite public policy in at least seventeen states and innumerable communities. Indeed, it would be difficult to find a recent Congressional enact-ment that equals in impact and scope this judicial holding. Whether one approves or disapproves of such judicial acts, it is clear that the court has undertaken a

* John P. Roche is Morris Hillquit Pro-fessor of Labor and Social Thought at Brandeis University; Milton M. Gordon   is Associate Professor of Sociology at Haverford College.—Editor

monumental project in the field of social engineering, and one obviously based on the assumption that morality *can* be legislated.

Opponents of the desegregation decision have, with the exception of a fringe of overt white supremacists, largely founded their dissent on the principle that law can not move faster than public opinion, that legal norms which do not reflect community sentiment are unenforceable. They cite the dismal failure of Prohibition as a case in point, urging that basic social change—however desirable—must come from the bottom, from a shift in "grass-roots" convictions.*

On the other hand, the court's supporters maintain that virtually every statute and judicial decree is, to some extent, a regulation of morality. Indeed, they suggest, if the moral standards of individuals were not susceptible to state definition and regulation, we would never have emerged from primitive barbarism.

In this article, we shall examine from the viewpoint of the social scientist the evidence on both sides of the question, and see if it is possible to extract any meaningful conclusions.

First of all, we must delve into the relationship that exists in a democratic society between law and community attitudes. While this is a treacherous area, full of pitfalls for the unwary generalizer, it seems clear that, as distinguished from a totalitarian society, law in a democracy is founded on consensus. That is to say that the basic sanctions are applied not by the police, but by the community. The jury system institutionalizes this responsibility in such cases as "mercy killings" or those involving "the unwritten law" by finding citizens who have unquestionably killed "not guilty."

Conversely, juries applying other sections of the criminal code—notably those penalizing subversion—will often bring in verdicts of "guilty" based not so much on technical guilt as upon the proposition that the defendant should be taken out of circulation. In another area of the law, insurance companies, faced with damage suits, have learned to shun juries like the plague. Indeed, they will frequently make

---

* See, e.g., Board of Public Instruction v. State, 75 So. 2d 832 (Sup. Ct. Fla., 1954): ". . . When desegregation comes in the democratic way it will be under regulations imposed by local authority who will be fair and just to both races. . . . If it comes in any other way it will follow the fate of national prohibition and some other 'noble experiments.' If there is anything settled in our democratic theory, it is that there must be a popular yearning for laws that invade well settled concepts before they will be enforced. The U.S. Supreme Court has recognized this." Concurring in State ex rel Hawkins v. Bd. of Control of Univ. of Florida, 83 So. 2d 20 (Fla. 1955), Terrel, J. said: "In a democracy, law, whether by statute, regulation, or judge made, does not precede, but always follows a felt necessity or public demand for it. In fact when it derives from any other source, it is difficult and often impossible to enforce. The genius of the people is as resourceful in devising means to evade a law they are not in sympathy with as they are to enforce one they approve. The early patriots turned Boston harbor into a teapot one night because they did not like the tax on tea. President Jackson is said to have once defied the order of the Supreme Court and challenged them to enforce it. He did not subtract from his fame or his integrity in doing so. Our country went to war to overthrow the Dred Scott decision and prohibition petered out, was made a campaign issue and was repealed because sympathy for it was so indifferent that it could not be enforced."—Editor

unjustified out-of-court settlements in preference to facing a jury that begins its labors with the seeming assumption that no insurance company of any standing would miss $100,000.

From this it should be clear that in the United States law is a great deal more, and simultaneously a great deal less, than a command of the sovereign. Thus one can safely say that no piece of legislation, or judicial decision, which does not have its roots in community beliefs, has a chance of being effectively carried out.

To this extent, it is undeniable that morality cannot be legislated; it would be impossible, for example, to make canasta playing a capital offense *in fact,* even if the bridge-players' lobby were successful in getting such a law on the books. This is a fanciful example, but in our view the Volstead Act and the Eighteenth Amendment were no less unrealistic in objective: like H. L. Mencken's friend, Americans seem willing to vote for Prohibition as long as they can stagger to the polls.

Excluding these extreme efforts to legislate morality, which are obviously unsound, we now come to the heart of the problem: Under what circumstances will an individual accept distasteful regulation of his actions? To put it another way: What are the criteria which lead an individual to adjust his acts to the demands of the state?

Specifically, why do people pay taxes when they disagree strongly with the uses to which the money will be put? A large-scale tax revolt, as the French have recently discovered, is almost impossible to check without recourse to martial law and police state methods, but the average taxpayer grouses and pays. While Americans are not, by and large, as law-abiding as their British cousins, it is probably fair to say that most of us obey most laws without even reflecting on their merits.

This problem of the basis of legal norms has proved a fascinating one to sociologists. In the past fifteen years some significant new thinking on the subject has grown out of empirical research, more incisive analysis, and general observation of large-scale experiences with legal desegregation in important areas of American life such as employment, public housing and the Armed Forces.

The older categorical view stated in classic fashion by the sociologist William Graham Sumner, was that law could never move ahead of the customs or mores of the people—that legislation which was not firmly rooted in popular folkways was doomed to failure. The implication was that social change must always be glacierlike in its movement and that mass change in attitudes must precede legislative action.

The newer viewpoint is based on a more sophisticated and realistic analysis of social processes. In the first place, it questions the older way of stating the problem in terms of all or nothing. Any large, complex society, with its multiplicity of social backgrounds and individual experiences, contains varying mores and attitudes within itself. On any given piece of legislation there will not just be supporters and enemies; rather there will be many points of view, ranging from unconditional support, through indifference, to unmitigated opposition.

Thus, the degree of success that will attend such an enactment is the result of a highly complex series of interactions and adjustments among people with diverse attitudes toward the measure itself and toward the imposition of legal authority. Furthermore, it is predictable that a large segment of the population will be basically neutral, if not totally indifferent.

To put the matter in an even broader framework, the prediction of behavior must take into consideration not only the attitudes of the individual but also the *total social situation* in which his behavior is to be formulated and expressed. For instance, people with ethnic prejudice are likely to express themselves in a social clique where, say, anti-Semitic jokes are *au fait*, but will restrain themselves in a group where such remarks are greeted with hostility. Once the bigot realizes that he must pay a social price for his anti-Semitism, he is likely to think twice before exposing himself to the penalty.

In this connection, Robert K. Merton, Columbia sociologist, has set up an incisive classification, suggesting that four major groups can be delineated:

(1) The all-weather liberal, who can be expected to oppose prejudice and race discrimination under any set of social conditions; (2) the fair-weather liberal, who is not himself prejudiced, but who will stand silent or passively support discrimination if it is easier and more profitable to do so; (3) the fair-weather illiberal, who has prejudices, but is not prepared to pay a significant price for expressing them in behavior, preferring rather to take the easier course of conformity; and (4) the all-weather illiberal, who is prepared to fight to the last ditch for his prejudices at whatever cost in social disapproval.

If we apply this classification to such a problem as desegregation, it immediately becomes apparent that the critical strata, so far as success or failure is concerned, are groups two and three. Group one will support the proposal with vigor and group four will oppose it bitterly, but groups two and three will carry the day.

But because groups two and three are not crusaders, are not strongly motivated, they are particularly susceptible to the symbolism of law. Thus the fact that fair employment practices have been incorporated into law, or that the Supreme Court has held school segregation unconstitutional, will itself tend to direct their thinking toward compliance.

The symbols of state power are to the undedicated non-revolutionary mighty and awesome things, and he will think long and hard before he commits himself to subversive action. Consequently the law tends to become in another of Merton's phrases, a "self-fulfilling prophecy"; that is, a statute tends to create a climate of opinion favorable to its own enforcement. As John Locke long ago pointed out, the great roadblock to revolution is not the police but the habits of obedience which lead the law-abiding majority to refrain from even legitimate and justified resistance.

American experience over the past decade and a half seems to confirm this hypothesis. By legislative action, executive order and judicial decision, the race prejudices of Americans have been denied public sanction. Fair employment practices commissions, of national scope during the war and subsequently operative in a number of states and municipalities, integration of the Armed Forces, integration of many segregated schools, elimination of "white primaries" and removal of racial restrictions in many professional associations—all these have provided a living laboratory for the study of the impact of law on the mores.

At virtually every stage in the development, strong voices were raised to plead that morality could not be legislated, that an end to discrimination must await an unprejudiced public. Yet, the results indicate a high degree of compliance, some covert evasion, and only a few instances of violent resistance.

Moreover, it should be kept in mind that the success of desegregation laws or orders need not be measured against a hypothetical standard of 100 per cent but against the usual standards of law enforcement. Even laws against homicide and rape, which have overwhelming community support, are occasionally violated.

But, while laws may restrain behavior, is there any evidence to indicate that attitudes are affected? Here the evidence seems clear: the law itself plays an important part in the educational process. Again the key to analysis is the social situation.

Legislation and administrative orders which have prohibited discrimination in such areas as employment, the Armed Forces, public housing, and professional associations have brought people of various races together—often with initial reluctance—in normal day-to-day contact on an "equal-status" basis where the emphasis is on doing a job together. Contact of this kind gives people a chance to know one another as individual human beings with similar interests, problems and capabilities. In this type of interaction racial stereotypes are likely to be weakened and dispelled.

Such a favorable change of attitude as a result of personal contact has been reported in a number of studies. In one carefully designed research project, Morton Deutsch and Mary Evans Collins found that white housewives who had been assigned to public housing projects which were racially integrated tended to develop favorable attitudes toward Negroes, while the vast majority of those who occupied segregated housing tended to remain the same in their racial views. A study of integration in the Army reached a similar conclusion.

Findings such as these support a considerably broader and more complex conception of the relations between legal norms and human acts and attitudes than did the older, simpler Sumner thesis. In this more comprehensive analysis, law itself is seen as a force which, in its impact, does more than prohibit or compel specific behavior. Indeed, in its operation, law actually provides the setting for types of social relationships—relationships which may have a profound effect on the very attitudes which are necessary to adequate enforcement of the statute in question.

We thus come down to the final and crucial problem. It is plain that under some circumstances morality can be legislated, while under other conditions, the laws prove impotent. But what are the specific factors which must be evaluated? What criteria can be offered as a guide to intelligent and effective action in these touchy areas of belief, superstition and vested prejudice? The following four considerations are suggested as a beginning:

First, the amount of opposition and its geographical spread. If a random of 15 per cent of the population, roughly gauged, oppose some regulation, there will probably be little difficulty in gaining public acceptance and enforcement. However, and this is particularly relevant to the desegregation problem, if the 15 per cent all live in one compact geographical area where they constitute a majority, control local government and supply juries, the magnitude of the problem is much greater.

Second, the intensity of opposition. This is a qualitative matter, for, to paraphrase George Orwell, while all Americans are created equal, some are more equal than others. A proposal which is militantly opposed by "opinion-formers" in the American community—for example, ministers, lawyers, newspaper editors—will have much harder sledding than a nose-count of the opponents would seem to justify, and, conversely a measure which receives the support of this key group, or significant segments of it, can overcome a numerically large resistance.

Much of the success of the Negro in overcoming his legal, social and economic disabilities has been an outgrowth of the strong stand on his behalf taken by church leaders, journalists, trade unionists, business men and politicians who have created a climate of opinion favorable to Negro claims and who have based their assertions on the values which constitute the American Creed: equality of treatment under law and human brotherhood under God. With this quality of support, much can be accomplished even against great numbers.

Third, the degree to which sanctions can be administered. Here we turn to the practical problems of enforcement, and it is at this point that Prohibition really should have run aground long before it was incorporated into public policy. Home manufacture of alcoholic beverages has, according to well informed sources, even survived in the Soviet Union, and if the M.V.D. is incapable of banning private brew, there is little reason to suspect that a democratic society could handle the job.

It can not be emphasized too often that general principles of morality are no stronger than the instruments by which they are implemented; it would thus be legislative folly to try to prohibit people from disliking Jews, Negroes, Catholics, or Protestants. However, making gin in the bathtub, or disliking minorities, is not action equivalent to segregating school children on the basis of their pigmentation.

Because it is nearly impossible to regulate what goes on in millions of private homes, it does not follow that enforcement of desegregation in public institutions will be equally difficult. In sum, false and misleading analogies must be avoided, and each proposal must be examined on its merits to determine whether or not it is enforceable.

Fourth, the diligence of enforcement. It is extremely important that enforceable regulations be diligently enforced. This is particularly true in the initial period when public attitudes (specifically, the attitudes of Merton's groups two and three) are in the process of formation. Flagrant refusal to obey usually is designed as a symbolic act to rally the undecided, and strong action at such a time will convince many wavering minds that the best course is compliance. . . .

In short, to ask, "Can morality be legislated?," is actually to pose the wrong question. What types of morality, under what conditions, and with what techniques for enforcement are qualitative considerations which fragment the question into more answerable units. Our analysis suggests that, although large-scale local considerations may call for special circumstances of implementation, the majesty of the law, when supported by the collective conscience of a people and the healing power of the social situation, in the long run will not only enforce morality but create it.

EDITORIAL NOTE: LAW-ENFORCEMENT SANCTIONS; the SANCTIONS for DESEGREGATION

Enforcement Sanctions in General. The question of enforcement of the Supreme Court's decrees in the School Segregation cases raises a general problem of law enforcement which concerns not only judge-made law, but also statutes and administrative orders and regulations. Ordinarily, of course, legal sanctions are not called into play, since most people obey the law most of the time. In particular they obey, as well as they are able, the final judgments of courts: custom, respect for the courts, the knowledge that the force is there, and the conviction that even unsuccessful litigation is better than a private war, make unnecessary any step beyond the final judgment in most cases. But behind the judgments, the statutes, and the regulations lies ready for use a whole arsenal of enforcement weapons.

It is surprising how little attention has been paid to this "sanctions" aspect of law in society. As Landis has said: "Sanctions, or the methods that exist for the realization of policies, may be thought of as constituting the armory of government. But even a catalogue of that armory is not in existence. Far worse, no knowledge exists of the fields in which its weapons have been employed. And the weapons themselves are many. The criminal penalty, the civil penalty, the resort to the injunctive side of equity, the tripling of damage claims, the informer's share, the usefulness of mere publicity as a means for coercing action, the license as a condition of pursuing certain conduct, the confiscation of offending property—these represent only a few of the many weapons in that armory. Their effectiveness to control conduct in one field, their ineffectiveness to achieve that same control in another field have never been scientifically stated. Why is it, for example, that the informer's share, a method commonly employed in colonial legislation, has generally disappeared from the statute books but nevertheless still survives in the field of customs collection? What leads to the device of permitting a litigant to recover triple damages for certain injuries, and how effective is that claim to bring about enforcement of the law by this effort to stimulate individual initiative? Questions such as these, which can so readily be put, have as yet failed to stir research. Far less have they received even tentative answers." Landis, The Administrative Process 90-1 (1938).

In the case of most statutes, the legislature normally finds it sufficient to provide a single method of enforcement instead of multiple methods. A criminal penalty for violation may be imposed and that will be all. Or no criminal penalities may be specified, but the statute may simply create rights and duties which private individuals are left to enforce by the ordinary processes of suing each other for damages (or perhaps for an equitable order of specific performance). Or a commission or other administrative agency may be set up to see that the statute is enforced by investigating complaints, holding hearings, and making orders which, when backed up by a court judgment, are enforced as all judgments are enforced. And, of course, throughout the range of judge-made law, the phenomenon of multiple sanctions which is to be found in the case of a great deal of legislation, does not occur at all. The cases terminate in a court judgment or order and that is all. There are some exceptions to this statement, but they are not important enough to be noted here. The point is that the compulsions developed by the common law and the machinery for imposing them were (and still are) ordinarily very simple, and that the business of law enforcement began to grow more complex and to take on new forms with the coming in of legislation, particularly in modern times.

Legal Sanctions for School Desegregation. Multiple sanctions of varying practical utility are available to enforce public school desegregation in the face of recalcitrance or obstruction on the part of (1) school officials; (2) private individuals; or (3) state legislators and Governors. We shall attempt to give only a brief sketch of a legal situation which is quite technical and complex.

(1) *Against school officials.* School officials in the South, reflecting community sentiment hostile to desegregation, have been slow to initiate the formulation of desegregation plans or to implement those which have been launched. And courts, in judging the reasonableness of delays, "have exhibited great diversity in according weight to the administrative factors enumerated in the Brown decree [see the second Brown opinion in Chapter 3, sec. 2 above—Editor] and in the scope of review accorded the [school] boards' action." "The cause of this diversity appears to be the response of the courts and the school boards to the factor of community hostility. Although this factor is not expressly considered in the Brown decree beyond the statement that 'disagreement' cannot alone prevent ultimate enforcement, since the Court ordered retention of jurisdiction of the cases by the lower courts it seems probable that in some instances the Court contemplated a protracted period of transition. Some courts and commentators have found that the Brown decree forecloses consideration of actual or potential local hostility in determining the need for delay, and that only the enumerated elements of administrative difficulty may be weighed in determining the need for delay in plans for desegregation. On the other hand, several courts have [relied] on hostile community attitudes in order to justify delay." Note, 71 Harv. L. Rev. 485, 488-489 (1958).[1] It should here be noted that the Supreme

---

[1] The writer goes on to say: "Even when the courts have not expressly relied on this ground, three types of decisions manifest sub silentio consideration of hostile community attitudes. First, some courts have decided that the administrative difficulties put forward by the board justify extensions of time, but the delays granted seem too

Court refused to delay desegregation in Little Rock because of community hostility found to have been engendered by state executive and legislative officials. Cooper v. Aaron, 358 U.S. 1 (1958).

What may a court do when it brooks no further delay? Federal district courts have (a) ordered the school board to submit a desegregation plan, which has then been adopted, modified or rejected by the court; or (b) ordered a general termination of segregation; or (c) if necessary, issued their own plans or even assigned specific Negro children to specific schools. Note, 47 Cal. L. Rev. 126, 131-132 (1959). To undertake the specific assignment of students forces the court "to administer a school system" and "requires innumerable lawsuits to obtain a very small degree of desegregation." Id. at 132, n. 33; 133.

To enforce their desegregation orders, the courts rely largely on their powers to imprison for contempt of court. When a civil contempt proceeding is instituted, the disobedient officials may be imprisoned until, and only until, such time as they comply with the court's order (they carry the "keys to the jail in their pockets"); or they may be subjected to a fine which is removed when they obey or to a fine designed to compensate the plaintiffs for damages suffered. While the civil contempt proceeding is regarded as remedial in purpose, the criminal contempt proceeding is designed to punish the officials' willful violations of the court's orders and may be instituted even after obedience has been exacted. Both the civil and criminal contempt sanctions may be imposed by the judge without a trial by jury. (In some cases, other than school desegregation decrees, statutes may require that criminal contempts be tried by jury).

Enforcement action may also be taken under the federal Civil Rights statutes. The latter make it a crime for anyone willfully to subject another "under color of any law, statute, ordinance, regulation or custom" to the deprivation of rights, privileges, or immunities guaranteed by the federal Constitution and laws. 18 U.S.C. § 242. They also make it a crime for two or more persons to conspire to impair a citizen's free exercise of such federal rights, 18 U.S.C. § 241, but it is doubtful whether this section will be interpreted to protect 14th Amendment rights. U.S. v. Williams, 341 U.S. 70 (1951) (the Court was evenly divided on this point). Civil remedies are also available under the Civil Rights statutes. An action for damages or

great to be supported on administrative grounds alone. . . . Second, several courts, upon finding that a prompt and reasonable start towards compliance has been made by the school board, have deferred to the board's exercise of discretion in formulating the plan unless the plan appeared 'unreasonable'. . . . Finally, several courts have framed decrees that either enjoin segregation without designating an effective date for the operation of the restraint, or simply order the defendant to proceed, without issuing an injunction. In this case, since no plan is required by the court, total discretion is left in the school board. It may base unlimited delays upon its judgment of community hostility subject only to a later determination, on the renewed application of the plaintiff, that further delay is unreasonable. . . ." Id. at 489-490.

injunction may be brought against anyone who, under color of law, subjects another to a deprivation of 14th Amendment rights. 42 U.S.C. § 1983. It seems unlikely that these criminal and civil sanctions will be very effective to enforce school desegregation in the face of community hostility, because they may be imposed only after a jury trial and juries drawn from the community are not likely to impose them. This is why the contempt power is so important.

(2) *Against private individuals.* Sanctions are available to prevent private persons—members of a threatening mob, for example,—from interfering with the course of school desegregation. In Hoxie v. Brewer, 238 F. 2d 91 (8th Cir. 1956), a school board adopted a desegregation plan without waiting to be ordered to do so by a court. When a mob threatened to resort to violence against both the board members and the Negro students, the board sought and obtained an injunction prohibiting the mob leaders from interfering with the process of desegregation. The Court held that as state officials sworn to uphold the Constitution, the board members had a right, which the federal courts could protect, to be free from this kind of coercive attempt by private individuals to force them to violate their constitutional duties and deprive the Negro children of their constitutional rights.

Until the passage of the Civil Rights Act of 1960, it was generally thought that even a school board under order of a federal court to desegregate would have to seek a court injunction to halt obstruction by private individuals. See Kasper v. Brittain, 245 F. 2d 92 (6th Cir. 1957), cert. den., 355 U.S. 834 (1957). And even then, it was doubtful whether the injunction would bind anyone except those individuals against whom it was directed by name. The Civil Rights Act of 1960 seeks to discourage general mob action against school desegregation by providing:

"Whoever by threats or force, willfully prevents, obstructs, impedes, or interferes with, or willfully attempts to prevent, obstruct, impede, or interfere with, the due exercise of rights or the performance of duties under any order, judgment, or decree of a court shall be fined not more than $1,000 or imprisoned for not more than one year, or both. No injunctive or other civil relief against the conduct made criminal by this section shall be denied on the ground that such conduct is a crime." 18 U.S.C. § 1509.

Again, it should be pointed out that the effectiveness of this section may be reduced by the fact that its sanctions can be imposed only after a trial by jury. Nor does the section cover the situation in Hoxie v. Brewer, *supra,* which will continue to be of great importance to school boards which may decide to desegregate without waiting for a lawsuit and court order compelling them to do so. In any case, this provision of the Civil Rights Act of 1960 should make it generally unnecessary to invoke the federal executive power to call out the federal troops in aid of school desegregation. This power to meet emergencies, however, always remains in reserve.

On September 23, 1957, when mob action at the Central High School in Little Rock, Arkansas obstructed the carrying out of the desegregation orders of the federal district court, President Eisenhower, acting primarily under 10 U.S.C. §§ 332-334,[2] issued Proclamation 3204, 22 Fed. Reg. 7628, commanding "all persons engaged in such obstruction of justice to cease and desist therefrom, and to disperse forthwith." Two days later, he issued an Executive Order (E.O. 10730, 22 Fed. Reg. 7628) stating that the Proclamation had not been obeyed and instructing the Secretary of Defense to "order into the active military service of the United States as he may deem appropriate to carry out the purpose of this Order, any or all of the units of the National Guard . . . and of the Air National Guard . . . within the State of Arkansas to serve in the active military service of the United States for an indefinite period and until relieved by appropriate orders." The Secretary of Defense was directed to take appropriate steps to enforce the court's desegregation orders and authorized to make use of the National Guard units, and "such of the armed forces of the United States as he may deem necessary." Secretary of Defense Wilson and Secretary of the Army Brucker acted immediately to call the Army and Air National Guard units in Arkansas into federal military service. These units effectively prevented mob interference with Negro students entering and leaving the Central High School.

(3) *Against state legislators and governors.* When Governor Faubus of Arkansas used the National Guard to prevent Negro children from enter-

[2] These sections read:

332. *Use of militia and armed forces to enforce Federal authority.* Whenever the President considers that unlawful obstructions, combinations, or assemblages, or rebellion against the authority of the United States, make it impracticable to enforce the laws of the United States in any State or Territory by the ordinary course of judicial proceedings, he may call into Federal service such of the militia of any State, and use such of the armed forces, as he considers necessary to enforce those laws or to suppress the rebellion.

333. *Interference with State and Federal law.* The President, by using the militia or the armed forces or both, or by any other means, shall take such measures as he considers necessary to suppress, in a State, any insurrection, domestic violence, unlawful combination, or conspiracy, if it—

(1) so hinders the execution of the laws of that State, and of the United States within the State, that any part or class of its people is deprived of a right, privilege, immunity, or protection named in the Constitution and secured by law, and the constituted authorities of that State are unable, fail, or refuse to protect that right, privilege, or immunity, or to give that protection; or

(2) opposes or obstructs the execution of the laws of the United States or impedes the course of justice under those laws.

In any situation covered by clause (1) the State shall be considered to have denied the equal protection of the laws secured by the Constitution.

334. *Proclamation to disperse.* Whenever the President considers it necessary to use the militia or the armed forces under this chapter, he shall, by proclamation, immediately order the insurgents to disperse and retire peaceably to their abodes within a limited time.

The President also cited the authority vested in him by the Constitution and Statutes, including 3 U.S.C. 301 (a general authorization for the President's delegation of functions to heads of executive departments or agencies, or officials whose appointment requires Senate ratification).

ing the Central High School, the United States, as amicus curiae, obtained a supplementary injunction restraining the Governor and the National Guard officers from further interference with the desegregation decree. Aaron v. Cooper, 156 F. Supp. 220, aff'd sub. nom. Faubus v. United States, 254 F. 2d 797 (8th Cir. 1958), cert. den., 358 U.S. 829 (1958). The Circuit Court relied on Sterling v. Constantin, 287 U.S. 378, 393 (1932), in which the Supreme Court said: ". . . where state officials, purporting to act under state authority, invade rights secured by the Federal Constitution, they are subject to the process of the federal courts in order that the persons injured may have appropriate relief. . . . The Governor of the state in this respect, is in no different position from that of other state officials." Governor Faubus obeyed the court's command and withdrew the National Guard from the school. President Eisenhower then called the Guard into federal service, as previously described.

The Supreme Court strongly affirmed the principle announced in Sterling v. Constantin when it refused to approve the suspension of the Little Rock school board's desegregation plan. Cooper v. Aaron, 358 U.S. 1 (1958). It proclaimed that the requirements of the Constitution, as interpreted in the School Segregation cases, were, by virtue of Article VI of the Constitution, the "Supreme Law of the Land"; that "every state legislator and executive and judicial officer is solemnly committed by oath taken pursuant to Article VI, clause 3, "to support this Constitution"; that the "Constitutional rights of children not to be discriminated against in school admission on grounds of race or color . . . can neither be nullified openly and directly by state legislators or state executive or judicial officers, nor nullified indirectly by them through evasive schemes for segregation whether attempted 'ingeniously or ingenuously.' " The school board's difficulties were the result of state action and "those difficulties, as counsel for the Board forthrightly conceded . . . can also be brought under control by state action."

To date, no state official has defied a federal court order addressed to him. The federal government has ample power to make its authority prevail. In the last analysis, the armed might of the United States stands behind the court's order and no President of the United States has ever refused to enforce an order of a Federal court. Nevertheless, one can only hope, in the interest of the ideal of racial equality itself, that such a clash between Federal and state power will be avoided.

What, then, is the outlook for the future of school desegregation enforcement? As one writer has said, "in those states where the populace, school officials, and state government combine to oppose desegregation, the most that can be hoped for is some assignments of a small number of Negro students to white schools. In many areas the residential pattern will cause most schools to continue to serve only or predominantly the members of one race. Furthermore, the antagonism shown by white students to the newly entering Negro students and the economic pressures exerted by the community on Negro parents will discourage many Negro children from attending schools now exclusively serving white students. In addition in some areas the more well to do portion of the white population may turn to bona fide private schools. It seems that true acceptance of the principles of integration, in education, as well as in other phases of life, must be based upon the acceptance of the ideals underlying the fourteenth amendment and not upon court decrees. Nevertheless, the Brown decisions may very well bring at least token desegregation to every state in the Union. The decisions will bring substantial desegregation to those communities ready to accept it but which have formerly been prevented from adopting it due to state law. In addition Brown I has provided the moral leadership which has brought widespread integration to Washington, D.C., some of the border states, and to those Northern communities that still had segregated facilities in 1955." Note, 47 Calif. L. Rev. 126, 143 (1959).

This assessment ignores the possibly accelerative effect on the progress of desegregation, of actions which the Congress may take in the future but which so far have not been politically feasible. Acting under the power granted to it by the 14th Amendment to enforce its guarantees, Congress may, for example, set up a federal administrative agency to plan, supervise, and facilitate the transition to a racially nondiscriminatory system of public education. And it may empower the Attorney General to bring lawsuits to compel desegregation instead of depending upon the initiative of Negro parents who are often intimidated from taking such action.

See generally, Foster, 1960: Turning Point For Desegregation? Saturday Review, Dec. 17, 1960; and the following articles by Professor Auerbach— How Congress Can Speed Integration, The New Leader, Dec. 22, 1958; Little Rock and the Law, *id.,* Sept. 30, 1957; Jury Trials and Civil Rights Cases, *id.,* April 29, 1957; and John Kasper and the Civil Liberties Union, *id.,* April 1, 1957.

The availability of sanctions, we know, is not a guarantee of compliance with law. The community must not be pressed too far. There are, in Pound's famous phrase, certain "limits of effective legal action"; and one of these limits is the point at which compliance is being forced upon too many persons who resist because of deep contrary conviction. What the "too much" point is depends upon the total culture and will therefore vary with geography and time. Both fundamentalists and radical reformers have from time to time discovered that even the state could not do everything they wanted. If for any reason the habit of obedience to a particular law is absent for long periods the law will break down and will either be repealed (like National Prohibition and the Fugitive Slave Law) or be disregarded (like the "Blue Laws" in some states). Such cases are not numerous because a democratic government is not likely very often or for long to attempt to impose policies or conduct which its people strongly disapprove. Enforcement of the desegregation decision presents such a heartbreaking problem because it pits a section of our national community against the whole. It presents that border-line situation which Roche and Gordon referred to when they said that "large-scale local considerations may call for special circumstances of implementation." The Supreme Court well appreciated this when, in formulating its judgment, it allowed for time and flexibility to solve the most urgent of the domestic problems facing our country.

NOTES AND QUESTIONS

1. Concerning the President's role in facilitating the process of desegregation, note the following from the newspaper column of James Reston, N.Y. Times, August 22, 1958: "In his news conference yesterday, President Eisenhower gave a revealing definition of what he regarded as his proper course in the public school integration controversy.

"It is his duty, he said, to see that the final orders of the Supreme Court are carried out, but it is completely unwise for him to state his personal opinion about whether the court's integration decision was good or bad.

"As a concept of Presidential responsibility, this goes back to the days when some of General Eisenhower's predecessors thought the primary function of the President was, as the President emphasized yesterday, merely to 'defend the Constitution of the United States and execute its laws.'

"It is, however, in conflict with the new conceptions of Presidential leadership personified by the two Roosevelts and Woodrow Wilson, and with the theory that Government in general and the Presidency in particular should be an active, reforming force in the life of the nation. . . .

"Wilson wrote as follows in his Blumenthal Lectures given at Columbia University in 1907:

" 'He [the President] can dominate his party by being spokesman for the real sentiment and purpose of the country, by giving direction to opinion, by giving the country at once the information and the statements of policy which will enable it to form its judgments alike of parties and men.

" 'His is the only national voice in affairs . . .

" 'Some of our Presidents have deliberately held themselves off from using the full power they might legitimately have used, because of conscientious scruples, because they were more theorists than statesmen. The President is at liberty, both in law and conscience, to be as big a man as he can.

" 'His is the vital place of action in the system, whether he accept it as such or not, and the office is the measure of the man—of his wisdom as well as of his force.' "

"Roosevelt within a few days of his first election put his conception of the Presidency this way:

" 'The Presidency is not merely an administrative office. That is the least of it. It is pre-eminently a place of moral leadership.

" 'All of our great Presidents were leaders of thought at times when certain historic ideas in life of the nation had to be clarified. Washington personified the idea of Federal Union. Jefferson practically originated the party system as we know it by opposing the democratic theory to the republicanism of Hamilton. This theory was reaffirmed by Jackson.

" 'Two great principles of our Government were forever put beyond question by Lincoln. Cleveland, coming into office following an era of great political corruption, typified rugged honesty. Theodore Roosevelt and Wilson were both moral leaders, each in his own way and for his own time, who used the Presidency as a pulpit.

" 'That is what the office is—a superb opportunity for reapplying, applying to new conditions, the simple rules of human conduct to which we always go back. Without leadership alert and sensitive to change, we are bogged up or lose our way.' . . ."

In what ways, if any, can the President help to facilitate the progress of school desegregation?

2. The variety of, and limitations upon, various penal and non-penal sanctions are discussed in 2 Simpson and Stone, Law and Society 1489-1592 (1949). On sanctions for school desegregation, see Note, Legal Sanctions to Enforce Desegregation in the Public Schools: The Contempt Power and the Civil Rights Acts, 65 Yale L.J. 630 (1956); Note, Implementation of Desegregation By the Lower Courts, 71 Harv. L. Rev. 486 (1958); Note, The Law, The Mob and Desegregation, 47 Calif. L. Rev. 126 (1959). See also the symposium on desegregation problems in 34 The Notre Dame Lawyer 607 (1959).

3. The statistical status of desegregation in education in the southern and border states was reported to be as shown on pages 326-327 by the Southern Education Reporting Service, as of November, 1960:

PUBLIC ELEMENTARY AND HIGH SCHOOLS

	White	Negro	Total	% Negro
Enrollment	10,165,246	3,097,534	13,262,780	23.4
Teachers	370,881*	99,008*	494,054	20.0*

*Maryland not included in racial breakdown

COLLEGES AND UNIVERSITIES

	Predominantly White	Predominantly Negro	Total	% Negro Schools
Public Institutions	228	49	277	17.7
Enrollment	528,606	57,886	586,492	9.9

STATUS OF SEGREGATION-DESEGREGATION

Public Schools, State	School Districts			Enrollment		In Desegregated Districts		Negroes in Schools with Whites	
	Total	Bi-racial	Deseg.	White	Negro	White	Negro	No.	%
Alabama	114	114	0	516,135**	271,134**	0	0	0	0
Arkansas	422	228	10	317,053†	105,130†	52,126	12,639	113	.107
Delaware	93	51	24	67,145	15,061	48,505	8,665	6,734	44.7
District of Columbia	1	1	1	24,697	96,751	24,697	96,751	81,392	84.1
Florida	67	67	1	776,743	202,322	133,336*	27,502*	27	.013
Georgia	198	196	0	682,354**	318,405**	0	0	0	0
Kentucky	211	171	128	593,494**	41,938**	445,000*	32,000*	16,329	38.9
Louisiana	67	67	1	422,181**	271,021**	37,490	51,113	4	.001
Maryland	24	23	23	449,879*	134,379*	406,286**	114,682**	28,072**	20.9
Mississippi	151	151	0	287,781**	278,640**	0	0	0	0
Missouri	1,889	214*	200*	758,000*	84,000*	—	75,000*	35,000*	41.7
North Carolina	173	173	10	816,682**	302,060**	117,404	54,746	82	.027
Oklahoma	1,276	241	189	504,125*	40,875*	266,405	30,725	9,822	24.0
South Carolina	108	108	0	352,164**	257,935**	0	0	0	0
Tennessee	154	143	6	670,680*	157,320*	87,393	19,644	342	.217
Texas	1,531	720	130	1,840,987*	288,553*	800,000*	85,000*	3,500*	1.21
Virginia	130	128	11	668,500	211,000	177,731	52,286	208	.099
West Virginia	55	43	43	416,646	21,010	416,646	21,010	14,000*	66.6
Totals	6,664	2,839	777	10,165,246	3,097,534	3,013,019††	681,763	195,625	6.3

*Estimated   **1959-60   †1958-59   ††Missouri not included.

Teachers. Public school faculties remain segregated in nine states, including five that have desegregated classes. Eight other states and the District of Columbia reported some degree of desegregation among teachers, although in five of these states several Negro teachers lost their jobs in the change to bi-racial schools.

Higher Education. Of the 228 predominantly white tax-supported colleges and universities in the region, 138 in 13 states are desegregated in practice or principle. Fifteen of the 49 predominantly Negro schools are desegregated. This makes 153 of 277 institutions of higher learning that will accept students of another race. The number of students, white and Negro, involved in the desegregation at this level is unknown since most of the border states no longer report enrollment by race.

Litigation. The summary lists 174 court cases filed in federal and state courts on segregation, desegregation and related issues.

Legislation. Legislatures of 15 states have adopted almost 300 new laws and resolutions to prevent, restrict or control school desegregation. Most of the legislation has been added to statute books since 1954, although a few laws were enacted in anticipation of the U.S. Supreme Court's 1954 decision. Only Oklahoma has taken legislative action to encourage desegregation. The Missouri and West Virginia legislatures removed racial designations from their school laws, recognizing desegregation as an accomplished fact. In 1959, Maryland ratified the 14th Amendment to the U.S. Constitution, giving approval to the amendment on which the desegregation decisions were based. Alabama, Georgia, Louisiana, Virginia and North Carolina adopted tuition grant laws. Legislatures in Alabama, Arkansas, Florida, Louisiana, Mississippi, North Carolina, Tennessee, Texas and Virginia set up pupil placement plans. Alabama, Arkansas, Florida, Georgia, Louisiana, Mississippi, South Carolina and Virginia legislators approved interposition resolutions.

Section 4

PRIVATE CONTRACTS, PUBLIC POLICY, and STATE ACTION

LITTLE ROCK AND FORT SMITH RY. CO. v. EUBANKS
48 Ark. 460, 3 S.W. 808 (1886)

By Court, SMITH, J. Appellee, as administratrix of J. C. Eubanks, sued appellant in the Franklin circuit court, alleging that she was the mother of the deceased, and administratrix, etc.; that on the seventh day of October, 1884, her intestate was employed under a contract as brakeman on appellant's railway; that on or before that time appellant's railway, at the town of Ozark, was in a defective condition, in this: "The defendant had constructed on its said road, and as a part of it on the track thereof at said place, a switch, and a frog, which was so worn, ill-constructed, and defective as to render it unsafe and unfit for use." The complaint alleges knowledge by appellant of these defects, and that by reason thereof, and the unsafe condition of the road at that point, and appellant's negligence, her intestate, while in the performance of his duty as brakeman under his contract, was thrown from the car, run over, and killed.

The answer denies that the switch or frog was defective, ill-constructed, or unfit for use, or that plaintiff's intestate was thrown from the car and killed by reason of any such defects; denies that the deceased was free from negligence, and alleges that his death was caused by negligence on his part. The answer also sets up and relies upon the following contract, executed by the deceased before his employment by the defendant, as a release of liability.

"Clinton Eubanks, having been employed, at his request, by the Little Rock and Fort Smith Railway in the capacity of brakeman, hereby agrees with said railway, in consideration of such employment, that he will take upon himself all risks incident to his position on the road, and will in no case hold the company liable for any injury or damage he may sustain, in his person or otherwise, by accidents or collisions on the trains or road, or which may result from defective machinery, or carelessness or misconduct of himself or any other employee and servant of the company."

The issues were submitted to a jury, which returned a verdict for the plaintiff for $9,360; upon which judgment was entered. A motion for a new trial was subsequently overruled; and a bill of exceptions was signed, saving the points hereinafter noticed.

The execution of the contract copied above was admitted by the plaintiff. But the court refused this prayer of the defendant: "If you find that before entering the service of defendant, deceased executed the release, a copy of which is set out in defendant's answer, you are instructed that by reason of said release plaintiff will be precluded from recovering anything in this suit, and you will find for defendant."

A common carrier, or a telegraph company, cannot, by pre-contract with its customers, relieve itself from liability for its own negligent acts. This, however, may be on the grounds of its public employment. . . .

The validity of the contract before us is not affected by such considerations. The relation existing between the parties to it is essentially a private relation,—that, namely, of master and servant. And the question is, whether a servant employed in the operation of dangerous machinery can waive in advance the duties and liabilities which the master owes him, and which do not depend on contract, but spring out of the relation itself. Of course, if he can waive them so as to bind himself, a waiver will also bar his personal representative for the personal representative only succeeds to the right of action which the deceased would have had but for his death.

In 1880, the English Parliament passed the "employer's liability act," the object of which was to make employers liable for injury to workmen, caused by the negligence of those having the supervision and control of them. In Griffiths v. Earl of Dudley, L.R. 9 Q.B.D. 357, it was held that a workman might contract himself and his representatives out of the benefits of this act.

An opposite conclusion has been reached by the supreme courts of Ohio and Kansas. They hold that it is not competent for a railroad company to stipulate with its employees, at the time of hiring them, and as a part of the contract, that it shall not be liable for injuries caused by the carelessness of other employees: Lake Shore & M.L.R.R. Co. v. Spangler, Sup. Ct. Ohio, 1886; Kansas Pacific R'y Co. v. Peavey, 29 Kan. 169. . . . This, however, is not precisely the same question we have to deal with. For the negligence of a fellow-servant is not in fact and in morals the negligence of the master, although by virtue of a statute it may be imputed to the master. It is impossible for the master always to be present and control the actions of his servants. Hence a stipulation not to be answerable for their negligence, beyond the selection of competent servants in the first instance, and the discharge of such as prove to be reckless or incompetent, might be upheld as reasonable, notwithstanding a statute might abolish the old rule of non-liability for the acts and omissions of a co-servant.

But the supreme court of Georgia has, in several cases, sustained contracts like the one before us as legal and binding upon the employee, so far as it does not waive any criminal neglect of the employer. The effect of these decisions is, that the servant of the railroad company, for instance, not only takes upon himself the incidental risks of the service, but he may, by previous contract, release the company from its duty to furnish him a safe track, safe cars, machinery and materials, and suitable tools to work with: Western and Atlantic Ry. Co. v. Bishop, 50 Ga. 465; Western and Atlantic Ry. Co. v. Strong, 52 Id. 461; Galloway v. Western and Atlantic Ry. Co., 57 Id. 512.

On the other hand, in Roesner v. Hermann, 10 Biss. 486, 8 Fed. Rep. 782, [Federal Circuit Court, District of Indiana] a contract by a master against his own negligence was declared to be void as against public policy. Gresham, J., saying: "If there was no negligence, the defendant needed no contract to exempt him from liability; if he was negligent, the contract set out in his answer will be of no avail."

Compare Memphis etc. R.R. Co. v. Jones, 2 Head, 517, [Tenn.] where it was decided that such a contract would not protect the master against gross negligence.

It is an elementary principle in the law of contracts that modus et conventio vincunt legem,—the form of agreement and the convention of parties override the law. But the maxim is not of universal application. Parties are permitted, by contract, to make a law for themselves only in cases where their agreements do not violate the express provisions of any law, nor injuriously affect the interest of the public: . . .

Our constitution and laws provide that all railroads operated in this state shall be responsible for all damages to persons and property done by the running of trains: Const. 1874, art. 17, sec. 12; Mansfield's Digest, sec. 5537.

This means that they shall be responsible only in cases where they have been guilty of some negligence. And it may be questionable whether it is in their power to denude themselves of such responsibility by a stipulation in advance. But we prefer to rest our decision upon the broader ground of considerations of public policy. The law requires the master to furnish his servant with a reasonably safe place to work in, and with sound and suitable tools and appliances to do his work. If he can supply an unsafe machine, or defective instruments, and then excuse himself against the consequences of his own negligence by the terms of his contract with his servant, he is enabled to evade a most salutary rule.

In the English case above cited, it is said this is not against public policy, because it does not affect all society, but only the interest of the employed. But surely the state has an interest in the lives and limbs of all its citizens. Laborers for hire constitute a numerous and meritorious class in every community. And it is for the welfare of society that their employers shall not be permitted, under the guise of enforcing contract rights, to abdicate their duties to them. The consequence would be that every railroad company, and every owner of a factory, mill, or mine, would make it a condition precedent to the employment of labor, that the laborer should release all right of action for injuries sustained in the course of the service, whether by the employer's negligence or otherwise. The natural tendency of this would be to relax the employer's carefulness in those matters of which he has the ordering and control, such as the supplying of machinery and materials, and thus increase the perils of occupations which are hazardous even when well managed. And the final outcome would be to fill the country with disabled men and paupers, whose support would become a charge upon the counties or upon public charity.

NOTES AND QUESTIONS

1. The basis for the lawsuit: Plaintiff here sues as the representative of the estate of a person killed by the alleged wrong conduct of defendant; plaintiff is "administratrix" of the estate, the one who administers the estate. The person killed is referred to as the "intestate" because he died without leaving a will to govern the disposition of his estate; i.e., he died intestate. Though not referred to by the court, the right to bring such a lawsuit as this, after the death of the injured person, depended on a statute. The statute permitting the administratrix to sue does not, however, affect the question of the validity of the contract purporting to release the employer from liability for future injury; the court has to decide that question on other bases.

2. Does the Eubanks case recognize any power in private individuals to fix, by mutual agreement, the standards and rules that will govern their relations? Where do private individuals get such a power? Where do courts get their power (in the Eubanks case, for example) to refuse to enforce such an agreement? Why should they exercise this power? Does the Eubanks case support or refute the views of Professor M. R. Cohen as to the basis of contract expressed in the excerpt which follows these Notes?

In reflecting upon these questions, consider the following statements:

Sir George Jessel, M.R., in Printing and Numerical Registering Co. v. Sampson, (1875) L.R. 19 Eq. 462, 465: "It must not be forgotten that you are not to extend arbitrarily those rules which say that a given contract is void as being against public policy, because if there is one thing which more than another public policy requires, it is that men of full age and competent understanding shall have the utmost liberty of contracting and that their contracts when entered into freely and voluntarily shall be held sacred and shall be enforced by courts of justice. Therefore, you have this paramount public policy to consider—that you are not lightly to interfere with this freedom of contract."

Sutherland, J., in Adkins v. Children's Hospital, 261 U.S. 525, 545-546 (1923): "That the right to contract about one's affairs is a part of the liberty of the individual protected by this clause [the due process clause of the 14th Amendment, U.S. Constitution] . . . is no longer open to question. . . . There is, of course, no such thing as absolute freedom of contract. It is subject to a great variety of restraints. But freedom of contract is, nevertheless, the general rule and restraint the exception; and the exercise of legislative authority to abridge it can be justified only by the existence of exceptional circumstances. . . ."

Are Sir George Jessel and Mr. Justice Sutherland expressing identical doctrines? Are their views as to the basis of contract the same as or different from those expressed by Professor Cohen in the excerpt following these Notes?

The Adkins case, *supra*, which invalidated a District of Columbia minimum wage law for women, was overruled in West Coast Hotel Co. v. Parrish, 300 U.S. 379 (1937), in which the majority said, regarding freedom of contract: "What is this freedom? The Constitution does not speak of freedom of contract. It speaks of liberty and prohibits the deprivation of liberty without due process of law. In prohibiting that deprivation, the Constitution does not recognize an absolute and uncontrollable liberty . . . (T)he liberty safeguarded is a liberty in a social organization which requires the protection of law against the evils which menace the health, safety, morals, and welfare of the people. Liberty under the Constitution is thus necessarily subject to the restraints of due process, and regulation which is reasonable in relation to its subject and is adopted in the interests of the community is due process."

3. State of the authorities: The Eubanks decision is in accord with the great weight of common law authority. See 6 Corbin on Contracts, Pt. VIII, especially s. 1472 (1950). It seems that this particular issue was never presented directly to the Wisconsin court, but there is no indication that it would depart from the weight of authority in this matter.

In 1955, the Supreme Court of the United States held that a contract clause releasing a tugboat from negligence liability for damages to its tow was invalid because contrary to public policy and explained: "This rule is merely a particular application to the towing business of a general rule long used by courts and legislatures to prevent enforcement of release-from-negligence contracts in many relationships such as bailors and bailees, employers and employees, public service companies and their customers. The two main reasons for the creation and application of the rule have been (1) to discourage negligence by making wrongdoers pay damages, and (2) to protect those in need of goods or services from being overreached by others who have power to drive hard bargains." Bisso v. Inland Waterways Corporation, 349 U.S. 85, 90-91 (1955).

4. Is the Eubanks decision consistent with the theory of implied contract advanced by the courts as the rationale of the fellow-servant and safe-place doctrines?

M. R. COHEN, *LAW AND THE SOCIAL ORDER*
69, 103-108 (1933)

The Basis of Contract. The cardinal error of the traditional individualistic theories of contract is their way of speaking as if the law does nothing but put into effect what the contracting parties originally agreed on. The best that can be said for this is that it may sometimes be true. But even if that were more generally the case, we should still have to attach more importance to the factor of enforcement than the prevailing theories do. The fact that two people agree to do something not prohibited by the public criminal law and carry out their agreement, or fail to do so, does not of itself bring the law of contract into being. A large number of important agreements, even in business, as in social, political, and religious matters, are left to be directly regulated by other agencies, such as the prevailing sense of honour, individual conscience, or the like. It is an error, then, to speak of the law of contract as if it merely allows people to do things. The absence of criminal prohibition will do that much. The law of contract plays a more positive role in social life, and this is seen when the organized force of the state is brought into play to compel the loser of a suit to pay or to do something. Doubtless most people live up to their promises or agreements either through force of custom or because it is in the long run more advantageous to do so. But there can be no doubt that the possibility of the law's being invoked against us if we fail to do so is an actual factor in the situation. Even if the transactions that come to be litigated are atypical, their judicial determination is still influential in moulding the legal custom. For the ruling in a case that departs from the mode supports or opposes some direction of variation and thus fixes the direction of growth of what becomes customary. The fact, then, that in the general run of transactions people do not resort to actual litigation is certainly in part due to the fact that they know in a general way what will be the outcome of that process. The law of contract, then, through judges, sheriffs, or marshals puts the sovereign power of the state at the disposal of one party to be exercised over the other party. It thus grants a limited sovereignty to the former. In ancient times, indeed, this sovereignty was legally absolute. The creditor acquired dominion over the body of the debtor and could dispose of it as he pleased. But even now, when imprisonment for debt has been, for the most part, abolished, the ability to use the forces of the state to collect damages is still a real sovereign power and the one against whom it can be exercised is in that respect literally a subject.

From this point of view the law of contract may be viewed as a subsidiary branch of public law, as a body of rules according to which the sovereign power of the state will be exercised as between the parties to a more or less voluntary transaction.

The first rules of public law, generally called constitutional law, regulate the conduct of the chief state officials by indicating the scope of their powers. Within this scope legislatures use their discretion or wisdom to enact certain statutes; and judges, by following precedents, elaborate certain rules as to when and how the power of the state shall be exercised. Among these rules we have the laws of partnership, leases, agreements for services, contracts of surety or insurance, and the like. Now, just as the rules of constitutional law are general and leave blanks to be filled in by the legislature, courts, and administrative officials (whose rules and habitual practices are law to those over whom they have authority), so do the rules of contracts allow men to formulate for themselves, within the prescribed limits, certain rights and duties governing certain transactions between them; and when the parties have thus formulated their agreements, the latter become a part of the law of the land, just as much as do treaties between our nation and others, compacts between states, contracts between a state or division thereof and a private corporation, or the grant of a pension to the widow of a former President. When a state or a municipality makes a contract with a public service corporation for gas or transportation at a given price to the consumer, no one doubts that such an agreement is part of the legal order. But so are private agreements that the law sanctions. Thus, when a trade union makes an agreement with an association of employers, or even with a single employer, the result is law not only for those "represented" at the signing of the papers but for all those who wish to enter the industry at any time that the agreement is in force. This is in general true of all more or less permanently organized partnerships, companies, corporations, or other groups; and enforceable agreements between individuals, no matter on how limited a scale, are similarly part of the law by virtue of the general rules of state action that apply to them.

If, then, the law of contract confers sovereignty on one party over another (by putting the state's forces at the disposal of the former), the question naturally arises: For what purposes and under what circumstances shall that power be conferred? Adherents of the classical theory have recognized that legal enforcement serves to protect and encourage transactions that require credit or reliance on the promises of others. But we also need care that the power of the state be not used for unconscionable purposes, such as helping those who exploit the dire need or weaknesses of their fellows. Usury laws have recognized that he who is under economic necessity is not really free. To put no restrictions on the freedom to contract would logically lead not to a maximum of individual liberty but to contracts of slavery, into which, experience shows, men will "voluntarily" enter under economic pressure—a pressure that is largely conditioned by the laws of property. Regulations, therefore, involving some restrictions on the freedom to contract are as necessary to real liberty as traffic restrictions are necessary to assure real freedom in the general use of our highways. . . .

Consider, for instance, the position of the man who has to ship his goods. Shall we leave him to bargain with the railroad company? That would certainly not add to the security of business. Experience has shown the necessity of the government's standardizing the transaction in regard to rates and other incidents. Similar considerations hold in regard to life and fire insurance. . . .

Contracts are standardized not only by statutory enactments such as the New York legislation on life insurance, by orders of commissions such as the Interstate Commerce Commission and the like, but also by the process of interpretation that courts apply to human transactions and to their formulated agreements. All agreements, if they are to hold for any length of time, must be constantly revised or supplemented. When disputes arise and courts are appealed to, the latter, by the process of interpretation, do this work of supplementing the existing agreements, just as they generally engage in subsidiary legislation when they interpret statutes. When courts follow the same rules of interpretation in diverse cases, they are in effect enforcing uniformities of conduct.

We may thus view the law of contract not only as a branch of public law but also as having a function somewhat parallel to that of the criminal law. Both serve to standardize conduct by penalizing departures from the legal norm. Not only by decrees of specific performance or by awards of damages, but also by treating certain contracts as void or voidable and thus withholding its support from those who do not conform to its prescribed forms, does the law of contract in fact impose penalties. Thus even when certain practices like gambling, illicit sex relations, or agreements in restraint of trade are not criminal offences, the law regards them with sufficient disfavour to refuse them the protection of its enforcing machinery.

The function of the law of contract in promoting the standardization of transactions is at all times an important one. And the more developed and complicated transactions become, the more there is need for eliminating as much uncertainty as possible by standardization. This is certainly true today. Consider the case of a man who wants to publish a book, to buy an insurance policy or a letter of credit, to ship his goods or to store them in a warehouse, to lease an apartment, to have gas or electricity or telephone service supplied to him, to mortgage his house, or to obtain a surety bond—in all these and in many other relations his freedom to contract is facilitated by standard forms moulded by past law and custom. Naturally, standardized contracts, like other laws, serve the interests of some better than those of others; and the question of justice thus raised demands the attention not only of legislatures but also of courts that have to interpret these standard forms and of administrative bodies that have to supervise their enforcement. In a changing social order these standards or forms must grow or become modified; and to make them function more serviceably it is not sufficient to wait until trouble develops and is brought before the courts for adjudication. The need of intelligent anticipation that can be affected by initiating inquiries cannot be met by our traditional court procedure, and this has compelled the joining of administrative with judicial power in the hands of bodies like the Interstate Commerce Commission and our various state public service commissions.

EDITORIAL NOTE: CUSTOM, CONTRACT, and STATE ACTION: IS THERE a SPHERE of PRIVATE ACTION for WHICH the STATE IS NOT RESPONSIBLE?

Most recently, the cases involving the enforceability of restrictive covenants have raised acutely the questions concerning the basis of contract discussed by the late Professor Cohen. In Shelley v. Kraemer, 334 U.S. 1 (1948), 30 out of a total of 39 owners of property in a certain area of St. Louis signed an agreement that no part of the property, for a period of 50 years, "shall be . . . occupied by any person not of the Caucasian race, it being intended hereby to restrict the use of said property . . . against occupancy . . . by people of the Negro or Mongolian Race." One of the parcels in the area, owned by one of the 30 signers, was sold to a real estate dealer who acted as agent for the Shelleys—a Negro couple. Other property owners in the area then brought suit to restrain the Shelleys from taking possession of the property. The trial court refused to grant the relief requested, but the Supreme Court of Missouri reversed the trial court. The Supreme Court of the United States reversed the Supreme Court of Missouri, holding that the contemplated judicial enforcement of the private agreements imposing the restrictions in this case would constitute *state action* depriving the Shelleys of the equal protection of the laws in violation of the 14th Amendment. For the same reason, the Court held that it would be unconstitutional for a state court to enforce a restrictive covenant by awarding damages to a covenantor against a co-covenantor who broke the covenant by selling property to a Negro. Barrows v. Jackson, 346 U.S. 249 (1953) (which we have had occasion to consider in another connection in Chapter 5).

It should be recalled that the 14th Amendment provides only that *no state* shall "deprive any person of life, liberty, or property, without due process of law" or "deny to any person . . . the equal protection of the laws." It is not, in terms, directed against *private* action. So the Supreme Court was careful to point out in the restrictive covenant cases that entering into the covenants was not itself illegal and if the parties adhered to them voluntarily, they would suffer no legal consequences.

The remaining materials in this chapter consider the background and still uncertain, but broad, implications of the restrictive covenant decisions.

COMMENT, THE IMPACT OF SHELLEY v. KRAEMER ON THE STATE ACTION CONCEPT
44 California Law Review 718 (1956)

. . . This Comment will present (1) a review of the "state action" concept prior to Shelley, (2) an analysis of the doctrine of Shelley v. Kraemer and its logical implications, (3) a presentation of the treatment of the doctrine by subsequent cases and (4) suggestions of the problems created and a possible solution, though without any attempt to be definitive.

"State Action" and the Fourteenth Amendment

Any analysis of the fourteenth amendment must begin with the understanding that its prohibitions apply only to "state action," not to the acts of private persons.

State action under the fourteenth amendment was early recognized to include not only the actions of state legislatures, but actions of the executive and judicial branches, as well as the activities of political subdivisions of the state. However, alongside these apparent situations of applicability, the courts prior to Shelley v.

Kraemer had broadened the definition of the state action doctrine in order to give greater effect to the amendment: (1) State action was held to include situations where state officials acted either in violation of or in excess of their authority ("color of law" theory)[9] and (2) state action was found to include even the acts of private persons under particular circumstances ("instrumentality" theory).[10]

The rationale of the "color of law" doctrine is that state officials, even when acting without authority, are so clothed with governmental power that they can effectively deprive persons of rights guaranteed under the fourteenth amendment. Acceptance of this doctrine was not immediate because of an obvious dilemma; if the state has given no authority, logically the state cannot be considered to have acted. However, this position has been rejected on the ground that where by virtue of their general authority to act for the state, persons have within their power the use of the means of government, the protection of the amendment is necessary against the unlawful means.

The reasoning behind the instrumentality theory, somewhat akin to the "color of law" approach, is that admittedly private persons, as distinguished from state officials, are sometimes in such a position that the "means of government" are open to them so that they also must be placed under the same constitutional restrictions as the government. The major difficulty of this doctrine is the problem of identifying the standards by which "private action" is converted into "state action" without obliterating the distinction between the two. As a preliminary step three questions can be asked. The affirmative answer to any of these is a warning at least that the situation is within the problem area of the instrumentality theory:[13] (1) Did the government grant any aid to the private person? [14] (2) Did the government give any authority to him? (3) Is he carrying on a "function of a governmental nature?" Given an affirmative answer, then the difficult task ensues of having to determine whether there is enough aid or "authority" or "function" to make the private person into some sort of "state instrument" by reason of an affinity to the government.

Consider the inter-play of factors arising from two similar cases where affirmative answers to the first and third questions are possible. In Kern v. City Comm'rs

---

[9] Iowa Des Moines Bank v. Bennett, 284 U.S. 239 (1931); Greene v. Louis & Interurban R.R., 244 U.S. 499 (1917); Home Tel. & Tel. Co. v. Los Angeles, 227 U.S. 278 (1913); see Screws v. United States, 325 U.S. 91 (1945). But see the concurring opinion of Frankfurter, J., in Snowden v. Hughes, 321 U.S. 1, 16-17 (1944).

[10] See, e.g., Marsh v. Alabama, 326 U.S. 501 (1946); Rice v. Elmore, 165 F. 2d 387 (4th Cir. 1947), cert. denied, 333 U.S. 875 (1948); Kerr v. Enoch Pratt Free Library, 149 F. 2d 212 (4th Cir. 1945), cert. denied, 326 U.S. 721 (1945); Lawrence v. Hancock, 76 F. Supp. 1004 (S.D.W. Va. 1948); Kern v. City Comm'rs of Newton, 151 Kan. 565, 100 P. 2d 709 (1940); Culver v. City of Warren, 84 Ohio App. 373, 83 N.E. 2d 82 (1948).

[13] See Note, 29 Ind. L.J. 125 (1953). For a discussion of the constitutional problem of the delegation of public authority to private groups, see Comment, 67 Harv. L. Rev. 1398 (1954). The situations discussed are ones where the instrumentality theory could well be applicable.

[14] No decision was found where the granting of government aid without more was held sufficient to give effect to the instrumentality theory.

of Newton[15] a swimming pool built at public expense was leased for an entire season to a private party who refused admission to Negroes. Plaintiff, a Negro, sued the city for a writ of mandamus to compel the city to prevent such discrimination. The city defended on the fact that the pool was leased to a private party. The Kansas Supreme Court held that the discrimination violated the fourteenth amendment and that mandamus was a proper remedy. Despite the fact that this was a bona fide lease to a private party and the lessee had the full duties of upkeep and control, the situation was treated as if the pool had retained its public characteristics. At the other extreme, in Harris v. St. Louis[17] the Missouri Court of Appeals refused to find state action in the discrimination practiced by the short-term lessee of a city auditorium. The city itself practiced no discrimination since it leased to both white and Negro groups, and the brevity of the lease ("several weeks") plus the lessee's limited control of the auditorium were not enough to impute any "governmental function" to the lessee. In each of these cases government aid was provided in the leasing of government property; the character of the leasehold determined whether there was a "governmental function." [19]

A striking example of a grant of authority converting the actions of a private party into governmental action is shown in Betts v. Easley.[20] Anti-Negro discrimination practiced by a union certified under the Railway Labor Act as the sole bargaining agent of all carmen, including Negroes, in a certain shop was held by the Kansas Supreme Court to be "governmental action" in violation of the fifth amendment.[21] Because the authority the union had over the Negro carmen arose

[15] 151 Kan. 565, 100 P. 2d 709 (1940); accord, Lawrence v. Hancock, 76 F. Supp. 1004 (S.D.W. Va. 1948); Culver v. City of Warren, 84 Ohio App. 373, 83 N.E. 2d 82 (1948) (decided after Shelley v. Kraemer). Compare Kerr v. Enoch Pratt Free Library, 149 F. 2d 212 (4th Cir. 1945), cert. denied, 326 U.S. 721 (1945), with Norris v. Baltimore, 78 F. Supp. 451 (D. Md. 1948) (decided after Shelley v. Kraemer).

[17] 233 Mo. App. 911, 111 S.W. 2d 995 (1938).

[19] An additional factor, at first not isolated from the others, has become recognized as an independent consideration in the leasing cases: Was the intent to discriminate a primary motivation in making the lease? Compare Tate v. Department of Conservation and Development, 133 F. Supp. 53 (E.D. Va. 1955) (discrimination invalidated because intent to discriminate was primary factor in making the lease), with Easterly v. Dempster, 112 F. Supp. 214 (E.D. Tenn. 1953) (financial reasons being the motive for the lease, discrimination by lessee not restrained); see Note, 42 Va.L.

Rev. 291 (1956). Should intent be a factor when in fact—intent or no—property bought with public funds is leased to a private party and discrimination takes place on what is still public property?

[20] 161 Kan. 459, 169 P. 2d 831 (1946); see Steele v. Louisville & N. Ry., 323 U.S. 192, 198 (dictum), and Murphy, J., concurring at 208 (1944).

[21] As with the fourteenth amendment, the fifth amendment does not prohibit the acts of private persons. Corrigan v. Buckley, 271 U.S. 323, 330 (1926). The problem of whether there has been private or governmental action is equally present. See Betts v. Easley, 161 Kan. 459, 467, 169 P. 2d 831, 838 (1946). But see Noreen v. Van Dyke, 133 F. Supp. 142, 146-47 (D. Minn. 1955) (dictum), where actions by a government official in his "capacity as an employer" were said not to be encompassed by the fifth amendment. Would not this mean that the scope of "state action" under the fourteenth amendment is broader than that of "governmental action" under the fifth?

by virtue of the government certification, the union had in effect become an agent of the government in this matter and subject to constitutional limitations.

The most significant developments under the instrumentality theory are found in the primary election cases[22] and in Marsh v. Alabama.[23] In the former the continuing attempt of southern state Democratic parties to keep Negroes out of primary election participation by step-by-step withdrawal of state collaboration with the parties has been paralleled by concurrent step-by-step extension of the instrumentality doctrine to meet the challenge. The logical culmination prior to Shelley v. Kraemer was Rice v. Elmore.[24] In South Carolina all statutes regulating primary elections had been repealed so that there was neither state prohibition of Negro voting, state authorization of political parties to choose their own members, a state requirement for holding primaries, nor state regulation even if a primary were held. Nonetheless, relying on Smith v. Allwright[29] for the proposition that it was not so much the actual state collaboration that was fundamental as the nature of the governmental function served by the political party in the Democratic primary, party rules barring Negroes from voting were held by the United States Court of Appeals for the Fourth Circuit to be violations of the fourteenth and fifteenth amendments.[30]

Undoubtedly the most provocative case raising the issue of the instrumentality theory is Marsh v. Alabama.[31] The community of Chickasaw, Alabama was a company-owned town, a few feet off the public highway but on private property. The community provided complete living and business facilities for its inhabitants.

[22] The important pre-Shelley cases include Smith v. Allwright, 321 U.S. 649 (1944); Rice v. Elmore, 165 F. 2d 387 (4th Cir. 1947), cert. denied, 333 U.S. 875 (1948); Chapman v. King, 154 F. 2d 460 (5th Cir. 1946), cert. denied, 327 U.S. 800 (1946). See note 30 infra for a discussion of the post-Shelley decisions.

[23] 326 U.S. 501 (1946).

[24] 165 F. 2d 387 (4th Cir. 1947), cert. denied, 333 U.S. 875 (1948).

[29] 321 U.S. 649 (1944).

[30] But see Chapman v. King, 154 F. 2d 460 (5th Cir. 1946), cert. denied, 327 U.S. 800 (1946). This decision finding state action was based squarely on state collaboration and expressly rejected criteria such as were relied on in Rice v. Elmore. The latter decision, written by Parker, J., voiced disapproval of the Chapman approach. Thus up to Shelley v. Kraemer the instrumentality theory had failed to determine in the election field whether the action of the individuals per se or the state collaboration created the "state action."

After Shelley v. Kraemer Judge Parker reasserted his position in Rice v. Elmore by holding that discrimination practiced by private political clubs, where in fact the club elections determined the winners in both the party primaries and the general election, was in essence no different than discrimination by the Democratic party and hence a violation of the fifteenth amendment. Baskin v. Brown, 174 F. 2d 391 (4th Cir. 1949).

Terry v. Adams, 345 U.S. 461 (1953), would appear to uphold Judge Parker. Seven justices in two opinions agreed that the acts of private electoral associations themselves could be state action. Though for different reasons Justice Frankfurter's position is akin to that taken by the court in Chapman v. King, while Justice Minton's dissent disagreed with the idea that just because a private electoral association was successful it should be placed in the state action category. Does the state action characterization depend on the success of the organization involved?

[31] 326 U.S. 501 (1946). But cf. Watchtower Bible & Tract Soc'y v. Metropolitan Life Ins. Co., 188 Misc. 978, 69 N.Y.S. 2d 385 (Sup. Ct. 1947).

The managers of the town maintained the right to prohibit any solicitation within Chickasaw unless a permit were obtained from them. After a refusal of a permit, plaintiff continued to distribute religious literature on a street of the town and was convicted under a state criminal trespass statute. The United States Supreme Court reversed the conviction, finding a violation of the fourteenth amendment. The problem is, what was the violation? Was it the court conviction based on the acts of private persons,[32] or was it the refusal of the managers to grant a permit? [33] The holding of the case was:[34]

"Insofar as the State has attempted to impose criminal punishment on appellant for undertaking to distribute religious literature in a company town, *its* action cannot stand."

But the decision speaks in broader terms:[35]

"Whether a corporation or a municipality owns or possesses the town the public in either case has an identical interest in the functioning of the community in such a manner that the channels of communication remain free. . . . *The managers appointed by the corporation cannot curtail the liberty of press and religion of these people consistently with the purposes of the Constitutional guarantees,* and a state statute, as the one here involved, which enforces *such* action by criminally punishing those who attempt to distribute religious literature clearly violates the First and Fourteenth Amendments. . . ."

Since the activities of individuals, without more, cannot violate the fourteenth amendment, the town managers must have been "governmental" in some manner to be able to "curtail the liberty of press and religion."

Thus prior to Shelley v. Kraemer the state action doctrine of the fourteenth amendment had been considerably broadened without being rendered meaningless. Despite the fact that "state action" had burst out of traditional bounds, the doctrine was so delineated that the scope of what was permissible "private action," not within the restrictions of the fourteenth amendment, was still foremost and without any real danger of obliteration.

Shelley v. Kraemer—The New Concept of "Judicial Enforcement"

. . . [The argument that] *judicial enforcement* of the covenants was barred

---

[32] This would place the case squarely as precedent for Shelley v. Kraemer. See Comment, 45 Mich. L. Rev. 733 (1947); cf. Lathrop, The Racial Covenant Cases, 1948 Wis. L. Rev. 508. But see Note, 44 Mich. L. Rev. 848, 852 (1946).

Shelley uses Marsh v. Alabama in this sense: "[I]t would appear beyond question that the power of the State to create and enforce property interests must be exercised within the boundaries defined by the Fourteenth Amendment. Cf. Marsh v.

Alabama. . . ." Shelley v. Kraemer, 334 U.S. 1, 22 (1948). (Emphasis added.)

[33] This would equate the action of the managers, private persons, to that of a municipality refusing to grant permits. Cf. Martin v. Struthers, 319 U.S. 141 (1943). See Notes, 44 Mich. L. Rev. 848 (1946), 1947 Wis. L. Rev. 121, 1 Wyo. L.J. 142 (1947).

[34] Marsh v. Alabama, 326 U.S. 501, 509 (1946). (Emphasis added.)

[35] Id. at 507-08. (Emphasis added.)

as being prohibited state action under the fourteenth amendment [while] very similar to the settled application of the rule that judicial activity in violation of the fourteenth amendment was invalid, . . . was distinct in one way. In the cases exemplifying "orthodox" judicial violation the prohibited activity was practiced by the judge himself. For example, in the famous decision of Powell v. Alabama failure of the judge to allow defendants adequate counsel was found to be a denial of due process. However, in this new approach the discrimination originated with private persons; the impartial "enforcement" of the discrimination had to be tainted by it and become prohibited. . . .

. . . [The Shelley court] forged the vital link—showing that judicial enforcement of private discrimination is prohibited state action—by presenting an argument based on the effect of the judicial activity:[53]

> "[T]hese are cases in which the States have made available to [private] . . . individuals the full coercive power of government to deny [defendants] . . . , on the grounds of race or color, the enjoyment of property rights. . . . Nor is the Amendment ineffective simply because the particular pattern of discrimination, which the State has enforced, was defined initially by the terms of a private agreement. State action [under] . . . the Fourteenth Amendment, refers to the exertions of state power in all forms. And when the effect of that action is to deny rights subject to the protection of the Fourteenth Amendment, it is the obligation of this Court to enforce the constitutional commands."

What does this reasoning imply? For some it has meant that *any* judicial "aid" to privately enforced activity (including a denial of remedy against such activity), when the state could not so act under the fourteenth amendment, is state action in violation of that amendment.[54]

But interspersed with these broad words of interpretation were words of caution:[55]

> "We conclude, therefore, that the restrictive agreements standing alone cannot be regarded as violative of any rights. . . . *So long as the purposes of those agreements are effectuated by voluntary adherence . . . it would appear clear that there has been no action by the State. . . .*
>
> "But here there was more. These are cases in which the purposes of the agreements were secured *only* by judicial enforcement of the state courts. . . ."

And further:[56]

> It is clear that *but for* the active intervention of the state courts . . . [defendants] would have been free to occupy the properties without restraint.
>
> "These are not cases . . . in which the States have merely abstained from action, leaving private individuals free to impose such discrimination as they see fit."

[53] 334 U.S. at 19-20.
[54] . . . Ming, Racial Restrictions and the Fourteenth Amendment: The Restrictive Covenant Cases, 16 U. Chi. L. Rev. 203, 234, 235 (1949) . . .
[55] 334 U.S. at 13-14. (Citations omitted; emphasis added.)
[56] *Id.* at 19. (Emphasis added).

These words have led to a search for a limit to Shelley. Granted that some form of judicial recognition of private activity is state action under the fourteenth amendment, does this apply in every case where judicial activity has become part of the scheme of private activity? Does it make a difference if suit is brought to end the private activity rather than to give it greater effectiveness? Shall the failure of a state court to give a remedy against private action be classified as similar to providing a remedy for the benefit of private action?

The Subsequent Treatment of Shelley v. Kraemer

. . . [A]nalysis of the decisions subsequent to Shelley v. Kraemer indicates a marked reluctance to apply its theory within its broad implications. Where the problem of private action and the fourteenth amendment has arisen the courts usually have sought to fit the case into one of the pre-Shelley doctrines. Failing in this most courts still refuse to give effect to the full scope of the decision, many of them either ignoring Shelley or summarily rejecting it.

Cases concerning racially restrictive covenants, the major exception to the general trend, have usually followed the Shelley doctrine in the broadest sense. But even here—because of the dictum in Shelley that the covenants per se were not invalid—the exact legal status of the covenants is still unclear. Those cases where equitable relief against covenant violations was prayed for were easily disposed of by reference to Shelley. The question of whether Shelley is available as a defense in suits for damages for a breach of a racially restrictive covenant was settled affirmatively in Barrows v. Jackson, the Supreme Court re-emphasizing the scope of the "judicial enforcement" doctrine. However, other problems are not settled. Since the covenant itself is "valid," may it be raised as a defense against an assertion of title by a Negro purchaser? [63] And since the covenant is unenforceable,

[63] Only one reported case has been found dealing with this problem in regard to racial restrictions against sale and use of land. Clifton v. Puente, 218 S.W. 2d 272 (Tex. Civ. App. 1948), denied the right to raise the covenant as a defense against a purchaser's assertion of ownership. "It is as much an enforcement of the covenant to deny to a person a legal right to which he would be entitled except for the covenant as it would be to expressly command by judicial order that the terms of the covenant be recognized and carried out." Id. at 274.

But see Rice v. Sioux City Memorial Park Cemetery, 245 Iowa 147, 60 N.W. 2d 110 (1953), aff'd per curiam without opinion by an equally divided court, 348 U.S. 880 (1954), but judgment vacated, 349 U.S. 70 (1955), 44 Calif. L. Rev. 153 (1956). Plaintiff had signed a contract with defendant cemetery to bury her Indian husband. The contract contained a covenant against the burial of non-Caucasians. When it learned of the deceased's ancestry the defendant refused to perform and escaped liability by defending on the covenant. "[A]ll of the previous decisions may be distinguished from our present case in that they disclose the exertion of governmental power *directly* to aid in discrimination, or other deprivation of right. Certainly, that factor is not presented here where the state has maintained neutrality." And further, "It is clear that state action . . . has only been expanded to direct action . . . to aid in the enforcement of restrictive or discriminating acts or agreements." Id. at 155, 157, 60 N.W. 2d at 115, 116. Are Clifton and Rice contrary in their uses of the Shelley doctrine? Is it not significant that in Clifton a refusal to follow Shelley would have resurrected defunct private discrimi-

should its mere presence be allowed as a means to aid a Negro purchaser in repudiating a contract to buy? [64] These are only some of the issues remaining concerning racially restrictive covenants.[65]

Aside from the restrictive covenant cases, the general attitude of the courts is illustrated in another decisional area. Dorsey v. Stuyvesant Town Corp.[66] presents a clear example of how a court first found the instrumentality theory inapplicable and then avoided the application of the doctrine of judicial enforcement. Pursuant to a state law designed to give impetus to the building of housing by private business firms, the defendant Metropolitan Life Insurance Company contracted with the city of New York to build through Metropolitan's subsidiary, defendant Stuyvesant Town Corporation, a housing project capable of accommodating about twenty-five thousand people. No state policy was announced as to the restriction of tenants, and the defendants excluded Negroes. Plaintiffs, Negroes, sued to enjoin such discrimination on the grounds that it violated the fourteenth amendment. Despite the facts that the erection of the project was part of a state policy to create housing and effect land rehabilitation, that the state gave aid in the nature of eminent domain, loans and tax exemptions, and that the state supervised through regular inspections, maximum rentals and financing regulations, a majority of the New York Court of Appeals were unwilling to find sufficient state action to bring defendants' acts under the amendment. Resting its decision on the statutory declaration that no state subdivision was authorized to engage in housing of the Stuyvesant variety, the court concluded that while there was government aid and control, there was no government intervention—hence no state action in the project itself.[67]

Whether or not one agrees with this analysis,[68] the important point to remem-

---

nation while in Rice such refusal served only to admit the existence of private discrimination otherwise effective?

[64] Savage v. Parks, 100 A. 2d 450 (Mun. App. D.C. 1953), allowed a Negro purchaser, who signed his contract after the rendition of Hurd v. Hodge, 334 U.S. 24 (1948), to rescind upon learning of the existence of a restrictive covenant in the chain of title. This fact was held material, even though this covenant was "unenforceable," since the purchaser would not be forced to "borrow trouble" from the unsettled condition of the racially restrictive covenant. Accord, Cohn v. Trawick, 60 A. 2d 926 (Mun. App. D.C. 1948) (contract signed prior to Hurd v. Hodge but suit subsequent to it).

[65] See also Claremont Improvement Club v. Buckingham, 89 Cal. App. 2d 32, 200 P. 2d 47 (1948) (refusal to render a declaratory judgment on the validity of a covenant per se) and Gaddis Investment Co. v.

Morrison, 3 Utah 2d 4, 278 P. 2d 284 (1954) (refusal of real estate agent to consummate a sale in violation of a covenant until he received approval from a local real estate board was not as a matter of law an abandonment of his contract and forfeiture of his commission).

[66] 299 N.Y. 512, 87 N.E. 2d 541 (1949), cert. denied, 339 U.S. 981 (1949); . . . cf. Johnson v. Levitt, 131 F. Supp. 114 (E.D. Pa. 1955).

[67] "The aid which the State has afforded to [defendants] . . . and the control to which they are subject are not sufficient to transmute their conduct into State action under the constitutional provisions here in question." 299 N.Y. at 536, 87 N.E. 2d at 551.

[68] Three judges dissented in Dorsey. Fuld, J., presents a concise picture of cooperation between the State and the defendants. Though it cites Shelley v. Kraemer several times, the dissenting opinion is concerned, not with the judicial enforcement theory,

ber is that its thrust goes only toward disproving that neither by state aid, nor by the exercise of a public function, were the acts of the defendants considered acts of the state. The court in Dorsey fails to meet the proposition that, by failing to provide plaintiffs with a remedy against the discrimination and thus giving sanction to the discrimination, the court itself denied plaintffs the equal protection of the laws under the doctrine of judicial enforcement.

But of far more interest than the cases where pre-Shelley doctrines might have fit are those where they would not. Where activities forbidden the states by the fourteenth amendment are carried on by purely private parties, activities which the older theories are incapable of reaching, has the Shelley doctrine been used to protect civil rights? Many commentators proclaimed Shelley would have an important effect here, drawing, for example, close parallels between restrictive covenants and other private means of restricting land ownership, such as the fee simple determinable with the right of reverter or the right of re-entry upon breach of a condition subsequent. Here again the courts have been reluctant to give effect to the doctrine of judicial enforcement.

The cases most clearly illustrating the problem are three decisions in which suits were instituted to determine the validity of the privately created discrimination and in which the courts recognized the validity of such private action.[74] One of these is especially indicative. In Charlotte Park and Recreation Comm'n v. Barringer[75] the plaintiff, a corporate public body, received *inter alia* as a deed of gift from the individual defendant certain property to be used as a public park on the condition that it be restricted to the exclusive enjoyment of "persons of the white race." The deed provided that if this condition were violated the property would revert to the grantor, his heirs or assigns, provided he paid a certain sum. Plaintiff sued for a declaratory judgment on the validity of the discriminatory condition in the deed. Emphasizing the fact that the deed created a possibility of reverter, by which title returned to the grantor with no activity required by him or the court, the North Carolina supreme court upheld the trial court's declaratory judgment that there was no state action in violation of the fourteenth amendment. Since the decision merely declared the validity of the reverter, it does not directly allow racial discrimination since the commission, a public body, may not discriminate under orthodox state action concepts and, realistically, is probably

but only with its disagreement with the majority opinion on the application of the instrumentality theory. See also Note, 29 Neb. L. Rev. 470 (1950).

[74] Gordon v. Gordon, 332 Mass. 197, 124 N.E. 2d 228 (1955), cert. denied, 349 U.S. 947 (1955) (gift-over if legatee married outside Hebrew faith); Charlotte Park and Recreation Comm'n v. Barringer, 242 N.C. 311, 88 S.E. 2d 114 (1955), cert. denied, 350 U.S. 983 (1956) (deed requiring property to revert to grantor if used by non-Caucasians); United States Nat'l Bank v. Snodgrass, 202 Ore. 530, 275 P. 2d 860

(1954) (gift-over if legatee married person of Catholic faith); cf. Junkins v. Local 6313, Communications Workers, CIO, 263 S.W. 2d 337 (Mo. 1954) (court refusal to review action of a labor union because it is not a private party).

[75] 242 N.C. 311, 88 S.E. 2d 114 (1955), cert. denied, 350 U.S. 983 (1956). See Notes, 27 Miss. L.J. 145 and 3 U.C.L.A.L. Rev. 243 (1956), where it is argued that the decision violates the doctrine of judicial enforcement. But see Notes, 13 Wash. & Lee L. Rev. 28 (1956) and 17 U. Pitt. L. Rev. 478 (1956).

forced to return the property. But this point aside, it is submitted that the decision leaves unanswered certain questions raised by Shelley v. Kraemer. Though the Barringer decision attempts to meet Shelley squarely and to distinguish it along the lines of the judicial enforcement doctrine, it fails in its task: the problem of state action here is not merely whether title passes independently of a court decision; the questionable state action in this case is the *declaratory judgment* by which —in apparent violation of Shelley—the court applies its sanction to a discriminatory instrument. Furthermore, if in a subsequent case a grantee of a deed subject to this sort of provision (or his non-white purchaser) refused to give up possession to the grantor, would not Barringer be used to substantiate an argument that since title has already returned to the grantor, the courts may ignore the discriminatory reasons for the return and aid him in his suit for repossession? If so, is not the "full coercive power of government" being made available to individuals to further their discriminatory acts?

Thus an analysis of the cases subsequent to Shelley v. Kraemer makes it clear that, aside from the racially restrictive covenant cases, the courts will not carry out the doctrine that court aid to all private discrimination is state discrimination. If the situation appears to fit within the pre-Shelley doctrines of state action, the courts will analyze it along those lines and decide only on those grounds, either ignoring or failing to meet Shelley. If the case concerns what was undoubtedly private action before Shelley, private action it remains. Admittedly the Supreme Court has not determined the matter. But certiorari was denied to Dorsey v. Stuyvesant Town Corp. in 1949 and to Gordon v. Gordon[81] in 1955. And note that Rice v. Sioux City Memorial Park Cemetery[82] was affirmed (if only by an equally divided court) in 1954 though this judgment was later vacated. Admittedly, little can be drawn from a denial of certiorari in any single case, and two denials may not establish a trend, but nonetheless in absence of other evidence it is reasonable to conclude that the Supreme Court is reluctant to carry Shelley forward.

What Is the Value of Shelley v. Kraemer Today?

"Since there is a growing public and professional interest in the role of legal institutions in the solution of contemporary social problems, the Court's decisions [in the restrictive covenant cases] should be evaluated in terms of their effect on racial segregation and the constitutional theories with respect to the protections afforded to members of minority groups." [84]

These words, written by a proponent of the full implications of the decision in Shelley v. Kraemer, fix attention on the fact that there is more involved in the case than placing a further limitation on racial discrimination. Also present are important issues of constitutional theory. The sharpest illustration of the prob-

[81] . . . see note 74 *supra* . . .
[82] . . . see note 62 *supra*. . . .
[84] Ming, Racial Restrictions and the Four-

teenth Amendment: The Restrictive Covenant Cases, 16 U. Chi. L. Rev. 203, 207 (1949).

lem facing us is the fact that, as shown above, of the cases subsequent to Shelley, aside from the restrictive covenant cases, not one reported decision has been found that followed the doctrine of judicial enforcement. In light of Shelley many of these cases are "illogical." But this very reluctance to follow Shelley should warn the legal commentator that before he can condemn these cases he must give consideration to the reason behind their position. It is submitted that the reasons for this judicial attitude is that Shelley, as a result of the potentially broad sweep of its doctrine, raises grave constitutional problems in two areas. (1) It upsets the balance of federal-state relationships by giving an enormous opportunity for federal activity in the civil rights area; (2) it poses definite problems concerning the relationship of the individual to his government.

Recent history has produced enough on the first problem; this Comment need not discuss it further. Suffice it to say that this would not be the only area where the federal-state relationship has been "upset." But consider this one question: If failure to provide a judicial remedy, an example of inaction, is now a form of state action, are other forms of state inaction also to be so included, thus giving the federal government greater authority to act under the "enabling clause" of the fourteenth amendment? [89]

The other problem involves issues which deserve more consideration here. If obtaining court aid to carry out "private" activity "converts" such private action into "state" action, then there could never be any private action in any practical sense. So entwined are our lives with the law[90] that the logical result would be that almost *all* action, to be effective, must result in state action.[91] Thus all private activity would be required to "conform" with the standards of conduct imposed on the states by the fourteenth amendment. Under the guise of protecting civil rights by "strengthening" due process and the equal protection of the laws, is it not possible that Shelley creates a means of *restricting* civil liber-

---

[89] U.S. Const. amend. XIV, § 5 ["The Congress shall have power to enforce, by appropriate legislation, the provisions of this Article"] . . . But note these words in Shelley: "These are not cases, as has been suggested, in which the States have merely abstained from action, leaving private individuals free to impose such discriminations as they see fit. Rather, these are cases in which the States have made available to such individuals the full coercive power of government. . . ." Shelley v. Kraemer, 334 U.S. 1, 19 (1948). Is the inference that if the state had "abstained from action" that the fourteenth amendment would not have been violated, or are these words to be taken only as emphasis, as contrast to the Court's conclusion? One writer concludes the former is correct. Huber,

Revolution in Private Law? 6 S.C.L.Q. 8, 29-30 (1954).

[90] Professor Hyman points out that there are other means of law enforcement of private action, besides that of the courts, that would be state action under the Shelley approach. Hyman, Segregation and the Fourteenth Amendment, 4 Vand. L. Rev. 555, 565-67 (1951).

[91] See Lathrop, The Racial Covenant Cases, 1948 Wis. L. Rev. 508, 513-15, and Scanlan, Racial Restrictions in Real Estate, 24 Notre Dame Law, 157, 172-74 (1949), which espouse the doctrine that the enforcement of "private law" is state action. If so can there ever be any significant "private action" in any practical sense? The issue is not the logic of the proposition but whether we wish to adopt it.

ties, making possible far greater government control of individual activity than desired.[92]

Given these dangers, does the doctrine of Shelley v. Kraemer itself provide internal limitations? The writers have presented primarily three theories of limitation: (1) That Shelley means only that one person cannot use the courts to compel another person to commit an act forbidden the states by the fourteenth amendment;[93] (2) that Shelley applies only if a court fails to provide a remedy for a right protected by that amendment where the state had the constitutional power to provide a remedy in other ways;[94] (3) that Shelley is inapplicable "where the necessity of protecting the property right [or any other personal activity?] outweighs the need for safeguarding the civil right," a "balancing of interests" approach.[95]

The first of these three is the only concrete limitation, for it excludes from application situations where the individual wants to use a court to enforce his own prejudicial action without requiring another to discriminate also. This would explain Rice v. Sioux City Memorial Park Cemetery and Dorsey v. Stuyvesant Town Corp., the instrumentality theory having failed. But while definite, is this a realistic limitation considering the wide terms in which Shelley speaks? [98] Even Professor Hyman expresses a doubt: "[T]here is the question whether this limitation goes far enough to serve the purposes of the Fourteenth Amendment." [99]

[92] Professor Cahn points out that we must distinguish between "official and unofficial" discrimination, the latter being tolerable even in a political democracy. "When we resolve to observe the principles of the Constitution in every activity that is sponsored or controlled by government, our ability to do so in a willing and congenial manner may well depend on our being free, spontaneous, and unhampered in the remainder of our relationships. . . . Discrimination in regard to corporate advantage (such as transportation, housing, employment, political franchise, or educational opportunity) violates the American promise; but discrimination in the choice of friends and associates may furnish the very safety valve that many Americans require for psychic health." Cahn, Jurisprudence, 30 N.Y.U. L. Rev. 150, 156 (1955). Considering the phrase "psychic health," note the irrational reaction in many Southern quarters to the School Segregation Cases, a reaction that goes beyond mere disagreement on constitutional or policy grounds. For a discussion similar to Professor Cahn's, but in another area, see United States Nat'l Bank v. Snodgrass, 202 Ore. 530, 536-39, 275 P. 2d 860, 863-64 (1954).

But cf. Wilson, The Merging Concepts of Liberty and Equality, 12 Wash. & Lee L. Rev. 182 (1955) . . .

[93] Hyman, Segregation and the Fourteenth Amendment, 4 Vand. L. Rev. 555, 569 (1951); cf. Vinson, C. J., dissenting in Barrows v. Jackson, 346 U.S. 249, 260 (1952) . . .

[94] Hyman, Segregation and the Fourteenth Amendment, 4 Vand. L. Rev. 555, 569-71 (1951).

[95] Comment, 48 Colum. L. Rev. 1241, 1244-45 (1948); see Hale, Freedom through Law 370-72, 376, 380-81 (1952); Comment, 96 U. Pa. L. Rev. 402, 413-14 (1948) . . .

[98] "The difference between judicial enforcement and nonenforcement of the restrictive covenants is the difference to [defendants] between being denied rights of property available to other members of the community and being accorded full enjoyment of those rights on an equal footing." Shelley v. Kraemer, 334 U.S. 1, 19 (1948) . . .

[99] Hyman, Segregation and the Fourteenth Amendment, 4 Vand. L. Rev. 555, 569 (1951).

The other two proposed limitations lack all the virtue of the first. What is the limit of the state's power to prevent private violations of rights protected by the fourteenth amendment? And how does one decide that the violation of a civil right is to be countenanced in order to preserve the freedom of some personal action? These are problems the courts have long had to deal with, and limitations having these problems as their foundation create only ephemeral delineations.

The writer submits, however, that there is another theory of limitation to be found within the doctrine of judicial enforcement as espoused by Shelley v. Kraemer. This approach is submitted in the belief that it reconciles Shelley with its subsequent decisions and presents a guide by which the courts may be able to apply the doctrine of judicial enforcement instead of avoiding it.

It is submitted that the doctrine of judicial enforcement as interpreted by Shelley is applicable only when the court action abets private discrimination which in the absence of such judicial aid would be ineffective. Judicial enforcement of private discrimination, not judicial recognition, is prohibited. Where the private activity, admitted in Shelley to be valid in itself, is already effective, it is not to be said that the court, in recognizing or failing to abolish the activity, is itself an arm of the discrimination; the situation has remained the same, court action or no. It is only where the proponents of discrimination, unable to further their ends privately, seek court aid is the state itself causing discrimination under Shelley.

In Shelley the status quo was non-discriminatory, that is, the Negroes were already in control of the disputed property as a matter of right. The only bar to their title and control was the discriminatory clause, *now ineffective*. Only by court action could the occupants be ousted. But the cases subsequent to Shelley presented the converse situation. Private discrimination was always a *fait accompli*, effective without court aid. In Dorsey, for example, the plaintiffs had already been effectively deprived of entrance before the complaint was ever filed. In Barringer the status quo was discriminatory, that is, the parties injured thereby had already been effectively deprived by the private acts. The declaratory judgment, while carrying the force of law, only admitted what Shelley expressed, that the private action was in itself valid.

The recent Supreme Court decision of Black v. Cutter Laboratories[105] may be an indication that a view such as this may be adopted. Plaintiff was discharged from her employment on the grounds that her continuing membership in the Communist Party was "just cause" for dismissal under a collective bargaining agreement. The Supreme Court of California held such a discharge to be valid under local contract law. The Supreme Court dismissed the writ of certiorari for want of a federal question, reasoning that only a question of local law was involved. The dissent, written by Justice Douglas, urged that a classification based on party membership is forbidden the government under the Constitution so that when a state court recognized such a classification, a violation of the fourteenth amendment occurred. Admitting the major premise of the dissenting argument, it is not necessary to conclude that the Shelley doctrine has been violated: Here was a clear case of private discrimination being effective without state action.

[105] 351 U.S. 292 (1956).

And since the majority in the Black case must have been aware of the dissenting argument, is not the holding that there was no federal question in reality a decision that in such a situation Shelley will not be applied?

Conclusion

Shelley v. Kraemer, though standing as a landmark decision in our constitutional history, has thus far been denied much practical judicial importance by its treatment in subsequent cases. The reason is clear: the wide sweep of the doctrine of judicial enforcement has caused judge and writer alike to wonder. Given the present judicial attitude—a failure to give us a guide by which Shelley can be used—the case is of no use as an important constitutional decision outside the field of racially restrictive covenants, for no court may be willing to apply it elsewhere. Yet so important a decision should not be lost. It is suggested that much can be done to preserve its importance by an analysis along the lines herein suggested. In this way it may be possible that the decision can remain a powerful weapon for the protection of civil liberties without remaining a potential danger as a limitation on personal activity.

NOTES AND QUESTIONS

1. In Chapter 3 we briefly discussed Prof. Wechsler's complaint that the School Segregation decisions exhibited a lack of clearly elaborated "neutral principle" in their reasoning. His complaint extended also to Shelley v. Kraemer.

"Assuming that the Constitution speaks to state discrimination on the ground of race but not to such discrimination by an individual even in the use or distribution of his property, although his freedom may no doubt be limited by common law or statute, why is the enforcement of the private covenant a state discrimination rather than a legal recognition of the freedom of the individual? That the action of the state court is action of the state, the point Mr. Chief Justice Vinson emphasizes in the Court's opinion is, of course, entirely obvious. What is not obvious, and is the crucial step, is that the state may properly be charged with the discrimination when it does no more than give effect to an agreement that the individual involved is, by hypothesis, entirely free to make . . . What is the principle involved? Is the state forbidden to effectuate a will that draws a racial line, a will that can accomplish any disposition only through the aid of law, or is it a sufficient answer there that the discrimination was the testator's and not the state's? [He here cites Gordon v. Gordon, 332 Mass. 197, cert. denied, 349 U.S. 947 (1955)]. May not the state employ its law to vindicate the privacy of property against a trespasser, regardless of the grounds of his exclusion, or does it embrace the owner's reasons for excluding if it buttresses his power by the law? Would a declaratory judgment that a fee is determinable [i.e., that one's title to land is subject to termination —Editor] if a racially restrictive limitation should be violated represent discrimination by the state upon the racial ground? [He here cites Charlotte Park and Recreation Comm'n v. Barringer, 242 N.C. 311, cert. denied, 350 U.S. 983 (1956).] Would a judgment of ejectment?" (Wechsler, Toward Neutral Principles In Constitutional Law, 73 Harv. L. Rev. 1, 29-30 (1959)).

Does any of the theories set forth in the Comment just preceding these Notes embody "neutral principles" capable of answering Prof. Wechsler's questions?

2. Responding to Prof. Wechsler, Prof. Pollak (whose article was also referred to in Chap. 3) says:

"As a starting point, it may be useful to revert to the Gordon case, and to Professor Wechsler's query whether the state is 'forbidden to effectuate a will that draws a racial line.' Reflection suggests that the hypothesized 'will that draws a racial line' really embraces two quite different kinds of situations—and the difference between them may have vital implications.

"In one of these situations the state power is exerted—or, if not exerted, waits in the wings—to induce compliance by others with the discriminatory behavior patterns favored by the testator. This was what happened in Gordon, where the state power to terminate the son's interest in his father's estate was utilized as a means of restraining the son from marrying a non-Jew.

"In the second situation the state's acquiescence in the testator's prejudices extends only to the point of learning his purpose—not to the point of using state power to compel conformity by others with the discriminatory pattern. Thus, let us suppose that in Gordon the testamentary limitation barred any share in the estate to a child who had, before learning the terms of his father's will, married a non-Jew. Under these circumstances, the probate court's necessary inquiry would be confined to identifying which of the children were the intended beneficiaries of the testator's prejudice. A determination that the son had previously married a Catholic and thereby disqualified himself would not be coercive of the son's or anyone else's present or future behavior. Here judicial enforcement of the limitation would no more adopt the testator's prejudices than would enforcement of a will dividing the testator's property among three named persons all of whom are Jews and selected for that reason—an exercise of private prejudice the fourteenth amendment can hardly be thought to interfere with.

"What marks the line between these cases? The line sought to be drawn is that beyond which the state assists a private person in seeing to it that others behave in a fashion which the state could not itself have ordained. [The author here assumes that the state itself could not validly prohibit racial intermarriage—Editor]. The principle underlying the distinction is this: the fourteenth amendment permits each his personal prejudices and guarantees him free speech and press and worship, together with a degree of free economic enterprise, as instruments with which to persuade others to adopt his prejudices; but access to state aid to induce others to conform is barred." (Pollak, Racial Discrimination and Judicial Integrity, 108 U. Pa. L. Rev. 1, 12-13 (1959)).

Is the Pollak theory like any of those treated in the Comment preceding these Notes? Is this a conservative or radical theory? E.g., would it permit a court to enforce a landowner's prejudice in excluding only Negro trespassers? Or to enforce exclusion by a private business (e.g., an ice-cream parlor) of Negro customers? Or to enforce a private cemetery owner's contract to bury Caucasians only? See id. at 14-15.

3. Compared with the Shelley "judicial enforcement" theory, the "government instrumentality" theory of state action has potentialities of extension far beyond the "company town" situation in Marsh v. Alabama. It has been suggested that the large centers of private power in our society—e.g., the big corporation and the big labor union—might eventually be treated as government instrumentalities subject to the constitutional restrictions imposed on state action. Professor Berle has made the suggestion as to corporations. Berle, Constitutional Limits on Corporate Activity—Protection of Personal Rights From Invasion Through Economic Power, 100 U. Pa. L. Rev. 933, 948-953 (1952) and Economic Power and the Free Society 17-18 (1957). The Kansas court in Betts v. Easley referred to in the Comment preceding these Notes took the first step toward applying the suggestion to labor unions.

Indeed, once we go so far we are faced with an even broader problem. It is clear that the state and federal governments together have broad powers to regulate the affairs of corporations and trade unions and certainly to prohibit them from discriminating on racial grounds in their employment or membership practices, as the legislatures of many states have already done. It is clear, too, that the state may prohibit the practice of racial discrimination by owners of public accommodations, including ice-cream parlors, which many legislatures have done. Shall we say, then, that when the state chooses not to exercise its power to prohibit racial discrimination, it is sanctioning such discrimination and that such inaction constitutes state action subject to constitutional commands?

Certainly the exercise of power by corporations and labor unions, for example, affects the lives of individuals as much as a good many rules of law promulgated by the courts and legislatures. Why then should not the exercise of this power (and the exercise of power by all other non-official agencies of social control) be regarded as the exercise of delegated state power? Professor Patterson tells us that Bentham "appears to have been the first modern writer to assert that the rules laid down by a subordinate power-holder are 'laws' of the sovereign." Patterson, Jurisprudence 171 (1953), citing Bentham, The Limits of Jurisprudence Defined 104-105 (Everett ed. 1945, from MS. of 1782). A similar view seems to be implicit in Professor M. R. Cohen's conception of the basis of contract.

Yet is not "the maintenance of a realm of individual activity within which the state does not intrude . . . an essential attribute of the freedom of the individual as against the state"? Patterson at 172. To answer this question in the affirmative does not mean that the state's public policy is such a separate matter that the trade union or corporation may call upon the state to enforce internal rules which are contrary to this policy. Nevertheless, to impose responsibility upon the state for *all* existing rules of conduct promulgated by every agency of social control is to encourage the state to exercise its authority to change them. This could provide a legal basis for threatening all autonomous private associations, the existence of which distinguishes our free society from totalitarian societies.

Where to draw the line which sets the limits to state intervention will, therefore, continue to present a perplexing problem to the official law-making agencies of society and particularly to the Supreme Court in its efforts to translate our constitutional ideals into reality. Theoretically, it may be possible to draw the line so as to subject to constitutional restraints only those non-official agencies of social control, like the corporation and the trade union, which both exercise great power and are allowed by the state to enjoy significant privileges. It should also be noted that to the extent that the concept of state action is broadened to include the acts of private power-holders, the Supreme Court is compelled to review these acts from the point of view of their consistency with the Constitution, even in situations in which the state and federal legislatures may not yet have announced their policies. Yet there is serious question whether the courts, rather than the legislatures, should be called upon to assure, in the first instance, the just exercise of private power. (Consider again Mr. Justice Brandeis's views in the Associated Press case, discussed in the Chapter 4 Editorial Note on overruling decisions, page 181). And again, it should be emphasized that the legislature may exercise its power to this end even if the action of the private power-holder is not regarded as state action.

4. Further discussions of the "state action" problem will be found in Greenberg, Race Relations and American Law, 46-61 (1959); Abernathy, Expansion of the State Action Concept Under the Fourteenth Amendment, 43 Cornell L.Q. 375 (1958); Horowitz, The Misleading Search for "State Action" Under the Fourteenth Amendment, 30 So. Calif. L. Rev. 208 (1957); Note, State Action—A Study of Requirements Under the Fourteenth Amendment, 1 Race Rel. Rep. 613 (1956); Lewis, The Meaning of State Action, 60 Colum. L. Rev. 1083 (1960).

CHAPTER Eight

The MECHANICS and THEORY
of JUDICIAL DECISION

Section 1

SOME QUESTIONS of MECHANICS

EDITORIAL NOTE: The MECHANICS of JUDICIAL
DELIBERATION: The SUPREME COURT EXAMPLE

In the overwhelming majority of cases, access to the Supreme Court of the United States is via a petition for a writ of certiorari, which requests the Court to exercise its discretion to hear the case. Only a small percentage of these requests is granted. Each Justice reviews each petition, which is then formally passed upon in a conference of the Justices. It is the practice of the Court to grant a petition on the vote of 4 or more Justices.[1]

The Supreme Court is in session, on the average, during thirty-six weeks of the year—from the first Monday in October to the Monday in mid-June when the Court usually adjourns.[2] During this time, the Court alternates between listening to oral argument for a two-week period and private study of the cases for a two to three week period. Oral argument is usually heard for four hours a day from Monday through Thursday. To transact their business, the "Justices meet in private conference every Friday following a week of oral argument and every other Friday preceding a Monday on which opinions or orders are to be announced" (p. 86).

In the Friday conference following a week of oral argument, a tentative vote is taken on the merits of each case argued during that week. The vote is, of course, preceded by discussion. The Chief Justice, who presides over the conference, opens the discussion by stating the case, the questions he thinks are raised by it, and his views on these issues. Thereafter, each Justice, in the order of his seniority, has his say.[3] The reverse order of seniority is followed in voting; the junior justice is the first to cast his vote.

---

[1] On the so-called "rule of four," see the dissenting opinions of Justices Frankfurter and Harlan in Ferguson v. Moore-Mc-Cormack Lines, 352 U.S. 521 (1957); and Leiman, The Rule of Four, 57 Col. L. Rev. 975 (1957).

[2] The account of the Court's internal decision-making process is based in large part on Hart, The Supreme Court, 1958 Term, Foreword: The Time Chart of the Justices, 73 Harv. L. Rev. 84 (1959). Unless otherwise indicated, the quotations and citations of pages in the text are from this article.

[3] See Frankfurter, Of Law and Men 111-143 (Elman ed. 1956).

Professor Hart estimates that the "average amount of time which the average Justice can be expected to spend in private study of the average case prior to casting his vote in the Friday conference" is two hours (p. 91). This is in addition to the 20-30 minutes spent by the average Justice on the same case at the stage of preliminary application (e.g., reviewing the petition for a writ of certiorari), the few minutes spent by him at the conference at which it was voted to consider the case fully (e.g., grant the petition for a writ of certiorari), and the one to two hours spent in listening to oral argument of the case (p. 91).

At the end of each two-week period of oral argument, the Chief Justice assigns each of the cases voted on, in which he is in the majority, to one of the Justices for the writing of the opinion. If the Chief Justice is in the minority, the "next senior justice of those in the majority does the assigning." [4]

When Hughes was Chief Justice, we are told: "The procedure was for each Justice to put his opinion in the case assigned to him in page proof and circulate it amongst the other Justices, who then would return the proof with a concurrence, with suggested changes, or perhaps with a wholly new opinion of their own suggested by way of substitution. When the views of every Justice on an opinion had been expressed in this fashion, the case would be called for the last time at Saturday [now Friday] conference and the final majority opinion would be agreed upon." [5] Each Justice may of course decide to write and publish an individual concurring or dissenting opinion.

Opinions are usually made public on a Monday; a summary is announced orally from the bench by the Justice speaking for the Court; and printed copies of the full opinion are distributed.

Professor Hart estimates that the average time spent by the average Justice in the writing of an opinion, including individual concurring and dissenting opinions, is 24 hours (p. 92). He explains that it is obvious that many opinions "have absorbed vastly more than 24 hours of working time in research and writing" and concludes that the extra time must have been spent during the 16-week summer recess (pp. 93-94).

It should also be noted at this point that the Chief Justice may avail himself of the services of three law-clerks; the other Justices of two each. The number available is generally employed, though Justice Douglas is content with only one law clerk.[6] The law clerks are usually recent law-school graduates who serve for one-year periods; some Justices have employed permanent law clerks.

On the whole, Professor Hart deplores the quality of the Court's recent work, and blames the lack of time for adequate deliberation and the internal

[4] Id. at 136.

[5] McElwain, The Business of the Supreme Court as Conducted by Chief Justice Hughes, 63 Harv. L. Rev. 5, 19, n. 26

(1949).

[6] See Frank, Marble Palace; the Supreme Court in American Life 115-116 (1958).

process of reaching decisions. He urges the Court to reduce the number of cases to which it grants a full hearing so that it may devote more time to collective deliberation, which he thinks is necessary if the Court's opinions are to be of a quality that will "genuinely illumine the area of law with which they deal" (p. 100).

Mr. Justice Douglas, on the other hand, derides as a "myth" the "idea that the Court is overworked, that if the Court were only relieved by statute or by voluntary action of some of the cases it would make 'better' decisions." [7] The Justice produces statistics to show that over the past twenty years the number of opinions written each term has declined markedly, as has the number of hours of oral argument heard by the Court. He points out that this decrease in the volume of work made it possible in 1955 to shorten the week reserved for oral argument from 5 to 4 days. The Justice acknowledges that the number of cases in the Supreme Court has increased substantially, but attributes this to the growing number of cases filed by indigent persons convicted of crime. The claims in these cases, he states, "are for the most part frivolous" and can be disposed of summarily (p. 407). "I do not recall any time in my twenty years or more of service on the Court," Justice Douglas concludes, "when we had more time for research, deliberation, debate and meditation" (p. 411). He agrees, however, that the difficulty of the cases coming to the Court has increased.

Even if it is accepted that the Justices have sufficient time to handle the current volume of the Court's business, Professor Hart's suggestion for more effective collective deliberation would require consideration. Hart makes the point that the vote on a case, which comes at the end of the week in which it is argued, is treated "as ordinarily final even though in theory tentative" (p. 124). This means, he maintains, "that positions tend to jell before any member of the Court, in the usual case, has yet had an opportunity to make an intensive study of the problem" (p. 124). "It means that the opinion-writing Justices, who make the only intensive study which the cases receive, work not only under a regrettable pressure of time but under the further handicap that their nonwriting brothers have already disabled themselves from dealing with uncommitted minds with the difficulties which intensive study turns up. It means that the limited time available for scrutiny of draft opinions and for final discussion in conference must necessarily tend to be employed largely in firming up positions already taken and shoring up lines already drawn rather than in thoughtful and dispassionate reconsideration of the issues as they have finally been exposed to view" (p. 124).

Professor Hart, therefore, recommends that "the votes which in practice are decisive" should come "at the end rather than at the beginning of the Court's intensive study of cases" (p. 124). "To call upon judges to vote on complex and often highly controversial issues after only a couple of hours, more or less, of private study of briefs and record is to invite

[7] Douglas, the Supreme Court and Its Case Load, 45 Cornell L.Q. 401, 402 (1960).

votes which are influenced more strongly by general predilection in the area of law involved than they are by lawyerlike examination of the precise issues presented for decision. If the votes which in practice are decisive came at the end rather than at the beginning of the Court's intensive study of cases, it seems unlikely that the voting records of the Justices would lend themselves quite as readily as they now do to neat pigeon-holing in the charts of professors of political science and sociology who believe that you can lump together votes in all civil-liberties cases, in all anti-trust cases, in all employment-injury cases, and the like, and find out how a Justice thinks. If the postponement of the effective vote were accompanied by a general recognition of the obligation that rests upon the Court as an institution to compose its differences wherever possible, it seems unlikely that there would be as many individual concurring and dissenting opinions as there are now. If the postponement were accompanied, in addition, by a recognition that an opinion of the Court is the responsibility of the whole Court and not simply of the Justice who writes it, it seems likely also that the opinions would be more accurate in their formulation of the issues and better reasoned in their disposition of them than many of the opinions in recent terms have been" (pp. 124-125).

Thurman Arnold ridicules the hopes Professor Hart lodges in more extensive collective deliberation, and charges that it reflects "an ignorance of the rules of elementary psychology." [8] Arnold insists that there "is no such process" as the "maturing of collective thought," upon which Hart relies, and that "there never has been." On the contrary: "Men of positive views are only hardened in those views by such conferences. . . . I have no doubt that longer periods of argument and deliberation, and more time to dissent, would only result in the proliferation of opinions of which we already have too many."

Responding to Arnold, Dean Griswold of the Harvard Law School has said [9] that Arnold's "answer rests on Judge Arnold's *ipse dixit,* fortified by his own judicial experience."

With great respect, I venture the thought that this is not enough. It is true that it has been supported by Justice Douglas in his Cornell address. . . . But Justice Stewart is in dissent, though perhaps he did not expect his remarks (addressing the 1960 annual dinner of the Yale Law Journal) to be reported. . . .

To a complete outsider, whose knowledge comes perhaps largely from the burden on his time and intellectual capacity which he finds in merely reading and trying to digest the opinions of the Court, the weight of this argument is clearly with Professor Hart. The volume of the work of the Court is staggering. When one adds to that the factual complexity, the intellectual and legal intricacy of many of the questions, the public importance of the problems, and the difficulties inherent in reaching mutual understanding in any group of nine men, the burden seems to me to be insupportable, and to be a fair explana-

[8] Arnold, Professor Hart's Theology, 73 Harv. L. Rev. 1298, 1313 (1960).
[9] Griswold, Foreword: Of Time and Atti-
tudes—Professor Hart and Judge Arnold, 74 Harv. L. Rev. 81, 84-85 (1960).

tion of the source of some of the problems that some thoughtful persons have found in the work of the Court in recent years . . .

. . . I must confess that I feel rather sorry for the outlook reflected in [Arnold's] statement. My own work in the law has been an exciting intellectual experience. I am not known for mildness of view, or for hesitance in expressing what views I have. But many times clearly held views of mine have been radically changed by discussions with associates or colleagues, often people with very different outlooks from mine . . . To me "the maturing of collective thought" is a profound reality . . .

EDITORIAL NOTE: WHY WRITTEN OPINIONS or DISSENTING OPINIONS?

Scope of the practice of writing and publishing judicial opinions. In Rochin v. California, 342 U.S. 165, 170, n. 4 (1952), Justice Frankfurter quotes Edmund Burke on the judicial practice of rendering opinions, as follows: "Your committee do not find any positive law which binds the judges of the courts in Westminster-hall publicly to give a reasoned opinion from the bench, in support of their judgment upon matters that are stated before them. But the course hath prevailed from the oldest times. It hath been so general and so uniform, that it must be considered as the law of the land." Report of the Committee of Managers on the Causes of the Duration of Mr. Hasting's Trial, 4 Speeches of Edmund Burke 200-201 (1816).

Burke was talking of the practice of English judges to render oral opinions from the bench. In this country, the constitutions of some states require the judges of courts of last resort to state the reasons for their decisions in writing. Written opinions are the general practice even in the states which do not have this constitutional requirement. But in the absence of such a requirement, not every decision of the highest court in a state is accompanied by a written opinion. Written opinions are usually reserved for cases involving the more important issues. Similarly, the Supreme Court of the United States does not write an opinion in every case. It disposes of the great bulk of its cases finally by denying certiorari, without opinion. Furthermore, the Supreme Court often grants certiorari and simultaneously affirms or reverses the judgment below, which may be that of a federal court of appeals or the highest court of a state, without the benefit of briefs or arguments upon the merits. Such actions of the Court are accompanied by per curiam opinions, unsigned opinions on behalf of the Court, which either give no reasons for the decisions or state them in a few sentences only.

The reasons for requiring judges to give written opinions were aptly stated by Mr. Samuel M. Wilson of California during the course of the 1879 debates on the article of the California constitution adopting such a requirement, as follows: ". . . The importance of requiring the Court to give written opinions cannot be overrated. They not only become the settled law of the State, and are precedents for subsequent cases, but in many cases where the litigation is not ended by the decision of the Supreme Court, and new trials are consequent upon a reversal, the decision of the Supreme Court should be given in writing, and reasons assigned, for they are instructions to the Court below, and are the controlling rule in the subsequent litigation. . . . Undoubtedly it [the requirement that written opinions be delivered] will . . . result in well considered opinions, because they must come before the jurists of the country and be subjected to the severest criticism. . . . It tends to purity and honesty in the administration of justice." 2 Debates and Proceedings of the Constitutional Convention of the State of California (1880) 949 et seq., quoted in Radin, The Requirement of Written Opinions, 18 Calif. L. Rev. 486 (1930).

Professor Max Radin in his article criticizes the imposition upon judges, by constitution or custom, of the obligation to write an opinion in every case. He thinks it results in "an inevitable and increasing delay in the final disposition of causes," and requires the lawyers to purchase and read an overwhelming mass of material each year. Professor Radin suggests that the written-opinion requirement be imposed only when the court of last resort reverses the decision below (courtesy alone then requiring a written explanation) or affirms the decision below in a case in which a majority of the judges thinks it sufficiently important to warrant a reasoned, written opinion.

Radin's feeling that reversals require written opinions is a common one. Professor Ernest J. Brown has severely criticized the practice of per curiam reversals employed by the U.S. Supreme Court. Brown, Foreword: Process of Law—The Supreme Court 1957 Term, 72 Harv. L. Rev. 77 (1958). Although the Court presumably takes such action only when it thinks the decision below "is so clearly erroneous as to make argument before the Court a waste of time," (Stern & Gressman, Supreme Court Practice 155-156 (2d ed. 1954)), Professor Brown doubts whether some of the recent cases of summary reversal which he examines can fairly be said to fall into this category. He is primarily concerned that the Supreme Court may be reversing judgments below without giving the parties who won below adequate opportunity to be heard. His colleague, Professor Sacks, is also disturbed by the summary nature of such per curiam opinions and thinks there is "some ground for questioning whether the Supreme Court is giving sufficient attention to the need for explanation, even in cases where the justices find the result easy to reach" and even when they affirm the judgment below. Sacks, Foreword—The Supreme Court, 1953 Term, 68 Harv. L. Rev. 95 (1954).

Lower court judges accompany their decisions with written opinions in a much lower percentage of the cases than do judges of the highest courts. Furthermore, while the written opinions of courts of last resort are, invariably, published, the written opinions of the lower courts in many states, including Wisconsin, are not published at all. Rule 52 of the Federal Rules of Procedure requires the judges of the federal district courts sitting without a jury to "set forth the findings of fact and conclusions of law which constitute the ground" of their actions. In cases in which they deem it warranted, federal district judges will also write full, reasoned opinions. In the main, the written products of their efforts are also published. For an attack upon the Rule 52 requirement, see Hanson, Findings of Fact and Conclusions of Law: An Outmoded Relic of Stage Coach Days, 32 A.B.A.J. 52 (1946).

The controversy over the dissenting opinion. We have already encountered the phenomenon of the dissenting opinion in these readings (see, e.g., the opinion of O'Neall, J. in the Murray case in Chap. 2), and we shall encounter more such opinions hereafter. We shall consider the advantages and disadvantages of this judicial practice of giving reasons for disagreement with the majority (or reasons, in the case of a concurring opinion, for agreement with the result but not the grounds for the result). In general, both the advantages and disadvantages will be lessened to the extent that dissents or concurrences are merely noted without opinion, or are written but not published.

Criticism of the United States Supreme Court in recent years has often been based on the increase in its split decisions. The ratio of such decisions to total decisions was 11% in 1930, 28% in 1940, 61% in 1950, and 76% in 1957. (See analysis in ZoBell, Division of Opinion in the Supreme Court: A History of Judicial Disintegration, 44 Cornell L.Q. 186, 205 (1959)). The practice of writing dissenting or concurring opinions goes back to the early years of the Supreme Court, and no one seriously expects it to be abolished by the Court. There has, however, been some attempt at state statutory control of the publication of minority opinions (see 24 Fordham L. Rev. 450 (1955)); and recently the Chief Justice of the Pennsylvania Supreme Court successfully prevented publication of a dissent by a member of his court.[1]

Perhaps the most common defense of minority opinion publication is the argument that it helps shape the law of the future. As the late Chief Justice Hughes of the Supreme Court put it: "A dissent in a court of last resort is an appeal to the brooding spirit of the law, to the intelligence of a future day, when a later decision may possibly correct the error into which the dissenting judge believes the court to have been betrayed. Nor is this

[1] "Associate Justice Musmanno of the Pennsylvania Supreme Court sought a writ of mandamus in a county nisi prius court to compel the official reporter to print his (Musmanno's) dissent in a case, when the Chief Justice had ordered that it not be included with the official report. Musmanno v. Eldridge, 1 Pa. D.&C. 2d 535 (Ct. of C.P., 1955). (Counsel for defendant reporter included former U.S. Supreme Court Justice Owen D. Roberts—who, one would suppose, well knew the value of separate opinions—and ex-U.S. Senator George Wharton Pepper.) Musmanno appealed an adverse judgment to the Pennsylvania Supreme Court. After ruling against his motion that all the Justices disqualify themselves as interested parties, the Court affirmed. Musmanno v. Eldridge, 382 Pa. 167, 114 A. 2d 511 (1955), 24 Ford. L. Rev. 450 (1957). Musmanno later published what amounts to a brief for his position in the case. Musmanno, 'Dissenting Opinions,' 60 Dick. L. Rev. 139 (1956). See also Freedman, 'The Dissenting Opinions of Justice Musmanno,' 30 Temp. L.Q. 253 (1957)." ZoBell, *supra* at 209-210, note 120.

appeal always in vain. In a number of cases, dissenting opinions have in time become the law." (Hughes, The Supreme Court of the United States 68 (1937 ed.)) No doubt also the threat of publication of a persuasive minority opinion prods the majority into writing a more careful, defensible opinion. Indeed, "the argument is often met with, and seems sometimes to have weight, that the very fact of a dissent proves peculiarly careful consideration [by the majority] and should therefore strengthen rather than weaken the case as an authority." (Llewellyn, The Bramble Bush, 63-64 (Oceana ed., 1951)).

It is also possible that the circulation and study of draft majority and minority opinions within the Court may cause members of the tentative majority to change their minds. Chief Justice Vinson of the United States Supreme Court attested to the fact that this sometimes happened. (Address, 20 Okla. B.A. J. 1269 (1949)). While Chief Justice Stone did not emphasize this possibility, he acknowledged that it had occurred during his tenure. Stone, Dissenting Opinions Are Not Without Value, 26 J. Am. Jud. Soc'y 78 (1942).

A minority or concurring opinion may also serve to clarify the majority opinion. For example, in the Murray case referred to above, the majority was silent on whether there was any express agreement between employer and employee covering liability in this type of case, but the concurring opinion made clear that there was not. Often a minority opinion contributes a more substantial clarification than this—either to the facts in the record, or to the nature of the problem, or about the consequences of decision.

A rather different kind of clarification may also result from minority opinions: by revealing the precise differences among the judges, a clearer basis is presented for predicting later decisions by the same court. The division on a court, said Supreme Court Justice Robert Jackson, should "be forthrightly exposed so that the profession will know on what narrow grounds the case rests and can form some estimate of how changed facts may affect the alignment in a subsequent case." (37 A.B.A.J. 801, 863 (1951)). In a 1955 bar association discussion, Justice Walter Schaefer of the Illinois Supreme Court agreed that minority opinions contributed to legal certainty and pointed out that the unanimous opinion may actually conceal considerable uncertainty in the minds of the judges. A judge who is not fully convinced of the majority's position may choose to bury his doubts because he does not feel strong or articulate enough to dissent. Even positive and certain language in the opinion may have psychological roots in the need to cover up the writer's doubts. "When you get through, you see, you swing in, you swing in hard. The matter that was extremely close, extremely doubtful to you, becomes an 'argument without merit,' you know—and 'the contention is unsound,' and so on—and adverbs, whenever you see an opinion sprinkled with adverbs, look out for it because that is the easiest way there is to cover up, and . . . it gives such a degree of conviction, you see, and it is so reassuring. . . ." (Schaefer, Remarks at American Bar Association Panel Discussion, August, 1955).

Those who oppose the extensive use of minority opinions argue principally that they impair public confidence in the authority of the court. The highly respected Judge Learned Hand, speaking of the division of opinion in the Supreme Court on certain constitutional issues, contended that this "is disastrous because disunity cancels the impact of monolithic solidarity on which the authority of a bench of judges so largely depends." "People become aware that the answer to the controversy is uncertain, even to those best qualified, and they feel free, unless especially docile, to ignore it if they are reasonably sure that they will not be caught. The reasoning of both sides is usually beyond their comprehension, and is apt to appear as verbiage designed to sustain one side of a dispute that in the end might be decided either way, which is generally the truth. . . ." (Hand, The Bill of Rights 72-73 (1958)).

Justice Musmanno, whose legal fight for publication of his own dissenting opinion was recounted above, replied to Judge Hand in the pages of the Harvard Law School Record for March 1958. He argued that "monolithic solidarity" would tend to obstruct legal change; that "lawless persons will defy the law whether it is laid down by a Court speaking through a 9 to 0 majority, or a Court speaking through a 5 to 4 majority"; and that judicial controversies cannot "generally be decided either way—that is, honestly."

In the last analysis, the issue is not whether minority opinions should be written and published, but to what extent and under what conditions. This is a question each judge must decide for himself. It goes without saying that a minority opinion is not to be used "for intemperate denunciation of the judge's colleagues, violent invective, attributing of bad motives to the majority of the court, and insinuations of incompetence, negligence, prejudice, or obtuseness of fellow members of the court." (Pound, Cacoethes Dissentiendi: The Heated Judicial Dissent, 39 A.B.A.J. 794, 795 (1953)). Perhaps also it should not be used to record disagreement with the majority's determination of facts rather than of the law. One attempt to state a controlling principle is Canon 19 of the Canons of Judicial Ethics adopted by the American Bar Association in 1924: "It is of high importance that judges constituting a court of last resort should use effort and self-restraint to promote solidarity of conclusion and the consequent influence of judicial decision. A judge should not yield to pride of opinion, or value more highly his individual reputation than that of the court to which he should be loyal. Except in case of conscientious difference of opinion on fundamental principle, dissenting opinions should be discouraged in courts of last resort." It was this spirit which moved Justice Brandeis to withhold issuance of many dissenting opinions "replete with the most exquisite detail of citation and the most comprehensive of footnotes." For "Brandeis was a great institutional man." "He realized that the Court is not the place for solo performances, that random dissents and concurrences weaken the institutional impact of the Court and handicap it in the doing of its fundamental job. Dissents and concurrences need to be saved for major matters if the Court is not to appear indecisive." (Frank, Book Review of Bickel, The Unpublished Opinions of Mr. Justice Brandeis, 10 J. Legal Ed. 401, 403 (1958)).

In conclusion, since much of the current discussion of minority opinions centers around the U.S. Supreme Court, one should note that the greater frequency of such opinions in the latter Court than in state appellate courts is to be expected. In the main, only cases which present important and close questions on which other courts are divided or on which reasonable men may differ come to the Supreme Court for review.

NOTES AND QUESTIONS

1. On the basis of your own experience with student committees, fraternal or political groups, or club meetings, would you agree with Arnold's negative view on the "maturing of collective thought"? Was your role in the group different enough from that of a Supreme Court Justice's role in a court conference to affect the usefulness of the comparison?

2. Do you think the School Segregation decisions would have met with more resistance if they had not been unanimous? Consider that when Lincoln denounced the Dred Scott decision, he pointed out that judicial "decisions are of greater or less authority as precedents according to circumstances"; and one of the important circumstances he listed as detracting from the authority of this decision was the fact that it had not been made "by the unanimous concurrence of the judges." (Quoted from Nicolay and Hay, Abraham Lincoln, 2:85-86, in Hicks, Materials and Methods of Legal Research 105 [3rd rev. ed. 1942]).

3. In the article quoted above, Judge Musmanno also asked: "If there are to be no dissenting opinions in the courts, then why should the Congressional Record carry the speeches of those who voted against the bill which has now become law?" Do you think his analogy is apt?

4. Revealing descriptions of the give and take in Supreme Court conferences will be found in A. T. Mason's Harlan Fiske Stone: Pillar of the Law (1956). Detailed data on the mechanics of decision of American appellate courts in general are presented in the Preliminary Report of the Institute of Judicial Administration on the Internal Operating Procedures of Appellate Courts (1957). For illustrations of the inner thoughts of a trial judge about the cases before him, see Ulman, A Judge Takes The Stand (1933).

5. For references to discussions of the dissenting opinion, see ZoBell, Division of Opinion in the Supreme Court: A History of Judicial Disintegration, 44 Cornell L.Q. 186 at notes 98, 123, 124. For a comparative survey, see Nadelmann, The Judicial Dissent— Publication v. Secrecy, 8 Am. J. Comp. L. 415 (1959), which portrays the unwillingness of courts in non-English speaking countries to identify and publish dissents.

6. The principles which Hart called for in his "Time Chart of the Justices" article discussed above were "impersonal" (as well as "durable") principles. A similar stress on impersonality or neutrality had been put by Wechsler in his "Towards Neutral Principles of Constitutional Law" 73 Harv L. Rev. 1 (1959) which we have discussed in prior connections. This aspect of the Hart and Wechsler articles has given rise to a growing literature on the meaning and possibility of "neutrality" in legal principle. See, e.g., Miller and Howell, The Myth of Neutrality in Constitutional Adjudication, 27 U. Chi. L. Rev. 661 (1960); Mueller and Schwartz, The Principle of Neutral Principles, 7 U.C.L.A. L. Rev. 571 (1960); Henkin, Some Reflections on Current Constitutional Controversy, 109 U. of Pa. L. Rev. 637 (1961).

Section 2

THEORIES of JUDICIAL DECISION

This section reviews some of the major themes presented in Part 1, particularly the relation between the "logical," "analytic," or "doctrinal" aspects of the judicial process and its "sociological," "ethical," or "policy" aspects. This relationship is the focal point of much writing by legal philosophers. Increasingly, American legal theory emphasizes the social roots, social consequences, and the ends or values sought to be attained by legal rules.

Theorists have pointed out that the syllogistic form of judicial reasoning reflected in the judicial opinion—in which the major premise is a rule of law, a general statement of the kinds of factual conditions upon which stated legal consequences depend; the minor premise states that the case at bar satisfies the specified conditions, and the conclusion is a prescription of the stated legal consequences for the case at bar[1]—has a deceptive simplicity or mechanical quality about it. We have had occasion to see that the selection of the major premise involves creative choice by the judge; that the factors influencing his choice include the ends or values he seeks to realize; and that no "realistic" analysis can be made of how judges in fact function, or should function, by concentrating on the syllogism alone.

This point of view no longer seems as radical as it did in the early '30's when Jerome Frank and Karl Llewellyn were spearheading an intellectual movement which came to be known as "legal realism." There were maverick elements in this movement—such as Jerome Frank's Freudian hypothesis that the persistence of the "myth of legal certainty" might be explained in terms of the "Father-image" symbolized by the Law; or Underhill Moore's extremist view of the role of social facts in shaping judicial decision; or the tendency of some researchers to view "fact-research" as an end in itself, rather than as a means of testing hypotheses and a pre-condition for value-analysis. But the dominant social emphasis of this movement—away from "mechanical jurisprudence" or the "slot-machine theory" of the judicial process—has come to characterize American legal thought.

Controversy continues, but largely over matters of emphasis: *to what extent* is the judge free to choose his premises; *how much* is he restricted by the "taught tradition of the law"; is he *more* free in some kinds of cases than in others and, if so, in *what* kinds; is his opinion merely a rationalization of a result reached on policy grounds and, if so, is the opinion worthless as a means of predicting the future course of decision; *to what extent* are the policy grounds chosen deliberately by the judge or apprehended intuitively by him; *to what extent* should the opinion articulate the relevant policy or ethical considerations which governed the decision?

---

[1] See Michael and Adler, The Trial of An Issue of Fact, I, 34 Colum. L. Rev. 1224, 1241-1244, 1248-1252 (1934).

COKE* *ON LITTLETON*
(1628) 97b

For reason is the life of the law, nay the common law itself is nothing else but reason; which is to be understood of an artificial perfection of reason, gotten by long study, observation, and experience, and not of every man's naturall reason; for, *nemo nascitur artifex* [no one is born a craftsman]. This legall reason *est summa ratio* [is the highest reason]. And therefore if all the reason that is dispersed into so many severall heads, were united into one, yet could he not make such a law as the law in England is; because by many successions of ages it hath beene fined and refined by an infinite number of grave and learned men, and by long experience growne to such a perfection, for the government of this realme, as the old rule may be justly verified of it, *neminem opportet esse sapientiorem legibus:* no man out of his own private reason ought to be wiser than the law, which is the perfection of reason.

DICKINSON,† *THE PROBLEM OF THE UNPROVIDED CASE*
81 University of Pennsylvania Law Review 115, 116-121 (1932)

In the seventeenth and the early part of the eighteenth century, when many of the lines of our present legal processes were laid down, it is fair to say that the problem of the unprovided case was taken for granted and not clearly envisaged as a problem at all. The bulk of litigation of the time lay in the field of real-property law where the rules had already been elaborated to great fullness and required little more than direct application to the cases. . . . Whenever an issue arose which seemed to the judges to call for relief not directly warranted by precedent, the case was apt to be decided on broad and vague grounds of "natural justice" and an unanalyzed sense of right and wrong, and of what was fair and just from a lay point of view. There is astonishingly little close legal reasoning in our modern sense; there are very few instances of an elaborate chain of analysis and deduction anywhere in the old reports. Toward the middle of the eighteenth century the tendency to decide unprovided cases on the basis of so-called natural justice increased, and many of the most famous decisions of Lord Mansfield can

---

* Sir Edward Coke was born on February 1, 1551 or 1552. A lawyer, he became Solicitor-General in 1592, a member and speaker of the House of Commons in 1593 and Attorney-General in 1594. He was made chief justice of the Common Pleas by James I in 1606 and of the King's Bench in 1613. Because of his resistance to the King and Court of Chancery, he was removed from his office in 1616 and committed to the Tower of London. Coke was again returned to Parliament in 1621 and died in 1633. His principal works are the so-called Institutes of the Laws of England, of which his Commentary on Littleton's Treatise on Tenures is a part. For an excellent biography of Coke, see Bowen, The Lion and the Throne (1957).—Editor

† John Dickinson, General Counsel and Vice President of the Pennsylvania Railroad, taught history, economics, and government at Amherst, Harvard, and Princeton, 1919-21, 1927-29, and has taught law at the Univ. of Penn. since 1929. He was Assistant Secretary of Commerce, 1933-35, Assistant Attorney General of the United States, 1935-37. His books include Administrative Justice and the Supremacy of Law (1927) and Hold Fast the Middle Way (1935).—Editor

be reduced in the last analysis to no other grounds than the opinion of that great Judge that fairness and convenience required the result arrived at. It was this characteristic of Lord Mansfield's decisions which antagonized the latent desire of the bar for more settled and definite grounds of decision, and which justified the reaction under Lord Kenyon toward a more technical and closely reasoned jurisprudence.

The first half of the nineteenth century witnessed a splendid outburst of intellectual effort in the field of the common law which shaped the basic assumptions still current among the legal profession in common-law countries as to the nature of law and the technique of its application. This effort is associated with the names of such jurists as Kent and Story and Parsons in this country and Chitty, Sugden, Williams and Blackburn in England. Carrying forward the thought of the jurists of continental Europe in the preceding century, they conceived law as a system or "science" in the sense of a body of rules all rationally related to and connected with one another in such a way that any given rule can be deduced by a process of logic from other rules already known.[4] The bearing of this conception on the problem of unprovided cases was direct, and its influence enormous. It formed the attitude toward the problem which still prevails, and what has become even more dominant through the influence of the case-method of teaching in the law schools.

The notion that legal rules are so connected rationally that one can be deduced from others leads to the conclusion that in the last analysis there is no such thing as an unprovided case. If the rules which are already established grow out of one another inevitably by a mere process of reasoning, it seems to follow that rules which have never yet been applied because their application has not chanced to be called for are yet fully implicit in the body of existing rules,[5] and that if a new case arises which calls for a hitherto unapplied rule, this rule can at once be deduced from the body of existing rules in the same way in which those rules themselves are supposed to have been deduced. There was thus consciously affirmed the doctrine of the "logical completeness" of the law, with the corollary that when an unprovided case arises the existing law already contains the proper legal ground of decision in spite of the fact that that ground of decision has never been applied in any preceding case. The theory is thus that it is not necessary to go outside the boundaries of existing law to find the ground of decision of new cases; that the law, being complete, is necessarily self-contained, and that the ground of deci-

---

[4] These views resulted from the attempt to treat law as a kind of geometry, possessing mathematical certainty, which was prompted by the great advance of the mathematical sciences in the 17th century and the resulting tendency of other lines of intellectual activity to borrow from mathematics. See Dickinson, Administrative Justice and the Supremacy of Law (Cambridge, 1927) 115, note 15. Quite comparable was the borrowing by other disciplines of the concept of biological evolution in the later 19th century.

[5] "It is supposed that the law contains within itself the materials for the decision of every case, however novel in its circumstances; and accordingly when the judges have a new case before them, they do not profess to arrive at the law by reasoning, by theory, or by philosophical inquiry, but they profess to discover it by searching among the records of former decisions." Lord Westbury, Speech on Revision of the Law, in Wambaugh, The Study of Cases (2d ed. 1894) 75.

sion of new cases is to be sought not in something outside the precedents, like natural justice or a common-sense opinion of right or wrong, but within the body of technical law itself as expressed in the precedents. . . . The process thus indicated was sufficiently technical to satisfy the demands of lawyers who were discontented with a crude appeal to lay considerations of natural justice and fair dealing, and on the other hand promised sufficient flexibility to make the law adaptable to the new cases which were constantly being presented by a progressive and changing civilization. . . .

It is a striking fact that this conception of law as self-contained, and as making it unnecessary to seek grounds of decision for new cases outside existing technical law, took possession of the jurists of Continental Europe during the same period, although the legal environment in which they were working was as different as possible from that of the American and English legal systems during the nineteenth century. The Continental jurists in a country like France were concerned with applying not a system of unwritten rules based on precedents, but a detailed Code which had been adopted in its entirety at a single moment. Nevertheless they took the view that this Code constituted a complete and scientific system of law precisely as the nineteenth century English and American jurists looked on the common law as constituting such a system, and the resulting attitude toward the problem of unprovided cases was the same. . . .

. . . [A]t the end of the nineteenth century . . . again the legal thought of Continental European countries and of common-law countries marched in the same direction at the same time. The rapid changes which were taking place throughout western civilization in prevalent conceptions as to some of the most fundamental human relations and institutions: the position of woman; the institution of marriage and divorce; the relation of parent to child; of employer to employee; of owner to property; the rapid evolution of new types of economic activity and organization; the growth of corporations; the development of banking, and the emergence of new methods of production and transportation, all created an unprecedented mass of novel situations for courts and lawyers to deal with. The attempt to deal with these situations strictly on the basis of rules deduced from pre-established and existing rules created dissatisfaction among jurists. . . .

What chiefly dissatisfied the newer thinkers was the idea that already existing rules of established positive law contained within themselves, and without resort to outside aids, the proper legal solution of all cases that might arise. In France the technique of the great commentators on the Code was challenged on the ground that it made the law too rigid and did not sufficiently permit its adaptation to meet problems which not only were never heard of by the authors of the Code, but would have been inconceivable to them. In Germany the revolt expressed itself in an extreme form in the movement for so-called "free judicial decision" which recommended leaving the decision of cases substantially to the discretion of the judge on the basis of the merits of each case. In the United States, where the older method was felt by many to have led to manifest injustices in the field of the law of husband and wife, master and servant, and constitutional law, the new tendency emerged in the so-called "sociological jurisprudence" sponsored by Dean Pound. The central idea of "sociological jurisprudence" was that the grounds of decision of unprovided cases should be sought not purely in deductions from existing rules but also in the study of social ends and purposes, of current views as to moral and economic values, and in a knowledge of the facts and methods of social and business life which would indicate the appropriate legal devices for attaining the results felt to be socially desirable.

Cardozo, *THE NATURE OF THE JUDICIAL PROCESS*
14-16, 18-25, 28, 30-32, 40-43, 66-67, 161-167 (1921)

Before we can determine the proportions of a blend, we must know the ingredients to be blended. Our first inquiry should therefore be: Where does the judge find the law which he embodies in his judgment? There are times when the source is obvious. The rule that fits the case may be supplied by the constitution or by statute. If that is so, the judge looks no farther. The correspondence ascertained, his duty is to obey. The constitution overrides a statute, but a statute, if consistent with the constitution, overrides the law of judges. In this sense, judge-made law is secondary and subordinate to the law that is made by legislators. . . .

. . . We reach the land of mystery when constitution and statute are silent, and the judge must look to the common law for the rule that fits the case. He is the "living oracle of the law" in Blackstone's vivid phrase. Looking at Sir Oracle in action, viewing his work in the dry light of realism, how does he set about his task?

The first thing he does is to compare the case before him with the precedents, whether stored in his mind or hidden in the books. I do not mean that precedents are ultimate sources of the law, supplying the sole equipment that is needed for the legal armory, the sole tools, to borrow Maitland's phrase, "in the legal smithy." Back of precedents are the basic juridical conceptions which are the postulates of judicial reasoning, and farther back are the habits of life, the institutions of society, in which those conceptions had their origin, and which, by a process of interaction, they have modified in turn. None the less, in a system so highly developed as our own, precedents have so covered the ground that they fix the point of departure from which the labor of the judge begins. Almost invariably, his first step is to examine and compare them. If they are plain and to the point, there may be need of nothing more. *Stare decisis* is at least the everyday working rule of our law. I shall have something to say later about the propriety of relaxing the rule in exceptional conditions. But unless those conditions are present, the work of deciding cases in accordance with precedents that plainly fit them is a process similar in its nature to that of deciding cases in accordance with a statute. It is a process of search, comparison, and little more. Some judges seldom get beyond that process in any case. Their notion of their duty is to match the colors of the case at hand against the colors of many sample cases spread out upon their desk. The sample nearest in shade supplies the applicable rule. But, of course, no system of living law can be evolved by such a process, and no judge of high court, worthy of his office, views the function of his place so narrowly. If that were all there was to our calling, there would be little of intellectual interest about it. The man who had the best card index of the cases would also be the wisest judge. It is when the colors do not match, when the references in the index fail, when there is no decisive precedent, that the serious business of the judge begins. He must then fashion law for the litigants before him. In fashioning it for them, he will be fashioning it for others . . . The sentence of today will make the right and wrong of tomorrow. If the judge is to pronounce it wisely, some principles of selection there must be to guide him among all the potential judgments that compete for recognition.

In the life of the mind as in life elsewhere, there is a tendency toward the reproduction of kind. Every judgment has a generative power. It begets in its own image. Every precedent, in the words of Redlich, has a "directive force for future cases of the same or similar nature." Until the sentence was pronounced, it was as yet in equilibrium. Its form and content were uncertain. Any one of many principles might lay hold of it and shape it. Once declared, it is a new stock of descent. It is charged with vital power. It is the source from which new principles or norms may spring to shape sentences thereafter. If we seek the psychological basis of this tendency, we shall find it, I suppose, in habit. Whatever its psychological basis, it is one of the living forces of our law. Not all the progeny of principles begotten of a judgment survive, however, to maturity. Those that cannot prove their worth and strength by the test of experience, are sacrificed mercilessly and thrown into the void. The common law does not work from pre-established truths of universal and inflexible validity to conclusions derived from them deductively. Its method is inductive, and it draws its generalizations from particulars. The process has been admirably stated by Munroe Smith: "In their effort to give to the social sense of justice articulate expression in rules and in principles, the method of the lawfinding experts has always been experimental. The rules and principles of case law have never been treated as final truths, but as working hypotheses, continually retested in those great laboratories of the law, the courts of justice. Every new case is an experiment; and if the accepted rule which seems applicable yields a result which is felt to be unjust, the rule is reconsidered. It may not be modified at once, for the attempt to do absolute justice in every single case would make the development and maintenance of general rules impossible; but if a rule continues to work injustice, it will eventually be reformulated. The principles themselves are continually retested; for if the rules derived from a principle do not work well, the principle itself must ultimately be re-examined." *

---

* Cf. Levi, An Introduction to Legal Reasoning (1949) 2, 3: ". . . if . . . the doctrine of precedent meant that general rules, once properly determined, remained unchanged and then were applied, albeit imperfectly, in later cases . . . it would be disturbing to find that the rules change from case to case and are remade with each case. Yet this change in the rules is the indispensable dynamic quality of law. It occurs because the scope of a rule of law, and therefore its meaning, depends upon a determination of what facts will be considered similar to those present when the rule was first announced. The finding of similarity or difference is the key step in the legal process. . . . The problem for the law is: When will it be just to treat dif-

The way in which this process of retesting and reformulating works, may be followed in an example. Fifty years ago, I think it would have been stated as a general principle that A. may conduct his business as he pleases, even though the purpose is to cause loss to B., unless the act involves the creation of a nuisance. Spite fences were the stock illustration, and the exemption from liability in such circumstances was supposed to illustrate not the exception, but the rule. Such a rule may have been an adequate working principle to regulate the relations between individuals or classes in a simple or homogeneous community. With the growing complexity of social relations, its inadequacy was revealed. As particular controversies multiplied and the attempt was made to test them by the old principle, it was found that there was something wrong in the results, and this led to a reformulation of the principle itself. Today, most judges are inclined to say that what was once thought to be the exception is the rule, and what was the rule is the exception.† A. may never do anything in his business for the purpose of injuring another without reasonable and just excuse. There has been a new generalization which, applied to new particulars, yields results more in harmony with past particulars, and, what is still more important, more consistent with the social welfare. This work of modification is gradual. It goes on inch by inch. Its effects must be measured, by decades and even centuries. Thus measured, they are seen to have behind them the power and the pressure of the moving glacier. . . .

In this perpetual flux, the problem which confronts the judge is in reality a two-fold one: he must first extract from the precedents the underlying principle, the ratio decidendi; he must then determine the path or direction along which the principle is to move and develop, if it is not to wither and die. . . .

The directive force of a principle may be exerted along the line of logical progression; this I will call the rule of analogy or the method of philosophy; along the line of historical development; this I will call the method of evolution; along the line of the customs of the community; this I will call the method of tradition; along the lines of justice, morals, and social welfare, the mores of the day; and this I will call the method of sociology.

I have put first among the principles of selection to guide our choice of paths, the rule of analogy or the method of philosophy. In putting it first, I do not mean to rate it as most important. On the contrary, it is often sacrificed to others. I have put it first because it has, I think, a certain presumption in its favor. Given a mass of particulars, a congeries of judgments on related topics, the principle that unifies and rationalizes them has a tendency, and a legitimate one, to project and extend itself to new cases within the limits of its capacity to unify and rationalize. It has the primacy that comes from natural and orderly and logical succession. Homage is due to it over every competing principle that is unable by appeal to history or tradition or policy or justice to make out a better right. All sorts of deflecting forces may appear to contest its sway and absorb its power. At least, it is the heir presumptive. A pretender to the title will have to fight his way. . . .

The directive force of logic does not always exert itself, however, along a single and unobstructed path. One principle or precedent, pushed to the limit of its logic, may point to one conclusion: another principle or precedent, followed with like logic, may point with equal certainty to another. In this conflict, we must choose between the two paths, selecting one or other, or perhaps striking out upon a third, which will be the resultant of the two forces in combination, or will represent the mean between extremes. Let me take as an illustration of such conflict the famous case of Riggs v. Palmer, 115 N.Y. 506. That case decided that a legatee who had murdered his testator would not be permitted by a court of equity to enjoy the benefits of the will. Conflicting principles were there in competition for the mastery. One of them prevailed, and vanquished all the others. There was the principle of the binding force of a will disposing of the estate of a testator in conformity with law. That principle, pushed to the limit of its logic, seemed to uphold the title of the murderer. There was the principle that civil courts may not add to the pains and penalties of crimes. That, pushed to the limit of its logic, seemed again to uphold his title. But over against these was another principle, of greater generality, its roots deeply fastened in universal sentiments of justice, the principle that no man should profit from his own inequity or take advantage of his own wrong. The logic of this principle prevailed over the logic of the others. I say its logic prevailed. The thing which really interests us, however, is why and how the choice was made between one logic and another. In this instance, the reason is not obscure. One path was followed, another closed, because of the conviction in the judicial mind that the one selected led to justice. Analogies and precedents and the principles behind them were brought together as rivals for precedence; in the end, the principle that was thought to be most fundamental, to represent the larger and deeper social interests, put its competitors to flight. I am not greatly concerned about the particular formula through which justice was attained. Consistency was preserved, logic received its tribute, by holding that the legal title passed, but that it was subjected to a constructive trust. A constructive trust is nothing but "The formula through which the conscience of equity finds expression." Property is acquired in such circumstances that the holder of the legal title may not in good conscience retain the beneficial interest. Equity, to express its disapproval of his conduct, converts him into a trustee. Such formulas are merely the remedial devices by which a result conceived of as right and just is made to square with principle and with the symmetry of the legal system. What concerns me now is not the remedial device, but rather the underlying motive, the indwelling, creative energy, which brings such devices into play. The murderer lost the legacy for which the murder was committed because the social interest served by refusing to permit the criminal to profit by his crime is greater than that served by the preservation and enforcement of legal rights of ownership. My illustration, indeed, has brought me ahead of my story. The judicial process is there in microcosm. We go forward with our logic, with our analogies, with our philosophies, till we reach a certain point. At first, we have no trouble with the paths; they follow the same lines. Then they begin to diverge, and we must make a choice between them. History or custom or social utility or some compelling sentiment of justice or sometimes perhaps a semi-intuitive apprehension of the pervading spirit of our law, must come to the rescue of the anxious judge, and tell him where to go. . . .

Logic and history and custom have their place. We will shape the law to conform to them when we may; but only within bounds. The end which the law serves will dominate them all. . . . I mean that when [judges] are called upon to say how far existing rules are to be extended or restricted, they must let the welfare of society fix the path, its direction and its distance. . . .

Our survey of judicial methods teaches us, I think, the lesson that the whole subject-matter of jurisprudence is more plastic, more malleable, the moulds less definitively cast, the bounds of right and wrong less preordained and constant, than most of us, without the aid of some such analysis, have been accustomed to believe. We like to picture to ourselves the field of the law as accurately mapped and plotted. We draw our little lines, and they are hardly down before we blur them. As in time and space, so here. Divisions are working hypotheses, adopted for convenience. We are tending more and more toward an appreciation of the truth that, after all, there are few rules; there are chiefly standards and degrees. It is a question of degree whether I have been negligent. It is a question of degree whether in the use of my own land, I have created a nuisance which may be abated by my neighbor. It is a question of degree whether the law which takes my property and limits my conduct, impairs my liberty unduly. So also the duty of a judge becomes itself a question of degree, and he is a useful judge or a poor one as he estimates the measure accurately or loosely. He must balance all his ingredients, his philosophy, his logic, his analogies, his history, his customs, his sense of right, and all the rest, and adding a little here and taking out a little there, must determine, as wisely as he can, which weight shall tip the scales. If this seems a weak and inconclusive summary, I am not sure that the fault is mine. I know he is a wise pharmacist who from a recipe so general can compound a fitting remedy. But the like criticism may be made of most attempts to formulate the principles which regulate the practice of an art. W. Jethro Brown reminds us in a recent paper on "Law and Evolution" that "Sir Joshua Reynolds' book on painting, offers little or no guidance to those who wish to become famous painters. Books on literary styles are notoriously lacking, speaking as a rule, in practical utility." After the wearisome process of analysis has been finished, there must be for every judge a new synthesis which he will have to make for himself. The most that he can hope for is that with long thought and study, with years of practice at the bar or on the bench, and with the aid of that inward grace which comes now and again to the elect of any calling, the analysis may help a little to make the synthesis a true one.

In what I have said, I have thrown, perhaps too much, into the background and the shadow the cases where the controversy turns not upon the rule of law, but upon its application to the facts. Those cases, after all, make up the bulk of the business of the courts. They are important for the litigants concerned in them. They call for intelligence and patience and reasonable discernment on the part of the judges who must decide them. But they leave jurisprudence where it stood before. As applied to such cases, the judicial process, as was said at the outset of these lectures, is a process of search and comparison, and little else. We have to distinguish between the precedents which are merely static, and those which are dynamic. Because the former out-number the latter many times, a sketch of the judicial process which concerns itself almost exclusively with the creative or dynamic element, is likely to give a false impression, an overcolored picture, of uncertainty in the law and of free discretion in the judge. Of the cases that come before the court in which I sit, a majority, I think, could not, with semblance of reason, be decided in any way but one. The law and its application alike are plain. Such cases are predestined, so to speak, to affirmance without opinion. In another and considerable percentage, the rule of law is certain, and the application alone doubtful. A complicated record must be dissected, the narratives of witnesses, more or less incoherent and unintelligible, must be analyzed, to determine whether a given situation comes within one district or another upon the chart of rights and wrongs. The traveler who knows that a railroad crosses his path must look for approaching trains. That is at least the general rule. In numberless litigations the description of the landscape must be studied to see whether vision has been obstructed, whether something has been done or omitted to put the traveler off his guard. Often these cases and others like them provoke difference of opinion among judges. Jurisprudence remains untouched, however, regardless of the outcome. Finally there remains a percentage, not large indeed, and yet not so small as to be negligible, where a decision one way or the other, will count for the future, will advance or retard, sometimes much, sometimes little, the development of the law. These are the cases where the creative element in the judicial process finds its opportunity and power. It is with these cases that I have chiefly concerned myself in all that I have said to you. In a sense it is true of many of them that they might be decided either way. By that I mean that reasons plausible and fairly persuasive might be found for one conclusion as for another. Here come into play that balancing of judgment, that testing and sorting of considerations of analogy and logic and utility and fairness, which I have been trying to describe. Here it is that the judge assumes the function of a lawgiver. I was much troubled in spirit, in my first years upon the bench, to find how trackless was the ocean on which I had embarked. I sought for certainty. I was oppressed and disheartened when I found that the quest for it was futile. I was trying to reach land, the solid land of fixed and settled rules, the paradise of a justice that would declare itself by tokens plainer and more commanding than its pale and glimmering reflections in my own vacillating mind and conscience. I found "with the voyagers in Browning's 'Paracelsus' that the real heaven was always beyond." As the years have gone by, and as I have reflected more and more upon the nature of the judicial process, I have become reconciled to the uncertainty, because I have grown to see it as inevitable. I have grown to see that the process in its highest reaches is not discovery, but creation; and that the doubts and misgivings, the hopes and fears, are part of the travail of mind, the pangs of death and the pangs of birth, in which principles that have served their day expire, and new principles are born.

THE HOLMESIAN VIEW

1. [The Common Law 1 (1881)] The object of this book is to present a general view of the Common Law. To accomplish the task, other tools are needed besides logic. It is something to show that the consistency of a system requires a particular result, but it is not all. The life of the law has not been logic: it has been experience. The felt necessities of the time, the prevalent moral and political theories, intuitions of public policy, avowed or unconscious, have had a good deal more to do than the syllogism in determining the rules by which men should be governed. The law embodies the story of a nation's development through many centuries, and it cannot be dealt with as if it contained only the axioms and corollaries of a book of mathematics. . . .

2. [Codes and the Arrangement of the Law, 5 Am. L. Rev. 1 (1870), reprinted in 44 Harv. L. Rev. 725 (1931)] It is the merit of the common law that it decides the case first and determines the principle afterwards. Looking at the forms of logic it might be inferred that when you have a minor premise and a conclusion, there must be a major, which you are also prepared then and there to assert. But in fact lawyers, like other men, frequently see well enough how they ought to decide on a given state of facts without being very clear as to the ratio decidendi. In cases of first impression Lord Mansfield's often-quoted advice to the business man who was suddenly appointed judge, that he should state his conclusions and not give his reasons, as his judgment would probably be right and the reasons certainly wrong, is not without its application to more educated courts. It is only after a series of determinations on the same subject-matter, that it becomes necessary to "reconcile the cases," as it is called, that is, by a true induction to state the principle which has until then been obscurely felt. And this statement is often modified more than once by new decisions before the abstracted general rule takes its final shape. . . .

3. [The Path of the Law, 10 Harv. L. Rev. 457, 465-466 (1897)] The training of lawyers is a training in logic. The processes of analogy, discrimination and deduction are those in which they are most at home. The language of judicial decision is mainly the language of logic. And the logical method and form flatter that longing for certainty and for repose which is in every human mind. But certainty generally is illusion, and repose is not the destiny of man. Behind the logical form lies a judgment as to the relative worth and importance of competing legislative grounds, often an inarticulate and unconscious judgment, it is true, and yet the very root and nerve of the whole proceeding. You can give any conclusion a logical form. You always can imply a condition in a contract. But why do you imply it? It is because of some belief as to the practice of the community or of a class, or because of some opinion as to policy, or, in short, because of some attitude of yours upon a matter not capable of exact quantitative measurement, and therefore not capable of founding exact logical conclusions. . . . I think that the

judges themselves have failed adequately to recognize their duty of weighing considerations of social advantage. The duty is inevitable, and the result of the often proclaimed judicial aversion to deal with such considerations is simply to leave the very ground and foundation of judgments inarticulate, and often unconscious, as I have said.

4. [Law in Science and Science in Law, 12 Harv. L. Rev. 443, 455, 460 (1899)] I am immensely struck with the blind imitativeness of man when I see how a doctrine, a discrimination, even a phrase, will run in a year or two over the whole English-speaking world. Lately have we not all been bored to death with *volenti non fit injuria,* and with Lord Justice Bowen's remark that it is *volenti* and not *scienti?* * I congratulate any State in whose reports you do not see the maxim and its qualification repeated. I blush to say that I have been as guilty as the rest. Do we not hear every day of taking the risk—an expression which we never heard used as it now is until within a very few years? Do we not hear constantly of invitation and trap—which came into vogue within the memory of many, if not most of those who are here? Heaven forbid that I should find fault with an expression because it is new, or with the last mentioned expressions on any ground! Judges commonly are elderly men, and are more likely to hate at sight any analysis to which they are not accustomed, and which disturbs repose of mind, than to fall in love with novelties. Every living sentence which shows a mind at work for itself is to be welcomed. It is not the first use but the tiresome repetition of inadequate catch words upon which I am observing,—phrases which originally were contributions, but which, by their very felicity, delay further analysis for fifty years. That comes from the same source as dislike of novelty,—intellectual indolence or weakness,—a slackening in the eternal pursuit of the more exact.

The growth of education is an increase in the knowledge of measure. To use words familiar to logic and to science, it is a substitution of quantitative for qualitative judgments. The difference between the criticism of a work of art by a man of perception without technical training and that by a critic of the studio will illustrate what I mean. The first, on seeing a statue, will say, "It is grotesque," a judgment of quality merely; the second will say, "That statue is so many heads high, instead of the normal so many heads." His judgment is one of quantity. On hearing a passage of Beethoven's Ninth Symphony the first will say, "What a gorgeous sudden outburst of sunshine!"—the second, "Yes, great idea to bring in his major third just there, wasn't it?" Well, in the law we only occasionally can reach an absolutely final and quantitative determination, because the worth of the competing social ends which respectively solicit a judgment for the plaintiff or the defendant cannot be reduced to number and accurately fixed. The worth, that is, the intensity of the competing desires, varies with the varying ideals of the time, and, if the desires were constant, we could not get beyond a relative decision that

* "Volenti non fit injuria": one may not recover for an injury to which he has consented or the risk of which he has voluntarily undertaken. This is the "assumption of risk" doctrine which we have seen talked of in the fellow servant cases. "It is volenti and not scienti": i.e., the reason for barring relief is that the injured party chose to run the risk, and not simply that he knew of it.—Editor

one was greater and one was less. But it is of the essence of improvement that we should be as accurate as we can. Now to recur to such expressions as taking the risk and *volenti non fit injuria,* which are very well for once in the sprightly mouth which first applies them, the objection to the repetition of them as accepted legal formulas is that they do not represent a final analysis, but dodge difficulty and responsibility with a rhetorical phrase. When we say that a workman takes a certain risk as incident to his employment, we mean that on some general grounds of policy blindly felt or articulately present to our mind, we read into his contract a term of which he never thought; and the real question in every case is, What are the grounds, and how far do they extend? The question put in that form becomes at once and plainly a question for scientific determination, that is, for quantitative comparison by means of whatever measure we command. When we speak of taking the risk apart from contract, I believe that we merely are expressing what the law means by negligence, when for some reason or other we wish to express it in a conciliatory form. . . .

My object is not so much to point out what seem to me to be fallacies in particular cases as to enforce by various examples and in various applications the need of scrutinizing the reasons for the rules which we follow, and of not being contented with hollow forms of words merely because they have been used very often and have been repeated from one end of the union to the other. We must think things not words, or at least we must constantly translate our words into the facts for which they stand, if we are to keep to the real and the true. I sometimes tell students that the law schools pursue an inspirational combined with a logical method, that is, the postulates are taken for granted upon authority without inquiry into their worth, and then logic is used as the only tool to develop the results. It is a necessary method for the purpose of teaching dogma. But inasmuch as the real justification of a rule of law, if there be one, is that it helps to bring about a social end which we desire, it is no less necessary that those who make and develop the law should have those ends articulately in their minds. I do not expect or think it desirable that the judges should undertake to renovate the law. That is not their province. Indeed precisely because I believe that the world would be just as well off if it lived under laws that differed from ours in many ways, and because I believe that the claim of our especial code to respect is simply that it exists, that it is the one to which we have become accustomed, and not that it represents an eternal principle, I am slow to consent to overruling a precedent, and think that our most important duty is to see that the judicial duel shall be fought out in the accustomed way. But I think it most important to remember whenever a doubtful case arises, with certain analogies on one side and other analogies on the other, that what really is before us is a conflict between two social desires, each of which seeks to extend its dominion over the case, and which cannot both have their way. The social question is which desire is strongest at the point of conflict. The judicial one may be narrower, because one or the other desire may have been expressed in previous decisions to such an extent that logic requires us to assume it to preponderate in the one before us. But if that be clearly so, the case is not a doubtful one. Where there is doubt the simple tool of logic does not suffice, and even if it is disguised and unconscious the judges are called on to exercise the sovereign prerogative of choice.

5. [Dissenting Opinion in Lochner v. New York, 198 U.S. 45, 74 (1905)] General propositions do not decide concrete cases. The decision will depend on a judgment or intuition more subtle than any articulate major premise . . .

6. [Dissenting Opinion in So. Pacific Co. v. Jensen, 244 U.S. 205, 221 (1917)] . . . I recognize without hesitation that judges do and must legislate, but they can do so only interstitially; they are confined from molar to molecular motions. A common-law judge could not say I think the doctrine of consideration a bit of historical nonsense and shall not enforce it in my court. No more could a judge exercising the limited jurisdiction of admiralty say I think well of the common-law rules of master and servant and propose to introduce them here *en bloc.* . . .

FRANK, *LAW AND THE MODERN MIND*
65, 66, 101-104 (1930)

[Consider] the slavish adherence of lawyers to that instrument of reasoning which was worshipped by all men of the Middle Ages—formal logic. How that logic "has kept students of the law going about in circles" is neatly set forth in a recent writing of Professors Oliphant and Hewitt, partly summarized in the following paragraphs:

The school board of Seattle is reported to have insisted that all teachers, as a condition of procuring employment in the Seattle schools, should sign a contract by which they would agree not to join a teachers' union. Suppose that a suit were brought to compel the school board to hire teachers without imposing this condition. If a court were to decide such a suit in favor of the school board, an analysis of its opinion would show that its reasoning was apparently based upon a "fundamental principle." The court would argue that one who is under no duty to enter into a contract with another may stipulate any condition he pleases as a condition to entering into a contract. This principle the court would take as its major premise. It would then state, as a minor premise, that the school board is under no duty to enter into a contract with any particular teachers. The court would then reason syllogistically—that is, it would apply its major premise to its minor premise—and thus reach the conclusion that the school board has a right, as a condition to entering into contracts with teachers, to impose any terms which it pleases, including the stipulation that teachers are not to become members of the teachers' union.

The court would find its major premise in one of two ways. It might state that this liberty of contract was an "abiding and eternal principle of justice,"—a method of finding major premises which many courts employ. Or the court might refer to prior decisions not involving teachers or contracts with governmental officials, and purport to derive this principle "indirectly" from such decisions.

But however the principle is derived, this method of syllogistic reasoning, which is that of formal logic, is the method used by the courts to-day. Because of its use, the courts' conclusions appear inescapable and inevitable. This seeming machine-like certainty, however, is artificial and conceals a fatal weakness. For a decision against the school board might have been rendered and, if so, could have been justified, with reasoning which would have seemed similarly inevitable. The court could have argued thus: Officials administering the trust of public office may not unreasonably discriminate between applicants for employment. That is an eternal principle of justice or a principle to be found in numerous earlier cases. (There is your major premise.) To deny employment to a teacher because he refuses to agree not to join an organization of teachers is an unreasonable discrimination. (And there is your minor premise.) The ineluctable conclusion is that the school board cannot rightfully refuse to hire a teacher because of his refusal to sign a contract by which he agrees not to become a member of the teachers' union.

The weakness of the use of formal logic is now exposed. The court can decide one way or the other and in either case can make its reasoning appear equally flawless. Formal logic is what its name indicates; it deals with form and not with substance. The syllogism will not supply either the major premise or the minor premise. The "joker" is to be found in the selection of these premises. In the great run of cases which come before the courts, the selection of principles, and the determination of whether the facts are to be stated in terms of one or another minor premise, are the chief tasks to be performed. These are difficult tasks, full of hazards and uncertainties, but the hazards and uncertainties are ordinarily concealed by the glib use of formal logic. . . .

While driving at a reckless rate of speed, a man runs over another, causing severe injuries. The driver of the car is drunk at the time. He is indicted for the statutory crime of "assault with intent to kill." The question arises whether his act constitutes that crime or merely the lesser statutory crime of "reckless driving." The courts of several states have held one way, and the courts of several other states have held the other.

The first group maintain that a conviction for assault with intent to kill cannot be sustained in the absence of proof of an actual purpose to inflict death. In the second group of states the courts have said that it was sufficient to constitute such a crime if there was a reckless disregard of the lives of others, such recklessness being said to be the equivalent of actual intent.

With what, then, appears to be the same facts before them, these two groups of courts seem to have sharply divided in their reasoning and in the conclusions at which they have arrived. But upon closer examination it has been revealed by Tulin that, in actual effect, the results arrived at in all these states have been more or less the same. In Georgia, which may be taken as representative of the second group of states, the penalty provided by the statute for reckless driving is far less than that provided, for instance, in Iowa, which is in the first group of states. If, then, a man is indicted in Georgia for reckless driving while drunk, the courts can impose on him only a mild penalty; whereas in Iowa the judge, under an identically worded indictment, can give a stiff sentence. In order to make it possible for the Georgia courts to give a reckless driver virtually the same punishment for the same offense as can be given by an Iowa judge, it is necessary in Georgia to construe the statutory crime of assault with intent to kill so that it will include reckless driving while drunk; if, and only if, the Georgia court so construes the statute, can it impose the same penalty under the same facts as could the Iowa courts under the reckless driving statute. On the other hand, if the Iowa court were to construe the Iowa statute as the Georgia court construes the Georgia statute, the punishment of the reckless driver in Iowa would be too severe.

In other words, the courts in these cases began with the results they desired to accomplish: they wanted to give what they considered to be adequate punishment to drunken drivers: their conclusions determined their reasoning.

But the conception that judges work back from conclusions to principles is so heretical that it seldom finds expression. Daily, judges, in connection with their decisions, deliver so-called opinions in which they purport to set forth the bases of their conclusions. Yet you will study these opinions in vain to discover anything remotely resembling a statement of the actual judging process. They are written in conformity with the time-honored theory. They picture the judge applying rules and principles to the facts, that is, taking some rule or principle (usually derived from opinions in earlier cases) as his major premise, employing the facts of the case as the minor premise, and then coming to his judgment by processes of pure reasoning.

Now and again some judge, more clear-witted and outspoken than his fellows, describes (when off the bench) his methods in more homely terms. Recently Judge Hutcheson essayed such an honest report of the judicial process. He tells us that after canvassing all the available material at his command and duly cogitating on it, he gives his imagination play, "and brooding over the cause, waits for the feeling, the hunch—that intuitive flash of understanding that makes the jump-spark connection between question and decision and at the point where the path is darkest for the judicial feet, sets its light along the way. . . . In feeling or 'hunching' out his decisions, the judge acts not differently from but precisely as the lawyers do in working on their cases, with only this exception, that the lawyer, in having a predetermined destination in view,—to win the law-suit for his client —looks for and regards only those hunches which keep him in the path that he has chosen, while the judge, being merely on his way with a roving commission to find the just solution, will follow his hunch wherever it leads him. . . ."

And Judge Hutcheson adds: "I must premise that I speak now of the judgment or decision, the solution itself, as opposed to the apologia for that decision; the decree, as opposed to the logomachy, the effusion of the judge by which that decree is explained or excused. . . . The judge really decides by feeling and not by judgment, by hunching and not by ratiocination, such ratiocination appearing only in the opinion. The vital motivating impulse for the decision is an intuitive sense of what is right or wrong in the particular case; and the astute judge, having so decided, enlists his every faculty and belabors his laggard mind, not only to justify the intuition to himself, but to make it pass muster with his critics." Accordingly, he passes in review all of the rules, principles, legal categories, and concepts "which he may find useful, directly or by an analogy, so as to select from them those which in his opinion will justify his desired result."

We may accept this as an approximately correct description of how all judges do their thinking. But see the consequences. If the law consists of the decisions of the judges and if those decisions are based on the judges' hunches, then the way in which the judge gets his hunches is the key to the judicial process. Whatever produces the judge's hunches makes the law.

What, then, are the hunch-producers? What are the stimuli which make a judge feel that he should try to justify one conclusion rather than another?

DICKINSON, *LEGAL RULES: THEIR FUNCTION IN THE PROCESS OF DECISION*
79 University of Pennsylvania Law Review 833, 846-848 (1931)

One of the objections brought against legal rules is that . . . in fact the judge reaches his decisions on the basis of his personal reaction towards a case as a whole in its individual uniqueness, and then simply casts about and finds one or another of the forms of words called legal rules which he can attach to his conclusion for the purpose of rationalizing it. This argument against the effectiveness of legal rules is much in the mouth of law-school teachers. The reason why it appeals to them is not far to seek. It is approximately true when applied to decisions of appellate courts which establish creative precedents, and these are precisely the decisions which find their way into "case-books." Here a court in deciding a new case to which one or more rules seem applicable with equal plausibility purports to bring the case under one rule rather than another, and it is quite true in such instances that it is not a rule of law but some nonlegal consideration which ultimately accounts for the decision. This type of case, however, by no means exhausts or even fairly represents the operation of legal rules, and even in cases of this type the influence of rules has often a somewhat larger part than at first sight appears.

There is, however, a large and important class of cases in which it is not too much to say that the outcome is in fact directly dictated by a legal rule without the intervention of judicial discretion in the smallest degree. Suppose, for example, that a purported will is offered for probate which bears the signature of but one witness in a jurisdiction where two are required by the statute. The rule of law which requires that the witnesses shall be two operates with the deadly inevitability of a guillotine to decide the question of probate. Similarly where land is claimed under a deed from a married woman not signed by her husband, in a jurisdiction where the law requires the husband to join in the deed. The automatic operation of direct specific rules of law of this character is seldom sufficiently brought home to professional teachers of law and students in law schools. It does not always appear from a study of litigation, because cases where the rule thus leaves absolutely no doubt are seldom litigated. But this does not mean that the automatic operation of legal rules in situations of this kind is not of the utmost importance from the standpoint of the value of law as an agency of social order. It is one of the great preventives of litigation. It enables counsel to advise their clients with an assurance which does not need to be tested by resort to the courts in every instance. It operates with equal value in another way. Clean-cut and specific rules make it possible for men to accomplish in their business dealing the legal results they intend without the necessity of constant recourse to the courts to resolve doubts. Thus it is well established that a deed expressed in certain words and executed, acknowledged and recorded in a certain way will have the legal effect of transferring land from one person to another without having to be adjudicated. Similarly a check will serve to transfer a right to money in such a way that no doubt will arise about the validity of the transfer. These results are made possible by the practically automatic operation of legal rules which are so simple and specific that legal scholars do not ordinarily find them interesting.

Where the bar is reasonably well educated, cases which reach the stage of litigation are all cases presenting a substantial element of doubt. This doubt is not necessarily, however, as to the legal rule or rules applicable; often the rule is clear, but doubt exists as to the facts of the situation to which it is sought to be applied. . . . Such a case will almost never get beyond a lower court except on a point of evidence or procedure; and therefore the vast mass of litigation of this character is seldom impressed on the attention of teachers who teach from case-books. The conditions of their work invite them, unless consciously vigilant, to overlook the obvious.

In a third variety of cases, which includes most of those decided by appellate courts, the issues are relatively more complex. They involve the application not of a single rule, but of a number of rules. In these cases the part played by any particular rule in determining the decision is less mechanical than in those hitherto considered. Any one rule may dictate or aid in determining the decision of a particular issue which will affect the ultimate decision of the case as a whole without necessarily determining it. Thus a legal rule applicable to one issue frequently operates merely to determine whether or not there are other issues in the case which are entitled to determination. For example there is a New Jersey rule that whether or not certain kinds of fraud afford ground for dissolving a marriage depends on whether or not the marriage was consummated. Here the rule requires that the fact of nonconsummation must be established before it becomes important to determine whether or not fraud of the character in question has been committed. Only if the marriage has [not] been consummated is the fraud material. Similarly in actions against carriers, where the plaintiff has taken a bill of lading with a clause exempting the carrier from liability, the legal rule allowing or denying effect to such an exemption stands guard at the outset of the case to determine whether or not the issues relating to the cause and nature of the damage are entitled to influence the decision.

In cases of any complexity it may thus be said that legal rules, even of a highly specific character, operate on the decision mainly by determining whether or not any issues, and if so which ones, remain to be decided in order to reach an ultimate decision of the case—operate, that is by guiding the attention of the adjudicating official to certain particular issues rather than others, and by making his ultimate decision of the case as a whole meet the test of consistency with the decisions which are determined or influenced by the pertinent rules as to these particular issues. In the absence of rules, the attention of the official would be free to wander at large over the manifold elements of the case so that the ultimate decision might be reached on the basis of any factor or factors which for the time being loomed largest to the judge's mind. The operation of rules is to make certain factors the primary elements before the judge's attention, and to push other considerations into the background until he has reached conclusions on those which the rules single out as primary. It thus helps him to decide without making the ultimate decision for him; it supplies a structure for his thought to follow, it draws a sketch map for him of the way into and through a case. . . .*

LLEWELLYN, *REMARKS ON THE THEORY OF APPELLATE DECISION*
3 Vanderbilt Law Review 395-398 (1950)

One does not progress far into legal life without learning that there is no single right and accurate way of reading one case, or of reading a bunch of cases. For

(1) Impeccable and correct doctrine makes clear that a case "holds" with authority only so much of what the opinion says as is absolutely necessary to sustain the judgment. Anything else is unnecessary and "distinguishable" and non-controlling for the future. Indeed, if the judgment rests on two, three or four rulings, any of them can be rightly and righteously knocked out, for the future, as being thus "unnecessary." Moreover, any distinction on the facts is rightly and righteously a reason for distinguishing and therefore disregarding the prior alleged holding. But

(2) Doctrine equally impeccable and correct makes clear that a case "holds" with authority the rule on which the court there chose to rest the judgment; more, that that rule covers, with full authority, cases which are plainly distinguishable on their facts and their issue, whenever the reason for the rule extends to cover them. Indeed, it is unnecessary for a rule or principle to have led to the decision in the prior case, or even to have been phrased therein, in order to be seen as controlling in the new case: (a) "We there said . . ." (b) "That case necessarily decided. . . ."

These divergent and indeed conflicting correct ways of handling or reading a single prior case as one "determines" what it authoritatively holds, have their counterparts in regard to the authority of a series or body of cases. Thus

(1) It is correct to see that "That rule is too well settled in this jurisdiction to be disturbed"; and so to apply it to a wholly novel circumstance. But

(2) It is no less correct to see that "The rule has never been extended to a case like the present"; and so to refuse to apply it: "We here limit the rule." Again,

(3) It is no less correct to look over the prior "applications" of "the rule" and rework them into a wholly new formulation of "the true rule" or "true principle" which knocks out some of the prior cases as simply "misapplications" and then builds up the others.

---

* Professor Walter Wheeler Cook regarded legal rules as "tools with which to work; as tools without which we cannot work effec- tively." Cook, The Logical and Legal Basis of the Conflict of Laws, 33 Yale L.J. 457, 487 (1924).—Editor.

In the work of a single opinion-day I have observed 26 different, describable ways in which one of our best state courts handled its own prior cases, repeatedly using three to six different ways within a single opinion.

What is important is that *all* 26 ways (plus a dozen others which happened not to be in use that day) are correct. They represent not "evasion," but sound use, application and development of precedent. They represent not "departure from," but sound continuation of, our system of precedent as it has come down to us. The major defect in that system is a mistaken idea which many lawyers have about it—to wit, the idea that the cases themselves and in themselves, plus the correct rules on how to handle cases, provide one single correct answer to a disputed issue of law. In fact the available correct answers are two, three, or ten. The question is: *Which* of the available correct answers will the court *select*—and *why?* For since there is always more than one available correct answer, the court always has to select.

True, the selection is frequently almost automatic. The type of distinction or expansion which is always *technically* available may be psychologically or sociologically unavailable. This may be because of (a) the current tradition of the court or because of (b) the current temper of the court or because of (c) the sense of the situation as the court sees that sense. (There are other possible reasons a-plenty, but these three are the most frequent and commonly the most weighty.)

The *current tradition* of the court is a matter of period-style in the craft of judging. In 1820-1850 our courts felt in general a freedom and duty to move in the manner typified in our thought by Mansfield and Marshall. "Precedent" guided, but "principle" controlled; and nothing was good "Principle" which did not look like wisdom-in-result for the welfare of All-of-us. In 1880-1910, on the other hand, our courts felt in general a prime duty to order within the law and a duty to resist any "outside" influence. "Precedent" was to control, not merely to guide; "Principle" was to be tested by whether it made for order in the law, not by whether it made wisdom-in-result. "Legal" Principle could not be subjected to "political" tests; even legislation was resisted as disturbing. Since 1920 the earlier style (the "Grand Style") has been working its way back into general use by our courts, though the language of the opinions moves still dominantly (though waningly) in the style (the "Formal Style") of the late 19th century. In any particular court what needs study is how far along the process has gotten. The best material for study is the latest volume of reports, read in sequence from page 1 through to the end: the current mine-run of the work.

The *current temper* of the court is reflected in the same material, and represents the court's tradition as modified by its personnel. For it is plain that the two earlier period-styles represent also two eternal types of human being. There is the man who loves creativeness, who can without loss of sleep combine risk-taking with responsibility, who sees and feels institutions as things built and to be built to serve functions, and who sees the functions as vital and law as a tool to be eternally reoriented to justice and to general welfare. There is the other man who loves order, who finds risk uncomfortable and has seen so much irresponsible or unwise innovation that responsibility to him means caution, who sees and feels institutions as the tested, slow-built ways which for all their faults are man's sole safeguard against relapse into barbarism, and who regards reorientation of the law in our polity as essentially committed to the legislature. Commonly a man of such temper has also a craftsman's pride in clean craftsman's work, and commonly he does not view with too much sympathy any ill-done legislative job of attempted reorientation.[1] Judges, like other men, range up and down the scale between the extremes of either type of temper, and in this aspect (as in the aspect of intellectual power and acumen or of personal force or persuasiveness) the constellation of the personnel on a particular bench at a particular time plays its important part in urging the court toward a more literal or a more creative selection among the available accepted and correct "ways" of handling precedent.

More vital, if possible, than either of the above is *the sense of the situation as seen by the court*. Thus in the very heyday of the formal period our courts moved into tremendous creative expansion of precedent in regard to the labor injunction and the due process clause. What they saw as sense to be achieved, and desperately needed, there broke through all trammels of the current period-style. Whereas the most creative-minded court working in the most creative period-style will happily and literally apply a formula without discussion, and even relief, if the formula makes sense and yields justice in the situation and the case.

So strongly does the felt sense of the situation and the case affect the court's choice of techniques for reading or interpreting and then applying the authorities that one may fairly lay down certain generalizations:

A. In some six appealed cases out of ten the court feels this sense so clearly that lining up the authorities comes close to being an automatic job. *In the very process of reading* an authority a distinction leaps to the eye, and that is "all" that that case holds; or the language of another authority (whether or not "really" in point) shines forth as "clearly stating the true rule." Trouble comes when the cases do not line up this clearly and semi-automatically, when they therefore call for intellectual labor, even at times for a conclusion that the law as given will not allow the sensible result to be reached. Or trouble comes when the sense of the situation is not clear.

B. Technical leeways correctly available when the sense of the situation and the case call for their use cease to be correctly available *unless used in furtherance of what the court sees as such sense*. There is here in our system of precedent an element of uprightness, or conscience, of judicial responsibility; and motive becomes a factor in determining what techniques are correct and right. Today, in contrast with 1890, it may be fairly stated that even the literal application of a thoroughly established rule is not correct in a case or situation in which that application does not make sense unless the court in honest conscience feels forced by its office to make the application.

---

[1] Intellectually, this last attitude is at odds with the idea that reorientation is for the legislature. Emotionally, it is not. Apart from the rather general resistance to change which normally companions orderliness of mind, there is a legitimate feeling that within a team team-play is called for, that it is passing the buck to thrust onto a court the labor of making a legislative job make sense and become workable.

C. Collateral to B, but deserving of separate statement, is the proposition that *the greater the felt need, because of felt sense, the wider is the leeway correctly and properly available in reshaping an authority or the authorities.* What is both proper and to be expected in an extreme case would become abuse and judicial usurpation if made daily practice in the mine-run of cases. All courts worthy of their office feel this in their bones, as being inherent in our system of precedent. They show the feeling in their work. Where differences appear is where they should appear: in divergent sizings up of what is sense, and of how great the need may be in any situation.

One last thing remains to be said about "sense."

There is a sense of the *type of situation* to be contrasted with the sense of a *particular controversy* between particular litigants. Which of these aspects of sense a court responds to more strongly makes a tremendous difference. Response primarily to the sense of the particular controversy is, in the first place, dangerous because a particular controversy may not be typical, and because it is hard to disentangle general sense from personalities and from "fireside" equities. Such response is dangerous in the second place because it leads readily to finding an out *for this case only*—and that leads to a complicating multiplicity of refinement and distinction, as also to repeated resort to analogies unthought through and unfortunate of extension. This is what the proverb seeks to say: "Hard cases make bad law."

If on the other hand the type of situation is in the forefront of attention, a solving rule comes in for much more thoughtful testing and study. Rules are thrust toward reasonable simplicity, and made with broader vision. Moreover, the idiosyncrasies of the particular case and its possible emotional deflections are set for judgment against a broader picture which gives a fair chance that accidental sympathy is not mistaken for long-range justice for all. And one runs a better chance of skirting the incidence of the other proverb: "Bad law makes hard cases."

EDITORIAL NOTE: "IMPLIED" CONTRACT TERMS
and OTHER LEGAL FICTIONS

In the fellow-servant cases, the courts "implied" conditions in the contract of employment—that the employee agreed to assume the risk of injury from a fellow-servant's negligence—to which, as the courts themselves acknowledged, the injured employee had not agreed either expressly or, in fact, impliedly. As Shaw stated in the Farwell case, the implication rested on the usual "basis on which implied promises are raised, being duties legally inferred from a consideration of what is best adapted to promote the benefit of all persons concerned, under given circumstances." The implied "promise" was itself a legal fiction, used to promote what was deemed to be justice. And because it was deemed just to permit an employee to recover damages under the circumstances calling for the application of the "safe-place and safe-equipment" rule, the fiction was invoked that the injury was caused by the employer's "own" negligence or that the employer "impliedly agreed" to be liable in such cases.

A colorful analogy to the use of legal fictions is supplied by this passage from Pound, Law in Books and Law in Action, 44 Am. L. Rev. 12 (1910):

When Tom Sawyer and Huck Finn had determined to rescue Jim by digging under the cabin where he was confined, it seemed to the uninformed lay mind of Huck Finn that some old picks the boys had found were the proper implements to use. But Tom knew better. From reading he knew what was the right course in such cases, and he called for case-knives.* "It don't make no difference," said Tom, "how foolish it is, it's the *right way*—and it's the regular way. And there ain't no other way that I ever heard of, and I've read all the books that gives any information about these things. They always dig out with a case-knife." So, in deference to the books and the proprieties, the boys set to work with case-knives. But after they had dug till nearly midnight and they were tired and their hands were blistered, and they had made little progress, a light came to Tom's legal mind. He dropped his knife and, turning to Huck, said firmly, "Gimme a case-knife." Let Huck tell the rest:

"He had his own by him, but I handed him mine. He flung it down and says, 'Gimme a *case-knife*.'

"I didn't know just what to do—but then I thought. I scratched around amongst the old tools and got a pickaxe and give it to him, and he took it and went to work and never said a word.

"He was always just that particular. *Full of principle*."

Tom had made over again one of the earliest discoveries of the law. When tradition prescribed case-knives for those tasks for which pickaxes were better adapted, it seemed better to our forefathers, after a little vain struggle with case-knives, to adhere to principle—but use the pickaxe. They granted that law ought not to change. Changes in law were full of danger. But, on the other hand, it was highly inconvenient to use case-knives. And so the law has always managed to get a pickaxe in its hands, though it steadfastly demanded a case-knife, and to wield it in the virtuous belief that it was using the approved instrument.

There are many classic instances of the law's adopting Tom's logic of fictions. Four illustrations are given below.

1. *Corporations and Diversity-of-Citizenship Suits in Federal Courts.* The following observations are from Frank, Law and the Modern Mind 24 (1930):

Under our Federal constitution and statutes the Federal courts may hear only a limited class of cases. If the subject matter of a dispute is not within any of these classes, the parties cannot ordinarily seek relief in the Federal as distinguished from the state courts. It is expressly provided, however, that, regardless of the nature of the subject matter, suit may be brought in the Federal courts whenever the controversy is one "between citizens of different states."

In other words, whatever the nature of the dispute, Jones, a citizen of Massachusetts, can sue Smith, a citizen of Rhode Island in the Federal courts.

* "Case-knife": "a knife carried, or such as is kept, in a sheath or case, such knives formerly being often used at table; hence, sometimes a table knife." Webster's New International Dictionary.—Editor

Early in its career the United States Supreme Court was called on to consider whether, for the purpose of such suits, a corporation is a "citizen": If Jones of Massachusetts brings suit in the United States District Court against the Smith Corporation, organized in Rhode Island [*Note:* Every corporation is organized under the statutes of some particular state, and is said to be "incorporated" in such state—Editor], can it be said that there exists a controversy "between citizens of different states"? No, said the Supreme Court. The controversy is between a citizen and a corporation. A corporation is obviously not a citizen. Therefore there is no controversy between citizens of different states and we cannot hear the case.

Subsequently other cases arose in which, in spite of the earlier ruling, the Court felt constrained, for practical reasons, to permit such suits. And gradually the Court evolved a rule that, while a corporation is not a citizen, yet in actual effect and for this special purpose, it will be treated exactly as if it were a citizen of the state in which it is incorporated. The Court, to all intents and purposes has abandoned its original doctrine. But, by the use of involved verbal processes (set forth . . . below) it still adheres to its original statement that a corporation is not a citizen.*

2. *Effect of Gross Negligence.* As well known an example of fictions as Frank's above example is the following development in the law of personal injury:

(a) The courts early decided that if defendant intentionally damaged plaintiff, defendant could not set up the defense that plaintiff had been guilty of negligence which contributed to cause the damage.

(b) But if defendant merely negligently damaged plaintiff, defendant could set up the defense that plaintiff had likewise been guilty of negligence which contributed to cause his injury. This defense of contributory negligence was held to bar plaintiff's recovery for any part of the damage done

---

* A general outline of the course of reasoning pursued by the court is as follows:

(1) In the first case, the court held that a corporation was not a citizen.

(2) In a later case, where a Rhode Island corporation was sued by a Massachusetts citizen, it was shown that all the stockholders of the corporation were citizens of Rhode Island. The court held that it would peer behind the corporation to observe the real parties, the Rhode Island stockholders, who were being sued in the guise of a corporation. Thus viewing the facts, the opposing parties to the suit were seen to be citizens of different states and the suit was allowed to be maintained in the Federal court.

(3) Then the following type of case arose: A Rhode Island corporation was sued by a citizen of Massachusetts. It appeared that some of the stockholders of the Rhode Island corporation were also citizens of Massachusetts, i.e., of the same state as

the plaintiff. The corporation argued that, pursuant to the rule laid down in case (2), the suit could not be maintained because the court should peer behind the corporation to the real parties; if it did so, then the suit would appear to be between citizens, to be sure, but citizens of the same state. The court refused to accept that "logically" correct position, but avoided it by creating a new rule, holding that in such a case it would be conclusively presumed, regardless of the actual facts, that all the stockholders of the Rhode Island corporation were citizens of Rhode Island. On the basis of such a presumption [a fiction, because not rebuttable], the suit was one between a Massachusetts citizen on the one side and Rhode Island citizens on the other side and the suit could be maintained in the Federal court. In other words, the court was in truth abandoning the rule laid down in case (1) without so admitting . . .

him even though plaintiff's contributory negligence was only a small part of the cause of injury and defendant's negligence was a much greater cause of the injury.

(c) But finally the courts were confronted with cases where the defendant's own negligence was of a peculiarly objectionable type, especially where defendant, though not actually intending to hurt plaintiff, had acted with knowledge of the danger and in conscious or reckless disregard of it. Then the courts ruled that the defendant "must be deemed" to have intentionally injured plaintiff. Defendant was thus liable under rule (a) above.

3. *Effect of Recording a Deed.* When a deed or mortgage is recorded with the proper public official, a person who later buys the property in good faith, not knowing that there has been a previous deed or mortgage, is said to have had "constructive" notice of the prior deed or mortgage and to be bound thereby, and he is not allowed to prove that in fact he did not know of it.

4. *Jurisdiction of Court of Exchequer.* In England the Court of Exchequer was a court which originally had jurisdiction over controversies affecting the King's property and his revenue. But, by an evolution of doctrine, eventually if a plaintiff wished to bring an ordinary personal action against the defendant in the Court of Exchequer, he would allege that he, the plaintiff, was indebted to the King, and that the defendant had refused to discharge a liability to the plaintiff, whereby the plaintiff is the less able (quo minus: whence the writ by which the proceedings were begun was known as a "writ of *Quominus*") to pay the King. Since there was a question of the royal revenues involved, the court had jurisdiction. Finally it became unnecessary for the plaintiff to prove the allegation of his indebtedness to the King, and the allegation was regarded as intended simply to confer jurisdiction on the court.

Plainly, when legal rules and judicial opinions make such assertions—that all stockholders of a Wisconsin corporation are Wisconsin citizens, that, in paragraph 2(c), the defendant must be deemed to have intended to harm plaintiff, or that the purchaser who was in fact innocent must be deemed to have had knowledge of the prior deed or mortgage, or that the plaintiff owes a debt to the King but he needn't prove it—they are relying on statements which they know are, or may be, false. It does not seem reasonable to suppose that such statements are "lies": a lie is an assertion contrary to fact, known to be untrue and made with the intention of deceiving others. Are such statements made to deceive the lawyers, the parties, or the general public? Are they likely to do so for long? Then are the judges deceiving themselves? No: they understand, for example, that it is not invariably true that the stockholders of a corporation organized in Wisconsin are citizens of Wisconsin.

Such statements do not seem, then, to be "lies" (untrue assertions made to deceive others) or "myths" (untrue assertions made in self-deception, i.e., where the speaker does not know himself that his assertion is false). They are "fictions": statements which are not true in fact, but are made with conscious recognition of their falsity. If such statements are not made through the judges' or lawyers' own ignorance, or are not made as lies, to deceive others, why are they made?

Morris R. Cohen suggested [(1931) 6 Encyc. Soc. Sci. 228]:

> The answer is partly that the practical convenience of brevity outweighs the theoretic gain of greater accuracy. But more important is the fact that at all times . . . the law must grow by assimilating new situations to the old, and in moments of innovation we cling all the more to old linguistic forms. The latter minister to the general feeling of security especially where the prevailing myth or make believe is that the judge merely declares the law and cannot change or extend it. That we can obey the law even when making it grow is more than the legal profession itself can often grasp.
>
> From the point of view of social policy fictions are, like eloquence, important in giving emotional drive to propositions that we wish to see accepted. They can be used . . . to soften the shock of innovation or to keep up a pleasant veneration for truths which have been abandoned, as when new allegoric or psychologic meaning is given to old theologic dogmas that we no longer believe. But if fictions sometimes facilitate change they often hinder it by cultivating undue regard for the past. If the social interest in truth were to prevail, we should in our educational and social policies encourage greater regard for literal accuracy even when it hurts national pride and social sensibilities. But no one has seriously suggested penalizing rhetoric and poetic eloquence in the discussion of social issues. The interest in truth is in fact not as great as in the preservation of cherished beliefs, even though the latter involve feelings which while temporarily pleasant prove ultimately to be illusions.

PATTERSON, *JURISPRUDENCE—*
MEN AND IDEAS OF THE LAW
579-594 (1953)

§ 5.05—*Judicial Techniques: The Hardship Case; the Unprovided Case.* From the time when the law student begins to cut his professional eye teeth on into his years of professional advocacy and counseling he is engaged in observing judicial techniques (i.e., types of arguments) as employed in the official opinions of Courts justifying their conclusions. Pound has long emphasized the importance of judicial techniques.[66] Llewellyn has explored judicial reasons and pseudo-reasons with the enthusiasm of an anthropologist studying the behavior of a savage tribe.[67] Professor Paton has recently presented a thorough and well-balanced account of judicial method.[68] Professor Julius Stone's valuable exploration of the "fallacies of the

---

[66] See The Spirit of the Common Law (1921), Ch. VII, "Judicial Empiricism"; An Introduction to the Philosophy of Law (1922), III.

[67] This objectivity seems to me to be implicit in his comments on seven varieties of equivocation in the use of precedents. [47 Yale L.J. 1243, 1244-1246]. See also his report on a study of the cases decided by the New York Court of Appeals on a single day in 1940. (1940) 14 U. Cinc. L. Rev. 203, 208-217.

[68] Paton, A Text-Book of Jurisprudence (1946), Ch. VII; (1951) Ch. VIII.

logical form" in English judicial opinions[69] is more critical of judicial techniques and more skeptical than those others of the influence of avowed legal premises on the mental process by which the decision is reached. . . .

One of the favorite arguments of the nineteenth century was reductio ad absurdum. *Assuming* that a certain proposed decision of the instant case would imply a certain proposition, the judge would then subsume other facts under this proposition and derive a conclusion which was patently untenable or absurd, from which it followed that the initial proposition, and hence the proposed decision should both be rejected. Lord Ellenborough used this argument to support the rule that an offer by mail is ordinarily accepted by the mailing of a letter of acceptance; for if the acceptance is not effective until it is received by the offeror, then why should not the offeree be entitled to receive notice of such receipt?—and so on ad infinitum.[72] Here the argument leads to *practical* consequences, which would be absurd. In arguing (unsuccessfully) against the rule of that case Baron Bramwell later argued that it would produce inconsistency in the legal system, since in other situations of fact a notice is not legally effective until received.[73] In the famous (eventually infamous) case first holding that a master is not liable to pay damages to his servant for injuries resulting from the negligence of his fellow-servant, Lord Abinger argued that to hold the master liable in such a case would make him pay damages to the footman because the carriage-maker had made a defective carriage, and other absurd consequences.[74] This example and several others were cases in which the master would not be liable even if the fellow-servant rule were rejected: The carriage-maker is not a fellow-servant of the footman but an independent contractor for whose faults the master would not be vicariously liable. These inaccuracies on the part of a careful and conscientious judge indicate that he was emotionally upset. Still the rule of "common employment," despite these errors of technique in its origin, continued to be the law in England until modified by statute. In Adams v. Lindsell the argument to absurd consequences was used to justify a right-creating rule; in Priestly v. Fowler, it was used to negate a right. Usually it seems to have been used for conservative ends. The way to refute it was shown in two recent cases in which the court rejected the contention that a certain interpretation of a complex written contract would lead necessarily to certain absurd interpretations in reference to other situations, by saying that it would deal with these other situations when they arose.[75] This argument, too, has its limitations, for some foresight of the future consequences of its holdings is an essential part of the reasoning of an appellate court in English and American law. The reductio ad absurdum argument when cloaked in sarcasm or rhetoric is often a crushing blow. Its vulnerability can be unmasked by stating it in syllogistic form, so that its premises can be attacked separately.

[69] Stone, The Province and Function of Law (1946), Ch. VII.

[72] Adams v. Lindsell, 1 B.&A. 681 (1818).

[73] Household Fire, etc., Co. v. Grant, 4 Exch. Div. 216, 234 (1879).

[74] Priestly v. Fowler, 3 M.&W. 1 (1837).

[75] Sarnia Steamships, Ltd., v. Continental Grain Co., 125 F. 2d 362 (C.C.A. 7 1941) (shipping contract): Johnson v. Maryland Casualty Co., 125 F. 2d 337 (C.C.A. 7 1942) (liability insurance).

Two types of cases bring out the ingenuities of judicial argument: The hardship case and the "unprovided" case.

1. *The Hardship Case.* As the term is here used this type of case is one in which the legal doctrine applicable to the facts is clearly established and yet the consequences of its application are felt to be harsh and unjust or highly inexpedient. Three questions arise as to the hardship case: How does the court recognize a hardship case? By what techniques does it seek to relieve the hardship? What effect does an appellate court's reported decision in such a case have on previously recognized legal doctrine?

Since every appellate judicial decision tends to impose a burden on or deny a claimed benefit to someone, is not every case a hardship case? A sensitive layman might have twinges of conscience on making every decision, no matter which way he decided it. Not so an experienced judge. Even as sensitive a judge as Cardozo concluded that nine-tenths of all the cases that come before an American appellate court are predestined to be decided just one way.[77] In other words, it seems that in this judge's experience nine-tenths of the cases were in the groove and evoked no feeling of hardship. Some of the others are hardship cases: The feeling of decency or the sentiment of rightness[78] or the sense of injustice[79] of one or more of the judges arouses in them a drive to prevent the consequences that would follow from the routine application of established law to the facts. Why should a judge, trained to reason like a lawyer, feel outraged by the results of that reasoning in particular cases? Professor Cahn regards the sense of injustice as partly rational and partly emotional, and so it is in the sense that it includes "the capacity to recognize oppression of another as a species of attack upon himself." Here it is considered to be primarily emotional. In many of the hardship cases some characteristic of the individual claimant's situation which indicates weakness (but which is legally irrelevant in private law under the principle of "equality before the law") arouses sympathy for him or her: The widow who bought from the banker her deceased husband's worthless note, giving her valuable promise;[82] the poor city youth who found his precarious recreation on the springboard projecting over the river from the wealthy railroad's right-of-way;[83] the poor manual worker who loyally crippled himself for life in order to save his employer from injury;[84] a veteran of a recent war, seeking a desperately needed home for his family and himself, who made a contract on Sunday for the purchase of a house.[85] Now these special circumstances were not legally relevant in the first three cases; and in each

---

[77] The Growth of the Law, (1924) 60.

[78] Riezler, Das Rechtsgefühl (1946).

[79] See Cahn, The Sense of Injustice (1949), 13.

[82] Newman & Snell's State Bank v. Hunter, 243 Mich. 331, 220 N.W. 665 (1928).

[83] Hynes v. New York Central R. Co., 231 N.Y. 229, 131 N.E. 898 (1921) (a 4 to 3 decision). The poverty of the deceased was not mentioned in the opinion and is inferred by the present writer from the

place where he went swimming.

[84] Webb v. McGowin, 27 Ala. App. 82, 168 So. 196 (1935), certiorari denied 232 Ala. 374, 168 So. 199 (1936). The poverty of the plaintiff does not appear in the official report; it is inferred from his being a manual laborer.

[85] Chadwick v. Stokes, 162 F. 2d 132 (C.C.A. Pa., 1947). That the plaintiff was a war veteran with a family was here a legally relevant fact.

of them the rule that denied the claim was one which aroused no emotional appeal:
The requirement of consideration (in the first and third); the rule that a landowner's only duty to a trespasser is not wilfully to injure him; and the Sunday
statute. One might explain the court's sense of injustice in the first three cases
rationally by saying that the court saw in the strict award of commutative justice
a violation of distributive justice (§ 4.23). Yet these courts do not give judgment
for plaintiffs just because they are hard up—as rural justices of the peace are
said to do. So the hardship case, as our illustrations reveal it, is jolted out of the
judicial groove by some emotional drive caused by facts which are in many instances legally irrelevant, according to the prevalent norms.

How does the court know about these legally irrelevant facts? If the bits of
evidence in the record were carefully purified of all logically irrelevant facts and
if the opinion of the court were as desiccated as that of a French court, the court
would never know and the reader of its reports would never know of the hardship
factor. Indeed, when the court sternly rejects the appeal of hardship, it usually
reduces the dramatic appeal of the facts, as in the North Carolina case where the
kind neighbor woman saved the defendant from having his head split open by his
irate wife and yet was denied recovery on defendant's gratuitous promise to indemnify plaintiff for injuries sustained.[86] The moral obligation to make recompense
sufficiently appears from the bare facts. At any rate the looseness of trial procedure plus inferences from facts of common knowledge make it possible in some
cases for these extraneous facts to get in. The troublesome thing about relieving
such hardship cases is that the production of emotive facts is necessarily somewhat
chancy, and the risk of unequal treatment of different litigants at different times
is a substantial one.

Now as to techniques: The widow's promise was held not binding because
her deceased husband's worthless note was not "consideration" for it [supra, note
82]. The court resorted to the equivalency concept of consideration which was
ordinarily rejected during the nineteenth century. This technique involved no
torturing of the facts, yet it was not a good professional job because it gave
reasons which the court later could not adhere to. The self-sacrificing employee
was allowed to recover judgment on his employer's promise to pay him a small
pension, on the ground that the moral obligation of the employer to the employee
was a sufficient consideration [supra, note 84]. Here again the technique would
hardly be deemed respectable by most English and American courts. The decision
can scarcely be quarreled with, for the emergency left the employee no time for
bargaining; a better professional job could be done by quasi-contract arguments.[90]
Judge Cardozo's technique in the springboard case [supra, note 83] was far more
subtle: The railroad company did owe a duty of ordinary care to a passerby on
the public waters of the Harlem River; and the boy standing at the end of the
springboard poised to dive was over the public water and not a trespasser when

[86] Harrington v. Taylor, 225 N.C. 690,
36 S. E. 2d 227 (1945); cf. Webb v.
McGowin, *supra*, n. 84.
[90] The opinion referred to the right of a
physician to be paid for his services rendered in an emergency to a man accidentally rendered unconscious. . . .

the railroad's electric wires (negligently maintained, or so the jury might find) fell upon him and killed him. Cardozo's later explanation of the case also emphasized the policy of protecting the person as against the policy of leaving landowners free to take no precautions for the protection of trespassers. In the Sunday law case the court found the veteran's purchase of a home for his family was a "work of necessity" and hence within an exception to the Sunday statute [supra, note 85]. The statute itself provided an exception for hardship cases of "necessity or charity"; yet some stretching of the exception appears.

What effects do hardship cases have on the law? The common maxim, "hard cases make bad law," expresses the view that they establish precedents for legal propositions that do not work well when applied in other cases, or that conflict with other propositions in the legal system. Yet the ratio decidendi of a case can be narrowly or broadly interpreted and if the material facts, using Professor Goodhart's method, are construed narrowly enough the hardship case will be readily distinguishable. Professor Paton ascribes the narrow interpretation that English courts place on their precedents to the necessity of distinguishing inconvenient cases which they do not have power to overrule.[93] Under this view of precedent and even under the looser American method the court's technique of justification in the hardship case would determine the material facts as viewed by the court, and would thus limit the scope of the precedent. Thus if the emergency requiring instantaneous action to save human life were made a part of the material facts in the case where the workman saw his employer below just as he pushed the huge block of wood over the edge, [Supra, note 84] then the precedent would be narrowed to such emergency situations. Cardozo's technique in the Hynes case [Supra, note 83] limited the scope of that case to a narrow interpretation of trespasser. . . . Yet this hedging-in of prior legal doctrine indicates probable further limitations by the same court on future legal doctrine; in short it increases uncertainty. The technique of the widow's-note case [Supra, note 82] seems the worst of those cited, since it places no limit on the scope of judicial supervision of the equivalence of exchange in bargains. Does it apply only to a widow, or to a widow vis-a-vis a banker, or to other kind-hearted relatives? On the whole it would seem better that courts, whether trial or appellate, should not write opinions in hardship cases.

2. *The Unprovided Case.* The term "unprovided case" has been used to refer to a situation of fact for which no law is provided in the present legal system which is jurisdictionally controlling. At the outset it may be asked, how can there be such a case under a mature legal system? Either there are principles, policies or analogies which can guide the court to a decision and provide it with justifications, or, if this be not so, then the procedural rule that the claimant has the burden of establishing his claim in both law and fact would suffice to deny the claim. The term "unprovided case" is here used to mean one for which no close analogy on the facts can be found. Now a modest-violet type of court might deny the claim on the basis of the procedural rule suggested above; yet ordinarily in appellate courts other reasons are given. An example is the claim of a mother

[93] Paton, Jurisprudence (1946) or (1951), § 44, p. 161.

to recover damages from one who alienated the affections of her minor son.[99] The court could find no precedent in American or in English law for enforcing such a claim; yet it said the absence of a precedent was not conclusive. Analogies there were, such as the father's right to recover damages for the seduction of his minor daughter; yet there a claim of loss of services was conventional even if often fictitious. The court concluded that it could find no good reason for enforcing such a claim. Is this "unprovided case" now provided for? The decision denying it established a negative precedent for that jurisdiction.

A more recent unprovided case was the claim of a minor child to recover damages from a woman who had enticed away the father from the family home. The court could find no precedent for enforcing such a claim either in Illinois (whose law was controlling) or in any other Anglo-American court of last resort. However, the court held the claim enforceable, relying formally on an equivocal provision of the Illinois constitution.[1] There were some remote analogies: The liability of one who unjustifiably induces another to commit a tort which harms a third person.[2] The opinion does not rely upon them but rather upon the court's belief that the claim ought to be allowed. This was judicial law-making scarcely disguised. A later case in Minnesota which enforced the minor child's claim against a man who enticed away the mother did a somewhat more cautious professional job.[3] The courts that denied the claim found the case was otherwise provided for in existing law. . . .

§ 5.06—*The Psychology of Judicial Decisions.* The title of this section is an overworked cliche, often used to refer to common sense observations about the mental processes of judges rather than to anything that would be recognized by a psychologist as falling within his science. In the last section the feeling of rightness or the sense of injustice was referred to as the emotional drive in the recognition by a judge of a hardship case, and yet this discussion employed no techniques of psychology. Nor were any employed in drawing the inference that Lord Abinger was emotionally disturbed from the circumstance that he used clearly inaccurate analogies in his reductio ad absurdum. A skillful advocate, about to argue before an appellate court a case that will likely divide the court, and aware that a certain doubtful judge will respond favorably to a certain argument, will make that argument unless it will be likely to alienate other judges who are believed to be favorably predisposed because of other arguments. A judge's attitude toward marriage and divorce may have some bearing upon his decisions in some cases.[8] No course in psychology is needed to observe such influences on judicial behavior.

---

[99] Pyle v. Waechter, 202 Iowa 695, 210 N.W. 926 (1926).

[1] Daily v. Parker, [152 F. 2d 174 (7 Cir. 1945)].

[2] See (1947) 12 Mo. L. Rev. 358, commenting on Johnson v. Luhman, 330 Ill. App. 598, 71 N.E. 2d 810 (1947).

[3] Miller v. Monsen, 228 Minn. 400, 37 N.W. 2d 543 (1949). The court examined the policy arguments of decisions that had rejected such a claim. (There were five decisions contra).

[8] A judge who had for years suffered a heavy matrimonial burden was avoided by lawyers representing wives in matrimonial matters, yet these alleged prejudices may well be exaggerated. Botein, Trial Judge (1952), 189.

While the law student should have his attention called to instances of various kinds of influences on judicial decisions, it remains doubtful whether any useful set of generalizations about them can be made in a law school. Perhaps two exceptions must be made: A course in professional ethics can deal with the permissible limits of advocacy and a course in forensic advocacy can develop the generalizations of an art.

Still, common sense observation can go sadly astray, and psychology has made some discoveries about human nature and conduct and about the technique of observing it. The trained psychologist may prevent the law-trained observer from making some mistakes; and psychology may give the latter some clues by which to interpret and analyze his observations. . . . We shall try to compress our present discussion of the subject under five headings:

1. *Reason and Emotion in the Judicial Process.* American legal realism, like its counterpart in Europe, the "free-law" movement of the early twentieth century, was a revolt against the prevailing belief that judicial decisions resulted inexorably from the logical application of the law to the facts. To show that choices of value were involved in this process and that the preferences of a judge or judges for one value over another were often decisive and were in some sense "emotional" was not very difficult. The movement went further, however, and asserted the dominance of emotion over reason, or made reason a mere ritual. Thus Ehrlich, arguing for judicial freedom of decision, uttered the half-truth: "There is no guaranty of justice save the personality of the judge." [9] Now it is true that a crooked judge or a biased judge can often find ways of circumventing legal norms; yet it is also true that he can sometimes be caught, and that pure-hearted judges sometimes make bad decisions as well as bad law. The anti-rational revolt was strengthened by the view, put forward by Rignano, that all concepts, even those of geometry, are determined by affectivity, a psychologist's attenuated name for emotion.[10] Such a generalization does not help beyond pointing out that one cannot think about anything or make decisions and take action without something that *moves* one. The nature of the mover is still open to question. The English philosopher Hume contended that "reason is, and ought only to be the slave of the passions, and can never pretend to any other office than to serve and obey them." [11] Now it is true that "reason," in the sense of formal logic, is empty of content, that its conclusions are determined by its premises and that in moral reasoning the ultimate major premises are not chosen merely by logic nor merely by observation, but partly by emotion or by authority. Still the question remains, is it possible that a judge's loyalty to the judicial technique in which he has been trained and to the law which he has sworn to uphold can overcome the contrary emotional pulls of particular factual situations or of his political or ethical beliefs which

[9] Ehrlich, (E.), "Judicial Freedom of Decision: Its Principles and Objects" in The Science of Legal Method (1917), 65.

[10] See Rignano, The Psychology of Reasoning (1923), 81, 109: "Every common noun, every concept, is essentially merely an *affective* grouping."

[11] Hume, A Treatise of Human Nature (Oxford, 1896), 415, quoted and discussed in Cairns, Legal Philosophy from Plato to Hegel (1949), 365. Cf. views of James and Dewey, *supra*, § 4.53, n. 81, n. 82.

run contrary to prevailing legal doctrine? It seems not only possible but fairly common that this occurs.[12] To the cases of conscious emotional tension may be added the great bulk of litigation in which the judge has no strong feeling one way or another, in which his principal drive is to do a good professional job. In another sense, too, reason can control emotion: The "cardiac promptings of the moment," to use Cardozo's caustic phrase, can be overcome by reflection and search for long-range and distant consequences of a decision one way or the other. Reflective thinking can be backed by emotions which dominate other emotions. Yet one need not go so far as to expect that the judge will, like Kant's saintly man of pure will, decide in accordance with reason *and not* take satisfaction in so doing.

2. *The Prediction of Judicial Decisions.* The stimulus-response analogy of behaviorism gave Oliphant the clue to a mode of interpreting judicial precedents, which has considerable value, even though it requires one to ignore the opinions of the judges. Given a case involving some genuine doubt about labor unions or monopolies or freedom of speech, during most of the past thirty years, and a shrewd counselor could guess how four to six Supreme Court justices would *vote* on the case with a probability value better than even. (This is, of course, the present writer's estimate.) That is not to say that the justices would all give the same reasons or concur in the same opinion. For clients who expect to have further litigation (such as large corporations and large labor unions) reasons are still important. More recently Professors Lasswell and McDougal have put forward the thesis that a technique of prediction of judicial decisions can be developed. "As scientist, the legal scholar will conceive that the response of any court is affected by two sets of factors: environmental and predispositional." [15] The former refers to what goes on when a case is tried; the latter to factors that existed before the case came before the judge. Here the authors reveal their own predilections by including in the predisposing factors the judge's biases and his attitudes toward the commerce clause or the opinions of Mr. Justice Brandeis, and by omitting the fact that the judge has studied, practiced and read something called "law." They seem to regard "legal norms" as mere conventional justifications contrived for losing counsel and higher courts or as having similar perfunctory uses. Since this nascent science of prediction has been presented publicly only in the terminology stage, one could only conjecture what it would eventually be. As to the trial of issues of fact before a jury (especially under the general verdict plan), Judge Frank's prediction that the outcome will never be predictable[17] seems correct. Even if the predisposing factors of judge and jurymen could be ascertained, could be assigned accurately their quantitative values and placed in a mathematical determinant or similar complex formula for solution by a computing machine, the judge and the jury might assert their independence by responding

[12] My elderly law partner used to dread trying a case before a Federal judge who was a good friend of his, because the judge always leaned over backwards to avoid partiality. Judges who have talked to me about their cases *before they had decided* exemplified the statement of the text. See also Botein, Trial Judge (1952), 309-10.

[15] Lasswell and McDougal, "Legal Education and Public Policy," (1943) 52 Yale L.J., 203, 238-241.

[17] Frank, Courts on Trial (1949), 202-204.

differently. On the other hand the case that comes before a multiple-judge appellate court (where several judges can read the record) has its factual issues drawn and settled and its legal issues drawn; the vagaries of witness-proof and jury-response and trial-judge-response are all past. If, as seems correct, eighty to ninety per cent of the cases taken to appellate courts[18] are predestined to be decided just one way,[19] then it seems that a shrewd and expert counselor, presupposing a skilful advocate on each side, could predict the outcome of appellate litigation with a probability much better than half.

3. *The Relations of Legal Norms to the Mental Processes of the Judge.* The prior discussions of this theme exemplify its difficulties and suggest the answers which here need only be summarized. Legal norms are used as fact-selectors in pleadings and proof and thus set the framework of litigation. They are used to narrow the issues of fact and law so that these become manageable in scope. This framing process reduces the need and the opportunity for judicial creativeness, and increases predictability. Furthermore, the statement of legal issues in terms of competing rules, principles or policies aids in the crucial decision. How does one know that legal norms play any such important parts in the mental processes of judges? Only by what honest men have said. The "hunch" theory of judicial decision was at one time thought to have disposed of the thesis just stated; yet the chief protagonist of that view has corrected that impression.[22] Expert intuition employs generalizations which are not made explicit in consciousness (§ 4.53). Now judges do not, it seems, formulate complete syllogisms, and the judicial stream of consciousness, one may venture to suppose, contains a good deal of non-legal flotsam and jetsam. Men are not transformed psychically when they don judicial robes but they are transformed morally, i.e., in their dominant loyalties. Some judges decide on the whole case first and then proceed to the analysis of reasons; others by analysis build slowly toward a decision. The flash of insight that brings conviction may occur in an instant; yet the preparatory steps are none the less important.

4. *The Relations of the Opinion to the Decision.* . . . Now it seems true that the opinion of a court, even a rather poor specimen, is orderly and clear as compared with the turbulent stream of consciousness of a judge who is thinking toward the decision of a case: The opinion is not a replica of the mental process. Who would want a judicial opinion to imitate the literary style of James Joyce or even of Marcel Proust? In a multiple-judge court, *whose* stream of consciousness should be exhibited in the opinion? The public functions of a judicial opinion call for selection of reasons and for conciseness and clarity in the formulation of them. That the more recent justices of the Supreme Court have been more prolific

---

[18] This figure would include, I suppose, those in which no opinion is written.

[19] Cardozo said nine-tenths are predetermined (The Growth of the Law, 60) and Judge Frank has said this was "perhaps not too wide of the mark." (1948) 13 Law & Contemp. Prob. 369, 374. Cf. Llewellyn in (1940) 14 U. Cinc. L. Rev. at p. 219: "something more than 80 per cent of those cases were clearly predictable in outcome."

[22] *Supra*, § 5.03, n. 46. [The reference is here to Judge Hutcheson's remarks in 14 U. Cinc. L. Rev. 203, 248, 272.—Editor]

in opinions, both concurring and dissenting, than their predecessors is due to their desire to be candid with the bar and the public about their mental processes on important public issues. The opinion of the court may give as "reasons" such vague or garbled concepts as to justify the inference that it does not adequately express the "real" reasons for the decision; yet this does not necessarily signify some dark secret prejudice or sin or frustration of the judge: He may be a poor opinion-writer, or he may have been hurried. Still, a judge's opinion occasionally betrays his emotional disturbance. Lord Abinger, whose opinion in the leading case that originated the fellow-servant rule (a boon to nineteenth century industrial employers) gave evidence of his agitation,[27] was, it seems,[28] concerned about his position as head of the household of a suburban country estate rather than about his investments in industrial enterprises.

The late Professor Edward S. Robinson, a distinguished psychologist who familiarized himself with judicial opinions, gave the best account of the rationalization theory that has yet appeared. Whether the reasons given for the defense of a decision are accurate statements of motivations or are fictitious is a question of fact that cannot be answered "by the loose, lazy and frequently cynical use of such terms as *unconscious complexes* and *rationalization*." [29] "Psychologists are becoming increasingly suspicious of the dark secret urges that are supposed to underlie overt behavior." [Ibid., 175] One can look back into one's motivations and discover "reasons" which were implicit in the mental process; these are not mere post-rationalizations. The individual self is not a lone wolf; its content is "largely social," and so the feeling that a critic will be examining one's conduct makes one prepare a defense. Especially with the appellate judge the need for writing an opinion (not universal) brings the search for justifications into the process of deciding, and thereby both guides and clarifies it. . . .

5. *Individual Personality Factors and Group Pressures.* That some individual personality factors of judges have some influence upon some decisions is a statement which will not here be denied. One of the early proofs of this thesis was Professor C. G. Haines' study of the decisions of New York city magistrates. In 1916, for instance, 17,075 persons were charged (before the magistrates) with intoxication and 92 per cent were convicted; yet one judge discharged 79 per cent of those accused.[32] From these and like statistics Haines drew the conclusion that something else besides "the law" [33] and "the facts" was motivating some magistrates' decisions, though he did not determine what it was. From these cases he went on to the conclusion that the social and economic beliefs of some justices of the United States Supreme Court had more to do with their votes on the regulation of employer-employee relations than the words of the Constitution or the

---

[27] *Supra* § 5.05, n. 74.

[28] The present writer made a study of the life of Lord Abinger some years ago, with a view to determining whether he represented industrialists. All of the evidence that I could find indicated a negative answer.

[29] Robinson, Law and the Lawyers (1935), 174.

[32] Haines, "General Observations on the Effects of Personal, Political and Economic Influences in the Decisions of Judges," (1922) 17 Ill. L. Rev. 96, 106.

[33] The chief examples he used were "intoxication" and "disorderly conduct," neither a model of legal clarity.

Court's precedents. Neither of these examples necessarily shows that the beliefs of judges on politics or any other theme have significant influences in the decision and justification of the vast majority of appellate decisions.

An additional ground for this belief is to be found in the tendency of consultation and discussion among the members of the court to reduce the extreme positions which individual judges might take at the outset. This view, put forward by Oliphant, found some confirmation in experiments conducted by Professor F. H. Allport.[34]

The judicial process will continue to be of great interest to lawyers, to judges, to law teachers and to law students. Case law will continue to be the staple diet of legal education; the method of casuistry can be introduced into the teaching of subjects that are codified. The legal profession can contribute to the improvement of the judicial process in many ways: By not waiting until the last minute to prepare their cases for trial; by not hurling at an appellate court every legal rubric and every citation that has a remote bearing on the case and by not expecting an appellate court to discuss thoroughly every point made. Judges of appellate courts can improve the judicial process by ruthlessly reducing the number of cases in which opinions are written, in order to have time to write opinions selectively and concisely. The public (meaning the voters) could help by getting more able men into judicial office. The law teachers can help by teaching their students that the judicial process must keep on trying to be reason without passion, even though they know that it will never quite make it.

NOTES AND QUESTIONS

1. What does Coke mean by "reason"? Does he mean by it the logic of the syllogism? What does Holmes mean by "logic" in his famous statement that the "life of the law has not been logic: it has been experience"? Does he mean by "logic" what Coke means by "reason"? Or what Frank means by the "formal logic" he disparages? In what sense does Holmes use the term "experience"?

2. Would Coke have agreed with Cardozo that the method of the common law is inductive and that it "draws its generalizations from particulars"? Would Holmes agree? To what extent would you say that the cases we have studied so far support Cardozo's view?

3. Which of the judicial methods described by Cardozo were used in the Priestley, Farwell, the two Chamberlain, and the Wedgwood cases?

4. In what sense should we take Cardozo's statement that "back" of precedents "are the habits of life, the institutions of society"?

5. What, in fact, is the extent of judicial creativeness according to (a) Cardozo; (b) Holmes; (c) Frank; (d) Dickinson; and (e) Llewellyn? To what extent do these writers agree? Is it possible to generalize about this question for all periods in our history? Is there reason to think that the extent of judicial creativeness has been declining in the last fifty years? Do you think the personality of the judge is as important, in this connection, as Llewellyn makes out?

6. What does Holmes mean when he says: "We must think things not words"? Is it

[34] See Allport, Social Psychology (1924), 277-278.

possible, literally, to do so? On the basis of the excerpts from Holmes reprinted above, would it be fair to criticize him, as some writers have done, for seeking to eliminate ideals or values from the law?

7. In discussing the predictability of judicial decision, the writers presented in this section are thinking primarily of predictability on the appellate, not the trial, level. We have touched on the difficulty, if not impossibility, of prediction on the trial level (partly because of the jury) in Chapter 6. On the appellate level, should we be concerned about the predictability of judicial reasoning or judicial decision? Is not Frank asking too much when he demands the former? Is it not sufficient, in the drunken driver case he gives, that we are able to predict severe punishment in every state?

8. After maintaining that "Whatever produces the judge's hunches makes the law," Frank states that the crucial question is "What . . . are the hunch-producers"? Would it be wrong to regard the "taught tradition of the law," with which the judge is imbued, as one of the "hunch-producers"?

In any case, does Frank's explanation exclude the influence of authority? Recall how Judge Dixon acted in the second Chamberlain case. Can his action best be explained by his "hunch" or by the weight of authority?

9. Note how closely Frank's view of the judicial opinion as largely rationalization resembles Arnold's scoffing at the "maturing of collective thought." Again we must ask whether the group process of appellate decision-making and the court's obligation to state the reasons for its decision in writing, may not often lead individual judges to discard their "hunches" and alter their initial views?

10. List all the factors that you can think of, including the "legal rules" which may influence a judicial decision. How can one determine the *relative* strength of the factors? Recall, once more, the material presented in Chapter 3.

11. What difference would one's position in the above-surveyed controversy of the role of logic in judicial opinions make for one's work as an advocate?

12. Justice Frankfurter has had occasion to say that Cardozo's book gave "me very little help in deciding any case that came before the [Supreme] Court," because "the business out of which Mr. Justice Cardozo's experience came when he wrote that book . . . was very different business from that with which the United States Supreme Court is now concerned." Frankfurter, Some Observations on Supreme Court Litigation and Legal Education (The Ernst Freund Lecture at the University of Chicago Law School 5, 1953).

13. Do you think courts should continue to resort to the deliberate contrary-to-fact assumption which is the legal fiction? What function does it perform? Would it be accurate to describe daylight-saving time legislation as based on a legal fiction? Can you think of a more effective and painless way of accomplishing the same objective?

14. For further analysis of legal reasoning, see Stone, The Province and Function of Law, chaps. VI and VII and bibliography, pp. 401-411 (1946); Levi, An Introduction to Legal Reasoning (1949); Jensen, Nature of Legal Argument (1957); Dewey, Logical Method and Law, 10 Cornell L.Q. 17 (1924).

For some specific comparisons between a "functional" and "non-functional" approach in judicial reasoning, see Note, Consent, Liability and Guilt: A Study in Judicial Method, 7 Stan. L. Rev. 507 (1955); Note, The Void and Voidable Marriage: A Study in Judicial Method, 7 Stan. L. Rev. 529 (1955).

Black, The People and the Court (1960)
Siffin, The Legislative Council in the American States (1959)
Acheson, A Citizen Looks at Congress (1957)
Griffith, Congress, Its Contemporary Role (1956)
Gross, The Legislative Struggle (1953)
Schriftgiesser, The Lobbyists (1951)
Truman, The Governmental Process (1951)
Hurst, The Growth of American Law 23-85 (1950)
Bentley, The Process of Government (1949 reissue)
Bailey, Congress Makes a Law (1949)
Burns, Congress on Trial (1949)
Newman and Miller, The Control of Atomic Energy (1948)
Galloway, Congress at the Crossroads (1946)
Key, Politics, Parties and Pressure Groups (1942)
Wilson, Congressional Government (1885)

For an excellent bibliography on the interpretation of statutes, see Sanders and Wade, Legal Writings on Statutory Construction, 3 Vanderbilt Law Review 569 (1950).

CHAPTER Nine

EMPLOYERS' LIABILITY LEGISLATION and ITS JUDICIAL CONSTRUCTION

Section 1

HISTORY and BACKGROUND of the LEGISLATION

EDITORIAL NOTE: SUMMARY of COMMON LAW DOCTRINES CONCERNING EMPLOYERS' LIABILITY *

1. *Liability of employer to employee for employer's personal conduct:* The employer, if a natural person, was held liable to an employee (1) if he intentionally and without justification inflicted harm on the employee; or (2) if he unintentionally but negligently inflicted harm on the employee.

2. *Liability of employer to an employee for harm inflicted by another employee:*

a. Though an employer might be generally liable towards strangers for injury inflicted by the negligence of its employees, it was not liable on the same bases to one of its employees for injury negligently inflicted upon that employee by a second employee. The employer here enjoyed three possible defenses:

(1) The fellow-servant rule: the employer was not liable to Servant One for injury negligently inflicted upon Servant One by Servant Two, even though at the time Two was acting in the course of his employment. The rule was subject to important qualifications: (a) A principal problem of the development of the rule was the reconciliation of the defense with the equally established duty of the employer, described below, to furnish a safe place and safe facilities for work. (b) The scope of the defense was also narrowed in some jurisdictions by the "departmental" and "vice-principal" rules: rules that the employer was liable to Servant One if Servant Two was in a different department of the business from One (and hence in this sense was not a fellow-servant of One), or if Two was in a position of authority over One (and so in this sense was not a fellow-servant of One). Despite some wavering in the cases, the Wisconsin court seems generally to have rejected emphasis on these factors.

(2) Assumption of risk: The employee could not recover for injury

* Before reading this Note, the student should reread the related material in Chap- ter 2, section 2, note 4, following Priestley v. Fowler.—Editor

arising out of ordinary, continuing risks of the employment of which he in fact knew or reasonably could have known. The employer's duties to furnish to an inexperienced employee, or one unfamiliar with the particular working conditions, information of risks involved modified somewhat the scope of the defense. (See the extract from Shearman and Redfield, below).

(3) Contributory negligence: "Contributory negligence" defeated many actions. If the plaintiff employee had been guilty himself of any negligence which was a contributing cause of the injury, he was barred from recovery entirely. The effectiveness of "contributory negligence" as a bar to an action was heightened in some jurisdictions by rulings to the effect that it was not matter of defense, the burden of proof of which would rest on defendant, but that the burden of proof was on the plaintiff, as part of his original case, to prove that no negligence of his had contributed to his injury.

b. The employer, however, was under a duty "to use reasonable or ordinary care to secure the safety of the servant while engaged in the service, and to that end:

"(1) To use reasonable or ordinary care to provide and maintain safe places to work and safe ways of passage over his premises.

"(2) To use ordinary care to provide and maintain reasonably safe machinery, tools and appliances; not including, however, liability for secret defects, not discoverable by ordinary care in selection and inspection.

"(3) To establish and promulgate rules and regulations for the reasonably safe conduct of a dangerous or complex service.

"(4) To give special instruction where youth, inexperience, unusual methods of operation, dangerous work out of the course of employment, or new devices in machinery, reasonably require it.

"(5) To use reasonable or ordinary care to provide competent co-employees and an adequate number of them; and to employ those only who are competent." 1 Shearman and Redfield, Law of Negligence (6th ed. 1913) 437-438.

3. *Effect of agreements between employer and employee regarding injuries to employee in the course of employment:* (1) It was a frequent practice for an employee to give his employer, in consideration of the employment, an advance agreement or release, that the employer should not be liable to the employee for any injury happening to the employee in the course of the employment. At common law, the courts differed as to the legal effectiveness of such agreements; many courts, as we saw, refused to enforce these agreements on the ground that they were contrary to public policy. (2) Apart from such agreements purporting to regulate the parties' relation regarding possible future injuries, the courts confronted problems of the validity of a release of liability given as part of a settlement or compromise

reached after an injury had occurred. In the absence of fraud or physical duress on the part of the employer, or in some cases material mistakes of fact or misunderstandings of facts by the employee, such settlement agreements were valid.

4. *Recovery of damages by the survivors of an employee who died of his injuries:* A serious limitation upon the scope of common law relief for injuries for which the employer was otherwise liable was the common law doctrine that a cause of action for personal injury wrongfully inflicted by another or for which another was legally responsible did not survive the death of the injured person. This meant that his estate could not sue for damages for the injury, pain, and suffering undergone by the injured person after the injury and before his death. Further, the common law refused to recognize any separate right of action in the surviving spouse, children, or relatives of the decedent for damage caused directly to them by the wrongful death, even though they had been dependent on the decedent for support.

5. *Method of recovery by injured employee:* The injured employee at common law could obtain recompense for the harm done him by bringing a lawsuit, which would be tried before a judge and jury. The jury determined the amount of damages to which the plaintiff was entitled, and could give damages based not only on loss of time and loss of future working capacity, but also for pain and suffering as well as medical expenses. The existence of damages was determined on the basis of evidence introduced at the trial. As we have seen, the "general verdict" form of the jury's determination gave the jury considerable power to deviate from the letter of the judge's instructions; and, on the other hand, procedural devices were available (e.g., demurrers, nonsuits, motions in arrest of judgment, motions to set aside verdicts) enabling a judge to forestall or override this exercise of jury power.

EDITORIAL NOTE: SUMMARY of EMPLOYERS' LIABILITY LEGISLATION PRECEDING the WORKMEN'S COMPENSATION ACT

After 1875 the legislature of Wisconsin, like the legislatures of other states, began to pass laws pertaining to the problem of industrial accidents. Enacted piecemeal, these statutes represented no general or coherent attack upon the problem. Fundamental points in the relation of such legislation to the common law were these:

1. *Basis of employer's liability:* Liability under this legislation was still based primarily on fault, either the personal fault of the employer, or the fault of the employee who caused the accident.

2. *Definition of the employer's duty to furnish a safe place and safe equipment for work:* Much of the legislation pertaining to conditions of

work laid down specific duties of care with reference to particular places or tools of work, and in this way served in some degree to render more definite the general "safe place" duty of the employer.

3. *Statutory changes in employer's defenses:* In the period between 1875 and 1910 the defenses of the fellow-servant rule and assumption of risk were abolished or modified as to some types of industries. The defense of contributory negligence was generally permitted to stand. Some statutes declared to be illegal any agreements of employees releasing the employer from liability for injuries which might occur.

4. *Recovery of damages by survivors of an employee who died of his injuries:* Legislation was enacted widely permitting recovery by certain dependents or next of kin not only of damages which the employee might have recovered had he lived, but also of damages for the loss suffered by the survivors through the employee's death.

5. *Method of recovery:* Under the employers' liability legislation, as at common law, the injured employee or his dependents sought relief by an action at law for damages; the suit was tried by a judge and jury; and the jury determined the amount of damages, except that in an action by survivors (see paragraph 4, above) the amount of recovery was limited by the terms of the statute permitting the action.

The following excerpts from a standard treatise on the history of workmen's compensation place the Wisconsin employers' liability legislation in the setting of developments in the United States and Great Britain.

Dodd,* *ADMINISTRATION OF WORKMEN'S*
COMPENSATION
11-19 (1936)

[In England by 1870] . . . dissatisfaction with the fellow-servant defense grew apace and soon spread beyond the class which it particularly affected. In 1877, the House of Commons appointed a committee to investigate the subject and it reported in favor of modifying the law. Three years later, in 1880, the English Employers' Liability Act was passed. It applied, in general, to all manual laborers, except domestic servants. It provided, among other things, that where a workman suffered a personal injury because of defects in the machinery or plant, or from the negligence of anyone in the service of the employer who was entrusted with any superintendence, or from the negligence of an employee who controlled any signal, locomotive engine, or train on a railway, such workman (or his dependents in case of his death), should have the same remedies against the employer as if he had not been a workman—in other words, the remedies a stranger had against the employer. However, a worker could not recover for injuries caused by defects in plant or machine unless such defects arose from, or were not remedied through,

---

* Walter F. Dodd taught political science at the Universities of Illinois and Chicago, was on the Yale Law School faculty, 1927- 33, practiced law in Chicago, and authored several well-known works, particularly in the field of constitutional law.—Editor

the negligence of the employer or superintending servant. The workman, by the terms of the act, was required to give notice of his injury to his employer within six weeks after its occurrence, and to bring action within six months thereafter. The amount of recovery was not to exceed a sum equivalent to the estimated earnings, for the three years preceding injury, of a person in the same grade of a similar employment in the same district. Personal injury suits were triable in the county courts.

The statute effected a modification, rather than the abrogation, of the fellow-servant rule, and did not touch upon the other two defenses. It provided that the clause "person who has superintendence" meant one whose sole duty was superintendence and who was not engaged in manual labor. If, then, a workman was injured by the negligence of a fellow employee of the same rank, he could not recover against the employer. The injured employee still must prove negligence on the part of the employer or superintendent, and he was still held to assume the risk of employment, except the negligent acts of a directing employee. The act did reach those masters who did not personally direct the work in their establishments but delegated such duties to others.

Just one year and a half after the Employers' Liability Act took effect in England, the courts held that it was competent for a workman to contract with his employer not to claim compensation for personal injuries under the act, such contract not being against public policy. Thus, what little protection the law had afforded the injured laborer was soon undermined by judicial decision.

In the United States, prior to 1880, five states—Georgia, Iowa, Kansas, Wisconsin, and Wyoming—had enacted statutes which made railway companies liable to employees, as to strangers, for injuries caused by the negligent acts of the railways' servants. Georgia, in 1855, was the first state to pass such a law. In 1873 the Territory of Montana placed on its statute books an act declaring a railroad corporation liable for injuries to all servants who were acting under the orders of superiors, thus confining the law's application to railroads alone. But in 1896 Montana's constitution was held to annul the act. Shortly after the passage of the English Employers' Liability Act in 1880, Alabama and Massachusetts enacted laws modeled thereon. Massachusetts expressly excluded domestic servants and farm laborers from its law's operation. The application of the Alabama law was general and there was an added proviso that it should not be regarded as contributory negligence or assumption of risk for a servant to remain in employment after knowledge of a defect in plant or machinery, unless he were an employee whose duty it was to remedy such defect. In 1893 Indiana passed an employers' liability law which was somewhat similar to that of England. It applied to all corporations except municipal corporations, but not to firms or individuals; but later the act was held unconstitutional, except as to railroads. In 1891 Colorado enacted a statute which was noteworthy as being the first one which entirely abrogated the fellow-servant doctrine in respect to all employments. In some other particulars, the Colorado law was also based on the English statute, and so was that of New York in 1902. The New York law applied to all employments.

In the period between 1885 and 1910, most of the states of the United States

enacted some form of employers' liability law. A few of these were merely codifi-
cations of the rules as to a master's duties to his servants which were already
embodied in the law of these states through judicial decision. The majority of the
statutes, however, effected a modification or abrogation of the fellow-servant doctrine, but their application was to railway companies only.[51] Maryland's law, on
the other hand, included only mining companies, while the laws of Oklahoma and
Montana covered both mines and railroads, and that of Nevada applied to railroads,
mines, and mills.

Some of the state statutes modified the defense of contributory negligence on the
part of the employee by providing that it should not bar recovery where the negligence of the employer in violating a safety statute was the ground of action. Ohio
and the District of Columbia adopted the rule of comparative or proportional
negligence as to all employments. The effect of this was to set off the negligence
of one party against that of the other and to allow the injured employee's negligence, if less than that of the employer, to lessen the amount of damages, rather
than to bar recovery altogether. Nevada applied this doctrine to actions of employees injured in mines, smelters, and ore mills; Maryland to coal mines and
clay works; Oregon to building operations; and nine states and the Federal Government to railroads.[61] Indiana made contributory negligence on the part of the
plaintiff an affirmative defense, to be pleaded and proved by the employer.

Many states by judicial decision adopted the rule that employees did not assume
the risk of their employers' violation of a safety or penal statute passed for the
employees' protection. Ohio, Iowa, and the United States enacted this holding into
law. The Iowa and Ohio statutes applied to all employments. New York provided
that the employee assumed only the ordinary risks of his work, that is, those
inherent in the business, and no others. And Alabama provided that if an employee remained in employment after he had knowledge of a defect in the plant
or machinery, etc., assumption of risk was not a defense. Oregon, South Carolina,
and Virginia applied the Alabama doctrine to railroad employees.

Almost all the states with employers' liability acts, except those whose laws
were based on the English statute, provided that agreements between employees
and employers to exempt the latter from liability were illegal or void. The federal
act also contained this provision. Thus these jurisdictions made certain that their
courts did not follow the English decision permitting contracts of exemption from
liability.

The first Federal Employers' Liability Act was adopted in 1906 and applied
to all employees of common carriers engaged in interstate or foreign commerce

[51] These states were Arkansas (which later included all corporations and mining companies), Florida, Georgia, Iowa, Kansas, Minnesota, Massachusetts, Nebraska, North Carolina, North Dakota, Ohio, Oregon, South Carolina, South Dakota, Texas, Virginia, Wisconsin, and Wyoming.

[61] Georgia, Iowa, Michigan, Nebraska, Nevada, North Dakota, South Dakota, Texas, Wisconsin and the United States.

or in trade or commerce in the District of Columbia or in any territory. This act was held invalid because applicable to employees not engaged in interstate commerce. The act was subsequently held valid as applicable to the District of Columbia and to the territories, and the Federal Employers' Liability Act of 1908 was enacted with respect to such employees of common carriers as are engaged in interstate or foreign commerce. The federal acts included substantially all the modifications of common law defenses contained in previous state statutes, and amount in effect to a codification of statutory gains up to the time of their passage. They were regarded as important forward steps at the time of their passage. If the employee was contributorily negligent, his damages were diminished in proportion thereto, but recovery was not barred; nor was contributory negligence allowed as a defense where the employer violated a safety statute. The employee did not assume the risk of his employer's violation of such a law. Railroads were liable to injured employees for the negligence of their officers, agents, or other employees, or because of defects due to negligence in cars, engines, machinery, tracks, etc. And contracts of exemption from the law's operation were prohibited.

The state and federal employers' liability acts, with all their changes in favor of the employee, succeeded only in lessening the severity of the defenses interposable in industrial injury suits. It was still as necessary for the employee to prove fault on the part of the employer in order to recover as it was under the unmodified common law. The method of procedure which the employee must adopt to gain his rights, namely, court action, remained the same. It was apparent in England, soon after 1880, that the liability law had increased litigation, and at the same time failed to reach many industrial accidents. A bill was introduced in the House of Commons in 1893 which entirely abolished the fellow-servant rule, removed the limit of damages recoverable, and prohibited contracting out of liability. But it left the defenses of contributory negligence and assumption of risk untouched. This bill was criticized on the ground that it did not go far enough, and it failed of passage. Sentiment was expressed in the House of Commons even at that time in favor of a law fixing liability on the employer for industrial accidents without his fault, and pressure for such legislation continued to grow. Stress was laid on the successful operation of the German workmen's compensation insurance laws, which at that time had been in effect for about twelve years. In 1897, representatives of the government in the House of Commons stated in regard to the liability act of 1880:

"The present law is notoriously inadequate; it fails to compensate for accidents if caused by fellow-servants, if contributed to by the injured, and if resulting from the risks of co-occupation; it causes costly litigation, 35 per cent of the amount recovered being legal expense; it leaves the employer ignorant of what his liability is. . . ."

SCHMIDT,* *HISTORY OF LABOR LEGISLATION*
IN WISCONSIN
2-19 (1933)

Wisconsin has changed since the Civil War from a wholly agricultural state to one in which, by 1930, industry was economically more important than agriculture. . . .

Before 1900 . . . we find little to break the purely agricultural character of Wisconsin. Those engaged in industrial occupations in 1900 constituted only 24.1 per cent, or about one-fourth of the population. This proportion had increased since 1880, but still agriculture dominated the state. Labor unions had been organized during the 'eighties, but many of these unions had been weakened by the depression of the early 'nineties and had turned to political action. The Wisconsin State Federation of Labor was seven years old in 1900. Lumber processing and flour milling were still the chief industries, but the manufacture of machines had already indicated its future possibilities of growth. After 1900 industrial development proceeded more rapidly. The period from 1900 to 1930 has also been the period during which all that is significant of Wisconsin's labor legislation has been enacted. The occupations of Wisconsin workers have shifted so that in 1920 and 1930 more were employed in industry than in agriculture. Lumbering and flour milling have fallen from first place in 1900 to tenth and twenty-third places in 1929, and a new industry, the manufacture of automobiles and automobile parts, has taken first place. Without doubt the labor legislation of these thirty years has been a necessary result of the shift from a purely agricultural economy to one in which industry is at least as important as agriculture.

The industrial development of Wisconsin has been concentrated in the east and southeast sections of the state. Milwaukee has been the only large city in the state, with a population in 1930 of 578,249. There have been eighteen cities in the state in the 10,000 to 50,000 class since 1900, with Racine in 1920 and Racine, Madison and Kenosha in 1930 just above 50,000. Much of the manufacturing has been done in the Milwaukee-Racine-Kenosha area. The industrial area which contains these three cities and of which Milwaukee is the center is best measured by considering Milwaukee, Racine and Kenosha counties, since the cities are close together and much manufacturing is done outside the city limits, but still within the three counties.[15] Even in 1880, this area produced 41.7 per cent of the value of the products of the state. This proportion has increased steadily so that in 1929, 54 per cent of the products of the state came from the Milwaukee industrial area.

Other sections of the state have developed industrially, although on a smaller and less concentrated scale than the Milwaukee-Racine-Kenosha area. Sheboygan, Green Bay, Appleton and Oshkosh, north of Milwaukee, comprise an important

---

* The excerpts reprinted are from an unpublished doctoral thesis on deposit at the Library of the University of Wisconsin. The author's statistical tables have been omitted.—Editor

[15] The Census of Manufactures for 1929 adopts, for the first time, the same classification of "Milwaukee industrial area."

industrial area, but still one in which agriculture employs a fair proportion of the population. With the exception of the Milwaukee area, this scattering of small industries through agricultural districts is characteristic of Wisconsin.

The concentration of a large part of Wisconsin industry in the Racine-Milwaukee-Kenosha area and the scattering of the remainder through districts which are both agricultural and industrial gives Wisconsin only one purely industrial section. Only the Milwaukee-Racine-Kenosha area is dominated by industry as are the industrial areas of the eastern states. The rest of Wisconsin's industrial population lives closer to the farm. Manufacturing establishments are small, and in many towns one plant offers the only available industrial employment. Workers shift from farm to city and back again. As a result, the farmers have had political influence in Wisconsin, which is more than proportional to their economic importance.

Section 2

LEGISLATION MODIFYING or ABROGATING the FELLOW-SERVANT RULE; ASPECTS of STATUTORY CONSTRUCTION; LEGISLATIVE ROLE of the EXECUTIVE

LAWS, 1857, Chapter 71

The people of the State of Wisconsin, represented in Senate and Assembly, do enact as follows:

§ 1. That whenever the death of a person shall be caused by a wrongful act, neglect or default, and the act, neglect or default is such as would (if death had not ensued) have entitled the party injured to maintain an action and recover damages in respect thereof; then and in every such case, the person who, or the corporation which would have been liable, if death had not ensued, shall be liable to an action for damages, notwithstanding the death of the person injured, and although the death may have been occasioned under such circumstances as constitute an indictable offence; *Provided,* That such action shall be brought for a death caused in this State, and in some court established by the constitution and laws of the same.

§ 2. Every such action shall be brought by and in the name of the personal representative of such deceased person; and the amount recovered shall belong and be paid over to the husband or widow of such deceased person, if such relative survive him or her; but if no husband or widow survive the deceased, the amount recovered shall be paid over to his or her lineal descendants, and to his or her lineal ancestors in default of such descendants; and in every such action the jury may give such damages, not exceeding $5,000, as they shall deem fair and just in reference to the pecuniary injury resulting from such death to the relatives of the deceased specified in this section; *Provided,* Every such action shall be commenced within two years after the death of such deceased person.

Approved, March 6, 1857.

NOTES AND QUESTIONS

1. Why was this statute necessary?

2. Is this, strictly speaking, an "employers' liability" act?

3. Is the statute of any benefit to the survivors of an injured employee if the employer was not in fact personally responsible for the situation giving rise to the accident?

4. Is it an accurate summary to say that the statute permits recovery by the estate of the damages which the injured employee might have recovered, had he lived?

5. Here the right to bring a lawsuit is defined in a statute; previously we have seen the right to bring a lawsuit defined in judicial decisions. Compare the manner in which the boundaries of the right to sue are marked out in the one method and the other.

6. The present form of this legislation will be found in Wis. Stat. 1959, §§ 331.01-331.04.

LAWS, 1875, Chapter 173

An Act to define the liabilities of railroad companies in relation to damages sustained by their employes.

The people of the State of Wisconsin, represented in Senate and Assembly, do enact as follows:

Section 1. Every railroad company operating any railroad or railway, the line of which shall be situated in whole or in part in this state, shall be liable for all damages sustained within this state by any employe, servant or agent of such company while in the line of his duty as such, and which shall have been caused by the carelessness or negligence of any other agent, employe or servant of such company, in the discharge of or for failing to discharge their proper duty as such; but this act shall not be construed so as to permit a recovery where the negligence of the person so claiming to recover materially contributed to the result complained of.

Section 2. That no contract, receipt, rule or regulation between any employe and a railroad company shall exempt such corporation from the full liability imposed by this act.

Section 3. This act shall take effect from and after its passage and publication.

Approved March 4, 1875. [Published March 18, 1875.—Editor]

NOTES AND QUESTIONS

1. Subsequent history: The act was held constitutional as not involving an unreasonable classification of businesses affected, in Ditberner v. C.M.&St.P.Ry. Co., 47 Wis. 138, 2 N.W. 69 (1879). It was construed not to be retroactive, in Schultz v. C.M.& St.P.Ry. Co., 48 Wis. 375, 4 N.W. 399 (1879). It was repealed by L. 1880, ch. 232. L. 1875, ch. 173 was embodied in Wis. Rev. Stat. 1878 as section 1816 and will, hence, be found cited as section 1816 in most of the cases which arose during its operation.

2. What changes did L. 1875, ch. 173 effect in the common law pattern of liability revealed in the Wisconsin materials previously studied? Is the statute consistent with the fellow-servant rule? Does it abrogate the fellow-servant rule? Does it impose

liability upon the employer without fault? Does it preserve the defense of contributory negligence?

3. Suppose that the plaintiff employee's injury came about not only through defendant's negligence but also through plaintiff's violation of a practicable, enforced safety rule of the company; what would be the company's argument on the basis of language in Section 1? What would be the plaintiff's argument on the basis of Section 2? Consider, in this connection, the Collins safety-rule case in Chapter 7 above—and the fact that the Collins case was decided under a later statute that preserved a contributory negligence defense and also had a section corresponding to Section 2 of this statute. How can the Collins decision be reconciled with the Section 2 language?

4. In Brabbits v. C.&.N.W. Ry. Co., 38 Wis. 289, 299 (1875), the court ruled that the defendant employer was liable for injury caused plaintiff employee by the negligence of a "co-employee" shop foreman in permitting a defective locomotive to continue in service (a case referred to in Chap. 4 in connection with the Wedgwood and Heine cases). The court said, in part:

> "We have considered and determined the case upon common law principles, because, when the plaintiff was injured, there was no statute affecting the liability of the defendant. But since that time, ch. 173, Laws of 1875, has been enacted. . . . In all cases which have arisen since the enactment of that law, or which may hereafter arise, in which a railway company is or may be the defendant, the question here determined cannot arise. And because nearly all actions of this character are brought against railway companies, the question above considered [whether the foreman's negligence barred plaintiff's suit, under the fellow-servant rule—Editor] has become of comparatively little practical importance in this state. We have, however, extensively examined and carefully considered the authorities cited in the arguments of the respective counsel, and only refer to the legislation of 1875 as a reason why we do not deem it our duty in the present case to comment on those authorities at length. Our conclusion is sustained by many of the best considered cases, and we follow them because we believe they rest upon sound principles of law. And perhaps we follow them a little more freely because they accord with the policy of the state in this behalf, as declared and established by the legislation of 1875."

Did the court base its decision against the employer upon the statute? Would it have been proper for it to do so? If not, what legal relevance did the statute have in this case? Why did the court cite it and what use did it make of it?

LAWS, 1889, Chapter 438

An Act to define the liability of railway corporations in relation to damages sustained by their employes.

The people of the state of Wisconsin, represented in Senate and Assembly, do enact as follows:

Section 1. Every railroad corporation doing business in this state, shall be liable for damages sustained by any employe thereof within this state, without contributory negligence on his part, when such damage is caused by the negligence of any train dispatcher, telegraph operator, superintendent, yardmaster, conductor or engineer, or of any other employee, who has charge or control of any stationary signal, target point, block or switch.

Section 2. This act shall take effect and be in force from and after its passage and publication.

Approved April 16, 1889.

QUESTIONS

1. Was the 1889 statute more favorable to employees or less so than the 1875 statute?

2. What effect would you expect the sequence of legislative action from 1875-1889 to have on the way courts would interpret the 1889 statute?

HARTFORD v. NORTHERN PACIFIC R.R. CO.
91 Wis. 374, 64 N.W. 1033 (1895)

[Deceased was a machinist, employed in defendant's repair shops at Waukesha, Wisconsin. Tait was the repair shop foreman. It became necessary, in the course of repairing an engine, to turn the center pair of drive wheels of the engine as it stood in the shop. Tait, in the cab of the engine, applied steam, while deceased applied a steel bar to the wheels. Tait applied steam at a moment when deceased was not prepared, the drive wheels turned and caused the steel bar to strike deceased in the chest. From a judgment entered on a verdict for plaintiff—administratrix of deceased, defendant appeals.—Editor]

MARSHALL, J. Under the most favorable view that can be taken of this case, respondent is not entitled to recover unless the foreman of the repair shops, Mr. Tait, who, it is claimed, applied the steam, was a superintendent within the meaning of ch. 438, Laws of 1889 (S.&B. Ann. Stats. sec. 1816a). As stated, in effect, by counsel for respondent in their printed argument, the action was brought on the theory that Tait was such a superintendent; that he was negligent; and that such negligence was the proximate cause of the injury which resulted in the death of the deceased. On that theory the cause was tried, submitted to the jury, a verdict rendered in plaintiff's favor, and judgment entered, from which this appeal was taken. It follows that, if the construction given to the act by the court below, upon which counsel relies, is wrong, then the judgment is wrong and must be reversed. . . .

The question here presented is not what definition the railroad company now gives to the word "superintendent," or how Webster defines it; but in what sense did the legislature use the word in the act in question? To properly determine such question, resort must be had to the established rules for the judicial construction of statutes. It is said that: "The true rule is to look at the whole and every part of the statute, and the apparent intent derived from the whole, to the subject matter, to the effect and consequences, to the reason and spirit of the law, and thus to ascertain the true meaning of the legislature, though the meaning so ascertained conflict with the literal sense of the words; the sole object being to discover and give effect to the intention of its framers." Ogden v. Glidden, 9 Wis. 46. . . . Applying this test to the act in question, it clearly appears that the legislative intent was to provide a remedy for the negligence of officers and employees that have to do with the operating department of the road, the movement of trains and cars. Each of those specifically named fits persons that, as a matter of common knowledge, are responsible for the proper movement of trains and cars, "train dispatcher, telegraph operator, superintendent, yard master, conductor, or engineer." And following these designations there is the general clause covering various other persons engaged in the same line of work, but who are not so well and commonly known by any specific name applied to their positions, "or of any other employee, who has charge or control of any stationary signal, target point, block or switch." Now, if such was the intent of the framers of the law, and we think it was, then the word "superintendent" cannot be made to apply to a foreman of the repair shop.

Again, it is laid down as an elementary principle in the construction of statutes that the common usage of words at the time of the enactment is a true criterion by which to determine their meaning. Smith, Stat. & Const. Law, § 482. The reason of this rule is that what was in the minds of the framers of the law at the time of its enactment, their thoughts, their specific intent, on the subject, must be sought out and given effect, in order to give to the law correct judicial interpretation. Applying the foregoing, there were, at the time of the enactment of the law in question, and had been for a long period of years theretofore, and have been subsequently, in railroad service everywhere in this country, as a matter of common knowledge, officers known as "superintendents" in the operating department of the road, general superintendents of the whole line, and superintendents of divisions. The general duties of such superintendents are intimately connected with the movement of trains and cars. Now, it must be presumed that the legislature used the word as it was commonly used. They had in mind the officers of railroads to whom the term was generally applied. The position of superintendent in the railway service is as definitely and well known as that of train dispatcher, telegraph operator, conductor, or engineer. It could not be sincerely claimed that the word "conductor" can be applied to the foreman of a section gang or of a bridge crew, because he merely conducts or manages the work; or that it can be applied to any other conductor than the one who manages the railroad train; and yet the act does not say "train conductor." It could not be sincerely claimed that the word "engineer" can be applied to the engineer who locates tracks and does engineering work of that kind, or who runs some little stationary pumping engine, or to any one of many other persons connected with railroad service that might properly be called "engineers"; and yet the act does not say "locomotive engineer." And the same illustration might be given in respect to each of the persons specifically named in the act. It may thus be clearly seen that to apply the word "superintendent" to the mere foreman of a repair shop would be entirely inconsistent with the obvious purpose of the act.

Again, if it could be held that Mr. Tait was a superintendent at the time of the accident, he was certainly not engaged in his work as such at the time in question, but was merely assisting Hartford and his helper to turn the wheels of the engine. He was working in a common employment with Hartford and as his fellow-servant. Stutz v. Armour, 84 Wis. 623. The rule, in effect, is laid down thus: "Whether a person is to be considered a vice principal of another or a co-employee and fellow-servant of such other depends, not upon the rank or grade of such person, but upon the work then being performed by such person and such other." So, in this case, in order to establish the liability under the act of 1889, it is necessary, not only to show that the person whose negligence is complained of was a superintendent within the meaning of that act, but that he was engaged in his line of work as such at the time of the accident. Here, according to the undisputed evidence, it was not part of Mr. Tait's duties as a foreman of the shops to do or to have anything to do with the work he and the deceased were engaged in at the time of the injury. He merely took hold as a volunteer, to assist in doing the work. Hartford, the deceased, was really the one in charge, and they were, for the time being in any view of the case, fellow-servants and nothing more. Though there is much conflict of authority on this subject in other jurisdictions, the rule here adopted has become thoroughly imbedded in the jurisprudence of this state. . . .

From the foregoing it follows that the judgment must be reversed.

By the Court.—Judgment reversed, and cause remanded for a new trial.

NOTES AND QUESTIONS

1. Why, as the court puts it, "under the most favorable view that can be taken of this case," was plaintiff not entitled to recover unless Tait was a "superintendent" within the meaning of the statute?

2. Precisely why is defendant found not liable under the statute? Consider the scope of the opinion. Does the court confine itself to deciding just so much as is necessary to dispose of the case? Evaluate the opinion from the standpoint of sound judicial technique. Of the two major principles invoked by the court, which, if any, is mere dictum?

3. What does the opinion indicate to be the proper function of the court in relation to the legislature and its handiwork?

4. List carefully the separate sources of information resorted to by the court for the interpretation of the statute. Consider the justification for relying on each of these sources and whether each source yielded information in favor of or against the decision reached.

5. What rules or canons of construction or interpretation did the court invoke? Consider the justification for invoking each of these rules and the effect each had on the court's decision.

6. What argument for or against the decision in the Hartford case can be based upon a comparison of the language in the 1875 statute and that in the 1889 statute?

7. Stutz v. Armour, 84 Wis. 623, 54 N.W. 1000 (1893), cited by the court in its interpretation of the statute, was an action for the recovery of damages for personal injuries, received by plaintiff while in the employ of the defendant, from a fall from a scaffold on the side of defendant's ice-house, due to the alleged negligence of defendant's foreman in helping plaintiff shift a plank on the scaffold. The opinion of the court, so far as here relevant, reads: "At the time the plaintiff received the injury of which he complains, and which he imputes to the negligence and improper direction of the foreman, they were both engaged in adjusting the three planks resting on the brackets of the scaffolding, and the foreman was doing, in connection with the

plaintiff, the work of a common laborer. The foreman was not, within the rule established in this state, a vice-principal, but was a mere fellow-servant with the plaintiff of a common master in doing the work in question, and the plaintiff in thus working with him assumed the hazard of the alleged negligence of Meinski [the foreman] . . . Whether Meinski is to be considered as a vice-principal of the defendant, or a co-employee and fellow-servant of the plaintiff depends, not upon his rank or grade, but upon the work then being performed by him. The act of Meinski in question was not one that the law implied a contract duty upon the part of the master to perform, and Meinski's negligence or improper performance of it cannot, therefore, be imputed to the master. . . ."

Note that this was a common-law decision. Why was the statute inapplicable? Was it proper for the court, in interpreting the statute in the Hartford case, to resort to common-law authority?

8. Can it be said that the Hartford court's attitude of resorting to the common law will always result, in statutory cases, in decisions adverse to employees? See Dugan v. C.M.&O. Ry. Co., 85 Wis. 609, 55 N.W. 894 (1893): "The jury found that the plaintiff's injury was caused by the negligence of the defendant's engineer in charge of the locomotive at the time. . . . Such engineer being the plaintiff's co-employee at the time, it is contended that there would have been no liability at common law, and hence that his right of action, if any, is purely statutory. The statute applicable reads: 'Every railroad corporation doing business in this state shall be liable for damages sustained by any employee thereof within this state, *without contributory negligence on his part,* when damage is caused by the negligence of any . . . engineer. . . .' [Emphasis is the court's] Ch. 438, Laws of 1889. . . . The contention is that under this statute the plaintiff was bound to prove, as a condition precedent to recovery, that he was without contributory negligence on his part. It is, in effect, conceded that independent of this statute the burden of proving contributory negligence, when not disclosed by the evidence on the part of the plaintiff, was purely a matter of defense. Hoye v. C.&N.W.R. Co., 67 Wis. 15. . . . The defense of contributory negligence has frequently been sustained to a right of action given by statute where none previously existed, notwithstanding the statute was silent on the subject of contributory negligence. . . . Holum v. C.M.&St.P.R. Co., 80 Wis. 303, and cases there cited. The mere fact that the legislature embodied in the act in question the words, 'without contributory negligence on his part,' when the courts would necessarily have supplied the same by construction had they not been so embodied, cannot operate to change the burden of proof from the defendant to the plaintiff. It will be observed that such words were not so embodied for the purpose of giving to the plaintiff a right of action, but for the purpose of more certainly securing to the defendant a defense in case of such contributory negligence. The case is clearly distinguishable from that line of cases where the right to recover is based wholly upon an exception in the statute, as, for instance, where the statute expressly prohibits all right of recovery except upon one condition, and the plaintiff seeks to bring himself within such exception. The supreme court of Minnesota has recently held that a similar statute in that state did not change the rule as to the burden of proving contributory negligence. Lorimer v. St. Paul C.R. Co., 48 Minn. 391. . . ."

9. Compare Lagage v. C.&N.W. Ry. Co., 91 Wis. 507, 65 N.W. 165 (1895): ". . . The only negligence on the part of the defendant's servants disclosed by the evidence is the failure of the head brakeman to get upon and ride the cars so kicked down on the main track, and control their speed by the use of the brake thereon. But such negligence of the head brakeman is not alleged in the complaint. . . . Had it been alleged and proved, it would simply have been the negligence of a co-employee, and, as such co-employee is not expressly named in ch. 438, Laws of 1889 (sec. 1816*a*, S.&B. Ann. Stats.), it is quite certain there could not have been recovery. . . ."

Does not this interpretation give a weight to the actual words of the statute which was denied them in the opinion in the Hartford case? Is not the brakeman's activity in the operation of the railroad within the "reason and spirit" of the statute, which the Hartford opinion stresses as properly to be considered by the court? Is there anything about the language of the 1889 statute that might justify this difference in judicial attitude?

10. Accepting the court's interpretation of the statute and its purpose, could a reasonable argument have been made that Tait was an "engineer" within the meaning of the statute? Why do you think this argument was not even mentioned by the court? Should it matter that plaintiff's attorney did not advance this argument? Is plaintiff's attorney subject to justifiable criticism for not making this argument?

LAWS, 1893, Chapter 220

An Act to define the liability of railroad companies in relation to damages sustained by their employes.

The people of the state of Wisconsin, represented in Senate and Assembly, do enact as follows:

Section 1. Every railroad or railway company operating any railroad or railway, the line of which shall be in whole or in part within this state, shall be liable for all damages sustained within this state by any employe of such company, without contributory negligence on his part; first, when such injury is caused by any defect in any locomotive, engine, car, rail, track, machinery or appliance required by said company to be used by its employes in and about the business of such employment, when such defect could have been discovered by such company by reasonable and proper care, tests or inspection, and proof of such defect shall be presumptive evidence of knowledge thereof on the part of such company; second, or while any such employe is so engaged in operating, running, riding upon or switching, passenger or freight or other trains, engines or cars, and while engaged in the performance of his duty as such employe and which such injury shall have been caused by the carelessness or negligence of any other employe, officer or agent of such company in the discharge of, or for failure to discharge his duties as such.

Section 2. Chapter 438, of the laws of 1889, is hereby repealed.

Section 3. No action or cause of action now existing shall be affected by this act.

Section 4. No contract, receipt, rule or regulation between any employe and a railroad company, shall exempt such corporation from the full liability imposed by this act.

Section 5. This act shall take effect and be in force from and after its passage and publication.

Approved April 17, 1893.

NOTES AND QUESTIONS

1. The Message of the Governor to the Legislature convened in 1893 had recommended to the legislators' attention the problem of the fellow-servant rule in connection with railroad operations, and had expressed hope for a new law "that will meet the just demands of this large special class of workmen." Assembly Journal, 1893, p. 16.

2. Was the 1893 statute more favorable to employees or less so than the 1889 statute?; than the 1875 statute?

3. Does the statute preserve the common law pattern of liability?

4. In Andrews v. C.M.&St.P. Ry. Co., 96 Wis. 348, 71 N.W. 372 (1897) it was held that the 1893 statute did not abrogate the defense of assumption of risk. Does this decision represent an unreasonably strict interpretation?

MEDBERRY v. CHICAGO, MILWAUKEE & ST. PAUL RY. CO.
106 Wis. 191, 81 N.W. 659 (1900)

CASSODAY, C. J. This is an appeal from an order sustaining a demurrer to a complaint for personal injury, alleging in effect, that the plaintiff at the time of the injury, and for twenty-five years prior thereto, had been in the employment of the defendant as a conductor in charge of a train running between Elkhorn and the village of Eagle; that such train was known as a combination mixed or passenger train, consisting of freight and passenger cars, engine, etc.; that during all of the time of the plaintiff's employment as such conductor it was a part of his regular duty to see to the making up of such train at the terminal points, and to get the same in readiness to leave such points upon scheduled time; that December 23, 1896, the plaintiff, in the regular discharge of his duties as such conductor, was engaged in the making up of his train preparatory to leaving Elkhorn on one of its regular trips; that it became necessary for the plaintiff, in the discharge of his duties as such conductor, to have a certain car, which was to compose and become a part of such train, unloaded at the freight depot at the station at Elkhorn prior to the leaving of the train; that in the performance of such duty as such conductor the plaintiff caused such car to be put into the train and drawn up beside the freight depot at the station at Elkhorn for the purpose of having the freight then in the car unloaded upon the platform; that it was the plaintiff's duty to see that the door of the car was properly closed and fastened after such freight had been unloaded, and to give proper signals to the engineer of the train when such work should be accomplished; that two co-employees of the plaintiff were engaged in taking out the freight in the car, and that the plaintiff, while in the performance of his duty as such conductor, was standing by the side of the car so being unloaded for the purpose of watching an open switch easterly from the train connecting the main lines of the railway with the track upon which the plaintiff's train was standing, and for the purpose of closing the car door when the freight should be unloaded, and for the purpose of signaling the engineer of the train when the work should be accomplished, and while so engaged the plaintiff was, by the carelessness and negligence of such employees of the defendant engaged in unloading the car, struck by a long, heavy bale of hair felt, which was carelessly and negligently thrown out of the car by the co-employees of the plaintiff engaged in unloading the same; that the injury was occasioned solely by the careless and negligent manner in which the co-employees of the plaintiff handled and manipulated the heavy bale of material, and without fault or negligence on the part of the plaintiff; that by reason of being struck as aforesaid the plaintiff was then and there seriously injured, and became sick and disabled, and that such injury had been progressive and had rendered him permanently disabled.

As indicated, the complaint expressly alleges that the plaintiff was injured solely by being struck by "a long, heavy bale of hair felt" carelessly and negligently thrown by the defendant's employees, who were co-employees of the plaintiff, engaged in unloading a freight car containing such bales. It is well settled that, in the absence of a statute giving the right, there can be no recovery from the master by reason of the sole negligence of such co-employee. . . . The only statute which is claimed to give any such right of action to the plaintiff in the case at bar declares. . . . Sec. 1816, Stats. 1898. [L. 1893, ch. 220.—Editor] As the complaint alleges that the plaintiff was free from contributory negligence, he is entitled to recover if the facts alleged bring the case within the provisions of the statute quoted.

That statute has been in force since April 22, 1893, and has repeatedly been before this court for construction. In Smith v. C., M.&St.P.R. Co., 91 Wis. 503, it was held, in effect, that a car repairer and a yard switchman were fellow-servants, and that the statute did not apply to an injury sustained by a car repairer through the negligence of such yard switchman in causing a car to be kicked against the stationary car in which such repairer was at work. In that case Mr. Justice Marshall, speaking for the whole court, said: "The words, 'while engaged in the performance of his duties as such employee,' refer to the words, 'while operating, running, riding upon, or switching passenger or freight or other trains, engines, or cars.' This, we think, is very clear. It is a familiar principle that statutes in derogation of the common law should be strictly construed, and not given any effect beyond the plain legislative intent. . . . The legislative idea of that part of the law under consideration plainly is to give a right of action to the class of employees engaged in operating and moving trains, engines, and cars while actually so engaged; and the words used to express such idea are too plain to leave any room for a resort to the rules for judicial construction to determine their meaning." Page 506. In Ean v. C., M.&St.P.R. Co., 95 Wis. 69, it was held that "a freight handler, while actually engaged in moving a freight car along the track to the freight house in the course of his employment, was engaged in operating and moving the car, within the meaning of the statute quoted." In that case Smith v. C., M.&St.P.R. Co. was expressly sanctioned, and some of the language quoted above repeated. In Hibbard v. C., St.P., M.&O.R. Co., 96 Wis. 443, it was held that "a warehouseman of a railroad company, who was injured, while sealing the doors of a car attached to an engine, through the negligence of an engineer or fireman in suddenly moving the engine, was not employed in 'operating, running, riding upon, or switching' trains or cars, within the meaning of" the statute quoted. In that case Mr. Justice Winslow, speaking for the whole court, said: "That the plaintiff was not at the time of his injury engaged in 'operating, running, riding upon, or switching' a car is so plain that argument of the question is unnecessary. Sealing the door of a car plainly is not operating or running it. This view is in harmony with the previous decisions of this court construing this statute."

In the case at bar it became necessary to have the freight car containing the heavy bales of hair felt unloaded at the freight depot at the station in Elkhorn, in order that it could be taken as a part of the train to Eagle. For that purpose the plaintiff caused that car to be put into the train and drawn up to such freight depot. After that car was unloaded, it would have been the duty of the plaintiff, had he not been injured, to see to it that the door of the car was properly closed and fastened, and to have signaled the engineer of the train when the work should be completed. While the plaintiff was standing by the side of the car so being unloaded, watching an open switch easterly from the train, and waiting to so close the door of the car when it should be unloaded, he was struck by the long, heavy bale of hair felt, and injured. In our judgment, the plaintiff was not, at the time of his injury, engaged in "operating, running, riding upon, or switching" the train, engine, or car, within the meaning of the statute quoted, as construed by this court. It is unnecessary to consider what has been decided by other courts under different statutes.

By the Court.—The order of the circuit court is affirmed.

Dodge, J. I find myself unable to concur in the decision reached by the court, which seems to me to very materially emasculate the statute (sec. 1816, Stats. 1898), [L. 1893, ch. 220.—Editor] and to thwart the purpose of the legislature in enacting the same. The ancient doctrine excusing the employer from liability for an injury to an employee occasioned by negligence of a co-employee grew up at a time when the employees of the same master were few in number and closely connected in their employment, and when, therefore, the opportunity of the employee to know as to the characteristics for caution, intelligence, etc., of his co-employee, and to guard himself against any lapses therein, was much better than those of the employer. The extension of that doctrine to the greatly modified industrial relations of the present day has carried it far beyond the reasons which led to its original adoption, until in modern times it has been applied to men ordinarily having no contact with each other, no opportunity to observe each other, indeed no knowledge of the existence or employment one of the other. This strain on the doctrine has perhaps been stronger in the case of railroad employees than any others. The conductor or the engineer residing at one end of a hundred miles of railroad has no opportunity to know of the qualifications of the switch-tenders, flagmen, track-layers, section-men, or station agents who may from time to time be scattered by his employer along that stretch of track. The stress of haste and expedition resting upon them precludes them from taking precautions against acts of negligence of these various other employees along the route, and almost, if not entirely, negatives the existence of the reasons which led to the adoption of the co-employee doctrine originally.

Legislatures of many of the states have recognized the inapplicability of this doctrine to certain modern situations, and to those of railroad employees more than others. After several experiments in this and other states, sec. 1816 was adopted in 1893 as an attempt to legislatively define those whose duties were of such a character as to make the application of the co-employee doctrine improper. The statute, doubtless, was not perfect, and there may well be other instances as much entitled to legislative regard as those to which the statute is addressed;

but to the extent to which it went it was positive and left to the courts nothing of policy but merely ascertainment of the facts. It created a class of employees whom it declared exempt from the application of this doctrine, and described that class as employees "engaged in operating, running, riding upon, or switching passenger, freight, or other trains, engines, or cars, while engaged in the performance of his duty as such employee." In the first case which arose—Smith v. C., M.&St.P.R. Co., 91 Wis. 503, 506,—this construction was declared, and the company was held not liable to an employee injured by reason of the running of engines and cars, because he was not in that class, he being a mere car repairer, engaged in making some repairs upon a car standing in the yard; he was not an "employee engaged in running or operating trains or cars." A similar holding was made in Hibbard v. C., St.P., M.&O.R. Co., 96 Wis. 443, as to a yard employee who was sealing the door of a car standing on the track, although he, too, was injured by reason of the moving of an engine.

These decisions were clearly in accord with the statute, for these men were not in the class of employees exempted by the legislature from the co-employee doctrine. Certain employees, however, must have been in the minds of the legislators as coming within the language of the statute, and most surely there must have been included the train crew, namely, the engineer, the fireman, the conductor, and the brakemen. These employees are, by the statute, exempted from peril from negligence of any others "while engaged in the performance of their duties as such employees." Can it be doubted that a brakeman is in the class so exempted because he may be repairing or fastening a door of a car while the train is in the course of its trip? Is he not then in the performance of his duty as such employee, to wit, as a brakeman? If not, what kind of an employee is he? Has he become a car repairer or a yard man? Shall a fireman, while in the midst of his run, although the engine be for a moment stationary, be held not engaged in the performance of his duty as such employee while oiling the engine or tightening a nut upon it, because, forsooth, a mechanic in the shop would not be within the statute if he were doing the same thing? It is a safe inference that this class was selected because its members are obliged to do many of the things which at times are done by other employees, under circumstances which subject them to greater peril. A part of the duty of the conductor and of the brakeman while operating their train is the giving of signals to the engineer and throwing of switches, to accomplish which the crossing of tracks and the exposure of themselves to perils thereby are absolutely necessary, and under such haste as to exclude them from the precautions that might be exercised by yard men in doing the same things. To my mind, a conductor does not cease to be such employee the moment his train stops, nor is he any the less operating it when standing on the platform to signal the engineer than when sitting in the caboose between stations. The situation presented by this case illustrates the propriety of our statute. The conductor's duty of expedition required his presence in such proximity to the car door that he might close it without delay, and his duty to care for his train by watching the open switch required a division of his attention, so that he could not exercise the precautions which might have been available to an employee of a different class, not burdened with the duty of operating the train. The Iowa statute has been so construed as to give right of recovery under circumstances here presented. Akeson v. C., B.&Q.R. Co., 106 Iowa, 54. That statute, while differing from our own, resembles it in some respects, and was much considered in formulating ours. I think decisions upon it are worthy of consideration.

To summarize my views: I think a conductor is one of the class of employees engaged in operating trains, etc.; that while standing beside his train to close a car door and signal the engineer he is "engaged in the performance of his duties as such employee," to wit, as a conductor, and also that he is engaged in operating his train; and therefore may recover for injuries caused by negligence of a co-employee. The rule of strict construction invoked by my brethren does not justify the court in repudiating the clear intent of legislation. That seems to me the result of the decision in this case.

WINSLOW, J. I concur in the foregoing opinion by Mr. Justice DODGE.

NOTES AND QUESTIONS

1. Explanation of procedure in the case: "This is an appeal from an order sustaining a demurrer to a complaint. . . ." When plaintiff filed his complaint, alleging the facts which he claimed to be able to prove and on the basis of which he asserted himself entitled in law to recover damages from defendant, defendant here did not choose at once to go to trial on the question of whether the facts were as plaintiff claimed. Instead, defendant demurred—i.e., defendant filed a motion, called a "demurrer," which asserted that, assuming for the sake of argument that all the facts were as set out in the complaint, yet those facts did not constitute a situation in which, under the applicable rules of law, defendant was liable to plaintiff. Cases previously studied have involved other procedural ways of thus segregating the issues of whether the facts are as plaintiff claims, and whether on the facts the rules of law entitle plaintiff to a recovery. Compare, e.g., (1) the motion in arrest of judgment, in Priestley v. Fowler; (2) the case stated, or facts stipulated, for the court's decision on the law, in Farwell v. Boston and Worcester R.R. Corp.; (3) objection to the charge to the jury, Chamberlain v. Milwaukee & Mississippi R.R. Co.; (4) objection to the introduction of any evidence by plaintiff, in the first Wedgwood case; (5) motion for a non-suit at the close of plaintiff's evidence, or at the close of all evidence, in the second Wedgwood case, and in Heine v. C.&N.W. Ry. Co.; (6) objection to the admission of evidence on a specific issue, Boyce v. Wilbur Lumber Co.

2. The compilation and publication of statutes: The statute laws of the state are printed in separate volumes, published at the close of each session of the legislature. These are known as the "Session Laws" and are cited by year and chapter, each statute passed constituting a separate chapter, in the given volume of the session laws: e.g., L. 1893, ch. 220. At more or less irregular intervals (1849, 1858, 1878, 1898) the legislature provided for the compilation of the session laws into compiled editions. These compilations, known as the Revised Statutes, were supposed to contain an ordered presentation of all general laws of the state in force at the time of their publication. Each general law in the session laws was fitted into what was thought the most appropriate place in the Revised Statutes, and was given a section number in the Revised Statutes. Thus L. 1893, ch. 220 became Stats. 1898, sec. 1816. Each revision had to be supplemented at any given time by the separate volumes of session laws published since the revision, in order to make any accurate appraisal of the statute law. Since 1909 the primary business of statutory compilation and revision has been entrusted to an official known as the Revisor of Statutes, whose office is

continuously at work in preparing for submission to the Legislature "revisors' bills" providing for the better ordering of the statutes, the correction of errors, and the elimination of deadwood. Under the direction of the Revisor, the general statutes of the state are now published in one or two compiled volumes shortly after the end of each biennial session of the legislature. These volumes are cited as Wisconsin Statutes 1955, 1957, etc. The statutes passed at a given session are still published in a separate volume of session laws for that session, but in addition, under certain statutory directions, the Revisor fits the new general laws passed into the current edition of Wisconsin statutes.

The general state practice in this regard is set forth in the following excerpt from American State Legislatures, Report of the Committee on American Legislatures of the American Political Science Association (1954) 152-153, 155-156:

"In recent years a large and increasing number of states have established permanent agencies to provide formal revision of the law, that is, to consolidate overlapping provinces; correct inaccurate, prolix, or redundant expressions; eliminate obscurities and conflicts; and collect and enact the whole into a logical, compact arrangement without change in effect. The enacting, of course, is accomplished by the legislature, passing upon the completed revision.

"Wisconsin led the way in this field with the establishment in 1909 of the office of revisor. By 1952 half of the states had authorized permanent revision facilities; some are engaged in making initial bulk revisions of their statutes. Others, having completed their bulk revisions, now are engaged in continuous revision—fitting new enactments into the code, spotting inconsistencies and bringing them to legislative attention, counseling with legislative bill sponsors and legislative committees to eliminate or alter unconstitutional and inconsistent matter from pending legislation, and performing similar tasks designed to maintain a consistent and logical pattern in the statutes. . . .

"All of the states now utilize some method of permanent statutory publication. These range all the way from the publication of the statutes in bulk at long intervals (ten to twenty or even more years apart in some instances) to methods that effectively keep the permanent laws of the states currently available—through pocket parts, supplemental volumes, looseleaf or loosepart replacements, or through frequent publication, perhaps at biennial intervals, of the statutes. Although most of the states at one time followed the practice of publishing their permanent statutes at long intervals with no intervening supplements, only six states—Delaware, Maine, New Hampshire, Pennsylvania, Rhode Island, and Vermont—still rely upon this method. At the opposite extreme are several states—Wisconsin, Illinois, Florida, Iowa, Kentucky, and Minnesota—that publish the entire body of statutory law every two to four years. The latter method, although initiated by Wisconsin in 1911, took hold only within the past decade.

"Various factors such as cost, ease of reference, and mass or bulk of statutes have led the several states to utilize different publication policies. The overwhelming majority of the states have found, however, that publication only in bulk and only at long intervals is unsatisfactory, and that the other methods indicated above are more satisfactory. . . ."

The Committee recommended (p. 162) that all states "establish permanent facilities and programs for carrying on continuous formal revision of the statutes" and "policies for permanent statute publication."

3. Judging from the Medberry opinion, what role does judicial precedent play in the process of statutory interpretation? Should it play any role in this process? Is the

decision in this case consistent with the interpretation of the statute in the other cases decided and cited by the court?

4. Would it have been more difficult, or less so, for the court in the Medberry case to rule the way it did if the Medberry case had been the first to arise under the 1893 statute?

5. Is the dissenting opinion guilty of an attempt to introduce wholly irrelevant considerations when it cites the Iowa court's construction of an Iowa statute?

6. What general principle of statutory construction is invoked by the majority? What attitude does the principle reflect toward the relation between legislation and the common law? What considerations cited by the dissenting opinion would tend to belittle the applicability of the principle to this case?

7. Did the court in Medberry give sufficient weight to the "reason and spirit" of the statute which was stressed in Hartford?

8. Accepting the court's interpretation of the statute, could a reasonable argument have been made that the plaintiff was engaged in "switching" within the meaning of the statute? Why do you think this argument was not even mentioned by the court? Should it matter that plaintiff's attorney did not advance this argument? Is plaintiff's attorney subject to justifiable criticism for not making this argument?

9. Documents on file at the office of the Secretary of State of Wisconsin reveal that in the form in which it was originally introduced, bill 180-A, which became L. 1893, ch. 220, provided: "Section 1. Every railroad company operating any railroad or railway, the line of which shall be situated in whole or in part in this state, shall be liable for all damages sustained within this state by an employee, servant or agent of such company while in the line of his duty as such, and which shall have been caused by the carelessness or negligence of any other agent, employee or servant of such company, in the discharge of or for failing to discharge his proper duty as such, but this act shall not be construed so as to permit a recovery where the negligence of the person so claiming to recover materially contributed to the result complained of." The bill, before passage, was amended to the form in which it appears above.

An amendment which was offered to the bill as introduced, and which was rejected, would have added to the above the following proviso: "provided that such railroad company shall not be liable for damages sustained by any employee, servant or agent of such company while engaged in working in any railroad office or car shop or other railroad shop in which the risk to life is no greater than in other shops of a like character, and which damages shall have been sustained on account of the carelessness or negligence of any other employee, agent or servant of such company in the discharge of, or for failing to discharge his proper duties as such while engaged in his ordinary employment in such office or shop. . . ."

Might the offering of such an amendment to the bill as introduced be argued to cast any light on the purpose behind the changing of the introduced bill to the form in which it was finally adopted? How might this argument affect the appraisal of the Medberry case?

Another amendment which was proposed after the bill had been amended to the form in which it was finally adopted, read as follows: "provided such damages were sustained by reason of the negligence of such company, or some agent, servant or employee thereof, not engaged in the same department or class of work with the person damaged." This amendment was rejected.

Might this fact be argued to cast any light on the problem of construction in the Medberry case?

JONES,* *SOME CAUSES OF UNCERTAINTY IN STATUTES*
36 American Bar Association Journal 321-322 (1950)

Every lawyer who holds himself out as a legislative draftsman dreams of one perfect job. Let the painter aspire to his one flawlessly balanced composition, the composer to his one consummate harmony, and the big league pitcher to that one crowning game at which no opposing batter will reach first base. The draftsman of bills will be ready to pronounce his *nunc dimittis* the day he sees enacted into law a statute of his devising that leaves no contingency unprovided for and that is clear and unambiguous in its direction as to each and every conceivable fact situation which may take place in the world of affairs.

Unhappily, the gap between aspiration and accomplishment stretches as wide in legislative craftsmanship as in any other professional field. The draftsman can narrow the area of statutory uncertainty by painstaking fact-gathering and intensive study of every facet of existing case and statute law bearing on the matter at hand. He can reduce the incidence of statutory ambiguity by conjuring up hundreds of hypothetical fact-situations which may arise in the future for decision under the statute. But, when the job is done and the bill added to the statute books, there will still be cases for which the statute affords no certain guide. It is the purpose of this sketch to suggest a few of the reasons why any statute, however carefully and imaginatively drawn up, must fall short of the goal of perfect certainty.

Certain of the draftsman's difficulties are not unique to legislative work but arise in connection with the preparation of all legal documents. The draftsman must express his understanding and purpose in words, and words are notoriously imperfect symbols for the communication of ideas. Justice Cardozo was speaking for our entire word-bound profession when he began his little classic, *The Paradoxes of Legal Science,* with the mournful exclamation, "They do things better with logarithms." What makes the legislative draftsman's job more trying than the task of the draftsman of a contract or a will is that the words of the statute must communicate the intention to at least three crucial classes of readers; the legislators who are to examine the bill to decide whether it is in accordance with their specifications, the lawyers who must make use of the statute in counseling and litigation, and the judges who will give the statute its final and authoritative interpretation. One does not have to be an expert in semantics to know that words rarely mean the same thing to all men or at all times. An intent that seems "plainly" expressed to the legislative experts on a standing committee may be ambiguous to affected persons and their lawyers and quite unintelligible to judges with no special knowledge or experience in the field of regulation.

Unforeseen cases account for the great majority of the instances of statutory

* Harry W. Jones, Cardozo Professor of Jurisprudence at Columbia Law School, has also taught at Washington University and University of California. He was Editor-In-Charge, Department of Legislation, American Bar Association Journal during 1948- 51, is Directing Editor of the University Textbook Series, Foundation Press, and edited the second edition of Dowling, Patterson and Powell, Materials for Legal Method (1952).—Editor

uncertainty. The problem here is that the typical drive for legislative action originates not in a desire for an over-all codification of the law but in some felt necessity for a better way of dealing with some specific situation or group of situations. The draftsman must make effective provision for the specific needs which are urged upon him, but he must write the statute in the form of a proposition of general applicability. In our legal system we have a long-standing distrust of legislation so narrowly drawn as to affect only designated persons or a few particularized situations. Inequality in the application of legislation is the evil aimed at in such provisions of the Federal Constitution as the Equal Protection and Bill of Attainder Clauses, and the same general idea is reflected in the provision of most state constitutions against local and special legislation. The policy is sound, beyond any question at all, but it leaves to the draftsman of statutes the hard task of formulating a general rule that adequately takes care of the specific situations before the legislature without including in its apparent scope unthought-of cases somewhat similar in fact content but distinguishable on policy grounds.

Case-minded judges and lawyers might be a little less caustic in their comments on the ambiguity of statutes if they were to reflect that the problem of uncertainty in relation to the unthought-of case arises also in the use of case precedents. Every first year law student learns that he must distinguish between the *holding* of a case and the *dicta* which may be set out in the court's opinion. In our common law tradition, we take as binding precedent only the decision of the court on the material facts of the case actually before it. All else we disregard as *dictum*—persuasive, perhaps, but not authoritative. This immemorial common law distinction between *holding* and *dictum* is based on a recognition that even the finest judge is at his best only when dealing with the facts of the case at hand, the issues on which he has had the benefit of argument of counsel. The same is true of the statute-law maker and his technical drafting assistants. If the draftsman is respectably skilled and careful, he will make unmistakably clear provision for the specific situations called to his attention at committee hearings and in other ways. If he is at all imaginative, he will anticipate and take care of other situations within the reach of reasonable anticipation. But human foresight is limited and the variety of fact-situations endless. Every generally worded statute, sooner or later, will fail to provide a certain direction as to the handling of those inevitable legislative nuisances, the cases nobody thought of.

So far in this sketch, the problems of the legislative draftsman have been considered without reference to the political realities of the legislative process in Congress and the state legislatures. But legislative drafting is not a branch of art for art's sake. After the statute has been drafted it has to be passed, and there are many stages in the process of enactment at which uncertainty may be introduced into the most tightly drafted legislative proposal. The sponsoring legislator or the responsible standing committee is likely to make changes in the bill without having the time to consider the effect of the changes on the articulation of the bill as a whole. An amendment from the floor may add confused or inconsistent provisions which fit awkwardly into the statutory pattern. It sometimes becomes necessary as a matter of political compromise to eliminate some precise key-word in the bill and substitute for it some less exact term, chosen deliberately to leave a controversial issue to the courts for decision. In short, it is wholly unrealistic to read a statute as if it were the product of wholly scientific, detached and uneventful deliberation. . . .

NOTES AND QUESTIONS

1. Professor Jones tells us that a statute speaks to the legislators, the lawyers, and the judges. Should it not also speak to the ordinary person whose behavior it seeks to control? What are the expectations regarding statutory language of these groups of people? Are they the same? If not, how can a statute ever be drafted to satisfy the different expectations?

2. While Professor Jones argues that legislative draftsmen should try to anticipate all possible applications of a proposed statute, Professor Frank C. Newman maintains that they are justified in resorting to "deliberate ambiguity" if they think "certain disputes should not be anticipated in the legislature for the reason, perhaps, that committee doubts or floor conflict might jeopardize the basic program." Newman, A Legal Look at Congress and the State Legislatures, in Legal Institutions Today and Tomorrow 75, The Centennial Conference Volume of the Columbia Law School (Paulsen ed. 1959).

Do you think Professor Newman has advanced a sound argument for "deliberate ambiguity"?

3. In what ways do the cases on statutory interpretation considered so far illuminate the main points made by Professor Jones?

Jones, *STATUTORY DOUBTS AND LEGISLATIVE INTENTION*
40 Columbia Law Review 957-974 (1940)

Comparative statistics are unavailable, but a glance through the case reports will suggest that judges are called upon to consider the application of statutory directions to the cases which come before them at least as often as they are required to fashion a controlling rule from the precedents which are the sources of the common law. Already the development has gone so far that it has been said of American and of English courts that they tend more and more to approximate "the civil law ideal of courts as agencies for the application and administration of the legislative precept."[5]

It is evident that this increasing reliance upon legislation must be given its full weight in a jurisprudence originally formulated with particular reference to the common law judicial process. One may question, for example, the adequacy of a case method of legal instruction which has, as its apparent major objective, the training of prospective lawyers in the shaping and manipulation of case-law precedents. Most significantly, the evolution of the statute law to a position, at least, of parity with the judge-made law demands the reexamination of judicial methods developed during periods in which the chief concern of the judges was to build up an interpretative technique by which occasional, ad hoc legislative directions might be fitted, neatly and without disturbance, into the general fabric of common law.

[5] Horack, In the Name of Legislative Intention (1932) 38 W. Va. L.Q. 119.

The general judicial attitude at the time of the original pronouncement of the traditional rules of statutory interpretation is indicated by the charge of a great common lawyer, the late Sir Frederick Pollock,[7] that many of those rules-of-thumb known as canons of construction ". . . cannot well be accounted for except upon the theory that Parliament generally changes the law for the worse, and that the business of the judge is to keep the mischief of its interference within the narrowest possible bounds."

Probably the most significant evidence of judicial recognition of the real place of legislation in modern American law is found in those judicial opinions which reveal the striving of judges to develop an interpretative technique keyed to the essential characteristics of the modern law-making process. Analysis of the decisions discloses that the federal courts, and to a less degree the state courts, are coming increasingly to determine the application of statutes by reference to their legislative history and to their underlying objectives, rather than by the mechanical, and hence more convenient, employment of the traditional canons or rules of construction. . . .

It must be admitted . . . that one who essays an analysis of the judicial process in the application of statute law finds more conflict in legal literature than inconsistency in the judicial decisions. The underlying conception in our theory of statutory interpretation, that of a communicable "legislative intention," has been denounced as a fraud by Radin,[11] defended forcefully by Landis,[12] and subjected to analytical attrition by de Sloovere.[13] Professor Horack,[14] by way of compromise, suggests that there is no such thing as a real "legislative intention" but that it is useful in cases of statutory interpretation to act as if there were. In this essay, it seems the part of prudence to postpone our discussion of the reality of "legislative intention" and to suggest first an analysis of the problems which judges encounter in the use of statutory directions as premises for reasoning in the decision of particular controversies, that is, of the interpretative doubts which courts customarily decide by reference to "legislative intention."

Logical Certainty and the Statute Law. In his land-mark essay, "The Path of the Law," [15] published before the turn of the century, Justice Holmes called attention to the fallacy of "the notion that the only force at work in the development of the law is logic." Typically, judicial opinions have been cast approximately in the form of syllogistic demonstrations, as if to suggest that the conclusion to

---

[7] Essays in Jurisprudence and Ethics (1882) 85.

[11] Statutory Interpretation (1930) 43 Harv. L. Rev. 863.

[12] A Note on "Statutory Interpretation" (1930) 43 Harv. L. Rev. 886.

[13] "The phrase, 'intention of the legislature,' therefore connotes no more than the most satisfactory meaning that the words will honestly bear in view of the actual conditions and evils toward the elimination of which the particular statute was di-

rected." de Sloovere, Extrinsic Aids in the Interpretation of Statutes (1940) 88 U. Pa. L. Rev. 527, 538.

[14] In the Name of Legislative Intention (1932) 38 W. Va. L.Q. 119.

[15] (1897) 10 Harv. L. Rev. 457, Collected Legal Papers (1920) 167. For a stimulating analysis of Holmes' attitude towards the place of logic in law see John Dewey, Logical Method and Law (1924) 10 Cornell L.Q. 17.

which the judges have come, in each instance, has involved little more than the discovery of a general proposition of law, embodied somewhere in the pre-existing doctrine, and the deduction from it of a rule of decision for the particular case. In judicial opinions, as in other forms of argument, the syllogistic form tends to obscure the actual mental operations performed in the making of decisions. It has been the chief thesis of modern critical jurisprudence that judicial thinking is more than mere discovery and deduction, that the judge, upon occasion, is more a legislator than a syllogistic calculator. In a sense, this essay is an effort to apply that jurisprudential thesis specifically to an analysis of the judicial process in statutory interpretation.

At the outset, it would appear that the application of the statute law to particular situations of fact should be vastly more certain and predictable than the application of the case law. The judge who makes use of a statute needs not labor to develop a general principle of law by painstaking induction from ambiguous and perhaps conflicting particular precedents. The statute, itself, is in the form of a general proposition, and all that the judge would seem to have to do is to derive, by deduction from that general proposition of law, a particular rule which will control the decision of the given controversy. The tone of assurance in which many opinions involving the statute law are written appears to give support to a theory that the application of statutes involves only simple deductive operations from which the personal judgment of the members of the court can be excluded.

Experience has shown, however, that judicial decisions involving the interpretation of statutes are by no means as certain and predictable as they would be if the judicial process in this aspect were nothing more than simple deduction. There are innumerable instances of differences of opinion which have existed between trial and appellate courts, and among the several members of appellate courts, with respect to the effect of statutes in particular cases. A large proportion of the important statutory cases decided by the Supreme Court have been handed down by divided benches. Indeed, not even the authors of legislative proposals are always able to predict the conclusions which the courts will reach in the application of the statute law. A famous instance is Caminetti v. United States,[19] in which a majority of the Supreme Court arrived at an interpretation of the Mann Act which was in direct conflict with an explicit assurance made by its author to the members of the House of Representatives.*

[19] 242 U.S. 470 (1917). . . .

* This case involved the White Slave Act (or Mann Act) of 1910, which made it a criminal offense knowingly to transport or cause to be transported in interstate commerce, any woman for purposes of prostitution or debauchery or for "any other immoral purpose." Caminetti's conviction under this law was for transporting a woman from Sacramento, California to Reno, Nevada where she was to become, in the court's words, his "concubine and mistress." A minority of the Supreme Court was persuaded that the statute had been erroneously applied to this case of non-commercialized vice, in view of the narrow legislative intent shown by the title of the act and the legislative reports, and in view of the encouragement of blackmail that would be given by the broader reading of the statute. But the majority saw no strong reason against a literal reading of "any other immoral purpose." It declared, in upholding the conviction, that "the language being plain, and not leading to absurd or wholly impracticable consequences, it is the sole

It could hardly be asserted that such persistent deviations from the norm of predictability are due either to stubborn disregard by judges of the directions of statutes or to the inability of judges to reckon simple logic sums. There are inherent difficulties in the process which make impossible of attainment such dreams as Bentham's hope of securing perfect legal certainty through universal codification. Inasmuch as judicial opinions, characteristically, are written in logical form, it seems advisable to formulate this analysis of the most frequently encountered problems of interpretation in terms borrowed from the discipline of logic. The suggestion is not that judges, unlike other men, are perfectly logical beings. The point is rather that in their reflective thinking judges, like other men, must make use of propositions, in this case those embodied in statutory enactments. The problems of statutory interpretation, considered from this point of approach, are problems inherent in any attempt to apply general or universal propositions to the concrete facts of actual experience.

When a judge is called upon to determine the effect which a statute shall have in a case presented to him for decision, the mental operation which he performs is, essentially, the extraction of a particular rule of decision from a general proposition of law embodied in the statute. If a concrete case is to be decided by reference to the statute law, the following essentials, at least, must be met: (1) the language of the statute must be reduced to the form of a general proposition of law; (2) the terms of the statutory proposition must be defined, that is, their meaning determined; and (3) if there be conflicting general rules or propositions in the body of statute law, a choice of one of them as the governing proposition must be made by the deciding court. These three essentials suggest three major classes of interpretative problems which arise in the judicial application of statute law. . . .

The problem of interpretation which judges most often face is that of determining the meaning, that is the denotation or connotation[22] of some general term used in a statute. It is frequently open to serious question whether a particular object, event, or other fact-circumstance, involved in a given case, may properly be classified within the general term or concept which the statutory draftsman has employed. To suppose a case which will be used for illustrative purposes throughout this discussion, the facts of a controversy may raise the question of the applicability of a "motor vehicle" licensing law to aeroplanes. An appellate decision sustaining the applicability of the statute could conceivably be written in the form of a rough syllogism:

> Every "motor vehicle" must be licensed.
> An aeroplane is a motor vehicle.
> An aeroplane must be licensed.

evidence of the ultimate legislative intent."
—Editor

[22] "A term may be viewed in two ways, either as a class of objects . . . or as a set of attributes or characteristics which determine the objects. The first phase or aspect is called the denotation or extension of the term, while the second is called the connotation or intension." Cohen & Nagel, An Introduction to Logic and Scientific Method (1934) 31.

It is evident, however, that a judicial opinion written in the form above would state merely the ultimate result of judicial thinking and nothing of the actual process by which that result was reached. The first and third propositions of the syllogistic statement above—that is, the statutory general principle and the particular rule deemed to control the decision of the case—may be regarded as logically connected by the syllogism only if the middle term, "motor vehicle" is common to the major and minor premise. Thus, the real issue in the case, the essential problem of interpretation, is whether aeroplanes may properly be classified as "motor vehicles" within the meaning of that term as used in the statute.

It should be observed that a statutory definition, however carefully drawn, cannot be an exhaustive catalogue of all of the possible attributes of the general term or class referred to in the statute; all that the legislative draftsman can do is to include in the definition the common attributes of the particular objects of which he has thought. Thus, in McBoyle v. United States,[23] which involved an interpretative issue much like the one under immediate consideration here, the statute included the following definition:

> "The term 'motor vehicle' shall include an automobile, automobile truck, automobile wagon, motor cycle, *or any other self-propelled vehicle not designed for running on rails.*"

What would be the helpfulness of this definition in the supposed case involving the applicability of a "motor vehicle" licensing law to aeroplanes?

In the first place, it is clear that aeroplanes possess both of the attributes mentioned in the statutory definition of the general term "motor vehicle," that is, aeroplanes are "self-propelled" and "not designed for running on rails." If the attributes mentioned in the definition be considered the sole essential attributes of the class, "motor vehicles," it follows that aeroplanes fall within the class and within the scope of the statute. But a further attribute, that of "running on the ground," is possessed in common by the particular vehicles which seem to have been in the mind of the draftsman at the time the general term was employed. The court, in our supposed case, faces the interpretative problem of determining whether an attribute possessed in common by the particular referents suggested to the members of the legislature by the general term "motor vehicle" should be regarded as an essential attribute of the class designated by the term, although the draftsman had not, by including it within the definition, expressly made it so. A comparable problem may be presented whenever a particular case involves the applicability of a statute to a fact-situation which the legislative draftsman has not foreseen and made express provision for. . . .

Inasmuch as statutes, if they are to be general in their operation, must contain general or class terms, it is evident that interpretative doubts of this second type are inevitable in the decision of particular cases by reference to the statute law. . . .

The cases present [another] type of interpretative problem, which is comparable to that created in common law judicial decision by the existence of conflicting precedents. Statute law is constantly undergoing revision, often without adequate

[23] 283 U.S. 25 (1931).

legislative examination of the existing statute law, and inconsistent statutory directions may raise difficult problems of construction. Frequently, even though the interpreting judge has determined that a particular situation of fact is within the terms of one statutory proposition, it is found that the situation is also within the general terms of another statute existing in the body of the law. The countless cases in which there have been expounded the rules of judicial policy with respect to repeals by implication illustrate the interpretative difficulties of this character and the common law judicial approach to their solution.

Interpretation as the Discovery of Legislative Meaning. In our legal and political theory it is a fundamental though inexact, generalization that the originative function of law-making is the province of the legislative department and that the judicial function is but the application of pre-existing law to particular controversies. This conception of the respective roles of legislators and judges may be seen as the background of the constantly repeated doctrine that in the decision of cases by reference to the statute law judges are bound to discover and to follow "legislative intention." According to this theory, interpretative doubts, whether arising from the confusion of statutory language, from the generality of statutory terms, or from the existence of conflicting statutory directions, are to be resolved by judicial resort to an "intention" entertained by the members of the lawmaking body at the time of enactment.

Here again, our supposed case involving the applicability of a "motor vehicle" licensing act to aeroplanes can be used for illustrative purposes. If the court is bound to follow the "legislative intention," and if "intention" is understood as synonymous with "meaning," the court must assign a denotation or connotation to the term "motor vehicle" which is consistent with the understanding of the legislators as to the meaning of that term. It may be that the judge will be able to discover that the draftsmen of the statute used "motor vehicle" with the specific understanding that aeroplanes were to be included within its denotation. If it cannot be determined whether the legislators meant specifically that "motor vehicles" should be taken to include aeroplanes as well as land vehicles, the judge would be bound to discover the connotation which that term suggested to the legislators and to determine the applicability of the statute in the light of that connotation. Some of the inherent difficulties in this process have been suggested in the foregoing discussion.

If the interpretation of statutes is really an operation by which the judges attempt to reproduce the thought in the minds of the members of the legislature, that is, the reference which the legislature sought to communicate through the medium of language, statutory interpretation is practically the same, in its approach, as the interpretation involved in such diverse fields as theology and literary criticism. A classic definition of interpretation is that stated by Lieber in his Legal and Political Hermeneutics:[31]

> "Interpretation is the art of finding out the true sense of any form of words, that is the sense which their author intended to convey, and of enabling others to derive from them the same idea which their author intended to convey."

[31] (3d Ed., 1880) 11.

Analysis of the actual procedures which courts follow in determining characteristic interpretative problems discloses, however, that judicial practice is by no means always consistent with the theory that statutory interpretation involves a judicial endeavor to discover the idea or reference which the members of the enacting legislature meant to convey through the statutory language. The principle that "legislative intention" is the controlling consideration in statutory interpretation is greatly qualified, at least in judicial theory, by the co-existence of the "plain meaning rule," that "if the words of the statute are plain and unambiguous, and do not lead to absurd results, they must be applied," [32] without regard, it will be observed, to "the sense which their author intended to convey." Such established doctrines as the presumption against repeal by implication, the rules of strict construction, and such canons as *expressio unius* and *ejusdem generis** are not really guides to the legislative will or understanding but rather rules of judicial policy which, irrespective of subjective legislative intention, may be given controlling effect in the application of statutes. The increasing use of extrinsic aids in statutory construction does suggest, however, that judges are usually willing to interpret the words of a statute in "the sense which their author intended to convey," if the actual understanding of the legislators can, in fact, be discovered.

As the first step in any effort to appraise the reality of the concept of "legislative intention" it is necessary to consider the difficulties which are involved in an attempt to reconstruct the state of mind of the members of a legislative body at the time of the enactment of a statute. The judicial problem is, to begin with, bound up with the inherent limitations of words as symbols for the communication of ideas. . . . It is unnecessary here to prove that words do not mean the same thing to all men, or at all times. It is well to recall the characteristic words of Justice Holmes:[36]

> "A word is not a crystal, transparent and unchanged, it is the skin of a living thought and may vary greatly in color and context according to the circumstances and the time in which it was used."

It follows that any serious effort on the part of judges to discover the thought or reference behind the language of a legislative enactment must be based upon a

[32] See Chamberlain, The Courts and Committee Reports (1933) 1 U. Chi. L. Rev. 81. There are discussions of the root assumptions of the plain meaning rule in Hopkins, The Literal Canon and the Golden Rules (1937) 15 Can. B. Rev. 689; and in the writer's The Plain Meaning Rule and Extrinsic Aids in the Interpretation of Federal Statutes (1939) 25 Wash. U.L.Q. 2.

* "Expressio unius, exclusio alterius": the expression of one thing implies the exclusion of the other; e.g., if the legislature provides that a municipality may petition the public service commission to secure a rate reduction from the local electric company, this may be taken to imply that no one besides the municipality may bring such a petition. "Eiusdem generis": if a statute contains a list of particular subjects covered and concludes the list with a general phrase or "catch-all clause," the general phrase or clause is to be interpreted as embracing only subjects of the same general character as those in the specific list.—Editor

[36] Towne v. Eisner, 245 U.S. 418, 425 (1918).

painstaking effort to reproduce the setting or context in which the statutory words were employed. Judicial reference to such extrinsic aids as committee reports and records of legislative history may be considered, from this point of view, as a technique by which to gather the original context of statutory language, and so to facilitate discovery of the psychological reference which the members of the legislature meant to communicate.

It would be difficult enough to discover "legislative intention," in the sense of the meaning which the words used bore to their author, if the law-maker were a single individual. But the task of the courts in the interpretation of statutes is even further complicated. The typical legislative authority, federal and state, is composed of two houses, each with a comparatively large membership. It has been vigorously contended, by Professor Radin[38] among others, that it is absurd to speak of an "intention" entertained in common by the numerous members of the typical bicameral legislature. From this contention, the argument has been made that judges, in the interpretation of statutes, should be guided only by their own notions as to the respective social results of the alternative decisions open to them in close cases.[39]

With respect to the finer points of statutory meaning it is, of course, wholly unrealistic to deny that differences of opinion or understanding may exist among the numerous members of a single house, or as between the respective members of the two houses.[40] Moreover, in view of the degree of specialization which has attended the development of the committee as the dominant force in the American legislative process, it is quite probable, as to the overwhelming majority of statutory enactments, that only the members of the particular committee in charge of a statutory proposal will be familiar with its technical phraseology. If "legislative intention" is supposed to signify a construction placed upon statutory language by every individual member of the two enacting houses, it is obviously a concept of purely fictional status. One who would defend the concept as a real or a useful one must be content with something less than unanimity.

In their day-to-day decision of cases, however, judges must make use of the most reliable sources of guidance which happen to be available to them. Notwithstanding the objections of theory which can be urged against the reality of "legislative intention," judges do, in fact, make use of legislative sources for whatever clues such sources may afford on questions of doubtful statutory meaning. By the examination of such records as committee reports and the history of amendments accepted or rejected during the course of the passage of an enactment, it is quite often possible to discover that at some stage of the legislative process committee members or other interested legislators had, in fact, come to an understanding with respect to the essential interpretative issue of a given case.

[38] Statutory Interpretation (1930) 43 Harv. L. Rev. 863. . . .

[39] For a strongly-worded criticism of this point of view, see Landis, A Note on "Statutory Interpretation" (1930) 43 Harv. L. Rev. 886, originally directed as a rebuttal to the Radin article in the same issue of the Review.

[40] And the approving executive also figures in the legislative process. One may speculate as to the effect of judicial discovery of a conflict of understanding as between the legislature and the executive. . . .

Such a discovered "intention" will normally be given full effect by an interpreting judge, although it cannot be shown conclusively that that understanding was shared by each and every member of the legislative authority.

The methods of interpretation employed by the federal courts in the interpretation of Congressional enactments are particularly suggestive. The increasing judicial tendency to accept the "intention" of Congressional committees as the controlling "intention" is certainly justified as a proper recognition of the facts with respect to the functional organization of Congress. This tendency is illustrated by a highly realistic statement of Judge Learned Hand:[45]

> It is, of course, true that members who vote upon a bill do not all know, probably very few of them know, what has taken place in committee. On the most rigid theory possibly we ought to assume that they accept the words just as the words read, without any background of amendment or other evidence as to their meaning. But courts have come to treat the facts more really; they recognize that while members deliberately express their position upon the general purposes of the legislation, as to the details of its articulation they accept the work of the committees; so much they delegate because legislation could not go on in any other way.

The concept of "legislative intention" can be said to possess validity in the theory and practice of statutory interpretation, if proof of unanimity of understanding be dispensed with for practical reasons. Thus it would seem that a judge is but following the best available evidence if he adopts a construction shown to have been put upon an enactment in one house of Congress, although there is no evidence either way as to whether that meaning was, in fact, understood in the other house. As a matter of probability, it is surely more likely that the same construction will have been put upon a statutory proposal in both houses than that a construction reached by a judge, unaided and perhaps years after the event, will be consistent with the legislative understanding in both houses, or in either of them.

The drafting of statutes by executive and administrative officers, or by other expert draftsmen who are not members of the enacting legislature, raises a question of practical as well as of theoretical significance. Judicial research into the legislative sources may fail to disclose any evidence of "legislative intention," in the sense of an understanding by the legislators, or by any of them, with respect to the interpretative issue of a given case. Under such circumstances, should an interpreting court give any weight to an expressed "intention" or understanding of the non-legislative draftsman? The writer has encountered a few cases in which judges have given consideration to the explanations of non-legislative draftsmen, but the theory upon which such attention was paid seems not to have been made clear. . . . It would seem, as to the interpretation of all statutes, that a strong argument for judicial consideration of nonlegislative "intention" of this character can be premised upon the need for basic consistency of direction in the judicial exposition of integrated legislative policies.

[45] SEC v. Collier, 76 F. (2d) 939, 941 (C.C.A. 2d, 1935).

Originative Aspects of Judicial Thinking in Interpretation. Up to this point, the discussion has been concerned primarily with the difficulties involved in judicial discovery of "legislative intention," in the sense of the construction put upon statutory language by those responsible for its adoption. The assumption has been that at least a few immediately interested legislators had, in fact, foreseen the essential interpretative issue raised in a given case, had actually come to a conclusion with respect to it, and had sought to communicate their will as to the effect to be given to the statute. Even upon the level of discovery of a pre-existing legislative understanding, more or less specific with respect to particular interpretative issues, the judicial application of statute law is far from a mechanical deductive process.

In the majority of cases circumstances demand more of the judge than the discovery of an earlier, actually entertained, legislative understanding. The thought of the members of the legislature, or any of them, may never have been directed, even in the most general outline, to the essential interpretative issue of a case at bar. For example, if the controversy is one in which the interpretative problem involves a choice between two possibly applicable and conflicting statutes, the probability is that the thought of the legislators, with respect to the later statute, included no reference at all to the earlier enactment. If the legislators had been aware of the possible conflict between the two statutes, they would doubtless have made clear their will as to which should be given controlling effect.

By way of further illustration of the limitations of the process of discovery in statutory interpretation, one final use can be made of the supposed case in which a court is called upon to decide whether the mandate of a "motor vehicle" licensing law applies to aeroplanes. If it be assumed for the moment that the statute in question had been enacted before the development of air transportation, it is clear that judicial reproduction of the construction placed upon the statutory terminology would afford no certain indication as to whether or not aeroplanes should be classified as "motor vehicles," within the meaning of the statute. Obviously the legislators could not be said to have used the term, "motor vehicles" with the understanding that aeroplanes, then unknown, were within its denotation. Moreover, mere judicial discovery of the connotation which the term, "motor vehicle" bore to the legislators would not greatly assist the court in determining the proper classification of aeroplanes, since, by the nature of the case, the thought of the members of the legislature could never have been directed to the question whether "running on the ground" should be taken as an essential attribute of all of the particular objects within the statutory class, "motor vehicles."

In short, it is impossible to say that the members of a legislative body have had any "intention," in the sense of a construction placed upon the language of a statute, with respect to interpretative issues raised by the existence or occurrence of objects, events, or other circumstances which were not in existence at the time of the enactment. Other objects or events, which were in existence at the time, may never have come to the attention of the legislators. . . . Thus, the most difficult questions of statutory construction are those in which it cannot be said that the legislators have had any "intention" at all, in the sense of an understanding of the meaning or legal effect of the statute with respect to particular interpretative issues.

From the language which judges employ in cases involving the application of the statute law, it would seem that they consider their action to be but the search for and application of a single true meaning, which has a real and ascertainable existence in the statute, or rather in the legislative mind. It has been shown, however, that in a great many cases the most diligent of judicial research, including careful examination of the legislative records, will not reveal any conclusive evidence either way as to the understood effect of a statute in particular situations of fact. In such cases the theory that the judge is always bound by pre-existing rules of law is as inappropriate as it has been shown to be in certain areas of common law decision. The conclusion of the judge, as to the meaning and effect of the statute, is in no sense predetermined; it is clearly originative judicial action.

The conception here advanced that judges must frequently act legislatively in determining the legal effect to be given to a statute is not really inconsistent with one line of established doctrine expressed in the American and English cases. The phrase, "legislative intention," may be taken to signify the teleological concept of legislative *purpose,* as well as the more immediate concept of legislative *meaning.* In the famous sixteenth-century opinion in Heydon's Case, which gave classic formulation to the doctrine that statutes should be interpreted in the light of the evil and the remedy, the duty of judges was said to be "to *add* force and life to the cure and remedy, according to the true *intent* of the makers of the act." * Similarly, in many modern cases, the principle that courts are bound to follow "legislative intention" has been taken to mean that in determining the effect of a statute in cases of interpretative doubt, the judge should decide in such a way as will advance the general objectives which, in his judgment, the legislators sought to attain by enactment of the legislation.

Every considered statute, in effect, embodies a decision on the part of the responsible legislators that a certain projected ordering of conduct will be just and socially beneficial. For example, the much litigated British housing legislation reflected a value judgment of a Parliamentary majority that the social interest in decent housing is great enough to justify severe interference with common law property rights. A judge will often differ with the conclusions of fact or with the judgments of value which have caused the members of a legislative body to adopt a controversial statutory policy. The principle that doubtful questions

---

* 3 Co. 7a, 7b, 76 Eng. Rep. 637 (K.B. 1584): ". . . for the sure and true . . . interpretation . . . of all statutes in general (be they penal . . . or beneficial, restrictive or enlarging of the common law), four things are to be discerned and considered: 1st, what was the common law before the making of the Act? 2nd, what was the mischief and defect for which the common law did not provide? 3rd, what remedy the Parliament hath resolved and appointed to cure the disease of the commonwealth? And 4th, the true reason of the remedy; and then the office of all the Judges is always to make such . . . construction as shall suppress the mischief, and advance the remedy, and to suppress subtle inventions and evasions for continuance of the mischief, and *pro privato commodo,* and to add force and life to the cure and remedy, according to the true intent of the makers of the Act, *pro bono publico.*"—Editor

should be resolved in accordance with "legislative intention" requires, in this significance of "intention" that the judge interpret the statute not in the light of his own personal notions of justice and expediency but in the light of the legislative conceptions of justice and expediency which underly the policy of the enactment.

It must be kept in mind that so-called interpretation, on issues which were wholly beyond the foresight of the draftsmen of a statute, is, itself, legislative in character. The substantial issue is whether the inevitable judicial legislation is to forward the policy of the legislative authority or to retard its fulfillment. The judge, when he must act as a law-maker to fill in the gaps of a statute, exercises not original legislative power but delegated power, comparable to that conferred upon administrative officers possessed of rule-making or subordinate legislative authority. Each has the duty of implementing the general policy of an enactment with detailed rules applying that policy to the infinite variety of unforeseeable particular situations of fact. The circumstance that judicial legislation is, in effect, retroactive, is but another reason for insisting upon the necessity of its consistency with the general legislative policy.

The writer does not mean to suggest that legislatures consciously delegate subordinate legislative power to the courts, although, as a matter of compromise in the legislature, the exact meaning of doubtful phrases is occasionally left to the courts by legislators unable to agree upon the exact formulation of difficult or highly controversial statutes. The fact is simply that the exercise of subordinate legislative power in certain cases is inevitable. Judges, in this creative phase of statutory interpretation, must discover the facts needed as the basis of action in such sources as the hearings and reports of investigatory committees and commissions and the records of legislative proceedings and debates. As a *delegate,* the judge should guide his action by the policy or purpose which the legislative majority has deliberately adopted, and his need for understanding of that policy requires that he discover the conclusions of fact and the judgments of value which seemed compelling to the legislators. As a *legislator,* the judge must have sufficient comprehension of the conditions and activities which his interstitial legislation will affect to enable him to make effective implementing rules, in the form of the particular decisions handed down in the "interpretation" of the act.

In our law the courts, for the most part, have rejected the civil law notion that the general principles drawn from statutes may be made use of as bases for analogy in the decision of cases which do not fall within the broadest possible meaning of statutory language.* But the application of the statute law has never been restricted solely to the fact situations actually and specifically foreseen by the members of the enacting legislature. Within the range of the broadest and narrowest possible meaning of statutes judges must make law, because there is no pre-existing law to discover. Even today, the greater number of the legal rules which courts apply are of legislative origin. If the growth of the law is to be consistent in its direction, judges must approach the statute law scientifically,

---

* But see section 4, *infra.*—Editor

sympathetically, and with full comprehension of its legislative and social backgrounds.

NOTES AND QUESTIONS

1. In McBoyle v. United States, to which Professor Jones alludes, the Supreme Court held that the National Motor Vehicle Theft Act of 1919, the crucial language of which is quoted by Jones, prohibited only the interstate transportation of stolen land vehicles and not stolen airplanes. The Court recognized that "etymologically it is possible to use the word [vehicle] to signify a conveyance working on land, water or air . . ." But it thought that the underlying statutory policy to cover only land vehicles was clear. It stressed the facts that airplanes were not mentioned in the legislative history; that "in everyday speech 'vehicle' calls up the picture of a thing moving on land"; that the specific examples of vehicles listed in the definition quoted by Jones were all land vehicles. In addition, the Court pointed to the fact that this was a criminal statute and hence should not be construed to require a course of conduct not clear from the face of the statute. The principle that penal statutes are to be strictly construed in favor of the defendant is one of the classic canons of construction.

Can you reconcile the decision in the McBoyle case with the decision in the Caminetti case, which is also mentioned in the Jones article? Do we have any clue as to when a court will be guided by the "literal" or "plain" meaning of statutory language and when it will choose instead to be guided by the "reason and spirit" and "obvious purpose of the act," to quote the Hartford opinion? In this connection, consider the following two cases also.

2. Holy Trinity Church v. United States, 143 U.S. 457 (1892), involved the federal Alien Labor Act's prohibition against contracting with an alien for "labor or service of any kind" prior to his importation into this country. In spite of the breadth of the quoted phrase if construed literally (and in spite of the fact that exemptions were limited to certain specified groups [e.g., actors, singers, lecturers, domestic servants] which did not expressly include "ministers") the Supreme Court determined that the statutory prohibition did not extend to a New York church's contracting with an English clergyman to come to this country to render services as the church's minister. "It is a familiar rule," said the Court, "that a thing may be within the letter of the statute and yet not within the statute because not within its spirit. . . . Frequently words . . . are . . . broad enough to include an act in question, and yet a consideration of the whole legislation, or of the circumstances surrounding its enactment, or of the absurd results which follow from giving such broad meaning to the words, makes it unreasonable to believe that the legislator intended to include the particular act." Hence, after considering certain matters of legislative history and pointing out that imputing an anti-religious action to Congress would fly in the face of the country's traditions, the Court concluded, "We cannot think Congress intended to denounce with penalties a transaction like that in the present case."

The dissenting Justices in the Caminetti case relied upon the Holy Trinity Church case. Can these cases be distinguished?

3. In United States v. Alpers, 338 U.S. 680 (1950), the federal prohibition against interstate shipment of any "obscene . . . book, pamphlet, picture, motion picture film, paper, letter, writing, print, or other matter of indecent character" was held applicable to obscene phonograph records. This was in spite of certain features of legislative history, in spite of the canon concerning strict construction of penal statutes, and in spite of the *"eiusdem generis"* canon. The majority regarded the plain meaning of the catch-all clause as coinciding with the "obvious purpose of the legislation," namely, "to prevent the channels of interstate commerce from being used to disseminate any matter that, in its essential nature, communicates obscene, lewd, lascivious or filthy ideas."

Is this case consistent with the McBoyle and Holy Trinity cases? Does this group of cases, taken together, make any over-all sense?

4. Jones referred to the plain-meaning rule and various other canons of construction as "qualifying" the principle of the primacy of legislative intent. Could one plausibly suggest a different kind of relation between the canons and the legislative intent?

5. The use of legislative history will be considered at greater length in Part 3.

HORACK,* COOPERATIVE ACTION FOR IMPROVED
STATUTORY INTERPRETATION
3 Vanderbilt Law Review 382, 388-394 (1950)

Statutory Interpretation: Where Extrinsic Aids Are Insufficient or Nonexistent. Practically all state legislation and most of the older Congressional legislation fall within this category. It would be a fair guess to say that 99% of the state statutes and 50% of federal statutory law reach a court without the benefit of any adequate legislative history officially recorded in hearings, reports or journals. Considering the fact that many interpretative questions will arise which even the best legislative histories will not settle with finality, it is clear that for many years to come courts will deal with statutes which do not have the benefit of extrinsic aids, even if all legislatures immediately provide official reports and records for all future legislation.

Obviously, it is insufficient to say that in these cases the statute should be literally construed, for this is no more than to say that the court is satisfied with the result which it reaches by such a process. It is equally clear that it is insufficient to say that the court should look for the legislative intent if by that is meant any objectively discoverable evidence of the applicability of the statute to the question in issue, for by hypothesis if that were available the question would be settled. Certainly if there are committee hearings and reports, amendments proposed and accepted or rejected, statutes *in pari materia* that provide keys to meaning, if there is prior administrative or judicial construction, a court will hesitate to ignore them or to depart from consistent enforcement patterns which they may have established.

However, with a case before the court, the court must decide; and even a determination that the "intention" of the legislature cannot be determined amounts to a decision—a decision that the statute does not apply to the situation at issue. Thus, at this point courts should not continue the fiction that they are interpreting the statute, but frankly recognize that their decision amounts to a partial exercise of the legislative function.

An application, however, of the modern view of separation of powers which the courts have applied to the other branches of the government fully justifies them in exercising a limited legislative function. Admonishing that the "whole power"

* Frank E. Horack, Jr., late Professor of Law at Indiana University, was the editor of the 3rd edition (1943) of Sutherland, Statutory Construction, probably the most widely used treatise in its field. He held advisory posts with federal and state agencies, and published casebooks in various fields, including legislation and land-use controls.—Editor

of one branch of the government cannot be usurped and exercised by another, the Supreme Court has nevertheless affirmed the proposition that the exercise of some powers other than the primary power is permissible when it accords with "common sense and the inherent necessities of governmental coordination."[27] The necessary legislative effect of many interpretative decisions is so clear that it hardly can be imagined how the court might discharge its judicial functions without interstitially exercising a limited legislative function. And this judges have on occasion admitted. Thus, a court in deciding an issue which arises under a statute the applicability of which cannot be determined by available legislative or quasi-legislative[29] sources, must decide not only whether the statute should apply, but also whether the court should make this legislative decision.

The court in determining whether it will exercise a limited legislative function must recognize that in our form of government we have consciously placed the primary lawmaking function in that branch of the government most responsive to the wishes of a majority of the people. Thus a court should hesitate to make a legislative determination which will result in a change in basic and broadly applicable legislative policies; but conversely it should not hesitate to decide where the amendatory effect of its decision is minor and obviously consistent with well accepted legislative policies in related fields.

To what extent should a court consider the inadequacies of judicial procedure for raising questions basically legislative in nature? All but the most immediately affected persons may be unaware of the case. Even the *amicus* brief may not provide a means for the presentation of argument of indirectly affected persons, not able to present their position. The "factual brief" may be a comparable tool for the presentation of material normally heard in legislative hearings; but legitimate lobbying and interest-group representation are foreign to and totally out of place in judicial proceedings, yet such activity might have determinative effect with the legislature. Balanced against these serious obstacles is the fact that the court must make a decision, but the decision is not final. If the court has improperly determined the legislative policy, the legislature, . . . may overrule the court—here, by statutory amendment. . . .

The policy questions which a court faces are, indeed, limitless. Will the decision reverse judicial decisions long relied upon as properly interpreting the statutory enactment?[32] Has legislative silence after prior court construction confirmed the propriety of the original construction?[33] Should the court consider in its determination the possibility that the legislature has not given effect to the "real opinion" of the electorate?[34]

Should the court withhold review, if possible, when it perceives that proper

---

[27] J. W. Hampton, Jr. & Co. v. United States, 276 U.S. 394, 48 Sup. Ct. 348, 72 L. Ed. 624 (1928).

[29] Such as administrative rules and administrative and judicial decisions relating to the statute.

[32] See People v. Olah, 89 N.E. 2d 329 (N.Y. 1949).

[33] Horack, Congressional Silence: A Tool of Judicial Supremacy, 25 Texas L. Rev. 247 (1947).

[34] This would appear to be real usurpation of legislative function. . . .

interpretation depends upon administrative experience and the act has not had sufficient operation for that experience to accumulate? Should the court consider that its interpretation of the statute may impose new administrative duties, change well established administrative practices, or stimulate litigation to determine the effect of its new rule on other possibly similar situations? [35]

Granted that one of the risks of living in society is the risk of having rights and duties improperly determined, to what extent should a court consider, particularly in a criminal case, that its decision may place the entire burden of improper construction on a single individual? If legislatures should customarily provide compensation for persons improperly fined or imprisoned should the court treat actions of this character differently?

To what extent should the court exercise its limited legislative function as a means of encouraging or "forcing" the legislature to take action? Some, for example, have advanced this hypothesis in defense of the decision in Christoffel v. United States.[36]

If a court has passed these and other hurdles and concludes that it should exercise its legislative power, the question remains, what standards other than those implicit in the answers to the above questions should the court follow? If extrinsic aids are nonexistent or insufficient, then legislative intent is of no aid. Under these circumstances it would seem most consistent with constitutional theory, and the subordinate position of the court in matters legislative, if the court sought a result similar to that which a legislature would reach.

But what legislature? The legislature that passed the act; the legislature that last had an opportunity to amend the act; or even the legislature convened next after the court's decision? When formal rules of interpretation are announced in opinions courts usually assert that their interpretation must be limited to the statute as enacted. Nevertheless, the results obtained in many cases cast doubt upon the actuality of the rule. For although courts have frequently asserted that this is the principal difference between constitutional and statutory interpretation, the distinction seems of doubtful merit so long as the court is not attempting to make basic changes in legislative policy in non-constitutional cases.

Historically this position is understandable. Originally there was no distinction between statutory and constitutional interpretation—both were limited to a literal application of the instrument. However . . . courts soon discovered that as the time of constitutional adoption receded, a literal or historical interpretation became impractical. This reason, of course, did not apply to statutes, because legislatures were, at least, in biennial session.

Today, many of our statutes have the same antiquity as our constitution. And while it is true that the legislature is in a position to revise them and keep them up-to-date it is equally obvious that on minor points where ambiguity may arise from the very lapse of time, the minuteness of the problem almost insures that it will not be called to legislative attention. Thus, there is real merit in the argument that if the court is exercising a legislative function secondarily, and

---

[35] E.g., Dobson v. Comm'r, 320 U.S. 489, 64 Sup. Ct. 239, 88 L. Ed. 248 (1943).

[36] 338 U.S. 84, 69 Sup. Ct. 1447, 93 L. Ed, 1349 (1949).

auxiliary to its judicial function, it should in forming its decision weigh the shift in social, economic and governmental philosophy, accept the facts of invention and improvement in the things upon which law operates, and should avoid a decision which will necessitate immediate legislative amendment of existing statutes.

The analogy between interpreting a constitution as a living and ever growing document and similarly interpreting a statute is subject to one serious objection. Generally speaking, a constitution restricts the powers of government and confers protections upon individuals, whereas statutes tend to restrict the powers of individuals and confer powers on the government or on classes of individuals. Arguably, if this is the character of legislation, the act of legislating should be reserved to the popularly elected representatives. The argument is, however, not conclusive. It goes rather to the propriety of the exercise of the power in particular cases rather than to its existence.

From the foregoing discussion it is clear that at least for new legislation the most effective contributions to the interpretation problem can be made by the legislatures themselves. Some steps are so obvious they scarcely require comment: improvement in the mechanics of determining legislative policy, better legislative records and improved drafting. Certainly the Caminetti, Holy Trinity Church, McBoyle and Alpers cases (to mention but a few) would not have reached the Supreme Court if the apparent legislative policy had been more accurately stated and had been paralleled by statutory language sufficient for the task.

In Alpers v. United States, for example, the apparent policy of Congress to bar from interstate shipment "matter of an indecent character" would have been reasonably clear, even with an inconclusive committee report, if the draftsman had not particularized items all visual in character—i.e., "books, pamphlets, pictures, motion picture film, papers, letters, writing, print." . . .

In situations of this character the courts must recognize not only that legislators attack problems from particulars and then generalize, but also that administrators and law enforcement officers in case of doubt rely on particulars to guide their conduct. Thus, statutes drafted in general terms may fail of enforcement even if they escape the threat of being held void for vagueness. Conversely, legislatures must recognize that frequently courts are unwilling to enforce statutes beyond particulars, and if they expect the particulars to be merely illustrative of a more general policy they are under a duty to say so expressly.

Many legislatures have undertaken to give guidance on questions of this character. The first chapter of most state codes and of the United States Code[47] set forth definitions of terms generally used in statutes and rules of interpretation which the legislature directs the courts to apply if definitions or rules of interpretation have not been set forth in particular statutes. But state and federal courts generally have paid but scant attention to these chapters, and occasionally a case arises which discloses that the court and counsel are all unaware of the existence of such statutory material.

---

[47] See, e.g., Rev. Stat. § 1 (1875), 1 U.S.C.A. § 1 (1948); N.Y. Stat. § 71 (1909); Ill. Am. Stat., c. 131, § 1 (Supp. 1949); Iowa Code Ann. § 4 (Supp. 1949); Mass. Ann. Laws, c. 4 (Supp. 1948). [See Wis. Stats. 1959, c. 990.—Editor]

Often there is real doubt as to the applicability of these acts to the statutes in question. Frequently, the specific problem is not covered by the legislatively adopted rules of interpretation. In Alpers, for example, the Congressional act is silent on the interpretation of words *ejusdem generis*. . . .

Unfortunately, when state legislatures have enacted general interpretative statutes or provided definitions and interpretative standards in specific acts they have done so without realization of the judicial problems involved. For example, the common provision that "all general provisions, terms, phrases and expressions shall be liberally construed in order that the true intent and meaning of the legislature may be fully carried out," is of little usefulness to a court in deciding specific cases. Legislatures can no more solve the problems of interpretation by the enactment of canons and maxims than can courts. Only care in the preparation and drafting of the statutes will contribute to the judicial use of legislative materials.

When the legislature fails in its task then the courts must assume responsibility. It is here that a court's conscious recognition that it is exercising a legislative function as well as a judicial one would be helpful.

If the court follows one approach in McBoyle and Holy Trinity Church and another in Caminetti and Alpers, the legislature has little on which to build its own drafting practice, and administrators will remain in doubt as to the limits of their enforcement obligation. To avoid these consequences courts must in deciding cases give some consideration to the effect their decisions will have upon the legislative process.

Custom and tradition have separated the legislative and judicial institutions so sharply that it is too much to hope that realistic standards of statutory application can be worked out cooperatively by the two branches; but it may be hoped that in some states where judicial and legislative councils are active, they may bridge the chasm. Likewise, it might not be impossible for courts, as they have done with rules of procedure, to define the basic standards of interpretation which they will apply. But that day will not be soon, and even if it should arrive it is not clear that such rules would not create as many questions as they would cure.

For now, the most hopeful improvement in "statutory interpretation" seems to be in a frank judicial recognition that in cases of real doubt the problems are not ones of interpretation but call for a limited exercise of the legislative function by the court. Judicial opinions drafted in these terms would be helpful to litigants and legislators, alike.

CURTIS, *A BETTER THEORY OF LEGAL INTERPRETATION*
3 Vanderbilt Law Review 407, 413-416, 424 (1950)

. . . Gray [it] seems to me . . . is talking cynically.

"A fundamental misconception prevails, and pervades all the books as to the dealing of the courts with statutes. Interpretation is generally spoken of as if its chief function was to discover what the meaning of the Legislature really was. But when a Legislature has had a real intention, one way or another, on a point, it is not once in a hundred times that any doubt arises as to what its intention was. If that were all a judge had to do with a statute, interpretation of statutes, instead of being one of the most difficult of a judge's duties, would be extremely easy. The fact is that the difficulties of so-called interpretation arise when the Legislature has had no meaning at all; when the question which is raised on the statute never occurred to it; then what the judges have to do is, not to determine what the Legislature did mean on a point which was present to its mind, but to guess what it would have intended on a point not present to its mind, if the point had been present." [29]

It is somewhat surprising to find the Supreme Court canonizing this analysis by Gray of "what the judges have to do" when there is no legislative intention, turning what Gray said the judges could not help doing into a judicial duty to do it. The smile with which Gray so often wrote as well as talked would have burst into a laugh if he had seen his "have to" turned into an "ought to," his statement of fact transmuted into legal doctrine. Yet this is just what the Court did in the case of Vermilya-Brown Co. v. Connell. [30] It was a matter of applying the Fair Labor Standards Act to Bermuda.

This Act, which was passed in 1938, covered "any Territory or possession of the United States" as well as the United States themselves. Two years later, and quite unexpectedly to Congress, we leased Bermuda from Great Britain as a military base. Did the Act apply to employees of contractors working on the base? Yes, said the Court, five of them, over the vehement dissent of Jackson, Chief Justice Vinson, Frankfurter, and Burton; and this is what the Court said about the point of statutory construction:

> "The point of statutory construction for our determination is as to whether the word 'possession,' used by Congress to bound the geographical coverage of the Fair Labor Standards Act, fixes the limits of the Act's scope so as to include the Bermuda base. The word 'possession' is not a word of art, descriptive of a recognized geographical or governmental entity. What was said of 'territories' in the Shell Co. Case, 302 U.S. 253; at 258, 58 Sup. Ct. at page 169, is applicable:
>
> " 'Words generally have different shades of meaning, and are to be construed if reasonably possible to effectuate the intent of the lawmakers; and this meaning in particular instances is to be arrived at not only by a consideration of the words themselves, but by considering, as well, the context, the purposes of the law, and the circumstances under which the words were employed.'
>
> "The word 'possessions' has been employed in a number of statutes both before and since the Fair Labor Standards Act to describe the areas to which various congressional statutes apply. We do not find that these examples sufficiently outline the meaning of the word to furnish a definition that would include or exclude this base. While the general purpose of the Congress in the enactment of the Fair Labor Standards Act is clear, no such definite indication of the purpose to include or exclude leased areas, such as the Bermuda base, in

---

[29] Gray, The Nature and Sources of the Law 172-73 (2d ed. 1921).

[30] Vermilya-Brown Co. v. Connell, 335 U.S. 377, 69 Sup. Ct. 140 (1948).

the word 'possession' appears. We cannot even say, 'We see what you are driving at, but you have not said it, and therefore we shall go on as before.' Under such circumstances, our duty as a Court is to construe the word 'possession' as our judgment instructs us the lawmakers, within constitutional limits, would have done had they acted at the time of the legislation with the present situation in mind." [31]

If our courts are going to decide our cases on what they think our legislatures would have done, would they not be better occupied with what the present legislature or the next legislature will do than turn themselves into a historical society reading papers on what some past legislature might then have done?

This doctrine of guessing at what the legislature would have done is no better than asking what the legislature intended. It too puts the court back to the time when the statute was passed, shoving the whole process of interpretation as far back into the past as possible. It has the same archaic, regressive ring as the orthodox doctrine.

As soon as a statute is enacted, it joins the rest of the law, and together with all the rest it speaks to the judge at the moment he decides a case. When it was enacted, to be sure, it was a command, uttered at a certain time in certain circumstances, but it became more than that. It became a part of the law which is now telling the judge, with the case before him and a decision confronting him, what he should now do. And isn't this just what the legislature wanted? The legislature had fashioned the statute, not for any immediate occasion, but for an indefinite number of occasions to arise in an indefinite future, until it was repealed or amended. It was to be used and applied to any such occasion, not only to the variety which might arise out of the particular situation out of which the statute itself had arisen and which had stimulated the legislature to pass it. If that were all the legislature had wanted, or if you please, intended, to do, it could have and should have used more specific terms.

The legislature which passed the statute has adjourned and its members gone home to their constituents or to a long rest from all lawmaking. So why bother about what they intended or what they would have done? Better be prophetic than archaeological, better deal with the future than with the past, better pay a decent respect for a future legislature than stand in awe of one that has folded up its papers and joined its friends at the country club or in the cemetery. Better that the courts should set their decisions up against the possibility of correction than make them under the shadow of a fiction which amounts to a denial of any responsibility for the result.

There are lawyers who will call this a crude alternative, my suggestion that the courts would do better to try to anticipate the wishes of their present and future masters than divine their past intentions. It seems crude, partly because lawyers prefer the past to the future, partly because it is candid, and candor is more formidable than any let's pretend. What the courts do, or at any rate say now they do, is not crude. It's rococo. Let the courts deliberate on what the present

[31] 335 U.S. at 368-88.

or a future legislature would do after it had read the court's opinion, after the situation has been explained, after the court has exhibited the whole fabric of the law into which this particular bit of legislation had had to be adjusted. The legislature would then be acting, if it did act, in the light of the tradition of the whole of law, which is what the courts expound and still stand for. . . .

So the meaning of words is to be sought, not in their author, but in the person addressed, in the other party to the contract; not in the grantor but in the grantee; not in the testator but in the executor or the legatee; in the defendant who is charged with violating the statute, in the conduct of any person who is acting under the authority and either within or without the authority of the words to be interpreted. Words are but delegations of the right to interpret them, in the first instance by the person addressed, in the second and ultimate instance by the courts who determine whether the person addressed has interpreted them within their authority. . . .

FRANKFURTER, *SOME REFLECTIONS ON THE READING OF STATUTES*
47 Columbia Law Review 527, 533, 535-546 (1947) *

Even within their area of choice the courts are not at large. They are confined by the nature and scope of the judicial function in its particular exercise in the field of interpretation. They are under the constraints imposed by the judicial function in our democratic society. As a matter of verbal recognition certainly, no one will gainsay that the function in construing a statute is to ascertain the meaning of words used by the legislature. To go beyond it is to usurp a power which our democracy has lodged in its elected legislature. The great judges have constantly admonished their brethren of the need for discipline in observing the limitations. A judge must not rewrite a statute, neither to enlarge nor to contract it. Whatever temptations the statesmanship of policy-making might wisely suggest, construction must eschew interpolation and evisceration. He must not read in by way of creation. He must not read out except to avoid patent nonsense or internal contradiction. . . .

. . . Judges may differ as to the point at which the line should be drawn, but the only sure safeguard against crossing the line between adjudication and legislation is an alert recognition of the necessity not to cross it and instinctive, as well as trained, reluctance to do so.

In those realms where judges directly formulate law because the chosen lawmakers have not acted, judges have the duty of adaptation and adjustment of old principles to new conditions. But where policy is expressed by the primary lawmaking agency in a democracy, that is by the legislature, judges must respect such expressions by adding to or subtracting from the explicit terms which the lawmakers use no more than is called for by the shorthand nature of language.

* This paper was first delivered as the Sixth Annual Benjamin N. Cardozo Lecture before the Association of the Bar of the City of New York, March 8, 1947. It is based, Justice Frankfurter tells us, upon an examination of the opinions of Holmes, Brandeis and Cardozo.—Editor

Admonitions like that of Justice Brandeis in the Iselin* case that courts should leave even desirable enlargement to Congress will not by itself furnish the meaning appropriate for the next statute under scrutiny. But as is true of other important principles, the intensity with which it is believed may be decisive of the outcome.

The Process of Construction.

Let me descend to some particulars.

The text.—Though we may not end with the words in construing a disputed statute, one certainly begins there. You have a right to think that a hoary platitude, but it is a platitude not acted upon in many arguments. In any event, it may not take you to the end of the road. The Court no doubt must listen to the voice of Congress. But often Congress cannot be heard clearly because its speech is muffled. Even when it has spoken, it is as true of Congress as of others that what is said is what the listener hears. Like others, judges too listen with what psychologists used to call the apperception mass, which I take it means in plain English that one listens with what is already in one's head. One more caution is relevant when one is admonished to listen attentively to what a statute says. One must also listen attentively to what it does not say.

We must, no doubt, accord the words the sense in which Congress used them. That is only another way of stating the central problem of decoding the symbols. It will help to determine for whom they were meant. Statutes are not archaeological documents to be studied in a library. They are written to guide the actions of men. As Mr. Justice Holmes remarked upon some Indian legislation, "The word was addressed to the Indian mind." [17] If a statute is written for ordinary folk, it would be arbitrary not to assume that Congress intended its words to be read with the minds of ordinary men. If they are addressed to specialists, they must be read by judges with the minds of the specialists.

And so we assume that Congress uses common words in their popular meaning, as used in the common speech of men. The cases speak of the "meaning of common understanding," "the normal and spontaneous meaning of language," "the common and appropriate use," "the natural straightforward and literal sense," and similar variants. . . .

Sometimes Congress supplies its own dictionary. It did so in 1871 in a statute defining a limited number of words for use as to all future enactments. It may do so, as in recent legislation, by a section within the statute containing detailed definitions. Or there may be indications from the statute that words in it are the considered language of legislation. "If Congress has been accustomed to use a certain phrase with a more limited meaning than might be attributed to it by common practice, it would be arbitrary to refuse to consider that fact when we come to interpret a statute. But, as we have said, the usage of Congress simply shows that it has spoken with careful precision, that its words mark the exact spot at which it stops." [19] Or words may acquire scope and function from the history of events which they summarize or from the purpose which they serve.

---

* Iselin v. United States, 270 U.S. 245, 250-251 (1926).—Editor
[17] Fleming v. McCurtain, 215 U.S. 56, 60 (1909).

[19] Boston Sand & Gravel Co. v. United States, 278 U.S. 41, 48 (1928).

"However colloquial and uncertain the words had been in the beginning, they had won for themselves finally an acceptance and a definiteness that made them fit to play a part in the legislative process. They came into the statute . . . freighted with the meaning imparted to them by the mischief to be remedied and by contemporaneous discussion. . . . In such conditions history is a teacher that is not to be ignored." [20]

Words of art bring their art with them. They bear the meaning of their habitat whether it be a phrase of technical significance in the scientific or business world, or whether it be loaded with the recondite connotations of feudalism. Holmes made short shrift of a contention by remarking that statutes used "familiar legal expressions in their familiar legal sense." [21] The peculiar idiom of business or of administrative practise often modifies the meaning that ordinary speech assigns to language. And if a word is obviously transplanted from another legal source, whether the common law or other legislation, it brings the old soil with it.

The context.—Legislation is a form of literary composition. But construction is not an abstract process equally valid for every composition, not even for every composition whose meaning must be judicially ascertained. The nature of the composition demands awareness of certain presuppositions. For instance, the words in a constitution may carry different meanings from the same words in a statute precisely because "it is a constitution we are expounding." The reach of this consideration was indicated by Mr. Justice Holmes in language that remains fresh no matter how often repeated:

"[W]hen we are dealing with words that also are a constituent act, like the Constitution of the United States, we must realize that they have called into life a being the development of which could not have been foreseen completely by the most gifted of its begetters. It was enough for them to realize or to hope that they had created an organism; it has taken a century and has cost their successors much sweat and blood to prove that they created a nation. The case before us must be considered in the light of our whole experience and not merely in that of what was said a hundred years ago." [22]

And so, the significance of an enactment, its antecedents as well as its later history, its relation to other enactments, all may be relevant to the construction of words for one purpose and in one setting but not for another. Some words are confined to their history; some are starting points for history. Words are intellectual and moral currency. They come from the legislative mint with some intrinsic meaning. Sometimes it remains unchanged. Like currency, words sometimes appreciate or depreciate in value.

Frequently the sense of a word cannot be got except by fashioning a mosaic of significance out of the innuendoes of disjointed bits of statute. Cardozo phrased this familiar phenomenon by stating that "the meaning of a statute is to be

[20] Mr. Justice Cardozo in Duparquet Co. v. Evans, 297 U.S. 216, 220, 221 (1936).
[21] Henry v. United States, 251 U.S. 393,

395 (1920).
[22] Missouri v. Holland, 252 U.S. 416, 433 (1920).

looked for, not in any single section, but in all the parts together and in their relation to the end in view." [23] And to quote Cardozo once more on this phase of our problem: "There is need to keep in view also the structure of the statute, and the relation, physical and logical, between its several parts." [24]

The generating consideration is that legislation is more than composition. It is an active instrument of government which, for purposes of interpretation, means that laws have ends to be achieved. It is in this connection that Holmes said "words are flexible." [25] Again it was Holmes, the last judge to give quarter to loose thinking or vague yearning, who said that "the general purpose is a more important aid to the meaning than any rule which grammar or formal logic may lay down." [26] And it was Holmes who chided courts for being "apt to err by sticking too closely to the words of a law where those words import a policy that goes beyond them." [27] Note, however, that he found the policy in "those words"!

Proliferation of Purpose. You may have observed that I have not yet used the word "intention." All these years I have avoided speaking of the "legislative intent" and I shall continue to be on my guard against using it. The objection to "intention" was indicated in a letter by Mr. Justice Holmes which the recipient kindly put at my disposal:

> "Only a day or two ago—when counsel talked of the intention of a legislature, I was indiscreet enough to say I don't care what their intention was. I only want to know what the words mean. Of course the phrase often is used to express a conviction not exactly thought out—that you construe a particular clause or expression by considering the whole instrument and any dominant purposes that it may express. In fact intention is a residuary clause intended to gather up whatever other aids there may be to interpretation beside the particular words and the dictionary."

If that is what the term means, it is better to use a less beclouding characterization. Legislation has an aim; it seeks to obviate some mischief, to supply an inadequacy, to effect a change of policy, to formulate a plan of government. That aim, that policy is not drawn, like nitrogen, out of the air; it is evinced in the language of the statute, as read in the light of other external manifestations of purpose. That is what the judge must seek and effectuate, and he ought not to be led off the trial by tests that have overtones of subjective design. We are not concerned with anything subjective. We do not delve into the mind of legislators or their draftsmen, or committee members. Against what he believed to be such an attempt Cardozo once protested:

> "The judgment of the court, if I interpret the reasoning aright, does not rest upon a ruling that Congress would have gone beyond its power if the purpose

---

[23] Panama Refining Co. v. Ryan, 293 U.S. 388, 433, 439 (1935) (dissenting).

[24] Duparquet Co. v. Evans, 297 U.S. 216, 218 (1936).

[25] International Stevedoring Co. v. Haverty,

272 U.S. 50, 52 (1926).

[26] United States v. Whitridge, 197 U.S. 135, 143 (1905).

[27] Olmstead v. United States, 277 U.S. 438, 469 (1928) (dissenting).

that it professed was the purpose truly cherished. The judgment of the court rests upon the ruling that another purpose, not professed, may be read beneath the surface, and by the purpose so imputed the statute is destroyed. Thus the process of psychoanalysis has spread to unaccustomed fields. There is a wise and ancient doctrine that a court will not inquire into the motives of a legislative body. . . ." [28]

The difficulty in many instances where a problem of meaning arises is that the enactment was not directed towards the troubling question. The problem might then be stated, as once it was by Mr. Justice Cardozo, "which choice is it the more likely that Congress would have made?" [29] While in its context the significance and limitations of this question are clear, thus to frame the question too often tempts inquiry into the subjective and might seem to warrant the court in giving answers based on an unmanifested legislative state of mind. But the purpose which a court must effectuate is not that which Congress should have enacted, or would have. It is that which it did enact, however inaptly, because it may fairly be said to be imbedded in the statute, even if a specific manifestation was not thought of, as is often the very reason for casting a statute in very general terms.

Often the purpose or policy that controls is not directly displayed in the particular enactment. Statutes cannot be read intelligently if the eye is closed to considerations evidenced in affiliated statutes, or in the known temper of legislative opinion. Thus, for example, it is not lightly to be presumed that Congress sought to infringe on "very sacred rights." [30] This improbability will be a factor in determining whether language, though it should be so read if standing alone, was used to effect such a drastic change. . . .

Search for Purpose. How then does the purpose which a statute expresses reveal itself, particularly when the path of purpose is not straight and narrow? The English courts say: Look at the statute and look at nothing else. . . .

. . . The rigidity of English courts in interpreting language merely by reading it disregards the fact that enactments are, as it were, organisms which exist in their environment. One wonders whether English judges are confined psychologically as they purport to be legally. The judges deem themselves limited to reading the words of a statute. But can they really escape placing the words in the context of their minds, which after all are not automata applying legal logic but repositories of all sorts of assumptions and impressions? Such a modest if not mechanical view of the task of construction disregards legal history. In earlier centuries the judges recognized that the exercise of their judicial function to understand and apply legislative policy is not to be hindered by artificial canons and limitations. The well known resolutions in Heydon's Case,[33] have the flavor of Elizabethan English but they express the substance of a current volume of U.S. Reports as to the considerations relevant to statutory interpretation. To be sure, early English legislation helped ascertainment of purpose by explicit recitals; at least to the extent of de-

[28] United States v. Constantine, 296 U.S. 287, 298, 299 (1936) (dissenting).
[29] Burnet v. Guggenheim, 288 U.S. 280, 285 (1933).

[30] Milwaukee Social Democrat Publishing Co. v. Burleson, 255 U.S. 407, 438 (1921) (dissenting).
[33] 3 Co. 7a 76 Eng. Rep. 637 (1584).

fining the mischief against which the enactment was directed. . . . Judicial construction certainly became more artificial after the practice of elucidating recitals ceased. It is to be noted that Macaulay, a great legislative draftsman, did not think much of preambles. He believed that too often they are jejune because legislators may agree on what ought to be done, while disagreeing about the reasons for doing it. At the same time he deemed it most important that in some manner governments should give reasons for their legislative course.[35] When not so long ago the Parliamentary mechanism was under scrutiny of the Lord Chancellor's Committee, dissatisfaction was expressed with the prevailing practise of English courts not to go outside the statutes. It was urged that the old practise of preambles be restored or that a memorandum of explanation go with proposed legislation.[36]

At the beginning, the Supreme Court reflected the early English attitude. With characteristic hardheadedness Chief Justice Marshall struck at the core of the matter with the observation "Where the mind labours to discover the design of the legislature, it seizes everything from which aid can be derived."[37] This commonsensical way of dealing with statutes fell into disuse, and more or less catchpenny canons of construction did service instead. To no small degree a more wooden treatment of legislation was due, I suspect, to the fact that the need for keeping vividly in mind the occasions for drawing on all aids in the process of distilling meaning from legislation was comparatively limited. As the area of regulation steadily widened, the impact of the legislative process upon the judicial brought into being, and compelled consideration of, all that convincingly illumines an enactment, instead of merely that which is called, with delusive simplicity, "the end result." Legislatures themselves provided illumination by general definitions, special definitions, explicit recitals of policy, and even directions of attitudes appropriate for judicial construction. Legislative reports were increasingly drawn upon, statements by those in charge of legislation, reports of investigating committees, recommendations of agencies entrusted with the enforcement of laws, etc. When Mr. Justice Holmes came to the Court, the U.S. Reports were practically barren of references to legislative materials. These swarm in current volumes. And let me say in passing that the importance that such materials play in Supreme Court litigation carry far-reaching implications for bench and bar.

The change I have summarized was gradual. Undue limitations were applied even after courts broke out of the mere language of a law. We find Mr. Justice Holmes saying, "It is a delicate business to base speculations about the purposes or construction of a statute upon the vicissitudes of its passage."[38] And as late as 1925 he referred to earlier bills relating to a statute under review, with the reservation "If it be legitimate to look at them."[39]

---

[35] Lord Macaulay's Legislative Minutes 145 et seq. (Dharker ed. 1946).
[36] Laski, Note to the Report of the Committee on Minister's Powers, Cmd 4060, Annex V, 135 (1932).
[37] United States v. Fisher, 2 Cranch 358,

386 (U.S. 1805).
[38] Pine Hill Coal Co. v. United States, 259 U.S. 191, 196 (1922).
[39] Davis v. Pringle, 268 U.S. 315, 318 (1925).

Such hesitations and restraints are in limbo. Courts examine the forms rejected in favor of the words chosen. They look at later statutes "considered to throw a cross light" upon an earlier enactment.[40] The consistent construction by an administrative agency charged with effectuating the policy of an enactment carries very considerable weight. While assertion of authority does not demonstrate its existence, long-continued, uncontested assertion is at least evidence that the legislature conveyed the authority. Similarly, while authority conferred does not atrophy by disuse, failure over an extended period to exercise it is some proof that it was not given. And since "a page of history is worth a volume of logic," [41] courts have looked into the background of statutes, the mischief to be checked and the good that was designed, looking sometimes far afield and taking notice also as judges of what is generally known by men.

Unhappily, there is no table of logarithms for statutory construction. No item of evidence has a fixed or even average weight. One or another may be decisive in one set of circumstances, while of little value elsewhere. A painstaking, detailed report by a Senate Committee bearing directly on the immediate question may settle the matter. A loose statement even by a chairman of a committee, made impromptu in the heat of debate, less informing in cold type than when heard on the floor, will hardly be accorded the weight of an encyclical.

Spurious use of legislative history must not swallow the legislation so as to give point to the quip that only when legislative history is doubtful do you go to the statute. While courts are no longer confined to the language, they are still confined by it. Violence must not be done to the words chosen by the legislature. Unless indeed no doubt can be left that the legislature has in fact used a private code, so that what appears to be violence to language is merely respect to special usage. In the end, language and external aids, each accorded the authority deserved in the circumstances, must be weighed in the balance of judicial judgment. Only if its premises are emptied of their human variables, can the process of statutory construction have the precision of a syllogism. We cannot avoid what Mr. Justice Cardozo deemed inherent in the problem of construction, making "a choice between uncertainties. We must be content to choose the lesser." [42] But to the careful and disinterested eye, the scales will hardly escape appearing to tip slightly on the side of a more probable meaning.

Canons of Construction. Nor can canons of construction save us from the anguish of judgment. Such canons give an air of abstract intellectual compulsion to what is in fact a delicate judgment, concluding a complicated process of balancing subtle and elusive elements. All our three Justices* have at one time or another leaned on the crutch of a canon. But they have done so only rarely, and with a recognition that these rules of construction are not in any true sense rules of law. So far as valid, they are what Mr. Justice Holmes called them, axioms of

---

[40] United States v. Aluminum Co. of Amer., 148 F. 2d 416, 429 (C.C.A. 2d 1945).

[41] New York Trust Co. v. Eisner, 256 U.S. 345, 349 (1921).

[42] Burnet v. Guggenheim, 288 U.S. 280, 288 (1933).

* The reference is to Holmes, Brandeis, and Cardozo.—Editor

experience.[43] In many instances, these canons originated as observations in specific cases from which they were abstracted, taken out of the context of actuality, and, as it were, codified in treatises. . . .

Fair Construction and Fit Legislation. The quality of legislative organization and procedure is inevitably reflected in the quality of legislative draftsmanship. Representative Monroney told the House last July that "ninety-five percent of all the legislation that becomes law passes the Congress in the shape that it came from our committees. Therefore if our committee work is sloppy, if it is bad, if it is inadequate, our legislation in ninety-five percent of the cases will be bad and inadequate as well." [44] And Representative Lane added that ". . . in the second session of the 78th Congress 953 bills and resolutions were passed, of which only 86 were subject to any real discussion." [45] But what courts do with legislation may in turn deeply affect what Congress will do in the future. Emerson says somewhere that mankind is as lazy as it dares to be. Loose judicial reading makes for loose legislative writing. It encourages the practise illustrated in a recent cartoon in which a senator tells his colleagues, "I admit this new bill is too complicated to understand. We'll just have to pass it to find out what it means." A modern Pascal might be tempted at times to say of legislation what Pascal said of students of theology when he charged them with "a looseness of thought and language that would pass nowhere else in making what are professedly very fine distinctions." And it is conceivable that he might go on and speak, as did Pascal, of the "insincerity with which terms are carefully chosen to cover opposite meanings." [46]

But there are more fundamental objections to loose judicial reading. In a democracy the legislative impulse and its expression should come from those popularly chosen to legislate, and equipped to devise policy, as courts are not. The pressure on legislatures to discharge their responsibility with care, understanding and imagination should be stiffened, not relaxed. Above all, they must not be encouraged in irresponsible or undisciplined use of language. In the keeping of legislatures perhaps more than any other group is the well-being of their fellow-men. Their responsibility is discharged ultimately by words. They are under a special duty therefore to observe that "Exactness in the use of words is the basis of all serious thinking. You will get nowhere without it. Words are clumsy tools, and it is very easy to cut one's fingers with them, and they need the closest attention in handling; but they are the only tools we have, and imagination itself cannot work without them. You must master the use of them, or you will wander forever guessing at the mercy of mere impulse and unrecognized assumptions and arbitrary associations, carried away with every wind of doctrine." [47]

Perfection of draftsmanship is as unattainable as demonstrable correctness of

---

[43] Boston Sand & Gravel Co. v. United States, 278 U.S. 41, 48 (1928).

[44] 92 Cong. Rec. 10040 (1946).

[45] 92 Cong. Rec. 10054 (1946).

[46] Pater, Essay on Pascal in Miscellaneous Studies 48, 51 (1895).

[47] Allen, Essay on Jeremy Bentham in The Social and Political Ideas of the Revolutionary Era 181, 199 (Hearnshaw ed. 1931).

judicial reading of legislation. Fit legislation and fair adjudication are attainable. The ultimate reliance of society for the proper fulfilment of both these august functions is to entrust them only to those who are equal to their demands.

QUESTIONS

1. Why should courts consider themselves bound to effectuate the intent of the legislature in their interpretation of statutes? Do Jones, Horack, Curtis, and Frankfurter agree or disagree that courts should be so bound?

2. Is the "intent" of the legislature ascertainable? Whose or what "intent" is the legislative "intent"? Do our authors agree in answering these questions? If the legislative intent is as fictional as has been claimed, how can its use as a standard be justified?

3. Do our authors agree on the extent to which statutory interpretation is, in fact, a creative judicial act? Do they agree on how far judges should feel free to interpret statutes so as to reach results in accord with their own notions of public policy? What other guides to decision do they have?

4. Do you agree that the problem of interpreting a statute differs from that of interpreting the Constitution and that the courts should approach these two problems with different attitudes? Why?

5. How do you think our authors would have decided the Lagage case referred to in number 9, Notes and Questions, page 415.

MESSAGE OF GOVERNOR ROBERT M. LA FOLLETTE TO THE 46TH REGULAR SESSION OF THE LEGISLATURE (1903)
Assembly Journal 102-104 (1903)

. . . To your careful consideration I recommend the question of more efficient protection to employees of railroad companies who may be injured in the discharge of their duties through carelessness or negligence of other employees or agents of the company. Of itself the employment is in most instances extremely hazardous to the employee. In the discharge of his duties he is frequently required not only to risk his life to save other lives, but he must jeopardize it to protect the property of the company and of the public. The duties of these men are quasi-public. The most efficient service that they can give is due to the public in protection of life and property, the safety of which depends upon their fidelity and courage. No man should be called to the discharge of such duties without assured compensation for injuries which he may receive through no fault of his own, or without reasonable provision for the support and maintenance of wife, children or other dependents, if his life be destroyed in the performance of his duty. While it is recognized that the service of these men under existing law, as a rule, is faithfully and honestly performed, there can be no doubt that just provision for himself in case of injury, or for those dependent upon him in the event of his death, would afford a consideration that would increase the efficiency of the service and redound to the benefit of the travelling public in addition to being a proper exercise of simple justice to a worthy class of citizens.

The statute on this subject has been inadequate since the year 1880. Section 1816 of the Revised Statutes of 1878, enacted by the Legislature of 1875, treated the subject comprehensively and offered substantial remedy. . . .

This law was repealed in 1880 through the influence and in the interest of railway companies, although it had been declared a valid enactment by the Supreme Court of the State. From that time till 1889 there was no State law pertaining to the subject. In the latter year a slight modification of the common law was enacted. It did not remedy the wrong. In 1893 the Legislature passed the present law. . . . It was a make shift provision. The first subdivision of the section is virtually a re-enactment of the common law on the subject and gives no practical remedy to the employee which he did not have before it was enacted. The remaining subdivision, which contains all there is of protection to the employee . . . restricts the right to recover by the employee within very narrow limits and does not approach in sufficiency the law repealed in 1880. Under this Act no employee can recover for injuries sustained unless engaged in the specific character of employment stated, and then only when the injury is caused by the carelessness of another employee, officer or agent while he is acting in the discharge of or in a failure to discharge his specific duties as such.

This statute has been strictly construed and restricted within these narrow limits by the decisions of the courts as being in derogation of the common law. It has been held that while a switchman and car-repairer were fellow-servants, if by the carelessness of the switchman another car was kicked against the stationary car in which the repairer was at work in the discharge of his duty, and the latter injured, he could not recover because his case was not within the express words of the statute. It has been decided that a railroad conductor, standing by a car for the purpose of watching a switch and closing the car door after it was unloaded, who was struck and injured by a bundle negligently thrown by a co-employee was "not engaged in operating, running, riding upon or switching trains, engines or cars" and was not within the provision of the law. The unloaded car was to be attached to the train which the conductor was to take out. It was his duty to close the door of the car in question, and yet he could not recover because no statute embraced his case. The negligence for which a recovery can be had must be the negligence of a co-employee in the discharge of his specific duty. If it be caused by the negligence of a fireman who is discharging the duty of an engineer, or of a superintendent who negligently performs the duty of a laborer or other employee, a conductor or brakeman in the discharge of any other duty than that to which he has been assigned by the company, the statute is held not to cover the case, and there can be no recovery.

The plan of this legislation was cunningly devised and the statute artfully drawn. It was enacted in the interest of the companies with the purpose of modifying as little as possible the common law on the subject. It was passed in the face of the public demand for a much more effective law giving ample protection to men engaged in this work.

I recommend that it be repealed and that section 1816 of the Statutes of 1878 be re-enacted.

NOTES AND QUESTIONS

1. Wisconsin Constitution:

"ARTICLE IV. Section 1. The legislative power shall be vested in a senate and assembly.

"ARTICLE V. Section 1. The executive power shall be vested in a governor. . . .

"Section 4. The governor . . . shall communicate to the legislature, at every session, the condition of the state, and recommend such matters to them for their consideration as he may deem expedient. . . .

"Section 10. Every bill which shall have passed the legislature shall, before it becomes a law, be presented to the governor; if he approve, he shall sign it, but if not, he shall return it, with his objections, to that house in which it shall have originated, who shall enter the objections at large upon the journal and proceed to reconsider it. . . . If, after such reconsideration, two-thirds of the members present shall agree to pass the bill, . . . it shall be sent, together with the objections, to the other house, by which it shall likewise be reconsidered, and if approved by two-thirds of the members present it shall become a law. . . . If any bill shall not be returned by the governor within six days (Sundays excepted) after it shall have been presented to him, the same shall be a law unless the legislature shall, by their adjournment, prevent its return, in which case it shall not be a law."

2. United States Constitution: "ARTICLE II, Section 3. He [the President] shall from time to time give to the Congress information of the state of the union, and recommend to their consideration such measures as he shall judge necessary and expedient." . . .

Article V, section 10 of the Wisconsin Constitution, *supra*, is modelled almost word for word upon Article II, section 7, paragraph 2 of the United States Constitution.

3. What functions does a governor's message perform in the legislative process? How much influence should it have on the subsequent interpretation of the statute enacted? See Johnson v. Southern Pacific Co., 196 U.S. 1, 19 (1904) where the Supreme Court of the United States, in interpreting a federal statute as requiring railroads to provide automatic couplers on cars, stated in support of its interpretation: "That this was the scope of the statute is confirmed by the circumstances surrounding its enactment, as exhibited in public documents to which we are at liberty to refer . . . President Harrison, in his annual messages of 1889, 1890, 1891 and 1892, earnestly urged upon Congress the necessity of legislation to obviate and reduce the loss of life and the injuries due to the prevailing method of coupling and braking. . . ."

4. How radical was LaFollette's message? Does he blame the courts for the inadequacies in the existing law to which he calls the legislature's attention?

EDITORIAL NOTE: The LEGISLATIVE ROLE
of the EXECUTIVE

The message of Governor LaFollette, reprinted above, introduces the question of the executive's role in legislation, which we shall come back to from time to time. In his stimulating book, The Legislative Struggle (1953), Bertram M. Gross, who was staff adviser to various committees of the United States Senate and executive secretary to the Council of Economic Advisers from 1946 to 1952, emphasizes that it is a fiction to think that government serves the "public interest" by standing above the struggle among the competing groups and interests in society. He quotes James Madison who, in the Federalist Paper No. 10, asked, "What are the different classes of legislators but advocates and parties to the causes which they determine?" (*Ibid.* at 92). It may be argued that what Madison said of legislators is true of the executive, as indicated by the LaFollette message and the history of the American Presidency.

The President, says Gross, in addition to his other duties as head of state, Commander in Chief of the armed forces, party chief, and conductor of our foreign relations, is "the most important single legislative leader in the Government." (*Ibid.* at 101). The Constitution, of course, expressly imposes upon the President various duties in connection with the legislative process. To discharge the responsibility imposed upon him by Article II, section 3, the President, at the beginning of each year, sends to Congress (1) a State of the Union Message; (2) an Economic Report; and (3) a Budget Message. Each of these messages contains proposals for legislation. The Budget Message is confined, of course, to proposals for appropriation acts. In addition, special messages dealing with particular legislative matters flow from the White House to Capitol Hill throughout the legislative session.

The President's ability to effectuate his program is based not only on his express constitutional powers but also, as Gross points out, on such informal means as conferences and correspondence with the leaders and members of Congress, the manipulation of patronage, the allocation of Federal funds and projects, the handling of constituents' cases in which members of Congress are interested, and direct appeal to the voters at large. (*Ibid.* at 102). It is Gross's principal thesis that the relative strength of the President and Congress at any particular time depends upon the strength of the groups in society which seek to achieve their aims principally through the one rather than the other institution of Government. Thus he thinks that farm groups (and the business groups supported by them) look primarily to Congress because, under our electoral system, farm groups are over-represented in Congress, relative to the urban population. And because they are under-represented in Congress, organized workers and racial minorities, who may hold the balance of power in presidential elections, tend to look to and give strength to the Presidency. (*Ibid.* at 103).

LAWS, 1903, Chapter 448

AN ACT to define the liabilities of any railroad company in relation to damages sustained by its employees and amendatory of subdivision 2 of section 1816 of the statutes of 1898.

The people of the state of Wisconsin, represented in Senate and Assembly, do enact as follows:

SECTION 1. Subdivision 2 of section 1816 of the statutes of 1898 is hereby amended by striking out all of said subdivision 2 and inserting in lieu thereof the following as said subdivision 2. "2. When such injury is sustained by any officer, agent, servant or employee of such company, while engaged in the line of his duty as such and which shall have been caused by the carelessness or negligence of any other officer, agent, servant or employee while in the discharge of, or for failure to discharge his duty as such, provided, that such injury shall arise from a risk or hazard peculiar to the operation of railroads. No contract, receipt, rule or regulation between any employee and a railroad corporation shall exempt such corporation from the full liability imposed by this section." So that said section and subdivision when so amended shall be and read as follows: Section 1816. Every railroad company operating any railroad which is in whole or in part within this state shall be liable for all damages sustained within the same by any of its employees without contributory negligence on his part:

1. When any such injury is caused by a defect in any locomotive, engine, car, rail, track, machinery or appliance required by said company to be used by its employees in and about the business of their employment, if such defect could have been discovered by such company by reasonable and proper care, tests or inspection; and proof of such defect shall be presumptive evidence of knowledge thereof on the part of such company.

2. When such injury is sustained by any officer, agent, servant or employee of such company, while engaged in the line of his duty as such and which shall have been caused by the carelessness or negligence of any other officer, agent, servant or employee while in the discharge of, or for failure to discharge his duty as such, provided, that such injury shall arise from a risk or hazard peculiar to the operation of railroads. No contract, receipt, rule or regulation between any employee and a railroad corporation shall exempt such corporation from the full liability imposed by this section.

SECTION 2. Any act or part of act conflicting or in any manner inconsistent with the provisions of this act is hereby repealed.

SECTION 3. This act shall take effect and be in force from and after its passage and publication.

Approved May 22, 1903.

QUESTIONS

1. To what extent did the Legislature accept the recommendations of Governor LaFollette?

2. Was the 1903 statute more favorable to employees, or less so, than each of the preceding statutes? To what extent did it retain the common law pattern of liability?

MESSAGE OF GOVERNOR ROBERT M. LA FOLLETTE TO THE 47TH REGULAR SESSION OF THE LEGISLATURE (1905)
Assembly Journal 82-83 (1905)

. . . The importance of providing for protection which is justly due to railroad employees and their families is again urged upon the law-making body. In the biennial message sent to the legislature in 1903, this subject was discussed somewhat at length. I have not since that time changed my views in reference to this matter, and again recommend that suitable provision as suggested in that message be made for such protection.

Chapter 448, of the laws of 1903, was enacted and became the law by my approval. Its provisions fall far short of doing justice to the railroad employee. I attached a memorandum to the bill expressing my views of it at the time I approved it, as follows:

[Headings: May 22, 1903]

"At the beginning of the session I had the honor to recommend that the present statutes, respecting the right of recovery under what is known as the co-employee law for the benefit of railroad employees be so amended as to afford a more substantial benefit to those engaged in that service.

"Pursuant to this recommendation, a bill much more favorable to railroad employees than the present law was passed by one branch of the legislature, but it has been so modified by amendment that its scope and value are much narrowed, as it now comes to me for executive action. While it falls far short of the full measure of relief, recommended in the message, as justly due to railroad employees, nevertheless, it seems to embrace within its provisions a somewhat larger number of those engaged in this important service than are now within the protection of the existing statute. I am aware that this bill is unsatisfactory to those who expected a more liberal measure and who in their disappointment, would at this time prefer that it should not become a law, but I am impressed with the great difficulties which such legislation encounters, and regard it as wise to secure for the present whatever ground has been gained at this session. For these reasons I approve this bill.

[Signature]

Chapter 448 of the Laws of 1903 ought to be repealed, and Bill No. 554, A., introduced into the assembly of 1903, or some bill equally strong, affording at least as high a degree of protection to the persons employed in the railroad service, ought in my judgment to become a law.

THE FEDERALIST
No. 78:456-462 (Lodge's ed. 1778)

[This paper was written by Alexander Hamilton under the name of "Publius" in support of the proposed constitution.—Editor]

The third ingredient towards constituting the vigor of the executive authority, is an adequate provision for its support. It is evident that, without proper attention to this article, the separation of the executive from the legislative department would be merely nominal and nugatory. The legislature, with a discretionary power over the salary and emoluments of the Chief Magistrate, could render him as obsequious to their will as they might think proper to make him. They might, in most cases, either reduce him by famine, or tempt him by largesses, to surrender at discretion his judgment to their inclinations. These expressions, taken in all the latitude of the terms, would no doubt convey more than is intended. There are men who could neither be distressed nor won into a sacrifice of their duty; but this stern virtue is the growth of few soils; and in the main it will be found that a power over a man's support is a power over his will. If it were necessary to confirm so plain a truth by facts, examples would not be wanting, even in this country, of the intimidation or seduction of the Executive by the terrors or allurements of the pecuniary arrangements of the legislative body.

It is not easy, therefore, to commend too highly the judicious attention which has been paid to this subject in the proposed Constitution. It is there provided that "The President of the United States shall, at stated times, receive for his service a compensation *which shall neither be increased nor diminished during the period for which he shall have been elected; and he shall not receive within that period any other emolument* from the United States, or any of them" . . .

The last of the requisites to energy, which have been enumerated, are competent powers. Let us proceed to consider those which are proposed to be vested in the President of the United States.

The first thing that offers itself to our observation, is the qualified negative of the President upon the acts or resolutions of the two houses of the legislature; or, in other words, his power of returning all bills with objections, to have the effect of preventing their becoming laws, unless they should afterwards be ratified by two thirds of each of the component members of the legislative body.

The propensity of the legislative department to intrude upon the rights, and to absorb the powers, of the other departments, has been already suggested and repeated; the insufficiency of a mere parchment delineation of the boundaries of each, has also been remarked upon; and the necessity of furnishing each with constitutional arms for its own defence, has been inferred and proved. From these clear and indubitable principles results the propriety of a negative, either absolute or qualified, in the Executive, upon the acts of the legislative branches. Without the one or the other, the former would be absolutely unable to defend himself against the depredations of the latter. He might gradually be stripped of his authorities by successive resolutions, or annihilated by a single vote. And in the one mode or the other, the legislative and executive powers might speedily come to be blended in the same hands. If even no propensity had ever discovered itself in the legislative body to invade the rights of the Executive, the rules of just reasoning and theoretic propriety would of themselves teach us, that the one ought not to be left to the mercy of the other, but ought to possess a constitutional and effectual power of self-defence.

But the power in question has a further use. It not only serves as a shield to the Executive, but it furnishes an additional security against the enaction of improper laws. It establishes a salutary check upon the legislative body, calculated to guard the community against the effects of faction, precipitancy, or of any impulse unfriendly to the public good, which may happen to influence a majority of that body.

The propriety of a negative has, upon some occasions, been combated by an observation, that it was not to be presumed a single man would possess more virtue and wisdom than a number of men; and that unless this presumption should be entertained, it would be improper to give the executive magistrate any species of control over the legislative body.

But this observation, when examined, will appear rather specious than solid. The propriety of the thing does not turn upon the supposition of superior wisdom or virtue in the Executive, but upon the supposition that the legislature will not be infallible; that the love of power may sometimes betray it into a disposition to encroach upon the rights of other members of the government; that a spirit of faction may sometimes pervert its deliberations; that impressions of the moment may sometimes hurry it into measures which itself, on maturer reflection, would condemn. The primary inducement to conferring the power in question upon the Executive is, to enable him to defend himself; the secondary one is to increase the chances in favor of the community against the passing of bad laws, through haste, inadvertence, or design. The oftener the measure is brought under examination, the greater the diversity in the situations of those who are to examine it, the less must be the danger of those errors which flow from want of due deliberation, or of those missteps which proceed from the contagion of some common passion or interest. It is far less probable, that culpable views of any kind should infect all the parts of the government at the same moment and in relation to the same object, than that they should by turns govern and mislead every one of them.

It may perhaps be said that the power of preventing bad laws includes that of preventing good ones; and may be used to the one purpose as well as to the other. But this objection will have little weight with those who can properly estimate the mischiefs of that inconstancy and mutability in the laws, which form the greatest blemish in the character and genius of our governments. They will consider every institution calculated to restrain the excess of law-making, and to keep things in the same state in which they happen to be at any given period, as much more likely to do good than harm; because it is favorable to greater stability in the system of legislation. The injury which may possibly be done by defeating a few good laws, will be amply compensated by the advantage of preventing a number of bad ones.

Nor is this all. The superior weight and influence of the legislative body in a free government, and the hazard to the Executive in a trial of strength with that body, afford a satisfactory security that the negative would generally be employed with great caution; . . .

It is evident that there would be greater danger of his not using his power when necessary, than of his using it too often, or too much. An argument, indeed, against its expediency, has been drawn from this very source. It has been represented, on this account, as a power odious in appearance, useless in practice. But it will not follow, that because it might be rarely exercised, it would never be exercised. In the case for which it is chiefly designed, that of an immediate attack upon the constitutional rights of the Executive, or in a case in which the public good was evidently and palpably sacrificed, a man of tolerable firmness would avail himself of his constitutional means of defence, and would listen to the admonitions of duty and responsibility. In the former supposition, his fortitude would be stimulated by his immediate interest in the power of his office; in the latter, by the probability of the sanction of his constituents, who, though they would naturally incline to the legislative body in a doubtful case, would hardly suffer their partiality to delude them in a very plain case. I speak now with an eye to a magistrate possessing only a common share of firmness. There are men who, under any circumstances, will have the courage to do their duty at every hazard.

But the convention have pursued a mean in this business, which will both facilitate the exercise of the power vested in this respect in the executive magistrate, and make its efficacy to depend on the sense of a considerable part of the legislative body. Instead of an absolute negative, it is proposed to give the Executive the qualified negative already described. This is a power which would be much more readily exercised than the other. A man who might be afraid to defeat a law by his single VETO, might not scruple to return it for reconsideration; subject to being finally rejected only in the event of more than one third of each house concurring in the sufficiency of his objections. He would be encouraged by the reflection, that if his opposition should prevail, it would embark in it a very respectable proportion of the legislative body, whose influence would be united with his in supporting the propriety of his conduct in the public opinion. A direct and categorical negative has something in the appearance of it more harsh, and more apt to irritate, than the mere suggestion of argumentative objections to be approved or disapproved by those to whom they are addressed. In proportion as it would be less apt to offend, it would be more apt to be exercised; and for this very reason, it may in practice be found more effectual. It is to be hoped that it will not often happen that improper views will govern so large a proportion as two thirds of both branches of the legislature at the same time; and this, too, in spite of the counterposing weight of the Executive. It is at any rate far less probable that this should be the case, than that such views should taint the resolutions and conduct of a bare majority. A power of this nature in the Executive, will often have a silent and unperceived, though forcible, operation. When men, engaged in unjustifiable pursuits, are aware that obstructions may come from a quarter which they cannot control, they will often be restrained by the bare apprehension of opposition, from doing what they would with eagerness rush into, if no such external impediments were to be feared. . . .

EDITORIAL NOTE: PRESIDENTIAL APPROVAL of BILLS and EXERCISE of the VETO POWER

The Constitution gives the President three choices in handling bills approved by both Houses of Congress—(1) "If he approve he shall sign it,"; (2) "but if not he shall return it, with his Objections to that House in which it shall have originated,"; (3) "If any Bill shall not be returned by the President within ten Days (Sundays excepted) after it shall have been presented to him, the Same shall be a Law, in like Manner as if he had signed it, unless the Congress by their Adjournment prevent its Return, in which Case it shall not be a Law." (Article I, section 7, paragraph 2).

Gross points out that many methods have been devised by our Presidents to indicate the degree of their approval of a bill which they have signed. To underscore the importance of a bill fully approved of, a full-fledged ceremony, duly photographed and often televised, may surround the act of signing. Or a statement calling public attention to the new law may be issued by the President. This statement may also constitute the first and most important interpretation of the new law, setting the course of administration policy. (Gross, The Legislative Struggle [1953] 404).

Presidential statements may also be used to explain why the President signed a bill although he was reluctant to do so. Governor LaFollette's memorandum, set forth above, is an example of this type of statement on the state level. Gross cites similar actions by Presidents Taft and Truman. (*Ibid.* at 405). Both these statements, as did Governor LaFollette's, recommended further action.

Sometimes, the President may accompany his approval of a bill with a message explaining his understanding of ambiguous provisions of the bill. President Truman did so when he approved the Hobbs Anti-Racketeering Act of July 3, 1946 (P.L. No. 486, 79th Cong., 2d Sess.) and the Portal-to-Portal Act of May 14, 1947 (P.L. No. 49, 80th Cong., 1st Sess.). Will such a message be part of the legislative history that will guide the courts in construing the statute in question? Professor Corwin thinks it should not be. "For a court to vary its interpretation of an act of Congress in deference to something said by the President at the time of signing it would be to attribute to the latter the power to foist upon the houses intentions that they never entertained, and thereby to endow him with a legislative power not shared by Congress." (Corwin, The President: Office and Powers, 1787-1957 [1957] 284.) Do you agree?

From the purely statistical view, the Presidential veto appears to be of little consequence. The total number of vetoes from 1789 to 1950 was only 2,002; and from 1921 to the end of 1948, the total number of vetoed bills was only about two-tenths of one percent of all bills enacted into law. (*Ibid.* at 406). President Franklin D. Roosevelt, who was most active in this regard, vetoed 505 bills by the close of his second term. (Robinson, The Veto Record of Franklin D. Roosevelt, 36 Am. Pol. Sci. Rev. 75 (1942)). As of July 1, 1960, President Eisenhower had vetoed 169 bills during his two terms of office. (The New York Times, July 2, 1960, p. 1, col. 8).

However, statistics of use alone do not measure the significance of the Presidential veto, which is "normally effective in nine cases out of ten." (Corwin, *supra* at 282. President Eisenhower's record is even better. In only two cases—a public works bill in 1959 and a bill in 1960 to give pay increases to 1,500,000 federal employees—was his veto overridden.) Professor Neustadt writes that "to FDR the veto power was among the presidency's greatest attributes, an independent and responsible act of participation in the legislative process, and a means of enforcing congressional and agency respect for presidential preferences or programs." (Neustadt, Presidency and Legislation: Growth of Central Clearance, 48 Am. Pol. Sci. Rev. 641, 656 (1954)).

The mere possibility of a veto, as Hamilton predicted, often may be sufficient to enable the President to secure from Congress the kind of legislation he wishes. And the constitutional provision for the pocket veto puts the President in a very strong position regarding bills sent to him during the ten days before adjournment because there is no possibility of overriding action by Congress unless, of course, Congress postpones its adjournment.

Gross reports that for every three regular vetoes, there have been, on the average, two pocket vetoes. (*Ibid.* at 411). Until 1934 it was not customary for a President to explain publicly why he used the pocket veto, but President Franklin D. Roosevelt broke this precedent in 1934 when he issued public statements explaining why he pocket-vetoed 53 bills. President Truman and President Eisenhower have followed this practice.

MESSAGE OF GOVERNOR JAMES O. DAVIDSON TO THE 48TH REGULAR SESSION OF THE LEGISLATURE (1907)
Assembly Journal 60-61 (1907)

. . . The present co-employee law consists of two clauses,—the first, in respect to defective appliances; the second, respecting injuries received by the negligence of co-employees. This law does not change the common-law rule which the United States supreme court has criticised and gives no increased protection. The second clause is so limited in the construction given it by the courts that it leaves many employees without protection at all. Under this statute the railroads have two defenses against claims for damages as a result of injuries to their employees. The supreme court has construed the law to apply only to train crews when actually operating the train and apparently while the train is in motion. The railroads also have the defense of contributory negligence which has been strictly enforced by the courts. The defense of contributory negligence often works injustice in a construction where the slightest degree of contributory negligence bars a recovery.

I recommend the passage of a law which will permit railway employees to recover damages for injuries, if it is found that their negligence was less than that of the railroad or that of a co-employee contributing to the injury, and that in all cases there shall be submitted to the jury the question of the existence of contributory negligence and the comparison of the negligence as between the railroad and the employee. It seems no more than just that where the negligence of the railroad contributed to the injury the company should bear a proportionate share of the loss.

LAWS, 1907, Chapter 254

AN ACT to amend section 1816 of the statutes, relating to liability of railroad companies for injuries sustained by employes.

The people of the state of Wisconsin, represented in senate and assembly, do enact as follows:

SECTION 1. Section 1816 of the statutes is amended to read:

SECTION 1816. Every railroad company . . . shall be liable for . . . damages . . . for all injuries whether resulting in death or not, sustained by any of its employes, subject to the provisions hereinafter contained regarding contributory negligence on the part of the injured employe:

1. When . . . such injury is caused by a defect . . . in any locomotive, engine, car, rail, track, roadbed, machinery or appliance . . . used by its employes in and about the business of their employment. . . .

2. When such injury . . . shall have been sustained by any officer, agent, servant or employe of such company, while engaged in the line of his duty as such and which such injury shall have been caused in whole or in greater part by the . . . negligence of any other officer, agent, servant or employe, of such company, . . . in the discharge of, or . . . by reason of failure to discharge his duties as such. . . .

3. In every action to recover for such injury the court shall submit to the jury the following questions: First, whether the company, or any officer, agent, servant or employe other than the person injured was guilty of negligence directly contributing to the injury; second, if that question is answered in the affirmative, whether the person injured was guilty of any negligence which directly contributed to the injury; third, if that question is answered in the affirmative, whether the negligence of the party so injured was slighter or greater as a contributing cause to the injury than that of the company, or any officer, agent, servant or employe other than the person so injured; and such other questions as may be necessary.

4. In all cases where the jury shall find that the negligence of the company, or any officer, agent or employe of such company, was greater than the negligence of the employe so injured, and contributing in a greater degree to such injury, then the plaintiff shall be entitled to recover, and the negligence, if any, of the employe so injured shall be no bar to such recovery.

5. In all cases under this act the question of negligence and contributory negligence shall be for the jury.

6. No contract or receipt between any employe and a railroad company, no rule or regulation promulgated or adopted by such company, and no contract, rule or regulation in regard to any notice to be given by such employe shall exempt such corporation from the full liability imposed by this act.

7. The phrase "railroad company," as used in this act, shall be taken to embrace any company, association, corporation or person managing, maintaining, operating, or in possession of a railroad in whole or in part within this state whether as owner, contractor, lessee, mortgagee, trustee, assignee or receiver.

8. In any action brought in the courts of this state by a resident thereof, or the representative of a deceased resident, to recover damages in accordance with this act, where the employe of any railroad company owning or operating a railroad extending into or through this state and into or through any other state or states shall have received his injuries in any other state where such railroad is owned or operated, and the contract of employment shall have been made in this state, it shall not be competent for such railroad company to plead or prove the

decisions or statutes of the state where such person shall have been injured as a defense to the action brought in this state.

9. The provisions of this act shall not apply to employes working in shops or offices.

Approved June 19, 1907.

NOTES AND QUESTIONS

1. Schmidt, History of Labor Legislation in Wisconsin (1953) (Unpublished doctoral thesis, deposited in the Library of the University of Wisconsin) pp. 53-57: "The Railroad Brotherhoods were not satisfied with the 1903 law and came to the 1905 session with demands for modifications. They wanted a more effective abrogation of the fellow-servant defense, and a substitution of the rule of comparative negligence for that of contributory negligence. . . . Railroad workers throughout the country were working at this time for the adoption of the rule of comparative negligence. In 1906 it was incorporated in the Federal Employers' Liability Act, and in 1907 eight states adopted it. In his message to the legislature in 1905, Governor LaFollette pointed out the need for a new employers' liability law for railroad workers. The Railroad Brotherhoods employed an attorney to state their case before the legislative committees. The railroad lobbies fought the measure vigorously, and were successful in having the bill defeated in the senate. The effectiveness of Progressive support for these measures both in 1903 and 1905 was weakened somewhat by the fact that in those years two other issues on which they had been fighting the railroads for a number of years were settled. The railroad taxation law of 1903 and the rate regulation law of 1905 were two of the Progressives' most important victories in those years. They supported the Railroad Brotherhoods in the demand for an employers' liability law, but it was characteristic of LaFollette tactics to concentrate the greatest effort on a few issues in each year, leaving others for subsequent legislative sessions. In 1907 Governor Davidson succeeded LaFollette . . . as the Progressive candidate for governor. Davidson was elected, and turned his attention to carrying out the remainder of the LaFollette program. . . . The railroad lobbies opposed the employers' liability bill of 1907, as they had been opposing similar bills since 1875 and as they had fought LaFollette's taxation and rate regulation programs, but this time Progressive support of the Railroad Brotherhoods was effective, and the law was enacted. . . ."

2. To what extent did the Legislature accept the recommendations of Governor David-son?

3. Was the 1907 statute more favorable to employees, or less so, than each of the preceding statutes? Did it retain the common law pattern of liability?

4. Did the employees ultimately retain everything the Legislature seemed to give them? See Kiley v. C.M.&St.P. Ry. Co., 138 Wis. 215, 119 N.W. 309 (1909) (previously considered in connection with the second Wedgwood case, Chap. 6,) which upheld the constitutionality of the 1907 statute. Even after Kiley, would a greater or lesser number of cases get to the jury under the 1907 law than under the prior statutes?

5. Do the foregoing materials—the progression of statutes affecting the fellow-servant rule, the governor's messages, the history summarized in note 1, above—suggest anything regarding the justification, or lack of justification, for a "rule" of strict construction of these statutes? Do these materials suggest any basis for a general presumption favoring strict construction of statutes in derogation of the common law?

6. How would you compare the ways in which law is shaped and declared by the legislature and by the courts?

a. Consider the two processes in terms of the relative efficiency of their responses to community needs and pressures, the relative certainty or fluctuation of legal rules arrived at, haphazard or planned development of the law, breadth or narrowness of presentation of the conflicting interests involved.

b. In answering these questions, it may be helpful to consult Dicey, Law and Public Opinion in England (2d ed., 1914) 361-370 and Horack, The Common Law of Legislation (23 Iowa L. Rev. 41, 41-49, 53-56 (1937). Do you think the materials we have considered thus far tend to support or refute Dicey's observation that "If a statute . . . is apt to reproduce the public opinion not so much of to-day as of yesterday, judge-made law occasionally represents the opinion of the day before yesterday." Do you think they tend to support or refute Horack's conclusions that (1) "Continuity of legislative policy is in degree similar to judicial precedent"; (2) one can therefore "predict within similar degrees of error the development of statutory rule"; (3) "case by case statutory expansion has paralleled the judicial technique of deciding questions as they arise"; (4) like courts, legislatures, before reaching their decisions, afford the essentials of a trial (notice, hearing, adversary presentation of evidence) which in some respects (e.g., responsibility for getting at the facts) is superior to the judicial trial; and (5) the "standard which guides the actions of each (legislatures and courts) is little more than judgment concerning desirable social controls."

c. Looking back at the modifications which the Wisconsin legislature made during the period 1875-1907 in the common law, so far as the railroad industry was concerned, do you think it would have been proper for the Wisconsin courts to effect these same modifications in the absence of any legislation? Could such court action have rested upon a "reasoned elaboration of the law" which Professor Hart tells us is the "distinctive function" of the courts? Henry M. Hart, Jr., Comment on Courts and Lawmaking, in Legal Institutions Today and Tomorrow 43 (The Centennial Conference Volume of the Columbia Law School, 1959).

d. Consider Professor Hart's following comments in the same volume at p. 42: "Do we or do we not want the general body of our law at the end of the next half century to rest upon a coherent and intelligible fabric of principle? Do we or do we not want it to have the qualities of understandability, of acceptability, and of susceptibility to being reasoned about which only a body of law that is founded on such a fabric of principle can have? If this is what we want, then we will have to depend heavily upon the courts to give it to us. No other agency of lawmaking is equipped to do the job without the assistance of the courts.

"The basic reason why this is so is that there is no substitute for the intensive analysis and the creative exposition of principles and policies at the point at which general propositions come into contact with concrete situations, so that they can be tested there. The courts are the only institution of solid authority in our society engaged in making decisions at this point.[42] In addition to this, the courts are the only institution which is manned by personnel with the training that is requisite, and which operates by the procedure that is appropriate, for the authoritative exposition of principle."

MC KIVERGAN v. ALEXANDER & EDGAR LUMBER CO.
124 Wis. 60, 102 N.W. 332 (1905)

This action was brought to recover damages which plaintiff claims to have suffered by the negligence of defendant.

[42] Administrative agencies engaged in adjudication may be thought to be an exception to this statement. But each agency deals only with a specialized segment of the law. Nor, for the most part, have administrative judges shown themselves to be adept or persuasive expositors of principle. Perhaps for this reason, their expositions do not enjoy a prestige with the public comparable to that of the courts.

The defendant is a corporation under the laws of Wisconsin, "organized for the purpose of carrying on a general logging, lumbering, and manufacturing business, buying and selling real estate and merchandise." In connection with defendant's business it operates a private railroad. The operation of its railroad business extends from Iron River, Bayfield county, to a place one mile west of Brule—a distance of about twelve miles over the tracks of the Northern Pacific Railway Company, and thence over their private side track for about four miles, with spurs projecting into adjacent timber lands. In conducting its railroad it used two geared locomotives in hauling logs to the sidetracks, and two regular locomotives in hauling timber to its mill at Iron River. It also used Russel logging and other cars for this purpose, part of which were leased from the Northern Pacific Railway. The Northern Pacific track used by defendant is a part of its main line, and while running over its track defendant operates under orders of the Northern Pacific Company. It used this track daily for the passage both ways of two or three trains of from twelve to sixteen cars.

At the time of the accident complained of, plaintiff was in defendant's employ and engaged as brakeman in the operation of defendant's logging trains. The injury occurred while plaintiff was in the discharge of his duty as such brakeman, and while in the act of making a coupling between one of defendant's logging cars and the engine. It is alleged that while plaintiff was exercising ordinary care in performing his duty, in attempting to place and adjust the link to make the coupling, the engineer carelessly and negligently caused the cars to move towards plaintiff and against the logging car, causing the injury to his fingers and hands.

The case was tried and submitted to a jury, who found for the plaintiff and awarded him damages. Thereafter the defendant moved for judgment in its favor notwithstanding the verdict, which motion the court granted, and awarded judgment accordingly. This is an appeal from such judgment. . . .

SIEBECKER, J. The court awarded judgment dismissing the complaint, notwithstanding the verdict, for the reason that no actionable negligence had been shown against defendant. The ruling was based upon the ground that the liabilities established by the provisions of sec. 1816, Stats. 1898, [L. 1893, ch. 220.—Editor.] did not attach to defendant. . . .

It is contended by plaintiff that in construing this statute the phrase "railroad company," as used in this section, is to be applied as the phrase "railroad corporation" is used in sec. 1861, Stats. 1898, which is as follows:

"The phrase 'railroad corporation' as used in these statutes, may be taken to embrace any company, association, corporation or person managing, maintaining, operating or in possession of a railroad, whether as owner, contractor, lessee, mortgagee, trustee, assignee or receiver."

Adopting this interpretation leads us to the inquiry, Upon whom did the legislature intend to impose the liabilities prescribed by the terms of sec. 1816, Stats. 1898? Were its terms only to apply to railroad corporations doing a public service, commonly known as "commercial railroads," or was it intended to impose these liabilities on every person, company, or corporation operating trains, engines, or cars, regardless of whether such business was in the nature of a public service as common carrier, or devoted exclusively to a private enterprise, including no public service? The question is not so clear and plain as to be free from all difficulties. If the statute be held to apply to the character of the employment, then no valid reason is suggested why it should not be held to cover all classes of public and private railroads, regardless of the nature of their business. The contents of this particular section might in its literal sense, permit of such an application. This, however, would put it out of harmony with the other provisions of ch. 87, Stats. 1898, covering legislation "on railroads" in this state. The best way to ascertain the legislative intent, under such circumstances, is to consider all the legislative provisions on the subject of which the provision is a part; keeping in view the occasion and necessity of the law and the object sought to be accomplished.

An examination of the provisions of this chapter discloses numerous provisions pointing to the fact that the legislation therein contained referred exclusively to railroad corporations doing the usual business of a public or commercial railroad. Among some of its provisions are those prescribing equality of rates for the transportation of persons or of property for a like service; the obligation to furnish cars for the transportation of property within a reasonable time after notice; the obligation to follow the regulations prescribed for the shipment of grain, carrying of live stock, the stopping of trains, the maintenance of guards and fences, and other requirements for the protection and safety of the public. An important and distinguishing characteristic of railroads included within the purview of this chapter is the grant to every corporation organized under it of the power of exercising the right of eminent domain in its quasi-public character. In the case of Chicago & N.W.R. Co. v. O., A. & B.W.R. Co., 107 Wis. 192, 83 N.W 294, it was held, in effect, that these provisions make it clear, and must remove any doubt, that in the legislative intent a railroad corporation, within the provisions of this chapter, is one engaged in a general railroad business "for the carriage of passengers and freight—a common carrier in its fullest sense—and to it [are] given the fullest provisions for condemnation of lands, as compensation for the great public duties imposed upon and assumed by it." The difference between such a railroad and one used as an incident to conducting a private business is readily perceived and understood without elaboration. The objects and uses of the one are far removed from those of the other, though the instruments of operation, such as tracks, cars, and engines, may be common to both.

Since the provisions of all these sections of this chapter, aside from sec. 1816, plainly and unmistakably include commercial railroads only, is there any conceivable ground for holding that this section includes private as well as commercial railroads or common carriers? We have discovered nothing which would warrant the court in enlarging the meaning of the terms of this section beyond the plain meaning of the same terms in the other provisions of this chapter. Every argument for so extending its terms applies with equal force to their use throughout other provisions on this subject. We must conclude that sec. 1816 is intended to embrace within its provisions only such railroad companies as are contemplated by ch. 87, Stats. 1898, namely, one engaged in a general railroad business for the carriage of passengers and freight; that is, a common carrier in the fullest sense. From this it necessarily follows that defendant does not come within the terms of the statute. . . .

The case of Roe v. Winston, 86 Minn. 77, 90 N.W. 122, is cited to our attention. In this case it appeared that plaintiff was injured in this state while in defendant's employ as brakeman on a private train used in connection with defendant's business of general railroad construction work, and the court held he was entitled to recover under the provisions of sec. 1816. His right to recover was predicated on the ground that the provisions of this section applied to a private railroad business. The decision follows the construction adopted by the court in construing a similar Minnesota statute, holding that it was applicable to the business of a private as well as a public service railroad. We are unable to avoid the conclusion that this construction is opposed to the manifest intent of the legislature, as embodied in this section and the other legislation on this subject.

By the Court.—The judgment is affirmed.

JONES v. MILWAUKEE ELECTRIC RY. & L. CO,
147 Wis. 427, 133 N.W. 641 (1911)

TIMLIN, J. . . . [Plaintiff, administratrix of a deceased employee] argues that the words "railroad company" in ch. 254, Laws of 1907, amending sec. 1816, Stats. (1898) [L. 1893, ch. 220.—Editor] were intended to include electric interurban railways, and hence that the defense of assumption of risk and that of the fellow-servant's negligence are not available to defendant. The phrase "railroad company" is defined in this act "to embrace any company," etc., "managing, maintaining, operating or in possession of a railroad." In one sense an electric interurban road is a railroad. The cars run on rails. But we think it is not a railroad within the meaning of this act. The amendatory act purports to amend sec. 1816, Stats. (1898), and this section is found in the chapter relating to the ordinary steam-driven commercial railroad which is operated by a corporation organized under a statute different from that under which defendant is organized and which imposes different duties and grants different powers. Again, many of the provisions of the chapter on railroads in which occurs sec. 1816 are entirely inapplicable to electric interurban roads. In various acts of the legislature, such as chs. 282, 580, and 582, Laws of 1907; ch. 475, Laws of 1909; and ch. 366, Laws of 1911, by specially naming electric interurban railways instead of attempting to cover them by general laws relating to railroads, the legislature has to some extent indicated its understanding that something more definite than the general term "railroads" or "railroad companies" was requisite to identify as the object of the legislation these electric interurbans. Next, the history of the statute, sec. 1816, Stats. (1898), and the popular use of the word "railroad" as indicating something other than an electric interurban railway, and what we conceive to be the general understanding of the legal profession, and the expressions of this court in McKivergan v. Alexander & E.L. Co., 124 Wis. 60, 102 N.W. 332; Gould v. Merrill R.&L. Co., 139 Wis. 433, 121 N.W. 161; State ex rel. Vilter Mfg. Co. v. M.,

B.&L.G.R. Co., 116 Wis. 142, 92 N.W. 546, and other cases, all tend to negative this construction. It would be quite a stretch of construction for this court to hold that the heavy burdens of sec. 1816 were intended by the legislature to be imposed on electric interurban railways under the term "railroads," when the legislature could use and is accustomed to use the more specific description in legislation concerning the interurbans. Where a statute is drastic and its burdens heavy it is not permissible to bring within its terms by latitudinarian construction those not named therein. This merely recognizes the intention which ordinarily accompanies any such command, and this principle lies at the basis of what is called strict construction. The effect of assumption of risk by the employee of an interurban railways company is not changed by this statute.

WEITZMAN v. BISSELL LUMBER CO.
193 Wis. 561, 214 N.W. 353 (1927)

OWEN, J. The first question to be determined is whether by sub. (5), sec. 192.27, Stats., the defendant was under a legal duty to maintain the warning sign at the crossing of the railroad track over the highway in question. It is the contention of the respondent that this statute applies only to common carriers and not to a private corporation such as the defendant, which simply maintains and operates a railroad in connection with its own private business. Sec. 192.27 is found in ch. 192 of the Statutes, which relates to the general regulations and liabilities of railroads. From a perusal of the general provisions of this chapter it is apparent that a great portion of the regulations therein contained applies only to common-carrier railroads. For instance, it prescribes passenger fares, penalizes passengers who do not provide themselves with a ticket before boarding a train, requires every railroad corporation operating a road to receive any and all grain offered to it and to deliver to the shipper or consignor the usual bill of lading for such grain; much the same regulations with reference to live stock; requires the maintenance of stations at certain places, and many other similar regulations which undeniably apply only to common-carrier railroads.

Ch. 180, Stats., provides for the organization of domestic corporations, and provides, among other things, that such corporations may be organized for the purpose of "building, constructing, maintaining and operating private steam logging railroads for use in carrying on and conducting a logging and lumbering business," etc. Ch. 190 provides specifically for the organization of corporations "for the purpose of constructing, maintaining and operating a railroad for public use in the conveyance of persons or property," etc.

Generically speaking, therefore, there is an obvious difference between a common-carrier railroad and a private logging road such as that operated by the defendant.

Prior to the passage of ch. 291, Laws 1923, the present chapters 190, 191, and 192 of our present statutes formed a part of ch. 87 of the Wisconsin Statutes. By sec. 1861, then a part of ch. 87, it was provided, "The phrase 'railroad corporation,' as used in these statutes, may be taken to embrace any company, association, corporation or person managing, maintaining, operating or in possession of a railroad, whether as owner, contractor, lessee, mortgagee, trustee, assignee or receiver." It is to be noticed that this definition does not provide that the phrase "railroad corporation" *shall* be taken to embrace any company, etc. It simply says that the phrase "railroad corporation" *may be* taken to embrace any company, etc. Now what was the purpose of this provision in the nature of a definition of the phrase "railroad corporation?" Certainly it did not mean that the phrase "railroad corporation" should at all times be construed as therein provided. It laid down a rule, but not a hard-and-fast rule, of construction. Manifestly it was intended to be an elastic rule, and one which would enable the courts to give effect to the legislative intent.

The major part of the regulations of ch. 87 were appropriate only to common-carrier railroads. As a rule, by the statutory language quite consistently implied throughout the chapter, the regulations were made to apply to "any railroad corporation." However, a perusal of said ch. 87 discloses regulations quite as appropriate to private corporations operating private railroads as to public railroads. This would seem true with reference to safety regulations. This is also true of sec. 1836, for example, which requires every corporation constructing, owning, or using a railroad to restore every stream of water, watercourse, street, highway, etc. along which such railroad may be constructed to its former state of usefulness. In this section the duty is not laid on every "railroad corporation," the general expression used throughout the chapter, but upon every corporation constructing, owning, or using a railroad.

It will at once be seen that this regulation is as appropriate to private railroads as to common carriers. Not only that, but the language of the section plainly expresses the legislative intent to comprehend private as well as public railroads. Sec. 1809, a part of former ch. 87, provides that "any railroad company or corporation operating a railroad in this state" shall not run its trains faster than therein provided. Obviously this regulation relates not only to public railroads but to private corporations operating railroads as well. These provisions are cited to illustrate that all the regulations included in the old ch. 87, most of which are now to be found in chapters 190, 191, and 192, were not intended to apply exclusively to public or common-carrier railroads. It seems obvious, therefore, that the rule of construction embodied in sec. 1861 (now sec. 192.74) was prescribed for the purpose of enabling the court to construe the term "railroad corporation" to include not only any other kind of corporations but any person or individual, where such was the evident legislative purpose.

This conclusion is further strengthened by consideration of the decision of this court in McKivergan v. Alexander & Edgar L. Co., 124 Wis. 60, 102 N.W. 332, and the legislation following that decision. In that case sec. 1816 of the Statutes, which provided that "Every railroad company operating any railroad which is in whole or in part within this state shall be liable for all damages sustained within the same by any of its employees without contributory negligence on his part," etc., was construed as applying exclusively to public or common-carrier railroads. In the course of the opinion the court said: "An examination of the provisions of this chapter discloses numerous provisions pointing to the fact that the legislation therein contained referred exclusively to railroad corporations doing the usual business of a public or commercial railroad." The court not only held that the provisions of sec. 1816 referred exclusively to such railroads, but it took occasion to say, obiter, that the provisions of the entire chapter applied exclusively to such railroads. It did not undertake to say what was meant by the rule of construction provided by sec. 1861. However, we apprehend that the rule of construction there laid down is sufficiently clear to obviate the necessity for elucidation. The decision in the McKivergan Case was rendered January 31, 1905. Although the legislature was in session in 1905 it apparently took no notice of the decision. However, said sec. 1816 was revised by ch. 254, Laws of 1907, and the legislature expressly wrote into this section the construction embodied in sec. 1861. Here certainly is a most emphatic legislative declaration that said sec. 1861 (now sec. 192.74) is intended to apply to other than public railroad companies.

Recurring to the provisions of sub. (5), sec. 192.27, we cannot proceed upon the theory that all regulations of railroads formerly embodied in ch. 87 applied exclusively to public railroads, and we are required to determine not only from the language employed, but from the subject matter and the purpose of the legislation, whether that section, requiring warning signs at railroad crossings, applies to the defendant. The opening portion of that section reads as follows: "No railroad company or corporation operating a railroad in this state and whose line of road extends into or through any incorporated city or village, shall run a train or locomotive faster than fifteen miles an hour," etc. Then sub. (5) of said section, the provision with which we are here concerned, provides: "Every such railroad company or corporation shall erect and maintain at all times at every place where its railroad track crosses a public highway or street" the warning sign prescribed therein. It would seem that the legislature ex industria not only included within this regulation railroad corporations but private corporations operating a railroad. Furthermore, when we refer to the purpose of this legislation, no reason is apparent why a logging railroad should be excluded from the duties therein imposed.

It is said that logging railroads do not run their trains as fast, nor operate trains as heavy, as commercial roads. However, logging railroads frequently run through undeveloped country and cross highways where the vision is greatly obscured, and although they do not run as fast or operate as heavy trains, they are quite as much a menace to the traveler upon the highway as the heavier and faster-moving trains of the commercial railroads. We conclude that it was the duty of the defendant to maintain the warning sign required by sub. (5), sec. 192.27, at this highway crossing and that its absence constituted negligence on its part. . . .

[Eschweiler, J., dissented without opinion on the interpretation of the statute.— Editor]

NOTES AND QUESTIONS REGARDING THE FOREGOING THREE CASES

1. Define precisely for each case the reasons and sources of information relied on by the court in determining the legislative intention. Are these cases further illustrations of the rule of strict construction of statutes in derogation of the common law? Are they consistent?

2. How does the Weitzman court's looking at other statutes in the same chapter differ from the way in which the McKivergan and Jones courts looked at other statutes in the same chapter?

Note that the court in McKivergan thought its duty was to keep "in view the occasion and necessity of the law and the object sought to be accomplished." The court in Weitzman similarly regarded its obligation—to consider "the subject matter and the purpose of the legislation."

Should it matter in this connection that all parts of ch. 87, Revised Statutes 1898, were not enacted at the same time?

3. A law punished by a fine of between $10 and $25, driving an auto on a "public highway" at more than 12 miles per hour. Defendant exceeded the limit on a toll road operated by a private corporation under certain statutes. Other statutes had differentiated between toll roads and public highways (e.g., when a private owner abandoned a toll road, it became a public highway; and there was a procedure for public acquisition of toll roads to make them public highways). Defendant's conduct was held covered by the speeding law. Can the decision be reconciled with the private railroad cases above, particularly with reference to the practice of looking for guidance to other statutes? Can the decision be reconciled with the "plain meaning" rule? See Weirich v. State, 140 Wis. 98 (1909).

4. What justification, if any, is there for the rule of construction relied upon by the court in Jones that where "a statute is drastic and its burdens heavy it is not permissible to bring within its terms by latitudinarian construction those not named therein"?

5. Is the legislative usage exemplified by the laws of 1907, 1909, and 1911, relied upon by the court in Jones, relevant to the question before the court in that case?

6. How would Jones, Horack, and Curtis decide the Jones case?

7. How persuasive is the court's reliance in Weitzman upon the legislative events following the decision in McKivergan?

8. Documents on file at the office of the Secretary of State of Wisconsin reveal that proposed substitute amendment 2-S to the bill finally passed as L. 1907, ch. 254, would have defined "railroad corporation" "to embrace any . . . person . . . operating . . . a railroad in whole or in part within this state, whether as owner, contractor, lessee, mortgagee, trustee, assignee or receiver, engaged in business as a common carrier." Reported out without approval of the committee charged with the bill, this amendment was rejected by vote of the Senate. Sen. Jour. (1907) 789. How would you appraise these cases in the light of this information? Note that this bit of history was not referred to by the court in Weitzman.

9. Could the problems here resolved by judges have been anticipated by the draftsmen?

Section 3

LEGISLATION CONCERNING the EMPLOYER'S DUTY to PROVIDE a "SAFE PLACE" for WORK; FURTHER ASPECTS of STATUTORY CONSTRUCTION

EDITORIAL NOTE: SUMMARY of LEGISLATION

Beginning with L. 1893, ch. 220, the legislation on injuries to railroad workers contained declarations regarding the employing railroad's duty to furnish a safe place and safe instruments for work. No systematic effort was made until shortly before the passage of the first workmen's compensation act to alter the common law defenses as to non-railroad workers in the state's industries, but from an early date there were enacted, more or less haphazardly, various statutes pertaining to the employer's duty to provide a "safe place" for work. Thus there was provision for fire escapes and outward-opening doors in factories (L. 1878, ch. 212; L. 1885, ch. 50; L. 1885, ch. 190; L. 1887, ch. 46; L. 1895, ch. 355; cf. L. 1868, ch. 44), laws regulating hours of labor for women and children (e.g., L. 1867, ch. 83; L. 1891, ch. 190; L. 1899, ch. 274; L. 1901, ch. 182; L. 1903, ch. 402; L. 1903, ch. 349; L. 1907, ch. 523), requiring provision of seats for women workers (L. 1899, ch. 77), regulating the number of persons who might be employed in certain building areas, and the conditions of labor pertinent to sanitation (e.g., L. 1887, ch. 549; L. 1895, ch. 279; L. 1899, ch. 79; L. 1899, ch. 232), providing for safe scaffolding, etc., in building construction (L. 1901, ch. 257; L. 1909, ch. 163), requiring provision of speaking tubes or other means of communication between the engine and machine rooms of factories (L. 1891, ch. 266), and regulating the use of emery wheels (L. 1899, ch. 189; L. 1907, ch. 115). Several important statutes were passed providing for a system of factory inspection.

So far as one can judge from the published sources, the part of the state's "safe place" legislation which was most involved in closely contested litigation was the series of statutes dealing with injuries caused by rapidly moving machinery—"belting, shafting, gearing, hoists, fly-wheels, elevators and drums. . . ." There were three important enactments in this field—L. 1887, ch. 549; L. 1905, ch. 303; L. 1911, ch. 396 (cf. L. 1907, ch. 112. Compare also L. 1889, ch. 123, regarding safety devices on railroad "frogs"). These statues regarding the safety of machinery are involved in the materials printed below.

Regarding general industrial accident legislation prior to 1911, consider the comments in Schmidt, History of Labor Legislation in Wisconsin (1933) 60: "If the workers in other industries could have secured a law like that for railroad employees which was passed in 1907, they would probably have been well satisfied. But the railroads were at that time the subject of legislative attack on other questions. [Railroad taxation and regulation, and the legislation designed to limit the power of political bosses, who were, in many cases, connected with the railroads.—Author's Footnote]. Also the unfairness of the law of employers' liability was clearest for the workers on railroads. A similar law for local industries, against whom no political battles were being fought, and in which the law of employers' liability seemed less unjust, would probably have been regarded as too drastic at that time. It is clear, however, that the gains which the railroad workers made in 1907 influenced the demands of other workers when a general scheme of workmen's compensation was being considered. [See especially the State Federation of

Labor's insistence on the workers' right of suit with the defense modified.
—Author's Footnote.]"

LAWS, 1887, Chapter 549

AN ACT to regulate factories, workshops and other places of employment.

The people of the state of Wisconsin, represented in senate and assembly, do enact as follows:

SECTION 1. No person, persons or corporation shall employ and put to work in any factory, workshop or other place of employment, or in any room or other part of such factory, workshop or other place of employment, more persons than the laws of health will warrant, as shall be determined by the board of health.

SECTION 2. Every stationary vat, pan or other structure with molten metal or hot liquids shall be surrounded with proper safeguards for preventing accidents or injury to those employed at or near them. All belting, shafting, gearing, hoists, fly-wheels, elevators and drums of manufacturing establishments so located as to be dangerous to employes when engaged in their ordinary duties shall be securely guarded or fenced so as to be safe to persons employed in any such place of employment.

SECTION 3. Any person, company or corporation who shall refuse or fail to comply with the provisions of this act, shall forfeit not to exceed twenty-five dollars for each offense, and every day's failure after the first conviction shall constitute a separate offense, after due notice by the state factory inspector.

SECTION 4. This act shall take effect and be in force from and after its passage and publication.

Approved April 15, 1887.

WISCONSIN STATUTES OF 1898

SECTION 1636j. No person or corporation shall employ and put to work in any factory, workshop or other place where labor is performed, or in any part of any such place, a larger number of persons than can be kept at work there without doing violence to the laws of health. The local board of health shall have power to determine any question arising under this provision, and its written determination shall be conclusive upon all parties to any action or proceeding under the same. The owner or manager of every place where persons are employed to perform labor shall surround every stationary vat, pan or other vessel into which molten metal or hot liquids are poured or kept with proper safeguards for the protection of his employees, and all belting, shafting, gearing, hoists, fly-wheels, elevators and drums therein which are so located as to be dangerous to employees in the discharge of their duty shall be securely guarded or fenced. Any person or corporation which shall neglect for thirty days after the receipt of written notice from the state factory inspector to provide a suitable place for the persons employed by him to work in or who shall fail to make and maintain such safeguards as this section requires, and as said inspector shall specify, shall forfeit not to exceed twenty-five dollars for each offense, and every day's neglect or failure, after a conviction hereunder, shall constitute a separate offense.

proximity of uncovered machinery. The defendant was entitled to an instruction which should inform the jury of the extent and limit of the defendant's duty to the plaintiff in respect to the safety of the place where his work was to be performed, and the rule of negligence in relation to that situation. The defendant asked this instruction on that point: "The court instructs you that if the defendant furnished a place which was as safe and free from danger as other persons of ordinary care, prudence, and caution, engaged in like business and in like circumstances ordinarily furnish, then you must find that the defendant furnished to the plaintiff a reasonably and ordinarily safe place to work." This proposed instruction undeniably states the law of negligence as applicable to the duty of the master to furnish a safe place to work, and to the facts of the case, with substantial accuracy. It should have been given as asked. It was error to refuse it, unless it was substantially given in the general charge. It was in fact given in the general charge, in substantially the same language but with the addition of a proviso or qualification which utterly perverts its force, and destroys its meaning, and leaves the jury utterly without a guide or standard by which to test the defendant's performance of the duty which it owed to the plaintiff. It gave correctly the general rule or definition of negligence as "a lack of ordinary care, or such care as men of ordinary care ordinarily use," and that "neither party to this action was bound to use extraordinary care, such care as those use who are more careful, cautious, or prudent than the great mass of mankind ordinarily use." But, as relating specifically to the duty of the defendant to furnish a reasonably safe place for the plaintiff to do his work in the instruction was: "If the defendant furnished plaintiff a place which was as safe and free from danger as other persons of ordinary care engaged in like business and under like circumstances ordinarily furnish, then you will find for the defendant on such fact; but not if you find that places provided by such other employers of labor for their workmen or servants are not reasonably safe places in which their men are obliged to work. It is for you to say, from the whole evidence, whether such is the fact or not, as you, and not myself, are the judges of the fact."

No doubt the test of negligence is the presence or absence of that degree of care which ordinarily prudent persons are accustomed to observe about the same or similar affairs in the same or similar circumstances. The doctrine of a safe place to work has little application, as against known dangers. The employer may carry on his business in such place as he pleases, and with such machinery and appliances as he may choose, provided only he does not violate the positive law of the land, nor expose his employees to unknown dangers. The employee is deemed to accept the place furnished, with the risk of such dangers as he knows or can discover by the exercise of ordinary attention. Having observed such degree of care as ordinarily prudent men engaged in the same business observe, the law is satisfied, and no liability arises from accidents which may then happen, although they might have been prevented by the exercise of a greater degree of care. No person is required to exercise a greater degree of caution and prevision than is exercised by the mass of mankind. More care than that is usually impracticable. Ordinarily, the very highest degree of care possible will defeat the success of the enterprise. The

law aims to be practical and to favor what is practicable. The standard by which
the liability of the defendant is to be tested is the standard which the law has
provided. The jury may not be allowed to make a new one, to suit their inclination, in the particular case. The defendant in the particular action may not be
required to have been wise and prudent beyond all his fellows. That is the vice
of this instruction. It plainly informed the jury that they were not limited by
the law of negligence, but could make the law, for the case, according to their
own notion of what was right. It is often easy, after the accident, to see how it
might have been prevented. The retrospect has this advantage. Human prevision is limited. This was a fundamental error, which must require a reversal of
the judgment.

WEST v. BAYFIELD MILL CO.
144 Wis. 106, 128 N.W. 992 (1910)

BARNES, J. . . . The first question in the special verdict was as follows:

"Did the defendant ever securely guard the gearing of the machine at which
the deceased, Philip La Pointe, was injured before said accident?"

In reference to this question the court charged the jury, among other things:

"By securely guarding it is meant that the defendant should guard the gearing safely, that the persons who work about the building *should be secure
against danger or violence while performing their work.*"

Exception was taken to the portion of the charge quoted and error is predicated
thereon.

We will first consider whether the charge was erroneous, and, if it was, then
whether it was prejudicial. The language used is not qualified in any way elsewhere
in the charge. We think the jury would naturally understand from this charge
that it was the defendant's legal duty to so guard this gearing that injury to an
employee could not result therefrom. The language of the court is that the gearing
should be so safely guarded that the employee *"would be secure against danger
or violence while performing his work."* Even though the guard was an ordinarily
safe one, or an extraordinarily safe one for that matter, still, if injury or violence
resulted therefrom, then the guard was unsafe under the instruction. The instruction practically made the defendant an insurer of the employee against injury
from the gearing. It has been decided by this court that this is not a correct statement of the duty of the defendant under sec. 1636j, Stats. (1898). This section
as construed by this court does not require the employer to insure his employees'
safety against the possibility of injury, nor does it require of him infallibility nor
omniscience. It requires him first to decide whether the gearing is so situated as to
be dangerous to employees in the discharge of their duty, and, second, to securely
guard or fence it if dangerous. He must use ordinary care and prudence in deciding
the first question, and decide it as ordinarily careful and prudent employers under
like circumstances, in honest exercise of their judgment, would decide it. If such

an employer could reasonably apprehend that injury might result to an employee in the discharge of his ordinary duties from the unguarded gearing, then it is dangerous and must be guarded, and he must also proceed to furnish such a guard, or at least as effective a guard as such ordinarily careful and prudent employers under like circumstances would and do deem it their duty to furnish. This is a secure guard within the meaning of the law. Guinard v. Knapp-Stout Co., 95 Wis. 482, 70 N.W. 671. . . . The only exception to the last proposition is that if the guard so ordinarily furnished be obviously dangerous it will not be deemed sufficient. Yazdzewski v. Barker, 131 Wis. 494, 111 N.W. 689. . . .

There can hardly be any justification for the claim that, while the employer must exercise only ordinary care in discovering whether a gearing or a shaft should be fenced or guarded, yet, having discovered that a guard must be put in place, such guard must afford an absolute protection to the employee at all times and under all circumstances when he is engaged in the line of his employment. If only ordinary care is required in the first place in discovering a defect, ordinary care is all that is necessary in guarding it.

If this rule be wrong, then the court was wrong in holding in Koltz v. Power & M.M. Co., 136 Wis. 107, 116 N.W. 770, that, while sec. 1636jj, Stats. (Laws of 1905, ch. 303), took away the defense of assumption of hazard where sec. 1636j, Stats. (1898), had been violated, still the "employer's right to the defense of other phases of contributory negligence" was not taken away; and the court was in error again in approving of this decision in Lind v. Uniform S.&P. Co., 140 Wis. 183, 120 N.W. 839.

If it be the duty of the master to insure the employee against danger from an unguarded gearing, and to make it so safe that the employee cannot get hurt therein, then the servant has a perfect right to rely on this legal duty and to assume that it will be performed, and in the nature of things he cannot be guilty of any act of negligence that would defeat a recovery. He might, as against any kind of a guard, manage to injure himself if he set about to do so, but this would not be negligence. The principle involved is very closely analogous to the principles held applicable to the common-law duty of an employer to furnish to an employee a safe place to work. That duty is to furnish a place reasonably safe; i.e., a place as safe and free from danger as other persons of ordinary care and prudence in like business and under like circumstances ordinarily furnish, subject only to the limitation as to obviously unsafe places above indicated. . . . So the true rule, subject to the limitation referred to, is that, if the employer furnish such a guard as is in general use among employers of ordinary caution in the same line of business and under the same circumstances, he has discharged the duty imposed upon him, and the guard so furnished is in a legal sense reasonably safe and the dangerous machinery has been securely guarded within the meaning of the statute. This rule of law requires the master to exercise ordinary care in providing a guard or fence for such machinery as is required to be guarded or fenced. That given by the trial court required something beyond even extraordinary care, in that it held him liable if injury resulted. There are cases in which the trial court has referred to the language of sec. 1636j without attempting to explain the meaning thereof. There are cases in which this court has done likewise. But in no case in this court, where the question was squarely raised and presented, has the court decided that the rule established by the cases cited herein is not good law, and in no case has it been said that machinery and appliances are not securely guarded when the owner exercises the degree of care in reference thereto called for by the established rule. We conclude that the trial court erred in giving the instruction under consideration.

The judgment should not be reversed, however, unless it appears that the erroneous instruction has affected the substantial rights of the defendant. Ch. 192, Laws of 1909 (sec. 3072m. Stats.). Did it do so? At best, the question was a close one as to whether the defendant was guilty of any act of negligence in providing the guard in question. The defendant strenuously contends in this court that the evidence does not support the finding of the jury in this behalf. The court submitted the first question to the jury presumably because it dealt with a disputed question of fact, and we are satisfied that upon the evidence the jury might well have found that the defendant was free from negligence. So we have a vital question in the verdict on which the jury might have found in favor of either party. It seems to us that the instruction, in effect, took this question from the jury and left it nothing to decide, if the jury paid any heed to it, and in view of the conclusion reached this court cannot say that the instruction was not a controlling factor with the jury. If the machine should be so guarded that the deceased would be "secure against danger or violence," then clearly the defendant was at fault, because the deceased was injured by reason of the failure of the master to provide a guard that would protect him. The process of reasoning by which the jury would naturally reach the conclusion which it did is simple, direct, and well nigh obvious. The master should have provided a guard that would have prevented the injury. He did not do so. Therefore he did not perform his duty by properly guarding the gear. A contrary conclusion could not well have been reached unless the jury wholly disregarded the instruction. The prejudice that might result from the instruction was further emphasized by the receipt of testimony, against objection, showing that a sheet-iron guard could be placed over the gearing and securely fastened without impairing the usefulness of the machinery. If an erroneous instruction can be regarded as prejudicial in any case, we fail to see any escape from the conclusion that the error we are considering was substantial and that there must be a new trial because of it. . . .

The witness Elfstrom testified that the gearing could have been guarded by using a sheet-iron covering instead of hemlock boards; that such a guard could have been fastened on the roller bed; and that so fastened it would not have interfered with the use of the machine. The evidence was objected to and exception taken to the rulings of the court holding it competent. The evidence was not competent and should not have been received. . . . It is not competent to show that some kind of a guard should have been used which in the judgment of a witness might be more efficient than that provided. So long as the master uses the ordinary appliances commonly used by ordinarily prudent men, and has disobeyed no law of the land, he has fulfilled his duty, unless, perchance, such appliances are obviously dangerous. Guinard v. Knapp-Stout & Co., 95 Wis. 482, 70 N.W. 671. . . .

By the Court.—The judgment of the circuit court is reversed, and the cause is remanded for a new trial. . . .

TIMLIN, J. (dissenting) . . . It seems quite plain that if the gearing is in fact such gearing as the statute describes, viz., one so located as to be dangerous to employees in the discharge of their duty, the duty to guard or fence it is mandatory; and the manner in which it shall be guarded or fenced is in like case covered by mandatory statute, viz., it shall be "securely guarded." There should be no great difficulty in the construction of such a statute if we approach it with judicial equanimity. There is no contention in this case that the statute makes the employer an insurer. There is no contention that it takes away the defense of contributory negligence. Panic on these two propositions, self-suggested, seems to be responsible for the extraordinary construction first attempted to be given to this statute in Guinard v. Knapp-Stout & Co., 95 Wis. 482, 70 N.W. 671, and returned to and revived with additional and accumulated error by the majority opinion in the instant case, notwithstanding many cases in this court later than the Guinard Case and inconsistent therewith. . . .

The majority opinion in the instant case puts forward as an excuse for departing from the statute that otherwise the venerable and valuable defense of contributory negligence might or would be excluded and that otherwise the statute might make the employer an insurer of the safety of his employee. These twin specters of the imagination are also disposed of by former cases in this court.

> "This court has distinctly held that where the law requires some particular thing to be done by a person to guard the personal safety of others, a failure to perform the duty so imposed constitutes actionable negligence at the suit of a person of that class, injured by such failure of duty, without contributory negligence on his part." Smith v. Milwaukee B.&T. Exch., 91 Wis. 360, 64 N.W. 1041. . . .

In Van de Bogart v. Marinette & M.P. Co., 132 Wis. 367, 106 N.W. 805, an instruction to the jury concerning the statute in question and containing this sentence was approved:

> "The failure to guard or fence a set-screw on a shaft so located as to be dangerous to employees while in the discharge of their duty would be negligence."

This, as I understand it, makes the negligence of the employer a matter of law, provided the shafting is so located, and therefore that decision is in conflict with the decision in this case. Given a shaft so located as to be within the calls of the statute, if the failure to guard it is negligence per se, or if the duty to guard it is a duty imposed by law, then it follows that it is no excuse for the defendant that other persons also disregard this legal duty or commit other acts which also constitute negligence per se.

In Walker v. Simmons Mfg. Co., 131 Wis. 542, 111 N.W. 694, judgment for the plaintiff was affirmed notwithstanding this instruction given to the jury:

"The law requires that the employer shall securely guard or fence shafting which is so located as to be dangerous to employees in the discharge of their duties, and if you find that the shafting in question, under all the facts and circumstances proven, was so located as to be dangerous to the plaintiff in the discharge of his duties in the line of his employment at the time of the injury to him, you should answer this question 'No.'"

The question so peremptorily directed to be answered in the negative was this: "Was such place so furnished by the defendant a reasonably safe place in which to do his work?" Here is a direct instruction making it a matter of law that the place was unsafe if the shaft was so located as to be dangerous to employees in the discharge of their duty and unguarded. . . . In Anderson v. Horlick's M.M. Co., 137 Wis. 569, 119 N.W. 342, the court said:

"What would constitute a reasonable guarding of an elevator entrance under the circumstances *was determinable with reference to the mandate of the statute that it must be securely guarded. Nothing short of that would be a reasonable guarding.*"

This is also in conflict with the opinion in the instant case. Now if we compare what was said by this court in these decisions with what was said by the court below in the instant case to the jury for which the judgment below was reversed, not selecting a detached sentence from the instructions below as is done in the majority opinion, but giving the context, we will find that the instruction given by the court below was but a paraphrase of the foregoing language quoted from this court in Klatt v. N. C. Foster L. Co., *supra;* Van de Bogart v. Patten P. Co., *supra;* Walker v. Simmons Mfg. Co., *supra;* and Anderson v. Horlick's M.M. Co., *supra.* The instruction in the instant case in the court below was as follows:

"The law requires the employer of labor, where the laborer is required to work about dangerous gearing which is so located as to be dangerous to the workmen, to securely fence or guard the same. It was the duty under this statute for the defendant to securely guard the gearing of the machine in question. The evidence of the plaintiff, the plaintiff claims, tends to prove that the defendant was guilty of negligence in not complying with the law in this respect. The defendant claims that its evidence tends to prove that the gearing of the machine in question was securely guarded. *By securely guarding it is meant that the defendant should guard the gearing safely, that the persons who work about the gearing should be secure against danger or violence while performing their work.* The statute in relation to this question reads as follows:" (reads statute to the jury).

That sentence from the foregoing instruction criticized by the majority opinion, and for the giving of which the judgment was reversed, in substance means, and could only be taken to mean, that by "securely guarding it" is meant the defendant should securely guard the gearing in question. It is not very instructive, but at the same time it is not harmful or misleading. Great stress is laid on the closing words of the sentence, "that persons who work about the gearing should be secure against danger or violence while performing their work." It is said, unfairly I think, that this makes the master an insurer of the safety of his servant. To me it merely says that a secure guard is one so constructed that persons who work about the gearing should be secure against danger or violence while performing their work. Not a very enlightening or accurate definition, it is true, but it will compare very favorably with many definitions found in the reports of this court. I can see no harm in this extemporaneous attempt of the circuit court. The plain meaning of the whole instruction is not that the employee should be secure against danger or violence from other things than the unguarded gearing, and not that he should be secure against danger or violence from this latter in case of his contributory negligence, because the question of contributory negligence was also separately submitted to the jury under proper instructions. If circuit judges are to be held down to such technicalities in instructing the jury, and judgments reversed for the use of language in such instructions which is the substantial equivalent of the language used by this court in its opinions on the same subject, we are extending mere technicalities beyond reason and disregarding ch. 192, Laws of 1909 (sec. 3072m, Stats.) [see majority opinion for statement of section 3072m.—Editor] because it cannot be fairly said that any jury could be misled by the subtile and hypercritical distinctions which might be traced out between the language employed by the circuit court in this case and the disposition of the same subject in the above cited decisions of this court. . . . I do not remember to have ever seen an opinion of a court of last resort containing so many erroneous statements of law as the majority opinion in the instant case. . . .

. . . Employers as a class have duties imposed upon them by this statute. All employers is a large class and necessarily includes "employers of ordinary caution in the same line of business and under the same circumstances." So that if employers of ordinary caution, etc., disregard this statute and set it at naught, or even if all employers disregard the statute and set it at defiance, each one when sued for damages may escape under this decision by proving that the others did not comply with the statute. This grants an extraordinary class privilege. It nullifies the statute if employers wish to nullify it. I regard this as a wholesome statute, and I believe it is generally so regarded. How can the legislature ever enact statutes which shall be sufficient for the amelioration of the condition of the laboring men, or to lessen the annual slaughter of employees engaged in the manufacturing industries, if such statutes are to be whittled away by construction in this manner. I say whittled away, because the decision places the liability of an employer with reference to dangerous machinery precisely upon the same ground that it would occupy at common law in the absence of this statute. . . . No person can excuse his noncompliance with statutory duties on the ground that in the effort to obey the statute he exercised "such care as the great mass of mankind ordinarily exercise under the same or similar circumstances."

"However rigidly a court may uphold the right of a master to follow general usage, it is clear that evidence of a custom to disregard a law requiring employers to use an appliance calculated to preserve their servants from some particular danger can never be admissible where the question of the exercise of due care on the employer's part is raised." 1 Labatt, Mast. & Serv. § 47, citing Cayzer v. Taylor, 10 Gray, 274, 69 Am. Dec. 317.

It does not, however, require authority to support such a self-evident proposition. Yet the opinion criticized will bear no other reasonable construction than that an employer commanded by sec. 1636j, Stats. (1898), to cover a gearing in fact located as therein described is not absolutely required to do so, but only to decide whether the gearing is so situated and use ordinary care and prudence in so deciding, and decide it as ordinarily careful and prudent employers under like circumstances, in honest exercise of their judgment, would decide it. This means that the employer might urge in justification of his disregard of this statute that he honestly decided not to cover the gearing because he thought it not so located as to be dangerous, although as a matter of fact it may be so located, and that he did so as ordinarily careful and prudent employers under like circumstances, in honest exercise of their judgment, would decide it. He and they decide upon what is their duty under the statute. Next, the statute says that the gearing shall be securely guarded, but the opinion says No, that the employer is only required to furnish "at least as effective a guard as such ordinarily careful and prudent employers under like circumstances would and do deem it their duty to furnish." This results in giving to a class designated in a statute as the subjects of regulation the right to determine the diligence of its own members by comparisons among themselves, and thus to decide whether or not they will comply with the statute, and whether or not, having arrived at the conclusion that a guard is required, they will conform to the statute and provide a secure guard, or merely one which they and others of their class "would and do deem it their duty to furnish." This is, to say the least, extraordinary. It is neither good law nor justice nor good sense. . . .

I cannot too vigorously emphasize the fact that the majority opinion brushes away the statute entirely and places the liability of the master on the same ground and subject to the same limitations and the same defenses as at common law.

I am authorized to say that Mr. Justice SIEBECKER and Mr. Justice KERWIN concur in this dissent.

LAWS, 1911, Chapter 396

AN ACT to amend section 1636jj of the statutes, relating to the assumption of risk and guarding machinery.

The people of the State of Wisconsin, represented in Senate and Assembly do enact as follows:

SECTION 1. Section 1636jj of the statutes is amended to read: Section 1636jj. *1.* In any action brought by an employee or his legal representative to recover for personal injuries, if it appear that the injury was caused by the negligent omission of his employer to guard or protect his machinery or appliances, or the premises or place where said employee was employed, in the manner required in the foregoing section, the fact that such employee continued in said employment with knowledge of such omission, shall not operate as a defense.

2. The duty to guard or protect the machinery or appliances, or the premises or place where said employee was employed, in the manner required in the foregoing subsection, as well as the duty of maintaining the same after installation, shall be absolute. The exercise of ordinary care on the part of the employer shall not be deemed a compliance with such duties.

Approved, June 16, 1911.

KRUECK v. PHOENIX CHAIR CO.
157 Wis. 266, 147 N.W. 41 (1914)

[Wisconsin Statutes, 1898, section 1636j was also amended at the 1911 session (L. 1911, Ch. 470) to include "saws" and "any revolving appliances" among the devices for which the employer had to provide guards as declared in section 1636j. Subsequent to the effective dates of the 1911 amendments to sections 1636j and 1636jj, in 1912, plaintiff was injured while in the employment of defendant operating a grooving saw. A special verdict found, among other things, that the unguarded saw was so located as to be dangerous to plaintiff in discharging the duty of his employment, which he was performing when injured; and that defendant's failure to guard the saw was a proximate cause of the injury. The trial court gave judgment for plaintiff on the verdict. Defendant complains because (1) the trial court refused to submit to the jury the question, "Could the defendant's grooving saw on which the plaintiff was injured be used for the work being done at the time he was injured if guarded?"; (2) the trial court refused to instruct the jury, as requested by defendant, that "if it was impossible to do the work of grooving chair backs on defendant's grooving saw machine as plaintiff was doing at the time of his injury, when the saw on said machine was guarded, then the defendant was not required by law to guard said saw"; and (3) instead, the court instructed the jury that it need not consider whether any guard could be devised which would not materially impair the efficiency or working capacity of the saw. Defendant also complains because the trial court refused to admit testimony of an expert witness, Kaems, to the effect that the machine could not be guarded and still be practically operated, or testimony of witnesses Wolff and Van de Loo, which was offered to show, apart from the question of practicability of a guard, that defendant was not negligent in not furnishing one.—Editor]

TIMLIN, J. At the threshold of this inquiry some doubt is suggested with reference to what statutes apply to the case, although appellant contends that under either statute it was entitled to a directed verdict. It is argued that sec. 1636j, Stats., as amended by ch. 470, Laws of 1911, [a corrected version of L. 1911, ch. 396.—Editor] approved June 28, 1911, published June 29, 1911, was repealed by implication by ch. 485, Laws of 1911, approved and published June 30, 1911. Repeals by implication are not favored. Where there is nothing inconsistent or conflicting in the statutes in question there is no repeal by implication. . . . Sec. 1636j has been construed as not requiring such fencing or guarding as would prevent the practical operation of the machine. Lind v. Uniform S.&P. Co., 140 Wis. 183, 120 N.W. 839. . . .

Premising that under the statute as it read when this injury occurred the duty to guard or protect is absolute; and that the exercise of ordinary care on the part of the employer cannot be deemed a compliance with such absolute duty, yet the statute is not to be construed to require the performance of that which is impossible. A mandate to guard, fence, or protect an appliance in use assumes the continued use of that appliance. The imposition of an absolute duty to guard is not the same as the imposition of a duty to guard absolutely. If it be said that the employer must, in order to comply with this statute, wholly discard any appliance of the class mentioned which cannot be securely guarded or fenced, or that he must forgo their use altogether, that is, we think, deriving from the statute a consequence not contemplated. The statute, sec. 1636j, contemplates the continued use of the described appliance, but of course guarded, fenced, or protected. It therefore means that the appliances shall be guarded or fenced as safely and securely as is possible consistent with the continued practical use of such appliances. This does not mean that the employer may insist on some particular form or style of machine, which particular form or style it is impossible to guard, when machines of a similar nature and capable of efficiently performing the same function may be had which it is perfectly feasible to guard; but (for illustration) the employer is not obliged to discontinue the use of circular saws because it might be impossible to place a stationary guard over the cutting edge thereof, although it might be his duty, when practical, to adopt as a guard the ordinary disappearing saw. In other words, the duty to guard might carry with it the duty to change the setting or frame of the saw so as to make a guard possible and practicable. In Besnys v. Herman Zohrlaut L. Co., ante, p. 203, 147 N.W. 37, the appliance could be guarded and still be operated. Mere difficulty, or inconvenience, or impracticability falling short of preventing the practical operation of the machine, is not sufficient excuse for failure to comply with the statutory duty. Willette v. Rhinelander P. Co., 145 Wis. 537, 130 N.W. 853.

Ch. 485, Laws of 1911 (secs. 2394—41 to 2394—71, Stats.), requires the employer to furnish to his employees a place of employment as free from danger as the nature of the employment will reasonably permit. This is not contradictory of or in conflict with sec. 1636j as construed by this court, and, applying ch. 485, supra, the industrial commission made a general order to the effect that all circular saws must be guarded, etc., except while specific work is being done, where it is impossible to do the work when the saw is guarded. There is therefore no inconsistency between these statutes; one is specific and the other is general, but covering cases which might come under both with like effect so far as the instant case is affected. Whether ch. 485, supra, has in some other aspects a broader scope need not be decided. Whether it is possible to cover a saw so as not to interfere with its practical operation and at the same time so as to prevent the injury sustained, must in most cases be a question of fact. In the instant case appellant's counsel argues that the impossibility of so doing is apparent, while respondent's counsel in argument proposes an ingenious plan of guarding which he considers perfectly feasible. The fact that respondent's counsel felt it necessary to make such argument is a subconscious impeachment of the judgment he is endeavoring to support. Expert investigation might weaken or destroy either claim. Unless the defendant failed in its duty to guard the saw in question, no negligent act or omission creating liability for this injury appears. It seems quite manifest that the judgment appealed from cannot be supported because of the ruling excluding the testimony of the witness Kaems and because of the given instruction quoted and the requested instruction quoted and denied, unless we are prepared to say it appears clearly that the saw could have been guarded or protected without preventing its practical use, and therefore these rulings were not prejudicial. We are not prepared to say this. Neither could we uphold the request to direct a verdict for defendant unless it appeared clearly that the saw could not have been guarded or protected without preventing its practical use. Neither of these conditions is conclusively established.

The questions for trial on this point were: (1) whether the saw was so located as to be dangerous to employees in the discharge of their duty; (2) whether it was securely guarded or fenced, considering the form of the carriage, the exposure or nonexposure of the saw, and the covering position of the chair back; (3) whether it was possible to further guard or fence the saw as to prevent injuries similar to that received by plaintiff without at the same time preventing the practical operations of the saw. There was therefore error in excluding the testimony of the witness Kaems, in giving the quoted instruction, and in the refusal to give the requested quoted instruction. The ruling excluding the testimony of the witnesses Wolff and Van de Loo rests upon a different ground. The testimony sought to be elicited from these witnesses went not to the impossibility of furnishing a guard or protection which would permit the saw to be used and at the same time protect the plaintiff, but to the question of defendant's negligence in not furnishing a guard. This last is a defense barred by the statute in force governing this case, and the exclusion of this testimony must be upheld. . . .

By the Court.—Judgment reversed, and cause remanded for a new trial.

BARNES, J. (dissenting). . . . By the opinion of the court the 1911 law is made to read that the duty to guard shall be absolute if it is practicable to guard and still use the device. In other words, an absolute duty is held to mean a conditional one. I think the exception written into the law by judicial construction is unwarranted and that the statute means what it says, and that if it is desirable to amend it the work should be left to the legislature. It was in fact rendered obsolete by the repeal of sec. 1636j in 1913, but this is no reason why those who were injured while it was in force should not have the benefit of it.

If it was the purpose of the legislature to prohibit the employer from using any saw unless it could be securely guarded, I do not know of a more appropriate word in the English language to use than the word "absolute." It admits of no exception. It is synonymous with "unconditional," "unlimited," "infallible," and "peremptory." Webster's Dict.; Cent. Dict.; Standard Dict. The definition given by lexicographers and that by the courts is the same. "Absolute" means "unrestricted," "unconditional." Columbia W.P. Co. v. Columbia E.S.St.R., L.&P. Co., 172 U.S. 475, 19 Sup. Ct. 247. . . .

This 1911 statute was passed to change the rule adopted in a line of cases beginning with Guinard v. Knapp-Stout & Co., 95 Wis. 482, 70 N.W. 671, and ending with West v. Bayfield M. Co., 144 Wis. 106, 128 N.W. 992, decided in December, 1910, a short time before the amendment was passed. . . .

Sec. 1636j was originally enacted in 1887. It simply required certain safeguards to be adopted and prescribed a penalty for failure to comply with such require-ments. How far it affected the civil liability of employers was a mooted question. Twenty-four years after the act was passed it was thought it had not been con-strued so as to carry out the legislative intent, or else that conditions had changed so as to demand that the law be made more drastic. The latter supposition is probably the more correct one, as the legislature was in session when the Guinard Case was decided, and neither then nor during the six succeeding sessions was any attempt made to change the rule of that case. Be this as it may, the legislature of 1911 had the decision of the court before it, as well as the views of the minority of the court as expressed in the dissenting opinion, and concluded that inasmuch as the law did not accord with the views of the minority it should be changed so as to do so.

Ch. 485, Laws of 1911, was introduced in the legislature March 22, 1911. It required every employer to furnish as safe a place to work in as the nature of the employment would reasonably permit.

Ch. 396 was not introduced until April 19th. It made the duty to guard saws and some other machinery absolute. These two acts were carried along and con-sidered at the same time. Ch. 396 was published on June 20th, and ch. 485 ten days later. It is apparent that as to the appliances covered by ch. 396 it was in-tended to impose greater obligations on the employer than were imposed by the proposed laws applying to occupations generally, which is now ch. 485. One im-posed an absolute duty to guard certain machinery; the other required the place of employment to be made as safe as its nature would reasonably permit. Under the construction now placed on ch. 396, it means no more than does ch. 485, and the act was wholly useless.

Construing sec. 1636—81, [requiring provision of safe scaffolding—Editor] which is not as mandatory in its terms as is sec. 1636jj, in the Koepp Case (Koepp v. Nat. E.&S. Co.), 151 Wis. 302, 313, 139 N.W. 179, the court said the statute made the employers "absolute insurers," except as against assumption of risk and contributory negligence. This language is in substance repeated in Van Dinter v. Worden-Allen Co., 153 Wis. 533, 543, 138 N.W. 1016, 142 N.W. 122, and in Rosholt v. Worden-Allen Co., 155 Wis. 168, 176, 144 N.W. 650, it is said, "the word *absolute,* as used in these decisions, must mean *without limitation unless limitation is expressly made.*" There is no limitation expressed in sec. 1636jj.

The plain language of the statute itself and the plain language of our decisions is against the construction adopted by the court.

To the well informed person making a retrospective survey of our decisions a few years hence, the present one will I think be regarded as being more narrow and technical than was the decision in the Guinard Case.

Ch. 396 was not passed for the benefit of the employer, and his needs did not particularly concern the legislature. As was suggested in the dissenting opinion in the case referred to, it was passed "to lessen the annual slaughter of employees engaged in manufacturing industries." That opinion was perhaps calculated to induce the legislature to go to extreme lengths, but the purpose of the amendment was surely laudable, and nothing should be done to hamstring the act so as to defeat that purpose.

It is improbable that there was a single member of the 1911 legislature who had not seen saws in operation many times. Individually and collectively they knew that the cutting edge of a saw could not be securely guarded and used at the same time. A saw so exposed as to cut an inch board will cut off a man's finger. One that will cut a stick of cord wood will cut off a man's arm, and one that will cut a saw log will cut a man's body in twain. Knowing these facts, as we must assume the legislature did, the exception now incorporated in the decision was not incorporated in the law. The tendency of the court has been to construe these safety laws so that the employee will get all the benefit from them that the legislature intended, and I know of no reason why we should single this one out for different treatment.

The legislature has plainly said to employers: You must guard your saws. If you cannot or do not do so, you become insurers of the safety of employees working around them, and liable for injury caused thereby, unless the injured party is guilty of contributory negligence. There is nothing remarkable about this statute, considering the state of public opinion when it was passed. The Workmen's Compensation Act (ch. 50, Laws of 1911) had become a law seven weeks before ch. 396 was passed. In it the legislature went as far as it was deemed safe from a constitutional standpoint in the direction of compelling employers generally to become insurers. Ch. 396 related to extra hazardous machinery, and it was no doubt thought that the state in the exercise of its police power might go to the extent of prohibiting the use of such machinery entirely or of making the employer an insurer as to injuries caused thereby. . . .

I do not think a mandate to guard an appliance assumes the continued use of it. I think it here means that if you use such an appliance you must guard it. It may be impossible to guard a machine, but it is not impossible to discontinue its use.

NOTES AND QUESTIONS REGARDING THE FOREGOING THREE CASES

1. Is the source of the plaintiff's rights to sue in the Guinard, West, and Krueck cases the common law or statute? Is there any sense in which the claims of the plaintiffs may be said to have been based upon the safety statutes? Compare in this respect, the railroad legislation previously studied. Would the application of the derogation rule preclude basing plaintiffs' claims to any extent upon the statutes?

Regarding the proposition relied on in Justice Timlin's West case dissent as being established law in Wisconsin—namely, that violation of the safety statute was in itself negligence—see James, Statutory Standards and Negligence in Accident Cases, 11 La. L.

Rev. 95 (1950); Morris, The Role of Criminal Statutes in Negligence Actions, 49 Colum. L. Rev. 21 (1949); Thayer, Public Wrong and Private Action, 27 Harv. L. Rev. 317 (1913).

2. Did the court in Guinard apply the derogation rule in construing the applicable statute? Expressly?

3. What data did the majority in West rely upon for its interpretation of the statute? How strong are the precedents adduced in the minority opinion? Did Justice Timlin make effective use of them?

4. Did the court in West apply the same standard in construing "securely guarded" that the court in Guinard used in construing "so located as to be dangerous"?

5. How sound a precedent is Guinard for the decision in West? Would the minority position have had the effect, as the majority in West claimed, of abolishing the contributory negligence defense?

6. What may the enactment of L. 1911, ch. 396 and the fact that the Guinard decision was permitted to stand until 1911, show as to the validity of the interpretation of the statute made in the Guinard and West cases? Might it be argued with force that the interpretation adopted was correct in 1897 but wrong in 1910? Recall the discussion of this problem by the writers on statutory construction previously presented. The intent of which legislature should the court in West have tried to ascertain?

7. What effect, if any, did the Krueck decision give to L. 1911, ch. 396? Was the rule of strict construction of statutes in derogation of the common law applicable in Krueck? Can the words of the statute reasonably bear the interpretation put upon them by the court in Krueck? Did the court exceed the bounds of judicial propriety in the interpretation of statutes?

8. Did the majority in Krueck give sufficient weight to the argument of the dissenters based on L. 1911, ch. 485 (safe place statute) and L. 1911, ch. 50 (workmen's compensation act)?

On the issue of implied repeal of L. 1911, ch. 396, by L. 1911, ch. 485, consider the possible significance of the fact that, in the Assembly, bill 482-S, which became L. 1911, ch. 396, was, upon receipt from the Senate, referred to the Assembly Committee on Workmen's Compensation, which was the committee which also considered both the workmen's compensation and the Industrial Commission bills. That committee recommended the passage of bill 482-S. Ass. Jour. 1196 (1911).

9. Documents on file with the Secretary of State of Wisconsin reveal that in the form in which it was originally introduced, the bill which became L. 1911, ch. 396, read, in part: "The duty to guard or protect the machinery or appliances, or the premises or place where said employee was employed, in the manner required in the foregoing section, as well as the duty of maintaining the same after installation shall be absolute, provided that evidence of the exercise of ordinary care on the part of the employer, when admissible, shall not be deemed controlling on either question; and in case of injury to an employee, the question whether such duties, or either of them, have been performed shall be a question of fact for the jury to be determined by the evidence." The Senate Committee on Judiciary, to which the bill had been referred, recommended the bill for passage with Amendment 1-S, striking out the provisos; and the bill was passed by the Senate and concurred in by the Assembly in the form thus recommended. How might this history be relevant to the problem of interpretation presented in the Krueck case?

10. Should the express repeal of Wisconsin Statutes, 1898, section 1636j by L. 1913, ch. 223, be deemed relevant in reaching the proper interpretation of 1636j in the Krueck case? Consider the fact that this left L. 1911, ch. 485 outstanding.

11. Note the reversal of the roles of Justices Timlin and Barnes in the West and Krueck cases. Is each of them consistent? Would it make sense to ascribe the differences between them in the two cases to the fact that one was politically more conservative or more liberal than the other?

EDITORIAL NOTE: The CANONS of STATUTORY INTERPRETATION

The judge or lawyer confronted with the problem of applying a statutory provision to a particular fact situation will often, and perhaps typically, find that he has nothing to guide him beyond the text of the statute itself. The possible use of legislative history of the statute (data on which have been brought to the student's attention in the foregoing materials wherever available) is reserved for more intensive study in Part 3.

Particularly when there is a paucity of extrinsic material revealing the legislative intent, judicial opinions and legal treatises suggest the application of certain canons or rules of statutory construction which presume a particular legislative intention in given situations. Several of the more important and more frequently cited of such rules have appeared in the cases cited in this chapter. The following readings deal with the use of these canons.

FORDHAM* AND LEACH,† *INTERPRETATION OF STATUTES IN DEROGATION OF THE COMMON LAW*
3 Vanderbilt Law Review 438, 439, 447-453 (1950)

The inquiry upon which this paper is based has led to the opinion that we should discard all rules of interpretation in the nature of presumptions. We would apply this with emphasis to the canon which calls for strict construction of a statute derogating from the common law. . . .

While the derogation canon has been freely criticized by text and periodical writers, there has been scant suggestion of judicial dissatisfaction with it. Many courts, on particular occasions, have found the rule inapplicable or overcome, but seldom has a court attacked it as ill-conceived or undesirable. . . . As long ago as 1888, the Court of Appeals of New York was prepared to assert that the canon was so firmly established that it would take legislation to break its hold. . . .[48]

Is interpretation legislation the answer? What reception might one expect the courts to accord it?

---

* Jefferson B. Fordham, Dean of the Law School of the University of Pennsylvania since 1952, was Dean of the Ohio State University College of Law, 1947-52, has taught at West Virginia, Louisiana State, and Vanderbilt, and has served as a federal government attorney. He is the author of Local Government Law (1949); A Larger Concept of Community (1956); The Legal Profession and American Constitutionalism (1957); and The State Legislative Institution (1959).

† J. Russell Leach is Reference Librarian, College of Law, Ohio State University.— Editor

[48] Fitzgerald v. Quann, 109 N.Y. 441, 445, 17 N.E. 354 (1888).

Interpretation Statutes

. . . It hardly need be stated that interpretative measures are, themselves, subject to interpretation. Equally obvious is the fact that while a fiction may be used to say that a later act was adopted with reference to an interpretive statute, subsequent legislatures are not bound to submit to that statute.

Any serious suggestion at this day that since interpretation is a judicial function a general interpretive act, applicable only to future statutes, would be unconstitutional, could hardly be taken seriously.[50] In both England [51] and America we have long proceeded on the basis that, although ultimate interpretation is for the courts, it is within the legislative province to lay down rules of interpretation for the future.[52] The National Conference of Commissioners on Uniform State Laws has even undertaken the preparation of a Uniform Statutory Construction Act.[53]

While we do not perceive that general interpretive acts should be denied prospective application to existing statutes, there is adverse authority.[54] Actually, if the legislation does not dress a change in meaning in the form of an interpretive provision but merely provides an aid in determining meaning there should be no more objection than in the case of its application to a future statute.

If it is thought to effect a change in meaning, is not the true question whether the process of amendment was regular? If an interpretation act could not be made to apply to the future operation of existing statutes its usefulness would obviously be very greatly limited. At the same time, one must consider the impact upon the judicial mind of a general interpretation clause designed to cover a great body of existing law. In 1947, the Ohio General Assembly inserted a separability clause in its more than 13,000-section General Code.[56] The clause purports to make each section and part of a section separable. This is so unrealistic in terms of the actual situation as to interdependence of existing code sections that it is likely to carry little authority or weight.

A truly retrospective interpretation act involves some additional considerations. If it purports to control interpretation in a pending case already decided and does that with respect to the very matter then in litigation it would surely meet with judicial disfavor as an effort to interfere with the independence or finality of judicial decision.[57] Even in the absence of that factor, an interpretive act would not, generally speaking, be given effect by the courts as to past transactions.

Forty-one states and three territories have statutes abrogating the rule of strict

[50] While no cases have been found which expressly deny this statement, the opinions in two Pennsylvania cases which involved retrospective interpretive acts contain language broad enough to condemn all interpretive acts as violative of separation of powers. Commonwealth ex rel. Roney v. Warwick, 172 Pa. 140, 33 Atl. 373 (1895); Titusville Iron-Works v. Keystone Oil Co., 122 Pa. 627, 15 Atl. 917 (1888). Examples of courts applying interpretive statutes to later acts are too numerous to mention.

[51] Interpretation Act, 1889, 52 & 53 Vict. c. 63.

[52] 2 Sutherland, Statutory Construction § 3003 (3d ed., Horack, 1943).

[53] Nat. Conf. of Comm'rs on Uniform State Laws, 1944 Handbook 240.

[54] Note, 86 U. Pa. L. Rev. 189, 196 (1938).

[56] Ohio Gen. Code § 26-2 (1948).

[57] People ex rel. Mutual Life Ins. Co. of New York v. Board of Supervisors, 16 N.Y. 424 (1857).

construction of statutes in derogation of the common law in regard to all or part of their legislation. The form and extent of these interpretive statutes vary. Two states, for example, have statutes providing that certain acts shall not be limited by any rules of strict construction but rather that they shall be liberally construed.[59] All of the other statutes hereafter mentioned state the common law rule of construction and expressly provide that it shall not be applicable to designated codes or acts. Many of these statutes further provide that the acts should be "liberally construed with a view to effect their objects and to promote justice." [60]

The abrogating provision has been used with reference to single acts, certain subdivisions of the state statutes or even to the entire statute law of the state. Examples of its application to single acts are found in the Uniform Partnership Act[61] and the Uniform Limited Partnership Act.[62] It has likewise been applied to an article on workmen's compensation[63] and a chapter dealing with the relationship of husband and wife.[64] Such a provision has been widely employed in civil practice acts.[65] Ohio has a clause of this character applicable to Part III of its General Code.[66] While Part III is entitled "Remedial," it appears to be largely procedural. In other states we find the device applied to civil codes,[67] all civil statutes,[68] a political code[69] and a probate act.[70] Twelve states have substantially abrogated the old canon with respect to all of their legislation.[71] Of these Pennsylvania alone has ordained expressly that the old canon should remain in force as to statutes enacted prior to the interpretation act.[72]

[59] Ind. Stat. Ann. § 2-4703 (Burns, 1933); Wash. Rev. Stat. Ann. § 144 (1932).

[60] See, e.g., Idaho Laws Ann. § 73-102 (1949).

[61] Uniform Partnership Act § 4 (1). See, e.g., N.Y. Partnership Law § 4; Ohio Gen. Code Ann. § 8105-4 (Supp. 1949); Tenn. Code Ann. § 7843 (Williams, 1934). Only Utah of the 29 states which have enacted the Uniform Partnership Act has omitted this section.

[62] Uniform Limited Partnership Act § 28 (1). See, e.g., N.Y. Partnership Law § 117; Tenn. Code Ann. §7909 (Williams, 1934). Only Iowa, Missouri and Utah of the 29 states enacting the Act have omitted this section.

[63] Md. Ann. Code Gen. Laws, art. 101, §78 (1939).

[64] Wash. Rev. Stat. Ann. § 6898 (1932). This provision was aimed at chapter 183 of the Washington Code of 1881. The provisions of that chapter are now embodied in Title 42 of the Revised Statutes.

[65] See, Ark. Stat. Ann. § 27-131 (1947); Cal. Code Civ. Proc. Ann. § 4 (1949); Ill. Ann. Stat., c. 110, § 128 (1948); Ky. Code Civ. Prac. § 733 (1948); Neb. Rev. Stat. § 24-2218 (1943); N.J. Stat. Ann.

§ 2:27-2 (1939); N.Y. Civ. Prac. Act § 3; S.C. Code Ann. § 902 (1942); Wyo. Comp. Stat. Ann. § 3-102 (1945).

[66] Ohio Gen. Code Ann. § 10214 (1948).

[67] Cal. Civ. Code § 4 (1949); Canal Zone Code, tit. 3, § 4 (1934).

[68] Tex. Rev. Civ. Stat. Ann., art. 10 (8) (1947).

[69] Cal. Polit. Code § 4 (1944).

[70] Ill. Ann. Stat., c. 3, § 159 (1941).

[71] Idaho Laws Ann. § 73-102 (1949); Iowa Code § 4.2 (1946); Kan. Gen. Stat. Ann. § 77-109 (1935); Ky. Rev. Stat. Ann. § 446.080 (1943); Mo. Rev. Stat. § 645 (1939); Mont. Rev. Code Ann. § 12-202 (1947); N.D. Rev. Code § 1-0201 (1943); Okla. Stat., tit. 12, § 2, tit. 25, § 29 (1941); and Pa. Stat. Ann., tit. 46, § 538 (1941); S.D. Code § 65.0202 (1) (1939); Utah Code Ann. § 88-2-2 (1943). It is of interest that the Supreme Court of Pennsylvania borrowed from the statutory construction act to declare that the derogation canon shall not be applicable to the rules of the court. Rule 130 of the Pennsylvania Supreme Court Rules of Procedure, 332 Pa. lxix (1939).

[72] Pa. Stat. Ann., tit. 46, § 558 (8) (1941).

The effectiveness of the statutes is very difficult to determine. Presumably, if followed in good spirit they would bring about wider applications of primary statutes but this can hardly be demonstrated in fact. One cannot be sure that, absent the interpretive provision, the result would have been different in a particular case. We can say that they, by and large, have served to take away one formulation otherwise available to explain a restrictive interpretation. The statutes have not universally achieved even this much. There have been cases where they were ignored and the old canon applied. As has already been noted, moreover, interpretive statutes have generally been restricted in application to later legislation. The effectiveness of these interpretive provisions has been limited in other ways.

The Supreme Court of Montana has concluded that the construction statute does not overcome the proposition that the rules of the common law are not to be overturned except by clear and unambiguous language.[76] By a strict construction of a liberal interpretation statute the court was able to declare, in effect, that once a statute has been found to be in derogation of the common law, it will be liberally construed, but the legislative intent to derogate must first appear from clear and unambiguous language. We suggest that the court was making a false distinction; the determination whether there is a change in the common law is the very stuff of the matter.

Another method of avoiding the statute is to give it lip service and then proceed to use the old rule anyway. It would not be fair to say that there had been many instances of this approach. In an Iowa case a broad statutory rule of liberal interpretation did not deter the court from holding that a statute which enabled a married woman to prosecute in her own name actions in tort or for the enforcement of any legal or equitable right did not permit her to sue her husband. Nor did the statute deter the court from asserting: "The relations of husband and wife to each other are essentially different from those of all other persons, and statutes dealing therewith should be clear and explicit in meaning, particularly when abrogation of a rule of the common law is involved." [77]

A third, and closely allied, method of restricting the application of the primary statute is to give a strict construction in determining the persons or classes of persons entitled to its benefits and a liberal construction in applying the statutes in their favor.[78] This looks like a hybrid combination of the old restrictive canon and the equally familiar rule that statutes which are procedural or remedial, in the strict sense, should be liberally construed.

In his edition of Sutherland's treatise on Statutory Interpretation Professor Horack says, "These general interpretive provisions have generally effectuated their purpose. . . ." [79] This we are constrained to doubt. The demonstration that they carried decisive weight in any of the cases he cited would be no mean performance.

[76] Conley v. Conley, 92 Mont. 425, 15 P. 2d 922 (1932).

[77] In re Dolmage's Estate, 203 Iowa 231, 212 N.W. 553, 555 (1927). See also Schwartz v. Inspiration Gold Mining Co., 15 F. Supp. 1030 (D. Mont. 1936) (Mont. statute); Hill v. Halmhuber, 225 Ky. 394, 9 S.W. 2d 55 (1928).

[78] Whittlesey v. Seattle, 94 Wash. 653, 163 Pac. 193 (1917). See also Estate of De Laveaga, 4 Coffey's Prob. Dec. 423, 429 (Cal. 1899).

[79] 3 Sutherland, Statutory Construction § 6205 (3d ed., Horack, 1943).

It is our belief that criticisms of the derogation canon and the enactment of legislation to discard or modify it have been directed more at the attitude of hostility to legislation reflected in the canon than its weakness as a tool of interpretation. Many of the pertinent statutes call for liberal construction to effect the objects of the laws construed and to promote justice. It is not a serious reflection upon the bar and the judges to say that a statutory exhortation in favor of liberal construction is not calculated to extirpate deep-seated attitudes. The most hopeful possibilities here lie, we believe, in the realm of legal education. . . .

As for techniques of interpretation, we reiterate that should a court wish to construe a statute strictly, it would find an abundance of tools remaining to replace the one withdrawn. We have already referred to three methods of avoiding the interpretive statute. In addition various "sets of words (more or less) well-played" are at hand. It may simply be said that the court cannot extend the meaning of a section further than the "clear intendment" of the statute,[80] or that the words of a section may not be extended beyond their "plain import."[81] Again we may be told that a liberal construction does not permit "supplying words omitted,"[82] or that the right must be found in the statute itself "fairly construed."[83] Oft-repeated is the observation that it is the duty of a court to administer the law as it is written, and not to make the law.[84] Nor does the interpretive statute abrogate the rule that "one claiming to be within the protection of the act must so show."[85] Liberal construction may not, it is said, extend a statute so as to require the performance of duties impossible of performance.[86]

As we have already seen, some of the interpretive statutes attempt to reverse the situation by substituting liberal for restrictive interpretation. In other words, they adopt a new presumptive rule with a different emphasis. As a general canon applicable to a great variety of statutes it is vulnerable to two of the major objections to the derogation canon: (1) it assumes too much when applied generally without discrimination and (2) it is, at best, little more than a formulation for use by way of apology instead of a guide to decision. Why, as a general proposition, put a statute at the plate with one strike already called, or, conversely, allow four strikes instead of three?

LLEWELLYN, *REMARKS ON THE THEORY OF APPELLATE DECISION AND THE RULES OR CANONS ABOUT HOW STATUTES ARE TO BE CONSTRUED*
3 Vanderbilt Law Review 395, 398-406 (1950)

On the case-law side . . . we ought all thus to be familiar with the fact that the right doctrine and going practice of our highest courts leave them a very real

---

[80] Niblock v. Salt Lake City, 100 Utah 573, 111 P. 2d 800, 804 (1941).

[81] Young v. Kipe, 38 Pa. D.&C. 434, 437 (1940).

[82] The Peterson Co. v. Freeburn, 204 Iowa 644, 646, 215 N.W. 746, 748 (1927).

[83] Farmers' & Mechanics' Nat. Bank v. Hanks, 104 Tex. 320, 137 S.W. 1120, 1123

(1911).

[84] *Ibid.*

[85] Stringer v. Calmes, 167 Kan. 278, 205 P. 2d 921, 925 (1949).

[86] Gorges v. State Highway Commission, 137 Kan. 340, 343, 20 P. 2d 486, 487 (1933).

leeway within which (a) to narrow or avoid what seem today to have been unfortunate prior phrasings or even rulings; or (b), on the other hand, to pick up, develop, expand what seem today to have been fortunate prior rulings or even phrasings.

It is silly, I repeat, to think of use of this leeway as involving "twisting" of precedent. The very phrase presupposes the thing which is not and which has never been. The phrase presupposes that there was in the precedent under consideration some one and single meaning. The whole experience of our case-law shows that that assumption is false. It is, instead, the business of the courts to use the precedents constantly to make the law always a *little* better, to correct old mistakes, to recorrect mistaken or ill-advised attempts at correction—but always within limits severely set not only by the precedents, but equally by the traditions of right conduct in judicial office.

What we need to see now is that all of this is paralleled, in regard to statutes, because of (1) the power of the legislature both to choose policy and to select measures; and (2) the necessity that the legislature shall, in so doing, use language —language fixed in particular words; and (3) the continuing duty of the courts to make sense, under and within the law.

For just as prior courts can have been skillful or unskillful, clear or unclear, wise or unwise, so can legislatures. And just as prior courts have been looking at only a single piece of our whole law at a time, so have legislatures.

But a court must strive to make sense *as a whole* out of our law *as a whole*. It must, to use Frank's figure,[2] take the music of any statute as written by the legislature; it must take the text of the play as written by the legislature. But there are many ways to play that music, to play that play, and a court's duty is to play it well, and in harmony with the other music of the legal system.

Hence, in the field of statutory construction also, there are "correct," unchallengeable rules of "how to read" which lead in happily variant directions.

This must be so until courts recognize that here, as in case-law, the real guide is Sense-for-All-of-Us. It must be so, so long as we and the courts pretend that there has been only one single correct answer possible. Until we give up that foolish pretense there must be a set of mutually contradictory *correct* rules on How to Construe Statutes: either set available as duty and sense may require.

Until then, also, the problem will recur in statutory construction as in the handling of case-law: *Which* of the technically correct answers (a) *should* be given; (b) *will* be given—and Why? . . .

II

One last thing is to be noted:

If a statute is to make sense, it must be read in the light of some assumed purpose. A statute merely declaring a rule, with no purpose or objective, is nonsense.

If a statute is to be merged into a going system of law, moreover, the court must do the merging, and must in so doing take account of the policy of the statute—

[2] Frank, Words and Music: Some Remarks on Statutory Interpretation, 47 Colum. L. Rev. 1259 (1947).

or else substitute its own version of such policy. Creative reshaping of the net result is thus inevitable.

But the policy of a statute is of two wholly different kinds—each kind somewhat limited in effect by the statute's choice of measures, and by the statute's choice of fixed language. On the one hand there are the ideas consciously before the draftsmen, the committee, the legislature: a known evil to be cured, a known goal to be attained, a deliberate choice of one line of approach rather than another. Here talk of "intent" is reasonably realistic; committee reports, legislative debate, historical knowledge of contemporary thinking or campaigning which points up the evil or the goal can have significance.

But on the other hand—and increasingly as a statute gains in age—its language is called upon to deal with circumstances utterly uncontemplated at the time of its passage. Here the quest is not properly for the sense originally intended by the statute, for the sense sought originally to be *put into it,* but rather for the sense which *can be quarried out of it* in the light of the new situation. Broad purposes can indeed reach far beyond details known or knowable at the time of drafting. A "dangerous weapon" statute of 1840 can include tommy guns, tear gas or atomic bombs. "Vehicle," in a statute of 1840, can properly be read, when sense so suggests, to include an automobile, or a hydroplane that lacks wheels. But for all that, the sound quest does not run primarily in terms of historical intent. It runs in terms of what the words can be made to bear, in making sense in the light of the unforeseen.

III

When it comes to presenting a proposed construction in court, there is an accepted conventional vocabulary. As in argument over points of case-law, the accepted convention still, unhappily, requires discussion as if only one single correct meaning could exist. Hence there are two opposing canons on almost every point. An arranged selection is appended. Every lawyer must be familiar with them all: they are still needed tools of argument. . . .

Plainly, to make any canon take hold in a particular instance, the construction contended for must be sold, essentially, by means other than the use of the canon: The good sense of the situation and a *simple* construction of the available language to achieve that sense, *by tenable means, out of the statutory language.*

Canons of Construction. Statutory interpretation still speaks a diplomatic tongue. Here is some of the technical framework for maneuver.

[NOTE: Llewellyn then presents a table of 28 "thrusts" and "parries," of which we have reproduced, below, approximately half. In each instance he cited footnote authorities, which we have deemed it unnecessary to reproduce—except for illustrative purposes in the cases of the first two pairs of maxims.—Editor]

THRUST   BUT   PARRY

2. Statutes in derogation of the common law will not be extended by construction.[5]

4. Where a foreign statute which has received construction has been adopted, previous construction is adopted too.[9]

6. Statutes *in pari materia* must be construed together.

7. A statute imposing a new penalty or forfeiture, or a new liability or disability, or creating a new right of action will not be construed as having a retroactive effect.

11. Titles do not control meaning; preambles do not expand scope; section headings do not change language.

12. If language is plain and unambiguous it must be given effect.

2. Such acts will be liberally construed if their nature is remedial.[6]

4. It may be rejected where there is conflict with the obvious meaning of the statute or where the foreign decisions are unsatisfactory in reasoning or where the foreign interpretation is not in harmony with the spirit or policy of the laws of the adopting state.[10]

6. A statute is not *in pari materia* if its scope and aim are distinct or where a legislative design to depart from the general purpose or policy of previous enactments may be apparent.

7. Remedial statutes are to be liberally construed and if a retroactive interpretation will promote the ends of justice, they should receive such construction.

11. The title may be consulted as a guide when there is doubt or obscurity in the body; preambles may be consulted to determine rationale, and thus the true construction of terms; section headings may be looked upon as part of the statute itself.

12. Not when literal interpretation would lead to absurd or mischievous consequences or thwart manifest purpose.

---

[5] Devers v. City of Scranton, 308 Pa. 13, 161 Atl. 540 (1932); Black, Construction and Interpretation § 388 (2d ed. 1911); Sutherland, Statutory Construction § 573 (2d ed. 1904); 25 R.C.L., Statutes § 281 (1919).

[6] Becker v. Brown, 65 Neb. 264, 91 N.W. 178 (1902); Black, Construction and Interpretation of Laws § 113 (2d ed. 1911); Sutherland, Statutory Construction §§ 573-75 (2d ed. 1904); 59 C.J., Statutes § 657 (1932).

[9] Freese v. Tripp, 70 Ill. 496 (1873); Black, Construction and Interpretation of Laws § 176 (2d ed. 1911); 59 C.J., Statutes, §§ 614, 627, (1932); 25 R.C.L., Statutes § 294 (1919).

[10] Bowers v. Smith, 111 Mo. 45, 20 S.W. 101 (1892); Black, Construction and Interpretation of Laws § 176 (2d ed. 1911); Sutherland, Statutory Construction § 404 (2d ed. 1904); 59 C.J., Statutes § 628 (1932).

THRUST	BUT	PARRY
15. Words are to be taken in their ordinary meaning unless they are technical terms or words of art.		15. Popular words may bear a technical meaning and technical words may have a popular signification and they should be so construed as to agree with evident intention or to make the statute operative.
16. Every word and clause must be given effect.		16. If inadvertently inserted or if repugnant to the rest of the statute, they may be rejected as surplusage.
17. The same language used repeatedly in the same connection is presumed to bear the same meaning throughout the statute.		17. This presumption will be disregarded where it is necessary to assign different meanings to make the statute consistent.
19. Exceptions not made cannot be read.		19. The letter is only the "bark." Whatever is within the reason of the law is within the law itself.
20. Expression of one thing excludes another. [*expressio unius, exclusio alterius*]		20. The language may fairly comprehend many different cases where some only are expressly mentioned by way of example.
22. It is a general rule of construction that where general words follow an enumeration they are to be held as applying only to persons and things of the same general kind or class specifically mentioned (*ejusdem generis*).		22. General words must operate on something. Further *ejusdem generis* is only an aid in getting the meaning and does not warrant confining the operations of a statute within narrower limits than were intended.
23. Qualifying or limiting words or clauses are to be referred to the next preceding antecedent.		23. Not when evident sense and meaning require a different construction.
25. It must be assumed that language has been chosen with due regard to grammatical propriety and is not interchangeable on mere conjecture.		25. "And" and "or" may be read interchangeably whenever the change is necessary to give the statute sense and effect.
26. There is a distinction between words of permission and mandatory words.		26. Words imparting permission may be read as mandatory and words imparting command may be read as permissive when such construction is made necessary by evident intention or by the rights of the public.

[Llewellyn's full table by no means exhausts the list of available canons of construction. Thus, one of the best known canons of all, which he omits, is that a penal statute should be construed strictly (with the inevitable "parry" that this rule is "not an inexorable command to override common sense and evident statutory purpose." United States v. Brown, 333 U.S. 18 (1948). Again, it is often said that if the statutory words lend themselves to alternative interpretations, one of which would result in raising a doubt about the statute's constitutionality, the construction should be chosen which avoids the constitutional doubt. Still, the "canon of avoidance of constitutional doubts must, like the 'plain meaning' rule, give way where its application would produce a futile result, or an unreasonable result 'plainly at variance with the policy of the legislation as a whole.' " Shapiro v. United States, 335 U.S. 1, 31 (1948).—Editor]

Section 4

STATUTES as a SOURCE of COMMON LAW and the "UNION of JUDGE-MADE with STATUTE LAW"

JOHNSTON v. FARGO
184 N.Y. 379, 77 N.E. 388 (1906)

GRAY, J. The plaintiff, while in the employment of the American Express Company, the defendant, sustained personal injuries, for which he has recovered this judgment in the Municipal Court of the city of Syracuse; which has been affirmed by the County Court of Onondaga county and by the Appellate Division of the Supreme Court, in the fourth department. The latter court was divided in opinion and has permitted the defendant to further appeal to this court, upon the ground that there was a question of law in the case, which ought to be reviewed by us. The injuries were occasioned by the plaintiff's falling with an elevator, or lift, in the barn of the express company, while it was being used for carrying down some vehicles, and the complaint charges that it was in a defective condition and that the occurrence was due to the fault, or negligence, of the defendant. . . . The one question for discussion upon this appeal is the sufficiency of the defense made by the company upon an agreement, which the plaintiff, upon entering the defendant's employment, executed and delivered to it. It was in these words:

"I do further agree, in consideration of my employment by said American Express Company, that I will assume all risks of accident or injury which I shall meet with or sustain in the course of such employment, whether occasioned by the negligence of said company, or any of its members, officers, agents or employees, or otherwise; and that, in case I shall at any time suffer any such injury, I will at once execute and deliver to said company a good and sufficient release, under my hand and seal, of all claims, demands and causes of action arising out of such injury or connected therewith, or resulting therefrom; and I hereby bind myself, my heirs, executors and administrators with the payment to said express company, on demand, of any sum which it may be compelled to pay in consequence of any such claim, or in defending the same, including all counsel fees and expenses of litigation connected therewith."

In submitting the case to the jury, the trial judge charged as follows, with respect to this defense: "There is a clause in the contract which provides that the plaintiff shall release the defendant from any injuries which he might suffer by reason of the negligence of the defendant. I shall hold as matter of law that that clause in that contract is void as being without consideration and as against public policy." At the Appellate Division the judgment was upheld, on this point, upon the ground that the agreement was contrary to public policy, and, therefore, invalid. . . .

The question of the validity of such a contract between an employer and a person in his employment, as affected by reasons of public policy, it must be conceded, is a debatable one. In support of the right to make the agreement we have respectable authority in decisions of the courts of England and of the state of Georgia. (Griffiths v. Earl of Dudley, L.R. [9 Q.B. Div.] 357; Western, etc., R.R. Co. v. Bishop, 50 Ga. 465, Same Co. v. Strong, 52 Ga. 461.) The great weight of authority in decisions of the courts of the various states, however, sustains the view that such an agreement is contrary to public policy. . . . [The opinion here cites numerous decisions, including L.R.&F.S.Ry. Co. v. Eubanks, 48 Ark. 466, reprinted above.—Editor] The preponderance of authority adverse to the validity of such contracts is such as greatly and properly influences our view of the question. In Griffiths v. Earl of Dudley, (supra), where such an agreement was held to be quite consistent with public policy, the view of the English court, as expressed by Justice FIELD, was that "the interest of the employed only would be affected" and not that of "all society," and "that workmen, as a rule, were perfectly competent to make reasonable bargains for themselves." It is to be observed, however, with respect to the situation in England, that subsequently, in 1897, an act of Parliament was passed, entitled "The Workingmen's Compensation Act," which, in effect, declares the public policy of the state. By that act, in reality, though not in form, the right of the workingman to contract away his right to recover compensation from his employer is nullified; inasmuch as such a contract is only valid when, as between employer and employed, there exists a general scheme for compensation, which secures to the workingman benefits as great as those he would derive from a proceeding under the Compensation Acts.

The attitude of this court, with respect to the freedom to contract for immunity from the consequences of negligence, has been, from an early day, very firm, where the contracts of common carriers are concerned; as may be seen by reference to Kenney v. N.Y.C.&H.R.R.R. Co., [125 N.Y. 422], where the cases establishing the rule were reviewed; but to extend the application of the doctrine in such cases to the relations of the employer and the employed involves considerations so closely touching the general welfare of the community, that the state must be, necessarily, deeply concerned. [In the Kenney case, it was broadly declared that under the common law of New York a common carrier might validly contract for freedom from liability for injury to a passenger or property carried, caused by negligence of the carrier's employees.—Editor] . . .

Contracts are illegal at common law, as being against public policy, when they are such as to injuriously affect, or subvert, the public interests. . . . If it were true that the interests of the employed, only, would be affected by such contracts as the present one, as it was held by the English court, in Griffiths v. Earl of Dudley, (supra), it would be difficult to defend, upon sound reasoning, the denial of the right to enter into them; but that is not quite true. The theory of their invalidity is in the importance to the state that there shall be no relaxation of the rule of law, which imposes the duty of care on the part of the employer towards the employed. The state is interested in the conservation of the lives and of the healthful vigor of its citizens, and if employers could contract away their responsibility at common law, it would tend to encourage on their part laxity of conduct in, if not an indifference to, the maintenance of proper and reasonable safeguards to human life and limb. The rule of responsibility at common law is as just as it is strict and the interest of the state in its maintenance must be assumed; for its policy has, in recent years, been evidenced in the progressive enactment of many laws, which regulate the employment of children and the hours of work, and impose strict conditions with reference to the safety and healthfulness of the surroundings of the employed, in the factory and in the shop. The employer and the employed, in theory, deal upon equal terms; but, practically, that is not always the case. The artisan, or workman, may be driven by need; or he may be ignorant, or of improvident character. It is, therefore, for the interest of the community that there should be no encouragement for any relaxation on the employer's part in his duty of reasonable care for the safety of his employes. That freedom of contract may be said to be affected by the denial of the right to make such agreements, is met by the answer that the restriction is but a salutary one, which organized society exacts for the surer protection of its members. While it is true that the individual may be the one, who, directly, is interested in the making of such a contract, indirectly, the state, being concerned for the welfare of all its members, is interested in the maintenance of the rule of liability and in its enforcement by the courts.

To a certain extent, the internal activities of organized society are subject to the restraining action of the state. This is evidenced by the many laws upon the statute book, in recent years, which have been passed for the purpose of prohibiting, restricting, or regulating, the conduct of a private business; either because regarded as hurtful to the health, or welfare of the community; or because deemed from its nature, or magnitude, affected with a public interest. It has been observed that it is still the business of the state, in modern times, to defend individuals against one another and, though the proposition is a broad one, when considered with reference to penal legislation and all legislation intended for the promotion of the health, welfare and safety of the community, it is not without truth. It is evident, from the course of legislation framed for the purpose of affording greater protection to the class of the employed, that the people of this state have compelled the employer to do many things which at common law he was not under obligation to do. Such legislation may be regarded as supplementing the common-law rule of the employer's responsibility and is illustrative of the policy of the state. Therefore it is, when an agreement is sought to be enforced, which suspends the operation of the common-law rule of liability and defeats the spirit of existing laws of the state, because tending to destroy the motive of the employer to be vigilant in the performance of his duty towards his employes, that it is the duty of the court to declare it to be invalid and to refuse its enforcement.

I think that the judgment below was correct and should be affirmed, with costs.

CULLEN, Ch. J., Edward T. BARTLETT, HAIGHT, VANN, Willard BARTLETT and CHASE, JJ., concur.

Judgment affirmed.

NOTES AND QUESTIONS

1. What is the source of the court's authority in Johnston to refuse to enforce the contract?

2. Compare the analysis and authorities relied on in the opinion of the New York Court of Appeals and in the opinion of the Arkansas court in the Eubanks case in ch. 7, sec. 4. Are they the same?

3. As noted in the Johnston opinion, for many years prior to that decision the New York court had ruled that under the common law of New York a common carrier might validly contract that it should not be liable for injury to passengers or property carried, caused by the negligence of the carrier's employees. How reconcile the Johnston decision with such rulings? What made the difference?

Would the New York court have reached the same result if New York judicial precedent had upheld the validity of the type of contract involved in Johnston? Cf. F. A. Straus & Co., Inc. v. Canadian Pacific Ry. Co., 254 N.Y. 407, 173 N.E. 564 (1930).

4. Compare the attitude of the court in Johnston with the attitude of the Wisconsin court in West (previously considered) toward the relationship between the common law and statute.

5. Do you think the court in the Lagage case (note 9, page 415, following the Hartford case in section 2 of this chapter) could have used the 1889 statute as a reflection of public policy warranting the exercise of its common law powers to decide the case the other way?

STONE,* *THE COMMON LAW IN THE UNITED STATES*
50 Harvard Law Review 4, 11-16 (1936)

* * *

. . . for a few moments I propose to recall the part which statutes have played in the development of the common law of this country.

If one were to attempt to write a history of the law in the United States, it would be largely an account of the means by which the common-law system has been able to make progress through a period of exceptionally rapid social and

* Harlan Fiske Stone (1872-1946) was Chief Justice of the U.S. Supreme Court 1941-46, having previously served as associate justice since 1925. He began teaching at Columbia Law School in 1899, was Dean from 1910 to 1923, and president of the Association of American Law Schools in 1919. He was Attorney-General of the U.S. in 1924. Among his notable writings are Law and Its Administration (1915) and the lecture here partly reprinted, which was delivered in 1936 at the Harvard Law School, as part of the ceremonies celebrating the tercentenary of the founding of Harvard College.—Editor

economic change. Law performs its function adequately only when it is suited to the way of life of a people. With social change comes the imperative demand that law shall satisfy the needs which change has created, and so the problem, above all others, of jurisprudence in the modern world is the reconciliation of the demands, paradoxical and to some extent conflicting, that law shall at once have continuity with the past and adaptability to the present and the future. Science, invention, and industrial expansion have done more than all else to change the habits of life of the people of this continent, and the striking development in those fields has taken place since the Civil War. In the brief space of about seventy years our law has been called upon to accommodate itself to changes of conditions, social and economic, more marked and extensive in their creation of new interests requiring legal protection and control than occurred in the three centuries which followed the discovery of America. Rapid social change, more than all else, puts to the test a legal system which seeks its inspiration and its guidance in a past which could make no adequate prophecy of the future.

To have kept pace with the rapid developments in the American commonwealth since the Civil War, any type of judge-made law must have possessed the qualities of flexibility and adaptability to a unique degree, and certainly to a far greater extent than had in fact been exhibited by the common law as it had developed in the United States, largely under the tutelage of the Blackstonian conceptions. His was the notion prevailing during most of the nineteenth century that the common law was a complete and perfect system, in the administration of which it was only needful for the judge to "find the law" by diligent search of the precedents. There was little scope in such a system so administered for the creative task of framing legal doctrine adequate to the needs of a new and rapidly changing experience.

Judge-made law, which at its best must normally lag somewhat behind experience, was unable to keep pace with the rapid change, and it could find in the law books no adequate pattern into which the new experience could be readily fitted. It was inevitable that the attempt should be made to supply the unsatisfied need by recourse to legislation. So it has become increasingly our habit to look for the formulation of legal doctrine suited to new situations not to the courts, as through most of the life of the common law, but to the legislatures; and the primary record of the most important changes in the law in our own time is to be found in the statute books.

It is the fashion in our profession to lament both the quantity and quality of our statute making—not, it is true, without some justification. But our role has been almost exclusively that of destructive critics, usually after the event, of the inadequacies of legislatures. There has been little disposition to look to our own shortcomings in failing, through adaptation of old skills and the development of new ones, to realize more nearly than we have the ideal of a unified system of judge-made and statute law woven into a seamless whole by the processes of adjudication.

The reception which the courts have accorded to statutes presents a curiously illogical chapter in the history of the common law. Notwithstanding their genius for the generation of new law from that already established, the common law courts have given little recognition to statutes as starting points for judicial lawmaking comparable to judicial decisions. They have long recognized the supremacy of statutes over judge-made law, but it has been the supremacy of a command to be obeyed according to its letter, to be treated as otherwise of little consequence. The fact that the command involves recognition of a policy by the supreme lawmaking body has seldom been regarded by courts as significant, either as a social datum or as a point of departure for the process of judicial reasoning by which the common law has been expanded.

Their attitude toward statute law presents an interesting contrast to that of the civilians, who have been more ready to regard statutes in the light of the thesis of the civil law that its precepts are statements of general principles, to be used as guides to decision. Under that system a new statute may be viewed as an exemplification of a general principle which is to take its place beside other precepts—whether found in codes or accepted expositions of the jurists—as an integral part of the system, there to be extended to analogous situations not within its precise terms. With the modern practice of drawing a statute as a statement of a general rule, I can perceive no obstacle which need have precluded our adoption of a similar attitude except our unfamiliarity with the civilian habit of thought. The Scottish law, with its Roman law foundation, took this position, and the House of Lords, common-law learning and background notwithstanding, found no difficulty in approving it as applied to local statutes, in passing on appeals from the Scottish courts.

But quite apart from such a possibility, I can find in the history and principles of the common law no adequate reason for our failure to treat a statute much more as we treat a judicial precedent, as both a declaration and a source of law, and as a premise for legal reasoning. We have done practically that with our ancient statutes, such as the statutes of Limitations, Frauds, and Wills, readily molding them to fit new conditions within their spirit, though not their letter, possibly because their antiquity tends to make us forget or minimize their legislative origin. . . . Apart from its command, the social policy and judgment, expressed in legislation by the lawmaking agency which is supreme, would seem to merit that judicial recognition which is freely accorded to the like expression by judicial precedent. But only to a limited extent do modern courts feel free, by resort to standards of conduct set up by legislation, to impose liability or attach consequences for the failure to maintain those or similar standards in similar but not identical situations, or to make the statutory recognition of a new type of right the basis for the judicial creation of rights in circumstances not dissimilar. . . . [T]he legislative function has been reduced to mere rule making by the process of narrow judicial interpretation of statutes, and in consequence of the renunciation by the courts, where statutes are concerned, of some of their own lawmaking powers.

That such has been the course of the common law in the United States seems to be attributable to the fact that, long before its important legislative expansion, the theories of Coke and Blackstone of the self-sufficiency and ideal perfection of the common law, and the notion of the separation of powers and of judicial independence, had come to dominate our juristic thinking. The statute was looked upon as in the law but not of it, a formal rule to be obeyed, it is true, since it is the command of the sovereign, but to be obeyed grudgingly, by construing it narrowly and treating it as though it did not exist for any purpose other than that embraced within the strict construction of its words. It is difficult to appraise the consequences of the perpetuation of incongruities and injustices in the law by this habit of narrow construction of statutes and by the failure to recognize that they are as significant as recognitions of social needs and rightly as much a part of the law as the rules declared by judges. A generation ago no feature of our law administration tended quite so much to discredit law and lawyers in the lay mind. A narrow literalism too often defeated the purpose of remedial legislation, while a seeming contest went on with the apparent purpose of ascertaining whether the legislatures would ultimately secure a desired reform or the courts would succeed in resisting it.

Happily the abrasive effect of the never-ending judicial labor of making a workable system of our law, so largely composed of statutes, is bringing about a more liberal attitude on the part of the courts. Fortunately, too, law schools have begun to study and investigate the problem involved in an adequate union of judge-made with statute law. They are developing the underlying principles for its solution, which rest basically on a more adequate recognition that a statute is not an alien intruder in the house of the common law, but a guest to be welcomed and made at home there as a new and powerful aid in the accomplishment of its appointed task of accommodating the law to social needs. But there still remains much to be done. The better organization of judge-made and statute law into a co-ordinated system is one of the major problems of the common law in the United States. I would invite those who doubt to survey almost any new field of legislation and particularly to consider the published studies of the Law Revision Commission of the State of New York, disclosing the results of its five years' search of the laws of New York for inequitable and anachronistic rules.

Unfortunately we cannot revise *ab initio* our philosophy of interpretation of statutes, but we can still give them a more hospitable reception as an aid and not a detriment to the system of judge-made law, and we can turn to better account than we have our theory that statutes are commands, and the illusion that in interpreting them our only task is to discover the legislative will. We can at least let the statute reveal more fully the reasons for its enactment, and we can let its command prescribe the treatment which courts are to accord to it. I observe in recent statutes a revival of the ancient practice of stating in them the reasons for their enactment. The reasons were addressed, it is true, to the removal of constitutional doubts, but the practice can similarly be made an aid to construction. As the force of judicial decision is enhanced by the reasons given in support of it, so the union of statutes with judge-made law may be aided by the statement of legislative reasons for its enactment, or by a more adequate preservation of the record of them in its legislative history. On occasion legislatures have made so bold as to direct that a statute shall be extended to cases plainly within its reason and spirit though not within the strict letter, a practice which, if skillfully employed, may yet restore to courts a privilege which they renounced only because they have mistakenly regarded statutory enactments as in some degree less a part of the law than their own decisions.

Pound, *COMMON LAW AND LEGISLATION*
21 Harvard Law Review 383, 385 (1908)

Four ways may be conceived of in which courts in such a legal system as ours might deal with a legislative innovation. (1) They might receive it fully into the body of the law as affording not only a rule to be applied but a principle from which to reason, and hold it, as a later and more direct expression of the general will, of superior authority to judge-made rules on the same general subject; and so reason from it by analogy in preference to them. (2) They might receive it fully into the body of the law to be reasoned from by analogy the same as any other rule of law, regarding it, however, as of equal or co-ordinate authority in this respect with judge-made rules upon the same general subject. (3) They might refuse to receive it fully into the body of the law and give effect to it directly only; refusing to reason from it by analogy but giving it, nevertheless, a liberal interpretation to cover the whole field it was intended to cover. (4) They might not only refuse to reason from it by analogy and apply it directly only, but also give to it a strict and narrow interpretation, holding it down rigidly to those cases which it covers expressly. The fourth hypothesis represents the orthodox common law attitude toward legislative innovations. Probably the third hypothesis, however, represents more nearly the attitude toward which we are tending. The second and first hypotheses doubtless appeal to the common law lawyer as absurd. He can hardly conceive that a rule of statutory origin may be treated as a permanent part of the general body of the law, but it is submitted that the course of legal development upon which we have entered already must lead us to adopt the method of the second and eventually the method of the first hypothesis.

Landis,* *STATUTES AND THE SOURCES OF LAW*
Harvard Legal Essays 213 (1934)

[In the opening pages of this essay, Dean Landis argues that "common-law courts at an early stage developed the doctrine of the equity of the statute." This doctrine was a "double-edged device." "Under its authority exceptions dictated by sound policy were written by (English) judges into loose statutory generaliza-

* James M. Landis was Dean of the Harvard Law School, 1937-46, after having taught there from 1926 to 1934. He was a member of the Federal Trade Commission, 1933-34, member of the Securities and Exchange Commission, 1934-37 (chairman from 1935), chairman of the Civil Aeronautics Board, 1946-47, Director of the Office of Civilian Defense, 1942-43, Director of American Economic Operations and Minister to the Middle East, 1943-45. He practises law in Washington and New York from which he is currently on leave to act as Special Assistant to the President. Landis is author of The Administrative Process (1938), The Business of the Supreme Court (with Felix Frankfurter) (1927), and a casebook on labor law.— Editor

tions and, on the other hand, situations were brought within the reach of the statute that admittedly lay without its express terms." Secondly, the doctrine enabled judges "to distil from a statute its basic purpose and employ it to slough off the archaisms in their own legal structure." "Even general legislation could thus be made to yield a meaning for law beyond its expressed operative effect. The class of situations to which the statutory remedy was expressly made applicable were but illustrative of other analogous cases that deserved to be governed by the same principle. The extension of one remedy beyond its recognized common-law area by the statute justified judges in giving another remedy the same expansive effect. The imposition of liability in a defined series of circumstances was not exhaustive, but offered a reason for fastening liability upon similar conduct."

[English judges in the 18th century, Dean Landis maintains, came to deny that they possessed the authority rightfully to employ statutes in the broad fashion made possible by the principle of the equity of the statute. He attributes this change in judicial attitude to a number of factors—(1) the recession, during the 18th century, "from the earlier periods of pronounced major legislative activity"; (2) the 18th-century acceptance of the "growing fact of the separation of powers" as a political dogma (which the American courts later imposed as a principle of constitutional law and which theoretically "divorced legislative powers from the judiciary, and led as a matter of logical verity to the conception of judges as passive agents, impotent to do otherwise than merely 'find' law"); and (3) the Blackstonian conception of the common law "as a fully matured system," leading to "the view that changes in that ideally self-sufficient system should not be lightly countenanced."

[The importance of these influences, Landis concludes, was heightened during the first half of the 19th century when legal thought was dominated by the analytical theories of jurisprudence which tended to view judges as merely discovering the command of the sovereign expressed in law, and by the historical jurists who regarded the common law as embodying the underlying spirit and customs of the people, not to be readily tampered with by legislative change. These currents of thought were congenial to conservative judges disturbed by the increasing popular demand for social reform.

[Landis then traces similar trends in American judicial attitudes occurring "much later in point of time."

[The accuracy of Dean Landis's reading of the early sources has been sharply challenged by Thorne, The Equity of a Statute and Heydon's Case (1936) 31 Ill. L. Rev. 202. But the verdict in this controversy over the significance of the earliest sources does not affect the validity of Dean Landis's description of contemporary judicial use of statutes by analogy, which follows.—Editor]

II

Courts to-day have avowedly rejected as part of their technique the doctrine of the equity of the statute. Whatever significance statutes possess to govern results, they achieve by virtue of being interpreted to include the particular situation. Under the guise of interpretation, however, much is accomplished that upon analysis reveals the court as true to the more ancient doctrine of the equitable application of statutes. The results of such dissembling are doubly unfortunate. They discredit the conception that there is any science of interpretation; but they also prevent the development of an appropriate juristic approach towards statutes as a source of "common law." Obviously there is something intrinsic in the attitude toward legislation that was once phrased by reference to the equity of the statute, that cannot be exorcised from the law. To confine to interpretation the judicial development of law from legislation will not suffice; an approach must be made to the problem of the place that statutes should occupy in judicial administration in terms other than hermeneutic [interpretative] theories as to the meaning of legislative enactments.

Certain factors peculiar to modern life make the problem more pressing. Both the profession and the schools are now demanding something more adequate than the traditional method of developing law purely from earlier judicial precedents. Even though the process permits a slow infiltration of wisdom from other branches of sociological effort, some more open liaison is required. Legislation, too, is assuming both a volume and a creative aspect of purpose that makes it impossible to ignore. But at the same time civilization is achieving a complexity that outstrips this effort to embrace its multitudinous activities by rules, while the traditional attitude of courts toward the legislative process insists upon confining that process to the making of rules. Changes in attitude, points of departure, germinating principles —these the judicial process reserves to itself and places beyond the scope of legislative power. On the other hand, the last few decades have seen the steady development of better methods of legislation. Not only has there been progress in the art of draftsmanship, but the growing use of experts and the committee system, itself tending toward an empiric efficiency, has meant much in the advancement of legislative method. A realization of this fact has already made for greater reliance upon the legislative process as an aid to statutory interpretation.* Also, there is a growing comprehension that wide modifications have been effected by recent legislation in the structural content of the law. The realization of their full significance is far from complete, for effort is now bent only towards unearthing and classifying the mass of materials dormant in our statute books. Clearly these factors negative the possibility of relegating the legislative process to the role of mere rule-making and of confining the relationship between courts and legislatures merely to the interpretation of statutes.

One well recognized field exists where statutes have been commonly relied upon by courts to determine whether certain types of conduct are to be regarded as tortious. Legislatures in striking at action deemed by them to be undesirable often fail to think beyond the imposition of a criminal penalty for pursuing forbidden acts. The very prohibition, however, carries with it a judgment of culpability. Courts have generally recognized this fact, and have enlarged the area of tort liability by giving the statute the effect of attaching culpability to action in dis-

* I.e., there has been increasing readiness in the courts to cite evidence contained in committee hearings and reports and pub-lished legislative debates to show the meaning of a statute.—Editor

regard of the statute.* . . . The relevance of the legislature's judgment as to the desirability of particular conduct is obvious. In the unfettered choice open to a heterogeneous assembly the pressure of the various interests making for or against penalizing certain action finds a ready reflection. What remains for the judicial process in such cases is the extent to which the indirect pressure of civil liability shall be employed to compel conformance to the legislative rule.

Legislation in this field is only permitted by courts to exercise a limited function, that of crystallizing recognized principles of liability into more rigid rules to cover recurring type situations. A more extensive use of like statutory material can fairly ask indulgence.† The statutory rule may have pricked out for reprobation only a limited number of examples from a wide field of not essentially dissimilar instances; but unless the enacted rule covers the particular type of conduct in issue, the traditional technique ignores the legislative treatment of analogous cases. The reasons for this neglect are difficult to grasp. The method of judicial evaluation of the conflicting claims which finally results in the enunciation of a rule has only very generalized and indefinite standards to guide it. Reliance is placed in the main upon particulars which consist of analogous cases decided by other courts, and which consequently reflect only a limited contact with the problem. The judgments of legislatures as expressed in statutory rules often represent a wider and more comprehensive grasp of the situation and yet are practically neglected. . . .

The arguments adduced for neglecting such statutory material generally do little more than pour contempt upon the legislative process. Legislation is presumed immune to "principle"; its judgments represent merely the political pressure of a

---

* A is driving his automobile after sunset without headlights. A hits B. B sues A for negligence in driving without his lights on. A argues that it was still light enough so that a reasonable and prudent driver would not have thought it necessary as yet to turn on his lights. A statute declares that one who drives without lights after sunset shall be punished by a fine. The statute, however, does not say anything as to what shall be the effect in a civil action for damages, of the fact that the person causing the injury was driving without lights after sunset. But, assuming it was shown that the absence of lights was in fact a cause of the accident, the Wisconsin court today, as most courts, would rule that the fact that A's conduct violated a penal statute established that A was negligent. A will not be heard to argue whether or not it was light enough so that it was reasonably prudent to drive without lights, since the legislature has decided that lights should be on after sunset. Even though the legislature spoke only regarding the criminal law and said nothing about private suits for damages, the standard set in the penal statute will be held determinative of what is the standard of conduct to be applied in the private damages suit.—Editor

† Suppose that the only statute regarding headlights after sunset has to do with automobiles. What if A, riding a bicycle without a headlight, after sunset, hits B? What if A, driving a horse and wagon without a headlight, after sunset, hits B? What if A is driving a motorboat around the lake and hits B's sailboat? Dean Landis in this paragraph is critical of the courts because in situations like these they would be likely to fail to draw on the automobile headlight statute as helpful in determining what was careful conduct in driving a bicycle, wagon or motorboat. True, the statute does not provide for bicycles, etc. But it does express a judgment from an authoritative body as to what is careful conduct in an analogous situation. As such, Dean Landis would urge, it should be used in determining a common law rule re bicycles, wagons or motorboats.—Editor

special class; it is both ignorant and perverse. Criticisms such as these, of course, have substance, but statutes are of all types. The task of distinguishing between the deliberate and the ad hoc pronouncements of a legislature is not too difficult. A course of legislation dealing continuously with a series of instances can be made to unfold a principle of action as easily as the sporadic judgments of courts. Deliberate and conscientious preferment of competing claims can be shown to underlie the enacted rule, while the wide generality of such a choice can be evidenced by the legislation of other jurisdictions. Only jejune conceptions of both the judicial and the legislative process stand in the way of the appropriate use of such statutory material.

III

Another field, somewhat less apparent, reveals courts giving effects to statutes far beyond their express terms. Doctrines of common law dealing with the relationship between individuals will often be seen to hinge upon a conception as to the position that one party is to occupy in our social structure. This becomes solidified into a concept of status.* But obviously status has no meaning apart from its incidents. These incidents, often so numerous as to escape description, have a varying importance in shaping the nucleus of a status. The alteration of some of them possesses no importance beyond the change itself; the alteration of others, however, may call for a radical revision of the privileges or disabilities that have generally been attached to a particular status. The common-law incidents of status, that in their origin have themselves been of empiric growth, must then give way before the new aims deducible from such a basic alteration.

Changes of this nature are commonly the product of legislation. The statutes that express them rarely directly make or alter a status as such; nor do the statutes often see the seamlessness of the pattern that they seek to change. The task of modifying the existing body of the law to fit the structural changes must of necessity be left to courts with the hope that given an end they will mould substantive doctrine to make it effective. Such was the method pursued in the married women's legislation of the last century.[23] The statutes themselves were quite terse, generally granting to married women merely powers to hold and convey property and to sue and be sued.[24] Obviously they swept away the contra-

---

* "Status": i.e., about certain relationships there cluster groups of rights and duties, as "landlord and tenant," "master and servant," "husband and wife." Also, persons occupy certain general legal positions with reference to the community as a whole: one is a "minor" or an "adult," a "legitimate child" or an "illegitimate"; an "alien" or a "citizen." The problem posed is: Assume that a statute has changed some particular feature of one of these legal positions or statuses. May that statute be given effect, as a matter of common law, in altering other features of the status which the statute does not itself purport to affect?— Editor

[23] See Lush, Changes in the Law Affecting the Rights, Status, and Liabilities of Married Women, being Chap. IX of A Century of Law Reform (1901); Dicey, Law and Public Opinion in England (1926) 371-395.

[24] For an attempt to achieve equality of rights and powers by blanket legislation, see 1921 Wis. Acts. c. 529, ["Women shall have the same rights and privileges under the law as men in . . . freedom of contract . . . holding and conveying prop-

dictory common-law limitations,* but their terms did not directly control numerous allied questions. The resolution of these demanded consideration of how far the change made by the statutes in one incident of the status should affect doctrine developed under a different conception of the married woman's position in society.

The incidental results of the married women's acts are to be seen in decisions dealing with such questions as the liability of the husband for the torts of his wife,[25] his responsibility for crimes committed by her in his presence,[26] . . . The

erty . . . and in all other respects. . . ."] construed in First Nat'l Bk. of Wisconsin v. Jahn, 179 Wis. 117, 190 N.W. 822 (1922) and Selts Investment Co. v. Baireuther, 202 Wis. 151, 231 N.W. 641 (1930) to enable a wife to become surety for her husband; in . . . Fontaine v. Fontaine, 238 N.W. 410 (Wis. 1931) to enable a wife to sue her husband in tort; in Sparks v. Keiss, 195 Wis. 378, 216 N.W. 929, 218 N.W. 208 (1928) to enable a wife to become a business partner of her husband; in Aaby v. Citizens Nat'l Bank, 197 Wis. 56, 221 N.W. 417 (1928) to abolish estates by the entirety. Cf. Ansorge v. Green Bay, 198 Wis. 320, 224 N.W. 119 (1929).
* I.e., at common law upon marriage a woman lost legal capacity to make contracts and to acquire or dispose of property. In general, her husband acquired full control of her economic affairs.—Editor
[25] The bases for the common-law doctrine imposing liability upon the husband for torts unconnected with the wife's separate estate that have been suggested are: (1) that as a matter of procedure the wife could not be sued separately, . . . ; (2) that the husband should be subjected to such an obligation because he became the owner of the wife's personal property and received the rents and profits from her realty, . . . ; (3) that the husband possessed a limited power of chastisement over the wife, . . . ; (4) that the wife in committing such torts acted under the superior will and influence of the husband, . . . The Married Women's Act swept away the first two grounds, and the third has disappeared. Giving effect to the policy of the acts should therefore have resulted in the abrogation of the common-law rule, except insofar as the fourth ground may be valid. In the main such abrogation has resulted. See cases collected in 1 Schouler, Marriage, Divorce, Separation and Domestic Relation-

ships (6th ed. 1921) §§ 130-131; Tiffany, op. cit. 101-104. Cf. Edward v. Porter (1915) A.C. 1. The contrary decisions have since generally been abrogated by statute. See 1883 Me. Laws, c. 207; 1897 Minn. Laws, c. 10; 1915 Mo. Acts, p. 269; 1890 N.Y. Laws, c. 51; § 2; 1921 N.C. Laws, c. 10; 1921 Tex. Laws, c. 130; 1931 W. Va. Code 48-3-§ 20. Cf. Moore v. Doerr, 199 Mo. App. 428, 203 S.W. 672 (1918); Marcus v. Rovinsky, 95 Me. 106, 49 Atl. 420 (1901). The common-law liability of the husband for the antenuptial contracts and torts of his wife presents an even clearer instance where the effect of the Married Women's Acts should be to overturn earlier doctrine based upon a different conception of marriage. Resting, as the rule did, upon the fact that the husband acquired the wife's personalty and the income from her realty together with the right to her earnings, the Acts removed the bases for such liability. Courts thus generally absolved the husband of personal liability. See 1 Schouler, op. cit., § 82. Contrary decisions were quickly abrogated by express legislative enactment. Kies v. Young, 64 Ark. 381, 42 S.W. 669 (1897); overruled by 1899 Ark. Acts, p. 4; Connor v. Berry, 46 Ill. 370 (1868), overruled by 1869 Ill. Laws, p. 255, as construed in Howarth v. Warmser, 58 Ill. 48 (1871); Alexander v. Morgan, Root & Co., 31 Ohio St. 546 (1877), overruled by series of statutes detailed in Y.&O. Coal Co. v. Paszka, 20 Ohio App. 248 (1925); Platner v. Patchin, 19 Wis. 333 (1865), overruled by 1872 Wis. Laws, c. 155; Berley v. Rampacker, 5 Duer 183 (N.Y. 1856), rendered innocuous by 1853 N.Y. Laws, c. 576.
[26] The common law presumed that a wife committing a crime in the presence of her husband did it under his compulsion. The same presumption applied at common law

statutory grant to the wife of the power to sue, though admittedly concerned with her rights against third persons, has been an important factor in determining what torts committed by one spouse against the property or person of another should give rise to a right of compensation.[32] The specific results that courts have reached in these cases need not here be detailed. It is the method that is significant. There has been general recognition that the married women's acts embodied principles which were of wider import than the statutes in terms expressed and thus necessitated remoulding common-law doctrines to fit the statutory aims. Judgments that sought to retain older common-law limitations hostile to the aim of the statutes were overruled by subsequent legislation, more attuned to the principles of the married women's acts than the courts that professed to be controlled by "principle." The result is an impressive edifice of law resting upon statute and yet not depending upon the express terms of the statutes for its content.

A similar development can be seen in bastardy law. In the early nineteenth century American states quite generally sought to alleviate the unfortunate position that the common law accorded the illegitimate child as a *filius nullius*.* These statutes generally made him the heir of his mother, while some states provided means for the subsequent legitimation of children born out of wedlock. In terms the statutes did not touch the nature of such children as "children" within the

to torts committed by the wife in the husband's presence. For these the husband was solely liable. . . . In both situations the reason for the common law rests upon the generalization that the acts are done under duress from the husband. For an early application of this principle, see Laws of Ine, 57, Attenborough, Laws of the Earliest English Kings (1922) 55. The Married Women's Acts thus of themselves do not strike at the basis for the rule. In advancing the economic independence of married women, the Acts may indirectly have challenged the truth of the early generalization. But the question hinges upon a wide issue of fact, and does not follow as a deduction from a change in economic status. Courts have, however, concluded that the Acts of themselves abrogated the common-law rule. . . .

Not unlike the issues here involved are those raised by the effect of the Married Women's Act upon the common-law doctrine that neither spouse could be guilty of a crime against the property of the other spouse. The separate economic existence given married women by the Acts would make for the abrogation of such a rule. Considerations of the undesirability of permitting resort to the criminal law in intra-familial matters would seem rightly to be subordinated, in the more serious crimes, to the desirability of maintaining inviolate the married woman's rights to her property. The trend has thus been to consider the Acts as having changed the common-law rule. . . .

[32] General agreement exists that the Acts enable the wife to sue the husband for torts committed against her separate property, though the authorities divide upon whether the action should be legal or equitable. See McCurdy, Torts Between Persons in Domestic Relation (1930) 43 Harv. L. Rev. 1030, 1038. Disagreement exists where the tort is of a personal nature. That the issue in these cases is not one of statutory interpretation but one of developing a rule appropriate to the institution of marriage as altered by statute, see McCurdy, supra. . . .

* "Filius nullius": Lat., literally, "the (legal) child of no one"; at common law an illegitimate child was not, in general, the subject of any of the rights and duties existent between parents and legitimate children. Especially, the illegitimate child had no rights of inheritance from either parent.—Editor

terms of a will, nor were they correlated with the contemporaneous wrongful death acts that gave "children" and "parents" reciprocal rights for compensation for injuries resulting in death. The course of decision in these two situations is worth elaborating.

Statutes which allow the illegitimate child to inherit from its mother, in terms apply only to the situation upon intestacy.* Whether the illegitimate child should take as a "child" under a will rested theoretically upon the intent of the testator. That intent was fashioned for testators by courts imbued with a morality which rigorously excluded the illegitimate child. That morality found its expression in the common-law concept that the bastard had no inheritable blood. This the statutes swept away, and so they should have been given the effect of throwing into the discard an interpretative attitude based upon that policy. With some exceptions the statutes were so utilized, and courts either adopted the presumption that the illegitimate child is to be considered the "child" of the parent from whom he has inheritable rights[36] or, throwing aside any presumption, sought to give effect to the true intent of the testator by inquiry into the *de facto* relationship as to the particular child.

American wrongful death acts commonly provide that a "child" may maintain an action for the death of its "parent" and vice versa, or else give the personal representative of the deceased a right to sue for the benefit of the next of kin. The latter type of act plainly draws upon principles of intestate distribution in order to fix the incidence of the injury caused by death, and distributes compensation in accordance with such a general plan. Changes in the principles of intestate distribution, whether made prior or subsequent to the death statute, should therefore carry through into the distribution of compensation effected by the death acts. Thus legislation giving the illegitimate child inheritable rights should make him one of the "next of kin" entitled to compensation by the death statute. Such a result has almost uniformly been reached by the courts. But strangely enough courts have on occasion shrunk from designating illegitimate children as "children" in death statutes that framed their plans of distributive compensation in such language.[39] Here, as distinct from the problem of interpreting "children" in testamentary dispositions, considerations of de facto relationships play no part, and the issue turns only upon legal and moral conceptions of the reciprocal duty

---

* "Intestacy" is the situation when a person has died without leaving a will; in this case a statute describes what persons shall be entitled to his property. If the deceased left a will, theoretically the descent of his property will be according to his wishes as expressed in the will. But what if he simply willed property to "my children"? In interpreting what he meant by "children," the courts applied presumptive rules of intention which expressed their ideas of sound public policy.—Editor

[36] In Wisconsin the presumption that "children" means legitimate children has since the bastardy statutes, been "impaired but not destroyed." Will of Kaufer, 203 Wis. 299, 234 N.W. 504 (1931); Will of Scholl, 100 Wis. 650, 76 N.W. 616 (1898). . . .

[39] . . . The fact that the American decisions reaching this result come uniformly from southern states suggests that the mulatto child has something to do with the result. It should be noted, however, that Florida and Texas are among the other jurisdictions in which contrary results have been reached. . . .

of support. The illegitimate child statutes have definitely moulded these relationships, and only adherence to doctrine, now devoid of substance, can be adduced for failing to carry out the principle of this legislation. . . .

The interplay between legislation and adjudication has been generally explored from the standpoint of interpretation. The function of the legislature as, in essence, a supreme court of appeal constantly busying itself with correcting the aberrations of the judicial process has been largely ignored. Cases, so far as their doctrinal content go, are overruled at almost every legislative session. The deeper import of such action has yet to be appreciated. A decent respect for the legislative process would strike a more favorable balance between legislative and judicial development of law.

One phase of the problem assumes importance especially in a nation with forty-eight coordinate but common legal systems. One jurisdiction faced with the same problem earlier decided by another jurisdiction has to weigh the significance to be attached to a statute repudiating the judicial solution made of the problem. To the narrow traditionalist the statute itself is a datum which reinforces the fact that the overruled decision is evidence of the common law, and so error perpetuates itself. But the simplicity of such a conception of the common law is slowly passing. A better understanding now exists of the nature of the judicial process and the nicety of the choices that sway judgment and thus result in law. Plainly, then, the statute is pertinent. Bench and bar have been prone to neglect this aspect of legislation. Cases are relied upon as authoritative without cognizance of the fact that in the jurisdiction that gave them birth they have already been repudiated.[69] An editorial criticism of a decision is relied upon as an excuse for refusing to follow it, while the judgment of a legislature overturning its effect is neglected.[70] Judicial reversals avowedly based upon the social inexpediency of the earlier conclusion stifle its germinating powers, but the same sober judgment of a representative assembly merely adds virulence to the poison of judicial unwisdom. Indeed, at times the process portrays a fantasy more than fit for a new Erewhon. . . .

---

[69] See, for example, Hammond, J., in Vegelahn v. Guntner, 167 Mass. 92, 44 N.E. 1077 (1896) relying on Reg. v. Druitt, 10 Cox C.C. 592 (1867); Reg. v. Hibbert, 13 Cox C.C. 82 (1875), then repudiated by the Criminal Law Amendment Act, 1871, 34 & 35 Vict. c. 31, and the Conspiracy & Protection of Property Act, 1875, 38 & 39 Vict. c. 86.

[70] In Pavesich v. New England L. Ins. Co., 122 Ga. 190, 50 S.E. 68 (1905), which recognized a right in privacy despite the contrary decision in Roberson v. Rochester Folding Box Co., 171 N.Y. 538, 64 N.E. 442 (1902), the court relies strongly upon an editorial in (1902) 36 Am. L. Rev. 636, and articles in other legal periodicals con-

demning the Roberson decision, but makes no mention of 1903 N.Y. Laws, c. 130, where the legislature promptly repudiated the Roberson rule. The statute finds no mention in any case that, like the Paversich case, refused to adopt the law of the Roberson case. Munden v. Harris, 153 Mo. App. 652, 134 S.W. 1076 (1910); Edison v. Edison Polyform Mfg. Co., 73 N.J. Eq. 136, 67 Atl. 392 (1907), Kunz v. Allen, 102 Kan. 883, 172 Pac. 532 (1918). But cf. Vanderbilt v. Mitchell, 72 N.J. Eq. 910, 67 Atl. 97 (1907). Strangely enough the statute is mentioned in a case which followed the Roberson case. Henry v. Cherry & Webb, 30 R.I. 13, 73 Atl. 97 (1909).

IV

The present attitude responsible for our cavalier treatment of legislation is certain to be a passing phenomenon. The consciousness that the judicial and legislative processes are closely allied both in technique and in aims will inevitably make for greater interdependence in both. The beginnings of such a movement are already clearly discernible in the process of statutory interpretation where courts, returning to an earlier attitude, seek to interpret expressions of policy in the light of the manifold circumstances responsible for the statutory formulation. Grammatical interpretation is giving way to functional construction. The distrust of legislative intervention is subsiding with the important advances made in the mechanics of law-making. Our prevailing philosophy makes us less certain that we have seized upon universals, and the search for pragmatical truth carries us naturally to seek for wisdom in the many sources of experience. Black-letter learning has rarely been characteristic of the legislative process, and its importance to adjudication is disappearing with the rise of the social scientific method.* And the consciousness that that method, though often in its crudest form, underlies legislation makes for tolerance with the product.

Circumstances militating against a freer use of statutory materials, apart from the passing juridical conception that negates the creative qualities intrinsic in the judicial process, are chiefly technical. The methods of statute-making still fail fully to disclose the operative forces behind legislation. Adequate records that give the lineage of a statute are, for the most part, non-existent. Often the assurance that respectable impulses have underlain its passage is wanting. Doubt may exist as to whether there has been a thorough exploration of the issues upon which choices have been made. Under the pressure of the legislative mechanics of an earlier generation, statutes have been stripped of everything save normative and compulsory provisions. Reasons for the legislature's action, once incorporated in unwieldly preambles, have been eliminated or expressed only in an incidental fashion where sterile judicial technique forbids their examination. Though the older preamble hardly offers the solution, some means of formulating in an authoritative manner the conceptions of policy upon which the statute is based are necessary. Statute books, too, are encumbered with a mass of detailed administrative regulation that tends to bring the entire process into contempt.

Finally, the profession and the schools are at fault for not affording the bench better technical aids. These United States present a most extraordinary laboratory for comparative legislative study. But while the precedents of even our *nisi prius* courts are carefully catalogued, analyzed, and weighed, no scientific concern is manifested over our constantly accumulating legislation. Texts and source-books thread their way through the welter of our decisions, throwing off statutes as excrescences upon the body of the law. Under the impulse of great law-teaching a national attitude toward the common law has arisen to counterbalance the

---

* "Black-letter learning": reliance simply upon logically symmetrical development of rules found in the reported decisions. The reference is to the style of printing in the Year Books, the earliest English Reports.— Editor

centrifugal forces of our many states. But even the idea that the same spirit can control legislative law is wanting. The task of its development promises to be a chief concern of tomorrow.

KUHL MOTOR COMPANY v. FORD MOTOR COMPANY
270 Wis. 488, 71 N.W. 2d 420 (1955)

MARTIN, J. The following facts are disclosed by the complaint. Plaintiff is a corporation located in the city of Milwaukee engaged in the business of selling and servicing motor vehicles. Defendant is a manufacturer of motor vehicles, parts, and accessories. On December 12, 1938, plaintiff and defendant entered into a written "Ford Sales Agreement," which provided that it could be terminated at any time at the will of either party by sixty days' written notice. On April 17, 1954, plaintiff received from the defendant a notice of its intention to terminate the agreement. Plaintiff alleges:

"6. That the writing hereto attached, marked Exhibit E, has been served upon the plaintiff by the defendant, contrary to the provisions of section 218.01 (3) paragraphs 16 and 17 thereof, of the Wisconsin statutes, in that it has been done unfairly without due regard to the equities of the plaintiff and without just provocation, and if acted upon by the defendant, unless enjoined by this court, will operate to put the plaintiff out of business and confiscate its good will, all and singular to its irreparable damage; that the cancellation of this franchise granted by the defendant to the plaintiff in and by Exhibit A hereto attached as amended, is within the scope and purview of section 218.01 (8) paragraph (d) of the Wisconsin statutes, and that the plaintiff has no adequate remedy at law or by administrative action."

Defendant demurred to the complaint on the grounds (1) that it does not state facts sufficient to constitute a cause of action, and (2) that the court has no jurisdiction of the subject of the action.

It was held by the trial court, first, that, disregarding sec. 218.01, Stats., the agreement of December 12, 1938, was valid and the notice of April 17, 1954, effectively terminated said agreement, basing its opinion on Bushwick-Decatur Motors, Inc., v. Ford Co. (2d Cir. 1940), 116 Fed. (2d) 675; Buggs v. Ford Motor Co. (7th Cir. 1940), 113 Fed. (2d) 618; Biever Motor Car Co. v. Chrysler Corp. (2d Cir. 1952), 199 Fed. (2d) 758; and Martin v. Ford Motor Co. (D.C. Mich. 1950), 93 Fed. Supp. 920.

In the last-named case, at page 921, it was held:

"The agreement in this case was not for a fixed period but was terminable at any time at defendant's will upon compliance with the requirement as to notice. It is beyond the power of the judiciary to engraft conditions upon the exercise of such a contractual right. . . .

"In the instant case it is clear that Martin's dealership was to continue no longer than either he or the Ford Motor Company desired it to continue and that its right to terminate it was subject to no conditions as to good or bad faith, motive, intent, or results, except as to the requirement of advance notice if such termination was desired by the Ford Motor Company."

Sec. 218.01 (3), Stats., so far as material, provides:

"(a) A license may be denied, suspended, or revoked on the following grounds: . . .

"16. Being a manufacturer of motor vehicles, factory branch, distributor, field representative, officer, agent, or any representative whatsoever of such motor-vehicle manufacturer or factory branch, who has attempted to induce or coerce, or has induced or coerced, any automobile dealer to enter into any agreement with such manufacturer, factory branch or representative thereof, or to do any other act unfair to said dealer, by threatening to cancel any franchise existing between such manufacturer, factory branch, or representative thereof and said dealer.

"17. Being a manufacturer, factory branch, distributor, field representative, officer, agent, or any representative whatsoever of such motor-vehicle manufacturer or factory branch, who has unfairly, without due regard to the equities of said dealer and without just provocation, canceled the franchise of any motor-vehicle dealer. The nonrenewal of a franchise or selling agreement without just provocation or cause shall be deemed an evasion of this section and shall constitute an unfair cancellation."

This statute was in effect at the time the agreement herein was made. In 1945 sec. 218.01 (8) (d), Stats., was enacted, providing:

"*Penalties.* Any person, firm, or corporation violating any of the provisions of this section shall be deemed guilty of misdeameanor and upon conviction thereof shall be punished as follows:

"(d) Any person or persons violating subsection (3) (a) 15, 16, and 17, may in addition to, or in lieu of, the general denial, suspension, or revocation penalties in said subsection, be subject to a fine of not more than $5,000 or be subject to a suspension or revocation sentence of not more than a year effective only in the territory formerly served by the unfairly canceled dealer, or by both such fine and suspension or revocation, except that in a metropolitan area serviced by several dealers handling the same motor vehicle, the suspension or revocation order shall not be applicable to the remaining dealers."

This action is not a proceeding under ch. 218, Stats., which sets forth the administrative procedure to be followed to invoke the penalties for unfair cancellation of a motor-vehicle manufacturer-dealer contract. Plaintiff seeks to enjoin termination of the contract on the ground that pars. 16 and 17 of sec. 218.01 (3), Stats., define public policy and constitute a valid exercise of the police power of the state to prohibit unfair cancellations of sales agreements.

On this question the trial court held:

"The legislature of the state of Wisconsin in enacting chapter 218 undoubtedly was of the opinion that because of the economic advantages which a motor manufacturer enjoys over a dealer the latter should be protected against harsh treatment when a manufacturer exercises his right under the contract to cancel his sales contract with the dealer.

"In order to deter the manufacturer from acting harshly or without cause in canceling his contract with the dealer the legislature sought to accomplish said purpose by visiting certain penalties upon the manufacturer if the latter cancels his contract with the dealer without cause. The legislation in question is intended to act as a deterrent against any harsh treatment of the dealer by the manufacturer.

"There is no indication in the legislation in question of any intent on the part of the legislature to change or to declare illegal or void any term of the contract in question."

In discussing the attitude of the judiciary toward the importance of the individual's right to contract, it is stated in 12 Am. Jur., Contracts, p. 670, sec. 172:

"As the right of private contract is no small part of the liberty of the citizen, the usual and most important function of courts of justice is rather to maintain and enforce contracts than to enable parties thereto to escape from their obligations on the pretext of public policy, unless it clearly appears that they contravene public right or the public welfare. Rules which say that a given agreement is void as being against public policy are not to be extended arbitrarily, because 'if there is one thing which more than any other public policy requires it is that men of full age and competent understanding shall have the utmost liberty of contracting, and that their contracts, when entered into freely and voluntarily, shall be enforced by courts of justice.' The paramount public policy is that freedom to contract is not to be interfered with lightly."

Any impairment of that right must be specifically expressed or necessarily implied by the legislature in a statutory prohibition and not left to speculation. The general rule to be applied in this case is expressed in 17 C.J.S., Contracts, p. 558, sec. 202, as follows:

"It would seem that in all cases the true rule is that the question is one of legislative intent, and the courts will look to the language of the statute, the subject matter of it, the wrong or evil which it seeks to remedy or prevent, and the purpose sought to be accomplished in its enactment; and if from all these it is manifest that it was not intended to imply a prohibition or to render the prohibited act void, the courts will so hold and will construe the statute accordingly."

The intent expressed in the introductory language of sec. 218.01 (3) (a), Stats., is that of a regulatory measure. No words are used in pars. 16 and 17 requiring the conclusion that the legislature intended to prohibit unfair cancellation of sales contracts. They simply state that a manufacturer who engages in such a practice is subject to penalty under the prescribed administrative procedure. And an inference of invalidity does not necessarily follow from the fact that the statute prescribes a penalty. The statute must be judged by itself as a whole. . . . Where the legislature has intended to impress certain terms upon contracts, as, for instance, the omnibus coverage clause in automobile liability insurance contracts, it has expressly so provided. But here it has used no language "prohibiting" unfair cancellations, making them "void" or directing that every sales contract shall contain provision for cancellation only "with just provocation" or "for cause." Nor are there any specific provisions insuring enforcement of such a "prohibition." Obviously, the legislature recognized that the right of a manufacturer to terminate might be exercised without just provocation and without due regard to the equities of the dealer, but it did not declare invalid a clause permitting such an act. What it did was to make such act unprofitable by imposing the penalty of suspension, revocation, or fine. As pointed out by the learned trial court, it is apparent that the legislature recognized the inequality in bargaining power between an automobile dealer and an economically powerful manufacturer such as the defendant and that it desired to furnish him some protection by deterring unfair cancellation.

But we see no declaration of public policy in the statute. This court stated in Huber v. Merkel (1903), 117 Wis. 355, 366, 94 N.W. 354:

> "Where laws which are supposed to be enacted in the exercise of the police power interfere with the citizens' liberty or rights of property, they can only be justified upon the ground that they in some manner secure the comfort, safety, or welfare of society. It is on this principle that drainage laws are sustained. Donnelly v. Decker, 58 Wis. 461, 17 N.W. 389. And conversely, if it appear from the law itself that its purpose is primarily to benefit private owners, they are condemned. In re Theresa Drainage District, 90 Wis. 301, 63 N.W. 288. It must appear that the interests of the public generally require the restriction, and not the interests of private individuals. State ex rel. Zillmer v. Kreutzberg, 114 Wis. 530, 90 N.W. 1098."

What is the public welfare sought to be served? This is a business contract for the sale of motor vehicles, its purpose the mutual economic benefit of both dealer and manufacturer. There is nothing inuring to the benefit of the public in the representation of a manufacturer by a certain dealer nor is there anything immoral or dangerous to the public welfare in the termination of the relationship between a particular dealer and manufacturer. While there does exist in that relationship the possibility that the dealer may suffer personal economic loss if the manufacturer arbitrarily terminates it, his loss does not adversely affect the public interest. An inequality of bargaining power is present in many contractual relationships, but the law does not attempt to equalize it by impairing the basic right to contract.

Plaintiff cites a number of cases which arose out of moratorium legislation which was enacted during the depression. Such legislation, however, was designed to protect the general welfare; it inured to the benefit of all citizens during a period of national emergency.

Plaintiff relies for its cause of action on sec. 218.01, Stats., but the statute affords it no remedy. Its purpose being purely regulatory, the only benefit any particular automobile dealer receives from its provisions is the same benefit that all other such dealers receive—its effect of deterring unfair exercise by manufacturers of their right to terminate sales agreements at will. If it desires to take advantage of its opportunity to receive that indirect benefit, it must proceed as provided by ch. 218, Stats.; but it cannot maintain an action in equity to invalidate one of the terms of a contract it voluntarily entered into by resorting for its cause of action to the penalty provisions of a regulatory measure.

By the Court.—Order affirmed.

GEHL, J. (concurring). I would affirm upon the sole ground that, in so far as the statute may be construed to authorize the relief demanded by plaintiff, it is unconstitutional and void as infringing upon the right to contract. . . .

True, the right to make contracts is not absolute. It is subject to certain limitations which the state may impose in the exercise of its police power. . . .

When a restriction is made under the authority of the police power "it must appear that the interests of the public generally require the restriction, and not the interests of private individuals," Huber v. Merkel, 117 Wis. 355, 366, 94 N.W. 354. . . .

I am not convinced that the interests of the public require that any particular Ford agency be continued in business. I do not believe that the welfare of the public would be affected by the substitution by Ford of the "XYZ" Motor Company for the Kuhl Motor Company as its agent. I doubt that I could be convinced that the interests of the public would be affected by the cancellation of the Kuhl contract and Ford's omission to grant a substitute franchise. I doubt that it can properly be said that the public is affected solely because Ford is a large institution and Kuhl is a relatively small one. If the relative size of the parties to the contract is to be held controlling, at what stage does a contracting party become too large to be permitted to require that it may terminate its contract upon giving a sixty-day notice, and when is the other party to be considered too small to be allowed to consent that cancellation may be so made although by the terms of the contract it is given the right to terminate without notice?

I am authorized to say that Mr. Justice BROADFOOT and Mr. Justice STEINLE join in this concurring opinion.

CURRIE, J. (dissenting). I must respectfully dissent from the court's opinion in this case. Sec. 218.01 (3)(a) 17, Stats., [and] Sec. 218.01 (8)(d) . . . made it crystal clear that the unfair cancellation of a dealer's franchise without provocation and without considering the dealer's equities is against the public policy of this state.

. . . The latest pronouncement of our court on this subject was made in Pedrick v. First Nat. Bank of Ripon (1954), 267 Wis. 436, 439, 66 N.W. (2d) 154, wherein it was declared:

> "'An agreement is against public policy if it . . . violates some public statute, . . .' 12 Am. Jur., Contracts, p. 663, sec. 167. '. . . courts of justice will not recognize or uphold any transaction which, in its object, operation, or tendency, is calculated to be prejudicial to the public welfare, to sound morality, or to civic honesty. *The test is whether the parties have stipulated for some-*

thing inhibited by the law or inimical to, or inconsistent with, the public welfare.' Id., pp. 662, 663 (Italics ours.) Unquestionably, according to the complaint the parties here stipulated for something inhibited by the law, namely, the appointment by a corporate executor of the attorney for the estate. Agreements against public policy or prohibited by public law '. . . cannot be enforced by one party against the other, either directly by asking the court to carry them into effect or indirectly by claiming damages or compensation for breach of them.' 12 Am. Jur., Contracts, p. 715, sec. 209."

The majority opinion states that secs. 218.01 (3) (a) 17, and 218.01 (8) (d), Stats., do not expressly prohibit unfair cancellation of dealers' contracts by auto manufacturers, but only subject manufacturers who engage in such practice to a penalty for so doing. The same argument might be advanced against many of the criminal statutes of this state, which do not in express words prohibit people from doing certain acts but only state that if they do perform such acts a penalty will be inflicted. Sec. 346.06 (1)[1] relating to bribery of officers is an example of such type of criminal statute. However, it is doubtful if anyone would have the temerity to seriously contend that a contract to bribe an officer would not be illegal and against public policy.

Par. 17 of sec. 218.01 (3) (a), Stats., was enacted in 1937, and the dealer's contract entered into between the defendant and the plaintiff corporation was executed on December 12, 1938. Any dealer's franchise contract entered into between an automobile manufacturer and a Wisconsin dealer applicable to business to be transacted in Wisconsin would be subject to the provisions of such statute, and any provision of such contract which violated the statute would be against public policy and void under the authorities above cited. If the provision of the agreement permitting the Ford Motor Company to terminate the franchise upon sixty-days advance notice is to be interpreted as authorizing the Ford Motor Company to unfairly cancel the same without just provocation, then such provision would be void. On the other hand, if such termination provision of the contract can be interpreted in the light of the statute as being operative upon giving the sixty-day notice so as to permit a cancellation upon any ground except one which

---

[1] Sec. 346.06 (1). Any person who shall corruptly give, offer, or promise to any executive, judicial, legislative, administrative, or other officer of the state, or of any county, town, city, village, school district, or of other municipal corporation or subdivision therein, after his election or appointment, and either before or after he shall have been qualified or shall have taken his seat, any gift or gratuity, or any money, goods, thing in action, personal or real property, or any thing of value, or any pecuniary or other personal advantage, present or prospective, with intent to influence his vote, opinion, judgment, or action upon any question, matter, cause, or proceeding which may then be pending or which may by law come or be brought before him in his official capacity, and any such officer who shall corruptly accept or receive any such gift, gratuity, money, goods, thing in action, personal or real property, or any thing of value, or any such pecuniary or other personal advantage, present or prospective, under any agreement or understanding that his vote, opinion, judgment, or action should be thereby so influenced shall be punished by imprisonment in the state prison not more than five years nor less than one year, or by fine not exceeding one thousand dollars nor less than two hundred dollars.

contravened the statute, then such cancellation clause would not be void *in toto*. It is this latter interpretation which the law favors and which I believe should be adopted by this court.

The majority opinion in effect holds that if the statute were to be construed as prohibiting automobile manufacturers from entering into franchise contracts with Wisconsin dealers, which would restrict the right of the manufacturer to cancel the same, the statute would be unconstitutional as violating the Fourteenth amendment. The reason advanced for such conclusion is that interference with the right to contract can only be grounded upon the exercise by the state of its police power to promote the general welfare, and the statute was not enacted in the interest of the general public but only to benefit a particular small class of citizens, viz., auto dealers.

The United States supreme court, as early as 1887, in Mugler v. Kansas (1887), 123 U.S. 623, . . . expressly laid down the overriding doctrine that neither the defense of impairment of existing contracts nor the taking of property without just compensation is a defense to the acts of the state when done under the authority of its police power if that power is otherwise validly exercised.

In discussing the extent of the police power the United States supreme court in Berman v. Parker (1954), 348 U.S. 26, 32, . . . declared:

> "Public safety, public health, morality, peace and quiet, law and order— these are some of the more conspicuous examples of the traditional application of the police power to municipal affairs. *Yet they merely illustrate the scope of the power and do not delimit it.*" (Emphasis supplied.)

One of the latest pronouncements of the United States supreme court toward the exercise of police power by the states is to be found in Williamson v. Lee Optical Co. (1955), 348 U.S. 483, 488, . . . wherein it was stated:

> "The day is gone when this court uses the due-process clause of the Fourteenth amendment to strike down state laws, regulatory of business and industrial conditions, because they may be unwise, improvident, or out of harmony with a particular school of thought. [Citing cases.] We emphasize again what Chief Justice WAITE said in Munn v. Illinois, 94 U.S. 113, 134 [24 L.Ed. 77], 'For protection against abuses by legislatures the people must resort to the polls, not to the courts.'"

It would seem reasonably clear that one of the chief objectives of the legislature in enacting sec. 218.01, Stats., in so far as it seeks to regulate the dealings between automobile manufacturers and dealers, is to promote fair dealing, which, of course, is a legitimate exercise of police power. Petition of State ex rel. Attorney General (1936), 220 Wis. 25, 264 N.W. 633. In stating the underlying reason for such conclusion it would be difficult to improve upon the forceful language of Mr. Chief Justice HUGHES in his dissent in Moorehead v. New York ex rel. Tipaldo (1936), 298 U.S. 587, 627, . . . :

> "We have had frequent occasion to consider the limitations of liberty of contract. While it is highly important to preserve that liberty from arbitrary

and capricious interference, it is also necessary to prevent its abuse, as otherwise it could be used to override all public interests and thus in the end destroy the very freedom of opportunity which it is designed to safeguard."

The fact that the persons to be benefited by this regulatory measure are confined to one class of our citizens, auto dealers, does not militate against the same being a legitimate exercise of the police power. As the Connecticut court recently stated in Amsel v. Brooks (1954), 141 Conn. 288, 297, 106 Atl. (2d) 152, 157:

> "A statute which is otherwise within the police power or serves a public purpose is not unconstitutional merely because it incidentally benefits a limited number of persons."

While all the citizens of the state are entitled to be protected against unfair dealing by others, this does not mean that the legislature must by one sweep prohibit all unfair dealing and cannot proceed piecemeal to remedy particular types of unfair dealing which manifest themselves in particular occupations or industries. On this point it is only necessary to quote further from Williamson v. Lee Optical Co., supra (348 U.S. 488):

> "Secondly, the district court held that it violated the equal-protection clause of the Fourteenth amendment to subject opticians to this regulatory system and to exempt, as sec. 3 of the act does, all sellers of ready-to-wear glasses. The problem of legislative classification is a perennial one, admitting of no doctrinaire definition. Evils in the same field may be of different dimensions and proportions, requiring different remedies. Or so the legislature may think. Tigner v. Texas, 310 U.S. 141. . . . Or the reform may take one step at a time, addressing itself to the phase of the problem which seems most acute to the legislative mind. Semler v. Dental Examiners, 294 U.S. 608. . . . The legislature may select one phase of one field and apply a remedy there, neglecting the others. A.F. of L. v. American Sash Co., 335 U.S. 538. . . . The prohibition of the equal-protection clause goes on no further than the invidious discrimination."

A convincing argument in favor of the legislature exercising the state's police power to protect automobile dealers against unfair dealing on the part of automobile manufacturers is provided in the following statement by Mr. Justice BLACK in his dissenting opinion in Ford Motor Co. v. United States (1948), 335 U.S. 303, 323, . . . :

> "At the time the decrees were entered, Ford made and sold about 25 per cent of all cars in the United States, Chrysler 25 per cent and General Motors 44 per cent. Ford and the others sell to dealers about four billion dollars' worth of cars yearly, requiring cash on delivery. The dealers then sell to retail customers. About 60 per cent of the retail sales are on credit. Dealers not permitted to sell other makes of cars are wholly dependent upon Ford's, G.M.'s, or Chrysler's favorable treatment for their business lives. The dealer agencies are for one year,

but the agency contracts can be canceled on short notice and without cause. The dealers are thus economic dependents of the company whose cars they sell." *

The instant appeal reaches us on the pleadings. I would reverse with directions to overrule the demurrer so that a trial might be had on the issue of fact of whether the reasons underlying the Ford Motor Company's attempt to cancel the plaintiff's franchise were unfair, without due regard to plaintiff's equities, and without just provocation.

I am authorized to state that Mr. Chief Justice FAIRCHILD and Mr. Justice BROWN join in this dissent.

*   *   *

A motion for rehearing was granted on September 16, 1955, and oral argument was heard October 14, 1955. . . .

The following opinion was filed November 8, 1955.

PER CURIAM (*on reargument*). Mr. Justice BROADFOOT announces that he withdraws his concurrence in the concurring opinion and that he now joins in the prior dissenting opinion. By reason of this, such prior dissenting opinion now becomes the majority opinion in this case. Mr. Justice MARTIN, Mr Justice GEHL, and Mr. Justice STEINLE dissent therefrom for the reasons already stated in the original majority and concurring opinions.

The previous mandate is vacated. The order appealed from is reversed, and cause remanded with directions to overrule the demurrer.

BERLE,† *THE 20th CENTURY CAPITALIST REVOLUTION* 77-82 (1954)

Thus, in one field the right of appeal against this kind of absolute power (if it is absolute) is beginning to be recognized by custom.‡ Let us take the very unromantic level of the dealer-distributor who sells the product of the large corporation.

We must approach this group of people with more respect than is presently accorded salesmen in current literature. There are, for example, about 47,000 dealer-agents of automobiles in the United States; the largest single group of these na-

---

* Consider this case in the light of the following excerpt from Berle, The 20th Century Capitalist Revolution (1954). Notes and Questions on the case follow the Berle excerpt.—Editor

† Adolf A. Berle, professor of law at Columbia since 1927, has been Assistant Secretary of State, 1938-44, Chamberlain of New York City, 1934, Ambassador to Brazil, 1945-46, and representative of the United States at various international conferences. He also practices law in New York City. He is the author of The Modern Corporation and Private Property (with G. C. Means) (1932), a famous analysis of the separation of ownership from control in the modern corporation; New Directions in the New World (1940), Power Without Property (1960), and a number of casebooks in the field of corporation law and finance.—Editor

‡ Professor Berle is referring to the exercise of absolute power by our giant corporations; absolute in the sense that there is no "keeper of conscience, to whom appeal [from the corporate decision] can be made, by whom inquiry and a fair hearing must be provided, and from whom a humanely fair decision can be had."—Editor

turally are the agents of the so-called "Big Three" motor corporations—General Motors, Ford, and Chrysler. It is not easy to calculate the total capital assets of this group. General Motors requires that any dealer-agent appointed by it shall have a minimum capital, said to be about $100,000. One may hazard the estimate that the total assets of automobile dealer-agents in the United States aggregate more than three billion dollars—probably a good deal more than that. They are also the nuclei of business and organization in every substantial town in the country. The shop, garage, service facilities, and so forth, grouped around the businessman who has the Ford agency, the Chrysler agency, or the General Motors agency are familiar and substantial elements of American business.

The basis of the position of each of these dealer-agents is a "contract," frequently known as a franchise, with the automobile corporation whose cars he sells. The contract itself is a framework rather than a definition. Under it, there is a general understanding that the company will sell to the dealer; the dealer will buy cars from the company for resale. No fixed number of cars are mentioned; the wholesale and retail prices are to be fixed from time to time; the dealer is not "bound" to buy the cars and resell them (though, of course, he is out of business if he does not); the company has quite ample escape clauses so that it does not need to deliver cars to him. The dealer is not "the agent" and certainly not the employee of the company. In effect, a loose relationship is established.

The "contract" is cancelable. Some companies permit cancellation at will by either side. Others permit cancellation on ninety days' notice. For practical purposes, the company has the overriding position. After a contract is canceled, the dealer's investment in good will, advertising, sales arrangements, servicing facilities, and so forth, goes by the board. Cancellation by the company may easily put him out of business; it would not be simple for him to get another agency. Against this must be set the fact that the companies themselves rely in large measure on "dealer relationships." Cancellation of a dealership makes ill will in the community, frightens other dealers, and if resorted to arbitrarily will adversely affect sales. Everything considered, however, the preponderance of power is overwhelmingly on the side of the company.

The company can, accordingly, fix what amount or quota of cars the dealer must sell. These may, and frequently do, include new types of cars which the community serviced does not particularly want and which the dealer finds it difficult to dispose of. To secure the necessary number of four-door sedans which perhaps are readily salable, he may have to order a couple of pick-up trucks, station wagons, or two-tone convertibles, which his constituency does not take. Since the dealer has to pay cash outright, this amounts to a real burden and frequently to a considerable risk. If he is unable to dispose of a particular type of car before a new model is announced, he may find himself in very bad shape indeed. He is accordingly under pressure and his business policies must conform more or less to that pressure. The extreme penalty of failure to conform is loss of the contract, and corresponding, often crushing, loss of investment and business status. Less extreme penalty may be failure to secure full allotment of readily salable vehicles, diminishing the dealer's possible profit. The apparent legal relationship is such that the dealer has no enforcible rights; in any case the economic relationship is such that he cannot afford to quarrel.

And yet, in the presence of this power a limiting custom has grown up. The extreme penalty—cancellation of contract—is not normally invoked by the company except for cause, such as bankruptcy, extreme misconduct of the dealer, attempt to assign the contract, or the like. Where it is imposed, General Motors, for one, has established an administrative board of review. A dealer whose contract is canceled is given the right to appeal against the cancellation; the board accords him a hearing at which the dealer may show that the action is unjustifiable; and the board may reverse the cancellation. So it seems that in this relationship at least the lacuna in the system—the need of a *Curia Regis* to give effect to the conscience of the king—is beginning to be filled in.

There are, of course, important defects in this arrangement. Appeal from company action is a matter of grace and not of right—but then, appeal to the *Curia Regis* and the exercise of the conscience of the king also was originally a matter of grace. It is of interest that in at least one state—Rhode Island—the right granted by General Motors has crystallized into explicit statute law. Under the Rhode Island legislation, cancellation of an agency may be appealed to a state administrative board, and the board after review may reverse the cancellation and direct that the relationship be restored.

This homely illustration perhaps sufficiently indicates the existence of a principle of far wider application. A habit of mind crystallizing into a commercial custom which can demand review of the power of cancellation of an agency contract, apparently prevails outside the automobile business. It was reported some time ago that a dealer in General Electric products publicly questioned the right of General Electric to terminate a dealer relationship with that company. One would expect to find a trend toward limitation on arbitrary power gradually appearing through the entire field—whether it concerns franchises granted by Coca-Cola to a manufacturer-salesman, or dealer-company relationships prevailing between farm machinery companies and their outlets, or other like arrangements through the entire range.

Tiny though the indication may be, it indicates a tropism in the emerging American corporate system. Power to deal at will with other men's property and occupations, however absolute it may be as a matter of technical contract law, is subject to certain limitations. They still lie in the field of inchoate law: we are not as yet able to cite explicit case and statute law clearly stating these limitations. We can only say that in this field a matrix of equity jurisdiction is beginning to appear. . . .

NOTES AND QUESTIONS

1. Justice George R. Currie, *Some Aspects of Appellate Practice Before the Wisconsin Supreme Court*, 1955 Wis. L. Rev. 554, 565:

"After a lawyer has striven his best to obtain a favorable result for his client, but nevertheless the appellate court has rendered an adverse decision failing to see the case in what counsel considers its true perspective, the question of whether to move for a rehearing arises. While the percentages are overwhelmingly against success in such an undertaking, nevertheless the Wisconsin court on occasion has been known to change its mind. . . .

"Success upon a motion for rehearing is almost entirely dependent upon convincing the court that an erroneous result was reached because the court overlooked some controlling authority, statute, or material fact, which, if it had been considered, would have required the court to reach the opposite conclusion from that stated in its opinion. Unless a lawyer is in a position to ground his brief in support of a motion for rehearing on such an oversight by the court, his chances of securing a reversal are practically nil. An illustration of a situation which probably presents the most hopeless example of possible success on a motion for rehearing is that in which a dissenting opinion was filed presenting the arguments upon which losing counsel must rely for success on such motion."

Is Kuhl the exception that proves the rule?

2. To what extent was the plaintiff's right in Kuhl grounded upon (a) the common law; (b) the statutes referred to in the opinion?

Could the court have properly reached the same conclusion in the absence of these statutes? Should it have?

Did the eventual majority apply the approach suggested by Landis? The approach of the Johnston case, on page 501?

3. Assume with the eventual majority that the court should accept and be guided by the public policy embodied in these statutes. Does it necessarily follow from this policy that the court should have held that the plaintiff (if he was able to show that the defendant's attempt to cancel the franchise was unfair, was without due regard to plaintiff's equities, and without just provocation) would be entitled to enjoin the Ford Motor Co. from terminating the franchise? Do the statutes reflect a public policy that the relationship between automobile manufacturer and dealer, under these circumstances, should be continued rather than that the dealer should merely receive compensatory damages for the wrongful cancellation?

4. What argument, based on legislative intent, can be made for the ultimate dissenters in Kuhl, which was not squarely considered in either of the two opinions?

Compare the Rhode Island statute cited by Berle which specifically authorizes an administrative board, which may entertain dealer appeals, to order the manufacturer not to terminate the franchise.

Compare, too, the federal Automobile Dealer Franchise Act, 70 Stat. 1125 (1956), which authorizes a dealer to bring suit in the appropriate federal district court to recover damages sustained by him because of the failure of the automobile manufacturer "to act in good faith in performing or complying with any of the terms or provisions of the franchise, or in terminating, canceling, or not renewing the franchise with" the dealer. "Good faith" is defined by the statute as the duty of the manufacturer "to act in a fair and equitable manner toward [the dealer] so as to guarantee the [dealer] freedom from coercion, intimidation, or threats of coercion or intimidation from the [manufacturer]."

Could a dealer appropriately seek, under this Act, to enjoin the manufacturer from canceling the franchise? Suppose the legislative history of the statute showed a Congressional intent to make the remedy of damages exclusive? Suppose the legislative history was itself inconclusive on this question?

Note that neither the majority nor the minority opinions in Kuhl cite any legislative history in connection with their discussions of the relevant statutes.

On the federal act, see McHugh, Automobile Dealer Franchise Act of 1956, and Fulda, A Dissent, 2 Antitrust Bull. 353 (1957); Kessler and Brenner, Automobile

Dealer Franchises: Vertical Integration by Contract, 66 Yale L.J. 1135 (1957). See also Brown & Conwill, Automobile Manufacturer-Dealer Legislation, 57 Colum. L. Rev. 219 (1957).

5. Did the Wisconsin legislature give the courts very much guidance for the administration of the statutes involved in Kuhl? How is it to be determined whether the manufacturer has cancelled the franchise "unfairly" or "without due regard to the dealer's equities" or "without just provocation"? See A.F.L. Motors, Inc. v. Chrysler Motors Corp., 183 F. Supp. 56 (E.D. Wis. 1960).

6. An amicus curiae brief in Kuhl argued that the Ford Motor Co. had "waived" any claim of unconstitutionality of the statutes because it applied for and obtained a license under them. One cannot, as some cases put it, attack a statute under which one has sought and received benefits. Ford's reply was to cite Wis. Stat. 227.20(2) (Chap. 227 is on "Administrative Procedure and Review") declaring that an appellant's right to challenge the constitutionality of any act or its application to him "shall not be foreclosed or impaired by the fact that he has applied for or holds a license, permit or privilege under such act." If the statute applies only to appeals from administrative determinations, Ford's reply is inadequate. But could not Wis. Stats. 227.20(2) properly be used by analogy? Another statute, sec. 269.56(2) declares that no one shall be foreclosed from a declaratory judgment on the validity of a statute or ordinance by the fact that he holds a license or permit thereunder. "Although this is not an action for a declaratory judgment," said the Court in Town of Yorkville v. Fonk, 274 Wis. 153, 158 (1956), that enactment is a declaration by the legislature as a matter of public policy that the general rule announced in the Wendlandt Case ['that, as a general principle, one may not enjoy the benefits and privileges of a statute and, after so doing, escape its burdens by attacking its validity'] should not be strictly followed in all cases." (Note that both the majority and minority in the Kuhl case did consider the constitutional question).

7. In Ross v. Ebert, 275 Wis. 523 (1957), the Wisconsin Supreme Court (one judge dissenting) held that the courts could not compel the Masons and Bricklayers Labor Union to accept two Negroes as members, even though the Negroes were qualified for membership and were excluded solely because of their race and color.

Wisconsin's Fair Employment Code at this time declared that it was "the public policy of the state to encourage and foster to the fullest extent practicable the employment of all properly qualified persons regardless of their race, creed, color, national origin, or ancestry." The Code authorized the state Industrial Commission to investigate complaints of racial discrimination in employment, make recommendations to the parties interested, and publicize its findings and recommendations.

The two Negro bricklayers complained to the Industrial Commission which, after investigation, found the union guilty of racial discrimination and recommended that the union admit the men to membership. When the union disregarded the recommendation, the Commission publicized the case. The men then instituted their lawsuit.

The Wisconsin Supreme Court emphasized that the legislature, in the Fair Employment Code, did not provide any remedy for persons discriminated against on racial grounds other than resort to the procedure of the Industrial Commission described above. "Where the law gives a new remedy to meet a new situation, the remedy provided by the law is exclusive." (The quoted principle, which had been invoked in Wisconsin cases prior to the Kuhl Motor case, was not even considered by the eventual majority in the Kuhl case. Why not?)

The Court in the present case also pointed out that (1) the bill which became the Code gave the Industrial Commission power to order violators to cease and desist and gave the courts power to review and enforce such orders, but that the provision granting these powers was deleted prior to the bill's passage; and (2) two unsuccessful attempts were made in subsequent sessions of the legislature to grant these powers.

The Wisconsin Supreme Court also took the position that the action of the union, a private voluntary association, was not action of the state and therefore not reachable under the Fourteenth Amendment to the United States Constitution. (See the materials in Chapter 7, sec. 4, considered in connection with Shelley v. Kraemer.)

Under these circumstances, do you think the Wisconsin Supreme Court should have used the Code and the Fourteenth Amendment as analogies to overturn the common law doctrine—which it reaffirmed—that trade unions, like voluntary associations, may impose such requirements for admission as its members deem fit and proper and that courts will not in any way review these requirements at the behest of a person excluded?

8. See further on the use of statutes by analogy, Page, Statutes As Common Law Principles, 1944 Wis. L. Rev. 175; Note, Reasoning by Analogy from Statute in Pennsylvania, 43 Dick. L. Rev. 234 (1939); Gellhorn, Contracts and Public Policy, 35 Colum. L. Rev. 679 (1935); U.S. v. Lennox Metal Mfg. Co. 225 F. 2d 302, 318-319 and cases cited (2 Cir., 1955); National City Bank of New York v. Republic of China, 348 U.S. 356 (1955).

CHAPMAN v. ZAKZASKA
273 Wis. 64, 76 N.W. 2d 537 (1956)

GEHL, Justice.

The facts are not in dispute. On April 5, 1954, plaintiff, a motor vehicle dealer, sold to defendant for the price of $1,695, plus a second-hand car, a used Nash automobile. Before the sale plaintiff had changed the speedometer reading on the Nash car to 21,000 miles. It had in fact traveled about 60,000 miles. A judgment note was given for a part of the purchase price. Judgment was taken upon the note. Defendant obtained an order setting aside the judgment and granting him leave to answer. He answered alleging that the sale was illegal because plaintiff had violated the provisions of sec. 218.01 (7a) (a), Stat., which are as follows:

"No used motor vehicle shall be offered for sale by any motor vehicle dealer or motor vehicle salesman unless the speedometer reading thereon shall be turned back to zero." [Except that, the statute goes on to say, "speedometers need not be set back to zero if readings thereon are indicated in writing by owners when selling or trading their cars to dealers and subsequently shown to purchasers."—Editor]

Violation of the requirements of the act is declared a misdemeanor.

By its answers to two of the questions of the special verdict a jury found that the value of the car as it existed at the time of the sale was $1,050, and that its value had it been as represented by the speedometer reading would have been $1,695. The court made findings of fact and conclusions of law and on July 11, 1955, entered judgment dismissing the complaint. The court was of the opinion that plaintiff's violation of the provisions of the statute rendered the contract wholly illegal so as to require that it be held that plaintiff may have no recovery whatever. Whether the trial court was correct in that conclusion is the sole issue presented upon this appeal.

Not all such contracts are void. Murphy v. Paull, 1927, 192 Wis. 93, 212 N.W.

402. To determine whether a statute such as that with which we are concerned is intended to render unenforceable contracts which conflict with its provisions the intent and purpose of the legislature should be considered and ascertained.

In Laun v. Pacific Mut. Life Ins. Co., 1907, 131 Wis. 555, at page 563, 111 N.W. 660, at page 663, 9 L.R.A., N.S., 1204, quoting from Pangborn v. Westlake, 36 Iowa 546, we said:

> " 'We are therefore brought to the true test, which is that while, as a general rule, a penalty implies a prohibition, yet the courts will always look to the language of the statute, the subject-matter of it, the wrong or evil which it seeks to remedy or prevent, and the purpose sought to be accomplished in its enactment; and, if from all these it is manifest that it was not intended to imply a prohibition or to render the prohibited act void, the courts will so hold, and construe the statute accordingly.' "

Speaking of the rule often stated, and very often by way of dictum, that contracts made in violation of a statute are unenforceable, it was said in Menominee River Boom Co. v. Augustus Spies Lumber & Cedar Co., 1912, 147 Wis. 559, 132 N.W. 1118, 1125, quoting from Deming v. State ex rel. Miller, 23 Ind. 416:

> " 'It is a grave error to regard it as a merely arbitrary rule applicable to *all* contracts which are prohibited by statute.' "
>
> "Legislative intent must be sought in each particular case, and though it is generally true that the imposition of a penalty for entering into a bargain or performing an act that is the subject matter of the bargain makes the bargain illegal, that is not invariably the case." Rest. Contr. sec. 580, Comment a.

For the proper construction of the statute it is not enough that only its terms be considered. Its effect must be deduced from a consideration of it and other statutes on the same subject, . . . and the applicable rules of the common law.

The facts establish the making by plaintiff of an express warranty relating to the automobile within the definition contained in sec. 121.12, Stats. The remedies for a breach thereof are set forth in sec. 121.69. Having elected to keep the car defendant impliedly chose to "set up against the seller [plaintiff], the breach of warranty by way of recoupment in diminution or extinction of the price." Sec. 1216.9 (1) (a), Stats. For the breach of the warranty this is his sole and limited remedy. Nowhere in the sales act is it provided that in such case the buyer may keep the goods warranted, which the defendant did in this case, and be relieved entirely of the obligation to pay the purchase price without a showing that he has actually been damaged in an amount equal to or greater than the purchase price or that the article sold has proved to be worthless.

The facts are also such as to permit recovery in an action for fraudulent misrepresentation. The measure of damages in an action so based is also clearly established in this state, that is, the difference between the value of the property as it was when purchased and what it would have been had it been as represented. . . .

The consequences of a violation of sec. 218.01(7a)(a) are defined therein. It would seem that if the legislature had intended to extend or enlarge those consequences by enlarging the remedies long and exclusively afforded to the buyer in case of breach of warranty or of a fraudulent misrepresentation it would have so declared.

The statute does not purport to create a new civil violation, nor to prohibit the sale of used cars. It is unlike those which, for instance, prohibit gambling, the sale of contraband goods, bargains made in violation of Sunday laws, et cetera. Unlike the situation in those cases the illegality in the instant case does not permeate the contract so as to furnish the reason for it and the foundation upon which it rests so as to make applicable the rule so generally and sometimes unnecessarily broadly stated that all contracts prohibited by statute are void and unenforceable. It is our opinion that the statute was intended to impose upon the violator an additional penalty, not to enlarge the rights of the other party to the contract.

We conclude that the court erred in holding the contract unenforceable. The jury found the automobile to have been worth at the time of the sale $1,050, or $645 less than it would have been as represented. Plaintiff should therefore have judgment for the amount of its note, less the sum of $645, and plus interest to be computed.

Judgment reversed. The cause is remanded with directions to enter judgment in accordance with this opinion.

CURRIE, J., dissenting.

NOTES AND QUESTIONS

1. Why was there no reference to the Kuhl case? In what respects are the problems in the two cases similar or dissimilar? In what respects is the present case similar or dissimilar to the Johnston case considered previously in this section?

2. If the dissenting justice had chosen to write an opinion, along what lines of argumentation should it have proceeded?

3. For rather analogous cases involving violations of federal anti-trust statutes, see Bruce's Juices v. American Can Co. 330 U.S. 743 (1947); Kelly v. Kosuga, 358 U.S. 516 (1959). See generally, Annotation, "Validity of Contract in Violation of Statute Imposing Criminal Sanction but Not Specifically Declaring Contract Invalid," 55 A.L.R. 2d 481 (1957). Both the Chapman and the Kuhl Motor cases are discussed in this annotation.

CHAPTER Ten

The MAKING of a LAW—LEGISLATIVE HISTORY of the WORKMEN'S COMPENSATION ACT in WISCONSIN

EDITORIAL NOTE: ORIGINS of WORKMEN'S COMPENSATION

In his treatise on Workmen's Compensation Law, Arthur Larson emphasizes that workmen's compensation is not merely an extension of the common law or of employers' liability legislation but the expression of an entirely new social principle having its origins in nineteenth-century Germany. He traces these origins and the development of the workmen's compensation principle in the United States in the following selection.

LARSON,* THE LAW OF WORKMEN'S COMPENSATION
33-39 (2 vols., 1952)

In 1838, one year after Lord Abinger announced the fellow-servant rule, and four years before Judge Shaw of Massachusetts popularized the defense of assumption of risk, Prussia enacted a law making railroads liable to their employees (as well as passengers) for accidents from all causes except act of God and negligence of the plaintiff. In 1854, Prussia required employers in certain industries to contribute one-half to the sickness association funds formed under various local statutes. In 1876 an unsuccessful voluntary insurance act was passed, and finally in 1884 Germany adopted the first modern compensation system, thirteen years before England, twenty-five years before the first American jurisdiction, and sixty-five years before the last American state.

It is interesting to inquire into the conditions which gave birth to the compensation idea. As to the intellectual origins: both philosophers and politicians played a part. Frederick the Great contributed both a profound conviction that "it is the duty of the state to provide sustenance and support of those of its citizens who cannot provide sustenance for themselves," [30a] and a completely uninhibited

---

* Arthur Larson is at present Professor of Law and Director of the World Rule of Law Center at Duke University. He has been a special assistant to President Eisenhower, Under Secretary of Labor, and Dean of the University of Pittsburgh Law School. He has taught at Cornell and Tennessee and been an attorney with federal agencies. He is author of Know Your Social Security (1955), A Republican Looks at His Party (1956), co-author of Towards World Prosperity (1947), and co-editor of a casebook on corporation law.—Editor.

[30a] Fourth Special Report of the Commissioner of Labor, 1893, pp. 25-6.

view of the state's power and right to bring this protection about by any means. Among the philosophers, probably Fichte was most responsible for propounding the idea that many of the misfortunes, disabilities and accidents of individuals are ultimately social and not individual in origin, and that the state is therefore "not to be negative nor to have a mere police function, but to be filled with Christian concern, especially for the weaker members." [30b] Lassalle, Sismondi, Winkelblech, Wagner and Schaeffle developed this general conception into insistent and eloquent arguments for the only mechanism which could effectively implement this ideal: industrial insurance. At the same time, especially during the years following the war of 1870-71, Bismarck began to be concerned about the increasing strength shown in elections by the Marxian type of socialists as against the practical socialists of the school of Lassalle, who favored the co-operative association type of development. Accordingly, in 1881 he met the situation by laying before the Reichstag his far-reaching plan for compulsory insurance, which was enacted in various measures between 1883 and 1887. [31] Thus, while Workmen's Compensation has a "socialistic" origin in the philosophical sense of the term associated with the views of Fichte and Hegel, it also has an anti-socialistic origin if the term is used in the Marxian sense.

The exact form taken by the German system should be specially noted, because it was significantly different from the English and American systems, and because it is continuing to exert a strong influence on the form taken by social legislation of all kinds. The distinguishing feature of German insurance (apart from its much greater comprehensiveness) was that contributions by the workman himself were an integral part of the system. Broadly, the German plan fell into three parts: the Sickness Fund (workers contributing two-thirds, employer one-third) paid benefits for the first thirteen weeks of either sickness or disability due to accident; the Accident Fund (contributions by employers only) paid for disability after the first thirteen weeks; and Disability Insurance (workers contribute one-half) provided for disability due to old age or other causes not specifically covered elsewhere. The plan, though compulsory, was thus essentially based on mutual association. The administration was placed in the hands of representatives of employers and employees under government supervision. The striking resemblance of this plan to the present British system is at once apparent.

It seems paradoxical on the surface that Germany, with its more socialistic philosophical tradition, should produce a system which is more individualistic in the sense that the workman in effect purchases in his own right an insurance policy against sickness and disability, with the employer sharing the premium; while America followed what might appear to be a more radical line by imposing unilateral liability without fault upon the employer, and by making him bear the entire burden of any insurance against that liability. There are several reasons for this. The choice of this mechanism in Germany was dictated largely by the existence of already successful schemes on this pattern within the German guilds (Knappschafts-

[30b] *Id.* p. 20.
[31] Fundamental Law of 1884 (Industry, Transport, Trades, Telegraph, Army and Navy); Agricultural Law, 1886; Building Law, 1887; Marine Law, 1887.

kassen). For hundreds of years these guilds had sponsored benefit societies and associations which provided disability, sickness and death benefits. In a highly developed system, such as the miners' societies, there were benefits on the insurance principle for sickness, accident, and burial, and pensions for orphans, widows and invalids.[33] The system was administered by a committee made up half of employers and half of employees, and contributions were in the same proportion, with the employer paying the "premium" and deducting the employee's half from his next wage payment.

The New York Commission whose report of March, 1910, was the basis for New York's Compensation Act studied the German plan, and made the following report:[34]

"Could we see a practical way to put a scheme of compensation in force in which the employer's share will be the 50 per cent of earnings recommended in our bills, and the workmen's contribution say 25 per cent above that, and the benefits insured to him thereby changed to three-fourths earnings during disability, we would recommend it. The German system on some such lines seems admirable. But practically we see no way to accomplish this by force of compulsory law."

The American pattern, then, became that of unilateral employer liability, with no contribution by employees. The issue is by no means dead, however, what with the contributory principle appearing in the British comprehensive system, in the state non-occupational disability plans that have been adopted, and, of course, in old age and unemployment legislation. It is most significant, therefore, to note that the New York Commission rejected the employee-contribution system only because of doubt that compulsory contributions could constitutionally be exacted, and that but for this doubt they would have recommended it. No doubt the American pattern was also influenced by the fact that such recovery for industrial injury as the employee had obtained in the past had always taken the form of an adversary imposition of liability upon the employer, so that it was perhaps natural to conceive of even this totally new principle of employee protection in terms of the old mechanism of employer liability.

By the end of the nineteenth century, as shown above, the coincidence of increasing industrial injuries and decreasing remedies had produced in the United States a situation ripe for radical change, and when, in 1893, a full account of the German system written by John Graham Brooks was published as the Fourth Special Report of the Commissioner of Labor, legislators all over the country seized upon it as a clue to the direction which efforts at reform might take. Another stimulus was provided by the enactment of the first British Compensation Act in 1897, which later became the model of state acts in many respects.

A period of intensive investigation ensued, carried on by various state commissions, beginning with Massachusetts in 1904, Illinois in 1907, Connecticut in 1908 and a legislatively-created commission of representatives, industrialists and other experts in New York in 1909. By 1910 the movement was in full swing,

[33] Fourth Special Report of the Commissioner of Labor, 1893, p. 37.

[34] New York Senate Documents, Vol. xxv, No. 38 [1910] 67.

with commissions being created by Congress and the legislatures of Massachusetts, Minnesota, New Jersey, Connecticut, Ohio, Illinois, Wisconsin, Montana and Washington. In 1910 also there occurred a conference in Chicago attended by representatives of all these commissions, at which a Uniform Workmen's Compensation Law was drafted.[36] Although the state acts which followed were anything but uniform, the discussions at this conference did much to set the fundamental pattern of legislation.

As to actual enactments, the story begins modestly with a rather narrow co-operative Accident Fund for miners passed by Maryland in 1902,[37] which quietly expired when held unconstitutional in an unappealed lower court decision.[38] In 1909 another miners' compensation act was passed in Montana,[39] and suffered the same fate.[40] In 1908 Congress passed a compensation act covering certain federal employees.[41]

In 1910 the first New York Act[42] was passed, with compulsory coverage of certain "hazardous employments." It was held unconstitutional in 1911 by the Court of Appeals, on the ground that the imposition of liability without fault upon the employer was a taking of property without due process of law under the state and federal constitutions.[43]

At the present time, with the constitutionality of all types of compensation acts firmly established, there is no practical purpose to be served by tracing out the elaborate and violent constitutional law arguments provoked by the early acts.[44] One important practical result did, however, flow from these preliminary constitutional setbacks: the very fear of unconstitutionality impelled the legislatures to pass over the ideal type of coverage, which would be both comprehensive and compulsory, in favor of more awkward and fragmentary plans whose very weakness and incompleteness might ensure their constitutional validity. And so, beginning with New Jersey, "elective" or "optional" statutes became common, under which employers could choose whether or not they would be bound by the compensation plan, with the alternative of being subject to common-law actions without benefit of the three common-law defenses. Similarly, a number of states limited their coverage to "hazardous" employments because of doubt as to the extent of the police power, and while several have since broadened their scope,[45] there remain nine states with this limitation.[46]

In New York, the Ives decision was answered by the adoption in 1913 of a

[36] See account of this conference in Boyd, Compensation for Injuries to Workmen [1913], pp. 17-22.

[37] Md. Laws 1902, ch. 139.

[38] Franklin v. United Railways and Electric Co. of Baltimore, 2 Baltimore City Rep. 390 [1904].

[39] Mont. Laws 1909, ch. 67.

[40] Cunningham v. Northwestern Improvement Co., 44 Mont., 180, 119 Pac. 554, 1 N.C.C.A. 720 [1911].

[41] 35 Stat. 556 [1908].

[42] Chapter 675, Laws of 1910.

[43] Ives v. South Buffalo Railway Co., 201 N.Y. 271, 94 N.E. 431 [1911].

[44] See, for example, Boyd, Compensation for Injuries to Workmen [1913] pp. 153-204.

[45] Arizona, Illinois, New Hampshire and New York.

[46] Maryland, New Mexico, Washington, Wyoming ("extrahazardous"); Louisiana, Oklahoma, Oregon ("hazardous"); Kansas ("especially dangerous"); and Montana ("inherently hazardous"). See §55.10.

constitutional amendment permitting a compulsory law, and such a law was passed in the same year. In 1917 this compulsory law,[47] together with the Iowa elective-type[48] and the Washington exclusive-state-fund-type law,[49] was held constitutional by the United States Supreme Court, and, with fears of constitutional impediments virtually removed, the compensation system grew and expanded with a rapidity that probably has no parallel in any comparable field of law.

By 1920 all but eight states had adopted Compensation Acts, and on January 1, 1949, the last state, Mississippi, came under the system.

Extension of coverage has taken the form, not only of adding jurisdictions, but of broadening the boundaries of individual acts, as to persons, employments, and kinds of injury (particularly occupational disease) covered. At the same time, where election is permissible, the percentage of employers choosing compensation coverage has constantly increased until in most states the non-electing employer is exceptional.

Arthur H. Reede, in his detailed study of compensation coverage entitled "Adequacy of Workmen's Compensation," concludes, after an analysis of coverage by states, that in 1915 the percentage of all gainful employees (excluding unemployed and self-employed) covered by compensation acts was 41.2; in 1920, 67.4; in 1930, 75.2; and in 1940, 81.5.

The principal occupational groups not yet brought within compensation acts are domestic and agricultural workers, who are excluded from almost all acts. Other exclusions are accounted for by small firms (since most acts exempt employers with less than a stated minimum number of employees), "casual workers," and workers who do not come within the classes of hazardous employment in states containing that limitation. The percentage of coverage looks slightly better if interstate rail employees, considered excluded in the above calculation, are included, since they have the protection of the Employers' Liability Act, which is regarded by some segments of railway labor as preferable to Workmen's Compensation Acts. The enactment of the Mississippi act also improves the coverage figure somewhat.

Section 1A

ACTIVITY of UNOFFICIAL AGENCIES: The LEGISLATIVE ROLE of POLITICAL PARTIES; The CASE of WISCONSIN LABOR LEGISLATION

WISCONSIN PARTY PLATFORMS

Democratic Platform, 1906: We favor the enactment of a law establishing the doctrine of comparative negligence in all personal injury cases.

[47] New York Central R. Co. v. White, 243 U.S. 188, 37 S. Ct. 247, 61 L. Ed. 667, L.R.A. 1917D, 1 Ann. Cas. 1917D, 529 [1917].
[48] Hawkins v. Bleakley, 243 U.S. 210, 37 S. Ct. 255, 61 L. Ed. 678 [1917].
[49] Mountain Timber Co. v. State of Washington, 243 U.S. 219, 37 S. Ct. 260, 61 L. Ed. 685, Ann. Cas. 1917D, 642 [1917].

Republican Platform, 1906: Railway employes are engaged in a public service most hazardous in its nature. Legislation should be enacted providing that negligence of an injured employe shall not bar a recovery of damages by him if the jury shall find that the negligence of the railway company is greater than his.

Socialist Platform, 1906: [pledged itself to] 3. Enact a law granting every wage worker over 60 years of age, who has earned less than $1000 a year and has been a citizen of the U.S. for fifteen years at least, a pension of not less than $12 a month for the rest of his life.

. . . 14. . . . The removal of the principle of contributory negligence from our statutes, and the enactment of laws to compensate workmen when injured when employed.

Republican Platform, 1908: We pledge ourselves to insure to the laboring classes of this state equality of opportunity in industry and equality of rights before the courts. We favor legislation which will assure to every workman the broadest equality in industrial controversies. In the matter of employer's liability and the protection of the life and health of workmen, Wisconsin should have as strong and as certain laws as those of any state or country.

Social Democratic Platform, 1908: The Social Democratic party . . . pledges itself to the following measures.

Eighteenth. . . . The removal of the principle of contributory negligence from our statutes, and the enactment of laws to compensate workmen when injured while employed.

Democratic Platform, 1910: The Democratic party always has a profound interest in the welfare of the laboring people and favors the enactment of a law providing for industrial insurance which shall justly compensate employes in case of injury received in their employment and justly compensate their families in case of death caused by such injuries, such enactment to be so framed as to do full justice as near as may be alike to the employes and employers.

Republican Platform, 1910: Losses occasioned by bodily injuries in industrial accidents should be borne by the industry in the first instance rather than by the disabled wage-earner or his dependents. We pledge immediate enactment of employers' liability laws, so framed as to meet the requirements of present conditions and to the immediate creation of a system of workmen's compensation. We favor a thorough investigation of the subject of occupational diseases, with a view to the early enactment of suitable legislation.

Social Democratic Platform, 1910: That the state legislature, the governor and our representatives in congress shall take such action as is calculated:

Eighth. To establish life insurance by the national government, and also insurance against sickness, accident, and loss of employment.

Nineteenth. . . . Also the removal of the principle of contributory negligence from our statutes, and the enactment of laws to compensate workmen when injured while employed.

SCHMIDT, *HISTORY OF LABOR LEGISLATION IN WISCONSIN*
19-27 (1933)

Before Robert M. LaFollette Sr. formed the group . . . known as "Progressive Republican," Wisconsin was ruled by the old Republican party. Occasional Democratic candidates challenged Republican supremacy, notably George W. Peck, who was Governor in 1890 and 1892, but this competition was not serious, nor was Democratic government very different from Republican. At that time the Republican party was dominated by a small group of bosses, recognized as the "machine" and rulers of the state. Only once, in 1888, when the farmers, organized in the Grange, secured the Governorship for William B. Hoard on the Republican ticket, was the bosses' control of the Republican Party broken.

LaFollette began fighting the Republican machine in 1880 when he ran for district attorney of Dane county.[17] His campaigns for a seat in Congress and for the governorship during the next twenty-five years were all battles with the machine. In this he went directly to the farmers, tapping the same sources of rebellion that had developed into the Granger movement in the 'seventies and the 'eighties. The issue was true representative government. The bosses controlled the party nominating conventions, and by the use of railroad passes, franks, and other inducements they made secure their control of the legislature. LaFollette directed his reforms at the conditions which gave the machine power, and with the support of the farmers won several victories over the old machine. Among the first laws which he secured after he became governor of the state were a limitation on the use of passes and franks, the corrupt practises act, and the direct primary. These were all victories for representative government over the machine and the farmers in Wisconsin were traditionally advocates of democratic government.

The railroads had been the worst offenders in the corruption of politics. They were also condemned by the farmers and small business men for the high and discriminatory rates which they charged and for the advantage accorded them in the tax laws of the state. Several attempts were made before 1900 to apply an ad valorem tax to railroads which the railroad lobby defeated, but not until LaFollette's administration in 1903 was such a law enacted. The railroad commission law, enacted in 1905, gave the state the power to pass on railroad rates. In these issues the railroad workers supported LaFollette, for they too were fighting the railroads, although on a different issue. The other workers of the state, to the extent that they were organized in unions, had by the time that LaFollette became Governor a different allegiance.

The industrial workers of the 'eighties and 'nineties were almost wholly in Milwaukee. Many of them were Germans, immigrants of the 'sixties and 'seventies and veteran German Socialists. "Milwaukee Socialism," which started as an organized movement during the 'seventies, was at first an off-shoot of German Socialism. . . . It was Victor L. Berger who accomplished the Americanization of German Socialism in Milwaukee and the change to the distinctive brand of "Milwaukee Social-

[17] Autobiography of Robert M. LaFollette Sr., "LaFollette and Wisconsin" by John R.   Commons, New Republic, vol. 40, pp. 63-67, Sept. 17, 1924.

ism." Victor Berger came to the United States in 1878, and in 1893 began to edit "Vorwärts" in Milwaukee. Berger's plan was one of cooperation with the trade unionists, and, ultimately, with the farmers and small business men. In 1894, under the leadership of Berger, the Socialists in Milwaukee formed an alliance with the People's Party (populist), which was then popular with trade unionists. . . .

By January 1897, the Socialists had broken with the Populists and had begun to concentrate their efforts on winning the direct support of the trade unions. In 1898 a number of trade unions were represented at the Socialist city convention, and a year later the leadership of the Federated Trades Council and many of its constituent unions was in the hands of the Socialists. With this trade union backing, the Socialists formulated a program which advocated a number of immediate reforms, such as public bathing houses, free school books, free medical and legal service provided by the city for the poor, and equal tax and water rates for small property owners and big corporations. Their first plank, municipal ownership of public utilities, and the emphasis on municipal activity in all the reforms preserved a Socialistic flavor, but the platform was far removed from the early days of doctrinaire Socialism. The emphasis on municipal reform, both in the Socialist platforms and in the activities of the party in Milwaukee developed still further. The platform statement in favor of municipal ownership of utilities was modified in 1904 to present a more favorable appeal to the citizens of Milwaukee, and in 1908 the popular reform principles of home rule for cities and the initiative and referendum and recall were adopted by the Milwaukee group . . . and in 1910, Emil Seidel, the first Socialist mayor of Milwaukee, was elected.

Milwaukee Socialism has been, as Mr. Frank J. Weber of the Wisconsin State Federation of Labor has often stated, the political organization for the workers whose economic organizations were the trade unions. There has been no direct endorsement of the Socialist party by the trade unions, but in Milwaukee, the center of trade unionism in the state, the same men have been leaders in both groups. Milwaukee trade unionists have been elected to the state legislature since 1905 on the Socialist ticket, and these Socialist trade unionists have been the first sponsors of the legislation desired by the trade unions. Frederick Brockhausen, Secretary-treasurer of the Wisconsin State Federation of Labor who served his first term in the legislature in 1905, was the first of these Socialist trade union legislators. Brockhausen and Mr. Frank J. Weber, general organizer of the Federation, were both elected to the state legislature in 1907, 1909 and 1911 as Socialists. . . .

When the Milwaukee Socialists turned to municipal reform in 1904 they had more in common with the LaFollette Progressives than they had had since their alliance with the People's Party in 1894. The Socialists made clear, however, the difference between their concern with immediate reforms in which they might often agree with the Progressives, and their ultimate objectives which made them a distinct party. . . .

The Progressives too . . . have often demonstrated that they are fundamentally a party of farmers and small business men, in spite of the occasions on which they have made common cause with the Socialists. The leaders have often been convinced of the desirability of certain kinds of labor legislation, in which their

"Progressivism" has led them closer to Socialism and the trade unions, but there has always been the necessity of holding the rural members in line, as a history of these measures will show.

In 1911-1914, when Francis B. McGovern was governor of the state, Socialist and Progressive cooperation in Wisconsin reached a height which it had never attained before, and has not equalled since. The Socialists were willing to work with the Progressives because the latter were ready to consider the measures which the Socialists had been advocating for the past decade. Progressive interest in labor measures is not so easily explained. Much of it came as the culmination of a long effort for social legislation on the part of a number of liberal groups, and can best be understood by considering the history of the particular measures which were enacted. Considering here only the make-up of political groups, the addition which McGovern's position in state politics brought to the Progressives should be mentioned. McGovern came from Milwaukee, and from 1901 to 1909 he had served in the district attorney's office there, for four years as assistant and for four years as district attorney. In these same years, the Socialists were gaining strength in their campaigns for municipal reform in Milwaukee, and as district attorney McGovern took an effective part in the fight for clean city government. When McGovern became governor of the state in 1911, he undoubtedly brought greater experience and interest in industrial problems as well as more support from the industrial population of the state than had characterized the leadership of the Progressives before.

Throughout the United States the Progressive movement reached its height during these years. In Wisconsin, the farmer-labor cooperation symbolized by the LaFollette-McGovern leadership of the Progressives was remarkably effective. But it did not last long. First political dissension and then war broke the national progressive movement of which Wisconsin Progressivism was an outstanding example. As a political unit, Wisconsin Progressivism split on a national issue. In the presidential campaign of 1912, the LaFollette group endorsed Wilson, and the McGovern group Roosevelt. Then the criticism of LaFollette during the war and the subordination of Progressive issues to the immediate problems of war caused a further eclipse of the Wisconsin Progressive movement. . . .

NOTES AND QUESTIONS

1. The industrial accident plank in the Republican platform of 1910 should be considered in connection with the excerpt hereafter reprinted from the Autobiography of Mr. Justice Marshall.

2. What hypothesis as to the role of the Social Democratic party as a pressure group is suggested by comparison of the platform planks reprinted above? How much do the various planks differ from each other? How might a lawyer reasonably make use of these planks in suggesting to a court the attitude it should take towards the interpretation of workmen's compensation legislation thereafter enacted?

3. In the light of Miss Schmidt's account, as it may be supplemented, confirmed, or contradicted by your knowledge from other sources, consider:

a. Is the political party apt to be the initiating force in the demand for legislation?

To what extent is an American political party likely to be the representative of a single interest in the community? How else than through the parties may interested groups seek their ends?

b. How may the political necessity of reconciling the interests of farmers and workers, as allies, affect the molding of legislation? May this give rise to problems of constitutionality?

EDITORIAL NOTE: The LEGISLATIVE ROLE of POLITICAL PARTIES on the NATIONAL SCENE

While it is true that our major political parties seek to appeal to the same variety of groups in society, the interests of which may be in conflict, this in itself is no reason to conclude, as do some writers about the American party system, that there are no significant differences in the aims and policies of our parties. For, as Bertram Gross has pointed out, the "two major parties have never been based upon an identical combination of groups and interests." (Gross, The Legislative Struggle 64 [1953]). To compare the major parties meaningfully at any particular time, it would be necessary to identify the various groups in society from which each party derives principal support. This would, of course, reveal to which party each group looks to fulfill its own aims. (See Key, Politics, Parties and Pressure Groups (1947) and Holcombe, Political Parties of Today (1924)).

Yet, Gross maintains, the political party as such does not play a decisive role in effectuating policy. "In the great majority of legislative struggles," he says, "the major parties are observers on the side lines" (*ibid.* at 67). He ascribes this lack of party control to a variety of factors—(1) party candidates appeal to voters not only on the basis of the party platform, but also on the basis of their personalities and do not, therefore, always regard themselves as bound by the party platform; (2) party platforms and policies are often too general to cover the real issues that arise when bills are debated and therefore are no sure guide to party representatives in Congress; (3) even Presidential candidates often take positions during the campaign which conflict with the platforms of their parties and other candidates as well may make conflicting promises to different groups; (4) the major parties do not promulgate national platforms for mid-term elections and so even this guidance is lacking for party representatives elected at that time; (5) often the party which has elected the President may not control both houses of the Congress; (6) groups within the same party may be so antagonistic to each other as to make the party leadership powerless to effectuate party policy; and (7) the principle of seniority by which chairmen and ranking members of legislative committees are selected makes these men a center of power different from and often opposed to the party leadership (*ibid.* at 65-67).

This, as Gross recognizes, does not deny that the parties play a legislative role. They serve to unify the efforts of party leaders, party members in Congress, and the executive branch when under the same party control and this becomes a crucial function when legislative issues do arise which split the members of Congress along purely party lines. By nominating candidates, the parties furnish the key participants in the legislative struggle. The party platforms may, at the least, give impetus to campaigns for the enactment of specific legislation. And in organizing the electoral campaigns, the parties bring together groups whose joint efforts may continue into the legislative struggles following the campaigns.

Many suggestions have been made to reform the party system with the aim of attaining greater "party responsibility" for effectuating party policy. See, for example, the Report of the Committee on Political Parties of the American Political Science Association (1950); Marx, Party Responsibility and Legislative Program, 50 Col. L. Rev. 281 (1950); and the excellent discussion of the various proposals in Gross, *op. cit.,* at 69-91. For the limited progress in this direction made by the two major parties' Senate Policy Committees (created in 1946 by an item in the Legislative Branch Appropriation Act, 60 Stat. 911, 79th Cong., 2d sess., after a similar item in the 1946 Legislative Reorganization Bill for both houses had been deleted by the House), see Bone, An Introduction to the Senate Policy Committees, 50 Am. Pol. Sci. Rev. 339 (1956).

See, too, Bailey, The Condition of Our National Political Parties (The Fund for the Republic Inc., 1959). Professor Bailey proposes nine political reforms to bring about a system "that will make parties compete vigorously to find the right answers; that will organize political power at the national level so that it is adequate to carry out those answers; and that will make this power ultimately accountable to popular majorities."

Section 1B

ACTIVITY of UNOFFICIAL AGENCIES: LOBBYING;
The CASE of WISCONSIN LABOR LEGISLATION

SCHMIDT, *HISTORY OF LABOR LEGISLATION IN WISCONSIN*
28-45 (1933)

1. *Wisconsin State Federation of Labor*

The Wisconsin State Federation of Labor was organized in 1893. Among the unions which first joined, Milwaukee unions and craft unions affiliated with the American Federation of Labor were dominant. Mr. Frank J. Weber, a member of the Seamen's Union who had been active in Milwaukee unions, was responsible for bringing them together in the State Federation of Labor. The purposes of the new organization were to bring about greater unity in the work of the unions in securing labor legislation, and in organizing new unions. At that time, Weber felt most strongly the need for cooperation in legislative work. He had represented Milwaukee unions at the state capitol on several occasions and had been impressed with their weakness in the state legislature. There was no agreement among the unions on what they wanted; their representatives were inexperienced and made a poor showing. In contrast, the railroads knew how to make the most of their political power. They had money, and no scruples about how they spent it. Weber believed that if the workers were better organized their lobbyist would have more influence, even without money to spend, because of the voting power behind him.

More than any one man, Weber has been the dominant personality in the Wisconsin State Federation of Labor. In 1893 he was elected president, and he continued as the chief officer until 1917, when he retired in favor of a younger man. . . .

Frederick Brockhausen of Milwaukee was another important figure in the early years of the Federation. Brockhausen was a cigarmaker by trade. He became secretary-treasurer in 1900, and served until 1912, when he retired to go into business. Since 1900 the Federation has had only two men in each of its chief offices. Mr. J. J. Handley, a member of the Ironmoulders Union, succeeded Brockhausen in 1912, and Mr. Henry Ohl Jr., a member of the Typographical Union, took Weber's place in 1917. . . .

The Wisconsin State Federation of Labor has always had a definite legislative program. The preamble to its constitution expresses in general terms some of these objectives. More important are the programs drafted at annual conventions. The program for the 1895 legislative session included better enforcement of child labor laws, sanitary inspection of factories, modification of employers' liability, repeal of the anti-boycott law of 1887, a law against "Pinkertonism," and "collective ownership of the means of production." [23] Since 1895, the Federation has presented a program to every legislature, with varying success.

When the first legislative program was drawn up, the Federation did not have the machinery for presenting it that was later developed. In the first years, Weber represented the Federation in Madison during the legislative sessions. When Brockhausen became secretary-treasurer he worked with Weber as a lobbyist. In 1905, Brockhausen was elected to the legislature, and in the three following sessions both of these Federation representatives were members of the assembly. These two men, with the help of occasional union legislators, handled most of the Federation's legislative work before 1911.

In 1915 a step was taken towards the more elaborate lobbying method which is used by the Federation today. The executive board appointed a committee of three to direct the legislative work of the Federation. Mr. J. J. Handley was a member of the legislative committee in 1915, and as the Federation's legislative work has developed Mr. Handley has done an increasing share of it. In 1915 a special effort was made by the Federation to organize local legislative committees to work with the state committee. They were used to present labor's issues to local candidates before election, and to push bills by local agitation and letter writing during the legislative session. These were used until 1920, when the emphasis was shifted to local "farmer labor leagues." Local leagues were organized for several legislative sessions, but after 1925 were of less importance because of the greater

[23] Proceedings of the first conventions are not available. This account is taken from an article by Mr. J. J. Handley in The Wisconsin Labor Yearbook for 1924.

effectiveness of another method of securing local participation in the legislative work of the Federation.

In 1919, the Federation called its first legislative conference in Madison. Local unions sent delegates and the conference met during the first part of the legislative session. Since 1919 similar conferences have been held for every session. Held early in the legislative session, they have demonstrated the concern of the unions of the state with legislation before legislative action has been taken, but yet not so long before as to permit the legislators to forget the unions. Joint action on many bills with the Railroad Brotherhoods has also been secured at these conferences. They have served an additional important purpose of acquainting the delegates to the conferences with the legislation which the Federation has endorsed. The need for such education is clear when the complicated nature of the changes which have been proposed, for example, in the law of labor disputes and in workmen's compensation, are considered. The conference proceeds by the method of rejecting or endorsing the bills which are presented to it by the executive board of the Federation. The method is democratic, but because many of the bills are part of programs which have already been adopted at conventions and because so much of the legislation proposed cannot be intelligently criticized by the delegates, the conference is dominated by the executive board. They have been valuable chiefly as an expression of organized labor's political strength at a strategic time, and as a means of pointing out important issues in the Federation's programs to constituent unions.

The experience of the Federation's secretary-treasurer, Mr. J. J. Handley, in legislative matters should be emphasized. Mr. Handley has held this office since 1912, and during most of this time has been the Federation's legislative representative. His experience in supporting proposals for legislation, and the recognition which both he and President Ohl are given as the accredited representatives of organized labor in the state are an important asset in the legislative work of the Federation.

As the legislative work of the Federation has developed, it has become necessary for the executive board to draft and criticize an increasing number of bills. In the early years Weber and Brockhausen, with help from people in the University, the Capitol, and after 1904 in the Legislative Reference Library, drafted the bills. Not only for organized labor, but for all the interests who submitted bills to the legislature, lawyers were less important in legislative work than they are now. The Federation had its lawyers on whom it depended, but their services were used in fighting cases. Mr. W. B. Rubin, a member of the Cigarmakers Union, was the Federation's lawyer in this field, and handled many of the early strike cases in Wisconsin.

In drafting bills, workmen's compensation was the first problem which was sufficiently complicated to require the services of a lawyer. To help in working out a bill satisfactory to labor, the Federation engaged Mr. Daniel Hoan, for a long time Socialist mayor of Milwaukee. Hoan resigned in order to run for a city office before the work was completed, and Mr. Michael Levin, a Milwaukee attorney, took his place. Since 1920, the Federation has had an arrangement with Mr. Joseph A. Padway of Milwaukee, under which he is counsel for the Federation. . . .

2. Employer Organizations

a. *Milwaukee Merchants' and Manufacturers' Association.* There was no state wide organization of manufacturers, comparable in legislative activities to the Wisconsin State Federation of Labor, until the Wisconsin Manufacturers' Association was formed in 1910. Even then it was largely a paper organization, and did not begin active work until 1915. The manufacturers' association which appeared most frequently before that, and especially during the important period for labor legislation between 1909 and 1913, was the Milwaukee Merchants' and Manufacturers' Association. This organization was, as the name implies, an organization of Milwaukee men, both manufacturers and those engaged in other businesses. But since the manufacturing of the state was so largely concentrated in Milwaukee, the organization served adequately as the legislative representative of Wisconsin manufacturers until its functions were taken over by the Wisconsin Manufacturers' Association.

The Milwaukee Merchants' and Manufacturers' Association was formed in 1894 by a consolidation of the Merchants' Association and the Manufacturers' Club. The former was the older organization, dating from 1861, and at first dominated the affairs of the new association. The Manufacturers' Club was only three years old at the time of the consolidation. The Merchants' and Manufacturers' Association had from the date of its organization a legislative committee which was instructed to follow developments in the state capitol, but it was not at first especially interested in labor legislation, having rather the interests which are now characteristic of commercial and civic clubs. Chief among the concerns of the Merchants' and Manufacturers' Association during its first years were the promotion of Milwaukee by the building of an auditorium, by city fairs, and by the extension and improvement of railroad service. It was also interested in securing advantages for Milwaukee business men in railroad rates, taxes and insurance rates.

In 1904 and 1905 Mr. Frederick W. Sivyer, President of the North West Malleable Iron Company, was president of the Association, and in 1905 Mr. A. J. Lindeman was made chairman of the legislative committee. These men were prominent metal manufacturers, and because of the conflicts with unions in their industry were awake to the importance of the "labor problem." The leadership of metal trades manufacturers, the strikes which had been going on in Milwaukee in the metal trades, and the growing interest of liberal groups in Milwaukee in protective legislation for working women and children directed the efforts of the Association from their former concentration on civic projects to a concern with labor problems and labor legislation. . . .

From 1907 through 1913 the Merchants' and Manufacturers' Association sent representatives to every legislative hearing on labor questions. Mr. Lindeman, Judge A. T. Carpenter, and General Otto H. Falk, who was president in 1910, were its most frequent representatives. On the question of legislation for women and children Milwaukee employers were at this time aroused, and the Association fought them vigorously. On workmen's compensation, as will be seen more fully below, the Association fought certain details of the proposals, but was convinced, perhaps not of the desirability, but of the inevitability of legislation. Following the practice of other employer and public groups of the period, the Association sent its secretary to England and Germany in 1910 to study the systems of compensation there. Whatever the motives of the members of the Association in taking part in the hearings on workmen's compensation they did make possible, for the first time in the state, a bargaining process with the Wisconsin State Federation of Labor in drafting the law. This bargaining process has since been repeated many times by the Wisconsin Manufacturers' Association and the Federation of Labor under the guidance of the Industrial Commission.

b. *Wisconsin Manufacturers' Association.* The Wisconsin Manufacturers' Association was organized in 1910, but did not become active until 1915. The plan of the organizers was to create an organization which would include manufacturers outside of Milwaukee, deal with problems which affected the entire state, and represent manufacturers to the exclusion of commercial and civic interests. In its first years it endorsed the work of the Merchants' and Manufacturers' Association, and as it has developed it has supplanted that organization in its legislative work. . . .

The chief policy of the Wisconsin Manufacturers' Association, as stated by its secretary, is to make Wisconsin a more attractive and profitable place for industry. In the field of labor legislation, which with taxation has been the Association's chief interest, the Association contends that laws which are not greatly in advance of other states are desirable, but any which impose an additional burden on Wisconsin manufacturers which is not found in other states are undesirable. Considering the Association not by its pronouncements but from its actions of the past eighteen years, it can best be characterized as an organization which represents the interests of its members, but whose leaders realized that under certain conditions a good compromise with the labor group is to their interest. . . .

3. *Welfare and Reform Organizations*

The third important group of lobbying organizations which has been interested in labor legislation in Wisconsin is one which does not represent an economic interest but approaches the question from the point of view of public welfare. . . .

The first and most effective of these organizations was the Consumers' League. The first Consumers' League in this country was that organized in 1891 in New York City. The movement spread to other eastern cities and in 1898 the National Consumers' League was formed. The Wisconsin Consumers' League was organized in Milwaukee in 1899 at the time of a meeting of the National Federation of Women's Clubs. League membership in Wisconsin grew rapidly in the first few years of its existence. The first efforts of the League were directed towards influencing employers directly, that is by granting the League label to employers who complied with the League's standards for working conditions, and by educational campaigns such as the one which they conducted in Milwaukee in 1900 for Saturday afternoon closing of department stores. The League's first legislative work was for an improved child labor law. Somewhat later its members turned their attention to laws for women, so that by 1913 when the Industrial Commission set up an advisory committee on women in industry the Consumers' League was recognized as the outstanding advocate of labor legislation for women. . . . It was largely through the efforts of the Consumers' League, for example, that a rate was set under the minimum wage law for women after a delay of six years. Since 1920, with a change in the leadership of the Consumers' League and the great development of women's clubs, the Consumers' League has been less effective. Many of the women's clubs of more recent origin have continued the support which the Consumers' League gave to labor legislation for women, but unlike the Consumers' League, have not been pioneers in labor legislation. None of them, however, are organizations whose first purpose is the improvement of working conditions but rather, like the League of Women Voters, the American Association of University Women, and Business and Professional Women's Clubs, are concerned with labor legislation only when it touches on the primary purposes for which they were organized. . . .

The American Association for Labor Legislation has done much, in Wisconsin as in other states, to stimulate interest in labor legislation. Its secretary, Mr. John B. Andrews, has appeared at a number of legislative hearings on labor measures in Wisconsin. Also the Association has done a great deal in setting standards, both for legislation and administration. In recent legislation in Wisconsin the Association has played an especially important part in the drafting of laws on the subjects of labor disputes and unemployment insurance.

PROCEEDINGS OF ANNUAL CONVENTIONS OF THE WISCONSIN STATE FEDERATION OF LABOR

[The following excerpts are taken from the published Proceedings of the annual conventions of the Wisconsin Federation of Labor. An effort has been made to present the significant references bearing on the Federation's promotion of a workmen's compensation act.—Editor]

1905. *Annual Report of the Secretary-Treasurer*

[Secretary Frederick Brockhausen urges labor to rely on and elect its own legislators. As a part of his argument, he urges:] But let us not forget our friends, the railroad employes, who for years have been induced to stand pat with the Republican party, and who, session after session, have pleaded and begged for favorable legislation to protect themselves only in case of accidents. They had the administration leaders to plead for them, and what they got for deserting their fellow wage-workers at the ballot-box is well known at this time. Of course they will blame the terrible Stalwarts for the throwdown, but let me say that the bait offered by the Half-breeds was not worth the sacrifice of their class interests, either now or in the future.

For years the State Federation has made demands for legislation in the interest of workingmen in cases of accidental injury and death. This should fully satisfy the railroad employes and induce them to make common cause with the Federation, instead of bargaining and begging for special legislation. [Proceedings, 1905, p. 30].

1907. *Annual Report of the Secretary-Treasurer*

[Commenting on labor's dissatisfaction with legislation, Secretary Brockhausen had the following to say about the Merchants and Manufacturers Association of Milwaukee. Compare references in subsequent materials to the attitudes of the Federation and the Association towards each other after they had come together in conferences regarding compensation legislation.]

This association is equipped in an up-to-date style to oppose any and all legislation against its interests, and not a single bill escapes the scrutiny of its paid lawyers and officers; and its tactics to kill our bills were at times dishonorable. The association is made up of all sorts of employers of labor, lawyers, politicians and school teachers. I understand that the teachers and other well-meaning people were induced to join the association to give it an air of public confidence and respectability. It's an old method of sugarcoating a game of the grafters. This association, of course, makes easy prey of the legislators with capitalistic minds. [Proceedings, 1907, p. 22].

1907. *Report of Committee on Education*

[A rather detailed proposal for a workmen's compensation act was submitted to the Federation's 1907 convention in a communication from Charles V. Schmidt, of Milwaukee, and was printed in Proceedings, 1907, pp. 45-48. The proposal was referred to the Committee on Education (there was apparently no standing committee on legislation until 1908; see Proceedings, 1908, p. 16). That committee made the following recommendation, which was adopted by the convention.]

Your committee also recommends that the incoming Executive Board draft a bill, to be known as the compensation bill, to conform with the lines laid down in the communication received from Charles V. Schmidt; the Executive Board to place said bill before the convention of the Federation for discussion and, if found satisfactory, to present same to the next session of the legislature of the State of Wisconsin. [Proceedings, 1907, p. 57].

1908. *Annual Report of the Secretary-Treasurer*

At the last convention there was submitted a plan from Charles V. Schmidt, of Milwaukee, for compensation to employes for injuries or death, by a system of taxation levied on all industries which menace life or limb of any member of society; this was referred to the incoming Executive Board upon the following recommendation by the Committee on Education: [Secretary Brockhausen here quotes the recommendation reprinted above].

At its semi-annual session your Executive Board instructed the Secretary to submit the entire matter to the firm of Rubin and Zabel of Milwaukee for the purpose of having a bill drafted, in conformity with the recommendations of the convention committee. The firm submits an opinion and gives advice, which is before you in a separate pamphlet. In the same pamphlet will also be found an opinion by Attorney Daniel W. Hoan. During the past year I have learned that certain people at Madison also have various plans to aid workingmen along the lines suggested by Mr. Schmidt. Prof. John R. Commons, of the American Association for Labor Legislation, Max A. Lorenz, Deputy Labor Commissioner of Wisconsin, and others have, as I understand, propositions to aid workingmen on the lines above suggested. Therefore I believe that the State Federation of Labor should take steps to bring all the parties interested together as soon as possible, in order that all may unite in some plan to be presented to the next legislature; and I suggest that this convention instruct the incoming Executive Board to act accordingly. [Proceedings, 1908, pp. 26-27].

1908. *Annual Report of the General Organizer*

. . . the labor measures that were introduced in the 1907 legislature were mostly relegated to the legislative waste-basket on account of opposition to the measures by the members from the agricultural districts, who are not familiar with the wants of the industrial workers in the industrial centers of the state. It is therefore necessary that an educational campaign be energetically prosecuted by the State Federation of Labor in the rural districts of the state, so that the agricultural producing classes will recognize the justice of our demands and the righteousness of our cause. [Proceedings, 1908, p. 36. Convention Resolution No. 22, providing for presentation of labor's point of view to the farmer, was adopted pursuant to this recommendation of General Organizer Frank J. Weber. Id., 79-80].

. . . Accidents to men, women and children while engaged in their daily labor in the factory, shop, mines, etc., make one of the most important questions that should receive consideration by organized labor of the state.

Under our present system of production, the employers of labor have found it beneficial and profitable to have their employes insured against accidents, in some private accident insurance company. By insuring his employes the employer is relieved of all responsibility for accident to them; for, whenever any accident happens to any of his employes, all he is required to do is to report it at once to the representative of the insurance company in the locality, when his responsibility ceases, as the representative takes the matter in hand, gathers the evidence and calls immediately upon the injured worker, who, in ninety-nine out of a hundred cases is yet in a weak and delirious condition and has no realization of anything he may say or accept. The representative of the accident insurance company takes advantage of the abnormal mental condition of the worker, and with false promises, intimidation, threats, and in many instances coercion, he tries to get the worker to acknowledge that he was responsible for the accident; if he fails in this then the next attempt he makes is to get the worker to accept a few dollars in final settlement of the case. What is true of these private accident insurance companies also applies to public service corporations, as the representatives of the claim departments of the public service corporations are just as unscrupulous in their work as the representatives of the private companies.

I recommend that the incoming legislative committee, in conjunction with the Executive Board, prepare and have introduced in the next session of the legislature a law which will protect the workers, in accident cases, against the sharks representing private insurance companies and public service corporations. [Proceedings, 1908, 45-46].

1908. *Proceedings of the Convention*

The following report of the Committee on Legislation was adopted: "(1) We recommend that the 'Legal Opinions on Compensation Bill' and the drafting of a compensation bill be referred to the incoming Executive Board. . . . (5) We endorse the recommendation of the General Organizer relating to accidents to workers, and recommend its adoption." [Proceedings, 1908, p. 63].

1909. *Annual Report of the General Organizer*

Ever since the Wisconsin State Federation of Labor inaugurated an aggressive agitation for the enactment of a state compensation law, the employers of labor have been very busy to prevent the enactment of such a law and to substitute therefor what is known as industrial insurance. The system of industrial insurance which the employers advocate would leave them the same profits on the products of their industries as at present, while the workers, the consumers of the products and the taxpayers of the state as a whole would be the ones to contribute all that is necessary to establish a state fund with which the killed or injured employes in the industries may be buried or cared for.

The system of industrial insurance which the employers would like to see enacted into law is simply a subterfuge to defeat a compensation law which would compel the industry to bear the burden of the compensation to be paid by law for the injury or death of a workingman caused by the industry.

The only just system of insurance for the workingman is a compensation law that would establish the following principles:

First—That every workingman should be compensated for any injury received while engaged in any industry.

Second—That each industry be compelled to pay a certain amount for every workingman killed while engaged in the industry.

Third—The amount to be paid for death and each class of injury should be specifically stated in the compensation law, so that the amount could be collected from the state without resorting to the slow process of the courts.

If the trade unions of the state and country would spend less time in forming death and accident benefit associations in co-operation with their employers, and would give more of their time for the election of working class representatives to be sent to the legislative halls of our country—representatives who would enact a law for a workingman's compensation act—the conditions of the workingman would be made much nearer the ideal than under the present system. [Proceedings, 1909, pp. 35-36.]

1909. *Report of Committee on Legislation*

. . . We recommend that the principles embodied in Assembly Bill No. 18A [introduced by Assemblyman Brockhausen in 1909; see later references to bills introduced] be endorsed by this convention; and further recommend that the incoming Executive Board be empowered to take full charge of this matter, including the employment of such legal advice as they may deem necessary. [Adopted, Proceedings, 1909, 74; cf. id., 69-70—adoption of recommendation approving General Organizer's report].

1910. *Annual Report of the Secretary-Treasurer*

At the closing of the Eau Claire convention [1909] the new Executive Board referred to me the matter of keeping informed on the meetings and actions contemplated by the state special committee on industrial insurance [i.e., a committee of the state legislature].

As far as practical, I have endeavored to keep in touch with the committee and its proceedings, both in Milwaukee and Madison. Because of the election of Mr. Daniel W. Hoan, our former attorney, to the public office of city attorney of Milwaukee, Mr. Michael Levin is now engaged as the Federation's attorney.

With the new attorney and Bro. Frank J. Weber, I have attended a number of conferences and committee meetings in the interest of compensation legislation. Relative to the bills submitted by the State Committee on Industrial Insurance, I can report that none of them came up to our expectations. The first bill went so far as to destroy the points of protection at law conceded to railroad employees. In its recent issue of bills the committee says in substance that its bills are tentative and that no final action will be taken until employers, employes, and others have been heard at the public meetings arranged by the committee.

As this position of the committee suggested that if those interested wanted more definite action within a reasonable time, and as the next session of the legislature is drawing near, it appeared to be of importance to have, if possible, some agreement between at least the parties directly interested for submission to the legislature. . . .

With this situation staring us in the face, your Executive Board on June 5, 1910, instructed me to write the M. & M., the Merchants and Manufacturers Association of Milwaukee, suggesting a conference toward aiding the state committee and above all to arrive at some definite conclusion preparatory to the next session of the legislature for the purpose of getting a good start out of our present chaotic and rotten system of liability insurance and by enacting at least a fair start of a direct compensation system.

Our suggestion to the M. & M. was not in vain and I believe I am justified in stating to you that the legislative committee of the M. & M. is inclined to be fair in the matter and to aid in keeping our state in the lead of a practical solution of a most undesirable system of dealing with industrial accidents.

As inferred, a conference was agreed to and just previous to the closing of this report, July 1, 1910, an informal conference was held discussing the situation for several hours. But owing to a semi-executive meeting arranged for July 12, and for several days succeeding, by the state committee at Madison, it was decided as advisable to await the results of the state committee meeting before any further joint conferences were held and any action taken. . . . [Proceedings, 1910, pp. 22-23].

1910. *Annual Report of the General Organizer*

That there is an urgent need in this state and country for the enactment of a law for an adequate system of accident insurance for workingmen is conceded by both the employers and employes. As this subject of accident insurance is a thing of education, I would suggest that the incoming Executive Board send out a circular to the unions and their members, setting forth the essentials why it has become necessary. . . . I realize that the subject is an educational one and that the workingmen of the state cannot act intelligently on the question without possessing the preliminary education as to its application. [Proceedings, 1910, p. 44; adopted, id., 63. The convention heard speeches on "industrial insurance" by attorneys Michael Levin and W. B. Rubin. Id., 51, 52].

1911. *Legislative Report*

[Beginning with this convention, a separate report regarding activities of the Federation and its representatives before the state legislature is printed for each convention. The 1911 report was by Frederick Brockhausen.]

The 1911 session of the Wisconsin State Legislature has given more consideration to labor legislation than any of its predecessors. There were certain reasons for this. In the first place, the last state campaign proved that money had lost a lot of its former influence which resulted in the election of a considerable number of reform Republicans and a few reform Democrats to the State Legislature.

But the most remarkable part of the election was that Milwaukee County elected fourteen Social Democrats.

This fact, together with the further fact that the labor unions of the state had for years made demands upon the legislature for labor legislation, no doubt, caused the old party conventions to inject into their platforms some of the longstanding demands of labor. When the legislature met it then became a matter of the reformers to make good, because the presence of the Social Democrats prevented any further shirking of platform and campaign promises.

This legislature was the first in the history of the state to have within it a noticeable element for human rights.

The business elements together with the political farmers were, of course, the strongest numerically, and strongly inclined for the commercial interests only, but as inferred above, some of the many broken promises had to be fulfilled. And even that required strong efforts on the part of the Socialist and other friends of labor.

The first law to be enacted was the Workmen's Compensation Act, which is now Chapter 50, Laws of 1911.

But here I wish to remind you that the 1909 session gave the legislation its first real start by appointment of a special committee. Its chairman, Senator W. Sanborn, of Ashland, Senator John J. Blaine of Boscobel and Assemblyman Taylor Freye of Eau Claire (Republicans) deserve special credit for their activities in the enactment of this law.

The Democrats, almost to a man, acted as obstructionists in the entire matter.

Attorney Michael Levin, of Milwaukee, worked very industriously with the special committee, guarding your interests wherever possible.

Your attention is also called to the fact that while your officials did introduce compensation acts in several sessions of the legislature in the past, your executive board decided at this session to keep neutral for the reason that the Republican party had assumed all responsibility in the matter. However, fearful of results, we did introduce bills to abolish two of the defenses of the employers and to change the rule of negligence to comparative negligence.

These bills were killed and the compensation act passed. . . . [Proceedings, 1911, p. 40ff].

ACTIVITIES OF THE MERCHANTS AND MANUFACTURERS ASSOCIATION OF MILWAUKEE

[The following excerpts are from reports of activities of the Association contained in its monthly "Bulletin" (published after 1910 under the heading "Civics and Commerce"). The accounts published in the Bulletin are not as detailed as the reports published in the Proceedings of the Wisconsin State Federation of Labor, but an effort was made here, as in the previous materials regarding the Federation, to reprint enough to give all of the essential accounts contained in the Bulletin of the Association's activity with reference to the compensation act. —Editor]

1909. *"Industrial Insurance" Smoker, January, 1909*

[Economic, social, and legal aspects of the idea of a system of workmen's compensation were discussed at an evening "smoker" staged by the Association, with talks by Professors John R. Commons and Walter Wheeler Cook, of the economics and law faculties of the University of Wisconsin; Hon. J. D. Beck, Commissioner, and Dr. Max Otto Lorenz, of the Wisconsin Bureau of Labor and Industrial Statistics; and Mr. William Duff Haynie, Illinois representative of the United States Steel Corporation].

1909. *Annual Report of Committee on Legislation*

One of the most important measures ever presented to the legislature will deal with the question of industrial insurance. This subject has been dealt with by students in economics and sociology for some years, but it was not until the past year that it was taken up in this country with any degree of earnestness. The older countries have worked out systems of a more or less satisfactory character. Whether any of these systems can be adapted to our conditions is problematical. At any rate, the average manufacturer stands ready at this time to consider the question and to give his support to such a measure as may be equitable to both employer and employee.

Speaking prospectively, it may be said that the state legislature is now in session, and that a flood of bills has already been poured into the legislative mill. There will be much work for the Committee during the current session. As in former years there will be much objectionable as well as desirable legislation. All bills will have to be examined and a vigorous objection will have to be made against all crank legislation, while laudable measures will have our earnest support. [Bulletin #25, Feb. 1909, p. 22. Bulletin #30, July 1909, p. 16 carries a news item of the first hearing by the legislative committee and the participation of Association representatives therein.]

1910. *Annual Report of Committee on Legislation*

Industrial Insurance. There is on file with the secretary a complete list of the bills acted upon by the committee with the report of such action. Of these bills the first to receive serious attention was a bill tentatively prepared in January by J. D. Beck, State Commissioner of Labor and Industrial Statistics, providing for industrial insurance in the State of Wisconsin. At the same time a similar bill was prepared by Attorney Daniel W. Hoan, representing the Federated Trades Council. Both of these bills were eventually introduced into the legislature.

The committee [i.e., the Association's Committee on Legislation] invited all who were interested in legislation pertaining to industrial insurance to appear for a general discussion of these bills on January 23d, 1909. Attorney Hoan presented arguments in favor of the Federated Trades Council bill, a liability measure founded upon the English compensation act which it resembled very clearly in many of its provisions.

The bill formulated by the Commissioner of Labor and Industrial Statistics provided for the creation of an industrial commission with authority to manage an industrial insurance system in this state, which would offer to employers of labor a choice of four methods of insuring employees. The bill incorporated certain compulsory measures, some of which have since been eliminated.

Prominent liability insurance men of the city appeared before the committee with numerous objections to both bills, but it developed that a prevailing sentiment favored the enactment of industrial insurance legislation providing a measure could be devised which would meet all the necessary requirements and eliminate the objectionable features found in the proposed legislation.

Realizing that the question could not find a satisfactory solution within the time limit set for the introduction of bills and that the question could hardly be satisfactorily disposed of during the present session of the legislature the committee recommended that all industrial insurance legislation follow a course suggested at that time by certain members of the legislature by which this and the questions of income tax, state highways, inland waterways and guarantee of bank deposits be referred to joint committees for report at an adjourned session of the legislature. Lacking assurance that such action would be taken, the committee formulated a bill providing for the creation of a temporary committee to thoroughly investigate the subject of industrial insurance and to report at the regular session of the legislature in 1911, which bill would be actively supported in case the matter was not referred to a joint committee.

Special Committees Appointed. The legislature adjourned in June after appointing special committees to investigate the important questions of industrial insurance, income tax, guarantee of bank deposits, inland waterways and highways.

The special committees were instructed to report at a special session to be called by the governor in the spring of 1910.

Immediately following the adjournment the [legislative] committee organized and held hearings in Milwaukee and other cities of the state to which the members of your committee were invited. After several hearings in Milwaukee the Committee on Industrial Insurance conferred with members of your committee and formulated a schedule of inquiry which was sent to all the manufacturers of the state in an effort to obtain data upon this subject. The large amount of material gathered as a result of these inquiries has shown to the members of the Industrial Insurance Committee that it will be impossible to tabulate the replies and adequately to cover the actuarial phase of the subject in time to make a final report before the regular session in 1911.

In the meantime the committee has considered three industrial insurance measures, the most important of which was introduced by Assemblyman Ingram. This bill provides a scheme of industrial insurance which it is planned to make acceptable to manufacturers and employers of labor only by removing all of the present legal safeguards which they now have. While there are features in this bill which should meet general approval there are other features which will doubtless be obnoxious to employers of labor and impose upon the industry of this state heavy burdens not borne by those of other states. Should a special session be called, the Committee on Industrial Insurance will doubtless submit a preliminary and tentative report, recommending that the results of their labors be reoffered to a commission to thoroughly study the subject and prepare a measure to be introduced at the regular session of the legislature in 1911. . . .

In conclusion, the committee wishes to acknowledge with no small degree of pleasure, the cordial co-operation accorded its members by the various committees of the legislature. Our delegates in every instance have found the legislators eager to learn the attitude of the committee on all important questions and it may safely be said that never before has the influence and prestige of the Association been more potent in directing legislation than at present. [Bulletin No. 33, March, 1910, pp. 24-26.]

'Bulletin' Comment, April, 1910

[The following excerpt is from an editorial-news comment in the Association's Bulletin setting out certain objections to proposed tentative bills before the legislative committee.]

At the hearings [before the legislative committee] the Association was represented by Judge Paul D. Carpenter [a lawyer], Mr. A. T. Van Scoy [Vice-Chairman, International Harvester Co.], and Attorney M. W. Babb [Counsel, Allis-Chalmers Co.], who thoroughly reviewed the bill clause by clause, suggesting many changes and improvements that would be necessary, before a satisfactory measure could be formulated. It was urged upon the special committee that in view of the short time which they have had to prepare the measure it could not be expected that a satisfactory bill would be offered and it was urged that more time and care be given to a thorough investigation of the subject in its broadest aspects such as might be made by a permanent commission, collecting and deducing their facts from data and material obtained from manufacturers in this and other states; bearing in mind the desirability of providing a measure that will give to the employee guaranteed compensation at a cost to the manufacturer not greatly in excess of that already borne by him in the normal defense of his rights under the present conditions.

In this effort the committee was aided by many manufacturers of Milwaukee who expressed the same views and their influence was augmented by representatives of the Wisconsin Federation of Labor who were also dissatisfied with the bill submitted. . . . [Bulletin No. 34, April, 1910, pp. 18-19. Following this item, Civics and Commerce, (the new name of the Bulletin) No. 2, August, 1910, pp. 14-16, described at length the recently enacted New York compensation legislation; and Civics and Commerce, No. 3, Sept., 1910, pp. 7-17, contained an article by William G. Bruce, secretary of the Assocation, describing data gathered in a tour of Europe in investigation of foreign compensation plans. Mr. Bruce's analysis was basically favorable to the compensation idea.]

'Civics and Commerce' Comment, October, 1910

[Civics and Commerce, No. 4, Oct., 1910, pp. 7-10, carried an editorial-news story describing a meeting of Wisconsin manufacturers on October 20, in response to a call by the legislative committee of the Association to discuss tentative compensation bills proposed by the committee of the legislature. Those leading discussion included Judge Carpenter of the Association, Senators Sanborn (chairman) and Fairchild of the Committee of the legislature, and Senator Brazeau. The item also records the first formal steps taken to organize the statewide Manufacturers Association].

'Civics and Commerce' Comment, March, 1911

[Civics and Commerce, No. 7, Jan., 1911, p. 20, carried a brief news note of further legislative committee hearings at which the Association was represented; and a similar report was made in No. 8, Feb., 1911, p. 11. No. 9, March, 1911, p. 20, had the following to say of the final draft of the bill sent to the legislature:] The work on it has been carried on so systematically and carefully by Senator A. W. Sanborn and his fellow committeemen that it is believed it will encounter little opposition in either house. . . . The importance of the proposed legislation cannot be gainsaid, but the Legislative Committee of this Association feels assured that the measure in its new form will not work injustice to Wisconsin employers or employees.

NOTES AND QUESTIONS

1. List the different kinds of activities in which the Federation of Labor and the Merchants and Manufacturers Association engaged in the course of the struggle for a workmen's compensation act in Wisconsin. Are they typical of lobbying activities today? Note the role of the lawyer in representing a client before the legislature and its committees. Compare the respective roles of the parties to a lawsuit with the roles played by the Federation and the Association.

2. Which group was more effectively organized to achieve its objectives—the Federation or the Association? Why?

3. Enumerate the various groups concerned about the proposed workmen's compensation act in Wisconsin. Compare the number and diversity of claims pressed upon legislators with those pressed upon judges. What does this comparison suggest as to the extent of sifting and compromising of issues which necessarily precede (a) enactment of a statute and (b) a judicial decision.

Reconsider, in this connection, the influence of pressure groups upon the judicial process, which we have previously mentioned. Professor Glendon A. Schubert regards the amicus curiae brief filed by a pressure group as a technique for "judicial lobbying." (Schubert, Constitutional Politics 70 [1960]). To what extent is this view valid? Compare this technique with the methods employed by legislative lobbies. Are there significant differences?

4. Note Brockhausen's criticism, in 1905, of the political strategy of the railroad unions. Does not every pressure group have to resolve or moderate internal conflicts of interests?

Recall, too, the evolution of railroad and general legislation regarding industrial accidents. Consider the implications of pressure group activities upon the possibility of achieving a well-rounded growth of statute law. See Cary, Pressure Groups and the Revenue Code: A Requiem in Honor of the Departing Uniformity of the Tax Laws, 68 Harv. L. Rev. 745 (1955) and Dykstra, Legislative Favoritism Before the Courts, 27 Ind. L.J. 38 (1951).

5. How might a lawyer make proper use of the foregoing materials from the Federation and Association publications in a lawsuit involving the constitutionality of

the Workmen's Compensation Act ultimately passed? In a lawsuit involving its interpretation?

EDITORIAL NOTE: The LEGISLATIVE ROLE of PRIVATE ORGANIZATIONS on the NATIONAL SCENE

The proliferation of voluntary private associations seeking to further the interests which their members think they have in common is a measure of our democracy. Aware of the potential power which democratic government places in the hands of mass organizations, these voluntary associations have been depending, increasingly, upon the electoral and legislative processes to accomplish their aims. Undoubtedly they have been responsible, in significant measure, for the intervention by government, through law, in so many phases of life in the United States since the 19th century. In turn, increasing government intervention has made it essential for private groups to intensify their participation in the electoral and legislative processes to protect gains already won and to extend them. It is possible, therefore, to look upon the legislative process, as Arthur F. Bentley did in his pioneer work, The Process of Government, and as Bertram Gross, developing Bentley's theme, does in The Legislative Struggle, as primarily an arena for combat among private organizations.

Gross identifies the following private organizations participating in the legislative process on the national scene: organizations of businessmen (corporations, trade associations, and the associations purporting to represent "business as a whole," i.e., the National Association of Manufacturers and the United States Chamber of Commerce); organizations of workers (the individual craft and industrial unions and the major national organizations, the American Federation of Labor and Congress of Industrial Organizations, the independent International Brotherhood of Teamsters, and the independent United Mine Workers of America); and organizations of farmers (associations of growers of particular agricultural commodities and the four major associations which purport to represent "farmers as a whole"—the American Farm Bureau Federation, the National Grange, the National Farmers Union, and the National Council of Farmer Cooperatives). (Gross, op. cit. at 20). While these are probably the most significant ones, they do not, by any means, exhaust the list of private associations which seek to influence the legislative process, among which should be mentioned the organized churches, veterans groups, nationality and racial groups (The National Association for the Advancement of Colored People), professional groups, associations of women, youth, the aged, and the physically handicapped, and non-party political groups such as Americans for Democratic Action and the Committee for Constitutional Government. (Id. at 20, 21)

The scope of these private associations is further described in the following law-review comment:*

---

* Comment, Exhaustion of Remedies in Private, Voluntary Associations, 65 Yale L.J. 369, n. 1 (1956).

"In 1949, there were at least 4,000 national trade, professional and civic associations in the United States. U.S. Dept. of Commerce, National Associations of the United States vii (1949). At the local level, there were 12,000 trade associations, 4,000 chambers of commerce, 70,000 labor unions and 15,000 civic service groups. *Id.* at viii. Fraternal organizations reported more than seventeen million members. *Id.* at 483. In 1951 the membership figure for trade unions was 15,300,000; in 1940 it was 8,500,000; in 1930, 3,392,800. Peterson, American Labor Unions 62 (rev. ed. 1952). The new AFL-CIO will have fifteen million members. N.Y. Times, Dec. 3, 1955, p. 1, col. 1. Total church membership in 1953 was 94,842,845. A Guide To The Religions of American 196 (Rosten ed. 1955).

"Most professional men are members of an association. The American Medical Association in 1953 claimed a membership of more than 140,000. Practically all doctors belong to a local society, and nearly all societies are affiliated with the national Association. Comment, 63 Yale L.J. 938, 939 (1954). In 1954, the American Bar Association claimed a membership of more than 52,000. American Bar Association, 79th Annual Report 151 (1954)."

To evaluate the role of these private groups in the legislative process, it is necessary, Gross explains, to appreciate that every organization is subject to internal struggles for positions of leadership and no one group has a monopoly of the loyalty of its members or even leaders because the members and leaders often belong to a number of different associations whose objectives may not always be compatible. While this fact may exacerbate conflict within the group, at the same time it helps to reduce tension among groups. (Gross, *op. cit.* at 22)

In addition, the strength of any particular organization may be judged by the following factors in combination—(1) its wealth, (2) its numbers, (3) its leadership and organization, and (4) its strategic position. (*Id.* at 143-149). These factors are related. Wealth cannot be equated with power if not combined "with numbers, organization and leadership, and strategic situations." Numbers may provide a source of wealth and the raw materials for organization and leadership and put a group in a legally strategic position by enabling it to monopolize certain types of skills or services. Only "through organization can the full advantage of wealth or numbers be exploited" and "a high degree of organization can often compensate for serious deficiencies in either wealth or numbers." But organization, in turn, is the product of leadership. (*Ibid.*)

Finally, each private group does not operate in isolation; the organization of blocs to effectuate immediate objectives is a normal occurrence. The exchange of legislative support, Gross acknowledges, has often been denounced as a kind of log-rolling practice which is against the public interest. But he argues that the process of swapping support—with all that it involves in the bringing about of mutual understandings and adjustments and whether it implies a temporary relationship or a long-standing coalition—can be regarded as an essential part of the democratic process. (*Id.* at 149) See for a generally similar attitude, with illustrations of log-rolling or alliances among different interest-groups with respect to particular bills, Truman, The Governmental Process 362-368 (1951).

EDITORIAL NOTE: The REGULATION of LOBBYING

1. *The Federal Regulation of Lobbying Act*

This Act (Title III of the Legislative Reorganization Act of 1946, 60 Stat. 839, 2 U.S.C.A. 261) was the first attempt in our history to deal by law with Congressional "lobbying." In spite of its title, the Act, as the House Select Committee on Lobbying Activities pointed out, "does not regulate lobbying in any way, but merely requires public disclosure of lobbying activities and the identity of those who finance efforts to influence legislation." [Final Report of the Committee, H. Rep. No. 3239, 81st Cong., 2d Sess. (1951)]

Section 308 requires any person (defined in section 302(c) to include "an individual, partnership, committee, association, corporation, and any other organization or group of persons") who "shall engage himself for pay or for any consideration for the purpose of attempting to influence the passage or defeat of any legislation" by Congress, to register with the Clerk of the House of Representatives and the Secretary of the Senate. "Legislation" is defined in section 302(e) to mean "bills, resolutions, amendments, nominations, and other matters pending or proposed in either House of Congress" and to include "any other matter which may be the subject of action by either House."

At the time he registers, the lobbyist is required by section 308 to report the following on a prescribed form (1) the name and address of the person by whom he is employed and in whose interest he appears or works; (2) the duration of his employment; (3) how much he is paid and is to receive; (4) by whom he is paid or is to be paid; and (5) how much he is to be paid for expenses, and what expenses are to be included. In addition, he is required to report quarterly (1) all money received and expended by him during the previous quarter in carrying on his work; (2) to whom paid; (3) for what purposes; (4) the names of any papers, periodicals, magazines, or other publications in which he has caused to be published any articles or editorials; and (5) the proposed legislation he is employed to support or oppose. These reports must be published quarterly in the Congressional Record.

Sections 305 and 307, furthermore, require any person who by himself, or through any agent or employee or other person, directly or indirectly solicits, collects, or receives money or any other thing of value to be used "principally to aid, or the principal purpose of which person is to aid" the passage or defeat of any Congressional legislation or influencing, directly or indirectly, the passage or defeat of any Congressional legislation, to file quarterly a statement containing the following: (1) the names and addresses of all contributors of $500 or more; (2) the total sum of all the other contributions made during the calendar year; (3) the total sum of all contributions made during the calendar year; (4) the names and addresses of all persons to whom expenditures of $10 or more were made during the calendar year and the amount, date, and purpose of each such expenditure; (5) the total sum of all other expenditures made during the calendar year; and (6) the total sum of all expenditures made during the calendar year. These statements must be filed with the Clerk of the House of Representatives who is required by section 306 to preserve them for a period of two years and make them available for public inspection.

Section 303 requires every person who solicits or receives contributions to any organization or fund for the purposes "hereinafter designated" (influencing legislation) (1) to keep a detailed and exact account of (a) all contributions; (b) the names and addresses of all contributors of $500 or more, including the date of each such contribution; (c) all expenditures made by or on behalf of the organization or fund; and (d) the names and addresses of the persons to whom the expenditures were made, including the date of each expenditure; (2) to obtain and keep a receipted bill, stating the particulars, for each such expenditure in excess of $10; and (3) to preserve all such accounts and bills for a period of at least two years.

Exempted from the Act by sections 307 and 311 are practices or activities regulated by the Federal Corrupt Practices Act, political committees as defined by that Act, and duly organized State and local committees of a political party. Section 308, furthermore, exempts from its requirements "any person who merely appears before a committee of the Congress . . . in support of or opposition to legislation." In United States v. Slaughter, 89 F. Supp. 205 (D.D.C., 1950), this exemption was held to extend to "any person who helps to prepare the witness for his appearance before the Committee, either in gathering material, preparing a statement to be given by him, or in any other way." Section 308 also exempts public officials acting in their official capacity and publishers of newspapers and periodicals.

Violations of the Act are subject, under section 310, to criminal penalties and to "disbarment" from lobbying (after conviction for a violation) for a period of three years.

The House Select Commitee on Lobbying Activities, which was created pursuant to H. Res. 298, 81st Cong., 1st Sess. (1949) to investigate all lobbying activities, concluded that "the Act is basically sound as it stands," but made a number of suggestions for "minor improvements." The Republican minority on the Committee, however, attacked the present act as "vague, ambiguous, uncertain and seriously in need of amendment." The Democratic majority regarded as an important forward step the fact that beginning in August 1948, when the Department of Justice completed its survey of compliance with the Act, such organizations as the Chamber of Commerce of the United States, American Federation of Labor, Congress of Industrial Organizations, National Association of Manufacturers, Association of American Railroads, began filing reports under the Act, whereas the earlier filings had been by individual lobbyists. But the Republican minority thought it was seriously open to question whether any lobbying statute should go further than to require "individuals whose principal purpose is to attempt to per-

suade individual members of Congress to follow a certain course of action
. . . to identify themselves and their source of support." The Republican
minority regarded group expenditures to influence public opinion and, indirectly thereby, legislation, as the exercise of "constitutionally protected
freedom of speech."

The final report of the Select Committee was issued before the Supreme
Court decided United States v. Rumely, 345 U.S. 41 (1953) interpreting the
scope of a Congressional resolution for investigating lobbying and considered
in some detail at a later point in this Chapter. This case tended to support
the views of the Republican minority by intimating that, in the light of the
First Amendment's protection of free speech, the Court was not likely to construe the Lobbying Act to cover "efforts of private individuals to influence
public opinion through books and periodicals," but only to cover "lobbying
in its commonly accepted sense," that is, "representations made directly to
the Congress, its members, or its committees." In his concurring opinion,
Justice Douglas pointed out that Rumely and the Committee for Constitutional Government had registered as lobbyists, but had not disclosed the
names of contributors of $500 or more earmarked for the public distribution
of CCG books and pamphlets or the names of persons who had bought CCG
books and pamphlets in bulk. The subpoena which Rumely had refused to
obey (and successfully, since the Court majority held the Congressional investigative resolution was not intended to reach these activities) ordered him
to disclose the names and addresses of these contributors and purchasers.

The intimations of the Rumely case were made express when the Supreme
Court decided United States v. Harriss, 347 U.S. 612 (1954), holding that
section 307 of the Lobbying Act covered only "direct communication with
members of Congress on pending or proposed federal legislation." Pointing
out that the Act should be construed to avoid constitutional doubts (as to
vagueness and as to First Amendment freedoms to speak, publish, and petition the Government) the Court further narrowed the Act's scope by ruling
that the basic disclosure requirements (Secs. 305, 308) were applicable only
to a person who "solicits, collects or receives" contributions for lobbying
(Sec. 307), as distinguished from a person who merely spends money for
lobbying, without such solicitation, etc. In another respect, however, the
Court seemed to broaden the literal meaning of the statutory words: The
coverage provision, in Sec. 307, refers to the person who solicits, collects,
or receives money or any other thing of value "to be used principally to aid,
or the principal purpose of which person is to aid, in the accomplishment
of" the lobbying purposes. This meant, said the Court, that "one of the
main purposes of such 'person', or one of the main purposes of such contributions" must be to influence the passage or defeat of Congressional legislation. If construed "otherwise—if an organization . . . were exempted because lobbying was only one of its main activities—the Act would in large
measure be reduced to a mere exhortation against abuse of the legislative
process."

Interpreting the Act in this manner, the Court, speaking through Chief Justice Warren, upheld its constitutionality as an exercise of Congress's "power of self-protection." Although the District Court, in dismissing the information, had held the "disbarment" penalty provided by section 310 to be unconstitutional as a violation of the First Amendment, the Court did not pass on the question. It did not do so because the provision imposing the penalty "has not yet been applied to the appellees, and it will never be so applied if the appellees are found innocent of the charges against them" and even if the penalty provision were invalid, the Act's separability clause would allow the remaining provisions to be effective.

Justice Douglas wrote a dissenting opinion, in which Justice Black concurred, arguing that the Act on its face was unconstitutional because too vague and indefinite, and there was "no warrant in the Act for drawing the line, as the Court does, between 'direct communication with Congress' and other pressures on Congress." Justice Jackson also dissented, protesting that in the latter respect and in the other two major rulings above summarized, the Court had engaged in "rewriting" the Act.

In evaluating the views of the justices of the Supreme Court on the constitutionality of legislation requiring public disclosure of "indirect" lobbying activities, consider the following statements of a group of political scientists: "In determining what form government control of lobbies should take, it must be emphasized that channels of mass communications serve as powerful informational and educational media that are effectively used by pressure groups in influencing the formulation of public policy. Effective lobbying today is not confined to button-holing of legislators by paid agents in the corridors of the capitol or in their private offices. Modern effective techniques are directed primarily to the grass roots, where large numbers of influential and rank-and-file citizens are reached. A specific piece of proposed legislation may be debated in a campaign involving mass pamphleteering, high volume sale of low-priced books, editorial newspaper advertising, mass letter writing, sponsored and unsponsored radio and television programs." American State Legislatures 215 (1954).

During the 84th Congress, President Eisenhower, even though he said he agreed with the objectives of H.R. 6645, the bill to exempt producers of natural gas from federal regulation, vetoed the bill because of the scandal created when a lobbyist for the natural gas industry offered Senator Case of South Dakota a campaign contribution of $2500, thinking the Senator was in favor of the bill. The Senator rejected the contribution and disclosed the whole matter during the debate on the bill. In his veto message, the President indicated that he deemed this lobbying effort "so arrogant and so much in defiance of acceptable standards of propriety as to risk creating doubt among the American people concerning the integrity of governmental processes." (New York Times, Feb. 18, 1956, p. 1)

The Harriss case, discussed above, and the natural gas bill scandal led the Senate to form another special committee to study the possibilities of revising the Federal Regulation of Lobbying Act. (S. Res. 219, 84th Cong., 2d Sess. (1956), extended by S. Res. 47 and S. Res. 128, 85th Cong., 1st Sess. (1957)). The Special Committee conducted extensive hearings and issued its final report on May 31, 1957. (Hearings Before Special Committee to Investigate Political Activities, Lobbying and Campaign Contributions, 84th Cong., 2d Sess. [1956] and 85th Cong., 1st Sess. [1957]). The bill which it drafted and recommended for adoption (S. 2191, 85th Cong., 1st Sess. [1957]) was referred to and studied by the Senate Committee on Government Operations. (Senate Committee on Government Operations, Staff Memorandum No. 85-1-38, June 20, 1957; No. 85-1-39, June 21, 1957; No. 85-1-44, July 3, 1957). But Congress did not revise the Act.

For an analysis of the provisions of S. 2191, see Lyon and Stanhagen, Lobbying, Liberty, and the Legislative Process: An Appraisal of the Proposed Legislative Activities Disclosure Act, 26 Geo. Wash. L. Rev. 391 (1958). See also Senator John F. Kennedy, Congressional Lobbies: A Chronic Problem Re-examined, 45 Geo. L.J. 535 (1957) and Nutting and Sell, Modern Lobbying and its Control, 26 Rocky Mt. L. Rev. 401 (1954).

The natural gas bill experience also revealed the close connection between the problems of controlling lobbying and the financing of political campaigns. The latter question will be considered shortly.

2. *State Lobbying Acts*

For a summary of the state laws regulating lobbies, see American State Legislatures 215-239 (1954). According to this report, as of 1953, 38 states and Alaska imposed public disclosure requirements of one sort or another upon lobbyists. California, Michigan, and Wisconsin "made the most significant recent contributions to the statutory regulation of lobbying." The California law goes furthest in imposing standards of conduct for lobbyists. Sec. 9910, ch. 66 of the California Government Code provides that a lobbyist is:

1. Not to engage in any activity as a legislative advocate unless he be registered as a legislative advocate, and not to accept compensation for acting as a legislative advocate except upon condition that he forthwith register as a legislative advocate.
2. To abstain from doing any act with the express purpose and intent of placing any Member of the Legislature under personal obligation to him or to his employer.
3. Never to deceive or attempt to deceive any member of the Legislature of any material fact pertinent to any pending or proposed legislation.
4. Never to cause or influence the introduction of any bill or amendment thereto for the purpose of thereafter being employed to secure its passage or defeat.
5. To abstain from soliciting any employment as a legislative advocate except on the basis of his experience, or knowledge of the business or field of activity in which his proposed employer is engaged or is interested.

6. To abstain from any attempt to create a fictitious appearance of public favor or disfavor of any legislative proposal or to cause any communication to be sent to any Member of the Legislature, the Lieutenant Governor, or the Governor, in the name of any fictitious person or in the name of any real person except with the consent of such real person.

7. Not to encourage the activities of or to have any business dealings relating to legislation or the Legislature with any person whose registration to act as a legislative advocate has been suspended or revoked.

8. Not to represent, either directly or indirectly, through word of mouth or otherwise, that he can control or obtain the vote or action of any Member or committee of the Legislature, or the approval or veto of any legislation by the Governor of California.

9. Not to represent an interest adverse to his employer nor to represent employers whose interests are known to him to be adverse.

10. To retain all books, papers, and documents necessary to substantiate the financial reports required to be made under this chapter for a period of two years.

For the current Wisconsin legislation, which was amended subsequent to the time when the report of the political scientists was written, see Wis. Stats., sec. 13.61 et seq.

3. *Some Suggestions for Revising Existing Lobbying Controls*

S. 2191, previously mentioned, would have retained the basic public disclosure approach of the Federal Act but would have extended its coverage to include direct communications with any committee, officer, or employee of Congress, and with any agency or department of the federal government —when the purpose of the communication is to influence legislation. Indeed, there is little reason not to impose disclosure requirements upon lobbyists appearing before government departments and agencies to influence decisions within their own provinces. Existing statutes in Louisiana and Wisconsin do so to some extent. (Louisiana Rev. Stats. 1950, 49: 71-76; Wis. Laws 1959, ch. 97.023)

S. 2191 would also have covered certain types of *indirect* communications by imposing the disclosure requirements of the Federal Act upon persons who (1) request or procure any other person to effect direct communication to influence legislation when (a) such request or procurement is in writing and addressed to or distributed to more than 1000 persons; or (b) the cost of such communication is paid or agreed to be paid by the person making the request or procurement and more than 25 persons are solicited to make such a communication; or (2) spend $50,000 or more during a 12-month period to influence public opinion with respect to pending legislation or the introduction of legislation. These proposals would raise questions of constitutionality under the Harriss case.

Describing the experience under the Federal Act as "disillusioning," Gross doubts the efficacy of disclosure requirements as a means of educating the public or inhibiting large-scale lobby operations. (The Legislative

Struggle at 46-48). But he points out that the disclosed information can and will be put to use by the various participants in the legislative process (members of Congress, executive officials, and the leaders and lobbyists of private groups) to further their own ends. Thus "the information could, to some extent, serve to deprive some participants, particularly the stronger ones, of the advantages achieved through more complete secrecy and add a minor increment to the power of the weaker participants."

The suggestion that misrepresentation in propaganda about legislation should be prohibited by law is rejected by Gross because the distinction between 'good' and 'bad' and 'true' and 'false,' in this area is so difficult to draw on an objective basis. (*Id.* at 47). It might be added that the effectuation of this proposal would also raise serious constitutional doubts because of its potential infringement of freedom of speech. Gross rejects the suggestion that contingent-fee contracts between lobbyists and their employers be prohibited, since he thinks there is no sound basis for special regulation of the remuneration for "a legitimate form of employment"; and judicial redress can be obtained against exorbitant fees in particular cases. However, it should be noted that in 1874, the Supreme Court of the United States held a contingent-fee lobbying agreement "illegal and void." Trist v. Child, 21 Wall. 441, 22 L. Ed. 623 (U.S. 1874). See Note, 56 Yale L.J. 304, 315 (1947). Contingent-fee lobbying is made expressly illegal in many states. (See, e.g., Wisconsin Statutes, Section 346.19).

Gross approves the suggestion that former members of Congress be denied access to the floor of the Senate and the House if they attempt to appear there as lobbyists, but doubts that Congress is likely to take such action because of "the desire of incumbent members themselves, when no longer in office, to be able to visit the scenes of their former glory, whether to indulge in nostalgia or to carry on personal business." (*Id.* at 48)

More fundamentally, it has been proposed that since the participation of private groups in the processes of government is not only inevitable but desirable, these groups should be formally incorporated into the structure of government, thereby making present methods of lobbying unnecessary. There is no general agreement as to how this should be done, but the proposals are of two kinds—to place representatives of private groups (1) in positions of formal power or (2) merely in advisory roles.

As "totally impractical" proposals of the first type, Gross mentions (*Id.* at 54-55) (1) that made by Harvey Walker in his book, Legislative Process; Lawmaking in the United States (1948) 134, to organize Congress, or at least one house of Congress, along economic, rather than geographical, lines; (2) that made by Benjamin A. Javits in his book, The Commonwealth of Industry (1936), to supplement the present structure of Congress with a new body (Javits's "National Economic Council") set up along functional lines; and (3) that made by Clinton S. Golden and Harold J. Ruttenberg in their book, The Dynamics of Industrial Democracy (1942), to bring conflicting economic groups directly into individual agencies of government. Some of these proposals smack of the "corporative state" theories developed by Italian Fascism and apart from questions of their practicability or constitutionality, raise the serious question whether it is wise in a democratic society to delegate substantial governmental authority to private groups. Possibly in time of war, when government controls supersede collective bargaining as the method of determining the relations between labor and management, a good case can be made for the formal participation of labor and management representatives within the government agency exercising the controls. This, of course, actually took place during World War II and the Korean War through the setting up of tripartite boards, representing labor, management and the public, to administer the wage controls and handle labor disputes. But this direct participation by private groups in administration will not necessarily do away with private group lobbying before the legislature.

The use of private group representatives as advisors to government agencies is not new. As we shall see, advisory committees representing labor, management, and the public help the Wisconsin Industrial Commission to fix safety standards for industry. It has often been suggested that this principle be extended and private group representatives "be brought together in some council or federation which would provide a forum for the reconciliation of intergroup controversies" and enable Congress to be advised on the areas of agreement. (Galloway, Congress at the Crossroads (1946) 309). Gross thinks that one of the earliest of such proposals was advanced by Senator Robert M. LaFollette, Jr., who, in 1931, introduced legislation to set up a National Economic Council, composed of 15 persons appointed by the President from lists submitted by industrial, financial, labor, agricultural, and transportation organizations. (The Legislative Struggle, at 56). This idea was basically endorsed by Senator Joseph C. O'Mahoney when Chairman of the Temporary National Economic Committee (Final Report and Recommendations of the Temporary National Economic Committee, Sen. Doc. No. 35, 77th Cong., 1st Sess. (1941) 48). It was tried under the War Mobilization and Reconversion Act of 1944, 50 U.S.C.A. App. 1651-1663. The War Mobilization and Reconversion Board established under that Act was composed of 12 members with equal representation for the representatives of business, farm groups, labor groups, and the public. But Gross reports that many of the high hopes held out for the agency were disappointed. (*Id.* at 56). Because the deliberations of the Board were necessarily secret, they did "little or nothing to bring private pressures out into the open." (*Ibid.*) Often, when Board members agreed among themselves, they were unable to gain the consent of their own organizations. And by the time the Act expired in 1947, "many of its members had wearied of attending meetings." (*Id.* at 57).

Soon after his inauguration, President Kennedy appointed an Advisory Committee on Labor-Management Policy, composed of representatives of labor, management and the public, to advise him on wage-price policy and the handling of labor disputes.

Professor Paul R. Hays is one of the few to strike a hopeful note in this area. (Hays, Comment on Legislative Process, in Legal Institutions Today and Tomorrow 101-104, The Centennial Conference Volume of the Columbia Law School, 1959). He sees the development of "legislative professionalism" —the "progressive institutionalization of the work of preparing legislation and legislative programs" through the medium of the professional, civil service staffs employed by Congress and the state legislatures, and by federal and state administrative agencies. This, he thinks, will lead to a desirable "institutionalization of lobbying." Hays writes:

"What appears to be needed is more lobbying rather than less. On the one hand, as the staffs of committees and departments become more important in the legislative process there should be more opportunity afforded for consultation on suggestions for new legislation on pending bills. Legislative proposals should be more widely circulated among the interested parties who should be encouraged to comment and criticize. Public hearings should be held where they are appropriate. By the time the legislative committee is ready to hold hearings, the bill should have been perfected in form, and the real issues which it raises should have been carefully defined and fully canvassed.

"More lobbying is surely necessary in the case of unrepresented or under-represented groups. With respect to legislation in the fields of criminal law, health, education, recreation, social security, and generally, consumer protection, there is now insufficient provision for making certain that all important points of view are adequately presented to those who are in charge of preparing legislation. Increasing professionalization will of itself tend to improve this situation, but other institutional methods must be devised such as a required prescreening of legislative proposals by designated public and private organizations." (*Id.* at 102-103.)

EDITORIAL NOTE: The CONTROL of CORRUPT PRACTICES

1. *Control of Campaign Contributions and Expenditures*

The election of legislators sympathetic to the aims of a particular group is, of course, the most effective way the group can influence legislation. And financial contributions to the campaigns of one thought to be sympathetic are made in the hope that they will cement the bond between the group and the legislator. State and federal laws seek to deal with this problem, but opinion is fairly unanimous that they have failed.

The Federal Corrupt Practices Act, 2 U.S.C.A. 241-256, together with other statutory provisions, restricts the amounts which may be spent by candidates in Congressional elections and amounts which may come from certain other permitted sources. It also imposes requirements as to filing and disclosure and prohibits contributions altogether from some sources.

a. *Election expenditures by the candidate.* The candidate's own election campaign expenditures are subject to the following maxima, unless the laws of his state prescribe lesser ones: $10,000, if a candidate for Senator, and $2,500 if a candidate for Representative, but these may be raised to $25,000 and $5,000 respectively under certain conditions which could be met by most states.[1] The stated incorporations of any more restrictive limits imposed by the states is significant: in Wisconsin, for instance, the $25,000 federal limit, under the second alternative, upon a Senator's election campaign may not come into play, since the state limit for the election campaign is $10,000.[2] These limits of the federal law can be highly misleading, because the law declares that in determining whether the candidate's expenditures have exceeded the sums fixed by Sec. 248 (b) of the federal law as his limit, there shall *not* be included his expenditures for "necessary personal traveling, or subsistence expenses, or for stationery, postage, writing, or printing (other than for use on billboards or in newspapers), for distributing letters, circulars, or posters, or for telegraph or telephone service," or the filing, etc. fee levied by the state.

It should be noted that the specified federal maxima, like all the other provisions of the Act, apply only to election, not primary, campaigns. But state laws may impose separate limits on expenditures in primary campaigns. Neither federal nor state law, however, covers expenditures by candidates for the presidency in primary or election campaigns.

b. *Ceiling on political contributions.* Contributions to or on behalf of candidates for federal elective office, or to or on behalf of a committee or organization supporting such a candidate, are subject to a $5,000 ceiling (18 U.S.C. 608). This limitation is made specifically inapplicable, however, to contributions "to or by a State or local committee or other State or local organization." Added to this loop-hole is the fact that sums much larger than $5,000 might readily be parcelled out, as to source, among different members of the same family.

c. *Ceiling on certain political committees' receipts and expenditures.* Any "political committee" which is not of a wholly local nature[3] must not "receive contributions aggregating more than $3,000,000 or make expenditures aggregating more than $3,000,000 during any calendar year." (18 U.S.C. 609) The obvious means of evading this barrier is the creation

---

[1] The alternative maximum, as set forth in 2 U.S.C. 248 is: "An amount equal to the amount obtained by multiplying three cents by the total number of votes cast at the last general election for all candidates for the office which the candidate seeks, but in no event exceeding $25,000 if a candidate for Senator or $5,000 if a candidate for Representative, Delegate or Resident Commissioner."

The Senatorial vote in the general election of 1958 in Wisconsin was 1,194,601 (Wis. Blue Book, 1960, p. 695). Multiplied by three cents this would give over $35,000.

[2] For the Wisconsin Corrupt Practices Act,

originally enacted in 1911, See Wis. Stats., ch. 12.

[3] The phrase, "political committee" is defined in 18 U.S.C. 591 to include any organization accepting contributions or making expenditures to influence the election of federal candidates "(1) in two or more States, or (2) whether or not in more than one State if such committee, association or organization (other than a duly organized State or local committee of a political party) is a branch or subsidiary of a national committee, association, or organization."

of numerous committees (or seeing to it that a committee does not have national or multi-state affiliation).

d. *Filing and disclosure.* The "political committee" above referred to is required to make sworn quarterly reports to the Clerk of the House, in addition to sworn reports shortly before the general election, showing the total of contributions and expenditures, identification by name, address, amount and date, of the contributors of $100 or more, and similar identification of those to whom expenditures of $10 or more were made. Anyone other than a "political committee" making expenditures (other than by contribution to a "political committee") of $50 or more to influence "in two or more States" the election of Congressional candidates must file a similar statement. The candidate himself, shortly before and after the election, must file a sworn statement with the Clerk of the House or Secretary of the Senate identifying each contribution, by amount and name of contributor, and the expenditures made, together with the names of persons receiving them (though no such breakdown need be given for certain specified items, including postage, printing, traveling) and a statement of any job-pledges made to procure support for his candidacy (which pledges are made unlawful by another section). These statements are preserved by the Clerk of the House and Secretary of the Senate for two years and are open to public inspection. (2 U.S.C. 242-247)

Limits on the effectiveness of these disclosure requirements are apparent. For example, the requirements apply only to the general election campaign, not to the primary election campaign; they do not cover loans as distinguished from gifts; not all committees or other campaign organizations are covered; the volume and detail of the material filed is such that its utility is limited in the absence of prompt auditing and analysis, and prompt publication in the affected States.

e. *Prohibited sources of contribution.* A member of the Senate or House (or candidate for such office), or other federal employee cannot solicit or receive political contributions from other federal officers or employees or persons compensated for services from the U.S. Treasury (18 U.S.C. 602); and this prohibition is broadened so as to apply to solicitation or receipt by *any* person, of political contributions from persons known to him to be compensated by federal relief funds. (18 U.S.C. 604). Nor can any *contractor* with the federal government make political contributions to candidates, parties or others "during the period of negotiation for, or performance under such contract. . . ." (18 U.S.C. 611)

More significant are the prohibitions on corporate and labor union contributions and expenditures. Until 1947 the Corrupt Practices Act had prohibited (1) national banks and corporations organized under federal law from making contributions in connection with *any election;* and (2) *any* corporation from making contributions in connection with *federal* elections. In 1947, Sec. 304 of the Taft-Hartley Act expanded these prohibitions so as to make them apply to "expenditures" as well as contributions, and to primaries, conventions, and caucuses as well as elections (whereas, as we have seen, the other Corrupt Practices Act restrictions still are limited to elections); and this broadened prohibition as to contributions and expenditures in federal elections, primaries, etc., was imposed upon "labor organizations" as well as corporations. (18 U.S.C. 610)

Since the prohibition of "expenditures" may prohibit activities regarded as the exercise of the right of free speech and a free press, questions of constitutionality have been raised. In order to avoid passing upon the constitutional question, the Supreme Court has held that the publication and distribution of an issue of the "C.I.O. News," published with union funds, urging all members of the C.I.O. to vote for a certain candidate for Congress in Maryland, did not constitute an "expenditure" within the meaning of the 1947 provision. United States v. C.I.O., 335 U.S. 106 (1948). "If," said Mr. Justice Reed, speaking for the Court, "S. 313 (of the Federal Corrupt Practices Act) were construed to prohibit the publication, by corporations and unions in the regular course of conducting their affairs, of periodicals advising their members, stockholders or customers of danger or advantage to their interests from the adoption of measures or the election to office of men, espousing such measures, the gravest doubt would arise in our minds as to its constitutionality." (*Id.* at 121). Justice Reed seemed to regard as immaterial the source of the union funds used for publication—whether they came from subscriptions, advertising revenues, returns from per copy sales or from union dues. He did observe that the indictment did not charge "an expenditure by the C.I.O. in circulating free copies to nonsubscribers, nonpurchasers, or among citizens not entitled to receive copies of the 'C.I.O. News', as members of the union" (*Id.* at 111). Justice Rutledge wrote a concurring opinion in this case, in which Justices Black, Douglas and Murphy joined, arguing that the majority incorrectly read the statute and misapplied its policy; and that the statute, read to apply the congressional policy, was unconstitutional in the light of the First Amendment.

However, in United States v. International Union, U.A.W., 77 S. Ct. 529 (1957), the Supreme Court reversed the judgment of a federal district court in Michigan dismissing the indictment, under 18 U.S.C. 610, charging the UAW-CIO with sponsoring out of its general treasury fund a series of television shows urging the election of certain candidates to the Senate and House of Representatives in 1954. The district court held that such sponsorship was not an "expenditure" within the meaning of the statute. The Supreme Court disagreed.

Speaking for the Court, Justice Frankfurter distinguished United States v. C.I.O., *supra,* because the C.I.O. "neither directed nor delivered" its communication to "the public at large." It "merely distributed its house organ to its own people." "The evil at which Congress has struck," the Justice concluded, "is the use of corporate or union dues to influence the public at large to vote for a particular candidate or a particular party."

Having decided the question of statutory interpretation, the Court refused to pass on the constitutionality of the statute until after the trial of the U.A.W. Justice Frankfurter suggested that the following questions of fact might be material at the trial: ". . . was the broadcast paid for out of the general dues of the union membership or may the funds be fairly said to have been obtained on a voluntary basis? Did the broadcast reach the public at large or only those affiliated with appellee (U.A.W.)? Did it constitute active electioneering or simply state the record of particular candidates on economic issues? Did the union sponsor the broadcast with the intent to affect the results of the election?"

Justice Douglas wrote a dissenting opinion, in which Chief Justice Vinson and Justice Black joined, arguing that the Act, as construed by the majority, was clearly unconstitutional under the First Amendment. Justice Douglas indicated that he would also hold the prohibition of expenditures by corporations to be unconstitutional. Though the ban on contributions is unobjectionable, the fear of "undue influence," he maintained, "cannot constitutionally form the basis for making it unlawful (via the prohibition on expenditures) for any segment of our society to express its views on the issues of a political campaign."

To protect "union members from the use of their funds in supporting a cause with which they do not sympathize," legislation might be passed, Justice Douglas pointed out, "permitting the minority to withdraw their funds from that activity," as the United Kingdom has done since 1913.

At the trial which followed the Supreme Court's decision, counsel for the U.A.W., Mr. Joseph L. Rauh, Jr., took careful heed of Justice Frankfurter's position. He introduced evidence to show that the nine telecasts in question, costing $5,985, in which the U.A.W. radio and television director had interviewed various Democratic candidates and union officials, (1) were part of a year-round TV educational program of the Union, called "Meet the UAW-CIO," which dealt with many subjects other than those directly related to elections; (2) were aimed primarily at union members and any effect they might have had on persons outside the U.A.W. was incidental; and (3) were financed from the union's general fund (dues) but only after delegates to the union's constitutional conventions had expressly approved the expenditures for this precise purpose.

The jury returned a verdict of not guilty.[4]

[4] N.Y. Times, Nov. 6, 1957. In International Association of Machinists v. Street, 81 S. Ct. 1784 (1961), the United States Supreme Court held that section 2, Eleventh, of the Railway Labor Act, which empowers railway labor unions and carriers to enter into union-shop agreements, does not authorize the unions under such agreements to spend a union member's money (given in the form of periodic dues, initiation fees and assessments) over his objection, for political causes which he opposes, even though such union expenditures are not made in violation of the Federal Corrupt Practices Act or any state corrupt practices legislation.

Justices Black and Douglas were of the opinion that a statute authorizing such union expenditures violates the freedom of speech guaranteed by the First Amendment.

*   *   *

It seems generally agreed that the attempt to impose limits on campaign contributions and expenditures has led to subterfuge and evasion. Various contradictory proposals have been made to change the statutory restrictions thus far considered: e.g., to increase the ceiling on contributions and expenditures to more realistic levels; to discontinue all prohibitions, requiring only public disclosure; to enforce the existing prohibitions more vigorously; and to have the federal and state governments subsidize some or all of the campaign expenses of all candidates for office, particularly in the form of free television and radio time. In a few states, a pamphlet printed and distributed to all voters by the State government serves to give candidates publicity that costs the candidate nothing or an amount much less than its value.

See, generally, Schaffter, Summary of Recommendations Concerning Campaign Funds Made by Congressional Committees, 1905-1956, in S. Rep. No. 395, 85th Cong., 1st Sess. 275 (1957); Newman, The Supreme Court, Congressional Investigations and Influence Peddling, 33 N.Y.U.L. Rev. 796, 808 (1958); Newman, Reflections on Money and Party Politics in Britain, 10 Parl. Affairs 308, 326 (1957); Peters, Political Campaign Financing: Tax Incentives for Small Contributors, 18 La. L. Rev. 414 (1958); and McKesson and Dickey, Financing Political Campaigns, 34 S. Cal. L. Rev. 165 (1961).

2. Maintenance of Ethical Standards by Legislators

The federal Criminal Code of course outlaws the taking and giving of bribes by or to members of Congress as well as other officials (18 U.S.C. 201-205). A member of Congress may not take anything of value for assistance in obtaining a Government contract (18 U.S.C. 216) or for services in any proceeding before a federal agency in which the United States is a party or is directly or indirectly interested (18 U.S.C. 281). Neither may he receive "any salary in connection with his services as such an official" of the United States from any non-federal source (except as may be contributed from a state, county or municipal treasury (18 U.S.C. 1914).[5] Pertinent here also is Rule VIII of the House of Representatives

Justices Frankfurter and Harlan dissented on the ground that the majority's interpretation of the Railway Labor Act was erroneous and that authorization of such union expenditures did not abridge anyone's freedom of speech.

[5] The provisions above listed apply also to executive or administrative officials. The latter are subject in addition, to certain other restrictions: e.g., one who is an officer of, or interested in the contracts or

profits of, a company may not as a government official transact business with that company (18 U.S.C. 434). Nor may a federal official assist in prosecuting a claim against the United States "otherwise than in the proper discharge of his official duties" or receive any gratuity or share of interest in the claim, in return for such assistance (18 U.S.C. 283); nor may he within two years from termination of his employment with a federal agency, act as attorney or

which provides that every House member "shall vote on each question put, unless he has a personal or pecuniary interest in the event of such question." Yet only rarely has the Speaker decided that because of personal interest, a member should not vote. And House members have not asked for enforcement of the Rule, nor for its extension to cover committee as well as floor action. (Gross, The Legislative Struggle 40 [1953])

These and other phases of the problem of ethics in government were considered in the 1951 report of the Subcommittee of the Senate Committee on Labor and Public Welfare, of which Senator Paul Douglas of Illinois was chairman. Among the recommendations were that the Criminal Code be amended (1) to broaden the definition of "bribe" to include "other considerations just as useful to bribers as hard cash," such as any "emoluments, fee, profit, advantage, benefit, position, future position, employment, future employment, opportunity, future opportunity, advancement or future advancement"; (2) to cover public officials who "receive things of substantial value not for doing things which come within their official capacity, but for using their influence with other persons in the government"; (3) to prohibit convicted bribers from participating in any substantial business activity with the federal government (the bribed are now subject to disqualification from henceforth holding an office, honor, or trust under the United States); and (4) to increase the penalties. (Ethical Standards in Government, Report of Subcommittee to Study Sen. Conc. Res. 21, Sen. Comm. on Public Welfare, 82d Cong., 1st Sess. [1951])

A number of other recommendations were made with respect to controlling the conduct of executive and administrative officials, the creation of a citizens' organization for improvement of government service, and creation of a Commission on Ethics In Government. The latter body would (1) investigate and report to Congress on the moral standards of those doing business with or seeking to influence Government, in relation to the moral standards prevailing in society; (2) recommend measures for improvement of the moral level of official conduct in the Government and of all those participating in the conduct of public affairs. A major recommendation of the subcommittee, pertinent to the present survey, was that members of Congress as well as other high officials of the Government and of the national political parties be required to make annual reports to the Comptroller General, disclosing their income by source and amount, their assets, and their dealings in securities and commodities.

Many are skeptical about the chances that these suggestions have for

---

agent for prosecuting any claim against the United States "involving any subject matter directly connected with which such person was so employed. . . ." (18 U.S.C. 284). See generally, McElwain and Vorenburgh, The Federal Conflict of Interest Statutes, 65 Harv. L. Rev. 955 (1952); Davis, The Federal Conflict of Interest Laws, 54 Colum. L. Rev. 893 (1954); Conflict of Interest and Federal Service (Report of the Special Committee on Federal Conflict of Interest Laws of the Association of the Bar of the City of New York, Harvard Univ. Press, 1960); U.S. v. Bergson, 119 F. Supp. 459 (D.C. 1954).

passage in Congress or about their effectiveness even if passed. Partly to make Congressmen less tempted to succumb to the more obvious forms of corruption, Congressional salaries were substantially increased in 1955 (from $12,500 to $22,500) along with other benefits, including retirement pay (2 U.S.C. 31-53; 5 U.S.C. 693-1).

On April 27, 1961, President Kennedy submitted a Message to the Congress relative to Ethical Conduct in the Government. (H. Doc. No. 145, 87th Cong., 1st Sess.). The proposals advanced by the President were based on the work of a panel composed of Judge Calvert Magruder, retired chief judge of the First Circuit Court of Appeals, Dean Jefferson B. Fordham of the University of Pennsylvania Law School and Professor Bayless Manning of the Yale Law School and appointed by the President soon after his inauguration.

The President proposed an Executive Employees' Standard Act embodying a comprehensive revision of the various "conflict-of-interest" statutes now on the books which, the President explained, "permit an astonishing range of private interests and activities by public officials which are wholly incompatible with the duties of public office"; and "on the other hand . . . create wholly unnecessary obstacles to recruiting people for Government service."

The President also stated that he would take action, under his own powers as Chief Executive (1) to prohibit every Government employee from (a) accepting any gift which "is, or appears to be, designed to influence official conduct"; (b) using for private gain official information which is not available to the public; (c) using the authority of his position to induce another to provide him with anything of economic value whenever the employee has reason to believe that the other person's private interests may be affected by the actions of the employee or his agency; and (d) engaging in outside employment which is incompatible with his Government employment; and (2) in addition, to prohibit officials appointed by the President from accepting outside compensation for (a) any activity within the scope of official duty; and (b) any lecture, article, public appearance, etc., devoted to the work of the department or based on official information not yet a matter of general knowledge; and to subject them to standards governing the ownership of property which will insure that no conflict of interest can exist.

On May 6, 1961, the President issued Executive Order No. 10939, 26 Federal Register 3951, imposing all these prohibitions upon all heads and assistant heads of departments and agencies, full-time members of boards and commissions appointed by the President, and members of the White House staff. The expectation is that these officials will, in turn, impose similarly appropriate prohibitions upon all subordinate Government employees.

The President also indicated in his Message to the Congress that he would designate, in the Executive Office of the President, a single officer charged with responsibility for coordinating the administration of ethical standards and reporting directly to the President.

None of the President's actions and proposals apply to the judicial or legislative branches of the Government. "Existing laws relating to the judiciary," said the President in his Message, "are deemed adequate." And "the adequacy and effectiveness of laws regulating the conduct of Members of Congress and congressional employees should be left to strictly congressional determination."

The question posed by the various suggestions for legislative reform is like one of the questions posed by the Supreme Court desegregation decision: can ethical standards be effectively raised by law? There are those who claim that "you can't legislate morality" and there are those who, at the opposite pole, are quick to urge "there ought to be a law" at the first signs of a social problem. The truth is that cynicism and immorality in public life are not wholly unrelated to the level of private morality in the society generally; and that the legal weapon must be supplemented by others if the fight is to be effective. At any rate, one should remember that the question is not whether proposed legal and other weapons will be completely effective. The question is whether they will produce a situation that is enough better than the existing one to justify the effort involved.

HORSKY,* *THE WASHINGTON LAWYER*
53-58 (1952)

[Mr. Horsky points out that although lobbying is the "chief role" of the Washington lawyer in the legislative process, it is not his only work in the legislative field. His other tasks include (1) advice to clients appearing before legislative committees; and (2) advice to clients on legislative developments, including interpreting and evaluating proposed bills. As part of the lobbying function, Horsky includes the lawyer's contacts or communications not only with specific legislators and legislative committees, but also with interested government agencies to secure their approval and cooperation in presenting and securing the passage or defeat of a bill. In performing this function, the Washington lawyer, says Horsky, is called upon to do a variety of legal work—drafting proposed legislation, testifying for a client before a legislative committee, and helping a client to prepare testimony which the client will deliver. A good deal of the lawyer's work may be "off the record" in the sense that his contacts with legislators and administrative officials, his assistance in the preparation of speeches for friendly Congressmen or in the preparation of legislative committee reports may never come to public attention. The author then considers the question whether a line can or should be drawn between the proper and improper in relation to such non-public activity.—Editor]

* Charles A. Horsky is a member of the firm of Covington and Burling, Washington, D.C. The book, which the student would do well to read in its entirety, consists of a series of lectures delivered under the auspices of the Julius Rosenthal Foundation at Northwestern University School of Law, in April 1952.—Editor

The direct guide is none too helpful. Canon 26 of the Canons of Professional Ethics of the American Bar Association reads as follows:

A lawyer openly, and in his true character, may render professional services before legislative or other bodies, regarding proposed legislation and in advocacy of claims before departments of government, upon the same principles of ethics which justify his appearance before the Courts; but it is unprofessional for a lawyer so engaged to conceal his attorneyship or to employ secret personal solicitations, or to use means other than those addressed to the reason and understanding, to influence action.

This Canon has had no pertinent official interpretation.

Let us leave until later the application of the canon to advocacy of claims before the government departments and now look at its application to lobbying. One matter is clear: an attorney who engages in any of the activities we have described, cannot, with propriety, conceal his attorneyship. This is plainly and rightfully condemned. But there clarity ends. What is the significance of the phrase in the first section of the Canon that the lawyer may render professional servces "before legislative . . . bodies"? Does the reference to "bodies" mean to exclude all contact with the individual member of Congress? To state the extreme case, does it mean that a client cannot with propriety request his Washington lawyer to accompany him in his attempt to persuade his own Congressman or Senator to introduce a bill which he has drafted? And does it mean that only at the risk of being accused of unprofessional conduct may a Washington lawyer visit an individual member of Congress for discussion of the merits of a bill?

We get no help from the second "thou shall not" section of the Canon. Its clauses are in the disjunctive, and there is an unqualified ban on "secret personal solicitations." Does "secret" mean to prohibit everything except appearances before committees? Specifically, does it prohibit a discussion with a member of Congress in his office, at which the lawyer attempts to persuade him by reasoned arguments? Does the word "personal" in the phrase "secret personal solicitations" mean that it bans only those non-public contacts where personal influence or favors, and not the merits, are the basis of the appeal?

The latter interpretation certainly sounds more reasonable, but if it is to be accepted it means that the whole clause simply duplicates the clause which immediately follows it—that no means shall be used "other than those addressed to the reason and understanding." For that matter, what does that mean? Literally, it means that a lawyer must close his eyes to the fact that lawmaking is a political process—unless "reason and understanding" implies that a lawyer may attempt to make clear to the members of Congress the political facts of life.

In truth, the Canon is either so strict as to be impossible, or so vague as to be useless. Washington lawyers do all of these things, and in my opinion properly so. Both the public and the non-public aspects of such work call for his legal abilities, and for the wisdom, understanding and judgment that can come only from experience in many cases, many victories and defeats, over many years.

The reader is no doubt saying to himself—all this is very well, but in view of the daily press, is it not more to the point that you speak of the improprieties than of the proprieties? My excuse, which I hope is recognized, is that it is important to know what Washington lawyers do, and to know that there are manifold ways in which they can properly engage in activities designed to affect legislation—can lobby, as we use the term. Perhaps I make my bow to the current state of public opinion in acknowledging that such a proposition requires exposition.

Certainly, I cannot vouch for the ethical standards among Washington lawyer-lobbyists. I think they are generally high, and that the principal criticism of lobbying activities is in fact directed at the non-lawyer lobbyists, who outnumber the lawyers perhaps ten to one. But neither do I challenge the assertion that there are, and will be, lawyers who recognize no limits. Vague as the ethical standards may be, there is clearly a line that no lawyer should pass. Fundamentally, there can be no more basis for a lawyer to obtain the vote of a member of Congress on the basis of friendship, or on the basis of past, present or future favors, than there is for a lawyer to obtain a vote from a judge or a juror on the same basis. The lawyer stands on a different footing from his client. John Smith, the voter, and also the man who favors H.R. 10,000, can with propriety tell his Congressman that the price of Smith's next vote or his next campaign contribution is the Congressman's own vote for H.R. 10,000. But it is the essence of democracy, it seems to me, that voters should be able to tell a member of Congress what they want, and to tell the member that if he disagrees, he will lose that voter's support in the next campaign.

The Washington lawyer, or any other lawyer, for that matter, is not the voter. He is retained, and paid, for professional advice and services. But when he is retained, or paid, for his influence or alleged influence over a member of Congress, regardless of the merits of the issue, he is no longer acting as a lawyer.

This is summary treatment of a complex and controversial part of the mechanics of democratic government. . . .

J. COHEN,* *THE "GOOD MAN" AND THE ROLE OF*
REASON IN LEGISLATIVE LAW
41 Cornell Law Quarterly 386, 396-398 (1956)

* * *

Now, granted that the legislative process involves the struggle over competing group interests in which irrational *and* rational forces are at work, in which legislative machinery may be manipulated for good *and* evil ends, and in which motivations are for private *and* public gain, what should be the nature of the lawyer's representational role in the legislative forum? Ideally, his function would parallel that of the lawyer in the judicial forum performing in the highest traditions of his profession. There, though he represents private clients before the court, he

* Julius Cohen, Professor of Law, Rutgers University, has served in various federal and state governmental posts, and is the author of Materials and Problems on Legislation (1949) and a contributor to Freedom and Authority in Our Time (1953), and to Symbols and Values (1954).—Editor

serves in a higher public capacity as an officer of the court. Here, too, his public duty as an officer of the legislature would transcend his immediate duty to his clients. He would lend his talents primarily to the task of helping policy-makers strike a proper balance between private group needs and the welfare of the community. Because present legislative procedures for independent fact-finding are woefully inadequate, he would bring to the legislative forum the best evidentiary materials that could be gathered for predicting the consequences of a policy proposal. He would, by logical analysis, endeavor to determine whether the consequences would be in harmony with the existing system of values; he would explore the need for correcting the existing system when it is not in tune with the basic aspirations of the community. Precedent and analogy would play an important role in helping to develop a sense of proportion and perspective,[27] and a critical eye would search out and expose errors and the various types of "crooked thinking"[28] that might be employed by the unscrupulous to influence legislative policy makers. Discounting institutional differences, this is essentially the pattern of the lawyer's role in the judicial arena whenever the court is called upon to legislate judicially—when it is asked, for example, to rule on questions concerning the meaning or the constitutionality of a statute. One of the distinguishing factors is that in the judicial forum, salient policy issues are too often beclouded by impressive legal jargon and symbolism;[29] in the legislative forum, the insulation of legal symbolism is more apt to be stripped off, and the policy considerations more likely to be laid bare. In addition, a lawyer appearing before a court is usually *representing* his client; but before a legislative body, he is apt to be *lobbying* for his client. But to the extent that lobbying involves alerting legislators to problems that might need attention in the legislative forum it is salutary. Petitioning for redress of grievances is, after all, a right that is granted under the Constitution. To the extent that it involves *private* hearings on the merits or demerits of pending proposals, it serves the useful function of bringing to the attention of policy makers information that could shed significant light on policy proposals. The difficulty, of course, with such a procedure is that all competing views are not given an equal chance to be heard. For private hearings require access to policy makers, and too often this is a privilege that is not accorded equally to all who knock at private legislative doors.

Besides the preparation of rigorous arguments for the justification or criticism of a policy proposal, the legislative lawyer should acquaint himself with the intricacies of legislative machinery, procedures, and sources of power. Without such knowledge, the most convincing argument could go for naught. . . . He must, for example, know who the real legislative judges of a policy issue would be, so as to know whom to persuade; he must have a keen sense of timing; he must be skilled in devising parliamentary strategy for use by a friendly Congressman or Senator;

---

[27] See Horack, "The Common Law of Legislation," 23 Iowa L. Rev. 41, 42-45 (1937).

[28] This is Thouless' term. Thouless, Straight and Crooked Thinking (1932).

[29] The import of legal symbolism is developed more fully in my article on "The Value of Value Symbols in Law," 52 Colum. L. Rev. 893 (1952).

he must know enough about legislative draftsmanship to make sure that the policy that is sought will not be perverted or otherwise defeated by improper legislative language; finally, he must be adept in the art of compromise, of knowing how best to reach a position not as good as the one hoped for, but considerably better than if the opposition forces clearly had their way.

All this, of course, is an account of the *ideal* view of the lawyer's representational role in the legislative forum. What are the practical difficulties in fulfilling this role? There are, indeed, many. The pressure for quick decision, the low level of competence of many legislators, the elements of bias and prejudgment, the factor of manipulation, the unwillingness of many to recognize the relationship between immediate and long-range goals, the impatience with the tedium of rigorous analysis, the high-pitched, volatile emotionalism that often pervades the legislative scene all combine to discourage anyone inspired to stride forth in the role of the idealist.[30] Other factors becloud the scene from a practical point of view. First of all, to amass rigorous empirical data in support of a legislative cause requires financial resources that only the more wealthy clients can afford to make available; the less affluent, accordingly, must suffer. Secondly, there are too many areas— especially those involving social behavior—in which reliable information is unavailable concerning consequences of proposed legislative action—areas in which conjecture and hunch must, of necessity, hold sway. . . . What then must the less gifted lawyer do under such circumstances? Perhaps he is left with no other recourse save that of presenting the justification for his cause as an hypothesis, and adducing whatever evidence, however slim, is available to sustain its plausibility. He would push his case to the hilt, and so would his adversary; out of the heat of conflict might emerge some basis upon which the policy maker could fashion a reasonably intelligent guess. . . .

NOTES AND QUESTIONS

1. Should the lawyer confine his legislative activities to those suggested by Professor Cohen?

2. Professor Frank C. Newman raises the following questions with respect to the last three paragraphs of the Horsky excerpt, *supra:* "If the favors come from the client and not the lawyer, is the lawyer governed by the same proscriptions that apply to judicial cases? Is it truly unethical for a lawyer to tell a legislator that the price of the client's next vote is the legislator's vote? Or might it rather be malpractice were that fact of political life left unmentioned? In general, should we not argue that for a politician the facts of political life quite properly are included among 'those addressed to the reason and understanding'?" Newman, A Legal Look At Congress and the State Legislatures, in Legal Institutions Today and Tomorrow 67, 78 (The Centennial Conference Volume of the Columbia Law School, 1959).

3. The person who offered Senator Francis Case $2,500, while the natural gas bill which President Eisenhower vetoed was before the Senate, was a lawyer. The Senate investigating committee concluded that even though "the offer of the contribution was

---

[30] Many of these factors are discussed in Cohen, "Hearing on a Bill: Legislative Folklore," 37 Minn. L. Rev. 34 (1952), and Cohen and Robson, "The Lawyer and the Legislative Hearing Process," 33 Neb. L. Rev. 523 (1954).

for the purpose of influencing the Senator's vote . . . there was neither a bribe nor an attempt to bribe." S. Rep. No. 1724, 84th Cong., 2d Sess. 9 (1956). The lawyer involved was later charged with failure to file as a lobbyist. Assuming he had filed, was his action ethical? Is it helpful to be told by the investigating committee that "lobbying is proper; contributions are proper—but they must not be combined for an ulterior purpose"?

4. Senator Clifford P. Case of New Jersey has answered some of these questions forthrightly: "I . . . question whether it is proper for a client, let alone a lawyer on behalf of his client, to suggest to me that my vote on a pending measure will determine his vote in the next election, or, more specifically, his willingness to open his pocketbook to me for a political contribution. In practice I would throw any person who made such a threat to me out of my office, even if I needed the money very much." Case, Comment on Legislative Process, in Legal Institutions Today and Tomorrow, *supra*, at 99.

Do you think Senator Case's position would be taken by most federal and state legislators? Should it be?

The late Senator Richard L. Neuberger of Oregon wrote: "The threat of retaliation at the polls is certainly a rightful attempt at influence in American politics—perhaps the most rightful of all." Neuberger, When Influence Is Good—And Bad, The New York Times Magazine, July 27, 1958, pp. 9, 22. Nor was the Senator certain that the acceptance of campaign contributions from people with an interest in specific legislation was improper. *Ibid.*

5. Special problems are faced by lawyers who are also legislators. Professor Newman reports that lawyers recently comprised 66% of the United States Senate, 56% of the House of Representatives, 58% of the New York legislature and 32, 30, 21, and 18% of the California, Illinois, Missouri, and Minnesota legislatures respectively. Newman, *supra* at 69. While serving as legislators, they also practice their profession. To what extent should they be permitted to represent clients having dealings with the government? Federal statutes, as we saw, impose certain curbs on their activities. In 1945, Michigan made it a felony for legislators to be employed by persons interested in pending bills at higher compensation than the reasonable value of the services if performed by non-legislators, even though the employment had nothing to do with the pending bills. Would you recommend such legislation for general enactment? Does it go too far? Or not far enough?

Of course it would be illegal in most states for a lawyer-legislator to represent any client in connection with the passage or defeat of bills. Furthermore, the Committee on Professional Ethics of the American Bar Association has held that "a law firm could not accept employment to appear before a legislative committee while a member of the firm is serving in the Legislature." It went on to say: "A full disclosure before the committee would not alter this ruling nor would it be changed by the fact that the member of the Legislature would not share in the fee received thereby." (Opinion 296, Aug. 1, 1959, 45 A.B.A.J. 1272 (1959). The opinion was based upon Canons 26 and 32. Canon 32 provides, in part: "No client, corporate or individual, however powerful, nor any cause, civil or political, however important, is entitled to receive, nor should any lawyer render, any service or advice involving disloyalty to the law whose ministers we are, or disrespect of the judicial office, which we are bound to uphold, or corruption of any person or persons exercising a public office or private trust, or deception or betrayal of the public."

6. Other aspects of the problems raised by Mr. Horsky and Professors Newman and Cohen, which involve fundamental questions about the nature of the legislative process, will be considered again at the close of this chapter.

Section 2

ACTIVITY of OFFICIAL AGENCIES OUTSIDE the LEGISLATURE

WISCONSIN BUREAU OF LABOR AND INDUSTRIAL STATISTICS, THIRTEENTH BIENNIAL REPORT
(1907-1908)

[This Bureau was created in 1883. The first commissioner of labor statistics made no attempt to enforce the labor laws on the books, but confined his activities to the collection of statistics. Subsequent legislation grudgingly added to the Bureau a deputy, some clerks, and a number of factory inspectors, and the effort to enforce factory safety legislation became important in the work of the Bureau. In 1907 the Commissioner of the Bureau was Hon. J. D. Beck, who was later one of the first members of the Industrial Commission, established to administer workmen's compensation and other labor legislation. Pages 1-143 of the 1907 Report of the Bureau were devoted to a factual study of the problem of industrial accidents in Wisconsin, based primarily upon accident statistics for the two years, October 1, 1905-October 1, 1907, the first period under the first Wisconsin legislation providing for the report and collection of accident statistics (L. 1905, ch. 416). A footnote at the opening of this report acknowledges the "invaluable assistance" of Professor John R. Commons in its preparation. The following passage is the "General Summary and Conclusions" which closed the Report on Industrial Accidents.—Editor]

A. *Summary*

1. *Statistics of Accidents.* Wisconsin physicians are requested to report accidents as they do births and deaths. These reports, while not complete, give valuable information regarding all classes of accidents. In the year ending October 1907, 13,571 accidents were reported, of which 53 per cent happened to workmen while at work. These reports show clearly the effect of the development of modern industrial methods on the number of accidents. The growing importance of industrial as distinguished from railway accidents is shown by the statistics of cases in the Supreme Court of Wisconsin.

2. *Money Cost of Accidents.* The money aspect of industrial accidents is considered in three aspects: (1) *To the state,* the cost of settling cases cannot on the whole be considered excessive, but the cost per case is large compared with the cost under a system of workmen's insurance. (2) *To the employer,* the cost of the existing system varies with the industry but averages from five-tenths to six-tenths of one per cent on the wage bill and from $2.50 to $2.80 per man per annum. This is chiefly for liability insurance premiums. Less than half of this money reaches the victims of accident. As explained in chapter III, the amount now spent by employers probably would, with an economical administration of funds, pay considerable relief in every case of accidents to employees, regardless of negligence. This consideration is confirmed by a study of rates charged by in-

surance companies in England under the workmen's Compensation Act of 1897. (3) *To the workman*, a study of individual cases shows that the instances of positive financial distress resulting from accidents are numerous, and seldom are the damages collected adequate. It is plain that workmen ought to carry accident insurance.

3. *Liability Insurance*. There has been a remarkable development in the business of insuring employers against claims resulting from accidents. Collective workmen's insurance has made little progress. A study of employers' liability policies shows one interesting condition: One of the companies permits the employer to make immediate payments (within limits) according to his own judgment, and then reimburses him up to 80 per cent of what he has paid out.

4. *Mutual Aid Societies*. An account is given of twelve mutual aid societies in Wisconsin, but the development is slight.

5. *Opinions of Employers and Federation of Labor*. There is a variety of opinions among employers. Some do more than is now required by law and would welcome a system of workmen's compensation.

The State Federation of Labor wishes some system that will give certain and definite compensation in all cases, but thinks the state should bear the burden, by means of a tax on industries according to the hazard.

6. *Wisconsin Legislation*. The modifications in the common law in Wisconsin indicate that the employers' defenses will be still further weakened in the future unless some system of workmen's insurance is adopted. This would mean higher rates to be charged by the liability companies.

7. *Foreign Systems*. Foreign countries have very generally provided insurance for workmen in case of accidents. A summary is given of the English, German and French systems.

B. *Proposed Reforms: I. The Prevention of Accidents*

It is more important to prevent accidents than to compensate the injury. In addition to being compelled to provide safe appliances and ways, employers should be supported in enforcing reasonable rules for doing the work, and employees should be constantly warned regarding the kinds of accidents that experience has shown are likely to happen. A special bulletin on the prevention of accidents is now being prepared. But when all that is possible has been done, there will still be many accidents.

[B. *Proposed Reforms:*] *II. The Compensation for Accidents*

1. *The Burden of Compensation*. No one will deny that when a man is injured he needs money. Where shall he get it:

(1) The answer of Great Britain: The British Parliament has said, the employer must pay damages to every one of his workmen who is injured.

(2) The answer of Germany: Germany compels its workers to be provident. The workman must contribute to an old age and sick insurance fund, and the latter

includes disability for accidents for 13 weeks. But the cost of insuring the workman further against accidents falls solely upon the employer.

(3) The answer of France: The employer must pay a specified compensation in practically all cases of injury.

(4) The burden rests entirely upon the employer in all of the following additional countries: Belgium, British Columbia, Cape of Good Hope, Denmark, Finland, Italy, Netherlands, New Zealand, Norway, Queensland, Russia, South Australia, Spain, Sweden, Western Australia.

(5) The burden is divided but rests largely on employers in the following additional countries: Austria, Greece, Hungary, Luxemburg.

(6) In the United States the workman must rely largely on his own savings, or personal insurance, or on the charity of employer, the public, or fellow workmen, because in the majority of cases, the employer cannot be proved negligent.

2. *Considerations For and Against Putting the Burden of all Accidents on the Employer.* (1) The experience of other countries seems to indicate that this is a practicable way of solving the problem.

(2) Some people are troubled by the proposal to give a man compensation when he has been negligent. But suppose you carry an accident policy and are negligent in stepping from a street car. Do you not expect the insurance company to pay? If you negligently overturn a lamp and your house burns, do you not expect the fire insurance company to pay? That is what insurance is for—to guard against the slips and mistakes that are characteristic of human nature. In cases of gross violation of rules, an exception might be made.

Before granting a pension do we ask whether a man used due care in dodging the bullets, or do we plead that he voluntarily assumed the risk? Then why, when a man courageously volunteers to do the dangerous work in transportation, mining, building, etc., should it seem wrong to grant him or his dependents compensation in case of accidents? The workers of our industrial army should be insured.

(3) Would workmen feign incapacity if compensation were certain? A manager of one of the prominent liability companies of England (Mrs. S. Stanley Brown) says that this is not a serious objection to the English law. Fraud must be contended against in fire and every other kind of insurance.

(4) Would the burden be a handicap in interstate competition? That depends entirely on the amount of benefits allowed under the insurance system. If $20,000 were allowed for every death and other payments in proportion, the burden might be seriously felt. But one state could begin such a reform alone if moderate benefits only were allowed.

(5) The industry is responsible for more than half the accidents, and putting the burden on the employers is, to the extent that they can shift that burden to the consumer in the shape of higher prices, one way of making the industry responsible. All of the burden may not be shifted, but is exact justice ever attainable?

(6) It is sometimes said that another way of making the industry bear the burden would be to have each workingman demand sufficiently high wages before entering a hazardous industry, and then buy his own accident insurance. As a

matter of fact workingmen do not succeed in doing this to any great extent at present. It may be said, however, that no system of compensation removes the duty on the part of the workingman to provide against accidents; the compensation which the employer would be asked to pay will not pay more than the barest necessities during incapacity from work; there always will be the desirability of having the workingman take out additional insurance at his own expense.

(7) Granted that as a general rule we should not make one person pay money for the benefit of another, are there not many exceptions? The Legislature has many times in the past put employers to expense for the sake of the public welfare. Factory inspectors are constantly ordering employers to introduce safety devices, sometimes at a high cost to the employer. No one seriously questions the propriety of the policy, and yet this expenditure is largely for the immediate good of the laborer, not of the employer. It has been argued that if it is fair to say to the employer, you shall not engage in a dangerous business unless you are willing to guard your machinery, it is also fair to say to the employer, you shall not engage in a dangerous business unless you are willing to pay for accidents which will inevitably or probably happen to any reasonably careful body of men whom you employ. This is not altogether convincing. To guard machinery is absolutely essential to prevent accidents, and public welfare demands such prevention. But is burdening the employer the only and necessary way to compensate for accidents?

(8) Would it be constitutional to require all employers to compensate for all injuries? Freund, in his work on the Police Power, (Sec. 634) has pointed out a line of argument according to which absolute liability might be held constitutional. Further, the Supreme Court of Wisconsin has upheld absolute liability regardless of negligence when imposed as a penalty. In Quackenbush, Adm'x vs. W.&M.R.R.Co., (62 Wis. 411, and 71 Wis. 472) a statute was upheld which made railroad companies absolutely liable for damages occasioned to a person or animal by want of a fence, reversing a previous decision in Curry v. C.&N.W.Ry.Co., (43 Wis. 665) which in turn had reversed earlier cases. Whether such liability would be constitutional when not imposed as a penalty, is certainly doubtful. This is a question for the lawyers. If such an act would be unconstitutional, an amendment to the State Constitution would not avail, because the Federal Constitution also protects property.

(9) The certain payment of definite compensation by the employer would deprive the individual workingman of the chance which he now has of obtaining very large damages. But, on the other hand, under present conditions, workingmen, taken as a whole, have no chance of obtaining adequate compensation; they have the certainty of obtaining inadequate compensation; they get less than half the money the employer pays out, and what they do get is not distributed either according to needs or merit.

As explained in the introduction, it may not appear logical to make the employer pay in all cases if we assume that every man is to be held responsible only for the consequences of his own conduct; but most countries seem to regard it as expedient to do so. Shall we follow suit?

3. *A Solution Adapted to American Conditions.* The views of those who think

our present law of negligence is inherently just and of those who think we should follow the modern European practice, are both given consideration in the following suggested principle: Let the employer contribute an amount which he probably would have to pay if he continued with the law of negligence, release him from liability to damage suits, and then distribute that money on the insurance principle, the employee being encouraged to carry as much additional insurance as he could. This contains nothing of class legislation, charity or confiscation.

4. *What Would Be the Cost if We Continued with the Law of Negligence?* Employers' liability insurance costs now in Wisconsin from 12 cents per $100 of wages in knitting mills to at least $9.00 in some building operations—an average of 50 or 60 cents. But it is very probable that this expense would be increased in the near future by weakening the defense of the employer in the courts. In the railroad industry, the fellow servant doctrine has been abolished in this state, and the doctrine of contributory negligence has been seriously modified. Similar modifications are practically inevitable for other hazardous industries if the present system of liability is retained. That means that the liability companies will charge more and more for a liability policy. But in addition where there is no legal liability, employers are appealed to for charity.

One absurdity of our present law is that it says: A railroad brakeman cannot wholly be barred from compensation by the defense of contributory negligence, but a structural steel worker or a worker in a sewer (both in very hazardous employments) can be debarred from compensation by that defense. The reason for this is that the accidents in the railroad industry were the first to attract attention. But that other classes of accidents are now relatively more important, is shown by the following analysis of Wisconsin Supreme Court cases involving claims by injured workmen against their employers. Before 1890, three-fourths were railway cases; since 1890, less than one-fourth are railway cases.

5. *What Could Be Paid with this Money if Distributed on the Insurance Principle?* The cost of the present system would be sufficient to inaugurate a general system of compensation if properly administered. The following estimate, which has been explained in Chapter III, is made on the basis of Wisconsin accident statistics:

To pay regardless of negligence for each fatal industrial accident three times the annual earnings, and for non-fatal accidents one-half wages during disablement after the second week up to one year, together with an additional payment of $500, or less according to the degree of the injury, to those permanently injured, and for all cases first medical aid, would cost at a maximum as follows for manufacturing establishments reported in the Federal Census of 1905 for Wisconsin:

Fatal accidents at three years' earnings	$164,290.80
Non-fatal during total disability for one year after	
the first two weeks at one-half wages	83,880.37
Permanent disability-additional	150,125.00
Medical fees, first aid at $5.00 per case	20,525.00
Administrative (15 per cent)	73,909.62
Total	$492,730.79

This would be approximately 68.9 cents per $100 of the wages bill or $.325 per man per annum, employed, on an average. In some industries it would be less and in some more. If these same manufacturers had been insured at existing employers' liability rates, the cost would have been about $416,204.61, which is 58 cents per $100 of wages of $2.75 per man per annum. That this last estimate is a reasonable one, appears from the following (explained in detail in chapter III): The bureau received reports from 540 establishments regarding their expenses on account of industrial accidents and wages in the year 1906. The result shows an average expense of from 53 cents to 58 cents per $100 of wages on the wages bill, and from $2.50 to $2.80 per man employed. The difference between the two estimates of $492,730 and $416,204 is not enough to prevent the adoption of a system of workmen's compensation on the ground of expense.

6. *Moderate Compulsory Liability or a Voluntary Cooperative Insurance Fund?*
(1) Compulsory liability. The preceding suggestions would be substantially carried out by the English system with the scale of benefits paid under the act of 1897. This would mean that little further governmental machinery would be necessary. The law would make employers in certain occupations liable for a given amount of damages in case of accidents to their employees without regard to ordinary negligence or assumption of risk, and employers would insure themselves as at present with employers' liability insurance companies. There are two objections to this plan: first, as already suggested, it may be unconstitutional, and second, it would retain the wasteful system of employers' liability insurance under competitive conditions.

(2) A voluntary cooperative insurance fund. Another plan for embodying the preceding suggestions would be as follows: Employers and employees would be allowed to make a contract whereby the employer would be relieved of the liability for damage suits on account of industrial accidents to his employees on condition that he paid into a fund, to be managed by the State Insurance Commissioner, or some special commission, an annual payment about equal to the present cost of employers' liability insurance in his industry. From this fund workingmen who had entered the scheme would receive a benefit (specified by law) in case of injury regardless of negligence (except in case of gross misconduct) without making any contribution themselves.

The state could probably not guarantee the fund without an amendment to the constitution. In other respects such a solution of the problem would be similar to the Illinois Commission plan, explained in the appendix. It would, however, have some advantages over that plan. The expenses of administration would probably be less because part of the administrative work could be borne by the state. Considering the public advantages of such a system, the state could very properly contribute something in this way indirectly. It would give the state more complete information regarding accidents than if it simply asked private companies for reports. Direct state supervision of this kind would inspire confidence and would guarantee fairness in the rates charged.

A clear advantage over the Illinois plan is that the conduct of liability insurance by private companies has proved excessively wasteful. As explained in chapter

III, they charge about two and one-half times as much as they pay out in losses. The plan here outlined could certainly be managed for much less than that. The administrative expenses of the German accident insurance system as already stated are now 13.50 per cent of total expenditure, and probably will be less in the future; and the experience of Wisconsin local fire mutuals indicates that the administrative expenses of the fund need not be more than 15 or 20 per cent.

To promote economy and speed in settlement, use might be made of the device employed by the Ocean and Accident Guarantee Corporation, elsewhere fully explained, whereby the employer might settle all small cases immediately according to his own interpretation of the law, and be reimbursed from the insurance fund up to 80 or 90 per cent of what he paid out.

7. *How the Workman May Be Encouraged to Provide for Himself.* It might be made a part of the conditions of the organization of the mutual insurance fund mentioned in the preceding section, that workmen who paid additional premiums (either directly or by having them deducted from their wages) into this fund, should receive additional benefits.

Or it might be advisable to separate these two features, and organize a system of workingmen's accident insurance on the plan now being tried for life insurance and annuities in Massachusetts, through the efforts of Mr. Louis D. Brandeis. The plan is as follows:

By an Act of the Massachusetts legislature in 1907, savings banks are permitted to established departments for the issue of life insurance. These departments (two of which have been organized at the present time) are to be conducted at a minimum expense, no solicitors being allowed. The waste in industrial insurance as now conducted by private companies is very great. It is the thought of this Massachusetts plan to supply good insurance at a low price to those who want it. It is only when such an opportunity is offered that one can reasonably adopt the principle of "let each man look out for himself."

Similarly the attitude, frequently expressed, "Let each man buy his own accident insurance in the same way that he buys his fire insurance," will only then be a reasonable one when the workingman is given an opportunity to buy this article without feeling that he is being robbed.

8. *Conclusion.* The foregoing considerations made inevitable the conclusion that the existing method of settling the claims arising out of accidents to workingmen while at work can be greatly improved. In some manner we should introduce the idea of insurance, which practically disregards the idea of negligence. Perhaps it would be best first to test the constitutionality of making all employers liable to moderate benefits, amounting on an average to about as much as they would pay under the present system, in all cases of accidents, and then releasing them from the liability to damage suits when these benefits have been paid. But if this is inadvisable, it would be desirable to have permissive legislation, as outlined in preceding sections, combining the idea of encouraging cooperation between employers and employees, state supervision of insurance funds to guarantee fairness, and the opportunity for workingmen to provide adequately for themselves.

In fact, a number of bills might be passed, each capable of standing alone, yet supplementing the others. Such bills would be in substance as follows: (1) Extend the law regarding the railway industry given on page 84 (ch. 254, L. of 1907) to other employments; (2) Give the workmen the option of proceeding under the law of negligence or under a law of compulsory liability that disregards negligence, but not under both; (3) Provide for a voluntary cooperative insurance fund as above outlined; (4) Require complete reports from employers' liability insurance companies. The combining and choosing of these plans is the work of the legislator.

NOTES AND QUESTIONS ON THE ROLE OF EXECUTIVE AND ADMINISTRATIVE AGENCIES IN THE LEGISLATIVE PROCESS

1. Compare, once again, the data upon which legislative law-making is based with the data relied upon in judicial law-making and the sources of data available in each of the law-making processes.

2. Did the Wisconsin Bureau of Labor and Industrial Statistics exceed the limits of its authority in making the foregoing report? Sec. 1021 (e) of the Wis. Stats. 1898, the organic act of the Bureau at the time the report was published, provided: "Said commissioner [of labor and industrial statistics] shall collect, collate and publish statistical and other information relating to the manufacturing interests, industrial classes and material resources of the state; he shall especially examine into the relations between labor and capital, the means of escape from, and the protection of life and health in, factories and workshops, the employment of children, the number of hours of labor exacted from them and from women, the educational, sanitary, moral and financial condition of laborers and artisans, the cost of food, fuel, clothing and building material, the causes of strikes and lockouts, and other kindred subjects pertaining to the welfare of the industrial interests and classes."

3. Administrative and executive agencies do not confine themselves to the writing of official reports proposing new legislation. They advise the Chief Executive in the preparation of his messages to the legislature recommending new legislation and in the exercise of his power to approve or veto bills passed by the legislature. They draft new bills on their own; their representatives appear before legislative committees to support or oppose passage of pending measures; they address memoranda to and maintain personal contacts with individual legislators; they make public statements about legislative matters; they seek informally to secure the agreement of affected private interests on the shape of proposed legislation and in this effort often negotiate compromises among these groups which are subsequently embodied in acts of the legislature.

Should the administrative and executive agencies be permitted to engage in the legislative process to this extent?

4. The close relations that developed over the years between the legislature and the various agencies threatened to make it impossible for the Chief Executive to coordinate the legislative policies of his Administration. On the federal level, a system has gradually developed by which all agency proposals for new legislation, agency views on proposed bills originating elsewhere, and agency recommendations for Presidential approval or veto of bills passed by Congress ("enrolled bills") must be cleared through the Bureau of the Budget, acting on the President's behalf. For the best single account of this development, see Neustadt, Presidency and Legislation: Growth of Central Clearance, 48 Am. Pol. Sci. Rev. 641 (1954).

Under its first Director, Charles G. Dawes, the Bureau of the Budget, in 1921, required the clearance only of fiscal legislation. The legal basis for this requirement was found in sec. 206 of the Budget and Accounting Act of 1921 which created the Bureau and forbade the departments to submit requests for appropriations or for increases in appropriations outside the President's budget, except at the request of Congress.

Clearance for non-fiscal, substantive legislation was first required in 1935 at the initiative of President Roosevelt. (Neustadt, *supra* at 648-649). The clearance agency for such legislation was, at first, the National Emergency Council, an enlarged Cabinet group which met from 1933 to 1936 under the President's chairmanship. In 1937, the clearance function was transferred to the Budget Bureau, then in the Treasury Department. In 1939 the Budget Bureau was transferred to the newly established Executive Office of the President. The legal basis for the requirement that non-fiscal legislation be cleared through the Budget Bureau is not statutory, but must be found in the constitutional powers of the President. See Wilkie, Legal Basis for Increased Activities of the Federal Budget Bureau, 11 Geo. Wash. L. Rev. 265 (1943).

So far as agency recommendations to Congress are concerned, the Budget Bureau requires that they be first submitted to it so that the agency may be advised "as to the relationship of the legislation, or of the report or recommendation thereon, to the program of the President." (Budget Circular A-19). Although the agency is not prevented from submitting to Congress a recommendation which is not in accord with the program of the President, it is required to notify the Congressional body or member of the advice it received from the Budget Bureau. In practice, conflicts between an agency and the Budget Bureau are likely to be resolved by appeal to some higher authority in the Executive Office of the President and finally to the President himself.

The Report of the American Political Science Association Committee, previously referred to, states that "Many states now provide similar if less formal clearance through the office of the governor with respect to both fiscal and policy matters"; and urges all states to adopt the practice. Zeller (ed.), American State Legislatures 168 (1954).

5. In its General Interim Report, the House Select Committee on Lobbying Activities likened the legislative activities of the executive and administrative agencies to "those conducted by private groups or lobbyists for private interests" and raised the following questions: "(1) Are such activities so extensive as to abuse our basic separation of powers? (2) Are they financed with funds appropriated for other purposes?" (H. Rep. No. 3138, Pt. V, 81st Cong., 2d Sess. [1950])

In its Final Report, however, the Select Committee rejected the proposal that the Lobbying Act be amended to cover executive officials, pointing out that "Congress, through the proper exercise of its powers to appropriate funds and to investigate conditions and practices of the executive branch, as well as through its financial watchdog, the General Accounting Ofice, can and should remain vigilant against any improper use of appropriated funds and any invasion of the legislative prerogatives and responsibilities of the Congress." (H. Rep. No. 3239, 81st Cong., 2d sess. 36 [1951])

The Republican minority commented as follows on the majority's conclusion: "This is the first time in our memory that a congressional committee has seen fit to defend lobbying by Government. It is a safe prediction that many of the obnoxious practices of Government officials designed to bring pressure on Congress will be intensified as a result of these statements by the majority of the Select Committee. . . ."

Is the majority or minority approach the wiser? What requirements of the Lobbying Act, if any, do you think should be made applicable to government officials? Consider the following provision of the U.S. Criminal Code (18 U.S.C. 1913): "No part of the money appropriated by any enactment of Congress shall, in the absence of express authorization by Congress, be used directly or indirectly to pay for any personal service, advertisement, telegram, telephone, letter, printed or written matter, or other device, intended or designed to influence in any manner a Member of Congress, to favor or oppose, by vote or otherwise, any legislation or appropriation by Congress, whether before or after the introduction of any bill or resolution proposing such legislation or appropriation; but this shall not prevent officers or employees of the United States or of its departments or agencies from communicating to Members of Congress, on the request of any Member or to Congress, through the proper official channels, requests for legislation or appropriations which they deem necessary for the efficient conduct of the public business."

6. Because executive and administrative officials participate so intimately in the legislative process, it has been suggested that the disclosure requirements of the lobbying acts be extended to cover the attempts of private groups to influence executive and administrative recommendations to the legislature. The House Select Committee on Lobbying Activities proposed that Congress authorize investigations of such private activity. (H. Rept. No. 3138 at 35). And in its 1951 report on Ethical Standards in Government, the (Douglas) Subcommittee of the Senate Committee on Labor and Public Welfare (p. 35) suggested that any person spending more than $10,000 a year in connection with representation before the executive and administrative agencies of the federal government be required to file details concerning the expenditures with the agency involved.

7. Gross tries to dispel the impression that a vast "Executive bureaucracy" has such great powers and influence that "the President can use it to dominate Congress and obtain whatever legislation he wants." (The Legislative Struggle at 104). He points out that no President has even been able to resolve all conflicts among the executive and administrative agencies themselves, some of which, like the Army Corps of Engineers, regard themselves as more responsible to Congress, or even to the private groups actively supporting their programs, than to the President. (Ibid.) We shall have further occasion to consider other limitations of Presidential control over administrative agencies in Part 3.

8. What use, if any, should reasonably be made of the foregoing report of the Wisconsin Bureau of Labor and Industrial Statistics in litigation attacking the constitutionality of the Workmen's Compensation Act ultimately passed?

9. What influence, if any, should the agency's participation in the process by which the statute it is administering became law have upon the attitude of the courts in cases contesting the agency's interpretation of the statute?

AUTOBIOGRAPHY OF ROUJET D. MARSHALL; THE LEGISLATIVE ROLE OF A "STRONG" JUDGE

[Hon. Roujet D. Marshall was a member of the Supreme Court of Wisconsin from 1895 to 1918. He wrote the opinion of the Court in Hartford v. Northern Pacific R.R. Co., reprinted in Chapter 9 above. The following passage is from Volume II of Mr. Justice Marshall's Autobiography (1931) 53. The footnotes are comments of Mr. Gilson G. Glasier, the editor of the autobiography, which was published after Mr. Justice Marshall's death.—Editor]

I think I am safe in claiming to have been largely the exciting cause of the establishment of the workmen's compensation law, a law which has saved more of public and private expense than any other that has ever been enacted in our state. . . .

By my efforts the following was, in 1909, made a part of the Governor's message to the legislature:

"*Industrial Accidents.* The problem of how to deal with the multitude of personal injuries incident to our industrial life challenges our attention. It is of such vast importance as to equal any subject dealt with by the law-making power in recent years, or waiting for legislative action. The present system which casts the entire burden upon the employer and relegates the injured to the courts for redress seems unadapted to modern conditions. At great public expense, and depressing, if not crushing, consequences to employers, it furnishes but partial returns to a small fraction of the injured ones for losses sustained. The cost in the aggregate is enormous. By the operation of economic laws, the whole burden, in the ultimate, by the increased cost of living, lessening of wages and opportunity for employment, finds its way on an ever ascending grade to a resting place upon the back of labor, moving the individuals of the most helpless class toward or over the boundary between comfort and want.

"To remedy the situation described, by a progressive course of casting the whole burden upon employers, tends to render opportunity for employment less and less as the burden increases. Such a course must, inevitably, in time, while benefiting the few to a small per cent of the total outlay, leave the greater number of unfortunates remediless, and move the whole nearer and nearer the point of capability for mere existence above the level of actual want.

"While the weakest and so most helpless, should be objects of the most earnest solicitude, it must not be lost sight of that, unless gainful occupations from the standpoint of employers is reasonably attractive, opportunity for employment will grow less, to the great detriment of the public at large.

"Every personal injury to an employe, not self-inflicted, is an involuntary contribution to the cost of production and distribution of those things administering to human needs and to the legitimate enjoyment of life. Why should that offering in any case be to the loss of the one least able to bear it? If it be left by law to rest where it first falls, will not the higher natural law move it on to be borne by the public at large, as suggested? Does not one's humanity rebel against a system which does so little for the unfortunate, and does that little with such waste?

"During the year 1909, judging from official records, we may expect 10,000 accidents to wage-earners in Wisconsin that will incapacitate them from work for an average period of four weeks each, which is equal to the full time of over 750 men. More than this, it is probable that 250 of these 10,000 accidents will be fatal. This, added to the 750 makes a total loss of the wages of 1,000 men per year. Based upon the average annual wage rate of $500 each, this means a loss of $500,000 yearly to wage-earners and those depending upon them, to say nothing about the loss in producing power (which, no doubt, amounts to a much larger sum) and the cost in court expenses to the taxpayers of the state arising out of the damage suits.

"When one sees that the nations of the Old World have dealt with this subject generally, and, in some cases, with most gratifying success during the past quarter of a century, he can but view with something akin to astonishment that so little has been done here, and that little has been wholly in the direction of increasing the burdens of employers, a course which in the most advanced of the older nations, was long ago abandoned as illogical and inefficient.

"Should not losses by personal injuries be laid, by some workable plan of mutual contribution, upon the whole body of the employers, the employees, and the public thus repairing, to the maximum of practicability, the individual misfortune, and minimizing the individual loss; if that should be done, then how best to do it, under our wise constitutional system, is the most inviting field for legislative study and action of the day. Humanity, and economic prosperity, as well, appeals for the best efforts of the best minds on this question. I most earnestly commend it to your consideration as a question of first importance." [1]

In 1910, largely through my efforts, the following clause was inserted in the State Republican platform: [The plank already reprinted is here quoted.—Editor] That was inspired by an independent opinion which I wrote.[2]

The incidents referred to made the enactment of a workmen's compensation law a matter of Republican political policy. They were followed by the appointment of a joint legislative committee at the first session of the legislature afterwards to consider the subject and report at the next session with a bill for a proposed law.

In the meantime I did all I properly could in an educational way to promote the movement. I did the rather extraordinary thing of indirectly addressing the legislature in writing opinions. I deemed the necessity for action so great that extraordinary methods of promotion were legitimate. It had come to pass that a great part of the time of all our courts was taken up with personal injury litigation and without any substantial gain to those who prevailed. The public and private waste was something enormous and was progressive in amount. The only way to meet it justly, to my mind, was a workingmen's compensation system which had been tried successfully in many countries, particularly in Germany.

While the question of adopting a workmen's compensation system was under consideration as indicated, I wrote the opinion in Houg v. Girard Lumber Company, 144 Wis. 337, (decided Jan. 10, 1911). It was a very distressing case in which, on legal grounds, the Court was compelled to reverse the judgment of the court below and remand the case with directions to dismiss the complaint, leaving the plaintiff remediless. Such course was necessary as the law stood. I could not part with the case without an appeal to the law-making power to do what the Court was powerless to do. I thought to thus stimulate legislative action and have the public appreciate that the fault was in the law; that the Court could not disregard judicial duty through sympathy, and it was too bad to permit a condition to remain which, through want of appreciation of judicial duty by the public,

---

[1] Wisconsin Senate Journal, 1909, p. 37. While this is a part of Governor Davidson's message to the Legislature, it is substantially Judge Marshall's language as anyone familiar with his style will readily recognize. Mr. Arthur A. McLeod, formerly Clerk of the Supreme Court, was then Marshall's secretary, and wrote this portion of the message at the Judge's dictation, personally taking it to the Governor's office. It was dictated by Judge Marshall at the Governor's request.

[2] It is believed that Judge Marshall here refers to an independent opinion which he wrote in the case of Monaghan v. Northwestern Fuel Co., 140 Wis. 457, 465, handed down in October, 1909. . . .

was constantly bringing criticism upon the Court, whose duty it was to stand guard over the law as it found it regardless of criticism. This situation was rapidly taking a political cast in the form of opposition to judges who were only performing their sworn duty. In that state of mind, after writing the opinion of the Court, I stepped aside and made this appeal:

"As the writer rests from speaking the foregoing for the Court, may he not, appropriately and beneficially, soliloquize briefly upon the law's uncharitableness with distressing losses like that here treated.

"Why should not such inevitable incidents of activities upon which all depend to satisfy demands of legitimate human desire be laid at once upon the subjects of consumption, where they must in the end inevitably go for final liquidation? Why not with a minimum of anguish instead of with the maximum thereof? Is is not for the whole, indirectly toiled for, but removed in general from the zone of danger, as well as those who present their bodies to the peril, that the latter be so? If so, why should an element as to either, involving no moral turpitude, be the deciding factor as to whether the one or the other shall be irreparably impaired? And moreover, why irreparably impaired at all, crushing human ambition, human hope, and human life as well? Why should not the sacrifices for all be taken at once as the burdens of all; not scattering by the way human wrecks to float as derelicts for a time, increasing the first cost till the accumulation disappears from view in the world of consumable things? Such losses, starting immediate victims,—particularly the weakest and humblest and often the most indispensable of them—to a lower level, go on by trackless ways till, enhanced by transition over the long road, the whole, disseminated so broadly as to be at last unappreciable, comes to rest as noiselessly, imperceptibly, and certainly as moves the 'breath of the summer night',—upon and is absorbed in, increasing the cost of subjects of human desire, there to be accounted for at the full money equivalent by the exchanges incident to consumption. Is not this a verity? Why then cannot such inevitable end occur without the added loss and arbitrary classification by which the majority of those who feel the misfortune most deeply, are not compensated at all, and the rest only by transfer in each instance to one engaged with the bodily sufferer in mutuality of general purpose and mutuality of risk from inadvertences which can only be minimized according to the degree of natural infirmities of the mutual actor? The courts cannot answer. They do not make the law. They only execute it and must do that with fidelity and with care without sympathy or fear or favor. Only the law-making power can answer. At its door lies the duty to do so, and will lie any sin there may be in not laboring to that end. To there in increasing volume points and will continue to point unrequited sorrow till there shall be a remedy. If these words shall help to render humanity's petition effective they will not have been spoken in vain."

I think these words sank deeply and efficiently into the legislative mind. They were read on the floor of the Senate at the final passage of the present workmen's compensation law, and will continue to influence legislative action long after the writer shall have been forgotten. . . .

NOTES AND QUESTIONS

1. In a subsequent chapter of Volume II of the Autobiography, written by Mr. Winter Everett, Mr. Everett remarks that "From the first, Judge Marshall was in close touch with this committee [the committee of the legislature named to study compensation] and from the writer's knowledge, it can almost be said that he practically acted as general counsel for the committee." [p. 242] "As a matter of fact there was hardly a clause in the law which was not gone over very carefully by Judge Marshall and upon which his opinion was not obtained, . . ."

2. Do you think it was proper for Justice Marshall to engage in these various activities to promote a workmen's compensation law? Does his concern for the good name of the judicial branch of government justify his efforts? Was it proper for the Justice subsequently to participate in the decision of the Wisconsin Supreme Court on the constitutionality of the workmen's compensation act?

3. Justices of the United States Supreme Court have, throughout the years, accepted a variety of "extra-curricular" assignments but doubt has always been expressed about the propriety of their doing so. See Mason, Harlan Fiske Stone: Pillar of the Law 704-719 (1956). In recent times, President Roosevelt drew upon the services of Justice Byrnes for assistance with war-time legislation and appointed Justice Roberts to head the commission of inquiry into the disaster at Pearl Harbor. (Id. at 707) President Truman named Justice Jackson as American Prosecutor at the Nuremberg War Crimes Trials, to the great displeasure of Chief Justice Stone. (Id. at 714-719) Chief Justice Stone himself declined President Roosevelt's request that he head a study of the nation's rubber supply and recommend ways of handling it. (Id. at 709-712) The Chief Justice also deflected a move to make him chairman of a War Ballot Commission or the designator of its members. (Id. at 713-714) He also rejected President Truman's invitation to head a committee on traffic safety. (Ibid.) Professor Mason reprints the Chief Justice's letters of refusal to President Roosevelt and Senator Vandenberg (concerning the War Ballot Commission) which he thinks "may, in time, become classic injunctions against extra-judicial service for members of the Supreme Court." (Id. at 720, 710-711, 713-714) It is interesting, in considering Justice Marshall's activities, that Stone wrote to President Roosevelt: "I assume that I would have no occasion to pass upon proposals involving questions of constitutional power or other questions which would be subject to review by the courts. That, of course, would be plainly inadmissible." (Id. at 710)

4. Consider again what limitations upon judicial law-making prevented the Wisconsin Supreme Court from so molding legal doctrine—in the absence of legislation—as to achieve the objectives of the workmen's compensation act.

5. Justice Marshall's efforts also indicate the crucial role a single individual can still play in the promotion of a particular piece of legislation. A most notable recent example is the heroic effort of Raphael Lemkin to obtain the adoption and ratification of the Genocide Convention by the nations of the world.

Section 3

ACTIVITY of the LEGISLATURE

EDITORIAL NOTE: The INTRODUCTION, SPONSORSHIP, and AUTHORSHIP of BILLS

Years before a measure reaches the stage at which there is sufficient support actively behind it to insure serious consideration, the legislative trend may be discernible in the evidence of bills introduced. Every legislative chamber keeps an official Journal in which one may find a list and an index of bills introduced at each session, and a history of the disposition of the bills. To find the text of bills introduced but not passed, one may learn the official number of the bill from the Journals, and then may locate the text of the bill by number in the bound volumes of bills introduced, which are kept by some agency in every state. For bills introduced in Congress, the Library of Congress will generally be found the most helpful source of information, though much is available in some of the better-equipped state libraries.

Thus an important part of the evidence of the consideration and efforts given to the development of a compensation act in Wisconsin may be found in the leading bills introduced on the subject. Bill 549A, 1905 (drawn by Mr. Charles McCarthy, of the Legislative Reference Library along lines favored by the Wisconsin State Federation of Labor, and introduced by Assemblyman Frederick Brockhausen; defeated after an unfavorable recommendation by the assembly committee); Bill 161A, 1907 (similar bill, under the same sponsorship, unfavorably recommended by committee, and defeated in the assembly); Bill 18A, 1909 (same sponsorship); Bill 189S, 1909 (sponsored by Senator Brazeau; neither this nor 18A received much consideration, due to the decision to turn the matter over to the legislative committee specially appointed to deal with the subject).

Wisconsin, incidentally, was a pioneer state in the creation of legislative reference services, now utilized by 44 states. (The Book of the States, 1952-53, pp. 114-124). "Although legislative research is the primary and most universal function of these agencies, bill drafting, statutory revision, the publication of analyses, summaries, and reports dealing with legislative and other subjects of interest to legislators, and providing a general information service for citizens are among the services rendered by a number of them" (Zeller, ed., American State Legislatures 143 [1954]). However, the practice of having bills drafted by a private attorney employed by the interest group has not completely disappeared with the creation of these services. This is true also on the federal level where both the Senate and the House have available the bill drafting services of the Office of Legislative Counsel.

It is important to separate the question of sponsorship and authorship of a bill; only a Senator or Representative can sponsor a bill in Congress but obviously few Congressmen actually draft the bills they introduce. Sponsorship carries with it a certain amount of personal responsibility; but some sponsors may regard responsibility lightly while others regard it as compelling them to assume leadership of the struggle for the bill's passage. (See Gross, The Legislative Struggle 180-185 [1953]). So far as authorship is concerned, Woodrow Wilson's observation is often cited approvingly, that legislation is a composite production whose precise origins and shaping factors cannot be isolated. (Wilson, Congressional Government 320 [1925]). Even after intensive research, it may be impossible to trace the source of an important legislative idea. Thus it has been said that though Stephen Bailey's history of the Employment Act of 1946 (Congress Makes A Law (1950)) was probably the most extensive attempt to trace the origins of a bill, Bailey had failed to discover the exact source of the proposal for a Council of Economic Advisers. (Gross, The Legislative Struggle 187 [1953]). You will find, after reading all of this chapter, that it is equally impossible to give a precise, straight-forward answer to the question "Who wrote the Wisconsin Workmen's Compensation Act?"

What Chamberlain wrote of the genesis of the New Deal legislation is probably true of most legislation: "Most of the great mass of regulatory legislation of the past decade, popularly dubbed New Deal legislation, had a well-defined prenatal history extending back several years before it was espoused by the Roosevelt administration. This is true not only of the more conventional fields such as banking, railroads, and taxation, but of the newer areas of social security, holding company regulation, and securities control. Congressional attention to these new fields had not been absent prior to the time the President made his specific recommendations. The normal process has been fairly uniform: an initial reference by one or a few individuals, then a gradually increasing volume of comment accompanied by numerous specific proposals coming from widely divergent sources. In some cases legislation results in a very short time, but more frequently the initial flurries of interest will subside, to be revived from time to time until finally culminating, perhaps with the help of the President, in a law. The long germination period detectable in the genesis of most laws is of the utmost importance: it constitutes one of the most valuable contributions that a legislative body can make." (Lawrence H. Chamberlain, The President, Congress and Legislation 462-463 [1946]).

QUESTIONS

1. What use, if any, can reasonably be made of the fact that a line of bills has been introduced on a particular subject and considered over a period of years, when the constitutionality of the act ultimately passed is subject to attack?

2. What use can be made of such a line of bills in litigation involving the interpretation of the act ultimately passed?

AN ACT relating to the committees of the legislature appointed to investigate the subjects of water powers, industrial insurance, the income tax, additional security for depositors in state banks, and state aid in the construction of highways and making an appropriation therefor.

WHEREAS, The legislature has by a joint resolution provided for five joint committees of the legislature to investigate the subjects of the control of water powers by the state and granting of franchises for the same, and the expediency of imposing a charge therefor, industrial insurance, the income tax, additional security for depositors in state banks and state aid in the construction of highways.

The people of the state of Wisconsin, represented in senate and assembly; do enact as follows:

Section 1. The committees of the legislature appointed under the provisions of such joint resolution are hereby authorized and empowered to do all things and perform all acts necessary and convenient to carry out the provisions of such resolution and the provisions of this act, and such authorization and power shall continue after the adjournment of this legislature. . . . One of such committees so appointed is hereby authorized thoroughly to investigate the subject of industrial insurance, and to report a bill or bills covering that subject. . . . The mention of any line of inquiry herein shall not in any way limit the field of investigation which each of said committees is empowered to enter upon and which it shall deem expedient in connection with the subject matter assigned to it for consideration.

Section 2. Each of said committees by a majority vote of the members thereof, is hereby vested with plenary powers to perform and discharge the duties by the said resolution and by this act enjoined. Any member of each of said committees shall have power to administer oaths to persons appearing before such committee.

Section 3. Each of said committees shall have power to employ such stenographers, clerks, assistants and experts as it may deem necessary and expedient for the proper discharge of the duties hereby assigned to it, and to fix the compensation of such persons as it shall employ.

Section 4. Each of said committees is authorized to print and send to each member of the legislature at least sixty days before the convening of the special session of the legislature referred to in said resolution, a copy of the proposed bills or bills framed, put together with a copy of the findings and recommendations of such committee.

Section 5. Each of said committees is authorized to hold such meetings at such places and at such dates as it shall deem most expedient.

Section 6. Each member of each of said committees shall be re-imbursed by the state for his actual necessary expenses, but shall receive no compensation for time devoted to the work of such committee.

Section 7. Each of said committees may by subpoena, issued over the signature of the chairman or acting chairman of said committee and served in the manner in which circuit court subpoenas are served, summon and compel the attendance of witnesses and the production of all books, papers, documents and records necessary or convenient to be examined or used by them in the course of the discharge of their duties.

Section 8. If any witness subpoenaed to appear before any said committee shall refuse to appear or to answer inquiries propounded, or shall fail or refuse to produce books, documents, papers, and records, within his possession or control when the same are demanded by said committee, such committee shall report the facts to the circuit court of the county in which such examination is being conducted and it shall be the duty of such court to compel obedience to such subpoena by attachment proceedings for contempt, as in case of disobedience of the requirements of a subpoena issued from such court, or a refusal to testify therein.

Section 9. A sum of money sufficient to carry out the provisions of this act and of the said resolution is hereby appropriated out of any money in the state treasury not otherwise appropriated. All bills for the expenses of any such committee, including witnesses fees, the compensation of stenographers, clerks, assistants and experts employed by each such committee, shall be approved by the committee certified by the chairman thereof and audited by the governor and by the secretary of state, who shall issue his warrant therefor upon the state treasurer.

Section 10. The provisions of this act shall also apply to the committee constituted under joint resolution No. 85, S.

Section 11. This act shall take effect and be in force from and after its passage and publication.

Approved June 17, 1909.

NOTES AND QUESTIONS

1. Provision had also been made for the special committees by Joint Resolution No. 8, Laws, 1909, p. 806. Authorization by statute was given, probably, to avoid any doubt as to the authority of the legislature to authorize by resolution the functioning of a committee after the adjournment of the session. Cf. 22 Op. Atty. Gen. (Wis.) 345; 24 *id.* 672.

2. Does every bill introduced come to the attention of a committee of the kind provided for by Laws 1909, ch. 518? Why such a committee in this case? See Editorial Note which follows.

3. Note the powers and machinery with which the statute endows the committee. Compare the powers of a court and note the provision for co-operation between the committee and the courts.

EDITORIAL NOTE: LEGISLATIVE COMMITTEE ORGANIZATION

In Wisconsin, the "senate has 9 standing committees and 3 procedural committees while the assembly has 23 standing committees. In addition there are 2 joint standing committees and 3 joint statutory committees. With 2 exceptions, appointments to senate committees are made by the senate upon the recommendation of a Committee on Committees, except that assignments of specific members of the minority party are made by the senate group of that party . . . The speaker of the Assembly appoints the committees of that body. Senate rules provide that each member shall serve on at least one of the standing committees, but in the assembly the rules are silent on the distribution of committee assignments, although customarily every member serves on at least one committee . . .

"In addition to the standing committees, special committees may be appointed . . . to study specific problems . . . [and] interim committees [have] functioned between legislative sessions. . . . Since 1947 almost all interim studies have been referred to the Legislative Council which coordinates the entire interim study and investigation program." (Wisconsin Blue Book 283, 285 (1960))

The Report of the American Political Science Association Committee on American Legislatures states: "It is generally recognized that the existing committee system of most state legislatures is poorly constituted to handle the large volume of important legislation." (Zeller (ed.), American State Legislatures 96 [1954]). It recommends, therefore, that (1) the number of standing committees be reduced substantially to a maximum of around 12; (2) each committee be assigned a broad area or related areas of legislation; (3) duplicate or companion committees be established in each house in order to facilitate joint meetings and hearings; (4) the number of committee assignments of members be reduced; (5) committee chairmen and members be selected more carefully, with due recognition of seniority, experience, and political and regional factors; (6) more adequate and competent committee staffs be provided; (7) regular, nonconflicting, and duly publicized schedules for committee meetings and hearings be adopted; (8) adequate committee records be kept; (9) workable discharge rules be established to enable a substantial minority of the house to secure floor consideration of a bill held by a committee beyond a reasonable length of time. (*Ibid.* at 104)

On the federal level, as is true also of the state level, much of the crucial legislative struggle takes place at the committee stage. Those interested in influencing the decisions of the legislature must also be, and are, interested in influencing the selection of personnel for standing committees and for conference committees (i.e., committees considering bills that have been passed in different forms by the two houses), in making a strong showing at committee hearings, and otherwise reaching the ears of committee members.

The Legislative Reorganization Act of 1946 reduced the number of Senate Committees from 33 to 15 and the number of House Committees from 48 to 19, and eliminated a large number of special committees whose jurisdictions conflicted with those of the standing committees. But the Act did not succeed in reducing significantly the total number of subcommittees. While there were 140 subcommittees in Congress immediately prior to the Act, there were 131 in 1950. (Galloway, The Operation of the Legislative Reorganization Act of 1946, 45 Am. Pol. Sci. Rev. 43 (1951)). Subcommittees have traditionally been created by the full committee chairman and do not need to be established by resolution of the full committee. Meyers v. United States, 171 F. 2d 800 (D.C. Cir., 1948), cert. den. 336 U.S. 912 (1949). The Act also specified the exact subject matter within the jurisdiction of each full committee, but did not succeed in eliminating jurisdictional conflict in view of inevitable overlapping and interrelatedness of legislative policies. (Gross, The Legislative Struggle 271 [1953])

The assignment of members of Congress to the various legislative committees is a complex process. Formally, each house elects the members of all its committees. Gross points out, however, that committee assignments are the responsibility of the major political parties, but within the bounds of the Legislative Reorganization Act which limits each Senator to membership on two standing committees and each Representative to membership on only one standing committee. In practice, however, this party function is performed by each party's Committee on Committees in each House. In the case of the Democratic Party in the House, the function of the Committee on Committees is performed by the Ways and Means Committee.

Chairmen of the Committees are chosen on the basis of seniority, a practice which has been severely criticized for tending to concentrate political power in the hands of those who are elected in election after election from constituencies which are free from real political competition, thereby making the chairman often unrepresentative of the trends which may have swept his party into power. (*Ibid.* at 278)

So far as committee staff is concerned, the Legislative Reorganization Act of 1946 authorized every standing committee of Congress to hire up to 4 professional staff members in addition to their clerical staffs. Committees, too, may avail themselves of the services of the Legislative Counsel's Office and the Legislative Reference Service in the Library of Congress. In practice, too, they are served by the staffs of executive agencies and private organizations. In 1950, the combined staff of both Houses, predominantly professional, totaled 673.

Selection of the professional staff members, according to the Legislative Reorganization Act, is "on a permanent basis without regard to political affiliations, and solely on the basis of fitness to perform the duties of the office." For a study of how this provision has actually operated in practice, see Kampelman, The Legislative Bureaucracy: Its Response To Political Change, 16 The Journal of Politics 539 (1954). Dr. Kampelman concludes that

". . . it is ridiculous to expect committee chairmen to surround themselves with staff people who hold views contrary to their own. Similarly, it is expecting the unreasonable to expect them to refrain from calling upon the technicians for assistance during the campaign. Congress is a thoroughly political institution and our government is a partisan government. To talk of experts as though they exist in a vacuum is to do a disservice to the cause of democracy. . . .

"Congress needs a technical staff. It needs a staff able to keep it informed so that it can adequately keep pace with the growth of the executive, which, up until a few years ago, had a near monopoly of expertise. But we destroy the value of experts and make it difficult to impress upon the Congress the need to employ experts, if we fail to recognize the fact that experts have opinions and judgments of their own, and that those personal opinions and judgments must be considered in the selection of experts by the Congress. It may be that the Democratic and Republican ranking members of a committee will agree on a policy. In that case, the same expert can serve both. An illustration of this is the Senate Foreign Relations Committee. It is more likely, however, that the ranking members of a committee will disagree along party lines. In that case, it is essential that both the majority and the minority have staff assistance available to serve their needs. This is as it should be. . . ."

The Legislative Reorganization Act also enlarged the investigating powers of the standing committees. Prior to its enactment "most Congressional investigations were conducted by special committees created for the specific purpose of making the inquiry, entrusted with the power of subpoena and directed to complete their task in a year or two. In 1946, however, each of the fifteen standing committees of the Senate was given the power to compel testimony and authorized [by sec. 134 (a) of the Act] to 'make investigations into any matter within its jurisdiction. . . .' And while the Rules of the House of Representatives authorize only three standing committees to issue subpoenas, that House has not hesitated to direct special investigations by its standing and select committees." (Maslow, Fair Procedure in Congressional Investigations: A Proposed Code, 54 Colum. L. Rev. 839-840 (1954)).

NOTES AND QUESTIONS ON LEGISLATIVE COMMITTEES' POWERS TO COMPEL TESTIMONY AND PRODUCTION OF PAPERS

1. Statutory powers similar to those which, we saw earlier in this section, were granted in 1909 to the special committees, are now vested in all legislative committees by Wis. Stats., 1959, ch. 13.

2. The principal corresponding federal provisions are as follows:

   a. 2 U.S.C. §192: "Every person who having been summoned as a witness by the authority of either House of Congress to give testimony or to produce papers upon any matter under inquiry before either House, or any joint committee established by a joint or concurrent resolution of the two Houses of Congress, or any committee of either House of Congress, wilfully makes default, or who, having appeared, refuses to answer any questions pertinent to the question under inquiry, shall be deemed guilty of a misdemeanor, punishable by a fine of not more than $1000 nor less than $100 and imprisoned in a common jail for not less than one month nor more than twelve months."

   b. 2 U.S.C. §193: "No witness is privileged to refuse to testify to any fact, or to produce any paper, respecting which he shall be examined by either House of Congress, or by any joint committee established by a joint or concurrent resolution of the two Houses of Congress, or by any committee of either House, upon the ground that his testimony to such fact or his production of such paper may tend to disgrace him or otherwise render him infamous."

   c. 2 U.S.C. § 194: "Whenever a witness summoned as mentioned in Section 192 fails to appear to testify or fails to produce any books, papers, records or documents, as required, or whenever any witness so summoned refuses to answer any question pertinent to the subject under inquiry before either House, or any joint committee established by a joint or concurrent resolution of the two Houses of Congress, or any committee or subcommittee of either House of Congress, and the fact of such failure or failures is reported to either House while Congress is in session, or when Congress is not in session, a statement of fact constituting such failure is reported to and filed with the President of the Senate or the Speaker of the House, it shall be the duty of the said President of the Senate or Speaker of the House, as the case may be, to certify, and he shall so certify, the statement of facts aforesaid under the seal of the Senate or House, as the case may be, to the appropriate United States attorney, whose duty it shall be to bring the matter before the grand jury for its action."

d. To insure honest testimony before legislative committees, statutes authorize the prosecution of witnesses who make false statements under oath as perjurers. See, for example, 18 U.S.C. §1621: "Whoever, having taken an oath before a competent tribunal, officer, or person in any case in which a law of the United States authorizes an oath to be administered, that he will testify, declare, depose, or certify truly, or that any written testimony, declaration, deposition, or certificate by him subscribed, is true, willfully and contrary to such oath states or subscribes any material matter which he does not believe to be true, is guilty of perjury, and shall, except as otherwise expressly provided by law, be fined not more than $2000 or imprisoned not more than five years, or both."

e. 2 U.S.C. §191 gives the President of the Senate, the Speaker of the House, a chairman of a committee of the whole, the chairman of any Committee of either House of Congress, and any member of either House of Congress the power to administer oaths to witnesses.

f. Increasingly significant federal provisions deal specifically with the power to compel testimony from witnesses who have claimed the constitutional privilege against self-incrimination. There are a number of "immunity statutes" in various areas of federal investigation and regulation which, in return for the evidence which is compelled by the federal agency in spite of the privilege, confer upon the witness an immunity from prosecution. One of these, 18 U.S.C. 3486, deals with witnesses before Congressional committees, grand juries and courts, in cases relating to the national security or defense. It is discussed in a subsequent Editorial Note in this section.

3. Is a statute or joint resolution necessary to confer the power to investigate upon a legislative committee? What other source of power may it draw upon?

4. Is a statute or joint resolution necessary to give a legislative committee the power to issue subpoenas to compel testimony or the production of papers? What other source of power may it draw upon for this purpose?

5. Must the legislature rely upon the courts to enforce its subpoenas in the event they are disobeyed? In Anderson v. Dunn, 6 Wheat. 204 (U.S., 1821), the Supreme Court held that each House of Congress has an inherent power to punish a recalcitrant witness for contempt by holding him in custody. What is the source of this inherent power? Is such punishment "inherently" a "judicial" function?

The Supreme Court has also indicated, Anderson v. Dunn, *supra* at 231, that the power of the House of Representatives to hold a recalcitrant witness in custody terminates upon adjournment. Because the Senate has been said to be a "continuing body," McGrain v. Daugherty, 273 U.S. 135, 180-82 (1927), its power in this respect may never terminate. In any case, Congress has, in the main, chosen to rely upon the courts to impose punishment for contempt, under the statutes set forth above. Jurney v. MacCracken, 294 U.S. 125 (1935) appears to have been the last time Congress exercised its inherent contempt power.

EDITORIAL NOTE: The LIMITS of LEGISLATIVE INQUIRY and the RIGHTS of WITNESSES before LEGISLATIVE COMMITTEES

The conduct of the post-World War II legislative investigations of subversive activities in the United States has evoked "wide concern, both in and out of Congress, over some aspects of the exercise of the congressional power of investigation."[1] It has been charged that (1) committees are not collecting information for purposes of legislation but are assuming an "informing function" not granted to Congress by the Constitution; (2) committees are functioning primarily as legislative courts to punish individuals by "exposing" them to public scorn; (3) the House Committee on Un-American Activities has compiled, and circulated, indiscriminately, dossiers on about a million Americans based on unevaluated reports of Communist connections; (4) under one pretext or another, private citizens having no connection with any government function have been compelled to make public avowal of their beliefs and associations; (5) individuals and organizations are being condemned on the basis of unsupported accusations and casual associations and contacts; (6) individuals and organizations are being stigmatized without being heard in their own defense; (7) in their quest for sensation, investigating committees have abandoned all sense of fair play and have converted committee hearings into public circuses.[2]

This criticism of the conduct of legislative investigations has brought to the fore once again the questions (a) whether there are and should be any constitutional limits upon the scope of the legislative power to investigate and to compel testimony during investigations; and (b) what are and should be the rights of witnesses before legislative committees. A great deal has been written on these problems in recent years and this note will undertake merely to outline their nature and the judicial approaches to them.[3]

---

[1] Mr. Justice Frankfurter in United States v. Rumely, 345 U.S. 41, 44 (1953).

[2] Maslow, Fair Procedure in Congressional Investigations: A Proposed Code, 54 Colum. L. Rev. 839 (1954).

[3] For more detailed consideration, consult the following writings in addition to others that will be cited in this editorial note: Ehrmann, The Duty of Disclosure in Parliamentary Investigation: A Comparative Study, 11 U. Chi. L. Rev. 1., 117 (1943); Nutting, Freedom of Silence: Constitutional Protection Against Governmental Intrusions in Political Affairs, 47 Mich. L. Rev. 181 (1948); Wyzanski, Standards for Congressional Investigations, 3 The Record of the Association of the Bar of the City of New York (1948); Symposium on Congressional Investigations, 18 U. Chi. L. Rev. 421 (1951); Westin, Do Silent Witnesses Defend Civil Liberties?, 15 Commentary 537 (1953); Fortas, Methods of Committees Investigating Subversion: A Critique, 29 Notre Dame L. Rev. 192 (1954); Newman, The Supreme Court, Congressional Investigations, and Influence Peddling, 33 N.Y.U. L. Rev. 796 (1958); Note, The Power of Congress To Investigate and To Compel Testimony. 70 Harv. L. Rev. 671 (1957).

A. *Are There Any Constitutional Limits Applicable to the Committee's Subject-Matter and Purposes?*

A court is called upon to consider this question only when an individual asks it for relief from punishment sought to be imposed upon him for refusing to answer questions or produce documents as requested. Such punishment may be imposed only when the investigating committee has exercised its power (through the subpoena) to compel disclosure. To date, however, the courts have assumed that the scope of the power to compel disclosure is coextensive with the power to investigate.

It has been argued that the Constitution limits the power to compel disclosure (1) in the course of an investigation into matters of thought, speech, or opinion because the only legislation that could come out of such an investigation would itself violate the rights guaranteed by the First Amendment to the Constitution of the United States or because the particular inquiries on the subject infringe such rights; or (2) if the private affairs of individuals are being investigated; or (3) if the purpose of the investigation is solely to expose individuals to public scorn and obloquy.

1. *The First Amendment.* The First Amendment to the Constitution of the United States commands Congress to "make no law . . . abridging the freedom of speech. . . ." But it cannot be assumed that an investigation into matters of thought, speech, and opinion will necessarily result in legislation violating this Amendment. The legislation ultimately passed might strengthen First Amendment rights or, though abridging them, might nevertheless be upheld by the Supreme Court, which does not view them as absolute.

In any case, only the Supreme Court may determine authoritatively whether an act of Congress is constitutional and only, as we have seen, when called upon to decide a "case or controversy". At the stage of investigation, neither statute nor case exists and discussion of constitutionality can have no meaningful context. Furthermore, even if it could be said that every piece of legislation Congress could possibly devise on the particular subject matter under investigation would be outside the scope of its existing constitutional authority—something almost impossible to imagine—the inquiry may still be in aid of legislation pursuant to Article V of the Constitution, under which Congress by a two-thirds vote of both houses may propose amendments to the Constitution.[4]

However, the manner in which a particular inquiry is conducted may result in the actual, present abridgement of the constitutional rights of particular witnesses. In United States v. Rumely,[5] which we have had occasion to consider in connection with the federal regulation of lobbying, the Supreme Court sustained the reversal by the court below of Rumely's conviction under 2 U.S.C. 192 (which imposes penalties for a refusal to make dis-

---

[4] See, however, Auerbach, The Communist Control Act of 1954: A Proposed Legal-Political Theory of Free Speech, 23 U. Chi. L. Rev. 182-204, particularly 194-195 (1956).

[5] 345 U.S. 41 (1953).

closures "pertinent to the question under inquiry") because the questions Rumely refused to answer were not pertinent to the inquiry which the House Select Committee on Lobbying was authorized to make by Congress.

H. Res. 298, 81st Cong., 1st Sess. (1949) authorized and directed the Select Committee to study and investigate "(1) all lobbying activities intended to influence, encourage, promote, or retard legislation. . . ." This resolution, said the Court, did not authorize the Committee to require Rumely (the Secretary of the Committee for Constitutional Government) to disclose the names and addresses of those who made bulk purchases of the books, pamphlets, and other writings sold by CCG, in order to make possible their further mass distribution.

In reaching this decision, Mr. Justice Frankfurter stated that the Court had "special regard for the principle of constitutional adjudication which makes it decisive in the choice of fair alternatives, that one construction may raise serious constitutional questions avoided by another." Thus the Court implied that if the resolution were read to empower the Committee "to inquire into all efforts of private individuals to influence public opinion through books and periodicals, however remote the radiations of influence which they may exert upon the ultimate legislative process," the resolution *would violate the First Amendment.* Accordingly, the Court construed "lobbying activities" in its "commonly accepted sense" to mean "representations made directly to the Congress, its members, or its committees," and to exclude attempts "to saturate the thinking of the community," with which Chairman Buchanan of the Select Committee charged the CCG.

Justice Douglas wrote a concurring opinion in which Justice Black joined, arguing that (1) H. Res. 298 did give the Select Committee authority to make the inquiry on which the contempt proceeding against Rumely was based but that (2) the resolution for that reason violated the freedoms of speech and press guaranteed by the First Amendment because "once the government can demand of a publisher the names of the purchasers of his publications, the free press as we know it disappears."

The Court also held that the First Amendment rights of Paul Sweezy (including his right to keep silent about his opinions and associations) were violated when the state of New Hampshire sought to punish him for refusing to answer questions. He had refused to talk about his affiliations with the Progressive Party (a political party *not shown to be subversive*) and about a lecture he gave to a class at the University of New Hampshire, other than to say he did not advocate the overthrow of the Government by force or violence.[6]

Similarly, the Court has held that it is unconstitutional for a state court to order the NAACP to disclose the names and addresses of its members in the state.[7] "It is beyond debate," Mr. Justice Harlan held, "that freedom to

[6] Sweezy v. New Hampshire, 354 U.S. 234 (1957). Cf. Uphaus v. Wyman, 360 U.S. 72 (1959).

[7] National Association for the Advancement of Colored People v. Alabama, 357 U.S. 449 (1958).

engage in association for the advancement of beliefs and ideas is an insep-
arable aspect of the 'liberty' assured by the Due Process Clause of the Fourteenth Amendment, which embraces freedom of speech." "This Court has
recognized the vital relationship between freedom to associate and privacy
in one's associations . . . Inviolability of privacy in group association may
in many circumstances be indispensable to preservation of freedom of association, particularly where a group espouses dissident beliefs." In this case,
the evidence showed that disclosure of membership in the NAACP would
subject those exposed to "economic reprisal, loss of employment, threat of
physical coercion, and other manifestations of public hostility." The Court
emphasized that the beliefs which the NAACP was organized to foster were
"beliefs which they admittedly have the right to advocate."

There is little question but that the Court would reach the same result if
the disclosure of the NAACP membership lists had been ordered by a legislative investigating committee.[8]

That there are limits to this First Amendment protection when inquiry is
made about membership in the Communist Party will be seen from the
Barenblatt case, discussed later herein.

2. *The Legislative Basis for Inquiry.* In an early case, Kilbourn v. Thompson,[9] the Supreme Court stated flatly that neither the House nor the Senate
"possesses the general power of making inquiry into the private affairs of the
citizen." In this case, the House sought to investigate a private real estate
pool or partnership in the District of Columbia in which Jay Cooke & Co.
was interested. Jay Cooke & Co. had become bankrupt and their estate was
in course of administration in a federal bankruptcy court in Pennsylvania.
Because the Secretary of the Navy had improvidently deposited United States
funds in the London Branch of Jay Cooke & Co., the United States was one
of the creditors. The trustee in bankruptcy had effected a settlement of the
bankrupts' interest in the pool with the associates of Jay Cooke & Co. The
House investigation of the pool and the settlement was started because the
United States and other creditors of Jay Cooke & Co. were dissatisfied with
the settlement. The resolution authorizing the investigation did not specify
any legislative purpose. Kilbourn disobeyed a subpoena duces tecum ordering him to produce all the papers and documents relating to the pool and
refused to divulge the names and addresses of the five members of the pool.
The House passed a resolution adjudging him in contempt and he was confined for 45 days in a District of Columbia jail. Upon his release, by a writ of
habeas corpus, Kilbourn brought an action for false imprisonment against
the Speaker, Clerk and Sergeant-at-Arms (Thompson) of the House and
members of the investigating committee.

The Court held that the House "not only exceeded the limit of its own
authority" by inquiring into private affairs, "but assumed a power which

---

[8] The Court reached the same result when a
municipal ordinance required the disclosure
allegedly to aid in the administration of a
system of occupational license taxes. Bates
v. Little Rock, 80 S.Ct. 412 (1960).
[9] 103 U.S. 168 (1880).

could only be properly exercised by" the courts, which alone could give "relief or redress" by setting aside the settlement in question. The House resolution, said the Court, "contains no hint of any intention of final action by Congress on the subject." "In all the argument of the case, no suggestion has been made of what the House of Representatives or the Congress could have done in the way of remedying the wrong or securing the creditors of Jay Cooke & Co., or even the United States. Was it to be simply a fruitless investigation into the personal affairs of individuals? If so, the House of Representatives had no power or authority in the matter more than any other equal number of gentlemen interested for the government of their country. By fruitless we mean that it could result in no valid legislation on the subject to which the inquiry referred."

Kilbourn v. Thompson was subjected to withering criticism by many writers and did not long survive the next round of great congressional investigations into the "personal affairs of individuals" thought to be of legitimate interest and concern to the United States. In 1927, in McGrain v. Daugherty,[10] "a bench better informed of the historic basis of the investigatory power and of the legislature's practical need of it in effect overruled the 1880 case." [11]

The congressional investigation in this case grew out of the Teapot Dome scandal. The resolution of Congress directed the committee to investigate the official conduct of Attorney General Harry M. Daugherty and his assistants in the Department of Justice. Mally S. Daugherty, the brother of Harry, and a bank president in Ohio, disobeyed a subpoena ordering him to appear before the committee and testify concerning the subject matter under consideration. The Senate passed a resolution that its president pro tempore issue his warrant commanding the Sergeant-at-Arms or his deputy to take Mally S. Daugherty into custody. The deputy (McGrain) took the witness into custody at Cincinnati, Ohio. The federal district court in a habeas corpus proceeding discharged the witness; but the Supreme Court, on a direct appeal, reversed.

The Court held that the object of the investigation and of the effort to secure the witness's testimony was to obtain information for legislative purposes, even though the resolution directing the investigation did not expressly say so. "Plainly the subject was one on which legislation could be had and would be materially aided by the information which the investigation was calculated to elicit. This becomes manifest when it is reflected that the functions of the Department of Justice, the powers and duties of the Attorney General and duties of his assistants are all subject to regulation by congressional legislation, and that the department is maintained and its activities are carried on under such appropriations as in the judgment of Congress are needed from year to year. . . . We think the resolution and proceedings give no warrant for thinking the Senate was attempting or

[10] 273 U.S. 135 (1927).   [11] Hurst, The Growth of American Law 35 (1950).

intending to try the Attorney General at its bar or before its committee for any crime or wrongdoing. Nor do we think it a valid objection to the investigation that it might possibly disclose crime or wrongdoing on his part."

Thus the Court made clear that an investigating committee had power to compel testimony in aid of an investigation of matters not pertinent to a proposal for legislation specified in the authorizing resolution of its parent body—even when these matters concerned the personal affairs of individuals and bore a judicial aspect—so long as they were matters on which legislation was possible.

Two years later, in Sinclair v. United States,[12] the Court reaffirmed its position. Sinclair was convicted of violating 2 U.S.C. 192 for refusing to answer a question of the Senate Committee on Public Lands and Surveys concerning a lease of government oil lands procured by the Mammoth Oil Company, which he owned. He refused to answer on the ground that pursuant to a joint resolution of Congress, the Government had instituted suit against the Oil Company and others, charging conspiracy and fraud and that a special grand jury was to investigate the making of the lease. The matter, therefore, into which the Committee sought to inquire was, Sinclair claimed, judicial and beyond the power of Congress.

"It may be conceded," said the Court, "that Congress is without authority to compel disclosures for the purpose of aiding the prosecution of pending suits;[13] but the authority of that body, directly or through its committees, to require pertinent disclosures in aid of its own consitutional power is not abridged because the information sought to be elicited may also be of use in such suits."

3. *The "Informing Function" of Inquiry.* Woodrow Wilson emphasized another purpose of congressional investigations—to discharge Congress's "informing function," which he saw principally as a means of exposing improprieties in the administration of the government.[14] Professor Hurst, however, points out that legislative inquiries, in fact, have reflected a broader view of the "informing function"—to bring to light "facts otherwise hidden or inadequately understood or weighed" and thereby contribute to the information and education of the public.[15]

Yet the Supreme Court has never accepted the view that public education in this broader sense is as legitimate a purpose of investigation, in which the power to compel disclosure is exercised, as possible lawmaking or the supervising of government operations.

On the contrary, in Watkins v. United States,[16] Chief Justice Warren, speaking for the Court, stated that a congressional investigation "is justified

---

[12] 279 U.S. 263 (1929).

[13] Cf. United States v. Icardi, 140 F. Supp. 383 (D.D.C. 1956); Young v. United States, 212 F. 2d 236 (D.C. Cir. 1954); and United States v. O'Connor, 118 F. Supp. 248 (E.D. Mass. 1953).

[14] Wilson, Congressional Government 297-304 (1885).

[15] Hurst, *supra* n. 9.

[16] 354 U.S. 178 (1957). The case was decided by a 6 to 1 vote, Justice Clark dissenting.

solely as an adjunct to the legislative process" and that investigations "conducted solely for the personal aggrandizement of the investigators or to 'punish' those investigated are indefensible." "We have no doubt," the Chief Justice concluded, "that there is no congressional power to expose for the sake of exposure"; the "informing function" of Congress is limited to informing the public "concerning the workings of its government" and may not "be inflated into a general power to expose where the predominant result can only be an invasion of the private rights of individuals." However, the Chief Justice added, the "motives alone" of the committee members "would not vitiate an investigation if Congress' legislative purpose is being served."

A full reading of the Watkins opinion will show that it "had the unmistakable air and sweep of the great case with the Court conscious of handling a great issue of policy, but in the end the decision was placed on a narrow and readily curable difficulty in the committee procedure" [17]—the failure of the committee to make clear to Watkins how the questions which he refused to answer were pertinent to the subject of inquiry.

The Supreme Court returned to the great issue in Barenblatt v. United States.[18] Upholding a probe of Communist infiltration into the field of education, the Court declared that the power to compel disclosure was limited by the Bill of Rights in the United States Constitution, but it held that the Bill of Rights did not protect Barenblatt, a former college teacher, from being compelled to reveal his associations. "Where First Amendment rights are asserted to bar governmental interrogation," wrote Mr. Justice Harlan for the majority, "resolution of the issue always involves a balancing by the courts of the competing private and public interests at stake in the particular circumstances shown." In this case, the public interests prevailed. The House Un-American Activities Committee, according to the majority of the Court, was not seeking to control what was taught in the universities but to ascertain the scope of a conspiracy dedicated to the ultimate overthrow of the United States Government, in the course of which it was proper for it to seek to identify a teacher-witness as a member of the Communist Party.

The majority agreed that an investigating committee had no power to expose individuals for the sake of exposure but denied that this was the committee's objective in this case. It pointed to the considerable body of legislation directed at the Communist movement which had resulted from the committee's investigations; and on the basis of the record, it could not "say that the unanimous panel of the Court of Appeals which first decided this case was wrong in concluding that 'the primary purposes of the inquiry were in aid of legislative processes.' " Moreover, Justice Harlan reiterated the

[17] Kalven, Mr. Alexander Meiklejohn and the Barenblatt Opinion, 27 U. Chi. L. Rev. 315, 319 (1960).

[18] 360 U.S. 109 (1959). The case was decided by a 5 to 4 vote; Justices Harlan, Frankfurter, Clark, Whittaker, and Stewart constituting the majority, and Chief Justice Warren and Justices Black, Douglas and Brennan, the minority.

Chief Justice's statement in the Watkins opinion that the motives of the committee members "alone would not vitiate an investigation which had been instituted by a House of Congress if that assembly's legislative purpose is being served."

Dissenting, Mr. Justice Black argued that Barenblatt's freedom of speech and association, protected by the First Amendment, was abridged by the Committee's resort to the weapons of "exposure, obloquy and public scorn." He objected to the majority's formulation of the issue before the Court as that of balancing Barenblatt's individual interest in privacy against the public interest in security, because it did not place the public's interest in freedom of speech and association on Barenblatt's side of the scale. This is a telling criticism, which has been elaborated by Professor Alexander Meiklejohn.[19] It repeats a warning given even earlier by Dean Roscoe Pound who wrote: "When it comes to weighing or valuing claims or demands with respect to other claims or demands, we must be careful to compare them on the same plane. If we put one as an individual interest and the other as a social interest, we may decide the question in advance in our way of putting it." [20]

Of course the public interest in political, social, and cultural progress, and the maintenance of free government itself, depends upon the preservation of freedom of speech and association. But it is debatable whether this public interest should be weighed only (or at all) on Barenblatt's side in this case, because precisely this public interest (and not only the public interest in security) is involved in the struggle against the Communist movement, which would destroy the basic freedoms if it came to power.[21]

Finally, Justice Black (and Mr. Justice Brennan in a separate dissenting opinion) asserted that the Committee's actual purpose, in fact, was not to decide whether to legislate or appropriate money, but to try, convict and punish persons suspected of Communist affiliations and, therefore, unconstitutionally to usurp the power of the courts. Professor Kalven is persuaded that the dissenters are correct in this judgment, but wisely comments: "Yet if Congress says it has a legislative purpose and if it occasionally legislates, what can the Court do with its knowledge of real life? How can it hear evidence on—and try the motives of Congress? It is not just idle etiquette that makes the Court go slow here. However much one admires the candor and gusto of the four dissenters on this point,—and I do—there remain real difficulties in translating their 'judicial notice' of committee reality into workable legal doctrine." [22]

These real difficulties might be obviated if the Supreme Court recognized what it has not yet fully recognized as a legitimate purpose of investigation —the "informing" or educating of the public. This would not necessarily

[19] Meiklejohn, Political Freedom and The Barenblatt Opinion, 27 U. Chi. L. Rev. 329, 336-37 (1960).
[20] Pound, A Survey of Social Interests, 57 Harv. L. Rev. 1, 2 (1943).
[21] See Auerbach, *supra* n. 4.
[22] Kalven, *supra* n. 15 at 326-327.

mean that the power to compel disclosure would be unlimited. Professor Kalven also suggests that the power to compel testimony or the production of documents should be narrower than the power to investigate and should be upheld only if actually needed to further a legitimate purpose of the legislature. "[I]t is surely absurd to assume," he writes, that Congress's "best route to legislative insight is to inventory the Communists in the United States one at a time." [23] (Of course, according to the broad view of the "informing function," another question would have to be answered before it could be determined whether the power to compel disclosure in cases like Barenblatt was properly exercised: Is it necessary, *in order to educate* the American people on the subject of Communism, to "inventory the Communists in the United States one at a time"?)

In any case, it is apparent from the Watkins and Barenblatt opinions that the Supreme Court has not yet spoken the last word on the constitutional limits of the legislature's powers to investigate and to compel disclosure in the course of investigation.

B. *Limits Imposed by the Legislature Itself and Some Constitutional Implications*

As we saw in United States v. Rumely, *supra,* a committee must stay within the area of inquiry delimited for it by the legislature itself and may not compel a witness to answer questions outside that area.[24] In the Watkins case, *supra,* the Supreme Court further held that "it is the duty of the investigative body, upon objection of the witness on grounds of pertinency," to describe for the record "what the topic under inquiry is and the connective reasoning whereby the precise questions asked relate to it." It reversed the conviction, under 2 U.S.C. 192, of Watkins, a UAW organizer, for contempt of Congress because a House Un-American Activities Subcommittee failed to discharge this duty.

In response to questions asking him to identify people whom he once knew to be members of the Communist Party, Watkins had refused to identify those who, to his best knowledge and belief, were no longer members. He was willing to identify those who, to his best knowledge and belief, were still Party members. Chief Justice Warren found the resolution authorizing the House Un-American Activities Committee to be of "such sweeping and uncertain scope" as to be afflicted with the "vice of vagueness," which remained uncured throughout the interrogation of Watkins. The Supreme Court itself, the Chief Justice stated, remained "unenlightened as to the subject to which the questions asked [Watkins] were pertinent." Watkins,

[23] *Ibid.*
[24] For other cases illustrating the views of courts on the pertinency question, see Sacher v. United States, 356 U.S. 576 (1958); United States v. Peck, 154 F. Supp. 603 (D.D.C. 1957); United States v. Lamont, 236 F. 2d 312 (2d Cir. 1956); and United States v. Kamin, 135 E. Supp. 382 (D.C. Mass. 1955) and 136 F. Supp. 791 (D.C. Mass. 1956).

therefore, was not "accorded a fair opportunity to determine whether he was within his rights in refusing to answer." Accused of the crime, under 2 U.S.C. 192, of refusing "to answer any questions pertinent to the question under inquiry" by the Congressional committee, he was deprived of the right guaranteed to all criminal defendants by the Due Process Clause of the Fifth Amendment to the United States Constitution, "to have available . . . information revealing the standard of criminality before the commission of the alleged offense."

This information, however, was available, the Court held, in the Barenblatt case, *supra,* sustaining the conviction of a former Vassar psychology instructor, under 2 U.S.C. 192, for refusing to disclose whether he was then or ever had been a member of the Communist Party. The entire "course of congressional actions" endorsing the work of the House Un-American Activities Committee, Justice Harlan stated, furnished a "definite content" to the terms of the authorizing resolution—to grant the Committee "pervasive authority to investigate Communist activities in this country," including the field of education.[25] Even though Barenblatt "raised no objections on the ground of pertinency at the time any of the questions were put to him," Justice Harlan went on to say, the pertinency of these questions was made apparent to him with "undisputable clarity." The Court was satisfied that Barenblatt understood that these questions were intended to elucidate the nature of his participation in, and his knowledge of, Communist activities at the University of Michigan during the years (1947-1950) he was a graduate student and teaching fellow there.[26]

There is little doubt that, in the light of the Watkins and Barenblatt opinions, an investigating committee can so conduct itself, no matter how broad and vague its mandate, as to obviate any objection based on lack of pertinency.

C. *Other Rights of Witnesses*

1. *The Fourth Amendment.*[27] Whether this Amendment guarantees that no citizen shall be subpoenaed to testify unless the Congressional investigating committee has probable cause to believe that he has information rele-

---

[25] In dissent, Justice Black argued that the "vice of vagueness" was not cured by the "mute acquiescence" of Congress in the Committee's activities.

[26] Perhaps Mr. Watkins too could have been found to understand the pertinency of the questions, in relation to un-American activities in the labor movement. "Are we to believe that the crucial failure in Watkins, a failure so prejudicial that it rose to the level of a constitutional defect, was the failure to mention that he was being asked about labor although he was

a labor leader and 23 of the 30 names he was asked about were clearly associated with labor?" (Kalven, *supra,* n. 15 at 322).

[27] The Amendment provides: "The right of the people to be secure in their persons, houses, papers and effects, against unreasonable searches and seizures, shall not be violated, and no warrants shall issue but upon probable cause, supported by oath or affirmation, and particularly describing the place to be searched, and the persons or things to be seized."

vant to the topic under inquiry has not been squarely decided by the Supreme Court. In the Barenblatt opinion, Justice Harlan noted the absence of evidence that Barenblatt's "appearance as a witness follow[ed] from indiscriminate dragnet procedures, lacking in probable cause for belief that he possessed information which might be helpful to the Subcommittee." The Court may soon have occasion to rule on this issue.[28]

2. *The Fifth and Sixth Amendments.* The Court in United States v. O'Connor, 240 F. 2d 404 (D.C. Cir., 1956) made clear that a Congressional committee's question might be so *vague* that punishing a witness for contempt for refusing to answer it would violate his *Sixth* Amendment right to be informed of the nature of the accusation; "the question set forth in the indictment [should] be definite enough to enable the accused to answer it with knowledge of its meaning."

This protection is related to that which we have seen established by the Watkins case on the ground of Fifth Amendment "due process": protection against contempt punishment for refusing to answer a Congressional committee's question whose *pertinency* to the inquiry had not, upon his objection, been revealed to him.

The aspect of the Fifth Amendment best known to the public is the privilege against self-incrimination. A witness before an investigating committee may refuse to testify or produce documents by claiming this privilege. The precise scope of the privilege has been litigated in a large number of cases involving grand jury as well as congressional investigations and is beyond our present purposes. Nor is it feasible here to consider the question whether adverse consequences should follow from the invocation of the privilege by a witness asked about his affiliations with the Communist Party. For example, should the assertion of the privilege be the basis for seeking the dismissal of a teacher, a government employee, a United Nations employee, a worker in a defense plant? Should it be grounds for disbarring a lawyer? Or depriving an individual of union membership? [29]

---

[28] In Shelton v. United States, 280 F. 2d. 701 (D.C. Cir. 1960), the courts rejected the applicability of the Fourth Amendment's probable cause requirement to the subpoena powers of a Senate Internal Security Subcommittee. A petition for certiorari is pending.

[29] See Slochower v. Board of Education, 350 U.S. 551 (1956); Beilan v. Board of Public Education, 357 U.S. 399 (1958); Lerner v. Casey, 357 U.S. 468 (1958); Nelson v. County of Los Angeles, 80 S. Ct. 527 (1960); Hook, Heresy, Yes— Conspiracy, No (1952); Byse, Teachers and the Fifth Amendment, 102 U. Pa. L.

Rev. 871 (1954); Note, Denying the Privilege Against Self-Incrimination to Public Officers, 64 Harv. L. Rev. 987 (1951); Brown, Lawyers and the Fifth Amendment, 40 A.B.A.J. 404 (1954); Horowitz, Loyalty Tests for Employment in the Motion Picture Industry, 6 Stan. L. Rev. 438 (1954), Margolis, The Plea Against Self-Incrimination by United Nation Employees, 40 Va. L. Rev. 283 (1954); Noonan, Inferences From Invocation of the Privilege Against Self-Incrimination, 41 Va. L. Rev. 311 (1955); Chafee and Sutherland, Letters to Harvard Crimson, Jan. 7, 1953, Reprinted in 99 Congressional

It should be mentioned that there are a number of federal "immunity statutes," applying in different situations. The only one now applicable to Congressional committees is the Immunity Act of 1954, 18 U.S.C. 3486, upheld in Ullman v. United States,[30] and the only committee hearings subject to the Act are those involving matters of national security. A witness who is compelled to make disclosure under this Act, after his rightful claim of the privilege, receives immunity from both state and federal prosecution for any matter concerning which he testifies. The committee cannot compel the testimony until after it votes to do so by at least a two-thirds vote, and obtains a federal court order compelling the testimony.

Many states, including Wisconsin, have immunity statutes.

3. *Privileges other than that against self-incrimination.* Claims of privilege before investigating bodies have also been made with varying success, to resist enforced disclosure of communications between husband and wife, attorney and client, clergyman and penitent, physician and patient, and newspaperman and informer. Where recognized, they have a common law or statutory rather than a constitutional basis. Executive officials have refused to respond to Congressional Committee subpoenas or demands for information of various kinds, on the theory that submission to these demands would violate the constitutional separation of powers.[31]

4. *Proposed codes of fair procedure.* So far as the conduct of the hearing before an investigating committee is concerned, a witness has no right (i.e., a claim which the courts will recognize and secure) to be accompanied and represented by counsel, to be given detailed advance notice of the specific charges being investigated, to confront the witnesses against him, to cross-examine them, or to call witnesses on his behalf, even if the material brought out might be the basis for instituting a criminal prosecution against him. [32]

To ensure that investigating committees will be fair in their procedures, bills have been introduced, based in the main on recommendations of local bar associations, which would require committees to follow a code of fair procedure. The House of Representatives has adopted a set of so-called "fair play" rules to govern the conduct of hearings by most House Committees.[33] A number of Senate Committees have adopted a similar code.

Record A 505-506, Feb. 6, 1953; Hook, Common Sense and the Fifth Amendment (1957).

[30] 350 U.S. 422 (1956).

[31] See the memorandum of Attorney-General Brownell to President Eisenhower, 100 Congressional Record 6621-23 (1954) and Study by Staff of the Committee on Government Operations, H. R. Committee Print, 84th Congress, 2d Session (1956).

[32] See Hannah v. Larche, 80 S. Ct. 1502 (1960). This involved the investigatory power of the Federal Commission on Civil Rights. The appendix to the majority opinion gives a tabular analysis of the authority and procedure of a representative group of administrative and executive agencies and congressional investigating committees.

[33] H. Res. 151, 84th Cong., 1st Sess. (1955); see also, Maslow, *supra* n. 2.

Rauh*, *REPRESENTATION BEFORE CONGRESSIONAL COMMITTEE HEARINGS*
50 The Journal of Criminal Law, Criminology and Police Science 219 (1959)

My subject—"*Representation* before Congressional Committee Hearings"—rather assumes that witnesses at these hearings do have legal representation akin to that of the courtroom. But, despite the fact that the rules of the various investigating committees almost invariably provide for counsel, his role before most committees is far too anemic to warrant the description "representation." Most committees take great pains to see that the witness knows he may have a lawyer with him and equal pains to see that the lawyer is unable adequately to protect his client's interests.

Before the House Un-American Activities Committee and Senate Internal Security Subcommittee—the two permanent investigating committees which have probably subpoenaed as many witnesses in the past decade as all the other Congressional investigating committees put together—counsel is not even allowed to address the Committee. Thus, the Rules of the former provide, in a show of concern for the Bill of Rights, that "at every hearing . . . every witness shall be accorded the privilege of having counsel of his own choosing"; but then the Committee turns around in its Rules and takes away most of the benefit of having counsel by providing as follows: "The participation of counsel during the course of any hearing and while the witness is testifying shall be limited to advising said witness as to his legal rights. Counsel . . . shall confine his activity to the area of legal advice to his client." Thus, before these committees, counsel is not even permitted to seek clarification of a question put to his client or to make objection to a question on grounds of lack of pertinence. All he can do is try and catch his client's attention and whisper an objection to him so that he can repeat it to the committee as nearly verbatim as possible.

The difficulty of a layman making legal objection on grounds of irrelevance after a whispered conversation with his lawyer will be obvious to anyone. An interesting case study of just what can happen in this situation is provided by Arthur Miller's contempt hearing. Mr. Miller's testimony before the passport investigation of the Un-American Activities Committee was an eloquent presentation of his personal beliefs which won him the praise of even some of the Committee members. He answered all the questions put to him except two which sought to elicit the names of certain Communist Party writers with whom he had attended meetings back in 1947 to discuss the relationship of Marxism to art and literature.

* Joseph L. Rauh, Jr. was Law Secretary to Mr. Justice Benjamin N. Cardozo and Mr. Justice Felix Frankfurter during the years 1936 to 1939. Prior to our entrance into World War II he was counsel to a number of Government agencies. More recently he has been in the general practice of law in Washington. He is Washington Counsel for the United Automobile Workers and the Brotherhood of Sleeping Car Porters, and does a good deal of professional work related to civil liberties and civil rights. This article was originally given as a lecture in the 1958 course for defense lawyers at Northwestern University.—Editor of the Journal

Mr. Miller told the Committee that his conscience would not permit him "to use the name of another person" and then went on to say, following a whispered conversation with counsel, that "my counsel advises me that there is no relevance between *this question* and the question of whether I should have a passport or whether there should be passport legislation in 1956." Since there were actually two questions before the Committee and the witness at that moment, a more precise objection would have been that there was no relevance between *these questions* and the subject of passports. But it still seems to me that Mr. Miller did pretty well in getting out as much of the whispered conversation as he did. Yet the Committee cited him for contempt, and the Government argued at the trial that Mr. Miller hadn't objected to the relevance of the first of the two questions because he said "this question" rather than "these questions." Believe it or not, the prosecution persuaded the District Judge to so hold, and Mr. Miller lived under the cloud of a criminal conviction for over a year until the Court of Appeals unanimously voted for his acquittal for want of a proper direction to answer by the Committee, without reaching the point at issue here.*

Lawyer Hamstrung by Committee. Lawyers not familiar with, and reconciled to, their feeble role at Committee hearings sometimes run into trouble. A subcommittee of the Senate Internal Security Subcommittee, in the person of Senator Eastland, was holding a hearing in New Orleans. John P. Kohn, a distinguished attorney from Montgomery, Alabama, appeared as counsel for a witness from Montgomery. Early in the course of the hearing, Mr. Kohn arose and asked the chairman if he would be allowed to cross-examine a witness who had accused his client. Then, according to the reporter from the *Montgomery Advertiser* who was covering the hearing, the chairman "frowned and growled that he had 'no intention of standing still for heckling during this hearing; it is unheard of for a witness before a congressional committee to be cross-examined. It will not be done here.' When Kohn pressed for an idea of the 'ground rules' for the investigation, Eastland snapped: 'I will decide those as we go along and announce them when I desire. Sit down, sir. You are out of order.'"

Before the McClellan (Labor-Management) and Harris (Legislative Oversight) Committees, which are the other two investigative committees most in the public eye today and which have allowed counsel wider scope of representation than the committees just mentioned, a lawyer is still not permitted to make opening or closing arguments, to put on his case as he deems best, to object to questions, or to cross-examine witnesses. The rules of the McClellan Committee expressly permit, and the Harris Committee would also undoubtedly permit, counsel to suggest to the Chairman that he put certain questions to the witness, but this is hardly a substitute for cross-examination. Even with the best of intentions on the part of the chairman—which is hardly to be expected towards a person under investigation by him—a question loses its impact when read haltingly by the chairman, and the follow-up counsel had in mind will seldom if ever be made.

Lawyer Plays Many Roles. Though a lawyer cannot give full representation be-

---

* 259 F. 2d 187 (D.C. Cir. 1958). The District Court opinion is at 152 F. Supp. 781 (D.D.C. 1957).—Editor

fore a congressional committee, he is not without value to his client. Actually a lawyer before a Congressional committee plays many roles—he might be described as part lawyer, part friend, part politician, part investigator and part public relations counsellor. These roles, of course, are often overlapping and may sometimes even conflict, as they did at the Goldfine hearing before the Harris Committee. The Washington lawyer, apparently thinking of the bad public relations involved in Mr. Goldfine's refusal to answer questions and particularly the bad public relations effect which a contempt citation would have on his client and the Administration, urged Mr. Goldfine to answer all questions of conceivable relevance. Boston counsel, less worried about bad public relations and the Administration and more worried about the adverse effect which answering all questions might have on Mr. Goldfine's tangled business affairs, advised the client to refuse to answer in cases where the relevance was not abundantly clear. Telling the Committee about his activities with the East Boston Company might very well have interfered with Goldfine's business affairs, increased his SEC troubles and weakened his defense in one or more lawsuits. Because of this and to the dismay of his Washington counsel, Mr. Goldfine settled the conflict by refusing to answer a number of questions and getting himself cited for contempt, with all the public obloquy that goes with both of those things. Ordinarily witnesses before an investigating committee cannot afford two sets of lawyers—one with an eye towards public relations, the other looking out for business affairs. Most witnesses have just one lawyer; the conflict goes on inside, which may explain the high ulcer rate of Washington attorneys.

The role of the lawyer, the friend and the public relations counsellor may all be present right at the outset of the hearing. Walking into the hearing room of the Senate Internal Security Subcommittee with a United Automobile Workers organizer, I saw my client blanch at the sight of the television and movie cameras. In a halting voice he told me that his daughter had graduated from high school the day before and that he could not bear to have her see him on the evening television newscast before going to her graduation dance that night. I knew that if he ever came forward and sat down in the witness chair, plenty of feet of film would be taken before we could get the cameras shut off. When my client's name was called by the Committee Chairman, I got up in the back of the room and announced that he would not come forward until the television and movie cameras had been turned off. In so doing we were simply exercising rights which we believed to be ours.[1] Yet the Chairman and his counsel were not easily so persuaded, and an unpleasant colloquy resulted. We held our ground, and the television and motion picture lights finally went out. Nothing one learns in law school trains a man to stand in the back of a crowded room and try to look dignified while the Chairman and his counsel, acting as prosecutors, judge and jury, demand that he bring his client to the witness stand. They probably don't care, but I understand that the girl had a lovely time at her graduation dance.

Lawyer as Investigator. Counsel's role as investigator may at times prove decisive. The hearings before the Harris Committee, which was investigating the granting

[1] United States v. Kleinman, 107 F. Supp. 407 (D.D.C. 1952).

of TV Channel 10 in Miami to National Airlines, went off on a tangent and began looking into the activities of the chief rival applicant, Mr. Katzentine. It developed that Mr. Katzentine had not been without political influence himself and indeed had persuaded a number of Senators to intervene with the FCC on his behalf. The leader of the attack on Katzentine was Congressman Wolverton, the ranking minority member of the Committee, who seemed quite outraged by any such Congressional intervention in a quasi-judicial proceeding. Things looked pretty black for Mr. Katzentine until his resourceful counsel, Paul A. Porter, himself a former FCC Chairman, turned up with a copy of a letter from Congressman Wolverton to the Commission in another case doing exactly what he had condemned in Mr. Katzentine. While most lawyers cannot hope to emulate Mr. Porter's feat in producing the clincher, there is always much preparation to be undertaken in reviewing earlier hearings and in outside investigation.

Lawyer as Politician. What the lawyer does as politician is, of course, quite obvious. He tries to persuade friendly members of the Committee, if any, to attend the hearing and give his client a little protection by timely interruption with a kind word or question; he tries to explain his client's case in advance to any member who may not yet have committed himself and to persuade him to take his client's side at the hearing. . . .

Public Relations Counsellor. I don't suppose one need say too much about the role of the lawyer as public relations counsellor. Ordinarily one's client isn't Mr. Goldfine and doesn't have the money to hire a model as a receptionist, Tex McCrary for prestige, and a raft of others for diversion, so the lawyer must take on this function, too. Since the client's reputation is generally at stake in the committee room, what the press and radio say before, during and after the hearing becomes all-important; so the method of presentation of a given point may be determinative.

Take the case of distinguished playwright Lillian Hellman. She was perfectly willing to tell the Committee everything she had ever done, but she was unwilling to inform on others with whom she had associated many years before. If she told the Committee all about herself, she would waive the privilege against self-incrimination and would either have to give the names of her former associates or stand trial for contempt. What she wanted to do was to let the public know that she had nothing to hide personally but was unwilling to turn informer on people she did not believe had ever been disloyal to our country. So Miss Hellman wrote the Un-American Activities Committee a respectful letter offering to waive her privilege against self-incrimination and tell all about herself, if only the Committee would refrain from demanding the names. The Committee responded with a curt rejection. When Miss Hellman appeared before the Committee and they began asking questions about her past, she promptly referred to her letter. The Chairman of the Committee brushed the letter aside and demanded that she answer the questions. But the press covering the hearing was vitally interested in the letter the Chairman was trying to hide and, while Miss Hellman was exercising her privilege against self-incrimination, the press was reading the exchange of letters which we handed out while she talked. For once the charging party, the Committee, did not get the headlines. The eloquence of Miss Hellman's explanation of her inability to bring bad trouble to others outranked her plea of the Fifth Amendment in the minds of the reporters present. . . .

Strictly Legal Role. What has gone before on the role of counsel as friend, politician, investigator and public relations counsellor was not intended to convey the impression that there is not a strictly legal role for counsel before a Congressional committee. A hasty look at this role may be of interest. . . .

If, as is the usual case, the client is a witness under investigation, there is much to be done beforehand in refreshing his recollection, helping him clear up in his mind things that he is psychologically anxious to forget, and indicating the phrasing of answers which will do the least damage to his reputation.

Once at the hearing, the plea of the Fifth Amendment will raise the most difficult legal questions. The Fifth Amendment can only be pleaded with impunity to those questions which, if answered, would serve as a link in the chain of evidence tending to incriminate the witness. If the answer would not tend to incriminate, and this decision is made by the Judge at the contempt trial a year or two later, a plea of the Fifth Amendment is of no avail. Consequently, the lawyer must make sure that the plea is not invoked until the questions reach the incriminating level. This has been made somewhat easier by the recent tendency of the courts to stretch the Fifth Amendment to questions which appear on their face to have little tendency to incriminate. Thus, a Court of Appeals' holding that a witness could not plead the Amendment when asked to state his residence,[3] was summarily reversed upon confession of error by the Solicitor General.[4]

But, just as counsel has to be careful about not letting his client plead the Fifth Amendment too early, he has to be equally careful that he not plead it too late. The right to claim the Fifth Amendment is waived by the admission of guilt or incriminating facts. As the Supreme Court put it in *Rogers* v. *United States*,[5] "Disclosure of a fact waives the privilege as to details." The Court there held that a witness who admitted to the holding of office in the Communist Party could not invoke the Fifth Amendment when asked to identify her successor in office, as the answer to that question would not subject her to any real danger of further incrimination. Following this decision, the Court of Appeals in the District of Columbia held that a Cornell professor who admitted past participation in a Marxist discussion group waived his right to plead the Fifth Amendment when asked whether persons identified as long-time Communists had attended these meetings.[6] Dave Beck's lawyers may not have been as silly as they seemed when they recommended that the Becks, father and son, keep their relationship to themselves.

On the other side of this problem, the courts are less willing to find a waiver when the witness denies guilt than when he makes admissions. Thus, Frank Costello's general denial of wrongdoing did not bar him from pleading the Fifth Amendment when asked about specific criminal acts.[7] Had some of the lawyers

[3] Simpson v. United States, 241 F. 2d 222 (9th Cir. 1957).
[4] Simpson v. United States, 355 U.S. 7 (1957).
[5] 340 U.S. 367, 373 (1951).

[6] Singer v. United States, 244 F. 2d 349 (D.C. Cir. 1957), rev'd on other grounds on rehearing, 247 F. 2d 535 (1957).
[7] Costello v. United States, 198 F. 2d 200 (2d Cir. 1952).

before the McCarthy Committee understood this rule a little better, it might have been harder for the Senator to have pulled off one of his favorite tricks. Very often, once a witness pleaded the Fifth Amendment on his relationship with Communism, Senator McCarthy would ask the witness whether he had ever committed espionage or sabotage. Afraid that a denial might constitute a waiver, lawyers very often had witnesses plead the Fifth Amendment to this question. Senator McCarthy would then pounce on this plea and lay claim to the catching of another spy. In the only reported case on this exact point, the District Court for the District of Columbia acquitted a witness who denied espionage and sabotage and pleaded the privilege on other matters.[8]

Another major area of legal assistance is on the issue of pertinence. Questions may be outside the authority of the Committee or not pertinent to the subject under inquiry at the particular moment. The lawyer will have to make a fast judgment on both authority and pertinence; in making this judgment he should recognize that the Committees themselves will seldom accept the answer that a question is unauthorized or irrelevant. As Mr. Goldfine so well knows, the Committee resolves doubtful issues of pertinence against the witness. To stand on a pertinence objection is to invite indictment, and, while the recent record of the committees in the courts is poor indeed, a lawyer who tells his client to plead lack of pertinence is asking for a federal case.

So much for the art, if it can be called one, of representing a witness before Congressional committees. I hope there are a few trade secrets left as this is pleasant work for one who enjoys combat. . . .

CHRONOLOGICAL RECORD OF MEETINGS OF SPECIAL COMMITTEE ON INDUSTRIAL INSURANCE, WISCONSIN LEGISLATURE

[The following record of the sessions of the legislative committee is reprinted from pp. 42-44 of the report made by that committee on January 10, 1911, to the Governor and Legislature. An outline of the contents of that report is reprinted in these materials at a later point.—Editor]

This committee, created under Chapter 518 of the Laws of 1909, was appointed in June, 1909, shortly before the Legislature's adjournment, Lieut. Gov. John Strange appointing Senators A. W. Sanborn of Ashland (chairman), E. T. Fairchild of Milwaukee, John J. Blaine of Boscobel, and Speaker Levi H. Bancroft of the assembly appointing Assemblymen Wallace Ingalls of Racine, Clarence B. Culbertson of Stanley, Walter D. Egan of Superior, and George G. Brew of Milwaukee.

Two weeks after its appointment the committee held its first meeting (July 10th, 1909) in Milwaukee, confirmed Senator Sanborn as chairman, and elected Paul J. Watrous of Milwaukee as secretary. At that time it passed resolutions favoring the attendence of its members at the first joint conference on employers' liability, at Atlantic City, July 30th and 31st and August 1st, which was participated in by members of the New York and Minnesota commissions. The next meet-

[8] United States v. Hoag, 142 F. Supp. 667 (D.D.C. 1956).

ing was held in Madison, August 20th. . . . The week of September 12th the committee held daily sessions, in the Plankinton house, Milwaukee, representatives of manufacturers and of organized labor also being in attendance. October 4th to 7th the committee held public hearings in the Milwaukee city hall, at which the opinions of various persons were heard by the members. This hearing was continued to October 12th.

November 22nd and 23rd a further hearing was held in Milwaukee, at which attorneys and employers appeared informally before the committee. February 16th a meeting was held in Madison, at which outlines of industrial insurance bills by Assemblyman Ingalls and Senator Blaine were discussed. At this meeting it was decided to publish tentative measures, one abrogating certain defences of employers, and the other providing a uniform scale of compensation to be covered by insurance. In drafting the two bills to be used as a basis for open discussion, the services of Mr. Reuben McKitrick of the Legislative Reference Library, were secured, and he was given directions for framing the tentative measures. These suggested forms of tentative bills were ordered printed at a meeting in Madison on March 10th, and a public hearing in Milwaukee was announced for April 12th. At this hearing the committee, through its chairman, asked for expressions on the tentative bills dated March 25th (see Appendix I) and for two days the committee heard expressions on various sections of the measures. At this meeting Mr. Daniel Hoan, then attorney for the Wisconsin State Federation of Labor, addressed the committee on his bill introduced in the legislature of 1909 by Assemblyman Fred Brockhausen of Milwaukee. He also submitted a brief. The following week, April 22nd, the committee met in Chicago with the Illinois commission on employers' liability for a joint discussion.

As a result of the Milwaukee and Chicago hearings, the committee directed the framing of revised measures, with the same underlying principles but with the insurance feature eliminated and on May 14th, in Madison, these new bills were ordered printed. At the same time it was decided to hold public meetings at LaCrosse, Eau Claire, Superior and Appleton, various organizations and individuals in these cities having requested hearings. The committee met May 31st at LaCrosse, and took as the basis of discussion its second tentative bills dated May 28th (see Appendix I). This meeting was held under the auspices of the LaCrosse Jobbers and Manufacturers' Club. The next day, June 1st, a hearing was held at Eau Claire, at the Eau Claire club. On June 2nd a hearing was held in the Commercial club at Superior, and on June 3rd the committee held a hearing in the city hall at Appleton. The same bills were taken as a basis for discussion at all these hearings.

The second joint conference of state commissions in Chicago, June 10th and 11th, was attended by several members of the committee, and the Wisconsin bills were critically discussed at considerable length.

On July 12th, when the committee met in Madison to act upon suggestions heard at the May and June hearings, it passed upon a third tentative bill, which combined the liability and compensation bills. This third tentative bill (see Appendix I) was printed August 4th, and, upon direction of the committee, was forwarded to authorities in all parts of the United States, with requests for written criticisms. These criticisms were received in large numbers, and were of great service in strengthening the later bill. From July 12th to November 15th the committee held no meetings, but, upon invitation, attended a conference in Milwaukee on October 20th, called by the Merchants' and Manufacturers' Association of Milwaukee. This meeting was attended by about two hundred employers from different parts of the state.

On November 15th the committee met to consider the new bill as drafted under the committee's direction, by Mr. Harry L. Butler of Madison. After making changes in this bill and directing Mr. Butler to revise certain sections, the committee ordered the printing of the fourth tentative bill (see Appendix I) dated Nov. 15th, 1910. The fourth tentative bill was the subject discussed at a public hearing in Milwaukee on November 29th. This hearing was attended by representatives of the Merchants and Manufacturers Association, the Wisconsin State Federation of Labor and by several attorneys and manufacturers of Milwaukee and of the state at large. Upon request the committee continued this hearing to December 5, at which time the meeting was resumed, the bill being reviewed section by section. Following the revision of the bill by Mr. Butler and others along the lines of suggestions laid down at the Milwaukee hearing, the committee met again in Madison, December 14, 15, and 16.

The committee's last meeting was held at Madison, December 29th. At this meeting the last draft of the bill and the report were read and finally approved by those present, copies being sent to the absent members for signature.

NOTES AND QUESTIONS

1. Consider the number of hearings afforded interested parties and the public and the diverse interests represented. Note that the Wisconsin measure was not produced in isolation from similar legislative movements in other parts of the country.

2. Previous materials have indicated that employer and employee groups, through their attorneys, came forward with precise draft suggestions for a bill. What new agency appears on the scene, in the committee's statement?

EDITORIAL NOTE: The PUBLICATION of COMMITTEE PROCEEDINGS and REPORTS

A stenographic transcript of most of the proceedings of the joint legislative committee on industrial insurance was made for the use of the committeemen and their drafting assistants. The typed transcript fills five large bound volumes, a set of which is on deposit at the Wisconsin Legislative Reference Library. There is also available the 148 page printed Report of the Special Committee on Industrial Insurance, rendered to the Governor and Legislature under date of January 10, 1911. One cannot expect to find such materials available with respect to state legislation in general.

Hearings are commonly held on all bills considered by committees of the Wisconsin Legislature, at which any interested parties are free to present their views. A formal record showing the date, time, and place of hearing, the committee members present, and the persons appearing for and against the proposed legislation is made with reference to each hearing; and this record will be found on file at the office of the Secretary of State together with copies of the bill introduced, amendments offered or adopted, and the final, official form of the bill as enacted into statute. This formal record of the hearing contains no statement of the arguments or testimony presented to the committee, and for most bills this is the only official record available regarding the hearing. It is only in connection with measures of unusual importance and public interest that one can expect to find preserved any detailed record, even in typed form, of the proceedings of the legislative committee. However, even the formal record which is the only official evidence of the hearing in the case of most statutes, may be of value; significant inferences may often be derived from the nature of the interested parties appearing for or against the bill, and reasonable deductions may often be made from the fact that the only appearances made were either for or against the bill. Although contemporaneous newspaper reports of hearings do not furnish evidence ordinarily competent in court, the lawyer must not overlook the possibility that newspaper accounts of a hearing in which he is interested may shed light on the background of a measure which may assist him indirectly in briefing a question of interpretation. Newspaper reports, of course, will be valuable to those (historians, political scientists, and sociologists) interested in the bill for non-legal purposes.

Similarly, it is the exception rather than the rule for a state legislative committee to render any detailed report commenting on a bill; and even if such a report is rendered it is only in the case of measures of unusual public interest that the report is likely to be printed.

The official, published materials bearing on the background of a Federal statute are much more generous than is true of state legislation. Proceedings at public hearings of Congressional committees are published in printed pamphlets in the case of most important measures. A committee report is rendered and printed regarding almost every bill enacted into law by the Congress. These materials are generally available at any library which is an official depository of U.S. public documents. They may also often be obtained through the Library of Congress or the clerk of the Congressional committee involved. If the hearings were not printed, it may be found that a stenographic transcript of the proceedings was made and is on deposit with the committee clerk.

FROM THE HEARINGS
OF THE INDUSTRIAL INSURANCE COMMITTEE

Milwaukee, Wisconsin October 13, 1909, two o'clock P.M.

The committee met pursuant to adjournment. Present: Senator Sanborn and Assemblyman Brew. [P. 340 ff.]

Max W. Babb, called as a witness herein, testified as follows:

Examined by the Chairman:

Q. You are the attorney of the Allis-Chalmers Company?

A. Yes, sir, and assistant secretary of the company.

Q. What do you manufacture in the state of Wisconsin?

A. We manufacture various kinds of heavy machinery, including Corliss engines, flour mill machinery, sawmill machinery, gas engines, steam turbines, electrical apparatus, and other machinery.

Q. And your principal plant is located in Milwaukee?

A. We have two plants in Wisconsin, both of which are located in Milwaukee county, one in the city of Milwaukee, and one in the city of West Allis.

Q. About how many men do you employ there?

A. In the two plants in Milwaukee at the present time we have in the neighborhood of 4500, that includes the force in our general offices which are at West Allis. This general office manages six plants, two of which are in Wisconsin and four of which are outside of the state of Wisconsin. . . .

Q. You employ a good many more men at West Allis?

A. Yes, we do . . .

Q. Now, do you know the number that you had injured in 1907 out there?

A. Yes, sir, I have got those figures here. I will just say in explanation of it first that we have a very complete system of reporting accidents. The report of every accident comes to me, and we have certain men in each of the works whose duty it is to make these reports, and they are instructed to report every accident of every kind that occurs, no matter how slight, because we have found that in our experience if a person gets their finger scratched, almost, and no attention is given to it, the next thing we know a case is brought against us for blood-poisoning, and there is no report of the accident and everybody has forgotten it had occurred, so our instructions are to have every accident of any kind reported.

Q. How many years have you got?

A. The last three years.

Q. I wish you would just give us those three years?

A. In 1906 there were 497 accidents in our Milwaukee plants. In 1907 595 accidents. And in 1908 443 accidents. . . .

Q. Do you keep any record as to the length of disability following those injuries?

A. We keep this kind of a record. We do not keep a record, but we keep particulars on the thing, keep it alive, in other words, coming before us until the man has returned to work, and then put it in the general files.

Q. You just keep particulars to keep track of it?

A. We keep it alive and watch the case until the man returns to work, and then close it up.

Q. Do you carry liability insurance?

A. Yes.

Q. Are there any objections to telling me what it costs you for liability insurance, grossly, per year?

A. No, I will tell you grossly, Mr. Kehoe [another company representative] has got those figures.

Q. Do you carry any system of insurance on benefits?

A. . . . There is a society called the Allis Mutual Aid Society which extends simply to the two Milwaukee plants, has nothing whatever to do with our other plants. Every person working for our company is eligible to membership in that Aid Society, although it is optional on their part. In joining that society they do not waive any claims whatever against the company or release the company in any way for any liability on account of things that occur. There is an initiation fee of 50 cents and the dues are 25 cents per month from each member. The company pays the Aid Society a sum equal to the total amount that it collects from its members; in other words, doubles the amount of the initiation fee and the amount it receives from members. Now, a member of the Aid Society, in case of sickness, or accidents, anywheres, disability from any cause whatever—

Q. Twenty-four hours exposure, any accident, whether it occurs in your works or not?

A. Yes, it is, because I would say whether it occurs in our works or not, because they are entitled to this in case of sickness. . . .

Q. Who manages the Aid Society?

A. They are managed altogether by the employees of the company.

Q. The company itself has nothing to do with it?

A. The company has nothing to do with it except that it contributes, it doubles the amount of their receipts. The company encourages it, helps it, and it believes the best interests of the Society are that they really govern themselves, because they handle their own money. . . .

[The witness continued at some length to describe the system and experience of operation of the form of plant insurance described. Thereafter, in response to a request for general suggestions as to the form of an act and problems in drafting it, the following exchange occurred.—Editor]

A. . . . I have always thought this, that the placing of a liability, placing of an absolute liability on a company for accidents, regardless of how they originate, would increase the number of accidents. That is, persons would endeavor to take advantage of the benefits, whether they are really hurt or not. I think there would be a tendency to increase the number of accidents. As I understand this matter it is one of the public reasons for wishing the passage of a law of this kind, that it will relieve the public to some extent of the necessity for providing for persons who are permanently injured and destitute. And also another reason is for the protection of the employees, and another reason for the protection of the employers, that is, to get a better adjustment of things so that better feeling exists and things work without any waste.

Q. Try to save the waste.

A. Now, with that thought in mind, it seems to me that any scheme that is evolved where the benefits go to three different elements like that, the expense should be borne by those three elements, in other words, I think both employees and public, the State, if you please, should contribute towards the maintenance of such a system. Now, I read over some plans which have been proposed in various places, and Mr. Kehoe here has figured out to some extent, out of curiosity, how some of those would operate with a plant like ours in case we were called upon to bear the total expenses, and the figures have been astounding as to how much it would increase the present cost; and of course you appreciate this fact and will, I know, give it careful consideration, that, if a system of industrial insurance is evolved in this state which greatly increases the expenses to manufacturers, that it will necessarily have the effect of cutting off new enterprises and not in driving those out, but reducing them.

Q. That is, you cannot compete with another state, or the manufacturers of any other state, that has not those burdens?

A. Our competitors are largely the Westinghouse Company, the General Electric Company, and different companies situated outside of Wisconsin, and, as I stated before, our company has six plants, two of which are in Wisconsin. We have separate files at each of our plants showing relatively the expenses of manufacture. If these figures should show that the expenses of manufacture in Wisconsin were greatly in excess of Illinois, or Indiana or Ohio, where our other plants are, the work would be done in those other states, because the object is to turn out the manufactured product at the least expense.

[The matters of employee contributions, and the relation to the competitive situation in other states, thus introduced at one of the earliest of the committee's hearings, were issues which ran consistently throughout the period in which the committee collected testimony.—Editor]

* * *

[Records of legislative committee hearings are ordinarily confined to public sessions at which interested parties appear to give their opinions and information. In the present case, the stenographic transcript also includes records of several executive sessions of the committee, at which no members of the public were present. The following excerpt is from one such session, pp. 506-527.—Editor]

Madison, Wis., February 17, 1910, 10 A.M. Present: Senator A. W. Sanborn, Senator E. T. Fairchild, Senator J. J. Blaine, Assemblyman Wallace Ingalls, Assemblyman Walter D. Egan, Assemblyman George J. Brew.

* * *

MR. INGALLS: Gentlemen, let us take up the matter. I was trying to recall the four points we discussed yesterday. First, as to whether it would be compulsory or optional; and the second proposition was the defenses that should be eliminated; and the third proposition was the occupations to which it should apply.

MR. BREW: The fourth was as to the State contributing towards it.

MR. INGALLS: Is there any objection to its applying to railways, other than the fact that something else might be better so far as the railways are concerned? Now, Judge Marshall only makes a suggestion of course—I was just talking with him a little while ago, but anything suggested by him is worthy of consideration. He has an idea of applying it generally.

SENATOR BLAINE: You would have to do that, if the State contributed, wouldn't you?

MR. INGALLS: He didn't make any suggestions that it would be necessary to apply it generally, because he says 'along the lines you are tending you are absolutely safe'; which, of course, is true.

THE CHAIRMAN [SENATOR SANBORN]: That is, as long as you are leaving it optional and preserving the employes' rights.

SENATOR BLAINE: If you leave it optional you can make almost any kind of a bill stand up.

MR. INGALLS: And the real secret of our success, if it does work out to be a success, the plan we have got, is the fact that everybody is being taken in and considered; and it is a mutual arrangement, in a sense, and that is what makes the German system so extremely successful. The Judge went on to comment on the English plan. He says one difficulty with the English plan is that it is aimed right at the manufacturers solely, and they insist upon the strictest sort of construction, and there is more or less contention and controversy . . . he says the later situation in Germany is that they have largely abandoned the contributions by employes at the request of the manufacturers; because they said it came out of them anyway.

[Discussion of the inclusion of railway employees followed; and then the question whether the committee should, at an already scheduled meeting that day with the governor, inform him that it would be able to present a bill in time for a special session. Senator Fairchild expressed the fear that the workmen's compensation bill might "get mixed up in the turmoil of a special session" which was also to deal with other controversial subjects and become the victim of "hostile trades and combinations." The matter was not finally determined at this meeting but a special session on the measure was never called.

[The Committee also decided that the chances of success for any new proposal would be maximized if it did not hurry its work but offered successive tentative bills for the criticism of interested parties at public hearings. This general strategy was followed.—Editor]

[The following excerpt, from another executive session of the committee, is presented as typical of exchanges between members in working out particular phraseology. "Mr. Butler" referred to is Mr. Harry L. Butler, attorney of Madison, who had been named counsel to the committee. The bill under discussion was a draft prepared under the instructions of the committee by the legislative drafting service of the Legislative Reference Library. The date of this session was May 10, 1910, pp. 1145-1147.—Editor]

SENATOR SANBORN: There is one thing I want to call to the attention of the committee, the way he worded that first part "It shall not be competent for the employer to plead or prove as a defense." I want to call Mr. Butler's attention to that too. Does that cut out the doctrine where it appears upon the plaintiff's showing that there is assumption of risk? Now, contributory negligence has been held to be a defense, but you do not have to plead those things.

MR. INGALLS: Neither would you have to plead assumption of risk.

SENATOR SANBORN: No, general denial would be sufficient.

MR. INGALLS: Suppose it appears on the plaintiff's showing that he assumed the risk. Does that fact, as an affirmative act upon his part, have to be pleaded or proven? Does that cover the proposition?

SENATOR SANBORN: That is what I want to get at, without any quibble in it.

MR. INGALLS: I know I expressed that in the bill I had to knock out assumption. [Mr. Ingalls refers to a bill previously introduced by him in the Assembly.] It was expressed differently, it was expressed something like this: "That no contract should be implied by reason of the employment that the servant assumed the risk." That was the substance of it. Of course, that is the definition. I used the definition of assumption of risk as laid down by all the decisions. . . .

SENATOR FAIRCHILD: That would still leave the assumption of risk, where it appears from the plaintiff's own showing, where it now is.

SENATOR SANBORN: . . . I was wondering whether it is not better to state that these two things shall not be a defense.

SENATOR BLAINE: I should think it would be better, that would be simpler. "Shall not be a defense in such action," and so on. . . .

SENATOR FAIRCHILD: It certainly would leave it altogether too much open. The Supreme Court might give us the meaning—

MR. INGALLS: They would be apt to construe it strictly.

SENATOR SANBORN: They might.

SENATOR BLAINE: Say it shall not be a defense.

MR. INGALLS: That would be better.

[The form of the bill finally adopted employs substantially the phraseology here finally agreed upon, with reference to the abrogation of defenses.—Editor]

NOTES AND QUESTIONS

1. The testimony of Mr. Babb: note that only two members of the committee were present. The style of questioning is that of the courtroom but more informal. And, of course, the witness is not subjected to cross-examination by employee representatives. Consider what different types of information such testimony as that of Mr. Babb furnishes a committee.

2. The executive sessions: note the evidence of Justice Marshall's influence and how concern for constitutionality and the customary attitude of judges towards the construction of statutes shape the drafting of a bill. Note, too, the ever present considerations of political strategy which entered into the discussion of the special session. Should executive sessions be abolished and all committee hearings be opened to the public?

3. Contrast these hearings with the kind of hearings Mr. Rauh writes about, *supra*, and which provoked the Watkins and Barenblatt cases.

EDITORIAL NOTE: FUNCTIONS of a COMMITTEE HEARING on a BILL

The legislative committee hearing on a bill of course plays an educational role, in bringing facts and arguments to the attention of committee members, other members of the legislature, and those members of the general public (including contending private groups) who are interested enough in the bill to pay attention to the hearing or the transcript thereof. But there are other less obvious functions served. The hearing furnishes a kind of proving ground for the bill—helping to reveal weaknesses which may be removed before consideration by the full legislature. Further, an interest-group is given an opportunity, by the hearing, to dramatize its position. Thus, the hearing has a "propaganda" as well as an "education" function.

This does not mean that private groups regard the public-hearing as their most effective educational or propaganda medium. Thus, for instance, in 1934 the general counsel of the Association of American Railroads wrote to railroad executives that, in effect: "Hearings before the Committees are largely matters of scenery to satisfy the public and . . . the effective work cannot be accomplished in . . . appearances before Committees. In his judgment [i.e., that of the association's chief staff officer] the effective work in opposition to bills harmful to railroads can only be done through personal interviews with Congressmen conducted by men personally acquainted with the Congressmen they interview and for whom the interviewed Congressmen would have a feeling of respect and confidence." [1]

Not only may there be media more important than the hearing, for the ultimate fate of the bill, but the hearing itself may fall short of accomplishing its ideal objectives. For instance, the transcript may not faithfully reflect what happened at the hearing. Thus the committee members may make, and may allow a witness to make off-the-record statements. Or the opportunity given to witnesses and committee members to correct their remarks before printing of the transcript may result in substantial deviations between what was said and what is printed. More significant as a shortcoming in some hearings is the fact that the chairman may have an axe to grind. Hence, he may not give full and fair opportunity for presentation of alternative views, or may so space the witnesses, and so time the sessions and recesses as to get maximum effect and news-value for a particular point of view. See, for interesting illustrations of this, in connection with investigating committee hearings, Truman, The Governmental Process 379-386 (1951); and on the general role of the hearing in the legislative process, Gross, The Legislative Struggle 284-308 (1953).

EDITORIAL NOTE: The REPORT of the SPECIAL COMMITTEE on INDUSTRIAL INSURANCE

The report of the committee to which a bill was referred for consideration is one of the most valuable sources of information regarding its background and objectives. It may be the principal source of data to

[1] S. Rep. No. 26, 77th Cong., 1st Sess., (1941), Pt. 2 at 63. For an interesting article on the roles of committee members, see Huitt, The Congressional Committee: A Case Study, 48 Amer. Pol. Sci. Rev. 340 (1954).

support the constitutionality of a statute. And it may contain the most explicit indications of the meaning of particular statutory provisions.

Space does not permit reprinting even a portion of the 148-page report of the Special Committee on Industrial Insurance. To give some concrete idea of its nature its contents are here outlined:

I. Foreword and Analysis of Bill (pp. 5-6 of the Report, setting out the objects to be attained as "1. To furnish certain, prompt and reasonable compensation to the injured employee. 2. To utilize for injured employees a large portion of the great amount of money wasted under the present system. 3. To provide a tribunal where disputes between employer and employee in regard to compensation may be settled promptly, cheaply and summarily. 4. To provide means of minimizing the number of accidents in industrial pursuits.")

II. The Bill as Recommended (pp. 7-34 set out the text of the committee's bill, each section of the bill accompanied by a comment explanatory of its meaning and of the considerations of policy underlying it. Some examples of this comment will be set out below).

III. General Statement (pp. 35-41 set forth the committee's basic conclusions as to the reasons of public policy which favor the substitution of a compensation scheme for the common law, and refer in some detail to the committee's activity in collecting new statistics, in conferring with interested groups, and in seeking the aid of other official bodies in other states and countries dealing with this problem).

IV. Chronological Record of Meetings (reprinted above).

V. Supplementary Statement by Wallace Ingalls, Vice-Chairman (pp. 45-50, further detailing the policy considerations thought to support the fundamental change in approach to the problem of loss from industrial accident).

VI. Counsel's Statement (pp. 51-58 contain a description of the bill, with some detailed comments on constitutional aspects and the meaning of certain portions of the bill, by Mr. Harry L. Butler of Madison, counsel to the committee).

VII. Appendix I: (pp. 59-67 with accompanying tables present the results of a study made especially for this committee of a limited number of industrial accident cases in Milwaukee county, to ascertain the practical effect of the injury upon the worker and his family).

VIII. Appendix II: (pp. 68-75, with accompanying tables, present further data from the study above mentioned).

IX. Appendix III: (pp. 76-85 give brief histories of 36 accident cases in Milwaukee county, stressing inadequate recoveries, no recoveries, delays).

X. Appendix IV: (pp. 87-126, with accompanying tables, give data as to several hundred cases, regarding wage-loss, causes of injury, nature of injury and length of disability, age, sex, marital status of the injured worker, disposition of suits).

XI. Appendix V: (pp. 127-145, copies of the four successive tentative bills submitted for public discussion by the legislative committee).

XII. Appendix VI: (pp. 146-148, bibliography on industrial accidents, employers liability, and workmen's compensation).

EDITORIAL NOTE: CONSIDERATION of a BILL on the FLOOR of the LEGISLATURE; The CASE of the WORKMEN'S COMPENSATION BILL

When a bill is reported by a legislative committee to the legislative house of which the committee is a part, two sorts of events may ensue which may furnish the lawyer with helpful material in subsequent litigation over issues of the constitutionality or interpretation of the bill as enacted into statute. Just as one may derive reasonable and helpful inferences as to the intention of the draftsmen from noting the ways in which the originally introduced bill may be amended in committee, so inferences may be drawn from amendments proposed on the floor of the legislative chamber during consideration of the measure, and there adopted or rejected.

In the second place, discussion of the bill may take place among members of the legislative chamber. The great bulk of bills enacted into law in the modern legislature receive their only substantial consideration in detail in the legislative committees, and the vote of the chamber in eventually passing or rejecting them is likely generally to follow the committee recommendations, without any open debate. Exchanges of arguments, comments, questions and answers as to the meaning of phraseology may, however, if they occur, often be most helpful in illuminating the significance of a statute. Unfortunately it has never become the practice of state governments, including Wisconsin, to take and preserve stenographic transcripts of proceedings on the floor of the legislature. Every state legislature keeps a Journal of the proceedings in each of its chambers, but the Journal contains only a record of motions made and votes taken upon the occasion of all the formal steps requisite in the consideration of a bill, and does not contain a record of debate. Some Journals, like that of the assembly and senate in Wisconsin, do contain copies of all Messages addressed to the legislature by the governor; and occasionally important committee reports.

In this matter, again, the material available regarding Federal statutes is much more generous, for the Congressional Record, an official publication, contains a verbatim report of all discussion as well as all formal official action which takes place on the floor of the Senate and House of Representatives of the United States.

If a measure considered in a state legislature is of particular importance, or gave rise to particularly lively discussion on the floor of either house of the legislature, contemporaneous newspaper accounts are likely to furnish some evidence of what took place. As a general rule, such newspaper accounts would not be admissible in evidence before a court regarding issues of constitutionality or interpretation, although it seems reasonably probable that such data may be admissible if it becomes relevant to consider the general history of the times in which a measure was passed. Even though such newspaper data may not be admissible in evidence, they are of considerable value to the non-lawyer interested in the statute and may furnish the lawyer help by suggesting leads for uncovering official sources of information regarding the passage of a bill and sound lines of argument to pursue on the basis of the available official materials.

We have examined the news accounts of the proceedings in the Wisconsin legislature on the proposed workmen's compensation act. Two unusual features mark the proceedings as reported in these accounts. The senate and assembly met jointly as committees of the whole to consider the bill, and representatives of various interested groups were given a final opportunity to appear before the full legislature and explain their positions on the measure.

According to the news accounts, only the advisability of setting up a new agency—an Industrial Accident Board—to administer the statute was seriously debated on the floor.

Following is an account of this controversy as it appeared in the *Madison Democrat,* January 20, 1911, under these headlines: "RAISE OBJECTION TO COMMISSION / ADMINISTRATION FEATURES OF WORKMEN'S COMPENSATION PROPOSALS ARE OPPOSED / SENATOR HUSTING AGAINST CENTRAL BOARD— FAVORS LOCAL COMMITTEES / SENATOR OWEN TALKS FOR MEASURE—FINAL HEARING THIS AFTERNOON.

Any material opposition to the workmen's compensation bill will be directed against the method of administration of the measure, which has been devised by the special committee. Sentiments expressed by legislators yesterday, indicate that the idea of a commission to administer the compensation law practically is the only objectionable feature of the bill.

Strong opposition to the establishment of any more state commissions was voiced at yesterday's joint hearing; the democrats being particularly averse to incurring any more expense to the state through the employment of high salaried commissioners. While the discussion was general in its nature, it is a fair index of the handling of the measure when it comes up for passage.

The bill as it now stands, provides for the creation of a commission of three members, which shall have the power to settle disputes between employers and employees in reference to the payment of claims under the compensation act. One member is to be appointed by the governor for a term of two years and one for a term of four years. The labor commissioner will be an ex-officio member. Salaries of $5000 per year have been provided for each member.

Many legislators favor the German plan, which provides for a local adjustment committee in each factory or shop where the law is in effect. This plan, they say, will do away with the expense of a special commission, will hasten the settlement of cases and will eliminate the expense which would be incurred by employees in coming to Madison to present their cases before the board.

They who favor this idea would not do away with the state commission plan entirely, but would have the administration powers vested in the bureau of labor, thus eliminating the expense of a new commission. It was suggested by Senator John J. Blaine that the labor bureau be done away with and the administration of all state labor laws be vested in the industrial insurance commission.

While the hearing was primarily a reviewing of the points of the bill for the information of the legislators, it rapidly evolved into a debate when the board question was opened by Senator Husting.

"What reason, outside of uniformity of rulings, has the special committee for favoring the central board instead of the local boards?" Senator Husting asked Senator Blaine.

It was stated that the committee aimed at simplicity in procedure. He said that Americans cannot do as the Germans do with their local boards because of the American spirit of personal independence. He asserted that in Germany the workmen do not question the fairness of the decisions of the local boards, because of the spirit of the race to bow to the authority of any who govern them. He said that the local board in America would only complicate matters because of the difficulty in securing decisions that would be satisfactory to all parties concerned.

An assemblyman stated that if he voted for the creation of an industrial insurance commission his constituents probably would hang him when he returned to his home. Senator Linley said that he had encountered a great amount of opposition among the legislators, to the commission idea.

This statement moved Senator Owen, who was presiding, to call Speaker Ingram to the desk and to take the floor to give the first exhibition of oratory of the session. He said:

"I have heard legislators, ever since I have been in the legislature, say that they are prejudiced against creating any more state commissions.

"It appears to me that, on this question, the merits of the bill should be taken into consideration and adequate means of its administration should be devised. We are wasting time haggling over prejudices regarding state commissions.

"We, as a nation, are making progress in legislation and more and more the necessity of commission government is felt. We are bound to have more state commissions, in spite of any prejudice against them.

"What experience have we had with commissions that we should have a prejudice against them? Would we want to abolish any one that we have? We must not defeat this great, humane measure because of a little difference over the manner of administration.

"Each county pays ten times more now in expenses for litigation than would comprise its share of keeping up the commission. This act will cut out a great amount of litigation and the enormous court expense attached to it."

The Milwaukee Free Press of January 21, 1911, reported that Senator Sanborn, chairman of the special committee, replied to criticisms of the proposed commission, as follows: "It is recognized," he said, "that in carrying out the economic reforms proposed these days the changes must be carried out by commissions. They are the most satisfactory administering agency. Any prejudice against commissions is not founded on logic, real experience or investigation of the subject. I ask these men from Milwaukee if they ever have heard any complaint against the tax commission or the railroad commission as to fairness in decisions?"

Both Hugh Ryan [attorney for Milwaukee employers] and Henry J.

Killilea [Wisconsin general attorney for the Milwaukee Road] spoke a loud "No." [Ryan and Killilea were on the floor at the time speaking in support of the bill.—Editor]

"In nearly every case of arbitration of disputes under the present law," continued Senator Sanborn, "we hear after the award that something was wrong; that there were prejudicial relations or adverse prejudice. We don't hear any talk like that about our commissions. If we are able to secure able, conscientious, studious men for the board as proposed, the administration of this bill will be just as satisfactory as the present administration of the railroad laws."

Only one amendment of substance to the bill as originally presented by the special committee was adopted by the legislature. This amendment, proposed by the special committee itself, added a separability clause to insure that if the courts held certain parts of the bill to be unconstitutional (particularly the provision that if the employee refused to come under the act, the employer could make use of the defenses of assumption of risk and negligence of a fellow-servant) the rest of the bill, without such parts, would remain standing.

The news accounts indicate that the manufacturers were bitterly disappointed by this amendment and decided, because of it, to contest the constitutionality of the entire measure. Senator Sanborn announced that he welcomed this test. The bill was approved by the Governor on May 3, 1911, and became effective on September 1, 1911.

KENNEDY,* THE CHALLENGE OF POLITICAL COURAGE
The New York Times Magazine, Dec. 18, 1955, p. 13

"People don't give a damn," a syndicated columnist told millions of readers not so many years ago, "what the average Senator or Congressman says. The reason they don't care is that they know what you hear in Congress is 99 per cent tripe, ignorance and demagoguery and not to be relied upon. . . ."

Earlier a member of the Cabinet had recorded in his diary: "While I am reluctant to believe in the total depravity of the Senate, I place but little dependence on the honesty and truthfulness of a large portion of the Senators. A majority of them are small lights, mentally weak, and wholly unfit to be Senators. Some are vulgar demagogues . . . some are men of wealth who have purchased their position . . . [some are] men of narrow intellect, limited comprehension, and low partisan prejudice . . ."

And still earlier a member of the Senate itself told his colleagues that "the confidence of the people is departing from us, owing to our unreasonable delays."

The Senate knows that many Americans today share these sentiments. Senators,

* John F. Kennedy, elected President of the United States in Nov. 1960, wrote this when he was Senator from Massachusetts. He had been a Representative from 1949-1953. The article was adapted from his book, Profiles in Courage (1955). He is also the author of The Strategy for Peace (1960) and Why England Slept (1940). —Editor

we hear, must be politicians—and politicians must be concerned only with winning votes, not with statesmanship or courage. Mothers may still want their favorite sons to grow up to be President, but, according to a famous Gallup poll of some years ago, they do not want them to become politicians in the process.

Does this current rash of criticism and disrespect mean the quality of the Senate has declined? Certainly not. For of the three statements quoted above, the first was made in the twentieth century, the second in the nineteenth and the third in the eighteenth (when the first Senate, barely underway, was debating where the Capitol should be located).

Does it mean then, that the Senate can no longer boast of men of courage?

Walter Lippmann, after nearly half a century of careful observation, rendered in his recent book a harsh judgment both on the politician and the electorate: "With exceptions so rare they are regarded as miracles of nature, successful democratic politicians are insecure and intimidated men. They advance politically only as they placate, appease, bribe, seduce, bamboozle, or otherwise manage to manipulate the demanding threatening elements in their constituencies. The decisive consideration is not whether the proposition is good but whether it is popular— not whether it will work well and prove itself, but whether the active-talking constituents like it immediately."

I am not so sure, after nearly ten years of living and working in the midst of "successful democratic politicians," that they are all "insecure and intimidated men." I am convinced that the complication of public business and the competition for the public's attention have obscured innumerable acts of political courage— large and small—performed almost daily in the Senate Chamber. I am convinced that the decline—if there has been a decline—has been less in the Senate than in the public's appreciation of the art of politics, of the nature and necessity for compromise and balance and of the nature of the Senate as a legislative chamber.

And, finally, I am convinced that we have criticized those who have followed the crowd—and at the same time criticized those who have defied it—because we have not fully understood the responsibility of a Senator to his constituents or recognized the difficulty facing a politician conscientiously desiring, in Webster's words, "to push [his] skiff from the shore alone" into a hostile and turbulent sea. Perhaps if the American people more fully comprehended the terrible pressures which discourage acts of political courage, which drive a Senator to abandon or subdue his conscience, then they might be less critical of those who take the easier road—and more appreciative of those still able to follow the path of courage.

The *first* pressure is a form of pressure rarely recognized by the general public. Americans want to be liked—and Senators are no exception. Realizing that the path of the conscientious insurgent must frequently be a lonely one, we are anxious to get along with our fellow legislators, our fellow members of the club, to abide by the clubhouse rules and patterns, not to pursue a unique and independent course which would embarrass or irritate the other members. We realize, moreover, that our influence in the club—and the extent to which we can accomplish our objectives and those of our constituents—are dependent in some measure on the esteem with which we are regarded by other Senators. "The way to get along," I was told when I entered Congress, "is to go along."

"Going along," it was clear, included fulfillment of my obligation to follow the party leadership whom I had helped select. All of us in the Congress are made fully aware of the importance of party unity (what sins have been committed in that name!) and the adverse effect upon our party's chances in the next election which any rebellious conduct might bring. Even the success of legislation in which a Senator is interested depends in part on the extent to which his support of his party's programs has won him the assistance of his party's leaders.

Finally, the Senator who follows the independent course of conscience is likely to discover that he has earned the disdain not only of his colleagues in the Senate and his associates in his party but also of the all-important contributors to his campaign fund.

It is thinking of that next campaign—the desire to be re-elected—that provides the *second* pressure on the conscientious Senator. It should not automatically be assumed that this is a wholly selfish motive—although it is not unnatural that those who have chosen politics as their profession should seek to continue their careers—for Senators who go down to defeat in a vain defense of a single principle will not be on hand to fight for that or any other principle in the future.

Defeat moreover is not only a setback for the Senator himself—he is also obligated to consider the effect upon the party he supports, upon his friends and supporters who have "gone out on a limb" for him or invested their savings in his career, and even upon the wife and children whose happiness and security—often depending at least in part upon his success in office—may mean more to him than anything else.

Where else, in a non-totalitarian country, but in the political profession is the individual expected to sacrifice all—including his own career—for the national good? In private life, as in industry, we expect the individual to advance his own enlightened self-interest—within the limitations of the law—in order to achieve over-all progress. But in public life we expect individuals to sacrifice their private interests to permit the national good to progress.

In no other occupation but politics is it expected that a man will sacrifice honors, prestige and his chosen career on a single issue. Lawyers, business men, teachers, doctors, all face difficult personal decisions involving their integrity—but few, if any, face them in the glare of the spotlight as do those in public office. Few, if any, face the same dread finality of decision that confronts a Senator facing an important call of the roll. He may want more time for his decision—he may believe there is something to be said for both sides—he may feel that a slight amendment could remove all difficulties—but when that roll is called he cannot hide, he cannot equivocate, he cannot delay—and he senses that his constituency, like the Raven in Poe's poem, is perched there on his Senate desk, croaking "Nevermore" as he casts the vote that stakes his political future.

Few Senators "retire to Pocatello" by choice. The virus of Potomac Fever, which rages everywhere in Washington, breeds nowhere in more virulent form than on the Senate floor. The prospect of forced retirement from "the most exclusive club in the world," the possibilities of giving up the interesting work, the fascinating trappings and the impressive prerogatives of Congressional office, can cause even the most courageous politician serious loss of sleep.

Thus perhaps without realizing it, some Senators tend to take the easier, less troublesome path to harmonize or rationalize what at first appears to be a conflict between their conscience—or the result of their deliberations—and the majority opinion of their constituents. Such Senators are not political cowards—they have simply developed the habit of sincerely reaching conclusions inevitably in accordance with popular opinion.

Still other Senators have not developed that habit—they have neither conditioned nor subdued their consciences—but they feel, sincerely and without cynicism, that they must leave considerations of conscience aside if they are to be effective. Not all Senators agree with them—but few would deny that the desire to be re-elected exercises a strong brake on independent courage.

The *third* and most significant source of pressures which discourage political courage in the conscientious Senator or Congressman—and practically all of the problems described apply equally to members of both Houses—is the pressure of his constituency, the interest groups, the organized letter-writers, the economic blocs and even the average voter. To cope with such pressures, to defy them or even to satisfy them, is a formidable task. All of us occasionally have the urge to follow the example of Congressman John Steven McGroarty of California, who wrote a constituent in 1935:

> "One of the countless drawbacks of being in Congress is that I am compelled to receive impertinent letters from a jackass like you in which you say I promised to have the Sierra Madre mountains reforested and I have been in Congress two months and haven't done it. Will you please take two running jumps and go to hell."

Fortunately or unfortunately, few follow that urge—but the provocation is there, not only from the unreasonable letters and impossible requests, but also from hopelessly inconsistent demands and endlessly unsatisfied grievances.

To my office, for example, comes a delegation representing New England textile mills, an industry essential to our prosperity. They want the tariff lowered on the imported wool they buy from Australia—but they want the tariff raised on the finished woolen goods imported from England with which they must compete. One of my Southern colleagues told me that a similar group visited him the same day with the same requests—but further urging that he take steps to (1) end the low-wage competition from Japan and (2) prevent the Congress from ending—through a higher minimum wage—the low-wage advantage they themselves enjoy to the dismay of my constituents.

Recently, two groups called me off the Senate floor—the first was a group of business men seeking to have a local Government activity closed as unfair competition for private enterprise; and the other was a group representing the men who work in that Government installation and who are worried about their jobs.

All of us in the Senate meet endless examples of such conflicting pressures, which only reflect the inconsistencies inevitable in our complete economy. If we tell our constituents frankly that we can do nothing, they feel we are unsympathetic or inadequate. If we try and fail—usually meeting a counteraction from other Senators representing other interests—they say we are like all the rest of the politicians. All we can do is retreat into the cloakroom and weep on the shoulder of a sympathetic colleague—or go home and snarl at our wives.

We may tell ourselves that these pressure groups and letter-writers represent only a small percentage of the voters—and this is true. But they are the articulate few whose views cannot be ignored and who constitute the greater part of our contacts with the public at large, whose opinions we cannot know, whose vote we must obtain and yet who in all probability have only a limited idea of what we are trying to do.

These, then, are some of the pressures which confront a man of conscience. He cannot ignore the pressure groups, his constituents, his party, the comradeship of his colleagues, the needs of his family, his own pride in office, the necessity for compromise and the importance of remaining in office. He must judge for himself which path to choose, which step will most help or hinder the ideals to which he is committed.

He realizes that once he begins to weigh each issue in terms of his chances for reelection, once he begins to compromise away his principles on one issue after another for fear that to do otherwise would halt his career and prevent future fights for principle, then he has lost the very freedom of conscience which justifies his continuance in office. But to decide at which point and on which issue he will risk his career is an overwhelming and frightening responsibility.

Why, then, does any man resist these pressures and speak out with courage and conscience? Perhaps those Senators whose acts of political courage are recounted in my forthcoming book were men who forgot all about themselves in their dedication to the public good. But, on the other hand, it is perhaps more likely that John Adams, surely as disinterested a public servant as we ever had, came much nearer to the truth when he wrote: "It is not true, in fact, that any people ever existed who love the public better than themselves."

If this be true, what then caused such statesmen to act as they did? It was not, it seems to me, because they "loved the public better than themselves." On the contrary, it was precisely because they did *love themselves*—because each one's need to maintain his own respect for himself was more important to him than his popularity with others—because his desire to maintain a reputation for integrity was stronger than his desire to maintain his office—because his conscience, his personal standard of ethics, his integrity or morality, call it what you will, was stronger than the pressures of public disapproval—because his faith that *his* course was the best one, and would ultimately be vindicated, outweighed his fear of public reprisal.

When the politician loves neither the public good nor himself, or when his love for himself is limited and is satisfied by the trappings of office, then the public interest is badly served. But when his regard for himself is so high that his own self-respect demands he follow the path of courage and conscience, all benefit.

Today, the challenge of political courage looms larger than ever before. For our everyday life is becoming so saturated with the tremendous power of mass communications that any unpopular or unorthodox course arouses a storm of protests. Our political life is becoming so expensive, so mechanized and so dominated by professional politicians and public relations men that the idealist who dreams of independent statesmanship is rudely awakened by the necessities of election and accomplishment.

And our public life is becoming so increasingly centered upon that seemingly unending war to which we have given the curious epithet "cold" that we tend to encourage rigid ideological unity and orthodox patterns of thought and to frown on insurgent individualism.

Thus, in the days ahead, only the very courageous will be able to take the hard and unpopular decisions necessary for our survival in the struggle with a powerful enemy—an enemy with leaders who need give little thought to the popularity of their course, who need pay little tribute to the public opinion they themselves manipulate, and who may force, without fear of retaliation at polls, their citizens to sacrifice present laughter for future glory. And only the very courageous will be able to keep alive the spirit of individualism and dissent which gave birth to this nation, nourished it as an infant and carried it through its severest tests upon the attainment of its maturity.

NOTES AND QUESTIONS

1. Does the fact that democratic government seeks to assure that the governors will be responsible to the governed mean that the representatives in a legislative body should act the way they think their constituents would have them act? Or should each representative follow his own best judgment?

Professors Wahlke and Eulau, editors of Legislative Behavior (1959) state, at p. 6, that "if responsibility is postulated as an appropriate end," the "classical, normative question" just put "becomes largely irrelevant." Rather, they write, the "problem is now to discover under what conditions the representative can afford to disregard the wishes of his constituents and still hope to maintain their confidence, or under what conditions the demands of constituents do, in fact, become mandatory."

2. In what sense is "responsibility" an end of democratic government? Do Wahlke and Eulau succeed in avoiding the "classical, normative question" by their formulation?

We shall return to some of these questions in the concluding section of this chapter.

EDITORIAL NOTE: The WISCONSIN WORKMEN'S COMPENSATION ACT

The various lines of interest and action suggested to some degree in the foregoing materials converged to produce the enactment of Laws, 1911, ch. 50, the basic workmen's compensation act in Wisconsin.

At the same session of the legislature, L. 1911, ch. 485, creating an Industrial Commission, was enacted, and the administration of chapter 50 was entrusted to this Commission, together with the administration of all labor (including industrial safety) legislation of the state.

It would require more space than is proportionate to the purposes of these materials to reprint the text of the original compensation act and the many important amendments made to it. From the outset, the act has been the subject of continued appraisal, questioning, addition, and remodelling by the legislature, under the pressure of interested groups, particularly organized employers and employees, insurance companies, and the Industrial Commission itself. The history of compensation legislation is a most striking example of the fact that the statute law, no less than the common law, has its processes of growth and that there is no "final" solution to any human problem.

Certain basic features of the workmen's compensation system may be outlined thus:

(1) *"Optional" versus compulsory system:* At the outset, both employer and employee were given, in terms, the right to elect whether they would come under the compensation act, or would continue to have their rights settled by litigation at common law. However, on the one hand, the common law defenses of the negligence of a fellow-servant, assumption of risk, and, in 1913, contributory negligence, were abrogated as to employers who did not choose to come under the compensation act; and, on the other hand, these defenses were left in effect as against an employee who elected not to come under the compensation act, if the employer had so elected. It was expected that, faced with this choice, both employers and employees would generally elect to come under the act; and this eventually proved to be the general experience. In 1931 the act was made compulsory, covering "every person . . . who usually employs three or more employees," (excepting farmers and farm labor) and all employees, except for a limited right of election left in epileptics and persons totally blind. If applicable, therefore, the act, now ch. 102 of Wis. Stats. 1961, completely supersedes the rights and liabilities of the parties as they existed at common law. Furthermore, exempted employers may elect to come under the Act.

For the rules applicable to court suits brought by workers *not* covered by the Act, see Wis. Stats., sec. 331.37.

(2) *The position of the railroad worker:* Railroad workers were held to be within the first workmen's compensation act upon election of their employer to come under the act, unless in any given case the employee had filed an election to retain his remedies of action at law under Laws, 1907, ch. 254, *supra.* In 1913, the compensation act was amended to provide that no railroad employee should be deemed within the act except by express election of both employer and employee. The 1931 law making the compensation act compulsory as to all employers who usually employ three or more employees also covered railroad workers and ended their special election rights.

Since 1908, however, when the Congress of the United States enacted a valid employers' liability act for railroad workers engaged in interstate commerce, no state law is applicable to injuries suffered by these workers.

Though the Federal Employers' Liability Act still requires proof of employer negligence in an ordinary court action (but abolishes the fellow servant and assumption of risk defenses and gives contributory negligence only the effect of proportionately diminishing damages, eliminating this defense entirely if the employer has violated a safety statute) it has been held to supersede not only state employers' liability legislation but also state workmen's compensation acts. The latter, therefore, apply—in the case of railroads—only to injuries suffered by railroad workers engaged in *intrastate* commerce.

(3) *The basis of liability:* Liability under the workmen's compensation act is not determined by fault, either on the side of the employer or his agent who may cause the injury, or on the side of the injured employee. However, the act provides for a 15% increase in the compensation award if the injury is caused by the employer's wrongful failure to comply with Industrial Commission safety regulations, and a 15% decrease in award if the employee is at fault in such respect. The confidence of proponents of compensation legislation that litigation would be greatly reduced by elimination of the fault issue has not been fully borne out, however, because liability under the act rests on statutory elements with reference to which there has been much dispute.

The statute's basic definition of the elements of liability (section 102.03) is that "Liability . . . shall exist against an employer only where the following conditions concur: (a) Where the employee sustains an injury. (b) Where, at the time of the injury, both the employer and employee are subject to the provisions of this chapter. (c) Where, at the time of the injury, the employee is performing service growing out of and incidental to his employment. . . . (d) Where the injury is not intentionally self-inflicted. (e) Where the accident or disease causing injury arises out of his employment. . . ." Most litigation arises under subsections (c) and (e). (The act was amended in 1919 to cover occupational disease as well as accident. This portion of the act has had a very complex history of litigation and amendment since. See, e.g., Rabinowitz, Compensation of Occupational Diseases from a Legal Viewpoint 12 Wis. L. Rev. 198 (1937).)

(4) *The amount of compensation:* Compensation is awarded in terms of definite schedules, of so many weeks of wage loss, for specified classes of injuries. In addition, more recently, the employer must pay the reasonable expenses of medical and surgical care.

(5) *The guaranty of payment of claims:* Every employer subject to the act must carry insurance to cover claims thereunder, unless he is permitted by the Industrial Commission to become a self-insurer under the regulations and supervision of the Commission. Mutual insurance companies locally organized have been very prominent in the provision of such insurance in Wisconsin since the enactment of the statute. The creation of a state insurance fund, such as exists in some states, has been several times proposed and defeated. The employee makes no direct contribution to the cost of

compensation insurance; but directly bears a substantial proportion of the immediate money loss of an accident because compensation at the most does not equal the employee's normal wages.

(6) *Administration:* The Industrial Commission consists of three members appointed by the governor with the advice and consent of the senate for overlapping terms, one term beginning each odd-numbered year. A Director of Workmen's Compensation manages this portion of the Commission's work. The injured employee does not go to court, but presents his claim to the Commission. A staff of examiners, supplemented on occasion by individual commissioners, travels throughout the state to hold hearings, on which reports are made in more or less detail to the commission at intervals. In the average case, the recommendation of the examiner who conducted the hearing will be made the decision of the commission. The orders of the commission are appealable to the Circuit Court of Dane County, and thence to the Supreme Court of Wisconsin.

Section 4

SCOPE and OBJECTIVES of LEGISLATIVE INTERVENTION and the PUBLIC INTEREST

AUERBACH,* *LAW AND SOCIAL CHANGE IN THE UNITED STATES*†
6 U.C.L.A. Law Review 516-532 (1959)

I. *General Introduction*

. . . Law is not merely a function of society. While social, economic, political and psychological factors affect the course of legal development, legal factors also affect man's behavior, his environment and even his attitudes. At a particular time and place, the legal system of a changing society may fail to meet its needs (as may be the case in many underdeveloped countries today) or, indeed, law may be used to alter or accelerate the course of social development, as may be the case in connection with the racial integration of our public schools.

II. *Function of Law in Society*

Our society entrusts two principal tasks to our law-making institutions—and by law-making institutions I mean the judicial, legislative, executive and adminis-

* Carl A. Auerbach is Professor of Law at the University of Minnesota, having taught at the University of Wisconsin from 1947 to 1961. He was a government attorney in a number of federal agencies, serving as Associate General Counsel in the Office of Economic Stabilization in 1946 and General Counsel at the Office of Price Administration in 1946-47. He received a Fulbright Advanced Research Award at the London School of Economics in 1953-54 and was a Fellow, Center for Advanced Study in the Behavioral Sciences in 1958-59.
† Delivered as The Second Annual Social Science Research Lecture at the University of California at Los Angeles, March 5, 1959.—Editor

trative agencies. These are, first, to establish the general framework, the rules of the game so to speak, within and by which individual and group life shall be carried on, and, secondly, to adjust the conflicting claims which different individuals and groups of individuals seek to satisfy in society.

A. *Allocation of Decision-Making between the Private and Public Spheres.* I should like to explain what I mean by this "general framework." The problem of ordering social life may be viewed as the problem of allocating the making of decisions concerning the conduct of individual and group life between "private" agencies (the individual himself, family, church, other voluntary associations, etc.) and "public-legal" agencies (the law-making institutions). The respective areas of private and public ordering of individual and group life that can be delineated in any particular society at any particular time are not, of course, isolated from each other. The private sphere would not exist if the law did not permit it a significant range of discretion in the making of final decisions affecting individual and group life. And even within this range, private decisions may need actual or potential legal enforcement to become effective.

The recognition of a private sphere implies that many of the conflicting claims which different individuals and groups seek to satisfy will be adjusted privately. But an individual or group which is dissatisfied with the adjustment-decision reached privately must be able to appeal to law for relief, just as the private decision-makers must be able to resort to law to enforce their decisions against non-conforming individuals and groups. Such appeal or resort to law must be made available as a substitute for the private use of physical force, which a legal order must severely circumscribe.

The legal institutions, therefore, must evolve principles, standards and rules laying down the conditions under which, and the way, they will enforce private decisions. Because they are public institutions, they must first decide whether the decisions sought to be enforced accord with public policy—public notions as to how the conflicting claims in question should be adjusted or how far the exercise of private discretion should be upheld without regard to the manner in which discretion is actually exercised in the particular case. In some cases, therefore, private decision will be enforced only within limits set by the legal institutions. (A liquidated damage clause in a contract will not be enforced if it seeks to impose a penalty. Compensatory damages will be allowed.) In other cases, the law-making institutions will remain "neutral"—they will not enforce the private decision but will tolerate private adherence to it. (The restrictive covenant situation.) The law-making institutions may, of course, go further and substitute decisions of their own for those which have been arrived at privately (minimum wage law supersedes wage agreement between employer and employee) or they may even require private individuals and groups to take initial action to effectuate decisions publicly reached (install devices to prevent air pollution).

By "private" decisions, then, I mean the decisions taken by individuals and groups falling within a significant range of decisions about the conduct of individual and group life which the law-making institutions will not set aside and which they may even stand ready to enforce. By "public" decisions, I mean the decisions taken by the law-making institutions enforcing, or refusing to enforce, limiting or displacing, private decisions or requiring certain initial action to be taken by individuals or groups.

I shall not attempt to describe, in any greater detail, the manifold relations between the private and public spheres in our society. But I do want to make a few, additional observations. Private decision-making is meaningful only in the context of the particular legal order, and public decision-making only in the context of the particular private order, which exists at a particular time. Secondly, law may and has been used to enlarge the area of private decision-making. And lastly, private decision-making itself affects the public sphere because, in a democracy, the people participate in the process by which public decisions are ultimately reached.

So, then, by the "general framework" which it is the task of the law to establish, I mean the over-all division of decision-making between the public and private spheres, including the relationships between the two spheres and the rules by which changes in the over-all division and these relationships are to be made. However, I do not mean thereby to regard as "law" the body of private decisions falling within the range of private discretion recognized by the law-making institutions. But I have no objection if anyone else chooses to call these decisions "law," whether taken by the head of a family, the officers of a corporation or trade union, the president of a private university or the coach of a football team. I shall reserve the term "law" for the decisions of those institutions in our society which monopolize the legitimate use of physical force and consequently make unlawful all other use of physical force without their concurrence. (Thus I would not call a father a law-making institution because the law permits him to use reasonable physical force to exact obedience from a child.)

B. *Adjustment of Conflicting Claims.* When the law-making institutions are called upon to adjust the conflicting claims of different individuals and groups, they need the information and the ideas which the social scientist can make available, yet which he is most reluctant to produce for this purpose. It is true that the process of adjustment often consists of arriving at some compromise which satisfies the contending parties for the time being. Decision also often demands a choice between conflicting claims, because the recognition of one requires the rejection of the other. In either case, the law-maker must be concerned with the ends which the legal order should seek to attain or, in other words, with the achievement of justice. For claims which are recognized by law become legal rights. They may as well be called realized ideals or values which have been chosen authoritatively.

We should not, of course, expect the social sciences to tell us *what* ought to be done. But this does not mean that they have nothing to tell us *about what* ought to be done. Analysis of the relationship between fact and value in this context should be a prime task of interdisciplinary research.

In struggling with the problem of values, the law-maker has an advantage over the moral philosopher, because it is the law's function to serve practical ends. So even if we grant that reason is powerless to settle conflicts about the ultimate ends of life, these are not the conflicts which the legal order is normally called upon to adjust. I do not, however, wish to imply that fact finding by the social scientist can ever displace the judgment of the law-maker, or of the individual citizen in a democracy, in the making of "effectual and responsible decisions concerning the direction of" individual and social life.[2] Or, since I value a free society, that it would be a good thing if this could be done and the responsibility for decision were turned over to the social scientist. I think this is what frightens ordinary people, including myself, about too literal talk of a "science" of human behavior. It implies that the so-called "behavioral" sciences should seek "to reduce man as a whole, in all his activities, to the level of a conditioned and behaving animal." [3] A more modest, and less frightening, aim of the social sciences would be to lay the informational and analytical bases for a more rational exercise of judgment and, possibly, also to contribute a "trained sense" when no definite knowledge can be said to exist about particular matters requiring decision.[4]

III. *Law and Social Change in 19th Century United States*

This long introduction to the question of the interrelationship between law and social change in the United States was intended to show why I shall approach the problem from the point of view of the changing adjustments made by law of the conflicting, changing claims which individuals and groups pressed for satisfaction over the course of our history and of the changing allocation of decision-making between the private and public spheres which the effectuation of these changing adjustments made necessary.[5]

A. *Significance of Political-Constitutional Framework.* It has become more or less fashionable of late to explain the bleak prospect for democracy in underdeveloped countries on the ground that these countries, though underdeveloped, are striving to become modern and industrialized as quickly as possible—an aspiration which only some form of totalitarian government can realize. Yet it is a fact

[2] Hart & McNaughton, Evidence and Inference in the Law, Daedalus (Journal Amer. Academy of Arts & Sciences), Vol. 87, No. 4. p. 64 (1958). Social scientists should find this entire essay to be worth reading.

[3] Arendt, The Human Condition 45 (1958).

[4] Hart & McNaughton, *op. cit. supra* note 2, at 63.

[5] For 19th century developments, I have relied heavily on the work of my colleague James Willard Hurst, Law and the Conditions of Freedom in the Nineteenth Century United States (1956); Law and the Balance of Power in the Community, 6 Record of the Bar Association of New York City, No. 4, p. 148 (Apr. 1951); excellent economic histories of a number of American states:

Handlin & Handlin, Commonwealth: Massachusetts, 1774-1861; A Study of the Role of Government in the American Economy (1947); Hartz, Economic Policy and Democratic Thought: Pennsylvania, 1776-1860 (1948); Kirkland, Men, Cities and Transportation (1948); Cadman, The Corporation in New Jersey (1949); Heath, Constructive Liberalism: The Role of the State in Economic Development in Georgia to 1860 (1954); Primm, Economic Policy in the Development of a Western State: Missouri, 1820-1860 (1954); and Karl Polanyi's account of British developments in the 19th century, The Great Transformation (1944). [See also Stone, The Myths of Planning and Laissez-Faire, 18 Geo. Wash. L. Rev. 1 (1949).—Editor]

that the American democracy became firmly rooted while the United States was still an underdeveloped nation. In 1789, the United States had a population of only four million people living mostly on farms. Poverty was pretty much their lot. At this time, if I may quote Stuart Chase: "Industry was in the handicraft stage of little mills on streams, little ironmasters, little shipbuilders; and George Washington's false teeth were made of wood." [6] Yet the leaders of this small pre-modern, underdeveloped society espoused a vigorous liberalism, resorted to violent revolution to win political independence and laid the foundation of a democratic republic. I think it would be equally true to say that politial democracy became rooted in Great Britain before the advent of the industrial revolution. When Karl Polanyi, in his book entitled *The Great Transformation,* tried to make us appreciate the depth of the social changes wrought by the industrial revolution in England, he asked us to think of its impact upon underdeveloped countries today.

Just as political democracy may precede industrialization, so there is no guarantee that it must follow industrialization, as the history of modern Germany woefully attests. One is tempted, therefore, to ascribe primacy to political factors in accounting for the rise of political democracy in the United States and Great Britain, as well as for the rise of totalitarianism in the Soviet Union and China.

The political fact, for example, that our federal union was based upon the Constitution of 1789 had profound consequences for the course of social change in the United States. The Constitution founded a democracy. By the middle of the 19th century, white manhood suffrage prevailed generally in the United States and no property qualifications for holding office were imposed. The Constitution gave the federal government ample power to deal with the exigencies of the future, yet prevented the centralization of over-all political power in the hands of the national government and of the federal government's power in the hands of any single branch within it. The Constitution created an independent judiciary to solve disputes within the federal structure peacefully and to enforce the constitutional guarantees of the freedom of speech and association and against arbitrary action by the federal government. The Civil War Amendments extended these guarantees to the individual in his relations with the states.

A form of government was thus established which made peaceful change possible, yet which imposed limits upon the temporary majority's treatment of the temporary minority. It therefore gave all groups in our society a greater stake in the rules by which peaceful change was to be effected than in the particular decisions reached by the law-making institutions at any particular time, no matter how adverse these decisions may have been to particular group interests. Having stated this generalization, I should hasten to point to the one great exception—the Civil War.

The very establishment of the federal union had more direct economic consequences also. With the constitutional provision for the admission of new states on a basis of equality with the old, it afforded the opportunity for the creation of an internal market of sufficient size for large-scale industrial growth—the importance

[6] Chase, No War, No Poverty? The Progressive, January 1959, p. 12.

of which has most recently been attested to by the European common market arrangements.

B. *Influence of Law in Preventing Consolidation of Social Life Antagonistic to Advent of Industrialization.* It is true that the advent of industrialization did not have the traumatic effect upon social and community organization in the United States which Professor Polanyi explains it had in Great Britain. English village life, ruled and protected by a hereditary landed gentry and an established clergy, and innately antagonistic to the march of industrialization, did not exist to be destroyed in the 19th century United States. The abundance of land in the United States led to the early abolition of primogeniture and feudal tenures and to the enactment of a policy favoring the free alienability of land. Farming was thus commercialized before industrialization came. The Constitution, of course, prohibited the federal government from establishing any church. And by 1833, no state in the Union had an established church. The drive to use the self-regulating market as the central mechanism for improving the material conditions of life in the United States thus never came into conflict with a system of strongly held, opposing values.

C. *Division between Private and Public Decision-Making.* 1. *Legal institutions creating and protecting the framework for private economic decision-making.* The American environment, as early as our colonial period, tended to encourage self-reliance and generate individual expectations of material improvement. Satisfaction of these expectations required the restriction of governmental power in certain areas of social life and its exercise in others.

a. *Eradication of mercantilist legal policy.* To release the productive energies of the individual, it was necessary, first, to sweep away the reflections in law of the colonial policy of Great Britain which severely restricted the scope of private economic decision-making. Colonial laws interfering with the free alienation of land, limiting wages, regulating prices and marketing practices and fixing standards of quality and measure were repealed.

b. *Legal protection of the market and facilitation of capital accumulation.* Then, to foster a self-regulating market economy, contract and criminal law doctrines were developed which safeguarded the claims to freedom of contract and the security of transactions and to private property and the security of acquisitions. The business corporation, probably the most significant legal invention of the century, enabled entrepreneurs to gather large aggregates of private capital for economic development. The accumulation of capital was further facilitated by the absence of any general federal or state income, gift, or inheritance taxes throughout the 19th century. The federal income tax of 1894 was declared unconstitutional by the Supreme Court.

2. *Promotion of economic development by law.* Government also intervened during the 19th century in order to promote economic development. The federal government subsidized agriculture by selling the best lands which it owned in small lots at low prices.

Government on all levels subsidized the construction of turnpikes, canals, railroads and river and harbor improvements.

Government aided the private credit facilities by delegating to them the power to issue banknotes.

Industry was sought to be aided by the protective tariff and, in many localities, by direct subsidies.

Through its policies with respect to banks, interest rates and the currency, the federal government sought indirectly to influence the allocation of scarce capital. The fact that capital was so scarce throughout the 19th century may explain why these policies provoked so much legal and political conflict.

To stimulate the import of capital, the Constitution embodied a number of provisions designed to protect foreign creditors. During the 19th century, too, the United States promoted immigration. And the states and municipalities pledged their tax revenues to back internal improvements for which it was sought to attract foreign capital.

3. *Social costs of economic development.* The achievements of the 19th century American capitalism were great. But its social costs were very high. The law did little to curb the extravagant exploitation of our natural resources. Forests were despoiled. Soil was permitted to erode. Game was exterminated. Air and water supplies were polluted and fish life destroyed. Natural gas was burned to get oil, which was squandered. Unplanned railroad development left a heritage of problems with which we are still struggling today.

Human resources were also cruelly used. The public health was nobody's concern. The workday and workweek were very long and earnings very low, though conditions of the American worker in the 19th century were probably better than the conditions of the worker anywhere else. Workers and their families bore the staggering costs of industrial accidents. The business cycle, which recurred throughout the 19th century, victimized farmers and workers.

As the pace of industrialization increased after 1870, the competitive process, central to the concept of the self-regulating market, began to destroy the basis of the competitive order by giving rise to big business and big finance.

Social unrest grew and found expression in the protest movements of the farmers; the railroad strikes of 1877 and 1894; the Haymarket bomb throwing in 1886; the Homestead strike riot of 1892 and Coxey's army of the unemployed in 1894. This unrest found political expression in the bitter Presidential campaigns of the 1890's.

Before the close of the 19th century, the law began to do something about these unintended consequences of rapid industrialization based upon private economic decision-making in order to allocate, in a more just and humane fashion, the material and human costs which did not show up in the acounts of any private firm.

Ironically, the ideology of individualism and laissez-faire reached its ascendancy in the United States only late in the 19th century when the developing economy became incompatible with the kind of society men like William Graham Sumner were extolling. Change always seems to outrun man's contemporaneous capacity to grasp its significance.

4. *Legal intervention to curb the exercise of private economic power.* To curb

the exercise of private economic power, Congress passed the Interstate Commerce Act in 1887 and the Sherman Antitrust Law in 1890. The Sherman Act was designed to safeguard the competitive order; the 1887 Act, to regulate the exercise of monopoly power in an industry in which it was thought not possible or not desirable to attempt to restore competition. To this day, both laws continue to provoke controversies which highlight the difficulty of weighing the effect of legal factors in the process of socio-economic development. And these controversies are carried on by economists who, of all social scientists, have been most successful in quantifying their analyses and their findings.

IV. *Law and Social Change in 20th Century United States*

A. *Legal Intervention to Curb the Exercise of Private Economic Power.* 1. *The anti-trust laws.* Great effort, for example, has been expended to show that the degree of concentration of industry has not increased since 1890. But the same degree of concentration may have greater significance, from the point of view of power in society, as the scale of industry grows larger, which, of course, has happened since 1890. And even the constancy of the relative degree of concentration may be due, as Professor Galbraith has pointed out, to the appearance of new industries since 1890.[7] It remains true that American industry is typified by a few large corporations and a fringe of small ones and that a small number of large corporations account for a very substantial proportion of industrial activity. Certainly, the anti-trust laws have not restored the kind of competitive order which Justice Brandeis desired and thought it was the aim of these laws to restore.

But would there not have been greater concentration if the Sherman Act had not been enacted? It is difficult to know how one should go about trying to answer such a question. We might adopt a comparative approach and find that in countries, like England and Germany, which up to recently had no anti-trust laws and tolerated cartels, single giant corporations or combinations came to dominate whole industries. It seems generally agreed that our situation of oligopoly is preferable, because it is more conducive than monopoly to technical progress and the development of countervailing power, to cite Professor Galbraith again. And it seems plausible to say that the anti-trust laws were responsible for the development of oligopoly, rather than monopoly, in the United States.*

It has also been argued that so long as the anti-trust laws do not facilitate concentration, they should be retained because they profess the ideal of a competitive order to which our people are still attached. But are they? My old boss, Leon Henderson, used to say that most businessmen clamor for competition in the things they buy but detest it when it comes to the things they themselves sell. But, more seriously, our economic strength, technical progress, our standard of living, our defense capabilities all depend upon the successful functioning of the large-scale

[7] Galbraith, American Capitalism 41-42 (1952).

* See generally, Whitney, Antitrust Policies:

American Experience in Twenty Industries (1958).—Editor

organization of business and labor. Would our people countenance its disruption? And is it desirable to cling to a myth which hides current reality?

2. *Public-utility-type regulation.* The Interstate Commerce Act raises similarly perplexing problems. It initiated the policy of subjecting the traditional "public utility" industries—those furnishing light, heat, power, water, transportation and communications—to legal control of the prices they charge and the quality and quantity of the services they render. The Act originally dealt with railroads, but now also covers road and water transport. Air transport and ocean shipping are subject to regulation under separate laws, as are the power, radio and television and telegraph and telephone industries. At first, regulation was justified on the ground that the industries subjected to it were monopolistic. Since the Great Depression of the 1930's, however, regulation has also been used to prevent too much or "cutthroat" competition from producing socially undesirable results. This, for example, explains the regulation not only of trucking but also of agricultural production, marketing and prices. American agriculture, in short, has become a "public utility."

How shall we assess the effects of this system of regulation? Some think it combines the worst features of both capitalism and socialism—that by divorcing authority from responsibility, it unites capitalism's lack of planning with socialism's bureaucratic rigidity. Of late—as the Goldfine-Adams case revealed—it has raised very serious problems of how to regulate the regulators.

Would we be better off without such regulation? Should we leave these industries in unregulated private hands? Or socialize them? How do we go about evaluating these alternatives? Could Congress and the states be persuaded to experiment —to try out the different alternatives in limited areas?

In any event, neither the anti-trust law nor public-utility-type regulation curbs the exercise of private economic power in many vital areas of the American economy. Should we be concerned about this fact? Whether or not our 20th century society can be justifiably described as affluent,[8] no one disputes the fact that the material conditions of life of our people have been greatly improved. We have also achieved a tolerable measure of social justice, distributing income about as equitably as do Great Britain and the Scandinavian countries. But the creditable performance of American capitalism in recent years cannot be attributed to the exercise of unchecked private economic power. I would agree with Galbraith that it is due, in large measure, to the development of centers of countervailing power, a process in which the law has played a most significant part.

3. *Organization of private countervailing power.* a. *Farmers' associations.* Thus, the farmers have organized buying and selling co-operatives to enable them to attain a more equal bargaining position vis-à-vis the oligopolies from which they buy and to which they sell. But only the buying co-operatives have succeeded.

Farmers as sellers remained in a weak position until the New Deal support price programs were launched.

b. *Chain stores.* Independent food stores and department stores have organized

[8] See, generally, Galbraith, The Affluent Society (1958).

co-operative buying organizations for similar reasons. The large chain retailers, which stand to gain by a policy of low prices and high sales volume, have attained sufficient power, by virtue of their size, to force large manufacturers to share the fruits of their economic power—to the consumer's ultimate benefit. Galbraith suggests that this may be the reason why consumer co-operatives have not prospered in the United States.

Twentieth century law has encouraged the organization of farmers' co-operatives. But it has shown hostility to the large chain retailer. Efforts have been made to cripple chains by taxation. And the A&P was prosecuted for violation of the anti-trust laws. If we accept Galbraith's analysis, a change in legal policy would be called for. But the law sees the chain not only as a center of power which countervails that of the oligopolist manufacturer, but also as a center of power which can overwhelm smaller retail competitors, as well as small manufacturers. How to deal with institutions which countervail the power of other institutions in our society yet, at the same time, also exercise overbearing power in other areas, has become a puzzling problem in our contemporary law.

c. *Trade unions.* The trade union is another vital center of countervailing power. It became such only after long and arduous struggle and the history of this struggle reveals the important role political and legal factors played in overcoming powerful business resistance to unionization. But again, it is difficult to weigh the purely legal factors. The voluntary association enables large numbers of people in a democracy to combine to exert political pressure in a legal fashion. The product of its efforts may be legislation which, in turn, enhances the power of the voluntary association itself. Difficult as it is to assess the influence of legislation under these circumstances, it seems to be agreed that the NRA and the Wagner Act (and the Clayton Act of 1914 before it) and the labor legislation and administration of World Wars I and II stimulated the growth of trade unions by recognizing them as essential institutions in a democracy.

The trade unions have forced the giants of American industry to share the fruits of their economic power with their workers. Equally important, the trade union has been responsible for the evolution of a rule of law in industry which has secured the individual worker's claim to the job and thereby given him a sense of status and community and independence.

B. *Legal Intervention Further Enlarging Scope of Public-Decision-Making.* The exercise of private countervailing power does not, of course, displace private economic decision-making. It merely enlarges the number of private individuals and groups participating in such decision-making. However, 20th century law has also greatly enlarged the scope of public decision-making in order to protect those who are not able to take care of themselves. In these cases, the law may be said to embody countervailing power. In order to achieve its ends, this body of legislation had to limit claims regarding the use and disposition of private property and the freedom of contract.

1. *To assure every individual the minimum standards of a decent life.* So government has stepped in to assure, by law, that every individual should enjoy the

material conditions necessary for a minimum decent life. Significant steps toward this goal were taken during the 19th century. A public school system was created by law. Factory safety legislation was passed. Conditions of labor for women and children were regulated, as were methods of wage payment generally. Laws for the relief of debtors were passed. Public care was provided for dependent and neglected children, old people and the insane and tax exemptions were granted private institutions undertaking these responsibilities.

Twentieth-century legislation took additional giant steps. Minimum wages and maximum hours were fixed. Child labor was abolished. A social security system was elaborated which now includes workmen's compensation and disability insurance, unemployment insurance, old age and survivors' insurance and programs of assistance to the old, dependent children and the needy. The losses suffered by the ordinary family as a result of illness (or accident not connected with the job) remain the major ones not covered by a universal system of insurance.

The legal institution of insurance makes it practical to spread losses incurred by individuals in the natural course of their lives over the community as a whole and, therefore, to reject the individualistic notion that these losses should be borne by the persons upon whom they happened to fall or by those who were legally at fault in causing them.

Our farm programs—price supports, federal crop insurance and rural electrification—are also part of the attempt to assure every individual a minimum decent life, as are the many state and federal laws designed to stimulate public and private housing.

I do not wish to imply that the protection of the law is so pervasive that it covers every individual in the United States whose interests are not furthered by a group having sufficient power to do so effectively. There are still more than two million hired farm workers who earn very low wages and have no strong unions to fight for them. In practically all states, these workers do not enjoy the benefits of workmen's compensation. And only in 1955 was a beginning made to bring them into the unemployment insurance system. The lot of the migratory farm worker is, of course, particularly bad. Because they are migratory, the American citizens among them cannot exert the pressure which usually accompanies the vote in a democracy. Clerks in retail and service establishments, government employees and even teachers could also use strong organization to protect their interests. In all, about 25% of our families—more than 10 million families in all—had incomes in 1957 of less than $3000 a year.* There is much unfinished business to take care of here.

2. *To guarantee every individual the rights of citizenship.* Legal intervention to protect the political and civil rights of women and of the Negro citizen reflects this same concern for the individual life. The wife became the equal of her husband when the law recognized her claim to hold property, enter into contracts and institute lawsuits and then liberalized the grounds for divorce. (The individuality

* See generally, Lampman, The Low Income Population and Economic Growth, Study Paper No. 12, Joint Economic Committee, 86th Cong., 1st Sess. (1959).—Editor

of the child, too, has been recognized by laws requiring vaccination and compulsory school attendance and making it possible to divorce a child from parents which mistreat it.)

In the case of the Negro citizen, we are witnessing an unprecedented legal effort to change the traditional behavior patterns of whole communities spread over large areas. Most serious questions have thereby been raised about the effective limits of law as an agency of this change.[9]

3. *To protect the individual as consumer and status-holder.* Law has also intervened to protect the individual as a consumer, in which capacity he seems unable to organize to protect the interests which tend to be ignored in our producer-minded economy. This intervention also began in the 19th century, with the enactment of public health legislation. It has been extended during the 20th century to include general pure food, drug and cosmetic laws; laws prohibiting false labeling and false advertising; and laws regulating the issuance of securities and the operation of the commodity and stock exchanges and insuring bank deposits.

Nineteenth century laws required fire and life insurance policies, mortgages and contracts for transportation to contain certain standard provisions to protect the contracting natural person. These laws exemplify the swing from contract to a kind of status which Dean Pound has called "The New Feudal System."[10] It is "new" because the relationship is entered into by contract but the law attaches certain rights and obligations to it, no matter what the parties to the relationship may have agreed upon—usually in order to protect the weaker party. Legal rights and obligations now surround the relationship between insurer and insured, mortgagor and mortgagee, common carrier and ticket holder, employer and employee, wife and husband, parent and child and even automobile manufacturer and dealer.

4. *To conserve and develop our natural resources.* Finally, legislation has also been enacted to conserve and develop our natural resources. To this end, we have not hesitated to resort to public ownership, as in the case of TVA and the Bonneville Power Administration.

5. *To maintain full employment.* I am aware that the control and offsetting of private economic power and the assurance of a minimum decent life for every individual contribute to, but do not guarantee, the maintenance of full employment and that the improvements in the general standard of life and the more equitable distribution of income to which I have alluded could not have taken place without full employment. But our government is now committed by law, the Employment Act of 1946, to maintain full employment and it seems fairly clear that neither political party will have much success unless it uses the governmental powers to tax and to spend and to regulate the banking, credit and currency system, so as to accomplish this objective.

* * *

Since the advent of the Industrial Revolution we have been struggling, it seems

[9] On this question generally, see Pound, Limits of Effective Legal Action, 27 Int'l J. Ethics 150 (1917).

[10] Pound, the New Feudal System, 19 Ky. L.J. 1 (1930).

to me, with the problem of determining what combination of public and private ordering of human activities is necessary to safeguard and enlarge individual freedoms and at the same time enable individuals to enjoy the potential benefits of modern science and technology. For classical liberalism, centralized political power was the principal danger to individual freedoms. So it insisted that the exercise of political power be limited by excluding economic decision-making from its scope. Classical liberalism failed to foresee that private economic power, when not checked either by private countervailing power or by political power, would itself come to endanger the freedoms of those subject to its exercise. Classical liberalism also underestimated the extent to which a modern, complex economy would require planning and coordination of private and public actions in order to make it an instrument of the general welfare. Socialism anticipated this need and because it regarded the exercise of private economic power as the principal danger to individual freedoms, it insisted upon the complete subordination of economic to political power. Thereby socialism failed to appreciate that the concentration of economic and political power in the same hands could endanger essential individual freedoms.

I do not propose, now, to enter into the controversy whether the public ownership of all the means of production and distribution will always result in tyranny, no matter how dedicated the people and its leadership may be to the maintenance of political democracy. It will suffice for present purposes to point out that our democracy has subjected, but not completely subordinated, private economic power to political power in a way Marxists did not believe to be possible. Markets—the arenas of private economic decision-making—continue to play a crucial role in reflecting consumer wants, in distributing the national income, in determining the rate of economic growth and in making possible the development of private, countervailing power. But these markets are no longer self-regulating; they are regulated by law to satisfy the claims and achieve the ends I have tried to describe.

A tolerable measure of social justice and individual freedom has thereby been achieved in our society as a result not of the pursuit of a vision of an ideal economic system but of the political struggle which individuals and groups have waged, according to the rules of democracy, to satisfy their claims.

Yet though we now have welfare corporations (big business), welfare trade unions (big labor) and a welfare state (big government), we cannot say that we have succeeded in controlling the power through the exercise of which alone welfare can be promoted. This task, in fact, becomes more difficult as the complexity and technicality of the problems requiring legal solution tax the understanding of our people, and big business, big labor and big government acquire effective means to manipulate the individual. The possibility of fuller individual participation in arriving at the decisions which affect the individual life appears to be getting remote. We seem, as a result, to be advancing from the idea of laissez-faire the individual to that of laissez-faire the group.

It is true that a minimum notion of justice requires that all claims made by individuals and groups should at least be heard and considered by the law-making authorities. This is why the freedom to speak and to associate with others in pursuit of common interests is so vital in a democracy dedicated to the achievement of justice. Furthermore, a larger measure of justice will be achieved if the law, as it has done, helps to assure that no single group becomes so powerful as to submerge the claims of all other groups in society, even if the law is then willing to accept the decisions reached as a result of private group conflict and adjustment.

But is this all justice should mean? Will the outcome of the struggle of groups roughly equal in power secure the interests of outsiders? Do groups always reflect the claims made by their individual members?

As we saw, we have used law directly to satisfy certain individual and social claims which could not be satisfied in any other way. So, for example, it seems generally agreed in western, democratic societies that law should intervene to make certain that every individual enjoys the material conditions necessary for a minimum decent life and to lessen the degree of inequality in the opportunities open to different individuals. Is this as far as law should go?

Thus, for example, the question may be raised as to why the corporate manager is the legitimate arbiter of the competing claims of stockholders, workers, consumers, the managers themselves and generations as yet unborn. A number of answers have been offered. Adolph Berle[11] of late is optimistic that we can rely on the growing social conscience of the industrial manager to perform this function equitably. A more acceptable answer may be that the divorce of ownership from management of large corporate enterprise has had the consequence of divorcing the inheritance of wealth from the inheritance of economic power. So long, therefore, as there is little prospect that a hereditary managerial elite will develop and the paths to managerial position remain reasonably open, the exercise of managerial power is tolerable.

Galbraith, of course, thinks the existing situation is tolerable only because the decisions of the corporate manager are checked by the countervailing power exerted by those with whom he deals and by government. But this answer only shifts the question of legitimacy to that of the proper scope of government intervention. Why, it may be asked, should corporate management and organized labor be permitted to enter into collective agreements which have even greater impact upon the public at large than do taxes imposed by governmental power? Is greater legal intervention, via direct wage and price controls, necessary to protect the public? Is it particularly required if we are to achieve the rate of economic growth needed to meet the exigencies of the Cold War without ruinous inflation?

It also may be said in answer to the question of legitimacy that the present system of decision-making reasonably satisfies the wants of our people. But Galbraith makes the fundamental objection that consumer wants are largely created by modern advertising and do not reflect the most urgent needs of our society and that our economic system is not, in fact, satisfying urgent needs. Though he calls our society affluent, Galbraith makes us acutely aware that we are poverty-stricken when it comes to the essential services which only government can provide.

[11] Berle, The 20th Century Capitalist Revolution (1954). [See also, Berle, Power Without Property (1959) and The Corporation in Modern Society (Mason, ed., 1959). —Editor]

The most persuasive answer to the question of legitimacy raised may be that no alternative decision-making process has been proposed which would not create even greater difficulties for a democratic society. But the imagination of the social scientist has not exhausted all the possible alternatives which might yet prove to be acceptable.

The problem remains, too, of preventing individuals or groups within each power-wielding association—corporation or trade union—from acquiring such a preponderance of power internally that they can ignore the wishes of the individuals who make up the association and block their full participation in the life of the association. This is the problem with which the Fund For The Republic is now wrestling.* As a minimum, legal intervention may be necessary to safeguard the individual claim to membership and participation in the association. Twentieth-century law already tends in this direction.

So far as the government bureaucracy is concerned, we seem more disturbed by its apparent ineffectualness than its potential power. We have not succeeded in developing a civil service of the calibre which the armed forces are creating. Apparently, the anti-bureaucratic bias, ever-present on the American scene, is expressed most strongly in popular attitudes toward the civil government bureaucracy (with the "labor bosses" a close second) rather than toward the business or the military bureaucracy. The difficulties which have recently afflicted our administrative agencies can be traced to these attitudes, as well as to the refusal of those regulated to accept the legitimacy of regulation.

Possibly, changes already under way, which we have not fully grasped, will help to solve our difficulties. Automation and low-cost power may enable us to enjoy a still higher standard of living with an even shorter work week. This could lessen the tensions that now surround the adjustment of economic claims and make possible more humane conditions of work and the use of leisure for the fuller development of the individual personality.

Even then, all our troubles would not be over. The "paradise of our domestic security," as Reinhold Niebuhr recently said, would still be "suspended in a hell of global insecurity." But the problem of reconciling the human race is not on our agenda. . . .

---

* The literature on private groups and private "governments" is voluminous. See, inter alia, Ferry, The Corporation and the Economy (The Fund For The Republic, 1959); Miller, Private Governments and the Constitution (The Fund For The Republic, 1959); Cox, The Role of Law in Preserving Union Democracy, 72 Harv. L. Rev. 609 (1959); Webb, Corporate Personality and Political Pluralism, and Pluralism and After, in Legal Personality and Political Pluralism (Webb, ed., 1958); Horn, Groups and the Constitution (1956); Wirtz, Government by Private Groups, 13 La. L. Rev. 440 (1953); Latham, The Group Basis of Politics (1952); DeGrazia, Public and Republic (1951); Drucker, The New Society (1950); Merriam, Public and Private Government (1944); Robbins and Hecksher, The Constitutional Theory of Autonomous Groups, 3 Journal of Politics 3 (1941); Hacker, Politics and the Corporation (The Fund For The Republic, undated).

EDITORIAL NOTE: The CONCEPT of the PUBLIC INTEREST

"Parliament," Edmund Burke wrote, "is not a congress of ambassadors from different and hostile interests; which interests each must maintain, as an agent and advocate, against other agents and advocates; but parliament is a deliberative assembly of one nation, with one interest, that of the whole, where, not local purposes, nor local prejudices, ought to guide, but the general good, resulting from the general reason of the whole." [1]

It is doubtful whether Burke, in this passage, was purporting to describe what the Parliament of his time actually was, rather than what it ought to have been. In any case, many of those who see the modern American legislature primarily as an arena for private group combat disagree with the Burke statement even if it is viewed as the statement of an ideal to be striven for. Arthur F. Bentley, for example, wrote: "Logrolling is . . . the most characteristic legislative process. When one condemns it 'in principle,' it is only by contrasting it with some assumed pure public spirit which is supposed to guide legislators, or which ought to guide them, and which enables them to pass judgment in Jovian calm on that which is best 'for the whole people.' Since there is nothing which is best literally for the whole people, group arrays being what they are, the test is useless, even if one could actually find legislative judgments which are not reducible to interest-group activities. And when we have reduced the legislative process to the play of group interests, then logrolling, or give and take, appears as the very nature of the process. It is compromise, not in the abstract moral form, which philosophers can sagely discuss, but in the practical form with which every legislator who gets results through government is acquainted. It is trading. It is the adjustment of interests. . . . There never was a time in the history of the American Congress when legislation was conducted in any other way." [2]

Issue may be joined on the following points:

1. Are legislators in fact guided, when they come to cast their votes on proposed measures, by some concept of the "public interest" or by the particular group-interests with which they identify themselves? If it is demonstrated, as President Kennedy tried to do in his book, Profiles in Courage, that the behavior of legislators is, in fact, motivated and influenced by their personal notions of the "public interest," then the "public interest" in this sense must be reckoned with by legislative students and practitioners alike.

2. Ought legislators to act on the basis of their own personal notions of the "public interest" when such action would conflict with the interests of the groups they purportedly represent? This question, too, is considered by President Kennedy.

[1] I Burke, Works 447 (Bohn ed. 1893).   [2] Bentley, The Process of Government 370-371 (1949 reissue).

3. Clearly Burke was not referring to these notions—which may differ from legislator to legislator—when he wrote of the "general good." Ought legislators, then, seek to determine "objectively"—by resort to reason and experience—what "is best literally for the whole people"? Is this search illusory?

There is a sense in which the search for the "public interest" or "general good" is not illusory, but rather grounded in the facts of our social experience. Is there not in fact substantial unanimity in this country on some of the ideals the realization of which is commonly referred to as being in the public interest? Could we not "define" the public interest in this sense?

It can be said that a legislative measure is in the "public interest" if there is, in fact, general agreement in society that the particular ends of the measure should be realized by the particular means proposed to be used, or, at least, if there is no substantial number of persons in the society irreconcilably opposed to the ends or the means. In other words, the "public interest" can be viewed as made up of the least common denominators that bind all the interest groups in our society. What these common interests are, at any particular time, is a matter for empirical investigation. A statement of some of them may be hazarded, in an order of decreasing certainty.

a. It is in the "public interest" that our nation be free from outside dictation in determining its destiny; that it have the power of self-determination. (Even this statement is not entirely free from doubt. The argument has been heard lately, for example, that it is better to surrender to the Soviet Union than run the risk of annihilation that the nuclear armaments race entails. In a broader frame of reference, our generation also questions whether there are not regional or world interests to which the national interest should be subordinated).

b. It is in the public interest to preserve the legitimated institutions through which conflicts in our society are adjusted and peaceful change effected, no matter how distasteful particular decisions reached by these institutions may be to particular groups in our society. In other words, the preservation of democracy—government with the freely-given consent of the governed—is in the public interest.

c. It is in the public interest that no group in our society should become so powerful that it can submerge the claims of all other groups.

d. It is in the public interest that all claims made by individuals and groups in our society should at least be heard and considered by the law-making authorities. This proposition, which calls for recognition of the freedom to speak and to associate with others in pursuit of group interests, is a fundamental assumption of the democratic order.

e. It is in the public interest that every individual enjoy a minimum decent life and that the degree of inequality in the opportunities open to different individuals be lessened.

Thus the definition of the public interest need not be as illusory as Bentley assumed. True, such generalized standards as these offer difficulties of interpretation and application. Greater difficulties arise when the legislative problems in question are not covered by these standards. Bentley's criticism becomes more pertinent (1) when there is no general agreement that the end in question is desirable and (2) when there is general agreement about the desirability of the end, but disagreement exists because the means proposed to achieve the end will make it impossible to achieve another generally agreed-upon end, thereby compelling a choice between ends.

At this point, the problem facing a legislature is no different from the problem facing the judge, and raises the same general question of the possibility of a rational choice of values that we explored in Section 3 of Chapter 3, which should be reread at this point. No general definition of the "public interest" can be formulated as a guide to action in every such situation. In such cases, it would be wiser to speak of "public interests" instead of *the* public interest. As Professor Sidney Hook has written, "what is in the 'public interest' can be determined only in respect to *specific* problems." [3] For example, Hook explains, "If there is a threat of plague, what the public interest requires is easy to tell even if it involves the destruction of property and the segregation of persons." [4] Considering this particular problem, there will be no disagreement as to how the choice between ends should be made. But it is questionable whether unanimity would prevail on whether the public interest required that compensation be paid the owner of the property destroyed or required him to bear the loss as the price of living in a civilized society.

When disagreement exists, special interest always seems to speak in the language of general interest. Each group tends to identify what it wishes to be done with the public interest, in order to make it more acceptable to others and to the authoritative decision-makers. This appeal to a concept other than self-interest is itself testimony of the indispensability of the need to define the public interest, which may or may not coincide with private interests, as a norm of decision in particular situations. (This is a task which, as we shall see, legislatures have imposed to an increasing extent upon administrative agencies.) [5]

[3] Hook, Political Power and Personal Freedom 371 (1959).
[4] *Ibid.*
[5] For writings on the concept of the "public interest," see Leys and Perry, Philosophy and the Public Interest (1959); Friedrich, Constitutional Reason of State (1957); de Jouvenal, Sovereignty, An Inquiry Into The Public Good (1957); Lippmann, The Public Philosophy (1955); Simon, The Philosophy of Democratic Government (1951); Herring, Public Administration and the Public Interest (1936); Dewey, The Public and Its Problems (1927); Schubert, The Public Interest in Administrative Decision-Making, 51 Amer. Pol. Sci. Rev. 346 (1957); Sorauf, The Public Interest Reconsidered, 19 J. of Politics 616 (1957); Cassinelli, Comments on Frank J. Sorauf's "The Public Interest Reconsidered," 20 J. of Politics 553 (1958); Cassinelli, Some Reflections on the Concept of the Public Interest, 69 Ethics 48 (1958).

CHAPTER Eleven

JUDICIAL REVIEW of the CONSTITUTIONALITY of LEGISLATION

Section 1

The CONCEPT of DUE PROCESS and the CONSTITUTIONALITY of the WORKMEN'S COMPENSATION ACTS

FROM THE CONSTITUTION OF THE UNITED STATES, AND AMENDMENTS

ARTICLE III. *Section 1.* The judicial power of the United States, shall be vested in one supreme court, and in such inferior courts as the Congress may from time to time ordain and establish. The Judges, both of the supreme and inferior courts, shall hold their offices during good behavior, and shall, at stated times, receive for their services, a compensation, which shall not be diminished during their continuance in office.

Section 2. The judicial power shall extend to all cases, in law and equity, arising under this constitution. . . .

In all cases affecting ambassadors, other public ministers and consuls, and those in which a state shall be party, the supreme court shall have original jurisdiction. In all the other cases before mentioned, the supreme court shall have appellate jurisdiction, both as to law and fact, with such exceptions, and under such regulations as the Congress shall make.

ARTICLE VI. . . . This constitution, and the laws of the United States which shall be made in pursuance thereof; and all treaties made, or which shall be made, under the authority of the United States, shall be the supreme law of the land; and the judges in every state shall be bound thereby, anything in the constitution or laws of any state to the contrary notwithstanding.

The senators and representatives before-mentioned, and the members of the several state legislatures, and all executive and judicial officers, both of the United States and of the several States, shall be bound by oath or affirmation, to support this constitution. . . .

Articles of Amendment to the Constitution of the United States

ARTICLE V. No person shall . . . be deprived of life, liberty, or property, without due process of law; nor shall private property be taken for public use, without just compensation.

ARTICLE IX. The enumeration in the Constitution, of certain rights, shall not be construed to deny or disparage others retained by the people.

ARTICLE X. The powers not delegated to the United States by the Constitution, nor prohibited by it to the States, are reserved to the States respectively, or to the people.

ARTICLE XIV. *Section 1.* All persons born or naturalized in the United States, and subject to the jurisdiction thereof, are citizens of the United States and of the State wherein they reside. No state shall make or enforce any law which shall abridge the privileges or immunities of citizens of the United States; nor shall any State deprive any person of life, liberty, or property, without due process of law; nor deny to any person within its jurisdiction the equal protection of the laws.

EDITORIAL NOTE: The CONCEPT of DUE PROCESS

It was settled, in Barron v. Baltimore,[1] that the first ten amendments to the United States Constitution, the so-called "Bill of Rights," restrict only the powers and activities of the federal government and not the states. While most of the states adopted similar provisions in their own constitutions, it was not till the Fourteenth Amendment to the federal Constitution was adopted at the close of the Civil War that the federal Constitution contained a "due process" clause restricting the states.

What, precisely, is the meaning of the phrase "due process of law"? The equivalent of the phrase as a declaration of rights is found in legal documents running far back into the Middle Ages. Its most famous equivalent in English legal history is in the 39th chapter of Magna Carta.[2] The phrase was probably used in general as some sort of guaranty that the power of the state would not be brought to bear in arbitrary fashion upon the subject or citizen. But none of the historic documents employing the term ever explained its meaning in more detail.

In the United States, the Supreme Court has attempted to give concrete meaning to the guaranty of due process. The Court first treated the due process clause of the Fifth Amendment to the Federal Constitution as a guaranty only of fair procedure: as insuring, for example, that a court should enter judgment against a person only if it had duly obtained juris-

[1] 7 Pet. 243 (1833).

[2] The "great charter" granted by King John to his rebellious barons at Runnymede in 1215, and afterwards, with some modifications, confirmed in Parliament by Henry III and Edward I is the foundation of English constitutional liberty. Its chapters include provisions for regulating the administration of justice, defining the jurisdictional boundaries between church and state, securing the personal liberty of the subjects and their property rights, the limits of taxation, the liberties and privileges of the church, etc. Ch. XXXIX reads: "No freeman shall be taken, or imprisoned, or be disseised [dispossessed] of his freehold, or liberties, or free customs, or be outlawed, or exiled, or any otherwise destroyed, nor will we go upon him, nor send against him, save by lawful judgment of his peers, or by the law of the land. We will not sell, nor deny, nor delay to any man either justice or right."

diction, and had afforded him due notice of trial and a fair opportunity to be heard.

The adoption of the Fourteenth Amendment gave the Court authority to subject state as well as federal legislation to the test of due process. For the first few years, the Court interpreted the new Amendment, as it had the Fifth Amendment, as principally a guaranty of fair procedure: and so far as it recognized the new Amendment as protecting any substantive rights, this extension was virtually confined to protection of the rights of the newly freed Negroes against racial discrimination. But towards the end of the 19th century the Court expanded the meaning of the due process guaranty to cover the substance of legislation and other governmental action generally, holding for example that if a statute affected the substantive rights of persons in an arbitrary or unreasonable way, it was invalid.[3]

The doctrine of "substantive" due process of law was used, as we shall see, to curb legislative regulation of private interests, including corporate interests. In 1886, the Court for the first time held that a corporation was a "person" within the meaning of the 14th Amendment, entitled to "due process of law."[4] To this day, Justices Black and Douglas have not made their peace with this decision,[5] which still represents the view of the Court.

The Supreme Court has also held that the concept of "due process" in the 14th Amendment does not include every one of the protections against federal government action embodied in the Bill of Rights.[6] In the Palko case, Mr. Justice Cardozo declared that only those specific guarantees in the first eight amendments which—like freedom of speech—are "of the very essence of a scheme of ordered liberty," embodying principles of justice "so rooted in the traditions and conscience of our people as to be ranked as fundamental," are included in the 14th Amendment.

Dissenting in the Adamson case,[7] Justices Black and Douglas criticized Justice Cardozo's " 'natural law' theory of the Constitution" and argued that the 14th Amendment was intended by its sponsors to make the Bill of Rights applicable to the states.

---

[3] For the development of the concept of substantive due process in the Supreme Court of the United States, see Cushman, The Social and Economic Interpretation of the Fourteenth Amendment, 20 Mich. L. Rev. 737 (1922); Corwin, Introduction, in Constitution of the United States, Annotated, esp. pp. xxii-xxvi (1952), Sen. Doc. 170, 82d Cong., 2d Sess.

[4] Santa Clara County v. Southern Pac. R.R. Co., 118 U.S. 394 (1886).

[5] See dissenting opinions of Justice Black in Connecticut General Life Insurance Co.

v. Johnson, 303 U.S. 77, 83 (1938) and of Justice Douglas in Wheeling Steel Corp. v. Glander, 337 U.S. 562, 576 (1949).

[6] Twining v. New Jersey, 211 U.S. 78 (1908); Palko v. Connecticut, 302 U.S. 319 (1937); and Adamson v. California, 332 U.S. 46 (1947). In these cases the Fifth Amendment's protection against double jeopardy and its privilege against self-incrimination were held not to be applicable to state criminal procedure.

[7] Supra, note 6.

EDITORIAL NOTE: The CONSTITUTIONAL ISSUE
in NEW YORK

It was the New York law which provided the occasion for testing the constitutionality of workmen's compensation in the Supreme Court of the United States.

New York Laws of 1910, c. 674, art. 14-a provided that in the case of certain "especially dangerous" employments, the employer shall be liable for any injury to an employee arising out of and in the course of the employment, by "a necessary risk or danger of the employment or one inherent in the nature thereof," except an injury "caused in whole or in part by the serious and wilful misconduct of the workman." Fault or negligence of the employer was not a prerequisite to his liability; and neither the fellow-servant defense nor the assumption of risk defense nor the ordinary contributory negligence defense was recognized. The law specified a scale of compensation for different classes of injuries and for death, which could be recovered by actions at law. This law was declared unconstitutional by unanimous decision of the New York Court of Appeals in Ives v. The South Buffalo Railway Company.*

Judged "by our common-law standards," said the New York court, the statute "is plainly revolutionary." As to the economic and sociological arguments urged in support of the law, the court said: "Under our form of government . . . courts must regard all economic, philosophical and moral theories, attractive and desirable though they may be, as subordinate to the primary question whether they can be moulded into statutes without infringing upon the letter or spirit of our written constitutions." Turning to the "purely legal phases of the controversy," the court held that it was within the legislative power to modify and even abolish the fellow-servant, the contributory negligence, and to a limited extent the assumption of risk, rules which were of judicial origin. But to impose liability without fault upon the employer violated the provisions of the Fourteenth Amendment and article 1, section 6 of the New York Constitution, which also guarantees all persons against deprivation of life, liberty, or property without due process of law. These guarantees, said the Court, embodied "those ancient and fundamental principles which were in existence when our Constitutions were adopted," one of which was that "no man who was without fault or negligence could be held liable in damages for injuries sustained by another." The imposition of absolute liability upon the employer in "its final and simple analysis . . . is taking the property of A and giving it to B" and therefore deprives the employer of the due process of law guaranteed by the Constitutions. Furthermore, said the court, the law could not be sustained as an exercise of the state's police power because it "does nothing to conserve the health, safety or morals of the

* 201 N.Y. 271, 94 N.E. 431 (1911).

employees" nor "to impose upon the enumerated employers any duty or obligation designed to have that effect."

This decision could not be carried to the Supreme Court for two reasons: (1) until 1914, the Judicial Code did not authorize Supreme Court review, even on certiorari, of a state court decision invalidiating a state statute because repugnant to the Federal Constitution; and (2) the decision also rested on the New York court's interpretation of the New York state constitution—an interpretation which would have remained unchanged even if the New York law was held to be consistent with the provisions of the Fourteenth Amendment.

Following the Ives decision, the New York Constitution was amended, effective January 1, 1914,[1] to authorize a workmen's compensation act which the New York Legislature enacted in December 1913,[2] and reenacted in 1914,[3] to take effect as to payment of compensation on July 1, 1914.

This Act was compulsory in the sense that it required every employer of employees in certain enumerated hazardous employments, whether or not he chose to come under it, to pay a prescribed compensation, based on earnings, for the disability or death of any employee resulting from an accidental personal injury arising out of and in the course of the employment without regard to fault as a cause—except where the injury (1) was occasioned by the wilful intention of the injured employee to bring about the injury or death of himself or of another, or (2) resulted solely from the intoxication of the injured employee while on duty. A "state insurance fund" was created, from premiums paid by employers, to insure employers against liability under the law and assure compensation to the persons entitled to it.

By insuring in the state fund, or, as he was allowed to do, with an authorized private company, or obtaining permission to act as a self-insurer, the employer was relieved from any further liability for personal injuries or death sustained by employees. A Workmen's Compensation Commission was authorized to pass upon claims to compensation and its awards were subjected to judicial review.

This act was sustained by the Court of Appeals as not inconsistent with the Fourteenth Amendment in Matter of Jensen v. Southern Pacific Co.[4] That decision was followed by the New York court in the case which reached the Supreme Court of the United States, and in which the Court sustained the act against the charge that it violated the Fourteenth Amendment, New York Central Railroad Co. v. White.[5]

"No person," said the Court, "has a vested interest in any rule of law entitling him to insist that it shall remain unchanged for his benefit." After citing a number of instances in which liability without fault is

---

[1] See N.Y. Const., I, 19.
[2] Laws 1913, c. 816.
[3] Laws 1914, c. 41.

[4] 215 N.Y. 514 (1915).
[5] 243 U.S. 188 (1917).

imposed by the common law (e.g., under the rule of respondeat superior), the Court held that the legislature, too, could, "upon proper occasion," impose such liability by abrogating the common-law fellow-servant, assumption of risk, and contributory negligence, doctrines. This was a "proper occasion" because New York provided a "reasonably just substitute" which in some ways limited and in other ways extended the common law rights of both employers and employees. The "new arrangement" could not be considered to be "arbitrary and unreasonable, from the standpoint of natural justice."

EDITORIAL NOTE: The CONSTITUTIONAL ISSUE in WISCONSIN

The Wisconsin workmen's compensation act and the provisions of the Industrial Commission Act relative to its functioning were sustained against constitutional objections in Borgnis v. Falk Co.,[1] approximately eight months after the decision was rendered in the Ives case and, of course, before the decision of the White case. The decision of the Wisconsin court was unanimous in favor of the act, although separate concurring opinions were filed by Barnes and Marshall, JJ, who objected to portions of the analysis of Winslow, C.J., who gave the opinion of the court. Note that Mr. Justice Marshall participated in the decision of the case. (Recall what we have seen of his role in getting the act passed).

The plaintiffs in Borgnis v. Falk Co. did not seek to carry the case to the Supreme Court of the United States.

(1) *The presentation of the case to the court:* Mr. Chief Justice Winslow, after declaring the court's reasons for considering the constitutional issues at this first opportunity, and investigating them broadly, says: "Impressed with this view of our duty under the circumstances, we advanced the present case upon the calendar, and invited argument upon the main question as to the constitutionality of the statute, not only from the Attorney General on behalf of the state, but from an attorney interested in the question. In pursuance of this invitation the Attorney General and the Industrial Commission filed briefs, and oral argument was made by the Deputy Attorney General."

The nature of the brief filed by the Industrial Commission in support of the statute is worth noting. The brief itself took 85 pages and in addition to considerable use of judicial precedent with reference to the constitutional issues, quoted, described, or called the court's attention to the following materials: (1) Report of the New York legislative committee; (2) condemnations of the common law rules regarding the bearing of the burden of industrial accident, as expressed by Winslow, C. J., and Marshall, J., in earlier opinions; (3) details of the history of workmen's compensation in various European countries; (4) Wisconsin political party

[1] 147 Wis. 327, 133 N.W. 209 (1911).

platforms regarding compensation; (5) Messages of Presidents Roosevelt and Taft to Congress regarding compensation; (6) Messages of Governors McGovern, of Wisconsin, and Woodrow Wilson, of New Jersey, on compensation; (7) findings of the Wisconsin Bureau of Labor and Industrial Statistics and of the Wisconsin legislative committee; (8) reports of the legislative committees in New York, Illinois, Minnesota, Washington, and other states; (9) declarations of the Wisconsin State Federation of Labor; (10) conclusions of a treatise by a member of the faculty of the University of Chicago. The brief was accompanied by an appendix containing these materials: (1) an editorial from the magazine, The Outlook, condemning the Ives decision; (2) a communication to the same publication, signed by 14 leading professors of constitutional law in law schools in the United States, condemning the Ives decision; (3) an article by Professor Ernst Freund, of the law school of the University of Chicago, criticizing the New York decision; (4) a brief by lawyers for the National Civic Federation, in support of the constitutionality of workmen's compensation; (5) the complete text of the report of the Wisconsin legislative committee; (6) copies of Chapters 50 and 485, Laws, 1911, with accompanying notes of the legislative committee and the first rules and regulations drawn thereunder by the Industrial Commission.

(2) *Presumption regarding validity of legislation; constitutionality of the election provision:* "In approaching the consideration of the present law we must bear in mind the well established principle that it must be sustained unless it be clear beyond reasonable question that it violates some constitutional limitation or prohibition." The Ives decision is noted, but no opinion is expressed on the basic ruling there, because "this is not a compulsory law."
". . . [W]e meet the objection that the law, while in its words presenting the employer and employee a free choice as to whether he will accept its terms or not, is in fact coercive, so that neither employer nor employee can be said to act voluntarily in accepting it. As to the employer, the argument is that the abolition of the two defenses is a club which forces him to accept; and as to the employee, the argument is that if his employer accepts the law the employee will feel compelled to accept also through fear of discharge if he does not accept. Both of these arguments are based upon conjecture. Laws cannot be set aside upon mere speculation or conjecture. The court must be able to say with certainty that an unlawful result will follow. We do not see how any such thing can be said here. No one can say with certainty what results will follow in the practical workings of the law. It may well be that many manufacturers, especially those employing small numbers of employees and in the less dangerous trades, will deliberately conclude that it will be better business policy to exercise greater care in guarding their employees from possible danger and greater discrimination in the employment of careful men, and reject the law entirely, running the risk of being able to prevent all or nearly all accidents. It seems extremely probable that the great bulk of workmen, especially of the unskilled classes, will be glad to come under

the act and thus secure a certain compensation in case of injury, in place
of that very uncertain and expensive thing, namely, the final result of a lawsuit. But whether this be so or not, it may be considered as reasonably certain
that very many will elect to come under the act voluntarily and freely, and
that those who do not will probably come from the ranks of skilled labor,
who will deem the rates of compensation under the law as entirely inadequate, or will be careful workmen in the less dangerous trades who will see
no gain in bartering their common-law rights for the restricted remedies
furnished by the statute. It cannot be said with any certainty that such men
will be discharged for their failure to voluntarily come under the law. The
probability would seem rather to be that they would be of a class which the
employer would wish to keep in his employ, notwithstanding their attitude
toward the law. These matters are, however, purely speculative and conjectural; none can say what the practical operation of the law will be. It is
enough for our present purpose that no one can say with certainty that it will
operate to coerce either employer or employee."

Section 2

The CONSTITUTIONAL BASIS for JUDICIAL REVIEW

EDITORIAL NOTE: HAS the SUPREME COURT BEEN GUILTY of JUDICIAL USURPATION?

Ever since Marbury v. Madison,[1] the Supreme Court has exercised the
power to declare acts of the legislative or executive branches of the government, state or federal, to be invalid when, in its opinion, they conflict with
the United States Constitution. Chief Justice Marshall justified this exercise
of power as an essential part of the judicial power to decide cases entrusted to
the Court by the Constitution. In his opinion in Marbury v. Madison he
explained:

"It is, emphatically, the province and duty of the judicial department, to say
what the law is. Those who apply the rule to particular cases, must of necessity
expound and interpret that rule. If two laws conflict with each other, the courts
must decide on the operation of each. So, if a law be in opposition to the
constitution; if both the law and the constitution apply to a particular case,
so that the court must either decide that case, conformable to the law, disregarding the constitution; or conformable to the constitution, disregarding the law;
the court must determine which of these conflicting rules governs the case;
this is of the very essence of judicial duty. If then, the courts are to regard the
constitution, and the constitution is superior to any ordinary act of the legislature,
the constitution, and not such ordinary act, must govern the case to which they
both apply."

Yet doubt may be expressed whether the case-deciding function of the
Supreme Court must include the power to determine the constitutionality
of relevant acts of Congress or the President. Certainly this function could

[1] 1 Cranch 137 (1803).

be performed even if the Court assumed that all such acts were constitutional. But then, Professors Hart and Wechsler ask:

"Does Congress in voting to enact the bill or the President in approving it actually make or purport to make . . . a determination [that a statute is duly authorized by the Constitution]? So far at least as concerns questions of the validity of a statute as applied in particular situations, how can they?

"Both Congress and the President can obviously contribute to the sound interpretation of the Constitution. But are they, or can they be, so organized and manned as to be able, without aid from the courts, to build up a body of coherent and intelligible constitutional principle, and to carry public conviction that these principles are being observed? In respect of experience and temperament of personnel? Of procedure for decision? Of means of recording grounds of decision? Of opportunity for close examination of particular questions?

"How important is it that such a body of constitutional principle should be developed? That people believe that the principles guide decision? . . .

"Does it follow from Marshall's reasoning that the executive and legislative departments have similar responsibility to interpret and apply the Constitution when that is relevant to the proper discharge of executive or legislative functions? . . ." [2]

In fact, different opinions have been expressed on whether the Congress should pass, or the President sign, a bill about the constitutionality of which either has doubts.[3]

In spite of the Supreme Court's long-standing practice, Judge Learned Hand contends that one "cannot find among the powers granted to courts [by the Constitution] any authority to pass upon the validity of the decisions" of the legislative and executive branches of the federal government.[4] Indeed, he claims the recognition of such authority is inconsistent with the concept of the separation of powers, under which each of the three branches of the government was to be independent of the others. Judge Hand reads Article VI—the Supremacy Clause—as requiring *state* courts, at times, "to decide whether state laws and constitutions, or even a federal statute, were in conflict with the federal constitution" [5] and, together with Article III, as requiring the Supreme Court "on some occasions . . . to decide whether a state court's construction of the constitution was correct." [6] But the explicit

---

[2] Hart & Wechsler, The Federal Courts and the Federal System 93 (1953).

[3] *Id.* at 93-4, citing President Roosevelt's letter of July 6, 1935 concerning a bill to regulate the bituminous coal-mining industry, 4 Public Papers and Addresses of Franklin D. Roosevelt 297-298 (1938); President Andrew Jackson's message of July 10, 1832, justifying his veto of the bill to continue the Bank of the United States in spite of Supreme Court decisions upholding its constitutionality, 2 Richardson, Messages and Papers of the Presidents 576, 582

(1896); and Lincoln's First Inaugural Address, March 4, 1861, 6 *id.* 5, 9.

[4] Hand, The Bill of Rights 4 (1958).

[5] *Id.* at 28. So far as review of federal statutes is concerned, Dean Rostow emphasizes that the language of Article VI makes the "laws of the United States" the "supreme law of the land" only when made "in pursuance of the Constitution." Rostow, The Democratic Character of Judicial Review, 66 Harv. L. Rev. 193, 194, n. 2 (1952).

[6] *Id.* at 5-6.

grant of power to the state courts implies a denial of "general authority" to the federal courts to declare legislative acts unconstitutional.

Nevertheless, Judge Hand thinks the assumption by the Supreme Court of authority "to keep the states, Congress, and the President within their prescribed powers," was essential to the successful operation of the constitutional scheme. If every branch of the Government had to assume that the acts of the other were constitutional, Congress would have become "substantially omnipotent." If each branch had the authority to decide for itself whether the acts of any other branch were constitutional, chaos would have resulted. So great, therefore, was the need for an "arbiter whose decision should be final" that it "was not a lawless act to import into the constitution such a grant of power" to the courts, which because of "the independence of their tenure" were the best Department in which to vest the power.[7]

Professor Wechsler is not satisfied with Judge Hand's analysis and maintains that the judicial power in question "is grounded in the language of the Constitution and is not a mere interpolation."[8] He reads the Supremacy Clause "as a mandate to all of officialdom including courts, with a special and emphatic admonition that it binds the judges of the previously independent states."[9] There is no basis in the language of the Supremacy Clause or Article III, Wechsler argues, for saying that the lower federal courts have a lesser obligation under the Supremacy Clause than the state courts, or that the Supreme Court has a lesser obligation when it reviews the judgments of the lower federal courts than when it reviews the judgments of the state courts. He points out that Congress could have chosen, under Article III, not to create any "inferior [federal] courts," in which case the state courts themselves would have had to handle "every case in which a constitutional issue could possibly arise,"[10] subject, in every case in which such an issue had arisen, to review by the Supreme Court. Surely, Wechsler concludes, it is not reasonable to read the text of the Constitution as limiting the power of the Supreme Court simply because Congress chose to create lower federal courts.

Controversy has raged not only over the proper reading of the text of the Constitution but over the question whether the Founding Fathers intended to give the Supreme Court the great power it has been exercising for more than 150 years. Judge Hand has concluded that "it is impossible to have any assurance how the [Constitutional Convention of 1787] would have voted at the time, had the question been put to it whether the Supreme Court should have a conclusive authority to construe the Constitution."[11] Louis Boudin was the leading exponent of the view that the Supreme Court usurped power by taking this function upon itself.[12] Professors Hart and Wechsler are persuaded that despite "the curiously persisting myth of usurpation," the understanding of the Constitutional Convention that the "grant of judicial power

[7] *Id.* at 29.

[8] Wechsler, Toward Neutral Principles of Constitutional Law, 73 Harv. L. Rev. 1, 2 (1959).

[9] *Id.* at 3.

[10] *Id.* at 4.

[11] Hand, *op. cit. supra* note 4, at 28.

[12] Boudin, Government by Judiciary (1932).

[by the Constitution] was to include the power, where necessary in the decision of cases, to disregard state or federal statutes found to be unconstitutional" emerges "from its records with singular clarity." [13]

Professor Crosskey suggests still another reading of the historical record. He concludes that "judicial review was not meant to be provided generally in the Constitution, as to acts of Congress, though it was meant to be provided generally as to the acts of the states, and a limited right likewise was intended to be given to the Court, even as against Congress, to preserve its own judiciary prerogatives intact." [14]

The difference of opinion between Judge Hand and Professor Wechsler is not merely of academic interest. Judge Hand concluded from his analysis that because the power to review the constitutionality of the actions of other branches of the government "is not a logical deduction from the structure of the Constitution but only a practical condition upon its successful operation, it need not be exercised whenever a court sees, or thinks that it sees, an invasion of the Constitution." "It is always a preliminary question how importunately the occasion demands an answer. It may be better to leave the issue to be worked out without authoritative solution; or perhaps the only solution available is one that the court has no adequate means to enforce." [15]

This abstention doctrine alarms Wechsler who, because he "finds the judicial power anchored in the Constitution" thinks "there is no . . . escape from the judicial obligation" to pass upon the issue of the constitutionality of federal or state legislative or executive action, whenever that issue is raised in a case which is otherwise proper for adjudication[16] and has not been committed by the Constitution itself to another agency of government.[17]

EDITORIAL NOTE: The POWER of CONGRESS to CONTROL the JURISDICTION of the SUPREME COURT*

During the first session of the 85th Congress, Senator Jenner introduced a bill, S. 2646, to deprive the Supreme Court of appellate jurisdiction in cases

[13] Hart & Wechsler, *op. cit. supra* note 2, at 14, citing Farrand, The Records of the Federal Convention (1911) and the Framing of the Constitution (1913); Beard, The Supreme Court and the Constitution (1912); and Warren, The Making of the Constitution (1937 ed). See too, Beard, The Supreme Court,—Usurper or Guarantee, 27 Pol. Sci. Q. 1 (1912); Corwin, The Basic Doctrine of American Constitutional Law, 12 Mich. L. Rev. 247 (1914); Haines, The Role of the Supreme Court in American Government and Politics, 1789-1935, at 16-26, 227-245 (1944) (presenting a view contrary to that of Hart and Wechsler).

[14] 2 Crosskey, Politics and the Constitution in the History of the United States 1007;

see 938-1046 (1953).

[15] Hand, *op. cit. supra* note 4, at 4.

[16] Wechsler, *supra* note 8, at 6.

[17] *Id.* at 7-8. Professor Wechsler here has in mind the doctrine elaborated by the Supreme Court that it will not pass upon "political" questions, even if they involve constitutional interpretation and arise in the course of litigation.

* This Note is based on the testimony of Mr. Joseph L. Rauh, Jr., before the Senate Internal Security Subcommittee on S. 2646, which Professor Auerbach helped to prepare. See Hearings before this Subcommittee of the Senate Judiciary Committee on S. 2646, Pt. 2, 39-70, 85th Cong., 2d Sess. (1958).

questioning the validity of (1) Congressional investigating committee proceedings;[1] (2) any federal loyalty-security program;[2] (3) state programs to control subversive activities within the state;[3] (4) public or private school programs to control subversive activities by teachers;[4] and (5) state regulation of the admission of persons to the practice of law within the state.[5]

The Jenner bill is not the first effort in our history to limit the appellate jurisdiction of the Supreme Court.[6] All such efforts, except one that will be mentioned shortly, have failed. But they pose perplexing constitutional problems.

So far as the language of Article III of the Constitution is concerned, it would seem that Congress has unlimited power to control the appellate jurisdiction of the Supreme Court. Recall that Article III specifies only the cases in which the Supreme Court shall have original jurisdiction and says that in all other cases the court shall have appellate jurisdiction "with such exceptions and under such regulations as the Congress shall make." Those who argue that Congress may, consistent with the Constitution, go so far as to eliminate the appellate jurisdiction rely on a decision of the Supreme Court itself, Ex parte McCardle.[7]

In 1868, the Radical Republican Congress passed a law withdrawing from the appellate jurisdiction of the Supreme Court review of certain kinds of judgments of the United States Circuit Courts in habeas corpus proceedings, in order to frustrate a Supreme Court determination of the constitutionality of post-Civil War reconstruction legislation. Even though the McCardle case had already been argued and was under consideration by the Court when the law was adopted, a unanimous Court held that Congress had validly deprived it of its authority to decide the case.

---

[1] The Supreme Court case in this category under attack by Senator Jenner and his adherents was the Watkins case, which we have previously considered.

[2] The cases under attack in this category were Cole v. Young, 351 U.S. 538 (1956), which held that the existing federal employee security program was properly applicable only to employees holding sensitive positions, and Service v. Dulles, 354 U.S. 363 (1957), which held that it was improper for the Secretary of State to discharge a State Department employee without following his own regulations in the process.

[3] The cases under attack were Pennsylvania v. Nelson, 350 U.S. 497 (1956) which invalidated Pennsylvania's "little Smith Act" because it conflicted with the federal Smith Act and the federal government's paramount interest in national security; and Sweezy v. New Hampshire, which we

have previously considered.

[4] The case under attack was Slochower v. Board of Education, 350 U.S. 551 (1956) which held that a college teacher may not be discharged automatically because he invoked the privilege against self-incrimination before a congressional investigating committee.

[5] The cases under attack were Schware v. Board of Bar Examiners of New Mexico, 353 U.S. 232 (1957) and Konigsberg v. State Bar, 353 U.S. 252 (1957) which held that the persons involved were, under the circumstances, arbitrarily deprived of their right to practice law.

[6] See Warren, Legislative and Judicial attacks on the Supreme Court of the United States—A History of the Twenty-Fifth Section of the Judiciary Act, 27 Am. L. Rev. 1, 161 (1913).

[7] 7 Wall. 506 (U.S. 1868).

Some writers have sought to explain the decision on the ground that the Court itself was relieved to be rid of its duty to decide the case on its merits. Be that as it may, no one can predict whether the present Court would read Ex parte McCardle as holding that Congress has power to eliminate the appellate jurisdiction of the Supreme Court, or even go as far as S. 2646 in this direction. It is difficult to reconcile the view that Article III gives the Congress unlimited power over the Court's appellate jurisdiction with the provision in Article III vesting in the Supreme Court and such inferior federal courts as the Congress may establish the "judicial power of the United States," which Article III extends to "all cases, in law and equity, arising under" the Constitution. Chief Justice Marshall intimated in an early case[8] that Congress could not constitutionally deprive the Supreme Court of *all* its appellate jurisdiction. Can it constitutionally deprive the Supreme Court of all its appellate jurisdiction, except a little that does not really matter?

One of the country's foremost students of our federal system, Professor Henry M. Hart, Jr., of the Harvard Law School, has suggested that the Constitution must not be read as authorizing its own destruction and that, therefore, Article III cannot reasonably be interpreted to permit Congress to make such exceptions from the Court's appellate jurisdiction as will "destroy the essential role of the Supreme Court in the constitutional plan." [9] If we accept Judge Hand's view that the essential constitutional role of the Supreme Court is "to keep the states, Congress and the President within their prescribed powers" there can be no question but that S. 2646 would deprive the Supreme Court of this role.

Professor Hart points out that the McCardle case did not involve such an exception from appellate jurisdiction as would destroy the Court's essential role—because even after the 1868 act was passed, the Supreme Court was empowered by other statutes to entertain a petition for a writ of habeas corpus filed with it in the first instance. In fact, following the McCardle case, a petition for habeas corpus seeking to test the constitutionality of the Reconstruction Acts was filed in the Supreme Court under the original Judiciary Act of 1789. This was the famous case of Ex parte Yerger,[10] in which the Court held that it had jurisdiction to grant the writ. A decision was again prevented, but this time only because Yerger was released from the challenged military custody and the case became moot.

Most professional opinion would agree that a bill like S. 2646, even if not unconstitutional, is at the very least "anti-constitutional." An example in another area may help to clarify this point. The Fifth Amendment provides that private property shall not be taken for public use without just compensation. But the constitutional doctrine of sovereign immunity says that the Government may not be sued without its consent. If Congress passed a law withholding this consent, private property could be taken with impunity

[8] Durousseau v. United States, 6 Cranch 307 (U.S. 1810).

[9] Hart, The Power of Congress to Limit the Jurisdiction of Federal Courts, 66 Harv. L. Rev. 1362, 1365 (1953).

[10] 8 Wall. 85 (U.S. 1869).

and the constitutional claim for just compensation could be defeated. Congress, however, has recognized its responsibility and has consented to this kind of suit.[11] A Congressional withdrawal of consent or refusal to appropriate funds to pay "just compensation" would be anti-constitutional, if not unconstitutional.

S. 2646 would be anti-constitutional in the sense also that it violates the basic assumption of the rule of law characterizing a free government—an independent judiciary. The Constitution created an independent federal judiciary by assuring life tenure and undiminished pay to the judges. Yet at times in our history Congress has sought to use its constitutional powers to curb this independence. In 1804-5, the Jeffersonians instigated the move to impeach Supreme Court Justice Samuel Chase whom they accused of harboring "dangerous opinions." John Marshall was their ultimate objective but to reach him the move against Chase had to succeed. Six of the Jeffersonian Senators,[12] however, broke with their party and joined with the Federalists in voting Chase's acquittal on all counts. The Senate thereby settled it as a matter of the practical political construction of the Constitution that it would not invoke its constitutional power to impeach because it disliked a federal judge's "political opinions, his conceptions of public policy, or his interpretation of the laws."[13] Since then and in spite of some recent posturing, no serious attempt has been made to impeach a federal judge for any of these reasons.

The movement for adoption of the doctrine of the recall of Supreme Court decisions invalidating acts of Congress, espoused by Theodore Roosevelt in 1912 and Senator Robert M. LaFollette in 1924, has also petered out.

It is Congress, too, which determines the number of Justices on the Supreme Court—a subject on which the Constitution is silent. However, when President Roosevelt urged that Congress exercise this constitutional power to enlarge the Court in 1937, substantial opinion throughout the country feared that the proposal would destroy the Court's independence. By defeating the so-called "court-packing" plan, which we shall examine at some greater length in the next section, Congress added another point of practical, political construction of the Constitution—that the number of Justices may not be increased solely to change the course of constitutional decision.

The independence of the federal judiciary would also be threatened if Congress exercised its power to deprive the Supreme Court of its appellate jurisdiction in cases in which Congress happened to disagree with the Court's decisions. Eminent lawyers have not been content to rely upon the practical, political construction of the Constitution in this respect. Led by the late Supreme Court Justice Owen J. Roberts, the Association of the Bar of the

---

[11] 28 U.S.C. 1346 (a) (2), 1491 (1) (Supp. 1952).

[12] Article I, Section 3 of the Constitution gives the Senate "the sole power to try all impeachments;" while Article I, Section 2 gives the House "the sole power of impeachment."

[13] Hurst, The Growth of American Law 136 (1950).

City of New York, the New York State Bar Association, and the American Bar Association have proposed that the Constitution be amended to deprive Congress of the authority to exclude any case arising under the Constitution from the appellate jurisdiction of the Supreme Court.[14] Whether such an amendment is regarded as advisable depends upon one's views about the function of the Supreme Court in our democracy—a subject that will be dealt with in the next section.

It should also be noted that S. 2646 did not purport to affect the jurisdiction of the lower federal courts or the state courts. However, if the Supreme Court's appellate jurisdiction were taken away in the five categories of cases specified above, the state and federal courts, by themselves, would be unable to achieve a uniform interpretation of the constitutional provisions applicable in these cases. An individual's rights would then depend upon the irrelevant circumstance of where he happened to bring his case—an outcome which violates fundamental notions of equal justice. Furthermore, passage of a bill like S. 2646 would constitute a thinly-veiled threat to the lower federal courts to disregard the Supreme Court's decisions in the five categories of cases in question. Even if the lower federal judges were determined to resist this threat, their independence would be jeopardized by the very fact that Congress—the creator (and potential abolisher) of the lower federal courts—had made the threat by passing such a bill.

The need for Supreme Court appellate jurisdiction to review the decisions of state courts in cases involving the assertion of rights under the federal constitution is even greater then the need to review lower federal court decisions. Only the Supreme Court is in a position in our federal system of government to act as the arbiter of the relations between state and nation and to assure that the states vindicate federal constitutional rights. This is why Justice Holmes once said he thought the Union would be imperiled if the Supreme Court could not declare laws of the several states unconstitutional and void. "For one in my place," Holmes wrote, "sees how often a local policy prevails with those who are not trained to national views." [15] Holmes did not think, it should be added, that the Union would come to an end if the federal courts, including the Supreme Court, were deprived of their power to declare acts of Congress unconstitutional.

Section 3

JUDICIAL REVIEW IN A DEMOCRACY

MR. JUSTICE MATTHEWS, *speaking for the court in HURTADO v. CALIFORNIA*
110 U.S. 516, 535-536 (1884)

It is not every act, legislative in form, that is law. Law is something more than mere will exerted as an act of power. . . . Arbitrary power, enforcing its edicts

---

[14] Roberts, Now Is the Time: Fortifying the Supreme Court's Independence, 35 A.B.A.J. 1 (1944).

[15] Holmes, Collected Legal Papers 295-296 (1920).

to the injury of the persons and property of its subjects, is not law, whether manifested as the decree of a personal monarch or of an impersonal multitude. And the limitations imposed by our constitutional law upon the action of the governments, both State and national, are essential to the preservation of public and private rights, notwithstanding the representative character of our political institutions. The enforcement of these limitations by judicial process is the device of self-governing communities to protect the rights of individuals and minorities, as well against the power of numbers, as against the violence of public agents transcending the limits of lawful authority, even when acting in the name and wielding the force of the government.

Cardozo, *THE NATURE OF THE JUDICIAL PROCESS* 93-94 (1921)

The great ideals of liberty and equality are preserved against the assaults of opportunism, the expediency of the passing hour, the erosion of small encroachments, the scorn and derision of those who have no patience with general principles, by enshrining them in constitutions, and consecrating to the task of their protection a body of defenders. By conscious or subconscious influence, the presence of this restraining power, aloof in the background, but none the less always in reserve, tends to stabilize and rationalize the legislative judgment, to infuse it with the glow of principle, to hold the standard aloft and visible for those who must run the race and keep the faith.

EDITORIAL NOTE: The 1937 PROPOSAL to "PACK" the SUPREME COURT

On February 5, 1937, President Roosevelt submitted to Congress a bill drafted by the Attorney General designed to expedite the work of the federal courts (a) by certain administrative and procedural changes, and (b) by providing in substance that when any federal judge (including those on the lower courts as well as the Supreme Court) had reached the age of 70, had served at least 10 years and had not elected to retire, an additional judge should be appointed to his particular court.

Of the nine Supreme Court justices six were in this category. If the bill were to pass and the six were to retire, their vacant positions would be filled by new appointees, and the Court's membership would remain at nine. But if the six elected to remain, six new appointees would be named, bringing the Court's membership up to fifteen. The President's message, and the Attorney General's letter accompanying it, discussed only questions of congested calendars, the need of adding to the judiciary when aged and infirm judges did not retire, etc. The fact that the Supreme Court, generally by a 5 to 4 vote, had held unconstitutional some of the most important legislation enacted in the preceding four years of the New Deal, was not mentioned. But it was instantly recognized that the real object of the bill was to deal with this situation; that all the rest was incidental.

After a protracted and bitter controversy the bill was defeated.[1] The American Bar Association, with a membership of 29,616 lawyers (out of over 150,000 in the U.S.), took a referendum vote in which 19,136 participated. The vote was about 6 to 1 against the "court packing" proposal.

At the hearings on the "court-packing" bill before the Senate Judiciary Committee the following statements, among a multitude of others, were made (they are among the best, if not the best, on the two sides).

STATEMENT OF ROBERT H. JACKSON*

When a situation exists in the Supreme Court which the President feels he cannot continue to ignore, it is to the Congress that he may properly bring the problem.

The responsibility upon Congress for seeing that the American people have a workable, harmonious and cooperative judicial system is so usually overlooked by those engaged in building up the tradition of judicial supremacy that the burden of constitutional responsibility on Congress deserves examination.

A sentiment has developed that sole responsibility for the functioning of the Supreme Court as an institution is upon the justices, and that their independence requires that a majority of them be let alone to shape the institution as they will. . . .

The power of Congress to exercise checks against the overreaching of the court is so generally overlooked or minimized that the alternatives that faced the Constitution writers deserve examination in detail.

1. The Constitution might have made the Supreme Court the sole custodian of judicial power. It did not. The judicial power is vested in the Supreme Court "and in such inferior courts as the Congress may from time to time ordain and establish."

2. The Constitution might have determined, or left to the Supreme Court to fix, its own jurisdiction. It did not. It has only a limited original jurisdiction and, except in cases affecting Ambassadors, Ministers and Consuls and those in which a State shall be a party, the Supreme Court has appellate jurisdiction only "with such exceptions and under such regulations as the Congress shall make."

3. The Constitution might have fixed the size of the Supreme Court or left the court to determine its own size, but the Constitution deliberately left the number of justices to be fixed from time to time by Congress.

4. The Constitution might have named the original members of the court or

---

[1] On the court-packing plan in general, see Hearings before Senate Judiciary Committee on S. 1392, 75th Cong., 1st Sess. (1937); the documents collected in S. Rep. No. 711, 75th Cong., 1st Sess. (1937); James M. Burns, Roosevelt, The Lion and the Fox, c. 15 (1956); Mason, Harlan Fiske Stone and F D R's Court Plan, 61 Yale L.J. 791 (1952); Cope and Krinsky,

Franklin D. Roosevelt and the Supreme Court (1952); and Jackson, The Struggle for Judicial Supremacy (1941).

* Then Solicitor General of the United States and later Associate Justice of the Supreme Court of the United States. Hearings before Senate Judiciary Committee on S. 1392, 75th Cong., 1st Sess. (1937), Pt. 1, p. 37.

might have given the court power to fill its own vacancies. It did not. The Constitution placed the continuing power of appointment in the President and in the Senate.

5. The Constitution left the amount of compensation of the justices entirely to Congress, with no restriction except in the provision that whatever compensation Congress may once give them shall not be diminished during their continuance in office.

6. The Constitution could have provided some source of revenue for the court, its justices, marshal, clerk and appointees. But it leaves it entirely to appropriations to be initiated in the House of Representatives.

7. The Constitution could have authorized the court itself to appoint the personnel necessary to execute and enforce court decrees. But it did not. For the enforcement of the court's decrees, the Congress and the Executive branch of the government must be relied upon.

8. The Constitution could have given to the court the power to judge the conduct of its own members. The power to judge the qualifications and to discipline its own members was given to each house of Congress. But the Supreme Court was entrusted with no such power to either accuse or judge its members. Impeachment can be only by the House and trial by the Senate.

When the Congress, as the supreme legislative and policy-making body of the United States, was granted such conclusive powers over jurisdiction and enforcement of decrees of the court, and over appointment and behavior of its personnel, it is idle to contend, as many of the advocates of judicial supremacy do, that it was ever intended that the Supreme Court should become a super-government.

From these powers it is apparent that Congress by failure to exert its checks and balances, assumes responsibility for the functioning of the court.

It is clear that Congress has the power to see that the personnel of the judicial system is adequate, both with respect to number and to neutrality of attitude.

It is a responsibility of Congress to see that the court is an instrumentality in the maintenance of a just and constitutional government and that it does not become an instrumentality for the defeat of constitutional government.

The duty of cooperation is not cast upon Congress and the Executive alone.

Congress, throughout our history, has made sparing use of its checks and balances against the court. It made one abortive attempt to use impeachment as a check. It once withdrew jurisdiction of the court to hear and determine a case that had already been submitted, and its power to do so was recognized.

Three times the device of constitutional amendment has been used to correct the court. Six times we have effected changes in the size of the court, with resulting changes in the court's attitudes.

Legislation creating or abolishing vacancies in the court is authorized in the Constitution and validated by historical practice as a method of bringing the elective and non-elective branches of the government back into a proper coordination.

Its frequent use has avoided amendments which would make the Constitution a document of patches and details. It does not change the constitutional powers of the Congress or the distribution of powers between the legislative and judicial branches. It does not eliminate any check or balance of the constitutional system.

Changing the size of the court has never deprived it of independence or prestige. It was obvious at the founding of the government that the court would not always remain of the same size, and that changes in its size would be made, as they have been made, at those times when its decisions caused dissatisfaction.

It is just as constitutional to add members to keep the court up with the country as it is to add members to keep the court up with its business. The power of the Congress to avert constitutional stagnation is as great as its power to prevent congested dockets.

And, whatever other motives have influenced the changes that have been made in the composition of the court, the dominant one has always been to keep the divergence between the court and the elective branches from becoming so wide as to threaten the stability of the government.

The amendment method to correct the court has been used three times: The Eleventh Amendment was adopted to correct the court on suits against the States; the Thirteenth, Fourteenth and Fifteenth Amendments to eradicate the philosophy of the Dred Scott decision and effectuate the policy of reconstruction; and the Sixteenth to alter the result produced by the court's ruling on income taxes.

I am not urging that the amendment method shall not now be tried. But I do point out certain problems which draftsmen and advocates of amendment will need to consider.

Experience has shown that it is difficult to amend a constitution to make it say what it already says. * * *

The Fourteenth Amendment was . . . a clarifying amendment intended to uproot the constitutional errors involved in the Dred Scott decision.

There is no doubt that the Congress which submitted, and the States which ratified, language which said, "Nor shall any State deprive any person of life, liberty or property, *without due process of law*," thought they were protecting the civil rights to a fair trial and hearing.

The Supreme Court extended the amendment to protect corporations, although its language only includes persons, and it then extended it from a guarantee of *procedural fairness*, to prevent the State from enacting almost any kind of economic legislation.

Thus the Fourteenth Amendment, far from clarifying the great constitutional principle of human rights, has brought forth a crop of new difficulties, and the amendment in the interest of freedom has brought forth new kinds of oppression.

The income-tax amendment was also intended to clarify the Constitution. An income tax had been levied and sustained during the Civil War. But in 1895, after one justice made a somewhat mystifying shift in his vote, the Supreme Court, by five to four, held the income tax to be constitutional to tax wages and salaries but unconstitutional to tax income from invested capital in the form of rent, interest and income from real or personal property.*

This inequality we attempted to correct by the Sixteenth Amendment, which

---

* Pollock v. Farmers' Loan and Trust Co., 157 U.S. 429 (1895); on rehearing, 158 U.S. 601 (1895).—Editor

provided: "Congress shall have the power to levy and collect taxes on incomes from whatever source derived * * *"

Despite its broad language, the courts now refused to apply it to their own salaries or to income from State and municipal bonds, or to salaries from State and municipal sources; or to stock dividends.

Even if this amendment were permitted to mean what it says, it gave us no more, after a delay of eighteen years, than could have been obtained if a single justice had stood by his original vote in the Pollock case.

Our constitutional history abundantly demonstrates that it is impossible to foresee or predict the interpretation or effect which may be given to any language used in an amendment.

The difficulty of enacting an amendment to overcome a single decision of the court, such as the Dred Scott decision or the income tax decision, becomes more difficult when the problem is not to meet a single concrete decision, but to meet a state of mind or mental attitude which pervades the whole course of recent judicial decisions. . . .

Judges who resort to a tortured construction of the Constitution may torture an amendment. You cannot amend a state of mind and mental attitude of hostility to exercise of government power and of indifference to the demands which democracy, attempting to survive industrialism, makes upon its government.

The outstanding development in recent constitutional history is the growing frequency with which the Supreme Court refuses to enforce acts of the Congress on the ground that such acts are beyond the constitutional powers of the Congress. . . .

In the seventy-one years from the adoption of the Constitution to the war between the States the Supreme Court so nullified only two acts of Congress. One of those two nullifications was the Dred Scott case which precipitated that war. . . .

Enumerated by decades, the number of laws of the United States nullified by the Supreme Court runs as follows:

Period	No.	Period	No.
1790-1800	0	1860-1870	4
1800-1810	1	1870-1880	9
1810-1820	0	1880-1890	5
1820-1830	0	1890-1900	5
1830-1840	0	1900-1910	9
1840-1850	0	1910-1920	7
1850-1860	1	1920-1930	19

But in just the last three years from the October (1933) term on, the court has refused to recognize the power of Congress in twelve cases. And five of these twelve decisions have occurred during a single year, i.e., the October (1935) term, four of the five by a sharply divided court.*

* For more detailed information about the statutes declared unconstitutional since 1790 and the cases in which they were invalidated, see The Constitution of the United

The outstanding constitutional development of the Roosevelt administration has been the increasing tendency of the Supreme Court to judge legislation according to the majority view of the wisdom of the legislation.

The early policy of judging constitutionality without weighing the wisdom of the act has departed, and the attitude that has come to prevail is that stated by Mr. Justice McReynolds (Nebbia v. New York, 291 U.S. 502, at 556):

> "But plainly, I think, this court must have regard to the wisdom of the enactment. At least we must inquire concerning its purpose and decide whether the means proposed have reasonable relation to something within legislative power—whether the end is legitimate, and the means appropriate."

Each success in thwarting Congressional power, or each effort that comes so near success as to lack but a vote or two, stimulates competing lawyers and aggrieved interests to new attack.

Nearly every newly organized institution of the government rests under a legal cloud. This is true of the Securities and Exchange Commission, the Social Security Board, the Public Works Administration, the Tennessee Valley Authority and the Labor Relations Board.

The acts of Congress involving the hopes and fears of a great proportion of the American people are likewise clouded in legal doubt. Old-age benefits, old-age assistance, unemployment compensation, the Securities Act, the Relief Acts, the Labor Relations Act, the Public Utility Holding Company Act, the Tennessee Valley Acts—as well as many taxing acts—are involved in litigation, and there is no definite assurance what their fate will be.

The whole program overwhelmingly approved by the people in 1932, 1934 and 1936 is in danger of being lost in a maze of constitutional metaphors.

For a century and a half it was settled doctrine that an act of Congress was a law to be obeyed until set aside by the Supreme Court; that even in that court it was presumed to be constitutional and a heavy burden rested on one who would prove it otherwise.

The Public Utility Holding Company Act was to take effect Dec. 1, 1935. Although the Supreme Court had not acted, and lower courts were in conflict, practically the entire industry, advised by eminent constitutionalists, refused

---

States, revised and annotated under the editorship of Professor Edward S. Corwin (1952) at 1241-1254.

The most significant of the 12 decisions referred to by Justice Jackson were Panama Refining Co. v. Ryan, 293 U.S. 388 (1935) and Schechter Poultry Corp. v. United States, 295 U.S. 495 (1935), holding basic provisions of the National Industrial Recovery Act of 1933 to be unconstitutional; Perry v. United States, 294 U.S. 330 (1935), declaring that a Joint Resolution of 1933 abrogating the gold clause in Government obligations was unconstitutional but barring recovery by the plaintiff on other grounds; Railroad Retirement Board v. Alton R.R., 295 U.S. 330 (1935), invalidating the Railroad Retirement Act of 1934; United States v. Butler, 297 U.S. 1 (1936), invalidating the Agricultural Adjustment Act of 1933; and Carter v. Carter Coal Co., 298 U.S. 238 (1936), invalidating the Bituminous Coal Conservation Act of 1935.—Editor

obedience unless and until the Supreme Court should have declared the law constitutional.

No more threatening development in law enforcement has occurred than the sight of the government, defied by the whole utility holding company industry, obliged to abdicate enforcement until a Supreme Court decision could be had.

If this attitude shall spread, then a subtle change has come about that transforms completely the function of the Supreme Court in our government.

Such an attitude reverses a century of legal opinion. It throws the burden on Congress of getting a favorable decision before its laws can be enforced. . . .

This attitude, if applied to Federal legislation, will hold up law enforcement and, in effect, require court approval, as well as Presidential approval, for acts of Congress with this important difference: the veto of the Executive can be overridden if a sufficient vote in the Congress favor it; the veto of the court has the finality of fate. . . .

It is often assumed that the powers which the court denies to the Federal Government fall to the State governments and that the Supreme Court is therefore a protector of the States. . . .

It was not Congress, nor the Executive, but it was the Supreme Court which denied the rights of any of the States of the Union to make any law whatever dealing with minimum wages, and it was in that case that the Chief Justice said:

> "And I can find nothing in the Federal Constitution which denies to the State the power to protect women from being exploited by over-reaching employers through the refusal of a fair wage as defined in the New York statute and ascertained in a reasonable manner by competent authority." [Morehead v. Tipaldo, 298 U.S. 587 (1936)].

He said further:

> "We have not yet arrived at a time when we are at liberty to override the judgment of a State to decide that women are not the special subject of exploitation because they are women and, as such, are not in a relative defenseless position."

The majority, however, not only overrode the State but overrode the Chief Justice of the court and three of its ablest members. Instead of saying the time has not yet arrived, the Chief Justice might properly have said: "The time has just this minute arrived."

Experiments by the States with laws to settle industrial disputes, minimum wage acts, and acts to regulate public utility and other business enterprises were frequently stopped by the Federal courts.† Had they been allowed to proceed, de-

---

† "Excluding the civil liberties cases, there were (during the period 1899-1937) 159 decisions under the due process and equal protection clauses in which state statutes were held to be unconstitutional, plus 16 in which both the due process and commerce clauses were involved, plus 9 more involving due process and some other clause or clauses." (Wright, The Growth of American Constitutional Law 154 (1942)). Professor Wright concludes that "less than a score of these decisions would have been

mands for the exercise of Federal power later would have been less imperative. . . .

The present controversy over the court reflects a controversy within the court. Neither Congress nor the President has sought the present dissension. Neither the Congress nor the Executive has in any manner sought to interfere with the judicial function, and neither has failed to obey any decision of the court.

A majority of the justices have made it apparent that the great objectives of this administration and this Congress offend their deep convictions and that the methods of this day violate their conceptions of good government.

Prediction of "impending moral chaos," grief over the fear that "the Constitution is gone," characterization of the Securities and Exchange Commission as a "star chamber," accusation that the Congress and the Executive have coerced farmers, taken freedom of contract away from working women and despoiled the States, indicate an implacable, although unquestionably sincere, opposition to the use of national power to accomplish the policies so overwhelmingly endorsed by the voters.

This frank hostility of these justices has been openly counted on by interested groups to defeat much important legislation.

On the other hand, a minority of the justices, whose patriotism and competence no one questions, have made it apparent that they feel that justice to their own records with posterity requires them to protest publicly and sharply against the overriding decisions of the majority.

Included among those who have seen fit to protect their place in judicial history by recorded protests are Chief Justice Hughes, Justices Holmes, Brandeis, Stone and Cardozo.

Under this stress and contention an inability to reach a decision developed in the case of the New York Unemployment Compensation Act, and the court split 4 to 4, one justice being absent from illness.

This left a cloud upon the social security program of many States and is a

possible" if the Supreme Court had adhered to the position it took in the Slaughter-House Cases, 16 Wall. 36 (U.S. 1873), that the due process clause of the 14th Amendment held out procedural safeguard only and was not a basis upon which the Court could pass on the reasonableness of state legislation.

Some of the more significant cases to which Justice Jackson alludes include Chicago, M. & St. Paul R. Co. v. Minnesota, 134 U.S. 418 (1890), holding that the reasonableness of public utility rate regulation "is eminently a question for judicial investigation, requiring due process of law for its determination;" Lochner v. New York, 198 U.S. 45 (1905), invalidating a New York statute limiting the hours of employment in bakeries; Coppage v. Kansas, 236 U.S. 1 (1915), invalidating a Kansas

statute outlawing the "yellow-dog" contract under which employers required their employees to agree not to join a union; Wolff Packing Co. v. Court of Industrial Relations, 262 U.S. 522 (1923), invalidating a Kansas statute calling for compulsory arbitration of labor-management wage disputes in the food, clothing, fuel, and transportation industries; Ribnik v. McBride, 277 U.S. 350 (1928), invalidating a New Jersey statute regulating fees charged by employment agencies; Williams v. Standard Oil Co., 278 U.S. 235 (1929), invalidating a Tennessee statute regulating the price of gasoline; New State Ice Co. v. Liebmann, 285 U.S. 262 (1932), invalidating an Oklahoma statute regulating the ice business; and Morehead v. Tipaldo, 298 U.S. 587 (1936), invalidating the New York minimum wage act for women.—Editor

possible threat to the Federal Social Security Act. Petition for rehearing has long awaited decision. . . .

When the decision of crucial constitutional issues may turn on the death or illness of a single justice, it would seem that our constitutional progress is governed by a blind fate instead of by human reason. . . .

Nobody, no matter where his sympathies lie, or what his views of constitutional doctrine may be, can view this situation with composure.

Even government victories by 5 to 4 decisions are unsatisfactory. A state of the law which depends upon the continuance of a single life, or upon the assumption that no justice will change his mind, is not a satisfactory basis on which the government may enter into new fields for the exercise of its power.

The climax was reached in the recent decision that "a State is without power by any form of legislation to prohibit, change or nullify contracts between employers and adult women workers as to the amount of wages to be paid" (Morehead v. New York ex rel. Tipaldo, 298 U.S. 587, 611).

In vain did the minority protest that "it is difficult to imagine any grounds, other than our own personal economic predilections, for saying that the contract of employment is any less an appropriate subject of legislation than are scores of others, in dealing with which this court has held Legislatures may curtail individual freedom in the public interest" (298 U.S. at 633).

Only ten days after the court had tossed aside the New York Minimum Wage Act, on the ground that the State was "without power by any form of legislation" to establish minimum wages for women, the Republican party pledged itself to support such legislation and avowed its belief that such legislation could be enacted "within the Constitution as it now stands."

This was exactly what the court said could not be done.

It thus becomes evident that there is a serious lag between public opinion and the decisions of the court. A majority of the justices have too frequently failed to recognize, as Justice Holmes so aptly stated, "what seemed to them to be first principles, are believed by half of their fellow men to be wrong."

The Supreme Court has never waited for a constitutional amendment when its majority wanted to overcome the effect of its past decisions. It has qualified and even expressly overruled important decisions on constitutional issues.

Conflict between Congress and the courts is in large part due to the refusal of the courts to permit Congress to have any share in defining the present day application of such indefinite terms as "general welfare," "due process," "commerce among the several States," and the things which directly affect it.

The court majority insists on a rigid, permanent and legalistic definition. . . .

If this split were decisively resolved by the addition of new members, the court could proceed to mark out a less ambitious course for itself and bring about greater harmony within the government.

The industrialization of society and the movement toward city dwelling, foreign political and economic dislocations, together with depression and distress, have generated an unrest which has put the whole complicated Federal system under severe strain. The ability of a federated form of government to withstand these pressures is greatly impaired by any dissension between branches that were intended to be cooperating and coordinate.

The Supreme Court's power over legislation is not defined or bounded, or even mentioned in the Constitution, but was left to lurk in inference.

As Mr. Justice Stone has well said:

> "The only check upon our exercise of power is our own sense of self-restraint." (United States v. Butler, 297 U.S. 1 at 79).

Chief Justice Hughes, when Governor of New York, put in a single sentence our whole constitutional law, when he said:

> "We are under a Constitution, but the Constitution is what the judges say it is."

I have attempted to review dispassionately some of the failures of judicial self-restraint by which the Constitution "as the judges say it is" has departed from the Constitution which Woodrow Wilson said "is not a mere lawyer's document; it is a vehicle of life, and its spirit is always the spirit of the age."

STATEMENT OF CHARLES C. BURLINGHAM *

The discussion which has been raging since the President sent his message to Congress on February 5 has been wholesome and enlightening, and we have not seen the end of it.

As I am against the President's proposal, perhaps I should begin by telling you that I am a Democrat, that I voted for Mr. Roosevelt twice for Governor and twice for President; that I am in sympathy with his policies and that I have been severely critical of some of the decisions of the Supreme Court.

What so many of us who have supported the President oppose is the method he is adopting to achieve his ends. The fundamental question before the people is not the minimum wage, the NRA, the AAA, or any other part of the New Deal. Nor is it the size of the court or the age of the judges; it is whether the Supreme Court is to be independent or controlled.

This is no new question; it is an American question fought out in Colonial days in the 17th and 18th centuries. The British Board of Trade and the royal governors insisted on controlling the judges, and the commissions of the judges issued by the King were not for life or during good behavior, but "at the King's pleasure." Again and again the Colonial Assemblies attempted to change this system. Here in New York in 1762, the Lieutenant Governor was induced, with difficulty, to sign an appropriation bill providing salaries for judges only on condition that they would acccept good-behavior commissions, but the British Board of Trade insisted on commissions at the pleasure of the King and ordered the salaries of the judges to be paid out of Crown revenues. The same sort of struggle went on in other

* Former President of the Association of the Bar of the City of New York. Hearings before Senate Judiciary Committee on S. 1392, 75th Cong., 1st Sess. (1937), Pt. 5, p. 1041.

American colonies. . . . When, in 1772, popular resistance to the King's judges was becoming more pronounced in Massachusetts, the British Parliament passed a law which gave the royal governor the right to transfer cases for trial to other colonies and even to England, and the Board of Trade made a rule that any decision of an American Colonial Court could be appealed to the board and heard in England.

But this was more than our forefathers would endure, and we all know the result. . . .

It was these experiences that led the signers to charge against George III in the Declaration of Independence: "He has made judges dependent on his will alone for the tenure of their offices and the amount and payment of their salaries." The founders knew what they were doing when they declared in our Constitution that there shall be one Supreme Court, whose judges shall hold their offices during good behavior and whose compensation shall not be diminished during their continuation in office.

I have briefly reviewed this story of the long fight for an independent judiciary because I find that many people, including some lawyers, do not seem to appreciate this blessing of a free country. And is it not amazing that citizens of foreign birth or parentage can forget that the courts of the Continent of Europe were controlled by the executives even before the advent of the Mussolinis, the Stalins, or the Hitlers, and do they not know that the Supreme Court is the protector of the liberties of the individual and the rights of minorities?

I am not here to defend all the decisions of the Supreme Court of the United States even in the matter of personal liberty. During the Civil War and again during the Great War there were lapses, but on the whole the Court, and especially the present Court, has stood strongly and consistently for free speech, free press, and free assembly.

It was the Supreme Court that in 1923 held a Nebraska statute which forbade the teaching of any language but English unconstitutional and reversed the conviction of a teacher for teaching German in a parochial school. It was the Supreme Court that in 1925 held unconstitutional the Oregon Compulsory Education Act, which required Catholics and Lutherans to take children out of their religious schools and send them to the public schools. . . . It was the Supreme Court that held that the Scottsboro boys did not have a fair trial. And in January of this year the Court . . . unanimously declared the criminal syndicalism law of Oregon unconstitutional and reversed the conviction of a man sentenced to prison for six years for merely attending a Communist meeting.

It cannot be necessary for a lawyer to present to an American audience an argument in favor of the independence of judges. And I have no doubt that the friends of the President's proposal will say that the President's bright young judges would be as solicitous of our hard-earned civil liberties as any of the "Nine Old Men." But President Roosevelt is not the last President of the United States; there will be others. All the Huey Longs are not dead, and as the political pendulum swings we may have reactionary presidents and reactionary senators who, with this bill as a precedent, may make a new court responsive to their will; and liberals and radicals, and labor, too, may curse the day when the Roosevelt bill was conceived.

The original reasons for increasing the number of the justices . . . have been abandoned. President Roosevelt is a very busy man, and he may have been misled by the Attorney General, whose letter published with the President's message was, to put it mildly, incorrect in every statement with regard to the business of the Supreme Court. The real purpose of the legislation proposed is to secure through additional judges a reversal of some of the recent decisions of the court. This is not the American, the democratic way. It was precisely what the Stuart Kings did in England in the 17th century, it is what the royal governors of the colonies tried to do here in America in the 18th century. It is not our way, and it is not the right way.

The right way is to proceed by a constitutional amendment and let the whole body of the people decide what they want, and not leave it to a Congress elected on other issues and dominated as this one is by the executive through patronage and refusal of patronage.

There are two kinds of amendments and they should be carefully distinguished—substantive amendments such as Senator Borah's, which would increase the power of the States and prevent indefensible decisions like that in the minimum wage case, or, to take another example, an amendment re-defining "interstate commerce" so as to include the production or distribution of commodities like coal, which compete with interstate commodities; and on the other hand amendments which concern only the Court itself, its size, its functions, and its powers.

Substantive amendments are hard to draft, and, as the President has said, hard to pass. Naturally so, for unless they are drawn with the utmost care and skill they may alter the form of our government. The extreme nationalists would like to concentrate the power of government in Washington, but the great mass of the American people believe in, and will not give up, a Federal system. That is the only sound form of government for a vast country like ours, with different characteristics and diverse needs.

But an amendment dealing with the Supreme Court itself is quite a different matter. Consider, for instance, the amendment introduced by Senator Burke of Nebraska, a good Democrat, who is as much interested in progressive legislation as is the President himself. That amendment provides for voluntary retirement of all federal judges at 70 and compels their retirement at 75. The exact age is not important. In this State and in many others (45 in all, the President says) judges must retire at 70. Such an amendment would do all that the President can do by his bill and do it in an orderly way in accordance with the provisions of the Constitution itself.

Senator Burke said the other day that he would add to his amendment a provision that of the present elderly Justices one only should be retired each year in the order of their seniority. It would disrupt the Court if six Justices were retired at one time.

The President, however, thinks that to proceed by amendment is too slow a process, and his docile Attorney General has found a quicker and easier way by pushing the old judges out; or, if they prefer to hang on, then let younger men take seats beside them, bring them up to date economically if possible, and if not, outvote them.

I have no right to an opinion on the length of time it will take to amend the Constitution. According to Senator Wheeler there will be little difficulty in bringing the opponents of the President's bill to agree on an amendment which, with the President's backing, he feels confident can be adopted within a reasonable time. The repeal of the 18th Amendment took only ten months. As most of the States of the Union have age limits for their own judges, their representatives in Congress would undoubtedly agree on an age limit for Federal judges. Do the people of the United States really want an independent judiciary? I think they do. Do they want a court filled up with President's men chosen because they are supposed to have the same views as the President as to what is good or bad in these times? I am sure they do not.

Why is the President in such a hurry? What crisis is upon us now? Has the Supreme Court been responsible for dust storms, for floods, for sit-down strikes? Why should the Court be made the whipping boy for all the ills that flesh is heir to?

And there is one thing more which is most important—the repute of this Court. If the bill should become law—I do not think it will, for I believe that the President will be reasonable enough to add his powerful support to some reasonable amendment suggested by the Senators—but if the bill should become law and the old justices receive this transfusion of Rooseveltian blood, how will the Court stand in the eyes of the people? When I say to my left-wing friends that the prestige and respect of the Court must be preserved, some of them reply that the Court has forfeited the respect of the people. I do not believe it. Criticism of courts and vilification of judges is no new thing in this country or in England, but in democratic countries it is essential that the people should have confidence in their courts, and especially in their highest court. It is my firm conviction that the appointment of a body of judges chosen for a specific purpose will not only lessen the confidence of the people in the Court, but will inevitably result in putting a stigma on these new judges themselves and make them objects of contempt, however conscientious or independent they may prove to be. They would be King's men.

FRANKFURTER, *MR. JUSTICE ROBERTS*
104 University of Pennsylvania Law Review 311, 313-317 (1955)

It is one of the most ludicrous illustrations of the power of lazy repetition of uncritical talk that a judge with the character of Roberts should have attributed to him a change of judicial views out of deference to political considerations. One is more saddened than shocked that a high-minded and thoughtful United States Senator should assume it to be an established fact that it was by reason of "the famous switch of Mr. Justice Roberts" that legislation was constitutionally sustained after President Roosevelt's proposal for reconstructing the Court and because of it. The charge specifically relates to the fact that while Roberts was of the majority in Morehead v. New York ex rel. Tipaldo, 298 U.S. 587, decided June 1, 1936, in reaffirming Adkins v. Children's Hospital, 261 U.S. 525 [1923] * and thereby invalidating the New York Minimum Wage Law, he was again with the majority in West Coast Hotel Co. v. Parrish, 300 U.S. 379, decided on March 29, 1937, overruling the Adkins case and sustaining minimum wage legislation. Intellectual responsibility should, one would suppose, save a thoughtful man from the familiar trap of post hoc ergo propter hoc. Even those whose business it is to study the work of the Supreme Court have lent themselves to a charge which is refuted on the face of the Court records. It is refuted, that is, if consideration is given not only to opinions but to appropriate deductions drawn from data pertaining to the time when petitions for certiorari are granted, when cases are argued, when dispositions are, in normal course, made at conference, and when decisions are withheld because of absences and divisions on the Court.

It is time that this false charge against Roberts be dissipated by a recording of the indisputable facts. Disclosure of Court happenings not made public by the Court itself, in its opinions and orders, presents a ticklish problem. The secrecy that envelops the Court's work is not due to love of secrecy or want of responsible regard for the claims of a democratic society to know how it is governed. That the Supreme Court should not be amenable to the forces of publicity to which the Executive and the Congress are subjected is essential to the effective functioning of the Court. But the passage of time may enervate the reasons for this restriction, particularly if disclosure rests not on tittle-tattle or self-serving declarations. The more so is justification for thus lifting the veil of secrecy valid if thereby the conduct of a Justice whose intellectual morality has been impugned is vindicated.

The truth about the so-called "switch" of Roberts in connection with the Minimum Wage cases is that when the Tipaldo case was before the Court in the spring of 1936, he was prepared to overrule the Adkins decision. Since a majority could not be had for overruling it, he silently agreed with the Court in finding the New York statute under attack in the Tipaldo case not distinguishable from the statute which had been declared unconstitutional in the Adkins case. That such was his position an alert reader could find in the interstices of the United States Reports. It took not a little persuasion—so indifferent was Roberts to misrepresentation—to induce him to set forth what can be extracted from the Reports.† Here it is:

"A petition for certiorari was filed in Morehead v. Tipaldo, 298 U.S. 587, on March 16, 1936. When the petition came to be acted upon, the Chief Justice spoke in favor of a grant, but several others spoke against it on the ground that

---

* In the Adkins case, the Supreme Court declared the District of Columbia minimum wage law for women to be unconstitutional. —Editor

† Mr. Justice Roberts gave me this memorandum on November 9, 1945, after he had resigned from the bench. He left the occasion for using it to my discretion. For reasons indicated in the text, the present seems to me an appropriate time for making it public. [Justice Frankfurter's note].

the case was ruled by Adkins v. Children's Hostpital, 261 U.S. 525. Justices Brandeis, Cardozo and Stone were in favor of a grant. They, with the Chief Justice, made up four votes for a grant.

"When my turn came to speak I said I saw no reason to grant the writ unless the Court were prepared to reexamine and overrule the Adkins case. To this remark there was no response around the table, and the case was marked granted.

"Both in the petition for certiorari, in the brief on the merits, and in oral argument, counsel for the State of New York took the position that it was unnecessary to overrule the Adkins case in order to sustain the position of the State of New York. It was urged that further data and experience and additional facts distinguished the case at bar from the Adkins case. The argument seemed to me to be disingenuous and born of timidity. I could find nothing in the record to substantiate the alleged distinction. At conference I so stated, and stated further that I was for taking the State of New York at its word. The State had not asked that the Adkins case be overruled but that it be distinguished. I said I was unwilling to put a decision on any such ground. The vote was five to four for affirmance, and the case was assigned to Justice Butler.

"I stated to him that I would concur in any opinion which was based on the fact that the State had not asked us to re-examine or overrule Adkins and that, as we found no material difference in the facts of the two cases, we should therefore follow the Adkins case. The case was orginally so written by Justice Butler, but after a dissent had been circulated he added matter to his opinion, seeking to sustain the Adkins case in principle. My proper course would have been to concur specially on the narrow ground I had taken. I did not do so. But at a conference in the Court I said that I did not propose to review and re-examine the Adkins case until a case should come to the Court requiring that this should be done.

"August 17, 1936, an appeal was filed in West Coast Hotels [sic] Company v. Parrish, 300 U.S. 379. The Court as usual met to consider applications in the week of Monday, October 5, 1936, and concluded its work by Saturday, October 10. During the conferences the jurisdictional statement in the Parrish case was considered and the question arose whether the appeal should be dismissed* on the authority of Adkins and Morehead. Four of those who had voted in the majority on the Morehead case voted to dismiss the appeal in the Parrish case. I stated that I would vote for the notation of probable jurisdiction. I am not sure that I gave my reason, but it was that in the appeal in the Parrish case the authority of Adkins was definitely assailed and the Court was asked to reconsider and overrule it. Thus, for the first time, I was confronted with the necessity of facing the soundness of the Adkins case. Those who were in the majority in the Morehead case expressed some surprise at my vote, and I heard one of the brethren ask another, 'What is the matter with Roberts?'

"Justice Stone was taken ill about October 14. The case was argued December 16 and 17, 1936, in the absence of Justice Stone, who at that time was lying

---

* Evidently he meant should be reversed summarily, since the Washington Supreme Court had sustained the statute. [Justice Frankfurter's note].

in a comatose condition at his home. It came on for consideration at the conference on December 19. I voted for an affirmance. There were three other such votes, those of the Chief Justice, Justice Brandeis, and Justice Cardozo. The other four voted for a reversal.

"If a decision had then been announced, the case would have been affirmed by a divided Court. It was thought that this would be an unfortunate outcome, as everyone on the Court knew Justice Stone's views. The case was, therefore, laid over for further consideration when Justice Stone should be able to participate. Justice Stone was convalescent during January and returned to the sessions of the Court on February 1, 1937. I believe that the Parrish case was taken up at the conference on February 6, 1937, and Justice Stone then voted for affirmance. This made it possible to assign the case for an opinion, which was done. The decision affirming the lower court was announced March 29, 1937.

"These facts make it evident that no action taken by the President in the interim had any causal relation to my action in the Parrish case." *

More needs to be said for Roberts than he cared to say for himself. As a matter of history it is regrettable that Roberts' unconcern for his own record led him to abstain from stating his position. The occasions are not infrequent when the disfavor of separate opinions, on the part of the bar and to the extent that it prevails within the Court, should not be heeded. Such a situation was certainly presented when special circumstances made Roberts agree with a result but basically disagree with the opinion which announced it.

The crucial factor in the whole episode was the absence of Mr. Justice Stone from the bench, on account of illness, from October 14, 1936, to February 1, 1937. 299 U.S. at iii.

* Perhaps Justice Roberts's explanation would not fully satisfy Professor Fred Rodell. For after stating as one of the two "big" factors in the defeat of the court-packing plan, "the sudden and self-saving about-face by the Court itself in its constitutional decisions" after the plan was proposed, he says: ". . . [It] was plain to lawyers and laymen alike that Roberts had simply switched sides. But . . . unnoticed was the most intriguing, and revealing, fact of all; the Washington minimum-wage case [West Coast Hotel Co. v. Parrish] though the decision came down in March, had been argued in Court and decided in conference in January— *before* the President proposed his plan. [The President formally proposed his plan on February 5, 1937.—Editor] Thus the circumstantial evidence is strong (Justices can, but very rarely do, change their votes after conference on a case is over) that Hughes [Charles Evans Hughes, then Chief Justice of the United States.—Editor] had begun to counter the plan and save his nine-man court a little ahead of when the plan was launched; for there can be no doubt that it was Hughes, as Chief, whose personal appeal, in the name of the Court's prestige, won Roberts away from the camp of the Four Horsemen. [Mr. Justices McReynolds, Van Devanter, Sutherland and Butler]. Whether there was a leak to Hughes from the Department of Justice where the plan was drafted, or whether, alerted by the election, he shrewdly foresaw what was coming, he got the jump, as few ever did, on Roosevelt." (Rodell, Nine Men (1955), 247-249).—Editor

For the view that Chief Justice Hughes's constitutional attitudes were uninfluenced by the Court plan, and that he had not pressured Roberts into changing his mind, see 2 Pusey, Charles Evans Hughes (1951), chaps. 70-71, particularly p. 757.—Editor

In Chamberlain v. Andrews and its allied cases, decided November 23, 1936, the judgments of the New York Court of Appeals sustaining the New York Unemployment Insurance Law were "affirmed by an equally divided Court." 299 U.S. 515. The constitutional outlook represented by these cases would reflect the attitude of a Justice towards the issues involved in the Adkins case. It can hardly be doubted that Van Devanter, McReynolds, Sutherland and Butler, JJ. were the four Justices for reversal in Chamberlain v. Andrews, supra. There can be equally no doubt that Hughes C. J. and Brandeis and Cardozo, JJ. were for affirmance. Since Stone, J. was absent, it must have been Roberts who joined Hughes, Brandeis and Cardozo. The appellants petitioned for a rehearing before the full bench, but since the position of Stone, as disclosed by his views in the Tipaldo case, would not have changed the result, i.e., affirmance, the judgments were allowed to stand and the petition for rehearing was denied. Moreover, in preceding Terms, Roberts had abundantly established that he did not have the narrow, restrictive attitude in the application of the broad, undefined provisions of the Constitution which led to decisions that provoked the acute controversies in 1936 and 1937.

Indeed, years before the 1936 election, in the 1933 Term, he was the author of the opinion in Nebbia v. New York, 291 U.S. 502, which evoked substantially the same opposing constitutional philosophy from Van Devanter, McReynolds, Sutherland and Butler, JJ. as their dissent expressed in West Coast Hotel Co. v. Parrish, supra. The result in the Nebbia case was significant enough. But for candor and courage, the opinion in which Roberts justified it was surely one of the most important contributions in years in what is perhaps the most far-reaching field of constitutional adjudication. It was an effective blow for liberation from empty tags and meretricious assumptions. In effect, Roberts wrote the epitaph on the misconception, which had gained respect from repetition, that legislative price-fixing as such was at least presumptively unconstitutional.* In his opinion in Parrish, the Chief Justice naturally relied heavily on Roberts' opinion in Nebbia, for the reasoning of Nebbia had undermined the foundations of Adkins.

Few speculations are more treacherous than diagnosis of motives or genetic explanations of the position taken by Justices in Supreme Court decisions. Seldom can attribution have been wider of the mark than to find in Roberts' views in this or that case a reflection of economic predilection. He was, to be sure, as all men are, a child of his antecedents. But his antecedents united with his temperament to make him a forthright, democratic, perhaps even somewhat innocently trusting, generous, humane creature. Long before it became popular to regard every so-called civil liberties question as constitutionally self-answering, Roberts gave powerful utterance to his sensitiveness for those procedural safeguards which are protective of human rights in a civilized society, even when invoked by the least appealing of characters. See his opinions in Sorrells v. United States, 287 U.S. 435, 453, and Snyder v. Massachusetts, 291 U.S. 97, 123.

Owen J. Roberts contributed his good and honest share to that coral-reef fabric

---

* In the Nebbia case, the Supreme Court upheld a New York law of 1933 creating a Milk Control Board to fix minimum and maximum prices for milk sold at retail.— Editor

which is law. He was content to let history ascertain, if it would, what his share was. But only one who had the good fortune to work for years beside him, day by day, is enabled to say that no man ever served on the Supreme Court with more scrupulous regard for its moral demands than Mr. Justice Roberts.

EDITORIAL NOTE: The SUPREME COURT after the COURT-PACKING PLAN

During the course of the Congressional debates on the court-packing plan, Congress passed the McCarran-Summers Act of March 1, 1937.[1] Prior thereto, a Justice of the Supreme Court who reached the age of 70 and had served on the federal bench for at least 10 years, could resign his office and become entitled to receive for life the salary he was getting when he resigned.[2] Under the new law, the Justices were given a more attractive alternative, one previously available to all other federal judges. Upon reaching the age of 70 with 10 years of service on the federal bench, they were permitted to retain their offices but to retire from regular active service on the Court. They would then be entitled to continue to receive the salary of the office and benefit from any salary increases granted by Congress to the active Supreme Court Justices.[3] As retired Justices, they also remained eligible for assignment by the Chief Justice to temporary judicial duties in the lower federal courts.

On June 2, 1937, while the debates were going on, Mr. Justice Van Devanter, normally counted in the majority which invalidated New Deal laws, retired and was succeeded by the then Senator Hugo Black of Alabama.[4] But even before Justice Black was able to tip the scales, Chief Justice Hughes and Justice Roberts joined with Justices Brandeis, Cardozo, and Stone to uphold vital New Deal legislation and effect a revolution in the Court's constitutional doctrine. On April 12, 1937, the Court upheld the constitutionality of the National Labor Relations Act in an opinion which reflected a sharp break with prior decisions which had restricted Congress's power over "commerce among the several states." [5] The Court's decision on March 29, 1937, sustaining minimum wage legislation, has already been considered.

On May 24, 1937, the Court sustained the scheme of old age benefits created by Social Security Act of 1935[6] in an opinion which can hardly be reconciled with its opinion invalidating the Agricultural Adjustment Act. On the

---

[1] 50 Stat. 24

[2] Act of April 10, 1869, 16 Stat. 44.

[3] The Retirement Act of Feb. 10, 1954, 68 Stat. 12, authorizes a Justice to retire on the same terms upon reaching the age of 65 with 15 years of service on the federal bench.

[4] Justice Sutherland retired Jan. 18, 1938 and was succeeded by Stanley Reed; Cardozo died July 9, 1938 and was succeeded by Felix Frankfurter; Brandeis retired Feb.

13, 1939 and was succeeded by William Douglas; Butler died Nov. 16, 1939 and was succeeded by Frank Murphy; McReynolds retired Feb. 1, 1941 and was succeeded by James Byrnes. Thus in the space of 4 years, the Roosevelt appointees constituted a majority of the Court.

[5] National Labor Relations Board v. Jones & Laughlin Steel Corp., 301 U.S. 1.

[6] Helvering v. Davis, 301 U.S. 617.

same day, it also upheld the unemployment compensation provisions of the Social Security Act,[7] in an opinion giving broad scope to the Congressional power to tax and to spend for the general welfare.

Whether this constitutional revolution would have occurred without the pressure of President Roosevelt's court reorganization plan is a question that had best be left to historians. From 1937 through 1956, only five federal statutes have been declared unconstitutional by the Court; in each of these cases the Court sought to protect "interests of personality as contrasted to property interests."[8] The Court has similarly refused to strike down state laws regulating economic affairs on substantive due process grounds. The present attitude of the Court was well expressed by Justice Douglas in an opinion upholding an Oklahoma statute prohibiting, *inter alia,* the duplication of lenses by an optician without a prescription from an optometrist or an oculist.[9] "The day is gone," said the Justice, "when this Court uses the Due Process Clause of the Fourteenth Amendment to strike down state laws regulatory of business and industrial conditions, because they may be unwise, improvident, or out of harmony with a particular school of thought. . . . 'for protection against abuses by legislatures the people must resort to the polls, not to the courts.' " It is significant that the Justice's quotation is from Munn v. Illinois,[10] the landmark case upholding the constitutionality of rate regulation of industries "affected with a public interest" and rejecting the substantive due process doctrine.[11]

EDITORIAL NOTE: The CONTROVERSY over the PREFERRED PLACE of FIRST AMENDMENT FREEDOMS

But controversy about the proper role of the Supreme Court has not been stilled. It now centers on the question whether the Court should strike down legislative acts infringing upon civil rights and liberties because in the words of the case quoted above, "they may be unwise, improvident, or out of harmony with a particular school of thought." As we saw previously, Justice Cardozo suggested in Palko v. Connecticut that there was reason for a different judicial attitude in this area. He was willing to read the First Amendment freedoms into the due process clause of the Fourteenth Amend-

---

[7] Steward Machine Co. v. Davis, 301 U.S. 546.

[8] Sutherland, The Law and The One Man Among Many 64, n. 1 (1956). The cases listed by Professor Sutherland are: Tot v. United States, 319 U.S. 463 (1945); United States v. Lovett, 328 U.S. 303 (1946); United States v. Cardiff, 344 U.S. 174 (1952); Bolling v. Sharpe, 347 U.S. 497 (1954); and Toth v. Quarles, 350 U.S. 11 (1950).

[9] Williamson v. Lee Optical of Oklahoma, 348 U.S. 483 (1955).

[10] 94 U.S. 113, 134 (1876).

[11] It should be mentioned that many state courts, acting under state constitutions, have not gone as far as the United States Supreme Court in refusing to pass upon the reasonableness of state legislation regulating economic affairs. See Hetherington, State Economic Regulation and Substantive Due Process of Law, 53 Nw.U.L. Rev. 13, 226 (1958).

ment because he regarded freedom of thought and speech as "the matrix, the indispensable condition, of nearly every other form of freedom."

One year after Palko v. Connecticut was decided, Chief Justice Stone in upholding a federal statute aimed at the adulteration of milk, and placing heavy reliance on the presumption of constitutionality of such legislation, wrote in a footnote: "There may be narrower scope for operation of the presumption of constitutionality when legislation appears on its face to be within a specific prohibition of the Constitution, such as those of the first ten Amendments, which are deemed equally specific when held to be embraced within the Fourteenth. . . .

"It is unnecessary to consider now whether legislation which restricts those political processes which can ordinarily be expected to bring about repeal of undesirable legislation, is to be subjected to more exacting judicial scrutiny under the general prohibitions of the Fourteenth Amendment than are most other types of legislation. . . .

"Nor need we inquire whether similar considerations enter into the review of statutes directed at particular religious . . . or national . . . or racial minorities . . . , whether prejudice against discrete and insular minorities may be a special condition, which tends seriously to curtail the operation of those political processes ordinarily to be relied upon to protect minorities, and which may call for a correspondingly more searching judicial inquiry . . ." [12]

Following this, Justice Rutledge was one of the first to speak of the "preferred place given in our scheme to the great, the indispensable democratic freedoms secured by the First Amendment" which "balanced" the "usual presumption supporting legislation." [13]

On the other hand, Justice Frankfurter has called for "vigilant judicial restraint" even when the Court must accommodate "liberty and order." [14] He has criticized the doctrine that all legislation touching matters related to liberties protected by the Bill of Rights is presumptively unconstitutional— a doctrine which he maintains "never commended itself to a majority of this Court." However, there is a sense in which even Justice Frankfurter gives First Amendment freedoms a "preferred place." Thus, he wrote:

"The ideas now governing the constitutional protection of freedom of speech derive essentially from the opinions of Mr. Justice Holmes.

"The philosophy of his opinions on that subject arose from a deep awareness of the extent to which sociological conclusions are conditioned by time and circumstance. Because of this awareness Mr. Justice Holmes seldom felt justified in opposing his own opinion to economic views which the legislature embodied

[12] United States v. Carolene Products Co., 304 U.S. 144, 152, note 4 (1938).

[13] Thomas v. Collins, 323 U.S. 516, 529-530 (1945). See also the eloquent opinion of Justice Jackson in West Virginia State Board of Education v. Barnette, 319 U.S. 624 (1943).

[14] Kovacs v. Cooper, 336 U.S. 77 (1949) (concurring opinion). The Court here upheld a municipal ordinance prohibiting the operation upon the city streets of vehicles equipped with sound amplifiers or other instruments emitting loud and raucous noises.

in law. But since he also realized that the progress of civilization is to a considerable extent the displacement of error which once held sway as official truth by beliefs which in turn have yielded to other beliefs, for him the right to search for truth was of a different order than some transient economic dogma. And without freedom of expression, thought becomes checked and atrophied. Therefore, in considering what interests are so fundamental as to be enshrined in the Due Process Clause, those liberties of the individual which history has attested as the indispensable conditions of an open as against a closed society come to this Court with a momentum for respect lacking when appeal is made to liberties which derive merely from shifting economic arrangements. Accordingly, Mr. Justice Holmes was far more ready to find legislative invasion where free inquiry was involved than in the debatable area of economics." [15]

There is little question but that the Supreme Court has disregarded the judgment of state legislatures by invalidating state action discriminating against and segregating racial minorities. Neither the presumption of constitutionality nor of unconstitutionality seems to have played a significant role in the judicial opinions in these cases. Nevertheless, judging from what the Supreme Court has done, it seems that discriminatory state action carries virtually a conclusive presumption of unconstitutionality.

Nor has the presumption of constitutionality or unconstitutionality played a significant role in the Court's opinions upholding Congressional acts aimed at subversive movements and individuals in the country. Strong dissents, however, have challenged the propriety of the Court's action in the light of the guarantees of the First Amendment. It is in this area that there is the sharpest controversy about the "preferred position" of the First Amendment.

The remaining materials in this Chapter are devoted to further consideration of the questions raised by the "preferred position" doctrine—questions which go to the heart of an understanding of the role of the Supreme Court in our democracy.

B. V. COHEN,* FROM AN ADDRESS COMMEMORATING THE TWENTIETH ANNIVERSARY OF JUSTICE WILLIAM O. DOUGLAS'S APPOINTMENT TO THE UNITED STATES SUPREME COURT
April 17, 1959

. . . There are those with respectable intellectual credentials who have suggested that these great issues of civil rights and liberties are essentially political or legisla-

---

[15] Id., at 95. Justice Frankfurter, however, was not willing to give sound trucks the constitutional rights accorded to the unaided human voice. His opinion traces the history of the "preferred position" doctrine to the time of his writing.

Judge Hand is in general agreement with Justice Frankfurter. See Hand, The Bill of Rights 51, 69 (1958).

* Benjamin V. Cohen is a distinguished lawyer with a record of outstanding public service which began during World War I. As an adviser to President Franklin D. Roosevelt, he assisted in drafting the Securities Act of 1933, the Securities Exchange Act of 1934, the Public Utility Holding Co. Act of 1935, and the Fair Labor Standards Act of 1938. During World War II

tive issues and those on the Court should defer to the legislative judgment. It has been suggested that the so-called activitists on the present Court may be accused, as the old guard on the Court during Roosevelt's first term was accused, of acting as a third legislative chamber and as such of encroaching on the powers of Congress.

But with all due respect to the learned men writing and lecturing on this subject I would suggest that there is a difference between the Court encroaching on the legislative function and the Court abdicating its own judicial function to the Congress or allowing the Congress to encroach on the judicial function. Even those or most of those who urge the greatest judicial self-restraint would draw the line somewhere. As a matter of fact the old guard on the Court in the twenties and thirties did not claim the right to act as a third legislative chamber; they took the view that the Bill of Rights embraced economic liberty and that *laisser-faire* was the essence of economic liberty. Twentieth century economic developments simply made their conception of economic liberty anachronistic. The old judicial guard stood not against transient passion and prejudice, but against the sober and reflective second, third and fourth thoughts of a whole generation.

There may well be debate as to what is or is not included in the Bill of Rights, as to what are the minimum standards which are "of the very essence of a scheme of ordered liberty," but once it is conceded that there is a serious question which involves the Bill of Rights, it seems quite unwarranted for the Court to abdicate its own judgment in favor of that of the legislature. Of course the Court should have regard for the reasons which may have supported the actions of the Congress, but that does not mean the Court should yield its own judgment to the transient pressures, prejudices and fears which may have induced legislative action.

It is true that other branches of government as well as the Court have a responsibility to uphold the principles of the Bill of Rights. But in this field in which the Court has and should have especial competence, the Court should not surrender its convictions to other branches of government without protest, without a clear and cogent statement of its position that will enable the people to appreciate the issues in historic perspective so that the people will not abandon, without knowing what they do to, the historic guarantees and safeguards of their freedom. Certainly when the First Amendment expressly denies to Congress the right to pass any law abridging freedom of speech or of the press, it is scarcely reasonable to believe that the founding fathers intended the Court to abdicate its judgment to the Congress.

We may differ as to what matters do or do not come within the Bill of Rights. We may find it useful to call the matters included in the Bill of Rights, preferred rights, natural rights or fundamental rights. But whatever we call them, I think we have a right to expect the Court to exercise and not abdicate its judgment concerning them. That duty the Court owes to the Congress as well as to the

he was assistant to the director of the Office of Economic Stabilization and general counsel of the Office of War Mobilization. After the war, he served as counselor of the Department of State, representative of the United States at various international conferences and delegate to the United Nations.

The address was printed privately.— Editor

people. Upon the maintenance of these rights the future of constitutional democracy depends.

It is no accident that the great judges before World War II—Holmes, Brandeis, Stone, Cardozo and Hughes—while allowing the greatest latitude to the legislature in the determination of legislative policy, did not abdicate their judicial judgment in favor of the legislative judgment in matters which they deemed within the Bill of Rights.

E. V. Rostow,* *THE SUPREME COURT*
AND THE PEOPLE'S WILL
33 Notre Dame Lawyer 573, 575, 576-580, 592-593 (1958)

. . . How can a society of majority rule condone the exercise of such far-reaching power by judges who are appointed for life? Is it true, as many have said, that the role of the Supreme Court in construing the Constitution makes it an oligarchic or aristocratic excrescence on our Constitution, to be abolished if possible, or at the least restricted to the narrowest possible jurisdiction?

This issue has been a matter of debate throughout our national history, and it is being vehemently debated today. Anxiety on this score has colored the temper in which some of our best judges have approached their work. Many have found in this issue a paradox impossible to reconcile with their faith as democrats. . . .

There is no substance in the supposed paradox of having appointed judges interpret the written constitution of a democratic society.

Popular sovereignty is a more subtle idea than the phrase "majority rule" sometimes implies.

The Constitution of the United States is the juridical act of the American people, not that of their Congress. It was, and is, a commitment to what the Founders called the republican form of government. Manhood suffrage was not universal in 1789 and equal manhood suffrage is not universal today. Equal manhood suffrage is, however, the ideal of the present stage of our constitutional theory as the ultimate source of sovereign authority in the American political system: the true base of what we should now identify as the republican form of government.

But universal manhood suffrage does not imply, in theory or in fact, that policy can properly be determined in a democracy only through universal popular elections, or that universal popular elections have or should have the capacity to make any and all decisions of democratic government without limits or delays of any kind. Representative government is, after all, a legitimate form of democracy, through which the people delegate to their elected representatives in legislatures, or in executive offices, some but not necessarily all of their powers, for a period of years. Neither the town meeting nor the Swiss referendum is an indispensable feature of democratic decision making.

The object of the men who established the American Constitution, like the

* Eugene V. Rostow, Professor of Law and Dean of the Law School, Yale University, is the author of Planning for Freedom　(1959) and A National Policy for the Oil Industry (1948).—Editor

object of democratic theorists in all countries, and at all times, was not omnicompetent popular government, but the freedom of man as an individual being within a free society whose policies are based ultimately upon his consenting will. The Constitution did not give Congress the full powers of the British Parliament. If that had been the Founders' idea, no written constitution would have been necessary. On the contrary, the Constitution provided for a federal system of divided and delegated powers. Not only the courts, but the desirable friction of contending authority—the President versus the Congress, the states versus the nation—were relied upon to help preserve an equilibrium and thus to enforce the grand design of the Constitution.

For the highest aim of our Constitution is that it seeks to protect the freedom and dignity of man by imposing severe and enforceable limitations upon the freedom of the State. Americans thought then, and their wisdom is confirmed by all our subsequent experience, that man can be free, that political processes can in truth be democratic only when, and only because, the state is not free.

Every plan for democratic government, and every democratic constitution, contains vital elements beyond its ultimate derivation from the will of a majority. The Constitution provides a significant self-limitation upon the amendatory powers of the people—that no constitutional amendment can deny a state its equal suffrage in the Senate without its consent.[5] Every democracy divides issues of policy into several categories, to be settled by different means. Some decisions are made, without violating the principle of ultimate popular sovereignty, by appointed officials to whom important powers are delegated; e.g., to the boards which license doctors and lawyers, innkeepers and chiropodists; to the Federal Reserve Board or the Tariff Commission, the armed forces and the Department of Agriculture. The President has wide authority in the conduct of foreign relations. Other classes of decisions in all systems of democracy are remitted to legislative or judicial bodies, or are reserved for decision to regular or special elections, or to constituent assemblies. Still others, in most democratic societies, are set apart and protected against the risk of hasty decision—issues of policy which are regarded as essential in assuring the division of functions among the branches of government, and the democratic character, over the long-run, of the decision-making process itself. Even a classic Vermont town meeting knows limits on its jurisdiction. The town meeting can fix the tax rate, embark on a school lunch program, or decide to buy a fire engine or a snow plow. But it cannot abolish the town meeting, nor delegate its powers to the selectmen. It cannot deny a resident citizen his right to vote, nor confiscate the land of a Democrat, nor impose a sentence of exile, nor try a law suit over boundaries or the habits of cattle. Any change in the basic procedures through which policy is made requires a longer and more carefully considered series of votes.

This pattern for decision-making is characteristic of all democratic communities, whatever devices they may use for accomplishing the goal. And it is a pattern entirely consistent with their democratic character. Laws fixing different procedures for different kinds of elections do not deny the people their ultimate power. The

[5] U.S. Const. art. V.

reason for practices of this kind is a fundamental one. For democracy is more, much more, than a commitment to popular sovereignty. It is also, and equally, a commitment to popular sovereignty under law. Sometimes the precautionary devices to assure the legality of particular classes of decisions by particular elections are declared in a written constitution. Sometimes they are enforced only by the pattern of custom, the weight of tradition, or the influence and the residual powers of institutions of special prestige, like the Crown in Great Britain and Sweden, or the Presidency in France, Germany and other countries.

Under our practice, limitations of this character determine the contours of the Constitution.

We often fall back, as Mr. Justice Frankfurter has recently and eloquently done, upon Chief Justice Marshall's pregnant dictum: "it is a constitution we are expounding." [6] Marshall's comment is usually read, and properly read, to stress the need for flexibility in constitutional interpretation. In this perspective, emphasis is put on the fact that the Constitution provides a plan for government designed to last for centuries. Such an arrangement must bend, we are reminded, if it is not to break. It must give all the elected branches of government wide ranging areas of discretion so that society may, by its own democratic decisions, adapt itself to circumstances and stresses vastly different from those of the isolated agricultural communities which put down their roots along the Atlantic coast during the seventeenth and eighteenth centuries.

All this is true enough. But Chief Justice Marshall's dictum cuts the other way with equal force. It is indeed a constitution we are expounding, a document to assure continuity as well as flexibility, boundaries of power as well as freedom of choice. Congress and the President must have enough authority under the Constitution to govern effectively, and they must be able to exercise their own political judgment in selecting among the alternative means available for dealing with the emergent problems of each new age. But it has never been supposed that elected officials had untrammeled discretion. The Constitution sets limits on their ambit of choice, and some of its limits can be enforced by the Courts. For until the people change it, the Constitution is a document intended to assure them that their representatives function within the borders of their offices, and do not roam at will among the pastures of power; that certain essential values in our public life be preserved, not ignored; and, in government's choice among the instruments of action, that those be selected which advance the cause of human freedom and those eschewed which threaten it. The idea was expressed by Bryce in these terms:

> The Supreme Court is the living voice of the Constitution—that is, of the will of the people expressed in the fundamental law they have enacted. It is, therefore, as some one has said, the conscience of the people, who have resolved to restrain themselves from hasty or unjust action by placing their representatives under the restriction of a permanent law. It is the guarantee of the minority, who, when threatened by the impatient vehemence of a majority, can appeal to this

[6] John Marshall and the Judicial Function, in Government Under Law 6, 8 (A. E. Sutherland ed. 1956).

permanent law, finding the interpreter and enforcer thereof in a Court set high above the assaults of faction.[7]

* * *

As the men of the eighteenth century knew well, following Locke and Montesquieu, the law is a continuing force in the process of public life. It has consequences, as well as causes. The changing dispositions of law respond to changing conditions in society itself. But in turn they profoundly influence the character of men, and of their society. The law is not a mere artifact, reflecting the pressure of events. It is and should be a vital element in the movement of society towards its ultimate goals. In this perspective, the constitutional decisions of the Court are more than a factor of continuity in protecting the democratic character of our political arrangements, and in protecting the individual against arbitrary action by the state. They are also among the significant forces influencing the evolution of our constitutional ideal itself. Montesquieu defined the ideal of law for each culture as the spirit of its laws—the cultural norm towards which each society aspires in the day-to-day processes of its law making. But, he pointed out, that spirit was not fixed and immutable, even for a given culture. It could and did evolve through time, for better or for worse, towards tyranny or towards the ideal of responsible freedom. And the principal function of law, in his view, is to serve as one of the educational and formative influences of the culture, not merely in bringing the law in action up to the standard of the existing ideal of law, but in perfecting the ideal of law itself. Thus, in construing and enforcing the basic purposes of the Bill of Rights, the Court is a leading participant in the endless striving of our culture to approach the goals of dignity and freedom for the individual whose grandeur dominates our Constitution. To preserve, to enrich, to further these values in the experience of our people is one of the first aims of the Constitution. . . .

HOOK,[*] *POLITICAL POWER AND PERSONAL FREEDOM*
252-257 (1959)

There is a root ambiguity in the word "liberal." It is reflected in the fact that its opposite is in some contexts "illiberal," which no one will own up to being, and in other contexts "conservative," to which, if it is kept in lower case, everyone in some respect can make a claim. A resort to history is not likely to be decisive in establishing the proper usage of "liberal," primarily because in the past the term was preempted by particular social and political programs. To this day in Europe

---

[7] The American Commonwealth 273 (1913) . . .

[*] Sidney Hook, Professor of Philosophy and Chairman of the Division of Philosophy and Psychology, Graduate School, New York University, is the author of Reason, Social Myths and Democracy (1940); The Hero in History (1943); Education for Modern Man (1946); Heresy, Yes, Conspiracy, No (1953); The Ambiguous Legacy: Marx and the Marxists (1955); Common Sense and the Fifth Amendment (1957); and has edited a number of other volumes.

The excerpts reprinted are taken from chapter 19, entitled Liberalism and the Law.—Editor

the predominant connotation of "liberal" is of laissez-faire economy, free trade, and opposition to government measures of welfare. And in the United States there are those who, like the adherents of the Liberty League in the 30's and the followers of Von Mises and Hayek today, regard freedom from government intervention as the key to all freedom.

Nonetheless there are two historical figures of the American past who in doctrine and temperament stand for what is commonly meant by liberalism: Jefferson and Lincoln. Jefferson is forever associated with the Declaration of Independence; Lincoln asserted that he had never had "a feeling, politically, that did not spring from the sentiments embodied in the Declaration of Independence." The Declaration was not only a pronouncement in favor of freedom but of equality. The notion that there is a necessary conflict between freedom and equality, current in their day as in ours, was dismissed by both Jefferson and Lincoln, perhaps too simply, as a prejudice of those who believed that nature itself was organized along aristocratic lines. There were certain *historical* reasons, however, that led many to fear that political equality could be achieved only at the cost of individual freedom. At any rate, no scheme of political equality is conceivable or practicable without some form of majority rule. That is why, among other reasons, both Jefferson and Lincoln were passionately devoted to the principle of majority rule. Lincoln, especially, recognized what some of the sophisticated critics of the principle, who feared the tyranny of the majority, have failed to see: that the only alternative to majority rule is either despotism or anarchy, the tyranny of the individual (or cabinet, mistress, junta, council, or court) or the tyranny of the mob.

At the same time neither Jefferson nor Lincoln believed that the majority was necessarily right or wise. Nor did they embrace Rousseauistic nonsense about the general will. For both of them a democracy which was not enlightened could not long remain free. It is this recognition of the importance of creative intelligence in the functioning and defense of a free society, and in the liberation of human personality, which constitutes the link between John Dewey and Thomas Jefferson.

American liberalism owes to Jefferson its acceptance of the principle of majority rule, its trust and faith in the free play of intelligence as the means by which not merely programs of political action emerge, but, beyond that, institutions fostering enduring sentiments of freedom. As Justice Frankfurter puts it: "This was the essence of Jefferson's social philosophy and the devotion of his life. It is the permanence of his meaning—to establish sentiments of freedom as the enduring habits of a people." These sentiments were not to be exercised vicariously or held in trust for the people by their betters.

From this principle Jefferson derived his well-known opposition to the doctrine of judicial supremacy. This opposition he bequeathed to contemporary liberalism; its most distinguished legal representative in our time, and possibly all time, was Justice Holmes. Although differing in their economic views, Holmes, Brandeis, Cardozo, and Frankfurter have been the great Jeffersonians on our bench. All of them recognize the necessity of a supreme *court* as well as a supreme *law*—else forty-nine different state legislatures and court systems would generate conflict and chaos. But at the same time they recognize that the supreme *law* in a democracy must express the legislative will of the nation as a whole and not merely the judicial will. The Constitution provides the guide lines to Congress, but cannot be made a fetish without violating the American spirit of government. . . .

What embarrasses the Jeffersonians on the bench, however, is that the Supreme Court, which is not responsible to the electorate, has the power, won for it by John Marshall, to nullify the acts of a Congress which is responsible to the electorate. No honest mind can contest Justice Frankfurter's reminder that "judicial review is a deliberate check upon democracy through an organ of government not subject to popular control." But the contention that such a check is necessary to prevent the tyranny of the majority, and that without such a check the civil liberties of minorities would necessarily be destroyed, is sheer rationalization: it was property, not freedom, that the Supreme Court safeguarded throughout most of its history. Nor has that history been distinguished by the valiant defense of civil rights.

In England, where a proposal to give the courts the power to pass on the constitutionality of an Act of Parliament would be regarded as comparable to restoring the doctrine of the divine rights of kings, civil liberties and minority rights flourish more luxuriantly than elsewhere. To be sure, majorities in a democracy may be foolish and tyrannical. But so may minorities if they have power. And the Supreme Court is the smallest of all minorities. If judges are to be our rulers, Morris R. Cohen used to say, they should be elected.

The Supreme Court has, of course, sometimes spoken out very effectively in behalf of civil rights, most notably in *Brown v. Board of Education,* which outlawed segregation in the nation's public schools. But let us not forget that in doing so it reversed the deplorable decision of *Plessy v. Ferguson* upholding "equal" and "separate" facilities, a decision that for fifty-eight years gave legal sanctification to a pattern which the more recent decision cannot easily modify. If the reasoning of the Court in 1954 had been followed in 1896, by this time we would be much closer to rectifying the social and civil injustices from which our Negro fellow citizens suffer—and not only in the South. And if history is relevant, there are few if any Supreme Court decisions on civil rights whose beneficial effects begin to compare in importance with the grievous consequences of the Supreme Court's decision in the Dred Scott case, which some historians regard as one of the causes of the Civil War. Only historical myopia can see in the Supreme Court a consistent defender of civil liberties.

Justice Holmes and his Jeffersonian colleagues have met the embarrassment in which their power to nullify acts of Congress has placed them by a severe self-restraint. They have resolutely refused to impose their own conception of social and economic policy on the country in the guise of interpreting the wisdom of Constitutional fathers who never even conceived of the character of contemporary problems and issues. What Justice Frankfurter says of Holmes is only in slightly lesser measure true of himself. "Probably no man who ever sat on the court was by temperament and discipline freer from emotional commitments compelling him to translate his own economic or social views into Constitutional commands." That is why he frequently speaks of the need for humility and detachment lest "limitations in personal experience are transmuted into limitations of the Constitution."

This has led to considerable criticism of Justice Frankfurter by a highly articulate group of liberals whose attitude toward the Supreme Court is frankly opportunistic —critical when they disagree with the Justices, as in the 30's, and approving when they agree, as in the present. Some of the unjust aspersions upon Justice Frankfurter's liberalism reflect the extent to which principles that should guide democratic *process* are conceived of merely as useful instruments toward specific *programs*. One reviewer, not the worst, of Justice Frankfurter's recent collection of miscellaneous papers and addresses[1] (from which I have already quoted) interprets his emphasis upon the need for "dominating humility" in judges as signifying that the judge "must not follow his own conviction but must derive his judgment as a spokesman, vicar, or proxy of some authoritative outside voice" (*New York Times Book Review*).

Nothing could be further removed from Justice Frankfurter's meaning. A judge who does not follow his own conviction is unworthy of his post, but his conviction must not be arbitrary or molded only by what he is familiar with in his personal experience. He must have a sense of the limits of his knowledge and of his power. He may, for example, be convinced that the free enterprise system is more efficient than any form of planned economy, and that all the freedoms of the Bill of Rights ultimately rest upon it, but he has no business reading that conviction into the Constitution by exegetical exercises on systematically ambiguous expressions like "due process." A judge without convictions should step down from the bench. But the conviction that he is not there to legislate; that the spirit of the democratic process gives this power to Congress; that on specific matters of policy he is not likely to be less foolish or more informed than most legislators; that although interpreting law is to some extent inescapably making law, there is a difference between adjudication and outright legislation—this according to Justice Frankfurter should be a judge's overriding conviction, and the source of his humility.

Justice Frankfurter pleads guilty to the charge of entertaining an "old-fashioned liberal's view of government and law." It is the liberalism with which we all grew up—even those who opposed it. If there has been any change, it has not been in Justice Frankfurter but in those sophisticated neo-Machiavellians who believe, despite the historical evidence, that in the long run courts are better guardians of the liberties and welfare of the people than a democratic legislature. They could well chew on his words: "If judges want to be preachers, they should dedicate themselves to the pulpit; if judges want to be primary shapers of policy, the legislature is their place." To make one's philosophy of judicial review dependent upon the composition of the Court at any definite time is cynical. Worse than cynical, it is foolish, for death and the pendulum of history are sure to place on the bench not merely conservatives but illiberals.

[1] Felix Frankfurter, Of Law and Men (New York, 1957).

Justice Frankfurter, like Holmes, recognizes the difference between what I have elsewhere called "the strategic freedoms," those upon which the functioning of the free market in ideas depends, like freedom of speech, press, and assembly, and those freedoms which are required, say, for the functioning of the free market in commodities. But since the strategic freedoms are themselves not absolute and on occasion conflict, it is sometimes necessary to abridge a particular freedom in order to safeguard the entire complex of freedoms on which the democratic way of life rests. Here is the really troublesome area in which the justification for judicial review of Congressional legislation seems most plausible. Where Congress clearly acts in haste or panic, or in anticipation of having the Supreme Court save it from its own folly while it reaps electoral dividends, the Justices of the Court can exercise with an easy conscience the power John Marshall won for them. Justice Frankfurter, as I read him, would no more hesitate than Justice Holmes, under the *existing powers* of the Court, to put a brake upon Congressional action, to nullify legislation that clearly violated the strategic freedoms, even though he believes that the best appeal from majority rule, drunk and unenlightened, is to majority rule, sober and enlightened.

Such cases, however, are extremely rare. The more usual cases are those involving, as does the Smith Act, conflict between legitimate concern for the security of our system of freedom and legitimate fear that one or another strategic freedom has been too tightly circumscribed. Here, according to Justice Frankfurter, the issue is not whether the legislation is wise or justified, or whether the individual Justice agrees or disagrees with the way Congress has resolved the conflict of rights and interests, but whether the legislation was sufficiently reasonable in the light of the evidence and the spirit of deliberation. If the Smith Act is unwise, amend or repeal it, but do not invalidate it on the ground that you as an individual Justice personally do not appraise the Kremlin and its fifth column as a serious threat, or that if you had been a Congressman you would have voted against it. It is even conceivable that a Senator Douglas may understand the nature of the Communist threat better than a Justice Douglas. There are obvious difficulties in interpreting the rule of "reasonableness," but they are less formidable than those involved in any alternative rule.

It betokens no lack of deference for the Supreme Court to recognize that Justices are capable of talking and writing nonsense like lesser mortals, including Congressmen; that the appearance of a Justice Holmes is the result of a mutation, not the operation of a rule; that many judges in the lower courts, such as Justice Learned Hand (whose opinion upholding the constitutionality of the Smith Act was much more profound than Justice Vinson's), know more law than do most Supreme Court Justices; and that the opinions of the Supreme Court are not unaffected by the winds of doctrine that blow in the market place. Every system of law needs a Supreme Court: but a truly democratic community does not need a Supreme Court as an arbiter of its destinies. . . .

AUERBACH, *THE COMMUNIST CONTROL ACT OF 1954:*
A PROPOSED LEGAL-POLITICAL THEORY
OF FREE SPEECH
23 The University of Chicago Law Review 173, 186-202 (1956)

[The current debate about the role of the Supreme Court has been provoked in large measure by its review of Congressional acts aimed at the Communist Party of the United States and its members. We have had occasion to consider the Court's attitude toward Congressional investigations of alleged Communist infiltration into various sectors of American life. In Dennis v. United States, 341 U.S. 494 (1951), the Court, by a 6 to 2 vote, upheld the conviction, under the Smith Act, of 11 top Communist leaders. These leaders were found guilty of conspiring to organize the Communist Party as a society, group, and assembly of persons who teach and advocate the duty and necessity of action to overthrow the United States government by force and violence, employing language reasonably and ordinarily calculated to incite persons to such action and with the specific intent of accomplishing their purpose at the earliest time that circumstances would permit.

[Chief Justice Vinson wrote the majority opinion in which Justices Reed, Frankfurter, Jackson, Burton, and Minton joined. Justice Clark did not participate in the decision. Justices Black and Douglas wrote dissenting opinions in which they argued that the conviction violated the First Amendment because it represented a "virulent form of prior censorship of speech and press" when there was no "clear and present danger" that Communist advocacy could succeed.

[The majority and dissenting opinions, discussed in the following excerpts, reflect opposing conceptions about the proper role of the Court in reviewing anti-Communist legislation. The article is particularly concerned with the proper role of the Court in relation to a later statute, outlawing the Communist Party.— Editor]

Assumptions Underlying the First Amendment—Movements Seeking To Crush Freedom Need Not Be Tolerated. Clear thinking about the First Amendment will heed Mr. Chief Justice Hughes' admonition that behind "the words of the constitutional provisions are postulates which limit and control." [42] In the opinion of Judge Learned Hand, the First Amendment "rests upon a skepticism as to all political orthodoxy, upon a belief that there are no impregnable political absolutes, and that a flux of tentative doctrines is preferable to any authoritative creed." [43] This skepticism and belief are also reflected in John Stuart Mill's defense of freedom of thought and expression in *On Liberty.* "We can never be sure," says Mill, "that

---

[42] Principality of Monaco v. Mississippi, 292 U.S. 313, 322 (1934). The historic antecedents of the First Amendment, as Mr. Justice Frankfurter has shown, also "preclude the notion that its purpose was to give unqualified immunity to every expression that touched on matters within the range of political interest." Dennis v. United States, 341 U.S. 494, 521 (1951). Mr. Jus-

tice Frankfurter points out, for example, that Jefferson, in opposing the Sedition Act, argued that the First Amendment reflected a limitation upon federal power, leaving the right to enforce restrictions on speech to the states.

[43] United States v. Dennis, 183 F. 2d 201, 207 (C.A. 2d, 1950).

the opinion we are endeavoring to stifle is a false opinion. . . . Complete liberty of contradicting and disproving our opinion, is the very condition which justifies us in assuming its truth for purposes of action;" however true a particular opinion may be, "if it is not fully, frequently, and fearlessly discussed, it will be held as a dead dogma, not a living truth," because "conflict with the opposite error is essential to a clear apprehension and deep feeling of its truth." "[T]hough the silenced opinion be an error," Mill adds, "it may, and very commonly does, contain a portion of truth; and since the general or prevailing opinion on any object is rarely or never the whole truth, it is only by collision of adverse opinions that the remainder of the truth has any chance of being supplied." [44]

To justify freedom of speech, however, it is not necessary to agree with Mr. Justice Holmes that "the theory of our Constitution" is that "the best test of truth is the power of the thought to get itself accepted in the competition of the market." [45] This view, which may at times also have been voiced by Mill, has the dangerous tendency to define truth in terms of what the market-place comes to accept.[46] Nor is it necessary to accept "the idealist view that what is true will survive," [47] because experience may refute this assumption. Yet the argument for the "clear and present danger" rule as elaborated by Holmes and Brandeis is based essentially on this pragmatist or idealist conception of truth and often the two merge since the idealist view will always be confirmed if the pragmatist definition of truth is accepted. While freedom to criticize may not guarantee the survival or victory of truth, it is sufficient to justify the First Amendment that it offers the only possibility of correcting error by the peaceful means of appeal to the reason of man. We may agree also with Professor Stone that in democratic countries the claims to free opinion and expression should "approach nearer absoluteness

[44] Mill, On Liberty, in 25 Harvard Classics 219, 222, 238, 249, 256.

[45] Dissenting opinion in Abrams v. United States, 250 U.S. 616, 630-631 (1919).

[46] Mr. Max Lerner has pointed out this weakness in Holmes' pragmatic view which has been termed the "survival" theory of truth—"the position that the idea which survives in the struggle of ideas is therefore the true one." Lerner, The Mind and Faith of Justice Holmes 290 (Modern Library ed., 1954). Lerner comments: "This is a dangerous position in a time when the manipulation of symbols has become as highly organized as under the Nazi regime, and in the working of Nazi propaganda outside of Germany." Ibid. For present purposes, I would substitute "Communist" for "Nazi" and "Soviet Union" for "Germany."

[47] Lerner thinks that this view, too, is implicit in some of Holmes' writings. Ibid. It is explicit, as he points out, in Milton: "And though all the winds of doctrine were let loose to play upon the earth, so truth be in the field, we do injuriously by licensing and prohibiting to misdoubt her strength. Let her and falsehood grapple; who ever knew truth put to the worse, in a free and open encounter?" Areopagitica, in The Portable Milton 199 (1949). It is the basis also of the famous quotation from Jefferson's First Inaugural in 1801: "If there be any among us who wish to dissolve this Union, or to change its republican form, let them stand undisturbed, as monuments of the safety with which error of opinion may be tolerated where reason is left free to combat it." Inaugural Addresses of the Presidents of the United States, H.R. Doc. No. 540, 82d Cong. 2d Sess. 12 (1952). See, too, the dissenting opinion of Mr. Justice Douglas in the Dennis case, 341 U.S. 494, 584 (1951). ("When ideas compete in the market for acceptance, full and free discussion exposes the false and they gain few adherents.")

than perhaps any other single claim" because "they are a vital prerequisite to the formulation and expression of human demands concerning the exercise of political authority. Indeed, insofar as we recognize that the function of law in a free community is the satisfaction of human demands for the time being, it is proper to point out that this function must be frustrated insofar as freedom of speech is not permitted to articulate these demands." [48]

Mill's classic argument, the eloquent statement of Judge Learned Hand and Professor Stone's formulation must all assume, it seems to me, one "impregnable" absolute—freedom itself. For if the theory that there are no political orthodoxies is taken to mean that we must also be skeptical about the value of freedom and therefore tolerate freedom's enemies, it will tend to produce, in practice, the very absolutism it was designed to avoid—as experience with modern totalitarianism demonstrates. When, therefore, Mill says that "we can never be sure that the opinion we are endeavoring to stifle is a false opinion," he could not consistently have been referring to the opinion that freedom of opinion itself should be suppressed.[49] There is a passage in *On Liberty* which, I think, supports this inference and has significance for our contemporary problem. Asking whether the law should enforce an agreement under which an individual sells himself, voluntarily, as a slave, Mill says no and argues: "The reason for not interfering, unless for the sake of others, with a person's voluntary acts, is consideration for his liberty. . . . But by selling himself for a slave, he abdicates his liberty; he foregoes any future use of it, beyond that single act. He therefore defeats, in his own case, the very purpose which is the justification of allowing him to dispose of himself. . . . The principle of freedom cannot require that he should be free not to be free. It is not freedom, to be allowed to alienate his freedom." [50]

So, in suppressing totalitarian movements a democratic society is not acting to protect the status quo, but the very same interests which freedom of speech itself seeks to secure—the possibility of peaceful progress under freedom. That suppression may sometimes have to be the means of securing and enlarging freedom is a paradox which is not unknown in other areas of the law of modern democratic states. The basic "postulate," therefore, which should "limit and control" the First Amendment is that it is part of the framework for a constitutional democracy and should, therefore, not be used to curb the power of Congress to exclude from the political struggle those groups which, if victorious, would crush democracy and impose totalitarianism. Whether in any particular case and at any particular time, Congress should suppress a totalitarian movement should be regarded as a matter of wisdom for its sole determination. But a democracy should claim the moral

---

[48] Stone, The Province and Function of Law 520-521 (1950).

[49] Nor does Mill's admonition that however true a particular opinion may be, "if it is not fully, frequently and fearlessly discussed, it will be held as a dead dogma, not a living truth," require toleration for the view that freedom of opinion should be suppressed. The value of freedom of speech and opinion will constantly prove itself as it is practiced to criticize the status quo in all fields of human thought and endeavor.

[50] Mill, *op. cit. supra* note 44, at 311-312.

and constitutional right to suppress these movements whenever it deems it advisable to do so.[51]

Objections to Position Taken. Does It Propose a Workable Criterion? Though Professor Riesman sees merit in the view that we should not tolerate the intolerant, because he thinks it implies that "its expounders have abandoned the unproven hope that their example of noninterference will convert the foes of civil liberties" in favor of the determination that "civil liberties constitute an active cause, deserving of protection against its enemies like any other and not above the battle," he rejects it because of "several ethical objections and insurmountable administrative difficulties." [52] Riesman objects that the suggested limit of tolerance is unworkable because of the difficulties of proving the true intentions and principles of totalitarian groups, like the Communists, who profess their affection for civil liberties and other democratic procedures.[53] But surely the difficulties of evaluating the historical forms of Fascist and Communist totalitarianism with which modern democracies have to cope are not insurmountable. Successive waves of events since the Bolshevik revolution should have removed all reasonable doubts about the true significance and intentions of the world Communist movement. Furthermore, as will be suggested, the determination of fact underlying the decision to proscribe a particular group, namely, that its objectives are totalitarian, should be reviewed by the Supreme Court in passing upon the constitutionality of the attempted proscription. This will not make the problem of proof less difficult, but will provide additional assurance that action will not be taken without proof.

In fact, Riesman concedes that if the totalitarians presented the only problem in the application of the suggested test, it "might somehow be manageable." [54] But, he argues, "many, if not most, American groups, as they admit or as can be inferred from their behavior or ultimate beliefs, would if they could deny certain civil liberties to some of their political opponents. . . . [Where] reactionary Catholics are in control, they seek to deny freedom of expression to 'Reds' (as defined by them), to atheists, to advocates of non-rhythmic birth control. Protestant fundamentalists have sought to silence evolutionists, and some from the same background would silence Catholics or Jews, and of course Negroes. Business groups, such as the National Association of Manufacturers, veterans' organizations, the Hearst opinion empire, have sought to curb civil liberties for critics of capitalism, as well as for critics of 'democracy' (as defined by them). The list is as endless as it is familiar." [55] But the position which Riesman here rejects is not that taken in this paper. It is not proposed that as a matter of public policy the government undertake to ferret out and suppress every intolerant group in the United States

[51] See I Popper, The Open Society and Its Enemies 265 n. 4 (2d ed., 1952) on the so-called "paradox of tolerance." As will become apparent, I am greatly indebted to Professor Popper's work and share his views about the implications of democracy.

[52] Riesman, Civil Liberties in a Period of Transition, in Public Policy 33, 52 (1942).

Though the parts of this article which I shall consider are those with which I do not in the main agree, my indebtedness to Riesman is great and I agree with his principal thesis.

[53] *Ibid.*, at 55.

[54] *Ibid.*, at 56.

[55] *Ibid.*, at 56-57.

which would, if it could, deny civil liberties to some other group. This policy may be unwise and unworkable. But the "reactionary Catholics," "Protestant fundamentalists," "Business groups," and "Veterans' organizations" of which Riesman speaks are not engaged in the struggle for political power as such. To the extent that they may exert pressure for the use of political power to enforce their intolerant private views, they can and should be resisted. But it is the "universality, or generality of the design" [56] of totalitarian movements seeking political power which makes them dangerous enough to warrant suppression.

Is It Consistent with Democratic Principles? The Paradox of Freedom. Riesman's "ethical objections" remain. He argues, first, that "any judgment that these radical groups [Fascist, Nazi and Communist] should be denied the right to urge their case—a case which includes as one of its features the denial of certain civil liberties to certain opponents—is in fact a concealed judgment concerning the worth of the total aims of these groups." [57] I do not agree, though I confess to regarding modern totalitarianism as an "absolute evil." [58] Even if the professed social aims of the totalitarians are regarded as desirable and it is thought possible to achieve them in a totalitarian state, there is implicit in the democratic creed "the conviction that the acceptance of even a bad policy in a democracy (as long as we can work for a peaceful change) is preferable to the submission to a tyranny, however wise or benevolent." [59] And this conviction may be the basis of the judgment to suppress totalitarian movements. In other words, because the democratic method of settling conflict keeps open the avenue of change so that wrongs may be righted peacefully, the citizens of a democracy have a greater stake in this method of settlement than in any particular outcome of any particular conflict. No group in our society, therefore, is justified in working for the destruction of democracy in order to achieve any particular ends, however meritorious they may, at the moment, seem to be.

Secondly, Riesman argues that "the denial of freedom of expression to those who disbelieve in it is inconsistent with orthodox, although perhaps erroneous, conceptions of the democratic theory. Under that theory, a majority is entitled to abandon traditional civil liberties if it follows the constitutional forms. Democrats for whom democracy means majority rule must therefore logically insist that this putative anti-civil-liberty majority should have the opportunity of hearing evidence that it would be better off in the absence of, say, freedom of speech and press." [60] It must be admitted that his "orthodox" conception of democratic theory underlies existing legislation against the totalitarian threat, as well as the judicial approach

---

[56] Livingston, Circuit Justice, in United States v. Hoxie, 26 Fed. Cas. 397, 401, No. 15, 407 (C.C.D. Vt., 1808). [For an analogy, see] Hurst, Treason in the United States, 58 Harv. L. Rev. 226, 395, 806 (1944-45), particularly at 411, 418, 428, 442, 808, 814, 818-825.

[57] Riesman, *op. cit. supra* note 52, at 54.

[58] See Arendt, [The Origins of Totalitarianism] 429-439, particularly at 433.

[1951].

[59] Popper, *op. cit. supra* note 51, at 125. Bertrand Russell quotes Democritus as having said: "Poverty in a democracy is as much to be preferred to what is called prosperity under despots as freedom is to slavery." The History of Western Philosophy 92, n. (1946).

[60] Riesman, *op. cit. supra* note 52, at 54.

to questions of the constitutionality of this legislation. Without exception, the courts seem to have assumed that the Communists have a "right," which the courts will protect, to pursue their aims by peaceful, "constitutional" means. For example, in his dissenting opinion in *Gitlow v. New York*,[62] Mr. Justice Holmes said: "If in the long run the beliefs expressed in proletarian dictatorship are destined to be accepted by the dominant forces of the community, the only meaning of free speech is that they should be given their chance and have their way." [63] Even Mr. Justice Jackson, in an opinion which showed an acute awareness of the aims of the Communist movement, thought it important to point out that "if they [the American Communists] can persuade enough citizens, they may not only name new officials and inaugurate new policies, but, by amendment of the Constitution, they can abolish the Bill of Rights and set up an absolute government by legal methods." [64] Judge Learned Hand was equally explicit in the *Dennis* case. In his opinion, the First Amendment "protects all utterances, individual or concerted, seeking constitutional changes, however revolutionary, by the processes which the Constitution provides. Any amendment to the Constitution passed in conformity with Article V is as valid as though it had been originally incorporated in it; the only exception being that no state, [without its consent] shall be denied 'its equal suffrage in the Senate.'" [65]

But any theory which equates democracy with majority rule is self-contradictory, as Professor Popper has conclusively shown. He tells us that Plato, by asking "What if it is the will of the people that they should not rule, but a tyrant instead?," was the first to pose this paradox of freedom.[66] The "orthodox" answer to this question, as we have seen, is that the people, that is, the majority of them, shall have their way. But then, Professor Popper replies, the principle of majority rule requires its adherents to oppose the new tyranny willed by the majority.[67] If any totalitarian party, using legal means, came to power in the manner prescribed by the Constitution and succeeded by constitutional amendment to inaugurate a totalitarian state, all partisans of democracy would have the moral right, recognized by the Declaration of Independence,[68] to use force and violence, if necessary,

---

[62] 268 U.S. 652 (1925).

[63] *Ibid.* at 673.

[64] American Communications Ass'n v. Douds, 339 U.S. 382, 429 (1950).

[65] 183 F. 2d 201, 206 (C.A. 2d, 1950).

[66] Popper, *op. cit. supra* note 51, at 123.

[67] *Ibid.*

[68] The "right of revolution" is usually based on the sentence in the Declaration beginning, "That whenever any Form of Government becomes destructive of these ends, it is the Right of the People to alter or to abolish it. . . ." But Professor Hook, [Does the Smith Act Threaten Our Liberties? 15 Commentary 63 (1953)] has called attention in this context to the next two sentences "Prudence, indeed, will dictate that

Governments long established should not be changed for light and transient causes; and accordingly all experience hath shown, that mankind are more disposed to suffer, while evils are sufferable, than to right themselves by abolishing the forms to which they are accustomed. But when a long train of abuses and usurpations, pursuing invariably the same Object, evinces a design to reduce them under absolute Despotism, it is their right, it is their duty, to throw off such Government, and to provide new Guards for their future security." These sentences support Mr. Chief Justice Vinson's statement in the Dennis case, 341 U.S. 494, 501 (1951), that "whatever theoretical merit there may be to the argument that there is

to overthrow the tyranny. Certainly then, it is inconsistent to maintain that the Constitution protects a totalitarian movement on its road to power, so long as it employs constitutional means, but once it comes to power, it becomes the moral right and duty of the people "to throw off such government." By then, too, an attempt to do so may be without hope of success. We can avoid these difficulties only by recognizing that democracy is not merely majority rule, but also embodies the principle of freedom and that, to paraphrase Mill, the principle of freedom cannot require that the people, or a majority of them, should be free to alienate its freedom. The principle of freedom requires that democratic policy be directed "to create, develop, and protect political institutions for the avoidance of tyranny," [69] which Professor Popper defines as a government "which the ruled cannot get rid of except by way of a successful revolution—that is to say, in most cases, not at all." [70] We should regard as a "democracy," therefore, not any government which is the product of the will of a majority, but only that government "which we can get rid of without bloodshed—for example, by way of general elections." [71] . . .

The rejection of the "orthodox" theory of democracy necessarily implies that one type of constitutional change in the constitutional system is excluded—"a change which would endanger its democratic character." [79] This, it is submitted, is the basic postulate which should control, not only the interpretation of the First Amendment, but also the amendment article (Art. V) of the Constitution. No one will maintain that the establishment of a totalitarian dictatorship in the United States by a constitutional amendment would not upset the basic scheme of things embodied in the Constitution as much as an amendment depriving cer-

---

a 'right' to rebellion against dictatorial governments is without force where the existing structure of the government provides for peaceful and orderly change." The "right to rebellion" in any case can only be a moral claim, never a legal right, because obviously no state can secure this claim. As Judge Learned Hand has said, "The advocacy of violence may, or may not, fail; but in neither case can there be any 'right' to use it. Revolutions are often 'right,' but a 'right of revolution' is a contradiction in terms, for a society which acknowledged it, could not stop at tolerating conspiracies to overthrow it, but must include their execution." 183 F. 2d 201, 213 (C.A. 2d, 1950). Even the moral claim to use force and violence to overthrow a tyranny is justified only if the action has as its exclusive aim the re-establishment of democratic institutions. The "use of violence is justified only under a tyranny which makes reforms without violence impossible and it should have only one aim, that is, to bring

about a state of affairs which makes reforms without violence possible." II Popper, *op. cit. supra* note 51, at 151.

[69] I Popper, *op. cit. supra* note 51, at 125.

[70] *Ibid.*, at 124.

[71] *Ibid.*, at 125. Bertrand Russell also defines democratic government "as a method of settling internal disputes without violence." The Practice and Theory of Bolshevism 98 (2d ed., 1949). Professor Riesman regards the "orthodox" conception of democracy as "perhaps erroneous" and admits it is plausible to argue that "one majority should have no right to preclude future majorities from reopening the issue and arriving at a different conclusion, and therefore no right—although all else is open to them—to tamper with the procedures of free opinion formation and electioneering which permit a present minority to become a future majority." *Op. cit. supra* note 52, at 54.

[79] II Popper, *op. cit. supra* note 51, at 161.

tain states without their consent of their equal representation in the Senate—which Article V expressly prohibits.[80] No democratic or constitutional principle is violated, therefore, when a democracy acts to exclude those groups from entering the struggle for political power which, if victorious, will not permit that struggle to continue in accordance with the democratic way.[81]

This view makes it irrelevant, for purposes of constitutional adjudication, whether a particular group is committed to the use of illegal means in the struggle for political power and will help to dissipate confusion resulting from the application of the clear and present danger rule to legislation forbidding the advocacy of the violent overthrow of the government. This conclusion is not based upon Riesman's view that such legislation "must fail of ethical justification, because it should never be assumed as a matter of course that a particular government deserves to stand, even if violence or the urging of violence is the only method by which, for all practical purposes, it can be overthrown." [82] The exercise of the Jeffersonian "right of revolution," upon which Riesman relies, has moral justification, as I have indicated, only if the government in power is a tyranny which closes all avenues of peaceful change and then only if the restoration of democracy is the sole objective.[83] Furthermore, resort to the violent seizure of power in a democratic state, even if intended to accomplish limited ends and not to destroy the democratic framework itself, is pernicious because the use of violence is "peculiarly calculated to create habits of despotism which would survive the crisis by

---

[80] Consult Corwin, The Constitution and What It Means Today 175 (11th ed., 1954): "Of the two exceptions to the amending power the first is today obsolete. This does not signify, however, that the only change that the power which amends the Constitution may not make in the Constitution is to deprive a state without its consent of its 'equal suffrage in the Senate.' The amending, like all other powers organized in the Constitution, is in form a delegated, and hence, a limited power, although this does not imply necessarily that the Supreme Court is vested with authority to determine its limits. The one power known to the Constitution which clearly is not limited by it is that which ordains it —in other words, the original, inalienable power of the people of the United States to determine their own political institutions." If I read Professor Corwin correctly, I infer that he would agree that even a majority of the people of the United States (and the people in the 36 ratifying states may constitute less than a majority) would have no constitutional right to exercise their power to determine their own political in-

stitutions so as to yield it to a totalitarian dictatorship, because this power is "original" and "inalienable."

[81] A democracy would thus have the right to suppress totalitarian movements whether they were committed to use (1) illegal means to come to power in a manner not prescribed by the existing constitution; or (2) illegal means (e.g., the terrorization of voters) to come to power in a manner prescribed by the existing constitution; or (3) legal means to come to power in a manner prescribed by the existing constitution, but once in power to use illegal means to overthrow the existing democratic order; or (4) legal means to come to power in a manner prescribed by the existing constitution and once in power, to use legal means (e.g., constitutional amendment) to inaugurate a totalitarian state. . . .

[82] Riesman, op. cit. supra note 52, at 60-61.

[83] See supra, note 68. This disposes of the argument that the suppression of the totalitarians will give them moral justification for using illegal means which they would otherwise lack, because their objective is to crush, not support, democracy.

which they were generated." [84] Therefore, because I agree with the legislative and judicial findings that the totalitarian Communist movement is committed to the use of force and violence, this fact alone, in my opinion, should support the congressional decision to outlaw the Communist Party. Nevertheless, there is reason to question the Supreme Court's finding that the conspiracy in the *Dennis* case created a clear and present danger of an attempt to overthrow the government by force and violence. We may agree, as I do, with Judge Learned Hand's determination that the gravity of the evil in the *Dennis* case (an attempt at overthrow), discounted by its improbability, was greater than the mischief of the repression. But we must agree with Mr. Justice Frankfurter that "[i]n all fairness, the argument [that "there is a constitutional principle . . . prohibiting restriction upon utterance unless it creates a situation of 'imminent' peril against which legislation may guard"] cannot be met by reinterpreting the Court's frequent use of 'clear' and 'present' to mean an entertainable 'probability.' " [85] Yet it is precisely this reinterpretation which has given rise to the fear that there are no longer any principles safeguarding freedom of speech.

Implications for the Clear and Present Danger Rule of Rejection of Orthodox Democratic Theory. If we accept the implications of the theory of democracy presented in this paper, the clear and present danger rule, whether as stated by Holmes,[86] Brandeis,[87] or Learned Hand,[88] will lose its significance in determining the constitutional limits upon the power of federal and state governments to exclude totalitarian movements from the arena of party struggle in a democracy. Some may still argue, however, that even if these implications are accepted, the First Amendment should be read as requiring that a totalitarian party be permitted to engage in the constitutional competition for political power until there is a "clear and present danger" that it may be victorious. All the objections that may be advanced against the clear and present danger rule as the test of constitutionality of legislation aimed at the use of force and violence as a means of political change also apply against the rule as the test of legislation aimed at totalitarian movements whether or not they are committed to the use of illegal means. In addition, it seems even more impossible to determine when there is a "clear and present danger" of

[84] Russell, The Practice and Theory of Bolshevism 92-93 (2d ed., 1949). . . .

[85] 341 U.S. 494, 527 (1951).

[86] "The question in every case is whether the words used are used in such circumstances and are of such a nature as to create a clear and present danger that they will bring about the substantive evils that Congress has a right to prevent. It is a question of proximity and degree." Schenck v. United States, 249 U.S. 47, 52 (1919).

[87] "To courageous, self-reliant men, with confidence in the power of free and fearless reasoning applied through the processes of popular government, no danger flowing from speech can be deemed clear and present, unless the incidence of the evil apprehended is so imminent that it may befall before there is opportunity for full discussion. If there be time to expose through discussion the falsehoods and fallacies, to avert the evil by the processes of education, the remedy to be applied is more speech, not enforced silence." Whitney v. California, 274 U.S. 357, 377 (1927).

[88] "In each case they [the courts] must ask whether the gravity of the 'evil,' discounted by its improbability, justifies such invasion of free speech as is necessary to avoid the danger." United States v. Dennis, 183 F. 2d 201, 212 (C.A. 2d, 1950).

a legal victory by a totalitarian party than of an attempt to overthrow the government by force and violence. The idealist and pragmatist assumptions at the basis of the views of the exponents of the clear and present danger rule enable them to avoid these difficulties, as becomes apparent when they attempt to meet the objection that this test[89] imposes the risk that it restrains action until it may be too late to prevent a totalitarian victory. "Our faith," says Mr. Justice Douglas, "should be that our people will never give support to these advocates of revolution, so long as we remain loyal to the purposes for which our nation was founded." [90] The pragmatist overtones of this expression of idealist faith are clear in Professor Nathanson's criticism of the *Dennis* case. "We expose our government," he writes, "to the apparent risk of successful revolution because we are confident that no government which is worth preserving can be seriously endangered by advocacy of the propriety or necessity of its violent overthrow. . . . [This] is a prophecy based essentially on faith in the democratic process." [91] Accordingly, even the success of the revolution should not be too disturbing because it would merely mean that the democracy overthrown, e.g., the Weimar Republic, Kerensky government or Czechoslovakian democracy, was not "worth preserving." But we value the democratic process, as has been pointed out, not because we assume that the policies of a democratic government are always the best or wisest or most just, but because it keeps open the path of non-violent change. And it is quite wrong, as Professor Popper warns, "to blame democracy for the political shortcomings of a democratic state. We should rather blame ourselves, that is to say, the citizens of the democratic state," because democracy only makes possible "the use of reason in the designing of new institutions and the adjusting of old ones. It cannot provide reason." [92]

It seems to me, too, that the current defenders of the clear and present danger rule, as stated particularly by Mr. Justice Brandeis, show an insufficient understanding of the nature and roots of modern totalitarianism. What Professor Wechsler said in criticism of legislation directed at the advocacy of violent overthrow of government can be said appropriately of the clear and present danger rule. "It represents an uncritical acceptance of a formula devised during the days when the Communist manifesto represented the technique of revolution; when revolutionaries operated by declaring rather than disguising their principles; when revolutionaries accepted rather than rejected the rule of reason; when they played upon the aspirations of men rather than upon their prejudices." [93] It is not necessary to

---

[89] "When conditions are so critical that there will be no time to avoid the evil that the speech threatens, it is time to call a halt." Mr. Justice Douglas, dissenting in Dennis v. United States, 341 U.S. 494, 585 (1951).

[90] 341 U.S. 494, 591 (1951). "I happen to believe," said Mr. Justice Black, dissenting in Carlson v. Landon, "that our free way of life enlists such respect and love that our nation cannot be imperiled by mere

talk." 342 U.S. 524, 555-556 (1952). See, too, Nathanson, The Communist Trial and the Clear and Present Danger Test, 63 Harv. L. Rev. 1167, 1174 (1950).

[91] Nathanson, *op. cit. supra* note 90, at 1175.

[92] I Popper, *op. cit. supra* note 51, at 126-127.

[93] Wechsler, Symposium on Civil Liberties, 9 Am. L. School Rev. 881, 888-889 (1941). "It does not follow," Judge Hand has said.

assume that the American people, too, have become apathetic and possessed of the psychological need to "escape from freedom" [94] and that mass propaganda, using the new facilities of mass communication, will lead them to succumb to the irrational appeal of totalitarianism, in order to agree with Riesman that "events have not shown that speech and writing, even those which begin as 'puny anonymities,' are incapable of promoting revolution," [95] and that the "job of wise statesmanship would seem to be to eliminate unnecessary gambles in the realm of public policy." [96] In any event, whether Mr. Justice Douglas' faith that "it can't happen here" is accepted as the basis of public policy at any particular time, it is difficult to see why such faith should become the basis of a constitutional doctrine limiting a democratic government's power to deal with totalitarian movements. Apart from the position that the question will never arise, it is inconsistent in principle, to say that the claim of a totalitarian movement to engage in the political struggle by legal means should be secured by the Constitution but that this protection should be withdrawn if the totalitarians approach victory by these means.

Judge Learned Hand interpreted the clear and present danger rule as involving "in every case a comparison between interests which are to be appraised qualitatively." [97] In each case, he wrote, the courts "must ask whether the gravity of the 'evil,' discounted by its improbability, justifies such invasion of free speech as is necessary to avoid the danger." [98] The interests he saw in conflict are those sought to be secured by free speech and the social interest in the general security sought to be protected by thwarting attempts to overthrow the government by force or violence. But so long as any test of constitutionality leaves it to the courts to estimate the gravity and probability of the evil—the attempt at forceful overthrow—it remains open to the criticism which Mr. Justice Frankfurter levelled against the view that "clear and present" means "imminent." "To make validity of legislation depend on judicial reading of events still in the womb of time—a forecast, that is, of the outcome of forces at best appreciated only with knowledge of the topmost secrets of nations—is to charge the judiciary with duties beyond its equipment." [99] Judge Hand, it seems to me, would not deny the validity of

---

that Brandeis would have been of the same opinion "if the conspirators had sought to mask their purposes by fair words, as they did in the case at bar." 183 F. 2d 201, 208 (C.A. 2d, 1950). The cases in which the "clear and present danger" test was elaborated all arose, as Mr. Justice Jackson has pointed out, "before the era of World War II revealed the subtlety and efficacy of modernized revolutionary techniques used by totalitarian parties." Dennis v. United States, 341 U.S. 494, 567 (1951). Consult, also, Russell, The Practice and Theory of Bolshevism 95 (2d ed., 1949).

[94] Consult Fromm, Escape from Freedom (1941).

[95] Riesman, op. cit. supra note 52, at 39.

The term "puny anonymities" was used by Mr. Justice Holmes in his dissenting opinion in Abrams v. United States, 250 U.S. 616, 629 (1919).

[96] Riesman, op. cit. supra note 52, at 40. "[I]n government, as in medicine or law," Riesman continues, "progress in the art is measured by the extent to which preventive measures are adopted before the point is reached at which only curative remedies are left." Ibid.

[97] 183 F. 2d 201, 212 (C.A. 2d, 1950).

[98] Ibid.

[99] Concurring opinion of Mr. Justice Frankfurter in the Dennis case, 341 U.S. 494, 551 (1951). Mr. Justice Jackson made the same point at 570.

this criticism, but would reply that the courts in the *Dennis* case at any rate had no choice but to make the forecast since the Smith Act made the courts the "surrogate" of Congress to do so.[100] To avoid the difficulty in Judge Hand's position, Mr. Justice Frankfurter calls essentially for a "candid and informed weighing of the competing interests"[101] without use of the clear and present danger formula. Thereby he makes explicit the legislative nature of the task which the courts have always had to perform in applying the clear and present danger rule. Recognition of this fact made it necessary for him to acknowledge that the legislature had the "primary responsibility"[102] to choose between competing interests and the courts must respect the legislative choice "unless outside the pale of fair judgment."[103]

Mr. Justice Frankfurter analyzed the conflicting interests as did Judge Hand and justified judicial deference to the legislative judgment solely because it was the judgment of the people's "representatives."[104] On both these points, it is submitted with respect, Mr. Justice Frankfurter's analysis does not go far enough and has been subjected to justifiable criticism.[105] Majority rule, as has been argued, does not exhaust the content of our constitutional democracy.[106] "The framers were not unaware," Mr. Chief Justice Stone has said, "that under the system which they created most governmental curtailments of personal liberty would have the support of a legislative judgment that the public interest would be better served by its curtailment than by its constitutional protection."[107] It is not "undemocratic" for the Court to resist the will of the majority in order to uphold the principle of freedom. But it is not inconsistent with this view to urge that the attitude of the Court toward anti-totalitarian legislation be similar to that which it takes toward legislation regulating economic affairs. Economic regulation, no less than anti-totalitarian legislation, involves the "paradox of freedom." It, too, limits the freedom of those subjected to it, but it may be upheld as constitutional not simply because of the deference due to the will of the majority, but in order to effectuate the principle of freedom; not because some interests other than those

---

[100] 183 F. 2d 201, 216 (C.A. 2d, 1950).

[101] 341 U.S. 494, 525 (1951).

[102] *Ibid.*

[103] *Ibid.*, at 540.

[104] *Ibid.*, at 552.

[105] Rostow, [The Democratic Character of Judicial Review, 66 Harv. L. Rev. 193 (1952)].

[106] In his first speech in the Virginia ratifying convention, Madison warned that in republics, the turbulence, violence and abuse of power of majorities have more frequently than any other cause produced despotism. 3 Elliott, The Debates in the Several State Conventions on the Adoption of the Federal Constitution 87 (2d ed., 1845), cited in Hurst, [Treason in the United States, 58 Harv. L. Rev. 406, n.

97]. Although Jefferson regarded "absolute acquiescence in the decisions of the majority as the 'vital principle of republics,'" he also invoked the "sacred principle" that the will of the majority "to be rightful must be reasonable; that the minority possess their equal rights, which equal law must protect and to violate would be oppression." First Inaugural in 1801, Inaugural Addresses of the Presidents of the United States, H.R. Doc. No. 540, 82d Cong. 2d Sess. 11-12 (1952). This strain runs through American thought otherwise as diverse as Calhoun, Lincoln, Thoreau and Emerson.

[107] Dissenting opinion in Minersville School District v. Gobitis, 310 U.S. 586, 604-605 (1940).

sought to be secured by freedom are considered more important by the legislature, but because economic regulation itself secures and expands the area of freedom. In other words, we have come to recognize that freedom means more than the absence of legal restraint and may require the removal of other restraints, like economic insecurity, which inhibit the individual personality. To enlarge the freedom of the economically weak, we see the necessity of limiting the freedom of the economically strong. Similarly, it is not interests other than those sought to be secured by freedom of speech which may be protected by anti-totalitarian legislation . . . but these very interests themselves. Concern for the national security in this case may not be concern for any existing institutions other than those which make possible non-violent change in a democratic framework. The principle of freedom, itself, therefore, requires that the Supreme Court uphold the judgment of Congress that totalitarian political organizations be proscribed.

However, this same principle of freedom, read into the First Amendment, requires that the Court review the congressional finding that a particular political organization sought to be proscribed is totalitarian in fact. . . . The important question is the scope of judicial review. In the *Dennis* case, Mr. Justice Frankfurter suggested that the Court ask whether the congressional determinations have "the warrant of substantial proof." [110] [Professor Auerbach then urged that the Court should uphold anti-Communist Party legislation only if it found to its own satisfaction that the Party was a totalitarian organization.—Editor] To the extent that deference to the principle of majority rule may make the courts reluctant to go this far, what has already been said on this question should, it is submitted, dispel the reluctance. Furthermore, the courts are as able as Congress or an administrative tribunal to evaluate the theoretical, historical and empirical data

[110] Concurring opinion in the Dennis case, 341 U.S. 494, 526 (1951). It does not help to determine the standard of review to talk about the "presumption" of constitutionality or unconstitutionality. Judge Learned Hand has held the "presumption of constitutionality" to be applicable not only when the courts are reviewing a legislative "choice of values," but also when the courts have "undertaken an inquiry as to the facts on which the validity of a statute turns." Borden's Farm Products Co. v. Ten Eyck, 11 F. Supp. 599, 600 (S.D.N.Y., 1935) on remand after Borden's Farm Products v. Baldwin, 293 U.S. 194 (1934), in which Mr. Chief Justice Hughes stated (293 U.S. 194, 209) that the presumption of constitutionality was a "presumption . . . of the existence of factual conditions supporting the legislation." To Judge Hand this meant that a court was to hold a law invalid not if "it finds to its own satisfaction that the necessary facts do not exist," but only if it

finds that "reasonable people could not believe that they did. . . ." 11 F. Supp. 599, 600 (S.D.N.Y., 1935). He then compared the function of the court in reviewing legislative findings to its function in reviewing a jury verdict or the findings of an administrative tribunal. This test of course comes very close to the test of the "warrant of substantial proof." Judging by his review of the legislative findings in the Carolene Products Co. case, it does not seem that Mr. Chief Justice Stone envisaged a lesser function for the judiciary when he suggested that the test of unconstitutionality was whether the legislation was "of such a character as to preclude the assumption that it rests upon some rational basis within the knowledge and experience of the legislators." United States v. Carolene Products Co., 304 U.S. 144, 152 (1938). See, too, Freund, On Understanding the Supreme Court 88 (1945).

involved in determining whether a particular political organization is totalitarian. In fact, [Congressional] findings are in large measure based upon judicial assessments of the Communist movement. . . .

NOTES AND QUESTIONS

1. On the basis of the evidence presented in this chapter and any other factors you deem relevant, what are the theories that might explain the Supreme Court's 1937 shift in constitutional attitude? Which do you regard as most plausible, and why?

2. What do you understand by the "preferred freedoms" doctrine? How can it reasonably be defended? How can it reasonably be attacked?

3. Regarding the Auerbach extract: What is his position on the proper scope of judicial review of constitutionality of anti-totalitarian legislation? How is this position similar or dissimilar to the preferred freedoms doctrine?

4. For discussions of the current role of the Supreme Court, see Symposium, Role of the Supreme Court, 6 J. Pub. Law 275 (1957); Freund, Storm Over the Supreme Court, 21 Mod. L. Rev. 345 (1958); Pritchett, The Supreme Court Today: Constitutional Interpretation and Judicial Self-Restraint, 3 S. Dak. L. Rev. 51 (1958); Symposium, Role of the Supreme Court, 33 Notre Dame Lawyer 521 (1958).

Davis, Administrative Law Text (1959)

Heady, The New Reform Movement in Regulatory Administration, 19 Public Administration Review 89 (1959)

The Independent Regulatory Agencies (Salomon ed. 1959)

Redford, National Regulatory Commissions: Need for a New Look (1959)

Schwartz, The Professor and the Commissions (1959)

Parker, Why Do Administrative Agencies Exist? A Reappraisal, 45 Georgetown Law Journal 331 (1957)

Arpaia, The Independent Agency—A Necessary Instrument of Democratic Government, 69 Harvard Law Review 483 (1956)

Symposium on Hoover Commission and Task Force Reports on Legal Services and Procedure, 30 New York University Law Review 1267 (1956)

Bernstein, Regulating Business by Independent Commission (1955)

Task Force Report on Legal Services and Procedure, [Hoover] Commission on Organization of the Executive Branch of the Government (1955)

Jaffe, The Effective Limits of the Administrative Process: A Reevaluation, 67 Harvard Law Review 1105 (1954)

Keeton, The Passing of Parliament (1952)

Task Force Report on Regulatory Commissions, [Hoover] Commission on Organization of the Executive Branch of the Government (1949)

Robson, Justice and Administrative Law (2nd ed. 1947)

Administrative Adjudication in the State of New York [Benjamin Report] (1942)

Report of the Attorney General's Committee on Administrative Procedure, Sen. Doc. No. 8, 77th Cong., 1st Sess. (1941)

Landis, The Administrative Process (1938)

CHAPTER Twelve

The ADMINISTRATIVE PROCESS in GENERAL—ADMINISTRATIVE ADJUDICATION

DUTIES OF THE INDUSTRIAL COMMISSION

Wisconsin Blue Book, Compiled by Wisconsin
Legislative Reference Library
345-354 (1954 ed.)

History. The Industrial Commission is the labor department of the state. Since the first labor law was passed in 1867, new laws on the subject have been enacted at every session of the legislature. The Bureau of Labor Statistics was created in 1887 to enforce all labor laws, but in 1911, when the Workmen's Compensation Law was passed, it was replaced by the Industrial Commission. This commission is composed of 3 persons appointed by the Governor for 6-year terms, subject to confirmation by the senate.

The commission's activities are carried out by the following divisions:

Apprenticeship Division. . . .

Employment Service. . . .

Fair Employment Practices. . . .

Safety and Sanitation. Wisconsin's interest in the safety of its people in public buildings and places of employment dates back to 1883. In that year a Bureau of Labor Statistics was created with one commissioner, who was required to "visit and examine factories and all other establishments where people are employed at any kind of labor, to see that all laws for the protection of the health and lives of operators in work shops and factories are enforced." The present Industrial Commission was created in 1911 and among the many responsibilities delegated to the commission by the legislature is one providing that all employments, places of employment and public buildings be made safe for all occupants and frequenters. The division of safety and sanitation was organized at that time, with the specific duty to supervise such places to see that they are safe.

The provisions of Chapter 101 of the Wisconsin Statutes, as they apply to safety and sanitation are relatively simple. They are merely enabling legislation to permit the Industrial Commission to enact its own standards and regulations. A portion of this chapter is commonly known as the "safe place statute," and can be called the core or basis of all safety requirements as far as an employer or owner of a

725

public building is concerned. This section places the responsibility for safety on each employer or owner.

Among its many duties, the commission was directed by the legislature: (1) to investigate, ascertain, declare and prescribe what safety devices, safeguards or other means or methods of protection are best adapted for providing safe employment and safe places of employment; (2) to ascertain and fix such reasonable standards and to prescribe, modify, and enforce such reasonable orders for the adoption of safety devices and safeguards as may be necessary to carry out all laws and lawful orders relative to the protection of the life, health, safety and welfare of employes and frequenters; (3) to ascertain, fix and order such reasonable standards, rules or regulations for the construction, repair, and maintenance of places of employment and public buildings as shall render them safe; and, finally, (4) to require the submission of proper plans and specifications for places of employment and public buildings as well as for elevators, toilets and other permanent equipment of such buildings.

Safety Codes. On the basis of authority thus granted, the Industrial Commission, since 1911, has enacted regulations comprising 26 separate safety codes. The general orders covered by these codes relate to: boilers; building; cleaning and dyeing; dusts, fumes, gases and vapors; electric fences; electricity; elevators; existing buildings; explosives; fire prevention; flammable liquids; heating, ventilation and air conditioning; industrial lighting; liquefied petroleum gases; manufacture of acetylene gas; mines; motor vehicle lights; quarries and pits; refrigerator plants; safety; safety in construction; school lighting; sanitary facilities in railroad terminals; sanitation; spray coating; tunnel, caisson and trench construction. One or more of these codes is constantly being revised to conform to existing conditions and to take advantage of changing methods of work. The orders thus promulgated have the same force and effect as statutes enacted by the legislature, except that statute laws can only be changed by the legislature while orders of the commission can be repealed, amended or modified by the commission itself.

The statutes also empower the Industrial Commission to appoint advisors who, without compensation, shall assist the commission in the execution of its duties. This authority is applied to the preparation and revision of all codes. As a result, every code which is issued or revised is the work of an advisory committee selected for this purpose. This means that every code has its own individual committee whose membership is composed of persons directly interested in the special problem at hand and particularly qualified along the lines needed for each individual regulation and standard. In its selection of committee members, the commission is careful to secure representation from all interested organizations, including industry, labor and the public in general. Each organization is requested to submit a list of 2 or more names from which the commission can appoint the committee members to represent each individual group. The committee thus selected meets as often as it deems necessary, and no order is recommended to the commission for adoption until the committee has unanimously agreed that such an order is reasonable as well as necessary.

When the order has been recommended by the advisory committee, the Industrial Commission arranges for public hearings in various cities throughout the state to which all interested persons are invited to be present and to submit any comments or criticisms on the proposed orders or revisions. At the conclusion of the hearings, the material thus gathered is referred to the advisory committee for its consideration and evaluation of all suggestions received as the result of the hearings. When this work has been completed, the code is then submitted to the commission with a recommendation for adoption which usually follows without any further question. Then, as required by statute, the new and revised orders are published in the official state newspaper and become effective 30 days after such publication.

This method of code preparation has proven exceedingly satisfactory over the more than 40-year period it has been in use. This is due especially to the fact that all interested organizations feel that they have had a part in the work and the public realizes that it also has had an opportunity to express its ideas. As a result, these various orders are recognized not only on a national basis but have, on request, been transmitted to many foreign countries. . . .

The enforcement of the safety orders thus prepared is vested in the safety and sanitation divison which, for this purpose, is subdivided into 8 sections or subdivisions. These sections are: boiler, building, elevator, electrical, factory, fire prevention, mining and quarrying, and safety education. . . .

Statistical Department. Through its statistical department the Industrial Commission collects, analyzes and publishes statistics relating to industrial conditions, including statistics on employment, industrial accidents and child labor. Index numbers of the volume of employment and payrolls are compiled monthly from reports voluntarily made by many employers, which are the best gauge of industrial conditions obtainable.

Unemployment Compensation. . . .

Woman and Child Labor; Wage Collection. . . .

Workmen's Compensation. The Workmen's Compensation Act provides for payment of compensation and for all necessary medical treatment to injured employees of employers subject to the compensation act, also for compensation to dependents of employes whose injuries result in deaths. During the year ended June 30, 1950, 54,000 industrial accidents and diseases were reported, of which 50,000 were found to call for payment of compensation over and above medical benefits. In about 90 per cent of these cases payments were made without formal order of the commission. In about 10 per cent, which involved more than one-half the total benefits paid during the year, the commission made formal order, either upon agreement of the parties or following hearing. Hearings are held in or near places where accidents occur or where the injured person resides. These hearings are conducted by examiners of the commission who draw orders, from which appeal may be taken to the commission as a body.

The advisory committee on workmen's compensation legislation advises with the commission on legislation affecting the workmen's compensation law. The committee consists of representatives of labor, employers, and compensation insurance groups. It is appointed by the Industrial Commission and meets upon call of the commission.

EDITORIAL NOTE: LEGISLATIVE, EXECUTIVE, and JUDICIAL FUNCTIONS of ADMINISTRATIVE AGENCIES

The Industrial Commission is only one of the many important administrative agencies in Wisconsin. And in every state, and above all, in the federal government, there is a similar network of commissions, boards, bureaus and other executive bodies having, in one form or another, power to make rules, or to decide controversies, or to grant licenses, or to render particular kinds of services, or to perform two or more of these functions. The Industrial Commission of Wisconsin exercises all of these functions. It makes rules for the safety of factories, etc. (see above under "Safety and Sanitation"). It decides controversies, under the Workmen's Compensation Act, for example (see above under "Workmen's Compensation"). It grants licenses (for example, to employment agents). And it renders particular kinds of services, as, for example, aiding wage earners to collect the wages due them.

When an administrative agency renders particular kinds of services, it is performing an executive function. When its field agents go out to make investigations (for instance, to see if the safety rules for factories are being obeyed) it is also performing an executive function. An executive function, under our form of government, is seeing to it that the laws are "executed"—that is, are carried out.

When an administrative agency makes rules or regulations, it is performing a legislative function. The function of the legislature, as we saw, is to enact rules and regulations which we call "statutes" or "laws," prescribing what shall or shall not be done. As the problems to be dealt with have become more and more complicated under the stress of the industrial revolution, legislatures have increasingly delegated to administrative agencies the task of formulating rules and regulations in particular fields (e.g., safety conditions in factories). The rules which administrative agencies make, within the scope of the powers delegated to them, have the force of law; the agencies which are granted these powers are really sublegislatures in the particular fields assigned to them; they are said to be "quasi-legislative" in nature.

When an administrative agency decides controversies it is performing a judicial function. The principal reason for assigning judicial functions to administrative agencies in particular fields, instead of to the courts, is practical. Professor Hurst reports that by the late 1920's "in a typical year, administrators [of workmen's compensation laws] were disposing of about 56,000 claims in Illinois, about 41,000 in Massachusetts, about 85,000 in Pennsylvania, about 21,000 in Wisconsin. A trifling percentage of these administrative decisions were reviewed in courts. In a typical year of the late 1920's review was sought in Illinois circuit courts in 237 (about four tenths of 1 per cent) of the 57,535 compensable accident cases reported; the Illinois supreme court granted further review in only 23 cases. In the same year, in Massachusetts review was sought in 183 out of 40,274 cases." (The Growth of American Law 389 [1950]). If only the cases contested before the administrative agency (which total about 5000 a year before the Wisconsin Industrial Commission) had to be tried in courts of law instead, there would be much delay and expense. Accordingly the legislature gave the Commission the power to hear and decide these cases, subject to a right of review in the courts; the agency is said to be acting in a "quasi-judicial" capacity.

When an administrative agency passes on applications for licenses, it has to decide what the facts are, just as a court does; but historically courts have been limited to issuing judgments and orders, and not to granting or denying licenses. Accordingly, this function can probably best be classified as executive.

We have previously had occasion to consider the great growth, in the twentieth century, of legislation regulating social and economic affairs. In the main, this legislation uses the administrative process to implement and carry out the policies embodied therein.

REPORT OF THE ATTORNEY GENERAL'S COMMITTEE ON ADMINISTRATIVE PROCEDURE
Senate Document No. 8, 77th Cong., 1st Sess. 7-20 (1941)

The Origins, Development, and Characteristics of the Administrative Process. The administrative process in the Federal Government is not new. On the contrary, it is as old as the Government itself; and its growth has been virtually as steady as that of the Statutes at Large. The growth has been pragmatic. Congress has enacted statutes, and it has resorted to the administrative device in the framing of statutes, in the practical effort to meet particular needs. Because the administrative process has developed in this fashion, it invites comprehensive study with a view to coordination and improvement. But for the same reason such study must be carried on with understanding of the deep roots which the process has in American history and with recognition of the practical judgments of successive Congresses and Presidents, and of the people, which it embodies. At the outset, therefore, it is appropriate to call attention to the origins of existing administrative agencies, to the reasons for their coming into being, and to some of their fundamental characteristics which must be taken into account in the formulation of proposals for improvement.

A. *Growth of Administrative Agencies*

Many different, and sharply varying, figures of the number of Federal administrative agencies have been current in popular discussion. The particular total arrived at depends, of course, on the unit to be taken as constituting an "agency" as well as on the concept applied in designating a particular agency as "administrative." The Committee has regarded as the distinguishing feature of an "administrative" agency the power to determine, either by rule or by decision, private rights and obligations. If the largest possible units be taken as "agencies," there are in the Federal Government nine executive departments and eighteen independent agencies which possess significant administrative powers of this character. An accurate picture is not drawn, however, by regarding each executive department as constituting but a single agency. That term may as appropriately be applied to subdivisions of departments—variously termed "bureaus," "offices," "services," and the like—which have a substantial measure of independence in the departments' internal organization and in the conduct of their adjudicatory or rule-making activities. The Federal Security Agency, moreover, consists in substance of three agencies—the Social Security Board, the Food and Drug Administration, and the Public Health Service.[1] By this mode of reckoning the total number of agencies may be considered to be increased from 27 to 51, of which 22 are outside the regular executive departments and 29 are within.[2]

Few agencies have been created at a stroke and have remained unchanged in organization and function. Some have been abolished; others have been merged; many have been transferred. Almost all have undergone changes of name and additions of function. In the account which follows of the origin of existing agencies, each agency has been placed in the period in which important powers of the kind which it now exercises were first authorized. . . .

From 1789 to the close of the Civil War.—Of the 51 administrative agencies or subdivisions of agencies discussed below, no less than 11 trace their beginnings to statutes enacted prior to the close of the Civil War. The first session of the First Congress enacted 3 statutes conferring important administrative powers, 2 of which are antecedents of statutes now administered by the Bureau of Customs in the Treasury Department and the third of which initiated the long series of pension laws now in the charge of the Veterans' Administration. In the next year "An act to promote the progress of useful arts" became the progenitor of the many later laws administered by the Patent Office (Department of Commerce), relating to applications for patents and their issuance and recordation: A few

---

[1] These agencies are now part of the Department of Health, Education and Welfare. —Editor

[2] The Office of Administrative Procedure has indicated that there are currently about 115-120 federal agencies with adjudicatory functions and, of course, almost every department and bureau of the executive branch, as well as every independent agency, engages in rule-making to some degree. Gardner, The Administrative Process, in Legal Institutions Today and Tomorrow, 111, The Centennial Conference Volume of the Columbia Law School, (Paulsen, ed. 1959).—Editor

years later, in 1796, "An act for establishing Trading Houses with Indian Tribes" made provision for trade with Indians "according to the rules and orders which the President shall prescribe": statutes dealing with such matters later became the concern of the Office of Indian Affairs which has existed in the Department of the Interior since the creation of the Department in 1849. Tax laws, of course, have been continuous since 1789; but the Bureau of Internal Revenue is perhaps best dated from the Act of July 1, 1862, which created the office of Commissioner of Internal Revenue and constituted the beginning of the system of general internal revenue taxation which has continued with modifactions to date. The six other agencies fairly to be dated from this period are the General Land Office established by the act of April 1, 1812, in the Treasury Department and transferred to the Department of the Interior in 1849; the Bureau of Marine Inspection and Navigation (Department of Commerce), which exercises functions first conferred upon the Steamboat Inspection Service created in 1838; the Passport Division (Department of State); the Office of the Chief of Engineers (War Department); the Office of the Comptroller of the Currency, established by the National Bank Act of February 25, 1863; and the Office of the Third Assistant Postmaster General, which administers the laws relating to formal classification of mail matter first provided by the Act of March 3, 1863. In this period also came the first of the Federal independent commissions, the California Land Commission created in 1851 by "An act to ascertain and settle the private land claims in the State of California"—an agency whose existence ended with the problems it solved.

From 1865 to the turn of the century.—Most spectacular of the administrative agencies created in the post civil-war period was, of course, the Interstate Commerce Commission established by the act of February 4, 1887. Five other agencies date from this period: The Office of the Solicitor in the Post Office Department, which administers the laws relating to mail frauds, dating from the act of June 8, 1872; the Bureau of Entomology and Plant Quarantine (Department of Agriculture), whose entomological work was well-established in the eighties; the Immigration and Naturalization Service, the first important functions of which trace back to the act of August 3, 1882; the Bureau of Animal Industry (Department of Agriculture) created by the act of May 29, 1884; and the Bureau of Fisheries, which dates for practical purposes from January 20, 1888, when a Commissioner of Fish and Fisheries was provided as a separate full-time officer.

From 1900 to the end of the World War.—Nine of the present Federal administrative agencies date from this period. The Bureau of Biological Survey in the Department of Agriculture was recognized as a permanent Bureau beginning with the appropriation act of 1905 and previously, as a Division, as far back as 1901. The Agricultural Marketing Service in the same department administers numerous statutes, of which important early ones were enacted in this period. The Public Health Service . . . was created in 1902, to administer quarantine statutes and regulations; in 1917, it was also given important powers to adjudicate medical questions in immigration cases. The present Food and Drug Administration goes back to the Pure Food and Drug Act of 1906. In 1913 the Federal Reserve System was established and a year later the Federal Trade Commission. In the year 1916 were created the United States Tariff Commission and the Shipping Board, predecessor of the present United States Maritime Commission.[3]

From 1918 to the beginning of the depression of 1929.—The post-war period, in addition to noteworthy extensions of the functions of existing agencies, witnessed the beginning of nine new agencies. The Federal Power Commission was established in 1920. The Grain Futures Act of 1922, was the beginning of what is now the Commodity Exchange Administration in the Department of Agriculture. The Immigration Act of 1924 resulted in the creation of the Visa Division in the Department of State. The Board of Tax Appeals was created by the revenue act of the same year. The Railway Labor Act of 1926 is the predecessor statute of the acts administered by both the National Mediation Board and the Railroad Adjustment Board; while from the Air Commerce Act of 1926 is derived what is now the Civil Aeronautics Administration in the Department of Commerce.[3a] The Radio Act of 1927 created the Federal Radio Commission, predecessor of the present Federal Communications Commission. Finally the Longshoremen's and Harbor Workers Compensation Act of 1927, and the District of Columbia Workmen's Compensation Act of 1928 set up deputy commissioners, acting under the general supervision of the United States Employees' Compensation Commission (which was itself created in 1916) to administer claims arising under these two acts.

From 1930 to 1940.—In the last decade belong 17 of the existing Federal administrative agencies. Listed in chronological order, they are:

Federal Home Loan Bank Board (1932).
Surplus Marketing Administration (Department of Agriculture) (1933).
Federal Deposit Insurance Corporation (1933).
Securities and Exchange Commission (1934).
Grazing Service (Department of the Interior) (1934).
Social Security Board (1935).
National Labor Relations Board (1935).
Commodity Exchange Commission (1936).
Public Contracts Division (Department of Labor) (1935).
Processing Tax Board of Review (Treasury Department) (1936).
Bituminous Coal Division (Department of the Interior) (1937).
Railroad Retirement Board (1937).
Sugar Division (Department of Agriculture) (1937).
Wage and Hour Division (Department of Labor) (1938).
Division of Controls (Department of State) (1939).
Selective Service Administration (Department of War) (1940).

---

[3] The work of the Maritime Commission is currently divided between the Federal Maritime Board and the Maritime Administration.—Editor

[3a] See note 5 following.

B. *Reasons for Resort to the Administrative Process*

What are the reasons why Congress thus resorted, continuously and with increasing frequency, to the administrative process as an instrument for the execution of the policies which it has enacted into law? No single or simple explanation can be given. The reasons are both varied and numerous, reflecting the variety and number of the agencies themselves. Discussion frequently requires classification in terms of the differing functions which the agencies perform.

1. *Advantages of administration as compared with executive action.*—One of the principal alternatives to the administrative process is the more extensive use of ordinary executive officers. This alternative appears in a distinctive field of governmental action, comprising those numerous functions which commonly are regarded, for historical or other reasons, as belonging peculiarly to the executive department. An instance is the issuance of passports, the task of the Passport Division in the Department of State. Another is the actual expenditure, as distinguished from the appropriation, of public funds. Congress itself cannot or should not issue passports or make payments of money. Nor have these been thought of as appropriate tasks for the courts. This being so, two alternatives, broadly speaking, are available. Congress can establish an administrative tribunal for the task. Or it can make use of executive officers, charged with acting substantially as officers of business enterprises act.

The difference between these alternatives is not easy of exact statement, yet it appears readily enough from a comparison of extremes. It can be illustrated by the contrast between the Works Progress Administration and the Veterans' Administration. Both agencies disburse benefits. The former, however, proceeds in fluid executive fashion under a statute so framed that it confers upon individuals no "rights" to relief in stated circumstances. It issues no regulations giving notice of how it will act or limiting its own discretion. The latter, administering law embodied in statute and regulations, adjudicates "rights" by a relatively formal hearing procedure. The former the Committee has not regarded as an "administrative" agency falling within its purview; the latter it has. In this and analogous situations weighty reasons may often lead Congress to frame statutes upon the executive, more broadly discretionary, pattern. But the alternative of administrative adjudication, where practicable, insures greater uniformity and impersonality of action. In this area of Government the administrative process, far from being an encroachment upon the rule of law, is an extension of it.

A substantial number of existing administrative agencies represent an effort to discharge in a fashion analogous to the judicial a function which might have been discharged executively or even legislatively. Many of these, as we have noted in the preceding paragraph, are concerned with disbursing what, in legal theory, have been regarded as benefits. The Patent Office, so far as concerns the issuance of patents, is an early illustration. So also came to be the General Land Office. The United States Employees' Compensation Commission—so far as concerns payment of benefits to Federal employees—is an administrative agency doing what Congress formerly did by private acts. The Veterans' Administration illustrates increasing application of the adjudicatory method in the evolution of pension policy. Most recently, in the field of general social security, Congress in creating the Social Security Board and the Railroad Retirement Board directed action by adjudication as a matter of course; indeed, establishment of these agencies would scarcely have been possible, politically, on any other terms.

Extension of the rule of law through resort to the administrative process is by no means confined to the disbursing of benefits. In the assessment of taxes, for example, the development of an administrative procedure through the Bureau of Internal Revenue and the Board of Tax Appeals[4] has operated in considerable measure to replace an executive procedure. The Public Contracts Division in the Department of Labor, in prescribing the wages which must be paid by employers contracting with the Government and enforcing the wage stipulations in these contracts, follows an administrative method of hearing and rule making sharply at variance with the executive methods by which other than labor terms of public contracts are determined. One of the most striking examples is the most recent—the Selective Service Administration with its relatively elaborate administrative process. . . .

2. *Constitutional limitations upon the powers of courts.* . . .

3. *The trend toward preventive legislation.*—If administrative agencies did not exist in the Federal Government, Congress would be limited to a technique of legislation primarily designed to correct evils after they have arisen rather than to prevent them from arising. The criminal law, of course, operates in this after-the-event fashion. Congress declares a given act to be a crime. The mere declaration may act as a deterrent. But if it fails to do so the courts can only punish the wrong-doer; they cannot wipe out or make good the wrong. Traditional non-criminal, private law operates for the most part in the same after-the-event fashion. A statute or the common law gives one individual a right to go into court and sue another. This procedure is likely to be expensive. It is uncertain. At best, in the ordinary action for money damages, it leads only to compensation for the injury, which is seldom as satisfactory as not having been injured at all. To be sure, courts of equity administer a substantial measure of preventive justice by giving injunctions against threatened injuries. But it is necessary to prove the threat, and other limitations confine the scope of this mode of relief. The desire to work out a more effective and more flexible method of preventing unwanted things from happening accounts for the formation of many (although by no means all) Federal administrative agencies.

The rate-making powers of the Interstate Commerce Commission afford an apt illustration. The common law, from time immemorial, recognized a right of action against a common carrier on account of an unreasonable rate. The shipper or the passenger could pay the charge and then sue to recover the unreasonable excess. Preference for a mechanism whereby reasonable rates could be established in advance was a principal factor leading to the Commission's establishment. A more recent example is the Securities and Exchange Commission. Within rather severe limits, the common law recognized a right in a purchaser of securities to recover damages from the seller resulting from false statements made in effecting the

[4] The Board of Tax Appeals is now the Tax Court.—Editor

sale. The importance of truth in securities led to a demand that honest statements, as well as fuller and more informative statements, be assured so far as possible in advance. If this end were to be accomplished, it could only be done by creating an administrative agency. A similar purpose, effected in a great variety of ways, underlies the formation of many other agencies. Thus, licensing is one of the most significant of all preventive devices. It would be possible to permit anyone to act as the pilot of a ship or a plane, and then to punish those whose incompetence led to accidents or to prohibit them from acting as pilots again. People have preferred, however, to attempt by a licensing method to assure competence in advance; and administrative agencies have had to be created to carry out the licensing system. Licensing of radio broadcasters has, among other purposes, a comparable object of securing advance assurance of conformity to certain standards of broadcasting, as well as the object of securing a ready means of dealing with departures from the standards. Licensing of any activity may be one of the most burdensome forms of regulation, since all who engage in the activity must be licensed in order that the persons who would probably act improperly may be controlled. But it is also one of the most effective, and it is particularly likely to be resorted to where the effort to effectuate policies is made with conviction.

4. *Limitations upon effective legislative action.*—Many of the functions of existing Federal administrative agencies obviously could not, in any view, be performed by Congress. Others, however, could. Thus, State legislatures once fixed rates by statute, although Congress seems never to have done so. Congress once disposed of all money claims against the United States by a private bill procedure; much, although not all, of this work has now been passed on to other agencies. Apart from instances of this character, the full range of rule-making activity of Federal administrative agencies represents work of a type which Congress could do if it had the time and deemed it wise to do it. Independently of the comparative advantages of administrative action, various inherent limitations upon its own functioning militate in these cases against action by Congress itself. The total time available is the most obvious. Time spent on details must be at the sacrifice of time spent on matters of broad public policy. Lack of specialized information is another; lack of a staff or a procedure adapted to acquiring it is a third. The complexity of the problems which have to be determined, even after basic policy has been settled, is the governing consideration. Even if Congress had the time and facilities to work out details, there would be constant danger of harmful rigidity if the result were crystallized in the form of a statute. Thus comes a steady pressure—which may, of course, be yielded to overreadily—to assign such tasks to the controlled discretion of some other agency.

5. *Limitations upon exclusively judicial enforcement.*—If Congress chooses to rely upon the courts instead of assuming the tasks itself . . . other limitations operate. The 94 Federal district and territorial courts are structurally incapable of the same uniformity in the application of law as a single centralized agency. The problem of uniformity, and other problems as well, arise also with respect to the initiative of enforcement which, of course, the judges themselves cannot assume. Action must be brought either in the name of the Government or by

private individuals. If brought by the Government, the 94 district and territorial attorneys will vary in their enforcement policy as will the courts in their decisions. If brought by private individuals, there is cast upon these individuals a burden which it is one of the prime purposes of administrative agencies to avoid. Certain agencies, it is essential to recognize, represent an effort, whether wise or unwise, to place upon the Government—rather than upon millions of people of often limited resources—a large share of the responsibility for making effective policies which the people through their Government have declared.

6. *The advantages of continuity of attention and clearly allocated responsibility.* —In contrast to the limitations of other agencies, just discussed, are certain advantages which administrative agencies, properly organized, may have. The need of bringing to bear upon difficult social and economic questions the attention of those who have time and facilities to become and remain continuously informed about them was recognized very early. In 1787, for example, the General Assembly of the State of Vermont recited that—

> Whereas it has been found by experience, that great advantage has been taken, by ferrymen demanding unreasonable prices for their services. And whereas this assembly cannot so well distinguish between the several rivers, and the several parts of said river, pond or lake, on account of distance, swiftness of water, number of travellers, etc. Therefore to prevent such impositions for the future:
>
> *Be it enacted by the general assembly of the State of Vermont,* That the magistrates, selectmen, and constables, of the several towns where ferries are needed, shall meet before the first day of August annually, at a time and place by them agreed upon, and appoint proper persons and places for ferries; and further regulate the price thereof, according to the profits of such ferries, and price of labour; to be varied from time to time as occasion shall require. . . .

One hundred years later problems arising from the rapid extension of railroads were pressing and national. Neither the courts nor Congress could exercise adequate control over rates and practices. The task, accordingly, was assigned to an administrative agency, the Interstate Commerce Commission. When in the course of time supervision over carrier operations was extended beyond rate control, the impossibility of direct legislative regulation and the need for an administrative system of control were merely emphasized.

The experience out of which came the Interstate Commerce Commission has been duplicated in other fields. Regulations of marine transportation and aviation presented problems not unlike those involved in regulation of the railroads and led to the Bureau of Marine Inspection and Navigation, the United States Maritime Commission, and the Civil Aeronautics Authority.[5] Control over water power and natural gas resources, after a period of unsatisfactory experiments, was given to

[5] The task of regulating the economic aspects of the air carrier industry is now entrusted to the Civil Aeronautics Board. The problem of air safety is now within the province of the Federal Aviation Agency, which has absorbed the Civil Aeronautics Administration.—Editor

the Federal Power Commission. Protection of commerce in agricultural products led to supervision of the instrumentalities of that commerce by the Department of Agriculture administering the Packers and Stockyards Act, the Commodity Exchange Act, and other regulatory statutes. Banks and banking presented complex problems calling for special knowledge and continuing and detailed supervision, not possible for either Congress or the courts, and now performed by the Federal Reserve System, the Federal Deposit Insurance Corporation, the Federal Home Loan Bank Board, and the Comptroller of the Currency. For radio communication only a limited air-space is available. The science has been from the first a rapidly developing one, demanding technical knowledge and expertness. Here complete legislative regulation was scarcely practicable. So Congress provided the principles of regulation and gave responsibility for administration to the Federal Radio Commission and its successor, the Federal Communications Commission. The financial collapse of 1929 and the years following focused attention upon the investment field. Delicate problems requiring at once an intimate knowledge of financial machinery and elasticity of treatment led Congress to delegate regulatory powers to the Securities and Exchange Commission. So, too, the administrative machinery of this Commission was availed of to perform the complex task of supervision and regulating the structure, finances, and management practices of public utilities.

Each of the agencies just mentioned specializes in the regulation of a single industry or phase of industry—railroad transportation, or shipping, or investment, or banking. But Congress has also employed the administrative process to perform specialized and continuing regulation not of particular industries but of activities cutting across many industries. For example, Congress, believing it necessary to supervise and check competitive practices which tended toward monopoly and restraint of trade, in 1914 created the Federal Trade Commission to prevent unfair methods of competition. In 1935 the National Labor Relations Board was established to prevent unfair labor practices. Both objectives were declared by Congress to embody a national policy. In the case of these two agencies, the factor of technical expertness plays a less important part than in the others; but the advantages of continuous attention and a clearly allocated responsibility are substantially the same. If the initiative for enforcement were to be left to the injured persons immediately concerned, they might often be too weak or timid or discouraged to bring the necessary proceedings, in which case, so Congress thought, the public interest would suffer, since the public interest called for the elimination of the particular practices.

The administration of the Walsh-Healey Act affords a similar example. This statute is enforced primarily by the Department of Labor, through its Division of Public Contracts. The statute provides in part that certain contractors with the Government must pay their employees not less than prescribed wages. If lower wages are in fact paid, a proceeding may be brought before the Division of Public Contracts by agents of the Department to recover for the employees the resulting deficiencies. The problems presented for determination in cases of this type do not require an expert tribunal for their proper solution. On the contrary, the issues involved resemble those which often appear in the courts. But the individual cases involve very small sums, and though the aggregate alleged to be due to all the workers may be substantial, each man's claim will normally be so small and his confidence in the security of his job so tenuous, that litigation will be out of the question for him. Therefore if the Act is to be enforced at all, official means of investigation and specialized procedure for the collection of numerous small claims must be provided.

The enforcement of the disciplinary provisions of the marine laws presents a problem not of acting for weak claimants in the public interest, but of acting against offenders in the wisest and most effective way possible. Meting out punishment for such offenses as intoxication, disorderly conduct, and the like is, of course, a function capable of execution by any magistrate, and technical complexities are absent. Yet discipline on vessels presents a special problem closely related to a whole scheme of regulation, inspection, and safety of the seas and waters. The relatively insignificant issue of whether a seaman was intoxicated is part of a much larger pattern over which there must be special regulation and to which special attention must be paid, and thus one finds the administrative process utilized to determine issues which elsewhere have been reserved for the judiciary.

It is thus apparent that varied types of subject matters, from rate control of railroad carriers to collection of employees' wages and disciplining of seamen, have been entrusted by Congress to administrative agencies at least in part for similar reasons: in order to assure continuous attention to and clearly allocated responsibility for the effectuation of legislative policies.

7. *The need for organization to dispose of volume of business and to provide the necessary records.*—The volume of cases arising under certain laws is very great. The Veterans' Administration, the Railroad Retirement Board, the Social Security Board, and the United States Employees' Compensation Commission, for example, each adjudicates annually thousands of comparatively small claims. The Veterans' Administration alone makes determinations in about 100,000 cases each year; the Social Security Board, it is estimated, will in the year 1940 have disposed of eight or nine times that number.[6] One need not labor the point that the present judicial structure would scarcely be equipped to handle this multitude of cases.

These same agencies illustrate another and related reason for employing the administrative process. This is the need of specialized staffs and machinery to keep and make available the records upon which judgment must be based. Before an agency such as the Social Security Board can disburse annually millions of dollars to hundreds of thousands of eligible claimants, a vast clerical machinery must be created. Complex records must be kept, classified, and made available. In the Railroad Retirement Board or the Veterans' Administration it may be necessary to call upon medical experts and occupational specialists. In the registration of securities the Securities and Exchange Commission must be organized to collect and collate huge masses of data available for immediate reference by clerks,

[6] The Social Security Administration receives over 2 million applications for old age and survivors benefits a year; in 1957, it assigned 12,737 appeals for hearing. 1956 Dep't of Health, Education and Welfare Ann. Rep. 28; 1957 Dep't of Justice, Office of Administrative Procedure Ann. Rep. 12 —Editor

accountants, analysts, oil and gas experts, engineers and the like. In part, also, the creation of these agencies with their staffs and accumulation of data is due to recognition by Congress that time is essential in the conduct of many business affairs. In the flotation of securities or the publication of a schedule of rates, it is important that procedures and staffs be available to investigate speedily the propriety of the proposed transaction, at least to the extent of suspending it for further study in formal procedure if serious question of public injury is raised.

C. *Some Characteristics of Administrative Agencies*

Certain characteristics of administrative agencies are of such fundamental importance in relation to the problems of their organization and procedure as to require specially emphatic statement.

1. *Size.*—Most administrative agencies are, of necessity, large organizations. For example, the Interstate Commerce Commission has a personnel of more than 2,500; the Securities and Exchange Commission, more than 1,200; the Social Security Board has some 9,000 employees in its Bureau of Old-Age and Survivors Insurance alone; the National Labor Relations Board and the Federal Power Commission each has a staff of more than 800; the Federal Communications Commission, more than 600; the Railroad Retirement Board, more than 2,500; and the Veterans' Administration, more than 36,000, of whom nearly 2,000 are engaged in adjudicating claims of various sorts.

The size of these staffs reflects both the nation-wide jurisdiction of the agencies and the character of the work they are called upon to perform. Each is charged by Congress with the work of continuing supervision of some field of activity throughout all the forty-eight States. . . .

2. *Specialization.*—Administrative agencies specialize in particular tasks and they include specialists on their staffs. The staffs may become such either by experience in the specialized work of the agency or by prior technical or professional training. In many cases a principal reason for establishing an agency has been the need to bring to bear upon particular problems technical or professional skills. A public health agency, for example, must be staffed with people who understand diseases, the Federal Communications Commission with technicans who comprehend the engineering and economic aspects of telegraph, telephone, and radio. In other instances recurring experience with the work of the agency, or with a particular phase of its work may develop specialists—such as are found, for instance, in the Veterans' Administration—who have an insight and judgment which a beginner would lack. In either event a central problem of organization is how best to utilize these skills of training and experience. This does not mean that the heads of the agencies should necessarily be specialists. The problem is rather how to bring into play the technical resources of the agency staff so as to reduce the ultimate points of contention, if such there be, to such compass and form that they can be presented upon an understandable record for decision by the heads of the agency and for review by the courts.

Specialization has further consequences in procedure. Because the members of an agency or of its staff—like persons of similar experience in private affairs—approach problems of administration with a considerable background of knowledge and experience and with the equipment for investigation, they can accomplish much of the work of the agency without the necessity of informing themselves by the testimonial process. It is in part for this reason that so many questions . . . can be disposed of by informal methods with the consent of the private interests involved. Only when differences do not yield to adjustment or when other considerations . . . make formal proceedings desirable need there be resort to the procedures of formal testimony, more familiar in judicial and legislative processes. Even if there is formal procedure, the characteristics of specialization may, . . . have an impact upon procedures for formal adjudication.

The same effects are felt in the procedures antecedent to rule-making. Here again the function of the formal hearing, in many instances, differs from its function in legislative and judicial methods. In the latter it is the instrument for gathering information. In many administrative rule-making situations, . . . the information may be and is obtained by direct investigation and the hearing is most useful as a method of subjecting it to the criticism of private interests affected and of obtaining the views of these interests upon the desirability of various methods of achieving all or some of the objects sought.

3. *Responsibility for results.*—An administrative agency is usually charged by Congress with accomplishing or attempting to accomplish some end specified in the statute. It may be to see that benefits of some sort are received by persons with whom the agency deals, or that transportation systems or communications systems, or various other business activities are conducted either so as to comply with certain negative requirements or so as to achieve positive results. Taken together, the various Federal administrative agencies have the responsibility for making good to the people of the country a major part of the gains of a hundred and fifty years of democratic government. This means that the agencies cannot take a wholly passive attitude toward the issues which come before them. Out of this fact flow perhaps the most difficult of the problems relating to the administrative process. Administrative agencies constitute a large measure of the motive power of Government; a problem of motive power is a problem also of brakes; but the necessity of both must be faced frankly when either is in question.

4. *Variety of administrative duties.*—No single fact is more striking in a review of existing Federal administrative agences than the variety of the duties which are entrusted to them to perform. This is true of many single agencies taken alone; it is true, above all, of the agencies taken as a group. This central and inescapable fact makes generalization in description difficult. It makes even more difficult generalization in prescription. For variety in functions means variety in the circumstances and conditions under which the activities of the various agencies impinge upon private individuals. A procedure which would be for the protection of the individual in one situation may be clearly to his injury in another. A set of standards evolved to meet one problem may fail wholly to meet another. One need look no further than a single agency—the Interstate Commerce Commission —to be impressed by the basic necessity of differing procedures for different types

of activities, and by the varying procedural patterns which the Commission has evolved to meet this necessity. . . .

Hurst, *THE GROWTH OF AMERICAN LAW*
379-380, 421-431 (1950)

The common use of words implied much of the history of executive power in the United States. What did people mean, when they talked about "the executive"?

(1) Certainly the executive was the President. In the states the executive was the governor; on this point common usage might be less emphatic, but it was no less sure. Ordinary meaning associated executive power with the idea of a chief executive.

(2) Thanks to Alexander Hamilton people early began to regard the Cabinet and the departments it represented as part of "the executive." In common expression the governor did not have a cabinet; and popular notions were hazy as to just who besides the governor made up the executive branch of state government.

(3) Even in the simple days before 1870 there were many people other than the handful named so far, whose business was to execute the law. Consider only local government: the police, the coroner, the public prosecutor, the town, city, and county clerks, the tax assessors, the village presidents and the city mayors; in a later day, the boards of tax assessment, the police and fire commissioners, the boards of zoning appeals, the boards of health, city managers. If pressed, common usage might concede that these officers wielded executive power. But it was a concession to schoolmaster's logic; everyday meaning did not feel that it jibed with the facts as everyday imagination saw them.

(4) In the twentieth century, common usage haltingly learned the term "administrative." As late as 1950 the word was ordinarily an adjective only; people did not easily refer to "the administrative" as they did to "the executive." They associated this new thing with the executive branch; they did not talk of "administrative" proceedings as a part of legislative or judical action. To this extent people had given the new phenomenon a location. But they had trouble in identifying what they were talking about. Hence they used "administrative" more readily to describe a quality of action than a distinct institution.

In all these respects, common usage fell short of describing reality, but nonetheless responded to some of its main currents.

(1) Measured by functions performed, the state executive branch as a whole overshadowed the governor, and the federal executive branch was at least of equal weight with the President. Yet the increasing importance of policy leadership steadily pushed the chief executive into higher responsibility and command.

(2) The Cabinet rarely had the coherence that the name implied, and the department heads' common responsibility to advise the President produced little co-ordination of policy among the departments. On the other hand, common usage was wholly correct in the distinction it drew between the national and the state governments. If there was a minimum of co-ordination of executive policy in the

national government, there was almost no centralized executive program in the states.

(3) People were ordinarily engrossed in the drama of Presidents and Cabinet members. But the law made itself felt in everyday living mainly through policemen, clerks, inspectors, and licensing officers. However, the common attitude pointed to two important realities. We so diffused the responsibility for executing the law that it was not easy to think of all law-enforcing officers as agents of a common task. And we allowed this to happen because usually we were not much interested in law enforcement.

(4) There is a temptation to talk about the growth of the administrative process as a separate development. In such great agencies as the Interstate Commerce Commission or the state industrial commissions, "the administrative" tended to become a distinct branch of government. Yet this was largely by accident—another reflection of our characteristic diffusion of responsibility and indifference toward implementing policy. A leading characteristic of the administrative process was its merger of legislative (policy-making), executive (policy-applying), and judicial (policy-determining) jobs in one agency. However, this equally marked the work of chief executives and heads of departments. There was much sense in the reluctance of common usage to treat "administrative" as a noun; the reality was much more that certain qualities or techniques of operation came to mark all major executive action. Separate discussion of "executive" and "administrative" agencies involves so much duplication as to point the moral. They were both aspects of a common task. We shall use the terms "executive" and "administrative" interchangeably to describe officers in the executive branch subordinate to the chief executive. . . .

[Professor Hurst then discusses the various tasks the executive has been called upon to perform in (1) carrying out "legislative and judge-made policy" for the regulation of people's affairs and the furnishing of services to the people and (2) promoting legislation. In the following excerpts, Hurst attempts "to mark certain features of structure which, in combination, identified the emphases in organization and technique which characterized 'administrative' agencies."—Editor]

2. *Specialization*. No aspect of structure more sharply distinguished administrative agencies than their specialized areas of action. In contrast, legislators, Presidents, governors, judges must deal with any questions of public policy that could be stated in terms of their procedures. By inheritance this was not only their right but also their duty.

Different reasons led to the creation of specialized agencies. In some fields there was a high premium on expertness. The expertness might derive from professional knowledge, or it might derive from the administrative job itself through the administrator's opportunity for concentrated, continuous experience in one area. . . .

Partisans of the administrative process were apt to overwork the explanation in terms of expertness. Much administrative work required specialized attention less because of its technical difficulty than because of its sheer bulk. . . .

The need for the expert and the need for specialized handling of vast detail were woven together in the creation of some of the most important administrative agencies. This was true of state public utility commissions, of the Interstate Commerce Commission, the Bureau of Marine Inspection and Navigation, the Patent Office, the Federal Communications Commission, the Federal Power Commission. It was true, also, in the administration of tax laws, workmen's compensation, and conservation policy. This combination of factors was implied in the "single generalization" which Louis L. Jaffe suggested could encompass the grounds of all delegated legislative power:

> Power should be delegated where there is agreement that a task must be performed and it cannot be effectively performed by the legislature without the assistance of a delegate or without an expenditure of time so great as to lead to the neglect of equally important business. [Jaffe, Essay on Delegation of Legislative Power, 47 Col. L. Rev. 359, 361 (1947)].

However, there were other reasons for administrative specialization. One related to policy planning. In the scanty legislative debates on administrative organization there stood out the persistent hope that administrative agencies might help the legislature construct long-range programs in their special areas of public interest.

Another reason touched the most controversial motive behind the resort to specialized enforcement of policy: the hope that from concentration of responsibility and energy, from the shaping of a single-purpose agency in the same heat in which was forged the policy of its governing statute, would come partisan zeal in implementing the statutory policy. This hope marked the creation of the early public utility commissions in the state; it was part of the history of the Interstate Commerce Commission, the Federal Trade Commission, the Securities and Exchange Commission, the National Labor Relations Board.

In this thinking there was a measure of naivete that carried the promise of disillusionment. An agency which specialized in the regulation of one industry, and through the sweep of its regulation entered into the industry's management decisions, was apt to learn a partner's rather than a prosecutor's attitude toward the industry's problems. An agency which specialized in problems that cut across many industries was not likely to run this course. But its more abstract specialization might lead it to fall prisoner to its own origins and precedents, robbed of imagination and initiative. Specialization did not guarantee long-lived vigor.

3. *Independence. a. Administrators and the Constitution.* In rare cases state constitution makers made an administrative body independent even of the legislature, when they established the administrative agency by constitutional fiat. Some state constitutions thus created commissions to regulate public utilities. The men who did this feared that they would lose power in the future, and that a legislature newly dominated by "the interests" would abolish or emasculate an agency which had only statutory authority. . . .

Experience indicated that administrative agencies, as such, had no special need of constitutional protection. In the absence of constitutional barriers, legislatures sometimes abolished offices. This might happen when changes in substantive policy made the offices no longer necessary. It happened in course of administrative reorganizations. Illegitimately, legislatures sometimes abolished an office as it existed under one title only to set it up again under a new name, to put jobs at the disposal of the dominant party. None of this had anything to do with the administrative process as such. No important administrative agency seems ever to have been destroyed because of objections to its distinctive characteristics as an administrative agency.

b. Administrators and the Legislature. Since the structure of administrative agencies was usually fixed by statute, it was the legislature in both the federal and state governments that ordinarily exercised basic control over administration. This was true at least until the 1920's. Then it began to be common for the chief executive to take the lead in administrative reorganization, under delegation from the legislature.

Once it was established, a major administrative agency enjoyed a large margin of freedom from legislative control. Top administrators were usually in office for more years than the average legislator. Legislators' and administrators' years of service overlapped, so that the legislature never confronted a wholly new array of administrators with whom it might make a fresh beginning. Administrative staffs gained experience and expertness in their fields which the average legislator could not match. Legislative committees generally lacked the knowledge, the time, or the staff to exercise any broad or thorough scrutiny of administrative activity. In fields like taxation administrators dealt with problems inherently so complicated as to guaranty the administrators practical freedom from any detailed legislative oversight.

In an unplanned way the appropriations committees grew to exercise the legislature's most regular and detailed check on administration.* The recurring hearings on the budget gave committeemen a strategic opportunity to question the administrators. Questions were often sharp and pointed, if haphazard and ill-balanced. So far as it went, this kind of legislative scrutiny made sense. It left general policy to the legislative committees assigned to deal with the major fields of public interest; on questions of general policy, these committees could ask the advice of informed administrators. On the other hand, the appropriations committees— concerned with concrete details of the budget—were logical agents to inquire into specific items of executive action.

Because it controlled the purse, the legislature inevitably had the residual power to question how policy was carried out. However, it was poorly suited to regular surveillance of the details of execution. As Robert Luce pointed out, legislators were not chosen for administrative capacity or experience. The range of problems that pressed on their attention did not give them time for details. They had ties to local constituencies and to party, and they must constantly be alert to the political battle; local, partisan, and personal aims were likely to impair their capacity to exercise objective supervision of an often intricate, technical pattern of administration. The most constructive development in the relation of legislator and administrator was the tendency toward the policy-making partnership that was

* See Macmahon, Congressional Oversight of Administration: The Power of the Purse, 58 Pol. Sci. Q. 161, 380 (1943)—Editor

effected through the interplay of statute, legislative committee, and administrative rule or order.

c. Administrators and the Chief Executive. In no respect was the twentieth century administrative agency more strikingly independent than in its relations to the chief executive. The chief executive appointed top administrators, but usually subject to the advice and consent of one of the chambers of the legislature. The statutes usually fixed the term of important administrators, and set it at a number of years greater than a single executive term of office. The laws often further hedged in the chief executive's choice by requiring that several-member commissions be bipartisan. In practice—and in law so far as Humphrey's Executor v. United States made it so—the chief executive could remove top administrators only for specified cause amounting to malfeasance. . . . Civil service rules further withdrew control of agency personnel from the chief executive. . . .

[Earlier Professor Hurst explained that in 1926, in Myers v. United States, 272 U.S. 52, the Supreme Court held that the postmaster general's removal, by direction of the President, of a first-class postmaster was valid, and that the statutory provision limiting the President's removal power by setting a term of office for first-, second-, and third-class postmasters and adding that these officers might be removed only with the advice and consent of the Senate, was unconstitutional because it violated the separation of powers. The Court announced that under Article II of the Constitution, the President could remove any "executive officers of the United States appointed by him," and that Congress could in no way limit this removal power. In the Humphrey case [Rathbun (Humphrey's executor) v. United States], 295 U.S. 602 (1935), the Supreme Court repudiated the broad dicta of the Myers opinion and held that the President could not remove a member of the Federal Trade Commission within the commissioner's statutory term of office for reasons not within those enumerated by statute as cause for removal. "The Federal Trade Commission," explained the Court, "is an administrative body created by Congress to carry into effect legislative policies embodied in the statute in accordance with the legislative standard therein prescribed, and to perform other specified duties as a legislative or as a judicial aid. Such a body cannot in any proper sense be characterized as an arm or an eye of the executive. Its duties are performed without executive leave and, in the contemplation of the statute, must be free from executive control."

[Most recently, the Supreme Court held that the President did not have the inherent power to remove a member of the War Claims Commission, even though the statute creating the Commission made no provision for the removal of a Commissioner. The Commission was established to adjudicate claims for compensation by civilian internees, prisoners of war and religious organizations who suffered personal injury or property damage at the hands of the enemy during World War II. President Eisenhower based his removal of the Truman-appointed commissioner on his desire to have "personnel of my own selection" on the Commission. The Court concluded that the task Congress set the Commission was of an "intrinsic judicial character" to be carried out free from executive control or influence. Therefore, the statute could not be construed impliedly to confer upon the President the power of removal he sought to exercise in this case. Wiener v. United States, 357 U.S. 349 (1958).

[The nature of the restriction upon presidential power imposed by the Humphrey and Wiener cases must be evaluated in the light of the fact that neither case prevents the President from filing charges of inefficiency or neglect of duty against a member of a commission or board entitled to the protection of these cases and, after a hearing, removing him. The courts are not likely to review the President's removal action to determine whether the charges against the member removed were, in fact, proved. See Cushman, The Constitutional Status of the Independent Regulatory Commissions, 24 Corn. L.Q. 163, 185 (1939). See too, Raffel, Presidential Removal Power: The Role of the Supreme Court, 13 U. Miami L. Rev. 69 (1958); Dawley, The Governors' Constitutional Powers of Appointment and Removal, 22 Minn. L. Rev. 451 (1938).—Editor]

After 1920, first in the federal government and later in the states the chief executive asserted a little more control of administrative policies and operating standards. The executive budget was the most effective instrument of this control. This required prior clearance by the chief executive for all requests for funds made to the legislature. During the administration of Franklin Roosevelt the Budget Bureau set up a Division of Legislative Reference whose function was to scrutinize legislative proposals made by departments and agencies to insure their consistency with the President's program. Committees of Congress on their own motion began to refuse to consider proposals that the Budget Bureau had not cleared. These tardily developed clearance procedures emphasized that full co-ordination of executive policy waited upon the provision of adequate staff facilities for the chief executive.

d. Administrators and the Courts. Lawyers, students, and publicists tended to give a disproportionate share of attention to the relations between administrative agencies and the courts. This was especially so in the generation of controversy that began about 1910 when the economy first felt the full new sweep of administrative regulation. For years after courses in "administrative law" first appeared in law school catalogs, they dealt almost exclusively with judicial review of administrative action. To case-trained lawyers judicial review had the attraction of a familiar landmark in new territory. To the pamphleteer it had the attraction of permitting him to import classic political concepts and bywords into novel controversies.

Of course, judicial review had deep roots in our legal tradition. The common law said that any private individual could hold liable in tort an official who abused public power to his damage. It had its classic, if narrowly circumscribed, writs by which to check on official arrogance—quo warranto, mandamus, certiorari. To the common law inheritance the United States added its peculiar stress on rights under written constitutions, declared and enforced by judges.

Actually, however, administrators disposed of the vast bulk of matters before them without contest. Of the minor percentage of contested matters, only a few went on to court review. Moreover, at most the courts did only the negative job of curbing abuse of power. They had neither the authority nor the equipment to superintend in any positive way the effectiveness with which the administrator did his work.

After 1850, in the first reaction against the pinch of expanded regulation, the courts used their reviewing power so broadly as to invade the proper sphere of the executive. The 1890's marked the high point of this judicial overreaching. Thereafter federal and state courts alike, of their own invention, imposed on themselves doctrines to restrain the substitution of judicial for executive discretion. That the courts were impelled to do this was perhaps the best evidence of how far the administrative process responded to urgent needs of modern government. Legislatures began to be more explicit in delegating freedom of choice to the executive, and in defining limits of judicial review. However, this legislation was guided by little formulated principle, and was usually vague enough to leave ample room for judicial invention.

Thus it was primarily judge-made law that fixed the basic doctrines affecting judicial review of administrative action. Three rules particularly concerned review of administrative adjudication. Only a person with defined legal standing, a clearcut interest in law and in fact in the matter contested, might attack administrative action. Courts generally . . . limited their review to deciding whether the administrators had substantial record evidence to support what they decided.

Where administrative legislation was drawn in question, the courts grew even more reluctant to disturb what the administrators had done. . . . The judges said . . . that a presumption of constitutionality like that which surrounded a statute also protected administrative legislation. If the challenge was not that the regulation was unconstitutional, but rather that it exceeded the power the legislature meant to delegate, still the courts usually gave the regulation the benefit of a presumption that it fell within the delegated authority.

The irony of politics dictated that just when administrative-judicial relations were achieving a workable pattern, demand should arise that legislatures enact codes of procedure for administrators, and that these codes should redefine the scope of judicial review. This pressure came out of the tensions that attended expansion of the government's role in the depression of the 1930's. The debaters talked of procedural reform. However, they lined up pretty much according to how they felt about the substantive merits of the policies that were being enforced by the agencies whose procedure was particularly in question.

The leading contest centered on federal legislation. Seven years of mounting controversy culminated in December, 1940, when President Roosevelt vetoed the Walter-Logan Bill. As a countermove, and to relieve the pressure to do something, the President appointed the Attorney General's Committee on Administrative Procedure. In 1941 a majority of that Committee recommended against any sweeping legislation. The war then shelved the matter. Renewed attention to the issue finally brought the federal Administrative Procedure Act of 1946. In the meantime North Dakota (1941) and Ohio and Wisconsin (1943) enacted administrative procedure codes of varying scope.

So far as judicial review was concerned, different people read the new laws to forecast quite different results. Some saw in the statutes mere declarations of previous judicial doctrine. Others saw an expansion of the scope of judicial review, particularly over the fact-finding aspect of administrative adjudication. How far the courts would take the legislation as warrant for opening a new chapter in their relations to the administrators remained to be seen.

4. *Merger of Functions.* The federal Administrative Procedure Act of 1946 dealt more with the internal structure and procedures of agencies than it did with judicial review of their actions. The fact was prophetic. The administrative process had apparently grown beyond the stages in which men were content to discuss it in terms of separation-of-powers doctrine and the scope of judicial review. At last they were prepared to give their attention to administrative organization itself and not just to its relations to other institutions of government. This development brought under examination what we noted as the third characteristic of administrative structure—the merger of legislative, executive, and judicial functions.

Attention to administrative structure was tardy and was at first moved more by desire to find political ammunition than to find facts. It was not surprising that there was little objective evidence accumulated by which to weigh even elementary problems. Nor was it surprising that emphasis was misplaced in defining the significant issues.

The choice between the single-member and the several-member agency was an example of an elementary problem on which evidence was lacking. In the early twentieth century the several-member commission became the model for the rapidly expanding administrative process. The precedent was set partly by the Interstate Commerce Commission, as the first great new federal agency; it was set partly by the successful Wisconsin Industrial Commission of 1911. Later opinion varied regarding the merits of the several-member commission. The consensus favored it for administrative legislation, but criticized it from an executive standpoint, as liable to internal division, inertia, and delay.

Wisconsin demonstrated experiments in administrative organization. Despite the early favorable precedent, it did not adhere rigidly to the several-member commission. By 1940 Wisconsin was employing (1) a single commissioner for insurance regulation, (2) a part-time commission with a full-time director for its Conservation Commission, its Board of Health, and its Department of Agriculture and Markets, (4) a full-time commission, with no separate administrative officer, for its Banking Commission, its Grain and Warehouse Commission, and its Labor Relations Board, and (5) a full-time commission with full-time executive officers for its Public Service Commission and its Industrial Commission.

In 1937 the President's Committee on Administrative Management recommended that all administrative functions except those of judicial type be assigned to the departments; the independent regulatory commissions would keep only the business of administrative adjudication. The recommendation was evidence that the question of the constitution of top administrative authority had become entangled with the thorny question of the separation of powers within agencies. The provision of separate executive officers in some Wisconsin agencies reflected the same mingling of problems, without the dogmatic sort of solution suggested by the President's Committee.

Demands for sharp separation of functions within agencies provided the outstanding example of misplaced emphasis in discussion of administrative structure. The demands usually boiled down, in particular, to insistence that agencies should not be both "prosecutor" and "judge." Critics sought moral weight for their plea by invoking the maxim that no man should be judge in his own case. Out of such thinking came the concrete suggestion that a staff wholly distinct from those who heard and decided questions of the application of law should do the inspecting and investigating, the bringing of charges, and the preparation and presentation of cases. . . .

The demand for a formal separation of administrative jobs ignored trends in practice which worked to the same ends, but in a fashion moulded and tested by experience. In natural response to a great volume of business, the larger administrative agencies developed a considerable division of labor within their organizations. The men who heard and decided contested matters were generally not in fact the same men who made inspections or investigations, who filed charges, or prepared cases for argument. Of course, in smaller agencies, typically in many state administrative offices, the volume of business did not warrant elaborate division of labor. . . .

How unreal was much of the argument for separation of the jobs of "prosecutor" and "judge" within administrative agencies was attested by a fact as familiar in the routine of a local prosecutor's office as in the operation of a major agency. The overwhelming bulk of questions that arose in the application of any law were inevitably disposed of by executive discretion. This was true whatever might be the formal divisions of functions for disposing of contested matters. Someone had to take the responsibility of deciding in countless instances whether to investigate or not to investigate, to file charges or to drop the matter, to withdraw or dismiss charges or to let them go to hearing, to negotiate an adjustment or to fight for the letter of the law. Such decisions were necessary incidents of carrying out legal policy. They made up most of the work of any administrative agency. In them there could be no division between executive and adjudicative functions.

5. *Judicial Analogies.* Demands that some administrators put on the judge's robe contrasted ironically with tendencies in the courts toward administrative organization and procedure.

The working partnership between public prosecutor and trial judge was a fact that experienced lawyers took for granted in many a court. It was the judiciary's oldest, continuing analogy to the administrative merger of functions. The reality of the partnership was reflected in the early-nineteenth-century insistence on the autonomy of the jury; the jury was the accused's reliance against an otherwise solid front of officialdom.

The pressures that produced the growth of the administrative process also affected the operation of the courts. The first impact was on policy making. The nineteenth-century judges had learned confidence in policy making out of the experience of building common law on the grand scale. When change speeded up in the 1870's, it was natural that the courts first ventured into closer participation in executive responsibility by assuming more burdens of general policy. Sometimes claiming authority by statute, sometimes building from common law, they made ill-advised efforts to engage in administrative regulation. Through the clumsy forms of lawsuits courts tried to regulate rates and services of public utilities. In actions to abate nuisances they did some limited and ex post facto land-use planning. On occasion they used mandamus to supervise collection of local taxes to pay arrears of interest on public bonds. They gave ready ear to taxpayers' suits to prevent alleged waste of public funds. They lent the prestige of the bench to the conduct of railroads by insiders who operated in the name of a receiver in equity. They were not reluctant to substitute their own weighing of evidence or policy for the judgment of administrators whose action was challenged by suit.

The courts did not have the investigative machinery, the time or specialized knowledge, the philosophy or the range of sanctions, to compete long with the executive in policy making. Their policy-making activity declined after 1900 as the legislature created new administrative agencies and added new duties and powers to older executive offices. . . .

Independence was a character which the courts inherited from their own particular history, with no borrowing from the rise of the administrative process. Specialization of function was a different matter. Through most of the nineteenth century, courts in the United States either held general jurisdiction, or at least jurisdiction over a considerable variety of matters. But the federal government developed its Court of Claims, its Court of Customs and Patent Appeals, its Tax Court, and its short-lived Commerce Court. The twentieth century produced state courts specially set up to handle small claims, domestic relations, traffic offenses, juvenile delinquents, and female offenders. Did these specialized courts represent any common principle, borrowed perhaps from administrative analogies? . . .

Not only in the immediate work of judges, but also in their dependence on new kinds of auxiliary officers, judicial developments raised questions of the force of administrative example. Tardily, and in limited measure, the courts began to use administrative assistance to check how effectively legal policy was executed in certain fields. . . .

Both legislatures and courts were slower to experiment with new machinery for disposition of criminal as compared to civil matters. There was little attention to the fixing of sentence, after the accused had been convicted. The trial judge determined sentence almost entirely at his discretion, according to his own philosophy, within such meager framework as the statutes might set. Once sentence was passed, the court's concern ended. This was the typical situation during most of the nineteenth century. From small beginnings at the end of the century there gradually developed a considerable administrative apparatus that affected the fixing and executing of sentence. In form the judge supervised, or was merely advised by, the administrative officers. In operation the administrators began to overshadow the court. They did so to an extent which suggested that sentence might finally

become an entirely separate administrative function, in the hands of special investigators, psychiatrists, probation and parole officers, and vocational and personal
affairs advisers, responsible to some central board. Trends in juvenile court administration pointed this way.

We need only recall here the . . . administrative assistance which legislatures
began to attach to some of the specialized state courts. Some domestic relations
courts had the help of staff social workers and doctors, as well as providing special
clerks to check compliance with decrees involving the payment of money. The
clerk of the small claims court helped suitors prepare cases, and sometimes staff
was provided to administer a financial settlement over a period of time between
debtor and creditors. In line with such developments, legal aid organizations tended
to integrate their work with that of other social agencies that dealt with problems
of the poor.

In some areas of twentieth-century economic regulation, Congress sought to
bring special administrative competence to the help of the courts. Thus it provided
that the federal courts might ask the help of the Federal Trade Commission in
preparing antitrust decrees. That this procedure was almost never used did not
disprove its inherent usefulness; the Commission failed to develop strength, and
during most of the years under the Sherman Act neither the Department of Justice
nor the courts showed energy or imagination in using the full range of means to
implement the antitrust laws. More significant was Congress's requirement that
the courts refer financial reorganization plans of distressed railroads or other corporations to the consideration of the Interstate Commerce Commission, or the
Securities and Exchange Commission, respectively. The judge could refuse to follow
the administrators' advice, but Congress required that he have that advice before
he took final action.

As a matter of judicial practice, courts began to recognize that they should
sometimes hear an administrative agency on a matter that came to court in the
first instance simply as a controversy between private parties. Where the private
suit involved laws with whose execution the administrator was charged, he might
ask to be heard as a friend of the court, or even as an intervening party; thus he
would have a voice in a matter contributing to shape the interpretation of the
policy with which he was concerned. On its own initiative, a court occasionally
asked administrators to participate in a private suit where public policy was in
issue. These various instances followed no plan and had limited effect. Even so,
they were one more way in which judicial administration drew closer to executive
practice. . . .

WISCONSIN MUTUAL LIABILITY COMPANY v. INDUSTRIAL COMMISSION
202 Wis. 428, 232 N.W. 885 (1930)

* * *

Appeal from a judgment of the circuit court for Dane county: August C. Hoppmann, Circuit Judge. Affirmed.

Action commenced May 2, 1929; judgment for defendants entered February 14, 1930. Plaintiffs appeal.

For the appellants there was a brief by Roehr & Steinmetz, attorneys, and C. J. Otjen of counsel, and oral argument by Ida E. Luick and Mr. Otjen, all of Milwaukee.

For the respondent Industrial Commission there was a brief by the Attorney General and Mortimer Levitan, assistant attorney general, and oral argument by Mr. Levitan.

FOWLER, J. The action was brought by an employer and its insurer to vacate an award made to the widow of an employee by the Industrial Commission under the workmen's compensation act. The employee, Gervase Hannon, was in the employ of a circus organization. The circus was about to move from Manitowoc. Its equipment was dismantled and loaded on wagons. Tractors were pulling the wagons to the railroad for loading on flat cars. A tractor ran over Hannon and killed him.

Two claims are made by appellants: (1) Hannon was not performing any service at the time of the accident. (2) A settlement entered into bars recovery in excess of the amount stipulated, which was less than the amount of the award.

(1) Hannon's duty was to load equipment on a wagon, see that the wagon was taken to the train, and stay with the wagon until it was loaded on the train. He was seen beside his wagon shortly before he was run over, waiting for it to be taken. He had probably lain down near it and gone to sleep and was run over while so lying. It seems plain enough that Hannon was on duty when injured, and if he was on duty he was performing service incidental to his employment. Under such circumstances "he also serves who only waits."

(2) On November 23, 1927, the widow, the show company, and its insurer entered into a stipulation for settlement. It provided that by way of settlement the second parties offer and the first party agrees to accept $1,650 in full payment and discharge, and states that all parties request the Industrial Commission to affirm the settlement and make an award thereon. Payment was not made pursuant to the stipulation. The stipulation was received by the commission shortly after December 1st. The commission on January 30, 1928, wrote the insurer that they wanted further information before acting on the stipulation, and on July 30th wrote that on their present information they could not approve the award. They made further investigation, however, and on February 23, 1929, the chairman of the commission wrote the insurer that "on Saturday last the commission gave consideration to the proposed compromise and unanimously agreed that it should not be affirmed," and citations for hearing to conclude the proceedings were thereupon issued. The insurer objected to further proceedings because of failure of the commission to approve or reject the compromise within one year from its receipt.

Sec. 102.16, Stats., provides that compromises "shall be subject to be reviewed by, and set aside, modified or confirmed by the commission within one year from the date such compromise is filed with the commission, or from the date an award has been entered, based thereon."

The appellants in support of their contention rely on this statute and the decision in Nowiny Pub. Co. v. Kappl, 187 Wis. 30, 203 N.W. 740. . . .

It is considered that the stipulation here involved is distinguishable. The parties did not treat it as an absolute settlement. They did not make and accept payment in accordance with it. They requested the commission to "affirm the settlement." These two things indicate that it was not intended as a settlement unless the commission should approve it; that it would become effective only in such case; in other words, that it was a conditional rather than an absolute settlement. The letter of July 30th above referred to clearly indicated that the commission had considered and taken action on the stipulation and that they did not "affirm" it and would not do so unless they received further information to cause a change of mind and reversal of action. We are of opinion that this was in effect a "review" and a "setting aside" of the stipulation within the meaning of the statute. Actions of the commission should be liberally construed to bring them within the purview of the statute and as effecting its purpose. The commission's action, "though somewhat informal in manner, was nevertheless action by" the commission. Hotel Martin Co. v. Industrial Comm., 182 Wis. 79, 84, 195 N.W. 865.

By the Court.—The judgment is affirmed.

EDITORIAL NOTE: PROCEDURE OF THE INDUSTRIAL COMMISSION IN THE HANNON CASE

[1. The following detailed account of the various steps that made up the proceeding in the above case is taken, largely verbatim, from the written opinion of the Industrial Commission.]

One Gervase Hannon, an employee of an itinerant carnival was run over and killed by one of its trucks in August, 1927. The commission first heard of the matter through a letter from the widow residing in Detroit, Michigan, inquiring about compensation. The commission immediately took up the case by telegraphing the employer at its headquarters in Montgomery, Alabama, asking for a report in the matter. Before information was received from this source, however, the insurance carrier, Wisconsin Mutual Liability Company, had seen the widow, Selma Hannon, at her home in Detroit. A stipulation and agreement, dated November 23, 1927, was entered into by her and the Rubin and Cherry Shows, Incorporated and the Wisconsin Mutual Liability Company and was filed with the Industrial Commission the early part of December, 1927.

This stipulation and agreement sets forth that a dispute exists as to whether the deceased employee was living with his wife at the time of the accident and whether he was performing service growing out of and incidental to his employment at the time of the accident; that the employer and insurance carrier agree to pay the sum of $1,650 in full release of all liability under the workmen's compensation act on account of such accident; that the Industrial Commission is requested to enter an award affirming the settlement. In a letter accompanying the stipulation, the insurance carrier indicated that it did not consider the deceased employee was in the course of his employment at the time of the accident and also stated that "from the information obtained it would appear that some sort of separation took place at the time he (the employee) left."

The commission advised the insurance carrier, under date of January 3, 1928, that it desired to investigate the question of whether or not the wife was in fact dependent. Since its investigation disclosed not the slightest evidence of estrangement, the commission wrote the insurance carrier, under date of January 30, 1928, requesting a detailed statement of the circumstances surrounding the accident. Some correspondence passed between the commission and the insurance carrier, and finally the commission advised the insurance carrier that it would be necessary to take the depositions of eye witnesses before it could properly dispose of the case. Because of the itinerant character of the employer and the rapid turnover in its labor force, much difficulty was experienced, but affidavits were finally obtained from J. Y. Nagata, one of the owners of the ferris wheel upon which the deceased was employed, and Frank J. Edwards, the foreman in charge of such ferris wheel. Copies of these affidavits were furnished the interested parties. The attention of the insurance carrier was called to the fact that both the secretary of Rubin and Cherry Shows, Incorporated, and the signers of these affidavits had indicated that they had previously been interviewed by a representative of the insurance carrier, and the insurance carrier was requested to furnish the commission with copies of any previous statements of these persons, if they were contradictory. The insurance carrier failed to submit any contradictory statements but requested an opportunity to take the testimony of the driver of the tractor which caused the accident. This driver could not be located but the secretary of Rubin and Cherry Shows, Incorporated, submitted a statement of one Charles Mangold, who was present at the time the accident occurred. A copy of this statement was furnished the insurance carrier, and the insurance carrier was again requested to furnish the commission with copies of statements which it had obtained from persons connected with the business of the employer. No reply was received to this letter and a few days later one of the commissioners personally requested copies of such statements but the insurance carrier still failed to submit them. In fact it has never submitted such statements, although it was again requested to do so on October 20, 1928.

On July 30, 1928, the commission wrote the insurance carrier advising that it could not approve of any settlement except for full liability. In reply to this letter the insurance carrier stated that it had located the tractor driver and "before going into this matter further" would like to have the opportunity of presenting his deposition. Thereafter, hearings were held at West Allis, Wisconsin; Reading, Pennsylvania; Detroit, Michigan; and Milwaukee, Wisconsin. At all of these hearings, with the exception of the one at Reading, Pennsylvania, a representative of the insurance carrier was present. A transcript of the testimony taken at Reading and Detroit was furnished the insurance carrier and the entire file submitted to the insurance carrier for examination and rebuttal. At the final hearing held March 19, 1929, the insurance carrier failed to submit any testimony, but filed a written objection to the proceeding, on the grounds that the commission was without jurisdiction inasmuch as more than one year had elapsed since the filing of the Stipulation and Agreement dated November 23, 1927. The position taken by the insurance carrier is that such Stipulation and Agreement is a compromise of a claim for compensation and that the commission has failed to review or to set aside, modify or confirm such compromise within one year from the date it was filed with the commission, as required by Section 102.16. The commission is of the opinion that the objection of the insurance carrier is without merit. The Stipulation and Agreement was not a compromise complete and of itself. It was merely an outline of the respective contentions of the parties and an agreement to settle on certain terms, if affirmed by the Industrial Commission. This view of the commission is supported by the very action of the insurance carrier in having failed to pay the amount, or any portion of the amount, specified in such Stipulation and Agreement. However, even though the Stipulation and Agreement were a compromise in the meaning of Section 102.16, the commission did review such compromise and set it aside within the year, notifying the insurance carrier of its action by letter on July 30, 1928. The commission does not believe that it is essential that such action be expressed in a formal order.

It is therefore necessary to consider this case on its merits. Upon the basis of the record, the commission makes the following Findings of Fact.

[Here followed a recital of the principal facts found by the Commission to be true, and the Award; the text of each will be set forth hereinafter.]

[2. We reproduce below affidavits, correspondence and testimony exactly as set forth in the printed proceedings filed with the Wisconsin Supreme Court at the time of the appeal from the Circuit Court's judgment. (Note: These printed proceedings did not fully reproduce all of the documents in the entire Record, but they listed in the left-hand margin the pages of the Record where the documents could be found).]

20 AFFIDAVIT OF J. Y. NAGATA

21 Copy of said affidavit.

Mr. Nagata was not near the scene of the accident but states that there was a rule requiring an employee such as Gervase Hannon to remain near the wagons until they were placed on flat cars. He attempts to state further that the accident happened on the show grounds and that Hannon was not intoxicated, but, as stated, he was not near the scene of the accident.

22 AFFIDAVIT OF FRANK EDWARDS

Stating in substance that Hannon was watching the ferris wheel; that he was on the fair grounds and that he was not intoxicated. Deponent states that he was not near the scene of the accident.

23 Copy of Edwards's affidavit.

*   *   *

55 COPY OF LETTER OF OCTOBER 8, 1927, FROM COMMISSION TO SELMA HANNON

In this letter the Commission advised the widow that she would be entitled to a death benefit of four times the husband's average annual wage, with a maximum wage of $30 a week.

"His wage is given as $18 per week. We do not know whether he had board and lodging in addition to the cash wage. If he did, then the wage would be taken at a somewhat higher figure than $18 per week.

"On the basis of a weekly wage of $18, the death benefit would be $3,600 and would be payable at the rate of $11.70 per week. The insurance carrier is the Wisconsin Mutual Liability Company of Milwaukee. In a letter from them they indicate doubt as to whether or not your husband was performing service at the time of his accident. However, we think their investigations are likely to indicate liability. . . . If your husband's wages average more than $18 per week, then the annual wage would be taken at a higher figure than $900 and your death benefit would be more than $3,600."

56-74 Correspondence.

75 LETTER OF DECEMBER 1, 1927, FROM WISCONSIN MUTUAL TO INDUSTRIAL COMMISSION

[Date, salutation, reference line]

We have made a further investigation in connection with this case and find our original information as to the cause of this man's death correct.

At the time in question, he was through with his work waiting for the rest of the show to be loaded and the train to move, he lay down next to the road and while sleeping was run over by a tractor. In addition, we find that while he was married to Mrs. Selma Hannon in April, 1926, they lived together until June 20, 1927. At that time, he left Detroit presumably to go West. They did not hear much from him until they were notified of his death. During this time, he did not send her any money towards support, in fact, she was obliged to support herself during this whole period.

From the information obtained, it would appear that some sort of a separation took place at the time he left. This show visited Detroit on Labor Day and the deceased's father as well as the wife were told the same story as to the cause of this accident as we have given above.

We feel confident that the accident did not occur in the course or grow out of his employment and in addition, we are very much in doubt as to whether his wife was living with him within the meaning of the law at the time of the accident. The widow was very anxious to have us make an offer of settlement. She was advised by the deceased's father and brother, who are operating a coal yard in Michigan and are familiar with the Compensation Act, that a settlement should be made. We offered to pay $1,650.00; $650.00 of which to take care of the funeral expenses which would give her $1,000.00. This was very acceptable to her, and we enclose herewith stipulations for your approval on that basis.

Trusting the award will come through in due course, we beg to remain.

[Signature: E. A. Piepenbrink]

* * *

81   LETTER, DECEMBER 17, 1927, SELMA HANNON TO COMMISSION

[Date, salutation]

On account of my own mother's poor health, I have come up here to be with her.

On November 16, Mr. Piepenbrink of the Wisconsin Mutual Liability Co. visited me in Detroit and explained the case of Gervase Hannon vs. The Rubin & Cherry Shows, Inc., and said his company was willing to make a settlement with me or I could take the matter through the court, so I decided on the settlement.

On November 23rd, I received the papers to be signed from their attorneys. I signed these and also had them signed by a notary public and another witness and returned them the same day. Mr. Piepenbrink explained to me that this would have to be taken up with you again and to date I have heard nothing more from them and I have been wondering what has been done in the matter.

*   *   *

83   Letter January 3, 1928, Commission to Wisconsin Mutual stating that the stipulation had been received and that they would like to have a more complete check-up.

84-85   Letter same date from Mr. Wilcox [member of the Commission] to Mr. Altmeyer [also a member] at Cleveland asking him to see the widow and mother of Hannon if he gets to Detroit.

86-88   Correspondence between Mr. Altmeyer and Mrs. Hannon making appointment.

89   Letter, January 24, 1928, Mr. Altmeyer to Mr. Wilcox enclosing copy of report of his interview with the wife and mother of Mr. Hannon.

90   [MR. ALTMEYER'S] REPORT

The following report represents an account of an interview with Mrs. Selma Hannon and Mrs. Nicholas Hannon, wife and mother, respectively, of the deceased Gervase Hannon, at Detroit, Mich., January 17, 1928. Both women answered all questions in the presence of each other. They are intelligent, English speaking, and evidently used to living in comfortable circumstances. The wife exhibited a marriage certificate, showing that she was married to the deceased on April 17, 1926. The given names were set forth as Angeline and Joseph. She stated that these were the correct names, but not the ones by which they were commonly known. The surname of the deceased was given as Hennen, instead of Hannon. The mother stated that this was the correct name, although the family was generally known as Hannon. The wife stated that she had known the deceased seven years before they were married, that they had used the less familiar names, so that when the application for marriage license was published their friends would not recognize the names, and that the parents knew of the marriage within a few hours. Neither the deceased nor the wife had ever been married before nor had any children.

For the first three or four months they occupied some light house-keeping rooms at 1027 (?) Perry Ave., Detroit. They then moved into a furnished apartment at 834 Calumet Ave., Detroit. The deceased went to Texas in September, 1926, to cook in a railway construction gang. From September, 1926, to November, 1926, the wife took a young couple as roomers. The wife then went to live with her husband's parents until he returned from Texas in December, 1926. They continued to stay with his parents until January, 1927, at which time they went back to the furnished apartment at 834 Calumet Ave., Detroit, Mich., where they stayed until the first week in June, 1927. They then rented a room from the wife's sister, who lived at 1382 Butternut St., Detroit, Mich.

The wife had started working again as a stenographer shortly after their marriage for the same employer for whom she had previously worked, the R. & H. Shoe Co., 336 Gratiot Ave., Detroit. She worked there continuously at a wage of $22.00 per week. She states that there was no exact distribution of the household expense. The deceased usually paid the rent and she spent most of her earnings on herself. The deceased was a painter by trade, but worked so irregularly that they saved practically nothing. However, she had $70.00 saved out of her own earnings in July, 1927, at which time the deceased left for Seattle, where an aunt of his lived. The wife gave him the $70.00, and he had altogether about $100.00 when he left.

The deceased wrote at least once a week to both his wife and mother, and each one read the other's letters. They heard from him at Cedar Rapids, Iowa, and Minneapolis, Minn. The mother then advised him not to go any farther because her sister had written that "things were quiet." At that time he joined the Rubin and Cherry Shows, Inc. According to his wife's statement, the deceased sent a five dollar bill to her from La Crosse, Wis. The mother states that at the time she was in Houghton, Mich., but when she returned the wife told her about receiving the money. The itinerary of the show indicates that it was in La Crosse, Wis., on August 1, 1927, and the mother gives July 29, 1927, as the date she went to Houghton, Mich., so the dates check.

The deceased sent a picture of himself, taken at a fair grounds, to his wife the day before the accident. This arrived after she received news of the accident. None of the letters from the deceased have been preserved by either the wife or mother, but the picture of the deceased is still in the possession of the wife and has been enlarged.

The mother states that her son and his wife never quarreled at any time to her knowledge, but on the contrary, appeared very happily married. The wife states that her sister had told her that when the deceased was saying goodbye, he remarked that he "had never seen any couple get along so well as he and Selma did."

*   *   *

93   LETTER, JANUARY 30, 1928, FROM COMMISSION TO WISCONSIN MUTUAL.
[Date, salutation]

We wrote you on January 3 that we were asking Mr. Altmeyer to interview the widow and the mother of the deceased and we are enclosing copy of Mr. Altmeyer's report.

We would like to have some more detailed statement of the circumstances surrounding this accident before we act on the stipulation.

94-95   Letter, February 2, 1928, Wisconsin Mutual to Commission giving information received by said company concerning the accident.

96-143   Correspondence.

144   COPY OF LETTER, JULY 30, 1928, COMMISSION TO WISCONSIN MUTUAL.
[Date, salutation, reference line]

You will recall that the writer discussed this case with you at Milwaukee a week or ten days ago and at that time it was his understanding that you were to send us copies of statements that you have obtained from various persons connected with the show and our file indicates that our secretary also wrote you on July 19th, asking that you send in these statements. However, they have not been received.

Upon the basis of the present record the commission is of the opinion that it cannot approve of any settlement except for full liability. All the information that it has indicates that the deceased was required to be where he was at the time of his injury and was in the course of his employment at the time of such injury. Even though there were no rule or custom that he should be where he was, the commission is of the opinion that he probably would still have been in the course of his employment, since he was associated with the business of his employer for practically the twenty-four hours of the day and the show grounds constituting the premises of the employer presented hazards peculiar to his employment.

We shall appreciate hearing from you at an early date.

[Signature, Voyta Wrabetz, Commissioner]

145-173   Correspondence.

174   LETTER, FEBRUARY 25, 1929, FROM COMMISSION TO WISCONSIN MUTUAL
[Date, salutation, reference line]

On Saturday last the commission gave consideration to the proposed compromise settlement and on the record unanimously agreed that it should not be approved. Mrs. Hannon is uneasy over the delay. Therefore, we would like to proceed as expeditiously as possible to get into the records everything that you and Mrs. Hannon may wish, preliminary to final disposition.

We have directed Mr. Altmeyer to issue a formal citation for hearing at Milwaukee in the near future. We will send the file to our Milwaukee office tonight by Mr. Kittleson, so that you may have opportunity to examine it and advise as to what, if any, of the letters and documents you desire copies of for rebuttal or other purpose.

[Signature, F. M. Wilcox]

175   Copy of letter Commission to Selma Hannon, enclosing copy of above letter and stating that it is not willing to enter an award on the compromise agreement.

* * *

180   DEPOSITION OF CHARLES MANGOLD TAKEN BY MR. WILCOX AT READING,
PENNSYLVANIA, SEPTEMBER 10, 1928

CHARLES MANGOLD, states in substance:

181   I have been working for Rubin & Cherry Shows since 1918. I knew Gervase
Hannon since he went on the show. I was in Manitowoc the night he was killed;
I was near him at the time he was killed, about fifty feet away. I signed the
deposition Mr. Reed took and that was true. All the riding device wagons went to
Belvidere, Illinois, and they pulled all the wagons down to the back of the Fair
Grounds like they do here. I happened to be down there and Hannon came down
with his wagon, the wagon he was supposed to take to the train. I went up to him
in a joking way and said: "Have you a bottle with you?" He said: "No, I wish
I did have." We were both tired out for want of sleep. Then I walked away from
the boy and went to the back of the grounds and was leaning up against a small
ticket office; that was about fifty feet away from Hannon; then I looked over and
saw the tractor and he hollered: "Oh, my God." Then I ran back and told the
tractor man he was on top of a man. He said: "What do you mean?" I said:
"Back off him quick." Then he backed off and there was Hannon, his whole right
side was open and his intestines and stomach were coming out of his right side. He
asked for a drink of water and nobody had a drink of water, but I think the man
who came down to the tractor gave him a bottle and I think there was some
whiskey in it. He only took one swallow but he should have had a gallon on account of the awful condition he was in. When he asked for a drink, he asked one
of the men whether he would live and he said: "I won't die; I am going to fight it
through." The fellow who gave him the whiskey asked his name and he spelled
his name and told where he lived. Then the ambulance came and took him to the
hospital and when they took him away he said: "Get a gun and shoot me." He was
in such agony. He was lying inside the Fair Grounds when I saw him but near
the road. He was on duty at the time. He was required to stay with the wagon. I
could not tell how he got run over; he must have sat down and must have gone to
sleep. Ten or fifteen minutes at the most elapsed from the time I left him. This
was between three and four o'clock in the morning and we had been up all day
Saturday working all day until twelve o'clock and several days before that. I heard
nothing about people being discharged that day on the grounds of drunkenness. I
am sure he was not drinking outside of when the man gave him a drink after he
was hurt. I know he was attentive to his job; he was a good worker. I could not
say how far back the wagon was at the time the tractor ran over him but I think
it was about three, four or five feet. I never heard from any one that this accident
occurred off the Fair Grounds. I never heard that Hannon was lying out in the
ditch in the road asleep. That is not a fact; at the time the tractor ran over him
he was inside of the Fair Grounds. I was the last man he spoke to before the
tractor went over him; I am sure there was no drink there except after he was
hurt.

*   *   *

184   Certificate

185   Synopsis of deposition of J. C. McCaffery, taken August 29, 1928, in which deponent states that Hannon was subject to call at all times and that the rule required all employees to stay on the lot in the immediate vicinity of their wagon until it is off the lot, and to stay on the fair grounds.

186   HEARING AT MILWAUKEE, MARCH 19, 1929

JOHN C. MCCAFFERY, sworn and testified. We will condense his testimony to a considerable extent since it is largely repetition and he was not in the immediate vicinity at the time the accident happened:

He testified in substance: I am general manager of Rubin & Cherry Shows and have been such for four years, and was such on August 27, 1927. We were in Manitowoc at that time and I recall a fatal accident. I made an investigation and to the best of my knowledge he had completed his work as to loading the wagons of the ferris wheel and he lay down on the grass somewhere within fifty or a hundred feet of the wagons, or a short distance away from the wagons, waiting for the wagons to be pulled off the grounds. The wagons were on a side road inside of the fair grounds. It was the duty of all employees of that class to stay with the wagons until they get off the load; in this case, I mean off the fair grounds. Most of our moving is done at night time. I think this accident happened around three or four o'clock in the morning. From my investigation, I think that Mr. Hannon was doing the thing he was supposed to do. I made an investigation with respect to whether or not Mr. Hannon was intoxicated or had been drinking and I got nothing definite, any more than hearsay. I was not able to obtain any definite evidence that he had been intoxicated or had been drinking before the accident. He was run over by a tractor, one of our tractors; I had notice of that before I left the grounds. Mr. Reed, the secretary, makes out the accident reports; if he reported Hannon's wage as $18 a week, I would say that was correct. I would say it was not necessary for Hannon to rent a room while he was traveling around; none of the employees receive meals. Our average season is about the first of April until the middle of November.

*   *   *

194   HEARING AT DETROIT, SEPTEMBER 15, 1928.

*   *   *

196   SELMA HANNON, testified in substance:

We were married April 17, 1926, and Mr. Hannon died August 27, 1927. There were no children. We were both twenty-five at the time of his death; no, he would not be twenty-five until September. There was no divorce and no disagreement. There had absolutely been no trouble between us. I saw him last on June 20th; that was when he left Detroit. I saw him last on the morning of the day he left Detroit when I went to work; I knew that he was going; his going was a matter of consent and agreement. I helped with the money which he took on the trip. I worked up until that time and worked since until last October; I have been with my mother most of the time. The burial expense exceeded $200. Mr. Hannon's mother advanced some money for the burial. I have no property. I got Mr. Hannon's picture the day after his body came home, there was no letter with it. It was a picture he had taken, a snapshot, and he mailed it on Friday. I know his handwriting. The last letter I had from him was a week before that. He said in that letter he would be home shortly. He was in Texas about three months from September to December, 1926; after he left in June, 1927, I had a letter from him at least once a week, and some weeks more.

* * *

202   Angeline Hannon, mother of the deceased, testified that she knew of no estrangement between her son and his wife; that the funeral expenses were considerably in excess of $200, and that she paid them.

* * *

205   Carlis Worden, driver of the tractor, testified in substance:

I was in the employ of Rubin & Cherry Shows in 1927 as a tractor driver. I knew Gervase Hannon and know of the accident which resulted in his death on August 27, 1927. I went up about 800 feet at the other end of the show lot and hooked on a wagon and hauled it over onto the hard road; I had to go about 300 feet on the other side of the hard road in order to haul the wagon onto the hard road and after it was on the hard road, I backed up the tractor about four or five feet and then after that I was off from him; I heard somebody yell; that was all that I saw of it; it was after it happened. At the time the accident happened, the wagons were almost all loaded and they were on the west side of the hard road; Hannon was lying about three or four feet off the hard road on the east hand side of the road at the time I run onto him with the tractor. That was a Holt ten-ton tractor and it makes a great deal of noise. A man if he were on duty ought to hear it half a mile. I had no knowledge of any of the employees being on the east side of the road at that time. There was grass on the east side of the road.

Examined by Mr. Wilcox.

* * *

211   I knew Hannon about eight or ten days before the accident; I think he was on the merry-go-round; I know he was working for the Jap, Nagata; I am not sure that he was actually the clutch man on the Ferris wheel. I know Frank Edwards; he was foreman on the Ferris wheel; the clutchman is supposed to be under orders of the foreman of the wheel; if Hannon was clutchman, then Edwards would be his superior. I never knew of any arrangement by which men were required to stay with their wagons. He might have had his orders; I don't know. Mr. Nagata ought to know what the arrangement with Hannon was; Mr. Edwards also. The hard road is inside the fair grounds; it was not a public highway; and the opposite side of the road was part of the fair ground. Rubin & Cherry Shows had been occupying both sides of the road. There had been nothing on the east side of the road for possibly four hours or more before the accident occurred. If Mr. Mangold told me that I was on a man and to pull off, I never heard it. I heard

Mr. Hannon say: "Why don't you kill me?" There were three men and a watchman around there then. They came from all over the lot; from three or four hundred feet. Everything has been a mystery to me; I don't know how it happened. Mr. Hannon was inside the fair grounds. I don't know whether he had been drinking; I did not hear anything to indicate that he had been drinking. There had been a lot of drinking going on at Manitowoc that day; I heard of some men being discharged, but I did not hear that Mr. Hannon had been drinking that day. I was not out on the lot until about eleven o'clock. At the time I ran onto Hannon, I was making a straight pull with the tractor; I had not started swinging it or turning it. I still had the other wagon hooked on at the time. I would not say that Hannon was watching the Ferris wheel wagon at the time I run over him; he might have been waiting for the wagon to come down but he was not with the wagon at the time. I don't know if the Ferris wheel wagon was down at the train or on the lot at the time of the accident. I don't know if it was on the hard road or over on the location or on the way down to the train; I don't know how close Mr. Hannon was to it at the time he was run down; I don't know if he was 80 or 800 feet. If he had been with the watchman and the other men that were there, unhooking the tractor and getting the trucks hooked onto the wagon, that would not have happened. The wagons were about forty, fifty feet from one another.

EDITORIAL NOTE: SANCTIONS and END PROCESSES in ADMINISTRATIVE PROCEEDINGS

The Commission made the following "Findings of Fact" in its opinion in the Hannon case:

"That on August 27, 1927, one Gervase Hannon, and the respondents were subject to the provisions of the workmen's compensation act, and that on August 27, 1927, said Gervase Hannon, was in the employ of the respondent, Nagata Brothers, subcontractors of Rubin and Cherry Shows, Incorporated, and while performing service growing out of and incidental to his employment, accidentally sustained injuries which resulted in his death on August 29, 1927; that the liability of the respondent, Nagata Brothers, under the provisions of the workmen's compensation act of Wisconsin, was uninsured; that the liability of the respondent Rubin and Cherry Shows, Incorporated, under the provisions of said act, was insured with the Wisconsin Mutual Liability Company; that said Gervase Hannon, deceased, was employed at an annual wage of $900; that the applicant herein, Selma Hannon, is the widow of said Gervase Hannon, deceased, and was living with him as his wife at the time of the accident and death; that she is therefore entitled to death benefit in the sum of $3,600, of which $1,006.20 has already accrued, and the balance of $2,593.80 is payable in monthly installments of $50.70; that Mrs. Nicholas Hannon paid funeral expenses in excess of two hundred dollars, and she is therefore entitled to reimbursement from the respondents and insurance carrier in the sum of $200." [1]

[1] It should be noted that the widow won the award of $3600 without incurring a cent of cost for attorney's fees or otherwise in the prosecution of the case before the commission and on appeal to the Circuit Court and Supreme Court.—Editor

The findings of fact were followed by the Commission's Award, reading as follows:

"Now, therefore, upon the facts so found, the commission makes the following [award:]

"That within ten days from date hereof, the respondent, Rubin and Cherry Shows, Incorporated, and its insurer, Wisconsin Mutual Liability Company, shall pay to the applicant Selma Hannon, the sum of One Thousand Six and Twenty-one Hundredths Dollars ($1,006.20), and on June 1, 1929, and on the first day of each month thereafter, shall pay the sum of Fifty and Seventy-One-Hundredths Dollars ($50.70), until such monthly installments shall equal the sum of Two Thousand Five Hundred Ninety-three and Eighty-One-Hundredths Dollars ($2,593.80), or until further order of the commission; that within like period the respondent and insurance carrier shall pay to Mrs. Nicholas Hannon, 13972 Mitchell Avenue, Detroit, Michigan, the sum of Two Hundred and No One-Hundredths Dollars ($200.00), as reimbursement for funeral expenses.

"Given under our hands of the City of Madison, Wisconsin, this 13th day of April, A.D. 1929. INDUSTRIAL COMMISSION OF WISCONSIN."

Notice the language of this Award. It uses words of command. The carnival company and its insurer "shall pay" so much to the widow, and "shall pay" so much to Mrs. Nicholas Hannon. How are these commands to be carried out? The Commission is not a court; it has no sheriffs to help carry out its orders; it has no power, like a court, to punish people for contempt; it has no authority to exert any kind of force on anybody. How, then, are its orders to be carried out? The legislature has seen to that in the following statutory enactment:

"102.20 *Judgment on award.* Either party may present a certified copy of the award to the circuit court for any county; whereupon said court shall, without notice, render judgment in accordance therewith; such judgment shall have the same effect as though rendered in an action tried and determined by said court, and shall, with like effect, be entered and docketed."

In other words, if the carnival company or the insurance company would not pay the widow, she could take her award to a circuit court and immediately get a court judgment for the amount of the award. And the judgment would be enforced for her by the sheriff, who has power, if necessary, to levy on the property of defendants who do not pay up. Of course, all this is in the absence of any proceeding to set aside the Commission's Award. What actually happened was that the carnival company and the insurance company at once started a proceeding to set aside the Award, and this automatically postponed the widow's remedy under section 102.20. In the final outcome, the circuit court found against the companies in their proceeding to set aside the award, and, at the widow's request made through the Commission, entered its judgment confirming the Award.

The point is that the Commission's order cannot itself be enforced. Only the judgment of a court can actually be enforced. Had the companies not gone to court themselves to try to get the Award set aside, the widow could have gone to court and gotten a judgment without any question and without any delay. Since the companies preferred to contest the Award, and had a right to do so, she had to wait until the contest was decided; then she got her judgment. Without a court judgment she would have had no enforceable rights, despite the commanding language of the Commission's Award.

The text of the Circuit Court's judgment, preceded by the last two paragraphs of Judge Hoppmann's opinion (reviewing and upholding the Commission's contentions), was as follows:

"It follows from the foregoing that the award must be affirmed and it is so ordered.

"The Attorney General may prepare the proper judgment in accordance with the foregoing, submitting same to opposing counsel before it is presented to the court for signature.

"Dated February 5, 1930. HARRY E. MANZER, Official Reporter."

"JUDGMENT. The above entitled matter coming on for hearing, before the court, without a jury, upon the return of the above named defendant, Industrial Commission of Wisconsin, Ida E. Luick of Roehr & Steinmetz appearing on behalf of the plaintiffs, and Mortimer Levitan, Assistant Attorney General, appearing on behalf of the defendant, Industrial Commission of Wisconsin, and there being no other appearances, and the court having heard the arguments of counsel, and being fully advised in the premises, and having taken the matter under advisement, and having, on the 5th day of February, 1930, filed its directions for judgment confirming the award of the Industrial Commission,

"Now, therefore, on motion of the said attorney for the Industrial Commission of Wisconsin,

"It is Adjudged, that the award of the Industrial Commission of Wisconsin, dated April 13, 1929, ordering the plaintiffs to pay certain sums as death benefits to the defendant Selma Hannon because of the death of her husband Gervase Hannon, be, and the same hereby is, in all respects confirmed.

"Dated at Madison, Wisconsin, this 14th day of February, 1930.

"By the Court: AUGUST C. HOPPMANN, Judge."

We may now note at least six different ways in which the force of law is put back of the orders of administrative agencies—

(a) As in the case of orders by the Wisconsin Industrial Commission, the person in favor of whom an order is made may file the order in court and get a judgment confirming it.

(b) The person adversely affected may start a court proceeding to set aside the order, and, if he loses, judgment confirming the order may be entered. As we have seen, this is what happened in the Hannon case. Under some statutes, if the person adversely affected does not start such a proceeding within a specified length of time, the order becomes automatically binding and enforceable.

(c) There are other statutes that place the initiative on the administrative agency: if its order is not obeyed nothing will happen unless the agency itself, generally within a specified time, applies to the court to get, if it can, a judgment confirming the order. This application, of course, can be resisted by the party adversely affected, and the court will then review the agency's proceedings in a hearing at which all parties are represented. This is the method which obtains in the case of the National Labor Relations Board and other agencies.

(d) Violation of commission regulations is sometimes made a crime by statute. When this is so, the person guilty of the violation may be prosecuted in an ordinary court, and if found guilty will be imprisoned or fined.

(e) If the business regulated is one requiring special license, the license may be taken away or suspended by the Commission until the concern complies. If it nonetheless carries on business without a license, it is generally guilty of a crime for which it may be prosecuted in the courts as for other crimes.

(f) An order operative in the future becomes a part of the law and controls the decisions of suits between private parties. Thus, if a railroad makes a shipper pay more for a shipment than the tariff (an order operative in the future) approved by the Interstate Commerce Commission calls for, the shipper may bring suit for the overcharge in the courts.

NOTES AND QUESTIONS

1. Note the actions taken by the Industrial Commission in the above case which no court of law would have taken. Make any other comparisons you can between the way this case was handled, from start to finish, and the way it would have been handled as ordinary litigation in a court of law.

2. It will be noted from the foregoing that the Industrial Commission in the Hannon case, for all practical purposes, was the initiator of the proceedings. At the same time it acted as judge of the truth of the facts. One might therefore argue that it was sitting in judgment on its own case. The same situation exists when the Commission first performs the executive function of filing a complaint against a factory owner (after an investigation) charging him with having violated the Commission's safety regulations, and then sits in judgment on this complaint. This mixture of executive and judicial functions is typical of a great many, if not most, administrative tribunals. Do you think administrative bodies should be allowed to sit in judgment in cases which they themselves have initiated? We shall have occasion to consider this question again later on.

3. From the record of the proceedings set forth above, it is apparent that the procedure before administrative tribunals, in comparison with that before courts, can be simple, informal, and flexible. The atmosphere, too, of administrative proceedings is more easygoing and informal than the atmosphere of a court-room; often the parties and witnesses and the commission's officials are seated around a table, and the hearing is more like a running conversation than a trial. Furthermore, many of the "rules of evidence" are not enforced in administrative proceedings. The "rules of evidence" are rules of exclusion: this type of testimony or that type of document cannot be "offered in evidence" either because its persuasiveness is not sufficient, or it is irrelevant and time-wasting, or because its content cannot be subject to cross-examination or it is thought to be apt to mislead the jury. In the early days when the rules of evidence were being developed by the judges, juries were composed of ignorant and uneducated people, and their capacity to weigh evidence was thought to be very limited. Hence numerous restrictions were laid down and developed into rules, relating to the kind of evidence which the jury should or should not be allowed to hear. For the most part, these rules do not obtain before administrative agencies, composed, as the latter are supposed to be, of experts, and sitting without juries.

EDITORIAL NOTE: A BRIEF CRITIQUE of WORKMEN'S COMPENSATION as a SYSTEM of ADJUDICATION

The above advantages, which it was thought the administrative process would have over the judicial process, gave rise to expectations that controversies, like those involved under the Workmen's Compensation Act, would be settled more quickly and cheaply by administrative agencies than by courts.

Whether these expectations have been realized is the subject of hot debate at the present time. Under the constant pressure of the legal profession, administrative agencies have tended to follow courtroom procedures more and more closely. Delay has been one of the consequences. Even the Hannon case is hardly a model of expedition, though the itinerant nature of the employer's activities created special difficulties for the Commission which a court might not have been able to obviate so successfully. Gervase Hannon was killed in August, 1927 and it was not until more than 3 years later that his widow received the compensation to which she was entitled. The case first came to the attention of the Commission in December, 1927. The Commission's award was issued April 13, 1929, approximately 16 months thereafter. The process of judicial review began May 2, 1929 and was concluded November 11, 1930, the date of the Supreme Court's decision, approximately 18 months thereafter. Again, it must be remembered that in 90% of the cases, payments are made under the Workmen's Compensation Act without even a formal order of the Commission.

Delay has not been the only basis for concern. In other respects too, the workmen's compensation system has not fulfilled all the expectations of its proponents. Every solution to a serious social problem seems to create difficulties of its own.

As will be recalled, the Federal Employers' Liability Act, not the state Workmen's Compensation Act, continues to govern compensation for occupational disabilities of railroad workers in interstate commerce. And no workmen's compensation scheme has been enacted to cover seamen—who are left to the traditional remedies which are afforded them by the general maritime law, modified in important respects by statute, but which require ordinary court litigation to be obtained. Yet to this day, the trade unions representing railroad workers and seamen have resisted the extension to them of any workmen's compensation system. This resistance has been cited by some as evidence that workmen's compensation has failed.

We shall not be able to deal in detail with the controversy concerning the respective merits of FELA and Workmen's Compensation, or with other controversies that have developed. We shall attempt merely to outline the general criticisms which have been directed against the workmen's compensation system, together with some brief indication of remedies:

a. The most serious criticism is that the amount of compensation provided by statute is generally inadequate to meet the needs of dependent families. Employers and the more "progressive" states also complain that the standards under the different state laws vary widely and that this variation tends to favor the location of industry in the less "progressive" states.

b. Rehabilitation has not yet become an integral part of the system.

c. The administrative and overhead costs of compensation insurance are much too high.

d. Excessive litigation is still the rule. We shall have occasion shortly to examine some other examples of such litigation, in addition to the Hannon case.

e. Studies have purported to show that workmen's compensation is more costly to administer than the system under the Federal Employers' Liability Act, which utilizes ordinary court procedures.

Some of these deficiencies are being met, partly, in a number of ways. The federal-state vocational rehabilitation program is vigorous and growing. Old-Age and Survivors Insurance benefits under the social security program often supplement workmen's compensation benefits. Some states (New York, New Jersey, California and Rhode Island) have adopted non-occupational disability insurance programs which also supplement workmen's compensation benefits. Some unions, too, have negotiated collective bargaining agreements which further supplement workmen's compensation benefits. The United Mine Workers Welfare and Retirement Fund is an outstanding example.

The argument that the cost of administration per dollar of benefit conferred is high compared to the cost under the Federal Employers' Liability Act does not prove the inefficiency of the workmen's compensation system itself. The high ratio of costs to benefits under the workmen's compensation system is understandable since benefits under the system are fixed by law at a relatively low level. Then, too, a larger proportion of FELA cases are settled (because of the high cost of court litigation), thus reducing the average cost of handling FELA claims. The disparity between the cost-benefit ratios under the two systems would diminish if legislatures increased the level of workmen's compensation benefits and took measures to reduce the volume of compensation litigation.

In an effort to reduce the volume of litigation under Workmen's Compensation Acts, the Department of Labor in 1956 drafted and sponsored a model state act to clarify the language in the existing statutes which has given rise to the bulk of the litigation.

The future of workmen's compensation is being debated, too, in the context of proposals for a comprehensive social insurance system which will safeguard the individual and his family against the hazards of wage loss whether due to sickness, accident, invalidism, or death, from an occupational or non-occupational origin, or to unemployment or old age.

For a defense of FELA, see Richter and Forer, Federal Employers' Liability Act—A Real Compensatory Law for Railroad Workers, 36 Cornell

L. Q. 203 (1951). For the argument in favor of a workmen's compensation scheme for railroad workers, see Pollack, Workmen's Compensation for Railroad Work Injuries and Diseases, 36 Cornell L. Q. 236 (1951). See, too, Symposium on the Federal Employers' Liability Act, 18 Law & Contemp. Prob. 107-431 (1953); Larson, The Future of Workmen's Compensation, 6 NACCA L.J. 18 (1950); Lenhoff, Social Insurance Replacing Workmen's Compensation in England, 5 NACCA L.J. 49 (1950); Conard, Workmen's Compensation: Is It More Efficient Than Employer's Liability? 38 A.B.A.J. 1011 (1952); Somers and Somers, Workmen's Compensation: Unfulfilled Promise, 7 Ind. & Lab. Rel. Rev. 32 (1953); Pollack, A Policy Decision For Workmen's Compensation, 7 Ind. & Lab. Rel. Rev. 51 (1953); and Riesenfeld, Contemporary Trends in Compensation For Industrial Accidents, 43 Colum. L. Rev. 531 (1954).

EDITORIAL NOTE: STATUTORY PROVISIONS for JUDICIAL REVIEW of ADMINISTRATIVE DETERMINATIONS of FACT

We have seen from the record of the proceedings in the Hannon case the kind of evidence the Industrial Commission had before it when it had to decide the circumstances under which Gervase Hannon was killed. The crucial fact questions were whether Hannon was on duty at the time he was killed, and whether Selma Hannon was living with him as his wife at that time. The Commission answered both questions in the affirmative. On review of the case in court, to what extent, if at all, should the court be authorized to upset the Commission's findings? The Commission had the benefit of hearing the witnesses, or most of them, and of being able to note their demeanor; and besides, the Commission was composed of experts in this type of case. How far should a judge, who has only the printed proceedings before him, be permitted to go in substituting his view of the facts for that of the Commission?

The legislature has attempted to answer this question in the following section, which also prescribes the method for reviewing the Commission's orders:

"102.23 *Judicial review* (1) The findings of fact made by the commission acting within its powers shall, in the absence of fraud, be conclusive; and the order or award . . . shall be subject to review only in the manner and upon the grounds following: Within thirty days from the date of an order or award . . . any party aggrieved thereby may commence, in the circuit court for Dane county, an action against the commission for the review of such order or award, in which action the adverse party shall also be made defendant. In such action a complaint, which need not be verified, but which shall state the grounds upon which a review is sought, shall be served with the summons. Service upon the secretary of the commission, or any member of the commission, shall be deemed completed service on all parties, but there shall be left with the person so served as many copies of the summons and complaint as there are defendants, and the commission shall mail one such copy to each other defendant. . . . The commission shall serve its answer within twenty days after the service of the complaint . . . With its answer, the commission shall make return to said court of all documents and papers on file in the matter, and of all testimony which may have been taken therein, and of its order, findings and award. . . . Said action may thereupon be brought on for hearing before said court upon such record by either party on ten days' notice to the other; . . . Upon such hearing, the court may confirm or set aside such order or award; . . . but the same shall be set aside only upon the following grounds:

"(a) That the commission acted without or in excess of its powers.

"(b) That the order or award was procured by fraud.

"(c) That the findings of fact by the commission do not support the order or award . . ."

The provisions for judicial review in the Workmen's Compensation Act should be compared with the similar provisions in the federal Administrative Procedure Act, 60 Stat. 237 (1946), 5 U.S.C.A. §1001 and in the Model State Administrative Procedure Act (see Handbook of the National Conference of Commissioners on Uniform State Laws).

Section 10 (e) of the federal Administrative Procedure Act provides:

"So far as necessary to decision and where presented the reviewing court shall decide all relevant questions of law, interpret constitutional and statutory provisions, and determine the meaning or applicability of the terms of any agency action. It shall (A) compel agency action unlawfully withheld or unreasonably delayed; and (B) hold unlawful and set aside agency action, findings, and conclusions found to be (1) arbitrary, capricious, an abuse of discretion, or otherwise not in accordance with law; (2) contrary to constitutional right, power, privilege, or immunity; (3) in excess of statutory jurisdiction, authority, or limitations, or short of statutory right; (4) without observance of procedure required by law; (5) unsupported by substantial evidence in any case . . . reviewed on the record of an agency hearing provided by statute; or (6) unwarranted by the facts to the extent that the facts are subject to trial de novo by the reviewing court. In making the foregoing determinations the court shall review the whole record or such portions thereof as may be cited by any party, and due account shall be taken of the rule of prejudicial error."

Section 12 (7) of the Model State Administrative Procedure Act provides:

"The court may affirm the decision of the agency or remand the case for further proceedings; or it may reverse or modify the decision if the substantial rights of the petitioners may have been prejudiced because the administrative findings, inferences, conclusions, or decisions are:

(a) in violation of constitutional provisions; or

(b) in excess of the statutory authority or jurisdiction of the agency; or

(c) made upon unlawful procedure; or

(d) affected by other error of law; or

(e) unsupported by competent, material, and substantial evidence in view of the entire record as submitted; or

(f) arbitrary or capricious."

Section 227.20 of the Wisconsin Uniform Administrative Procedure Act, which does not apply to the Industrial Commission in matters arising out of the Workmen's Compensation Act, provides:

"(1) . . . The court may affirm the decision of the agency, or may reverse or modify it if the substantial rights of the appellant have been prejudiced as a result of the administrative findings, inferences, conclusions or decisions being:

(a) Contrary to constitutional rights or privileges; or
(b) In excess of the statutory authority or jurisdiction of the agency, or affected by other error of law; or
(c) Made or promulgated upon unlawful procedure; or
(d) Unsupported by substantial evidence in view of the entire record as submitted; or
(e) Arbitrary or capricious.

"(2) Upon such review due weight shall be accorded the experience, technical competence, and specialized knowledge of the agency involved, as well as discretionary authority conferred upon it. . . ."

In spite of these legislative solutions, what the standards for judicial review of administrative findings of fact should be is still a subject of controversy. No undue reliance should be placed upon differences in statutory language dealing with the scope of review, because judges exercising the review power, as we shall see, manage to reach results they consider desirable regardless of the particular statutory language. Lawyers and students who are not sympathetic with the work and the objectives of administrative agencies, or who see in them a threat to the liberties of citizens, advocate trials de novo in the reviewing courts or giving the courts broad latitude in substituting their own views of the facts for those of the commissions. Those who tend to emphasize the value of the administrative process seek to prevent trials de novo and to give to administrative findings of fact as much finality and conclusiveness as possible.

HILLS DRY GOODS CO., INC. v. INDUSTRIAL COMMISSION
217 Wis. 76, 258 N.W. 336 (1935)

[In addition to regular compensation, the Commission here awarded the injured employee, a minor, treble damages under provisions of the act prohibiting the employment of such a minor in the running of an elevator and setting the award at treble the amount otherwise recoverable, if the minor was injured while engaged in a prohibited employment. In an action by the employer to review the award of treble damages, the circuit court for Dane county affirmed the award.—Editor]

Upon this evidence the commission found that Klicka at the time he sustained his injury was engaged in the operation of the elevator. The question to be determined is—Is the evidence sufficient to sustain that finding?

For the reason that in a large share of the cases coming to this court we are asked to say that the findings of the commission should be set aside because there is no evidence to support them, this is as appropriate a time as any to review briefly the law upon this subject.

In International H. Co. v. Industrial Comm., 157 Wis. 167, 147 N.W. 53, the whole matter of the power of the court to set aside an award of the Industrial Commission is considered, and it was held that by statute the findings of fact made by the commission within its power in the absence of fraud are conclusive;

that it was clearly outside of its power to find essential facts that had no support in the evidence, from which it follows that there must be some support in the evidence for findings of fact made by the commission.

In Oldenberg v. Industrial Comm., 159 Wis. 333, 150 N.W. 444, consideration was given as to what constituted "some evidence" sufficient to support a finding. It was said:

> "Manifestly a very clear case must be made to call for a ruling [that the order of the commission was made without any evidence to sustain it]. . . . All evidence which tends to render probable or improbable the existence of the facts which are the subject of inquiry is relevant, and conversely all relevant facts have this tendency. In order to support an argument to the effect that an ultimate conclusion of fact has no evidence to support it there must be shown an absence of all evidence or an absence of any such relevant evidence."

While the court evidently considered the finding was made against the weight of the evidence, it was nevertheless sustained.

While the language relating to the quantum of evidence varies somewhat, the terms used such as "credible evidence," "some evidence," and "evidence" are practically, as used, synonymous. . . . The real question is, in a particular case,—Is there or is there not evidence of the fact found? The test suggested by Mr. Wigmore is perhaps as good as any that can be suggested. As applied to Industrial Commission cases it is:

> "Are there facts in the evidence which if unanswered would justify a person of ordinary reason and fairness in affirming the existence of the facts which the claimant is bound to establish?" 5 Wigmore, Evidence, §2494.

The matter was carefully considered in Creamery Package Mfg. Co. v. Industrial Comm., 211 Wis. 326, 248 N.W. 140. In that case death benefit was claimed under the compensation act on the ground that deceased contracted typhoid fever while performing services in the course of his employment. He was a traveling man and traveled over four states. It was held:

> "Mere possibilities leave the solution of an issue of fact in the field of conjecture and speculation to such an extent as to afford no basis for inferences to a reasonable certainty, and in the absence of at least such inferences there is no sufficient basis for a finding of fact. It will not do to reach a conclusion in favor of the party on whom the burden of proof rests by merely theorizing and conjecturing. There must at least be sufficient evidence to remove the question from the realm of conjecture. [Citing case.] A finding of fact made by the commission cannot be based upon mere conjecture any more than a finding of fact by a court or jury. While it is within the province of the commission to draw inferences, they must be drawn from established facts which logically support them. If not so supported, the findings of the commission based on its inferences are mere conjecture in excess of its powers."

In this case there is no direct testimony that the claimant fell into the elevator shaft while operating, or attempting to operate, or even getting ready to operate, the elevator. Do the facts adduced upon the hearing permit of an inference that he was operating the elevator? In this connection an inference is to be clearly distinguished from a mere guess or conjecture. As was said in Creamery Package Mfg. Co., supra, "inferences . . . must be drawn from established facts which logically support them." In other words, they must be rational. The inference must not only be rational, but it must be a logical deduction from the established facts and not one of several inferences which might with equal propriety be drawn from the same facts.

In Belle City M.I. Co. v. Industrial Comm., 180 Wis. 344, 192 N.W. 1010, the commission found that a hernia was a personal injury sustained while claimant was performing services growing out of and incidental to his employment. The court said:

> "The mere fact that during the period covered by his employment the applicant discovered a protrusion through the inguinal tract is not sufficient to show any relation between his employment and his condition. It cannot be said that it must have come from his work. He may have slipped. He may have been engaged in work on his own account, or it may have come about in any of the numerous ways by which the manifestations of a congenital or acquired weakness are made manifest. There is no evidence of an injury, accidental or otherwise."

In this case the testimony of the claimant is to the effect that he did not pry the door of the elevator open; that he did not open the door; that he did not look into the elevator shaft to see where the elevator was; and that he does not know whether the door was open or closed. In fact, his recollection of everything that happened from the time he had the conversation with Roman about the box until after he was hurt is hazy. If the doors were open he may have fallen in accidentally. The elevator by the undisputed facts was on the fifth floor and not on the first floor. Whether he walked into the opening expecting to find the elevator there, as he said he thought it was, is at least a possibility. It perhaps is needless to speculate on the possibilities in connection with this case. The burden of proof was upon Klicka to establish by evidence that he was engaged in operating the elevator at the time he sustained his injury. We find no evidence which by any reasonable interpretation permits of inference that he was so engaged. When considered in connection with his denial that he opened the door or stepped into the elevator shaft, there is no room for a permissible inference that he was so operating the elevator and was injured while so doing. There are no preponderating probabilities in this case which turn the scale in favor of the claimant.

We may point out in this connection that application of the test suggested excludes the consideration of all questions relating to the weight of the evidence. When the test is applied and it is found that there are *facts in evidence which if unanswered* [italics supplied—Editor] would warrant the commisson in making the finding complained of, this court can go no further. The weight of the evidence and credibility of the witnesses under such circumstances are wholly for the commission. . . . If the commission finds against the great weight and clear preponderance of the evidence, or if it finds upon a given state of the evidence one way in one case and another way in another case, there being the requisite minimum evidence in each case, the matter is beyond the jurisdiction of this court. While findings made against the great weight and clear preponderance of the evidence justify the party against whom they are made in feeling that justice has not been done, this court has no power to set aside an award for that reason. The determination of the commission under such circumstances being final and conclusive, it should be reached in accordance with the established principles of law which are laid down in matters of this kind to enable tribunals charged with the duty of finding the facts to do justice between the parties to the controversy.

By the Court—The judgment appealed from is reversed, and cause remanded to the trial court, with directions to enter judgment setting aside the award of treble damages.

NOTES AND QUESTIONS

1. State all the issues which the Industrial Commission was called upon to decide in the Hannon case. Which of them raised questions of fact? Which, questions of law?

2. Did the Wisconsin Supreme Court lay down any standard for the judicial review of administrative fact-finding in the Hannon case? Compare the opinion in that case with the opinion in the Hills Dry Goods Co. case in this respect. Why the difference? Is the standard adopted by the court in the Hills case clearly derivable from the language of the Workmen's Compensation Act?

3. The Supreme Court of the United States has had occasion to explain the requirement in section 10 (e) of the federal Administrative Procedure Act that in determining whether administrative findings are supported by substantial evidence, "the court shall review the whole record or such portions thereof as may be cited by any party." Recall that the state Administrative Procedure Acts similarly require such determinations to be made "in view of the entire record as submitted." In Universal Camera Corp. v. N.L.R.B., 340 U.S. 474, 487-488 (1951), a case involving the Taft-Hartley Act which the Court stated imposed the same standard as section 10 (e), the Supreme Court said:

"Whether or not it was ever permissible for courts to determine the substantiality of evidence supporting a Labor Board decision merely on the basis of evidence which in and of itself justified it, without taking into account contradictory evidence or evidence from which conflicting inferences could be drawn, the new legislation definitively precludes such a theory and bars its practice. The substantiality of evidence must take into account whatever in the record fairly detracts from its weight. This is clearly the significance of the requirement in both statutes that courts consider the whole record." [This amended standard, however, was not] "intended to negative the function of the Labor Board as one of those agencies presumably equipped or informed by experience to deal with a specialized field of knowledge, whose findings within that field carry the authority of an expertness which courts do not possess and therefore must respect. Nor does it mean that even as to matters not requiring expertise a court may displace the Board's choice between two fairly conflicting views, even though the court would justifiably have made a different choice had the matter been before it de novo."

During the oral argument of the Universal Camera case, the Solicitor General of the United States stated that the federal courts, including the Supreme Court, had always applied the "whole record" test, even before enactment of the federal Administrative Procedure Act. Justice Frankfurter, who wrote the opinion in the case, disagreed and cited N.L.R.B. v. Nevada Consolidated Copper Corp., 316 U.S. 105 (1942), a per curiam decision in which the Court affirmed an NLRB decision "since upon an examination of the record we cannot say that the finding of fact of the Board is without support in the evidence." Justice Frankfurter then said to the Solicitor General: ". . . that means if I find something in the evidence which supports it, my case is at an end. That is what I thought I had been doing." The Solicitor General replied: "I cannot contradict your honor."

4. In Motor Transport Co. v. Public Service Commission, 263 Wis. 31 (1953), the Wisconsin Supreme Court interpreted the standard for review set forth in section 227.20 (1) (d) of the Wisconsin Administrative Procedure Act as follows: "We believe that the principles enunciated by the United States Supreme Court in the Universal Camera Corp. Case . . . are sound and are applicable to the proper interpretation of the phrase 'substantial evidence in view of the entire record' in sec. 227.10 (1) (d) . . . Since the adoption of our . . . Administrative Procedure Act in 1943 containing such provision it is no longer proper for a court in reviewing the findings of an administrative agency to affirm such findings by merely considering isolated testimony, which if standing alone, would be sufficient to sustain the findings, without considering other testimony in the record which impeaches the same."

The court then reached the conclusion that the standard for review laid down in the Workmen's Compensation Act, as interpreted in the Hills case, which the trial court in the Motor Transport Co. case had cited as authority, was precisely the same as the standard laid down in section 227.10 (1) (d), as now interpreted by it. The court stressed the words, italicized above, in the last paragraph of the opinion in the Hills case, and said: "Clearly the . . . words 'which if unanswered' . . . cannot mean uncontradicted by other evidence in the record in view of what is stated therein that this court has no power to pass upon the credibility of witnesses or the weight of the evidence. 'Unexplained' would seem to be a more accurate expression than 'unanswered.' " So, the court concluded, the scope of review under the Hills case was just as broad, after all, as that under the Universal Camera case, in spite of the differences in the language of the statutes involved.

5. What are the reviewing judges supposed to do to determine whether there is substantial evidence, in the light of the entire record, to support the administrative findings of fact? Must they read the entire record or all the portions thereof cited by the parties? Do you think that appellate judges are, in fact, doing so?

6. Since the Universal Camera case was decided, the Hoover Commission (appointed to inquire into and make recommendations regarding the operations of federal agencies) has received from its Task Force and submitted to Congress without majority endorsement, the proposal that the A.P.A. standard of review be changed to the standard applicable, under the Federal Rules of Civil Procedure, to appellate review of the fact findings of a trial judge sitting without a jury. In the latter situation, the findings are approved unless they are "clearly erroneous." In United States v. United States Gypsum Co., 333 U.S. 364, 395 (1948), the Supreme Court expounded the "clearly erroneous" rule as follows: "A finding is 'clearly erroneous' when although there is evidence to support it, the reviewing court on the entire evidence is left with the definite and firm conviction that a mistake has been committed."

While this standard has been viewed as giving greater lee-way or scope of review to the reviewing court than the "substantial evidence" rule (see Stern, Review of Findings of Administrators, Judges and Juries: A Comparative Analysis, 58 Harv. L. Rev. 70, 80-89 (1944)), others regard it as not much different, if at all, from the standard of substantial-evidence-on-the-whole-record. (See observations of Professors Jaffe, Cooper, and Schwartz in Symposium, Hoover Commission and Task Force Reports on Legal Services and Procedure, 30 N.Y.U.L. Rev. 1296, 1380, 1392-93 (1955)).

7. The student will be excused if he fails to detect the precise differences between the various formulas appellate courts use to explain their function in reviewing findings of fact made by other tribunals. Possibly the Report of the Attorney General's Committee on Administrative Procedure has a word of wisdom for us when it points out the wide discretion any form of language regarding the scope of review necessarily leaves to the judges, and the factors which enter into the exercise of this discretion: "In exercising their powers of review the courts have been influenced, it is commonly thought, by a variety of inarticulate factors: The character of the administrative agency, the nature of the problems with which it deals, the nature and consequences of the administrative action, the confidence which the agency has won, the degree to which the review would interfere with the agency's functions or burden the courts, the nature of the proceedings before the administrative agency, and similar factors." (S. Doc. No. 8, 77th Cong., 1st Sess. 91 [1941]).

Do you think a more precise standard of review is either possible or desirable?

8. The Hills Dry Goods case should be compared with the following cases: McCarthy v. Industrial Commission, 194 Wis. 198 (1927); McDonald v. Industrial Commission, 250 Wis. 134 (1947); A. O. Smith Corp. v. Industrial Commission, 264 Wis. 510 (1953).

CHAPTER Thirteen

RULE MAKING and OTHER ASPECTS of ADMINISTRATIVE LEGISLATION

WISCONSIN STATUTES, 1959, Chapter 101.
Industrial Commission

101.01. *Definitions of terms used.* The following terms as used in sections 101.01 to 101.29 of the statutes, shall be construed as follows:

(1) The phrase "place of employment" shall mean and include every place, whether indoors or out or underground and the premises appurtenant thereto where either temporarily or permanently any industry, trade or business is carried on, or where any process or operation, directly or indirectly related to any industry, trade or business, is carried on, and where any person is directly or indirectly employed by another for direct or indirect gain or profit, but shall not include any place where persons are employed in (a) private domestic service which does not involve the use of mechanical power or (b) farming. The term "farming" includes those activities specified in s. 102.04(4) and also includes the transportation of farm products, supplies or equipment directly to the farm by the operator of said farm or his employes for use thereon, if such activities are directly or indirectly for the purpose of producing commodities for market, or as an accessory to such production.

(2) The term "employment" shall mean and include any trade, occupation or process of manufacture, or any method of carrying on such trade, occupation or process of manufacture in which any person may be engaged, except in such private domestic service as does not involve the use of mechanical power and in farm labor as used in subsection (1).

(3) The term "employer" shall mean and include every person, firm, corporation, state, county, town, city, village, school district, sewer district, drainage district and other public or quasi-public corporations as well as any agent, manager, representative or other person having control or custody of any employment, place of employment or of any employe.

(4) The term "employe" shall mean and include every person who may be required or directed by any employer, in consideration of direct or indirect gain or profit, to engage in any employment, or to go to work or be at any time in any place of employment.

(5) The term "frequenter" shall mean and include every person, other than an employe, who may go in or be in a place of employment or public building under circumstances which render him other than a trespasser. . . .

(10) The term "welfare" shall mean and include comfort, decency and moral well-being.

(11) The term "safe" or "safety" as applied to an employment or a place of employment or a public building, shall mean such freedom from danger to the life, health, safety or welfare of employes or frequenters, or the public, or tenants, or firemen, and such reasonable means of notification, egress and escape in case of fire, and such freedom from danger to adjacent buildings or other property, as the nature of the employment, place of employment, or public building, will reasonably permit.

101.06. *Employer's duty to furnish safe employment and place.* Every employer shall furnish employment which shall be safe for the employes therein and for frequenters thereof and shall furnish and use safety devices and safeguards, and shall adopt and use methods and processes reasonably adequate to render such employment and places of employment safe, and shall do every other thing reasonably necessary to protect the life, health, safety, and welfare of such employes and frequenters. Every employer and every owner of a place of employment or a public building now or hereafter constructed shall so construct, repair or maintain such place of employment or public building, and every architect shall so prepare the plans for the construction of such place of employment, or public building as to render the same safe.

101.10. *Other powers, duties and jurisdiction of commission.* It shall also be the duty of the industrial commission, and it shall have power, jurisdiction and authority:

(1) To employ, promote and remove deputies, clerks and other assistants as needed, to fix their compensation, and to assign to them their duties; and to appoint advisors who shall, without compensation, assist the industrial commission in the execution of its duties. . . .

(3) To investigate, ascertain, declare and prescribe what safety devices, safeguards or other means or methods of protection are best adapted to render the employes of every employment and place of employment and frequenters of every place of employment safe, and to protect their welfare as required by law or lawful orders. . . .

(4) To ascertain and fix such reasonable standards and to prescribe, modify and enforce such reasonable orders for the adoption of safety devices, safeguards and other means or methods of protection to be as nearly uniform as possible, as may be necessary to carry out all laws and lawful orders relative to the protection of the life, health, safety and welfare of employes in employment and places of employment or frequenters of places of employment. . . .

(7) To adopt reasonable and proper rules and regulations relative to the exercise of its powers and authorities and proper rules to govern its proceedings and to regulate the mode and manner of all investigations and hearings.

[The commission is empowered, also, to investigate to discover violations of safety requirements, 101.11, and a penalty of a money fine is provided for violation of the statute or orders or rules issued thereunder, 101.28. Orders of the commission in conformity with law are declared prima facie valid, and subject to challenge only by proceedings for review as provided in the act, 101.13, 101.15, 101.17, 101.26, and the Administrative Procedure Act, chapter 227 of the statutes. —Editor]

WISCONSIN STATUTES, 1959, Chapter 102.
Workmen's Compensation

102.57. *Violations of safety provisions, penalty.* Where injury is caused by the failure of the employer to comply with any statute or any lawful order of the commission, compensation and death benefits as provided in this chapter [Workmen's Compensation] shall be increased fifteen per cent. Failure of an employer reasonably to enforce compliance by employes with such statute or order of the commission shall constitute failure by the employer to comply with such statute or order.

102.58. *Decreased compensation.* Where injury is caused by the wilful failure of the employe to use safety devices where provided in accordance with any statute or lawful order of the commission and adequately maintained, and their use is reasonably enforced by the employer, or where injury results from the employe's wilful failure to obey any reasonable rule adopted by the employer for the safety of the employe and of which the employe has notice, or where injury results from the intoxication of the employe, the compensation, and death benefit provided herein shall be reduced 15 per cent.

INDUSTRIAL COMMISSION, GENERAL ORDERS ON SAFETY
3-4, 7-11, 13 (Effective Oct. 3, 1949; reprinted 1954)

Introduction

Authority. The General Orders on Safety have been adopted by the Industrial Commission in discharge of its duties under Section 101 of the Statutes of Wisconsin.

History. The General Orders on Safety were the first general orders to be adopted by the Industrial Commission after its organization and originally became effective on May 3, 1912. In addition to the original code, revised editions were issued in 1915 and again in 1932.

The necessity for further and more extensive revision of these orders became evident, and, following its usual policy in such matters, the Commission in 1945 invited a number of interested organizations to nominate representatives to serve on a new advisory committee. The personnel of this committee together with their representation is as follows:

M. F. Biancardi, Allis-Chalmers Manufacturing Company, Milwaukee, representing Wisconsin Manufacturers' Association—(Chairman)

Leon DeBroux, Port Washington, representing Wisconsin State Federation of Labor

E. P. Gallenbeck, Malleable Iron Range Company, Beaver Dam, representing Wisconsin Manufacturers' Association

Robert Gess, Employers' Mutuals, Milwaukee, representing Insurance Interests

H. J. Grimm, Hardware Mutual Casualty Company, Stevens Point, representing Insurance Interests

Ralph Harrison, Edgerton, representing Wisconsin State Federation of Labor

R. J. Lederer, Milwaukee, representing Master Builders' Association of Wisconsin

E. M. Lindsay, Hamilton Manufacturing Company, Two Rivers, representing Wisconsin Manufacturers' Association

Malcolm S. Lloyd, Onalaska, representing Wisconsin State Industrial Union Council

Carlton Mauthe, Northern Casket Company, Fond du Lac, representing Wisconsin Manufacturers' Association

Harry A. Nelson, Madison, representing Industrial Commission of Wisconsin

O. T. Nelson, Madison, representing Industrial Commission of Wisconsin—(Secretary)

In addition to the general advisory committee, the Industrial Commission also appointed two special subcommittees representing the paper mill industry and the laundry industry. These committees rendered efficient service in preparing revised orders pertaining to their respective industries.

The general advisory committee held thirty meetings beginning on April 7, 1947 and concluding on April 14, 1949. The resulting revised code was then submitted to the public at hearings conducted by the Industrial Commission at Appleton, Wausau, Madison, Milwaukee, Superior, Eau Claire and LaCrosse.

After giving consideration to the comments and suggestions received at these hearings, the revised code was adopted by the Industrial Commission on August 15, 1949. Publication was made in the official state newspaper on September 3, 1949 and the code became effective on October 3, 1949.

Order 1. Definitions

Guarded. When used in these orders, the term "guarded" unless otherwise specifically provided, shall mean so covered, fenced or enclosed that a person in the course of employment, or a frequenter is not likely to come in contact with the point of danger and be injured.

Exposed to Contact. When used in these orders, the term, "exposed to contact," unless otherwise specifically defined, shall mean that the location of the mechanical contrivance is such that it is likely to cause injury to a person while in the course of employment, or to a frequenter.

Order 2. Standards and Specifications

(a) *Railings and Toeboards.* Where standard railings and toeboards are called for in these orders, they shall conform to the following specifications:

(1) Railings shall be 42 inches in height except where otherwise specified and shall be equipped with toeboards unless the space between the lower rail and floor is filled with material as specified in (b).

(2) They shall be of substantial construction, shall be permanently fastened in place, and shall be smooth and free from protruding nails, bolts and splinters. An intermediate rail shall be provided between top rail and the floor, unless this space is filled with substantial wire mesh work, expanded metal, or other suitable material complying with the requirements of Order 2 (b).

(3) If constructed of pipe, the inside diameter of the pipe shall not be less than 1¼ inch.

(4) If constructed of metal shapes or bars, each part shall have a cross section at least equal in strength to that of a 1½″ x ³⁄₁₆″ angle.

(5) If constructed of wood, the posts shall not be smaller than the sizes commercially known as 2″ x 4″ or 3″ x 3″. The top rail shall be at least as large as the size known as 2″ x 4″, unless it is constructed in the manner shown in Fig. 1. [omitted.—Editor] The dimensions shown in Fig. 1 are the nominal size, and the finished size after planing is usually only about 3¾″ x 1³⁄₁₆″. The intermediate rail shall not be smaller than the size commercially known as 1″ x 4″.

(6) Wooden posts and uprights shall be spaced no more than 8 feet apart, and if of steel, not more than 10 feet apart.

(7) Toeboards shall be at least 4 inches in height and be constructed of wood, metal, metal grill with openings not exceeding 1 inch or other suitable material.

(8) Intermediate rails and toeboards, and top rails which are attached to side of posts, shall be placed on the side of the posts away from the engine, belt, floor opening, etc., to be guarded, so that any blow or pressure against them will be taken up by the posts instead of tending to push the rails away from the posts.

(b) *Guards.* (1) If guards are made of wire mesh work, perforated or expanded metal, crossed strips or bars of wood or metal, etc., the width or diameter of the holes shall not exceed 2 inches (see note below). If parallel strips or bars of wood or metal are used, the space between them shall not exceed 1 inch. There shall be no opening more than ½ inch in width or diameter within 4 inches of any gear, belt, pulley or flywheel, or other dangerous moving part. Wood slats shall be smooth and free from splinters, and the holes in perforated or expanded metal shall be free from sharp, cutting edges.

Note: If the material of which the guard is constructed has openings wider than ½ inch, it shall be covered at all points within 4 inches of belts, etc., with wire, mesh work or sheet metal or some other suitable material having no openings wider than ½ inch. If the hole is diamond shape, the width shall be measured along one side of the opening. If the hole is oblong, the greatest dimension shall not exceed that specified for "width."

. . . .

(2) The thickness of material used for guards shall not be less than is specified in the following table:

Material	A Clearance from Moving Part at All Points	B Largest Mesh Opening Allowable	C Minimum Gauge (U.S. Stand.) or Thickness
Woven Wire	Under 4″	½″	½″-#16
	4″-15″	2″	2″-#12
Expanded Metal	Under 4″	½″	½″-#18
	4″-15″	2″	2″-#13
Perforated Metal	Under 4″	½″	½″-#20
	4″-15″	2″	2″-#14
Sheet Metal	Under 4″	—	#22
	4″-15″	—	#22
Wood or Metal Strip Crossed	Under 4″	½″	Wood ¾″
	4″-15″	2″	Metal #16
Wood or Metal Strip Not Crossed	Under 4″	½″ width	Wood ¾″ Metal #16
	4″-15″	1″ width	Wood ¾″ Metal #16
Solid Wood *	—	—	—

* If plywood is used it shall be not less than ⅜″ thick and not less than 3 ply.

Note 1. If the width or diameter of the opening is less than ½ inch, the thickness of the material shall be at least as great as is specified above for a ½ inch opening.

Note 2. The material commonly known as "chicken wire" is not suitable for guards and does not meet the requirements of this section.

(3) The supporting frames shall be of substantial construction, such as angles varying from 1″ x 1″ x ⅛″ to 1½″ x 1½″ x ³⁄₁₆″, or iron pipe with inside diameter varying from ¾ inch to 1½ inch, according to the weight of the filling material, the size of the panels, and the exposure of the guard to collision with trucks, etc. Any panel which measures more than 42 inches in both width and length shall be substantially supported across its narrowest dimension at intervals of not more than 42 inches.

(4) The filling material shall be bolted, riveted, or welded or otherwise securely attached to the frame in such a manner that no sharp points or edges will be exposed.

Bolts and rivets shall be at least ³⁄₁₆ inch in diameter and shall be spaced not more than 10 inches apart. Where welded construction is used, it shall be such as will give equivalent strength.

Flat bars or strips used for clamps shall not be smaller than ¾″ x ⅛″ of metal or 1″ x 1″ if of wood.

Perforated or solid sheet metal may be bolted, riveted or welded directly to the angle iron frames.

(5) Guards shall be securely and permanently fastened in place, except as specifically otherwise provided.

Order 3. Maintenance

(a) All equipment, machine tools and power driven machinery shall be maintained in safe condition.

(b) Hand tools shall be maintained in safe condition.

Order 4. Belts, Pulleys, Etc.

The provisions of this order shall cover all types of belts, chains, cables and ropes together with pulleys, sprockets and sheaves in connection therewith, and for the purpose of simplification shall be referred to as belts and pulleys.

(a) All vertical and inclined belts within 6 feet of floor or platform level, and all pulleys and all horizontal belts within 7 feet of floor or platform level, except flat belts that are one inch or less in width and single round belts ½ inch or less in diameter, that move so slowly and are so located that there is no possibility of danger, shall be completely enclosed or effectively guarded. Belts protected by railings shall be guarded in accordance with Order 2 (a). Belts protected by guards other than railings shall be guarded in accordance with Order 2 (b).

[Then follow some detailed provisions under the headings "Vertical and Inclined Belts," "Horizontal Belts," and "Cones, Pulleys and Belts."—Editor]

General Interpretations

(i) Where belts are so located with reference to other equipment or to parts of buildings that they are guarded just as effectively as would be by standard guards as herein prescribed, no further guards shall be required.

(j) Where belts and other transmission apparatus are located in locked enclosure not used for manufacturing or storage purposes, and are inaccessible except when the machinery is not in motion, such locked enclosures will be accepted in lieu of other guarding.

(k) Belts which are within 18 inches horizontally from the vertical plane of the edges of any balcony or working platform shall be subject to the same requirements as if they were directly over such balconies or platforms.

[Then follow some "illustrations and descriptive matter . . . intended to be helpful in meeting the requirements for the guarding of belts and pulleys."—Editor]

NOTES AND QUESTIONS

1. The General Orders on Safety, of which there are 83, form but one of numerous codes or bodies of regulations of the Industrial Commission in the field of safety. Other rules or orders concern mines; quarries and pits; elevators; explosives; flammable liquids; tunnel, caisson, and trench construction; cleaning and dyeing; electrical work; electric fences; dusts, fumes, vapors, and gases; spray coating; building construction; sanitation; boilers; refrigerating plants; acetylene gas; heating, ventilating, and air conditioning; and fire prevention.

2. Compare the provisions of the Industrial Commission Act and the Commission's General Orders on Safety, reprinted above, with the common-law safe-place rule, as administered by judge and jury. Which legal process do you think is likely to be more effective in achieving safety objectives? Why?

Compare the same provisions with the early safety legislation dealt with in Part II. Which of these alternatives is likely to be more effective in achieving safety objectives? Why?

3. By authorizing the Industrial Commission to formulate such bodies of rules, has the legislature abdicated, or unduly delegated, its legislative power to the Commission? Is such delegation constitutional? These problems are dealt with in the extract from Professor Hurst's book, reprinted beginning on page 789.

4. a. Documents on file at the office of the Secretary of State reveal that in the form in which it was introduced, the bill which was eventually enacted as L. 1911, ch. 485 read in part: "Sec. 1021b-1, (10): The term 'safe' as applied to the place of employment and to the equipment, surroundings, conditions or operation thereof shall mean and include such as are free from any danger to the employee in or the frequenter of such place of employment, and such as do not subject the employee or frequenter to any possible harm or injury while in such place of employment." Compare the definition of "safe" in 101.01, (11), which is substantially the same as the like provision enacted in 1911. Which is the stronger? Which the more definite? Why the change? Compare the terms of the early factory safety legislation and the decisions thereunder, studied in Part II. Would it not have been better draftsmanship, because more direct and simple, to have defined "safety" simply in terms of "reasonable" safety? Or why, indeed, encumber the statute with any definition of so well-known a term as "safety" anyway? See the excerpt from Commons's biography, reprinted below.

b. The bill which was to become the Industrial Commission Act, as originally introduced, required the employer to furnish not only a "safe" but a "hygienic" place of employment, and declared that "The term 'hygienic' as applied to the place of employment and to the equipment, surroundings, conditions or operation thereof shall mean and include such as shall be in no degree injurious to the health of the employee in or the frequenter of such place of employment and such as shall not subject the employee in or the frequenter of such place of employment to any loss of health or to any injury to his physical condition." These provisions were omitted from the bill as passed into law. Consider the significance of this alteration.

MYSELF, THE AUTOBIOGRAPHY OF JOHN R. COMMONS *
141-143, 153-160 (1934)

Here [during an investigation of steel industry accidents, in Pittsburgh.— Editor] I learned my first lesson in accident prevention. The United States Steel

---

* John R. Commons, 1862-1945, was Professor of Economics at the University of Wisconsin, 1904-1933, member of the Industrial Commission, 1911-13, the Wiscon-

Company was then just becoming a pioneer in this field. I followed this up and, when I became a member of the Wisconsin Industrial Commission, I attended conferences of the safety experts of the Steel Corporation brought together from different parts of the country. I decided then that a workman's accident compensation law, if properly drawn, would cost nobody anything. It would not raise prices for the consumers, and would actually increase the profits of the employers. It was amazing to me how greatly accidents could be prevented by safety experts if employers could be furnished an inducement to hire them for the purpose. I wanted all employers to be compelled by law to pay accident compensation as an inducement to accident prevention. Afterwards, in 1911, in drafting the Industrial Commission law for Wisconsin, I tied together, under one administrative body, the workmen's insurance and the accident prevention law. These had been conceived, in Wisconsin and other states, as two independent activities under two independent state boards, insurance to be shifted to consumers in higher prices, and safety to be enforced on employers by factory inspectors and criminal prosecutions with jury trials, where the employer was assumed to be innocent unless proved without a doubt to be guilty. Why not assume the opposite? The employer intends to do right but does not have sufficient inducement. Why not shape up legislation and administration on this assumption? Let the state furnish him with the inducements by taxing him proportionate to his employees' loss of wages by accidents, and then employ safety experts, instead of crime detectives and prosecutors, to show him how to make a profit by preventing accidents.

The experts of the Steel Company claimed, to my astonishment, that they could reduce the burden of accidents two-thirds, if they were supported, as they were, by the company. Obviously I wanted all employers to be forced by law to follow the lead of the Steel Corporation, and to make a profit by doing good, instead of defending themselves as alleged criminals for neglecting the safety of their employees. . . .

While working on the public utility law of 1907 I wondered why similar administrative machinery could not be set up for the conflicts of capital and labor. I came across, in the University library, the remarkable volumes by Hector Denis, professor of ethics and economics at the University of Brussels and leader of the socialist group in the Belgian parliament. These volumes, first published in 1897, as Histoire des Systèmes économiques et socialistes, enlightened me more than any other history of economic thought. Denis had organized, outside the parliamentary system, the Belgian Superior Council of Labor, composed of representatives of capital, labor and the public, quite similar to Easley's National Civic Federation. It was copied in France.

I immediately set one of my students, Francis H. Bird, from Dartmouth College, to writing for his doctor's dissertation, a history of this Belgian Council. I had an idea that something like this council, based on my experience with the Civic

sin Minimum Wage Board, 1919-1945. His books include History of Labor in the United States (with others) (1926-35); Legal Foundations of Capitalism (1957 reprint); Principles of Labor Legislation (with John B. Andrews) (1927); and Institutional Economics (1934).—Editor

Federation, could be incorporated into a Labor Department for the State of Wisconsin. In 1910, while I was at work on the Milwaukee survey, I placed Bird in charge of organizing my class in labor problems into a miniature world-wide council of capital and labor for the investigation of labor administration in all countries, and then incorporated what fitted the Wisconsin situation into an Industrial Commission law for the state. Then, in drafting such a bill on the initiative of the newly elected governor, Francis E. McGovern, Bird and I joined with McCarthy [Dr. Charles McCarthy, organizer and first chief of the Wisconsin Legislative Reference Library.—Editor] in his reference library, during the legislative session of 1911. All of the piece-meal labor laws of the state, going back to their beginnings in 1867, and including the new accident compensation law then before the legislature, were now to be brought together under a single council of capital and labor. The older laws were repealed, to take effect when the Commission issued its "orders."

Here the problem was, in part, the constitutional problem, already solved in the railroad commission law, of delegating by the legislature to an administrative body the power to make rules governing, in this case, the relations of employers and employees. The railroad and public utility laws dealt with monopolies. Here we were dealing with competitive industries. In the former laws it had been necessary only to delegate to the Commission authority to investigate, ascertain and fix "reasonable values" and "reasonable services," leaving to the Commission to find out, if it could, what was "reasonable," subject to review by the courts. But in the relation of employers and employees we had to shift the legal meaning of "reasonable" to cover, not values but practices. These practices came under such diverse headings as safety, health, child labor, moral well-being, wage-bargaining, hours of labor, minimum wages for women and children, labor disputes, and free employment offices. Here McCarthy came in with his acute and inescapable criticism. The word "reasonable," under judicial interpretation, meant just ordinary, average, or customary practices, and any effort of the Industrial Commission to raise the standards above that level would be declared by the courts to be unconstitutional as taking the property of employers without "due process of law." We spent much time endeavoring to overcome these criticisms by McCarthy. This was my ideal of "collective thinking." We wanted a definition of "reasonableness" that would be acceptable to the courts but would raise the standards above the ordinary. We assigned to Bird the research in law encyclopedias and court decisions to ascertain such a definition. After many conferences he came forward with the definition that reasonableness should mean the highest degree of safety, health, well-being of employees, etc., that the nature of the industry or employment would reasonably permit.

This definition of reasonableness I worked out afterwards, with my classes, during more than twenty years, as my meaning of "pragmatism" distinguished from "idealism." I find many applications in my Institutional Economics. Reasonableness is idealism limited by practicability. Practicability could be investigated and ascertained as actually in operation in the factories of the more progressive employers, and then the rules of the commission, sanctioned by law, could bring other employers up to their level.

Reasonable values and reasonable practices were entirely new words introduced into the theories of political economy. Often my students and sometimes my economist critics said that "reasonable" was something purely subjective, and there were as many meanings of reasonableness as there were individuals. Such a term placed the determination of reasonableness in the arbitrary mind of whatever individual happened to be in authority. But I considered this objection to be an inheritance from the subjective individualism of preceding economic theorists. A collectivistic theory of value derived from existing best practices, from custom, the common law, and the decision of courts, could make reasonableness "objective" and therefore capable of investigation and testimony, leading to the formation of working rules for collective action in control of individual action. I had in mind, all along, the accident prevention work of the United States Steel Corporation, but extended to all other best practices of other pioneer employers. . . .

But how could the Labor Council of Denis, or the Civic Federation of Easley, [a Foundation for the study of social and economic problems.—Editor] be incorporated in the industrial commission law for the investigation of "reasonable" practices? We were afraid that the legislature would provide that future governors, according to American practice, would appoint politicians instead of "industrialists" and trade unionists. The latter could be selected only by their own voluntary associations. Yet these associations could not lawfully select officials of government. So we left that selection to the Commission, and merely provided that the Commission might appoint "advisers without compensation," latterly interpreted by the Attorney General to include necessary expenses. We saw no job-seeking by political parties if there were no money in it from the state treasury. So it turned out. The Commission had, at one time, as many as two hundred advisers, either the well-known leaders themselves, or recommended by the leaders of voluntary associations, including employers, employees, insurance companies, physicians, consumers' leagues, social workers, professors, and others.

It became my assignment, after the Industrial Commission was organized, to initiate these advisory committees, while the other members had charge of the other activities of the commission. I remember my first committee, the committee on boiler safety. There were a manufacturer of boilers, a manufacturer-user of boilers, an insurance company's inspector of boilers, an employee operating boilers, and the deputy of the Commission, a former locomotive engineer who had been a factory inspector in the former labor department. We converted the factory inspectors into secretaries, organizers and investigators for these safety and other committees. The boiler committee met in Milwaukee as often as they decided. I looked in occasionally on their meetings. The Industrial Commission was getting, free of charge, the services of men who could not have been hired at $100 per day by the state and would not have worked at all with a political appointee of the Commission. It required this committee about a year to work out its "boiler code." We considered that, if a committee like this, representing several conflicting economic interests, could agree unanimously upon a code of safety rules, then that code would be considered "reasonable" by the courts. The code would not be "ideal" but it would be pragmatic, the best that the nature of the industry would permit; and it would enlist the better employers to support its enforcement instead of fighting it in the courts. We could always say to employers, "This code is not our work nor the work of the legislature. It is the work of your leading fellow employers." And we printed their names when publishing the codes.

Yet "reasonable safety" would be idealistic. It would not be the ordinary safety of the common law, but that ideal safety which was practicable. Boiler manufacturers learned to turn out boilers to meet the specifications of the code. When the code was completed the Commission printed it as a "tentative" code, and held a public hearing—to meet the requirements of "due process of law"—where anybody in the state could appear with his objections. Then the code was referred back to the advisory committee for revision, and the final code, as recommended, was issued as an "order" by the Commission. The old laws on boiler safety were then automatically repealed as dated forward by the enabling act of the legislature, and the new code became the law of the state. Eventually several hundred pages of similar codes, on this and other subjects, with revisions and improvements on earlier codes, were printed by the Commission, and these became, for the lawyers of the state, a part of their working libraries equivalent in authority to the "Wisconsin Statutes," the latter published after each session of the legislature. If a lawyer brought a suit in court involving the unreasonableness of these codes, the legislature had provided that he could bring in no testimony not previously presented to the Industrial Commission, and the court was required to send the case back to the Commission, which meant the advisory committee, to take into account this new testimony and make revision of the code if the committee saw fit. "Reasonableness" was now deemed to be ascertained, not by conflicting arguments and pleadings in court or legislature, nor by legal precedents, nor by ordinary custom, nor by opinions of judges, but by collective action of leading representatives of conflicting interests in the advisory committees. The court passed only on the "due procedure" of the Commission.

After the enactment of the Industrial Commission law in Wisconsin I was called upon at various times to appear before the legislatures, or legislative committees, of Ohio, New York, and Colorado, to explain the principles of the law which was in course of adoption by those states. Lawyers and courts naturally objected to its substitution of business men and labor leaders for lawyers in determining what was reasonable by cross-examinations in a trial court.

It was my participation in these proceedings that set me to investigating what the courts meant by "due process of law." I discovered in the Hurtado case, of 1884 [Hurtado v. California, 110 U.S. 516—Editor], developed in my Legal Foundations of Capitalism, that the Supreme Court of the United States changed the meaning of due process from the "due procedure" of the ancient common law to the meaning of "substantial justice" under changing conditions, and that this "justice" was equivalent to reasonableness. So I contended that, in economic conflicts, reasonable values and reasonable practices were not the subjective opinions of anybody, but were the collective opinion, expressed in action, of those whose economic interests were conflicting, but who investigated together and knew by experience all of the facts. This, I found afterwards was Peirce's "pragmatism." My boiler committee was my pragmatism in action. I am now told by a colleague in philosophy that it is "instrumental pragmatism," which philosophers were beginning to formulate. He quotes for me what I wrote in 1913 when I was in the midst of these experiments in methods of teaching economics: "Academic teaching . . . is merely brains without experience. . . . The 'practical' extreme . . . is experience without brains. One is half-baked philosophy—the other is rule-of-thumb."

HURST, *THE GROWTH OF AMERICAN LAW*
406-411 (1950)

After 1870 administrators had most influence on policy through the issue of rules or regulations under authority delegated by the legislature. Through such delegated legislation the executive branch as a whole probably had more effect on the everyday lives of people than through all its influence upon the legislature.

(1) *Federal Doctrine.* Constitutional theory first denied that there could be any lawful "delegation" of legislative power: The legislature could authorize the executive to find facts, on the existence of which the exercise of a statutory power depended; but the courts insisted that it was the exclusive right and duty of the legislature to decide what should be the law. As late as 1892, in Field v. Clark [143 U.S. 649] the Supreme Court repeated this rigid doctrine, though with incongruity typical in this area the Court there held that Congress could give the President discretion to remove from the free list certain products of a country whose own tariff the President found to be "reciprocally unequal and unreasonable."

In 1928, in Hampton v. United States [276 U.S. 394] Mr. Chief Justice Taft cast the principle into new form. There the Court sustained the Flexible Tariff Act of 1922, which authorized the President to adjust tariff rates up to 50 per cent where he found that existing rates did not "equalize . . . differences in costs of production in the United States and the principal competing countries. . . ." The Chief Justice tried to minimize the extent of discretion that this grant conferred. But he did not try to rationalize what Congress had done as merely a delegation to the President of a power to find "facts." Rather, he declared that "If Congress shall lay down by legislative act an intelligible principle to which the person or body authorized to fix such rates is directed to conform, such legislative action is not a forbidden delegation of legislative power." Five years later the new judicial frankness had progressed to the point at which Mr. Justice Cardozo, speaking for the Court, could refer to the 1922 statute as "in substance a delegation, though a permissible one, of the legislative power." [Nitrogen Products Co. v. United States, 288 U.S. 294, 305 (1933)].

Through the years when the Court insisted that legislative power could not be "delegated," it upheld all acts of Congress that were challenged before it on the ground of unlawful delegation. However, in two cases in 1935 the Court held that provisions of the National Industrial Recovery Act were an invalid abdication of legislative responsibility. [Panama Refining Co. v. Ryan, 293 U.S. 388 (1934); Schechter Poultry Corp. v. United States, 294 U.S. 495 (1935)].

The government lost these cases in an atmosphere so unfavorable to it as to cast doubt on the strength of the precedents so established. Congress passed the National Industrial Recovery Act in days of mingled despair, fear, and hope in a new administration. Concerned above all to save the country from economic disaster, Congress granted the President powers of wartime breadth to campaign against depression. The two lawsuits reached the Supreme Court after the country had recovered nerve. By then small businessmen and liberals alike were severely critical of the act, which they felt worked mainly to promote monopoly. A majority of the Justices were emotionally as well as intellectually opposed to the administration's broad intervention in the economy. On top of these factors, one of the lawsuits provided an object lesson in the dangers of loose administrative procedure. At the last minute the Government discovered . . . that the regulation under which the defendant was being prosecuted had by inadvertence been amended out of existence before the charged violations occurred.* Against this background the NIRA cases did not prophesy a fundamental change in the Court's general treatment of delegation. On the whole record, the doctrine limiting delegation of legislative power stood more as an admonition of principle than as a substantial curb on Congressional practice.

(2) *Federal Practice.* In its practical effect, constitutional doctrine reflected the realities of government as it was conducted from 1790 on. From the days of the first Congress there were examples of statutory delegation of rule-making

---

* The case referred to is United States v. Smith, 293 U.S. 633 (1934). The fact referred to was discovered by Special Assistant to the Attorney General M. S. Huberman to whom the Department of Justice had assigned the task of preparing the briefs in Panama Refining Co. v. Ryan and Amazon Petroleum Corp. v. Ryan, 293 U.S. 388 (1934). "On looking into the materials . . . Huberman . . . discovered to his astonishment that the provision of the petroleum code involved in the Amazon case, and which had been involved in the Smith criminal case, had been inadvertently dropped in the process of amending the code, and had not been in existence during the entire period of the litigation. Members of the Petroleum Board had learned of the omission shortly after it had been made, but, knowing it to have been unintentional, they apparently had assumed it to be of little importance. The Department of Justice, therefore, with Judge Stephens as its

spokesman, had to face the Supreme Court crippled by the mistakes of lawyers of another agency. Opposition counsel made the most of the situation. It was said, referring to the Smith case which had now been dismissed [the Government's appeal to the Supreme Court had, on the Government's motion, been dismissed], that 'Smith was arrested, indicted, and held in jail for several days and then had to put up bond for violating a law that did not exist.' A reporter stated that 'smiles appeared on the usually solemn faces of the Justices and the crowd of lawyers that filled the room when Mr. Stephens admitted that the trial court had sustained a demurrer to the indictment on the ground that the nonexistent section of the code was unconstitutional and that the Justice Department had appealed this decision to the Supreme Court'" Swisher, Federal Organization of Legal Functions, 33 Am. Pol. Sci. Rev. 973, 984 (1939).—Editor

powers to the executive. The subjects involved ranged from control of trading with the Indians to the collection of internal revenue, the appraisal of imported goods for tariff purposes, the taking of fire precautions on passenger and freight vessels, and the prevention of diseases imported from foreign places.

After 1870 government intervened more and more in economic affairs. As it did so, more and more rule-making power was delegated to the executive. This went on regardless of which political party was in power. Plainly the growth of delegated legislation responded to deep needs of government. By 1940 all but four or five of forty-nine major federal administrative agencies held authority to make rules to regulate matters under their jurisdiction; all of them held power to fix procedural rules to govern their disposition of business.

These rule-making powers grew to include areas of life that deeply concerned great numbers of people. . . .

(3) *State Doctrine and Practice.* In the states, after 1900, administrative legislation grew on a scale proportionate to its growth in the federal government. State legislators and administrators were partners in the progressive building of policies that concerned industrial safety, compensation for industrial accidents, the rates and services of public utilities, the issue of securities, and the conservation of natural resources. The relatively weak position of the governor allowed independent administrative agencies to play a larger role in policy making in some states than such agencies did in the federal government.

Though state and federal practice were parallel, constitutional doctrine had a somewhat different history in the state courts from that which it followed in the Supreme Court of the United States. Well into the 1930's some state courts still denied that there could be any lawful "delegation" of legislative power. Other state courts—for example, the Wisconsin court, in a much cited opinion by Mr. Chief Justice Rosenberry in 1928—went beyond the Supreme Court of the United States in frank recognition of the realities of delegated legislation. [State ex rel. Wisconsin Inspection Bureau v. Whitman, 196 Wis. 472, 220 N.W. 929 (1928)].

The conservatism of state court doctrine reflected a stiffer application of constitutional limits on delegation. It was not until 1935 that the Supreme Court of the United States upset an act of Congress on this ground. From 1850 on, state Reports were sprinkled with decisions which held state laws unconstitutional because they made unlawful delegations. The tone of opinions and the kinds of cases that provoked the opinions suggested that the judges often thus rationalized their distaste for the substantive policy of the disputed statute. This seemed particularly likely where the legislation regulated economic affairs.

On the whole the state courts tempered their strict doctrine with common sense in application. For example, they uniformly upheld administrative regulation of public utility rates. Sometimes the decisions which upset legislation made more sense than the opinions that went with them. If the judges looked skeptically on broad delegations of the power to license the practice of callings, perhaps they knew that licensing could serve to restrain competition as well as to protect public interest. If they showed distrust of broad delegations to make building codes, or fire regulations, or to set zones for business and residential property, perhaps they took heed of the dubious level of local government administration in such matters. There was little evidence that the state courts had more than delayed the extension of delegated legislation into any areas where the public interest required it.

(4) *Why Delegated Legislation?* What was behind this vast growth of delegated legislation? The range of human affairs involved made it unlikely that any one explanation would suffice. Observers emphasized various causes: the need for speed and flexibility in some fields of regulation; the need of more firsthand knowledge than a legislature could provide in areas of tangled, detailed, shifting problems; the value of the continuity, and tested expertness which experienced administrators could bring to the shaping of a policy in evolution; the release of the legislature from encumbering detail, to the consideration of general policy. One could match each of these explanations with examples—but how evaluate their relative force?

Sometimes legislators delegated rule-making power simply because they did not know what else to do, or because opposing forces were in such balance as to preclude putting into a statute anything except the most general declaration of principle. In this aspect delegated legislation was simply a more open form of a practice that the legislature had often followed with the help of the court. When legislators entrusted the enforcement of any broadly phrased statute to private or public lawsuits, this amounted to a delegation of rule-making power to the judges who would be called on to "interpret" the legislation. So accepted was this partnership of legislature and court that when objection was raised that the vague terms of the Sherman Act called on the judges to legislate, and hence violated the separation of powers, Mr. Chief Justice White summarily dismissed the argument: it was "clearly unsound." He declared that the argument "in substance denies the existence of essential legislative authority and challenges the right of the judiciary to perform duties which that department of the government has exerted from the beginning." [Standard Oil Co. v. United States, 221 U.S. 1, 69 (1911)]. This reply—either very naive or very sophisticated—skirted the fact that stood out in the legislative history of the act: namely, that Congress had passed the statute feeling it must do something, but unable to agree on anything tangible to do.

Much delegated legislation did what the more realistic judicial doctrine declared it to do; it specified rules within the framework of standards defined by the legislature. But even the remodeled judicial doctrine did not realistically describe all that was done by delegated legislation. Under many important statutes the administrators made first-rank policy as well as filling in the details under statutory standards. This was true of railroad regulation under the Interstate Commerce Act and the rules and orders of the Interstate Commerce Commission. It was true of the patterns of regulation spelled out by statute and administrative orders under the Public Utilities Holding Company Act, or under some aspects of the Fair Labor Standards Act.

"Delegation" once implied that a job within a fixed frame of policy had been turned over more or less finally to the administrators. However, as delegated legislation grew in importance, administrators and legislators more and more joined in a continuing process of policy making, by experiment and out of experience. The law that resulted was less and less the product of a definitive act of legislation. What happened oftener fitted this pattern: (1) The legislature entered a new field, with a broad declaration of standards and a delegation of rule-making power to an administrative agency. (2) Administrative legislation began to put content into the broad outlines of the basic statute. (3) In subsequent acts the legislature might refine, approve, or rebuke the administrative policy making. (4) More often, legislative committees heard administrators on their requests for appropriations or new authority, aired complaints about the operation of the law, sought explanations of things done or undone, and in such diverse ways contributed to shape evolving policy. (5) All of this activity following upon the original legislative decision to embark on a new course of policy making was given practical focus in the day-to-day work of administration—in fact finding, rule making, inspecting, form checking, negotiating, conciliating, arguing, warning, prosecuting, interpreting, deciding.

The policy-making partnership of legislator and administrator was largely an unplanned and wasteful accommodation to our failure to provide institutions properly organized and staffed to deal with twentieth-century issues. On the other hand, in some measure the partnership was inevitable. It responded to issues that were too new and too complicated for men to grasp and resolve at first impact in a completed program. Often the partnership was the only way by which law could begin to take hold of a problem while government waited on the growth of the understanding and public consent required for a sound and democratic choice of policy. The approach was not new in our law. As working partners, judges and lawyers, and judges and legislators had built many a principle of common law and court-glossed legislation. . . .

EDITORIAL NOTE: PUBLICATION of ADMINISTRATIVE LEGISLATION

The Government's embarrassment in the Panama Refining Co. case, referred to by Professor Hurst above, provoked the passage in 1935 of a Congressional statute establishing the Federal Register. All documents promulgated by any federal agency, other than a judicial or legislative agency, and having "general applicability and legal effect" or prescribing a penalty must be published in the Register. "No document required . . . to be published in the Federal Register," the statute says, "shall be valid as against any person who has not had actual knowledge thereof" until copies have been filed for publication with the National Archives Establishment. Filling in the Federal Register constitutes constructive notice of the contents of the document in all cases except those in which notice by publication is insufficient in law. See Federal Crop Insurance Corporation v. Merrill, 332 U.S. 380 (1947).

Many of the regulations published in the Federal Register have been codified in the Code of Federal Regulations, which consists of the original code (15 volumes), a cumulative supplement and annual supplements. See

J. H. Wigmore, The Federal Register and Code of Federal Regulations—How to Use Them, If You Have Them, 29 A.B.A.J. 10 (1943); F. C. Newman, Government and Ignorance—A Progress Report on Publication of Federal Regulations, 63 Harv. L. Rev. 929 (1950).

In 1955, Wisconsin passed similar legislation requiring the publication of all administrative "rules" in the newly created Administrative Code and Register. See Laws 1955, c. 221; Helstad New Law in Administrative Rule-Making, 1956 Wis. L. Rev. 407. For the situation in other states, see Harris, Administrative Practice and Procedure: Comparative State Legislation, 6 Okla. L. Rev. 29 (1953); Heady, Administrative Procedure Legislation in the States (1952); Moreland, State Administrative Rules, 9 The Book of the States 157 (1952-53).

EDITORIAL NOTE: PUBLIC PARTICIPATION in RULE MAKING

The federal Administrative Procedure Act does not attempt to establish uniform rule-making procedures to which all agencies must conform, but it does impose certain minimum requirements. Thus it requires every agency to accord any interested person the right to petition for the issuance, amendment, or repeal of a rule, but apparently does not require the agency to act on the petition. (5 U.S.C.A. 1004[d]). The Act does not itself require that a public hearing precede administrative rule making. But if rules are required by some other statute to be made on the record after opportunity for an agency hearing, it details a procedure which must then be followed. (5 U.S.C.A. 1004[b], 1007 and 1008). If no other statute requires a hearing, the Act requires that rule making be preceded by notice of the proposal in the Federal Register, which shall include "either the terms or substance of the proposed rule or a description of the subjects and issues involved." But even this requirement of notice is not to apply to (a) any military, naval, or foreign affairs function of the United States; (b) any matter relating to agency management or personnel or to public property, loans, grants, benefits, or contracts; (c) interpretative rules; (d) general statements of policy; (e) rules of agency organization, procedure or practice; and (f) any situation in which the agency for good cause finds that notice and public procedure thereon are impracticable, unnecessary, or contrary to the public interest. If notice is required, the agency must, thereafter, "afford interested persons an opportunity to participate in the rule making through submission of written data, views, or arguments with or without opportunity to present the same orally in any manner; and, after consideration of all relevant matter presented, the agency shall incorporate in any rules adopted a concise general statement of their basis and purpose." (5 U.S.C.A. 1004). State administrative procedure acts, like that in Wisconsin, contain similar provisions.

Although the federal Act does not deal with informal procedures and advisory committees, these methods of public participation are widely used by federal agencies and are specifically established in some federal statutes (e.g., see The Fair Labor Standards Act of 1938, 29 U.S.C.A. 208[a] [1946].) The Wisconsin act specifically states that the agency is not confined to the use of the designated formal procedures but may, in addition, continue to use informal conferences and consultations and is authorized "to appoint committees of experts or interested persons or representatives of the general public to advise it with respect to any contemplated rule making."

EDITORIAL NOTE: LEGISLATIVE REVIEW of ADMINISTRATIVE RULES

The legislature, of course, may exercise its power to review administrative rules by modifying or repealing the statute under which the agency operates. Often, however, it may not be feasible for the legislature to exercise this broad power to get at particular rules which may have aroused dissatisfaction, particularly if it has to run the gantlet of the executive veto. So, for example, Wisconsin Laws 1953, Chapter 331 authorized the legislature to invalidate any administrative rule by joint resolution. The Attorney-General, however, rendered an opinion to the effect that chapter 331 was unconstitutional because it violated Art. IV, s. 17 of the Wisconsin constitution which provides that "no law shall be enacted except by bill" and a bill must run the gantlet of a possible veto by the governor. (43 Ops. Att'y. Gen. 350 (1954).) The 1955 law on administrative rule-making, therefore, repealed the 1953 act. Instead, it created a special legislative committee, consisting of two senators and three assemblymen, to promote "adequate and proper rules by agencies and an understanding upon the part of the public respecting such rules." It is authorized to (1) investigate complaints with respect to rules and (2) "recommend to the rule-making agency responsible for the rules complained of, such changes in, deletions from or additions to the rules as they believe would make the rules to which objection was raised more equitable, practical and more in conformity with the public interest"; and (3) "report, biennially, to the legislative council, legislature and governor of its activities and include therein its recommendations." (S. 227.041).

No federal statute expressly requires any congressional committee to exercise functions similar to those of the Wisconsin legislature's special committee for review of administrative rules. Nevertheless, congressional committees do, in practice, perform these very same functions. This aspect of their work has aroused controversy and is discussed in the article by Newman and Keaton, which follows this note.

The Wisconsin law, outlined above, represents an attempt to make use of long-standing British practice, which Gellhorn and Byse, Cases and Comments on Administrative Law 189-91 (1960) describe as follows:

"For many years British statutes delegating power to make regulations usually, but not always, have required the regulations promulgated thereunder to be laid before Parliament for 'negative' or 'affirmative' action. If the 'affirmative' requirement is used, the regulation does not become effective unless it is approved. By far the more widely used is the 'negative,' which provides that if within a stated period—usually forty days—either House resolves that the regulation be annulled, it shall thenceforth have no effect, but without prejudice to any action which may have been taken under it. . . . Since 1944, a Committee on Statutory Instruments [administrative rules—Editor] has examined every statutory instrument laid or laid in draft before the House of Commons, with a view to determining whether the special attention of the House should be drawn to it. The Committee is not to consider questions of the policy or the merits of the instrument nor is it to determine issues of legal validity. But since it is empowered to draw attention to any 'unusual or unexpected use of the powers conferred by the Statute under which' the instrument was promulgated, the Committee 'has often found itself peeping over the fence at questions of policy merits, and vires. . . . Most frequently the Committee finds itself reporting instruments on the rather formal ground of unpunctuality (in publication or in laying) or of unintelligibility.' (C. T. Carr, Legislative Control of Administrative Rules and Regulations: II. Parliamentary Supervision in Britain, 30 N.Y.U.L. Rev. 1045, 1050 [1955].)

" 'During the first eight years of its existence the Committee examined 6,886 instruments and . . . [drew] attention of the House to 66.' [Carr, *supra* at 1050]. Aided during this period by Sir Cecil T. Carr, the highly respected Counsel to the Speaker who was for long the editor of Statutory Rules and Orders, the Committee often called upon administrative bodies to clarify and justify their proposed regulations. According to informed persons with whom the matter has been discussed in Britain, administrators have been induced by the Committee's mere existence to exercise great care in utilizing the powers delegated to them."

For further information on the British practice, see Kersell, Parliamentary Supervision of Delegated Legislation (1960); Griffith and Street, Principles of Administrative Law 84-99 (2d ed. 1957); and Jennings, Parliament 501-515 (2d ed. 1957).

A few states, other than Wisconsin (Alaska, Connecticut, Kansas, Nebraska, Michigan and Virginia), have also experimented with systems of legislative review inspired by British practice. For a discussion of these systems and their problems, see Schubert, Legislative Adjudication of Administrative Legislation, 7 J. Pub. L. 134 (1958); Howe, Legislative Review of Administrative Rules, in Current Trends in State Legislation, 1955-56, p. 167 (1957); and Schwartz, Legislative Control of Administrative Rules and Regulations: I. The American Experience, 30 N.Y.U.L. Rev. 1031 (1955); Rhode, Committee Clearance of Administrative Decisions (1959); Bernstein, The Job of the Federal Executive 93-99, 109-111 (1958); and Smith and Cotten, Administrative Accountability to Congress, 10 West. Pol. Q. 405 (1957).

The Research Report on Administrative Rule-Making of the Wisconsin Legislative Council (Vol. II, Part II, pp. 140-141) sums up the advantages and disadvantages of legislative review as follows:

"Among the *advantages* which have been cited for legislative clearance or review procedures are the following:

"(1) Such procedures tend to give the legislature greater control over the administration of the laws which it has enacted. Popular control over law making therefore is extended. According to the proponents of legislative clearance, this tends to bring administrative rule making into accord with constitutional theory.

"(2) Rules are apt to be more carefully drafted with a view toward complying with legislative intent if the administrator knows that the rules will be or are likely to be subjected to legislative scrutiny. Legislative clearance or review procedures therefore have a salutary effect on rule making which should redound to the benefit of legislators, administrative officials, and the public even without review procedures being invoked.

"(3) Administrative officials also might benefit from review or clearance procedures in that such procedures would tend to relieve the officials of the pressures for rule changes which sometimes are brought to bear by individual legislators on behalf of constituents or at least would enable administrative officials to point to established procedures as the proper means of obtaining changes in rules.

"A requirement that the legislature must pass on all rules before their becoming effective would have several *disadvantages:*

"(1) The burden of technical detail which the legislature must bear would be greatly increased. This would leave less time for important policy decisions and thus would tend to defeat the original purpose of delegation of power to agencies.

"(2) Many important and proper rules probably would die with the sine die adjournment of the legislature, simply because the legislature did not get around to acting on them.

"(3) If the power of disapproval is vested in a small legislative committee, the danger of abuse is greatly increased. A few legislators then could invalidate a rule even though the majority of legislators might have favored it if it had been brought to their attention. The objective of popular control over administrative rule making would be defeated.

"(4) A disadvantage which can be cited for all devices which place a burden on rule making is that the likelihood of agencies operating under informal or unpublished policies thereby is increased. Michigan experience seems to bear out this apprehension. Ninety rules were filed in 1945 prior to the imposition of clearance requirements for rules. By 1950, just 3 years after the imposition of clearance requirements, this figure had dropped to 18.

"Most of the disadvantages or limitations cited above can be overcome if the legislature is given a power of invalidating rules by disapproval rather than being required to approve rules before they become effective or being required to act on all rules which are adopted. The Michigan experience, however, indicates that this procedure is subject to one drawback. Since a rule is given legislative consideration only when someone complains about the rule, the hearings take on the form of adversary proceedings, the complainant being one party and the agency being the other party. Because of the limited scope of such hearings, many facts which should enter into considerations of policy making are likely to be omitted."

Newman* and Keaton,* *CONGRESS AND THE FAITHFUL
EXECUTION OF LAWS—SHOULD LEGISLATORS
SUPERVISE ADMINISTRATORS?*
41 California Law Review 565-578, 584-595 (1953)

"He [the President of the United States] . . . shall take Care that the Laws be faithfully executed. . . ." [1]

In 1953 the problem of legislative interference with administrative action became a headline issue. It is more than the problem dramatized by struggles between Executive and Legislative—between strong or weak Presidents and strong or weak Congresses. It is more than the problem whether the late Senator Taft, as Majority Leader, had too much control over foreign policy, or Representative Reed, through the Ways and Means Committee, too much influence on tax policy. It relates to a wide range of questions that arise when Congress, or committees of Congress, or individual Senators and Representatives take action intended to affect administrative rule making, administrative adjudication, and administrative management.

To illustrate: As citizens (and particularly as lawyer citizens) should we care when the Food and Drug Administration and the Department of Agriculture, allegedly because of pressure from the Senate Agricultural Committee, abandon their program of grain inspection? Or when the Air Force, allegedly because of a pending Senate investigation, cancels the Kaiser-Frazer contract for flying boxcars? Or when a Senator announces that he and other members of the Appropriations Committee intend to "knock out of the policy-making shops [of the State Department] . . . about a hundred or two hundred top people," for the reason that the incumbent Secretary refuses to purge these "hold-overs" from a prior Administration? [7]

Unhappily, fair comment on this kind of question is muddled by many commentators' failure to identify the exact issues that should cause concern. There is a tendency to overlook the distinction between (1) the merits of a controversy, and (2) the governmental powers and procedures that led to a decision on the merits. In the Kaiser-Frazer case, for instance, some people argue that senatorial interference was good or bad by reference to their opinions on Kaiser-Frazer's handling of the flying boxcar contract. As citizens we do care about the merits of flying boxcars, and of contracts for their production; but in this article the

---

* Frank C. Newman is Dean of the University of California (Berkeley) School of Law; Harry J. Keaton is a member of the California Bar. This article also constitutes Section 2 of Chapter 4 of Newman and Surrey's Cases and Materials on Legislation 223-249 (1955).

[1] U.S. Const. Art. II, §3; see Crosskey, Politics and the Constitution 433-43 (1953); cf. §136 of the Legislative Reorganization Act, 60 Stat. 832 (1946): "To assist the Congress in appraising the administration of the laws and in developing such amendments or related legislation as it may deem necessary, each standing committee of the Senate and the House of Representatives shall exercise *continuous watchfulness* of the execution by the administrative agencies concerned of any laws, the subject matter of which is within the jurisdiction of such committee. . . ." (Emphasis added.)

[7] The Alsops' column of April 17, 1953.

inquiry will be restricted to the powers and procedures problem. There will be no attempt to assess Kaiser-Frazer's performance, or to resolve the pros and cons of matters like grain inspection, or to defend or deprecate the "top people" in Dulles' State Department.

Even when the issue of powers or procedures has been isolated, many commentators forget that our Constitution plainly sanctions *some* Congressional interference with administrative action. Thus, aside from the merits of the controversies, *objection is not appropriate:*

(1) *When Congress by law revokes the authority of administrative officials, or prescribes their future action.* . . .

(2) *When Congress in reviewing the President's budget concludes that funds should not be appropriated for certain purposes, or that for other purposes the amounts budgeted are inadequate.* For example, the decision of a Congressional majority to slash foreign aid funds, or to reduce appropriations for enforcing the labeling laws, or to withhold grants "for further construction of the Garrison Dam until an investigation can be made," [12] is surely contemplated by the Constitution. Nor is there any usurpation of power if the majority decides we need a 143-wing and not a 120-wing air force, 21 instead of 17 teams of FCC field examiners, or $125 million instead of nothing for Franco Spain.

(3) *When the Senate, by refusing to approve a man nominated for high public office, in effect calls for more (or less) vigorous enforcement of the laws he would have administered.* This point is illustrated by the proceedings involving Tom Lyon, nominated by President Eisenhower to be Director of the Bureau of Mines,[18] and Leland Olds, nominated by President Truman for a third term on the Federal Power Commission.[19]

(4) *When the Senate and the House, or their committees, or individual Congressmen decide they ought to look into agency activities and make whatever comments are inspired by the inquiry.* For example: If there is a chance that subsidies were iniquitously granted to publishers favoring the Fair Deal, or that the Housing Expediter illicitly conspired with parties opposing the decontrol of rents, or that our fighting men were endangered by ammunition shortages in Korea, Congressmen are entitled (perhaps even obligated) to find out what the story is. If they become convinced that only a warped Secretary of Defense would say he was "not interested as a military project in why potatoes turn brown when they are fried," [24]

[12] See remarks of Rep. Burdick, 99 Cong. Rec. 3443 (April 20, 1953); cf. Davis, Administrative Law 55 n. 70 (1951) ("The CAB granted the certificate to American Export Lines. But Congress then refused the necessary appropriation for airmail subsidies.").

[18] Lyon, whose nomination was later withdrawn, told the Senate commitee that Congress never should have passed the mine safety law, which is "just that much more Federal control," but that if confirmed he would do his best to administer it. . . .

[19] See Joseph Harris, The Senatorial Rejection of Leland Olds: A Case Study, 45 Am. Pol. Sci. Rev. 674 (1951) ("The real issue was federal regulation of the price of natural gas. . . ."); cf. Joseph Harris, The Courtesy of the Senate, 67 Pol. Sci. Q. 36 (1952).

[24] See remarks of Rep. Engle, 99 Cong. Rec. A4007 (June 24, 1953). But cf. Rep. Andresen's comments, *id.* at 8038 (July 1, 1953) ("[A] great deal of money is being spent on research to get the proper dishes to go with the sterling silver that the Navy uses.").

or that an agency ought to formulate or publicize certain policies, or that "[t]he Interior Department should be concerned with only those functions or activities which private enterprise cannot or will not undertake . . . ,"[26] there is no reason why they should not tell us their views.

In summary, the mere fact that administrative action might be affected does not give rise to constitutional issues when Congressmen pass laws, make appropriations, reject nominations, or inquire, expose, comment, criticize, request, recomment, prod, cajole and castigate. The bothersome issues appear when we examine this kind of question:

    I. Are there any limits on scope?
    II. Are there abuses in method?
    III. What about the requirement of "advice and consent"?
    IV. What about Senator McCarthy?
    V. Do we need law reform?

I. *Are There Any Limits on Scope?*

There are a few situations where administrators are constitutionally immune from Congressional interference. Thus, the President's power to fire certain officials[27] and to retain others[28] cannot be abrogated, even by statute. And he apparently enjoys some autonomy in conducting military and foreign affairs, though no one knows just what the bounds are. Further, it seems that he and his subordinates have a right of privacy greater than that of mere citizens, though as yet this point remains untested. At most, however, these insulations are of limited significance, and in general the Constitution gives little immunity to the Executive.

Are there immunities apart from the Constitution? Can we find, for example, a doctrine of good government or principle of good sense to tell us when Congress intrudes illegitimately? Is some meddling with administrative affairs officious, though legal?

One point seems obvious. Congress goes too far if it spends so much time supervising that not enough time is left for legislating. Conversely, administrators can hardly do the jobs that statutes declare they must do if they have to spend most of their workweek on Capitol Hill, testifying before committees.

But can we pick and choose among the *subjects* of Congressional activity and as to some say to Congressmen, "Mind your own business"? People often assert that Congress should be concerned with high policy only, leaving the details to

[26] See statement of Sen. Hennings, 99 Cong. Rec. 7637 (June 27, 1953).
[27] See Myers v. United States, 272 U.S. 52 (1926); Corwin, The President as Administrative Chief, 1 J. of Politics 17, 42 (1939); Notes, 9 Geo. Wash. L. Rev. 703 (1941); 39 Mich. L. Rev. 1410 (1941).
[28] See United States v. Lovett, 328 U.S. 303 (1946); Schuman, American Government and Politics: "Bill of Attainder" in the Seventy-eighth Congress, 37 Am. Pol. Sci. Rev. 819 (1943); cf. attempt by House Republicans to cut off Acheson's salary as Sec. of State, N.Y. Herald Tribune, July 26, 1951, p. 1; Sen. Downey's threats against Reclamation Bureau chiefs, reported in Drew Pearson's column of Nov. 17, 1949.

agency discretion. But does this mean that statutes dealing with matters like price control and monopoly, where the standards are extremely vague, are always more wisely conceived than statutes like the Internal Revenue Code and the conservation laws, where Congress has dealt with a multitude of minutiae? And while normally we want experts to decide what kind of ships we need, to advise where dams ought to be built, and to manage the postal system, do we conclude that only a buttinsky Congress would ever inquire into oil tankers and supercarriers, or the merits of reclamation projects, or whether postal clerks should be made to check in and out when they go to the bathroom? Even President Eisenhower, perhaps the most expert Chief Executive we have had on military appropriations, has stated that of course he would not rule out the possibility that Congress, "without impairing national security," could find room for budget cuts. And regarding naval affairs, what happens to dead pets at sea is surely esoteric. Yet if the Navy's dead pet rule is stupid, requiring among other things radiograms and an inquisition by three commissioned officers,[44] is Congressional criticism *ultra vires?*

The New York Bar Report. Four years ago the Administrative Law Committee of the New York City Bar filed a thoughtful report called "Congressional Oversight of Administrative Agencies," which deals with a variety of problems of legislative supervision.[45] With respect to functions other than lawmaking, the Committee's conclusions on "scope" were as follows:

1. When an agency has requested that interested persons state their views on proposed substantive rules, informed Congressmen (specifically, members of the appropriate standing committees) should not hesitate to speak up.[46] Similarly, they

[44] See A.P. dispatch from Washington of July 2, 1953 ("Dead Navy Pets Cost Too Much, Congressman Thinks"), 99 Cong. Rec. 8170 (July 2, 1953); cf. the bill to restrict importation of certain giant snails, to which was added an amendment dealing with the impact of the hydrogen bomb on peanut growers in South Carolina, 96 Cong. Rec. 16786 (Dec. 15, 1950).

[45] 5 N.Y. Bar Record 11 (1950), summarized by Beryl Levy, chairman of the key subcommittee, in 36 A.B.A.J. 236 (1950); . . .

[46] 5 N.Y. Bar Record 18. The report seems to be silent on *existing* substantive rules. Aside from the merits of the particular controversies, we see no objection to items like these: (1) H. Con. Res. 98, urging "That the Federal Reserve Board . . . support the price of United States Government securities at par . . . as was done before the so-called Treasury-Federal Reserve accord which was announced March 4, 1951." See 99 Cong. Rec. 7846 (June 30, 1953); *id.* at 7534 (June 25, 1953); cf. N.Y. Times,

Oct. 11, 1953, p. L1, col. 1 (House Committee formally requests Sec. Benson to extend price supports to cattle). (2) Statements by the chairman of a committee investigating color T-V, requesting (A) that the NPA revoke its rule suspending the manufacture of color T-V sets, and (B) that the FCC comment on industry proposals calling for relaxed rules on color telecasting. See remarks of Rep. Wolverton, 99 Cong. Rec. A1483 (March 19, 1953); *id.* at A1744 (March 30, 1953), A5624 (Aug. 28, 1953); Gould, Color Video in 3 or 4 Months Forecast After F.C.C. Test, N.Y. Times, Oct. 16, 1953, p. C27, col. 6; cf. Plea Addressed to Treasury Secretary Humphrey for Temporary Suspension of Tariff on Aluminum by Representatives Blatnick, Celler, Deane, Eberharter, Fine, Forand, Morano, and Rodino, 99 Cong. Rec. A3113 (May 26, 1953). (3) Continued questioning by the chairman of the Joint Committee on Defense Production, indicating his doubts as to the legal authority for Defense Manpower Policy No. 4. See 99 Cong. Rec.

should feel free to suggest that agencies revise "procedures or internal organization." [47]

2. However, (A) "a Congress dissatisfied with agency interpretation of the governing statute should amend the statute, not coerce the agency to change its view . . .";[48] (B) legislative committees ought not suggest how the agency should decide particular cases or issues pending in those cases . . . [even as to] the manner in which [or the priority with which] [49] a particular case is being processed . . . ," [50] and (C) "the same constraints apply to comment on cases already decided by the agency where such comment is intended in any way to influence the agency to reverse its previous ruling or . . . to limit the trend indicated by that ruling." [51]

Are the constraints recommended in Point 2 really workable? The reasons for the Point 1 premise were first, that as to proposed substantive rules informed Congressmen can often "comment helpfully"; and second, that "[i]t is not practicable to process through a busy Congress a statute which does no more than change a procedural regulation or revise an agency's internal organization in some particular." [52] But do not these reasons similarly justify many of the Congressional attacks on agency interpretations, mentioned in Point 2A? Some Congressmen are remarkably well-informed as to the meaning of statutes;[53] also, there are countless

3364 (April 17, 1953). (4) Sen. Margaret Chase Smith's column of June 26, 1951, protesting "[T]he President's suspension, through an 'escape clause,' of a ban on foreign aid to countries trading behind the Iron Curtain." (5) A statement advising the Secretary of Agriculture that the members of a subcommittee of the California Delegation in the House, together with Senator Nixon and miscellaneous Congressmen from Oregon and Washington ("after conferences jointly with representatives of the . . . Department of Agriculture and of the affected industries"), all oppose "the policy of imposing Federal or Federal-State inspection services under the Federal Marketing Agreements and Orders for prunes, raisins, and walnuts." See attachment to Dried Fruit Association of California form-letter of June 30, 1950, addressed to all members. Cf. Albright, Nixon Making a Real Job of Vice President, reprinted in 99 Cong. Rec. A3893 (June 22, 1953) ("[Nixon] has instructed his staff not to handle any 'case work' involving intercession with Government agencies.").

[47] 5 N.Y. Bar Record 17.

[48] *Id.* at 22.

[49] Cf. these remarks of Sen. Langer, 99 Cong. Rec. 1154 (Feb. 8, 1953): "[A]ny lawyer practicing in North Dakota, no matter how young or old he may be, can do a better job than has been done in . . . [a named FTC monopoly case], in which 13 years have passed without the taking of action. . . . [Therefore,] if any member of the Commission has served on it for as long as 10 years . . . he should resign his office and should let a competent person take his place."

[50] 5 N.Y. Bar Record at 15-16. The committee was specifically concerned with Taft-Hartley cases. . . .

[51] 5 N.Y. Bar Record 17 (1950).

[52] *Id.* at 18.

[53] E.g., see NLRB v. Nina Dye Works Co., 198 F. 2 d 362, 365 (3d Cir. 1952), comparing Senator Taft's "Supplemental Analysis of Labor Bill [Taft-Hartley Act] as Passed" with Congressman Hartley's Our New National Labor Policy (1948); cf. notes 61-2 *infra*; *The Congress Should Watch and Correct the Interpretation of Statutes*, 33 A.B.A.J. 666 (1947); Jones, Legislature-Agency Disagreements Concerning the Construction of Regulatory Statutes, 36 A.B.A.J. 859 (1950).

instances where the interpretive question, like questions of procedure or organization, cannot efficiently be handled via an amendatory statute.[54]

Regarding Point 2B (cases which are pending), the Report states that since a legislature could hardly presume to tell judges how they should decide a case, like comment addressed to administrators is presumptuous. But legislators do speak up on issues in court cases (as do newsmen, law review writers, and many others); and one wonders—assuming an adjudicator of even moderate integrity—why a never-any-comment rule is necessarily desirable.

The difficulty in articulating such a rule is shown by this excerpt from the Report, concerning Point 2C (cases already decided):[58]

> Criticism of decided cases designed to influence future agency action under the existing statute, with respect to some doctrine the agency is evolving, intrudes upon the agency's area of responsibility in the same way as suggestions on how to decide pending cases.
>
> If, however, the [Congressional] committee is genuinely considering changing the terms of the statute, the committee's discussion of such proposed (or considered) changes may unavoidably involve criticism of agency decisions. Where there is this proper legislative objective of a general and constructive nature, such collateral criticism of decided cases is not objectionable. . . . The appropriate test would appear to be: *Is the criticism genuinely a phase of the committee's consideration of a legislative reorientation?* . . . Indeed, the same criterion might, in extraordinary instances, justify reference even to a pending case where such reference is integral to a bona fide contemplation of statutory change of a general policy nature and is *not intended to exert pressure on the agency to decide one way or the other.* . . .

Is it feasible to decide when criticism really is "genuinely a phase of the committee's consideration of a legislative reorientation" and "not intended to exert pressure on the agency to decide one way or the other"? Consider this plaint:[59]

[I]n the interest of all parties, I [a Representative from Michigan] respect-

---

[54] "[T]here are many reasons, other than to indicate approval of what the courts have done, why Congress may fail to take affirmative action to repudiate their misconstruction of its duly adopted laws. Among them may be the sheer pressure of other and more important business." Cleveland v. United States, 329 U.S. 14, 22 (1946); cf. Note, Congressional Reaction to Recent Supreme Court Decisions in Taxation and Criminal Law, 36 Geo. L.J. 48 (1947).

[58] 5 N.Y. Bar Record 17 (1950) (emphasis added). The report further states, "Traditional repugnance to special legislation would suggest, however, that recommendations for statutory change should not be

designed to secure a particular result in a particular case in aid of a special interest or litigant. . . ." *Id.* n. 5; . . . veto message in 96 Cong. Rec. 17077 (1951); Bowe, Congress or the Courts as Final Arbiter in Tax Disputes, *supra* note 38.

[59] Remarks of Rep. Shafer, 99 Cong. Rec. 3778-80 (April 23, 1953); cf. Hyneman, Bureaucracy and the Democratic System, 6 La. L. Rev. 309, 335 (1945) ("If Congressmen get close enough to the bureaucracy to get the information they need for proper legislative action, they are pretty certain to make suggestions as to how the department can do a better job of carrying out the intent of statutes . . ."); . . .

fully request that the Committee on Education and Labor of this House forthwith summon the Chairman of the NLRB, the General Counsel of NLRB, and such other person or persons as it deems necessary and proper, for questioning and explanation as to the actions of the Board in the case I have described [Albion Malleable Iron Co., 104 NLRB 31 (1953)]. Such action by the committee is, I believe, abundantly justified alike in the interest of securing the full facts in this case and *in the interest of determining the bearing of these facts upon proposed labor legislation now before the committee.* . . .

Not only the interests and rights of workers, management, and owners are urgently involved, but the hope of restoring confidence, stability, and tranquility to a small but typically American community is at stake. What is done, *or left undone,* in this matter will affect for good or ill the way in which many of my constituents and of your fellow citizens will read, in the future, those noble words: "Equal justice under law."

Is it ever an intrusion on administrative responsibility when Congressmen merely inquire and comment? If, for instance, the legislators who served on the Conference Committee are convinced that the Attorney General is undermining the Internal Security Act by "absurd interpretation," should they not say so—regardless of proceedings involving Italian opera stars, Spanish Falangists, and other aliens that may be pending? When Representative Smith vehemently denied that the Smith-Connally Act authorized the Montgomery Ward seizure, should his opinion have been kept secret? Did the Michigan congressional delegation exceed its jurisdiction when it sat in on the Pentagon's public hearing concerning the Kaiser-Frazer cancellation? Are any improprieties disclosed by the following report of incidents in the daily life of Congressman John F. Shelley? [64]

Several weeks ago, Shelley demanded an investigation of the Agriculture Department's secret sale of 80,000 tons of dried peas to three firms on the West Coast, for $2.4 million, not much more than half the price at which the peas had been offered to other grain dealers.

Shelley forced a probe by the House Agriculture Committee. It reported that it found no "political favoritism" in the deal, but the Agriculture Department promised not to make such secret deals again. Instead, it will give everyone a chance to submit "competitive bids" for surplus farm products.

II. *Are There Abuses in Method?*

The discussion of *scope,* above, indicates that it is not easy to fix limits on Congress' broad interests. If the heckling of agencies does not engulf their officials,

[64] Calif. AFL News Service dispatch in East Bay Labor Journal of July 10, 1953; cf. Sen. Williams' letter to RFC reprinted in 99 Cong. Rec. 3169 (April 14, 1953) (requests "complete record" of all loans made during past year contra to recommendation of Review Board, with explanation of why the loan was made). Beceause of facts disclosed in a 1952 congressional investigation of why, in 1949, certain liquor distillers were not prosecuted under the antitrust laws, the Department of Justice in 1953 decided to order its own investigation. N.Y. Times, Oct. 3, 1953, p. 25, col. 4.

time-wise, and if Congressmen reserve enough time and energy to enact the laws we need, not much in governmental affairs can be called out-of-bounds for Congress. We want our legislators to concentrate on major problems; but they can learn a great deal about major problems from a "case method" approach, and the instructive cases may range in significance from the gigantic to the minuscule.

As to *method*, we emphatically do not want a system where agency officials must prove they are not liars,[86] or have to shout in order to make themselves heard.[87] They should also be protected, as individuals, by organizational and procedural reforms that most observers now believe are requisite to fair committee hearings.

Are other reforms needed? It would be desirable if overlappings in committee jurisdiction could be minimized, and lines between legislative and appropriative policy drawn more sharply. Improvements in the staffing and administering of committees would help; and conflicts of interest and divided loyalties should be avoided—though complaints that the hiring of ex-administrators by Congress and ex-Congressional employees by the Executive violates separation of powers hardly seem justified. Congressional junketing has been scoffed at; but query whether we can censure, say, the dispatch of men like Senators Dirksen and Magnuson to the Far East, "for a country-by-country survey of military aid needs." [96]

The New York Bar conclusion that Congress should not "coerce" agencies to change their interpretations was quoted above. Perhaps we should frown on all forms of coercion (except, presumably, that resulting from duly enacted laws—including duly enacted appropriation bills). The difficulty lies in deciding at what point conduct becomes coercive. When a Congressman calls an agency on the telephone, is the presence or absence of "threat" to be determined by reference to what he says, or to his status, his tone of voice, his past practices, or the political richness of the proceeding? A memo prepared for the Senate's GOP Policy Committee credits Republican Appropriations committeemen with prodding the State Department to publish a 40-volume history of U.S. diplomacy under Roosevelt and Truman. This could be a product of coercion; but it could just as well be a valued addition to the nation's archives, to which legislators contributed either the original idea or the needed encouragement. A recent committee proposal that the Bonneville Administration buy supplementary power from private firms might have been thought coercive; but on the Senate floor one of the committeemen explained what seemed to him obvious, that the proposal's "validity is for the . . . [Administrator] to determine, both as to the wisdom and the legality." [99]

Congressmen sometimes threaten, and they sometimes make good their threats. The Douglas Committee on Ethical Standards in Government argued that "Pres-

---

[86] See 99 Cong. Rec. 2382-4 (March 25, 1953) (Knowland charges McCarthy with doubting the word of top officials, as well as Knowland's own veracity).

[87] Cf. U.P. dispatch from Washington of July 13, 1953, concerning Summerfield's row with the House Post Office Committee ("The Cabinet officer was game but vocally outclassed.").

[96] A.P. dispatch from Washington of May 16, 1953; cf. Carnahan, Congressional Travel Abroad and Reports, 289 Annals 120 (1953); N.Y. Herald Tribune dispatch from Washington of Aug. 9, 1953 ("Near-Record Schedule of Study Trips for Legislators").

[99] 99 Cong. Rec. 7580 (June 26, 1953).

sure through personal attacks or by hostile action in budgets or legislation is a kind of blackmail which is damaging to the public interest and which destroys satisfactory working relations between the legislative and executive branches." [101] Nonetheless, the Committee concluded that the only practicable control was "the self-restraint of Senators and Representatives." [102]

III. *What about the Requirement of "Advice and Consent?"*

One device used by legislators to keep tabs on administrators relates to the rule that the President make treaties and appoint men to high public office only "by and with the advice and consent of the Senate." [103] Recent Congresses seem to have liked variations of this device, and several statutes now declare that agency action on matters other than treaties and appointments requires legislative consent. Moreover, the consent called for is to be manifested not in a follow-up statute, but in a resolution of either or both Houses, or by vote of a committee or the endorsement of its chairman. [104]

Mr. Robert W. Ginnane, in a penetrating article titled "The Control of Federal Administration by Congressional Resolutions and Committees," contends (1) that prescribing consent-by-resolution is an unconstitutional by-passing of the President's veto power, and (2) that requiring committee consent is an unconstitutional delegation of Congress' law-making power. [105] His views were shared, at least in part, by both Roosevelt and Truman. [106]

These consent requirements, exploiting the force of law, differ from the samples of Congressional oversight we have already examined. Consent is demanded by law but is to be expressed not in the form of law but in another form, i.e., by simple or concurrent resolution or committee approval. Our premise has been that Congress has full power to pass laws, appropriate, inquire, and comment. Consent is a hybrid device. It parallels the treaty and appointment procedures, but is neither these nor law-making.

[101] Sen. Rep., [83d Cong., 1st Sess. (1951)] at 57; cf. *id.* at 29.

[102] *Id.*, The Committee also concluded, however, that measures could be taken to improve legislative-administrative relations in general. See particularly pp. 1-5, 29-30, and 57-8.

[103] U.S. Const. Art. II, §2; see Mike Mansfield, The Meaning of the Term "Advice and Consent," 289 Annals 127 (1953).

[104] See Ginnane, The Control of Federal Administration by Congressional Resolutions and Committees, 66 Harv. L. Rev. 569 (1953); cf. debate on 1953 extension of Reorganization Act of 1949 (providing that President's plans become effective unless either House disapproves within 60 days), where Congressmen discuss whether disapproval should be expressed by simple or

constitutional majority vote, 99 Cong. Rec. 791 (Feb. 2, 1953) (House); *id.* at 935 (Feb. 6, 1953) (Senate); *id.* at A445 (Feb. 3, 1953) (Rep. Holifield); also see *id.* at 7539 (June 25, 1953) (debate on bill subjecting contracts for disposal of government-owned rubber plants to disapproval by concurrent resolution).

[105] See Ginnane, *supra* note 104, at 593, 605.

[106] See Jackson, A Presidential Legal Opinion, 66 Harv. L. Rev. 1353 (1953); Ginnane, *supra* note 104, at 603; message disapproving H.R. 6839, which required Postmaster General to obtain committee approval before entering into lease-purchase agreements, 98 Con. Rec. A4945 (July 29, 1952).

This article is not the place for a review of Mr. Ginnane's findings, or a complementary study of Congress's experiments with the consent device. Regarding constitutionality, however: Has the veto power in fact been circumvented when the President could have vetoed the statutes that set up the requirement of consent? [107] Further, now that we accept tremendously broad delegations of power to public officials and private groups, can we sensibly hold that experimental delegations to the House and Senate, or to committees they trust, are void per se? A system whereby all agency action was to be approved by Congressmen would be hopelessly chaotic; but so would a system whereby all law was to be enacted by regulation, instead of statute. We have avoided the latter not because of constitutional restraints, but because our legislators have been wise enough to delegate their powers sparingly. Similar wisdom should protect us from capricious use of "consent." Under the Constitution, legislative-administrative liaisons have not been set rigidly. Efforts to develop new forms of liaison should not be squelched by a literalness of constitutional interpretation that we reject for most other problems.

When consent is not made essential, statutes requiring that administrators before taking action advise Congress or consult with its committees are surely not objectionable.[110] The "advice" requirement is merely an offspring of the power to inquire and comment. If Congress feels that the national parks would be better administered were the Secretary of Interior to report on all concessions and leases, it should so require.[111] Even when legislators argue that better administration requires their informal approval of items like concessions and leases there is no objection—so long as everyone understands that the approval really is informal, and that (unlike the "consent" situation discussed above) agencies are not bound by disapproval.

IV. *What About Senator McCarthy?*

Question: Didn't your subcommittee take over the function of the State Department by forcing the Greek shipowners to stop cargo shipments to Red China?

Answer: [114] We did not. The subcommittee kept well within the functions of a legislative body and we did not "force" any action. We merely persuaded the shipowners to agree voluntarily among themselves to discontinue trade with the enemy. Secretary of State Dulles praised our work in the shipping case and said our efforts "were in the national interest." Frank C. Nash, Assistant Secretary of Defense, testified March 31 before the subcommittee and said that even halting one ship "would be of great help," and that our persuading owners of 242 ships

---

[107] A statute setting up a consent requirement could, of course, have been enacted over the President's veto, or been approved by a predecessor President. But the veto power is a power of the office, not the man; and there would seem to be no circumvention if there has been an opportunity to exercise the power.

[110] Cf. Jones, Further Notes on the Presidential Power Issue, 37 A.B.A.J. 468 (1951); Jones, "Watchdog Committees" in the 80th Congress, 34 *id.* at 726 (1948).

[111] Cf. 99 Cong. Rec. 7575, 7578 (June 26, 1953).

[114] [The questions and answers under this heading are from] a news release, Senator McCarthy Answers Questions, 99 Cong. Rec. A3579 (June 11, 1953).

to stop such traffic "would be 242 times as much help." (Two hundred and forty-two ships had been removed from trade with Red China and between Soviet bloc countries at that time. The figure is now 295.) He added that our efforts "would meet with applause from the Department of Defense. . . ." [115]

Q.: Do you agree with the statement that recent developments of your Investigations Committee, for example, the transportation of Communist troops along the China coast during the Korean war by ships owned by British firms is [sic] increasing the existing tensions between the United States and Great Britain?

A.: First, we must examine the existing tensions before we can answer the question. I think one of the greatest contributing factors to existing tensions is the apparent lack of real unity among the western powers. Unquestionably it is extremely important to have complete unity of purpose among the western powers if world peace is to be attained. However, nothing would be gained by covering up and disguising a phony unity. Certainly there is nothing unreasonable in a request to our allies to stop supplying the sinews of war to a mutual enemy. Certainly all of the peoples of the so-called free world are entitled to have the facts brought to light when any of our allies flagrantly abuse a trust. . . .

Q.: Recently your committee has been checking all books by Communist authors which were purchased by the Acheson State Department and placed on the shelves of our libraries throughout the world. . . . What is the new administration doing about these books?

A.: Following the disclosure of the facts by our committee, the State Department, under its new leadership, ordered books by Communist authors removed from the shelves of our information centers in other countries. As fast as we disclose more information on Communist writers, the State Department has promised action in clearing out this Communist propaganda which cost the taxpayers hundreds of thousand of dollars. . . .

Q.: Have you ever sued anyone because of false statements about your Communist fight?

A.: Yes. I sued the Post-Standard, of Syracuse, N.Y., for libel. The result of this libel suit was a payment by them of $16,500 plus the printing of the following retraction: . . . [116]

> The editorial . . . also criticized Senator McCarthy for a financial transaction with the Lustron Co. The facts in this case are these:
>
> Senator McCarthy had prepared a book advising veterans how they could finance home purchases and obtain full advantage of all helps and provisions of Federal housing laws. He entered into an agreement with the Lustron Co., whereby they undertook to publish and distribute 100,000 copies of this book, to pay him 10 cents a copy for these and 5 cents a copy thereafter. This agree-

---

[115] McCarthy announced later that he felt he almost owed an apology to the Greek shipowners for "having encouraged them to get out of that profitable trade and then have it taken over by the British." U.P. dispatch from Washington of Aug. 4, 1953.

Cf. Solow, Those Resourceful Greek Shipping Men, 48 Fortune 142 (Oct. 1953).

[116] The retraction dealt with several matters of which the one mentioned here is especially pertinent.

ment was entered into after Senator McCarthy's party, the Republican Party, had been defeated in the 1950 elections and had lost control of Congress and Senator McCarthy was very unpopular with the Truman Administration. It is not possible, therefore, that Senator McCarthy could have been useful to the Lustron Co. with the Truman administration.[117] Lustron at that time was about to embark upon a large scale production of homes. There was no public indication that the RFC was about to foreclose. There has never been evidence presented before any committee or elsewhere that Senator McCarthy in any way attempted to intercede on behalf of Lustron. The Post-Standard is therefore convinced that Senator McCarthy's part in this transaction was on the same plane as the common practice among legislators of accepting fees for speeches and earning other fees from legitimate services. . . .

Q.: President Eisenhower recently set up a new loyalty-security program. . . . Was this program discussed with you before it was adopted?

A.: Yes, Senator Jenner, chairman of the Internal Security Committee, Congressman Velde, chairman of the House Un-American Activities Committee, and I, as chairman of the Senate Permanent Subcommittee on Investigations, were called to the White House where the matter was discussed in complete detail with us. . . .

These questions and answers reveal how Senator McCarthy himself regards outcries that he is usurping the duties of the Executive Branch. The writers of this article are inclined to accept his denial of usurpation.[119] For if people are convinced that what the Greek and British shipowners did was right, or that pressure on them should always be channeled through their governments, or that the deals the Senator made were less beneficial than what Mr. Stassen or Mr. Dulles could have negotiated, then those points—i.e., the merits—ought to be argued. Similarly, people who object to book burning or the loyalty-security program ought to stress the merits there—not whether the Senator's role was seemly. And those who believe that McCarthy had poor judgment, or is scheming, or ruthless, or fanatical, ought to debate at that political level—and not sweeten their rebukes with talk of *ultra vires*.

V. *Do We Need Law Reform?*

The climate of politics is tempestuous. But we should not wreck the framework of our government to get planks for storm shelters. McCarthy and his cohorts are by no means the only legislators who dabble, for example, with military and foreign affairs. Who would deny any Congressman his concern with the Korean War, disloyalty, European aid, and the aims of our allies, including the British? The law-making, appropriating, and investigating powers must stand—so far as they affect the Executive. If Congress wants to resolve that it favors a unified Germany we should acclaim its power to do so, though we might question the wisdom of the resolution.[121] How can there be "impropriety" in Senator Knowland's friendship

[117] Query.
[119] But readers should not infer that we generally endorse the Senator's views. . . .

[121] Sen. Con. Res. 36, 83d Cong., 1st Sess., 99 Cong. Rec. 8161 (July 2, 1953); . . .

for Free China, or in Congressman Multer's interceding with the Spanish Ambassador on behalf of children orphaned by Hitler's death mills?

The fracas in March 1953, preceding the confirmation of Charles F. Bohlen as Ambassador to Russia, caused much fussing about who can do what to whom. One highly respected newspaper editorialized as follows:[123]

> It is a generally understood principle of our three-faceted system of government that the President's appointees to the diplomatic service are untouchable except where glaring improprieties or misdemeanors are involved or, as Hamilton put it, where an obviously undesirable character has been chosen. The Senate's constitutional function in these matters, it has been said, is "confined to simple affirmation or rejection" of the President's nomination. It was not intended that appointments should be made the occasion of prolonged and debilitating debates.

The writers of this article disagree. The Senate's consent to the appointment of an ambassador should be an authentic consent. The majority normally will want to respect the President's judgment, but if there are doubts they ought to be aired, and no special cloture rules or like inhibitions should throttle the doubting Senators.

* * *

A variety of law reforms dealing with legislative supervision could be articulated —in Congressional rules, in statutes, in amendments to the Constitution. With few exceptions (e.g., those relating to the efficiency of Congress and the fairness of its hearings) the writers of this article believe such reforms are not needed.

That is not to say Congress is blameless. We could easily cite instances where Congressional interference has reflected the crassest kind of politics, and where personal interest has overwhelmed the public interest. Further, there is serious danger that Congressmen *are* becoming mired in trivia; and we can hardly be proud of their recurring failures to meet fiscal deadlines, or their frantic activities during adjournment week.

One wonders, though, where the most blame lies. If administrators play a scared-rabbit, hangdog role, salaaming whenever a legislator snaps his fingers, legislative-administrative relations will of course deteriorate. And even when their officials are stout-hearted, some agencies still knuckle under and then rationalize, "Only thus do we most benefit the public in the long run." One wonders what would happen if the attitude were rather: "All right, you are a bigshot on an important subcommittee. Yet *we* make the decisions—regardless of your inquiries, comments, criticisms, and requests, your exposés, proddings, harangues, and cajoleries. We listen respectfully but on the basis of all information do what to *us* seems best." Congressmen could respond, of course, by eviscerating the agency with amendments of its laws, or hamstringing it with inadequate appropriations, or decapitating it with refusals to consent to the appointment of its best leaders. But are drastic retaliations like these a real threat? At each step the administrator has a chance to defend and to rally his friends, in and out of Congress. If the issue is crucial

---

[123] Washington Post editorial of March 28, 1953; . . .

he can enlist even the President's aid. And it is not easy for a Congressman to persuade his colleagues, say, that appropriations should be cut $1,000,000 because the agency has denied the claim of one of his constituents (unless we assume log-rolling at its very worst).

A stiff backbone means that the merits of retaliatory action—laws, appropriations, appointments—are exposed. If such a course were routine, is it not conceivable that Congress would have to widen its perspective? Only a pampered overseer can afford to be dilettante; a responsible overseer has to be discriminate. If their bluffs were called, if they were forced to take public responsibility for their demands, more Congressmen might become decently discriminating in their choices. At least, is not the chance worth taking?

NOTES AND QUESTIONS

For views contrary to those expressed by Newman and Keaton, see, in addition to the Administrative Law Committee Report referred to in their article, Schwartz, Legislative Oversight: Control of Administrative Agencies, 43 A.B.A.J. 19 (1957) and O'Connor, Policing the Administrative Process, 43 A.B.A.J. 920 (1957).

Recently, Professor Newman has raised the question whether a lawyer should ask members of Congress to intercede before an administrative agency on his client's behalf, in order to assure the client "full administrative protection." Newman, A Legal Look At Congress and the State Legislatures, in Legal Institutions Today and Tomorrow 81-83, The Centennial Conference Volume of the Columbia Law School (Paulsen ed. 1959). He would not bar such intervention, but would make public all communications between members of Congress and members of the regulatory agencies on a specific case. However, Newman advises lawyers to "restrict their legislative appeals to those cases where administrative error seems clear and judicial relief is inadequate." Id. at 83.

Do you agree that such action by a lawyer is proper?

Horsky, *THE WASHINGTON LAWYER*
104-106, 133-145, 147-155 (1952)

. . . We have already discussed Canon 26 of the Canons of Professional Ethics in terms of non-public legislative activities. [See previous excerpt from Horsky reprinted in Chap. 10, sec. 1 above.—Editor] The Canon applies equally to "advocacy of claims before departments of government." The same ambiguities and difficulties inherent in the phrase "secret personal solicitation" also bedevil one who seeks an ethical evaluation of the activities of Washington lawyers in informal, non-public, agency proceedings. What was said before is equally applicable here— the Canon is so all-inclusive in scope and so vague in standard as to be largely unworkable.

Yet this much can be said. Where there is a formal administrative hearing, any informal, off-the-record contacts with the person who will make the decision should certainly be held to a minimum. Section 5(c) of the Administrative Procedure Act, which seeks to insulate, within each agency, the investigating and prosecuting personnel from those who are responsible for agency adjudication, is aimed at this objective, though it provides exemptions. The Civil Aeronautics Board has taken a still further step. Its principles of practice include the provision that in cases to be decided after hearing and on a record:

It is improper that there be any private communication on the merits of the case to a member of the Board or its staff or to the examiner in the case by any person, either in private or public life, unless provided by law.[17]

The objective, of course, must be to preserve the integrity of the quasi-judicial process, and at the same time not to endanger the viability of the administrative process as a whole. Everything I have said indicates the danger of generalization, and certainly I am not prepared to say that the Civil Aeronautics Board rule would work equally well in other agencies. The tripartite boards like the Wage Stabilization Boards raise questions all their own. On this problem, too, much more work is still to be done. . . .

When we reach . . . the conclusion that the Washington lawyer has a part to play in the processes of the federal government—we cannot avoid the next step. We must deal with the challenge which Chief Justice Stone put to the entire bar. To what extent, in other words, are the professional services of the Washington lawyer "directed toward the public interest?"

Probably no one would assert that Washington lawyers—or lawyers generally, for that matter—are as aware of the public interest as they should be. Three years ago, in defending the bar against criticism of its conservatism and its unawareness of the public concern with its activities, Robert T. Swaine admitted:

> . . . Probably too frequently our advice has been too limited to the technical validity of proposed action without regard to its social or economic implications. . . .[5]

Nonetheless, only one far more confident and far wiser than I would venture to say just where, and to what degree, the lawyer should temper the fundamental tenet of the profession—loyalty to the client—by economic, social and political considerations.

Yet there are some things that can be said. Let us state one aspect of the problem in terms of the Washington lawyer's legislative activity, for in that area it was posed many years ago by Mr. Justice Brandeis.[6] He stated the problem in terms of activities intended to affect legislative action—what we have called lobbying. After describing the situation in a judicial proceeding, where single-minded, vigorous advocacy is balanced by an adversary equally single-minded and vigorous, the Justice continues:

> But when lawyers act upon the same principle in supporting the attempts of their private clients to secure or to oppose legislation, a very different condition is presented. In the first place, the counsel selected to represent important private interests possesses usually ability of a high order, while the public is often inadequately represented or wholly unrepresented. That presents a condition of great unfairness to the public. As a result many bills pass in our legislatures which

---

[17] 16 Fed. Reg. 2932 (1951).

[5] Swaine, Impact of Big Business on the Profession: An Answer to Critics of the Modern Bar, 35 A.B.A.J. 89, 170-171

(1949).

[6] The Opportunity in the Law, 39 Am. L. Rev. 555 (1905).

would not have become law if the public interest had been fairly represented; and many good bills are defeated which if supported by able lawyers would have been enacted. Lawyers have, as a rule, failed to consider this distinction between practice in the court involving only private interests and practice before the legislature or city council where public interests are involved. Some men of high professional standing have even endeavored to justify their course in advocating professionally legislation which in their character as citizens they would have voted against. . . .[7]

In 1905, when that was written, Congress had not delegated widely to administrative agencies. Had the Justice written a half-century later, he would no doubt have included in his comment not only the legislature and the city council, but also the board, the bureau, and the agency. Except for the truly quasi-judicial agencies, most of the executive and administrative agencies and departments are equally subject, with the legislative branch, to what might be called ex parte approaches.

I recognize, as you will have, that the Justice has here brought in an additional problem—the possibility of injustice from loading all the legal competence on one side of a controversy. Put that aside for a moment, however, and look at the problem as the Justice poses it—the lawyer advocating professionally in a non-adversary proceeding, a position which, as a private citizen, he would oppose.

Were we to decree by canon that such conduct was unethical, we would certainly take a long step toward relieving the alleged congestion of the bar. Lawyers who represent clients in dealings with the government cannot be assumed to certify that the public interest is always best served by what they seek for their clients. If that appears to be too great a concession, consider the following:

In some areas where the Washington lawyer operates, neither the lawyer nor the client can possibly know enough to have an opinion on where the public interest lies. We now have controls over the use of scarce materials, the exact allocations being determined by facts relating to a wide variety of industrial uses and business situations, and by evaluation of such imponderables as the policy of containment of Communist aggression and the sociological consequences of scattered local unemployment. A brewery wants more tin plate allocated to beer cans, and retains a Washington lawyer to present its arguments to the officials in Washington who make the basic allocation. No one, I believe, would say that the lawyer, before he can properly accept the retainer, must satisfy himself that beer is more important than beans, or that glass bottles would not do equally well under all the circumstances. The government official, supplied with the facts upon which the lawyer makes his case for beer, but equally in possession of other materials which all the resources of government bring him for his guidance, assumes the responsibility for, and must make the decision on, the public interest.

Consider also the fact that in many areas what may seem to be ex parte proceedings are considerably tinged with adversary characteristics. My tinplate allocator is analogous to a judge, and as to him it is perhaps proper to regard my brewery

[7] *Id.* at 561.

lawyer as proceeding ex parte. But contrast a situation where a client retains a Washington lawyer to attempt to persuade the Wage-Hour Administrator that the Fair Labor Standards Act does not apply to a particular industry, or to a particular course of conduct because it is intrastate. Or consider the tax lawyer who is urging a position for his client upon the attorneys in the Bureau of Internal Revenue. Neither the Administrator nor the Bureau attorneys are judges; they are enforcement officers, and can properly be approached by the Washington counsel as an adversary party. . . .

Consider, too, the number of times when the lawyer is faced with a situation in which the goal—"the public interest"—is itself in issue. There certainly is no basis for a conclusive presumption that the government agency is always acting in the public interest. . . . Perhaps the issue is, in fact, no more than which part of the public is to be protected, as in the recent butter-margarine controversy. Fair trade acts, not long ago again in the arena of public debate because of the Supreme Court's decision in the Schwegmann case, present the problem of whether the consumer or the distributor requires more protection. Again, the need for revenue, certainly a public interest, conflicts with the public interest in agricultural cooperatives. The public interest in a domestic hemp supply, which would free us from reliance upon imports of a vital commodity, is met with the fact that the leaves of the plant provide a rich source of narcotics such as hashish. The debate over the "meeting competition" concept of the Robinson-Patman Act, as it is currently posed, is a debate on whether to protect competitors or to protect competition.

One of the reasons we have political parties, and disagreements within those parties, is that there is no agreement on where the public interest lies. Moreover, the present-day lawyer in Washington is often faced with a situation in which the goal—the "public interest"—is curiously vague and indeterminate. Just why does—or did—the Reconstruction Finance Corporation lend money to the snake farm and decorative cactus growers? We welter under a hodge-podge of confusing, conflicting, and ever changing ideas of what best serves the country.

But even though all this can be said, it is nevertheless not a complete answer. What Justice Brandeis had in mind was not a canon of ethics, but a personal standard by which we judge not only the clients we are willing to represent, but also the extent to which we will seek to include in our professional advice and assistance a consideration of national affairs. We have an obligation to do more than tell clients how they can lawfully do what they want to do. I do not refer only to the clients who want to urge positions so outrageous that no lawyer could advocate them and still maintain his self-respect. We should go beyond that. The public position of the bar suffers, and properly so, when it becomes apparent that there are Washington lawyers who are quite willing to ignore entirely the larger interests of the country and the basic standards of decency in the process of stringing together sets of legal loopholes to achieve some inordinate advantage. Because this is an area in which canons of ethics and Grievance Committees cannot operate is the more reason why all lawyers should be alert to the implicit, as well as the explicit, responsibilities which distinguish law as a profession, not merely a highly technical trade.

Now let us turn to the other aspect of Justice Brandeis's problem—the danger of weighting the scales against the public interest by concentrating all the legal ability on one side. That problem, on the surface, would appear to relate to a matter which is not within our present scope—the quality of government lawyers. In fact, its manifestations are much broader, and bear directly on the Washington lawyer himself. To state the matter summarily, one of the very important reasons why we do have able government lawyers—why the scales are not weighted as the Justice feared they would be—is that we have permitted government lawyers to leave the government and become Washington lawyers in private practice. Now, at least, the limitations imposed on the ex-government lawyer, while not ideal, are reasonable. The danger, however, which warrants some attention to the problem, is that recent developments will lead us into indiscriminate measures, which will seriously prejudice both the government lawyer and the private practitioner.

The danger arises from an aspect of Washington life which has been much in the news of late. "Influence-peddling" is not a very accurate term, and it covers a multitude of sins, but it is sufficiently descriptive to define what we are talking about. It has been publicized and condemned, and in some respects misunderstood. What I should like to suggest is that in our efforts to control lawyers who engage in it we do not adopt such drastic restrictions on the ex-government lawyer as to make it difficult, or impossible, for the government to continue to attract able lawyers for service in its legal positions.

To make my point clear, we must have a little background. There are a few matters on which all should agree. First, no one doubts that it is important to have competent lawyers in government. Where safeguards of the adversary sort do not exist, it will fall to the government official—frequently, the government lawyer—to see to it that there is an adequate consideration of all the sides of the question. That cannot be expected if only the waifs and strays of the legal profession—the lawyers who can't get jobs elsewhere because of their inadequate training or their basic incompetence—are the ones who serve the public. . . .

Second, I believe that we can agree that we do get very many competent lawyers in government, even with the low government salary scale. One of the reasons is the security of the position; short of a catastrophe, one can reasonably expect long tenure in any but the highest government legal positions. Another reason, too, especially in times like these, is patriotism. Many lawyers, some of whom can ill afford it, are making financial sacrifices because they did not feel that they could say no to a request for their services. Another reason is that in many ways the work is interesting, even exciting, and for many government lawyers there is a strong belief in the rightness of the institutions with which they are associated and the purpose of the statutes with which they deal. Esprit de corps is not an exclusive with the military.

These factors operate, with varying force, on all government employees. For lawyers in particular, another factor seems to me of even more importance. There has been a recognition, at least since the early 1930's, that legal ability is of more value to the government than legal experience. Most departments have operated on the wise premise that an appropriation of $10,000 can be better spent to employ three able young lawyers with $10,000 worth of ability, even if they are just out of law school, rather than to employ one older, experienced man. Consequently, Washington has been a strong magnet for young lawyers of very high talents, who could get pay as high or higher than they could command on entering private practice, and who would promptly be assigned to positions of considerable responsibility.

This is in essence a process of earning while learning. Its necessary correlative is that these young lawyers must later be able to use in private practice what they have learned. This they have done; a goodly proportion of Washington lawyers have served, for longer or shorter periods, in some government legal position. . . .

Third, let us agree that influence-peddling in its various forms does exist. . . .

Much as one would like to say the contrary, Washington lawyers no doubt have their share of influence-peddlers. Some are simply unscrupulous, some have only a warped sense of ethics, and a particularly thick skin. Just how far the debasement of the professional standards of the legal profession has gone, I cannot even guess.

Of course, this does not mean that everyone who peddles influence has it. Quite the contrary. Probably 999 times out of 1000 a client who employs a Washington lawyer who claims to have influence doesn't get what he thinks he does, and what he pays for. At best he gets a guide through the Washington labyrinth that any Washington lawyer can give him, or perhaps a hearing on his problem with a government official who might be difficult to see without an appointment. At worst, he gets less than nothing; his case is tainted by the ill-will with which most government employees will regard a known or apparent influence-peddler. Even if he escapes that, he probably gets nothing in the way of assistance, for the lawyer who is in the business of selling influence is either ipso facto incompetent or is not likely to trouble his mind about supplying helpful professional advice.

So much, then, for the background. Assuming agreement on those three points, let us consider what, if any, corrective measures are in order. There are many possibilities, and I do not propose to attempt a discussion of them all. The one which is relevant to our present topic is the current suggestion that we can minimize influence-peddling by more severe limitations on ex-government lawyers. If I am correct, and I am sure that I am, that a major attraction of government law practice to able young lawyers is an ability to utilize later what they learn in government, it is clear that we must move with caution or we may do irreparable harm. We have already gone quite a way in legislating ethical canons. Legislative control of morals, however, is dubious business at best, and in attempting to legislate against the occasional lawyer whose regard for the Canon of Ethics is minimal or nonexistent, we may well, as one article has stated, "surround the government service with so many snares, snags and spring-guns that only the unwary can be recruited." [10] It will be worth while to see whether the laws and regulations can

[10] McElwain and Vorenberg, The Federal Conflict of Interests Statutes, 65 Harv. L. Rev. 955 (1951).

be improved and strengthened, without at the same time putting the government lawyer who wants to enter private practice at such a disadvantage that few will be willing to serve in the first place.

At the present time, there are two major permanent statutes. The principal one[11] makes it a crime for a lawyer who has worked for the government to prosecute "any claim" against the government for two years after leaving government service if the claim involves "any subject matter directly connected with" the work in which the lawyer was employed or performed duty.

The statute has two weaknesses, both of which can be corrected without undue limitation on the Washington lawyer and without jeopardizing the attraction of government legal service. The word "claims," which defines what the lawyer may not prosecute, is open to the very narrow construction that it applies only to monetary claims. That is a wholly unnecessary and formalistic limitation. The real weakness of the statute, however, lies deeper. The real defect is that the law should appear to sanction a violation of Canon 36 of the Canons of Professional Ethics. That Canon provides:

> A lawyer, having once held public office or having been in the public employ, should not after his retirement accept employment in connection with any matter which he has investigated or passed upon while in such office or employ.

There is no limit as to time in Canon 36, and there should not be in the statute. Government does not move fast enough to warrant a legislative finding that things will always be different after two years.

The other statute applicable to ex-government lawyers, while more sweeping in its terms, has had but limited effect.[12] It forbids, for two years, a lawyer employed in any of the executive departments from prosecuting any claim against the government which was pending while he was employed. This is much too drastic, even if the word "claim" is construed narrowly, and it also contains the unfortunate two-year limitation. That it has not had more serious consequences is due to the fact that it carries no specific criminal sanctions, and has been applied only to prevent the lawyer from collecting a fee.

There is room here for improvement. There should be a permanent, rather than a temporary, ban on work by an ex-government lawyer so far as he may be involved in matters on which he worked while in the government. There are difficulties in the application of the phrase "matters on which he worked," and the language of the law should be carefully drawn to make the penumbra of doubtful cases as narrow as possible. Canon 36, which says about all there is need to say on the subject, is probably important enough in this area to be accorded criminal sanctions.

Indeed, it might be well to go further, and extend the permanent prohibition to representation before the agencies of government in any matters in connection with which the government lawyer had any immediate responsibility during his government employment. This is the approach that has been adopted in the Executive

---

[11] 18 U.S.C. § 284 (Supp. 1951). . . .   [12] Rev. Stat. § 190 (1875), 5 U.S.C. § 99 (1946).

Order issued under Section 710 of the Defense Production Act, 1950.[14] Here there are no doubt palpable and considerable subsequent disadvantages which might affect the quality of the upper stratum of government legal services. Nevertheless, lawyers in top government positions do have supervisory relationships which may affect problems being worked on by their subordinates, even though they do not have any direct contact with the matters themselves. If the law is carefully drawn, a more substantial limitation on lawyers who had wider government responsibilities would help materially to eliminate unfortunate intangible effects.

To meet this same problem there is also room for a temporary prohibition. Canon 36 does not cover the abuse of friendships and residual prestige of the lawyer who held a high place in the government. Senator Douglas's subcommittee, in reporting on "Ethical Standards in Government," concludes that "A public official of high rank who leaves a regulatory agency and then returns immediately to practice before it, can hardly avoid pleading with people who previously may have been his subordinates or associates." [15] The Committee recommended a two-year "sterilization" period, during which persons who had held a position in an agency with a grade of GS-15 or above ($10,000 per year or more) would be barred from acting before the agency in any matter whatever.[16] One might doubt whether the line is not drawn at a point somewhat too far down on the scale, but there appears to be justification for a rule which distinguishes on the one hand the situation of the lawyer who held an important place in the government, and on the other the situation of the vast body of government lawyers whose area of work and responsibility is limited in scope, and whose future livelihood may well depend on the right to continue to make use of their experience.

Finally, there is need for administrative regulations and enforcement of ethical standards. Because so many Washington lawyers are not members of the local bar, the only Grievance Committee to which they are amenable is that of their own bar, which may be remote, uninformed, and even uninterested. There is need for something equivalent to a local Washington Grievance Committee for such lawyers. This could be met by the general adoption of a regulation such as that of the Securities and Exchange Commission, which provides that the privilege of practicing before it may be denied to anyone who after hearing is found to be "lacking in character or integrity or to have engaged in unethical or improper professional conduct." [17]

But let us recognize that no matter how we perfect and refine the rules, we cannot legislate a moral attitude or a cure for influence-peddling. All influence-peddlers are by no means ex-government employees, and no statute or regulation will ever take the place of an individual sense of concern for moral standards and ethical conduct. Moreover, we must recognize that there is a distinction between

[14] Exec. Order No. 10, 182, pt. II, 15 Fed. Reg. 8013 (1950), as amended.

[15] Report of a Subcommittee of the Senate Committee on Labor and Public Welfare, 82d Cong., 1st Sess. 22 (1951).

[16] *Id.* at 51-52.

[17] 17 Code Fed. Regs. § 201.2(e)(2) (1949). This regulation was applied to a firm which was told it would violate Canon 36 if it permitted an ex-employee to work on a matter, wholly intra-office, on which he had worked while with the Commission. 3 CCH Fed. Sec. Law. Serv. § 63, 102.10 (1939).

influence-peddling and what, for lack of a better word, we may call reputation, or expertise. Any Washington lawyer who is worth his salt and who has practiced in Washington for any length of time will have at least a speaking acquaintance with many of the staff in any agency where he may specialize. If he has professional competence and individual integrity—if he is a good lawyer in the true sense of the words—he will not only be known, he will be known favorably. That status will give him undoubted advantages—it will make it easier for him to arrange a conference, or to obtain a hearing for his client, or to discuss and discover the agency's position on particular matters that may come up. The lawyer who appeared in that agency for the first time would not find similar achievements impossible, and his client would fare equally well, if sufficient perseverance were exerted and if sufficient time were available. But advantages based on reputation and experience are wholly normal and wholly proper. To condemn them is likewise to condemn the trial lawyer in Chicago whose clients are advantaged because he is known to the court clerks and familiar with the intimate workings of their offices. . . .

NOTES AND QUESTIONS

Do you agree with Mr. Horsky that it is wise for the Government to serve as an arena of experience for "young lawyers of very high talents" who will, eventually, seek their careers in private practice or private industry?

On the conflict-of-interest problems discussed by Mr. Horsky, recall the Executive Employees' Standard Act proposed by President Kennedy, referred to in Part 2, chap. 10, sec. 1.

EDITORIAL NOTE: JUDICIAL REVIEW of ADMINISTRATIVE RULES

Section 10 (e) of the federal Administrative Procedure Act and section 102.23 of the Wisconsin Workmen's Compensation Act, which have been set forth in the preceding chapter, also apply to the judicial review of administrative rules. The 1955 Wisconsin law on rule-making specifies the procedure by which judicial review of an administrative rule may be secured. It also provides that a rule may be held invalid if the court finds that it (1) violates constitutional provisions; or (2) exceeds the agency's statutory authority; or (3) was adopted without compliance with statutory rule-making procedures.

"Judging from information . . . obtained [from officials of 46 agencies] judicial review of administrative rules in Wisconsin has not been extensive and attacks based on the unreasonableness of rules have been rare. . . . It would appear . . . that the Wisconsin Supreme Court has accorded to rules of administrative agencies the same presumption of validity as is accorded a statute enacted by the legislature." Helstad, New Law on Administrative Rule Making, 1956 Wis. L. Rev. at 424, n. 75.

The case that follows is an example of a rule that was declared invalid by the court and raises the general question of the weight courts should give to the administrative construction of a statute—a question to which we shall return in the next chapter.

WENZEL & HENOCH CONSTRUCTION CO. v. INDUSTRIAL COMMISSION
202 Wis. 595, 233 N.W. 777 (1930)

NELSON, J. The facts are not in dispute. Willie Haney Alexander, applicant before the Industrial Commission, is the widow of James Alexander, who came to his death on September 19, 1928, while in the employ of Wenzel & Henoch Construction Company and while working at the bottom of an open trench being dug by said company on the east side of Lake Drive in Fox Point, Wisconsin. The trench was about sixteen feet deep and about twenty-seven inches wide. It was being excavated by a trenching machine which had a boom about thirty feet long on which was an endless belt or chain carrying digging buckets. The end of the boom was six feet above the surface of the ground, the lower end being at the bottom of the trench. The nature of the soil through which this trench was being dug was hard clay. The soil was not sandy or wet or liable to cave in as the word "liable" is ordinarily used. The sides of the trench were shored up with two-by-six maple planks placed in pairs and spaced about two or two and one-half feet apart along the sides of the trench, each pair of planks being supported by four hardwood struts or braces placed between them. At the time of the accident a brace had been placed about one and one-half feet from the lower end of the boom. From the last brace just mentioned there was exposed on each side of the trench above the boom a triangular surface about fourteen feet in length along the surface of the ground from the last brace to the point where the top edge of the boom came out of the ground. These triangular surfaces of the ditch were supported by a pair of braces placed six or seven feet ahead of the long perpendicular brace. These braces were five feet in length and were supported by hardwood struts between them. Alexander's work was to place the lower end of the new upright braces which were put in from time to time as the machine proceeded and to place the lower struts or braces between the upright planks. A new set of braces was about to be placed when the ground between the last set of upright braces and the short brace upon the triangular surface along the east side of the ditch caved in and fell upon the boom. The cave-in reached about seven feet along the trench and covered the lower end of the boom. A hard piece of ground rolled down along the boom and struck Alexander on the side of the head as he was backing up along the bottom of the trench, causing his death. The bracing that was used in this trench was that customarily and ordinarily used by the company and by other operators in the same community working in similar trenches and ground. The company had, before the day of the accident, completed more than two thousand feet of ditch through substantially the same kind of soil and had employed the same methods of shoring without any cave-in occurring.

On January 9, 1929, the commission entered its award directing the payment of the primary compensation to the applicant, but reserved the right to determine any liability for increased compensation because of any failure of the employer to comply with any law of the state or lawful order of the commission. Thereafter, on February 12, 1929, a hearing was held and the commission decided that increased compensation was payable to the applicant because of a violation of order No. 53. No question is raised herein as to the primary compensation.

The plaintiffs contend that the Industrial Commission was without authority to promulgate said order No. 53. That said order is, under the decisions of this court, an attempt at legislation and was beyond the power of the commission to promulgate. . . .

The part of said order which is claimed to be legislative and unreasonable is as follows: "All excavations which are located in sandy or wet soil, or any soil which is liable to cave in, must be securely shored up."

In order to justify the fifteen per cent penalty it must appear that the injury was caused "by the failure of the employer to comply with any statute of the state or any lawful order of the Industrial Commission." Sec. 102.09(5)(h), Stats. The plaintiffs contend that order No. 53, under the decisions of this court, was not a "lawful order." [The court recites the terms of sections 101.06, 101.01, (11), 101.10, (3) and (4), as reprinted above.—Editor]

. . . This court, in Bentley Bros. v. Industrial Comm., 194 Wis. 610, 614, 217 N.W. 316, construed these statutes conferring authority upon the Industrial Commission as follows:

"In other words, it is the duty of the Industrial Commission to ascertain what safety devices or safeguards will make various places of employment as free from danger as the employment or place of employment may reasonably permit, and to require the installation of such safeguards and safety devices. That is the duty enjoined upon the Industrial Commission, and it marks the extent of its authority."

Does order No. 53, when applied to ditch excavations, require the installation of such safeguards and safety devices as will make such places of employment as free from danger as the employment or place of employment may reasonably permit? The court has concluded that it does not and that this case is ruled by Bentley Bros. v. Industrial Comm., supra.

Order No. 53, requiring excavations to be "securely shored up," is as much of "an attempt at legislation, pure and simple," as was general order No. 3502 involved in the Bentley Case, which order was as follows: "Safe and appropriate scaffolds shall be provided for workmen in exposed or elevated places." As to said order No. 3502 this court held in Bentley Bros. v. Industrial Comm., supra, p. 613:

"The language of the Industrial Commission, however, is broader than the language of the statute. The statute requires every employer to furnish a safe place of employment (sec. 101.06), and defines the term 'safe,' as used in such connection, to mean 'such freedom from danger to the life, health, safety or welfare of employees . . . as the nature of the employment or place of employment . . . will reasonably permit.' Sec. 101.01(11). It will thus be seen that while the statute requires the place of employment to be as free from danger as the nature of the employment will reasonably permit, the order of the Industrial Commission lays out of consideration the question of reasonableness and assumes to require all scaffolds to be safe. That this is an attempt at legislation, pure and simple, is apparent. That it is ineffective, and beyond the power of the Industrial Commission, is just as manifest."

That order No. 53 is subject to condemnation for the same reasons stated in the Bentley Case clearly appears when the plain ordinary meaning of the words "securely shored up" is given consideration. Webster's New International Dictionary defines "secure" as follows: "Not exposed to danger; safe, as secure from foes." "So strong, stable, or firm as to insure safety; safe." The Century Dictionary and Cyclopedia defines "securely" as follows: "Without risk or danger; in security; safely." "Firmly, in such a manner as to prevent failure or accident; so that loss, escape, injury, or damage may not result; as, to fasten a thing securely." It appears that the words "safe" and "secure" are synonymous. If order No. 3502, which required the "scaffold to be safe," was beyond the power of the commission to promulgate, then it seems clear that order No. 53, which requires excavations to be securely shored up, is equally beyond the power of the commission to promulgate, because it is an attempt at legislation and assumes to require that all excavations "be securely shored up."

It also seems clear to the court that so much of order No. 53 as applies to excavations, requiring them to be securely shored up, is not a reasonable order. If order No. 53 is given its plain ordinary meaning as applied to ditch construction excavations, then it becomes equally apparent that every cave-in resulting in injury will inevitably justify the imposition of a fifteen per cent penalty, because a mere cave-in would prima facie at least make out a penalty case. The mere happening of the cave-in would probably justify the conclusion that the excavation was not "securely shored up." We do not think that the statute giving authority to the commission justifies the promulgation of the order in its present form. In other words, we think that sub. (3) and (4) of sec. 101.10 place upon the Industrial Commission the duty of ascertaining what devices or safeguards are reasonably necessary in a given situation. Order No. 53 is silent as to what safety devices or safeguards are reasonably required in the construction of sewer ditch excavations. It is also silent as to what device or safeguard is required in order to make the exposed triangular sections hereinbefore mentioned as free from danger as such place of employment may reasonably permit. Before a penalty should be imposed, an employer engaged in any work ought to be reasonably advised or informed as to what safety devices or safeguards are required in order that the question as to whether or not he is complying therewith may be at least reasonably clear. The fairness of this conclusion becomes apparent when we consider that the testimony in this case shows that the method of "shoring up" the ditch where deceased came to his death was the same safety method customarily and ordinarily used by the company and other similar operators engaged in similar work. It is undisputed that a representative of the Industrial Commission inspected the job prior to the accident while the company was working in the same kind of ground and using the same method of shoring and that no criticism of such method was suggested.

It further appears that the commission's own experts and investigators were not in accord as to whether the instant case was one in which the penalty should be inflicted. On September 25, 1928, Dennis J. Doyle, deputy, reported to the commission among other things as follows:

"It might be possible to shore the unprotected side walls on an angle with the boom to prevent such slides, especially on jobs where the depth of the trench is over ten feet."

In reply to this letter Mr. Satterfield, assistant engineer, wrote Mr. Doyle among other things as follows:

"We doubt the advisability of submitting this case under the conclusion that order No. 53 was violated. We have had a number of accidental injuries occurring in this way, and so far it has not been considered practical to shore that section of the trench walls immediately over the extended boom of the digging machine. It is the writer's opinion that to attempt the shoring in the way suggested would add an additional hazard in that the workman, in placing such shoring, would be subjected to contact with the moving conveyor."

It is therefore apparent that order No. 53 gave no definite information as to what would be a compliance therewith.

While the workmen's compensation act should be liberally construed, to which proposition we give our whole-hearted accord, we feel that orders promulgated by the Industrial Commission which necessarily and properly result in the infliction of a penalty, if violated, ought to be reasonably clear so as to give notice to employers as to what is reasonably expected of them in complying with such orders.

For the reasons stated it is held that so much of general order No. 53 as requires all excavations merely to be "securely shored up" was beyond the power of the commission to promulgate.

The Industrial Commission ought to have no difficulty in promulgating a new order as a substitute for order No. 53 condemned herein, which will not be legislative in character, will be sufficiently plain in its requirements to be reasonable and valid, and will give to employers notice as to what is required in order that they may comply therewith. Excavations in or through different kinds of soil undoubtedly require different kinds of shoring in order that a safe place of employment, as defined by secs. 101.06 and 101.01, sub. (11), may be furnished.

By the Court.—Judgment reversed, and cause remanded with directions to render judgment setting aside the fifteen per cent penalty award herein.

OWEN, J. (dissenting). The opinion of the court holds the provisions of Industrial Commission order No. 53, in so far as it requires "all excavations which are located in sandy or wet soil, or any soil which is liable to cave in, must be securely shored up," to be unlawful and beyond the power of the commission. To this I cannot assent. It is said that this conclusion is compelled by Bentley Bros. v. Industrial Comm., . . . I see no similarity between the two cases. The language of the order there under consideration was: "Safe and appropriate scaffolds shall be provided for workmen in exposed or elevated places." This order prescribed no "safety device, safeguard, or other means or methods of protection." It simply provided that all scaffolds should be safe. It did not say that scaffolds should be equipped with a railing, nor did it prescribe any other safeguard that should be adopted or employed for the purpose of making scaffolds a safe place upon which to work.

The situation here is altogether different. This order does specify a safeguard. It requires ditches to be shored up. It specifies something that is not specified in the statute. The statute merely prescribes that the trench shall be maintained as a reasonably safe place in which to work. The order of the Industrial Commission says that to make it such a reasonably safe place in which to work it shall be securely shored up. I cannot see why this is not in response to the duty which the statute lays upon the commission. . . . The opinion seems to assume that if the order had laid down specifications to which the shoring should conform, then it would have been a lawful order. This is laying upon the Industrial Commission an unnecessary if not an impossible burden. I apprehend that what constitutes secure shoring is well known to any person engaged as contractor in the business of digging ditches and that further definiteness is not required. It is as definite as the term "drunk and disorderly," or as the term "reckless driving," both of which are made punishable offenses under our statute.

As the opinion does not discuss the question of whether there was in fact a violation of the order, I express no opinion thereon. I dissent from the conclusion that the order is unlawful.

NOTES AND QUESTIONS

1. Is the court reading into the statute the common law standard of due care with reference to the employer's duty? Is there anything in the opinion reminiscent of the common law standard? Does the majority opinion effectuate the legislative intent as we can ascertain it from note 4 following the Commission rules reprinted earlier in this chapter and from Professor Commons' autobiography?

2. Does Order No. 53 subdelegate to the courts the authority which the legislature delegated to the commission and intended the commission to exercise? Does the dissenting opinion meet this difficulty? What further specification is called for by the requirement of Order 53 that the excavations in question "must be securely shored up"?

3. Can the same objection be made to any administrative rule or regulation which calls for judicial interpretation? Suppose Order No. 53 laid down specifications to which the shoring had to conform, but the employer contended that the excavation was not located in "sandy or wet soil, or any soil which is liable to cave in." Would the court have objected to the order on this ground? Should every case of "subdelegation" to the courts be legally objectionable? For an interesting discussion of these questions by Mr. Justice Jackson, see FTC v. Ruberoid Co., 343 U.S. 470 (1952).

MARYLAND CASUALTY CO. v. THOMAS FURNACE CO.
185 Wis. 98, 201 N.W. 263 (1924)

[Plaintiff is the insurance carrier of defendant Murphy Boiler Co., employer of the deceased workman. The Murphy Co. sent deceased to help repair a boiler at the plant of defendant Thomas Furnace Co., and in the course of that employment, the workman was overcome by gas which leaked into the boiler. The widow of the deceased was awarded compensation under the workmen's compensation act, which was paid by plaintiff. Plaintiff here sued the Furnace Co., apparently under Wisconsin Statutes 1923, section 102.29, which provided that "The making of a lawful claim against an employer or compensation insurer for *compensation . . .* for the injury or death of an employe shall operate as an assignment of any cause of action *in tort* which the employe or his personal representative may have against any *other* party for such injury or death; and such employer or insurer may enforce in their own name or names the liability of such other party for their benefit as their interests may appear. . . ." (Emphasis added.) Murphy Boiler Co., having refused to commence the action, was made a party defendant for the purpose of foreclosing any rights it might have. The trial court entered judgment dismissing the complaint.—Editor]

DOERFLER, J. . . . It appears from the evidence introduced by the plaintiff that during the two-week period while Mullens was engaged in his work, some gas was contained in the boiler. The valve in use was a patented device, and at the time of its installation was the best device known to furnace men engaged in a business similar to that of the furnace company. The president of the furnace company, Mr. Thomas, and the engineer of the company, both of whom have had long years of experience in the furnace business, knew of no better device. In addition to the valve, in order to further frustrate the escape of gas the packing of the flue above the valve with wet sand and ashes to a height of about fourteen to eighteen inches was also resorted to. It would appear almost conclusively that the means adopted by the furnace company to prevent the escape of gas were not only in accordance with the usual method adopted by furnace men, but that it constituted a method which was as safe as the business of the furnace company would reasonably permit. Under the provisions of the workmen's compensation and the industrial commission acts, the commissioners were vested with the supervision of every employment and place of employment in this state, and they were authorized, and in fact it was their duty, to adopt and enforce all proper orders, rules, and regulations for the protection of the life, health, safety, and welfare of every employee in such employment or place of employment. Members of the industrial commission are experts in matters of this kind, and it would appear that unless a member had special knowledge with respect to manufacturing industries he would not be in a position where he could adequately fulfil the requirements of his office. No rule, regulation, or order of the industrial commission requiring a different or better system to prevent the gas from escaping was called to our attention, and the evidence does not show that any effort whatsoever was made to provide a better system. The operation of a furnace like the one in question is one connected with unusual hazard to the life and health of the employees, and we assume that in adopting rules and regulations and in making and enforcing orders the commission would pay prompt and early attention to such a business. In the discharge of their duties the members of the industrial commission represent the public interest, which is designed to preserve life and health. Inquiry made at the office of the industrial commission and an inspection of the records of such commission by a member of this court yielded the information that at the time of the happening of the accident no order, rule, or regulation was in force by the commission which required a different method than that which was in operation at the plant of the defendant furnace company. We must assume that they had knowledge of the method employed, and, not having criticized the method or ordered or devised a different or better method, that this method had the approval of the commission.

It may be claimed, although such claim was made neither in the brief nor the argument, that it is a matter of common knowledge that a flue like the one in question can readily be so constructed as to be proof against the escape of gas, and that other methods such as ventilating systems may be introduced in order to purify the atmosphere in a boiler or other similar device. This, however, is a subject of which the court cannot take judicial notice. It is within the field of experts. Plaintiff's counsel did not introduce evidence upon this subject, and, as before stated, no such device was deemed necessary by the industrial commission, and the members of such commission are experts.

Work on boilers like that of the defendant furnace company is only performed at comparatively long intervals, when the boiler becomes out of repair or where a new boiler must be installed. The work of the deceased, Mullens, was not confined to the repair or replacement of furnace boilers, but to boilers in general. Adequate precaution had been imparted to the deceased with respect to his conduct in regard to his work in this boiler. He was the sole judge of the time necessary for recuperation in the open atmosphere. No evidence was introduced showing that employees prior to that time had either been overcome by gas or that any one had lost his life. Under these circumstances we can readily agree with the learned circuit judge when he directed a nonsuit upon the substantial ground that the place of employment was as safe as the business of the furnace company would reasonably permit.

. . . The judgment of the lower court is affirmed.

By The Court.—Judgment affirmed.

CROWNHART, J. (dissenting). The facts in this case have been fairly stated by the court. The safety statute has also been set out in the opinion. The decision turns on the question of common knowledge of which the court will take judicial notice.

In the course of judicial proceedings there has grown up the principle, which is firmly established by thousands of decisions, that those things which are of common knowledge in the jurisdiction of the court will be judicially noticed and accepted as facts in the trial of a case, without proof. In other words, the courts are presumed to possess the intelligence generally possessed by the people in the same judicial district. Juries have the same right to apply their common knowledge and experience in the consideration of their verdicts.

The question here to be determined was whether it is a matter of common knowledge that fuel gas can be readily and safely contained, and whether it is a matter of common knowledge that such gas could have been displaced by ventilation so as to have made the place of employment safe. I am of the opinion that both of these questions should be answered in the affirmative. I am unwilling to confess ignorance where such confession is self-abasement rather than modesty.

Fuel gas, which contains the dangerous monoxide gas, is and has been in common use in this state for very many years. It is used for light, heat, and power. It is safely contained in great tanks. It is piped into houses and used by housewives without danger. It is safely used for power in thousands of engines throughout the state. It is known by every one who comes in contact with gas that it can be safely controlled in metal containers, and by the proper use of simple contrivances the flow of gas can be completely regulated. This, then, was the situation when Mullens was sent to his death in a room filled with poisonous gas. The gas was lighter than the air, and was introduced at the bottom of the boilers, while Mullens was working at the top, where the gas would rise and make the place especially dangerous. It is admitted the gas was introduced through a flue which was closed by a butterfly valve similar to the damper in a stove. This butterfly valve allowed the escape of gas, and, to partially control the escape of gas, ashes and sand were placed on top of the valve. But it is admitted that this did not prevent the escape of gas through the butterfly valve and the sand and ashes, so that the place where Mullens worked was, continually, highly dangerous. On the day of the accident the workmen had been obliged to escape from the dangerous situation into the open air each half hour or so. Monoxide gas is cumulative in its effect; that is, a person inhaling a quantity of it at one time during the day would require less gas at a subsequent time to overcome him. It is tasteless and odorless. The workmen could only judge of its effect by reason of headaches that came on. Now, notwithstanding this highly dangerous situation, the defendant furnished this place of employment for workmen, and for work which was to continue over a period of weeks. It was to meet such situations that the safety statute, quoted in the opinion, was passed. That statute is more important to the health and welfare of workers than any other law that has been placed on the statutes of Wisconsin. It should not be whittled away or made ineffective, but on the contrary it should be fairly enforced and given every reasonable intendment to carry out its purpose. It is plain to my mind that this place of employment was not reasonably safe within the meaning of the statute, but, on the contrary, it was highly dangerous, and the danger could have been readily removed, and should have been removed, in the exercise of common prudence. Its danger could have been prevented, as I have said, by simple contrivances—for one thing, by a metal cap that would screw on or be fastened on tightly to the gas flue. For another thing, the valve could have been packed with substances that were not readily permeable by gas, like ashes and sand. A still more simple way, and one which has been pointed out by the industrial commission as early as 1913, was to introduce into the boiler housing pure air to displace the gas-laden air. Every manufacturer understands how this may be done, and it is a very simple thing, of which people have common knowledge.

An attempt is made in the opinion to excuse the defendant because the industrial commission had not provided a rule with reference to this particular place of employment. No such rule was required of the industrial commission. The statute furnishes the rule, but in the enforcement of the rule the industrial commission, from time to time, does make orders. But it should be noted that this was not an ordinary place of employment; it was a temporary condition, of which the commission might have no knowledge. But as early as 1913 the commission did issue General Order 2013, reading as follows:

"Order 2013. *Furnaces and forges.* All furnaces and forges which emit gas or smoke in such quantity as to be irritating, obnoxious, or injurious to health must be equipped with a ventilating system which will remove as much of the gas and smoke as the character of the work will permit."

And Order 2014:

"Order 2014. *Foundries, forge shops, and roundhouses—Ventilation.* All foundries, forge shops, roundhouses, and *other places* of employment in which smoke, gas, dust, or vapors are present in sufficient quantities to obstruct the vision, or to be irritating, obnoxious, or injurious to the health, must be equipped with a system of ventilation which will eliminate such smoke, gas, dust, or vapors in so far as the conditions of the industry will permit. . . ."

While these orders do not cover the exact situation here, they do sufficiently suggest a proper method to be used by the employer. The industrial commission does not run these plants, and the statute does not direct the industrial commission to furnish the safe place. It is the employer who is required to do this. He cannot, and ought not, be allowed to shift his responsibility onto the commission. Here is a great public-policy statute, important to employers, employees, and the public. It needs no apology and allows of no evasion. The attempt to show compliance by proof of common practice or claim of ignorance as to better methods should be frowned upon. That was the old rule that the statute is designed to escape. This statute aims to protect human health and life. A reasonable compliance with it would have saved the life of Mullens.

The plaintiff failed to show by evidence that there was any safer practice which could be reasonably adopted. Prudence on plaintiff's part might have suggested the danger of supposing that the court would take judicial knowledge that gas may be readily and easily contained, or that ventilation would overcome the danger. But plaintiff's failure to prove matters of common knowledge does not excuse the court from applying the rule of common knowledge, where such matters are in fact of common knowledge, to be judicially noticed.

For these reasons I respectfully dissent.

NOTES AND QUESTIONS

1. Note from the majority opinion how the court informed itself regarding the actions of the Industrial Commission. Was this proper?

2. Is the plaintiff's claim in this case based upon the common law or upon statute? Have you encountered similar situations previously in this book? Where?

3. Is the majority saying that a statute providing for the issuance of administrative rules on a particular matter is to be deemed of no legal effect until the rules have been issued? Is such a position warranted? Did the majority take it?

If the violation of an applicable administrative rule is deemed by the courts to show conclusively that the employer failed to provide a safe place of work, does it follow that the absence of an administrative rule requiring a change in the existing practice of an employer should be deemed by the courts to show conclusively that the commission regards the existing practice as providing a safe place? Why not? Is this what the majority is saying?

Precisely what legal effect is the majority giving to the absence of an administrative rule applicable, in their opinion, to the situation? Is the majority applying the common law standard of care?

4. What doctrine limiting the scope of judicial notice is the majority enunciating? Is Justice Crownhart, in dissent, suggesting an unwise extension of the scope of permissible judicial notice? Note that Justice Crownhart was the first chairman of the Industrial Commission, serving from 1911-1915.

5. Should the trial court have submitted the case to the jury? For what purpose?

6. What legal effect should the courts give to an employer's *compliance* with an applicable administrative rule? In Waterman v. Heinemann Brothers Co., 229 Wis. 209, 282 N.W. 29 (1938), plaintiff sued to recover for injuries sustained in falling down a stairway in defendant's store. Plaintiff claimed that the accident resulted from defendant's violation of the safe-place statute, section 101.06. The jury found, in favor of plaintiff, that the stairway was unsafe, due in part to insufficient lighting. Judgment below for plaintiff was reversed by the Supreme Court, and the record remanded with instructions to the trial court to dismiss the complaint. The court said, in part: "Under the undisputed evidence as to the lighting of the stairhead we consider that the plaintiff's claim of being blinded by light is in conflict with the physical facts and is utterly incredible. She may have been 'blinded,' but if she was, it was not from the lights in the store, but from failure of her eyes to function from physical causes. It is to be noted in this connection that the lighting here involved complied with the only order of the industrial commission that relates to lighting at stairheads. Order 3538 of the commission, so far as it relates to stairheads, reads: '*Illumination.* Natural or artificial illumination shall be provided at the head and foot of all stairs . . . which are open to use. . . . The following intensities of illumination in foot candles shall be considered a minimum for the location specified.' There is no claim or suggestion that the minimum illumination was not provided. When the commission has provided the necessary elements of safety applicable to a particular place it is not for the court or jury to establish others."

Do you agree?

CHAPTER Fourteen

JUDICIAL REVIEW of ADMINISTRATIVE INTERPRETATIONS of STATUTES and the USE of EXTRINSIC AIDS in INTERPRETATION

The materials in Part II showed how various unofficial and official bodies may contribute to the production of a particular statute, and that a particular statute may have behind it also an illuminating history of previous (actual and proposed) legislation and judicial decision. We have considered briefly the legal relevance of such legislative history. We shall once again examine the extent to which such "extrinsic aids"—including administrative interpretations of statutes—are legally admissible and practically useful in the interpretation of statutes. We have noted that our previous consideration of questions of statutory interpretation has been restricted to those cases, typical of the situation in the states, where little or no documentary evidence of the background of legislation is available. Nevertheless, important examples of the use of legislative history in statutory interpretation are contained in Part II and you should find and re-examine the use of (1) administrative construction; (2) committee hearings; (3) committee reports; (4) successive or related statutes; and (5) successive drafts or amendments to the same statute proposed in course of passage.

The cases that follow present the problem of the use of legislative history in connection with the interpretation of statutes which are implemented or enforced by administrative agencies. Therefore, they also illustrate how administrative agencies go about interpreting statutes and the weight accorded their views by the courts.

PELLETT v. INDUSTRIAL COMMISSION
162 Wis. 596, 156 N.W. 956 (1916)

Appeal from a judgment of the circuit court for Dane county: E. RAY STEVENS, Circuit Judge. Affirmed.

Action to set aside an award against the plaintiffs made by the Industrial Commission in favor of James Suffern, who on July 29, 1914, sustained an injury while in their employ . . . Plaintiffs brought an action in the circuit court for Dane county to set aside the award. The court made findings of fact and conclusions of law sustaining the award, and from a judgment entered accordingly the plaintiffs appealed. . . .

VINJE, J. . . . Plaintiffs also seek to set aside the award because it was procured by fraud. The allegations as to fraud on claimant's part are substantially these: (a) that Suffern testified before the Commission that he was totally disabled for six months, when in fact he was not, and that he settled with a casualty company in which he was insured for only one month of total disability; (b) that he concealed from the Commission that he was subsequently and within six months of his injury injured while in the employ of one Kennedy, resulting in total disability for ten days and partial disability for one week more. Plaintiffs also allege that they first learned of Suffern's representations to the casualty company January 11, 1915, and that the Commission refused to set aside the award because more than ten days had elapsed since it was made. Sec. 2394—17, Stats. 1915.

It will be seen the fraud complained of consisted of false testimony on the part of the claimant and of concealment by him of facts material to the issue before the Commission. Sec. 2394—19, Stats. 1915, provides that an award may be set aside on the following grounds: "(1) That the commission acted without or in excess of its powers. (2) That the order or award was procured by fraud. (3) That the findings of fact by the commission do not support the order or award." The question, therefore, presented is whether the fraud alleged, assuming it to be sustained by proof, constitutes a ground for setting aside the award. It may be conceded that the language of the statute upon an original construction, regardless of principles guiding equity in granting relief from judgments obtained by fraud as announced in Boring v. Ott, 138 Wis. 260, 119 N.W. 865; . . . and regardless of the intent of the legislature as expressed in the report of and discussions before the committee that drafted the Workmen's Compensation Act, is susceptible of the construction that the fraud meant by the act includes perjury or the concealment of material facts upon the hearing. It is also susceptible of the construction that it includes neither; that it was not contemplated that trial after trial should be had upon the question of whether a witness testified falsely, for if one award could be set aside upon that ground a subsequent one could also, and so on indefinitely. Happily there is as to this statute no doubt upon the subject. The report of the committee referred to and the discussions had before it conclusively show that it was the legislative intent that perjured testimony or concealment of material facts were not such fraud as the statute contemplates. In their report the committee said: "The fraud alluded to in the second ground will be only such as was perpetrated in securing the award, and will not include false testimony of any party, because such questions all will be decided by the board" (commission). This view is reinforced by the discussions before the committee, too lengthy to be here inserted. Such being the express legislative construction given the language used; and such construction, being repugnant neither to the language used nor to judicial principles, must control. That reference may be had to the report for the purpose of ascertaining the correct construction of the language used was held in Minneapolis St.P.&S.S.M.R. Co. v. Industrial Comm., 153 Wis. 552, 558, 141 N.W. 1119; Hoenig v. Industrial Comm., 159 Wis. 646, 648, 150 N.W. 996. The court therefore properly refused to receive evidence of the fraud alleged, since if established it could not affect the validity of the award.

By the Court.—Judgment affirmed.

NOTES AND QUESTIONS

1. What type of fraud, in the court's opinion, would justify setting aside an order or award of the Industrial Commission?

2. The court concluded that the language of the statute could reasonably bear the construction urged by the plaintiffs as well as that adopted by the court. Do you agree? What argument about the meaning of the crucial language could you make from the context in which it appears?

3. What "extrinsic aids" were relied upon by the court to support its interpretation of the statute? Would it be accurate to say that talk about "legislative intent" on the point in question is talk about a fiction? Recall the discussions of this question in Part II.

4. The Industrial Commission does not publish all its decisions and opinions under the workmen's compensation act. Those deemed especially important or valuable as a guide to Commission policy are published in the biennial report of the Commission on its workmen's compensation activity. A Commission chairman has been quoted as saying that the commission "refuses to enlarge the Reports sufficiently to include all case findings because it does not want precedents to play too dominant a role in the judicial work of the examiners." Merwin, Public Relations in Selected Wisconsin Administrative Departments 116 (Unpublished doctoral thesis, 1937).

Do you think this attitude of the Commission is warranted? Would you guess that the Commission, in fact, does or does not follow precedent? Do you think the courts should so review the judicial work of the Commission as to ensure that it does follow precedent? If not, do you think the courts should be concerned to know whether apparent inconsistency in Commission decisions is due to a change in policy (or in the interpretation of the statute) or represents a discriminatory action? Is the bar or the court in a position to know these things if all the decisions of the Commission are not reported?

For a comparison of the doctrine of stare decisis in the judicial and administrative processes, see Davis, Administrative Findings, Reasons and Stare Decisis, 38 Calif. L. Rev. 218, 242-258 (1950).

MILWAUKEE EL. RY. & L. CO. v. INDUSTRIAL COMMISSION
212 Wis. 227, 247 N.W. 841 (1933)

FRITZ, J. Plaintiff seeks judgment setting aside a death benefit awarded by the Industrial Commission for the death of Frank Forman, during the hours and in the place of his employment by the plaintiff. The evidence established that on September 8, 1930, Forman, who had taken a shower bath, as was permissible and usual during the last hour in his daily employment, had a heart attack while walking up the third or fourth step of a stairway in his place of employment. The stairway was in proper condition, and safe in all respects. He fell backward against the wall and down to the floor, which was either twenty-two or thirty-one inches below the step from which he fell. He lived for one-half hour after the fall. He sustained a fracture of the skull as the result of the fall, and that fracture was the cause of his death, which occurred one-half hour after the fall. He probably would not have died as the result of the heart attack. The commission found, in its formal order making the award, that Forman "accidentally sustained personal injury resulting in his death," while in the employ of plaintiff and "performing service growing out of and incidental to his employment." In the memorandum filed in connection with the formal order, the commission stated that it was satisfied that "the fracture of the skull resulted because of the height from which the applicant's husband fell, and that inasmuch as his employment caused him to be exposed to a fall from such a height as he did fall, that his death occurred because of his employment so as to entitle the applicant to death benefit herein.". . .

The circuit court affirmed the award. The only error assigned on this appeal is that the court erred in refusing to set aside the commission's findings and award "on the ground that the fall itself, and the resulting injury and ensuing death, did not 'grow out of' the employment." Inasmuch as the commission found, upon evidence that amply supports its finding, that Forman "accidentally sustained personal injury resulting in his death, . . . while in the employ of plaintiff," and "performing service growing out of and incidental to his employment," the award was clearly within the provisions of sec. 102.03, Stats. 1929, even though it may be debatable whether, as contended by plaintiff, that fall itself, and the resulting injury and ensuing death, grew out of the employment.

So far as "any personal injury accidentally sustained" is concerned, there is no provision in the statutes of Wisconsin because of which it is necessary that such an injury "grow out of" the employment in order to render the employer liable for compensation. In that respect there is a material difference between the statutes of this state and those involved in the cases upon which plaintiff relies, in contending that liability for compensation is conditioned upon the injury growing out of the employment. The cases in other jurisdictions which are cited in support of plaintiff's contention were decided under statutes which, by their express provisions, allowed compensation only for injury "growing" or "arising" out of the employment. That is not required by any provision in the statutes of Wisconsin. There are no words in our statutes which require, so far as "any personal injury accidentally sustained" is concerned, that the injury *grow out* of the employment in order to render the employer liable for compensation. In that respect the only provision in our statute is that "the employee is performing *service growing out of* and incidental to *his employment*," and as to the significance and scope of that provision, we have the legislative declaration, by an amendment in 1913 (ch. 599, Laws of 1913, p. 712), that:

> "Every employee going to and from his employment in the ordinary and usual way, while on the premises of his employer, shall be deemed to be performing service growing out of and incidental to his employment."

Thus as regards "any personal injury accidentally sustained," sec. 102.03, Stats. 1929, in prescribing the "Conditions of liability," provided, so far as here material:

> "Liability for . . . compensation . . . shall exist against an employer for any personal injury accidentally sustained by his employee, and for his death, in those cases where the following conditions of compensation concur:
>
> "(1) . . .
>
> "(2) Where, at the time of the accident, the employee is performing service growing out of and incidental to his employment.
>
> "Every employee going to and from his employment in the ordinary and usual

way, while on the premises of his employer, shall be deemed to be performing service growing out of and incidental to his employment. . . .

"(3) Where the injury is proximately caused by accident, and is not intentionally self-inflicted."

The only provision in that statute creating an exception from liability for "any personal injury accidentally sustained" by an employee, when he and his employer are otherwise within the provisions of the compensation act, and the injury is proximately caused by accident, is when the injury is intentionally self-inflicted. That exception is not applicable in the case at bar. On the other hand there is no provision in the statute which exempts the employer from liability because some physical affliction or disorder of the employee preceded the accident, which proximately caused the personal injury sustained by the employee.

It is true that although there were then no words in the statutes expressly to that effect, it was said in Hoenig v. Industrial Comm., 159 Wis. 646, 150 N.W. 996 [1915]:

"It seems quite clear that the injuries for which compensation is to be paid, under the act, are such as are incidental to and grow out of the employment."

[In Hoenig, the court upheld a Commission ruling that dependents could not recover for the death of an employee struck by lightning on the job when lightning was not a special hazard of the job.—Editor]

Although two prior decisions of this court were cited in support of that statement, nothing expressly to that effect was held in those decisions, and the decisions from other jurisdictions, which were then cited, were based upon statutes which, in this particular respect, were worded otherwise than the statutes of this state. That statement of the rule was assumed to be warranted under our statutes in several cases, such as . . . Eagle River Bldg. & S. Co. v. Industrial Comm., 199 Wis. 192, 225 N.W. 690, although in the last case the report of the legislative committee, which presented the original bill, was relied upon, in part, as basis for the rule. That report does state that one of the essential conditions for the payment of compensation is that "such *injury grew out of* and was incidental to *his employment.*" However, for some reason or another, that condition was not incorporated in the statutes, and the condition actually embodied therein, viz. "that the employee is performing *service growing out of* and incidental to *his employment,*" differs so materially in that respect that it affords no basis for holding that the statute requires that the injury grow out of the employment.

In this connection it should probably be noted that for a time, until the repeal thereof by sec. 39, ch. 403, Laws of 1931, an amendment by ch. 457, sec. 2, and ch. 668, Laws of 1919, sec. 102.35, Stats., provided that "the provisions of sections 102.01 to 102.34 . . . are extended so as to include, in addition to accidental injuries, all other injuries, including occupational diseases, growing out of and incidental to the employment." In so far as that amendment extended the provisions of the compensation act to "other injuries, including occupational diseases," than "personal injuries accidentally sustained," as to which compensation had theretofore been provided, the adjective clause "growing out of and incidental to the employment," which is in that amendment, operated to limit the "other injuries including occupational diseases" to those growing out of and incidental to the employment. But that limitation is confined to the "other injuries including occupational diseases" to which that amendment extended the act so as to provide for compensation in instances "in addition to accidental injuries." But even as to that limitation in sec. 102.35, Stats. 1919 to 1929, it must be noted as reflecting the public policy of this state as disclosed in its legislative enactments, that all of sec. 102.35 was repealed by sec. 39 of ch. 403, Laws of 1931; and that by amendments provided for in sec. 5 of that chapter, the rather extensive scope (as compared to similar statutory provisions in other states) of sec. 102.03, Stats., in so far as it described the kind of injuries which were compensable thereunder, was even enlarged. By these amendments, liability for compensation against an employer, when both he and his employee are subject to the provisions of the compensation act, and the employee, at the time of the injury, is performing service growing out of and incidental to his employment, was extended to any "disability" —instead of any "injury accidentally sustained" as in former statutes—sustained by an employee where the injury is not intentionally self-inflicted—instead of "where the injury is proximately caused by accident and is not intentionally self-inflicted," as in the former statutes.

Likewise, there is no exception under the statutes because the effect of the fall was no greater as a result of the industry itself than ordinarily under such circumstances, or because the conditions of exposure are no different by reason of the industry than they are ordinarily under similar circumstances. When any personal injury accidentally sustained by an employee is not self-inflicted, it makes no difference who was at fault or to blame. "The injury is compensable when it results from a hazard incidental to the industry," even though the hazard in an industry is no greater than it is ordinarily under a similar condition affecting human action. . . . It is not the nature of the hazard that is the determinative thing, but rather whether or not it is a usual or necessary incident to the employment. Schroeder & Daly Co. v. Industrial Comm., 169 Wis. 567, 173 N.W. 328. In the case at bar the height of three or four steps above the floor constituted the hazard. That hazard was a usual and necessary incident to the employment, and it constituted the "determinative thing" regardless of the nature or extent of the hazard, and regardless of whether it was or was not more dangerous than three or four steps usually are. It is sufficient that that hazard, such as it was, pertained to and was inseparably connected with the industry, and that death resulted,—not because of the heart attack, but because of the accidental injury, i.e., the skull fracture, sustained in falling the increased height which resulted from that hazard.

By the Court.—Judgment affirmed.

NOTES AND QUESTIONS

1. Correspondence in the files of the Industrial Commission is of interest in appraising the decision in Milwaukee El.Ry.&L.Co. v. Industrial Commission and the statutory amendment which followed it. Quotations given here are made with permission.

From a letter of May 11, 1933, from Mr. A. J. Altmeyer, then Secretary of the Industrial Commission, to Mr. Joseph A. Padway, then counsel to the Wisconsin State Federation of Labor: ". . . It seems very strange that the court should . . . bring about such a radical change in the underlying basis of the workmen's compensation act, especially when such an interpretation affects the constitutionality of the act as a whole . . . Apparently the question involved was not given consideration in the briefs and Mr. Levitan [Assistant Attorney General] tells me that the attention of the court was not called to the fact that Section 102.01 contains a definition of 'time of injury' which involves the element of causation. After you have had an opportunity to study these decisions, I should appreciate your letting me know what you think about asking the legislature to amend section 102.03, (1) as follows. . . ." Mr. Altmeyer then suggested an amendment substantially similar to that finally adopted and set forth in note 5 below.

a. Can the language of the statute reasonably bear the construction for which the Milwaukee El.Ry.&L.Co. contended?

b. Do you think the court's argument based on section 102.23 (3)—that the only statutory exception from employer liability is when the injury is intentionally self-inflicted —is valid? How would you counter this argument on behalf of the employer? Was it necessary for the legislature to specify this exception in the light of any reasonable interpretation of the preceding statutory language?

c. Section 102.01 (2) defines "time of injury" as "the date of the accident which caused the injury or, in the case of disease, the last day of work for the last employer whose employment caused disability." Does this definition validate the contention of the Milwaukee El.Ry.&L.Co., as Mr. Altmeyer and Mr. Levitan seemed to think?

d. What is the constitutional problem referred to by Mr. Altmeyer?

2. Was the language of the statute so clearly favorable to the employee's contention that the court was warranted in ignoring the report of the legislative committee which reflected a contrary legislative intent? Note the following letter from Mr. Padway to Mr. J. J. Handley, Secretary of the Wisconsin State Federation of Labor, a copy of which was sent by Mr. Padway to Mr. Altmeyer: May 29, 1933: ". . . When the Compensation Act was first passed it contemplated payment of compensation for injuries arising out of employment. This has been the interpretation of the act for all the years the act has been administered. However, the Supreme Court recently [radically changed] the basis of the Workmen's Compensation Act, in effect it holds that an injury occurring while in employment is to be compensated even though it does not arise out of the employment. For instance, if an office clerk with a bad heart died of heart failure while at his desk, his widow would receive compensation even though his death was in no manner connected with his employment. In other words, workmen's compensation is virtually turned into accident and health insurance. Whether this should be so or not is a matter that I would like to give much more study to and discuss at greater length. However, you as officers of the Federation of Labor, and I as its attorney, must look at this matter as it exists under the present situation and consider what is just and fair under the circumstances as they presently exist. The change came about through accident. It was not intended nor is it the result of a proposal urged by us or by agreement with the Commission or insurance companies. It seems, therefore, that the fair thing to do is to put the law back where it was than to take advantage of something that we did not request or agree upon, no matter how beneficial the change may be. I can conceive of a situation arising if the change is not made, which may upset rates, etc., and cause much havoc to employers and insurance companies—something I know the Federation does not desire to inflict upon any one. . . ."

3. What other "extrinsic aids" were available to the court on the meaning of the statute? Did the court use them properly? Particularly, was it justified in overruling an administrative construction of long standing which, apparently, the Wisconsin Supreme Court had previously upheld? Was it justified in ignoring the views of other states on

this question? Did the court make valid use of the history of the occupational disease clause from 1919 to 1931? Note that the 1931 law to which the court refers was originally a Revisor's Bill. Does this fact affect the soundness of the argument the court elaborates on the basis of the 1931 law?

Compare the role of "extrinsic aids" in this case with their role in the preceding Pellett case.

4. On May 19, 1933, Mr. Altmeyer wrote to Mr. Harold W. Story, counsel for the Allis-Chalmers Manufacturing Company, and to Mr. L. J. Parrish, of the A. O. Smith Corporation, inviting their advice with reference to the court's decisions and informing them that he had approached the State Federation of Labor and expected its cooperation in securing an amendment.

5. The opinion in Milwaukee El.Ry.&L.Co. v. Industrial Commission was filed April 11, 1933. Thereafter, by L. 1933, Chapter 402, the legislature amended Section 102.03 of the workmen's compensation act, prescribing the conditions of liability. L. 1933, Ch. 402 added clause (1), (e) to Section 102.03, providing that liability shall exist against an employer only "Where the accident or disease causing injury arises out of his [employee's] employment."

From Mr. Altmeyer to Mr. Padway, June 5, 1933: ". . . At the hearing last week, you also raised the question whether the phrasing 'arises out of' was broad enough. We made use of that phrase because it is found in about forty acts and has been given the legal interpretation that we have heretofore had in Wisconsin; e.g., it would cover cases of lightning, heat prostration, freezing, or any other hazard, even though it is not peculiar to the employment, if, as a matter of fact, the employment exposed the employee to such a hazard to a greater extent than the commonalty. If there is still any doubt in your mind as to the wisdom of the changes that have been made, will you please phone the writer . . . so that the bill may be changed before it is reported out of committee. . . ."

6. Note again the initiative taken by the administrative agency in bringing about legislative change. Note the considerations that entered into the drafting problem.

7. The 1933 legislation is but one of a multitude of cases in which legislatures have overruled judicial decisions, including decisions of the Supreme Court of the United States on matters of statutory interpretation. In a few cases, decisions of the Supreme Court construing the Constitution have been overcome by constitutional amendment. The Eleventh Amendment overruled Chisholm v. Georgia, 2 Dallas 419 (U.S. 1793) so as to make clear that a private party could not sue the state in a federal court without the state's consent; the 16th Amendment overruled Pollock v. Farmers' Loan & Trust Co., 157 U.S. 429 (1895) so as to permit Congress to tax all incomes.

NOTE, THE RE-EVALUATION OF THE USE OF LEGISLATIVE HISTORY IN THE FEDERAL COURTS
52 Columbia Law Review 125-134 (1952)

At least two members of the United States Supreme Court have recently questioned the propriety of extensive use of legislative history in judicial interpretation of federal statutes. In Schwegmann Bros. v. Calvert Corp.,[1] Mr. Justice Jackson, joined by Mr. Justice Minton, while concurring in the judgment of the Court, felt constrained to write an opinion expressing the view that the Court, in construing the Miller-Tydings Amendment,[2] should not have looked beyond the lan-

[1] 341 U.S. 384 (1951).   [2] 15 U.S.C. § 1 (1946).

guage of the statute.[3] Mr. Justice Frankfurter has been critical of the "spurious use of legislative history." [4] The opinion of the Court in United States v. C.I.O.[5] indicates that some of the members of the majority refused to consider the legislative history set forth in that opinion.[6]

Whether or not this reaction to apparently well-settled practice[7] presages a trend, it does invite an examination and re-evaluation of the purpose of judicial reliance on legislative materials in the interpretation of federal statutes, as well as the manner in which federal courts have used such materials. This inquiry is of special importance in view of the fact that construction of legislative enactments now constitutes the major part of the work of federal courts.

I. *The Judicial Function in the Interpretation of Statutes*

. . . the courts still view their primary function in the interpretation of statutes as that of so construing the language as to give effect to the intention of the legislature. This attitude reflects judicial recognition of the different roles assigned to the legislature and the courts in our society.

If "legislative intent" is taken to mean the existence in the mind of each legislator of an identical set of precisely defined fact situations to which the statute applies, "legislative intent" clearly is the fiction Radin labelled it. If, however, such intent is looked upon as a common agreement on the purpose of an enactment and a general understanding of the kind of situation at which it is aimed, to deny the existence of a legislative intention is to deny the existence of a legislative function.

Recognition of the existence of a legislative intention, and of a judicial obligation to ascertain and effectuate it, does not solve the problem of statutory interpretation. If laws were directed only to judges, this problem would not be easy of solution. But legislatures are concerned with guiding the conduct of laymen, and statutory language is the primary means to this end. The "plain meaning" rule appears to have been premised on the importance of the popular understanding of a statute. But it rests on a questionable assumption—the assumption that statutes

---

[3] See Schwegmann Bros. v. Calvert Corp., 341 U.S. 384, 395-397 (1951) (concurring opinion).

Earlier, Justice Jackson had attacked the use of extrinsic aids in statutory construction. See Jackson, The Meaning of Statutes: What Congress Says or What the Court Says, 34 A.B.A.J. 535 (1948); 8 F.R.D. 121 (1948).

[4] Frankfurter, Some Reflections on the Reading of Statutes, 47 Colum. L. Rev. 527, 543 (1947); see Shapiro v. United States, 335 U.S. 1, 48 (1948) (dissenting opinion); American Stevedores v. Porello, 330 U.S. 446, 460 (1947) (dissenting opinion); ICC v. Mechling, 330 U.S. 546, 585

(1947) (dissenting opinion).

[5] 335 U.S. 106 (1948).

[6] "Some members of the Court, joining in this opinion, do not place the reliance upon legislative history that this opinion evidences, but reach the same conclusion without consideration of that history." United States v. C.I.O., 335 U.S. 106, 120 (1948).

[7] . . . See Commissioner of Internal Revenue v. Church's Estate, 335 U.S. 632, 667, 687 (1949) (dissenting opinion). The appendix to the dissenting opinion lists well over 100 recent cases in which legislative history was decisive of the interpretation of a particular statutory provision. . . .

have a "plain meaning." There is an inherent difficulty in applying general statements, however clearly worded, to particular situations. Moreover, the language employed in legislative drafting is rarely either plain or clear.

There appear, then, to be two important considerations in the judicial construction of statutory language: (1) the intention of the legislature; (2) the extent to which that intention can be gathered from the statutory language by those whose conduct it affects. While these two factors do not ordinarily conflict, an over-emphasis on one may lead to a negation of the other. Perhaps the judicial conception of the relative importance of these two considerations explains, in part, the different techniques which have been employed in legislative interpretation.

For a long time the plain meaning rule dominated statutory construction in federal courts. When carried to the extreme,[21] this tended to obliterate the judicial obligation to the legislature. In the late 1930's, the Supreme Court adopted a philosophy of self-restraint toward legislative regulation in the economic area. This greater emphasis on Congressional will seems to have led to the extensive use of extrinsic aids for its ascertainment. Recent criticism of this technique of statutory construction stresses its tendency to detract from the guiding function of statutes, and seems to reflect a desire to return to the plain meaning rule.

II. *The Use of Legislative History by the Federal Courts*

A. Permissible Sources. Since the almost complete destruction of the "plain meaning" hurdle in 1940,[24] the use of legislative history in the interpretation of statutes has become standard practice in the federal courts. The term "legislative history" has become a catch-all for extrinsic evidence of Congressional intent. Some classification of the materials referred to is necessary for closer analysis. Helpful for this purpose is Sutherland's division of legislative history into three chronological categories: (1) The events leading up to the introduction of the bill; (2) consideration of the original bill from the time of its introduction to its final enactment; (3) the history of the statute since its enactment.[26]

1. *Events Leading up to Introduction of the Bill.* The circumstances which existed at the time the law was passed and the contemporaneous evils at which the statute was aimed, are considered appropriate objects of judicial inquiry.[27] In United States v. Carbone,[28] for example, the Supreme Court held that the Federal Kickback Act did not apply to the activities of union leaders since that statute was passed to protect the wages of laborers on Federal projects from employer coerced kickbacks.

[21] For a striking example, see Caminetti v. United States, 242 U.S. 470 (1917).

[24] "It would be anomalous to close our minds to persuasive evidence of intention on the ground that reasonable men could not differ as to the meaning of words. Legislative materials . . . can scarcely be deemed to be incompetent or irrelevant." United States v. Dickerson, 310 U.S. 554, 562 (1940). See United States v. American Trucking Ass'ns, 310 U.S. 534, 543 (1940).

[26] 2 Sutherland, Statutes and Statutory Construction § 5001 (3d ed. Horack 1943).

[27] See Collins v. Hardyman, 341 U.S. 651, 657, 661-662 (1951); Apex Hosiery Co. v. Leader, 310 U.S. 469, 489 (1940); United States v. Trans-Missouri Freight Ass'n, 166 U.S. 290, 319 (1897).

[28] 327 U.S. 633 (1946).

Presidential messages describing conditions which require Congressional regulation are generally admissible as evidence of the purpose of statutes enacted in response to such requests.[33] Thus, in construing a provision of the Emergency Price Control Act, the Supreme Court considered the message which President Roosevelt had sent to Congress before the introduction of the bill.[35]

2. *Consideration of the Bill from Time of Introduction to Final Enactment.* The reports of the committees in charge of the bill in both Houses of Congress, including conference committees,[36] are the most commonly used materials for the determination of legislative intent,[37] and are generally considered the most authoritative extrinsic aids.[38] Since most of the work of Congress is done in committee, and a committee report carefully explaining each section of a bill is presented to all the members of the legislature before general debate on the floor and final voting, reliance on the committee's explanation of the meaning of statutory language is well justified.[39]

The testimony of witnesses at committee hearings and statements made in general debate on the floor of Congress[41] are usually inadmissible to explain the meaning of particular statutory language. Since statements at hearings, unless adopted and included in the committee report, are not voted on by the legislature and may not even be brought to its attention, they cannot be taken to express the common understanding of Congress. Similarly, speeches of Congressmen normally represent individual views, and cannot be taken as indicative of the general position of the group.[42] But this rule has been qualified by many exceptions.

Testimony of the draftsman of the statute as to the nature and effect of the bill are often treated as evidence of legislative intent.[43] Further, where an amendment urged by a witness in a hearing is adopted, the testimony of that witness is regarded as evidentiary of its meaning.[44] Finally, testimony before Congressional commit-

---

[33] See New York Central R.R. v. Winfield, 244 U.S. 147, 150 (1917); Johnson v. Southern Pacific Co., 196 U.S. 1, 19 (1904).

[35] See Shapiro v. United States, 335 U.S. 1, 4 (1948).

[36] See NLRB v. Denver Bldg. Council, 341 U.S. 675, 686-687 (1951); Roland Electric Co. v. Walling, 326 U.S. 657, 672 (1946); FTC v. Staley Mfg. Co., 324 U.S. 746, 753 (1945).

[37] See, e.g., Algoma Plywood and Veneer Co. v. Wisconsin Employment Relations Bd., 336 U.S. 301, 306-309 (1949); Jones v. Liberty Glass Co., 332 U.S. 524, 530 (1947); McCullough v. Kammerer Corp., 331 U.S. 96, 98 (1947); Helvering v. N.Y. Trust Co., 292 U.S. 455, 466 (1934).

[38] See Gooch v. United States, 297 U.S. 124, 128 (1936); Duplex Printing Press Co. v. Deering, 254 U.S. 443, 474 (1921).

[39] Even Justice Jackson would not totally exclude committee reports. See Schwegmann Bros. v. Calvert Corp., 341 U.S. 384, 395 (1951) (concurring opinion).

[41] See Duplex Printing Press Co. v. Deering, 254 U.S. 443, 474 (1921); United States v. Trans-Missouri Freight Ass'n, 166 U.S. 290, 318 (1897); Goodyear Tire & Rubber Co. v. FTC, 101 F.2d 620, 623 (6th Cir. 1939); Abram v. San Joaquin Cotton Oil Co., 49 F. Supp. 393, 401 (S.D. Cal. 1943).

[42] See United States v. Trans-Missouri Freight Ass'n, *supra* note 41, at 318-319.

[43] See Elder v. Brannan, 341 U.S. 277, 284 (1951); Elgin, J.&E. R.R. v. Burley, 325 U.S. 711, 723-724 (1945).

[44] See Railway Labor Ass'n v. United States, 339 U.S. 142, 150-151 (1950); United States v. Zazove, 334 U.S. 602 (1948); United States v. Ogilvie Hardware Co., 330 U.S. 709, 716-717 (1947).

tees, although not admissible to explain the meaning of statutory language, is accepted as evidence of the general purpose of the law.[45]

The views of individual legislators are usually considered admissible when they seem to represent the common understanding of the group.[46] The statements of the Representative or Senator in charge of the bill,[47] or of the Congressman who introduced it,[48] are often used as evidence of legislative intent. When a question from the floor or a requested change leads to amendment of the bill, the reasons given by the proponent of the change are deemed persuasive of Congressional intention.[49]

In view of the numerous exceptions which limit the scope of the rule of exclusion, it may be questioned whether in actual practice there is a rule at all.

3. *History of the Statute Since Its Enactment.* Congressional acquiescence in the judicial or administrative interpretation of a statute is considered evidence of legislative intent at the time of enactment. Such acquiescence may be inferred from the refusal of Congress to change a judicial or administrative construction which is brought to its attention.[51] Thus, in determining that the Fair Labor Standards Act[52] applied to a daily newspaper one-half per cent of whose total circulation was out-of-state, the Supreme Court gave weight to the fact that several subsequent bills which were introduced to get exemption for such journals had failed of passage.[53]

[45] See Hilton v. Sullivan, 334 U.S. 323, 328 (1948); Ayrshire Collieries Corp. v. United States, 331 U.S. 132, 143 (1947); Bowles v. Goebel, 58 F. Supp. 686, 688 (D.N.D. 1945); Twin Ports Oil Co. v. Pure Oil Co., 26 F. Supp. 366, 373 (D. Minn. 1939); Petition of Bone, 19 F. Supp. 219, 222 (E.D. Mich. 1937); L.&I. Freight Lines v. Railroad Comm'n, 17 F. Supp. 13, 15 (S.D.Fla. 1936).

[46] See United States v. San Francisco, 310 U.S. 16, 22 (1940); Humphrey's Ex'r v. United States, 295 U.S. 602, 625 (1935); Goodyear Tire & Rubber Co. v. FTC, 101 F.2d 620, 623 (6th Cir. 1939); Abram v. San Joaquin Cotton Oil Co., 49 F. Supp. 393, 401 (S.D. Cal. 1943).

[47] See NLRB v. Denver Bldg. Council, 341 U.S. 675, 686 (1951); Algoma Plywood and Veneer Co. v. Wisconsin Employment Relations Bd., 336 U.S. 301, 309-310 (1949); United States v. C.I.O., 335 U.S. 106, 116-119 (1948); ICC v. Mechling, 330 U.S. 567, 575 (1947); FTC v. Staley Mfg. Co., 324 U.S. 746, 753 (1945).

[48] See Fong Haw Tan v. Phelan, 333 U.S. 6, 9 (1948); Williams v. United States, 327 U.S. 711, 720-721 (1946).

[49] See Ahrens v. Clark, 335 U.S. 188, 192 (1948); United States v. National City

Lines, 334 U.S. 573, 582-585 (1948); Roland Electric Co. v. Walling, 326 U.S. 657, 672 (1946).

[51] See NLRB v. Gullette Gin Co., 340 U.S. 361, 365-366 (1951); United States v. Shreveport Grain & Elevator Co., 287 U.S. 77, 84 (1932); McCaughn v. Hershey Chocolate Co., 283 U.S. 488, 492-493 (1931); United States v. Obermeier, 186 F.2d 243 (2d Cir. 1951). But see Girouard v. United States, 328 U.S. 61, 69-70 (1946).

Considerable weight is accorded to the construction of the agency charged with administering the law, even when it is not shown to have been specifically brought to the notice of Congress. See Brewster v. Gage, 280 U.S. 327, 336 (1930); Brooks Transp. Co. v. United States, 93 F. Supp. 517, 522 (E.D. Va. 1951); In re West Coast Cabinet Works, 92 F. Supp. 636, 664 (S.D. Cal. 1950); ICC v. Service Truck Co., 91 F. Supp. 533, 535 (E.D. Pa. 1950); ICC v. Weldon, 90 F. Supp. 873, 877 (W.D. Tenn. 1950).

[52] 52 Stat. 1069 (1938), 29 U.S.C. § 216 (b) (1946).

[53] See Mabee v. White Plains Publishing Co., 327 U.S. 178, 185 (1946).

B. Influence of Materials Used. It is extremely difficult to gauge the weight accorded to any particular legislative materials. There are relatively few holdings on the admissibility of legislative materials.[54] The few statements in judicial opinions which deal explicitly with the admissibility of such evidence do not indicate how much reliance is to be placed on any specific source. Moreover, an examination of Supreme Court cases during the last decade reveals that most statutory decisions rest on several kinds of legislative materials, with little indication of their relative influence.

III. *Criticism of the Use of Extrinsic Sources*

Legislative materials are often an amorphous mass, parts of which can easily be used to justify a variety of results: sometimes both the majority and the dissenting judges rely on legislative history but reach opposite results;[56] contrary results in fact have been based on resort to the same legislative materials.[57] The magic formula—"The legislative history shows . . ."—is at times invoked even when the legislative materials are not clear in relation to the problem before the court.[58] Moreover, there are no clear and comprehensive rules to guide judicial consideration of legislative history. Therefore, doubts have arisen as to the efficacy of extrinsic aids in statutory interpretation.

A. Mr. Justice Jackson's Position. Mr. Justice Jackson has taken the position that resort to legislative materials is justified only when "the face of the Act is inescapably ambiguous." [59] Even then, he would not look beyond the committee reports. The Justice advances a number of reasons for the proposed change of technique. He urges that the final enactment is the most accurate and the only conclusive statement of Congressional intent, since it is the statute itself which is considered and voted on by the whole legislature. Most legislative history contains statements of interested groups, as well as tentative and conflicting views expressed at various stages of the legislative process. Consideration of such materials, while appropriate for the legislature, involves the Court in political questions which are not proper subjects for judicial determination. Further, he points to the fact that when the President signs a bill, he approves only the words of the final draft; he does not "endorse the whole Congressional Record."

[54] For a rare instance of a square holding on the admissibility of legislative history, see Harrison v. Northern Trust Co., 317 U.S. 476 (1943) (reversible error for lower court to refuse to consider the legislative history of the statutory provision involved, even though the provision on its face seemed plain and unambiguous).

[56] See Schwegmann Bros. v. Calvert Corp., 341 U.S. 384 (1951); Shapiro v. United States, 335 U.S. 1 (1948); Williams v. Austrian, 331 U.S. 642 (1947); American Stevedores v. Porello, 330 U.S. 446 (1947); Hust v. Moore-McCormack Lines, 328 U.S. 707 (1946); Elgin, J.&E. R.R. v. Burley, 325 U.S. 711 (1945).

[57] See United States v. Ogilvie Hardware Co., 330 U.S. 709 (1947). The fact that reasonable men may reasonably differ in their interpretation of legislative materials may offer a partial explanation for this conflict in result.

[58] See Schwegmann Bros. v. Calvert Corp., 341 U.S. 384, 390 (1951); Shapiro v. United States, 335 U.S. 1, 8 (1948); American Stevedores v. Porello, 330 U.S. 446, 454 (1947).

[59] Schwegmann Bros. v. Calvert Corp., *supra* note 58, at 395 (concurring opinion).

Mr. Justice Jackson also emphasizes the practical effects on the bar of the present trend in statutory construction. He believes that since most law offices are not equipped with legislative materials or financial facilities for examining the legislative history of statutes, the use of these materials by the courts has serious consequences on the counselling task of the legal profession. And he contends not only that the materials necessary for such prediction are unavailable in most law offices, but that even the few adequately equipped offices in large cities can no longer advise clients on the meaning of statutes. He attributes this to the absence of any uniform criteria for the judicial evaluation of legislative materials. In a speech to the American Law Institute,[67] Mr. Justice Jackson suggested that the formulation of a set of uniform rules of interpretation would help both bench and bar in dealing with legislation.

There seems to be little indication that the Justice's position has been accepted by the other members of the Supreme Court. Although Mr. Justice Minton joined in Mr. Justice Jackson's concurring opinion in Schwegmann v. Calvert Corp., it is not clear whether he shares Mr. Justice Jackson's general rejection of the use of extrinsic aids, or was merely rejecting the relevance of the legislative history of the Miller-Tydings Amendment to the issue before the Court.

B. *Mr. Justice Frankfurter's Views.* Mr. Justice Frankfurther's criticism has been directed primarily at what he conceives to be the improper judicial use of legislative history,[70] rather than at the propriety of any use of extrinsic aids in the interpretation of statutes. He has attacked the judicial tendency to read into a committee explanation an independently derived construction when the committee report is silent or unclear on the issue litigated.[71] For example, in determining the scope of the word "damages" as used in the Public Vessels Act, the Supreme Court looked at the House committee report, and found reference to property damage only. The Court reasoned that statement of a purpose to permit actions for property damages does not preclude an intention to allow claims for personal injuries. From the absence of any repudiation of such a purpose, the Court concluded that Congress must have intended to include personal injury actions.[73]

Mr. Justice Frankfurter has also suggested that indiscriminate use of legislative materials encourages special interest groups to manufacture legislative history.[74] There does seem to be a tendency, perhaps because of extensive judicial resort to legislative history, to "plant" legislative intention for the courts to find and use.[75] He has warned, too, that the decreasing emphasis on the actual words of

[67] Jackson, The Meaning of Statutes: What Congress Says or What the Court Says, 34 A.B.A.J. 535 (1948), 8 F.R.D. 121 (1948).
[70] See Commissioner v. Church's Estate, 335 U.S. 632, 667 (1949) (dissenting opinion); American Stevedores v. Porello, 330 U.S. 446, 460 (1947) (dissenting opinion); ICC v. Mechling, 330 U.S. 567, 585 (1947) (dissenting opinion); Hust v. Moore-McCormack Lines, 328 U.S. 707, 745 (1946) (dissenting opinion); United States v. Carbone. 327 U.S. 633, 642, 644 (1946)

(dissenting opinion).
[71] See American Stevedores v. Porello, *supra* note 70, at 460 (dissenting opinion).
[73] American Stevedores v. Porello, 330 U.S. 446, 452-453 (1947).
[74] See Shapiro v. United States, 335 U.S. 1, 36, 48-49 (1948) (dissenting opinion).
[75] See Cox, The Labor Management Relations Act, 61 Harv. L. Rev. 1, 44 (1947); Dykstra, The Impact of Pressure Groups on the Legislative Process, 1951 Wash. U.L.Q. 306.

statutes will lead to poor drafting and lazy legislation—a trend which should be discouraged by the courts.[76]

C. Appraisal of Criticism. In view of the value of legislative history as an aid to the judicial effectuation of the will of the legislature, the present technique ought not to be abandoned unless the difficulties said to be involved in its use are inherent.

Mr. Justice Jackson has stated that the consideration of legislative materials necessarily involves the courts in political questions—and the decision of such questions is a function properly reserved to Congress. But when the meaning of general terms is in issue, the determination of legislative intent solely from the words of the statute seems much more susceptible of becoming a subconscious inquiry into what a reasonable or wise legislature would mean by such words, than is a factual search for the explanation given by the legislators. Even when the legislative documents are silent or ambiguous on the point in question, the very search for the actual legislative purpose tends to reinforce the judicial obligation in interpreting statutes, and decrease the probability of improper political judgments.

The argument that the words of a statute express the final legislative intention and should therefore be regarded as the sole authoritative source in ascertaining that intention is essentially fallacious. For it rests on the erroneous assumption that words have a fixed meaning.[78] Words are symbols used for communication—means, not ends, in the legislative process. To employ every available method of accurately determining the intended referents of the statutory language is not necessarily to vary or distort the symbols. The argument that the President approves the statutory words standing alone seems equally invalid. As leader of a major political party and active participant in the legislative process, the chief executive does not read the words as of first impression; he is usually familiar with the kind of situation at which a statute is aimed. The use of legislative history, therefore, may be as important in determining the President's understanding of the statutory language as it is in ascertaining the intention of Congress.

Finally, the practical effects of the use of legislative history on the bar and the general public must be considered. Legislative history materials are not generally available in law offices. But many important Congressional measures are given detailed coverage in the newspapers. The Congressional attitudes, statements, and explanations are often widely publicized. This information is not an exact substitute for legislative materials and cannot provide as reliable a basis for predictability. There is, however, no foolproof guide to prediction of the outcome of the litigation. Indeed, the result which Mr. Justice Jackson reached, in the Schwegmann case, looking only to the words of the Miller-Tydings Amendment, was con-

---

[76] See Frankfurter, *supra* note 4, at 545.

[78] "Words are not crystals." Towne v. Eisner, 245 U.S. 418, 425 (1918). ["A word is not a crystal, transparent and unchanged, it is the skin of a living thought and may vary greatly in color and content according to the circumstances and the time in which it is used." Justice Holmes is writing.—Editor] See Ogden and Richards, The Meaning of Meaning (1948 ed.) *passim*.

trary to the interpretation on which most businessmen of this country had relied in the conduct of their affairs for more than ten years.[79]

IV. *Conclusion*

If the evidentiary nature of legislative history is kept firmly in view, much of the abuse which has attended its extensive use may be eliminated. Thus, "manufactured" legislative history should be inadmissible on the ground that it is not competent evidence of Congressional intent. Legislative history which is of no evidentiary value on the point in question should be excluded as irrelevant. Legislative materials, if used with discrimination and flexibility, are valuable aids to statutory interpretation.

NOTES AND QUESTIONS

1. In Note, Trends in the Use of Extrinsic Aids in Statutory Interpretation, 3 Vand. L. Rev. 586 (1950), wherein the emphasis is on state courts, the conclusion is that "At the state level, where the most valuable types of extrinsic aids are still generally lacking, all indications from previous decisions and from the States which do have such aids are that the state courts are willing to make full use of all types of relevant materials which may be presented for their consideration. At both the state and federal levels there is a definite trend toward the more clear and careful drafting of statutes. If the 'plain-meaning rule' were consistently followed, then resort to extrinsic aids to interpretation would be reduced to the extent that greater numbers of 'clear and unambiguous' statutes are enacted in the future. In view of the great criticism of that rule, however, and in view of the general willingness of courts to avoid it, it may very well be that in the future even apparently 'clear and unambiguous' statutes will be interpreted in the light of extrinsic materials."

For the situation in Wisconsin, see Shearer, Statutory Construction—Use of Extrinsic Aids in Wisconsin, 1940 Wis. L. Rev. 453.

2. Mr. Justice Jackson, concurring in United States v. Public Utilities Commission of California, 345 U.S. 295 (1953), termed this case "a dramatic demonstration of the evil" of the practice of using legislative history materials for the "psychoanalysis of Congress" which he had condemned in the Schwegmann case. He reported that "Neither counsel who argued the case for the State Commission nor the Supreme Court of California had access to the material used by the Court today. Counsel for the Public Utilities

---

[79] See Schwegmann Bros. v. Calvert Corp., 341 U.S. 384, 402 (1951) (dissenting opinion). [In his dissenting opinion in the Schwegmann case, in which Mr. Justices Black and Burton joined, Mr. Justice Frankfurter said: "Not only is the view of the Court contrary to the words of the statute and to the legislative history. It is also in conflict with the interpretation given the Miller-Tydings Act by the Federal Trade Commission, by the Department of Justice, and by practically all persons adversely affected by the 'fair trade' laws." In July 1952, Congress passed the McGuire Act, P.L. 542, 15 U.S.C.A. 45, amending the Federal Trade Commission Act so as to overturn the effect of the decision in the Schwegmann case and make express what the dissenters thought was already clear in the Miller-Tydings Act, namely, that contracts and agreements establishing resale prices could be extended by state law to persons who are not parties to such contracts and agreements. Does this action by Congress demonstrate that the Supreme Court's decision in the Schwegmann case was erroneous?—Editor]

Commission of the state stated at the bar, and confirmed by letter, that he had tried without success over a period of four months to obtain the legislative history of s. 20 of Part I of the Federal Power Act. He obtained it only four days before argument, in Washington at the Library of this Court. He stated that the City and County Library of San Francisco, the Library of the University of California, and the Library of the largest law office in San Francisco were unable to supply it. The City and County Library tried to obtain the material by inter-library loan from the Library of Congress, but the request was refused. Counsel then attempted to obtain the material from the Harvard Law School Library, but it advised that 'our rules do not permit this kind of material to be sent out on loan.' " Justice Jackson then recalled the case of Panama Refining Co. v. Ryan which led to the establishment of the Federal Register and concluded: "Today's decision marks a regression from this modern tendency. It pulls federal law, not only out of the dark where it has been hidden, but into a fog in which little can be seen if found. Legislative history here as usual is more vague than the statute we are called upon to interpret."

Elizabeth Finley, the librarian for a large law firm in Washington, D.C., has written that while it is true that "there was no *compiled* history of the [Federal Water Power] Act and of the 1935 Amendments" involved in this case, a survey of libraries in the San Francisco area indicated that "everything cited by the Court, except the bills, *was* available." Finley, Crystal Gazing: The Problem of Legislative History, 45 A.B.A.J. 1281, 1283 (1959).

Miss Finley also states that The Library of Congress has several sets of congressional hearings and reports for the past fifty years which it is its policy to lend to any qualified library. However, the Library will not lend bills. But bills are usually reprinted in the debates, reports, or hearings. In any case, "if the request was for the 'legislative history of the Federal Water Power Act of 1920 as amended,' The Library of Congress might be justified in 'refusing.' Such a request amounts to passing a research chore from the borrower to the lender." *Ibid.* Miss Finley informs us that in the past twenty years, many law libraries have been assembling legislative histories; some of these histories have been published by the Government Printing Office; Matthew Bender & Co. has begun to publish a microcard edition of selected compiled histories; and since 1939, the West Publishing Co.'s U.S. Code Congressional and Administrative News has published at least one committee report on every federal statute.

How could Justice Jackson have been so misinformed?

3. Charles Nutting maintains: "The great reliance which is placed on extrinsic evidence of legislative intent by federal courts has made it relatively easy to draft a statute in broad or ambiguous terms and then to insert a statement in a committee report which will resolve the ambiguity in such a way as to support an interpretation which, if clearly expressed in the statute, might not have been accepted by the Congress." Nutting joins Reed Dickerson in denouncing this practice "not only as morally indefensible but also as usurping the legislative function." Nutting, [Dickerson's] Legislative Drafting: A Review, 41 A.B.A. J. 76 (1955).

Professor Newman disagrees. He detects "neither immorality nor usurpation of the legislative function." Newman, A Legal Look at Congress and the State Legislatures, in Legal Institutions Today and Tomorrow 76-77, The Centennial Conference Volume of the Columbia Law School (Paulsen ed. 1959). "Given the realities of legislative combat, I [Newman] would argue that a draftsman who is loyal to the legislators who are his 'clients' need not even flag the ambiguity, for the benefit of his clients' legislative opponents. . . . [F]air interpretations of vague language are legitimate ploys by whoever are authorized to edit the extrinsic documents. That does not imply, of course, that a judge or administrator is bound by those interpretations. On the contrary, his job is to interpret the words of the statute in the light of all available evidence." *Ibid.*

Do you agree with Newman or with Nutting and Dickerson?

4. In Commissioner of Internal Revenue v. Acker, 361 U.S. 87 (1959), the Supreme

Court held that a taxpayer who did not file a declaration of estimated tax could not be subjected to the penalty prescribed for one who has "substantially underestimated" his tax, *in addition to* the penalty for failure to file. A Treasury regulation provided that in the event of failure to file, the amount of the estimated tax, for the purpose of applying the additional penalty, should be taken as zero. The Senate and House Committee Reports supported the position taken by the Treasury. The Court refused to give any weight to these Reports on the ground that the statutory language was clear and should be given effect, particularly since a penal provision was involved, which called for a strict construction.

Justice Frankfurter (joined by Justices Clark and Harlan) dissented, saying: "The Court's task is to construe not English but Congressional English. Our problem is not what do ordinary English words mean, but what did Congress mean them to mean."

What do you think? Consider, too, the note that follows.

NOTE, ADMINISTRATIVE CONSTRUCTION AS A GUIDE IN THE INTERPRETATION OF STATUTES
40 Harvard Law Review 469 (1927)

It is very frequently the case that before a Congressional statute has been brought to the Supreme Court for interpretation, the officers charged with its administration have placed a certain construction upon it. To what extent is the executive practice taken into account in the decision? This question seems best answerable from the holdings and in the language of the Supreme Court itself. Two classes of cases have to be distinguished. In the first, there has been simply an executive ruling; in the second, after such a ruling there has been a substantial reenactment of the original law, and it is with the construction of the reenactment that the Court is faced. . . .

[I]t was decided as early as 1827, in Edward's Lessee v. Darby,[1] that the interpretation of the executive officers called upon to carry a law into effect "is entitled to very great respect." This decision has in general been followed wherever the statute is ambiguous and the administrative construction has been uniform and long-continued.

Nor has the Court failed to bring forward convincing arguments for its acceptance of the executive interpretation. If the legislature does not interfere with the administrative conduct, it is argued, there has been an implied recognition that the latter expresses the Congressional meaning. The Court cannot reason in vacuo as to the meaning of practical words intended to govern practical affairs, and therefore accepts the guidance of "able men and masters of the subject."[4] Members of the administrative are not infrequently draftsmen of the laws they are afterwards called upon to enforce, and therefore the legislature must have intended to accept their interpretation in passing the law. Since the layman who has to act under an ambiguous law will seek and rely upon undisturbed rulings as to the meaning of that law and will govern his affairs accordingly, the Court will be reluctant indeed to defeat the reasonable expectation of the general public by repudiating the construction upon which they have been acting.

---

[1] 12 Wheat. 206, 210 (U.S. 1827).

[4] United States v. Moore, 95 U.S. 760, 763 (1877), per Swayne, J.

The Court has, however, found cases where exceptions must be made. Rulings of a department cannot be followed where they are not uniform; where the statute is in the opinion of the Court clear and free from ambiguity, so that the administrative construction would substantially alter the law; where though the statute is somewhat doubtful, the rulings appear to the Court as unreasonable; or where the statute is in terms applicable to certain situations and the administrative has set itself up as a legislator to supply omissions and defects in the law by applying it elsewhere.

Where the Court is asked to interpret a statute which has reenacted in substantially similar form an earlier law that had been the subject of administrative construction, a different problem is presented. If it can be shown that Congress at the second passage was aware of the executive action, then it is fair to say that Congress silently approved and impliedly incorporated the construction as an integral part of the new statute. Congressional knowledge of the departmental rulings can be shown in the records of the debates in committee or on the floor of the house, or it may be presumed if the ruling was of long standing and general knowledge. Given such an implied incorporation, its acceptance by the Court becomes mandatory. The executive interpretation is no longer mere evidence of legislative intent to be accepted in lieu of better evidence if the Court considers it reasonable. By reenactment, the legislature has accepted the construction as its own. In such situations, therefore, the Supreme Court has held that the interpretation is not merely "entitled to great respect," but controlling.

Even here we must note a probable exception, . . . Where the statute originally and in its reenactment is unambiguous and specific, it has been held that an administrative construction which alters its scope will not be regarded as having been incorporated. It seems contrary to our technique of statutory construction to suppose that the legislature meant anything but what it said in plain terms; although a strong contrary argument could be made where there is proof, say from the legislative proceedings, that the inconsistent rulings were in fact approved of by those reenacting the bill. Moreover, the strongest reasons of policy preclude a means of construction which would prevent a layman from relying upon the plain text of a law. . . .

EDITORIAL NOTE: INFERENCES of LEGISLATIVE INTENT DRAWN from LEGISLATIVE HISTORY

In using extrinsic aids to interpret a statute, courts have indulged in a variety of conflicting inferences. They have inferred legislative approval of a prior administrative or judicial construction of a statute from the mere fact that no attempt was made to change it; or from the fact that efforts to change the construction failed in legislative committee. Toolson v. New York Yankees, 346 U.S. 356 (1953), which we have considered in Chapter 4, is an example of the latter inference. But in other cases, courts have thought that inferences from such legislative inactivity were too dangerous to make. See Girouard v. United States, 328 U.S. 61, 69 (1946), in which the Court said: "It is at best treacherous to find in Congressional silence alone [in this case proposed legislative changes had died in committee] the adoption of a controlling rule of law."

Courts are more inclined to infer legislative approval of a statutory construction if one or both Houses of the legislature rejected a proposal to adopt a contrary interpretation, made either during passage of the bill or subsequent to its enactment. See Youngstown Sheet & Tube Co. v. Sawyer, 343 U.S. 579, 586 (1952); Fox v. Standard Oil Company, 294 U.S. 87 (1935). But even in this situation, courts will sometimes refuse to make this inference. See Hecht v. Bowles, 321 U.S. 321 (1944). As stated in Fox v. Standard Oil Co., *supra* at 96: the rejection of a proposed amendment in the course of a bill's history "is doubtless not conclusive as to the meaning of the bill in the unamended form. . . . It is, however, a circumstance to be weighed along with others when choice is nicely balanced. . . ."

Contrary inferences have been drawn even from the adoption of an amendment, either in the course of the bill's passage or subsequent to its enactment. From such action, courts have often derived a strong indication of a legislative intent to change the bill or the statute. See, e.g., United States v. Plesha, 352 U.S. 202 (1957). Other courts, however, have refused to make such inference even in this situation. In Coplon v. United States, 191 F.2d 749 (App. D.C. 1951), the court was dealing with the FBI's power to make an arrest of Judy Coplon, a Department of Justice employee suspected of espionage. Another Circuit Court had already ruled that the statute applicable to FBI arrests gave no authority to make arrests, without a warrant, for the commission of felonies in the presence of the officer. Congress had then amended the statute so as to expressly grant such an authority. Dealing with the legal situation as it had existed prior to the amendment, the Court refused to conclude that the amendment itself showed a lack of the arresting authority prior to its passage. The amendment had simply "made unmistakable what we think was true before revision: that agents have the same power which private persons have to arrest without warrant for felonies committed in their presence. . . ." (p. 755). See also, United States v. Lowden, 308 U.S. 225, 239 (1939); and State v. Boliski, 156 Wis. 78 (1914).

In brief, the inferences we have been discussing in this Note are analogous to the "thrust-parry" maxims of statutory construction, analyzed in Chapter 9, sec. 3, *supra,* in this respect: They represent the same kind of "clues," "guides," or "counsels of caution" which the maxims have been said to represent; they point to a relevant consideration but do not compel the final conclusion, which must take account of all other relevant considerations as well.

EDITORIAL NOTE: JUDICIAL REVIEW of "MIXED" QUESTIONS of LAW and FACT

Questions which are referred to as "mixed questions of law and fact" —e.g., whether news-boys are "employees" within the meaning of the

Wagner Act—require the administrative agency not only to determine questions of fact (what do newsboys do, what are their relations with the newspapers?) but also to determine a legal question, i.e., to make a policy judgment or arrive at a standard as to what constitutes the employer-employee relationship within the meaning of the statute. In deciding whether the newsboy-newspaper relationship comes within the standard thus evolved, the agency is generally described as "applying" the law to the facts.

Professor Davis has suggested that a possible way to solve the problem of how far a court should review a so-called mixed question of law and fact decided by an administrative agency would be for the court to separate the parts of the question into law and fact, using the "substantial evidence" rule to review the fact determinations and making a fully independent redetermination of the question of law. But it is entirely clear, he writes, that such a simple solution does not fit the case law. Davis, Administrative Law—Cases-Text-Problems 559-560 (1960).

In fact, mixed-question determinations by administrative agencies have been given confusingly different types of review.[1] On occasion they have been treated like questions of law, i.e., given full, independent review. Thus, e.g., the court substituted its own judgment and rejected administrative constructions: in Social Security Board v. Nierotko, 327 U.S. 358 (1946), when it determined that the back-pay ordered by the Labor Board for reinstated employees qualified as "wages" under the Social Security Act; in Davies Warehouse Co. v. Bowles, 321 U.S. 144 (1944), when it determined that a particular warehouse was within the "public utility" exemption of the Emergency Price Control Act. On other occasions, mixed-question determinations by administrative agencies have been given the deference which is given to administrative determinations of fact. Examples are the judicial treatment of the I.C.C.'s application of the "undue preference" standard under the Interstate Commerce Act (United States v. Louisville & N.R.R., 235 U.S. 314 (1914)), and a compensation commission's application of the "arising out of or in the course of employment" requirement applicable to injuries under the Federal Longshoremen and Harbor Workers Act (O'Leary v. Brown-Pacific-Maxon, 340 U.S. 504 (1951)). In such cases the court may invoke this sort of proposition: that "so long as there is warrant in the record for the judgment of the expert body it must stand. . . . The judicial function is exhausted when there is found to be a rational basis for the conclusions approved by the administrative body." (Rochester Tel. Corp. v. United States, 307 U.S. 125 (1939), involving the

---

[1] In the federal courts, mixed-question determinations by a jury are given the same scope of review as are fact determinations; and those by a trial judge sitting without a jury are usually given the same scope of review as are determinations of law, i.e., the appellate courts feel free to give full review—to make a fully independent redetermination of the question of law. See, generally, Stern, Review of Findings of Administrators, Judges and Juries, 58 Harv. L. Rev. 70 (1944).

issue whether the Rochester Telephone Co. was "controlled by" another company within the meaning of the statute, so as to bring it within the statutory control of the F.C.C.) This "rational basis" formula, or other analogous formulae (e.g., that the Court should respect an agency's exercise of the "discretion" or "judgment" which has been "entrusted" to the agency by the legislature) eventuates in a limited type of review.

What determines whether one attitude or the other will be taken by the Supreme Court on these administrative determinations of mixed questions? Commentators are by no means in agreement, and a variety of factors have been suggested, including: whether the court or the agency is best qualified to decide the particular question involved; whether there is some indication in the particular statute that the legislature wished to delegate discretion over the matter to the agency; whether the determination would be generally applicable or limited to the particular facts of the case. Other factors may exercise a subtle or unconscious influence, such as whether the particular agency from its past record has earned the court's respect for the reliability of its determinations, or whether the instant determination is one which the court would itself have made. For a detailed discussion of these factors, with illustrations from cases and commentators, see Davis, Administrative Law Text, Chap. 30 (1959). See also Brown, Fact and Law in Judicial Review, 56 Harv. L. Rev. 899 (1943); Nathanson, Administrative Discretion in the Interpretation of Statutes, 3 Vand. L. Rev. 470 (1950); Jaffee, Judicial Review: Question of Law, 69 Harv. L. Rev. 239 (1955), Judicial Review: Question of Fact, 69 Harv. L. Rev. 1020 (1956).

CHAPTER Fifteen

REEVALUATIONS of the ADMINISTRATIVE
PROCESS

*HEARINGS BEFORE A SUBCOMMITTEE OF THE SENATE LABOR
AND PUBLIC WELFARE COMMITTEE TO STUDY SENATE
CONCURRENT RESOLUTION 21 ESTABLISHING A
COMMISSION ON ETHICS IN GOVERNMENT*
82d Cong., 1st Sess. 116, 224, 384 (1951)

MR. [HAROLD L.] ICKES, [Former Secretary of the Interior]. . . . These were
great days in the State of Wisconsin when, under a forceful and honest leadership
that did not know what it was to accept defeat, a social laboratory was set up out
of which came many models for the improvement of State government that other
States were eager to adopt. But who today believes that the public interest is served
by these State commissions? In the course of time the private utilities muscled
their way in by the usual methods with the result that the commissions, in effect,
became adjuncts, or at least they did so in many cases, of the private utilities,
despite the fact that the members of the commissions and their staffs were on the
public payroll.

On the lines of the Wisconsin model, in course of time the Federal Government
began to set up regulatory commissions with extensive administrative and quasi-
judicial powers which would have been highly beneficent if they had continued
to be exercised for the public good. But alas and alack, we have already reached a
stage of degeneracy in Washington, so far as some of the Federal commissions are
concerned, that calls for the purging of certain members of the commissions and
the reconstitution of the agencies on which they serve. But can this now be done?
Could the Commission on Ethics proposed by this resolution revitalize the commissions whose normal health is bad? Could it make its influence felt so that new
commissioners would really be zealous to represent the public and serve the public
welfare? I am inclined to doubt it, notwithstanding which the drafting of a code
of ethics and the setting up of a commission to measure the conduct of public
officials might help, at least for a while. But even so, it would be necessary to
guard zealously the source of the spring whose water at least was pure to begin
with. The main problem, as I see it, would be to try to do something that would
assure against the same type of degeneracy setting in that we have found in the
past in certain State and Federal commissions.

SENATOR [PAUL H.] DOUGLAS [of Illinois, Chairman of the Subcommittee].
I believe the disease has been called "administrativitis."

Mr. Ickes. Yes.

Senator Douglas. The characteristics of which are lethargy, indifference, and in some cases the domination by the very interests they are supposed to regulate.

Mr. Ickes. That is accurate.

* * *

Judge [Learned] Hand. . . . I think I am right in saying that the history of commissions is very largely this. When they start they are filled with enthusiasts; the problems are before them and they are themselves flexible and adaptive. Like all of us (and this as you know is the fault constantly charged, and properly charged, against courts) after they have proceeded a while they get their own sets of precedents, and precedents save "the intolerable labor of thought." So they fall into grooves, just as the judges are so apt to do. And when they get into grooves, then God save you to get them out of the grooves. It has become the customary way, and the safe way, and we find it so easy to follow the safe and customary way.

On the other hand, they do get an expertness and acquaintance with the subject matter that we judges cannot possibly have. The thing that teases me most, and I confess seems to be insoluble as far as I have been able to judge, is whereas the courts have a more widespread knowledge, it is nothing like the commissions' accurate knowledge of the precise subject matter. Where are the courts to intervene? I am perfectly satisfied that somewhere along the line you cannot leave the last word with an administrative tribunal; I am sure that that will run in the end into a sclerosis that will be fatal. But how shall the judges, who do not know the intricacies, know when to intervene; and where and how? Do not say the Supreme Court will do it; they could not possibly do it. The amount of it is far beyond the power of any conceivable nine men. It must be somewhere further down and for ordinary judges. I wish I had some light on it; frankly I feel bankrupt.

* * *

Mr. [Thurman] Arnold. . . . One of the things that happens to all administrative tribunals is that it first is opposed by the industry and then it becomes controlled by the principal industry. That does not have anything to do with corruption. That is due to the fact that young men in Government careers want to get the best jobs they can in the specialties and there is this social pressure to be a sound man, rather than an unsound man, because if you are an unsound man, you will never get a job in the industry. You cannot remove that. But I would have apart from those pressures an independent tribunal, whether you want to call it administrative courts or use your own courts, which would have sufficient dignity so people would not want to get off. I got off the bench and into private practice because of my peculiar temperament. But ordinarily people do not leave the bench. They like to get on and do not leave it.

I would make that a secure and dignified position that people would not want to leave.

NOTE

Reread, in this connection, the excerpts from Mr. Horsky's book reprinted in Chapter 13. Compare Mr. Horsky's views with those expressed by Judge Arnold.

TESTIMONY OF MARVER H. BERNSTEIN, HEARINGS BEFORE THE ANTITRUST SUBCOMMITTEE OF THE HOUSE JUDICIARY COMMITTEE ON MONOPOLY PROBLEMS IN REGULATED INDUSTRIES
84th Cong., 2d Sess., Pt. 1, Vol. 1 (Airlines) 59-64 (1956)

Mr. BERNSTEIN. I am Marver H. Bernstein, associate professor of politics, Princeton University.

One of the most significant developments in American politics during the last 100 years has been the growth and expansion of public regulation of economic life. Since the birth of the Interstate Commerce Commission in 1887, the independent regulatory commission has become a major institution of public regulation of economic affairs. The Commission has been widely regarded as an adequate, satisfactory, and even ideal instrument of governmental control. Reformers have relied upon it to correct abuses that had crept into the economy, and the regulated interests have generally accepted it as the most appropriate governmental instrument of regulation.

In general, the independent commission has been championed by those who believe that governmental regulation of business requires a high degree of expertness, a mastery of technical detail, and substantial continuity and stability in regulatory policies and administration. These requirements, it has been alleged, can best be met by a board of commissioners functioning in a neutral environment, free from partisan political considerations.

Congress itself has tended to regard the commission as a bulwark against excessive concentration of power in the executive branch of Government. Industries have preferred regulation by commission rather than by executive department in the belief that commissions can act more judicially and will treat them more favorably.

Supporters of the commission movement, nevertheless, have recognized that commissions have serious administrative deficiencies. They do not plan their operations satisfactorily; they tend to take a highly specialized view of regulatory matters with little consideration for the broader economic policies of Government. Their regulatory procedures are under almost constant attack on the ground that they fail to meet the tests of impartiality and fair treatment of respondents.

After nearly 70 years of experience with regulation by commission, the case for the independent commission has remained largely unchanged. . . .

The record of the regulatory commissions: A review of American regulatory experience since the 1880's reveals the principal characteristics of the independent commission.

1. Americans have shared a faith in commissions as efficient and effective agents of Government control. Although commissions have been attacked from time to time as inappropriate, there has been a remarkable predominance of the opinion that the commission is the best organizational device for governmental regulation of business.

2. Commissions have been supported by those who sought to insulate the process of governmental regulation from partisan political forces. Since corruption was identified with politics, it was believed that honest, competent administration could be achieved only in an atmosphere of judicial detachment. The advocates of commissions wanted to achieve statesmanship without politics, and they sought to avoid corruption by escaping presidential supervision.

3. The commission has had a profound faith in expertness and in rational solution of controversial regulatory problems. Regulation has been viewed largely as a matter of collecting facts and of deciding issues in an unbiased way, by examining the facts and applying a rule of law.

4. While American industry has undergone tremendous technological and structural changes, regulatory policies have evolved with painful slowness and hesitancy and bear the stamp of obsolescence and staleness. Commissions tend to be static and apathetic in contrast to the dynamic development and productive ingenuity of American industrial enterprise.

5. Although the commission was supported originally in part because it was regarded as superior to the courts in dealing with complex and intricate economic problems, it is now attacked most frequently on the ground that it is not sufficiently judicial in its operations. In the effort to meet charges of administrative absolutism and arbitrary action, commissions have become more and more like courts in their methods and procedures.

7. The general public knows very little and cares very little about independent commissions. Public concern with regulation usually declines sharply after the establishment of a commission. The regulatory problems are themselves so intricate and complex that they defy easy comprehension. The lawyers, moreover, have succeeded in turning regulation into a highly technical, legalistic process that presumably lies outside the layman's area of experience. And finally, attempts to take regulation out of politics by assigning regulatory responsibilities to commissions have failed to insulate regulation from politics, but they have removed the commission from the public spotlight and have allowed public support for regulation to wither and die.

8. Commissions operate in hostile environments, and their regulatory policies become conditional upon the acceptance of regulation by the regulated groups. In the long run, a commission is forced to come to terms with the regulated groups as a condition of its survival.

9. The vaunted independence of regulatory commissions is a device to escape popular politics. It facilitates maximum responsiveness of a commission to the

demands and interests of regulated groups. It provides maximum freedom from exposure to popular political forces. It tends to alienate the commission from sources of political strength in Congress and the Presidency. It reduces the effectiveness of regulation.

10. The presumed advantages of commissions have been conspicuous by their absence.

(*a*) Presidents have often been less than careful in making appointments.

Because any one member of a commission is less important than the administrator of a single-headed agency, the President may feel that he can afford to nominate mediocre persons. Appointments to commissions tend to fall below the general standard of presidential appointments.

(*b*) With respect to tenure and continuity of policy, the commission's record is mixed. In some commissions tenure has been excessively long with a consequent loss of vitality and strength. In other commissions, members rarely serve out their terms, and their average length of service is astonishingly short.

(*c*) Commissions tend to know more and more about less and less as their regulatory jurisdictions become narrower and narrower in relation to the general political and economic development of the country. They lack perspective, and their experts have a remarkable capacity for developing a type of professionalism that narrows the vision of the public interest. Economists, lawyers, accountants, and engineers become preoccupied with problems of their professional status and specialized points of view.

(*d*) In terms of general administrative capacity, the commissions have long tolerated antiquated methods of doing their business which could not possibly survive in the ordinary private business. Complacency, inertia, and apathy appear as inevitable developments in the careers of commissions. Although tradition, precedent, and custom can harden into blind, deadening routine in all type of social organization, the commission seems to be particularly susceptible to the hardening of the administrative arteries.

(*e*) And lastly, because of their acknowledged inability to plan their activities and provide constructive assistance to congressional committees in revising regulatory statutes, they gradually lose their sense of mission. In their mature stage, their concept of the public interest is hardly distinguishable from the views of the dominant regulated interests. . . .

Jaffe,* *THE EFFECTIVE LIMITS OF THE ADMINSTRATIVE PROCESS: A REEVALUATION*
67 Harvard Law Review 1105-1107, 1134-1135 (1954)

Many of the still current attitudes about the administrative process, and certain of the doctrines of administrative law, at least in their form and intensity, have been powerfully influenced by the immediate historic role of the administrative

* Louis L. Jaffe is Byrne Professor of Administrative Law, Harvard Law School. He taught law at University of Buffalo Law School, where he was Dean from 1948 to 1950, and has written extensively in the area of administrative law.—Editor

process. That history began, let us say, with the adoption of the Interstate Commerce Act of 1887. It reached its culmination in the New Deal with the creation of the Labor Board and the Securities and Exchange Commission. The administrative process was thought to have an inherent political or social orientation. There was more or less agreement as to its significance between those who hailed it and those who hated it. It was seen with hope by the one and fear by the other as capable of working continually progressive modification of the economy and the society. Supplanting private industry, it would take over the role of leadership in the "public interest." This was not, as we can see now, a just historical estimate if we were to push history far enough back. But it is both the strength and the weakness of the American that he is not history-minded. Very few great societies have had less history to contend with and have been so emboldened to bank upon an unmortgaged future. Our faith in a vigorous application of the administrative process has borne fruit. If we use the hopes of their proponents as the measure (not to try at this time to make absolute evaluations) the National Labor Relations Board and the Securities and Exchange Commission, to name but two, have been successful. They have, in their fields, made remarkable contributions to the reorientation of American society. They are only two evidences of a legislative and administrative movement which has profoundly changed our society, a change which can be set down beside the English Reform Movement of the nineteenth century as one of the great historical jobs of law-making. In taking stock of the administrative process today, it would compound the shortsightedness of the thirties if we forgot these achievements. But to accomplish this miracle with an unfettered, unquestioning spirit it may have been necessary to misunderstand the basic nature of our economy and to overlook the fact that history does not grant to any institution a fee in perpetuity. A long look at the administrative process might show some inherent potentialities, certain persistent functions, at least certain patterned recurrences and reincarnations, but it would also show that it can serve "reaction" as well as "progress," stability as well as change. Indeed those of us who took hope from the SEC were even at the time appalled by the Immigration Service, but this was not permitted to infect our general outlook. And now there are signs that we are readying ourselves for a Great Disillusion. There may be cause for disillusion, but I am afraid that we are in danger of drawing the wrong conclusions.

Let us begin by recalling how in 1938 a representative scholar was coming to envisage the role of the administrative process. I take an example from Dean Landis' eloquent series of lectures, The Administrative Process. Landis, speaking of the SEC, draws an analogy between its development and the ICC's: "As in the case of the Interstate Commerce Commission, it was not long before it became evident that the mere proscription of abuses was insufficient to effect the realization of the broad objectives that lay behind the movement for securities legislation. The primary emphasis of administrative activity had to center upon the guidance and supervision of the industry as a whole." [1] "[R]esort to the administrative process," he continues, "is not . . . simply an extension of executive power. . . .

[1] The Administrative Process 15 (1938).

In the grant to it of that full ambit of authority necessary for it in order to plan, to promote, and to police, it presents an assemblage of rights normally exercisable by government as a whole." [2] It thinks, he says, "in terms of the economic well-being of an industry." [3] "If the railroads are 'sick' we listen eagerly to what Commissioner Eastman may have to say upon the subject. . . . [T]he ills of the industry have become . . . [the ICC's] bailiwick. The policies they must formulate must now be directed toward broad and imaginative ends, conceived in terms of management rather than of police." [4] Thus the administrative process is seen evolving through two stages, one merging imperceptibly into the other: first the identification of the administrative process with the protection of the economically weak and unorganized against the oppression of the economically powerful; and then, because private industry has appeared to fail in its organizing function, the assertion of government responsibility to plan for the well-being of industry. This was the ultimate view that enthralled the New Dealer. This was the horrid specter that terrified the world of private industry.

We have come to see that both the thrill and the chill failed to take into account basic factors limiting the managing and "planning" potentialities of the administrative process. These factors are inherent in our industrial organization, in our conceptions of regulation, and in our political machinery. The planning thesis took almost no account of the character and the psychology of our administrators, a psychology which is a complicated product of these social factors, of the pattern of human nature in America, and of the special attitudes developed in the regulator by the fact of regulation itself. Let us turn then to a consideration of these factors. . . .

[Professor Jaffe then discusses the following limiting factors—(1) the tendency of the regulatory agency to be unduly influenced by the views of the regulated groups; (2) the tendency of administrators to favor regulation for its own sake; (3) the difficulties, in an industrial system characterized by dynamic change, of planning and making decisions in the area of management without assuming managerial responsibility; (4) the limits imposed by procedural safeguards that surround administrative action; (5) the difficulty of adequate and competent staffing.—Editor]

It is not then my purpose here, nor am I prepared, to draw out the conclusions from what has gone before. . . .

We have evolved our administrative system. We have worked out a great variety of basic forms and doctrines which have determined its structure and its relation to the other organs of government. But its operation in some respects has not been clearly foreseen. It is to these aspects of the system that we must now direct our energies. •

EDITORIAL NOTE: JAFFE on BERNSTEIN

Reviewing Professor Bernstein's book, Regulating Business By Independent Commission (1955) in 65 Yale L.J. 1068 (1956), Professor Jaffe analyzes

---

[2] *Id.* at 15.

[3] *Id.* at 16.

[4] *Id.* at 17, 13.

the elements in the current attack on the independent agency. His major concern is with the criticism that the agency's policy functions are independent of control by the Chief Executive. "The independent agency is criticized not only because it is politically irresponsible, but because from the total body of policy powers, most of which are committed to the President, it arbitrarily abstracts a segment and thereby impedes policy coordination."

Prof. Jaffe has a mixed reaction to these criticisms. He is sympathetic to the point made as to democratic control and policy coordination. Though realizing that complete Presidential coordination would be virtually impossible, still the "practical difficulties of coordination hardly warrant, except for strong and well-considered reasons, the creation of additional obstacles. It would seem to me, therefore, that at least in the future Congress should hesitate to set up further foci of independent, policy-making power." This presumption against an independent agency and in favor of a regular executive department or bureau does not extend however to the *adjudication* function. "Where the adjudicatory element is predominant, independence may be required or warranted. But this . . . may be a reason for stripping such an agency of as many of its executive and policy-making powers as is consistent with an adequate solution of the problem which the agency is being created to deal with."

As for the criticism that the independent agency tends to become industry-oriented, Jaffe is unimpressed. It has not been shown, he says, that these agencies are more industry-oriented than the executive agencies. "Anyone who follows the activities of the Department of Agriculture, for example, comes to feel (though this too is no doubt an exaggeration) that the Department is a glorified farmer's lobby." And there "is very little in our history, I think, to indicate that an executive agency will be much different from an independent agency in periods when public opinion or statutory policy is slack, indeterminate, or lacking in conviction. The odds are that it will respond in much the same way to the climate of opinion. The history of the antitrust division of the Department of Justice, for example, is one of alternation between strict and loose enforcement of the antitrust laws."

Moreover, "the critics' real quarrel, if they would but recognize and admit it, is with Congress" rather than the independent agency as such. The basic difficulty "is the radical lack of a meaningful statutory policy in many of the areas where the independent agencies function." Thus, the ICC "is criticized for being 'railroad-minded' and monopolistic. But can anyone find in the legislation of 1935 and 1940 an intention to establish competition as the presumptive norm of transportation regulation? . . . In radio . . . there never has been a statutory policy. The FCC was simply told to go ahead and regulate in 'the public interest.' . . . The Commission has lacked foresight, has often been timid and has sometimes been subservient, but to my mind this is the result of the absence of congressional guidance. [I]n the absence of a clear mandate, it is not only inevitable but appropriate that regulation take the form of an accommodation in which industry is the senior partner. This is the essence of 'industry orientation.' "

". . . My arguments, of course, do not make a case *for* the independent agency. As I have already indicated it seems to me sounder on balance that these policy-making agencies should be subject to presidential control. Rather, these arguments are intended to show that the critics of the agencies have attributed to the factor of agency independence all sorts of political ills and disappointments for which it bears no responsibility whatever."

It is interesting to note that Congress does not seem to be concerned with the difficulties of executive "coordination" but rather with the possibility that the Executive may be exercising too much control over the independent regulatory commissions. The Harris Subcommittee, for example, proposed to require, by statute, that the budget requests submitted to the Appropriations Committees of the Congress should disclose the original agency budget requests made to the Bureau of the Budget, the changes effected by the Bureau, and the Bureau's reasons for making these changes. It also recommended, cautiously, that Congress undertake a study "with a view to legislation that would require disclosure to Congress *both* of original agency legislative proposals *and* the views thereon of the Bureau of the Budget." H. Rep. No. 2238, 86th Cong., 2d Sess. 40-41 (1961). These Subcommittee suggestions were based on a report of its staff entitled "Budget Bureau Censorship and Control of Independent Agency Fiscal and Other Matters."

ETHICAL STANDARDS IN GOVERNMENT, Report of a Subcommittee of Senate Committee on Labor and Public Welfare
82d Cong., 1st Sess. 60-61 (1951)

A subtle malady which is apparently institutional rather than personal in its incidence is the tendency of the independent regulatory commissions not to die, but to fade away; with advancing age they tend to become the servants rather than the governors of the industries which they regulate, and attain a sort of dignified stability far from the objectives which they originally sought.

Proposals for dealing with this phenomenon vary greatly. They include: (1) separation of the responsibility for dynamic regulatory action from the function of finally hearing and deciding individual cases; (2) vesting the responsibility for the regulatory initiative, i.e., the selection and preparation of actions and the initiation of policy proposals, in appropriate executive departments; (3) making the residual commissions with their more limited adjudicative functions highly independent in status; (4) adopting the more limited plan of reorganization recommended by the Hoover Commission,* consisting chiefly of concentrating responsi-

---

* The reference here is to the first Hoover Commission, which reported in 1949. Commission on Organization of the Executive Branch of the Government, Report to the Congress on the Independent Regulatory Commissions (1949).—Editor

bility for administrative direction of the commission's work in the chairman; (5) an expanded judicial review of the decisions of regulatory commissions; (6) the creation of an administrative court of appeals to review cases from all regulatory agencies; and (7) the abandonment of the principle of maintaining independent regulatory agencies with a single clientele.

Although the apparent inability of the Government to establish independent regulatory agencies which maintain their original direction and momentum has its ethical aspect, the subcommittee believes that defects in organic structure are at the root of it. Probably a radical remedy (in the medical sense) is required. The necessary diagnosis and prescription should be made by another committee.

REPORT OF THE SPECIAL SUBCOMMITTEE ON LEGISLATIVE OVERSIGHT OF THE HOUSE COMMITTEE ON INTERSTATE AND FOREIGN COMMERCE
H.R. Rep. No. 2711, 85th Cong., 2d Sess. 9, 10, 21-23, 41 (1959)

II. *Recommendations*

To promote the fair and efficient administration of the law by the six independent regulatory commissions and agencies (referred to hereinafter as "commissions"), the subcommittee offers the following recommendations:

*   *   *

1. A code of ethics governing the conduct of commissioners, commission employees, practitioners, and others who appear before the commissions, should be enacted into law. Provision should be made for civil and criminal sanctions and for continuous enforcement.

2. Ex parte or extra record representations or communications, written or unwritten, not authorized by statute, made to any commissioner or commission employee for the purpose of influencing the decision or action in any proceeding or other matter involving necessity for commission decision or action should be prohibited in a law providing both civil sanctions and criminal penalties. Persons who aid and abet in the making of such unauthorized representations or communications should be included in the coverage of this law.

3. Written communications received by any commissioner or commission employee from any Member of the United States Congress or from any person in the executive branch pertaining to any proceeding or projected proceeding should be made forthwith a part of the public record. There should also be inserted in the public record a memorandum setting forth the substance of any nonwritten communication received from any Member of Congress or from any person in the executive branch. A copy of any such memorandum should be forthwith transmitted to the member or person who made such nonwritten communication.

4. Any communication, written or nonwritten, to or from a commissioner or commission employee, pertaining to any proceeding which by law or by commission rule or practice must be determined upon the record shall be included in the public

record. A memorandum containing the substance of any such nonwritten communication shall be included in such record.

5. Any written communication, to or from any member or employee of any commission, relating to any matter within the jurisdiction of the commission, shall be deemed an official communication. Any written communication to, and a copy of any written communication from, any member or employee of any commission shall be placed in the official files of the commission and shall not be removed therefrom except in accordance with law.

6. Any applicant, interested person or party, who represents himself in any proceeding before a commission; and any person, firm, corporation, association or organization, or agent or representative thereof, who for anything of value, received directly or indirectly, represents or acts on behalf of any such applicant, person, or party, in any proceeding before a commission, shall file with it a written notice of appearance, stating for whom he appears or acts and in what capacity. This notice of appearance shall be made forthwith a part of the public record. . . .

14. Each commission should be directed by law that the commission, or the majority of the commission, as the case may be, designate a commissioner to prepare or have prepared under his personal direction the opinion or decision of the commission, or of the majority of the commission, in any case submitted to the commission for decision, and that the commissioner thus designated shall sign his name to the opinion or decision. Care should be taken in such designation to rotate this responsibility among the commissioners so that every commissioner is designated to prepare opinions in all types of cases and to avoid specialization by individual commissioners.

III. *Reasons for the Recommendations*

* * *

The combination of executive, legislative, and judicial powers in one hand, as recognized in the deliberations which led to framing our Constitution, is bound to cause many of the difficulties we now experience in administrative law. The subcommittee makes no recommendation that the doctrine of separation of powers should be applied to the administrative regulatory commissions. Indeed our hearings contain testimony of experts in administrative law which shows the extreme difficulty of even fixing the line between the legislative and executive functions of the administrator. We believe, however, that the question of separation of powers merits further study. We may thereby arrive at some lasting answers to the problems generated from what certain authorities have referred to as "administrative absolutism."

When commissions are entrusted with the power to give licenses or franchises or authority worth millions of dollars, it is a foregone conclusion that selfish interests will begin to put on the pressure. If, to paraphrase Hamilton or Madison in The Federalist No. 61, the seekers after franchises were angels there would be no need for ethics or even criminal law. Unfortunately, our hearing record is replete with instances of improper ex parte pressures upon Commissioners. As we point out later, these pressures were made sometimes when the subject matter was under adjudication by the Commission and sometimes when the subject matter was in the so-called legislative process of rulemaking. The subcommittee's recommendations are to outlaw improper ex parte pressures, irrespective of whether they are made while the Commission is acting in a judicial, legislative, or executive capacity. . . .

A statutory code of ethics for all Federal agencies is needed. Laws alone may never lead to perfect ethical and moral standards in Government or in the men who appear before agencies; yet the existence of a statutory ethical code may well serve as a deterrent to the bad and a source of reassurance to the good as to the propriety of their conduct in doubtful situations.

The code should be formulated from the precepts contained in the codes of the American Bar Association and other association whose representatives appeared before us. Provisions should be made for effective enforcement. Extensive testimony has been taken pertaining to the ethical code. The subcommittee's jurisdiction, however, is limited. It does not extend to the executive agencies of Government. A statutory code of ethics should be of comprehensive application to the legislatively created regulatory agencies as well as to the executive agencies. Its provisions should be carefully interrelated to existing civil and criminal laws respecting conflict of interest and the obstruction of justice. It should set forth, among other things, standards of ethical conduct and procedures for enforcement against both lawyers and nonlawyers who appear before the various Federal agencies.

A code of ethics by itself is of little practical use. The ability and character of the administrators and the men appearing before them is of more importance. . . .

Individual responsibility of commissioners for commission decisions. The subcommittee has been impressed with the need for change in the practices followed by some commissions of letting the commission staff rather than individual commissioners assume responsibility for the preparation of commission decisions and opinions. It is the view of the subcommittee that inconsistencies in commission decisions over the years are traceable to a considerable extent to the failure of following the practice of having the commission, or the majority of the commission, designate individual commissioners to assume responsibility for the preparation of the decisions or opinions of the commission, or the majority of the commission. It is the view of the subcommittee that this practice, which is traditional with the courts and which has been followed by some commissions, should be adopted by all commissions. It is the hope of the subcommittee that this change will produce a sense of personal responsibility of individual commissioners for the decisions and opinions of the commission and will avoid the practice of having commission staffs assume the burden of reconciling inconsistent decisions reached by the commissions.

Conclusion

* * *

The vitality of our system of representative government depends upon the widespread confidence of the public in the fairness and integrity of the operations of governmental institutions. How this public confidence can be strengthened and given renewed vigor has been of great concern to the members of this subcommittee in all their deliberations.

We live in a highly developed form of society. Reasonable governmental regulation of economic and other power exercised by private persons and groups is necessary for the general public welfare. This is especially true in the fields of transportation, power, communications, fair business practices, and investment. Congress, as representative of the people, cannot engage in the day-to-day surveillance which is needed. Delegation of a certain amount of governing power must, therefore, be made to specialized and expert regulatory commissions. This delegation does not mean abdication. Rather it increases the responsibility of Congress. It must be constantly watchful and alert to insure that the laws enacted for the national public good are administered in accordance with their meaning and intent. Moreover, Congress must see to it that commissions are not permitted to be what the 1937 Report of the President's Committee on Administrative Management call "a headless 'fourth branch' of the Government, a haphazard deposit of irresponsible agencies and uncoordinated powers." Congress must also make certain that improper fraternization or pressures are not permitted. Otherwise, the administrative commissions may be converted into Washington branch offices of the regulated industry, or instruments of overaggressive seekers of special privileges. Sacrifices of the inborn vigor of the individual and of the incentive of reward for individual effort are not necessary in order to have more perfect functioning of our administrative regulatory commissions. These elements will continue to flourish if everyone concerned knows that the commissions will regulate without fear or favor and that a party substantially aggrieved may have a right of appeal and review. Strict adherence to the rules of the game and the elimination of advantages gained by underhanded deceits is absolutely essential.

One of the most effective steps, we believe, to strengthen the administration of law by commissions is to have as commissioners and key personnel, men of unquestioned ability and character. The entrustment of great discretionary power, in many instances nonreviewable by the courts, to persons having a modicum of qualifications invites trouble. We strongly urge that appointments to commissionerships be removed from politics and from the influences brought to bear by the more important members of the regulated industry. The national public interest requires that the Executive appoint as commissioners men of independence, experience, and attainment in the field of activities they are called upon to administer. The tenure and compensation of commissioners should be such as to attract to and keep in public service capable men and women. Public service should not be used as a stepping stone to more lucrative employment by a regulated industry.

While the Executive through the power of appointment has the opportunity to improve the administration of law by commissions, Congress itself has a similar opportunity.

Several of the statutes creating the major regulatory commissions do not provide detailed standards or even guidelines to channelize the broad discretionary powers conferred upon the commissions. Commissioners should not be turned adrift in a statutory sea of discretion with no channel markers in the form of standards to guide them. It is not enough to tell a commission that its decisions must be in the public interest, convenience, and necessity.

One of our important recommendations is that a thorough study be made of the various statutes conferring discretion upon a commission with a view toward establishing therein more precise standards or guidelines to control the exercise of such discretion.

NOTE

The most celebrated case in which the Committee charged improper ex parte pressures upon commissions involved the then Assistant to President Eisenhower, Sherman Adams, and Boston industrialist Bernard Goldfine. For the details, see H. Rep. No. 2580, 85th Cong., 2d Sess. (1958); and H. Rep. No. 2711 at 41-50, 65-70 and 73-76.

AUERBACH, *SHOULD ADMINISTRATIVE AGENCIES PERFORM ADJUDICATORY FUNCTIONS?*
1959 Wisconsin Law Review 95

Introduction

The administrative process is being attacked from opposite directions. Some critics see the mingling of judicial with legislative and executive powers as impeding the protection of private and public interests.[1] Others deplore the judicialization of the administrative process and think that the merger of powers is essential to the accomplishment of legislative objectives.[2]

Both schools of criticism are concerned for democratic values. The first bases itself upon the wisdom of the Founding Fathers and stresses the role of an independent judiciary in maintaining the supremacy of law.[3] The second emphasizes that the administrative agency is an instrument "for making good to the people of the country a major part of the gains of a hundred and fifty years of democratic government."[4] Any answer to the question thus posed by the different views must be judged by how well it finds the "balance between the public interest which

[1] . . . Report to the Congress on Legal Services and Procedure, Commission on Organization of the Executive Branch of the Government 84-85 (1955) [hereinafter cited as 2 H.C. Rep.]; Task Force Report on Legal Services and Procedure, Commission on Organization of the Executive Branch of the Government (1955) [hereinafter cited as TLS]; Proceedings of the House of Delegates of the American Bar Assoc., Midyear Meeting, Feb. 20-21, 42 A.B.A.J. 371 (1956); Report of the Special Comm. on Legal Services and Procedure of the American Bar Assoc., 81 A.B.A. Rep. 340 (1956).

[2] . . . . Bernstein, Regulating Business by Independent Commission (1955).

[3] The classic statements of the separation of powers doctrine are found in The Federalist No. 47 (Madison) and The Federalist Nos. 51, 68, 78 (Hamilton). Milovan Djilas has recently written of the incompatibility between totalitarianism and the rule of law applied by an independent judiciary. Djilas, The New Class 88-89, 92 (1957).

[4] Attorney General's Comm. on Administrative Procedure, Administrative Procedure in Government Agencies, S. Doc. No. 8, 77th Cong., 1st Sess. 20 (1941) [hereinafter cited as Att'y Gen. Rep.].

[administration] . . . promotes and the private interest which it disturbs." [5] . . .

Are the Reasons Why Agencies Were Given Adjudicatory Functions Still Valid?

The Elements of Adjudication. The process of adjudication requires the tribunal to determine the facts in the situation before it, formulate principles of law applicable to situations of this kind, and apply the principles to the facts. By writing an opinion generalizing the grounds of its decision, the tribunal also shapes the law for the future. The more general the controlling principle of law, the more discretion must be exercised in applying it and the greater will be the law-making role of the decision. The more precise it is, the less the discretion in applying it and the less significant will be the decision for the law's development.

Since the decision-making process seems to be essentially the same, whether performed by agency or court, why were courts by-passed?

The Fear of Judicial Bias Against New Legislative Policies. Agencies were created because legislatures were dissatisfied with the way courts handled or ignored particular social problems. Once new policies were adopted to solve these problems, legislatures feared that courts would not effectuate them zealously, because they would be more concerned for the private interests impinged upon than for the social interests sought to be protected.

It is difficult to know if this fear is still warranted.[27] Certainly, courts are "more conscious of current economic and social trends than they were two decades ago." [28] Yet, the question still remains whether the institutional framework within which they operate and the traditions which guide them do not tend, in time, to produce in all judges, whatever their background and previous experience, a bias in favor of private rights. Whether this bias is a good thing depends upon the extent to which the law otherwise protects the social interests involved. It does not by itself justify administrative adjudication.

Use of Rule-Making and Adjudication as Alternative Methods of Making Law. Particularly when it subjected an industry to regulation to promote its welfare as

---

[5] Comm. on Administrative Tribunals and Enquiries, Report, Cmd. No. 218, at 2, 5 (1957), which reflects similar concerns in a sister democracy. . . .

[27] We do not have the information necessary for intelligent judgment. We have some data about the prior political party affiliations of the men who become our federal judges and federal administrators. See, e.g., Miller, Politics and the Courts: The Struggle for Good Judges Goes On, 42 A.B.A.J. 939 (1956). But prior party affiliation is not a reliable basis upon which to predict future behavior of a judge or administrator. Mr. Miller expressed the confidence of the bar that "when the American lawyer becomes a judge he can and almost invariably does throw off all partisan ties and prejudices." Miller, *supra* at 939. Professor Bernstein concluded that there "is little evidence that commissioners divide on major policy issues according to their party affiliations." Bernstein, *op. cit. supra* note 2, at 104. [See, too, Schmidhauser, The Supreme Court, Its Politics, Personalities, and Procedures (1960).—Editor]

[28] Davison, An Administrative Court of the United States, 24 Geo. Wash. L. Rev. 613, 617 (1956). See also Schwartz, Administrative Justice and its Place in the Legal Order, 30 N.Y.U.L. Rev. 1390, 1400-01 (1955).

well as to protect the public from abuses, Congress gave the agency involved a "full armory of administrative weapons," [29] including rule-making and adjudication. This provided the agency with the flexibility needed to achieve the balance between rule and discretion which the particular situation demanded. . . . The Securities and Exchange Commission's choice of adjudication, rather than rule-making, to achieve flexibility in the regulation of inside trading in the course of the simplification of a utility system, was upheld in the celebrated *Chenery* cases.[31] The Federal Communications Commission has often been faced with a similar choice, deciding in favor of rule-making, for example, to regulate chain broadcasting, give-away programs, and multiple ownership of broadcast stations.[32] In each case, the rules were to be made effective through adjudication requiring, of course, the exercise of fresh discretion.[33] . . .

It may be granted that rule-making affords the greatest "freedom from unanticipated frustration of expectations" and "satisfies" elementary notions of fair play.[35] But in an area of regulation where "experience is yet to be won . . . premature rigidifying of policies may prove to be harmful in the extreme." [36] As experience accumulates, rule-making should play an increasingly important role in the regulatory process. But changes in the technology, structure, and practices of a regulated industry may always raise new problems requiring the more flexible case-by-case approach. Some problems, like ICC, CAB, and FCC licensing, which often require agencies to predict the future,[37] defy solution by precise rules. At best, these agencies have been able to develop criteria by which their decisions will be guided. But the weight given to each of the criteria will vary from case to case because of "the infinite variety of circumstances which may occur in specific instances." [38]

To transfer adjudication to courts, where it is an alternative law-making method, will deprive the rule-maker of adjudicatory experience and the judge of rule-making experience. Lacking overall responsibility, the rule-maker may be tempted either to make the rules too rigid in order to minimize the role of the judge or too general in order to "pass the buck" to him in difficult situations. . . .

[29] Note, SEC v. Chenery Corp.: A Case Study in Administrative Technique, 62 Harv. L. Rev. 478 (1949); See Landis, The Administrative Process (1938).

[31] SEC v. Chenery Corp., 332 U.S. 194 (1947); SEC v. Chenery Corp., 318 U.S. 80 (1943).

[32] National Broadcasting Co. v. United States, 319 U.S. 190 (1943); FCC v. American Broadcasting Co., 347 U.S. 284 (1954); United States v. Storer Broadcasting Co., 351 U.S. 192 (1956).

[33] See, e.g., Don Lee Broadcasting System, 14 F.C.C. 993 (1949), in which the FCC renewed licenses in spite of violations of the chain broadcast regulations. Since then, the FCC has been authorized to issue cease and desist orders against violations of its regulations. 48 Stat. 1086 (1934), 66 Stat. 716 (1952), 47 U.S.C. § 312(b) (1952).

[35] Note, *supra* note 29, at 482. The note writers, with reason, criticize the Chenery case, as does TLS, *supra* note 1, at 31.

[36] Att'y Gen. Rep., *supra* note 4, at 29; TLS, *supra* note 1, at 24. . . .

[37] "Every new bus route, new airplane service, new radio station, new stock issue, new pipe line, new power project, and so on, seeks its permissive certificate upon the basis of future possibilities." American Airlines v. CAB, 192 F. 2d 417, 420 (D.C. Cir. 1951).

[38] ICC v. Parker, 326 U.S. 60, 65 (1945). . . .

This may explain why the proposals for an Administrative Court do not deal with the FCC, the CAB, or the ICC, even though current dissatisfaction with the administrative process centers around the work of these agencies. In justifying its unanimous recommendations for an Administrative Court with tax and trade sections, the [Hoover Commission] Task Force explained that in these fields the adjudicatory process "has, through experience, acquired a characteristically judicial aspect, and the applicable law has by statute or by case-to-case development become well defined in content." [39] Messrs. McFarland, Stason, and Vanderbilt, as members of the Attorney General's Committee, were also loath to separate adjudication from rule-making in areas in which "the practice of administrative discretion is large." [40]

Use of Adjudication by a Specialized Agency as Principal Method of Making Law. Need for Discretion. The mingling of the functions of investigation, initiation of action, advocacy, and decision is attacked in areas, exemplified by the work of the Federal Trade Commission and National Labor Relations Board, where the legislature placed main reliance upon adjudication to elaborate the law.

The demand for the FTC came from those who wanted more effective enforcement of the antitrust laws than that promised by the judicially created rule of reason, and from businessmen who wanted greater certainty than the rule afforded. The FTC act itself is "unfinished law which the administrative body must complete before it is ready for application." [42]

In the process of deciding cases, the FTC was expected to formulate standards that would put flesh on the bare-bones concept of "unfair competition." It was to use adjudication, not primarily to determine the legality of past action, but to prevent unfair competitive methods from being used in the future. No sanction, therefore, was to accompany an FTC finding that a particular practice was "unfair"; the offending party was merely to be ordered to cease and desist from the practice.

However, the FTC has been criticized for failing to develop under its statute guiding criteria of legality, even though it has attempted to overcome some of the difficulties inherent in the case-by-case approach to its problems[44] through the trade conference procedure of announcing rules designed to prevent unfair competitive practices on an industry-wide basis.[45] Nevertheless, the Task Force maintains that the FTC is now guided largely by precedent, and in particular, judicial precedent.[46] A 1942 study similarly concluded that the great majority of FTC

[39] TLS, *supra* note 1, at 34.

[40] Att'y Gen. Rep., *supra* note 4, at 207.

[42] FTC v. Ruberoid Co., 343 U.S. 470, 485 (1952) (dissenting opinion of Mr. Justice Jackson).

[44] See, e.g., Moog Industries v. FTC, 355 U.S. 411 (1958) (per curiam), holding that it is not within the scope of the reviewing authority of the court of appeals to postpone the operation of a valid cease and desist order against a single firm until similar orders are entered against that firm's competitors.

[45] See FTC Trade Practice Conference Rules, 16 C.F.R., Subchapter B (1958 Supp.). There were 161 trade practice rules in force on June 30, 1957. Ann. Rep. FTC 59 (1957).

[46] TLS, *supra* note 1, at 253.

orders were merely warnings to lawbreakers who were well aware of the illegality of their acts.[47] But former FTC Chairman Robert E. Freer thinks that the assumption "that all unfair methods of competition are presently known and catalogued" is disturbingly irresponsible.[48] The first Hoover Commission Task Force called for a "rejuvenated" FTC to give "the policy of the statutes continuous vitality in terms of current conditions." [49]

These conflicting views reveal the hazards of generalizing about the FTC's work. Generalization about the NLRB is equally hazardous. For example, the proscription of employer unfair labor practices has been described as "primarily judicial" because the statute here is "fairly definite." [50] But the Board has the task of filling in the content of general terms in preventing union unfair labor practices.[51] In imposing the duty to bargain, the Board "exercises more of a regulatory power," [52] which it also does when it determines the appropriate bargaining unit.[53] The Board itself termed the supervision of the selection of employee bargaining representatives as an "investigatory" function.[54] In handling jurisdictional disputes, the Board is clothed with "rule making power in one of the most intricate areas of industrial relations," because nothing in the statute "offers even the slightest guidance in a problem of this kind, which has hitherto been within the domain of private arbitration." [55]

Yet, the bills that have been introduced to establish an Administrative Court would vest exclusive jurisdiction in its labor section to issue orders discontinuing employer and union unfair labor practices[56] and in its trade section to issue orders discontinuing unfair competitive practices under a number of statutes.[57]

Granted that wide discretionary powers in certain cases are still entrusted to both the NLRB and the FTC, why should agencies rather than courts exercise them?

Need for Specialization. The need to bring "to bear upon difficult social and economic questions the attention of those who have time and facilities to become and remain continuously informed about them" is a major reason for the creation of agencies.[58] It is doubtful whether the proposed Administrative Court will meet this need. The judges of each of the three specialized sections would be subject

---

[47] Chamberlain, Dowling & Hays, The Judicial Function in Federal Administrative Agencies 135-36 (1942).

[48] Freer, The Case Against the Trade Regulation Section of the Proposed Administrative Court, 24 Geo. Wash. L. Rev. 637, 653 (1956). . . .

[49] TRC, *supra* note 36, at 124-25.

[50] *Id.* at 134. . . .

[51] *Id.* at 135. . . .

[52] *Id.* at 135. . . .

[53] *Id.* at 136. . . .

[54] TLS, *supra* note 1, Part VI, I at 46. The Board stated that it disposes of 10,000 such cases a year.

[55] TRC, *supra* note 36, at 136. . . . The first Task Force thought that the regulation

of initiation fees . . . also required the exercise of discretion in the light of knowledge of the internal operations of trade unions. TRC, *supra* at 136.

[56] S. 2292, H.R. 8751, § 110(c), 85th Cong., 1st Sess. (1957). . . . This was the recommendation of the second Task Force, TLS, *supra* note 1, at 280-81. The ABA, however, recommended that the adjudication of representation cases also be transferred to the Labor Section. Proceedings, *supra* note 1, at 374.

[57] S. 2292, H.R. 8751, § 110(a), 85th Cong., 1st Sess. (1957). This was the recommendation of the second Task Force, TLS, *supra* note 1, at 34, 41, 249-50. . . .

[58] Att'y Gen. Rep., *supra* note 4, at 15.

to assignment to the other sections when needed.[59] The three sections would also pool their commissioners, upon whom much of the burden of work would fall.[60] These arrangements would suffice if the matters within their jurisdiction merely required finding facts and applying precedent. But if the policy must be shaped, the judges of the Administrative Court, even if each section were a separate court, would not have the specialized staffs which make the agencies expert. Furthermore, technical skill alone does not assure this expertness. Only day-to-day contacts with people in industry familiarize agency personnel with the technical and other problems they are expected to solve. Neither the judges nor the court commissioners of any Administrative Court would be expected to maintain these contacts. To avoid them is a major purpose for creating such a court.

Need for Accountability. Agencies must account for their policies to the legislature and the people. The legislature looks to the agency to be its principal advisor on legislation affecting its field. The people expect to be informed. An agency's actions may also have to be co-ordinated with those being taken elsewhere in the government. It may, therefore, wish to consult with the Chief Executive about "general questions, trends, and policies." [63] No court could have such relations with the legislature, the executive, other agencies, or the public. Yet, they may be essential if adjudication plays a law-making role.

Need for Uniformity. Uniformity, predictability, and equality in the application of law are ends universally sought in the administration of justice. It was thought that they could be more readily achieved by a single agency than by scattered trial courts set into motion only at the initiative of private individuals or public prosecuting attorneys. If adjudication calls for the exercise of broad discretion, the device of appeals to the court of last resort, even if it were not as time consuming and expensive as it is, cannot be relied upon to secure those ends.[66]

Whether the administrative process has, in fact, accomplished these objectives is debatable. Dean Pound has complained that agencies are prone to act "as if every case were unique" [67] and others charge that improper influences are exerted to produce inconsistent, arbitrary decisions.[68]

The proponents of the Administrative Court intend to achieve uniformity by continuing the FTC, NLRB, and Internal Revenue Service as investigating and prosecuting bodies and giving the specialized court sections the function of decid-

---

[59] S. 2292, H.R. 8751, § 104(a), 85th Cong., 1st Sess. (1957). The Task Force so recommended. TLS, *supra* note 1, at 248.

[60] S. 2292, H.R. 8751, § 107, 85th Cong., 1st Sess. (1957).

[63] This is what the first Hoover Commission Task Force urged the FTC to do. TRC, *supra* note 36, at 130.

[66] Landis, *op. cit. supra* note 29, at 33. For an illustration of this point in a wholly different field requiring the exercise of discretion, note that the Attorney General has repeatedly called to the attention of the Judicial Conference of the United States

the "problems created by disparities in sentences for similar crimes given to individuals with substantially the same background and prior record." 1957 Judicial Conference, Rep. 57. Connecticut, for example, has attempted to solve this problem by centralizing the final authority to sentence. Conn. Pub. Act 1957, No. 436.

[67] Pound, Administrative Law 40, 62 (1942).

[68] This seems to be the import of the charges made so far before the House Subcommittee on Legislative Oversight. Dean Landis recognized this danger. See Landis, *op. cit. supra* note 29, at 100.

ing only such cases as the agencies are unable to settle informally.[69] The ensuing division of responsibility between agency and court, however, may make it difficult to work out uniform policies. For this reason, Messrs. McFarland, Stason, and Vanderbilt thought that complete separation of prosecuting agencies would be tolerable only if the prosecuting agencies would, by rule-making, "so prescribe policies that any separate adjudicating tribunal will chiefly do no more than apply those policies to the facts of individual cases." [70] This situation is approximated in the tax field. But the FTC and the NLRB do not have significant rule-making powers and there is disagreement about whether they have prescribed such policies through the process of adjudication.

Furthermore, creating an Administrative Court will not assure solution of the problems that trouble the bar and the country about the administrative process. In important measure, functions will continue to be merged because decisions whether to prosecute or to settle informally are also adjudicatory acts. The NLRB General Counsel, for example, has been called "a prosecutor, an administrator, a policy maker," because his decision not to issue a complaint cannot be appealed to the Board or the courts.[71] It is also possible for improper influences to be brought to bear at these stages of administration even more easily than at the stage of formal adjudication.[72]

Use of Agency as Cheaper and Speedier Instrument for Applying Law. For a number of reasons, agencies were given adjudicatory functions even under statutes calling principally for the application and not the elaboration of law.

Agencies, but Not Courts, May Initiate Proceedings. Agencies were also created because their initiative was needed to vindicate the interests sought to be protected by statute. Current proposals for a specialized Administrative Court would not change this aspect of the agency's work.

Agency Procedure Would be Cheaper and Speedier Than Court Procedure. Expectations that administrative justice would be cheaper and speedier than court justice have largely been disappointed. To an extent, this is due to the judicialization of administrative procedure, upon which the bar has insisted. Nevertheless, it is appalling to learn that something less than one-half the total bill for workmen's compensation is accounted for by cash payments to injured workers; the remainder goes for expenses incurred in operating the system.[75] But there is little evidence that trial courts would do much better.[76]

---

[69] TLS, *supra* note 1, at 253-54, 281. The NLRB would also continue to certify labor unions, conduct elections, and determine conflicts over representation. *Id.* at 282.

[70] Att'y Gen. Rep., *supra* note 4, at 207. They advocated that complete separation be effectuated by creating independent administrative tribunals to perform the adjudicatory function. *Id.* at 205.

[71] TRC, *supra* note 36, at 139. For the status, powers and duties of the General Counsel, see 61 Stat. 139 (1947), 29 U.S.C. § 153(d) (1952). . . .

[72] See Landis, *op. cit. supra* note 29, at 106-07. 110.

[75] Conard & Mehr, Costs of Administering Reparation for Work Injuries in Illinois 33, 35 (1952); Somers & Somers, Workmen's Compensation 193-96 (1954). The results of the Conard and Mehr study are summarized in Conard, Workmen's Compensation: Is It More Efficient Than Employer's Liability?, 38 A.B.A.J. 1011 (1952).

[76] Professor Conard concluded: "It [the Illinois study] shows only that in Illinois

In any case, to choose between court and agency on the basis of whether judicial or administrative procedure is preferred, is to put the cart before the horse. Once it is determined what procedures are best fitted for particular adjudicatory tasks, they should be used by whichever tribunal is selected to perform them.[77]

Volume of Adjudication Involved. The existing federal and state court structures could not possibly handle the volume of administrative adjudication. Court congestion and delay is now "the most serious problem . . . confronting the profession."[79] Nor does the appointment of additional judges seem to be a practical answer.[80] Interestingly enough, the most promising suggestions for relieving congested trial calendars are based on the use of men who are not judges to share the burden of adjudication.[81]

The proponents of the Administrative Court think that its burdens will be manageable because its creation will result in more frequent and effective utilization of informal settlements. Others maintain that private interests will be subjected to greater harassment if the prosecuting agency is deprived of the power of formal decision. It is argued that even if the agency will not be interested in building a record based upon the number of cases it brings before the court, the agency will not know what policies the court may adopt and, consequently, will be remiss in its duty if it does not try everything. Furthermore, private persons will have an incentive to retry matters settled by the agencies in the hope that the Administrative Court will adopt different policies.

It is difficult to decide between these conflicting views. We know, for example, that the Tax Court, which consists of sixteen judges and avails itself of the services

the employers' liability system costs less [than the workmen's compensation system] *per dollar of benefit conferred*" (Emphasis supplied.) Conard, 38 A.B.A.J., *supra* note 75, at 1058. So, if workmen's compensation benefits were increased significantly, its efficiency, as measured by Conard, would increase proportionately. Conard states that "the Illinois study fails to prove that the high operating expense of the workmen's compensation system is caused by the structure of the system." *Ibid.*

[77] The proposed Administrative Court would be governed "to the extent practicable" by the rules of procedure governing federal district judges sitting without a jury. There would be no jury trial in the Administrative Court. See § 109(b) of S. 2292, H.R. 8751, 85th Cong., 1st Sess. (1957).

[79] Brownell, The Problem of Backlogs: A National Shortcoming in our Courts, 42 A.B.A.J. 1032 (1956). See also, Annual Rep. of the Proceedings of the Judicial Conference of the United States, 4-6, 49-57, 63-143 (1957); Rep. of Attorney General's Conference on Court Congestion and Delay

(1956); Report of ABA Committee on the Federal Judiciary, New York Times, February 24, 1958, p. 27, col. 4.

[80] The New Mexico Supreme Court admitted, for example, that in the last decade, the number of New Mexico district judges grew from 9 to 19, primarily because of the increasingly large load of workmen's compensation cases. Yet, dissatisfaction with the delays that accompanied judicial handling of these cases was great enough to produce the legislation [providing a system of workmen's compensation] which the majority declared unconstitutional. State ex rel. Hovey Concrete Products Co. v. Mechem, 63 N.M. 250, 316 P.2d 1069 (1957).

[81] La Brum, Congested Trial Calendars: It's About Time To Do Something About Them, 43 A.B.A.J. 311 (1957); Nims, The Law's Delay: The Bar's Most Urgent Problem, 44 A.B.A.J. 27 (1958); Nims, Backlogs: Justice Denied, 42 A.B.A.J. 613 (1956). Mr. La Brum would encourage arbitration; Mr. Nims, the use of temporary hearing officers or auditors and even temporary judges.

of more than that number by calling upon retired judges, disposes of 5,000 cases annually. Yet, that court has a backlog of 9,000 cases.[85] The Attorney General's Committee thought that there was unnecessary litigation because the collecting officials could not know what the Tax Court would do about particular questions of statutory interpretation; but the Committee did not estimate how much litigation is caused by this uncertainty.[86]

Against the possibility of an increase in formal litigation must be weighed the benefits that may be derived in various situations from transferring to courts the function of adjudication in contested cases. . . .

Conclusion

Analysis so far suggests, generally, that prosecuting agencies should exercise judicial powers only if the process of adjudication calls for the exercise of such broad discretion that it involves the making of law. Because the NLRB plays a law-making role in controversial areas of public policy and because the complete internal separation of prosecuting and deciding functions under the governing statute has not been critically evaluated,* its power to adjudicate contested cases should not be transferred to any court. Opinion differs more about the role of FTC adjudication and the effectiveness of its internal separation of functions.[112] However, since courts are performing major law-making functions in the antitrust field, there is less reason to oppose their exercise of original jurisdiction over contested FTC cases.[113] Furthermore, in view of the difficulty of predicting what will happen if one rather than another form of governmental organization is adopted,

[85] Gribbon, Should the Judicial Character of the Tax Court be Recognized?, 24 Geo. Wash. L. Rev. 619, 633 (1956).
[86] Att'y Gen. Rep., *supra* note 4, at 59. In 1939 the Treasury received 7,600,000 tax returns, but only 4,854 appeals were filed in the Board of Tax Appeals and 900 in the courts. *Id.* at 35.
* [But see Klaus, The Taft-Hartley Experiment, 11 Ind. & Lab. Rel. Rev. 371 (1958).—Editor]
[112] Section 5(c) of the Administrative Procedure Act, 60 Stat. 237 (1946), 5 U.S.C. § 1004(c) (1952), requires separation in the case of the FTC. Mr. Freer thinks FTC internal separation is effective and that the second Hoover Commission's recommendations are based "upon abstract theory and upon tradition" and are without documentation. Freer, The Case Against the Trade Regulation Section of the Proposed Administrative Court, 24 Geo. Wash. L. Rev. 650-51 (1956).
[Mr. Earl W. Kintner, a former General Counsel and Chairman of the FTC supports

Mr. Freer's objection to the transfer of the FTC's judicial functions to a Trade Court. See Kintner, The Trade Court Proposal: An Examination of Some Possible Defects, 44 A.B.A.J. 441 (1958) and The Trade Court, The ABA, The Lawyer and The Public Interest, Proceedings, ABA Section of Antitrust Law, Apr. 4-5, 1957, p. 72. For a view supporting the Trade Court proposal, see Berger, Removal of Judicial Functions from Federal Trade Commission to A Trade Court: A Reply to Mr. Kintner, 59 Mich. L. Rev. 199 (1960).—Editor]
[113] It has been argued that more effective antitrust enforcement would follow transfer of the FTC's antitrust functions to the Department of Justice and the courts. Simon, The Case Against the Federal Trade Commission, 19 U. Chi. L. Rev. 297 (1952). See also, Report of the Committee on Cartels & Monopoly, in Stocking & Watkins, Monopoly and Free Enterprise 559-60 (1951).

it would be instructive to try out the basic Hoover Commission—American Bar Association proposals in the trade practice field.

Instead of creating an Administrative Court for this purpose, it may be wiser to set up a special tribunal composed of regular district judges on special assignment.[114] This would satisfy the need for specialization and uniformity and still provide judges with broad knowledge and understanding of the law. If it were decided subsequently to return formal adjudication to the FTC, no problem would arise about the use of these judges.[115] . . .

But analysis cannot stop here. If it is true, as it is being charged, that the institutional framework within which administrators work makes it impossible for them to develop a judicial attitude of mind, reliance upon the administrative process to uphold the rule of law is illusory. Administrators have limited tenures[117] and are subject to pressures from other branches of the government. But it was expected that, in time, they would develop traditions of independence and methods of impartial thought, which are as important to rule-making as they are to adjudication.[118] It is possible that history "will probably find that the sharp critics in this generation have underestimated the fairness and skill with which these new agencies have performed their task." [119] Nevertheless, each generation has a duty to heed criticism that will improve the machinery of justice.

In the last analysis, the quality of justice depends upon the quality of the men who administer it. But all non-elected government officials cannot be given the tenure and status of federal judges. A number of things, however, can be done to secure the caliber of men needed. The ABA, and possibly other professional organizations, can undertake to pass on the qualifications of men considered for appointment to administrative office. Consideration should be given to rotating commissioners among different agencies, so that there can be continued injections of different but experienced viewpoints in each agency and new challenges to the energies of each commissioner. To protect agencies against improper influences, the legislature should enact codes of conduct for agency members and those who appear before them.

---

[114] *Cf.* the Emergency Court of Appeals, which was created by the Emergency Price Control Act of 1942, § 204(c), 56 Stat. 23, 32 (1942), and is composed of regular circuit and district judges selected by the Chief Justice of the United States.

[115] After abolition of the United States Commerce Court in 1913, controversy arose about the future of its judges; they were finally kept as roving circuit judges. . . .

[117] The average tenure of a commissioner on a regulatory agency is about half the length of a full, presidential term. Bernstein, Regulating Business by Independent Commission 107 (1955).

[118] Impartiality exists when "decision is is not motivated by any desire to deal with

the parties or their interest otherwise than in the manner which an objective appraisal of the facts and the furtherance of the public duty imposed upon the agency require." Att'y Gen. Rep., *supra* note 4, at 43. . . .

[119] Jackson, The Administrative Process, 5 J. Soc. Phil. 143, 146-49 (1940). [But *cf.* Mr. Justice Jackson dissenting in FTC v. Ruberoid Co., 343 U.S. 470, 485 (1952).] The then Mr. Robert Jackson added: "[W]e do not condemn the judicial process because judges err, but a large number of persons are condemning the administrative process just because administrators err." There are, of course, instances of corruption on the federal bench. . . .

But above all, we must review from time to time the need for regulation in particular areas. If the need is reaffirmed, the legislature should make every effort to enact policy standards which are as definite as the statutory purpose will allow. The task of regulation must then be accepted and supported by the public and not viewed as an alien intrusion upon American life. The administrator, like the judge, must come to be regarded as an instrument for the attainment of justice.

AUERBACH, *SOME THOUGHTS ON THE HECTOR MEMORANDUM*
1960 Wisconsin Law Review 183

In September 1959, Florida lawyer and businessman Louis J. Hector resigned as a member of the Civil Aeronautics Board after nearly two years of service. Since this is about the average term of office for members of our federal regulatory commissions, Mr. Hector's action would normally have escaped public notice. But he wrote a long farewell Memorandum to the President arguing that the "independent regulatory commission is not competent in these days to regulate a vital national industry in the public interest" and should, therefore, be broken up.[2]

Topping public disclosures which shook the prestige of the regulatory commission and subjected it to fierce attack in Congressional quarters and the press, Mr. Hector's Memorandum created a sensation. It was circulated by the President among all the regulatory commissions and, though not published officially,[*] it soon became available in Congressional offices in Washington. It has been read widely. Because it deals with basic issues which I discussed in a previous issue of this *Review*,[4] an addendum taking account of the Hector Memorandum may be in order.

Mr. Hector's General Position

Mr. Hector hurls three principal charges against the independent regulatory commission—(1) it is appallingly inefficient in policy-making, planning and administration; (2) it does not perform its adjudicatory functions fairly; and (3) it hinders the coordination of national economic policies.

Mr. Hector maintains that these faults of the independent regulatory commission are "organic" because they stem from the commingling of executive, legislative and judicial functions in one organization. The structure, not the personnel, of the commission is, therefore, responsible for its inadequacies. To remedy them, he would break up the commission as presently constituted and transfer "to an appropriate executive department the functions of policy-making and administration,

[2] Hector, Problems of the CAB and the Independent Regulatory Commissions, Memorandum to the President, Sept. 10 (Mimeographed). The quotation is at 1.
[*] Since this article was written, the Hector Memorandum has been published in 69 Yale L.J. 931 (1960) and two memoranda reflecting the views of the CAB on the Hector Memorandum have been published by the CAB in mimeographed form, dated March 29, 1960. See, too, Kintner, The Current Ordeal of the Administrative Process: In Reply to Mr. Hector, 69 Yale L.J. 965 (1960).—Editor
[4] Auerbach, Should Administrative Agencies Perform Adjudicatory Functions? 1959 Wis. L. Rev. 95.

to an administrative court or courts the adjudicatory responsibility in major litigated cases and appeals from administrative actions, and to the Department of Justice the prosecution functions." [5]

Mr. Hector would go further than Messrs. McFarland, Stason and Vanderbilt (the minority members of the Attorney General's Committee on Administrative Procedure), the Second Hoover Commission and the American Bar Association.[6] None of the proposals previously made would have separated the "judicial" from the "legislative" aspects of the licensing and rate determination work of agencies like the CAB, the FCC and the ICC.

Previously, too, the commingling of powers in the regulatory agency was attacked on the ground that it would result in the zealous prosecution of the public interest at the undue expense of the private interest. Now Mr. Hector blames commingling for the neglect of the public interest. It is possible, of course, that the organizational structure of the independent regulatory commission precludes it from promoting either the public or the private interest. But commissions are not being criticized for neglecting the private interest; they are being attacked for subordinating the public to the private interest.[7] If this criticism is warranted, organizational structure alone cannot be to blame. For if the commingling of powers permits the agency to sacrifice either the private or the public interest, factors other than commingling must determine which interest is chosen for the sacrifice.

Whether or not one agrees with Mr. Hector's recommendations, his analysis and views deserve the most serious attention.

Charge (1)—Policy Making, Planning and Administration Are Inadequate

I am inclined to agree with Mr. Hector's basic criticism that our independent regulatory commissions have failed to discharge their most important responsibility —"to formulate broad plans and general policies to ensure that the regulated segment of the economy operates for the public benefit as defined by Congress." [8] And that this failure is due to their preoccupation with the decision of individual cases. But I do not agree that the commingling of powers is the cause of the failure. In my opinion, the successful pressure exerted by the organized bar to force the agencies to consider policy matters primarily in a litigious context is more to blame. Former CAB Chairman James M. Landis, complaining of this pressure as early as 1948, wrote:

> When I was with the Board, I had the opportunity to inaugurate a series of studies on the weaker carriers with the aim of getting some knowledge of their weaknesses, whether these weaknesses lay in route patterns or management, and what could be done about them. But the legal traditions immediately seized

---

[5] Hector, *supra* note 2, at 66-67, 3.
[6] See Auerbach, *supra* note 4, at 102-03.
[7] Mr. Hector himself makes the general charge that agencies today "find it far too easy to think only of the industry they

regulate." Hector, *supra* note 2, at 73. For some of the examples he gives to back up this general charge, see *id.* at 56-60.
[8] Hector, *supra* note 2, at 4.

upon that effort. Instead of studies, they had to be investigations. And competitors under the whip of their lawyers insisted we could not benefit from these studies or utilize them in route or rate decisions, unless they could be mercilessly torn to pieces by cross-examination. The result, I gather, is that these investigations have now been buried, because their handling has become too difficult, too likely to create "error" for some gowned tribunal to pounce upon. And yet what more sensible way is there to approach this problem? [9]

Legal traditions have forced members of agencies to see themselves mainly in the image of the judge or referee and not the planner and policy-maker. As a result, judicial trial procedures have been used to handle tasks, like route planning, for which the procedures are not suitable. The misuse of judicial procedures accounts for the inefficiency and delay which Mr. Hector deplores in the typical cases he calls to our attention.[10] But the commingling of powers in the regulatory commission does not require that procedures be used which are not suited for the task at hand. Nor would the separation of powers and transfer of such planning jobs to the Executive branch of the Government, as Mr. Hector recommends,[11] guarantee that suitable procedures would be used.

Mr. Hector distinguishes between questions like "the type of subsidized local air service required in the public interest and selecting the cities to be served," which he thinks the Executive branch of the Government should determine, and questions like the "selection of carriers to perform this service," which should be decided by "a true administrative court" not burdened with other duties and using judicial trial procedures.[12] But is it possible to draw such a line? The CAB, for example, planned its international air routes pretty much as Mr. Hector would have wished.[13] But in the subsequent proceedings involving the selection of carriers, evidence was introduced to cause it to modify its plans in important respects.[14] The selection of the carrier affects the route to be chosen and vice versa. A particular route might even be described in such a way that only a single carrier could possibly operate over it.

This assumption—that a satisfactory way can be found to separate the "legisla-

---

[9] Landis, Air Routes under the Civil Aeronautics Act, 15 J. Air. L. & Com. 295, 299 (1948).

[10] Hector, *supra* note 2, at 4-8. Hector specifically mentions, *inter alia*, the Seven States Area Investigation, No. 7454, CAB, Feb. 13, 1959, which took 3 years to complete. He criticizes the inability of the Board to give any direction to the Hearing Examiner and of the Hearing Examiner to seek any Board guidance; the absence of any machinery to enable the Examiner "to actively seek out the information which he thought he needed," with the result that "he just sat and took what the interested towns and airlines brought him" and, on that basis and with "no assistance of any

kind except a secretary," had to come up with a route plan; the redoing of the Examiner's plan by the Board members personally on the basis, mainly, of "briefs and . . . their memory of the long oral argument," since "they could not utilize the services of the Examiner, nor any of the parties, nor even of the Board's own staff of experts."

[11] *Id*. at 8-9.

[12] *Ibid*.

[13] See Sweeney, Postwar International Route Planning By the Civil Aeronautics Board, 16 J. Air. L. & Com. 388 (1949).

[14] See, for example, North Atlantic Route Case, 6 C.A.B. 319 (1945).

tive" from the "judicial" aspects of the regulatory commission's work—lies at the heart of Mr. Hector's analysis and proposals. I will come back to it. But so far as the "legislative" aspects are concerned, the same procedural questions would seem to arise whether or not the agency which plans the air routes—to take Mr. Hector's example—also selects the carriers to operate over them. To what extent should states, localities, the carriers themselves, and other interested groups be permitted to participate in route planning? How should they participate? With respect to what kinds of issues raised in the process of route planning might trial-type procedures be useful? And the answers to these questions should be the same whether or not the route planning agency also selects the carriers.

Apart from procedural questions, Mr. Hector expects that an executive agency with no adjudicatory functions would be compelled to engage in active planning and policy-making.[15] This may be a reasonable expectation, even though there is scant evidence that our purely executive agencies have done a better job of planning and policy-making than our independent regulatory commissions.[16] But is there no way of accomplishing the desired result that would at the same time avoid the serious problems of coordination that would be created by the separation of "adjudication" from "policy-making"? [17]

Charge (2)—The Process of Adjudication Is Unfair

Mr. Hector charges that the independent regulatory commission performs its adjudicatory functions poorly and unfairly. Specifically, he discloses that the CAB does not decide litigated cases before it "on the basis of general principles and standards known to the parties and applicable to all cases," or "on the basis of the voluminous testimony and arguments advanced by the parties and this alone" and that the Board members do not "personally state the reasons for their decisions." [18]

There are no general administrative principles and standards to guide the decision of particular cases. This lack is, of course, a familiar and in the main justified complaint. But it is not a peculiar failure of the administrative agency. Even the Supreme Court of the United States is being criticized for not developing a coherent and intelligible body of constitutional principles.[20] As we saw, Mr. Hector expects

[15] Hector, *supra* note 2, at 72-73.

[16] Surely, it cannot be maintained that Mr. Hector's criticism of the independent regulatory commission for taking up so much time "with minor details" to the neglect of "major policy and planning matters" (*id.* at 12) does not apply to any of the executive departments.

[17] See Auerbach, *supra* note 4, at 101-03. Mr. Hector recognizes the difficulty of distinguishing between "policy" and "administration" even within the same agency when he discusses the failure of Reorganization Plan No. 13 § 1(a), 64 Stat. 1266 (1950), 5 U.S.C. § 133z-15 (1958), which trans-

ferred the "executive and administrative functions of the Board" to the CAB Chairman. Hector, *supra* note 2, at 14-18. In short, Mr. Hector tells us that the Plan failed because control over the executive and administrative functions, in the last analysis, entailed control over policy, which no member of the Board wished to relinquish.

[18] Hector, *supra* note 2, at 19-40.

[20] See, e.g., Wechsler, Toward Neutral Principles of Constitutional Law, 73 Harv. L. Rev. 1 (1959); and Hart, The Supreme Court, 1958 Term-Foreword: The Time Chart of the Justices, 73 Harv. L. Rev. 84 (1959).

the separation of the "legislative" from the "judicial" functions of the regulatory commission to remedy the situation. The Executive branch of the Government would establish the general policies to be applied by the administrative courts in specific cases.[21] The administrative court would then be "free from policy-making," even when it is deciding contested rate or licensing cases.[22]

The relationship which Mr. Hector envisages between the executive agency and the administrative court fails to take sufficient account of the multiple uses of adjudication—(1) to substitute for rule-making in the development of general principles and standards; (2) to accompany rule-making in the development of policy; (3) to handle situations in which it is difficult to develop general principles and standards because the discretionary element is so important; and (4) to apply pre-established principles and standards to particular cases which do not call for any appreciable exercise of discretion.

If all regulatory situations could be made to fall into category (4), Mr. Hector's proposals would suit them all. For only then would the policy-making element in adjudication, never totally absent in any case, be at a minimum. Yet none of the examples Mr. Hector gives of the CAB's failure to develop consistent standards is likely ever to be made to fall into this category.

It is understandable, for example, why any agency would prefer to use case-by-case adjudication, rather than rule-making, to determine such questions of policy as when (and how much) competitive air service should be permitted between particular cities and when and how new route awards should be used as a means of strengthening the financially weaker carriers. No principles or standards can be promulgated which will do more than set forth criteria to guide the exercise of the decision-maker's discretion in particular cases. And the decision-maker would wish to decide cases for a while before attempting to set down these criteria. Mr. Hector's proposed separation of powers would deprive the rule-maker in such cases of adjudicatory experience and the judge of rule-making experience, with the result that both rule-making and adjudication might be inept.

The analogy that Mr. Hector draws between his proposed executive agency-administrative court relationship and the general relationship between Congress and the courts is not sound.[23] In the case of legislation which does not involve an administrative agency, Congress has decided that its policy should be implemented by the ordinary process of law enforcement and case-by-case court adjudication. The "overlap between the legislative powers of the Congress and the judicial powers of the courts," which exists to the extent that the decision of cases involves policy-making under the statute, does no harm. The power of the courts to interpret and apply the statute is, to be sure, a check upon the legislature. But the legislature can have the last word.

Legislation turned over to an administrative agency, however, is, as Mr. Justice Jackson described the Federal Trade Commission Act, "unfinished law" which

[21] Hector, *supra* note 2, at 70.
[22] *Ibid.*
[23] *Id.* at 71: ". . . there has always been the same basic overlap between the legislative powers of the Congress and the judicial powers of the courts, and we have coped with that successfully for a century and three quarters."

must be completed by the agency "before it is ready for application." [24] Congress expected the legislation entrusted to the agencies Mr. Hector particularly has in mind—the CAB, the FCC, the ICC—to be completed by agency rule-making or adjudication or both in any combination experience indicated would be best. The agency is already subject to judicial and legislative checks. Will the situation be improved if additional checks are provided by dividing the task of implementing legislative policy in the first instance into two tasks—one labeled "legislative" and entrusted to an executive agency and the other "judicial" and entrusted to an administrative court? Though he thinks that separation will "compel active policy-making" [25] by the Executive branch, Mr. Hector is realist enough to know that this will not always happen. So he acknowledges that in cases in which the Executive has not promulgated any policies, the administrative court would be compelled "to interpret the broad Congressional mandate as best it could." [26] But even when the Executive branch has formulated general plans and policies, the administrative court would be empowered by Mr. Hector to ignore them if it thought they were not authorized by the applicable statute.[27] The possibility of conflict between the Executive branch and the administrative court, under Mr. Hector's scheme, would be very real. Whether we should risk it depends, of course, upon how bad we think the present situation is and the feasibility of other alternatives. An evil at hand always seems much worse than an imaginary one.

Agency heads do not decide on the basis of the record alone and do not write their own opinions. The same failure to distinguish the different situations in which adjudication is used mars Mr. Hector's criticism of the decision-making process in adjudicated cases. He approves the formulation of policy "on the basis of free, extensive, informal discussions with many interested and informed individuals or groups and on the basis of delegated staff work." [28] But he insists that adjudication requires "formalized procedures, the building of a record with opportunity for presentation and cross-examination of evidence, and final judgment on the basis of the record alone by the persons responsible for decision." [29] He thinks that these essentials of a proper adjudicatory process are currently lacking.

But again, Mr. Hector's sharp dichotomy does not allow for situations typical of the work of agencies like the CAB, the FCC and the ICC—in which policy is made by the adjudication of cases.

Mr. Hector attributes the inability of the heads of regulatory commissions to adopt the attitudes of the judge when they are deciding cases to the fact that they simultaneously perform legislative and administrative functions. But the attitudes of the judge may be improper for members of regulatory commissions which make policy via the adjudication of cases. And a trial-type hearing, such as Mr. Hector contemplates, may not be suitable for the disposition of many issues that arise in the course of such adjudication. Mr. Hector himself gives examples of this unsuitability.[30]

[24] FTC v. Ruberoid Co., 343 U.S. 470, 485 (1952) (dissenting opinion).

[25] Hector, *supra* note 2, at 72.

[26] *Ibid.*

[27] *Id.* at 71.

[28] *Id.* at 51.

[29] *Id.* at 52.

[30] *Id.* at 53. On this question generally, see 1 Davis, Administrative Law Treatise ch. 7 (1958).

Contrary to Mr. Hector's assumption, members of regulatory commissions in the past have shown that it is possible for the same men to keep separate their roles as "policy-makers" and as "judges," when separation is called for. But such separation is not always desirable. A commissioner should not drive "from his mind as a judge what he knows as an administrator." [31] Administrative agencies were created so that the commissioner's role as policy-maker might aid him in performing his role as adjudicator and vice versa.

To the extent that policy will continue to be made via adjudication, the creation of administrative courts will not succeed in separating the roles of "policy-maker" and "judge." It will, however, ensure that "the officers of administrative courts" will, as Mr. Hector wishes, "conduct themselves like judges" [32] and make bad policy. They will have no specialized staffs to advise them and no opportunity for day-to-day contact with the individuals and groups that will be affected by their policies. They will tend to think only of the parties appearing before them as adversaries. In short, judicial trial procedures and techniques will be used even more than they are today to solve problems for which they are not suited.

Surprisingly, Mr. Hector's analysis of the internal process of administrative decision-making neglects to consider its constructive potentialities. One must agree, however, that his description of that process in the CAB supplies a realistic antidote to any optimism that the affirmative possibilities will be realized. According to Mr. Hector, CAB members discuss a case on the basis of the examiner's decision, the briefs and oral argument, but virtually ignore the record. Then they vote and the result of the vote is announced publicly. Only thereafter is the job of opinion-writing turned over to a staff of opinion writers.

Because the Board members have no personal knowledge of the record and do not write their own opinions, Mr. Hector maintains that their votes are willy-nilly, shaped by extra-record influences—"memories of casual conversations, tid-bits of information picked up here and there, trade-press editorials, and Congressional or Executive views or desires." [33]

The task of the opinion-writing staff, according to Mr. Hector, is to comb the record "for facts and data to support a predetermined conclusion" so that it becomes "appeal-proof." [34] The staff does this job "with little or no guidance from the Board members" and does it so well that the Board members hardly ever have to rewrite, modify or even edit the final opinion.[35] "I know of no case," says Mr. Hector, "where the opinion-writers ever came back to the Board and said that the facts in the record of a case simply would not support a substantial decision previously made by the Board." [36] "It is too much to expect," he comments, "that the ultimate facts of record when dispassionately viewed will always support a decision previously reached without close personal knowledge of the record." [37]

I do not know whether Mr. Hector realizes how grave is the indictment which he seems to be making against the CAB lawyers on the opinion-writing staff. If I

[31] *Id.* at 54.
[32] *Id.* at 55.
[33] *Id.* at 65.
[34] *Id.* at 65, 37, n. 39.

[35] *Id.* at 37-38.
[36] *Id.* at 39.
[37] *Ibid.*

read him correctly, he charges them with writing opinions legally justifying action which they know cannot be so justified. This would constitute professionally irresponsible, if not unethical, conduct on their part.

Recently, Mr. Hector has written that the integrity of the decision-making process in the independent regulatory commission, even as it is now organized, could be restored by adopting the Harris Committee recommendation that commissioners write their own opinions "or at least . . . supervise personally the writing of their opinions." [38] I doubt that this is the answer. The administrative decision-making process may be weak precisely because of the increasing isolation of commission members from staff at the point of decision. This isolation, it seems to me, would be enhanced by Mr. Hector's proposal that each commissioner be given a personal staff to write his opinions, subject to "his detailed direction from the very beginning of the document-writing process." [39]

The Justices of the Supreme Court of the United States, of course, write their own opinions, with the aid only of their law clerks. Yet dissatisfaction with the quality of their opinions has been expressed and the cause attributed to the process by which the Justices collectively reach decisions. [40] Professor Hart concludes that "the most disturbing feature of the conditions under which the Court works . . . is not the shortness of time ordinarily available for the preparation of an opinion, disturbing though that is, but the shortness of time available and used for collective deliberation and for private study of argued cases prior to such deliberation." [41] . . .

Professor Hart's remedy is simple but penetrating. Let "the votes which in practice are decisive" come "at the end rather than at the beginning of the Court's intensive study of cases" and let the Justices recognize that "an opinion of the Court is the responsibility of the whole Court and not simply of the Justice who writes it." [43]

Professor Hart's suggestion could be made applicable to administrative decision-making. Although the burden of opinion-writing imposed upon an administrative agency is much greater than that carried by the Supreme Court or any other court, [44] the agency has a means not available to any court to assure that the quality of its decisions does not suffer. The agency can use its staff intelligently in the production of an institutional decision for which the agency heads are prepared to take full responsibility. [45]

The institutional decision does not mean, as Professor Davis points out, that procedures cannot be devised by which the agency heads will attain a "substantial

[38] Hector, Government by Anonymity: Who Writes Our Regulatory Opinions?, 45 A.B.A.J. 1260 (1959).

[39] Hector, supra note 38, at 1264. The 1952 amendments to the Communications Act went farthest in this direction, 66 Stat. 712, 721 (1952), 47 U.S.C. §§ 155(c), 409 (1958). Yet I wonder to what extent they may be responsible for the difficulties the FCC is currently experiencing.

[40] See Hart, supra note 20.

[41] Id. at 124.

[43] Id. at 124, 125.

[44] For some statistics, see 2 Davis, Administrative Law Treatise § 11.11 (1958).

[45] On the pros and cons of the institutional decision, see 2 Davis, Administrative Law Treatise ch. 11 (1958). I am in general agreement with Professor Davis' analysis and suggestions.

understanding of the record," even though they have not personally read it.[46] Staff memoranda can serve this purpose. The institutional decision does not require the "improper use of extra-record facts." [47] Procedures can be devised to give interested parties the opportunity to meet "in the appropriate fashion" all the material facts,[48] as well as the policy considerations that will guide decision. The institutional decision does not imply that improper political or personal influences will be brought to bear upon the agency heads. In fact, increased staff participation in the decision-making process will itself afford a guarantee that such influences will not prevail.

To bring the staff and agency heads together at the point of decision, a draft opinion, representing the judgment of the commission staff (and including dissenting views) could be presented to the commissioners *before* they vote on the disposition of the case.[49] This would, for example, free the CAB opinion-writing staff from the morale-shattering task of post-hoc rationalization and encourage it freely to discuss policies and their application to particular cases. The issues for decision would thereby be posed very sharply and careful deliberation on the part of the commissioners would be encouraged. There could be no objection then to making a commissioner responsible for personally writing or directing the writing of the final opinion. But the pressure of work may be so great as to make it inadvisable to require this by law in every case.[50]

Charge (3)—The Coordination of Policy Is Hindered

Mr. Hector blames the independence of each regulatory commission from Executive control for the absence of coordination of its plans and policies with those of other commissions and agencies of Government. Considering the examples Mr. Hector cites,[51] one may doubt whether the independence of the regulatory commissions concerned would thwart coordinated policies agreed upon by Congress and the President. It may be true, however, that independence inhibits the agency heads and staffs from thinking in terms of larger economic policies and goals and contributing to their development and coordination.

---

[46] 2 Davis, Administrative Law Treatise § 11.03 (1958). Mr. Hector throughout his Memorandum makes much too naive an assumption about the extent to which judges personally read records.
[47] 2 Davis, Administrative Law Treatise § 11.09 (1958).
[48] *Id.* at § 15.14. In Chapter 15 of his Treatise, entitled Official Notice, Professor Davis discusses the various fashions that are appropriate, depending upon the nature of the facts in question.
[49] I would exclude from the process of preparing the draft opinion, only those staff members who were engaged in earlier

stages of the case as investigators, prosecutors or advocates (in cases which are prosecutions).
[50] There are a number of ways by which an institutional decision can be reached and the interests of affected parties safeguarded. I have in mind, particularly, a process like that followed by the FCC prior to the 1952 amendments. See Att'y Gen. Comm. Ad. Proc. Monograph, FCC, S. Doc. No. 186, 76th Cong., 3d Sess. (1940). This process is briefly described in 2 Davis, Administrative Law Treatise § 13.07 (1958).
[51] Hector, *supra* note 2, at 41-45.

Just as Mr. Hector blames the commingling of functions for all the troubles of the regulatory commission, others blame its independence. . . .

Mr. Hector thinks that agency independence is itself a consequence of the commingling of powers because of the general insistence that the adjudicatory function be performed free from Executive interference.[55] He assumes that Executive control over agency policy-making will entail Executive control over agency adjudication. So he urges a separate adjudicatory body to prevent this and win acceptance for Executive policy-making.

Again, Mr. Hector ignores the policy-making aspect of adjudication. We should not be shocked by the notion that policy-making is and should be "political"—not, of course, in the invidious sense of being "corrupt, fraudulent, dishonest, and motivated by desire for private gain," [56] but in the sense that the basic issues arising out of the regulatory effort should be debated publicly and settled by the democratic process.

The introducton of "politics" in this sense need not destroy the "judicial mind" of the administrator. Unhappily, the independent status of the regulatory commission has not precluded current suspicions and charges of improper Executive influences on the adjudicatory process. If the President were given the clear authority, as well as responsibility, "to take care that the laws be faithfully executed," including the laws now turned over for administration to independent regulatory commissions, improper Executive influences upon the process of administrative adjudication might diminish. Agency independence may be a mask which hides the exercise of improper Executive influences; Presidential authority commensurate with responsibility would tear the mask away. At the same time, it might encourage the administrators to take the initiative in policy-making in the public interest.

No one can be sanguine that Congress will easily be persuaded to increase Executive authority and responsibility as a means of improving the administrative process. Professor Bernstein thinks that the regulatory commission's organizational independence "reflects such basic political factors as Congressional-presidential rivalries, the decentralization of political parties, the absence of party government, and the prevailing particularistic interests of Americans." [57] If we have to wait for change in these basic political factors before the independence of the regulatory commission will be curtailed in any manner, then every independent regulatory commission is here to stay.

This would be unfortunate. We know little about the effect that different forms of organizational structure have upon the quality of organizational decision-making and the likelihood of achieving organizational goals. We might learn something about this relationship if, for example, Congress would subject all the agencies now regulating the transport industries to Executive control by putting them into a new Department of Transportation or some existing Executive Department or Departments. But it is difficult for legislators to adopt an experimental attitude when they are made to feel the multiple pressures of the vested interests which inevitably grow up around any existing system of organization.

[55] Hector, *supra* note 2, at 49-50.

[56] Bernstein, *op. cit. supra* note 1, at 258.

[57] *Id.* at 168-69.

NOTES AND QUESTIONS

1. While Mr. Hector thinks that the current difficulties of the independent regulatory commission are due entirely to its structure, Judge Henry J. Friendly thinks they are due entirely to the lack of sufficiently high-calibre administrative personnel. Friendly, A Look At The Federal Administrative Agencies, 60 Colum. L. Rev. 429, 444-446 (1960).

Are there any research techniques available by which we could weigh and compare the importance of the factors of structure and personnel to the effective performance of an agency's statutory responsibilities? As a practical matter, should we rely entirely upon either Mr. Hector's or Judge Friendly's assumption?

2. Warner W. Gardner, a practitioner of administrative law of wide experience, does not think that the judicialization of the administrative process has proceeded to the extent that it can be called a principal cause of administrative delay. He points out that although the federal Administrative Procedure Act imposes certain procedural standards, it leaves "what is in fact if not in theory a complete freedom to adapt procedure to a particular need." Gardner, The Administrative Process, in Legal Institutions Today and Tomorrow 129 (Paulsen ed. 1959). Gardner deplores the efforts of the American Bar Association to change the law so that it will prescribe definite and uniform rules of procedure, without exception, for all agencies. Id. at 129-130. These efforts have had their effect on existing procedures, even though they have not yet culminated in the amendment of the statute.

At the same time, Gardner concludes: "We can all agree that the administrative process is slow, and often much too slow for effective government. The reasons are not hard to find: some of the issues are enormously complicated; there are often rising work loads coupled with static or dwindling appropriations; there is too much desk-to-desk movement producing certain delay and only uncertain supervision; and in some instances there is simple incompetence. These, however, seem to be vices inherent in government generally; not in the administrative process alone. A fifth reason, the willingness of most of our profession to harass and delay the tribunal which may favor the opponent, is a cross borne chiefly by the administrative agency." Id. at 120.

For Judge Friendly's views on administrative delay—its causes and cures—see Friendly, op. cit. supra at 432-438. The student would profit from reading both of these perceptive articles in their entirety.

REPORT OF JAMES M. LANDIS * TO PRESIDENT-ELECT KENNEDY ON THE FEDERAL REGULATORY AGENCIES
Senate Judiciary Committee Print, 86th Cong., 2d Sess. (Dec. 1960)

Delay, Costs and Agency Organization

The existing state of the organization of many of the agencies is one chief reason for their delays. Their reorganization to correct this situation is thus essential and can be accomplished best and most expeditiously by the Executive. His constitutional responsibility to see that the laws are faithfully executed calls upon him to do so. The Executive, moreover, is less beset by the vested interests in bureaucracy that too often find support from members of the Congress. To do this, however, he must be empowered to act.

* In one of his first acts after his election, President Kennedy requested Mr. Landis to make the study which culminated in the Report, excerpts from which are reprinted above. On December 29, 1960, President Kennedy named Mr. Landis as Special Assistant to the President to plan the effectuation of the suggested reforms.— Editor

The first step consequently is, at least, to revive powers heretofore granted the President under the Reorganization Act of 1949, under which the power of the President to submit reorganization plans expired on June 1, 1959. A simple statute can do this. It would be better, moreover, in view of the bureaucratic pressures that are capable of being organized, as was evidenced by the defeat of President Truman's Plan No. 7 for the reorganization of the Interstate Commerce Commission, to require that the veto powers by the Congress over reorganization plans submitted by the President should require a majority in both houses of Congress. The leadership of the President in these matters should be respected by the Congress unless he is palpably wrong. . . .

The Interstate Commerce Commission

Among the agencies principally calling for reorganization is the Interstate Commerce Commission. It lacks positive direction because of the absence of the position of a chairman who is other than a presiding officer. The theory of a rotating chairman, elected annually by the membership, may assuage the ambitions of its membership, but it deprives the commission of that leadership it so sadly needs. The informed public generally knows the names of the heads of our Executive departments and has some sense of the general policies that they advocate. But even the informed public within the railroad and trucking industries have no idea and care less who, for the time being, might be the chairman of the Interstate Commerce Commission. The selection of the chairman from among its membership is essential but it is equally essential that he be appointed to that office by the President and hold it at his pleasure. . . . His powers should include the appointment of all personnel to the agency, save the heads of the prime divisions or bureaus where the assent of his colleagues can be required and also reserving to his colleagues certain excepted positions necessary to enable them to perform thir individual tasks. He should have complete authority as to the internal organization of the agency, the divisions and bureaus into which it should be divided, and the complete responsibility, subject to the review of the Bureau of the Budget, for its budget. He should also be the spokesman for the agency before the Congress, the President and the Executive departments, although he naturally would advise with his colleagues on such matters as well as delegate to others matters that he believes can be better handled by them. He should not, however, restrict the free expression of views differing from his by his colleagues to the Congress, the President or the public.

The membership of the Interstate Commerce Commission, eleven in number and the largest of any regulatory agency, gives ground for concern.

Opinions of the Interstate Commerce Commission are presently in the poorest category of all administrative agency opinions.

Their source is unknown and the practice has grown up of parsimony in discussing the applicable law in making a determination. Lengthy recitals of the contentions of the various parties are made as a prelude to a succinct conclusion devoid of real rationalization. . . .

The creation of an opinion writing section has been urged by the managerial consultants hired to survey the commission. But opinion writing sections are not the answer even at their best as in the Securities and Exchange Commission.

Individual commissioners must be assigned the responsibility of expressing the conclusions of the commission. They will, of course, need help and appropriate help in the nature of law clerks such as now assigned to Federal judges, rather than the present practice of temporarily assigning attorneys from the staff of a bureau. Law clerks personally attached to a commissioner will take pride in their chief's performance just as the law clerks seek now to perfect the work of their judges. . . .

A major problem in the reorganization of the Interstate Commerce Commission, as in most other agencies, is the delegation of appropriate duties to persons below the commission level. . . .

Whether a reorganization plan could make final the decisions by single commissioners, hearing examiners, or employe boards in certain groups of cases might be debatable, but a reorganization plan could make them final subject to review akin to the selective review by certiorari now employed as the means by which the Supreme Court of the United States determines which decisions of the Circuit Court of Appeals it wishes to review.

A judicious use of such a scheme and an insistence on brief petitions for certiorari by counsel would cut down enormously the business demanding attention at the commission level. The legality of such a plan under the concepts of due process is not truly questionable. . . .

The Civil Aeronautics Board

The chief criticisms of the Civil Aeronautics Board center about (1) the inordinate delay in its disposition of proceedings, especially in route cases; (2) the fact that its procedures are such as to make extraordinarily complex the issues before it in various types of proceedings; (3) the intrusion of influences off the record that appear to be determinative of pending cases; (4) a failure to do forward planning of the type necessary to promote our air commerce to its desired level of efficiency.

The inordinate delay in its disposition of pending causes and the complexity of these proceedings arises out of the procedure it applies to them. Issues with regard to route extensions, new routes, and new services come before it for determination as a result of the filing of applications by carriers or would-be carriers.

The disposition of these matters pursues no pattern or plan. The result is that issues with regard to the desirability of new routes and new services are commingled with issues as to what carriers should fly what routes, calling for a final judgment that has to be based on political, economic, sociological, business and aeronautical considerations.

All the issues in such a proceeding are handled by the lengthy process of examining and cross-examining witness. This is a wasteful manner of establishing many of the basic facts.

Routes that in the public interest should be flown are capable of being determined without resort to proceedings of this character but as a result of staff studies carried on in a less formal manner.

Evidence now being presented in a formal manner as to the needs of various communities for service, as to the community of interest between communities, as to the desirability for increased competition or the existence of sufficient adequate surface transportation, as to the type of service required and the potentiality of generating a sufficient quantum of air traffic, can all be determined beforehand by less legalistic and reasonably scientific methods, leaving for a "judicialized" hearing only the question of which of the competing carriers is to be selected for certification on any particular route.

If necessary, hearings could be held on the staff study itself, which also could be of a less formal type. . . .

The lack of planning on the part of the board stems from the burden of its adjudicatory work. Planning has been so neglected over the past few years that a staff, fit to be called a planning staff, can hardly any longer be said to exist. At every point major issues of policy remain undecided. Cases being dealt with now are already so obsolete that they even fail to raise these issues, so that policy fails to evolve as fast as it should from the adjudicatory process.

Reorganization to make planning possible is a matter of internal organization. The only need for a "plan" within the meaning of the Reorganization Act lies in further increasing the powers granted to the chairman in 1950 to the full extent herein suggested for the Interstate Commerce Commission and to permit more flexibility in the delegation of those decisions which require no real ratiocination to hearing examiners or to bureau heads subject to a certiorari type of review by the board. . . .

The Federal Communications Commission

The Federal Communications Commission presents a somewhat extraordinary spectacle. Despite considerable technical excellence on the part of its staff, the commission has drifted, vacillated and stalled in almost every major area. It seems incapable of policy planning, of disposing within a reasonable period of time the business before it, of fashioning procedures that are effective to deal with its problems.

The available evidence indicates that it, more than any other agency, has been susceptible to ex parte presentations, and that it has been subservient, far too subservient, to the subcommittees on communications of the Congress and their members. A strong suspicion also exists that far too great an influence is exercised over the commission by the networks.

The quality of its top personnel is, of course, primarily responsible for these defects. The members of the commission do not appear to be overworked in the sense that the commission's docket is bulging with cases calling for disposition. Nevertheless disposition lags.

Only thirty-two cases, all dealing with broadcasting licenses, were decided by the commission during fiscal 1959, other than cases dismissed or in which the examiner's report became final. Commission action following the examiner's report in nine of these cases took from six to twelve months and in ten cases from one year to two years.

In broadcast license cases no criteria for decision have evolved. True, criteria of various different kinds are articulated but they are patently not the grounds motivating the decision. No firm decisional policy has evolved from these case-by-case dispositions. Instead the anonymous opinion writers for the commission pick from a collection of standards those that will support whatever decision the commission chooses to make.

Observers of the procedures employed by the commission agree that the issues litigated are unreal and a mass of useless evidence, expensive to prepare, is required to be adduced. The uselessness of much of this evidence derives from several causes.

The first is that programming proposed by applicants is of high-sounding moral and ethical content in order to establish that their operation of a radio and television station would be in the "public interest." The actual programming bears no reasonable similitude to the programming proposed.

The commission knows this but ignores these differentiations at the time when renewal of licenses of the station is before them. Nevertheless, it continues with its Alice-in-Wonderland procedures. Also because of the varying standards that the commission employs, a vast amount of unrealistic testimony is adduced to support each of these standards, incumbering the record with useless data.

On major policy matters, the commission seems incapable of reaching conclusions. The UHF [ultra-high-frequency television] débacle has been plainly apparent for some five to six years. Nothing of any substantial consequence has yet been accomplished by the commission to relieve the situation, although they are now purporting to make available additional VHF [very high frequency] channels in one and two TV-channel markets.

The procedures employed by the commission in adjudicatory matters as well as in purely exploratory matters seem primarily at fault for these deficiencies. Leadership in the effort to solve problems seems too frequently to be left to commercial interests rather than taken by the commission itself.

No patent solution for this situation exists other than the incubation of vigor and courage in the commission by giving it strong and competent leadership, and thereby evolving sensible procedures for the disposition of its business.

The Federal Power Commission

The Federal Power Commission without question represents the outstanding example in the Federal Government of the breakdown of the administrative process. The complexity of its problems is no answer to its more than patent failures. These failures relate primarily to the natural gas field, in the commission's handling of its responsibilities with respect to the transmission and the production of natural gas. . . .

These defects stem from attitudes, plainly evident on the record, of the unwillingness of the commission to assume its responsibilities under the Natural Gas Act and its attitude, substantially contemptuous, of refusing in substance to obey the mandates of the Supreme Court of the United States and other Federal courts.

The commission has exhibited no inclination to use powers that it possesses to get abreast of its docket. Thousands of rate cases dealing with independent gas producers clutter its docket.

Of this mass of cases Senator Paul H. Douglas of Illinois has pointed out that an exemption of producers of natural gas in interstate commerce for resale of less than 2,000,000,000 cubic feet per year would take 4,191 producers, whose total production of natural gas was only 9.26 per cent of the total volume of gas purchased by interstate pipeline companies in 1953, out of the jurisdiction of the commission. Nevertheless, no effort has been made by the commission to clear its docket of these inconsequential cases in order to come to grips with the relatively few remaining producers who do matter. . . .

Dissatisfaction with the work of the commission has gone so far that there is a large measure of agreement on separating from the commission its entire jurisdiction over natural gas and creating a new commission to handle these problems exclusively.

It is probably unnecessary to go this far. However, certain amendments to the Natural Gas Act are essential.

The commission might well be increased to seven members so as to permit it to sit in two panels of three, with final decision in each panel, so as to help it clear up its enormous backlog. But primarily leadership and power must be given to its chairman and qualified and dedicated members with the consumer interest at heart must be called into service to correct what has developed into the most dismal failure in our time of the administrative process. . . .

[Mr. Landis did not comment on the proposed transfer of the judicial functions of the FTC to a trade court. He recommended a return to the pre-Taft-Hartley Act organization of the NLRB, under which the General Counsel was subordinate to the Board.—Editor]

Personnel

The prime key to the improvement of the administrative process is the selection of qualified personnel. Good men can make poor laws workable; poor men will wreak havoc with good laws. . . . Good men are primarily attracted by the challenge inherent in a job. Salary is a secondary consideration, provided only that it is high enough to enable them to meet reasonable standards of living comparable to their positions in the society. Our universities have known and, indeed, traded on these facts. Tenure is another consideration of more importance than salary, for with tenure goes independence and the opportunity for long-range planning.

Basic challenges have been missing in the last decade. Good men cannot be attracted to agencies if they see that the colleagues with whom they are called upon to work, the staffs that they must utilize, are not measurable by standards they believe to be appropriate.

Such a condition implies a lack of concern or a lack of understanding of the regulatory process by the President, either or both of which are destructive of the very thing that could hold an appeal. The appeal of a job can also be destroyed if the President, through design or neglect, permits his prejudices in behalf of political associates or friends to dictate the disposition of individual items of business. No truly good man can submit to such interference. . . .

Compensation is a consideration. Present salaries for top administrative personnel are in the neighborhood of $20,000 per year. This is a reasonable salary for the present level of the cost of living. Increasing it by $2,500 or even $5,000 would not appreciably affect the situation.

But there are two things that could make these positions more attractive at a very reasonable cost. The first is the grant of a moderate entertainment allowance to the administrator. Like an ambassador, he needs to maintain a certain prestige with the industry. He should be able to entertain rather than be required to suffer entertainment. At conferences, which he not infrequently is required to call, luncheon breaks should provide something better than service from a Government cafeteria.

The second matter is an adequate retirement allowance. For unexplained reasons, the retirement allowance for Executive employes is considerably less than the allowances available to legislators. As an alleged servant of the Congress, the independent commissioner or his counterpart could be enfolded within the legislative scheme. This fringe benefit could well make a difference.

Chairmen, especially if their powers are enhanced, should be compensated on a better basis than their colleagues, for they have more to do. The present difference rarely runs over $500 a year, a sum which is neither sufficient to be compensatory nor to make for prestige. . . .

Longer tenures would mean opportunities for longer-scale planning, freedom from worry as to reappointment, and generally the concept of devotion to a career rather than that of a stepping stone to further political or professional advancement. Life tenure is, perhaps, too dangerous in these areas of dynamic activity but certainly a ten-year term is not too much to suggest. . . .

Administrative Procedure

In 1953, the President sent out a call for a conference on the subject of administrative procedure which was attended by representatives of the various federal regulatory agencies, and distinguished members from the bench, and bar and the universities.

One recommendation of the conference suggested that it, or something similar to it, be placed on a permanent basis and this recommendation was endorsed by the American and Federal Bar Associations as well as the Judicial Conference of the United States. On August 29, 1960, the President requested Judge [E. Barrett] Prettyman of the Court of Appeals for the District of Columbia Circuit to undertake the preliminary work of organizing such a conference. Judge Prettyman in turn appointed a committee of fourteen members and has ready a preliminary draft of by-laws for such an organization.

This work should be encouraged and Judge Prettyman, whose knowledge of and devotion to the subject is well-known, should be requested to continue his efforts. Much can come from this effort, including not merely revisions in our administrative procedures but also the making of our regulatory agencies into a system just as the Judicial Conference of the United States has made a system of what were once isolated and individual Federal courts.

But for a conference of this type to be effective it is essential that a permanent secretariat be established, which can follow the work of various committees, break out issues and problems that require exploration and research, arrange for appropriate publications, and act as liaison agent between the conference, the Congress and the Government generally.

The work and functions now lodged in the Office of Administrative Procedure in the Department of Justice should be transferred to this secretariat . . .

The Coordination of Agency Policy

In various areas, agency policies must be coordinated and welded into an integrated whole. Certain areas such as transportation, communication and energy are obvious areas where such coordination is essential.

It has not infrequently been suggested that something akin to a ministry or department of transportation with Cabinet rank should be created. Many other countries have such departments and they are operated with considerable success. There are, however, striking differences between the situation in these countries and that which prevails in the United States. . . .

Plans and blueprints for mechanisms such as a department of transportation have been in existence for years and new ones are being devised. None have as yet received substantial Congressional or Executive support.

The blueprints, even the best of them, are unrealistic, beautiful in design but lacking in the appreciation of those earthy factors that are embedded in our regulatory transportation structure.

Most of them entail the concept of some person in the nature of a czar sitting astride the whole transportation structure and exercising through subordinate bodies many of the functions now vested in the regulatory agencies. Others conceive of splitting away the adjudicatory functions but consolidating other functions in an Executive department.

It may be that we can eventually attain some such goal but the means of reaching it or an equally satisfactory goal must still be developed. . . .

If we would build toward the goal of coordinating our transportation system and its problems, we should do this carefully and on the basis of accumulating experience not merely as to problems but as to mechanisms to deal with these problems. . . .

The evolution of a national transportation policy must have a close and intimate relationship to the President. To do so by the creation of an Executive department, however, means the imposition of presently undefined Executive duties in the head of that department. These duties could probably be more defined at a later date in the light of experience and then vested without too much controversy in an appropriate governmental unit. Meanwhile, development of the coordinating function could be placed in the Executive Office of the President. . . . The office would need no regulatory powers. It does need the constant personal support of the President and through him the President's Cabinet and the Bureau of the Budget.

Given these, a coordination of policy can be effected by such an office among the various regulatory agencies, implemented where necessary by Executive order. And, as experience demonstrates, coordination and consolidation of functions among them can be effected by the wise use of the President's power under the Reorganization Act. . . .

Similar approaches can be made by the creation of similar offices for the areas of communications and energy.

Relationship of the Agencies to the Executive and the Legislative

The development of detailed plans for the reorganization of the administrative agencies and continued oversight of these activities remains to be considered. Such oversight as is exercised by the Bureau of the Budget is at too low a level and extends substantially only to managerial functioning. The areas in which the agencies fail or hesitate to formulate policy presently tend to go unnoticed, as do those overlaps that have developed or are in formulation. . . .

The function of exercising oversight should be in firm but friendly hands and the office that exercises it a protagonist of the agencies before the Bureau of the Budget, the President and the Congress.

The person charged with these responsibilities should not be a mere inspector-general but also a source of imaginative and creative activity. Lodging that function in the Executive office of the President independently of the Bureau of the Budget and transferring to that office the functions now exercised by the Bureau of the Budget of managerial assistance is the solution.

Presidential concern with the work of the agencies is important both from the standpoint of the President's duty to see that the laws are faithfully executed and from the standpoint of the morale of the agencies, for they will then realize how important their activities are to the national scene. . . .

Summary and Conclusions

The present needs are too pressing to await the initiation of what would be a mammoth project of consolidation in the fields of transportation, communication, and energy, and even a huge project in any one of them. The prime and immediate need in these fields is for developing and coordinating policy immediately at a high staff level.

Operations for the moment can be left to the existing agencies, whose conduct should in the light of these recommendations show marked improvements. If experience later would dictate the desirability of the consolidation of certain operating functions, they will then have become sufficiently identified and understood to enable their intelligent consolidation in an appropriate departmental structure.

To attempt such consolidation in the absence of the experience that would be derived from determined effort to evolve policy through coordination directly under the President would be substantially to plan in vacuo. The creation of a mechanism for staff coordination can and should begin now.

With this thought in mind, the following recommendations are made:

1. Secure for the President from the Congress the right to propose reorganization plans pursuant to powers heretofore granted the President under the Reorganization Act of 1949, subject to veto by a concurrent resolution of both houses of the Congress. The powers to propose plans should be available for a minimum of two years but preferably for four years.

2. Propose a reorganization plan for the Interstate Commerce Commission whereby its chairman will be designated by the President and serve as chairman at his pleasure.

3. Propose a reorganization plan for the Federal Power Commission making clear that the tenure of its chairman is at the pleasure of the President.

4. Propose reorganization plans for the Interstate Commerce Commission, the Civil Aeronautics Board, the Federal Communications Commission, the Federal Power Commission, the National Labor Relations Board, the Federal Trade Commission and the Securities and Exchange Commission which will make clear that the chairman's authority extends to all administrative matters within the agency, including responsibility for the preparation and review of its budget estimates, the distribution of appropriated funds according to major programs and purposes, and the appointment of all personnel, except (I) those whose appointment is by statute vested in the President, (II) division heads whose appointment must be confirmed by a majority of the agency members, (III) special assistants, not in excess of three, to each of the members, which appointments shall be made by the respective members.

5. Propose reorganization plans for the same agencies providing for the delegation to panels of agency members, single agency members, hearing examiners or boards of employes for final determination all adjudicatory matters subject only to discretionary review by the agency en banc on petition by a party in interest.

6. Create within the Executive Office of the President with appropriate powers an office for the coordination and development of transportation policy to develop and implement a national transportation policy. This should be accomplished by a reorganization plan transferring to this office all the responsibilities now vested in the Under Secretary of Commerce for Transportation.

7. Create within the Executive Office of the President with appropriate powers an office for the coordination and development of communications policy and simultaneously by Executive order transfer to this office all powers relating to telecommunications now vested in the Office of Civil and Defense Mobilization.

8. Create within the Executive Office of the President with appropriate powers an office for the coordination and development of energy policy with authority to

propose to the President plans for the development of the energy resources of this nation.

9. Create within the Executive Office of the President with appropriate powers an office for the oversight of regulatory agencies which will assist the President in discharging his responsibility of assuring the efficient execution of those laws that these agencies administer.

10. Abolish the present President's Advisory Committee on Government Organization.

11. Abolish the positions of such special assistants to the President who have heretofore had as their major concern matters within the purview of the offices to be created under recommendations 6, 7, 8, and 9.

12. The offices mentioned in recommendations 6, 7, 8 and 9 can be substituted for the Office for Emergency Management which in its present form can be abolished.

13. Impose upon the Office for the oversight of regulatory agencies the duty to prepare for the President detailed reorganization plans for the regulatory agencies with prime emphasis on the Federal Power Commission, the Interstate Commerce Commission, the Civil Aeronautics Board, and the Federal Communications Commission.

14. Issue an Executive order dealing with the ethics of Government employes and their duty to reject and refrain from receiving ex parte presentations in pending matters before them for adjudication on the record . . .

15. Promote the organization of the Administrative Conference of the United States and . . . provide for the creation of a secretariat to the conference, transferring to that secretariat duties now performed by the Office of Administrative Procedure within the Department of Justice, which would thus be abolished and transferring from the Civil Service Commission to the secretariat duties now exercised by the commission with respect to the qualifications and grading of hearing examiners.

16. Require the submission to the Congress and President of annual reports by the offices created pursuant to recommendations 6, 7, 8 and 9.*

EDITORIAL NOTE: PRESIDENT KENNEDY'S
IMPLEMENTATION of the LANDIS REPORT

As this is written, it is too early to assess the work of President Kennedy in reforming the federal regulatory agencies.

On April 13, 1961, the President submitted a Message to the Congress Relative to the Regulatory Agencies of Our Government, which reiterated most of the Landis recommendations.

The President's appointments to the regulatory agencies have evoked both high praise and severe criticism. His imposition of high ethical standards

* For comments on the Landis Report, see McFarland, Landis' Report: The Voice of One Crying in the Wilderness, 47 Va. L. Rev. 373 (1961); and Carrow, Dean Landis and the Regulatory Process, 29 Geo. Wash. L. Rev. 718 (1961).—Editor

upon his appointees, to which we have previously referred, has been acclaimed. But the effectuation of the changes in internal agency organization suggested by Mr. Landis has encountered strong and successful opposition.

At the President's request, Congress extended the Reorganization Act of 1949 until June 1, 1963 (75 Stat. 41) but retained the provision that a majority vote in either house of Congress could defeat any reorganization plan submitted by the President thereunder. So far, the President has submitted six Reorganization Plans to permit the SEC, FCC, CAB, FTC, NLRB and Federal Home Loan Bank Board, to delegate authority to take final action in substantive matters, on behalf of the agency, to "a division of the Commission, an individual Commissioner, a hearing examiner, or an employee or employee board." The plans for all these agencies, except the NLRB, would also increase the administrative powers of their chairmen. To date, the plans for the FCC, SEC and NLRB were defeated by the Congress but those for the FTC and CAB were permitted to stand.

By Executive Order 10934, April 13, 1961 (26 Federal Register 3233), the President established the Administrative Conference of the United States. Under the leadership of Judge Prettyman, the Conference has embarked upon the task of assisting the President, the Congress and the administrative agencies and executive departments in improving existing administrative procedures.

The President has given no indication that he will create White House offices, as recommended by Mr. Landis, to coordinate and develop transportation, communications, and energy policies or to oversee the regulatory agencies.

TABLE OF CASES

(Case-titles in italics refer to cases reprinted in this volume. Those in roman type refer to cases cited in Editorial Notes or in the Notes and Questions.)

INDEX